PRINCIPLES OF OPERATIONS RESEARCH

With Applications
to
Managerial Decisions

PRENTICE-HALL INTERNATIONAL SERIES IN MANAGEMENT

PRENTICE-HALL, INC.
PRENTICE-HALL INTERNATIONAL, INC., *United Kingdom and Eire*
PRENTICE-HALL OF CANADA, LTD., *Canada*
J. H. DE BUSSY, LTD., *Holland and Flemish-speaking Belgium*
DUNOD PRESS, *France*
MARUZEN COMPANY, LTD., *Far East*
HERRERO HERMANOS, SUCS., *Spain and Latin America*
R. OLDENBOURG VERLAG, *Germany*
ULRICO HOEPLI EDITORE, *Italy*

HARVEY M. WAGNER

Department of Administrative Sciences
Yale University;
Consultant to the Firm
McKinsey & Company, Inc.

PRINCIPLES
OF
OPERATIONS
RESEARCH

With Applications
to
Managerial Decisions

Prentice-Hall, Inc., Englewood Cliffs, New Jersey

Current printing (last digit):

10 9 8 7 6 5 4

13–709576–7

Library of Congress Catalog Card Number: 76–82807
Printed in the United States of America

To my parents
and their favorite grandchildren,
Caroline and Julie

Preface

This book is written primarily for college students who have no previous background in operations research and who intend careers as administrators, consultants, executives, or managers in business, nonprofit enterprises, or government. The broad topic coverage also should make the text helpful for students who seek careers as teachers and researchers as well as for practitioners who desire an up-to-date review of operations research. The book can be used in half-year or full-year introductory courses for juniors, seniors, or graduates in business, economics, and engineering curricula.

The central goal of the book is to answer the question, "What are the *fundamental ideas* of operations research?" The text does not presuppose any *advanced* training in business administration, industrial engineering, mathematics, statistics, probability theory, or economics. Therefore, the main ideas do not rely on the reader's being expert in these areas. The text does assume, however, that the reader is not entirely naive about such subjects.

MATHEMATICS PREREQUISITES

We have consistently tried to motivate the technical developments and to make the mathematical logic clear. But, frankly, we did not try to make the mathematics palatable for a student who is congenitally adverse to science.

The differential calculus is employed only in Chaps. 14, 15, and 20, and the integral calculus only in Chap. 20 and Appendix III. Nevertheless, much of the text assumes a mathematical sophistication comparable to that acquired in standard college-level introductory calculus or a no-nonsense finite mathematics course. Elementary probability theory is first needed in Chap. 16. The three appendices and much of the optional material, designated by either an asterisk or smaller print, relate to technical details and often require a noticeably higher level of mathematical maturity.

vii

PRINCIPAL OBJECTIVES

Beginning students frequently ask, "What must I learn about operations research if I intend to become a manager rather than a specialist?" and "What must I learn about operations research given that I want to apply it to real problems?" Regrettably, a single introductory operations research course cannot completely answer either question. But such a course can better answer the first rather than the second question.

In the context of these two questions, the book's principal objectives are

- To introduce the important ideas in operations research which are both fundamental and long lasting.

- To provide those students not going beyond a single introductory course with enough understanding and confidence to appreciate the strengths and inherent limitations of the operations research approach.

- To prepare and motivate future specialists to continue in their study by having an insightful overview of operations research.

- To demonstrate the cohesiveness of operations research methodology.

COVERAGE AND EMPHASIS

Obviously, an author of an introductory text must exercise considerable judgment in selecting topics and in choosing the depth of treatment. In this regard, we have been influenced considerably by more than 15 years of first-hand experience in applying operations research to actual situations in business and government. The examples in the text often are scaled-down versions of real problems that we have encountered. Of equal importance in selecting topics is our accumulated experience teaching hundreds of undergraduates and graduates, many of whom now are using operations research to aid managerial decision making or are, in turn, educating other college students. The specific models that we chose, their complexity, and sequential development all reflect our observations of how most students come to appreciate and understand the pivotal concepts in operations research.

To permit an instructor to select the topics that are most appropriate for his class, we have included material at several different levels of complexity. *Any material designated by an asterisk or appearing between the symbols ▶ and ◀ and set in smaller print may be skipped without loss of continuity.*

Throughout, the book stresses the *insights* for decision making that stem from operations research analysis. The text puts into focus the value of information derived from an operations research solution and attempts to give an accurate representation of how a hypothetical example would be applied in a real situation.

The text develops the student's skill in formulating and building models and, specifically, in translating a verbal description of a decision problem into an equivalent mathematical model. The book also explains the importance and the degree of severity of a model's assumptions, the connection between the starting assumptions and the derived results, and the seriousness of the assumptions for practical purposes. Finally, the text demonstrates by means of important examples the process and usefulness of constructing analogies, finding multiple interpretations of models, and deriving significant special cases from general models.

SUGGESTIONS TO STUDENTS

If you have taken courses in both the calculus and elementary statistics or probability theory, you will recall that you could understand most of the calculus text without much help from the instructor whereas you needed the guidance of the instructor to fully understand the statistics or probability theory text. This is a very common occurrence among students. Can you suggest why? You will find operations research to be more like statistics and probability theory than the calculus in that you can expect, as a matter of course, to rely on your instructor to amplify the ideas and techniques in this book. Since the concepts can be intricate, you may have to study several pages before comprehending the full idea. So be prepared for patient reading and some rereading.

We have tried to avoid giving numerical examples that are so *misleadingly* simple that you are not sufficiently prepared for the exercises at the end of each chapter. As a result, you will find it advantageous to examine carefully the numerical illustrations in the chapters. Here and there, the text will ask you to verify certain calculations and conclusions. Obviously, the purpose of these suggestions is not to validate the accuracy of the author's arithmetic or logic. Rather, they are signals to guide you in learning the material. When studying a chapter for the first time, do not interrupt your reading to make these checks; but afterwards return to these points to ascertain that you have really understood the ideas.

If your instructor assigns the exercises at the back of the chapters, do not wait until the last minute to begin the problems. The numerical exercises, although straightforward, can be fatiguing if attempted in a single evening session. Most students find that formulation problems require a "gestation period," so allow yourself a few days to ponder such exercises.

Surprisingly, it is difficult to write a *verbal* description of an operations research problem that is completely unambiguous. More than once, thoughtful students have discovered vague wording in problems that we had assigned previously to other classes that experienced no difficulty in obtaining the intended solutions. Consequently, if you believe an exercise displays a troublesome ambiguity, try to resolve it in a sensible way and make explicit on your paper the specific assumption that you adopted. The purpose of the exercises (namely, to give you practice in mathematical formulation) is well served by this procedure.

SUGGESTIONS TO INSTRUCTORS

Clearly, the entire book is too large for even a full year's introductory course. This broad topic coverage has been purposely designed to give you considerable flexibility in choosing the subjects that you want to stress. The logical organization of the chapters is shown in Exhibit A.

In a one-term introductory survey course, where the students know elementary probability theory and the calculus, you can include Chaps. 1 through 6, 8, 10, 16, 17, 19 through 22, skipping all of the starred (*) sections and optional material in smaller print. If you do not want to use the calculus, then omit Chap. 20. If the students are unfamiliar with elementary probability theory, then you can assign Chaps. 1 through 8, 10, and choose topics from Chaps. 9 and 11 through 15.

To assist you in selecting other combinations, the "Immediate Predecessors" of each chapter are shown in Exhibit B. In general, the chapters become progressively more difficult. Thus, although you could cover dynamic programming (Chaps. 8, 9, and 10) prior to linear programming, the reverse sequence ordinarily would be preferable, because the dynamic programming chapters assume the student already is somewhat familiar with multivariate constrained optimization models and solution techniques.

The book contains more than 1000 exercises, many of which have multiple parts. The problems are grouped into four categories. The Review Exercises are keyed closely to the text and determine whether the student has understood the conceptual developments. The Formulation Exercises consist of "word problems" and test whether the student can translate a verbal statement into a precise mathematical model. The Computational Exercises provide practice problems for applying algorithms. The Mind-Expanding Exercises are primarily for advanced students—you also may want to pick some of these problems as topics for your lectures. There is "redundancy" in the multiple parts of many exercises, and consequently, you should examine the parts to ascertain which ones you want to assign.

In comparing this book with other elementary texts in operations research, you will notice a few differences in the standard list of chapter headings. We give extended treatment at an introductory level to several topics (such as dynamic programming over an unbounded horizon, integer programming, nonlinear programming, stochastic programming, and dynamic programming in Markov chains) that are covered only briefly, if at all, elsewhere. In contrast, we have not devoted entire chapters to the subjects of replacement theory and game theory. Important replacement models are included in the dynamic programming chapters. Game theory has been omitted, with the exception of the Fundamental Theorem of Two-Person, Zero-Sum Matrix Games given in exercise 35 of Chap. 5. In practicing operations research, we have found that game theory does not contribute any *managerial insights* to real competitive and cooperative decision-making behavior that are not *already* familiar to church-going

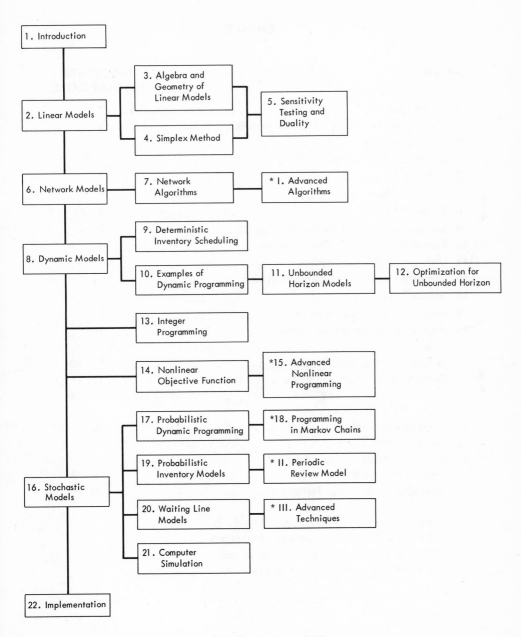

EXHIBIT A. Organization of Chapters.

Exhibit B

NOTE: Chaps. 16 through 21 require probability theory.
         Chaps. 14, 15, and 20 require differential calculus.
         Chap. 20 and App. III require integral calculus.
         ( ) indicates desirable but not essential.

poker players who regularly read the Wall Street Journal. (This is not to say, however, that the intricacies of real competitive economic behavior, such as price wars, advertising campaigns, mergers, and acquisitions, have yet become phenomena fully understood by scientists.)

ACKNOWLEDGMENTS

Throughout the four years of developing this text, I received many helpful suggestions from undergraduates and graduates at both Stanford and Yale Universities, and I benefited from the sage counsel of Professors William J. Carroll (Rutgers), C. West Churchman (University of California, Berkeley), Charles H. Falkner (University of Wisconsin), Oliver Galbraith, III (San Diego State College), Arthur M. Geoffrion (University of California, Los Angeles), Richard B. Hoffman (State University of New York at Buffalo), Robert E. Jensen (University of Maine), David Kendrick (Harvard), Leonard Lodish (Wharton School of Finance and Commerce), Lawrence L. Schkade (North Texas State University), Alan J. Seelenfreund (Stanford), Herbert A. Simon (Carnegie-Mellon), Matthew J. Sobel (Yale), Martin K. Starr (Columbia), Robert M. Thrall (University of Michigan), Donald M. Topkis (University of California, Berkeley), and Leon S. White (M.I.T.), many of whom bravely endured the inchoate mass of an unweildy typewritten edition. I especially want to acknowledge Professor Arthur F. Veinott, Jr. (Stanford) who considerably influenced my own thinking about the principles of operations research.

I also am grateful to Ernest C. Arbuckle, formerly Dean of the Stanford Graduate School of Business, who provided tangible long-term encouragement, and to the National Science Foundation, which supported the pioneering research underpinning many ideas in this text. In great measure, the managerial relevance of the book has been enhanced through my association since 1960 with McKinsey & Co., as a Consultant to the Firm, and particularly through the personal guidance of Dr. David B. Hertz, Douglas Watson, Warren M. Cannon, John G. Neukom, and Richard F. Neuschel.

A fine Instructor's Manual was patiently prepared by John Chamberlin, John M. Harrison, and Michael Saunders (all of Stanford University).

The secretarial skill and encouraging dispositions of Mrs. Sheila Hill (Stanford) and Mrs. Marcia Wheeler (Yale) triumphed admirably over the seemingly never-ending strain of typing redrafts and meeting deadlines. And we all can be thankful for the unsparingly, but deftly, employed red pencils of editors Mr. Will Harriss (RAND) and Mr. Kenneth Cashman (Prentice-Hall).

Amazing as it may seem, suddenly I am lost for words in trying to adequately express appreciation to my wife Ruthie for keeping a "togetherness" at home far longer than a reasonable planning horizon. Hence, I must resort (hopefully only this once in the book) to a cryptogram that is unambiguously decipherable only to her: $\dfrac{1}{\epsilon} \to \infty$.

HARVEY M WAGNER

New Haven, Connecticut

Contents

*Any material designated by an asterisk may be skipped without loss of continuity.

CONTENTS

CHAPTER **1**

The Art and Science
of Executive Decisions

1.1 BEFORE GETTING STARTED...

You may well be curious to know how a subject with so abstruse a name as *operations research* could beget a several hundred page introductory text purportedly dealing only with principles. The ambiguous term *operations research* was coined during World War II. At that time, it was an apt description of the subject matter. Unfortunately, the name stuck, even though present-day applications of operations research are considerably more diverse than they used to be.

Now there is a worldwide confederation of professional societies named Operations Research. The staffs of many industrial organizations bear the title. So do departments in leading universities, which have gone on to sanctify the term by granting advanced degrees bearing its name. These vested interests are so well entrenched that the name *operations research* is unlikely to be supplanted in our lifetime.

Disgruntled though we may be, saddled as we are with a title that is undescriptive if not downright misleading, we nevertheless must show our respect. After all, the scientists who originated the term were on the winning side of the war. (Who knows what might have happened if the other side had invented the approach first?)

1.2 BY ANY OTHER NAME

Numerous synonyms for operations research are in common use. The British like *operational research*. A frequent American substitute is *management science*. (The popularity of this name is fostered by yet another international professional society called the Institute of Management Sciences. The Operations Research Society and the Institute of Management Sciences regularly hold joint meetings, and their membership overlaps to a large extent.) As a beginning student, fortunately, you can afford to assume a lofty indifference to the whole matter, leaving this semantic bone of contention for your seniors to wrangle over.

For convenience, and with reasonable accuracy, you can simply define operations research as a scientific approach to problem-solving for executive management. An application of operations research involves:

- Constructing mathematical, economic, and statistical descriptions or models of decision and control problems to treat situations of complexity and uncertainty.
- Analyzing the relationships that determine the probable future consequences of decision choices, and devising appropriate measures of effectiveness in order to evaluate the relative merit of alternative actions.

It is sometimes believed that operations research refers to the constant monitoring of an organization's ongoing activities—and, in fact, decision and control problems often do concern certain daily "operations" of the organization. Examples of this sort include production scheduling and inventory control, facility maintenance and repair, and staffing of service facilities, to name a few applications.

But many operations research studies treat other kinds of decisions that bear on daily operations only indirectly. These studies usually have a planning orientation. Illustrations include determining the breadth of a firm's product line, developing a long-term program for plant expansion, designing a network of warehouses for a wholesale distribution system, and entering a new business by merger or acquisition.

It is bad enough that the word "operations" inadequately describes the diversity of present-day applications. To make matters worse, the word "research" creates the false impression that the method is a "blue-sky approach." On the contrary, in the past decade operations research has proved time and again to be a powerful and effective approach for solving critically real management problems. You will learn most of the reasons in this chapter, and you will know the full story after reading the main chapters of this book.

▶Of course, fundamental research in the *methods* of operations research continues, mainly at universities and at governmental and industrial research laboratories. Unlike the situation with basic research in other sciences, however, relatively little time elapses between an important discovery in operations research and its implementation by experienced practitioners in industrial groups.   ◀

Better decisions in a complex and uncertain environment. A preferable term to describe the subject of this book is *decision analysis*. An emphasis on making decisions or taking actions is central to all operations research applications.

Decision analysis separates a large-scale problem into its subparts, each of which is simpler to manipulate and diagnose. After the separate elements are carefully examined, the results are synthesized to give insights into the original problem. You may wonder why such complex decision-making problems arise in the first place.

One reason is that in today's economy, technological, environmental, and competitive factors typically interact in a complicated fashion. For example, a factory production schedule has to take account of customer demand (tempered by the likelihood of a price-cut by competitors), requirements for raw materials and intermediate inventories, the capacities of equipment, the possibility of equipment failures, and manufacturing process restrictions. It is not easy to make up a schedule that is both realistic and economical.

Other reasons for complexity in real decision-making situations are that the organization (perhaps only half-knowingly) may be pursuing inconsistent goals, the responsibility and authority for making the required decisions may be greatly diffused within the organization, and the economic environment in which the company operates may be uncertain.

To be successful, an operations research approach must improve the managerial decision-making process—the improvement being measured by the net cost of obtaining it. You should keep in mind the distinction between improved decision-making and improved performance, or more succinctly, between a good decision and a good outcome. For example, by all prior analysis, your betting on the Irish Sweepstakes may not appear to be a good decision (economically or morally); but *after* betting, the outcome will be good if you win. Improving decision analysis is important because the only thing *you* control is your decision prior to the uncertain outcome.

Distinguishing characteristics. There are many ways to approach management problems, and most of these ways are related. Certainly, there is no clear boundary line isolating the solutions derived by professional operations researchers from those derived by such people as industrial engineers, or economists specializing in economic planning, or accountants or financial analysts oriented toward management information systems. But most operations research applications possess certain distinguishing characteristics. Specifically, a suggested approach to a particular problem must contain all the following qualities before we would call it an operations research approach:

i. *A Primary Focus on Decision-Making.* The principal results of the analysis must have direct and unambiguous implications for executive action.

ii. *An Appraisal Resting on Economic Effectiveness Criteria.* A comparison of the various feasible actions must be based on measurable values that unequivocally reflect the future well-being of the organization. In a commercial firm, these measured quantities typically include variable costs, revenues, cash flow, and rate of return on incremental investment. A recommended solution must have evaluated the tradeoffs and have struck an optimum balance among these sometimes conflicting factors.

iii. *Reliance on a Formal Mathematical Model.* The procedures for manipulating the data should be so explicit that they can be described to another analyst, who in turn would derive the same results from the same data.

iv. *Dependence on an Electronic Computer.* This characteristic is not really a desideratum but rather a requirement necessitated by either the complexity of the mathematical model, the volume of data to be manipulated, or the magnitude of computations needed to implement the associated management operating and control systems.

In science we trust. To embrace operations research, a company must believe that applying the scientific method is relevant to the analysis of managerial decisions. This statement is not the platitude it may seem to be at first reading. The adoption of operations research calls for an act of faith in the benefits of a systematic approach to decision-making, and not all corporation executives are ready to make that act as yet.

It may sound strange, at this late date, to hear a plea for faith in science—and operations research is a science. After all, the legitimacy of the scientific method in the study of other subjects, such as physical phenomena, is hardly open to question. After hundreds of years of experience, chemists and physicists have developed efficacious laboratory techniques. But the virtue of applying scientific procedures to decision-making problems of significance is not so well-established; its recognition still calls for what the poet Coleridge described, in another context, as "the willing suspension of disbelief." Here is why.

Rarely, if ever, can a company perform what most people would regard as a bona fide "scientific" experiment to test the merit of an operations research solution. Consider a company that is contemplating using a mathematical model to arrive at its annual operating plan. Since the company's economic environment differs from year to year, it can never exactly repeat history, and therefore can never prove indisputably that the model solution will produce a realized improvement over the company's current planning approach.

Consider a second illustration. Suppose that an operations research model has been suggested for controlling a company's inventories. Again, testing whether the new system will definitely yield an improvement over the present approach is inherently limited. Although you could use historical data to compare how the suggested rule would have operated in the past, the comparison does not represent a truly scientific experiment with controlled variables. For one thing, you can only *assume* that historical data are indicative of what will happen in the future. For another, if the suggested rules improve service and customers recognize the improvement, then there may be an increase in customer demand. In other words, the very operation of the suggested policy can alter the environment.

Thus, the historical data may not be typical of the future. And because the decision system itself influences the environment, it is not really possible to operate both the present and new systems "in parallel." (Occasionally, you can run part of the system under the new set of rules and the other part under the old set of rules. Explain why this test, also, is not a truly controlled experiment.)

Of course, before a manager accepts a specific operations research solution, he should perform various tests of reasonableness, including historical comparisons. But at some point after making such tests, even in an ideal situation, the manager will have to accept as axiomatic that a scientific approach has intrinsic merit. We make three amplifying observations before leaving this conclusion.

First, even though a company may be convinced about the worthiness of the scientific method to aid decision-making, it need not accept the results of a particular operations research study as being valid. After all, the specific project may have been ill conceived or poorly executed.

Second, a trust in science does not imply the abandonment of hunch and intuition. On the contrary, the history of science itself is studded with cases of important discoveries made through chance, hunch, serendipity—even dreams. Behavioral scientists have not yet developed ways to induce such flashes of brilliance consistently. But most executives who use their hunches well also seem to possess a high level of knowledge and understanding about their activities. So the question is not when to apply science and when to rely on intuition, but rather how to combine the two effectively.

Third, the inherent difficulty of demonstrating that a suggested solution is a sure-fire improvement is not unique to operations research. Because of the inability to duplicate history, an act of faith is also required to accept any other proposed solution—including maintaining the status quo.

Past, present, and future. Although the term "operations research" was coined during World War II, the scientific origins of the subject date much further back. Primitive mathematical programming models were advanced by economists Quesnay in 1759 and Walras in 1874; more sophisticated economic models of a similar genre were proposed by Von Neumann in 1937 and Kantorovich in 1939. The *mathematical* underpinnings of linear models were established near the turn of the 19th century by Jordan in 1873, Minkowski in 1896, and Farkas in 1903. Another example of early development is the seminal work on dynamic models accomplished by Markov, who lived from 1856 to 1922. Two further illustrations are the innovative suggestions for economical inventory control, published in business and industrial engineering journals during the 1920's, and the pioneering studies of waiting line phenomena completed by Erlang, who lived from 1878 to 1929.

Even though these early starts received recognition and acclaim, only recently have mathematical models for decision analysis taken hold in business. Why? At least two factors are important. First, the competitive pressures of doing business have increased tremendously since World War II. Executives of large corporations now find it essential in maintaining profits to improve on the traditional ways of collecting and analyzing data. Second, the fantastic development and widespread adoption of high-speed electronic computers have fostered the growth of more sophisticated means for assessing decision alternatives.

There are many reasons to believe that the process of implementing operations-research-oriented systems will quicken. For example, new technological developments in what is called *time-shared computing* bring the power of an electronic computer literally into an executive's office. It is a pipedream to suppose that, in the next few years, most corporation presidents will have computer consoles on their desk tops for querying at a moment's notice. But already, financial vice presidents in several industrial companies do have such consoles to evaluate major investment alternatives. The future is getting closer all the time.

1.3 BOUNDARIES OF QUANTITATIVE ANALYSIS

As should be obvious, quantitative analysis can never provide the entire basis for *all* strategic decisions. It is inconceivable that the selection of a corporation president by a company's board of directors, for example, could (and should) ever rest solely on the manipulation of quantitative data, although some numerical information may be relevant.

It is probably less apparent that even when quantitative analysis is of central importance for a managerial decision process, an operations-research-oriented system never supplies all the information required for action, no matter how sophisticated the system's design. Furthermore, a truly successful implementation of an operations research system must apply behavioral as well as mathematical science, because the resultant system must interact with human beings. And finally, the very process of constructing an operations research system involves the exercise of judgment in addition to the logical manipulation of symbols and data. We discuss below each of these boundaries on quantitative analysis.

Problems solved and unsolved. As you read the chapters of this book, you will learn the ways an executive can be aided by the different operations research models that are treated. We therefore limit our comments in this section to more generally applicable remarks.

We have already mentioned that at the very inception of implementing an operations research system it is necessary for experienced executives to discern the relevance of the model. This alone is not enough, of course. Since the corporate owners hold these men responsible for wisely managing the firm, executives must continue to exercise their judgmental duty well beyond initial acceptance of the model. In one way or another, they must monitor the system to ensure that the underlying model remains valid, and in particular that it continues to be used properly to provide insights into the real decision-making problems of the company. (Managers must guard against thinking of the model as being reality, and hence of the accompanying answers as being sacrosanct.)

A newly implemented operations research system may well bring about a restructuring or an amplification of information. As a result, executives may act differently from how they might have acted without such information. There is no getting away from the fact, however, that an executive, not the model, takes the action.

In short, an operations research model is never sufficient unto itself; it cannot become entirely independent of judgment supplied by knowledgeable managers. This boundary on quantitative analysis is always manifest, because the number of questions that managers can pose is boundless, whereas the kinds of answers that a single model can provide are inherently limited.

Systems are for people. The above discussion also suggests that there is more to a successful implementation of an operations research system than the mere design of a mathematically correct model. Clearly, the system must operate in the larger context of managerial activity. The model must take account of the data sources, with respect both to quality of the data and to the goals and expertise of the people responsible for collecting the data. The system must also reflect the information requirements of the managers who review the analytic results, especially the needs for descriptive and interpretive commentary.

Most experienced practitioners of operations research know how to solve these so-called problems of communication. But there is a more fundamental limitation on quantitative analysis: rarely, if ever, is a suggested operations research system in perfect harmony with previously existing managerial attitudes and predilections. To ignore this fact is to invite internal conflict, subterfuge, and sometimes downright sabotage of a new system.

For example, a corporate planning model may call for the development of *realistic sales forecasts*. You would expect that marketing executives should ordinarily be entrusted to provide these figures; but the traditional orientation of the marketing department may make it impossible for these personnel to articulate anything other than *sales goals*. If the motivational drive of the sales organization is to set up targets and then try to meet them, and if it is then called upon to enunciate both targets *and* realistic forecasts, severe organizational conflicts may break out.

What can be done about this kind of limitation on quantitative analysis? Presently, considerable research is under way by behavioral scientists to discover successful means of instituting effective organizational change. Such developments in administrative science will certainly have a fundamental effect on the actual degree of success and speed of implementation of operations research systems.

The art of management science. The problem-solving ingenuity of professional operations researchers is still a limiting factor in the spread of quantitative analysis. Despite the enormous growth in the acceptance of management science models, there are preciously few "standard" applications. Even in areas of decision-making where the relevance of mathematical models has become well established, designing particular applications in specific companies requires significant skill on the part of the management scientist. Model formulations remain tailor-made to a large degree.

Conceivably, in the next decade some of the well-developed applications of operations research will have become so widely adopted that procedures for building these models can be codified, as many of the techniques in industrial engineering and managerial accounting have been. The unabated expansion of quantitative analysis into previously untouched areas of decision-making is so enormous, however, that the need for imaginative and talented problem-solving will remain undiminished for some time.

In other words, a considerable amount of "art" is still required for the successful practice of management science. This in turn means that whether you are a managerial user or a practitioner of operations research, you must have some facility with both the artistic and the scientific ingredients of the subject. A textbook, such as this one, can teach you many of the scientific aspects, and give you a modicum of practice in the art through the study of toy examples and the formulation and solution of small-scale problems. Unfortunately, however, it can do no more than make you aware of the artistic elements.

To help you understand this interplay between the art and the science of applying operations research, we offer an analogy with the fine arts. A knowledge of scientific principles, such as the chemistry of paint, the physiology of the eye, the physics of light, the psychology of color, and the laws of perspective, helps the artist master fully the craft of painting. Likewise, such knowledge also distinguishes the true connoisseur from the casual, albeit appreciative, Sunday museum-goer. By the same token, an understanding of the fundamentals of operations research is essential not only for the practitioner, but for the manager who wants to make truly effective use of the approach. If today's business world continues to become more complex, an executive will not be able to compete successfully in the role of a casual onlooker, or he himself may end up as a museum exhibit.

1.4 IMPORTANCE OF MODEL-BUILDING

If you study this text diligently, you will learn a considerable amount of mathematical technique. But a benefit that far transcends the mastering of specific algorithms is the facility you will gain in formulating, manipulating, and analyzing mathematical models. *Model-building is the essence of the operations research approach.* It is the counterpart to laboratory experimentation in the physical sciences.

Constructing a model helps you put the complexities and possible uncertainties attending a decision-making problem into a logical framework amenable to comprehensive analysis. Such a model clarifies the decision alternatives and their anticipated effects, indicates the data that are relevant for analyzing the alternatives, and leads to informative conclusions. In short, the model is a vehicle for arriving at a well-structured view of reality.

A mixed bag. The word "model" has several shades of meaning, all of which are relevant to operations research. First, a "model" may be a substitute representation of reality, such as a small-scale model airplane or locomotive. Second, "model" may imply some sort of idealization, often embodying a simplification of details, such as a model plan for urban redevelopment. Finally, "model" may be used as a verb, meaning to exhibit the consequential characteristics of the idealized representation. This notion conjures up in the mind those television commercials dramatizing how love and happiness will result after a single application of the sponsor's product.

In operations research, a model is almost always a mathematical, and necessarily an approximate, representation of reality. It must be formulated to capture the crux of the decision-making problem. At the same time, it must be sufficiently free of burdensome minor detail to lend itself to finding an improved solution that is capable of implementation. Striking a proper balance between reality and manageability is no mean trick in most applications, and for this reason model-building can be arduous.

You will find three pervasive and interrelated themes in operations research model-building. The first is an emphasis on optimization. Concentrating on decisions that are optimal according to one or more specified criteria has been the forcing wedge for attaining *improved* decision-making. Typically, the optimization is constrained, in that the values of the decision variables maximizing the stated objective function are restricted so as to satisfy certain technological restraints. Often, the model includes restrictions that mirror the impact of dynamic phenomena.

The second theme is derivation of the analytic properties of a mathematical model, including the sensitivity of an optimal solution to the model's parameters, the structural form of an optimal solution, and the operating characteristics of the solution. To illustrate, if you have a mathematical model leading to an inventory replenishment policy, you will want to know how the rule depends on forecasts of customer demand, the specification of the rule (such as, "when down to n, order again"), and the long-run frequency of stockouts and the average inventory level.

The third theme is explicit recognition of system interactions. One of the difficult tasks in writing an elementary text is to convey how, in real applications, the model-building effort is oriented toward management system considerations. The results of an operations research analysis must be integrated into the management information, decision-making, and control systems fabric of the organization. Operations research applications cannot be undertaken in isolation from the surrounding managerial environment. For these reasons, an operations research project should be regarded, at least in part, as a systems effort.

In one easy lesson. Many of the scientists who pioneered present-day applications of operations research are still alive and carry forward their individual banners of progress. One cannot help but be struck by the way each of these men treats nearly all of the significant decision-making problems he encounters by using his own specialty, such as linear programming, dynamic programming, inventory theory, or simulation, etc. This ability to apply a single solution technique or mathematical construct to a diverse range of problems—and to do so effectively—attests not only to the sheer genius of these innovators but to the flexibility of their approaches.

The experience of these scientists not withstanding, most operations research analysts, when faced with a difficult managerial decision problem, usually do not find it *self-evident* that a single solution technique or model is patently most appropriate. For example, an analysis of what markets a company should serve, what products it should manufacture, what investments it should undertake, or where it should locate its plants and warehouses rarely leads to an immediate selection of a linear programming, or a dynamic programming, or a simulation approach. This being the case, you may well wonder how you will go about building or selecting a model when faced with a particular decision problem.

We know that the notion of model-building, as described in a textbook, carries with it an aura of mystery. Regrettably, it is virtually impossible to provide you with a checklist for infallibly selecting and developing a model. But rest assured, there is considerable evidence that most students who have been trained in either the sciences, engineering, mathematics, business administration, or economics have little trouble building models in practice, provided they are inclined to do so. And nowadays, rarely, if ever, will you be faced with applying operations research unaided by an experienced practitioner. Therefore, you can count on being tutored at least the first time you use operations research.

1.5 PROCESS OF QUANTITATIVE ANALYSIS

We outline below the stages that are standard in applying quantitative analysis. An experienced practitioner takes these steps almost instinctively, and frequently does not attach formal labels to them. Actually, the components are not entirely distinct, and at any point in time, several of the phases proceed in concert. As a beginner, however, you will find it helpful to look over the entire process seriatim, so that you can plan ahead accordingly.

A prelude to a quantitative analysis of a decision problem should be a thorough qualitative analysis. This initial diagnostic phase aims at identifying what seem to be the critical factors—of course, subsequent analysis may demonstrate that some of these factors are not actually so significant as they first appear. In particular, it is important to attain a preliminary notion of what the principal decisions are, what the measures of effectiveness are among these choices, and what sorts of tradeoffs among these measures are likely to ensue in a comparison of the alternatives. There will be trouble ahead unless you get a good "feel" for the way the problem is viewed by the responsible decision-makers. Without this appreciation, you may encounter considerable difficulty in gaining acceptance and implementing your findings. What is worse, your results could very well be erroneous or beside the point.

Formulating the problem. The preceding diagnostic should yield a statement of the problem's elements. These include the controllable or decision variables, the uncontrollable variables, the restrictions or constraints on the variables, and the objectives for defining a good or improved solution.

In the formulation process, you must establish the confines of the analysis. Managerial decision-making problems typically have multifold impacts, some of them immediate and others remote (although perhaps equally significant). Determining the limits of a particular analysis is mostly a matter of judgment.

Building the model. Here is where you get down to the fine detail. You must decide on the proper data inputs and design the appropriate information outputs. You have to identify both the static and dynamic structural elements, and devise mathematical formulas to represent the interrelationships among these elements. Some of these interdependencies may be posed in terms of constraints or restrictions on the variables. Some may take the form of a probabilistic evolutionary system.

You also must choose a time horizon (possibly the "never-ending future") to evaluate the selected measures of effectiveness for the various decisions. The choice of this horizon in turn influences the nature of the constraints imposed, since, with a long enough horizon, it is usually possible to remove any short-run restrictions by an expenditure of resources.

Performing the analyses. Given the initial model, along with its parameters as specified by historical, technological, and judgmental data, you next calculate a mathematical solution. Frequently, a solution means values for the decision variables that optimize one of the objectives and give permissible levels of performance on any other of the objectives. The various mathematical techniques for arriving at solutions comprise much of the contents of this text.

As pointed out previously, if the formulation of the model is too complex and too detailed, then the computational task may surpass the capabilities of present-day computers. If the formulation is too simple, the solution may be patently unrealistic. Therefore, you can expect to redo some of the steps in the formulation, model-building, and analysis phases, until you obtain satisfactory results.

A major part of the analysis consists of determining the sensitivity of the solution to the model specifications, and in particular to the accuracy of the input data and structural assumptions. Because sensitivity testing is so essential a part of the validation process, you must be careful to build your model in such a way as to make this process computationally tractable.

Implementing the findings and updating the model. Unfortunately, most tyro management scientists fail to realize that implementation begins on the very first day of an operations research project. There is no "moment of truth" when the analyst states, "Here are my results," and the manager replies, "Aha! Now I fully understand. Thanks for giving me complete assurance about the correct decision."

We consider the entire process of implementation in Chap. 22. But we mention here the importance of having those executives who must act on the findings participate on the team that analyzes the problem. Otherwise, the odds are heavy that the project will be judged only as a provocative, but inconclusive, exercise.

It is common for an operations research model to be used repeatedly in the analysis of decision problems. Each time, the model must be revised to take account of both the specifics of the problem and current data. A good practitioner of operations research realizes that his model may have a long life, and so documents its details as well as plans for its updating.

What's it all about? Having learned the basic components of the quantitative analysis process, you should step back to see what the entire approach accomplishes.

The major effort is constructing a mathematical representation of a complicated situation, along with gathering the required data. The model is essentially approximate—elaborate enough to capture the essentials, yet gross enough to yield computable solutions. The balance between detail and tractability is found by a trial and error process, involving considerable examination of preliminary findings and extensive sensitivity analysis.

When operations research is applied in a planning context, the solution usually consists of a most favorable set of values for the decision variables, with some information as to the cost of deviating from these values. When management science is used for developing an operating system, such as a means for controlling inventories, then the solution consists of a set of decision rules. Often, these rules are embodied in a computer program. For an inventory system, the computer routines analyze historical demand data, permit judgmental adjustments if specified, signal when replenishment is to take place, and calculate the reorder amount.

Only rarely does an operations research solution represent a precise forecast of what will happen in the future. Such an accurate prediction would be of interest; but the crux of the decision problem is to select among alternatives, not to forecast. A well-built model makes a valid comparison among the alternatives. In case this distinction between accurately predicting an outcome and legitimately comparing alternatives is puzzling, consider the following illustration.

A company is about to decide whether or not to open a new plant in Europe. An operations research model is constructed that contains forecasts of sales, costs, and revenues; the resultant solution probably indicates anticipated production levels. If the economic advantage of opening this new plant is relatively insensitive to a range of reasonable values for the forecasted figures, then the company can make the correct expansion decision. It does *not* need to commit itself, at the same time, to production levels; they would be determined subsequently when more accurate demand forecasts are available.

1.6 OPERATIONS RESEARCH, LILLIPUTIAN STYLE

Before explaining how and why quantitative analyses have been valuable in aiding executive decision-making, we will examine a few highly simplified illustrations of operations research models. Since our only purpose is to show what mathematical decision models look like, we make no pretense about the realism of these formulations; you will find more practical versions in the subsequent chapters.

One-Potato, Two-Potato Problem. A frozen-food company processes potatoes into packages of French fries, hash browns, and flakes (for mashed potatoes). At the beginning of the manufacturing process, the raw potatoes are sorted by length and quality, and then allocated to the separate product lines.

The company can purchase its potatoes from two sources, which differ in their yields of various sizes and quality. These yield characteristics are displayed in Fig. 1.1. Observe that from Source 1, there is a 20% yield of French fries, a 20% yield of hash browns, and a 30% yield of flakes; the remaining 30% is unrecoverable waste. The figures for flakes and waste are also 30% for potatoes from Source 2, but the yield of French fries is relatively higher.

Product	Source 1	Source 2	Purchase Limitations
French fries	.2	.3	1.8
Hash browns	.2	.1	1.2
Flakes	.3	.3	2.4
Relative Profit	5	6	

FIGURE 1.1. Potato Yields for a Unit of Weight.

How many pounds of potatoes should the company purchase from each source? The answer depends, in part, on the relative profit contributions of the sources. These relative figures are calculated by adding the sales revenues associated with the yields for the separate products, and subtracting the costs of purchasing the potatoes, which may differ between the two sources. (We have used the term *relative profit contribution* because we are ignoring other variable expenses, such as sales and distribution costs. These depend only on the products and not the sources of the raw potatoes, and so do not affect the purchase allocation decision.) Suppose the relative profit contribution is 5 for Source 1 and 6 for Source 2. Even though Source 2 is more profitable, it does not follow that the company should purchase all of its potatoes from Source 2.

At least two other factors are relevant to the purchase decision: the maximum amount of each product that the company can sell, and the maximum amount that the company can manufacture—given its production facilities. To keep the

exposition simple, suppose that the two factors, in concert, imply that total purchases cannot exceed 1.8 for French fries, 1.2 for hash browns, and 2.4 for flakes,
where these constants are measured in terms of an appropriate unit of weight
(such as millions of pounds). These restrictions can be expressed mathematically as
follows.

Let P_1 denote the amount (in weight) of potatoes that will be purchased from

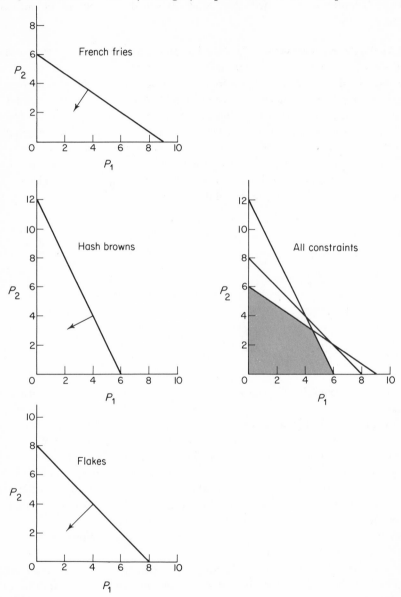

FIGURE 1.2. Feasible Purchasing Policies.

Source 1, and P_2 the amount from Source 2. Then the values for P_1 and P_2 are constrained by the linear inequalities

(1)
$$.2P_1 + .3P_2 \leq 1.8 \quad \text{for French fries}$$
$$.2P_1 + .1P_2 \leq 1.2 \quad \text{for hash browns}$$
$$.3P_1 + .3P_2 \leq 2.4 \quad \text{for flakes}$$
$$P_1 \geq 0 \quad \text{and} \quad P_2 \geq 0.$$

The nonnegativity restrictions $P_1 \geq 0$ and $P_2 \geq 0$ are imposed because a value such as $P_1 = -4$ would have no physical significance.

All the values for P_1 and P_2 satisfying (1) are shown in the shaded region in Fig. 1.2. Notice that each line in the diagram is represented by a restriction in (1) expressed as an equality. The arrow associated with each line shows the direction indicated by the inequality signs in (1). Explain why a pair of values for P_1 and P_2 that satisfies *both* the French fries and hash brown constraints will also satisfy the flakes constraint.

Optimal values for P_1 and P_2 are found by making the relative profit contribution as large as possible, consistent with the constraints. Therefore, the optimization problem is to

(2)   maximize $(5P_1 + 6P_2)$

subject to (1). In this simple problem, the solution can be exhibited graphically, as in Fig. 1.3.

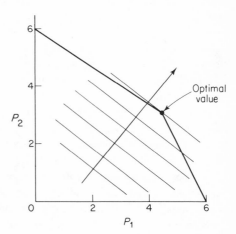

FIGURE 1.3. Relative
Profit.

Each of the parallel straight-line segments represents different combinations of P_1 and P_2 that give the same value for the linear objective function $5P_1 + 6P_2$. The highest segment still having a point in the feasible constraint region is the optimal value of the objective function, and such a point is an optimal solution. You can see in Fig. 1.3 that there is only one optimal solution in this example; it occurs at the intersection of the French fries and hash brown constraints. Con-

sequently, you can calculate the optimal values by solving the associated simultaneous linear equations

(3)
$$.2P_1 + .3P_2 = 1.8 \quad \text{for French fries}$$
$$.2P_1 + .1P_2 = 1.2 \quad \text{for hash browns.}$$

Verify that the optimal answers are $P_1 = 4.5$ and $P_2 = 3$, as shown in Fig. 1.3,
giving an objective-function value of 40.5.

This problem illustrates what is termed a *linear programming model*. Real applications of linear programming usually involve hundreds of constraints and thousands
of variables. You will learn how to formulate and solve such models in Chaps.
2 through 7.

Secretary Problem. An executive wishes to hire a new secretary, and
is about to ask a placement service to send qualified girls for him to interview. He
has found from past experience that he can determine from an interview whether
a girl, if hired, will turn out to be terrific, good, or just fair. He assigns a relative
value of 3 to a terrific secretary, 2 to a good one, and 1 to a fair one. His previous
experience also leads him to believe that there is a .2 chance of interviewing a
girl who will be a terrific secretary, a .5 chance that she will be a good one, and
a .3 chance that she will be a fair one.

He wishes to see only three girls at most. Unfortunately, if he does not hire a
girl immediately after an interview, she will take another job; hence, he has to
decide right away.

If the first girl he sees is terrific, he will hire her immediately, of course. And if
she is fair, he has nothing to lose by interviewing a second girl. But if the first girl
looks good, then he is not sure what to do. If he passes her by, he may end up with
only a fair secretary. Yet if he hires her, he surrenders the chance of finding a
terrific girl. Similarly, if he chooses to see a second girl, he will again face a difficult
decision in the event that she turns out to be good.

The selection problem can be displayed conveniently by a so-called *decision tree*,
shown in Fig. 1.4. The circled nodes represent the interviewed girls, and the
branches from these nodes show the chance events and their probabilities. The
boxes indicate where a decision must be made, and the number at the end of a
branch gives the relative value of stopping the decision process at that point.

The problem of finding an optimal decision strategy can be solved by what is
termed *dynamic programming*, and in particular, by a process known as *backward
induction*. You will study dynamic programming models and solution techniques in
Chaps. 8 through 12, and Chaps. 17 and 18. The solution process is so simple in
this example that you can compute the optimal hiring strategy very easily, as we
have done below.

Suppose that the executive does end up interviewing, and hence hiring, a third
girl. Then the expected value associated with the uncertain event is

(4)
$$3(.2) + 2(.5) + 1(.3) = 1.9.$$

In other words, the average value of a girl selected at random for an interview is

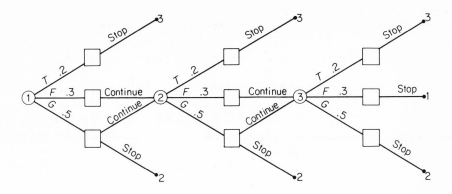

Legend:

T Terrific
F Fair
G Good

FIGURE 1.4. Decision Tree for Secretary Problem.

1.9. Assume that this expectation legitimately represents the executive's evaluation of the chancey event. Mark the number 1.9 above the circled Node 3 in Fig. 1.4.

Next consider what happens if the executive does interview a second girl, and she turns out to be good. If he decides to stop, then he obtains a value 2. But if he continues, then he can expect to receive only the value 1.9. So he should stop when the second girl looks good. Put an × on the branch indicating "Continue" when the second secretary is good; this signifies not to take that action.

Now you are ready to determine the correct decision if the first girl looks good. By stopping, the executive would obtain the value 2. But if he continues, then the expected value associated with the chancey outcome of the second interview, and possibly the third, is

$$(5) \qquad 3(.2) + 2(.5) + 1.9(.3) = 2.17.$$

The first term in (5) is for the event of seeing a terrific secretary, whom he hires; the second term is for the event of seeing a good secretary, whom he hires, as you already determined in the preceding paragraph; and the third term is for the event of seeing a fair secretary, and consequently continuing to the third chancey event that has a value of 1.9, given in (4). Since 2.17 is larger than 2, the executive should pass up the first girl if she turns out to be good. Mark 2.17 above the circled Node 2 in Fig. 1.4, and put an × on the branch indicating "Stop" when the first secretary is good.

To summarize, the optimal policy is to stop after the first interview only if the girl is terrific, and to continue after the second interview only if the girl is fair. The overall expected value of the interviewing process, given that the executive acts optimally, is

$$(6) \qquad 3(.2) + 2.17(.5) + 2.17(.3) = 2.336.$$

Explain why. Mark this number above the circled Node 1 in Fig. 1.4. Since the quantity 1.9, calculated in (4), also represents the expected value if the executive interviews only a single secretary and hires her, the difference $(2.336 - 1.9 = .436)$ is the incremental value from interviewing as many as two more girls.

Where-or-When Production Problem. The name of this problem arises from the observation that the associated mathematical model has several interpretations. One is in terms of deciding optimal production levels at each of several plants in a single time period; another is in terms of choosing optimal production levels at a single plant in each of several time periods. (The model also can be interpreted as a combination of the two problems, that is, as a where-and-when problem.)

Starting with the multiplant version, suppose a company has N plants, and must manufacture a total of D units of a single item during a stated time period. Hence, letting x_t denote the amount of production at Plant t, the levels $x_1, x_2, \ldots, x_N$ must satisfy the constraints

(7) $$x_1 + x_2 + \cdots + x_N = D \quad \text{and all} \quad x_t \geq 0.$$

Assume that the cost of producing x_t at Plant t is given by $(1/c_t)x_t^2$, where $c_t > 0$ is known from historical accounting information. Consequently, optimal values for the x_t are those that

(8) $$\text{minimize} \left(\frac{x_1^2}{c_1} + \frac{x_2^2}{c_2} + \cdots + \frac{x_N^2}{c_N} \right)$$

subject to (7).

This optimization problem can be solved by dynamic programming methods as well as by some simple nonlinear programming techniques, which are discussed in Chaps. 14 and 15. The numerical answers can be easily computed from the insightful formula

(9) $$\text{optimal } x_t = \frac{c_t \cdot D}{c_1 + c_2 + \cdots + c_N} \quad \text{for } t = 1, 2, \ldots, N,$$

which yields the associated minimum cost

(10) $$\frac{D^2}{c_1 + c_2 + \cdots + c_N} \quad \text{(optimal policy)}.$$

Turning to the multiperiod version, suppose you interpret x_t as being the level of production in a single plant during Period t. Notice that in this version, all the costs are due to production, and no storage costs are incurred while the units are inventoried from Period 1 to the end of Period N, when the demand requirement D must be met. Given this view, you can state what would be the optimal value for x_t if the preceding levels $x_1, x_2, \ldots, x_{t-1}$ were already determined [not necessarily by (9)], namely,

(11) $$\text{optimal conditional } x_t = \frac{c_t \cdot (D - x_1 - x_2 - \cdots - x_{t-1})}{c_t + c_{t+1} + \cdots + c_N}$$

$$(x_1, x_2, \cdots, x_{t-1} \text{ are specified}).$$

As you can verify, calculating $x_1, x_2, \ldots, x_N$ recursively (that is, successively, one by one, starting with x_1) from (11) yields the same values as computing each of them from (9).

Economic Order Quantity Problem. In Chaps. 9 and 19, and Appendix II you will study a variety of inventory replenishment models that have proved successful in practice. The formulation below is perhaps the simplest such model. Its precise assumptions are only rarely satisfied in real life. Nevertheless, the resultant solution turns out to be sufficiently close to optimal for many practical situations as to make it a very useful approximation.

Consider a company that consumes (or sells) an item at the rate of, say, M units per week. For simplicity, suppose there is no uncertainty about this consumption. Hence, if the inventory level is kM units, then this stock is depleted in exactly k weeks. Further, suppose the rate M is unchanging over time, so that the company must regularly place a replenishment order. The decision problem is to determine the most economical order quantity. (Assuming that the delivery time for an order is also known exactly, each replenishment action is initiated early enough so that the order arrives just when the inventory level falls to zero.)

Let the order quantity be denoted by Q. Then the level of inventory can be pictured by the sawtooth pattern shown in Fig. 1.5. Observe that each time a replenishment arrives, the inventory level shoots up by the order quantity Q. Then the level diminishes, as shown by the downward slope of the sawtooth, which equals $-M$.

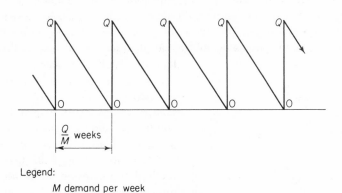

Legend:

   M demand per week
   Q order quantity

FIGURE 1.5. Pattern of Inventory Levels.

An optimal order quantity strikes a balance between the costs associated with replenishing and with holding inventory. Specifically, assume that a fixed setup cost K is incurred each time an order is placed, that a purchase cost c is paid for each item ordered, and that a holding cost h is assessed for each unit of inventory held per week. The setup cost is related to the effort expended in placing and receiving the order. The holding cost is associated with storage, insurance, and the capital tied up in inventory.

Let the economic criterion of effectiveness be measured as average cost per week. Then the contribution due to setup costs is $K(M/Q)$, since there are M/Q setups per week. The contribution due to purchase costs is cM, since M items are consumed per week. And the contribution due to holding costs is $h(Q/2)$, since $Q/2$ is the average level of inventory, as you can see in Fig. 1.5. Adding the components, you have

$$(12) \qquad \text{average cost per week} \equiv \text{AC} = \frac{KM}{Q} + cM + \frac{hQ}{2}.$$

The economic order quantity that minimizes AC is

$$(13) \qquad \text{optimal } Q = \sqrt{\frac{2KM}{h}},$$

which can be found by setting the derivative of AC with respect to Q equal to 0, and solving for Q. It follows from (13) that the optimal order quantity only doubles when the demand rate quadruples. Also note that the optimal quantity is determined by the *ratio* of setup to holding costs.

OR Airline Problem. The One-Ride Airline Company is opening a reservation service to be located in a suburban shopping center. A passenger making reservations will be able to telephone the office and state his request. The OR Airline Company wants to decide how many telephone lines to install for answering reservation calls. It can easily compute the telephone and personnel expenses that vary with the number of lines. But it also wishes to compare the level of service for several different numbers of lines. In particular, suppose the company seeks to determine the percentage of time all the lines will be busy and the average length of such busy periods.

This sort of analysis is classified as *queuing* or *waiting line theory*, and is explained in Chaps. 20, 21, and Appendix III. We could construct an explicit model and subject it to rigorous mathematical analysis, but instead, we explain here how the method of simulation can be used to determine the service figures. To keep the explanation easy, we present only a rudimentary technique, and suggest that you read Chap. 21 for a more detailed exposition of the simulation approach.

Suppose the company obtains data showing the statistical frequencies of minutes between successive incoming telephone calls. As a first approximation, assume that

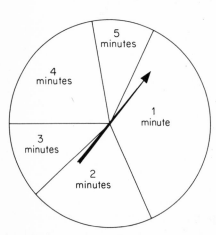

FIGURE 1.6. The Distribution of Telephone Interarrival Times.

these successive interarrival times are completely independent (such independence does not hold precisely if, for example, a passenger calls up, finds the lines busy, and immediately redials the number). A convenient way to summarize this distribution is to use a pie diagram, such as the one in Fig. 1.6, where we assume for simplicity that the time between incoming calls never exceeds 5 minutes.

Imagine a pointer, or spinner, affixed to the center of the pie diagram—the mechanism would look something like a wheel-of chance at carnivals, or a device that is often included in a child's game to determine how many advances a player's piece may take at each turn. You can simulate the traffic of incoming calls by giving the pointer a succession of sharp spins, and jotting down the resultant sequence of interarrival times.

In addition, suppose the company has a frequency distribution of the number of minutes that incoming calls require. Assume that these service times are independent of each other and of the interarrival times. Then another pie diagram and spinner mechanism can be constructed for generating the service times.

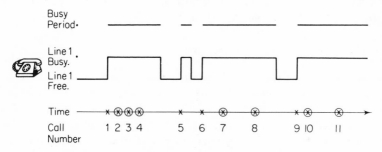

FIGURE 1.7. Simulated History for One Telephone Line.

You are now ready to simulate the system. To begin, suppose there is only a single telephone line. Then a simulated history may look like that in Fig. 1.7. The instants of incoming calls are recorded with ×'s on the time axis, and are determined by successive spins of the pointer mechanism for interarrival times. The telephone line becomes busy as soon as the first call arrives. The length of the busy period is determined by a spin of the pointer mechanism for service times. Notice that the calls arriving at the instants circled in Fig. 1.7 are not answered because the single telephone line is busy. You can obtain a good estimate of the percentage of time the line will be busy and the average length of a busy period by calculating the corresponding statistics for a fairly long simulated run.

Suppose next that there are two telephone lines. Then the same sequence of incoming calls can lead to a service history like that in Fig. 1.8. Observe that more incoming calls are answered. Here a busy period is defined to be a length of time during which both telephone lines are tied up. Note how these periods are shorter in Fig. 1.8 than in Fig. 1.7 for the particular history. As you can see, the same approach can be used to estimate service for any number of lines.

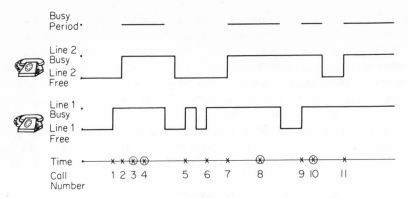

FIGURE 1.8. Simulated History for Two Telephone Lines.

Commentary. As we stated at the beginning of this section, the above examples illustrate how mathematical models are constructed to analyze decision problems. We have made no attempt to be "realistic" in these examples. But as you continue reading this book, you will discover how to build practical models, and learn ways to solve problems with them.

1.7 AT THE END OF THE RAINBOW

Today, virtually every major corporation employs personnel who are responsible for applying operations research. Usually, these people constitute a staff group at headquarters level. The group often reports to the controller, the chief financial officer, or the head of corporate planning; but with growing frequency, companies are also assigning operations researchers to report directly to line managers. In a parallel fashion, operations research activity has enjoyed a widespread growth within federal and local governments, as well as in other nonprofit organizations. This section tells why management science has succeeded so well.

Merits of a rational process. Obviously, executives must and do make decisions all the time. For a particular situation, an operations research model *may* yield the very same conclusion that an experienced manager would arrive at solely on intuitive grounds. Therefore, the benefits of using operations research have to be evaluated in terms of its long-run impact on the entire managerial process.

The proper comparison is well represented by the question, "If a company does not use operations research to guide the decision process, then what will it use, and will the answers be consistently as good?" Corporations that apply operations research—even when the approach does not meet all of the company's initial expectations—find that analyzing complicated managerial problems this way is a sounder method than traditional means. This assertion is amply borne out by the steadily increasing support given to operations research in both the private and public sectors.

Qualities inherent in this particular rational approach make it a valuable method, regardless of whether a company's operations research personnel attain the highest level of accomplishment for a specific project. These benefits include:

- Emphasis on assessing the system-wide interactions and ramifications of decision alternatives. Intrinsic in an operations research approach is the construction of a model that synthesizes the segments of an enterprise that are affected by a decision choice. Each individual part is constructed by personnel who are the most knowledgeable about the relevant data.
- Impetus to developing a full range of decision alternatives. The number of action possibilities that can be analyzed increases tremendously by the application of mathematics and computers.
- Focus on resolving the critical issues. The approach proceeds in the fashion of establishing implications of the form, "if Hypothesis H is true and Action A is taken, then Result R will occur." The method fosters interdepartmental communication. As a consequence, clashes of opinion within an organization can be sorted into disagreements over the probable truth of different hypotheses, and over the assumptions used in deriving the implications of different actions.

Important ancillary benefits emerge from the direction provided by the model for gathering data, quantifying the value of additional information, and documenting factual knowledge that may be required in subsequent decision analyses.

Having listed several of the important merits stemming from the rational analytic process of operations research, we hasten to point out that the advantages will occur to a greater or lesser degree, depending on the skill used in carrying out the study.

Managerial cutting edge. The preceding paragraphs dealt with *why* operations research is helpful in analyzing decision problems. Now we discuss *how* the approach is beneficial. We have classified the ways into four somewhat arbitrary and partially overlapping categories:

i. *Better Decisions.* Frequently, operations research models yield actions that do improve on intuitive decision-making. A situation may be so complex (because of intricate interrelationships among decisions, voluminous data pertinent to operations, and uncertainties of market activity) that the human mind can never hope to assimilate all the significant factors without the aid of operations-research-guided computer analysis.

Of course, in the past managers have made decisions in these situations without the aid of operations research. They had to. But the depth of their understanding and the quality of their decisions improve with the application of such models, as considerable experience has shown. Particular decisions may ultimately turn out to be wrong, but the improved decision-making process reduces the risk of making such erroneous decisions.

ii. *Better Coordination.* Sometimes operations research has been instrumental in bringing order out of chaos. The following example, drawn from an actual application, illustrates what can happen.

During special campaigns, a food manufacturer runs advertising that significantly increases sales volume. But manufacturing production facilities are limited, the supply of the foodstuff is limited, and the sales response is often erratic. In the past, consequently, the marketing and manufacturing divisions have been at opposite poles in terms of cooperative actions. An operations-research-oriented planning model becomes a vehicle for coordinating marketing decisions within the limitations imposed on manufacturing capabilities.

iii. *Better Control.* The managements of large organizations recognize that it is extremely costly to require continuous executive supervision over routine decisions. Operations research approaches combining historical experience with the scientific method have resulted in standardized and reliable procedures for handling everyday activities and for signaling dangerous trends. Executives have thereby gained new freedom to devote their attention to more pressing matters, except for those unusual circumstances which, when they arise, necessitate reviewing the the course of everyday action. The most frequently adopted applications in this category deal with production scheduling and inventory replenishment.

iv. *Better Systems.* Often, an operations research study is initiated to analyze a particular decision problem, such as whether to open a new warehouse. Afterwards, the approach is further developed into a system to be employed repeatedly. Thus the cost of undertaking the first application may produce benefits that are longer lasting than originally envisioned.

Where the action is. By this time, applications of operations research are so common in industry and government, and so diverse in the functional areas of decison-making, that we cannot hope to provide a complete survey. To give you some idea, however, we mention that there are numerous applications in industries such as aircraft, apparel, chemicals, cement, glass, computers, electronics, farm and industrial machinery, food, metal manufacturing and products, mining, motor vehicles, paper and wood products, petroleum refining, and pharmaceuticals, as well as in commercial banks, insurance companies, merchandising firms, public utilities, and transportation companies.

Depending on the industry, the applications pertain to extraction of natural resources, manufacturing, transportation and warehousing, plant size and location, inventory management, scheduling of men and machines, forecasting, new product development, marketing, advertising, cash management and finance, portfolio management, mergers, and both short- and long-range corporate planning.

Most companies' early operations research projects deal with monthly or quarterly scheduling, annual planning, inventory control, and other fairly well-defined areas of decision-making. After the operations research group demonstrates its capability in these areas, a company then applies its operations research talents to the study of high-level strategic problems, such as selecting new plant sites, entering new markets, acquiring overseas affiliates, and so forth.

Operations research has provided a significant advance in the techniques of long-range strategic planning. Even senior executives have difficulty piecing together all the important considerations involved in a well-designed long-range plan. What is more, the operations research approach lends itself to the formulation of contingency plans, that is, a complete strategy indicating which courses of action are appropriate for various future events. In addition, the findings may include directions for obtaining and then utilizing critical information about such future events. In this way, the operations research model suggests the actions to be taken immediately and the ones to be postponed, and when to undertake a reassessment. For these reasons, more and more frequently, boards of directors of large corporations find strategic proposals being justified on the basis of extensive operations research studies.

*Profitable applications in nonprofit organizations. The growth of operations research in government and nonprofit corporations has been phenomenal. A long succession of military applications began during World War II. Now governmental applications involve health, education, and welfare; air and highway traffic control; air and water pollution; police and fire protection; voter and school redistricting; and annual planning and budgeting by program, to name only a few.

Certainly, much of the credit for the great impetus in the adoption of operations research in the public sector goes to the RAND Corporation (located in Santa Monica). Many fundamental concepts and techniques in operations research can be traced to the innovative ideas of RAND scientists. At present, there are several other research organizations similar to RAND serving the Federal Government; a number of these (RAND among them) work on state and city management problems as well as on military projects.

How different is operations research applied in the public sector from that used in the private sector? The answer depends on the aspects of operations research you are considering. Specifically, the problem-solving characteristics, the ensuing benefits, the emphasis on model-building, the limitations of the scientific method, and the analytic process discussed above, all hold with equal validity in applications to governmental and nonprofit organizations.

There does seem to be a noticeable difference, however, in the sorts of solution techniques used. For example, linear programming has gained widespread acceptance in industry, but is employed only occasionally in governmental planning. The opposite has been true of simulation models.

Sometimes it is claimed that the lack of clear-cut objective functions to be optimized in nonprofit organizations raises a significant difference between applications in the private and public sectors. Industry most often measures improvement in terms of contribution to profit, but this criterion is by no means the only relevant one for decision-making. Businesses are always compromising among different objectives. Therefore, we feel that the absence of a profit measure is less important than it might seem at first glance.

Probably the most important difference between the public and private sectors concerns the exercise of decision-making responsibilities. The organizational structures of big corporations are complex, and the authority for taking actions may not always be precisely defined. But these structures are simple indeed in comparison with most governmental structures. The difference can be stated this way. In a commercial company, there is no one left to pass the buck to, once the necessity for making a decision reaches top management (or the board of directors). In an organization such as the Federal Government, even the President's decisions are subject to the review of—and thus become partly the responsibility of— Congressmen, who, along with the President, are publicly elected. Understand that diffuse responsibilities and authority only make it *difficult* to apply operations research outside of industry. As the record shows, plenty of applications are being made in governmental and nonprofit organizations.

1.8 IN THE BEGINNING...

Studying linear optimization models is an excellent way to begin learning about operations research. Hence, this subject is taken up in the next chapter and several to follow. As you read about linear and other models throughout the text, try to keep in mind the boundaries and the process of quantitative analysis (which we discussed in Secs. 1.3 and 1.4). By so doing, you will maintain a perspective on the strengths and limitations of operations research.

REVIEW EXERCISES

1 Using the stages in the process of quantitative analysis as outlined in Sec. 1.5, explain how you would apply such an approach to the decision-making problems below. Also state what you think would be the merits of applying a rational process and what would be the associated managerial cutting edge (as discussed in Sec. 1.7).

   (a) Exploring and drilling for crude oil.
   (b) Harvesting of timber lands.
   (c) Assigning customer orders to each of several steel rolling mills in a large steel corporation.
   (d) Establishing field warehouses for the distribution of canned food.
   (e) Locating and deciding the capacity of an ore reduction plant.
   (f) Market-testing a new packaged soap product.
   (g) Locating new sites for grocery stores.
   (h) Establishing an advertising budget for the promotion of a soft drink.
   (i) Determining the size of a bank balance for an aircraft company.
   (j) Selecting a portfolio of securities in an insurance company.

(k) Deciding whether to merge two railroads.
(l) Planning for future growth in a computer manufacturing company.
(m) Deciding whether to automate a post office.
(n) Allocating funds to urban renewal projects.
(o) Selecting an intercontinental ballistic weapon system.
(p) Designing an effective national welfare program.
(q) Selecting a route for a superhighway.
(r) Establishing a single nationwide telephone number for emergency police services.
(s) Determining the number and location of fire stations in a city.
(t) Deciding whether to unify two separate school districts.
(u) Allocating funds among participating agencies in the United Fund.

One-Potato, Two-Potato Problem (Sec. 1.6). In exercises 2 through 5, draw a diagram showing the feasible purchasing policies and the optimal solution. Also calculate optimal values for P_1 and P_2 and the associated value of the objective function. Assume all the data as given in Fig. 1.1 except for the specific change indicated below in each separate part of the exercise.

2 (a) Purchase limitation on French fries of 1.7. Of 1.9.
   (b) Purchase limitation on hash browns of 1.1. Of 1.3.
   (c) Purchase limitations on French fries of 1.7 and on hash browns of 1.1.
   (d) Purchase limitations on French fries of 1.9 and on hash browns of 1.3.
   (e) Purchase limitation on flakes of 2.5. Of 2.3. Of 2.1. Of 1.5.

3 (a) Relative profit of a unit from Source 2 of 7. Of 8.
   (b) Relative profit of a unit from Source 1 of 4.
   (c) Relative profit of a unit from Source 1 of 6 and from Source 2 of 2.
   (d) Relative profit of a unit from Source 1 of 6 and from Source 2 of 3.

4 (a) Yield of .25 French fries from a unit of weight from Source 1.
   (b) Yield of .2 French fries from a unit of weight from Source 2.
   (c) Yield of .3 hash browns from a unit of weight from Source 1.
   (d) Yield of .15 hash browns from a unit of weight from Source 2.

5 An additional restriction that
   (a) $P_1 \leq 4$.
   (b) $P_2 \leq 2.5$.
   (c) $P_1 \leq 4$ and $P_2 \leq 2.5$.
   (d) $P_1 \geq 5$.
   (e) $P_2 \geq 4$.
   (f) $P_1 \geq 5$ and $P_2 \geq 4$.

Secretary Problem (Sec. 1.6). In exercises 6 through 11, draw a decision tree, and find an optimal interviewing policy. Assume all the data as given in Fig. 1.4 except for the specific change indicated below in each separate part of the exercise.

6 The executive is willing to interview up to four girls. What is the incremental value of interviewing as many as three *more* girls instead of only one? What is the incremental value of interviewing as many as four girls instead of a maximum of three?

7 The executive is willing to interview up to five girls. What is the incremental value of interviewing as many as four *more* girls instead of only one?

8 The relative value of a terrific girl is 4. What is the incremental value of interviewing as many as two *more* girls instead of one?

9 (a) There is a .2 chance that an interviewed girl will be a good secretary, and a .6 chance that she will be a fair one. What is the incremental value of interviewing as many as two *more* girls instead of one?
  (b) There is a .1 chance that an interviewed girl will be a terrific secretary, a .4 chance that she will be good, and a .5 chance that she will be just fair. What is the incremental value of interviewing as many as two *more* girls instead of one?

10 (a) There is a *cost* of .15 for each interview.
   (b) There is a *cost* of .15 for each interview and the executive is willing to interview up to four girls.

*11 (a) What is the expected number of girls the executive interviews?
   (b) If the executive is willing to interview up to four girls, what is the expected number of girls the executive interviews? (Utilize your answer from exercise 1.6.)

Where-or-When Production Problem (Sec. 1.6). In exercises 12 through 16, assume the following data except for the specific change indicated below in each separate part of the exercise:

$$D = 100, \ N = 4, \ c_1 = 1, \ c_2 = 2, \ c_3 = 3, \ c_4 = 4.$$

Find the optimal value of each x_t and the associated minimum cost.

12 Assume the data as given above.

13 Let $D = 200$.

14 (a) Let $c_1 = 3$.
   (b) Let $c_4 = 2$.
   (c) Let $c_1 = 3$ and $c_4 = 2$.
   (d) Let $c_1 = c_2 = c_3 = c_4 = 2.5$.

15 (a) Let $N = 5$ and $c_5 = 5$.
   (b) Let $N = 5$ and $c_1 = c_2 = c_3 = c_4 = c_5 = 2$.

16 (a) Let $x_2 = 36$.
   (b) Let $x_2 = 4$.

Economic Order Quantity Problem (Sec. 1.6). In exercises 17 through 20, assume the following data except for the specific change indicated below in each separate part of the exercise: consumption rate $M = 5$, setup cost $K = 90$, and holding cost per unit $h = 4$. To simplify computations, let purchase cost $c = 0$.

17 Find the optimal economic order quantity, the associated average cost per week, and the corresponding number of weeks between successive orders.

(a) Assume the data as given above. Then draw a graph of the average cost per week as a function of the order quantity Q. Indicate the optimal value for Q on your graph as well as the minimum average cost per week. Draw a graph of the sawtooth pattern of inventory levels for the optimal policy, analogous to that in Fig. 1.5.

(b) Let $h = 16$.

(c) Let $K = 360$.

(d) Let $M = 20$.

(e) Let $h = 16$ and $K = 360$.

(f) Let $h = 16$ and $M = 20$.

(g) Let $K = 360$ and $M = 20$.

*18 (a) What is the average cost per week if you use an order quantity that is 10% larger than optimal?

(b) What is the average cost per week if you use an order quantity that is 10% smaller than optimal?

*19 (a) What is the *actual* average cost per week if you use the order quantity that is optimal for $h = 4$, but in reality $h = 16$?

(b) What is the *actual* average cost per week if you use the order quantity that is optimal for $h = 16$, but in reality $h = 4$?

*20 (a) What is the *actual* average cost per week if you use the order quantity that is optimal for $M = 5$, but in reality $M = 20$?

(b) What is the *actual* average cost per week if you use the order quantity that is optimal for $M = 20$, but in reality $M = 5$?

OR Airline Problem (Sec. 1.6). Suppose you simulate the arrivals and service of telephone calls as follows. Toss four coins and assign an interarrival time of three minutes when there are four heads, two minutes when there are three heads, one minute when there are two heads, four minutes when there is one head, and five minutes when there are no heads (four tails). For each call determine an associated service time (which occurs if the caller does not find all the telephone lines busy) by tossing two coins and letting the service time be one minute when there are two heads, two minutes when there is one head, and three minutes when there are no heads (two tails).

21 In each experiment below, simulate 20 calls. Calculate the average time between calls, the average service time of those calls that are answered, the number of calls not answered (because all the lines are busy), the fraction of time that all the lines are busy, and the average length of time when all the lines are busy. In performing the calculations, assume that all the lines are free at the start, that the system shuts down two minutes after the twentieth call (regardless of whether or not it is answered), and that no more arrivals occur within this final two-minute interval. Also, draw a diagram (such as in Figs. 1.7 and 1.8) to display the simulated history. Let the number of telephone lines be

(a) One.

(b) Two.

(c) Three.

*(d) Calculate the theoretical average time between successive arrivals.

*(e) Calculate the theoretical average service time, assuming that all calls are answered.

CONTENTS

CHAPTER 2

Formulation of Linear
Optimization Models

2.1 INTRODUCTION

Unquestionably, linear optimization models are among the most commercially successful applications of operations research; in fact, there is considerable evidence that they rank highest in economic impact. This chapter initiates your study of linear models.

Qualitative analysis. To set the stage, suppose we consider the operations of a large firm in a process-oriented industry such as petroleum, chemicals, metal working, or wood products. Specifically, let us choose a major integrated oil company. As depicted in Fig. 2.1, the critical decisions in this type of firm relate to the processes of:

- Exploring for oil deposits
- Producing crude oil
- Exchanging proprietary crude oil for other companies' crudes at different locations
- Purchasing additional crude
- Shipping the crude to any of several refineries
- Cracking the crude into several blending stocks
- Combining the stocks into several dozen petroleum products
- Shipping the manufactured products from the refineries to marketing areas.

A decision to install a new cracking unit at a refinery, of course, affects the refinery's operating efficiency. But equally important, such a decision can and often does have a decided impact on all the other operations listed. The design characteristics of the new unit influence the selection and allocation of crudes, as well as

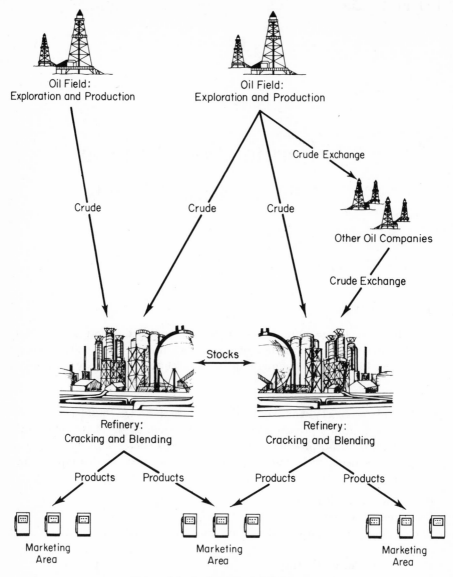

FIGURE 2.1. An Integrated Oil Company.

the relative composition and distribution of marketable products. Similarly, expanding the share of the market for gasoline products in a particular region has implications for setting refinery operating levels, for making crude-exchange agreements with other oil companies, and for deciding where to concentrate exploration activities.

For another illustration, we may look at a lumber manufacturing firm that owns raw timber resources, processes cut logs into various wood products, and distri-

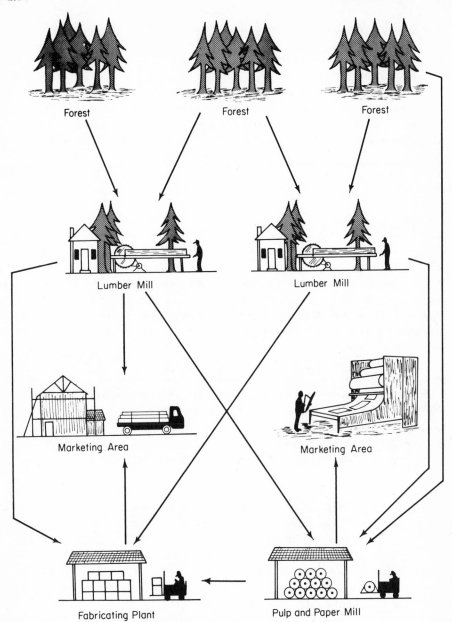

Forest   Forest   Forest

Lumber Mill   Lumber Mill

Marketing Area   Marketing Area

Fabricating Plant   Pulp and Paper Mill

FIGURE 2.2. Wood Products Firm.

butes these commodities over a widespread geographical area, as shown in Fig. 2.2. Just as with the petroleum firm, all strategic decisions must reflect the inherent constraint stemming from the nature of the raw material: any single log yields only a limited amount of each grade of sawn timber. To earn profits, the firm must carefully allocate these various grades to the different types of finished products.

As a practical matter, then, the company must produce a slate of products that fully utilizes the material in the logs; but within this mode of operation there is still considerable discretion for deciding the particular composition of the final products slate.

Although both of these illustrations were simplified, the resource allocation decision problems posed have close counterparts in actual companies. The complexities to be found in real situations magnify the effort required to provide a scientific economic analysis of various decision consequences. Nevertheless, these very decision problems are now being solved in many major companies with the aid of linear optimization models, usually called **linear programming models.**

Profit potential. Why do successful companies bother to use such mathematical aids? Are not management experience, know-how, and intuition sufficient to ensure sound decisions? Executives with a profit-making outlook have long realized that the comprehensive planning of future operations is important to their company's success, and it is a rare manager who neglects such planning. In a large enterprise, however, merely recording the factual information required for analyzing significant decisions can entail a tremendous effort. Consequently, available manpower for testing the likely economic impact of a plan is a limiting factor for a company.

As you will see, linear programming provides a breakthrough in amplifying the analytic abilities of a manager and his staff. The mathematical models you will study enable an executive to evaluate a wider range of resource allocation plans than he would ever have thought possible. As we pointed out in Chap. 1, it is important to realize that the results of these tests are not meant to substitute for the manager's experience and intuition. To the contrary, they provide the precise and comprehensive data he requires to apply his knowledge effectively.

The way it is. The purpose of this chapter is to introduce you to a variety of optimizing problems that lend themselves to a linear model formulation. In order not to detract from this purpose, the chapter will not deal with the numerical techniques for solving the models. That topic is treated in detail in Chap. 4.

If you want to learn how to apply linear programming, sooner or later you have to face up to the fact that real situations are much more complex than the One-Potato, Two-Potato Problem given in Chap. 1. Several other Lilliputian examples are in the Formulation Exercises at the end of the chapter; these will offer you an opportunity to refresh your abilities in writing and graphing linear relationships. But we think there is no point in our dillydallying with misleadingly simple toy problems. You need to become accustomed to models having more than two or three unknowns and restrictions, and the quicker, the better. Consequently, we have chosen to explain more typical-looking linear programming problems.

By the same token, you must learn to express decent-sized problems in algebraic terms, since, with plentiful data, graphical representations are out of the question.

In a real application you will have to rely on employing an electronic calculator to find a numerical solution. Such computer routines require that you specify the model in an algebraic fashion. Therefore, you will need facility in translating verbal problem statements into mathematical symbols. In short, you are about to see linear programming like it is.

The first two examples deal with product- and feed-mix selections, and are prototypes of many actual applications. The third example treats fluid-blending; it includes considerations found in both the mix selection problems and also imposes additional restrictions based on the manufacturing technology.

All three examples are called *static models* because they deal with decisions that occur only within a single time period. The formulation required for multiperiod or dynamic models is explored in Sec. 2.6.

An illustration of an important class of models known as *transportation problems* is given in Sec. 2.7. Many large-scale linear programming models combine transportation and mix selection problems, and are posed in a dynamic context.

We expect that as you continue reading this chapter you will become increasingly familiar with ways to specify a linear programming model. Hence, we present more detailed explanations in the first sections than we do toward the end of the chapter. Here and there, we advise you to verify certain statements, so you can check whether you have indeed been following the progression of ideas.

Study guide. In reading the examples below, ask yourself

1. What is the key decision to be made? What problem is being solved?
2. What makes the real decision environment so complex as to require the use of a linear optimization model? What elements of this complexity are embodied in the model? What elements are ignored?
3. What distinguishes a practical decision from an unusable one in this environment? What distinguishes a good decision from a poor one?
4. If you were a manager, how would you employ the results of the analysis? What would be your interpretation of the answers? In what ways might you want or need to temper the results because of factors not explicitly considered in the models?

After presenting these examples, we will return to a discussion of the application of linear programming models in today's business firms.

2.2 PRODUCT-MIX SELECTION

In product-mix selection, the decision-maker wishes to determine the levels for a number of production activities during a specified period of time. These levels are constrained by technological or feasibility considerations, given in the form of linear equalities or inequalities. Subject to these restrictions, management seeks to optimize a particular objective function. In the instance below, the objective will be maximum profit. In the subsequent examples, you will see other objectives, such as minimum cost.

Suppose the Knox Mix Company has the option of using one or more of four different types of production processes. The first and second processes yield items of Product A, and the third and fourth yield items of Product B. The inputs for each process are labor measured in man-weeks, pounds of Material Y, and boxes of Material Z. Since each process varies in its input requirements, the profitabilities of the processes differ, even for processes producing the same item. The manufacturer, deciding on a week's production schedule, is limited in the range of possibilities by the available amounts of manpower and of both kinds of raw materials. The full technology and input restrictions are given in Fig. 2.3.

Item	One Item of Product A		One Item of Product B		Total Availabilities
	Process 1	Process 2	Process 3	Process 4	
Man—weeks	1	1	1	1	≤ 15
Pounds of Material Y	7	5	3	2	≤ 120
Boxes of Material Z	3	5	10	15	≤ 100
Unit profit ($)	4	5	9	11	Maximize
Production level	x_1	x_2	x_3	x_4	

FIGURE 2.3. Knox Mix Product Selection.

We could jump immediately to taking the data in Fig. 2.3 and writing a linear formulation, just as we did for the One-Potato, Two-Potato Problem in Chap. 1. But this time we choose to be more contemplative. We consider what assumptions about the technology are needed to imply linearity.

Linear axioms. We will make two crucial technological and economic assumptions about how the production processes operate:

i. *Divisibility*. For each activity, the total amounts of each input and the associated profit are strictly proportional to the level of output—that is, to the activity level. In other words, each activity is capable of continuous proportional expansion or reduction. To illustrate, the direct effect of doubling the inputs of any process is the doubling of output and profits. In particular, to manufacture 10 units by Process 1 ($x_1 = 10$), there must be 10 man-weeks, 70 pounds of Material Y, and 30 boxes of Material Z allocated to the activity, and the accrued profits are \$40. The divisibility postulate further implies that the activity levels are permitted to assume fractional values as well as integer values. For example, we admit the technological possibility of $x_2 = 2.5$ or $x_4 = \frac{10}{3}$.

ii. *Additivity.* Given the activity levels for each of the decision variables x_j, the total amounts of each input and the associated profit are the sums of the inputs and profit for each individual process. To illustrate, in Fig. 2.3 one unit of Process 1 and one unit of Process 3 require 2 man-weeks, 10 pounds of Material Y, and 13 boxes of Material Z, and yield \$13 profit.

The assumptions of divisibility and additivity are equivalent to stating that the underlying mathematical model can be formulated in terms of linear relations. Strictly interpreted, the axioms imply constant returns to scale and preclude the possibility of economies or diseconomies of scale (in both the technology and profit aspects). As you can read in Chaps. 13, 14, and 15, suitable mathematical devices of an advanced nature often make it possible to introduce economies and diseconomies into a modified linear model. In real situations the above two postulates may hold only approximately, but nevertheless well enough, to permit useful application of the linear approach. For all the examples in the remainder of this chapter, we assume the legitimacy of the two assumptions.

In the specific example there is one linear inequality relation for each labor and material restriction, and one linear relation expressing profitability:

(1)　　　　　maximize profit $\equiv$ maximize $(4x_1 + 5x_2 + 9x_3 + 11x_4)$,

subject to the constraints

$$
\begin{aligned}
1x_1 + 1x_2 + 1x_3 + 1x_4 &\le 15 \quad \text{(man-weeks)} \\
7x_1 + 5x_2 + 3x_3 + 2x_4 &\le 120 \quad \text{(Material Y)} \\
3x_1 + 5x_2 + 10x_3 + 15x_4 &\le 100 \quad \text{(Material Z)}.
\end{aligned}
$$

(2)

There is no physical meaning to negative production levels, such as $x_1 = -4.2$, so we do not allow production to be "negative." We constrain each unknown production level to be either zero or positive, that is, to be **nonnegative,**

(3)　　　　　$x_1 \ge 0$　　$x_2 \ge 0$　　$x_3 \ge 0$　　$x_4 \ge 0$.

(A variable that is allowed *also* to assume negative values is said to be **unrestricted in sign.**)

Management's problem is to find values for all the unknowns x_j that satisfy the relations (2), (3), and also maximize profit (1). In general, such values need not be unique. There may exist **alternative optimal solutions.**

Rather than get side tracked at this juncture by discussing a method for calculating an optimal solution, the computational question will be postponed to Chap. 4. You will find it very helpful in reading Chaps. 4 and 5 to have a copy of Fig. 2.3, and we urge you to make one. Also, jot down now what you think may be an optimal solution to this example, so that you can check your guess against the answer given in Chap. 4.

We will demonstrate in Chap. 4 the remarkable fact that in linear programming problems having m restrictive relations (not including the nonnegativity constraints) and possessing finite optimal solutions, there is at least one best solution in which no more than m activity variables are employed at positive levels. Therefore in this example, there is an optimal solution using no more than three of the variables.

In addition to wanting optimal values for each x_j, management may also want to know how profit would be affected by increasing each input, by improving one of the technological processes, by a change in the cost of raw materials—and consequently a change in the profitability of the processes—or by some other resource used in the processes and heretofore not considered limited becoming scarce. In many real applications of linear programming models, these considerations are even more important than finding exact optimal values for each x_j. Techniques for such *sensitivity analysis* are presented in Chap. 5.

2.3 FEED-MIX SELECTION

The Hion Hog Farm Company may purchase and mix one or more of three types of grain, each containing different amounts of four nutritional elements; the data are given in Fig. 2.4. The production manager specifies that any feed mix for his livestock must meet at least minimal nutritional requirements, and he seeks the least costly among all such mixes. Suppose his planning horizon is a two-week period, that is, he purchases enough to fill his needs for two weeks.

Assuming divisibility and additivity, we write the linear formulation as

(1)   minimize cost $\equiv$ minimize $(41x_1 + 35x_2 + 96x_3)$,

Item	One Unit Weight of			Minimal Total Requirements Over Planning Horizon
	Grain 1	Grain 2	Grain 3	
Nutritional ingredient A	2	3	7	≥ 1250
Nutritional ingredient B	1	1	0	≥ 250
Nutritional ingredient C	5	3	0	≥ 900
Nutritional ingredient D	.6	.25	1	≥ 232.5
Cost per unit weight ($)	41	35	96	Minimize
Weight level	x_1	x_2	x_3	

FIGURE 2.4. Hion Hog Company Feed-Mix Selection.

subject to the constraints

$$2x_1 + \ 3x_2 + 7x_3 \geq 1250$$
$$1x_1 + \ 1x_2 \qquad\ \ \geq 250$$
(2) $\qquad\qquad$ $$5x_1 + \ 3x_2 \qquad\ \ \geq 900$$
$$.6x_1 + .25x_2 + 1x_3 \geq 232.5$$
$$x_j \geq 0, \quad \text{for} \quad j = 1, 2, 3.$$

Give a verbal interpretation of (1) and (2).

Note that in real applications of this model, as well as of the previous model, the number of activities can exceed the number of inequality restrictions. In the Product-Mix Selection Model, letting $x_j = 0$ for each variable is feasible in that all the constraints are satisfied; here the values $x_1 = 625$ and $x_2 = x_3 = 0$ provide one feasible solution. The optimal solution turns out to be $x_1 = 200$, $x_2 = 50$, and $x_3 = 100$, so that the minimum cost is 19,550.

The production manager may want information other than merely values for each x_j, since the model may be an oversimplified version of the real problem. For example, he may want to know how much it will cost him to use a nonoptimal value for a specific x_j, how much excess over each minimal total nutritional requirement an optimal feed mix provides, how much he would save by reducing the minimal nutritional requirements, or how much the cost of a new feed component must drop, say Grain 4, before he seriously considers using this grain in his mix. These questions fall in the realm of sensitivity analysis.

2.4 FLUID-BLENDING SCHEDULE

Another variant of mixture models is the economic problem associated with blending fluids, such as crude oils, molten metals, and other chemicals, into saleable intermediate or finished products. Instead of using specific numerical values as we did in the previous examples, here we make use of a generalized notation.

Suppose the Twobridge Company, a firm that sells various chemical products, is planning to prepare amounts of three such blends. Each of the products may be blended from at least one of two chemical inputs, subject to certain availability and mixture constraints. Define the unknown activity levels as

x_{ij} = number of gallons of Chemical i to be used in the blend of Product j,

and we assume $x_{ij} \geq 0$. Verify that in the example, we have $i = 1, 2$, and $j = 1, 2, 3$.

The first pair of constraints limits the amount of input of each of the chemicals

(1) $\qquad\qquad$ $$x_{11} + x_{12} + x_{13} \leq S_1$$
$$x_{21} + x_{22} + x_{23} \leq S_2,$$

where S_i is the amount (in gallons) of Chemical i available during the planning horizon period. The top constraint in (1) indicates that the sum of the number of gallons of Chemical 1 used in Products 1, 2, and 3 cannot exceed the amount S_1 that is available.

The second set of constraints expresses the requirement that production must be scheduled to at least meet specific minimal levels of customer demand for each of the products:

$$x_{11} + x_{21} \geq D_1$$
(2)
$$x_{12} + x_{22} \geq D_2$$
$$x_{13} + x_{23} \geq D_3,$$

where D_j is the minimal demand for Product j during the planning period. Assume there is no volumetric loss when the two chemicals are blended. So the first constraint in (2) requires that amounts of Product 1 to be blended from both Chemicals 1 and 2 must be at least as large as the minimal level of demand D_1.

The next restriction refers to a technological property to be satisfied by a mixture yielding Product 1. Suppose each input chemical contains a critical constituent. Specifically, a gallon of Chemical i has the proportion a_i of this constituent. The constraint is that in the blend of Product 1, the proportional content of this constituent must be at least the fraction r_1:

(3)
$$\frac{a_1 x_{11} + a_2 x_{21}}{x_{11} + x_{21}} \geq r_1.$$

An analogous restriction may hold for Product 2:

(4)
$$\frac{b_1 x_{12} + b_2 x_{22}}{x_{12} + x_{22}} \leq r_2;$$

here the fraction r_2 is a maximal limit. Check that after some algebraic manipulation both (3) and (4) may be rewritten in a standard *linear* form:

(5)
$$(a_1 - r_1)x_{11} + (a_2 - r_1)x_{21} \geq 0$$
$$(b_1 - r_2)x_{12} + (b_2 - r_2)x_{22} \leq 0.$$

Finally, there may be a simple minimal ratio to be observed between the two chemical inputs in the Product 3 blend:

(6)
$$\frac{x_{13}}{x_{23}} \geq r_3 \quad \text{or} \quad x_{13} - r_3 x_{23} \geq 0.$$

Letting p_{ij} be the profit associated with a unit of activity x_{ij}, we state the **objective function** as

(7)
$$\text{maximize profit} \equiv \text{maximize } p_{11}x_{11} + p_{12}x_{12} + p_{13}x_{13}$$
$$+ p_{21}x_{21} + p_{22}x_{22} + p_{23}x_{23}.$$

Examine how the model consisting of (1) through (7) is summarized in tabular form in Fig. 2.5. (From this point onward, we usually indicate zero coefficients of activities by blanks in the technology table.) *What questions would a manager want answered by this model?*

Item	One Gallon of						Restriction
	Chemical 1 in Product			Chemical 2 in Product			
	1	2	3	1	2	3	
Chemical 1 supply	1	1	1				$\leq S_1$
Chemical 2 supply				1	1	1	$\leq S_2$
Product 1 demand	1			1			$\geq D_1$
Product 2 demand		1			1		$\geq D_2$
Product 3 demand			1			1	$\geq D_3$
Product 1 technology	$a_1 - r_1$			$a_2 - r_1$			≥ 0
Product 2 technology		$b_1 - r_2$			$b_2 - r_2$		≤ 0
Product 3 technology			1			$-r_3$	≥ 0
Unit profit (\$)	p_{11}	p_{12}	p_{13}	p_{21}	p_{22}	p_{23}	Maximize
Activity level	x_{11}	x_{12}	x_{13}	x_{21}	x_{22}	x_{23}	

FIGURE 2.5. Twobridge Chemical Company Fluid-Blending Schedule.

In reviewing the blending model, notice that the supply and demand restrictions are similar to the restrictions you saw in the previous two examples. The technological restrictions are of a somewhat different complexity. It is possible in a model such as this that the entire set of restrictions does not admit a feasible solution. In other words, S_i, D_j, and r_j may be such that no set of values exists for the x_{ij} satisfying every constraint. For example, if $S_i = 5$ and $D_j = 10$ for all i and j, then total minimal demand would exceed total available supply.

*2.5 ARBITRAGE TRANSACTIONS

In certain exchange markets such as foreign currencies, stocks and shares, and commodities for spot and future delivery, it is possible to transact buying and selling agreements that yield a profit due to an imbalance in the pertinent exchange rates. Such a transaction is known as *arbitrage*. Suppose an arbitrageur named Jay Canes faces possible trades in six types of market commodities. Assume he may make, all in all, up to nine separate kinds of transaction agreements. Figure 2.6 illustrates the details of the situation.

For activity x_1, a sale of a unit of Market Commodity II yields r_{11} units of Market Commodity I. For activity x_7, a sale of a unit of Commodity I yields r_{37} units of Commodity III and r_{67} units of Commodity VI. The other activities are defined analogously. The r_{ij}, of course, may be fractional-valued. Note that activities x_j, for $j = 1, 2, \ldots, 5$, imply that any commodity may be exchanged into Commodity I. Also note the **sign convention** observed in Fig. 2.6. Since you

Item	Transaction Type									Market Position
	1	2	3	4	5	6	7	8	9	
Market commodity I	r_{11}	r_{12}	r_{13}	r_{14}	r_{15}	-1	-1			≥ 0
Market commodity II	-1					r_{26}			r_{29}	≥ 0
Market commodity III		-1					r_{37}	r_{38}		≥ 0
Market commodity IV			-1					-1	r_{49}	≥ 0
Market commodity V				-1				r_{58}		≥ 0
Market commodity VI					-1		r_{67}		-1	≥ 0
Transaction level	x_1	x_2	x_3	x_4	x_5	x_6	x_7	x_8	x_9	

FIGURE 2.6. Jay Canes' Arbitrage Transactions.

must distinguish between sales and receipts of each commodity, you can do this by letting a negative number denote an outflow, or sale, and a positive number denote an inflow, or receipt.

In the idealization of the market, envisage Canes as making all transactions simultaneously and instantaneously. The only constraints imposed are those ensuring that he is not short on any commodity. In other words, for each commodity, his sales must not exceed his purchases. Verify that in terms of linear constraints, the restrictions are

$$r_{11}x_1 + r_{12}x_2 + r_{13}x_3 + r_{14}x_4 + r_{15}x_5 - x_6 - x_7 \geq 0$$

$$-x_1 + r_{26}x_6 + r_{29}x_9 \geq 0$$

$$-x_2 + r_{37}x_7 + r_{38}x_8 \geq 0$$

(1) $$-x_3 - x_8 + r_{49}x_9 \geq 0$$

$$-x_4 + r_{58}x_8 \geq 0$$

$$-x_5 + r_{67}x_7 - x_9 \geq 0$$

$$x_j \geq 0 \quad \text{for} \quad j = 1, 2, \ldots, 9.$$

Assume his objective function is to maximize his net proceeds in terms of Market Commodity I:

(2)   maximize $(r_{11}x_1 + r_{12}x_2 + r_{13}x_3 + r_{14}x_4 + r_{15}x_5 - x_6 - x_7)$.

When all the right-hand sides of a set of linear inequalities are zero, as is true for (1), the system is termed **linear homogeneous**. Note that $x_j = 0$ for all j is a trivial feasible solution but yields zero net proceeds. Suppose there is some set of nontrivial values for the x_j that yields positive net proceeds. Then, because of the homogeneity of (1), kx_j would also be feasible for all $k \geq 0$, and the net proceeds would thereby be changed by a factor k. Thus in this model, if there exists any feasible solution with positive net proceeds, the value of the objective function can be made arbitrarily large. In such a situation, we state that there is an **unbounded optimal solution**.

We would mislead the reader if we purported that the above linear optimization model is a practical tool for an actual arbitrageur. In real commodity markets, a trader must be able to spot imbalances in rates very quickly since economic market forces correct such situations rapidly. Consequently, our primary purpose for citing this illustration is to show how a problem with an unbounded optimal solution can arise reasonably. Such a model is of independent interest to economists for gaining insights into the fundamental properties of multicommodity exchange markets.

2.6 DYNAMIC PLANNING—INTEGRATED PRODUCTION PLANNING EXAMPLE

Each of the examples you have investigated so far can be expanded into a planning problem extending over several time periods. To illustrate, in the Product-Mix Selection Model, if raw material and manpower availabilities as well as unit profits change over time, and if it is possible to store excess raw materials and finished goods from one period to the next, then the optimization problem is truly dynamic. It does *not* factor completely into separate period-by-period optimization problems. Similarly, in the Feed-Mix Selection Model, if the farmer permits mild relaxations of the nutritional requirements in one planning period on condition that compensations occur in subsequent periods, and if the grain costs vary over time, a dynamic planning problem results. Similar generalizations are possible in the blending and arbitrage models.

Common to all models in this category is that current decisions have their effects both presently and in subsequent periods. Consequently, the important economic tradeoffs are not only those between activities within a single time period, but also those between activities in different time periods. Typically, such tradeoffs become significant when the decision-maker can invest, expand capacity, or train personnel, with the effect of creating profit-making or cost-saving potentialities in future periods.

Qualitative analysis. Suppose the Great Auto Works Company is committed to supplying the amounts S_t, for $t = 1, 2, \ldots, T$, over an incipient **planning horizon** of T time periods. The activities in any period are to

- Utilize available workers to produce items for current and future demands,
- Build inventory to meet subsequent requirements,
- Increase or decrease the work force, or
- Leave idle some of the work force, while awaiting increased production in future periods.

Leaving some of the work force idle may be economical, provided the costs of firing and subsequently hiring workers exceed the cost of keeping workers idle for a limited amount of time. (In a real situation, the level of idleness may manifest itself in a slow-down or decrease in efficiency.) The linear technology of this problem can be summarized by showing the effects of the activities in Period t upon the constraining relations for Period t and subsequent periods. The time interrelations can be exhibited in a variety of ways. Experience and ingenuity with problems of this sort often enable one to arrive at a formulation giving the interrelations in terms of Period t and of only a limited number of future periods, rather than of the entire set of future periods. This idea will be made clear in the present example.

We pause a moment before launching into the detail. This example is the largest and most involved you have read so far. Go slowly, and plan to reread the explanation at least once or twice. It is worth the effort because many of the truly important applications of linear programming are dynamic models and have a structure similar to this example; that is why we chose it. Once you have gotten the hang of this problem, you will find it fairly easy to formulate other dynamic models, really.

Time-staged formulation. Figure 2.7 gives the essence of the *entire T* period technology in terms of the interrelations between only Periods t and t + 1. The nonnegative decision variables in Period t are

e_t = number of workers currently engaged in production (employment level activity)

s_t = inventory of items on hand at the end of Period t in excess of current requirements, in units of 25 items (stock level activity)

x_t = increase in number of workers at start of Period t (hiring activity)

y_t = decrease in number of workers at start of Period t (firing activity)

d_t = number of workers currently idle, in units of 10 workers.

Within each period there are two constraints to be observed, these being, in general terms, that (1) the *sales requirement S_t* is to be met, and (2) the production level is to be limited by the level of the work force.

Getting into the detail, observe that there are two ways of meeting the sales

Variables		e_t	s_t	x_t	y_t	d_t
Period t Relations	sales requirement	4	−25			
	workforce restriction	1		−1	1	10
Period $t+1$ Relations	sales requirement		20			
	workforce restriction	−1				−9
Unit Costs		c_t	i_t	h_t	f_t	n_t

Legend: e_t employment level
         s_t stock level
         x_t hiring
         y_t firing
         d_t idle-workers level

FIGURE 2.7. G.A.W. Company. Two-Period Interrelations.

requirement S_t, namely, through the output of workers currently engaged in production and from inventories *entering* Period t. Current production and entering inventories in excess of S_t become inventory at the end of Period t. From the e_t column of Fig. 2.7, you see that each employed worker produces four items during the period. The value of inventory s_t is measured in units of 25 items. Thus, if $s_t = 1$, 25 units remain at the end of Period t, or if $s_t = \frac{2}{5}$, only 10 units remain at the end of Period t. The fact that the coefficient of s_t in the Period t + 1 sales relation is 20 implies that spoilage of 5 units occurs from one period to the next whenever 25 items are inventoried. Note the **sign convention** employed for the technological coefficients. A positive number in a sales-requirement relation implies the inflow of items to meet the requirement, and a negative number implies an outflow of items that is in addition to the sales requirement.

The second set of restrictions applies to the work force. The inflow of work force entering Period t from the previous period may be augmented by hiring, and is then allocated as an outflow to the activities of producing, firing, and leaving workers idle. A sign convention is adopted to distinguish between the inflow of work force and the outflow or uses of it. For example, the coefficient of e_t in the work force restriction of Period t is $+1$ to denote a use of labor; the coefficient is -1 in the Period t + 1 restriction to signify an inflow of labor from Period t. The work force entering Period t + 1 consists of those persons engaged in production and those left idle during Period t. But note that the technology of the idle activity indicates that for every 10 men left idle in Period t, only 9 are available for possible work in Period t + 1. Presumably the reason for this shrinkage effect is that 1 out of 10 men left idle decides to leave the firm.

With the information in Fig. 2.7, you now may construct in a straightforward manner the full technology of the model, analogous to the technologies exhibited for earlier models. The entire structure appears in Fig. 2.8. The constant W_1 represents the level of the work force at the start of Period 1, before any Period 1 increase or decrease in the work force takes place. Let $W_1 = 0$ if the firm has just started business. A positive value for W_1 may be viewed as an exogenously given supply of work force, that is, a supply determined independent of the optimization process. If the G. A. W. Company has made other exogenous decisions to increase the work force by the amounts W_t, for $t = 2, 3, \ldots, T$, such positive numbers will appear in the work force equations instead of the 0 constants on the right-hand side. Exogenous decreases would be handled analogously using negative values for W_t.

For expository purposes, we list a few specific relations that are embodied in Fig. 2.8

Period 1 sales requirement: $S_1 + 25s_1 = 4e_1$
Period 1 work force restriction: $e_1 + 10d_1 = W_1 + x_1 - y_1$
Period 3 sales requirement: $S_3 + 25s_3 = 20s_2 + 4e_3$
Period 3 work force restriction: $e_3 + 10d_3 = e_2 + 9d_2 + x_3 - y_3$
Period T sales requirement: $S_T + 25s_T = 20s_{T-1} + 4e_T$
Period T work force restriction: $e_T + 10d_T = e_{T-1} + 9d_{T-1} + x_T - y_T.$

$e_1\,s_1\,x_1\,y_1\,d_1$	$e_2\,s_2\,x_2\,y_2\,d_2$	$e_3\,s_3\,x_3\,y_3\,d_3$	$e_4\,s_4\,x_4\,y_4\,d_4$	$\cdots$	$e_T\,s_T\,x_T\,y_T\,d_T$		Row
4 −25				$\cdots$		$= S_1$	1
1 −1 1 10						$= W_1$	2
20	4 −25			$\cdots$		$= S_2$	3
−1 −9	1 −1 1 10					$= 0$	4
	20	4 −25		$\cdots$		$= S_3$	5
	−1 −9	1 −1 1 10				$= 0$	6
		20	4 −25	$\cdots$		$= S_4$	7
		−1 −9	1 −1 1 10			$= 0$	8
$\vdots$	$\vdots$	$\vdots$	$\searrow$	$\searrow$	$\vdots$	$\vdots$	$\vdots$
				$\cdots$	4 −25	$= S_T$	$2T-1$
					1 −1 1 10	$= 0$	$2T$
$c_1\,i_1\,h_1\,f_1\,n_1$	$c_2\,i_2\,h_2\,f_2\,n_2$	$c_3\,i_3\,h_3\,f_3\,n_3$	$c_4\,i_4\,h_4\,f_4\,n_4$	$\cdots$	$c_T\,i_T\,h_T\,f_T\,n_T$	Minimize	

Legend: e_t employment level
s_t stock level
x_t hiring
y_t firing
d_t idle–workers level
S_t sales requirement
W_t exogenous change in work force

FIGURE 2.8. G.A.W. Company Dynamic Planning Example.

The above relations express the idea that, "*Total uses of resources or products must equal their total supply,*" or "*Total amount flowing in must equal total amount flowing out.*" For example, the Period 1 sales requirement states that the amount to be supplied in Period 1 (S_1), plus the inventory at the end of Period 1 ($25s_1$), must equal total production ($4e_1$) in Period 1. Similarly, the Period 3 sales requirement states that the amount to be supplied in Period 3 (S_3), plus the inventory at the end of Period 3 ($25s_3$), must equal inventory entering from Period 2 ($20s_2$), plus total production ($4e_3$) in Period 3. As a final illustration, the Period 3 work force restriction states the number of workers employed in Period 3 (e_3), plus the number left idle ($10d_3$), must equal the number employed in the previous period (e_2), plus the number left idle in Period 2 that still remain with the company ($9d_2$), plus the number hired in Period 3 (x_3), less the number fired in Period 3 (y_3).

Similarly, the objective form is written as

$$
\begin{aligned}
\text{minimize } [\,&(c_1e_1 + i_1s_1 + h_1x_1 + f_1y_1 + n_1d_1) \\
+ &(c_2e_2 + i_2s_2 + h_2x_2 + f_2y_2 + n_2d_2) \\
+ &(c_3e_3 + i_3s_3 + h_3x_3 + f_3y_3 + n_3d_3) \\
+ &\cdots \\
+ &(c_Te_T + i_Ts_T + h_Tx_T + f_Ty_T + n_Td_T)\,].
\end{aligned}
$$

(1)

As you can see, the above is a clumsy expression to write. In building your own models you certainly would not want to use such a drawn out way of expressing the idea that the objective function consists of the sum of each period's costs, starting with Period 1 and ending with Period T. Therefore, the lengthy expression can be abbreviated by employing the standard summation notation Σ (sigma) that you often find in statistics texts. Specifically, (1) can be rewritten as

$$(2) \qquad \text{minimize} \left[\sum_{t=1}^{T} \left(c_t e_t + i_t s_t + h_t x_t + f_t y_t + n_t d_t \right) \right].$$

From Fig. 2.8, you should be able to see what complexities arise in determining a dynamic plan. For example, a decision to increase the number of workers engaged in production during a period, of course, has an immediate impact on the costs of that period. But such a decision also may influence the number of workers required subsequently if the plan provides for inventories to be left over at the end of the period. Similarly, an exogenous increase in the sales requirement of a period may bring about a revision in the work force plan for several preceding periods. As a third illustration, a personnel policy that decreases the attrition arising when workers are idle can have a complicated overall effect in reducing the need to hire new workers. *In what ways do you think a manager would find such a planning model useful?*

▶ At the start of this section we mentioned there are alternative, but, of course, mathematically equivalent, ways of viewing such a model. We illustrate this point by transforming the relations in Fig. 2.8 into another meaningful equivalent representation. You proceed in the following manner. Add Row 1 to Row 3 to form a new Row 3′. Add the new Row 3′ to Row 5. Add the new Row 5′ to Row 7, and so forth. Similarly add Row 2 to Row 4. Add the new Row 4′ to Row 6. Add the new Row 6′ to Row 8, and so forth.

The results of these operations appear in Fig. 2.9. The legitimacy of the transformations follows immediately from the rule, "*Adding equals to equals yields equals.*" All you have done is to add one equation to another to yield a composite equation.

The sales restrictions are now stated in terms of cumulative sales. In any Period t*, total sales to date, plus spoilage losses, plus inventory at the end of Period t* equals accumulated production:

$$(i) \qquad \sum_{t=1}^{t^*} S_t + 5 \sum_{t=1}^{t^*-1} s_t + 25 s_{t^*} = 4 \sum_{t=1}^{t^*} e_t \qquad \begin{array}{l} \text{Period t*} \\ \text{sales requirement} \\ \text{Row } (2t^* - 1)'. \end{array}$$

Similarly, the work force restriction in Period t* appears as the initial work force, plus accumulated hirings, equals accumulated firings, plus accumulated shrinkages due to workers left idle, plus men currently engaged in production, and men currently left idle:

$$(ii) \qquad W_1 + \sum_{t=1}^{t^*} x_t = \sum_{t=1}^{t^*} y_t + \sum_{t=1}^{t^*-1} d_t + e_{t^*} + 10 d_{t^*} \qquad \begin{array}{l} \text{Period t*} \\ \text{work force restriction} \\ \text{Row } (2t^*)'. \end{array}$$

Test your facility in making transformations of this sort by revising Fig. 2.9 for the case in which no inventory spoilage occurs (therefore the -20 in Fig. 2.7 is changed to

$e_1\,s_1\,x_1\,y_1\,d_1$	$e_2\,s_2\,x_2\,y_2\,d_2$	$e_3\,s_3\,x_3\,y_3\,d_3$	$e_4\,s_4\,x_4\,y_4\,d_4$	$\cdots$	$e_T\,s_T\,x_T\,y_T\,d_T$		Row
4 −25				$\cdots$		= S_1	1'
1　−1 1 I0						= W_1	2'
4 −5	4 −25			$\cdots$		= $S_1 + S_2$	3'
−1 1 1	1　−1 1 I0					= W_1	4'
4 −5	4 −5	4 −25		$\cdots$		= $S_1 + \cdots + S_3$	5'
−1 1 1	−1 1 1	1　−1 1 I0				= W_1	6'
4 −5	4 −5	4 −5	4 −25	$\cdots$		= $S_1 + \cdots + S_4$	7'
−1 1 1	−1 1 1	1　−1 1 1	1　−1 1 I0			= W_1	8'
↓	↓	↓	↘	↖	$\vdots$	$\vdots$	$\vdots$
4 −5	4 −5	4 −5	4 −5	$\cdots$	4 −25	= $S_1 + \cdots + S_T$	$(2T-1)'$
−1 1 1	−1 1 1	−1 1 1	−1 1 1		1　−1 1 I0	= W_1	$(2T)'$
$c_1\,i_1\,h_1\,f_1\,\,n_1$	$c_2\,i_2\,h_2\,f_2\,\,n_2$	$c_3\,i_3\,h_3\,f_3\,\,n_3$	$c_4\,i_4\,h_4\,f_4\,\,n_4$	$\cdots$	$c_T\,i_T\,h_T\,f_T\,\,n_T$	Minimize	

Figure 2.9. G.A.W. Company Alternative Formulation.

−25) and no shrinkage in the number of workers left idle occurs (therefore the −9 in Fig. 2.7 is changed to −10). Then give a corresponding verbal interpretation of the revised equations (i) and (ii). ◀

2.7 PRODUCT ALLOCATION THROUGH
A TRANSPORTATION NETWORK

Many important linear programming models have what is termed a **network structure,** which yields a very simple kind of technology table. We provide a typical example below, and subsequently explain why it is equivalent to a network problem. But first let us mention what this special technology looks like, so you will know it when you see it.

For any activity variable in a network structure, the entire set of constraints contains no more than two nonzero entries, these coefficients being either +1 or −1, depending on the sign convention adopted. When there *are* two coefficients for an activity, then one is +1 and the other −1. When the technology of the model has this form, it is usually possible to interpret the optimization problem in terms of routing the flow of a single commodity through a network. Sometimes it is necessary to manipulate the equations of the model in order to establish the network structure of the problem. In Chap. 6 you will study network models in detail.

In case you forgot. We mentioned in the preceding section that employing the Σ (sigma) summation symbol considerably reduces the amount of writing to express lengthy expressions. You will see this claim borne out again in the model below. If you have never taken a statistics course, or did so long ago, you may need a brush up on the rules for using the Σ symbol. By means of examples, we present such a review next. (If you don't need this review, skip directly to the model.)

1. Consider the summation

$$c_1x_1 + c_2x_2 + c_3x_3 + c_4x_4 + \cdots + c_nx_n.$$

In Σ notation, this sum is written as

$$\sum_{j=1}^{n} c_jx_j,$$

where the so-called *index of summation*, in this case j, may be any conveniently chosen letter. Any other index would serve as well, such as

$$\sum_{t=1}^{n} c_tx_t.$$

2. The expression

$$c_1x_1 + d_1y_1 + c_2x_2 + d_2y_2 + c_3x_3 + d_3y_3 + \cdots + c_nx_n + d_ny_n$$

can be written in several ways, two of which are

$$\sum_{t=1}^{n} (c_tx_t + d_ty_t) \quad \text{and} \quad \sum_{t=1}^{n} c_tx_t + \sum_{t=1}^{n} d_ty_t.$$

3. Suppose that all the c_j in the above expressions are equal; for example, suppose every $c_j = 5$. Then

$$5x_1 + 5x_2 + 5x_3 + \cdots + 5x_n$$

can be written simply as

$$5 \sum_{j=1}^{n} x_j.$$

4. Consider the expression

$$a_{i1}x_1 + a_{i2}x_2 + a_{i3}x_3 + \cdots + a_{in}x_n.$$

Here the coefficient of each x_j is a_{ij}, where i is a fixed, but unspecified, number. This expression is written as

$$\sum_{j=1}^{n} a_{ij}x_j.$$

5. Suppose the summation involves two subscripts:

$$c_{11}x_{11} + c_{12}x_{12} + c_{21}x_{21} + c_{22}x_{22} + c_{31}x_{31} + c_{32}x_{32}.$$

Notice that the first subscript takes the values $1, 2$, and 3, and the second subscript takes the values 1 and 2; also, every combination of values for the first and second subscripts appears. This so-called *double summation* can be abbreviated as

$$\sum_{i=1}^{3} \sum_{j=1}^{2} c_{ij}x_{ij}.$$

The above examples cover almost all the applications of the Σ notation we use in this book.

Example. A large dairy firm, the Saur Milk Company, has m plants located throughout a state. Daily milk production at Plant i can supply at most S_i gallons, for $i = 1, 2, \ldots, m$. Each day the firm must furnish its n distributing warehouses with at least D_j fresh gallons, for $j = 1, 2, \ldots, n$, to meet demand requirements. The economic problem is to designate which plants are to furnish which warehouses so that total transportation costs are a minimum.

Let x_{ij} be the number of gallons shipped from Plant j to Warehouse j, and c_{ij} be the associated shipping cost per gallon. A mathematical specification of the model is

$$(1) \qquad\qquad \text{minimize} \quad \sum_{i=1}^{m} \sum_{j=1}^{n} c_{ij} x_{ij}$$

subject to the restrictions

$$(2) \qquad \sum_{j=1}^{n} x_{ij} \leq S_i, \quad \text{for} \quad i = 1, 2, \ldots, m \quad \text{(supply restrictions)}$$

$$(3) \qquad \sum_{i=1}^{m} x_{ij} \geq D_j, \quad \text{for} \quad j = 1, 2, \ldots, n \quad \text{(demand requirements)}$$

$$(4) \qquad\qquad\qquad \text{each } x_{ij} \geq 0.$$

Give verbal interpretations of (2) and (3), and write out in full (1), (2), and (3) for $m = 3$ and $n = 4$.

Figure 2.10 is a convenient tabular summary of the situation. If $\sum_{i=1}^{m} S_i \geq \sum_{j=1}^{n} D_j$, so that total supply is at least as large as total demand, it is always possible to find a *feasible* transportation schedule in which no more than $(m + n - 1)$ routes are utilized. As shown in Chap. 6, an *optimal* solution also exists in which no more than $(m + n - 1)$ routes are employed.

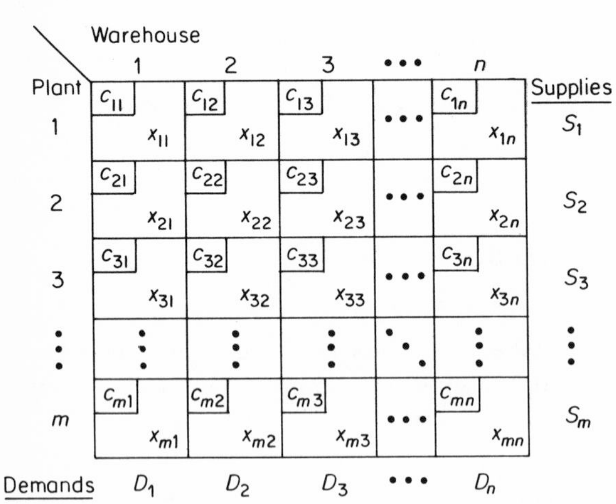

FIGURE 2.10. Transportation Table.

▶To construct one such feasible schedule with at most $(m + n - 1)$ routes, start at the upper-left corner, or, as it sometimes is called, the *northwest corner*, and allocate the available production S_1 to each demand requirement, beginning with D_1, until the

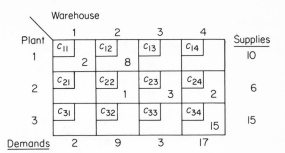

FIGURE 2.11. Initial Feasible Solution.

production is exhausted. Then continue the process with S_2, and so forth. Figure 2.11 illustrates the procedure with an example. Needless to say, this trial routing may be, and often is, far from optimal. ◀

Network equivalence. Suppose we multiply by -1 each warehouse demand-requirement relation in (3). Multiplication by a negative number reverses the sense of the inequalities. Then the technology can be written as in Fig. 2.12.

Shipping Activities

	x_{11}	x_{12}	x_{13}	$\cdots$	x_{1n}	x_{21}	x_{22}	x_{23}	$\cdots$	x_{2n}	$\cdots$	x_{m1}	x_{m2}	x_{m3}	$\cdots$	x_{mn}	
1	1	1	1	$\cdots$	1												$\leq S_1$
2						1	1	1	$\cdots$	1							$\leq S_2$
$\vdots$											$\cdots$						$\vdots$
m												1	1	1	$\cdots$	1	$\leq S_m$
1	-1					-1						-1					$\leq -D_1$
2		-1					-1						-1				$\leq -D_2$
3			-1					-1						-1			$\leq -D_3$
$\vdots$				$\ddots$					$\ddots$		$\cdots$				$\ddots$		$\vdots$
n					-1					-1						-1	$\leq -D_n$
	c_{11}	c_{12}	c_{13}	$\cdots$	c_{1n}	c_{21}	c_{22}	c_{23}	$\cdots$	c_{2n}	$\cdots$	c_{m1}	c_{m2}	c_{m3}	$\cdots$	c_{mn}	Minimize

Plant Supplies (rows 1–m), Warehouse Demands (rows 1–n).

FIGURE 2.12. Transportation Network Example.

Observe that in the column for each x_{ij} there are only two nonzero coefficients, $+1$ and -1, the former indicating an output at Plant i and the latter an input at Warehouse j. You can visualize the plants and warehouses as a set of points in space or, using network terminology, as a set of nodes. Each x_{ij} variable then corresponds to a flow along a directed link or arc between the Nodes i and j, and c_{ij} corresponds to the associated cost of a unit of flow. We draw the network for this

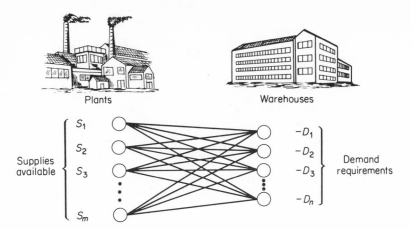

FIGURE 2.13. Transportation Network Schematic.

example as Fig. 2.13. To complete the network specification, we show each plant's supply and each warehouse's demand requirement. As a network flow problem, the task is to allocate the amounts at the positive nodes along the various arcs so as to meet the negative nodes' requirements at a minimum cost. In management science literature, this model is often referred to as the *Hitchcock-Koopmans Transportation Problem*.

It is a remarkable property of the network problem, described by (1) through (4), that if the model has a feasible solution, an optimal solution exists for which all the x_{ij} have integer values (provided S_i and D_j are integers). We elaborate on this result in Chap. 6. Network models involving the occurrence of gains and losses along the arcs generally do not possess this property of integer optimality.

*2.8 ROUTE SELECTION THROUGH A NETWORK

Here we consider a significant network problem, discussed in greater detail in Chaps. 6 and 10. Examine the network depicted in Fig. 2.14. Observe that it is possible to go from any Node i, for $i = 1, 2, 3, 4$, to any other Node j, provided that $j > i$. The route can be either direct or indirect by way of intermediate nodes

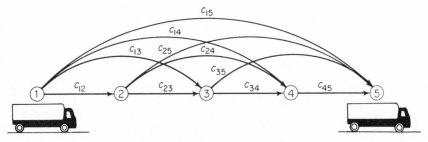

FIGURE 2.14. Shortest-route Model.

if $j - i > 1$. Thus a route from Node 1 to Node 5 can be direct, across the arc $(1, 5)$; or indirect, by way of $(1, 3)$ and then $(3, 5)$; or by $(1, 3)$, then $(3, 4)$, and finally $(4, 5)$; and so forth.

Assume each arc (i, j) has an associated cost c_{ij} for traversing it. There is no particular relationship between the value of c_{ij} and the pictorial representation of the length of the arc (i, j) in Fig. 2.14. In a particular application, for example, c_{15} could be either larger or smaller than $c_{13} + c_{35}$. Ordinarily $c_{ij} \geq 0$, but this assumption need not be made here.

One illustration of ow such a network can arise is the following. Suppose a trucking company needs to lease a particular amount of transportation equipment over a four-year period. The company can meet its requirements by leasing a new piece of equipment at the beginning of Year 1 and keeping it until the beginning of Year 5. The associated cost c_{15} is comprised of the rental fee plus the expected running and maintenance costs of this equipment for the four years. Another alternative is to lease a new piece of equipment at the beginning of Year 1 and keep it until the beginning of Year 3, then lease another new piece and keep it until the beginning of Year 5. The associated cost of the latter policy is $c_{13} + c_{35}$, where again these costs include rental fees plus running and maintenance costs. In most instances $c_{15} \neq c_{13} + c_{35}$. Obviously, there are other alternatives to be investigated in pursuit of the minimum-cost leasing policy. In this particular context, the network model of Fig. 2.14 is an example of a dynamic planning problem.

The specific questions to be answered for the network in Fig. 2.14 pertain to finding a best route from Node 1 to Node 5. We pose the questions in two distinct, albeit closely related, versions:

1. What is the *cost* of a least-cost route from Node 1 to Node 5?
2. What is the *route* of a least-cost route from Node 1 to Node 5?

It is intuitive that in answering one of these questions you concomitantly provide the answer for the other question. However, we will proceed by setting up a linear optimization model to solve each question separately and then analyze the connection between these two models. We start with question 1.

Cost of a least-cost route. Define for $i = 1, 2, 3, 4$,
$$y_i = \text{cost of a least-cost route from Node i to Node 5.}$$

Then you can find y_i by calculating for each Node j (where $j > i$) the cost of proceeding *directly* to Node j, and then continuing *optimally* from Node j to Node 5. The smallest of all these costs is the value for y_i. This approach can be stated mathematically as

(1) $\qquad y_i = \underset{j=i+1,\ldots,5}{\text{minimum}} [c_{ij} + y_j] \quad \text{for } i = 1, 2, 3, 4, \quad \text{and} \quad y_5 \equiv 0.$

In particular, for $i = 1$ you have

(2) $\qquad y_1 = \text{minimum } [c_{12} + y_2, c_{13} + y_3, c_{14} + y_4, c_{15}].$

Thus you can find the cost of a least-cost route from Node 1 to Node 5 if you know the cost of a least-cost route from Node 2 to Node 5, Node 3 to Node 5, and Node 4 to Node 5; for then it is simply a matter of comparing the cost of going directly from Node 1 to Node 5 with the cost of getting from Node 1 to each intermediate node and taking the best route from that node to Node 5.

The calculation in (2) can be expressed in terms of a linear optimization model as

(3)   maximize $1y_1$

subject to

$$1y_1 \leq c_{12} + 1y_2$$
(4) $$1y_1 \leq c_{13} + 1y_3$$
$$1y_1 \leq c_{14} + 1y_4$$
$$1y_1 \leq c_{15}.$$

The equivalence of (2) to (3) and (4) can be argued as follows. The value of y_1 can be no larger than the value of each $c_{1j} + y_j$, for $j = 2, 3, 4, 5$, by the definition of a minimum in (2). The constraints (4) express this fact. However, y_1 actually must be equal to at least one of the values $c_{1j} + y_j$, for $j = 2, 3, 4, 5$, and this property is ensured by the maximization in (3). Explain why.

Of course, you do not know the values of y_i, for $i = 2, 3, 4$, and if you limit yourself to questions 1 and 2 above, you have no particular interest in these values. But you can treat each y_i, for $i = 2, 3, 4$, as an unknown in (4) provided you apply relation (1) to yield the appropriate constraints:

$$1y_2 \leq c_{23} + 1y_3$$
(5) $$1y_2 \leq c_{24} + 1y_4 \quad \text{for } i = 2$$
$$1y_2 \leq c_{25}$$

(6) $$1y_3 \leq c_{34} + 1y_4 \quad \text{for } i = 3$$
$$1y_3 \leq c_{35}$$

(7) $$1y_4 \leq c_{45} \qquad \text{for } i = 4.$$

It is permissible but not necessary to strengthen (7) to an equality. For the sake of symmetry, we leave (7) as an inequality. Question 1 is answered by solving the model (3) through (7). Note that you do not constrain the y_i to be nonnegative. If all $c_{ij} \geq 0$, you could add nonnegativity conditions without loss, but even then you need not state them explicitly. The linear optimization model is summarized in Fig. 2.15.

▶Observe that although the optimal value of y_1 in the solution of (3) through (7) does indeed provide the optimal cost from Node 1 to Node 5, the other values of y_i, for $i = 2, 3, 4$, may not turn out to be the optimal cost from Node i to Node 5. This arises because (5), (6), and (7) do not fully embody the minimization operation indicated by (1). For example, suppose $c_{15} = 1$ and all other $c_{ij} > 1$. Then $y_1 = 1$ and $y_i = 0, i = 2, 3, 4$, solves (3) through (7). But $y_i = 0$, for $i = 2, 3, 4$, is *not* the cost of a least-cost route from Node i to Node 5. However, you always obtain all optimal y_i if you maximize $\sum_{i=1}^{4} y_i$.   ◀

Does solving this model answer question 2 as well? Yes. To avoid a lengthy description of the process for finding an optimal route having the minimal cost, we explain the approach using a simplified example. As you verified above, in an optimal solution at least one of the constraints in (4) will be satisfied as an equality. *Assume* there is a single such constraint, and that it is the one involving c_{13} and y_3. Next examine (6), the constraints for y_3. Again *assume* there is only one of these restrictions that is satisfied with an equality, and that it is the one involving c_{35}. Then the unique optimal route is along arcs $(1, 3)$ and $(3, 5)$.

It may puzzle you that although the problem to be analyzed involves a network, the technology exhibited in Fig. 2.15 seems inconsistent with the network problem as described at the start of Sec. 2.7. In particular, there are more than two nonzero entries in each of the columns. Look at the table more carefully. Do you observe any indication that the analysis above seems to have dealt with a *transposed* network technology? In pursuit of this idea, we turn now to a direct solution of question 2.

	y_1	y_2	y_3	y_4	
	1	-1			$\leq c_{12}$
	1		-1		$\leq c_{13}$
	1			-1	$\leq c_{14}$
	1				$\leq c_{15}$
		1	-1		$\leq c_{23}$
Arcs		1		-1	$\leq c_{24}$
		1			$\leq c_{25}$
			1	-1	$\leq c_{34}$
			1		$\leq c_{35}$
				1	$\leq c_{45}$
	1	0	0	0	Maximize

FIGURE 2.15. Least-cost Analysis.

Route of a least-cost route. Solving the route problem directly requires only a straightforward extension of the ideas used in the transportation network model of Sec. 2.7. As before, let

x_{ij} = amount of flow from Node i to Node j   for $i = 1, 2, 3, 4$ and $j > i$.

Impose the restriction $x_{ij} \geq 0$. To find the best route, make a unit of flow available at Node 1 and force it to flow out to the other nodes

(8) $1x_{12} + 1x_{13} + 1x_{14} + 1x_{15} = 1.$

Then ensure that any amount of flow entering Nodes 2, 3, and 4 must flow out to a higher numbered node

$$-1x_{12} + 1x_{23} + 1x_{24} + 1x_{25} = 0 \quad \text{(Node 2)}$$
(9) $$-1x_{13} - 1x_{23} + 1x_{34} + 1x_{35} = 0 \quad \text{(Node 3)}$$
$$-1x_{14} - 1x_{24} - 1x_{34} + 1x_{45} = 0 \quad \text{(Node 4)}.$$

Give a verbal interpretation of the Node 3 constraint.

You also could add a constraint stating that all the flow entering Node 5 must equal 1, but this relation actually is implied by (8) and (9), as can be seen by summing all these constraints. Therefore such a relation is **redundant.**

The objective function is

$$\text{minimize } c_{12}x_{12} + c_{13}x_{13} + c_{14}x_{14} + c_{15}x_{15}$$
$$+ c_{23}x_{23} + c_{24}x_{24} + c_{25}x_{25}$$
$$+ c_{34}x_{34} + c_{35}x_{35}$$
$$+ c_{45}x_{45},$$

which can be succinctly written with the $\sum$ notation as a double summation:

$$(10) \qquad \text{minimize } \sum_{i=1}^{4} \sum_{j=i+1}^{5} c_{ij}x_{ij}.$$

Thus the linear optimization model involves finding nonnegative values for x_{ij} satisfying (8), (9), and (10). The technology of the problem is shown in Fig. 2.16.

Now it is evident that this model satisfies the conditions for a network: for any variable, the entire set of constraints contains no more than two nonzero entries— these being either $+1$ or -1; when there *are* two coefficients for a variable, one is $+1$ and the other is -1. Consequently, among the optimal solutions to (8), (9), and (10) there is at least one that is integer-valued. In this instance, the integer property results in each x_{ij} being either 0 or 1. Explain why. It follows that if (8), (9), and (10) have a unique solution, then that solution must be integer-valued. For ease in exposition *assume* this uniqueness condition. Suppose that the optimal solution is $x_{13} = x_{35} = 1$ and all other $x_{ij} = 0$. Then the optimal route is along arcs $(1, 3)$ and $(3, 5)$.

Does solving this model yield the answer to question 1? Of course. In the illustration, the cost of the least-cost route is simply $c_{13} + c_{35}$.

Duality. By this point you will have discovered the interconnection between the two models exhibited in Figs. 2.15 and 2.16. The rows of Fig. 2.15 are the columns of Fig. 2.16, but the sense of optimization is opposite in the two models.

Nodes	x_{12}	x_{13}	x_{14}	x_{15}	x_{23}	x_{24}	x_{25}	x_{34}	x_{35}	x_{45}	
1	1	1	1	1							=1
2	−1				1	1	1				=0
3		−1			−1			1	1		=0
4			−1			−1		−1·		1	=0
	c_{12}	c_{13}	c_{14}	c_{15}	c_{23}	c_{24}	c_{25}	c_{34}	c_{35}	c_{45}	Minimize

FIGURE 2.16. Best-route Analysis.

▶ The inquisitive reader should try to show that if all $c_{ij} \geq 0$, then (8) and (9) can be written as ($\geq$) relations without loss, in which case the sense of the inequalities also is opposite in the two models. As we remarked previously, in this instance you can add without loss the restriction $y_i \geq 0$ in the first model.   ◀

The transposition phenomenon in Figs. 2.15 and 2.16 is referred to as *duality*. You will study it again in Chap. 5. It suffices to say here that every linear optimization model has a corresponding dual problem and, as you will verify later, solving one of the problems automatically furnishes a solution to its dual.

2.9 INDUSTRIAL IMPORTANCE OF LINEAR
OPTIMIZATION MODELS

The beginning of this chapter briefly discussed actual industrial applications of linear programming. Now that you have studied several small-scale models, you are ready to proceed with this topic in more detail.

We start again with the example of a major integrated oil company. This industry's use of linear optimization models deserves special attention for two important reasons. First, oil companies throughout the world have the best overall record of success in early and continued application of linear programming. Their experience amply demonstrates that it is practical and profitable to use mathematical models for planning purposes. Second, the oil companies, encouraged by their initial success, have pioneered the application of linear optimization methods to a wide variety of decision areas, and thus have demonstrated techniques for making this scientific approach workable in a competitive business environment.

Look back at Fig. 2.1 (p. 34) to review how the *flow* of material starts with the activity of pumping crude from the earth and ends with the activity of marketing gasoline at service stations. Linear programming models have been formulated and tested to aid in decision-making at every major point in this stream. Specifically, models have been developed to:

- Schedule production from a series of underground oil reservoirs so as to maximize profit, subject to equipment-capacity limitations and constraints imposed by physical pumping phenomena;
- Determine the net profitability of exchanging a proprietary crude for another company's crude, given the configuration of refineries and the associated economics of processing the exchanged crude;
- Calculate the incremental cost of increasing the amount of a product for a spot sale (for example, manufacturing a specified amount of jet fuel for a government contract), given the targeted quantities of other products to be manufactured;
- Plan weekly minimum-cost schedules for refinery unit operations and product-blending, taking into account crude availabilities, throughput constraints on the refining units, performance characteristics of each product (such as octane rating), and the pre-established shipping requirements for the products;
- Establish the return on investment of a proposed new refinery unit, realizing its full impact on existing units;
- Route products from several refineries to a number of marketing areas along least-cost transportation paths, recognizing factors of differential costs of manu-

factured products at the separate refineries, relative shipping charges, and
seasonal variations in customer demand;
- Construct an annual plan to integrate the major decisions of the entire company.

By no means have we exhausted all the linear programming applications, or
even all the important ones within an oil company. But the list is long enough to
convey the wide applicability of the approach.

Since each oil company has its peculiar characteristics, such as refinery location
and age configuration, marketing districts, crude-oil reserves, and so forth, firms
differ in their use of linear programming models. Some find it convenient to have
one or two comprehensive models that can be repeatedly employed to make several of the analyses described above. Other companies have constructed separate
models for each specific purpose, with differing degrees of complexity and detail.

Certain patterns of use are well established, however, and these can guide you
to an understanding of how linear programming is presently being employed in the
oil industry. Many refineries calculate optimal operating schedules on a weekly
or a monthly basis. A number of oil companies apply a linear programming analysis whenever they are considering a major agreement for the exchange of crude
or other products. More and more, oil firms are periodically analyzing their distribution patterns to discover transportation cost savings and profit potentials
for new or expanded markets. The leading firms are using linear optimization
models to test different strategies for long-term growth (e.g., five years). In the
dozen largest oil companies in the world, you will typically find 25 to 35 people—
and often two or three times that many—whose prime responsibility is to apply
linear programming to the analysis of important decisions.

Similar trends are developing in other major industries, including chemicals,
iron and steel, aluminum, wood products, food processing, and banking. The
applications include production planning, allocating customer orders to different
manufacturing plants, establishing cash flow requirements, scheduling work
force levels and composition, purchasing raw materials, and deciding whether
to make or buy a product. Some firms use linear programming as a performance-
control device to establish variable cost budgets for a plant with significantly
fluctuating output levels, and to compare actual cost performance with scientifically determined standards. Frequently, a linear optimization analysis is undertaken as a special study. For example, companies have used linear programming to
establish the number and location of warehouses and new plants, the profitability
of a particular line of business, and the appropriate capacity dimensions of a new
piece of heavy equipment.

Improving profit. It is no easy task, of course, to apply a linear optimization model to a real business problem; use of the model must be justified on the
basis of its potential, direct or indirect, contribution to the company's profits.
The principal costs incurred by utilizing this approach are associated with the
tasks below.

1. *Establishing the Appropriate Framework of Analysis.* It is a rare manager who immediately recognizes that solving his decision-making problem is tantamount to solving a linear programming model. Even the executive thoroughly trained in the *techniques* of linear optimization models finds it difficult to conclude at first glance that such methods will pay off. The reason is simply that a certain amount of skillful trial and error is usually required to determine whether the essence of a complex decision problem can be captured in a linear model. To illustrate, the analyst must consider thoroughly the proper selection of a criterion function to be optimized. In some instances he may test **multiple criteria**, that is, apply several different (perhaps incommensurable) objective functions, to see if they point toward significantly different strategies. He must also exercise care in depicting the relevant constraints to be imposed on the optimization. The dangers here are twofold: he must not overlook any significant constraining factor, but on the other hand, he must not impose so many restrictions that optimization becomes impossible. The latter danger has proved the more difficult to avoid. In fact, model formulation entails about a third of the effort required in applying linear programming.

2. *Obtaining the Required Data.* Applications of linear optimization to actual planning problems typically involve 100 to 200 constraints, with two to three times as many unknowns. And models with 500 to 1000 constraints are steadily becoming more common. These large-scale applications arise when a plan is to integrate several manufacturing plants, each represented by a medium-scale model, and when a firm wants to develop a long-term program of growth. Obtaining the necessary data for a model is by far the largest of all the tasks listed here. It can easily represent half the work required.

3. *Calculating and Analyzing the Trial Answer.* Once the model has been constructed with actual data, it is necessary to calculate an optimal result. Without high-speed electronic computers, it would be virtually impossible to solve realistic industrial linear programming models. However, in minutes, these devices perform operations that would consume the equivalent of decades or even centuries of manual computing. The cost of computing a linear programming solution is now the smallest portion of the entire expense involved.

4. *Testing the Validity and Sensitivity of the Answer. Modifying the Trial Model as Necessary.* Any mathematical model of a management decision problem is inherently an abstraction. Consequently, there is no guarantee that the first trial model will produce an answer that is practical, given the myriad considerations not *explicitly* taken into account in the analysis. The solution must be examined carefully for its soundness. Further, the answer must undergo sensitivity tests to determine whether it depends critically on the exact values of particular data. If it does, the analyst may need to improve the accuracy of his data before he can rely on the validity of the model's result. Chapter 5 discusses sensitivity analysis in detail.

By studying the examples in this chapter and answering the exercises below, you will gain considerable experience in translating the essence of a complex situation into the form of a linear optimization model. In the chapters to follow, you will be introduced to additional examples that will highlight certain problems with special structures.

From here on. In the next three chapters you will learn the fundamentals of linear optimization models. Chapter 3 summarizes the various algebraic techniques that assist in translating a verbal formulation of a linear program to an equivalent mathematical representation. The chapter also illustrates geometrical interpretations of a linear optimization model. Chapter 4 explains the most widely employed technique for solving a linear program. This material will not only deepen your knowledge of linear programming *per se*, but will also help you better understand many notions that are central to optimization methods. In Chap. 5 the discussion extends to an analysis of solution sensitivity to input data.

Chapters 6 and 7 focus on models of the network type. They discuss how the special structure of a network problem can be exploited both for deriving an understanding of the nature of these applications and for computing optimal solutions efficiently. The reason for an interest in special computational methods for network problems is plain. Recall the transportation network example in Sec. 2.7. In a real application the number of plants could easily be 25 and the number of warehouses 100. As a result there would be 2500 variables in the model. It would consume an excessive amount of computer time to handle such a problem by one of the methods in Chap. 4 instead of by a network approach.

Chapters 8 through 12 turn to optimization models that encompass dynamic phenomena and discuss fruitful points of view for analyzing these problems. In certain simple yet important situations, you can exploit the dynamic structure so as to be able to relax the requirements for linearity without seriously increasing the difficulty of finding a solution.

Chapter 13 deals with models in which the *divisibility axiom* of Sec. 2.2 is dropped. Only integer values for certain activity levels are permitted. The most general nonlinear optimization models studied in this book are treated in Chaps. 14 and 15.

Starting in Chap. 16, we introduce probabilistic uncertainty. Frequently, random variation in the structural specification of a model entails only an obvious extension of the deterministic analysis given in the preceding chapters. But in other situations, probabilistic elements present new considerations requiring careful analysis.

REVIEW EXERCISES

1 Four study-guide questions are posed at the end of Sec. 2.1. Discuss the answers to these questions in the context of each example treated in the chapter:

   (a) Knox Mix Company (Sec. 2.2).
   (b) Hion Hog Farm Company (Sec. 2.3).
   (c) Twobridge Chemical Company (Sec. 2.4).
*(d) Jay Canes' Arbitrage Problem (Sec. 2.5).
   (e) Great Auto Works Company (Sec. 2.6).
   (f) Saur Milk Company (Sec. 2.7).

2 One reason that the models treated in this chapter are approximations to reality is that the axioms of divisibility and additivity rarely hold exactly. How good do you think these approximations are when applied to situations such as the

   (a) Knox Mix Company (Sec. 2.2).
   (b) Hion Hog Farm Company (Sec. 2.3).
   (c) Twobridge Chemical Company (Sec. 2.4).
*(d) Jay Canes' Arbitrage Problem (Sec. 2.5).
   (e) Great Auto Works Company (Sec. 2.6).
   (f) Saur Milk Company (Sec. 2.7).

3 *Knox Mix Company* (Sec. 2.2). Using a diagram like Fig. 1.3 for the One-Potato, Two-Potato Problem discussed in Chap. 1, draw the feasible production policies, indicate an optimal policy, and calculate the associated value of the objective function *assuming* you can utilize only

   (a) Process 1 and Process 3 (so that $x_2 = x_4 = 0$).
   (b) Process 1 and Process 4 (so that $x_2 = x_3 = 0$).
   (c) Process 2 and Process 3 (so that $x_1 = x_4 = 0$).
   (d) Process 2 and Process 4 (so that $x_1 = x_3 = 0$).

4 *Knox Mix Company* (Sec. 2.2)

   (a) Suppose you let $x_2 = x_3 = x_4 = 3$. What is the best value for x_1?
   (b) Suppose you let $x_1 = x_2 = x_3 = 3$. What is the best value for x_4?
   (c) Suppose you let $x_1 = x_3$ and $x_2 = x_4 = 0$. What is the best value for x_1 (and x_3)?
   (d) Suppose you let $x_2 = x_4$ and $x_1 = x_3 = 0$. What is the best value for x_2 (and x_4)?
   (e) Suppose you let $x_1 = x_2 = x_3 = x_4$. What is the best value for x_1 (and each other x_j)?

5 *Hion Hog Company* (Sec. 2.3). Using a diagram like Fig. 1.3 for the One-Potato, Two-Potato Problem discussed in Chap. 1, draw the feasible purchase policies, indicate an optimal policy, and calculate the associated value of the objective function *assuming* you can utilize

   (a) Grain 1 and Grain 2 but not Grain 3 (so that $x_3 = 0$).
   (b) Grain 1 and Grain 3 but not Grain 2 (so that $x_2 = 0$).
   (c) Grain 2 and Grain 3 but not Grain 1 (so that $x_1 = 0$).
   (d) Grain 1 and Grain 2, after setting $x_3 = 100$ for Grain 3.
   (e) Grain 1 and Grain 3, after setting $x_2 = 50$ for Grain 2.
   (f) Grain 2 and Grain 3, after setting $x_1 = 200$ for Grain 1.

6 *Hion Hog Company* (Sec. 2.3).

   (a) Suppose you let $x_2 = x_3 = 50$. What is the best value for x_1?

(b) Suppose you let $x_1 = x_2 = 200$. What is the best value for x_3?
(c) Suppose you let $x_1 = x_2$ and $x_3 = 0$. What is the best value for x_1 (and x_2)?
(d) Suppose you let $x_1 = x_3$ and $x_2 = 0$. What is the best value for x_1 (and x_3)?
(e) Suppose you let $x_2 = x_3$ and $x_1 = 0$. What is the best value for x_2 (and x_3)?
(f) Suppose you let $x_1 = x_2 = x_3$. What is the best value for x_1 (and x_2 and x_3)?

7 *Hion Hog Company* (Sec. 2.3). Given that the optimal solution is $x_1 = 200$, $x_2 = 50$, and $x_3 = 100$, can the minimal total requirement for any of the ingredients be raised without also raising total cost? Justify your answer.

8 *Twobridge Chemical Company* (Sec. 2.4). Let $S_1 = S_2 = 100$ and $D_1 = D_2 = D_3 = 50$. Assume $r_3 = 1$. Either indicate a feasible solution or demonstrate that no feasible solution exists if

(a) $r_1 = .1$, $r_2 = .6$, $a_1 = .3$, $a_2 = .4$, $b_1 = .2$, and $b_2 = .5$.
(b) $r_1 = .5$, $r_2 = .6$, $a_1 = .3$, $a_2 = .4$, $b_1 = .2$, and $b_2 = .5$.
(c) $r_1 = .1$, $r_2 = .1$, $a_1 = .3$, $a_2 = .4$, $b_1 = .2$, and $b_2 = .5$.
(d) $r_1 = .1$, $r_2 = .6$, $a_1 = .5$, $a_2 = .6$, $b_1 = .2$, and $b_2 = .5$.
(e) $r_1 = .1$, $r_2 = .6$, $a_1 = .3$, $a_2 = .4$, $b_1 = .8$, and $b_2 = .4$.

*9 *Jay Canes' Arbitrage Problem* (Sec. 2.5). Demonstrate that there exists an unbounded optimal solution if

(a) $r_{11} = .75$ and $r_{26} = 2$.
(b) $r_{11} = 2$ and $r_{26} = .75$.
(c) $r_{11} \cdot r_{26} > 1$.

10 *Great Auto Works Company* (Sec. 2.6). In what ways do you think a manager would find such a planning model useful?

11 *Great Auto Works Company* (Sec. 2.6). Write the sales requirement and the work force restrictions for

(a) Period 2.
(b) Period 4.
(c) Period $T - 1$.

12 *Great Auto Works Company* (Sec. 2.6). Assume the planning horizon length is $T = 4$. Let $W_1 = 0$, and $S_1 = 100$, $S_2 = 200$, $S_3 = 100$, and $S_4 = 160$. To keep the computations simple, assume there is no spoilage of items inventoried from one period to the next; hence, the amount 25 should appear instead of 20 in Fig. 2.8. Also assume that there is no shrinkage effect in workers left idle; hence, the amount -10 should appear instead of -9 in Fig. 2.8. Devise a plan so that

(a) Every period keeps inventory at a minimum.
(b) The company hires as few workers as possible. Is there more than one such plan? Explain.
(c) Answer (a) and (b) for $S_3 = 160$ and $S_4 = 240$.

13 *Transportation Network* (Sec. 2.7). Write all the linear restrictions (2) and (3) and the complete objective function (1) for a transportation problem in which

(a) $m = 2$ and $n = 3$.

(b) $m = 3$ and $n = 2$.

(c) $m = n = 3$.

(d) $m = 3$ and $n = 4$.

*14 *Route Selection Through a Network* (Sec. 2.8)

(a) Find the cost and route of a least-cost route from Node 1 to Node 5 in Fig. 2.14, where

$$c_{12} = 2 \qquad c_{13} = 10 \qquad c_{14} = 16 \qquad c_{15} = 20$$
$$c_{23} = 9 \qquad c_{24} = 14 \qquad c_{25} = 17$$
$$c_{34} = 5 \qquad c_{35} = 9$$
$$c_{45} = 3.$$

(b) Given your answer to part (a), show feasible solutions to the linear programming problems in Figs. 2.15 and 2.16.

*15 *Route Selection Through a Network* (Sec. 2.8). Consider a network like that in Fig. 2.14 augmented by Node 6, which can be reached from each other Node i directly by an arc from that node. Draw the network showing all the arcs. State in full a linear programming model that obtains the cost of a least-cost route from Node 1 to Node 6.

16 Explain your understanding of the following terms:

linear programming model	alternative optimal solutions
divisibility	multiple criteria
additivity	sensitivity analysis
nonnegative variable	sign convention
variable unrestricted in sign	time-staged problem
feasible solution	planning horizon
objective function	network
optimal solution	*redundant relation
*unbounded optimal solution	*linear homogeneous system.

FORMULATION EXERCISES

17 The Tim Burr Company wants to best utilize the wood resources in one of its forest regions. Within this region, there is a sawmill and a plywood mill; thus timber can be converted to lumber or plywood.

Producing a marketable mix of 1000 board feet of lumber products requires 1000 board feet of spruce and 3000 board feet of Douglas fir. Producing 1000 square feet of plywood requires 2000 board feet of spruce and 4000 board feet of Douglas fir. This region has available 32,000 board feet of spruce and 72,000 board feet of Douglas fir.

Sales commitments require that at least 4000 board feet of lumber and 12,000 square feet of plywood be produced during the planning period. The profit contributions are $40 per 1000 board feet of lumber products and $60 per 1000 square feet of plywood. Let L be the amount (in 1000 board feet) of lumber produced and P be the amount (in 1000 square feet) of plywood produced.

(a) Express the problem as a linear programming model.
(b) Using a diagram like Fig. 1.3 for the One-Potato, Two-Potato Problem in Chap. 1, exhibit the feasible product mixes and indicate an optimal solution.

18 The Jericho Steel Company must decide how many pounds of pure steel x_1 and how many pounds of scrap metal x_2 to use in manufacturing an alloy casting for one of its customers. Assume that the cost per pound of pure steel is 3 and the cost per pound of scrap metal is 5 (which is larger because the impurities must be skimmed off). The customer's order is expressed as a demand for at least five pounds and the customer is willing to accept a greater amount if Jericho requires a larger production run.

Assume that the supply of pure steel is limited to four pounds and of scrap metal to six pounds. The ratio of scrap to pure steel cannot exceed 7/8. The manufacturing facility has only 18 hours of melting and casting time available; a pound of pure steel requires three hours whereas a pound of scrap requires only two hours to process through the facility.

(a) Express the entire problem as a linear programming model.
(b) Using a diagram like Fig. 1.3 for the One-Potato, Two-Potato Problem in Chap. 1, exhibit the feasible mixes of pure steel and scrap metal, and indicate an optimal solution.

19 The Flagg-Poole Advertising Company has announced that it can optimally allocate its client's advertising dollars by means of linear programming. The company's approach is to identify the various audiences the client wants addressed—such as teenagers, young married couples, the geriatric group, etc. Let the index i represent the ith audience. The client must specify a desired level of exposure E_i for each audience i. Then each advertising vehicle (such as Life Magazine, a prime-time television spot commercial, a color ad in a Sunday newspaper, etc.) is scored for its effectiveness in each of the identified audience categories. Let the index j represent the jth advertising vehicle, and a_{ij} the scored effectiveness for the ith audience of allocating a dollar to the jth vehicle.

Each decision variable is designated as x_j, which represents the total amount of dollars allocated to the jth advertising vehicle during a promotion campaign. The client's objective is to minimize its total advertising expenditure while still meeting its desired levels of product exposure.

(a) Assume that there are three audiences and five advertising vehicles. Write the linear programming model implied by the above description.
(b) Discuss whether you think this linear programming model is an appropriate approach for choosing an optimal allocation of advertising dollars.

20 The Best Tasties Corporation makes four different kinds of breakfast cereals: Noisies, Soggies, Bursties, and Reposies. Each of these is a composite of ingredients (grains, vitamins, sugar, and preservatives). Let the index i represent Ingredient i, where $i = 1, 2, \ldots, I$. Let a_{Ni} be the amount of Ingredient i in a pound of Noisies, and similarly a_{Si}, a_{Bi}, and a_{Ri} be the amounts for the three other cereals. Assume that M_i

is the maximum amount of Ingredient i available during the next month for making all of these breakfast cereals.

The profit contribution of a pound of Noisies is represented by p_N, and similarly, the profit contributions for the other cereals are represented by p_S, p_B, and p_R. Let x_N, x_S, x_B, and x_R represent the number of pounds of each breakfast cereal manufactured during the next month. At least 100,000 pounds of Noisies must be manufactured, as well as at least 125,000 pounds of Soggies, 30,000 pounds of Bursties, and 500,000 pounds of Reposies.

Show how an optimal production schedule can be obtained by a linear programming formulation.

21 The Turned-On Transistor Radio Company manufactures Models A, B, and C which have profit contributions of 8, 15, and 25, respectively. The weekly minimum production requirements are 100 for Model A, 150 for Model B, and 75 for Model C.

Each type of radio requires a certain amount of time for the manufacturing of component parts, for assembling, and for packaging. Specifically, a dozen units of Model A require three hours for manufacturing, four hours for assembling, and one hour for packaging. The corresponding figures for a dozen units of Model B are 3.5, 5, and 1.5, and for a dozen units of Model C are 5, 8, and 3. During the forthcoming week, the company has available 150 hours of manufacturing, 200 hours of assembling, and 60 hours of packaging time.

Formulate the production scheduling problem as a linear programming model.

22 The manager of the Boilen Oil Company wishes to find the optimal mix of two possible blending processes. For Process 1, an input of one unit of Crude Oil A and three units of Crude Oil B produces an output of five units of Gasoline X and two units of Gasoline Y. For Process 2, an input of four units of Crude Oil A and two units of Crude Oil B produces an output of three units of Gasoline X and eight units of Gasoline Y. Let x_1 and x_2 be the number of units the company decides to use of Process 1 and Process 2, respectively.

The maximum amount of Crude Oil A available is 100 units and of Crude Oil B, 150 units. Sales commitments require that at least 200 units of Gasoline X and 75 units of Gasoline Y are produced. The unit profits of Process 1 and Process 2 are p_1 and p_2, respectively.

Formulate the blending problem as a linear programming model.

23 The High Tail Airfreight Company, which operates out of a central terminal, has 8 aircraft of Type 1, 15 aircraft of Type 2, and 12 aircraft of Type 3 available for today's flights. The tonnage capacities (in thousands of tons) are 45 for Type 1, 7 for Type 2, and 4 for Type 3.

The company dispatches its planes to Cities A and B. Tonnage requirements (in thousands of tons) are 20 at City A and 30 at City B; excess tonnage capacity supplied to a city has no value. A plane can fly only once during the day.

The cost of sending a plane from the terminal to each city is given by the following table.

	Type 1	Type 2	Type 3
City A	23	5	1.4
City B	58	10	3.8

Let x_1, x_2, and x_3 denote the number of planes of each type sent to City A, and similarly, y_1, y_2, and y_3 the number sent to City B.

(a) Formulate a linear programming model of this routing problem.
(b) Discuss whether an answer so derived would represent an optimal solution to the actual routing problem.

24 The Glassey-Staire Television Network wants to establish competitive but profitable prices for advertising time. The following is a simplified version of its pricing problem. Assume there are three classifications of network advertising time: prime-evening, weekday, and Saturday/Sunday afternoon (before 6 p.m.). Let p_1, p_2, and p_3 be the price per minute for each of these time slots, respectively.

The network sells large blocks of time to K major advertisers who have a significant effect on the determination of the prices. The network knows that major advertiser k wants to purchase a package consisting of a_{1k}, a_{2k}, and a_{3k} minutes in the three time slots and is willing to pay up to A_k dollars for this package. The network also sells time to many smaller advertisers and figures that *in toto* it can sell M_1, M_2, and M_3 minutes of prime, weekday, and weekend time, respectively, provided that its prices are suitable with regard to the K major advertisers.

(a) Formulate the pricing problem as a linear programming model.
(b) Suppose Glassey-Staire wonders whether it should consider satisfying all but one of its major advertisers. How would you analyze this possibility?

25 *Trim Problem.* A mill of the Fine-Webb Paper Company produces so-called liner board in jumbo reels having a standard width of 70 inches. (Each reel has a fixed length.) The company's customers, however, order reels having smaller widths (and the same fixed length as the larger reel). Today's orders are for 100 reels of 22-inch width, 125 reels of 20-inch width, and 80 reels of 12-inch width. These smaller widths are to be cut from the larger standard size reel.

For example, the company can decide to slit a jumbo into two reels each 22 inches wide, and one reel 20 inches wide; this leaves 6 inches of trim waste from the 70-inch jumbo. The company wants to manufacture today's orders so as to minimize total trim waste.

(a) Find every possible way to slit a 70-inch jumbo reel into combinations of 22-inch, 20-inch, and 12-inch width reels. One such combination was already illustrated in the example. Calculate the trim waste for each combination. Label the combinations $1, 2, 3, \ldots$, and let x_i be the number of jumbo reels cut into Combination i.

(b) Formulate the problem as a linear programming model. (Note that if any smaller reels in excess of the customer requirements are produced, these too must be counted as waste.)

(c) Show that the objective function also can be written as

$$\text{minimize} \quad 70(x_1 + x_2 + \cdots).$$

26 *Trim Problem.* Answer the questions in exercise 25 assuming that the width of the jumbo roll is 105 inches, and that today's orders are for 100 reels of 25-inch width, 125 reels of 30-inch width, and 80 reels of 35-inch width. [Note that the coefficient in part (c) is no longer 70.]

27 *Trim Problem.* Answer the questions posed in exercise 25 assuming that the width of the jumbo roll is 200 inches, and that today's orders are for 100 reels of 30-inch width, 125 reels of 55-inch width, and 80 reels of 65-inch width. [Note that the coefficient in part (c) is no longer 70.]

28 The Fly-by-Night Airline must decide on the amounts of jet fuel to purchase from three possible vendors. The airline refuels its aircraft regularly at the four airports it serves.

The oil companies have said that they can furnish up to the following amounts of fuel during the coming month: 250,000 gallons for Oil Company 1; 500,000 gallons for Oil Company 2; and 600,000 gallons for Oil Company 3. The required amount of jet fuel is 100,000 gallons at Airport 1; 200,000 gallons at Airport 2; 300,000 gallons at Airport 3; and 400,000 gallons at Airport 4.

When transportation costs are added to the bid price per gallon supplied, the combined cost per gallon for jet fuel from each vendor furnishing a specific airport is shown in the table.

	Company 1	Company 2	Company 3
Airport 1	12	9	10
Airport 2	10	11	14
Airport 3	8	11	13
Airport 4	11	13	9

(a) Formulate the decision problem as a linear programming model.
(b) Is the model equivalent to a transportation or a network problem? Explain.

29 The Hayes Manufacturing Company produces a small component for an industrial product and distributes it to five wholesalers at a fixed *delivered* price of $2.50 per unit. Sales forecasts indicate that monthly deliveries will be 3000 units to Wholesaler 1; 3000 units to Wholesaler 2; 10,000 units to Wholesaler 3; 5000 units to Wholesaler 4; and 4000 units to Wholesaler 5.

The monthly production capacities are 5000 at Plant 1; 10,000 at Plant 2; and 12,500 at Plant 3. The direct costs of producing each unit are $1.00 at Plant 1, $.90 at Plant 2, and $.80 at Plant 3.

The transportation costs of shipping a unit from a plant to a wholesaler are given below.

	Whlslr. 1	Whlslr. 2	Whlslr. 3	Whlslr. 4	Whlslr. 5
Plant 1	$.05	$.07	$.10	$.15	$.15
Plant 2	.08	.06	.09	.12	.14
Plant 3	.10	.09	.08	.10	.15

Formulate a linear programming model to indicate optimal production amounts at each plant, and to show how many components each plant supplies each wholesaler.

30 The Kleen City Police Department has the following minimal *daily* requirements for policemen:

		Minimal Number of
Time of Day		Policemen Required
(24-Hour Clock)	Period	During Period
2–6	1	20
6–10	2	50
10–14	3	80
14–18	4	100
18–22	5	40
22–2	6	30

Note, you are to consider Period 1 as following immediately after Period 6.

Each policeman works eight consecutive hours. Let x_t denote the number of men starting work in Period t every day. The Police Department seeks a daily manpower schedule that employs the least number of policemen, provided that each of the above requirements are met.

Formulate a linear programming model to find an optimal schedule.

31 Around 435 B.C., Sparta decided to draft reserve troops to supplement its regular army. New warriors could be enlisted for 1, 2, 3, or 4 years. Let x_{1t}, x_{2t}, x_{3t}, and x_{4t} be the number of warriors enlisted in Year t for 1, 2, 3, and 4 years, respectively. The associated unit costs are c_{1t}, c_{2t}, c_{3t}, and c_{4t}. In each Year t, the minimal total reserve warrior strength was set at R_t; R_t varied from year to year.

As a Spartan general, you could find an optimal enlistment policy for the ensuing 20 years by solving the problem as a linear programming model. For simplicity, let $t = 1$ denote the year 435 B.C.

(a) Construct a table like that in Fig. 2.7 to exhibit the time interrelations for x_{1t}, x_{2t}, x_{3t}, and x_{4t} over Years t, t $+$ 1, t $+$ 2, and t $+$ 3.
(b) Exhibit the manpower constraints for Years 1, 2, 3, 4, and 5.
(c) Exhibit the manpower constraints for Years 16, 17, 18, 19, and 20.
(d) Exhibit the general form of a manpower constraint for Year t, where $6 \leq t \leq 15$.

32 The Feedem-Speedem Airline Company must decide how many new stewardesses to hire and train over the next six months. The requirements expressed as the number of stewardess-flight-hours needed are 8000 in January; 9000 in February; 8000 in March; 10,000 in April; 9000 in May; and 12,000 in June.

It takes one month of training before a stewardess can be put on a regular flight; so a girl must be hired at least a month before she is actually needed. Also, a trainee requires 100 hours of supervision by experienced stewardesses during the month of training so that 100 less hours are available for flight service by regular stewardesses.

Each experienced stewardess can work up to 150 hours in a month, and Feedem-Speedem has 60 regular stewardesses available at the beginning of January. If the maximum time available from experienced stewardesses exceeds a month's flying and training requirements, the regular girls work fewer than 150 hours, and none are laid off. Each month, approximately 10% of the experienced stewardesses quit their jobs to be married or for other reasons.

An experienced stewardess costs the company $800 and a trainee $400 a month in salary and other benefits.

(a) Formulate the hiring-and-training problem as a linear programming model. Let x_t be the number of stewardesses that begin training in Month t, where $x_0 = 60$. Define any additional symbols that you need to express the decision variables.

(b) The above statement of the problem assumes a six-month planning horizon. Suppose you add July's requirements to the model. Would the previous solution necessarily change? Explain.

33 The Holme Appliance Company produces refrigerators, stoves, and dishwashers. During the coming year, sales are expected to be the following.

| | Quarter | | | |
Product	1	2	3	4
Refrigerators	2000	1500	3000	1000
Stoves	1500	1500	1000	1500
Dishwashers	1000	3000	1500	3000

The company wants a production schedule that meets each of these quarterly demand requirements. Management also has decided that the inventory level for each product must be at least 100 units at the end of each quarter. There is no inventory of any product at the start of the first quarter.

During a quarter only 8500 hours of production time are available. A refrigerator requires .5 hour, a stove 2 hours, and a dishwasher 1.5 hours of production time. Refrigerators cannot be manufactured in the fourth quarter because the company plans to modify tooling for a new product line.

Assume that each item left in inventory at the end of a quarter incurs a holding or storage cost of 5. The company wants a production schedule that does not exceed the production-time limitation of each quarter, that meets the quarterly demand and inventory requirements, and that keeps the total cost of carrying inventory to a minimum.

Let R_t, S_t, and D_t be the number of refrigerators, stoves, and dishwashers manufactured in Period t. Define any other symbols that you need to represent the variables. Show how the problem can be solved by a linear programming model.

34 *Knox Mix Company* (Sec. 2.2). Assume that the technological data shown in Fig. 2.3 are valid for each of four consecutive time periods. Suppose you can store *excess* (or *unused*) Material Y and Material Z from one period to the next at a holding cost per unit per period of h_Y and h_Z, respectively. Formulate the product-mix selection problem as a dynamic planning problem. Be sure to define new symbols that indicate the time period for each production variable, and to specify the storage activities.

35 *Twobridge Chemical Company* (Sec. 2.4). Assume that the data in Fig. 2.5 are valid in each of T consecutive periods, except that the available supplies of chemicals, the demands for the products, and the profits of each activity vary from period to period. State how you would modify the model to permit excess supplies of Chemicals 1 and 2 in one period to be inventoried for possible use in succeeding periods, and to allow for

Products 1, 2, and 3 made in one period to be stored for meeting demands in sub-sequent periods. Be sure to define new symbols that indicate the time period for each production variable and to specify the storage activities.

36 The Expando Manufacturing Company, which produces a single type of item, wishes to enlarge its capacity over the next six periods (a period is three months). The company's objective is to have its production capacity as large as possible by the end of the sixth period.

Each item produced in a period requires d dollars (for the purchase of raw materials and the payment of wages), and one unit of plant capacity; it yields r dollars of sales revenue at the beginning of the *next* period.

In each period, the company can use either or both of two construction techniques to expand its plant. Each requires cash in the period the expansion is initiated, and one takes more time than the other. Specifically, building a unit of capacity by Expansion Method 1 requires b dollars when the construction activity is started and yields the added capacity by the beginning of the following period. Building a unit of capacity by Expansion Method 2 requires c dollars when the construction activity is started and yields the added capacity by the beginning of the period *after* the following one.

The company has D dollars to finance its production and expansion in Period 1, but requires that the subsequent production and expansion activities be self-funding (that is, no supply of cash will be forthcoming from *outside* sources after the first period). The plant capacity at the start of Period 1 is K.

For each period, t, let x_t denote the production level; u_t and v_t the levels of capacity expansion using Methods 1 and 2, respectively; w_t unused cash at the end of the period; and z_t unused plant capacity.

(a) Construct a table like that in Fig. 2.7 to exhibit the time interrelations.
(b) Show how the problem can be solved by a linear programming formulation.

MIND-EXPANDING EXERCISES

37 The Uptight Faucet Company has two factories, one on the East Coast and one on the West. Let the index i designate Factory i. To keep the explanation simple, assume that both factories produce the same type of faucet. The company wants to plan its production schedule for the next two quarters, which are designated as Periods 1 and 2. In each period, the production capacity at Factory i is L_i.

The company ships its faucets to two distributing warehouses, designated by the index j. The minimal demand requirement to be met by the end of Period t at Warehouse j is R_{tj}, where $t = 1$ and 2, and $j = 1$ and 2.

For each Factory i, let

$x_i \equiv$ amount produced *and shipped* by the end of the first quarter.

$y_i \equiv$ amount produced *and shipped* by the end of the second quarter.

$s_i \equiv$ amount produced *and stored* at Factory i at the end of the first quarter.

For each Factory i and Warehouse j, let

$z_{ij} \equiv$ amount shipped from Factory i to Warehouse j by the end of the first quarter.

$v_{ij} \equiv$ amount shipped from Factory i to Warehouse j by the end of the second quarter.

For each Warehouse j, let

$w_j \equiv$ amount stored at Warehouse j at the end of the first quarter.

Define any other symbols you need to represent the variables in the problem.

The company requires that the sum total of production for Factory 1 in both quarters combined be at least 80% of the like quantity for Factory 2. Because of limited storage space, no more than S_i faucets can be stored at Factory i at the end of the first quarter.

The production cost of a faucet at Factory i is p_i. The cost of a faucet stored at the end of the first quarter at Factory i is k_i; the cost of a faucet stored at the end of the first quarter at Warehouse j is h_j. Shipping an item from Factory i to Warehouse j incurs a transportation cost of c_{ij} per faucet. Assume that transportation time is virtually zero (as compared to the length of the quarter), so that an item shipped during a quarter arrives before the quarter is over.

Show how an optimal production and shipping schedule can be found from a linear programming formulation.

38 The Mighty Steel Corporation has two iron ore reduction plants, which are designated by the index r. Each of these plants processes iron ore into two different ingot stocks, which are designated by the index s. The ingot stocks are shipped to any of three different fabricating plants, which are designated by the index f. Each fabricating plant makes two products, which are designated by the index p. Over the forthcoming planning horizon, the company wants to minimize the total tonnage of iron ore processed in its reduction plants, subject to production and demand-requirement constraints.

Let the decision variables be

$x \equiv$ total tonnage of iron ore processed by both reduction plants.

$y_{sfr} \equiv$ total tonnage of iron ore processed into Ingot Stock s for shipment to Fabricating Plant f by Reduction Plant r.

$z_{spf} \equiv$ total tonnage of Ingot Stock s manufactured into Product p at Fabricating Plant f.

The technological data are

$a_{sr} \equiv$ tonnage yield of Ingot Stock s from one ton of iron ore processed at Reduction Plant r.

$b_{spf} \equiv$ total yield from one ton of Ingot Stock s manufactured into Product p at Fabricating Plant f.

$c_r \equiv$ maximum tonnage of iron ore that can be processed by Reduction Plant r.

$k_f \equiv$ maximum tonnage of all stocks that can be manufactured into products at Fabricating Plant f.

$D_p \equiv$ tonnage demand requirement for Product p.

The production and demand requirement constraints include

(i) The total tonnage of iron ore processed by both reduction plants must equal the total tonnage processed into ingot stocks for shipment to the fabricating plants by the reduction plants.

(ii) Total tonnage of iron ore processed by each reduction plant cannot exceed the plant's available capacity.

(iii) Total tonnage of ingot stock manufactured into products at each fabricating plant must equal the tonnage of ingot stock shipped to it by the reduction plants.

(iv) Total tonnage of ingot stock manufactured into products at each fabricating plant cannot exceed the plant's available capacity.

(v) Total tonnage of each product manufactured must equal its demand requirement.

(a) Formulate the problem as a linear programming model.

(b) Comment on the appropriateness of the objective function. Suggest an alternative objective function that might be more appropriate.

39 The Babylon Corporation finds its internal telephone communication network is failing to meet peak-load requirements because of limited transmission capacities. Two stations originate calls, and three stations receive the calls; more than one call can be sent or received by any station. The calls are transmitted through links and two switching nodes. Figure 2.17 illustrates the situation.

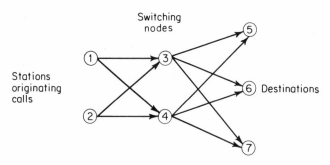

FIGURE 2.17

The decision problem is to increase the transmission capacity of the network in an economic manner. Increasing the capacities to handle the entire peak-load requirements may be too expensive, but some improvement in service is required.

Let a_{ij} be the daily peak-load requirements of messages originating at Station i and destined for Station j, where $i = 1$ and 2 and $j = 5$, 6, and 7. Let C_{kj} be the present link-transmission capacity between Switching Node k and Destination j, where $k = 3$ and 4, and $j = 5$, 6, and 7. Let S_k be the present transmission capacity for messages flowing through Switching Node k.

Define

x_{ikj} = the number of calls originating at Station i, destined for Station j, and passing through Switching Node k.

c_{kj} = new transmission capacity along the link between Switching Node k and Destination j.

s_k = new transmission capacity through Switching Node k.

The constraints to be satisfied are

(i) The total number of calls from each originating station to each destination cannot exceed the peak-load requirement for such calls.

(ii) The total number of calls passing along the link between a switching node and a destination cannot exceed the corresponding link-transmission capacity.

(iii) The total number of calls passing through any switching node cannot exceed the corresponding transmission capacity.

(iv) The new link and node capacities must be at least as large as at present.

The service-level requirement is specified as follows. The routing of calls must satisfy the restriction that the ratio of the *total* number of calls that are actually transmitted to the sum of all the peak-load requirements must be at least f (where $f < 1$).

The cost of increasing link-transmission capacity by one unit between Switching Node k and Destination j is d_{kj}, and of increasing node-transmission capacity at Switching Node k by one unit is d_k.

Show how a linear programming formulation can be used to find a minimum-cost plan for increasing link and node capacities, subject to the above-mentioned constraints.

CONTENTS

CHAPTER 3

Algebraic and Geometric Representations of Linear Optimization Models

3.1 INTRODUCTION

Chapter 2 scanned a wide assortment of linear optimization models. For the most part, the constraints were written as immediate translations of a verbal description. The chapter gave scant notice to the possible connections among different formulations, nor did it elaborate on how much flexibility you have in specifying a model. We provide this information here.

In the initial sections below, you will study how to manipulate linear constraints into different-appearing but mathematically equivalent statements. The techniques presented are helpful for two reasons. First, they enable you to prepare any particular problem you may have for numerical solution by the techniques discussed in Chaps. 4 and 5. Second, they permit you to formulate the model in a way that will subsequently enable you to see how to apply powerful mathematical analysis.

The remainder of the chapter deals with geometric representations of a linear optimization model. Of course, two- and three-dimensional geometric constructions are not sufficient for solving actual large-scale applications; however, these pictorial interpretations do aid you in developing intuition about the workings of a linear programming model.

In all honesty, though, if you are impatient to learn how to find numerical solutions to linear programming models, go ahead and read Chap. 4. You can come back later to read the material in this chapter.

3.2 GENERAL ALGEBRAIC FORMULATION

We can summarize the mathematical representations of the several models you studied in Chap. 2 in the following way. Letting x_j be the level of Activity j, for $j = 1, 2, \ldots, n$, you want to select values for x_j such that

$$p_1 x_1 + p_2 x_2 + \cdots + p_n x_n$$

is maximized, or minimized, depending on the context of the problem. The x_j are constrained by a number of relations, each of which is one of the following type:

$$a_1 x_1 + a_2 x_2 + \cdots + a_n x_n \geq a$$

$$b_1 x_1 + b_2 x_2 + \cdots + b_n x_n = b$$

$$c_1 x_1 + c_2 x_2 + \cdots + c_n x_n \leq c.$$

The first relation includes the possible restriction $x_j \geq 0$.

Such a constrained optimization problem may have

(i) no feasible solution, that is, there may be no values of all the x_j, for $j = 1, 2, \ldots, n$, that satisfy every constraint;

(ii) a unique optimal feasible solution;

(iii) more than one optimal feasible solution; or

(iv) a feasible solution such that the objective function is unbounded; that is, the value of the function can be made as large as desired in a maximization problem, or as small in a minimization problem, by selecting an appropriate feasible solution. (This can happen in the arbitrage model of Sec. 2.5.)

In a few instances, Chap. 2 indicated how there can be more than one explicit way to represent the linear relations characterizing a linear optimization model. For example, in the dairy company model of Sec. 2.7, the sense of the demand-requirements inequalities (3) was reversed by changing the sign of all the constants.

Changing the sense of the optimization. Any linear maximization model can be viewed as an equivalent linear minimization model, and vice versa, by accompanying the change in the optimization sense with a change in the signs of the objective function coefficients. Specifically,

$$\text{maximize} \sum_{j=1}^{n} c_j x_j \quad \text{can be treated as} \quad \text{minimize} \sum_{j=1}^{n} (-c_j) x_j$$

and vice versa. Of course, if V is the optimal value of the right-hand expression above, then $-V$ is the optimal value of the left-hand expression.

Changing the sense of an inequality. All inequalities in a linear programming model can be represented with the same directioned inequality since

(1) $$\sum_{j=1}^{n} a_j x_j \leq b \quad \text{can be written as} \quad \sum_{j=1}^{n} (-a_j) x_j \geq -b,$$

and vice versa. To illustrate, the following two inequalities are equivalent:

$$1x_1 - 1x_2 \leq -4 \qquad -1x_1 + 1x_2 \geq 4.$$

Converting an inequality to an equality. Any inequality in a linear model can be represented as an equality by introducing a nonnegative variable as follows:

(2) $\sum\limits_{j=1}^{n} a_j x_j \leq b$ can be written as $\sum\limits_{j=1}^{n} a_j x_j + 1s = b$ where $s \geq 0$

(3) $\sum\limits_{j=1}^{n} a_j x_j \geq b$ can be written as $\sum\limits_{j=1}^{n} a_j x_j - 1t = b$ where $t \geq 0$.

It is common to refer to a variable such as s in (2) as a **slack variable**, and t in (3) as a **surplus variable**.

To illustrate, in the Product-Mix Selection Example of Sec. 2.2, the constraint on the availability of pounds of Material Y was

$$7x_1 + 5x_2 + 3x_3 + 2x_4 \leq 120.$$

An equivalent way of viewing this restriction is

$$7x_1 + 5x_2 + 3x_3 + 2x_4 + 1y = 120 \quad \text{where} \quad y \geq 0,$$

where y is interpreted as left-over or unused pounds of Material Y. Here y is a slack variable.

Similarly, in the Feed-Mix Selection Example of Sec. 2.3, you can write the constraint on Nutritional Ingredient A as

$$2x_1 + 3x_2 + 7x_3 - 1a = 1250 \quad \text{where} \quad a \geq 0,$$

where a is viewed as the overfulfillment of the requirement for Ingredient A. Thus a is a surplus variable.

Converting equalities to inequalities. Any linear equality or set of linear equalities can be represented as a set of like-directioned linear inequalities by imposing one additional constraint. To motivate the idea, note that $x = 8$ is equivalent to the combination $x \leq 8$ and $x \geq 8$, which in turn can be written as the pair $x \leq 8$ and $-x \leq -8$. As you should check graphically, the equations $x = 1$ and $y = 2$ are equivalent to the combination $x \leq 1, y \leq 2$, and $x + y \geq 3$, which in turn can be expressed as $x \leq 1, y \leq 2$, and $-x - y \leq -3$. The idea generalizes as follows:

(4) $\sum\limits_{j=1}^{n} a_{ij} x_j = b_i$ for $i = 1, 2, \ldots, m$ can be written as

(5) $\sum\limits_{j=1}^{n} a_{ij} x_j \leq b_i$ for $i = 1, 2, \ldots, m$ and $\sum\limits_{j=1}^{n} \alpha_j x_j \leq \beta$

where

(6) $\alpha_j = -\sum\limits_{i=1}^{m} a_{ij}$ and $\beta = -\sum\limits_{i=1}^{m} b_i.$

Thus for $m = 1$, (5) is simply

(7) $\sum\limits_{j=1}^{n} a_{1j} x_j \leq b_1$ and $-\sum\limits_{j=1}^{n} a_{1j} x_j \leq -b_1.$

For an illustration, consider the system

$$1x_1 + 1x_2 \qquad\quad = 1$$
$$2x_1 \qquad\quad - 4x_3 = -5.$$

Apply (5) and (6) to verify that this system is equivalent to the system below:

$$1x_1 + 1x_2 \qquad \leq 1$$
$$2x_1 \qquad - 4x_3 \leq -5$$
$$-3x_1 - 1x_2 + 4x_3 \leq 4.$$

*Converting variables unconstrained in sign to nonnegative variables. When for some j, x_j is unconstrained in sign in a linear model, two transformations are helpful in finding a numerical solution. The first is to select a constraining *equality* containing x_j. This can always be done, possibly after converting an inequality to an equality. Then, using this relation as a *definition* for x_j, substitute for x_j in all the other linear relations, including the objective function, and simplify by collecting terms.

For example, if x_1 is unconstrained in sign and appears in relation 1, which is stated as an equality, write

$$(8) \qquad x_1 = \frac{1}{a_1}\left(b_1 - \sum_{j=2}^{n} a_{1j}x_j\right).$$

Then the right-hand side of (8) is substituted wherever x_1 appears in the model. As is easily seen, the resultant relations are still linear in the remaining variables.

During the optimizing computational process, the definitional relation for x_j may be completely ignored. *After* a solution for the remaining variables is obtained, x_j can be computed from its definitional relation.

The second transformation converts x_j into the difference between two nonnegative variables and substitutes this difference for x_j wherever x_j appears. Specifically,

$$(9) \qquad x_j \equiv x_j' - x_j'' \quad \text{where } x_j' \geq 0 \quad \text{and} \quad x_j'' \geq 0.$$

Thus this transformation expands the number of variables in the model, and preserves linearity of the original relations. The legitimacy of the substitution of (9) requires an argument, but the idea is simple enough and you may want to justify it for yourself.

▶ A third transformation, closely allied to the idea used in relations (4), (5), and (6), is to add only a single new nonnegative variable z and make the conversion

$$(i) \qquad x_j \equiv x_j' - z \quad \text{where } x_j' \geq 0 \quad \text{and} \quad z \geq 0$$

for each x_j unconstrained in sign.

Suppose x_j, for $j = 1, 2, \ldots, k \leq n$, is unconstrained in sign. Then the constraints

$$(ii) \qquad \sum_{j=1}^{n} a_{ij}x_j = b_i \quad \text{for } i = 1, 2, \ldots, m$$

become

$$(iii) \qquad \sum_{j=1}^{k} a_{ij}x_j' + \sum_{j=k+1}^{n} a_{ij}x_j - \alpha_i z = b_i \quad \text{for } i = 1, 2, \ldots, m,$$

where

(iv)
$$\alpha_i = \sum_{j=1}^{k} a_{ij} \quad \text{for } i = 1, 2, \ldots, m.$$ ◄

*Converting lower-bounded variables to nonnegative variables. When an x_j is bounded below by $b_j \neq 0$, it is possible to convert the model into one with a nonnegative variable (that is, where b_j is replaced with 0) by employing the relation

(10)
$$x_j \equiv b_j + x'_j \quad \text{where} \quad x'_j \geq 0.$$

Thus the right-hand side of (10) is substituted for x_j wherever x_j appears.

3.3 CANONICAL FORMS FOR LINEAR OPTIMIZATION MODELS

As you will see in later chapters, it is convenient to be able to write *any* linear optimization model in a compact and unambiguous form. The various transformations above allow you to meet this objective, although it is now apparent that there is considerable latitude in the selection of a particular canonical form to employ. We illustrate two such representations here.

Any linear optimization model can be viewed as

(1)
$$\text{maximize} \sum_{j=1}^{n} c_j x_j$$

subject to

(2)
$$\sum_{j=1}^{n} a_{ij} x_j \leq b_i \quad \text{for } i = 1, 2, \ldots, m$$

(3)
$$x_j \geq 0 \quad \text{for } j = 1, 2, \ldots, n.$$

Similarly, any linear optimization model can be written as

(4)
$$\text{minimize} \sum_{j=1}^{n} c_j x_j$$

subject to

(5)
$$\sum_{j=1}^{n} a_{ij} x_j = b_i \quad \text{for } i = 1, 2, \ldots, m \quad (b_i \geq 0)$$

(6)
$$x_j \geq 0 \quad \text{for } j = 1, 2, \ldots, n.$$

It is typical, although not required, that $n > m$ in (5).

3.4 GEOMETRIC INTERPRETATION

In undertaking the solution and mathematical analysis of linear optimization models in Chaps. 4 and 5, you will see that a grasp of the *algebraic* nature of this type of model is required. Your comprehension of the algebraic properties may be enhanced, however, through a geometric interpretation of the ideas. Accordingly, in order to deepen your understanding of the properties of linear optimization models, we turn to description of the geometry of these problems. So that you do not misconstrue the intent here, we emphasize that a geometric viewpoint usually affords very little help in obtaining numerical solutions to *actual* linear optimization models.

There are two geometric representations of a linear optimization model. One is called the *solution space representation* and is treated here. The other is called the *requirements space representation*; it is less important for a beginner to understand and is explained in the advanced Sec. 3.6.

Solution space representation—two dimensions (variables). You have already seen this representation in the One-Potato, Two-Potato Problem of Chap. 1. You may want to skim over the example to refresh your memory. Here we proceed directly to the consideration of a numerical example:

(1)   maximize $12x_1 + 15x_2$

subject to

(2) $4x_1 + 3x_2 \leq 12$

(3) $2x_1 + 5x_2 \leq 10$

(4) $x_1 \geq 0$ and $x_2 \geq 0$.

The problem is graphed in Fig. 3.1. Observe that both (2) and (3) are drawn as equations. Then each inequality is indicated by an arrow on the side of the line representing permissible values of x_1 and x_2. Since the two variables must be non-negative, the region of permissible values is bounded also by the two coordinate axes.

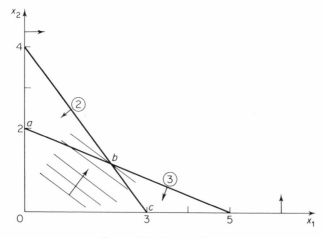

Figure 3.1. Solution Space.

Accordingly, the polygon $\overline{oabc}$ represents the region of values for x_1 and x_2 that satisfy all the constraints. This polygon is called the **solution set**. The set of points described by the polygon is **convex**, meaning that if any two points of the polygon are selected arbitrarily, then a straight-line segment joining the two points contains only points of the polygon. The vertices o, a, b, and c are referred to as the **extreme points** of the polygon in that they are not on the interior of any line segment connecting two distinct points of the polygon.

The parallel lines in the figure represent various values of the objective function. The arrow points in the direction of increasing values of the objective function. The optimal solution is at the extreme point b, where $x_1 = \frac{15}{7}$, $x_2 = \frac{8}{7}$, and $12x_1 + 15x_2 = \frac{300}{7}$.

Alternative optimal solutions. If the coefficients of the objective function are changed so as to alter the direction of the parallel lines in Fig. 3.1, it is clear that the optimal solution point may change, but in any case there is *always* an extreme-point optimal solution. Consider, in Fig. 3.2, a problem for one specific rotation of the parallel lines:

(5)   maximize $4x_1 + 10x_2$

again subject to the same constraints (2), (3), and (4).

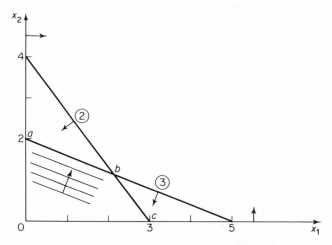

FIGURE 3.2. Alternative Optimal Solutions.

Now, all the points (an infinite number) on the segment $\overline{ab}$ are optimal. Thus $x_1 = \frac{15}{7}$ and $x_2 = \frac{8}{7}$ are still optimal. But so are $x_1 = 0$ and $x_2 = 2$, as well as any positive-weighted average of these two optimal solutions. The optimal value of the objective function is 20.

Unbounded optimal solutions. The third illustration, pictured in Fig. 3.3, is based on the model

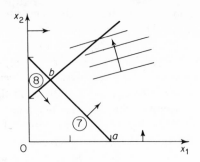

Figure 3.3.   Unbounded Optimal Solution.

(6)   maximize $-2x_1 + 6x_2$

subject to

(7) $-1x_1 - 1x_2 \leq -2$

(8) $-1x_1 + 1x_2 \leq 1$

(9) $x_1 \geq 0$ and $x_2 \geq 0.$

The solution set for this problem is *unbounded*. Check that it is convex, and verify that a and b are the only extreme points. The objective function for the problem can be made arbitrarily large. Given any value for the objective function, there always is a solution point having an even greater objective function value. And there always is such a point satisfying (8) with equality.

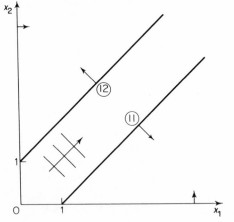

Figure 3.4. No Optimal Solution.

Infeasible problem. The fourth illustration, shown in Fig. 3.4, is based on the problem

(10)   maximize $1x_1 + 1x_2$

subject to

(11) $-1x_1 + 1x_2 \leq -1$

(12) $1x_1 - 1x_2 \leq -1$

(13) $x_1 \geq 0$ and $x_2 \geq 0$.

Figure 3.4 illustrates that the problem does not have a feasible solution.

Conclusion. We will summarize the results of the several geometric illustrations you have studied.

   (i) If the solution set is nonempty, it is convex and may be either bounded or unbounded.

  (ii) If the solution set is nonempty, the optimal value of the objective function may be finite or unbounded. If finite, then an optimal solution exists at an extreme point.

*3.5 SOLUTION SPACE REPRESENTATION IN HIGHER DIMENSIONS

We record here the vocabulary of the geometric representation of the solution space for models having more than two variables.

Assume that the linear optimization model is given by

(1) $\text{maximize } \sum_{j=1}^{n} c_j x_j$

subject to

(2) $\sum_{j=1}^{n} a_{ij} x_j \leq b_i$ for $i = 1, 2, \ldots, m$

(3) $x_j \geq 0$ for $j = 1, 2, \ldots, n$.

Then consider Euclidean n-space, which is comprised of points with n coordinate values $(x_1, x_2, \ldots, x_n)$. Since each $x_j \geq 0$, only the positive orthant of Euclidean n-space need be considered.

Each relation

(4) $\sum_{j=1}^{n} a_{ij} x_j = b_i$ for $i = 1, 2, \ldots, m$

corresponds to a **hyperplane** in n-space, and cuts this space into two **half-spaces**. When the inequality sign $\leq$ is restored to (4), the specified direction indicates which of the two half-spaces contains points satisfying that relation. The intersection of the corresponding m half-spaces comprises the set of feasible solutions. When nonempty, this set is convex and polyhedral, the faces being parts of the hyperplanes (4) and the edges and vertices being intersections of these hyperplanes. To ease exposition, assume that this **convex polyhedral set** is of full dimension n.

The objective function can also be viewed by means of a hyperplane in the solution space. More precisely, the set of all points in Euclidean n-space for which the linear objective function has some given value is a hyperplane. Further, these hyperplanes, one for each distinct value of the objective function, are parallel to each other. It follows that a point strictly interior to the solution set cannot be an optimal solution, for there exist neighboring points in the set lying on hyperplanes having improved values for the objective function. Therefore if the objective function value of an optimal solution is finite, an optimal solution must exist at an extreme point of the solution polyhedron. Further if two or more extreme points are optimal, then so are all the points on the edges or faces connecting them.

*3.6 REQUIREMENTS SPACE REPRESENTATION

We now investigate an alternative to the solution space representation of a linear optimization problem. You can picture a model in terms of the requirements space, which has dimension equal to the number of constraints (excluding nonnegativity conditions). The *set of coefficients* of each activity variable x_j, as well as the constants on the right-hand side of the constraints, are given a vector interpretation. The linear technology implies that each vector j is scaled by the amount $x_j \geq 0$, and the resultant vectors are then added. Consider the entire collection of points that can be formed from every possible sum of the vectors for the x_j, including sums in which the vectors have been scaled by a nonnegative factor. This set comprises what is called a **convex polyhedral cone** in the **requirements space.**

A feasible solution exists, provided the vector corresponding to the right-hand side does not lie outside the cone. The optimization objective may be stated as finding a best sum of vectors that lies within the cone and equals the right-hand-side vector. These geometric ideas will now be illustrated with several of the preceding examples.

Finite optimal solution. In Fig. 3.5 the requirements space is drawn for the model

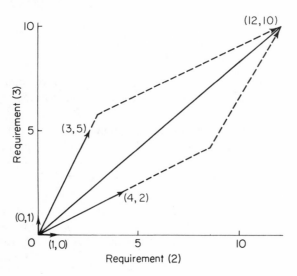

FIGURE 3.5. Requirements Space.

(1)   maximize $12x_1 + 15x_2$

subject to

(2) $4x_1 + 3x_2 \leq 12$

(3) $2x_1 + 5x_2 \leq 10$

(4) $x_1 \geq 0$ and $x_2 \geq 0,$

which you analyzed at the start of Sec. 3.4.

To represent fully the possible linear programming activities, add the slack variables, which become vectors lying along the coordinate axes. Thus, in algebraic form, the constraints of the problem to be illustrated correspond to

$$4x_1 + 3x_2 + 1x_3 \qquad = 12$$
(5)
$$2x_1 + 5x_2 \qquad + 1x_4 = 10$$

$$x_j \geq 0 \quad \text{for } j = 1, 2, 3, 4.$$

With the slack variables added, the requirements space cone consists of the entire nonnegative quadrant. The solution, as indicated by Fig. 3.1, is to add a multiple $x_1 = \frac{15}{7}$ of the vector $(4, 2)$ and a multiple $x_2 = \frac{8}{7}$ of the vector $(3, 5)$ to yield $(12, 10)$:

(6)
$$\left(\frac{15}{7}\right) \cdot \begin{pmatrix} 4 \\ 2 \end{pmatrix} + \left(\frac{8}{7}\right) \cdot \begin{pmatrix} 3 \\ 5 \end{pmatrix} = \begin{pmatrix} 12 \\ 10 \end{pmatrix}.$$

From Fig. 3.5 it is clear that you could also combine a positive multiple of $(1, 0)$ with $(3, 5)$ or with $(0, 1)$, and a positive multiple of $(4, 2)$ with $(0, 1)$ to yield $(12, 10)$. Check that it is not possible to add positive multiples of $(1, 0)$ and $(4, 2)$ to give $(12, 10)$.

Alternative optimal solutions. Suppose that the objective function in the above problem is altered to

$$\text{maximize} \quad 4x_1 + 10x_2$$

so that there are alternative optimal solutions. This does not change the requirements space representation.

Unbounded optimal solutions. Consider again the model

(7)   maximize $-2x_1 + 6x_2$

subject to

(8) $-1x_1 - 1x_2 \leq -2$

(9) $-1x_1 + 1x_2 \leq 1$

(10) $x_1 \geq 0$ and $x_2 \geq 0.$

Recall from Sec. 3.4 that in this model the objective function can be made arbitrarily large by utilizing x_1, x_2, and in effect the slack variable from relation (8). In Fig. 3.6 these variables correspond to the vectors $(-1, -1)$, $(-1, 1)$, and $(1, 0)$,

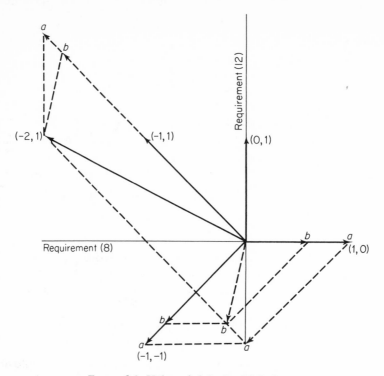

FIGURE 3.6. Unbounded Optimal Solution.

respectively. If you first add the vectors $(-1, -1)$ and $(1, 0)$, and then add the resultant vector $(0, -1)$ to the multiple $x_2 = 2$ of $(-1, 1)$, you obtain $(-2, 1)$, as shown:

$$(11) \qquad (1) \cdot \binom{-1}{-1} + (1) \cdot \binom{1}{0} + (2) \cdot \binom{-1}{1} = \binom{-2}{1}.$$

This vector addition is indicated by the points labeled a on Fig. 3.6.

Similarly, if you first add .8 of $(-1, -1)$ to .6 of $(1, 0)$, and then add the resultant vector $(-.2, -.8)$ to 1.8 of $(-1, 1)$, you obtain $(-2, 1)$:

$$(12) \qquad (.8) \cdot \binom{-1}{-1} + (.6) \cdot \binom{1}{0} + (1.8) \cdot \binom{-1}{1} = \binom{-2}{1}.$$

This vector addition is indicated by the points labeled b on Fig. 3.6. There is an infinite number of combinations of these three vectors, which, when added, yield $(-2, 1)$. Such a combination having a larger multiple of $(-1, 1)$ will give a larger value for the maximizing form.

Optimization. In the requirements space diagrams, we have not indicated so far any information pertaining to the objective function, that is, to the problem of what vectors should be summed to optimize the value of the linear objective function. The information can be added by introducing one more dimension. Consider the problem in (1) through (4), shown in Fig. 3.5. Add as a third dimension the coefficients of the maximizing function. Thus the vectors are (1, 0, 0), (4, 2, 12), (3, 5, 15), and (0, 1, 0), and span a polyhedral cone in 3-space. The requirement vector is (12, 10, Z), where Z is to be maximized over all the vectors in the polyhedral cone.

The illustration appears in Fig. 3.7. Having represented the requirements

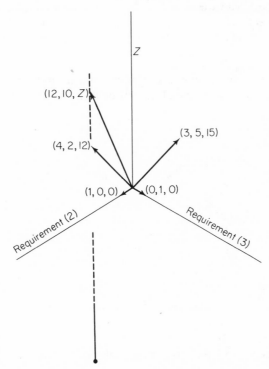

FIGURE 3.7.   Objective-
Function Representation in
Requirements Space.

vector parametrically as (12, 10, Z), draw it as a straight line parallel to the axis of the added dimension and piercing the cone. For some problems, the line may pierce the cone only once, and for others, not at all. In the latter case, there exists either an unbounded optimal solution or no feasible solution at all.

Assume that the line pierces the cone twice. Then an optimal solution corresponds to the "higher" point of intersection of the line with the cone. This point typically is within a face of the polyhedral cone, that is, on a plane spanned by several vectors. The variables corresponding to these vectors comprise an optimal set.

REVIEW AND COMPUTATIONAL EXERCISES

1 Explain your understanding of the following terms:

sense of optimization

sense of an inequality

slack variable

surplus variable

*lower-bounded variable

canonical form

solution space

solution set

convex set

extreme-point solution

*hyperplane

*half-space

*convex polyhedral set

*requirements space

*convex polyhedral cone.

In Secs. 3.2 and 3.3, you read that any linear programming model can be transformed into certain specified canonical forms. Two such representations are

$$\text{maximize} \sum_{j=1}^{n} c_j x_j$$

subject to   (Form 1)

$$\sum_{j=1}^{n} a_{ij} x_j \leq b_i \quad \text{for } i = 1, 2, \ldots, m$$

$$x_j \geq 0 \quad \text{for } j = 1, 2, \ldots, n,$$

and

$$\text{minimize} \sum_{j=1}^{n} c_j x_j$$

subject to   (Form 2)

$$\sum_{j=1}^{n} a_{ij} x_j = b_i \quad \text{for } i = 1, 2, \ldots, m, \quad \text{and where} \quad b_i \geq 0$$

$$x_j \geq 0 \quad \text{for } j = 1, 2, \ldots, n.$$

In exercises 2 through 5, transform each problem into Form 1 and Form 2.

2 Consider

$$\text{minimize } 3x_1 - 4x_2 + 1x_3$$

subject to

$$-1x_1 \qquad + 5x_3 = 50$$

$$2x_1 - 3x_2 \qquad \geq 12.$$

(a) Assume every $x_j \geq 0$.

*(b) Assume $x_1 \geq 4$, $x_2 \geq 0$, and $x_3 \geq 0$.

*(c) Assume $x_1 \geq 0$, $x_2 \geq -5$, and $x_3 \geq 0$.

3 Consider

$$\text{maximize } 1x_1 - 2x_2 + 3x_3$$

subject to

$$1x_1 + 1x_2 + 1x_3 \leq 7$$
$$1x_1 - 1x_2 + 1x_3 \leq -2$$
$$3x_1 \quad\quad + 2x_3 = 5$$
$$1x_2 - 1x_3 \geq 1.$$

(a) Assume every $x_j \geq 0$.
(b) Assume $x_1 \geq 0$, $x_2 \geq 0$, and $x_3 \leq 0$.
*(c) Assume $x_1 \geq 0$, $x_2 \geq 2$, and $x_3 \geq 0$.
*(d) Assume $x_1 \geq 0$, $x_2 \geq 0$, and x_3 is unconstrained in sign.
*(e) Assume $x_1 \geq 0$, $x_2 \geq 0$, and $x_3 \geq -4$.

4 Consider

$$\text{minimize} \quad -2x_1 + 5x_2 - x_3 + 6x_4$$

subject to

$$4x_1 \quad\quad - 2x_3 + x_4 = 2$$
$$2x_1 + x_2 + 4x_3 - x_4 \geq 12$$
$$-3x_1 + 2x_2 \quad\quad - 8x_4 = -31$$
$$x_1 + x_2 + x_3 + x_4 \leq 12.$$

(a) Assume every $x_j \geq 0$.
(b) Assume $x_4 \leq 0$ and every other $x_j \geq 0$.
*(c) Assume $x_4 \geq 2$ and every other $x_j \geq 0$.
*(d) Assume $x_4 \geq -2$ and every other $x_j \geq 0$.
*(e) Assume x_4 is unconstrained in sign and every other $x_j \geq 0$.
*(f) Assume $x_1 \geq 0$, $x_2 \geq -6$, $x_3 \geq 0$, and $x_4 \geq -2$.
*(g) Assume $x_1 \geq 0$, $x_3 \geq 0$, and x_2 and x_4 are unconstrained in sign.

5 Consider

$$\text{maximize} \quad -x_1 + 5x_2 + 5x_3 - 2x_4$$

subject to

$$-5x_1 + 3x_2 - 4x_3 + x_4 \geq -10$$
$$3x_1 + 6x_2 - 2x_3 - x_4 = 7$$
$$x_1 + 4x_2 + 4x_3 + 3x_4 \geq 15$$
$$2x_1 + x_2 + 2x_3 - 6x_4 = -11.$$

(a) Assume every $x_j \geq 0$.
(b) Assume $x_1 \leq 0$ and every other $x_j \geq 0$.
*(c) Assume $x_1 \geq 2$ and every other $x_j \geq 0$.
*(d) Assume $x_1 \geq -2$ and every other $x_j \geq 0$.
*(e) Assume x_1 is unconstrained in sign and every other $x_j \geq 0$.
*(f) Assume $x_1 \geq -2$, $x_2 \geq 0$, $x_3 \geq 0$, and $x_4 \geq -3$.
*(g) Assume $x_2 \geq 0$, $x_3 \geq 0$, and x_1 and x_4 are unconstrained in sign.

In exercises 6 through 20, draw the solution space representation. Identify all the extreme points. In each of the parts, indicate an optimal solution. State whether it is unique, and if it is not, give two more optimal solutions. Be sure you calculate optimal values for x_1 and x_2 and find the associated value of the objective function.

6 Consider the constraints

$$-x_1 + x_2 \le 1$$
$$6x_1 + 4x_2 \ge 24$$
$$x_1 \ge 0 \quad \text{and} \quad x_2 \ge 2.$$

(a) Minimize x_1.
(b) Minimize x_2.
(c) Maximize x_1.
(d) Maximize x_2.
(e) Minimize $x_1 + x_2$.

(f) Maximize $x_1 + x_2$.
(g) Maximize $-x_1 + 2x_2$.
(h) Maximize $x_1 - 2x_2$.
(i) Maximize $-3x_1 - 2x_2$.

7 Answer the questions in exercise 6 assuming also that $x_1 \le 5$.

8 Answer the questions in exercise 6 assuming also that $x_2 \le 4$.

9 Answer the questions in exercise 6 assuming also that $x_1 \le 5$ and $x_2 \le 4$.

10 Consider the constraints

$$-10x_1 - 15x_2 \ge -150$$
$$5x_1 + 10x_2 \ge 50$$
$$x_1 - x_2 \ge 0$$
$$x_1 \ge 2 \quad \text{and} \quad x_2 \ge 0.$$

(a) Maximize x_1.
(b) Minimize x_1.
(c) Maximize x_2.
(d) Minimize x_2.
(e) Maximize $x_1 + x_2$.

(f) Minimize $x_1 + x_2$.
(g) Maximize $x_1 + 3x_2$.
(h) Maximize $-2x_1 + x_2$.
(i) Maximize $-x_1 - 3x_2$.
(j) Maximize $-x_1 - 2x_2$.

11 Answer the questions in exercise 10 assuming the lower bound $x_1 \ge 5$.

12 Answer the questions in exercise 10 assuming the lower bound $x_1 \ge 15$.

13 Answer the questions in exercise 10 assuming the lower bound $x_1 \ge 20$.

14 Answer the questions in exercise 10 assuming the additional constraint $x_2 \le 5$.

15 Answer the questions in exercise 10 assuming the additional constraint $x_2 \ge 6$.

16 Answer the questions in exercise 10 assuming the additional constraint $x_2 \ge 8$.

17 Consider the constraints

$$x_1 + x_2 \geq 5$$
$$-7x_1 + 8x_2 \leq 0$$
$$3x_1 + 2x_2 \leq 18$$
$$0 \leq x_1 \leq 4 \quad \text{and} \quad 0 \leq x_2 \leq 6.$$

(a) Maximize x_1.
(b) Minimize x_1.
(c) Maximize x_2.
(d) Minimize x_2.
(e) Maximize $x_1 + x_2$.
(f) Minimize $x_1 + x_2$.

(g) Maximize $3x_1 + 5x_2$.
(h) Minimize $3x_1 + 5x_2$.
(i) Maximize $-2x_1 - x_2$.
(j) Maximize $-x_1 - 2x_2$
(k) Minimize $x_1 - 2x_2$.
(l) Minimize $2x_1 - x_2$.

18 Answer the questions in exercise 17 assuming the first constraint is $x_1 + x_2 \geq 6$.

19 Answer the questions in exercise 17 assuming the first constraint is $x_1 + x_2 \geq 4$.

20 Answer the questions in exercise 17 assuming the new bounds $0 \leq x_1 \leq 4.5$ and $0 \leq x_2 \leq 3$.

*21 Draw the requirements space representation for the constraints

$$x_1 + 4x_2 + x_3 \leq 1$$
$$1.5x_1 + x_2 + 3x_3 \leq 1$$
$$\text{every } x_j \geq 0.$$

*22 Draw the requirements space representation for the constraints

$$x_1 + 3x_2 - 2x_3 - x_4 \leq -1$$
$$5x_2 + 2x_2 - x_3 - 3x_4 \leq 2$$
$$\text{every } x_j \geq 0.$$

CONTENTS

CHAPTER 4

Simplex Method of Solution

4.1 THEORY IN PERSPECTIVE

You will probably never have to calculate manually the solution of a linear programming model in a real application, since an electronic computer will do the work for you. You may legitimately ask, then, "Why do I need to know the underlying *theory* of linear optimization models? Isn't it enough merely to have the skill to formulate them?" It is difficult to answer these questions convincingly for a student who has not *already* learned the fundamentals of linear optimization theory; but in the light of considerable experience in applying linear programming to industrial problems, we are persuaded that an executive must understand the principles explained here in order to make truly effective and sustained use of this management tool.

The following analogy may help win you over to our point of view. In learning to drive a car, it strains the intellect only mildly to learn to speed up, slow down, go forward or backward, turn, and so forth—in short, to master the skill of driving. To qualify as a topnotch driver, however, you need to know more. You should have an idea of how to care for the battery; otherwise you may make the mistake of playing the radio for a long time with the ignition off. If you drive on icy highways, a knowledge of the braking mechanism should help you control your car when it skids. If your engine overheats suddenly, an understanding of the radiator's function may suggest the correct remedy. Summing up, to be a good driver you must know more than how to handle your auto under ideal conditions. You must know enough about its mechanism to be able to skirt danger when possible. On the other hand, you can obviously be an excellent driver without the training of an automobile mechanic.

By the same token, the manager who resolutely avoids familiarizing himself with the basic mechanism of his operations research application is flirting with trouble. If he really wants to maintain control, he must nurture his insight to the approach. Only a modest effort is required to reach the appropriate level of knowledge; it does not entail your becoming an expert theoretician.

You may ask another serious question concerning the value of studying linear optimization theory: "Do I have any assurance that the methods I learn now will remain relevant in a few years, given the rapidity of new advances in technology?" Of course, we can only speculate about the future, but history offers guidance. Again, the automobile analogy is helpful in framing an answer. If you glance at a typical early-model car, you recognize at once that it *is* an auto. Despite the vast technological improvements in automobile design, much of the basic structure has remained unchanged.

The advances in methods for solving linear optimization models show a similar pattern. Each decade of development has brought substantial modifications in computer methods for solving linear programming problems. Nevertheless, certain fundamental ideas have withstood the test of time, and still provide the basic structure of all approaches. These are the principles you will learn next.

4.2 ASSESSMENT OF THE OBJECTIVE

In this chapter, you will examine a computational method—an **algorithm** —for deriving numerical solutions to linear programming models. The task goes beyond merely specifying steps that eventually lead to a solution. The goal is to discover a systematic method that permits you to analyze and fully understand a model and its complex interrelations. Such a goal is essential, for in actual applications of linear programming you always want more than a mere numerical answer. Usually, you want to know precisely how the answer depends on the input specifications, that is, how sensitive the solution is to the original data. The importance of sensitivity analysis is apparent since often the technological specifications are based on estimates and the constraints included may only be approximate. Further, a number of real constraints may be provisionally left absent from the model. And the objective function may not completely exhaust the factors of relevance in evaluating a solution.

An equally important objective is perceiving the basic structure of optimizing algorithms. By concentrating in this chapter on what is known as the *simplex technique*, you will become familiar with the algorithmic method. As a result, you will gain the insights needed for a sound understanding of approaches to other optimization models studied in subsequent chapters.

Rather than start with a full-blown statement of the simplex algorithm, we begin slowly with some simplifying assumptions. Otherwise, you might easily get bogged down in detail, and lose sight of the central ideas, which are very intuitive. Rest assured, by the time you finish this chapter, you will have learned all the details necessary to apply the algorithm to *any* linear programming model.

Preliminary analysis. Before exploring the simplex algorithm, we briefly examine a small linear programming model so as to appreciate the hurdles to be encompassed by a technique of solution. Consider the problem

(1)   maximize $2x_1 + 3x_2 + 7x_3 + 9x_4$

subject to

(2) $1x_1 + 1x_2 + 1x_3 + 1x_4 + 1x_5 \qquad = 9$

(3) $1x_1 + 2x_2 + 4x_3 + 8x_4 \qquad + 1x_6 = 24$

$$x_j \geq 0 \quad \text{for} \quad j = 1, 2, \ldots, 6.$$

As a start toward solution, try the maximal amount of x_4, the variable having the largest coefficient in the objective function. Check that this trial amount is $\frac{24}{8} = 3$ and is determined by the coefficients in (3). The associated objective function value is $9(3) = 27$. If you try instead the maximal amount of x_3, which you can verify to be $\frac{24}{4} = 6$, then the associated objective function value is the larger amount $7(6) = 42$. Thus, because of the constraining relations, it is not always best to use only a variable with the largest payoff per unit.

Check that letting $x_3 = 6$ implies that $x_5 = 3$. Since the latter variable does not contribute to the value of the objective function, we ask next whether we can improve the solution further by combining several other economic variables. Even in a problem as small as this, it would be wearisome to test various combinations unless some simple rules were available that allowed us to skip over clearly inferior solutions.

Suppose you guess next that an optimal solution contains x_2 and x_3 at positive levels, and all the other variables at zero levels. It is easy to verify whether this conjecture is valid. You need only be able to manipulate (2) and (3) by the usual method in elementary algebra for solving two simultaneous linear equations. In mathematics literature, the approach often is called **Gaussian elimination.**

As a preliminary, bring x_1, x_4, x_5, and x_6 to the right-hand side of the equality signs:

(4) $1x_2 + 1x_3 = 9 - 1x_1 - 1x_4 - 1x_5$

(5) $2x_2 + 4x_3 = 24 - 1x_1 - 8x_4 \qquad - 1x_6.$

Then eliminate x_2 from (5) by multiplying (4) by 2 and subtracting the result from (5) to obtain (7):

(6) $1x_2 + 1x_3 = 9 - 1x_1 - 1x_4 - 1x_5$

(7) $2x_3 = 6 + 1x_1 - 6x_4 + 2x_5 - 1x_6.$

Next *normalize* the coefficient of x_3 in (7) by dividing by 2, yielding (9):

(8) $1x_2 + 1x_3 = 9 - 1x_1 - 1x_4 - 1x_5$

(9) $1x_3 = 3 + \tfrac{1}{2}x_1 - 3x_4 + 1x_5 - \tfrac{1}{2}x_6.$

Finally, you should *eliminate* x_3 from (8) by subtracting (9) from (8), giving the pair of equations

(10) $$x_2 = 6 - \tfrac{3}{2}x_1 + 2x_4 - 2x_5 + \tfrac{1}{2}x_6$$

(11) $$x_3 = 3 + \tfrac{1}{2}x_1 - 3x_4 + 1x_5 - \tfrac{1}{2}x_6.$$

The combined normalizing and eliminating operation is sometimes called **pivoting**.

The present hypothesis is that $x_1 = x_4 = x_5 = x_6 = 0$. Then from (10) and (11) you can conclude that $x_2 = 6$ and $x_3 = 3$. [Check that these values satisfy (2) and (3).] For this solution, the value of the objective function (1) is $3(6) + 7(3) = 39$. Since you previously examined a solution ($x_3 = 6$) that gave an objective function value of 42, you know the current guess is not optimal. However, we are seeking a simple way to discover whether the current guess is optimal without referring to any *previous* trials.

To proceed in this pursuit, substitute the relations for x_2 and x_3 as given in (10) and (11) into the objective function:

(12)
$$\begin{aligned}
&2x_1 + 3(6 - \tfrac{3}{2}x_1 + 2x_4 - 2x_5 + \tfrac{1}{2}x_6) \\
&+ 7(3 + \tfrac{1}{2}x_1 - 3x_4 + 1x_5 - \tfrac{1}{2}x_6) + 9x_4 \\
&= 39 + 1x_1 - 6x_4 + 1x_5 - 2x_6.
\end{aligned}$$

It is evident from (12) that raising the value of either x_1 or x_5 from zero will increase the objective function beyond 39. In fact, according to the coefficients of x_1 and x_5 in (12), for each unit you introduce of either of these variables, the objective function goes up by 1.

Suppose you decide to increase x_1. How large can you make it? Looking at (10) and (11), which are merely rearranged versions of (2) and (3), you can check that if you increase x_1 and leave $x_4 = x_5 = x_6 = 0$, then x_2 will decrease by $\tfrac{3}{2}$ and x_3 will increase by $\tfrac{1}{2}$ for each unit of x_1 added. But for a feasible solution all $x_j \geq 0$. Therefore, x_1 can be made only as large as 4, at which point x_2 becomes 0. Further, according to (12), the corresponding value of the objective function is $39 + 1 \cdot 4 = 43$.

You are now ready to try your newest guess at an optimal solution, namely that x_1 and x_3 are positive and all the rest of the variables are zero. Check your understanding of the way we progressed from the pair (2) and (3) to the pair (10) and (11) by carrying out the analogous computations to solve for x_1 and x_3. You should obtain

(13) $$x_1 = 4 - \tfrac{2}{3}x_2 + \tfrac{4}{3}x_4 - \tfrac{4}{3}x_5 + \tfrac{1}{3}x_6$$

(14) $$x_3 = 5 - \tfrac{1}{3}x_2 - \tfrac{7}{3}x_4 + \tfrac{1}{3}x_5 - \tfrac{1}{3}x_6.$$

If you set $x_2 = x_4 = x_5 = x_6 = 0$, then $x_1 = 4$ and $x_3 = 5$. The value of the objective function is $2(4) + 7(5) = 43$. Notice the objective function equals $39 + 1(4) = 43$, as predicted by (12), and is an improvement on the previous guess.

To test for optimality, you can substitute as before the relations for the solution variables (13) and (14) into the objective function. Verify that this gives

(15) $$43 - \tfrac{2}{3}x_2 - \tfrac{14}{3}x_4 - \tfrac{1}{3}x_5 - \tfrac{5}{3}x_6.$$

Now you can see that if the variables x_2, x_4, x_5, or x_6 are utilized at *any* level above zero, the objective function must decrease from its current value 43. Thus the present solution is indeed optimal.

It is intuitive that the ideas in the preceding analysis could be distilled and formalized into a set of rules. The result would be an algorithm that would guide the selection of guesses to be tested and provide a criterion for ascertaining whether a particular trial solution was optimal. If you are eager to see this done, or if an optimizing algorithm is a new idea to you, then we advise that you skip the next section and come back to it after you have finished learning the simplex algorithm in Sec. 4.4. The questions raised in the next section will be more meaningful after you have studied an algorithm. But if you like proceeding from the general to the specific, then continue reading. Don't be too disturbed when some of the material seems vague at this first exposure—the fuzziness will disappear by the time you have finished the chapter.

4.3 THE ALGORITHMIC METHOD

You will study several types of algorithms throughout this book. By far, the type used most often is an iterative approach: at each trial solution, starting with the first, the instructions specify whether to stop the computations or to proceed to a new trial solution. It is essential to know when a suggested computational scheme is a bona fide algorithm for solving a problem.

Consider, for example, the process we used to solve the small problem above. Whenever we wanted to test the optimality for a specified pair of variables, we had no trouble in finding unique values for this pair that satisfied all the constraints. Was this only luck? We devised a simple procedure for testing whether a trial solution could be improved by introducing another variable. Does this approach always work? We found that bringing one variable into a trial solution caused only one other variable to leave the solution. Is this sort of uniquely determined substitution inevitable? We discovered an optimal solution rather rapidly. Is such speed typical?

You will find it helpful for understanding both the simplex method and other algorithms in subsequent chapters to have a general framework for viewing computational techniques. Specifically, to evaluate such algorithms, you should examine four interrelated characteristics.

1. **Completeness.** Are the algorithm's rules unambiguous? Is there a practical method for always obtaining a first trial solution to initiate the algorithm? Is the method described in terms of rules so well specified that they can be performed by a person or an electronic calculator having only the ability to read and follow the rules without exercising further judgment?
2. **Domain of applicability.** What mathematical problems does the algorithm purport to solve? How easy is it to determine whether a specific problem falls within this domain of applicability? When the calculations

terminate, does the final-trial answer invariably provide an exact solution to the problem? If not, is there an indication of the existence and cause of failure?

3. **Convergence properties.** Does the algorithm always converge? If so, does it unfailingly converge to a correct solution? Will the method terminate in a finite number of iterations? For actual problems, how many iterations occur until convergence? Do the trial solutions progressively improve the objective function value? If the calculations are stopped short of obtaining an optimal solution, is the final-trial answer usable?

4. **Computational requirements.** How severe is the computational burden needed to obtain a solution? How much numerical accuracy is required to ensure the method operates satisfactorily?

Establishing the answers to many of these questions is often a routine exercise for an operations researcher. But the most subtle category of questions is that relating to determining the convergence properties of an algorithm. Although the topic of convergence in algorithmic methods involves a number of intricacies, the ideas essential for the purposes here can be demonstrated simply. For the sake of illustration, suppose you are trying to maximize the value of an objective function, provided the solution satisfies certain constraints. This would be so if you were solving a linear programming model. The cases in Fig. 4.1 show how the value of the objective function might vary from one iteration to the next for a specific algorithm.

Case 1. At each iteration you observe a strict improvement in the objective function. Convergence to an optimal solution occurs after a finite number of iterations. In the example, the optimum is reached at iteration 7.

Case 2. At each iteration you observe a strict improvement in the objective function. However, convergence to an optimal solution does *not* occur in a finite number of iterations. At each trial, the solution gets a little bit better, but the improvements get progressively smaller.

Case 3. At each iteration you observe a strict improvement in the objective function. And, as in the preceding case, convergence does not occur in a finite number of iterations. But the objective function is tending to a limiting value that is *below* the true optimum!

Case 4. Convergence to an optimal solution occurs in a finite number of iterations, and each solution is at least as good as the preceding one. But at some iterations the objective function does not show a *strict* improvement. In the example, the objective function stalls at iterations 3, 7, and 8.

Case 5. Prior to convergence, the value of the objective function decreases for several iterations. In the illustration (*Case 5* of Fig. 4.1), this phenomenon occurs at iterations 4 and 5.

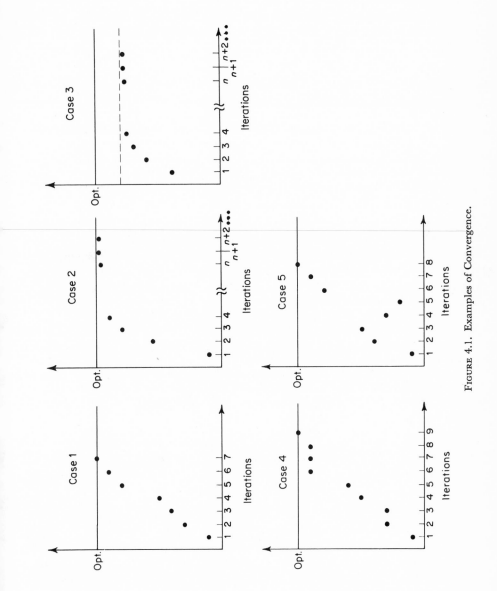

FIGURE 4.1. Examples of Convergence.

101

Thus the objective function in an algorithm may or may not converge to a limiting value in a finite number of iterations. If it does converge, the limiting value may or may not be the truly optimal value. And, in any case, the objective function may or may not show a strict improvement during the course of the iterations.

4.4 INTRODUCTION TO THE SIMPLEX ALGORITHM

Many different algorithms have been proposed to solve linear programming problems, but the one below has proved to be the most effective in general. Recognize, however, that if you are able to assume more about the form of the problem—such as that it has a network flow structure—then even better algorithms can be applied. We discuss these methods for special models in Chap. 7.

Let us verbalize the reasoning process used in Sec. 4.2 to solve the illustrative example. In that case, there were two equations. You examined trial solutions having two unknowns at positive levels and the remaining variables at zero levels. If the approach is to generalize, it is reasonable to suppose that in an m-equation model, you would choose m variables to have positive levels, and let the remaining variables equal zero. Assume for the time being that a feasible solution exists and the optimal value of the objective function is finite. We remove these restrictive assumptions later. Then the procedure appears to be the following.

Step 1. Select a set of m variables that yields a feasible starting trial solution. Eliminate the selected m variables from the objective function.

Step 2. Check the objective function to see whether there is a variable that is equal to zero in the trial solution but would improve the objective function if made positive. If such a variable exists, go to *Step 3*. Otherwise, stop.

Step 3. Determine how large the variable found in the previous step can be made until one of the m variables in the trial solution becomes zero. Eliminate the latter variable and let the next trial set contain the newly found variable instead.

Step 4. Solve for these m variables, and set the remaining variables equal to zero in the next trial solution. Return to *Step 2*.

Interestingly, after tidying up the language of these steps to remove certain ambiguities, the resulting algorithm in fact does find an optimal solution to a general linear programming model in a finite number of iterations. Often this method is termed *Dantzig's simplex algorithm*, in honor of the mathematician who devised the approach.

We first examine a "well-behaved" problem and explain the **simplex method** by means of this example. Afterwards we complete the presentation of the details.

Example. Consider the model

$$\text{maximize} \quad 4x_1 + 5x_2 + 9x_3 + 11x_4$$

subject to

$$1x_1 + 1x_2 + 1x_3 + 1x_4 \leq 15$$
$$7x_1 + 5x_2 + 3x_3 + 2x_4 \leq 120$$
$$3x_1 + 5x_2 + 10x_3 + 15x_4 \leq 100$$
$$x_1 \geq 0 \quad x_2 \geq 0 \quad x_3 \geq 0 \quad x_4 \geq 0.$$

You may recall that this is the Product-Mix Selection Example in Sec. 2.2. Did you jot down your guess of the optimal solution?

Let x_0 be the value of the objective function and add slack variables. Then write the system as

(1)
$$
\begin{aligned}
1x_0 - 4x_1 - 5x_2 - 9x_3 - 11x_4 &= 0 \quad &\underline{\text{Row 0}} \\
1x_1 + 1x_2 + 1x_3 + 1x_4 + 1x_5 &= 15 \quad &\underline{\text{Row 1}} \\
7x_1 + 5x_2 + 3x_3 + 2x_4 + 1x_6 &= 120 \quad &\underline{\text{Row 2}} \\
3x_1 + 5x_2 + 10x_3 + 15x_4 + 1x_7 &= 100 \quad &\underline{\text{Row 3,}}
\end{aligned}
$$

where *all* the variables must be nonnegative. Notice how the introduction of the variable x_0 in Row 0 permits us to express the objective function in equation form.

The task of *Step 1* is to find a starting feasible solution to (1). There are a large number of such solutions, but it is certainly most convenient to begin with $x_0 = 0$, $x_5 = 15$, $x_6 = 120$, $x_7 = 100$, and all other variables equal to 0. In other words, start with an all-slack solution. We term this an *initial basic solution*, and x_0, x_5, x_6, and x_7 are known as the **basic variables**, sometimes shortened to **the basis**. The remaining variables we call **nonbasic**.

The word *basic* stems from the mathematical property that the solution is represented by four variables, "four" being the number of linear relations, and that the values of these four variables are uniquely determined (and dependent on the constants on the right-hand side of the equations). As you will discover, the simplex method employs only trial *basic* solutions. Despite the restriction to this class of solutions, the simplex method nevertheless determines an optimal solution, provided one exists.

If you interpret x_0 as profits, then the current solution is certainly not very profitable. Undoubtedly you can improve it. A moment's reflection leads to examining the coefficients in Row 0 of those variables currently not in the basis. Specifically, look at the coefficients of $x_1, x_2, x_3,$ and x_4. Each negative coefficient represents how much x_0 will increase if you let the corresponding variable equal 1. This conclusion about the interpretation of the coefficients in Row 0 remains valid throughout the trial calculations, and we record the general principle here.

INTERPRETATION OF COEFFICIENTS IN ROW 0. Each coefficient represents the increase (for negative coefficients) or decrease (for positive coefficients) in x_0 with a unit increase of the associated nonbasic variable.

For *Step* 2 the simplex method adopts the following easy-to-apply rule for deciding the variable to enter the next trial basis.

Simplex Criterion I (Maximization). If there are nonbasic variables having a negative coefficient in Row 0, select one such variable with the most negative coefficient, that is, the best per-unit potential gain (say x_j). If all nonbasic variables have positive or zero coefficients in Row 0, an optimal solution has been obtained.

According to *Criterion I*, you should introduce x_4. Each unit of x_4 added brings about an increase of 11 in x_0. Clearly, the larger you make x_4, the more you increase x_0. But examine the constraints (1). Notice that as you increase x_4, you must decrease every current basic variable corresponding to a row wherein x_4 has a positive coefficient. Specifically, if x_4 is increased to the level 1, then verify in (1) that

(i) x_5 must be decreased by 1 so that the Row 1 constraint remains satisfied,
(ii) x_6 must be decreased by 2 so that the Row 2 constraint remains satisfied,
(iii) x_7 must be decreased by 15 so that the Row 3 constraint remains satisfied.

How big can x_4 become before one of the current basic variables reaches its lower bound 0? Check that this number is $x_4 = \frac{100}{15} = 6.66$, at which value you find $x_7 = 0$. Such being the case, introduce x_4 into the basis and remove x_7.

We summarize the preceding discussion by the following rule for *Step* 3.

Simplex Criterion II. (a) Take the ratios of the current right-hand side to the coefficients of the entering variable x_j (ignore ratios with zero or negative numbers in the denominator). (b) Select the minimum ratio—that ratio will equal the value of x_j in the next trial solution. The minimum ratio occurs for a variable x_k in the present solution; set $x_k = 0$ in the new solution.

The calculations indicated by *Criterion II* are performed in Fig. 4.2.

Now that you know x_4 is to replace x_7 in a trial basis, you perform *Step 4*. Rewrite the relations (1) so that x_4 has a coefficient of 1 in Row 3 and coefficients of 0 in Rows 0, 1, and 2, just as x_7 does in (1). The process by which this is achieved is known as a **change-of-basis** calculation, or a **pivot operation**. First divide Row 3 by 15, the coefficient of x_4,

Basic Variables	Current Solution	Coeffs. of x_4	= Ratios	Min.	Next Solution
x_0	0	−11	— —		
x_5	15	1	15		
x_6	120	2	60		
x_7	100	15	6.66	6.66	$x_4 = 6.66, x_7 = 0$

Figure 4.2. *Iteration 1: Criterion II for x_4 Entering Basis.*

$$(2) \quad \begin{array}{llll} 1x_0 - 4x_1 - 5x_2 - 9x_3 - 11x_4 & = 0 & \text{Row 0} \\ 1x_1 + 1x_2 + 1x_3 + 1x_4 + 1x_5 & = 15 & \text{Row 1} \\ 7x_1 + 5x_2 + 3x_3 + 2x_4 \quad + 1x_6 & = 120 & \text{Row 2} \\ \frac{1}{5}x_1 + \frac{1}{3}x_2 + \frac{2}{3}x_3 + 1x_4 \quad + \frac{1}{15}x_7 = \frac{20}{3} & & \text{Row 3.} \end{array}$$

By pivoting on 15, you have created the coefficient of 1 for x_4 in Row 3. Note that the mathematical manipulation is legitimate, for all you have done is divide equals by equals (both sides of Row 3 by 15). Create coefficients equal to 0 in Rows 0, 1, and 2 as follows:

Row 0: multiply Row 3 by 11 and add to Row 0,
Row 1: multiply Row 3 by −1 and add to Row 1,
Row 2: multiply Row 3 by −2 and add to Row 2.

The result is

$$(3) \quad \begin{array}{lll} 1x_0 - \frac{9}{5}x_1 - \frac{4}{3}x_2 - \frac{5}{3}x_3 & + \frac{11}{15}x_7 = \frac{220}{3} & \text{Row 0} \\ \frac{4}{5}x_1 + \frac{2}{3}x_2 + \frac{1}{3}x_3 \quad + 1x_5 & - \frac{1}{15}x_7 = \frac{25}{3} & \text{Row 1} \\ \frac{33}{5}x_1 + \frac{13}{3}x_2 + \frac{5}{3}x_3 \quad + 1x_6 - \frac{2}{15}x_7 = \frac{320}{3} & \text{Row 2} \\ \frac{1}{5}x_1 + \frac{1}{3}x_2 + \frac{2}{3}x_3 + 1x_4 & + \frac{1}{15}x_7 = \frac{20}{3} & \text{Row 3.} \end{array}$$

As before, the mathematical manipulations are legitimate, for all you have done is multiply equals by equals (both sides of each row by a constant) and then add equals to equals (one row to another row). Consequently, the relations (3), although appearing to be in different form from (1), are equivalent to (1). The usefulness of the form of (3) is that by letting $x_1 = x_2 = x_3 = x_7 = 0$, you see immediately the values for the new trial-basic solution, Fig. 4.3.

As a check of your understanding, observe that the new basic solution has profit $x_0 = \frac{220}{3}$, which can be calculated from the relation

x_0	$\frac{220}{3}$
x_5	$\frac{25}{3}$
x_6	$\frac{320}{3}$
x_4	$\frac{20}{3}$

FIGURE 4.3. Second Trial Basic Solution.

new profit = (profit from previous solution) + (number of units of new basic variable) × (per-unit potential gain from new basic variable, as was given by the previous coefficient in Row 0)

$$\frac{220}{3} = 0 + \frac{20}{3}(11).$$

You now are better able to interpret *Criterion II*. If x_5 (or x_6) is eliminated instead of x_7, then in finding new values for x_4, x_7, and x_6 (or x_5), you would obtain negative numbers, contrary to the nonnegativity constraints. Try to eliminate x_5 instead of x_7 for a second-trial solution and thereby verify these remarks.

Iteration 2. At this point the first iteration of the simplex method has been completed. On returning to *Step 2*, you are ready to determine whether an optimal solution has been obtained or if another simplex iteration is required.

Criterion I, which examines the nonbasic variables, indicates that a still better solution seems to exist. You might profitably enter into the basis either x_1, or x_2, or x_3. *Criterion I* selects x_1, since it promises the greatest gain per unit increase. Next perform the *Step 3* calculations, using *Criterion II* as shown in Fig. 4.4.

Basic Variables	Current Solution $\div$ Coeffs. of x_1		= Ratios	Min.	Next Solution
x_0	$\frac{220}{3}$	$\frac{9}{5}$	$--$		
x_5	$\frac{25}{3}$	$\frac{4}{5}$	$\frac{125}{12}$	$\frac{125}{12}$	$x_1 = \frac{125}{12}$, $x_5 = 0$
x_6	$\frac{320}{3}$	$\frac{33}{5}$	$\frac{1600}{99}$		
x_4	$\frac{20}{3}$	$\frac{1}{5}$	$\frac{100}{3}$		

FIGURE 4.4. *Iteration 2: Criterion II for x_1 Entering Basis.*

From Fig. 4.4. notice that x_1 will replace x_5 in the next trial solution. You must rewrite (3) to reflect the substitution. To make the change-of-basis calculation in *Step 4*, first divide by the pivot $\frac{4}{5}$ in Row 1, causing the coefficient of 1 to be removed from x_5 and to appear for x_1:

(4)
$$1x_0 - \tfrac{9}{5}x_1 - \tfrac{4}{3}x_2 - \tfrac{5}{3}x_3 \qquad\qquad + \tfrac{11}{15}x_7 = \tfrac{220}{3} \quad \text{Row 0}$$
$$1x_1 + \tfrac{5}{6}x_2 + \tfrac{5}{12}x_3 \qquad + \tfrac{5}{4}x_5 \qquad - \tfrac{1}{12}x_7 = \tfrac{125}{12} \quad \text{Row 1}$$
$$\tfrac{33}{5}x_1 + \tfrac{13}{3}x_2 + \tfrac{5}{3}x_3 \qquad\qquad + 1x_6 - \tfrac{2}{15}x_7 = \tfrac{320}{3} \quad \text{Row 2}$$
$$\tfrac{1}{5}x_1 + \tfrac{1}{3}x_2 + \tfrac{2}{3}x_3 + 1x_4 \qquad\qquad + \tfrac{1}{15}x_7 = \tfrac{3}{20} \quad \text{Row 3.}$$

Then to complete the pivot operation, create coefficients equal to 0 for x_1 in Rows 0, 2, and 3 as follows:

Row 0: multiply Row 1 by $\frac{9}{5}$ and add to Row 0,
Row 2: multiply Row 1 by $-\frac{33}{5}$ and add to Row 2,
Row 3: multiply Row 1 by $-\frac{1}{5}$ and add to Row 3.

The result is

(5)
$$1x_0 \qquad + \tfrac{1}{6}x_2 - \tfrac{11}{12}x_3 \qquad + \tfrac{9}{4}x_5 \qquad + \tfrac{7}{12}x_7 = \tfrac{1105}{12} \quad \text{Row 0}$$
$$1x_1 + \tfrac{5}{6}x_2 + \tfrac{5}{12}x_3 \qquad + \tfrac{5}{4}x_5 \qquad - \tfrac{1}{12}x_7 = \tfrac{125}{12} \quad \text{Row 1}$$
$$- \tfrac{7}{6}x_2 - \tfrac{13}{12}x_3 \qquad - \tfrac{33}{4}x_5 + 1x_6 + \tfrac{5}{12}x_7 = \tfrac{455}{12} \quad \text{Row 2}$$
$$\tfrac{1}{6}x_2 + \tfrac{7}{12}x_3 + 1x_4 - \tfrac{1}{4}x_5 \qquad + \tfrac{1}{12}x_7 = \tfrac{55}{12} \quad \text{Row 3.}$$

The third trial-basic solution appears in Fig. 4.5. Notice that at each iteration, the coefficients of any variable not in the trial solution have the interpretation that if a unit of this variable is introduced, the current basis variables will be changed by these amounts. In (3), for example, introducing each unit of x_1 will decrease x_5 by $\frac{4}{5}$, x_6 by $\frac{33}{5}$, and x_4 by $\frac{1}{5}$. Corroborate this statement with the values you have derived for the third solution, in which $\frac{125}{12}$ units of x_1 were actually introduced.

Also observe that prior to introducing x_1 into the basis, x_2 looked attractive in (3). Entering x_1 caused x_2 to change its indication in the present iteration (5).

Iteration 3. Having completed the second simplex iteration, once more examine the coefficients in Row 0 to ascertain whether you have discovered an optimal solution. It now appears favorable to enter x_3. The calculations to determine which variable leaves the basis are given in Fig. 4.6. You will find from these calculations that x_4, which entered at the first iteration, is now to be removed from the

x_0	$\frac{1105}{12}$
x_1	$\frac{125}{12}$
x_6	$\frac{455}{12}$
x_4	$\frac{55}{12}$

FIGURE 4.5. The Third Trial Basic Solution.

Basic Variables	Current Solution $\div$	Coeffs of x_3	= Ratios	Min.	Next Solution
x_0	$\frac{1105}{12}$	$-\frac{11}{12}$	$--$		
x_1	$\frac{125}{12}$	$\frac{5}{12}$	25		
x_6	$\frac{455}{12}$	$-\frac{13}{12}$	$--$		
x_4	$\frac{55}{12}$	$\frac{7}{12}$	$\frac{55}{7}$	$\frac{55}{7}$	$x_3 = \frac{55}{7}$, $x_4 = 0$

FIGURE 4.6. *Iteration 3: Criterion II* for x_3 Entering Basis.

basis. Frequently in applications of the simplex method, a variable enters the solution at one iteration and is removed at a later iteration. It is this possibility that prohibits stating a *helpful* upper bound on the number of simplex iterations necessary to solve any linear programming problem.

As with the preceding iterations, create a coefficient of 1 for the entering variable x_3 in Row 3 by dividing Row 3 by $\frac{7}{12}$. This gives

$$
\begin{aligned}
&1x_0 &&+ \tfrac{1}{6}x_2 - \tfrac{11}{12}x_3 &&+ \tfrac{9}{4}x_5 &&+ \tfrac{7}{12}x_7 = \tfrac{1105}{12} \quad \text{Row 0}\\
&1x_1 + \tfrac{5}{6}x_2 + \tfrac{5}{12}x_3 &&&&+ \tfrac{5}{4}x_5 &&- \tfrac{1}{12}x_7 = \tfrac{125}{12} \quad \text{Row 1}\\
&-\tfrac{7}{6}x_2 - \tfrac{13}{12}x_3 &&&&- \tfrac{33}{4}x_5 + 1x_6 + \tfrac{5}{12}x_7 = \tfrac{455}{12} \quad \text{Row 2}\\
&\tfrac{2}{7}x_2 + 1x_3 + \tfrac{12}{7}x_4 &&- \tfrac{3}{7}x_5 &&+ \tfrac{1}{7}x_7 = \tfrac{55}{7} \quad \text{Row 3.}
\end{aligned}
$$

(6)

Now create coefficients equal to 0 for x_3 in the remaining rows as follows:

Row 0: multiply Row 3 by $\frac{11}{12}$ and add to Row 0,

Row 1: multiply Row 3 by $-\frac{5}{12}$ and add to Row 1,

Row 2: multiply Row 3 by $\frac{13}{12}$ and add to Row 2.

The result is

$$
\begin{aligned}
&1x_0 &&+ \tfrac{3}{7}x_2 &&+ \tfrac{11}{7}x_4 + \tfrac{13}{7}x_5 &&+ \tfrac{5}{7}x_7 = \tfrac{695}{7} \quad \text{Row 0}\\
&1x_1 + \tfrac{5}{7}x_2 &&&&- \tfrac{5}{7}x_4 + \tfrac{10}{7}x_5 &&- \tfrac{1}{7}x_7 = \tfrac{50}{7} \quad \text{Row 1}\\
&-\tfrac{6}{7}x_2 &&&&+ \tfrac{13}{7}x_4 - \tfrac{61}{7}x_5 + 1x_6 + \tfrac{4}{7}x_7 = \tfrac{325}{7} \quad \text{Row 2}\\
&\tfrac{2}{7}x_2 + 1x_3 + \tfrac{12}{7}x_4 &&- \tfrac{3}{7}x_5 &&+ \tfrac{1}{7}x_7 = \tfrac{55}{7} \quad \text{Row 3.}
\end{aligned}
$$

(7)

At this iteration you have just seen another aspect to the computational rule in *Criterion II*. Had you attempted to eliminate a variable where a negative ratio occurred in Fig. 4.6—this would be x_6—then x_3 would have become negative. Since such a condition is not permitted, the negative coefficient causes the basic variable for the associated row to increase in value as the new variable is introduced into the solution. If you ever tried to eliminate a basic variable in a row where 0 occurs as the coefficient of the entering variable, you would not be able to carry out the prescribed pivoting manipulations. The very first operation would call for a division by 0, which is not permissible.

To sum up, *Criterion II* ensures that each new basic solution results only in zero or positive values for the trial values of the basis. Consequently, the solution remains feasible at *every* iteration.

x_0	$\frac{695}{7}$
x_1	$\frac{50}{7}$
x_6	$\frac{325}{7}$
x_3	$\frac{55}{7}$

FIGURE 4.7. Fourth Trial and Optimal Basic Solution.

Iteration 4. All the coefficients in Row 0 of (7) are nonnegative, and consequently *Criterion I* asserts you have found an optimal solution (Fig. 4.7). Thus the calculations are terminated in *Step 2*. Check that the values in Fig. 4.7 do indeed satisfy (1).

Summary. In brief the simplex method consists of

Step 1. Select an initial basis.

Step 2. Apply *Simplex Criterion I*. If the current-trial solution is not optimal, proceed to *Step 3*. Otherwise, stop.

Step 3. Apply *Simplex Criterion II*.

Step 4. Make a change of basis, and return to *Step 2*.

▶You can easily interpret the progress of the simplex method in the geometry of the solutions space. Each basis corresponds to a vertex of the convex polyhedral set of feasible solutions. Going from one basis to the next represents going from one extreme point to an adjacent one. Thus the simplex method can be said to seek an optimal solution by *climbing along the edges, from one vertex of the convex polyhedral solution set to a neighboring one.*   ◀

Optimality. It is a simple matter to demonstrate that you have in fact found an optimal solution. Since you have derived the final formulation (7) from the original equations (1) only by elementary operations, such as multiplying equals by equals and adding equals to equals, the two formulations are merely different-appearing views of the *same* problem. Suppose you had started with (7). Rearranging Row 0 slightly, you can write the objective function as

$$(8) \qquad \text{maximize } x_0 = \tfrac{695}{7} - \tfrac{3}{7}x_2 - \tfrac{11}{7}x_4 - \tfrac{13}{7}x_5 - \tfrac{5}{7}x_7.$$

If the nonbasic variables x_2, x_4, x_5, or x_7 have *any* feasible value other than zero, then the above relation shows that x_0 will be less than its present value of $\tfrac{695}{7}$.

The final Row 0 coefficients of the original variables are sometimes referred to as

relative or **shadow costs**. They represent the decrease in the optimal value of the objective function resulting from a unit increase in a nonbasic variable, assuming the final basis remains feasible. (The final Row 0 coefficients of the slack variables are sometimes called **shadow prices**, and their interpretation is discussed at length in the next chapter.)

For example, suppose you decided to set $x_2 = 1$; then the value of x_0 would decrease by $\frac{3}{7}$. The values of the basic variables would also change, and you could examine this effect in the same way you used for x_0. Consider the basic variable x_1 in Row 1 of (7):

$$(9) \qquad x_1 = \tfrac{50}{7} - \tfrac{5}{7}x_2 + \tfrac{5}{7}x_4 - \tfrac{10}{7}x_5 + \tfrac{1}{7}x_7.$$

By letting $x_2 = 1$, you decrease the value of x_1 by the amount $\frac{5}{7}$.

Alternative optima. You saw in Chap. 3 (Fig. 3.2) that a linear programming problem may have more than one optimal solution. The two-dimensional diagrammatics show that if more than one optimal solution exists, then an infinite number exist. The corresponding generalization to larger problems is valid.

To illustrate how this situation occurs, suppose there is an additional variable x_8 in the example above, and that it appears in the initial formulation (1) as

$$(10) \qquad \begin{array}{ll} -2x_8 & \underline{\text{Row } 0} \\[4pt] +1x_8 & \underline{\text{Row } 1} \\[4pt] +9x_8 & \underline{\text{Row } 2} \\[4pt] +.2x_8 & \underline{\text{Row } 3.} \end{array}$$

It is straightforward to check that at the final iteration, x_8 would appear in (7) as

$$(11) \qquad \begin{array}{ll} 0x_8 & \underline{\text{Row } 0} \\[6pt] +\dfrac{9.8}{7}x_8 & \underline{\text{Row } 1} \\[10pt] +\dfrac{2.8}{7}x_8 & \underline{\text{Row } 2} \\[10pt] -\dfrac{2.8}{7}x_8 & \underline{\text{Row } 3.} \end{array}$$

If you introduce x_8, then verify that x_1 leaves the basis according to *Criterion II*, and that the alternative basic optimal solution is

$$(12) \qquad \begin{aligned} x_0 &= \frac{695}{7} \\[6pt] x_8 &= \frac{50}{9.8} = 5.10 \\[6pt] x_6 &= \frac{3045}{7(9.8)} = 44.39 \\[6pt] x_3 &= \frac{679}{7(9.8)} = 9.90, \end{aligned}$$

where $x_1 = x_2 = x_4 = x_5 = x_7 = 0$. It is easy to show that any **positive-weighted average** of these two basic optimal solutions also yields an alternative optimal (feasible) solution:

$$x_0 = \frac{695}{7}$$

(13)
$$x_1 = w(\tfrac{50}{7}) + (1 - w)0$$
$$x_3 = w(\tfrac{55}{7}) + (1 - w)9.90$$
$$x_6 = w(\tfrac{325}{7}) + (1 - w)44.39$$
$$x_8 = w(0) + (1 - w)5.10,$$

where w is the **weighting factor** such that $0 < w < 1$. [Try $w = .5$ in (13) and calculate x_1, x_3, x_6, and x_8. Check that these values satisfy the original constraints and yield an objective function value of $\frac{695}{7}$.]

▶Frequently, in large-scale applications there are more than two alternative optimal basic solutions. This condition is indicated by a zero coefficient for two or more nonbasic variables in the final Row 0. Advanced techniques exist for determining *all* basic optimal solutions. Once these have been found, any positive-weighted average of the alternative solutions is also a solution. Note that the resultant *set* of variables does *not* constitute a basis. The set contains more variables than the number of constraining relations; consequently, listing which of the variables are in the set is not sufficient to *uniquely* determine their values. ◀

Conclusion. It is fair to say that the optimal solution to even the small problem in this section was not obvious from the start. In larger models, the importance of being able to approach an optimal solution in a systematic fashion is manifest. We turn next to an evaluation of the simplex algorithm in terms of the four characteristics discussed in Sec. 4.3; if you skipped that section, go back and read it now.

4.5 COMPLETENESS OF THE ALGORITHM

At some iterations, the operations stated in *Criteria I* and *II* of the simplex algorithm may be ambiguous as to the variable to introduce into or to remove from the basis. In *Criterion I*, when two or more variables appear equally promising, as indicated by the values of their coefficients in Row 0, an arbitrary rule may be adopted for selecting one of these. For example, use the lowest-numbered variable, or one suspected to be in the final basis.

In *Criterion II*, when two or more variables in the current basis are to fall simultaneously to the level zero upon introducing the new variable, only one of these is to be removed from the basis. The others remain in the basis at zero level. The resultant basis is termed **degenerate**. As we discuss in Sec. 4.7 below, a delicate question of theory is involved in the selection of a tie-breaking rule. Unless some care is given to the method of deciding which variable is to be removed from the basis, you cannot *prove* the method always converges. However, long experience with simplex computations has led to the conclusion that for all *practical* purposes, the selection can be arbitrary and the associated danger of nonconvergence is negligible.

If you find at some iteration in applying *Criterion II* that there is no positive coefficient in any row for the entering variable, then there exists an unbounded optimal solution. In this event, the entering variable can be made arbitrarily large, the value of x_0 thereby increases without bound, and the current basic variables remain nonnegative. Thus we now may drop the earlier assumption that the optimal value of the objective function is finite. The simplex algorithm provides an indication of when an unbounded optimal solution occurs. Reword *Criterion II* to cover this case.

Starting basis. Here we turn to the selection of an initial basis to begin the algorithm. Because each constraint in the example of the preceding section was of the form

(1) $$\sum_{j=1}^{n} a_{ij}x_j \leq b_i \quad \text{where } b_i \geq 0,$$

adding a slack variable to each relation and starting with an all-slack basic solution provided a simple way of initiating the simplex algorithm. As you recall from Chap. 2, relation (1) does not encompass all the constraints that may be found in a linear optimization model. But the discussion in Chap. 3 enabled us to assert that the constraints in any linear programming model can be written as

(2) $$\sum_{j=1}^{n} a_{ij}x_i = b_i \quad \text{for } i = 1, 2, \ldots, m \quad \text{where } b_i \geq 0.$$

In this form, if a variable appears only in constraining relation i and has a coefficient of 1, as would be the case for a slack variable, it can be used as part of the initial basis. But relation i may not have such a variable. (This would occur, for example, if the ith equation were linearly dependent on one or more of the other equations, such as being a sum of two equations.) Then we may employ the following approach.

Write the constraints as

(3) $$\sum_{j=1}^{n} a_{ij}x_j + 1y_i = b_i \quad \text{for } i = 1, 2, \ldots, m \quad \text{where } b_i \geq 0,$$

and where $y_i \geq 0$; then use y_i as the basic variable for relation i. (We have assumed, for simplicity, that every constraint requires the addition of a y_i.) The name **artificial variable** is given to y_i because it is added as an artifice in order to obtain an initial-trial solution. Is this approach legitimate? The answer is yes, provided you satisfy *Condition A*.

Condition A: To ensure that the final solution is meaningful, every y_i must equal 0 at the terminal iteration of the simplex method.

If the constraints admit of no feasible solution, it will be impossible to satisfy

Condition A. At the final iteration of the simplex algorithm, at least one y_i will be in the basis at a positive level, indicating the infeasibility condition. Thus you can remove the assumption made in Sec. 4.4 that a feasible solution exists. If one does not, the simplex algorithm will tell you so.

We can state at last that the instructions for carrying out the rules of the simplex method are complete. They can be, and, of course, have been, programmed for operation on every large-scale electronic computer.

▶We mention that in the most sophisticated computer programs of the simplex algorithm, the model designer is *not* required to write each restriction in the form (2) above. He may specify his constraints exactly as he originally formulates them. The computer program then automatically adds either a slack, surplus, or artificial variable to each relation and also guarantees *Condition A*. In some programs, the user may even preselect a particular set of variables to be the initial basis. This procedure is known as an **advanced start**, and is designed to reduce the number of iterations required. Other similar "hints" may be supplied the computer to indicate those variables that are the most likely candidates for the final basis. Adroit use of such devices for speeding convergence is part of the *art* of applying the simplex algorithm.   ◀

The Big M Method. There are a number of computational techniques for guaranteeing *Condition A*. Since they are of interest principally to operations research specialists, however, we do not delve into them here except to mention a simple but somewhat inelegant approach.

Add to the maximizing objective function each y_i with a large **penalty-cost coefficient**:

$$(4) \qquad x_0 - \sum_{j=1}^{n} c_j x_j + \sum_{i=1}^{m} M y_i = 0,$$

where M is relatively large. To initiate the algorithm, you first eliminate each y_i from (4) by using (3). This gives

$$(5) \qquad x_0 - \sum_{j=1}^{n} c_j x_j - M \sum_{i=1}^{m} \sum_{j=1}^{n} a_{ij} x_j = -M \sum_{i=1}^{m} b_i,$$

which simplifies to

$$(6) \qquad x_0 - \sum_{j=1}^{n} (c_j + M \sum_{i=1}^{m} a_{ij}) x_j = -M \sum_{i=1}^{m} b_i.$$

The very technique of optimizing drives the y_i variables to zero, *provided* there exists a feasible solution. (Incidentally, whenever a y_i drops from a basis at some iteration, you need never consider using it again, and can eliminate it from further computations.)

An example will clarify the approach. Consider the problem

$$(7) \qquad \text{maximize} \quad -3x_1 - 2x_2$$

subject to

$$(8) \qquad 1x_1 + 1x_2 = 10$$

$$(9) \qquad 1x_1 \qquad \geq 4$$

$$(10) \qquad x_1 \geq 0 \qquad x_2 \geq 0.$$

Then, after adding a surplus variable x_3 in (9), we can write the model as

$$\begin{array}{llll} x_0 + 3x_1 + 2x_2 & & = 0 & \underline{\text{Row 0}} \\ & 1x_1 + 1x_2 & = 10 & \underline{\text{Row 1}} \\ & 1x_1 & - 1x_3 = 4 & \underline{\text{Row 2.}} \end{array}$$

(11)

Next, we introduce artifical variables y_1 and y_2, and let $M = 10$, giving

$$\begin{array}{lllll} x_0 + 3x_1 + 2x_2 & & + 10y_1 + 10y_2 = 0 & \underline{\text{Row 0}} \\ & 1x_1 + 1x_2 & + 1y_1 & = 10 & \underline{\text{Row 1}} \\ & 1x_1 & - 1x_3 & + 1y_2 = 4 & \underline{\text{Row 2.}} \end{array}$$

(12)

To initiate the algorithm, you have to subtract ($M = 10$) times Row 1 and ($M = 10$) times Row 2 from Row 0 to eliminate y_1 and y_2:

$$\begin{array}{lllll} x_0 - 17x_1 - 8x_2 + 10x_3 & & = -140 & \underline{\underline{\text{Row 0}}} \\ & 1x_1 + 1x_2 & + 1y_1 & = 10 & \underline{\underline{\text{Row 1}}} \\ & 1x_1 & - 1x_3 & + 1y_2 = 4 & \underline{\underline{\text{Row 2.}}} \end{array}$$

(13)

What is the optimal solution?

4.6 DOMAIN OF APPLICABILITY

Many linear programming models have, as their objective, minimizing a linear function. They can be solved by changing the signs of the coefficients in the objective function, as was pointed out in Sec. 3.2. Then *Criterion I* (Maximization) is applied to the revised form. But we find it convenient to record here, for future purposes, a restatement of *Criterion I* when minimization is called for and the objective function is left in its original form.

SIMPLEX CRITERION I (MINIMIZATION). If there are nonbasic variables having a plus coefficient in Row 0, select one such variable with the most positive coefficient (say x_j). If all nonbasic variables have minus or zero coefficients in Row 0, an optimal solution has been obtained.

An example will clarify the procedure. Consider the trivial linear programming problem

(1)　　　　　　　　　minimize　$-2x_1 + 3x_2$

subject to

(2)　　　　　　　$0 \le x_1 \le 6$ and $0 \le x_2 \le 10$.

We could proceed to solve the problem by first changing both the signs of the coefficients in (1) and the sense of optimization:

(3)　　　　　　　　　maximize　$2x_1 - 3x_2$.

This transformation will give the same optimal values for x_1 and x_2. Then if we use the simplex algorithm format in the preceding section, we would start the iterations with the model

$$
\begin{array}{rll}
x_0 - 2x_1 + 3x_2 & = 0 & \underline{\text{Row } 0} \\
1x_1 \quad\quad + 1x_3 & = 6 & \underline{\text{Row } 1} \\
1x_2 \quad\quad + 1x_4 & = 10 & \underline{\text{Row } 2,}
\end{array}
$$

(4)

and enter x_1 into the basis according to *Criterion I* (Maximization).

But we can instead employ (1) directly by defining the variable x_0 equal to the objective function in (1), and setting up the initial formulation as

$$
\begin{array}{rll}
x_0 + 2x_1 - 3x_2 & = 0 & \underline{\text{Row } 0} \\
1x_1 \quad\quad + 1x_3 & = 6 & \underline{\text{Row } 1} \\
1x_2 \quad\quad + 1x_4 & = 10 & \underline{\text{Row } 2.}
\end{array}
$$

(5)

Here we would apply *Criterion I* (Minimization), so that at the first iteration we select x_1 to enter the basis, since its coefficient is $+2$ in Row 0.

In a minimization problem, no revision in *Criterion II* is needed, because this second rule is aimed only at keeping each basic solution feasible.

Property of an optimal solution. Let us summarize what you have learned about the simplex method so far:

(i) The algorithm applies to *all* linear optimization models.

(ii) At the final iteration, the terminal answer *is* an exact solution to the problem.

We have *not* yet established that the simplex algorithm terminates for all linear programming models. We discuss this point in the next section. But assuming that convergence can be established, you have discovered a remarkable proposition:

THEOREM OF THE BASIS: If a linear optimization model has a finite optimal solution, then there exists an optimal *basic* solution.

Recall that in a linear model with m constraints, a basis is a set of m variables having *unique* values that satisfy the constraints when all the other variables are assigned 0 value.

To see the full impact of this theorem, suppose you want to solve a linear programming model with 50 (linearly independent) constraints and 300 unknowns. If the hypothesis of the theorem holds, there is an optimal solution containing at most 50 variables at a positive level. Adding more variables may improve the optimal value of the objective function, but it will not increase the number of variables required for an optimal solution beyond 50. Notice that adding more linearly independent constraints to a model enlarges the size of the set of basic variables. Therefore, an optimal solution to the augmented model usually requires more variables to be at a positive level.

How do you know the Theorem of the Basis is correct? You know because when the hypothesis is true, the simplex method actually *constructs* such an optimal basic solution.

▶Historical remark: we have used the validity of the simplex method to prove the Theorem of the Basis. In the early literature on linear programming, you find the result proved independently as a nonconstructive *existence* theorem. The implication in turn is used to motivate the simplex method, which is viewed as a sequential search restricted to sets of basic variables. ◀

4.7 CONVERGENCE PROPERTIES

Establishing convergence is usually the hardest single task in the development of an algorithm. You will see why.

You know by the way *Simplex Criteria I* and *II* operate that each successive trial solution is feasible and the value of the objective function is no worse than at the previous solution. Suppose, for the moment, that at each iteration the objective function to be maximized actually increases. This information alone is not enough to establish convergence in a finite number of iterations. The objective function may improve by smaller and smaller amounts, as you saw in *Case 2* of Fig. 4.1 (p. 101). What is worse, the value of the objective function may not be approaching the optimum, as you saw occur in *Case 3* of Fig. 4.1.

But you can make use of more information about the algorithm. The simplex method proceeds from one *basic* solution to another. Since the values for any set of basic variables are uniquely determined, it is not possible to return to any previous basic solution, given the assumption that the objective function improves at each trial. There are only a finite number of basis sets—certainly no more than the combination of n things taken m at a time, $\binom{n}{m} = n!/[m!(n-m)!]$, for an m-equation and n-variable problem. Therefore only a finite number of iterations can occur, and we already have argued that *when* termination takes place, the final solution *is* optimal.

Now has convergence been established? Unfortunately, no. The argument in the preceding paragraphs *assumed* that the objective function increases at each iteration. However, in many linear optimization problems, the objective function actually *stalls* for several iterations. This occurs in the following way.

At some iteration, when *Criterion II* is applied the minimum ratio is zero. (Such an event can arise when, on the previous iteration, more than one variable in the basis is driven to zero as the new variable enters. Thus at the present iteration, one or more *basic* variables are at zero level, so that the basic solution is degenerate.) Therefore the new variable enters the basis at zero level, and all the remaining variables as well as the objective function remain unchanged. The change-of-basis calculation in *Step 4* does cause the Row 0 coefficients to be modified, and hopefully at the next iteration the new variable selected leads to a minimum ratio that is strictly positive. But it is conceivable that the objective function stalls again. This condition could persist for several iterations, until eventually a previous basis might reappear! Then the cycle would start all over again, and convergence would not occur.

To sum up, we almost have a finite convergence proof, and would have one if we could force the objective function to make a strict increase at each iteration. To put your mind at ease, we hasten to mention that a finite convergence proof can be devised. Using slightly more advanced mathematical analysis than is employed in this book, it is possible to demonstrate that the simplex method can be made to cause a strict increase in the objective function. In order to provide the proof, *Criterion II* must be revised slightly to eliminate the ambiguity over which variable to remove from the basis when a tie occurs, and the notion of a "strict increase in the objective function" has to be suitably defined.

In practice, degeneracy has not caused the number of iterations required until convergence to be a real problem. Considerable empirical evidence suggests that most actual applications are solved within the range of $1.5m$ to $3m$ iterations, where m is the number of constraints and the starting basis is comprised only of slack, surplus, and artificial variables.

▶In the example of Sec. 4.4, you saw that a variable, namely x_4, entered and later left the basis. It is this phenomenon that causes the number of iterations to exceed the number of equations. The following example will startle your intuition about what can happen in the course of iterations:

(i)   maximize $1y$

subject to

(ii)
$$3x - 2y + 4z + 1u = -2$$
$$3x - 8z + 1v = 6$$
$$15x + 6y - 12z + 1w = 222$$
$$1x + 4z + 1t = 12$$
$$x \geq 0 \quad y \geq 0 \quad z \geq 0 \quad u \geq 0 \quad v \geq 0 \quad w \geq 0 \quad t \geq 0.$$

Figure 4.8 shows the succession of trial solutions. Observe that in proceeding from the initial to the second solution, variable z replaces the variable t. Then in going from the

Current	Values of						
Solution	x	y	z	u	v	w	t
Initial		1			6	216	12
2		7	3		30	216	
3	6	13	1.5			72	
4	6	25	1.5	24			
5	2	32		56			10
6		37		72	6		12
7		43	3	72	30		

Note: Objective function = $1y$

Figure 4.8. An Example of Slow Convergence.

fourth to the fifth solution, t replaces z. Finally, in progressing from the sixth to the seventh solution, z replaces t again. The variable z starts outside the basis, later enters, then leaves, and finally enters again. The variable t starts in the basis, leaves, enters, and then leaves again. Notice also that variable x replaces v at the third solution, and later v replaces x at the sixth solution. All in all, the simplex method requires examining seven solutions to obtain convergence. (Note that the objective function, $1y$, does improve at each iteration.)

When we tried to establish finite convergence of the simplex method, recall we only stated that **cycling** is conceivable. We did not demonstrate that an example exists where cycling *does* occur if an arbitrary rule is used to break ties when degeneracy arises. Here is such an illustration. (It was discovered by sheer ingenuity.)

The example assumes the following arbitrary tie-breaking rule for *Criterion II*: If two variables are candidates to leave the basis, the variable with the smaller subscript is chosen. The model is

(iii) $$\text{maximize} \ \tfrac{3}{4}x_1 - 150x_2 + \tfrac{1}{50}x_3 - 6x_4$$

subject to

(iv)
$$\tfrac{1}{4}x_1 - 60x_2 - \tfrac{1}{25}x_3 + 9x_4 + x_5 \qquad\qquad = 0$$
$$\tfrac{1}{2}x_1 - 90x_2 - \tfrac{1}{50}x_3 + 3x_4 \qquad + x_6 \qquad = 0$$
$$1x_3 \qquad\qquad\qquad + x_7 = 1$$
$$x_j \geq 0 \quad \text{for} \quad j = 1, 2, \ldots, 7.$$

The sequence of trial solutions is shown in Fig. 4.9. At each iteration, there is no ambiguity in the application of *Criterion I*. Thus, for the initial solution, the variable x_1 is chosen to enter. Because of degeneracy, either variable x_5 or x_6 can be dropped from

Current Solution	Row 0 Coefficients of							Basic Variables Having Values			Objective Function Value
	x_1	x_2	x_3	x_4	x_5	x_6	x_7	0	0	0	
Initial	$-\tfrac{3}{4}$	150	$-\tfrac{1}{50}$	6	0	0	0	x_5	x_6	x_7	0
2	0	-30	$-\tfrac{7}{50}$	33	3	0	0	x_1	x_6	x_7	0
3	0	0	$-\tfrac{2}{25}$	18	1	1	0	x_1	x_2	x_7	0
4	$\tfrac{1}{4}$	0	0	-3	-2	3	0	x_3	x_2	x_7	0
5	$-\tfrac{1}{2}$	120	0	0	-1	1	0	x_3	x_4	x_7	0
6	$-\tfrac{7}{4}$	330	$\tfrac{1}{50}$	0	0	-2	0	x_5	x_4	x_7	0
7	$-\tfrac{3}{4}$	150	$-\tfrac{1}{50}$	6	0	0	0	x_5	x_6	x_7	0

Note: Optimal solution is $x_1 = \tfrac{1}{25}$, $x_3 = 1$, $x_5 = \tfrac{3}{100}$, and objective function $= \tfrac{1}{20}$

FIGURE 4.9. Example of Cycling.

the basis. The tie-breaking rule for *Criterion II* as enunciated above selects x_5. Observe that the seventh solution is identical with the initial solution, and consequently cycling ensues. Also note that the objective function is stalled at the value 0, whereas the optimal value of the objective function is $\frac{1}{20}$. The cycling is eliminated as soon as a mathematically sound tie-breaking rule is used.   ◄

*4.8 COMPUTATIONAL REQUIREMENTS

Most real applications of linear programming involve at least several dozen and quite often several hundred constraints. Therefore the computational burden of the simplex method must be discussed in the context of employing a high-speed electronic calculator. In the foregoing sections, we explained the fundamental steps of the algorithm. Any computer program of the simplex method achieves these steps in one way or another. However, there are variations in performing the steps within a computer. These secondary modifications can have a decided impact on the number of iterations required for convergence.

Some computer programs are coded to act like chess players: they look ahead several iterations and decide on an appropriate strategy for the next few basis changes. This device increases the amount of calculation required at any one step, but reduces the total number of iterations for convergence. In other computer codes, the search in *Criterion I* is restricted to only a subset of variables at any one iteration. When no further improvement is possible with this subset, a new subset is examined. Termination occurs when improvement is impossible for every subset. This approach reduces the computation involved at each iteration, but may increase the number of iterations for convergence.

Consequently, the total number of calculations required by the simplex method to solve a particular problem usually depends heavily on the computer program employed. For practical applications, several million arithmetic operations are usual. Considerable experience suggests that, as a *rough* approximation, the computational burden increases as the cube of the number of constraints. Thus a 200-equation problem is likely to require 8 times as many calculations as a comparable 100-equation model.

Realize that improvements in both electronic calculators and computer programs for linear optimization have now made it quite feasible to solve problems with hundreds of constraints. The newest advances in technology are opening up the realm of possibility to models with more than 1000 constraints.

If you have had any experience in manually solving small systems of simultaneous linear equations, say five equations in five unknowns, you know that round-off error can build rapidly. In fact, if you keep only two or three significant digits in your computations, the answer may be too inaccurate to use. For systems of equations as large as those to be found in linear programming applications, the danger of accuracy loss is severe. For that reason, most computer programs for the simplex method have built-in devices for controling round-off error. Even so, trouble does arise on occasion; so when you solve a linear optimization model, watch out for this possibility and check your answer in the original constraints.

Because computer codes keep only a limited number of significant figures in the calculations, some round-off error is inevitable. Therefore, it is necessary to allow for such inaccuracies in performing the tests in *Criteria I* and *II*. To illustrate, a computer code may terminate the algorithm when all Row 0 coefficients exceed $-.00001$.

*4.9 TABULAR REPRESENTATION

In proceeding from one trial solution to the next, it is both cumbersome and unnecessary to write $x_1, x_2, \ldots, x_n$ as we have throughout this chapter. Only the

Iteration	Basis	Current Values	x_1	x_2	x_3	x_4	x_5	x_6	x_7	Row
1	x_0	0	-4	-5	-9	-11				0
	x_5	15	1	1	1	1	1			1
	x_6	120	7	5	3	2		1		2
	x_7	100	3	5	10	$\boxed{15}$			1	3
2	x_0	$\frac{220}{3}$	$-\frac{9}{5}$	$-\frac{4}{3}$	$-\frac{5}{3}$				$\frac{11}{15}$	0
	x_5	$\frac{25}{3}$	$\boxed{\frac{4}{5}}$	$\frac{2}{3}$	$\frac{1}{3}$		1		$-\frac{1}{15}$	1
	x_6	$\frac{320}{3}$	$\frac{33}{5}$	$\frac{13}{3}$	$\frac{5}{3}$			1	$-\frac{2}{15}$	2
	x_4	$\frac{20}{3}$	$\frac{1}{5}$	$\frac{1}{3}$	$\frac{2}{3}$	1			$\frac{1}{15}$	3
3	x_0	$\frac{1105}{12}$		$\frac{1}{6}$	$-\frac{11}{12}$		$\frac{9}{4}$		$\frac{7}{12}$	0
	x_1	$\frac{125}{12}$	1	$\frac{5}{6}$	$\frac{5}{12}$		$\frac{5}{4}$		$-\frac{1}{12}$	1
	x_6	$\frac{455}{12}$		$-\frac{7}{6}$	$-\frac{13}{12}$		$-\frac{33}{4}$	1	$\frac{5}{12}$	2
	x_4	$\frac{55}{12}$		$\frac{1}{6}$	$\boxed{\frac{7}{12}}$	1	$-\frac{1}{4}$		$\frac{1}{12}$	3
4	x_0	$\frac{695}{7}$		$\frac{3}{7}$		$\frac{11}{7}$	$\frac{13}{7}$		$\frac{5}{7}$	0
	x_1	$\frac{50}{7}$	1	$\frac{5}{7}$		$-\frac{5}{7}$	$\frac{10}{7}$		$-\frac{1}{7}$	1
	x_6	$\frac{325}{7}$		$-\frac{6}{7}$		$\frac{13}{7}$	$-\frac{61}{7}$	1	$\frac{4}{7}$	2
	x_3	$\frac{55}{7}$		$\frac{2}{7}$	1	$\frac{12}{7}$	$-\frac{3}{7}$		$\frac{1}{7}$	3

FIGURE 4.10. Simplex Tableau for Product-Mix Selection Problem.

coefficients of the variables are needed in the computations. Once you have understood the straightforward logic of the simplex iterations, you can save yourself considerable writing effort by organizing the computations in a convenient tabular form called a **simplex tableau**.

Figures 4.10 and 4.11 depict two approaches for the example in Sec. 4.4.

Iteration	Basis	Current Values	x_1	x_2	x_3	x_4	Row
1	x_0	0	-4	-5	-9	-11	0
	x_5	15	1	1	1	1	1
	x_6	120	7	5	3	2	2
	x_7	100	3	5	10	$\boxed{15}$	3
			x_1	x_2	x_3	x_7	
2	x_0	$\frac{220}{3}$	$-\frac{9}{5}$	$-\frac{4}{3}$	$-\frac{5}{3}$	$\frac{11}{15}$	0
	x_5	$\frac{25}{3}$	$\boxed{\frac{4}{5}}$	$\frac{2}{3}$	$\frac{1}{3}$	$-\frac{1}{15}$	1
	x_6	$\frac{320}{3}$	$\frac{33}{5}$	$\frac{13}{3}$	$\frac{5}{3}$	$-\frac{2}{15}$	2
	x_4	$\frac{20}{3}$	$\frac{1}{5}$	$\frac{1}{3}$	$\frac{2}{3}$	$\frac{1}{15}$	3
			x_5	x_2	x_3	x_7	
3	x_0	$\frac{1105}{12}$	$\frac{9}{4}$	$\frac{1}{6}$	$-\frac{11}{12}$	$\frac{7}{12}$	0
	x_1	$\frac{125}{12}$	$\frac{5}{4}$	$\frac{5}{6}$	$\frac{5}{12}$	$-\frac{1}{12}$	1
	x_6	$\frac{455}{12}$	$-\frac{33}{4}$	$-\frac{7}{6}$	$-\frac{13}{12}$	$\frac{5}{12}$	2
	x_4	$\frac{55}{12}$	$-\frac{1}{4}$	$\frac{1}{6}$	$\boxed{\frac{7}{12}}$	$\frac{1}{12}$	3
			x_5	x_2	x_4	x_7	
4	x_0	$\frac{695}{7}$	$\frac{13}{7}$	$\frac{3}{7}$	$\frac{11}{7}$	$\frac{5}{7}$	0
	x_1	$\frac{50}{7}$	$\frac{10}{7}$	$\frac{5}{7}$	$-\frac{5}{7}$	$-\frac{1}{7}$	1
	x_6	$\frac{325}{7}$	$-\frac{61}{7}$	$-\frac{6}{7}$	$\frac{13}{7}$	$\frac{4}{7}$	2
	x_3	$\frac{55}{7}$	$-\frac{3}{7}$	$\frac{2}{7}$	$\frac{12}{7}$	$\frac{1}{7}$	3

FIGURE 4.11. Condensed Simplex Tableau for Product-Mix Selection Problem.

The columns for the *basic* variables in Fig. 4.10 are so simple that they could be eliminated with no danger of ambiguity arising. The resulting condensed version is given in Fig. 4.11; this smaller table requires changing one column heading for the new *non*basic variable at each iteration.

*4.10 MATRIX REPRESENTATION

In this chapter and the next, the simplex method and its variants are explained by arraying the full equations. Using matrix notation instead is a helpful device for exhibiting the *mathematics* in a condensed form.

The matrix statement of the problem is

(1) $$\text{maximize} \quad cx$$

subject to

(2) $$Ax \le b$$

(3) $$x \ge 0.$$

When converted to a tabular representation such as Fig. 4.10, the problem data are viewed as

(4) $$\begin{bmatrix} 0 & -c_1 & -c_2 & \cdots & -c_n & 0 & 0 & \cdots & 0 \\ b & A_1 & A_2 & \cdots & A_n & U_1 & U_2 & \cdots & U_m \end{bmatrix},$$

where $\begin{bmatrix} 0 \\ U_i \end{bmatrix}$ is a column with a 1 in Row i and zeros elsewhere. [As always, the top row of (4) is referred to as Row 0.] A further condensation is

(5) $$\begin{bmatrix} 0_{11} & -c & 0_{1m} \\ b & A & I_m \end{bmatrix},$$

where 0_{pq} is a matrix of zeros with p rows and q columns, and I_m is an m-dimensional identity matrix.

At any iteration, let $\begin{bmatrix} -c_B \\ B \end{bmatrix}$ represent the m columns of (5) associated with the current set of basic variables. The first column corresponds to the basic variable in Row 1 of that iteration, the second column to the basic variable in Row 2, and so forth. Then the simplex tableau for that iteration is

(6) $$\begin{bmatrix} c_B B^{-1} b & c_B B^{-1} A - c & c_B B^{-1} \\ B^{-1} b & B^{-1} A & B^{-1} \end{bmatrix}.$$

Thus the current tableau is simply (5) multiplied on the left by

(7) $$\begin{bmatrix} 1 & c_B B^{-1} \\ 0_{m1} & B^{-1} \end{bmatrix} = \begin{bmatrix} 1 & -c_B \\ 0_{m1} & B \end{bmatrix}^{-1}.$$

Simplex Criterion I (Maximization) searches for the most negative entry in $[c_B B^{-1} A - c \quad c_B B^{-1}]$, the term that represents Row 0 of (6). Suppose this entry occurs for variable x_j. Then *Simplex Criterion II* makes use of the coefficients of x_j in (6), which are

$$(8) \qquad \begin{bmatrix} c_B B^{-1} A_j - c_j \\ B^{-1} A_j \end{bmatrix} \equiv \begin{bmatrix} r_{0j} \\ r_{1j} \\ \cdot \\ \cdot \\ \cdot \\ r_{mj} \end{bmatrix}.$$

Note that if x_j is the ith slack variable, then $c_j = 0$ and $A_j = U_i$ in (8). Assume that the minimum ratio found by *Criterion II* occurs in Row k.

The ensuing change-of-basis calculation amounts to multiplying (6) on the left by

$$(9) \qquad E = \begin{bmatrix} 1 & 0 & \cdots & -r_{0j}/r_{kj} & \cdots & 0 \\ 0 & 1 & \cdots & -r_{1j}/r_{kj} & \cdots & 0 \\ \multicolumn{6}{c}{\cdots\cdots\cdots\cdots\cdots\cdots\cdots} \\ 0 & 0 & \cdots & 1/r_{kj} & \cdots & 0 \\ \multicolumn{6}{c}{\cdots\cdots\cdots\cdots\cdots\cdots\cdots} \\ 0 & 0 & \cdots & -r_{mj}/r_{kj} & \cdots & 1 \end{bmatrix},$$

where the ratios are placed in the $(k+1)$st column of E. Multiplication by E is often called an **elementary transformation**.

Notice that the values $B^{-1}b$ for the current basis are optimal when

$$(10) \qquad\qquad c_B B^{-1} A - c \geq 0 \qquad c_B B^{-1} \geq 0.$$

The corresponding value of the objective function is

$$(11) \qquad\qquad c_B B^{-1} b.$$

REVIEW EXERCISES

1 (a) Solve for x_1 and x_3 in (2) and (3) of Sec. 4.2, and verify the result in (14) and (15).
   (b) Substitute in the objective function the expressions for x_1 and x_3 from part (a) and verify the result in (16) of Sec. 4.4.

Exercises 2, 3, and 4 refer to the numerical example in Sec. 4.4 with certain specified changes in the data.

2 What variable do you enter into the basis at iteration 1 of the simplex method if the objective function to be maximized is

   (a) $14x_1 + 5x_2 + 9x_3 + 11x_4$?
   (b) $4x_1 + 5x_2 + 9x_3 + 8x_4$?
   (c) $4x_1 + 5x_2 - 9x_3 + 11x_4$?
   (d) $-4x_1 - 5x_2 - 9x_3 - 11x_4$?

3 Given that you enter variable x_4 into the basis at iteration 1 of the simplex method, what variable do you remove from the basis and what will the new value of x_4 be if

(a) The coefficient on the right-hand side of Row 2 is 20? Is 12?
(b) The coefficient on the right-hand side of Row 3 is 300? Is 75?
(c) The coefficient of x_4 in Row 3 is 20? Is 24? Is -15?
(d) The coefficient of x_4 in Row 2 is 24?
(e) The coefficients on the right-hand sides of Rows 1, 2, and 3 are 40, 60, and 20, respectively, and the coefficients of x_4 in these rows are -5, 10, and 2, respectively?

4 Assume that you enter variable x_4 into the basis at iteration 1. What are the new values of the basic variables if

(a) You remove variable x_5 instead of x_7?
(b) You remove variable x_6 instead of x_7?
(c) Are the values in parts (a) and (b) feasible? Explain.

Exercises 5 through 14 refer to the numerical example in Sec. 4.4. In each part of an exercise, certain coefficients are altered. Find an optimal solution and the associated value of the objective function. Think carefully about each problem, because you may find that it is not necessary to redo all the arithmetic. It may be possible to "salvage" many of the previous computations in Sec. 4.4.

5 Assume that the objective function to be maximized is

(a) $4x_1 + \frac{33}{7}x_2 + 9x_3 + 10x_4$.
(b) $5x_1 + 5x_2 + 9x_3 + 11x_4$.
(c) $5x_1 + \frac{33}{7}x_2 + 9x_3 + 10x_4$.

6 Assume that the coefficient on the right-hand side of

(a) Row 2 is 140.
(b) Row 2 is 60.
(c) Row 1 is 12.
(d) Row 1 is 10.
(e) Row 1 is 20.

7 Assume that the objective function to be maximized is $5x_1 + 5x_2 + 9x_3 + 11x_4$ and the coefficient on the right-hand side of Row 1 is 20.

8 Assume that the first constraint, prior to adding a slack variable, is stated as

$$2x_1 + 2x_2 + 2x_3 + 2x_4 \leq 30.$$

9 Assume that the coefficient of

(a) x_2 in Row 3 is 10.
(b) x_4 in Row 3 is 20.
(c) x_2 in Row 2 is 4.
(d) x_4 in Row 2 is 1.
(e) x_1 in Row 2 is 10.
(f) x_3 in Row 2 is 6.

10 Assume that the coefficients in Rows 0, 1, 2, and 3 of

   (a) x_1 are 40, 10, 70, and 30, respectively.
   (b) x_2 are 20, 4, 20, and 20, respectively.
   (c) x_3 are 90, 10, 30, and 100, respectively.

11 Suppose you require $x_4 = 4$.

12 (a) Consider the variable x_8 defined in (10) of Sec. 4.4. Calculate the coefficients of x_8 at each of the simplex iterations, that is, in (2) through (7) of Sec. 4.4.
   (b) Verify that if you enter x_8 into the basis found at iteration 4, the solution is given by (12) of Sec. 4.4.
   (c) Let $w = .5$ in (13) of Sec. 4.4 and calculate optimal values for x_1, x_3, x_6, and x_8. Check that these values satisfy the original constraints and yield an objective-function value of $\frac{695}{7}$.

13 Consider the variable x_8 defined in (10) of Sec. 4.4. Determine whether entering x_8 into the basis found at iteration 4 improves the solution if the coefficient of x_8 in

   (a) Row 2 is 8, instead of 9.
   (b) Row 2 is 10, instead of 9.
   (c) Row 3 is 1, instead of .2.
   (d) Row 3 is .1, instead of .2.

14 Suppose another variable z is added to the example in Sec. 4.4, and at iteration 4, the coefficients of z in (7) are -1 in Rows 0 through 4. What is an optimal solution? Exhibit a solution having an objective-function value 100.

15 Consider the example (7) through (10) in Sec. 4.5. In each part below, apply the Big M Method, with $M = 10$, and derive a starting set of equations analogous to those in (13).

   (a) Add the constraint $x_2 \geq 2$.
   (b) Let the first constraint be $5x_1 + 6x_2 = 56$, instead of (8).
   (c) Let the first constraint be $-5x_1 + 6x_2 = 16$, instead of (8).

16 For a given set of constraints, suppose an all-slack-variable basis provides a feasible initial solution. What variable do you enter into the basis at iteration 1 of the simplex method given that the objective function to be minimized is

   (a) $4x_1 + 5x_2 - 9x_3 + 11x_4$.
   (b) $-4x_1 + 5x_2 - 9x_3 + 11x_4$.
   (c) $-4x_1 - 5x_2 - 9x_3 - 11x_4$.
   (d) $4x_1 + 5x_2 + 9x_3 + 11x_4$.
   (e) Given your answers in each of the preceding parts and that the constraints of the problem are Rows 1, 2, and 3 in (1) of Sec. 4.4, state what slack variable drops from the basis.

17 Explain your understanding of the following terms:

   algorithm   positive-weighted average
   Gaussian elimination   weighting factor

algorithmic convergence
basis and basic solution
basic and nonbasic variable
change of basis
pivot operation (or pivoting)
relative (or shadow) costs
shadow prices

degenerate basic solution
artificial variable
penalty-cost coefficient
*cycling
*simplex tableau
*elementary transformation.

COMPUTATIONAL EXERCISES

18 *One-Potato, Two-Potato Problem* (Sec. 1.6). Apply the simplex method to solve

$$\text{maximize } 5P_1 + 6P_2$$

subject to

$$.2P_1 + .3P_2 \leq 1.8$$
$$.2P_1 + .1P_2 \leq 1.2$$
$$.3P_1 + .3P_2 \leq 2.4$$
$$P_1 \geq 0 \quad \text{and} \quad P_2 \geq 0.$$

19 Apply the simplex method to solve

$$\text{maximize } 15x_1 + 6x_2 + 9x_3 + 2x_4$$

subject to

$$2x_1 + x_2 + 5x_3 + \ .6x_4 \leq 10$$
$$3x_1 + x_2 + 3x_3 + .25x_4 \leq 12$$
$$7x_1 \qquad\qquad + \quad x_4 \leq 35$$
$$\text{every } x_j \geq 0.$$

(*Hint:* you should find an optimal solution in no more than three iterations.)

20 (a) Apply the simplex method to solve

$$\text{maximize } 30x_1 + 23x_2 + 29x_3$$

subject to

$$6x_1 + 5x_2 + 3x_3 \leq 26$$
$$4x_1 + 2x_2 + 5x_3 \leq 7$$
$$\text{every } x_j \geq 0.$$

(*Hint:* you should find an optimal solution in no more than three iterations.)

(b) Solve part (a), assuming that the two right-hand side coefficients are 31, instead of 26, and 20, instead of 7. (*Hint:* you should find an optimal solution in no more than four iterations.)

21 Apply the simplex method to solve

$$\text{maximize } 60x_1 + 26x_2 + 15x_3 + 4.75x_4$$

subject to

$$20x_1 + 9x_2 + 6x_3 + 1x_4 \leq 20$$

$$10x_1 + 4x_2 + 2x_3 + 1x_4 \leq 10$$

$$\text{every } x_j \geq 0.$$

(*Hint:* you should find an optimal solution in no more than five iterations.) Does the objective function increase at every iteration? Is there a unique optimal solution?

22 *Alternative Optimal Solutions*

(a) Apply the simplex method to solve

$$\text{maximize } 1x_1 + 1x_2$$

subject to

$$1x_1 + 1x_2 \leq 3$$

$$1x_1 \qquad \leq 2$$

$$1x_2 \leq 2$$

$$x_1 \geq 0 \quad \text{and} \quad x_2 \geq 0.$$

(b) Alter the coefficients of x_1 to be 10, instead of 1, in both the objective function and constraints. Apply the simplex method to solve.

(c) Alter the coefficients of x_2 to be 10, instead of 1, in both the objective function and constraints. Apply the simplex method to solve.

(d) In each of the above parts, indicate how you know at the final iteration that there are alternative optimal solutions. Using formulas analogous to those in (13) of Sec. 4.4, characterize *all* the optimal solutions.

23 *Unbounded Optimal Solution.* Consider the constraints

$$x_1 - x_2 \leq 1$$

$$-x_1 + x_2 \leq 1$$

$$x_1 \geq 0 \quad \text{and} \quad x_2 \geq 0.$$

Apply the simplex method and assume that the objective function is

(a) Maximize x_1.

(b) Maximize x_2.

(c) Maximize $x_1 + x_2$.

(d) In each of the above parts, indicate a solution having objective-function value 100.

24 Consider the constraints graphed in exercise 10 of Chap. 3:

$$-10x_1 - 15x_2 \geq -150$$

$$5x_1 + 10x_2 \geq 50$$

$$x_1 - x_2 \geq 0$$

$$x_1 \geq 0 \quad \text{and} \quad x_2 \geq 0.$$

(We have eliminated the explicit constraint $x_1 \geq 2$ which was shown in exercise 10 of Chap. 3.)

Use the Big M Method, with $M = 10$, to find an initial basis. Solve for an optimal solution by the simplex method and assume that the objective function is

(a) Maximize $x_1 + x_2$. (d) Maximize $-2x_1 + x_2$.
(b) Minimize $x_1 + x_2$. (e) Maximize $-x_1 - 3x_2$.
(c) Maximize $x_1 + 3x_2$. (f) Maximize $-x_1 - 2x_2$.
(g) State in each of the above parts whether there is a *unique* optimal solution, and if there is not, calculate an alternative optimal solution. (*Hint:* do *not* add an artificial variable for the first constraint.)

25 Consider the constraints graphed in exercise 6 of Chap. 3:

$$-x_1 + x_2 \leq 1$$
$$6x_1 + 4x_2 \geq 24$$
$$x_1 \geq 0 \quad \text{and} \quad x_2 \geq 2.$$

Use the Big M Method, with $M = 10$, to find an initial basis. Obtain an optimal solution by the simplex method and assume that the objective function is

(a) Minimize x_1. (d) Maximize $-x_1 + 2x_2$.
(b) Minimize $x_1 + x_2$. (e) Maximize $x_1 - 2x_2$.
(c) Maximize $x_1 + x_2$. (f) Maximize $-3x_1 - 2x_2$.
(g) State in each of the above parts whether there is a *unique* optimal solution, and if there is not, calculate an alternative optimal solution.

26 Answer the questions in exercise 25 assuming that $x_1 \leq 5$.

27 Answer the questions in exercise 25 assuming that $x_2 \leq 4$.

28 *No Feasible Solution.* In Sec. 3.4, you saw a simple example that had no feasible solution:

$$\text{maximize } x_1 + x_2$$

subject to

$$-x_1 + x_2 \leq -1$$
$$x_1 - x_2 \leq -1$$
$$x_1 \geq 0 \quad \text{and} \quad x_2 \geq 0.$$

Apply the Big M Method to see what happens in this case. (Show that *Condition A* in Sec. 4.5 cannot be satisfied, regardless of how large a value you assign M.)

29 *Redundancy and Degeneracy.* Consider the problem

$$\text{maximize } x_1 - x_3$$

subject to

$$5x_1 + 3x_2 + x_3 = 40$$
$$x_1 + x_2 + 4x_3 = 10$$
$$\text{every } x_j \geq 0.$$

Use the Big M Method to derive an optimal solution when the model is augmented by the constraint

(a) $6x_1 + 4x_2 + 5x_3 = 50$.
(b) $6x_1 + 4x_2 + x_3 = 50$.

CONTENTS

CHAPTER 5

Sensitivity Testing and Duality

5.1 POSTOPTIMALITY ANALYSIS

In Chap. 4 you studied the mechanics of obtaining an optimal solution to a linear programming model. As a result you learned the important considerations for understanding the algorithmic approach and acquired an initial insight into the mathematical structure of a linear model—discovering, for example, that if a linear optimization model has a finite optimal solution, there exists an optimal *basic* solution.

But recall that the stated goal has been to provide systematic methods by which you can fully analyze and comprehend the complex interrelations in a linear programming application. We pursue this objective here.

The experienced user of a linear programming model rarely confines his interest to the numerical values of an optimal solution, unless he has already applied the model so many times that he fully understands the range of validity of the answer. Typically, he wants to know how far the input parameter values can vary without causing violent changes in a computed optimal solution or the composition of a basis set. Such an investigation is termed a **sensitivity** or **postoptimality analysis**.

Many important postoptimality questions are easily answered, given the numerical information at the final simplex iteration. Three illustrative examples are, "If the profit contribution of a particular basic activity decreases, does the current solution remain optimal? What happens if resource availability is curtailed? What happens if a new activity is added?" Other sensitivity questions can be sufficiently complex to require an electronic computer for the analysis, but even then, most electronic computer codes make considerable use of the previous optimal solution, and do *not* solve the revised model from scratch.

In the sections to follow, we explore the fundamental ideas that underlie sensitivity analysis in linear programming. The methods we present relate to the model

$$(1) \qquad\qquad \text{maximize } \sum_{j=1}^{n} c_j x_j$$

subject to

$$(2) \qquad\qquad \sum_{j=1}^{n} a_{ij} x_j \leq b_i \quad \text{for } i = 1, 2, \ldots, m$$

$$(3) \qquad\qquad x_j \geq 0 \quad \text{for } j = 1, 2, \ldots, n.$$

The mechanics of sensitivity testing are straightforward, and rather than confuse the presentation with frightening-looking formulas, we explain the ideas in terms of the Product-Mix Selection Example that was solved in Sec. 4.4. We repeat here both the initial and final systems of equations, labeling them (I) and (F):

$$
\begin{array}{llll}
1x_0 - 4x_1 - 5x_2 - 9x_3 - 11x_4 & = 0 & \text{Row 0} \\
1x_1 + 1x_2 + 1x_3 + 1x_4 + 1x_5 & = 15 & \text{Row 1} \\
7x_1 + 5x_2 + 3x_3 + 2x_4 \quad + 1x_6 & = 120 & \text{Row 2} \\
3x_1 + 5x_2 + 10x_3 + 15x_4 \quad\quad + 1x_7 & = 100 & \text{Row 3,}
\end{array}
$$

(I)

and

$$
\begin{array}{llll}
1x_0 \quad + \tfrac{3}{7}x_2 \quad + \tfrac{11}{7}x_4 + \tfrac{13}{7}x_5 \quad + \tfrac{5}{7}x_7 = \tfrac{695}{7} & \text{Row 0} \\
1x_1 + \tfrac{5}{7}x_2 \quad - \tfrac{5}{7}x_4 + \tfrac{10}{7}x_5 \quad - \tfrac{1}{7}x_7 = \tfrac{50}{7} & \text{Row 1} \\
- \tfrac{6}{7}x_2 \quad + \tfrac{13}{7}x_4 - \tfrac{61}{7}x_5 + 1x_6 + \tfrac{4}{7}x_7 = \tfrac{325}{7} & \text{Row 2} \\
\tfrac{2}{7}x_2 + 1x_3 + \tfrac{12}{7}x_4 - \tfrac{3}{7}x_5 \quad + \tfrac{1}{7}x_7 = \tfrac{55}{7} & \text{Row 3,}
\end{array}
$$

(F)

where x_0 is being maximized.

We ask you to copy (I) and (F) on a sheet of notepaper to keep before you as you read the text below.

5.2 OBJECTIVE FUNCTION

First we investigate whether a previously optimal feasible solution remains optimal if the coefficients in the objective function are altered. Such alterations do not affect the feasibility of the previous solution; therefore, whenever an improved solution is possible, you need only reinitiate the simplex method computations, starting at the previous final iteration.

Consider the coefficients of the nonbasic variables x_2 and x_4 in Row 0 of (I). It is intuitive that if they are made less profitable, the current solution remains optimal. If you sufficiently increased their profitability, however, you could eventually improve on the current solution. At what level of unit profit for x_2 does the present solution become nonoptimal?

Suppose the unit-profit coefficient of x_2 is $(5 + \delta)$, where δ (delta) is nonnegative. Then Row 0 in (I) would be written:

(1) $\qquad 1x_0 - 4x_1 - (5 + \delta)x_2 - 9x_3 - 11x_4 = 0 \quad$ Row 0.

In performing each simplex iteration, you added a multiple of a row to Row 0. Consequently at the final iteration, Row 0 of (F) must be

(2) $\qquad 1x_0 + (\frac{3}{7} - \delta)x_2 + \frac{11}{7}x_4 + \frac{13}{7}x_5 + \frac{5}{7}x_7 = \frac{695}{7} \quad$ Row 0,

as you should verify. Thus, subtracting δx_2 in (1) causes δx_2 to be subtracted in all subsequent Row 0 equations.

You can see that if δ is greater than $\frac{3}{7}$, the coefficient of x_2 in (2) is negative. Then x_2 would enter the next basic solution, according to *Simplex Criterion I* (Maximization). Similarly, if the coefficient of x_4 were increased by more than $\frac{11}{7}$, the current basic solution would no longer be optimal.

Thus, the final Row 0 coefficients of the nonbasic variables represent the largest positive increments to the original objective function coefficients that leave the current solution optimal.

Suppose you substantially reduce the profitability of x_1 or x_3, which are in the basis. It is plausible that the current basic solution might not remain optimal. It is not so intuitive that if you *increased* one of these unit-profit coefficients, the current solution could become nonoptimal. Within what range can the profitability of x_1 vary before the present solution can be improved?

To answer this question, you proceed as before. Row 0 in (I) becomes

(3) $\qquad 1x_0 - (4 + \delta)x_1 - 5x_2 - 9x_3 - 11x_4 = 0 \quad$ Row 0,

and in (F) correspondingly becomes

(4) $\qquad 1x_0 - \delta x_1 + \frac{3}{7}x_2 + \frac{11}{7}x_4 + \frac{13}{7}x_5 + \frac{5}{7}x_7 = \frac{695}{7}.$

To draw any conclusions about a critical range for δ, you first must recreate a coefficient equal to 0 for x_1 in Row 0. This is achieved in the usual fashion. Multiply Row 1 of (F) by δ and add it to (4) to give

(5) $\quad 1x_0 + (\frac{3}{7} + \frac{5}{7}\delta)x_2 + (\frac{11}{7} - \frac{5}{7}\delta)x_4 + (\frac{13}{7} + \frac{10}{7}\delta)x_5 + (\frac{5}{7} - \frac{1}{7}\delta)x_7$
$$= \frac{695}{7} + (\frac{50}{7})\delta \quad \text{Row 0.}$$

Look carefully at (5), and check that for

(6) $$-\frac{3}{5} \le \delta \le \frac{11}{5},$$

the current solution remains optimal. If δ is less than $-\frac{3}{5}$, the coefficient of x_2 becomes negative. If δ exceeds $\frac{11}{5}$, the coefficient of x_4 becomes negative. Consequently, as soon as δ falls outside the range in (6), the present basis is no longer optimal.

▶So far, the sensitivity analysis has been explained for a change in the profit coefficient of a single basic or nonbasic variable. The same approach is applicable for changes in several profit coefficients of the basic variables. However, the expression corresponding to (5) will have several change-quantities δ_j in each coefficient modifying the nonbasic variables. All of these expressions must remain nonnegative. Thus instead of a single pair of inequalities such as (6), there will be a system of inequalities, one corresponding to each coefficient of a nonbasic variable.

Many computer programs of the simplex method automatically provide **ranging analysis** for the objective function coefficients. A few routines also can perform more extensive sensitivity analysis using devices known as **multiple objective functions** and **parametric programming.**

The option of multiple objective functions permits solving a succession of linear programming problems, each with a different criterion function. The computer code optimizes on the first function, then goes on to each other function, one by one, employing the previously optimal basis as an initial solution.

In a parametric programming analysis, the model has as its objective function the expression

(i) $$\sum_{j=1}^{n} (c_j + \delta c_j^*) x_j,$$

where δ is viewed as a parameter to be varied over a specified range. In the simplest case, all the c_j^* equal 0, except one which equals 1, and the analysis is merely an extensive ranging study. The device of parametric programming can also be used to test whether a *specific* alteration in the objective function coefficients leads to the same optimal solution. To do this, c_j^* is defined as the increment to c_j corresponding to the *specified* alternative coefficient. Then a test is made to see whether the current basic solution remains optimal for $\delta = 1$.   ◄

5.3 RIGHT-HAND-SIDE CONSTANTS

Now we investigate whether a previously optimal basis remains feasible if a constant on the right-hand side is altered. When the basis remains feasible, the new solution is optimal, because the coefficients in Row 0 are unchanged.

Consider the constant on the right-hand side of Row 2 of (I). Suppose you change it to $(120 + 1\delta)$. Observe in (F) that the *slack* x_6 for this row is in the final basis, and so x_6 will change by the amount δ. Give a verbal argument for this conclusion. Consequently from Row 2 of (F), the present solution remains feasible so long as $\delta \geq -\frac{325}{7}$. (What is the value of x_6 if $\delta = -\frac{325}{7}$?)

Next consider the constant on the right-hand side of Row 1 of (I). Suppose you alter it to $(15 + 1\delta)$. Over what range of δ does the current solution remain feasible?

You can determine the answer if, while performing the simplex arithmetic, you carry along the quantity 1δ on the right-hand side of the equations. Notice, however, that row for row the quantity 1δ added on the right of (I) is just like the quantity $1x_5$ already appearing on the left of (I). It follows that at any iteration, the coefficients of δ will be the same row by row as the coefficients of x_5. Hence at the final iteration you must have

(1)

$$1x_0 \quad + \tfrac{3}{7}x_2 \qquad + \tfrac{11}{7}x_4 + \tfrac{13}{7}x_5 \qquad + \tfrac{5}{7}x_7 = \tfrac{695}{7} + \tfrac{13}{7}\delta \quad \underline{\text{Row } 0}$$

$$1x_1 + \tfrac{5}{7}x_2 \qquad - \tfrac{5}{7}x_4 + \tfrac{10}{7}x_5 \qquad - \tfrac{1}{7}x_7 = \tfrac{50}{7} + \tfrac{10}{7}\delta \quad \underline{\text{Row } 1}$$

$$- \tfrac{6}{7}x_2 \qquad + \tfrac{13}{7}x_4 - \tfrac{61}{7}x_5 + 1x_6 + \tfrac{4}{7}x_7 = \tfrac{325}{7} - \tfrac{61}{7}\delta \quad \underline{\text{Row } 2}$$

$$\tfrac{2}{7}x_2 + 1x_3 + \tfrac{12}{7}x_4 - \tfrac{3}{7}x_5 \qquad + \tfrac{1}{7}x_7 = \tfrac{55}{7} - \tfrac{3}{7}\delta \quad \underline{\text{Row } 3.}$$

As always, setting the nonbasic variables x_2, x_4, x_5, and x_7 to zero yields the values for the basic variables, which are now expressed in terms of δ. For feasibility, all the constants on the right-hand side of (1) must be nonnegative; therefore, the current solution remains feasible for

$$(2) \qquad\qquad -\frac{50}{10} \le \delta \le \frac{325}{61},$$

as you should verify. If $\delta < -\frac{50}{10}$, the basic variable x_1 becomes negative, and if $\delta > \frac{325}{61}$, the basic variable x_6 becomes negative.

Suppose $\delta = 1$, which can be interpreted as augmenting the scarce resource in Row 1 by one unit. Then the value of the objective function increases by $\frac{13}{7}$, as you can see in Row 0 of (1), and all the basic variables remain nonnegative. In other words, $\frac{13}{7}$ is the incremental value of another unit of this resource at an optimal solution.

▶The approach in (1) generalizes to simultaneous changes in several of the right-hand-side coefficients. Suppose the Row 1 constant is $(15 + 1\delta_1)$, the Row 2 constant is $(120 + 1\delta_2)$, and the Row 3 constant is $(100 + 1\delta_3)$. Then, analogously to (1), there is a column for each δ_i, for $i = 1, 2, 3$, on the right-hand side of (F). After setting the nonbasic variables to zero, the system appears as

$$
\begin{aligned}
x_0 &= \tfrac{695}{7} + \tfrac{13}{7}\delta_1 && + \tfrac{5}{7}\delta_3 \\
x_1 &= \tfrac{50}{7} + \tfrac{10}{7}\delta_1 && - \tfrac{1}{7}\delta_3 \\
x_6 &= \tfrac{325}{7} - \tfrac{61}{7}\delta_1 + 1\delta_2 + \tfrac{4}{7}\delta_3 \\
x_3 &= \tfrac{55}{7} - \tfrac{3}{7}\delta_1 && + \tfrac{1}{7}\delta_3.
\end{aligned}
$$

(i)

The coefficients of each δ_i are the same as the coefficients of the corresponding slack variable in (F). The expressions for x_1, x_6, and x_3 in (i) must be nonnegative to preserve feasibility, and consequently, there is a set of three inequalities to be satisfied by δ_1, δ_2, and δ_3.

Many computer routines of the simplex method automatically perform ranging analysis on the right-hand-side constants. Several programs also permit obtaining a succession of solutions for **multiple right-hand sides**, analogous to the approach available for multiple objective functions. In addition, certain computer codes include a parametric programming device for tracing the solution to a model having right-hand-side constants $b_i + \delta b_i^*$. In this approach the quantity δ is viewed as a parameter that ranges over a specified interval.   ◀

5.4 DUALITY

The techniques you have learned so far in answering questions about the sensitivity of an optimal solution may have seemed logical but ad hoc. In the same way, we could continue to develop methods for testing the sensitivity to the technological coefficients a_{ij}, for deciding whether it would be beneficial to enter into the basis a newly added variable, and for altering the solution when new constraints are imposed.

But there *is* a unifying concept, namely, **duality**, that establishes the interconnections for all of the sensitivity analysis techniques. If you are like most beginning students, you will first think of duality as being an abstract idea and, consequently, somewhat puzzling and remote. The reaction of most beginners when they read the Dual Theorem below is, "That's nice. So what?" At this point in your understanding, the only reply we can give is, "Keep the faith, baby." If ever the maxim applies that "there is nothing more practical than a good theory," this is it. We would be less than honest if we did not admit that many effective practitioners of linear programming have managed to avoid understanding duality. The most successful, however, know it cold.

We begin with a statement of the duality relationships and give a few immediate implications. Then in the subsequent sections we show how to employ duality for sensitivity testing.

Primal and dual problems. Consider the pair of linear programming models:

(1) $$\text{maximize } \sum_{j=1}^{n} c_j x_j$$

subject to

(2) $$\sum_{j=1}^{n} a_{ij} x_j \leq b_i \quad \text{for } i = 1, 2, \ldots, m$$

(3) $$x_j \geq 0 \quad \text{for } j = 1, 2, \ldots, n,$$

and

(4) $$\text{minimize } \sum_{i=1}^{m} b_i y_i$$

subject to

(5) $$\sum_{i=1}^{m} a_{ij} y_i \geq c_j \quad \text{for } j = 1, 2, \ldots, n$$

(6) $$y_i \geq 0 \quad \text{for } i = 1, 2, \ldots, m.$$

For the sake of definiteness, we arbitrarily call (1), (2), and (3) the **primal problem** and (4), (5), and (6) its **dual problem**.

As an illustration, consider the following pair of problems:

(7) $$\text{maximize } 4x_1 + 5x_2 + 9x_3$$
subject to

$$1x_1 + 1x_2 + 2x_3 \leq 16$$
(8) $$7x_1 + 5x_2 + 3x_3 \leq 25 \qquad \underline{\text{Primal}};$$
$$x_1 \geq 0 \quad x_2 \geq 0 \quad x_3 \geq 0$$

and

(9) $$\text{minimize } 16y_1 + 25y_2$$
subject to

$$1y_1 + 7y_2 \geq 4$$
(10) $$1y_1 + 5y_2 \geq 5 \qquad \underline{\text{Dual}}.$$
$$2y_1 + 3y_2 \geq 9$$
$$y_1 \geq 0 \quad y_2 \geq 0$$

Loosely put, the dual problem can be viewed as the primal model flipped on its side:

(i) The jth column of coefficients in the primal is the same as the jth row of coefficients in the dual.

(ii) The row of coefficients of the primal objective function is the same as the column of constants on the right-hand side of the dual.

(iii) The column of constants on the right-hand side of the primal is the same as the row of coefficients of the dual objective function.

(iv) The direction of the inequalities and sense of optimization are reversed in the pair of problems.

The proposition of significance is the following:

DUAL THEOREM: (a) If both the primal and dual problems possess feasible solutions, then the primal problem has an optimal solution x_j^*, for $j = 1, 2, \ldots, n$, the dual problem has an optimal solution y_i^*, for $i = 1, 2, \ldots, m$, and

$$(11) \qquad \sum_{j=1}^{n} c_j x_j^* = \sum_{i=1}^{m} b_i y_i^*.$$

(b) If either the primal or dual problem possesses a feasible solution with a finite optimal objective-function value, then the other problem possesses a feasible solution with the same optimal objective-function value.

To start demonstrating the ramifications of duality, we show that *any* feasible solution to one problem provides a bound on the optimal value of the objective function for the other problem.

Let x_j actually satisfy the primal constraints, and y_i similarly satisfy the dual constraints. Multiply the ith constraint in the primal by y_i. Likewise multiply the jth constraint in the dual by x_j. Since $y_i \geq 0$ and $x_j \geq 0$, the directions of the inequalities are unchanged by the multiplication. Add all the resultant constraints from the primal to give

$$(12) \qquad \sum_{i=1}^{m} y_i \left(\sum_{j=1}^{n} a_{ij} x_j \right) \leq \sum_{i=1}^{m} b_i y_i,$$

and add all the resultant constraints from the dual to give

$$(13) \qquad \sum_{j=1}^{n} x_j \left(\sum_{i=1}^{m} a_{ij} y_i \right) \geq \sum_{j=1}^{n} c_j x_j.$$

Note that adding like-directioned inequalities preserves the inequality direction.

The calculated quantities on the left-hand sides of (12) and (13) are the same; therefore,

$$(14) \qquad \sum_{j=1}^{n} c_j x_j \leq \sum_{i=1}^{m} b_i y_i.$$

Consequently, the value of the objective function for a feasible solution to one of the problems bounds the objective-function value in the other problem for *any* feasible solution, including an optimal one.

For the example of the primal problem stated in (7) and (8), and its dual in (9) and (10), we can write (14) as

(15) $$4x_1 + 5x_2 + 9x_3 \leq 16y_1 + 25y_2,$$

for any feasible primal and dual solutions. A feasible solution to the primal problem is $x_1 = x_2 = 0$ and $x_3 = 8$, which has an objective-function value of 72. A feasible solution to the dual problem is $y_1 = 5$ and $y_2 = 0$, which has an objective-function value of 80. Therefore, the optimal objective-function value for *both* primal and dual problems lies within the range of 72 to 80. Explain why.

If one problem has an unbounded optimal solution, then the other problem cannot have a feasible solution. For example, suppose for any value of the primal objective function, *no matter how large*, there exists a feasible solution yielding this value. Then the dual problem can have no feasible solution. If it did, a contradiction would arise. By (14), the dual solution would provide an upper bound on the value of the primal objective function for *any* feasible primal solution. But we assumed that the primal objective can be made arbitrarily large.

We also point out that the Dual Theorem indicates the fundamental test for optimality of a trial feasible solution to the primal problem. If there is a corresponding feasible solution to the dual problem such that the values of both objective functions are equal, then the two solutions must be optimal in their respective problems. (Explain why in a sentence or two.)

▶An interesting corollary of the Dual Theorem is the following:

THEOREM OF COMPLEMENTARY SLACKNESS. Let x_j^*, for $j = 1, 2, \ldots, n$, and y_i^*, for $i = 1, 2, \ldots, m$, be corresponding feasible solutions to the primal and dual problems, respectively. Then both are optimal if and only if

$$y_i^* \cdot \left(\sum_{j=1}^{n} a_{ij}x_j^* - b_i \right) = 0 \quad \text{for} \quad i = 1, 2, \ldots, m$$

$$x_j^* \cdot \left(\sum_{i=1}^{m} a_{ij}y_i^* - c_j \right) = 0 \quad \text{for} \quad j = 1, 2, \ldots, n.$$

This implies that whenever a constraint in one of the problems holds with strict inequality, so that there is slack in the constraint, the corresponding variable in the other problem equals 0.

We used convenient canonical forms for stating the primal and dual problems in (1) through (6). For any particular problem, you may have to employ the methods in Chap. 3 to transform the original statement to conform with either (1), (2), and (3) or (4), (5), and (6). You will gain further perception of duality relationships by seeing the pair of problems stated in the following expanded canonical forms:

(i) $$\text{maximize} \sum_{j=1}^{n} c_j x_j$$

subject to

(ii) $$\sum_{j=1}^{n} a_{ij}x_j \leq b_i \quad \text{for} \quad i = 1, 2, \ldots, h \leq m$$

(iii)
$$\sum_{j=1}^{n} a_{ij}x_j = b_i \quad \text{for } i = h+1, h+2, \ldots, m$$

(iv)
$$x_j \geq 0 \quad \text{for } j = 1, 2, \ldots, k \leq n$$

(v)
$$x_j \text{ unrestricted in sign} \quad \text{for } j = k+1, k+2, \ldots, n,$$

and

(i')
$$\text{minimize } \sum_{i=1}^{m} b_i y_i$$

subject to

(ii')
$$\sum_{i=1}^{m} a_{ij}y_i \geq c_j \quad \text{for } j = 1, 2, \ldots, k$$

(iii')
$$\sum_{i=1}^{m} a_{ij}y_i = c_j \quad \text{for } j = k+1, k+2, \ldots, n$$

(iv')
$$y_i \geq 0 \quad \text{for } i = 1, 2, \ldots, h$$

(v')
$$y_i \text{ unrestricted in sign} \quad \text{for } i = h+1, h+2, \ldots, m.$$

The Dual Theorem is valid for the above pair of problems.

Test your facility with the idea of duality by this exercise. Take as correct the relationships (1) through (6). Then derive the correspondence between (iii) and (v') by employing the devices in Chap. 3. The duality relationships can be summarized as follows:

Primal (Maximize)	Dual (Minimize)
Objective function	Right-hand side
Right-hand side	Objective function
jth column of coefficients	jth row of coefficients
ith row of coefficients	ith column of coefficients
jth variable nonnegative	jth relation an inequality ($\geq$)
jth variable unrestricted in sign	jth relation an equality
ith relation an inequality ($\leq$)	ith variable nonnegative
ith relation an equality	ith variable unrestricted in sign.

5.5 SOLUTION TO THE DUAL PROBLEM

By now, you must be wondering how to *calculate* a solution to the dual problem. But like the character in Molière who is delighted to hear he has been speaking prose all his life without knowing it, you have already calculated dual solutions without knowing it.

OPTIMAL VALUES OF DUAL VARIABLES. (a) The coefficients of the slack variables in Row 0 of the final simplex iteration of a maximizing problem are the optimal values of the dual variables. (b) The coefficient of variable x_j in Row 0 of the final simplex iteration represents the difference between the left- and right-hand sides of the jth dual constraint for the associated optimal dual solution.

To illustrate, consider the Product-Mix Selection Example originally written as

$$\text{maximize} \quad 4x_1 + 5x_2 + 9x_3 + 11x_4$$

subject to

$$1x_1 + 1x_2 + 1x_3 + 1x_4 \leq 15$$
$$7x_1 + 5x_2 + 3x_3 + 2x_4 \leq 120$$
$$3x_1 + 5x_2 + 10x_3 + 15x_4 \leq 100$$
$$x_j \geq 0 \quad \text{for } j = 1, 2, 3, 4.$$

Verify that the dual problem is

(1) $\qquad\qquad$ minimize $\quad 15y_1 + 120y_2 + 100y_3$

subject to

$$1y_1 + 7y_2 + 3y_3 \geq 4$$
$$1y_1 + 5y_2 + 5y_3 \geq 5$$
(2) $\qquad\qquad 1y_1 + 3y_2 + 10y_3 \geq 9$
$$1y_1 + 2y_2 + 15y_3 \geq 11$$
$$y_1 \geq 0 \qquad y_2 \geq 0 \qquad y_3 \geq 0.$$

Look at the coefficients of the three slack variables in Row 0 of the final iteration, which we have been referring to as (F), given in Sec. 5.1. You can conclude from (a) above that the optimal values of the dual variables are

(3) $\qquad\qquad\qquad y_1^* = \dfrac{13}{7} \quad y_2^* = 0 \quad y_3^* = \dfrac{5}{7}.$

Copy these values as you will want to refer to them below.

First verify that the constraints in (2) are satisfied:

$$1(\tfrac{13}{7}) + 3(\tfrac{5}{7}) = \tfrac{28}{7} \geq 4$$
$$1(\tfrac{13}{7}) + 5(\tfrac{5}{7}) = \tfrac{38}{7} \geq 5$$
(4) $\qquad\qquad 1(\tfrac{13}{7}) + 10(\tfrac{5}{7}) = \tfrac{63}{7} \geq 9$
$$1(\tfrac{13}{7}) + 15(\tfrac{5}{7}) = \tfrac{88}{7} \geq 11.$$

Second, check that the value of the dual objective function is the same as the value of the primal objective function:

(5) $\qquad\qquad 15(\tfrac{13}{7}) + 120(0) + 100(\tfrac{5}{7}) = \tfrac{695}{7}.$

The values in (3) must be optimal, since they satisfy all the dual constraints and yield an objective-function value equal to the optimal primal value.

Finally, calculate the differences between the left- and right-hand sides of (4). For example, the second and third constraints give

$$\frac{38}{7} - 5 = \frac{3}{7}$$
(6)
$$\frac{63}{7} - 9 = 0.$$

These are the coefficients of x_2 and x_3, respectively, in Row 0 of (F), as claimed in (b) above.

By reference to the notion of duality, you now can deepen your understanding of what is really happening in the simplex method. Interpret the coefficients of the slack variables in Row 0 of the primal problem at each iteration as trial values of the dual variables. Likewise view the other coefficients in Row 0 as the difference between the left- and right-hand sides of (2), using these trial values for the dual variables. *Then the simplex method can be seen as an approach that seeks feasibility for the dual problem while maintaining feasibility in the primal problem.* As soon as feasible solutions to *both* problems are obtained, the iterations terminate.

*One more time. The preceding explanation of how to find the optimal values of the dual variables was predicated on the model being specified with all ($\leq$) inequality constraints. Suppose instead that it is written as

$$(7) \qquad\qquad \text{maximize} \ \sum_{j=1}^{n} c_j x_j$$

subject to

$$(8) \qquad\qquad \sum_{j=1}^{n} a_{ij} x_j = b_i \quad \text{for } i = 1, 2, \ldots, m$$

$$x_j \geq 0 \quad \text{for } j = 1, 2, \ldots, n.$$

For simplicity, assume that the variables have been arranged so that $x_1, x_2, \ldots, x_m$ is an optimal basis. Then you can find the optimal values of the dual variables by solving the m simultaneous linear equations

$$(9) \qquad\qquad \sum_{i=1}^{m} a_{ij} y_i = c_j \quad \text{for } j = 1, 2, \ldots, m.$$

▶The duality result is readily apparent when you employ the matrix notation that we developed in Sec. 4.10. In such terms, the dual pair of problems is

	maximize cx subject to	minimize yb subject to
(i)	$Ax \leq b$	$yA \geq c$
	$x \geq 0$	$y \geq 0.$

As you saw in Sec. 4.10, a primal solution can be written as

$$(ii) \qquad\qquad x_B = B^{-1}b.$$

The corresponding objective-function value is

$$(iii) \qquad\qquad c_B B^{-1} b,$$

and the accompanying conditions for optimality are

$$(iv) \qquad\qquad c_B B^{-1} A - c \geq 0 \quad c_B B^{-1} \geq 0.$$

To verify that the associated optimal dual solution is

$$(v) \qquad\qquad y_B = c_B B^{-1},$$

only observe that (iv) then demonstrates that the feasibility conditions for the dual problem are satisfied and (iii) shows that the values of the primal and dual objective functions are equal. Note also that if the primal constraints are equalities, then (v) continues to hold, but y_B no longer has to be nonnegative. ◀

5.6 MORE POSTOPTIMALITY ANALYSIS

We promised that if you studied the Dual Theorem, you then would be better able to understand and do sensitivity analysis. Now we make good on our word. To start, we review what you have already learned at the beginning of the chapter, this time making clear where duality enters the picture. Afterwards, we answer some new sensitivity questions.

Objective function. Recall in the Product-Mix Selection Example that the dual restriction corresponding to the primal variable x_2 is

(1) $$1y_1 + 5y_2 + 5y_3 \geq 5.$$

If the objective function coefficient of x_2 becomes $(5 + \delta)$, then $(5 + \delta)$ appears on the right-hand side of (1). Substituting the optimal values of the dual variables into (1), where $(5 + \delta)$ is used, yields

(2) $$1\left(\tfrac{13}{7}\right) + 5(0) + 5\left(\tfrac{5}{7}\right) \geq 5 + \delta,$$

or

(3) $$\frac{3}{7} \geq \delta.$$

Thus the current dual solution remains feasible provided δ does not exceed $\tfrac{3}{7}$. If δ is made larger than this fraction, the dual solution is no longer feasible, and consequently the primal solution is no longer optimal. This conclusion agrees with what we found in Sec. 5.2.

Right-hand-side constants. In Sec. 5.3, we derived in an ad hoc fashion that the coefficient of a slack variable in Row 0 of an optimal solution represents the incremental value of another unit of the resource associated with that variable. And in the preceding section we stated that the optimal value of a dual variable is the very same coefficient. Putting the two statements together, we have the following:

INTERPRETATION OF THE DUAL VARIABLES. The optimal value of a dual variable indicates how much the objective function changes with a unit change in the associated right-hand-side constant, *provided* the current optimal basis remains feasible.

This interpretation accords with the fundamental equality relation (11) of the Dual Theorem in Sec. 5.4, which states:

(4) optimal value of x_0
$$= \sum (\text{right-hand-side constants}) \times (\text{optimal dual variables}).$$

The optimal values of the dual variables are often called **shadow prices**. When the right-hand-side constants represent quantities of scarce resources, the shadow price indicates the unit worth of each resource as predicated on an optimal solution to the primal problem. For the Product-Mix Selection Example, the value $\frac{13}{7}$ is the shadow price for the first constraint (man-weeks), and similarly 0 holds for the second constraint (pounds of Material Y), and $\frac{5}{7}$ for the third constraint (pounds of Material Z). Therefore, an additional man-week increases the profit level by $\frac{13}{7}$; an additional pound of Material Z increases the profit level by $\frac{5}{7}$; but an additional pound of Material Y does not improve the profit level. Why? Because Material Y is already in excess supply, as evidenced by the slack variable x_6 being in the optimal basis.

In general, a resource in excess supply is indicated by the slack variable for that resource appearing in the final basis at a positive level. You would expect the corresponding shadow price to be zero, because *additional* excess supply is of no value. This is precisely what occurs. Since the slack is in the basis, its final Row 0 coefficient is zero.

Interpreting the values of the dual variables as shadow prices leads to an insightful view into the meaning of the dual problem. In the context of the Product-Mix Selection Example, think of each dual variable as representing the true marginal value of its associated resource, assuming that the company is acting optimally. Then (4) indicates that total profit is the same as evaluating the total worth of all the resources in scarce supply. Interpret each coefficient a_{ij} as the consumption of the ith resource by the jth activity. The summation $\sum_{i=1}^{m} a_{ij} y_i$ represents the underlying economic cost of using the jth activity, evaluated according to the shadow prices. The constraints of the dual problem ensure that at an optimal solution, the profit of an activity can never exceed its true economic worth. What is more, you will never employ an activity if its profit is less than its economic worth.

▶The following example shows why the above interpretation of the dual variables has to be qualified with the proviso that the current basis remains feasible. Consider

(i) $$\text{maximize} \ -x_1 - x_2$$

subject to

$$2x_1 - x_2 \le 2$$
(ii) $$-x_1 + 2x_2 \le 0$$
$$x_1 \ge 0 \qquad x_2 \ge 0.$$

The solution $x_1 = x_2 = 0$ is clearly feasible and thus is optimum. Why? [You may find it helpful to draw a two-dimensional diagram of the solution space implied by (ii) and single out the unique optimum.]

Add slack variables x_3 and x_4 to the inequalities in (ii). Then if you choose x_3 and x_4 to be basic variables, after pivoting, you will find that $x_3 = 2$, $x_4 = 0$, which is a degenerate solution. The corresponding dual variables are $y_1 = y_2 = 0$. Further, the associated Row 0 relation will be $x_0 + x_1 + x_2 = 0$, so that both nonbasic variables have strictly positive coefficients. If, instead, you choose x_1 and x_3 to be the basic variables, then after pivoting, you will find that $x_1 = 0$, $x_3 = 2$, and the corresponding variables are $y_1 = 0$, $y_2 = 1$. Further, the Row 0 relation will be $x_0 + 3x_2 + 1x_4 = 0$, so that both nonbasic variables have strictly positive coefficients. Thus, because the optimal solution leads to a degenerate basis, you have found different optimal values for (y_1, y_2), each set corresponding to one of the optimal bases. Suppose now the second constraint is

(iii) $$-x_1 + 2x_2 \leq \delta_2.$$

For δ_2 nearly zero, which value for y_2 indicates how the objective function will change? If $\delta_2 > 0$, then $x_1 = x_2 = 0$ is still optimal, and so $y_2 = 0$ is correct. The basis with x_1 and x_3 is not feasible for $\delta_2 > 0$ (x_1 has a negative value). If $\delta_2 < 0$, then $y_2 = 1$ is correct, for then you must have $x_1 > 0$ for feasibility.   ◄

Technological coefficients. To begin consideration of sensitivity tests on the a_{ij}, suppose an entirely new activity is added to the model. Is it advantageous to enter it into the basis? The easiest test is to check whether the associated dual constraint is satisfied by the current values of the dual variables. If not, the new activity should be introduced.

Consider the Product-Mix Selection Example, as given by (I) in Sec. 5.1. Suppose you add another variable:

(5)
$$+1x_8 \quad \underline{\text{Row 1}}$$
$$+\tfrac{2}{7}x_8 \quad \underline{\text{Row 2}}$$
$$+17x_8 \quad \underline{\text{Row 3.}}$$

Let the profit coefficient of x_8 in the objective function be c_8. At what value of c_8 is it attractive to enter x_8? The associated dual relation is

(6) $$1y_1 + \tfrac{2}{7}y_2 + 17y_3 \geq c_8.$$

Substitute the current optimal values of the dual variables in (6) to obtain

(7) $$1\left(\tfrac{13}{7}\right) + \tfrac{2}{7}(0) + 17\left(\tfrac{5}{7}\right) \geq c_8,$$

or

(8) $$14 \geq c_8.$$

Therefore, if c_8 exceeds 14, you should enter x_8 into the basis.

►Assume $c_8 = 20$. Then the coefficient of x_8 in Row 0 of (F) is $14 - 20 = -6$. What are the coefficients of x_8 in other rows of (F)? This question may be answered in the following way.

View the coefficients in (5) row by row as equivalent to the sum of 1 times the coefficients of x_5, $\tfrac{2}{7}$ times the coefficients of x_6, and 17 times the coefficients of x_7, as given in (I):

(iv)
$$[1(1) + \tfrac{2}{7}(0) + 17(0)]x_8 = \quad 1x_8 \quad \underline{\text{Row 1}}$$
$$[1(0) + \tfrac{2}{7}(1) + 17(0)]x_8 = \quad \tfrac{2}{7}x_8 \quad \underline{\text{Row 2}}$$
$$[1(0) + \tfrac{2}{7}(0) + 17(1)]x_8 = 17x_8 \quad \underline{\text{Row 3.}}$$

Then the coefficients of x_8 in (F) can be computed row by row as the same multiples of the corresponding coefficients of x_5, x_6, and x_7 in (F). Specifically,

(v)
$$[1(\tfrac{10}{7}) + \tfrac{2}{7}(0) + 17(-\tfrac{1}{7})]x_8 = -1x_8 \quad \underline{\text{Row 1}}$$
$$[1(-\tfrac{61}{7}) + \tfrac{2}{7}(1) + 17(\tfrac{4}{7})]x_8 = \quad \tfrac{9}{7}x_8 \quad \underline{\text{Row 2}}$$
$$[1(-\tfrac{3}{7}) + \tfrac{2}{7}(0) + 17(\tfrac{1}{7})]x_8 = \quad 2x_8 \quad \underline{\text{Row 3.}}$$ ◄

If x_j is a nonbasic variable, you can study the effect of changing its technological coefficients a_{ij} in exactly the same fashion. To illustrate, x_4 is nonbasic in the optimal solution of the Product-Mix Selection Example. Consider the possibility that its coefficient in Row 3 is altered by δ. Then the associated dual restriction is

(9) $$1y_1 + 2y_2 + (15 + \delta)y_3 \geq 11.$$

Substitute the current optimal values of the dual variables in (9) to obtain

(10) $$1(\tfrac{13}{7}) + 2(0) + (15 + \delta)(\tfrac{5}{7}) \geq 11$$

or

(11) $$\delta \geq -\frac{11}{5}.$$

Therefore, if δ is smaller than $-\tfrac{11}{5}$, you should enter x_4 into the basis.

If x_j is a basic variable, analyzing the effect of changing a technological coefficient is more complex. The analysis involves a simultaneous consideration of both the primal and dual problems. The derivation goes beyond the scope of this text, but can be found in several advanced books on linear programming.

5.7 SUMMARY

In Secs. 5.1 to 5.6, you have seen how to probe the sensitivity of an optimal solution of a linear programming problem to changes in the model formulation. In particular you studied how to

(i) Find the range of variation in each objective-function coefficient and right-hand-side constant over which the current basis remains optimal, provided the basis remains feasible.

(ii) Evaluate the economic impact of specific changes in the model's data.

(iii) Revise a previously optimal solution after adding new variables.

The mechanics for all these postoptimality analyses are straightforward extensions of the simplex-method arithmetic. But duality is the key idea that ensures the mechanics are correct.

Every linear optimization model has a dual formulation. In solving one of these problems, you automatically solve the other. As you progress in learning the fundamentals of operations research, you will find the notion of duality frequently reappearing.

*5.8 DUAL SIMPLEX ALGORITHM

Given the reciprocal relations between the primal and dual problems, another possibility for solving a linear program seems plausible. Consider an algorithm for the primal problem in which, until the final iteration, each trial primal solution is infeasible as it contains negative-valued variables; but the associated *dual* solution stays feasible at every iteration. This is the idea of the dual simplex algorithm.

There are at least two practical reasons for studying the dual simplex algorithm. One is that it sometimes permits you to easily select an initial basis without having to add any artificial variables. You will observe how this can happen in the example below. Second, it aids in certain types of sensitivity analysis, as you will see in the subsequent section.

We begin the discussion with an illustration. Examine the problem

(1)   minimize $2x_1 + 1x_3$

subject to

$$1x_1 + 1x_2 - 1x_3 \geq 5$$
(2) $$1x_1 - 2x_2 + 4x_3 \geq 8$$
$$x_1 \geq 0 \qquad x_2 \geq 0 \qquad x_3 \geq 0.$$

Here it is convenient to designate (1) and (2) as the primal problem, and so its dual is

(3)   maximize $5y_1 + 8y_2$

subject to

$$1y_1 + 1y_2 \leq 2$$
$$1y_1 - 2y_2 \leq 0$$
(4)
$$-1y_1 + 4y_2 \leq 1$$
$$y_1 \geq 0 \qquad y_2 \geq 0.$$

As before, if you let x_0 be the value of the objective function and add surplus variables to (2), you can write the primal problem as

$$1x_0 - 2x_1 \qquad - 1x_3 \qquad\qquad = 0 \quad \underline{\text{Row 0}}$$
(5) $$1x_1 + 1x_2 - 1x_3 - 1x_4 \qquad = 5 \quad \underline{\text{Row 1}}$$
$$1x_1 - 2x_2 + 4x_3 \qquad - 1x_5 = 8 \quad \underline{\text{Row 2.}}$$

A starting solution with x_0, x_4, and x_5 as basic variables is infeasible, since $x_4 = -5$ and $x_5 = -8$ when $x_1 = x_2 = x_3 = 0$. As a result, the current value $x_0 = 0$ is too small; you can see from (1) and (2) that x_0 will be positive when feasibility occurs. But notice that for this infeasible starting solution, the coefficients in Row 0 satisfy the optimality condition in *Simplex Criterion I* (Minimization) stated in Sec. 4.6. Therefore, we say that this initial basis is **dual-feasible**. [Verify that $y_1 = 0$ and $y_2 = 0$ satisfy the constraints (4).] In this method, we seek to maintain dual feasibility but remove the primal infeasibilities.

The method. Proceeding by analogy with the simplex algorithm, we construct a **dual simplex algorithm**. First we formulate a rule indicating which variable is to be *removed* from the current basis.

DUAL SIMPLEX CRITERION I. If there are basic variables having negative values, select one such variable that is most negative (say x_k). If all basic variables have nonnegative values, an optimal solution has been obtained.

To apply *Criterion I*, rewrite (5) after multiplying Rows 1 and 2 by (-1); this gives

$$
\begin{aligned}
1x_0 - 2x_1 \quad\quad - 1x_3 \quad\quad\quad\quad\quad &= \quad 0 \quad \text{Row 0} \\
- 1x_1 - 1x_2 + 1x_3 + 1x_4 \quad\quad\quad &= -5 \quad \text{Row 1} \\
- 1x_1 + 2x_2 - 4x_3 \quad\quad + 1x_5 &= -8 \quad \text{Row 2.}
\end{aligned}
$$

(6)

According to *Criterion I*, remove the basic variable x_5 since it is more negative than x_4.

Next we provide a rule selecting a variable to be *introduced* into the basis. Keep in mind that you want to preserve dual feasibility. After the change of basis, the coefficients in Row 0 are to remain nonpositive.

DUAL SIMPLEX CRITERION II (MINIMIZATION). (a) Take the ratios of the current coefficients in Row 0 of the nonbasic variables to the coefficients in the row of the currently leaving x_k (ignore ratios with zero or positive numbers in the denominator). (b) Select the minimum ratio, which occurs for a variable x_j.

Nonbasic Variables	x_1	x_2	x_3
Current Row 0 ÷	-2	0	-1
Coeffs. in Row 2 =	-1	2	-4
Ratios	2	$--$	$.25$
Minimum			$.25$

The calculations indicated by *Criterion II* are performed in Fig. 5.1. Since you know that x_3 is to replace x_5 in a trial basis, you can perform the same change-of-basis calculations as you do in the ordinary simplex method. Start the pivot operation on (-4), the coefficient of x_3 in Row 2; this yields

FIGURE 5.1. *Iteration 1: Dual Simplex Criterion II* for x_5 Leaving Basis.

$$
\begin{aligned}
1x_0 - 2x_1 \quad\quad - 1x_3 \quad\quad\quad\quad &= 0 \quad\quad \text{Row 0} \\
- 1x_1 - 1x_2 + 1x_3 + 1x_4 \quad\quad &= -5 \quad \text{Row 1} \\
\tfrac{1}{4}x_1 - \tfrac{2}{4}x_2 + 1x_3 \quad\quad - \tfrac{1}{4}x_5 &= 2 \quad\quad \text{Row 2.}
\end{aligned}
$$

(7)

Thus you have created a coefficient 1 for x_3 in Row 2. Next create coefficients equal to 0 in Rows 0 and 1:

Row 0: multiply Row 2 by   1 and add to Row 0,
Row 1: multiply Row 2 by -1 and add to Row 1.

The result is

$$
\begin{aligned}
1x_0 - \tfrac{7}{4}x_1 - \tfrac{2}{4}x_2 \quad\quad\quad -\tfrac{1}{4}x_5 &= 2 \quad\quad \text{Row 0} \\
- \tfrac{5}{4}x_1 - \tfrac{2}{4}x_2 \quad + 1x_4 + \tfrac{1}{4}x_5 &= -7 \quad \text{Row 1} \\
\tfrac{1}{4}x_1 - \tfrac{2}{4}x_2 + 1x_3 \quad\quad - \tfrac{1}{4}x_5 &= 2 \quad\quad \text{Row 2.}
\end{aligned}
$$

(8)

The corresponding basic solution is

(9) $$ x_0 = 2 \quad\quad x_4 = -7 \quad\quad x_3 = 2. $$

As the infeasibilities are removed, the objective function progresses toward the optimal value.

Iteration 2. Once again apply *Criterion I* and find that x_4 should leave the basis. Figure 5.2 exhibits the calculations for *Criterion II*. Observe that x_2 is to enter the basis in place of x_4. Carrying out the usual change-of-basis calculations transforms (8) into

(10)
$$1x_0 - \tfrac{1}{2}x_1 \qquad\qquad - 1x_4 - \tfrac{1}{2}x_5 = 9 \quad \underline{\text{Row 0}}$$
$$\tfrac{5}{2}x_1 + 1x_2 \qquad - 2x_4 - \tfrac{1}{2}x_5 = 14 \quad \underline{\text{Row 1}}$$
$$\tfrac{3}{2}x_1 \qquad + 1x_3 - 1x_4 - \tfrac{1}{2}x_5 = 9 \quad \underline{\text{Row 2.}}$$

The associated basic solution is

(11)
$$x_0 = 9 \qquad x_2 = 14 \qquad x_3 = 9.$$

Nonbasic Variables	x_1	x_2	x_5
Current Row 0 ÷	$-\tfrac{7}{4}$	$-\tfrac{2}{4}$	$-\tfrac{1}{4}$
Coeffs. in Row 1 =	$-\tfrac{5}{4}$	$-\tfrac{2}{4}$	$\tfrac{1}{4}$
Ratios	$\tfrac{7}{5}$	1	$--$
Minimum		1	

Figure 5.2. *Iteration 2: Criterion II for x_4 Leaving Basis.*

At this iteration all the basic variables are nonnegative, and consequently the calculations terminate with (11) as the optimal solution to the primal problem (1) and (2). The optimal values for the dual variables are *minus* the coefficients of the slack variables in Row 0 of the final iteration of a minimizing problem. Consequently, $[y_1 = -(-1) = 1]$ and $[y_2 = -(-\tfrac{1}{2}) = \tfrac{1}{2}]$ are optimal in (3) and (4).

Maximization. The algorithm has been explained for minimization problems and is easily altered for maximization problems. At each iteration, all the coefficients of the nonbasic variables in Row 0 are nonnegative. There is no change in *Dual Simplex Criterion I*, but you now apply the following.

Dual Simplex Criterion II (Maximization). (a) Take the ratios of the current coefficients in Row 0 of the nonbasic variables to the coefficients in the row of the currently leaving x_k (ignore ratios with zero or positive numbers in the denominator). (b) Select the maximum ratio, which occurs for a variable x_j.

Computational characteristics. We do not discuss the properties of the dual simplex algorithm as we did for the simplex method in Chap. 4. Most of this would be simply repetitious. For completeness, however, we do mention how the algorithm indicates when the primal problem has no feasible solution. In applying *Dual Simplex Criterion II*, if the coefficients in the row of the presently leaving x_k are *all* nonnegative, then the primal problem is infeasible. (In this instance, the dual problem has an unbounded optimal solution.)

We also call attention to one feature that can be a drawback to the dual simplex approach. If the iterations are stopped short of convergence, the current basic solution for the primal problem is *not* feasible.

Many advanced computer programs for linear optimization models include the dual simplex algorithm. In these codes, the computer automatically examines the constraints and objective function and decides whether to apply the dual method.

Comparison of primal and dual algorithms. We list the connections between the two methods we have examined for solving linear programming problems.

(i) Both methods progress from one basic solution to a neighboring one. At each iteration, there is only one change in the composition of the set of basic variables.

(ii) The value of the objective function at any iteration is at least as close to optimum as it was at the previous iteration.

(iii) For both methods, *Criterion I* seeks to reduce an infeasibility. In the simplex method, the rule eliminates a dual infeasibility. In the dual simplex method, the rule removes a primal infeasibility.

(iv) For both methods, *Criterion II* seeks to maintain feasibility. In the simplex method, the basic variables remain primal-feasible. In the dual simplex method, the coefficients in Row 0 stay dual-feasible.

These properties can be restated succinctly as follows.

(1) Applying the simplex method to a linear programming model is identical to the process of applying the dual simplex method to the dual problem.

(2) Applying the dual simplex method to a linear programming model is identical to the process of applying the simplex method to the dual problem.

*5.9 ADDITIONAL AND TIGHTER CONSTRAINTS

In real applications of linear programming, it is not unusual to want to add new restrictions after you have obtained a preliminary solution. At times you may find it necessary to impose additional constraints once you have examined the full implications of a trial optimal solution. On other occasions you may purposely omit some constraints from the initial formulation in order to lighten the computational burden. Empirical evidence suggests that the simplex method computations increase *roughly* as a cubic function of the number of constraints. Hence you actually are well advised to be conservative in deciding on the number of constraints to start with. Frequently, you have a priori knowledge that certain restrictions are not likely to be binding in an optimal solution. These conditions, which sometimes are referred to as **secondary constraints**, are added later only if required.

Testing whether a new constraint is satisfied by a current solution is the simplest case of postoptimality analysis. Merely insert the current optimal values for the basic variables and check whether the constraint is met. If not, the dual simplex method can be applied to restore feasibility.

To illustrate, consider the Product-Mix Selection Example, and suppose the following constraint is added to formulation (I):

(1) $$14x_1 + 7x_3 + 1x_4 + 1x_8 = 150 \quad \underline{\text{Row 4,}}$$

where $x_8 \geq 0$ is the slack variable for this relation. Given the current basic optimal solution, you see that

(2) $$14(\tfrac{50}{7}) + 7(\tfrac{55}{7}) + 1(0) + 1x_8 = 150,$$

or

(3) $$x_8 = -5.$$

The negative value for x_8 signals that the current solution does not satisfy the new constraint. Therefore, you proceed as follows.

Add x_8 to the basis set of the enlarged problem. By the usual pivot operations, eliminate the basic variables x_1 and x_3 from (1) by using Rows 1 and 3 of formulation (F). Specifically, multiply Row 1 by (-14) and Row 3 by (-7) and add the results to (1) to yield

(4) $$-12x_2 - 1x_4 - 17x_5 + 1x_7 + 1x_8 = -5.$$

Now apply the *Dual Simplex Criterion II* (Maximization). You find that x_2 enters the basis in place of x_8. The resultant ordinary change-of-basis calculation produces a feasible, and therefore optimal, primal solution:

(5)
$$x_0 = \frac{8325}{84} \qquad x_1 = \frac{575}{84}$$
$$x_6 = \frac{3930}{84} \qquad x_3 = \frac{650}{84} \qquad x_2 = \frac{35}{84}.$$

Note that in many problems you will need more than one iteration of the dual simplex algorithm to restore primal feasibility. By using the above approach, you can simultaneously add *several* new constraints.

Right-hand sides again. In the analysis of right-hand-side sensitivity in Secs. 5.3 and 5.6, we stopped short of stating what to do if a right-hand-side constant were altered so as to make the current optimal basic solution no longer feasible. In that case, a basic variable has turned negative and you would initiate the dual simplex algorithm, starting with the previous final iteration.

For example, you saw in the Product-Mix Selection Example that if the right-hand side of Row 1 is $(15 + 1\delta)$, then the optimal basis remains feasible only for $-\tfrac{50}{10} \leq \delta \leq \tfrac{325}{61}$, according to (2) in Sec. 5.3. Further, you learned that if δ lies below this range, then x_1 turns negative. To restore feasibility, you would remove x_1 from the basis, and apply *Dual Simplex Criterion II* (Maximization) to determine the variable to enter. You would use the same procedure if δ were above the permissible range.

*5.10 UPPER-BOUNDED VARIABLES

In many important linear optimization models, each variable is bounded above:

(1) $$x_j \leq u_j \quad \text{for } j = 1, 2, \ldots, n.$$

Since the scaling of x_j can be chosen freely, no loss in generality arises by assuming $u_j = 1$.

Of course, (1) can be included with the rest of the inequalities in solving such a model. But the simple form of (1) leads to a solution technique that avoids enlarging the model by the n constraints in (1). The method requires only a minor modification in the rules of the simplex method.

The relation (1) can be viewed as

$$(2) \qquad x_j + x_j' = 1 \quad \text{with } x_j' \geq 0,$$

where now u_j has been set equal to 1. As the iterations progress, it may be necessary to remove x_j by substitution using

$$(3) \qquad x_j = 1 - x_j'.$$

This substitution causes x_j' to appear explicitly in the model. At later iterations, it may be necessary to remove x_j' by using

$$(4) \qquad x_j' = 1 - x_j.$$

As a result, x_j then reappears explicitly.

We will state that an **upper-bound substitution** occurs whenever (3) or (4) is utilized.

The algorithm consists of the *Simplex Criterion I* (Maximization), stated without change, as well as *Simplex Criterion II* modified as follows.

SIMPLEX CRITERION II (BOUNDED VARIABLES). (a) Take only the ratios of the current right-hand side to the *positive* coefficients of the entering variable. Let r_1 be the value of the minimum ratio, which occurs for the basic variable in Row k. (b) Take only the ratios of (current right-hand side -1) to the *negative* coefficients of the entering variable. Let r_2 be the value of the minimum ratio, which occurs for the basic variable in Row k'. (c) Let $r = $ minimum (r_1, r_2). (d) If $r \geq 1$, do not perform any change-of-basis calculation. Make the upper-bound substitution for the entering variable. (e) Otherwise, if $r = r_1$, perform the standard change-of-basis calculation, pivoting in Row k. (f) Otherwise, if $r = r_2$, perform the standard change-of-basis calculation, pivoting in Row k'. Then make the upper-bound substitution for the variable previously basic in Row k'.

When the algorithm terminates, the model will contain explicitly either x_j or x_j'. If x_j appears as a nonbasic variable, its optimal value is 0. If x_j is a basic variable, then it is presently at its optimal value. If x_j' appears as a nonbasic variable, then the optimal value of x_j is 1. If x_j' is a basic variable, then the optimal value of x_j is $1 - x_j'$. An example is given below.

▶ With an equally simple alteration, the dual simplex algorithm can be made to accommodate upper-bounded variables. *Criteria I* and *II* are unchanged, but the upper-bound substitution is employed. State how you think the algorithm would work. As a starting point, take a solution that is optimal without the upper bounds (assume the optimum value is finite), but infeasible with respect to these bounds.   ◀

Example. Consider this problem

(5)   maximize $4x_1 + 10x_2 + 9x_3 + 11x_4$

subject to

$$1x_1 + 1x_2 + 1x_3 + 1x_4 \leq \frac{5}{2}$$

(6) $3x_1 + 5x_2 + 10x_3 + 15x_4 \leq \frac{275}{16}$

$$0 \leq x_j \leq 1 \quad \text{for } j = 1, 2, 3, 4.$$

Let x_5 and x_6 be the slack variables for the first and second inequalities. Note that these variables are not bounded by 1, but this will not cause any difficulties in the calculations.

The initial basic solution consists of the slack variables, and is shown as iteration 1 in the condensed tableau in Fig. 5.3 (this form was presented in Sec. 4.9). According to *Simplex Criterion I* (Maximization), variable x_4 enters the solution. Since there are no negative coefficients for x_4,

(7) $r = r_1 = \text{minimum} \left(\frac{5}{2}, \frac{275}{15 \cdot 16} \right) = \frac{275}{240} > 1.$

Therefore *Simplex Criterion II* (Bounded Variables) indicates that an upper-bound substitution is to be made for x_4, yielding the result labeled as iteration 2. Observe that the tableau contains the variable x_4' signifying the substitution, and the current values of the basic variables have been changed accordingly.

Next x_2 enters the solution. Once again, there are no negative coefficients and so

(8) $r = r_1 = \text{minimum} \left(\frac{3}{2}, \frac{17}{5 \cdot 16} \right) = \frac{17}{80};$

thus x_2 enters and x_6 leaves the basis. After the usual change-of-basis pivot step, the coefficients are shown as iteration 3.

At this point, x_4' is to be introduced, and

(9) $r_1 = \frac{103}{2 \cdot 80} \qquad r_2 = \frac{\frac{17}{80} - 1}{-3} \qquad r = r_2 = \frac{21}{80}.$

Hence x_4' enters the basis and x_2 leaves *at its upper bound*. Therefore, apply the change-of-basis pivot step, and then the upper-bound substitution for x_2. The result appears as iteration 4.

Verify that now x_1 enters the basis and x_5 leaves, since $r = r_1 < 1$, giving the values in iteration 5. Check that, as a result, x_3 enters the basis and x_4' leaves at its upper bound, requiring another upper-bound substitution. The final tableau is shown as iteration 6. The optimal values for x_1 and x_3 appear in the "Current Values" column; since x_2' is nonbasic, the optimal value of $x_2 = 1$.

In reviewing the iterations, be sure to observe how first x_4 enters the solution at its upper bound, necessitating an upper-bound substitution; then later on, x_4' enters the basis; and ultimately, x_4' leaves the basis at its upper bound, once again necessitating an upper-bound substitution and causing x_4 to appear in the final tableau.

Iteration	Basis	Current Values	x_1	x_2	x_3	x_4
1	x_0	0	-4	-10	-9	-11
	x_5	$\frac{5}{2}$	1	1	1	1
	x_6	$\frac{275}{16}$	3	5	10	15
			x_1	x_2	x_3	x_4'
2	x_0	11	-4	-10	-9	11
	x_5	$\frac{3}{2}$	1	1	1	-1
	x_6	$\frac{17}{16}$	3	5	10	-15
			x_1	x_6	x_3	x_4'
3	x_0	$\frac{105}{8}$	-2	2	11	-19
	x_5	$\frac{103}{80}$	$\frac{2}{5}$	$-\frac{1}{5}$	-1	2
	x_2	$\frac{17}{80}$	$\frac{3}{5}$	$\frac{1}{5}$	2	-3
			x_1	x_6	x_3	x_2'
4	x_0	$\frac{1449}{80}$	$-\frac{9}{5}$	$\frac{11}{15}$	$-\frac{5}{3}$	$\frac{19}{3}$
	x_5	$\frac{61}{80}$	$\frac{4}{5}$	$-\frac{1}{15}$	$\frac{1}{3}$	$-\frac{2}{3}$
	x_4'	$\frac{21}{80}$	$-\frac{1}{5}$	$-\frac{1}{15}$	$-\frac{2}{3}$	$\frac{1}{3}$
			x_5	x_6	x_3	x_2'
5	x_0	$\frac{1269}{164}$	$\frac{9}{4}$	$\frac{7}{12}$	$-\frac{11}{12}$	$\frac{29}{6}$
	x_1	$\frac{61}{64}$	$\frac{5}{4}$	$-\frac{1}{12}$	$\frac{5}{12}$	$-\frac{5}{6}$
	x_4'	$\frac{29}{64}$	$\frac{1}{4}$	$-\frac{1}{12}$	$-\frac{7}{12}$	$\frac{1}{6}$
			x_5	x_6	x_4	x_2'
6	x_0	$\frac{331}{16}$	$\frac{13}{7}$	$\frac{5}{7}$	$\frac{11}{7}$	$\frac{32}{7}$
	x_1	$\frac{9}{16}$	$\frac{10}{7}$	$-\frac{1}{7}$	$-\frac{5}{7}$	$-\frac{5}{7}$
	x_3	$\frac{15}{16}$	$-\frac{3}{7}$	$\frac{1}{7}$	$\frac{12}{7}$	$-\frac{2}{7}$

FIGURE 5.3. Condensed Simplex Tableau for the Bounded-Variables Example.

REVIEW EXERCISES

The problems in exercises 1 through 7 refer to the Product-Mix Selection Example in Sec. 4.4, with the initial system of equations being given by (I) and the final system by (F), as shown at the beginning of Sec. 5.1. Think carefully about each problem, because in many of the exercises you do *not* need to repeat *all* the computations of the simplex algorithm to obtain the answer.

1 (a) Assume the coefficient of x_2 in the original objective function is $4\frac{6}{7}$, instead of 5. Calculate the coefficients of x_2 in Row 0 at each iteration of the simplex method, and verify that at the final iteration the coefficient is $\frac{2}{7}(=\frac{3}{7}-\frac{1}{7})$.

(b) Answer part (a) for a coefficient of $5\frac{1}{7}$, instead of 5.

(c) Assume the coefficient of x_4 in the original objective function is 10, instead of 11. Calculate the coefficients of x_4 in Row 0 at each iteration of the simplex method, and verify that at the final iteration the coefficient is $\frac{4}{7}(=\frac{11}{7}-1)$.

(d) Answer part (c) for a coefficient of 12, instead of 11.

(e) Assume the coefficient of x_3 in the original objective function is $(9+\delta)$. Over what interval for δ does the basic solution in (F) remain optimal? What variable do you enter into the solution when δ lies below the interval? When δ lies above this interval?

(f) Assume the slack variable x_6 has a coefficient δ in the original objective function. Answer the questions posed in part (e).

2 Is the basic solution in (F) still optimal if the original objective function is to maximize

(a) $6x_1 + 5x_2 + 9x_3 + 12x_4$?

(b) $3\frac{3}{4}x_1 + 5\frac{2}{7}x_2 + 9x_3 + 12\frac{3}{7}x_4$?

(c) $3\frac{1}{2}x_1 + 5x_2 + 9x_3 + 12x_4$?

(d) $6\frac{1}{2}x_1 + 5\frac{2}{7}x_2 + 9x_3 + 11x_4$?

(e) $4x_1 + 5\frac{2}{7}x_2 + 8x_3 + 12\frac{3}{7}x_4$?

(f) $4x_1 + 5x_2 + 7\frac{1}{2}x_3 + 12x_4$?

(g) $4x_1 + 5x_2 + 13\frac{1}{2}x_3 + 12x_4$?

(h) $4x_1 + 5\frac{2}{7}x_2 + 13x_3 + 12x_4$?

(i) In each case above, if the basic solution in (F) is not optimal, state which variable you enter into the next basis.

3 Is the basic solution in (F) still optimal if the original objective function is to maximize

(a) $7x_1 + 8x_2 + 14x_3 + 18x_4$?

(b) $8x_1 + 9x_2 + 15x_3 + 21x_4$?

(c) $11x_1 + 16x_2 + 32x_3 + 46x_4$?

(d) $12x_1 + 17x_2 + 33x_3 + 45x_4$?

(e) $33x_1 + 50x_2 + 103x_3 + 163x_4$?

(f) In each case above, if the basic solution in (F) is not optimal, state which variable you enter into the next basis.

*4 Assume the coefficient of x_1 in the original objective function is $(4+\delta_1)$ and, similarly, the coefficient of x_3 is $(9+\delta_3)$.

(a) Using a manner analogous to the derivation of (5) and the resultant inequalities in (6), in Sec. 5.2, derive a set of inequalities for the pair (δ_1, δ_3) such that the basic solution in (F) remains optimal provided the pair satisfies all these inequalities.

(b) Draw a graph of the region implied by the set of inequalities in part (a).

(c) Assume the coefficient of x_1 in the original objective function is c_1, and similarly the coefficient of x_3 is c_3. Analogous to part (b), draw a graph of the region for (c_1, c_3) such that the basic solution in (F) remains optimal provided this pair of coefficients lies within the displayed region.

5 (a) Assume that the right-hand-side constant in Row 2 of (I) is 100, instead of 120. Calculate the right-hand-side constants in all the rows at each iteration of the simplex method, and verify that at the final iteration the constant in Row 2 is $\frac{185}{7}$ $(= \frac{325}{7} - 20)$.

(b) Answer part (a) for a constant $(120 - \frac{325}{7})$, instead of 120.

(c) Assume that the right-hand-side constant in Row 1 of (I) is 11, instead of 15. Calculate the right-hand-side constants in all the rows at each iteration of the simplex method, and verify that the basic solution in (F) is still optimal.

(d) Answer part (c) for a constant of 20, instead of 15.

(e) Assume that the right-hand-side constant in Row 1 of (I) is $(15 + \delta)$. Verify the assertion in (2) of Sec. 5.3 that the basic solution in (F) remains feasible provided δ satisfies $-\frac{50}{10} \leq \delta \leq \frac{325}{61}$.

(f) Assume that the right-hand-side constant in Row 3 of (I) is $(100 + \delta)$. Over what interval for δ does the basic solution in (F) remain feasible?

6 Does the basic solution in (F) remain feasible if the right-hand-side constants in Rows 1, 2, and 3 are, respectively,

(a) 20, 110, and 130?

(b) 25, 75, and 215?

(c) 15, 30, and 185?

(d) 18, 150, and 40?

(e) 22, 150, and 80?

(f) In each case above, indicate the optimal values of each variable and the objective-function value if the basic solution in (F) remains feasible. Otherwise, indicate the infeasibility.

*7 Assume that the right-hand-side constant in Row 1 is $(15 + \delta_1)$ and in Row 3 is $(100 + \delta_3)$.

(a) Derive a set of inequalities for the pair (δ_1, δ_3) such that the basic solution in (F) remains feasible provided the pair satisfies all these inequalities.

(b) Draw a graph of the region implied by the set of inequalities in part (a).

(c) Assume the right-hand-side constant in Row 1 is b_1, and, similarly, that the constant in Row 3 is b_3. Analogous to part (b), draw a graph of the region for (b_1, b_3) such that the basic solution in (F) remains feasible provided this pair of constants lies within the displayed region.

(d) How do your answers to the preceding parts change if the right-hand-side constant in Row 2 is 121? Is 119?

The problems in exercises 8 through 11 below refer to the Product-Mix Selection Example in Sec. 4.4, which is repeated at the beginning of Sec. 5.5.

8 In parts (a)-(h), modify the example as indicated and write the dual problem.

(a) The primal objective function to be maximized is $6x_1 + 8x_2 + 7x_3 + 12x_4$.

(b) The right-hand-side constants in Rows 1, 2, and 3 are 25, 80, and 150, respectively.

(c) The coefficients of x_3 in Rows 1, 2, and 3 are 1, 4, and 9, respectively.

(d) The coefficients of x_2 in Rows 1, 2, and 3 are 1, 6, and -8, respectively, and the objective-function coefficient is -3, instead of 5.

(e) There is an additional variable z having coefficients in Rows 1, 2, and 3 of 1, 1, and 18, respectively, and an objective-function coefficient of 13.

(f) There is an additional constraint $4x_1 + 7x_2 - 5x_3 - 6x_4 \leq 50$.

(g) All the modifications in the above parts are in effect.

(h) Examine the dual problem as given by (1) and (2) in Sec. 5.5. Specify two feasible solutions and the corresponding values of the objective function.

*9 Review the iterations of the simplex algorithm, as given in Sec. 4.4. At each iteration,

(a) What are the trial values for the dual variables?

(b) What are the associated infeasibilities in the dual problem, and the corresponding value of the dual objective function?

*10 Find optimal values for the dual variables, assuming that the basic solution in (F) of Sec. 5.1 is optimal and the objective-function coefficients of x_1 and x_3 are, respectively,

(a) 7 and 14.   (d) 12 and 33.
(b) 8 and 15.   (e) 33 and 103.
(c) 11 and 32.

11 (a) Assume the coefficient of x_4 in the objective function is $(9 + \delta)$. Use the dual constraint associated with x_4 to derive the largest value for δ that leaves the basic solution in (F) optimal.

(b) Find the optimal value of the primal objective function if the right-hand-side constants in Rows 1, 2, and 3 are, respectively,

16, 120, and 100   15, 120, and 101   16, 120, and 101   14, 121, and 101;
14, 120, and 100   15, 120, and 99   14, 120, and 99   16, 119, and 99.

*(c) Assume the right-hand-side constant in Row 1 is $(15 + \delta)$. Will the objective function increase by more or less than $\frac{13}{7}\delta$ for $\delta > \frac{325}{61}$? For $\delta < -\frac{50}{10}$? Give an economic justification of your answers using the context of the Product-Mix Selection Example.

(d) Suppose the coefficient of x_2 in Row 3 is $(5 + \delta)$. How small can δ be such that the basic solution in (F) remains optimal?

(e) Suppose the coefficient of x_2 in Row 1 is $(1 + \delta)$. How small can δ be such that the basic solution in (F) remains optimal?

(f) Suppose you add a variable z having coefficients in Rows 1, 2, and 3 of 1, 1, and 18, respectively. What is the smallest coefficient for z in the objective function such that the final basic solution in (F) remains optimal?

(g) Answer part (f) assuming the coefficient of z in Row 3 is 16.

*(h) What are the coefficients for z in Rows 1, 2, and 3 of (F), given the coefficients for z stated in part (f)? Answer the same question using the data in part (g).

*(i) Suppose the coefficient of x_1 in Row 3 is $(3 + \delta)$. Discuss how you would find an interval for δ such that the basic solution in (F) remains optimal.

*12 This problem refers to the example given in (1) and (2) of Sec. 5.8.

(a) What variable do you remove from the basis at iteration 1 if the right-hand-side constant in the second constraint of (2) is 10, instead of 8? If the constant in the first constraint is 10, instead of 5? If the constant in the first constraint is 15, instead of 5, and in the second constraint is 10, instead of 8?

(b) Assume that you remove x_5 from the basis at iteration 1. Determine which variable you enter into the basis, and what its new value will be if the objective-function coefficients of x_1, x_2, and x_3 are, respectively,

$$1, 0, \text{ and } 2 \quad 8, 8, \text{ and } 8 \quad 4, 1, \text{ and } 3 \quad \tfrac{1}{2}, \tfrac{1}{2}, \text{ and } \tfrac{1}{2},$$

instead of 2, 0, and 1.

(c) Answer part (b) where the coefficient of x_2 in the second constraint of (2) is 2, instead of -2.

(d) Answer part (b) where the coefficient of x_3 in the second constraint of (2) is 2, instead of 4.

(e) What occurs when you remove x_4 from the basis at iteration 1, instead of x_5?

*13 Determine whether the basic solution in (F) for the Product-Mix Selection Example remains feasible when the right-hand-side constant in the constraint (1) of Sec. 5.9 is

(a) 140.   (c) 170.

(b) 160.   (d) For each of the above parts, find an optimal solution.

*14 Suppose the right-hand-side constant in Row 1 of (I) for the Product-Mix Selection Example is 5, instead of 15. Find an optimal solution. Use the dual simplex algorithm and start with the equations (F), appropriately revised to reflect the change in the constant.

15 Explain your understanding of the following terms:

postoptimality analysis   primal and dual programs
sensitivity analysis   shadow prices
*ranging analysis   *complementary slackness
*multiple objective functions   *dual-feasible
*multiple right-hand sides   *secondary constraints
*parametric programming   *upper-bounded variables
duality   *upper-bound substitution.

COMPUTATIONAL EXERCISES

16 Consider the following problem

$$\text{maximize } -2x_1 - 1x_2 + 3x_3 - 2x_4$$

subject to

$$1x_1 + 3x_2 - 1x_3 + 2x_4 \leq 7 \quad \text{Resource A}$$

$$-1x_1 - 2x_2 + 4x_3 \qquad \leq 12 \quad \text{Resource B}$$

$$-1x_1 - 4x_2 + 3x_3 + 8x_4 \leq 10 \quad \text{Resource C}$$

$$\text{every } x_j \geq 0.$$

If you add x_5, x_6, and x_7 as slack variables, you have at the final iteration of the simplex method

$$\begin{array}{lllll} x_0 + \tfrac{7}{5}x_1 & & + \tfrac{12}{5}x_4 + \tfrac{1}{5}x_5 + \tfrac{4}{5}x_6 & = 11 & \text{Row 0} \\ \tfrac{3}{10}x_1 + 1x_2 & & + \tfrac{4}{5}x_4 + \tfrac{2}{5}x_5 + \tfrac{1}{10}x_6 & = 4 & \text{Row 1} \\ -\tfrac{1}{10}x_1 & + 1x_3 + & \tfrac{2}{5}x_4 + \tfrac{1}{5}x_5 + \tfrac{3}{10}x_6 & = 5 & \text{Row 2} \\ \tfrac{1}{2}x_1 & & + 10x_4 + 1x_5 - \tfrac{1}{2}x_6 + 1x_7 & = 11 & \text{Row 3.} \end{array}$$

(a) State optimal values for each x_j and the objective function. Is the optimal solution unique?

(b) For each nonbasic variable, give an interval for its objective-function coefficient such that the basic solution in part (a) remains optimal.

(c) Answer part (b) for each basic variable.

*(d) Assume the coefficient of x_2 in the objective function is $(-1 + \delta_2)$, and similarly, the coefficient of x_3 is $(3 + \delta_3)$. Derive a set of inequalities for the pair (δ_2, δ_3) such that the basic solution in part (a) remains optimal provided the pair satisfies all these inequalities. Draw a graph of the region implied by this set of inequalities.

(e) Give an interval for each right-hand-side constant such that the basic solution in part (a) remains optimal.

*(f) Assume that the right-hand-side constant for Resource A constraint is $(7 + \delta_1)$ and for Resource B constraint is $(12 + \delta_2)$. Derive a set of inequalities for the pair (δ_1, δ_2) such that the solution in part (a) remains feasible provided the pair satisfies all these inequalities. Draw a graph of the region implied by this set of inequalities.

(g) Write the dual problem. Indicate optimal values for the dual variables and *calculate* the associated value of the dual objective function.

(h) Write an economic interpretation of each dual variable and illustrate your interpretation with numerical examples.

(i) For each nonbasic variable, use the associated dual restriction to derive an interval for its objective-function coefficient such that the solution in part (a) remains optimal.

(j) Suppose two new variables x_8 and x_9 are added to the model. Assume the coefficients for x_8 in the constraints for Resources A, B, and C are 5, -3, and 1, respectively, and the objective-function coefficient is 2. Assume that the coefficients for x_9 in the constraints are -2, 10, and 12, and the objective-function coefficient is -4. Can the solution in part (a) be improved? If so, show how. If not, indicate what happens if x_9 is introduced into the basis.

*(k) Find the coefficients for x_8 and x_9 appropriate to the equations for Rows 0, 1, 2, and 3 shown above.

(l) Suppose the coefficient of x_1 in the Resource A constraint is $(1 + \delta)$. How small can δ be such that the solution in part (a) remains optimal? How large?

(m) Suppose the coefficient of x_1 in the Resource B constraint is $(-1 + \delta)$. How small can δ be such that the solution in part (a) remains optimal? How large?

(n) Answer the questions in parts (l) and (m) for the coefficients of x_4.

17 In each of the parts below, state optimal values for the decision variables and the objective function. For each variable, give an interval for its objective-function coefficient such that the basic solution at the final iteration of the simplex method remains optimal. Give an interval for each right-hand-side constant such that the basic solution at the final iteration remains optimal. Write the dual problem. Indicate optimal values for the dual variables and *calculate* the associated value of the dual objective function. For each nonbasic variable, use the associated dual restriction to derive an interval for its objective-function coefficient such that the final solution remains optimal.

(a) The One-Potato, Two-Potato Problem in Sec. 1.6 and exercise 18 of Chap. 4.
(b) The problem in exercise 19 of Chap. 4.
(c) The problem in exercise 20, part (a), of Chap. 4.
(d) The problem in exercise 20, part (b), of Chap. 4.
(e) The problem in exercise 21 of Chap. 4.

18 Suppose at some iteration in solving a linear programming model, you arrive at the relations shown in parts (a) and (b). Note that x_0 is being maximized and the variables x_4, x_5, and x_6 are the slacks in the constraints for Resources A, B, and C, respectively. Find an optimal solution and indicate whether it is unique. State how much an additional unit of each resource is worth. Give optimal values for the dual variables. Interpret the meaning of the dual variables, and illustrate your interpretation with numerical examples.

(a)

$$
\begin{array}{lll}
x_0 - 4x_2 \quad\quad - 1x_4 \quad\quad - 2x_6 = 100 & \text{Objective function} \\
\quad\quad - 1x_2 \quad + 6x_4 + 1x_5 + 3x_6 = 12 & \text{Resource A} \\
1x_1 + 5x_2 \quad + 10x_4 \quad\quad + 5x_6 = 20 & \text{Resource B} \\
\quad + 1x_2 + 1x_3 + 1x_4 \quad\quad + 10x_6 = 10 & \text{Resource C}
\end{array}
$$

(b)

$$
\begin{array}{lll}
x_0 - 2x_1 + 3x_2 \quad\quad - 1x_5 \quad\quad = 30 & \text{Objective function} \\
2x_1 - 2x_2 \quad + 1x_4 + 4x_5 \quad\quad = 6 & \text{Resource A} \\
2x_1 \quad + 1x_3 \quad + 4x_5 \quad\quad = 12 & \text{Resource B} \\
4x_1 + 4x_2 \quad\quad - 6x_5 + x_6 = 16 & \text{Resource C}
\end{array}
$$

19 Consider the problem

$$\text{maximize } -10x_1 + 24x_2 + 20x_3 + 20x_4 + 25x_5$$

subject to

$$-1x_1 + 1x_2 + 2x_3 + 3x_4 + 5x_5 \leq 19$$
$$-1x_1 + 4x_2 + 3x_3 + 2x_4 + 1x_5 \leq 57$$
$$\text{every } x_j \geq 0.$$

(a) Write the dual problem and verify that a feasible solution is $y_1 = 4$ and $y_2 = 5$.
(b) Use the information in part (a) to derive an optimal solution to both the primal and dual problems.

*(c) Suppose the constraint $x_1 + x_2 + x_3 + x_4 + x_5 \leq 20$ is imposed on the above problem. Find optimal primal and dual solutions.

20 Consider the problem

$$\text{maximize} -1x_1 + 7x_2 - 5x_3 + 14x_4$$

subject to

$$3x_1 + 4x_2 + 5x_3 + 6x_4 \leq 24$$
$$-1x_1 + 1x_2 - 2x_3 + 2x_4 \leq 4$$
$$\text{every } x_j \geq 0.$$

(a) Write the dual problem and verify that a feasible solution is $y_1 = 1$ and $y_2 = 4$.
(b) Use the information in part (a) to derive an optimal solution to both the primal and dual problems.
*(c) Suppose the constraint $x_1 + x_2 + x_3 + x_4 + x_5 \leq 8$ is imposed on the above problem. Find optimal primal and dual solutions.

21 Each part below refers to an example in Sec. 3.4. Write the dual problem, and draw a solution space represention. Indicate a solution to the dual problem on the graph, and calculate the corresponding values for the dual variables and the dual objective function.

(a) Relations (1) through (4).
(b) Relations (5), and (2) through (4).
(c) Relations (6) through (9).
(d) Relations (10) through (13).

*22 In parts (a) and (b), assume that x_1 and x_2 yield an optimal basic solution. State the dual problem and optimal values for the dual variables. Find the largest values for c_3 and c_4 that allow the assumption that x_1 and x_2 comprise an optimal basis.

(a) Maximize $-1x_1 + 18x_2 + c_3x_3 + c_4x_4$ subject to

$$1x_1 + 2x_2 + 3x_3 + 4x_4 \leq 3$$
$$-3x_1 + 4x_2 - 5x_3 - 6x_4 \leq 1$$
$$\text{every } x_j \geq 0.$$

(b) Maximize $-13x_1 + 24x_2 + c_3x_3 + c_4x_4$ subject to the same constraints as in part (a).

*23 Each problem below was solved in the exercises of Chap. 4 by the Big M Method. Find an optimal solution using the dual simplex algorithm.

(a) Exercise 24, part (b).   (e) Exercise 25, part (b).
(b) Exercise 24, part (e).   (f) Exercise 25, part (f).
(c) Exercise 24, part (f).   (g) Exercise 28, where you
(d) Exercise 25, part (a).   *minimize* $x_1 + x_2$.

*24 For each of the examples below from Chap. 4, use the dual simplex algorithm on the dual problem to find an optimal solution to the dual problem.

(a) The example in exercise 19.

(b) The example in exercise 20, part (a).

(c) The example in exercise 20, part (b).

(d) In each part above, show how to find an optimal solution to the primal problem from the system of equations at the terminating iteration.

(e) In each part above, compare the primal and dual trial solutions at each iteration of the simplex and the dual simplex methods.

*25 (a) Use the dual simplex algorithm to solve the dual of the Product-Mix Selection Example, given by (1) and (2) in Sec. 5.5.

(b) Consider the system of equations (I) for the Product-Mix Selection Example, as given at the start of Sec. 5.1. Introduce x_4 and remove x_5 from the basis. Verify that the resultant trial values of the dual variables are dual-feasible. Are the basic variables in the primal problem feasible? If so, indicate optimal primal and dual solutions. If not, apply the dual simplex algorithm to obtain optimal solutions.

*26 Consider the problem in exercise 16. In each part below, state whether the optimal solution for that problem remains feasible when the model is augmented by the specified constraint. Determine optimal primal and dual solutions.

(a) $x_1 + x_2 + x_3 + x_4 \leq 10$.

(b) $x_1 + x_2 + x_3 + x_4 \leq 6$.

(c) $x_2 + x_3 \leq 0$.

(d) $x_2 + x_3 \leq -1$.

(e) $x_1 + x_2 + x_3 + x_4 \geq 10$.

*27 Consider the following problem

$$\text{minimize } \sum_{t=1}^{T} y_t$$

subject to

$$y_T + y_1 \geq r_1$$
$$y_{t-1} + y_t \geq r_t \quad \text{for} \quad t = 2, 3, \ldots, T$$
$$\text{every } y_t \geq 0.$$

An example of this model is the Kleen City Police Department Problem, stated in exercise 30 of Chap. 2.

(a) Display the model in full for $T = 5$, where $r_1 = 8$, $r_2 = 7$, $r_3 = 10$, $r_4 = 10$, and $r_5 = 2$.

(b) Calling the above problem the dual, write the associated primal problem.

(c) Solve the dual by the dual simplex algorithm, and indicate the associated optimal primal solution. (*Hint:* you need no more than five iterations.)

(d) Solve the primal by the simplex algorithm and indicate the associated dual solution. (*Hint:* you need no more than five iterations.)

(e) Find optimal primal and dual solutions when $r_1 = 9$, instead of 8.

*28 Solve each problem by the bounded-variables algorithm in Sec. 5.10.

(a) Maximize $5x_1 + 14x_2 + 24x_3 + 20x_4$ subject to

$$1x_1 + 6x_2 + 12x_3 + 8x_4 \le 8$$
$$2x_1 + 2x_2 + 12x_3 + 4x_4 \le 4$$
$$0 \le x_j \le 1 \quad \text{for} \quad j = 1, 2, 3, 4.$$

(b) Maximize $9x_1 + 1x_2 - 15x_3 - 5x_4$ subject to

$$-3x_1 + 2x_2 + 9x_3 + 1x_4 \le 7$$
$$6x_1 + 16x_2 - 12x_3 - 2x_4 \le 10$$
$$0 \le x_j \le 1 \quad \text{for} \quad j = 1, 2, 3, 4.$$

MIND-EXPANDING EXERCISES

*29 *Duality and Complementary Slackness*

(a) Show that the Dual Theorem implies the Theorem of Complementary Slackness.
(b) Show that the Theorem of Complementary Slackness implies the Dual Theorem.

*30 Show how the Dual Theorem for the primal problem (1) through (3) and the dual problem (4) through (6) in Sec. 5.4 can be extended to cover the pair of problems (i) through (v) and (i') through (v') stated at the end of Sec. 5.4.

31 Consider the problem

$$\text{maximize} \sum_{j=1}^{n} (c_j + \delta c_j^*) x_j$$

subject to

$$\sum_{j=1}^{n} a_{ij} x_j = b_i + \delta b_i^* \quad \text{for} \quad i = 1, 2, \dots, m$$

$$\text{every } x_j \ge 0.$$

(a) Suppose you have found an optimal basic solution for a fixed value of δ, say $\bar{\delta}$. Derive upper and lower bounds for δ such that, for δ in that interval, the same set of basic variables remains optimal.
(b) Apply your answer in part (a) to the Product-Mix Selection Example where $\bar{\delta} = 0$, $c_1^* = -1$, $c_2^* = 0$, $c_3^* = 0$; and $c_4^* = 2$; and $b_1^* = 1$, $b_2^* = -20$, and $b_3^* = 0$.

32 *Sensitivity Testing.* Consider the linear programming problem

$$\text{maximize} \sum_{j=1}^{n} c_j x_j$$

subject to

$$\sum_{j=1}^{n} a_{ij} x_j \le b_i \quad \text{for} \quad i = 1, 2, \dots, m$$

$$\text{every } x_j \ge 0.$$

Let F be the optimal value of the objective function.

Suppose that the c_j, a_{ij}, b_i are not known with certainty but are known to lie within the intervals

$$c_j^- \leq c_j \leq c_j^+ \qquad a_{ij}^- \leq a_{ij} \leq a_{ij}^+ \qquad b_i^- \leq b_i \leq b_i^+.$$

Derive upper and lower bounds for F which make use of only the end points of the intervals.

*33 *Dual Simplex Algorithm*

    (a) Suppose all the constraints are inequalities. Derive a method for obtaining a dual-feasible solution.

    (b) Suppose some of the constraints are equalities. Derive a method using artificial variables for obtaining a dual-feasible solution.

*34 *Upper-Bounded Variables*

    (a) State how you would revise the dual simplex algorithm to accomodate upper-bounded variables.

    (b) Apply your method to the example in (5) and (6) in Sec. 5.10.

    (c) Apply your method to part (a) in exercise (28). To part (b).

35 *Two-Person, Zero-Sum Matrix Games.* Consider a game between Player I and Player II. Player I may select any one of m choices, indexed $i = 1, 2, \ldots, m$. Player II may select any one of n choices, indexed $j = 1, 2, \ldots, n$. If Player I selects i and Player II selects j, then Player I receives the amount a_{ij}, and Player II receives $-a_{ij}$. (Note that a_{ij} may be negative.)

For example, suppose each player can select the integer 1 or 2. If Players I and II both choose 1, then assume $a_{11} = 2$; if Players I and II both choose 2, then assume $a_{22} = 4$. If Player I chooses 1 and Player II chooses 2, then assume $a_{12} = -3$; and if Player I chooses 2 and Player II chooses 1, then assume $a_{21} = -3$. The payoffs a_{ij} to Player I can be displayed as the matrix

$$\text{Player II}$$
$$\text{Player I} \begin{bmatrix} 2 & -3 \\ -3 & 4 \end{bmatrix}$$

Suppose that neither player actually makes the selection himself, but transmits *instructions* for making his selection to an impartial referee. Both players know all the a_{ij}, but neither player knows the instructions of his opponent.

Assume each player is permitted to instruct the referee to make a choice by means of a random selection. Specifically, Player I provides selection probabilities $y_1, y_2, \ldots, y_m$, where each $y_i \geq 0$ and $\sum_{i=1}^m y_i = 1$, and, likewise, Player II provides selection probabilities $x_1, x_2, \ldots, x_n$, where each $x_j \geq 0$ and $\sum_{j=1}^n x_j = 1$. Each of these probability selections is called a *mixed strategy*.

    (a) Given probabilities x_j, let V_2 be the maximum expected value of Player I's payoffs among all his selections $i = 1, 2, \ldots, m$. Formulate a linear programming model for choosing x_j such that V_2 is as small as possible. An optimal solution is called Player II's *minimax strategy*.

    (b) Given probabilities y_i, let V_1 be the minimum expected value of Player I's payoffs among all of Player II's selections $j = 1, 2, \ldots, n$. Formulate a linear programming model for choosing y_i such that V_1 is maximized. An optimal solution is called Player I's *maximin strategy*.

(c) Apply the Dual Theorem to show that the minimum of V_2 equals the maximum of V_1. This result is referred to sometimes as *Von Neumann's Fundamental Theorem for Two-Person, Constant-Sum Matrix Games* and sometimes as the *Minimax Theorem*. Let the common value be V, which is called the *value of the game*. [*Hint:* You can assume without loss of generality that all $a_{ij} > 0$; see part (d).]

(d) Show that optimal values for x_j and y_i remain optimal when the payoffs are $a_{ij} + k$ for any constant k, and the associated value of the game is $V + k$.

(e) Show why feasible x_j and y_i always exist.

(f) Find optimal probabilities for the numerical example above.

(g) Verify that the expected value that Player I receives is

$$\sum_{i=1}^{m} \sum_{j=1}^{n} y_i a_{ij} x_j.$$

Show that this amount equals V when both players use optimal x_j and y_i found in parts (a) and (b).

(h) Show that both players need not assign *positive* probabilities to more than the smaller of (m, n) of their selection possibilities.

(i) Show that if, for optimal x_j,

$$\sum_{j=1}^{n} a_{ij} x_j < V,$$

then $y_i = 0$ is optimal. Similarly, if, for optimal y_i,

$$\sum_{i=1}^{m} y_i a_{ij} > V,$$

then $x_j = 0$ is optimal.

(j) Show that if $y_i = 1$ and $x_j = 1$ are optimal then a_{ij} equals both minimum $(a_{i1}, a_{i2}, \ldots, a_{in})$ and maximum $(a_{1j}, a_{2j}, \ldots, a_{mj})$. The element a_{ij} is called a *saddle point* for the payoff matrix. Further, if $a_{kl} = a_{ij}$, then $a_{il} = a_{kj} = a_{ij}$.

(k) Show that if $m = n$, $a_{ii} = 0$ for $i = 1, 2, \ldots, m$, and $a_{ij} = -a_{ji}$ (called a *skew-symmetric* matrix game), then $V = 0$, and $y_i = x_i$ in an optimal solution.

(l) Suppose b_{ij} are payoffs to Player II, where b_{ij} need not equal $-a_{ij}$, but where $a_{ij} + b_{ij} = k$. This is known as a *constant-sum* game. Show how to convert a constant-sum game to a zero-sum game having the identical optimal strategies.

36 *Warehouse Problem.* The partnership of Byer, Long, Celler, Short trades in the purchase and sale of agricultural commodities. It owns a large storage tank with a capacity of C gallons, in which it keeps soybean oil. At the start of the present period, designated Period 1, the firm owns G ($\leq C$) gallons. The firm wants a profit-maximizing plan for selling and purchasing soybean oil over a horizon of T periods. (To keep the formulation of the problem simple, assume the firm places no value on soybean oil left at the end of Period T.) This model is often referred to as the *Warehouse Problem*.

Suppose the firm can forecast for each Period t the selling price p_t as well as the purchase cost c_t for each gallon of oil. For a variety of economic causes, the selling price is sometimes larger and sometimes smaller than the purchase cost. Assume that a purchase in Period t is not delivered until the very end of the period (too late for a subsequent sale in that period); thus the firm is prohibited from "making a killing" by both purchasing and selling an unlimited amount in a period when the selling price exceeds the purchase cost.

Let w_t be the number of gallons sold and x_t the number of gallons purchased in Period t, where every $w_t \geq 0$ and $x_t \geq 0$. These amounts must satisfy two types of constraints. First, there are T capacity constraints that state the gallonage at the very end of each period cannot exceed the limit C. Thus, in Period 1 the restriction is that $G - w_1 + x_1 \leq C$, where G is a known constant. Similarly, in Period t, the amount G plus the difference between total purchases and total sales over Periods $1, 2, \ldots, t$, must not exceed the capacity C.

Second, there are T sales constraints that state the gallonage sold in Period t cannot exceed that which is on hand at the beginning of the period. Thus, in Period 1 the restriction is that $w_1 \leq G$. In Period t, the restriction is that w_t cannot be larger than G plus the difference between total purchases and total sales over Periods $1, 2, \ldots, t - 1$.

(a) Display the model in full for $T = 5$.

(b) For each Period t, let y_t be the dual variable for the capacity constraint and z_t the dual variable for the sales-quantity constraint. Display the dual problem for $T = 5$.

(c) Devise an algorithm for determining optimal values of the dual variables in the order $y_T, z_T, y_{T-1}, z_{T-1}, \ldots, y_1, z_1$. Given these optimal values, explain how to derive an optimal plan of selling and purchasing.

(d) Apply your method to the case where $C = 100$, $G = 75$, and

$$p_1 = 2 \quad p_2 = 3 \quad p_3 = 1 \quad p_4 = 2 \quad p_5 = 3$$
$$c_1 = 2 \quad c_2 = 1 \quad c_3 = 1 \quad c_4 = 4 \quad c_5 = 1.$$

How would your answer change if $C = 200$?

(e) Suppose gallonage at the end of Period t is charged an inventory holding cost of h_t per gallon. (Note that inventory at the end of Period t is G plus the difference between total purchases and total sales over Periods $1, 2, \ldots, t$.) Show how to modify your answers in parts (a), (b), and (c) to account for storage costs.

*(f) Characterize the form of an optimal policy for the *Warehouse Problem*.

*(g) Show how to modify the formulation when there are T liquidity constraints that limit the cash amount of a purchase in each period to be no larger than the accumulated cash over the preceding periods (assume K is the initial amount of cash at the start of Period 1).

CONTENTS

CHAPTER 6

Optimization in Networks

6.1 SIGNIFICANCE OF NETWORK MODELS

Network optimization models—usually special cases of linear programming models—have a twofold importance. They often pertain to problems of product distribution. Consequently, they are economically significant for many commercial enterprises that operate several plants and hold inventory in local warehouses. In addition, networks have a mathematical structure identical to that of other operations research models that seem unrelated at first glance. But these two reasons alone do not warrant your singling out network models to study in *greater* detail.

The key justification is that the mathematical characteristics of network models are so special that by exploiting these structural properties you can obtain major efficiencies in finding optimal solutions. In actual industrial applications, network models often contain thousands of activities and hundreds of constraints, so that using a streamlined algorithm is not only worthwhile but sometimes a practical necessity. By investigating networks, you also benefit from seeing how a variety of apparently disparate operations research models are amenable to an insightful unifying mode of analysis.

This chapter concentrates on network model formulation. The first several examples deal with planning decisions and will illustrate why network terminology provides a convenient graphical description of the optimization problems. You will easily recognize the connections between the components of the network and the elements of the actual problem. In the subsequent examples, the network representation is purely formal; for these you will have to rely on making abstract identifications to establish the counterparts.

In Chap. 7, you will focus on algorithms for finding optimal solutions to network models.

6.2 CLASSICAL TRANSPORTATION PROBLEM

The **transportation** (or **distribution**) **problem** was an early example of linear network optimization and is now a standard application for industrial firms having several manufacturing plants, warehouses, sales territories, and distribution outlets. The model's primary usefulness is for planning. In this instance, the strategic decisions involve selecting transportation routes so as to allocate the production of various plants to several warehouses or terminal points. You already saw an example of this sort in the Saur Milk Company Problem of Sec. 2.7. Some companies find it necessary to review their distribution decisions as often as every month, especially if their order mix is subject to considerable variation. But typically a firm draws up such a distribution plan yearly.

The mathematical description of the classical transportation problem is

$$(1) \qquad\qquad \text{minimize} \sum_{i=1}^{m} \sum_{j=1}^{n} c_{ij} x_{ij}$$

subject to

$$(2) \qquad\qquad \sum_{j=1}^{n} x_{ij} \le S_i \quad \text{for } i = 1, 2, \ldots, m \quad \text{(supply)}$$

$$(3) \qquad\qquad \sum_{i=1}^{m} x_{ij} \ge D_j \quad \text{for } j = 1, 2, \ldots, n \quad \text{(demand)}$$

$$(4) \qquad\qquad x_{ij} \ge 0 \quad \text{for all } i \text{ and } j.$$

The network and technology tables for this model are shown in Figs. 6.1 and 6.2. (You may find it helpful to review Sec. 2.7, where we first introduced this model.)

In the standard interpretation of the model, there are m supply points with items available to be shipped to the n demand points. Specifically, Plant i can ship at most S_i items, and Demand Point j requires at least D_j items. The S_i and D_j are fixed in reference to a stated time interval or *planning horizon*. The cost of shipping each unit from Plant i to Demand Point j is c_{ij}. The objective is to select,

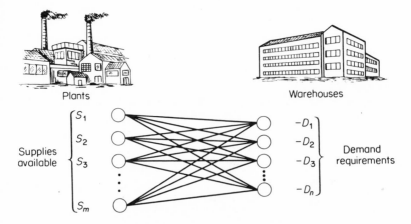

FIGURE 6.1. Network for Transportation Problem.

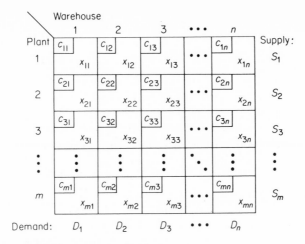

(a) Transportation Table.

Shipping Activities

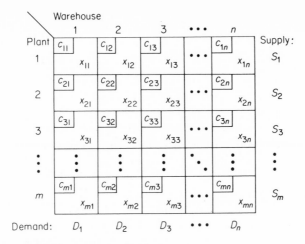

(b) Technology Table for a Transportation Problem.

FIGURE 6.2

for the duration of the horizon, a routing plan that minimizes total transportation costs.

A key result in network theory is that among all the optimal solutions to the model (1) through (4), there is at least one in which each x_{ij} is integer-valued, provided the S_i and D_j are all positive integers, which we assume from here on.

Therefore, strengthening (4) to

(5) $$x_{ij} = 0, 1, 2, \ldots$$

does not adversely affect the value of (1). What is more, the simplex method will find such an optimal solution. These results are demonstrated in Chap. 7.

If the unit cost of producing an item differs from plant to plant, then this cost is included in the determination of c_{ij}. If for physical or economic reasons a certain plant is inaccessible to a particular demand point, then the associated x_{ij} is eliminated or, if more convenient, the corresponding c_{ij} is defined to be arbitrarily large. To simplify the discussion, assume $c_{ij} \geq 0$. Then (3) can be rewritten with equalities.

For the model to possess a feasible solution, it certainly is necessary that total supply is at least as large as total demand, $\sum_{i=1}^{m} S_i \geq \sum_{j=1}^{n} D_j$. There are a number of applications in which you would expect to find the total supply in excess of the total demand requirements. For example, S_i sometimes represents the production *capacity* of Plant i during the planning horizon, rather than an amount of the commodity actually manufactured for distribution at the start of the period. In analyzing a standard transportation model and devising an optimizing algorithm, however, it is convenient to assume that total supply equals total demand:

(6) $$\sum_{i=1}^{m} S_i = \sum_{j=1}^{n} D_j.$$

Employing a simple-minded formal device permits you to assert (6) without any loss of generality: create a fictitious destination with a requirement of $\sum_i S_i - \sum_j D_j$. Then let this fictitious destination be labeled the nth. Let $c_{in} = 0$ so that the interpretation of x_{in} is "slack capacity at Plant i." The sum of the capacities now equals the sum of the requirements. Consequently, with this device the relations (2) can just as well be written as equalities. Therefore, *unless stated otherwise, hereafter assume* (6) *holds and* (2) *and* (3) *are equalities*, so the model is

(7) $$\text{minimize} \sum_{i=1}^{m} \sum_{j=1}^{n} c_{ij} x_{ij}$$

subject to

(8) $$\sum_{j=1}^{n} x_{ij} = S_i \qquad \text{for } i = 1, 2, \ldots, m \quad \text{(supply)}$$

(9) $$\sum_{i=1}^{m} x_{ij} = D_j \qquad \text{for } j = 1, 2, \ldots, n \quad \text{(demand)}$$

(10) $$x_{ij} = 0, 1, 2, \ldots \quad \text{for all } i \text{ and } j,$$

where all the S_i and D_j are positive integers satisfying (6).

Applying the model. Implicit in the mathematical description of the model (7) through (10) is the assumption that only a single type of commodity is being shipped. Why? Because in meeting the demand *requirements*, the model does not distinguish among the sources of supply. All the supply arriving at Demand Point j is commingled insofar as satisfying the demand constraint is concerned.

We emphasize the single-commodity assumption because it would seem to restrict the application of the model. After all, how many multiplant firms distribute only one product? Occasionally, a multiplant, multiproduct company can establish a separate routing pattern for each of its major commodities; but usually there is a decided economic advantage to restricting the number of plants that serve a warehouse or sales district. Therefore, most firms determine a complete distribution system by taking *explicit* account of the entire product line. As you can imagine, you have to use ingenuity to fit an actual distribution problem into the mold of a standard transportation model. It is impossible to catalog here all the devices that have proved successful for this purpose in actual practice. One approach is sketched below to illustrate the basic notions.

Establish the product mix required over the planning horizon at each Demand Point j. Designate the total amount D_j of all products in some convenient and meaningful common unit of measurement, such as tons. Analogously, specify S_i in the same units. To calculate c_{ij} *assume* that if Plant i ships a ton to Demand Point j, the ton is comprised of the precise product mix required at Demand Point j.

How usable and good will the resultant numerical solution be? To answer sensibly, you must keep two factors in mind. First, the essence of the solution is a *plan* for product distribution during a specified time interval. That is, the model provides an assignment of plants to demand destination points. The numerical values of the x_{ij} are inherently approximate, since in most real applications the values of D_j are only *forecasts* of requirements during the planning horizon. Therefore, the x_{ij} solution values do not represent amounts actually transported, but merely estimate the order of magnitude of future shipments. Second, the plan's relative merit must be judged against whatever practical alternatives the firm can devise, including, of course, the current routing. In line with these points, many companies have improved their profits significantly by adopting a distribution *plan* based on a standard transportation model solution.

What's in a name. We conclude with a word about the nomenclature of network models. All the network models discussed in this and the following chapters are examples of linear programming problems. With the exception of the two models at the end of this chapter, by an appropriate definition of symbols, all the problems can be shown to be examples of the model formulated above as (7) through (10). Therefore, in a formal mathematical sense, these are all illustrations of the classical transportation problem, even though they may have nothing to do with shipping a commodity. However, the category of transportation problems itself can be subdivided to give prominence to certain significant models in which additional assumptions are made. To illustrate, when $n = m$ and $S_i = D_j = 1$ for all i and j, the model is termed an *assignment problem*, for reasons made clear in Sec. 6.4. The assignment problem in turn encompasses an important subclass of so-called shortest- (or longest-) route models. These are illustrated in Secs. 6.5 and 6.6. To keep matters straight as you read, ask yourself what the additional structural assumptions are in each transportation model that make it convenient to narrow the problem's designation with a special term.

▶Several of the apparently restrictive assumptions of the transportation model are easily modified or eliminated by appropriate reformulations. To give you an idea of these extensions, a few are summarized.

Seasonal variation. The transportation model has been described as a method of finding a plan for a single time period, such as a span of 12 months. In certain instances, a company may want to shift its distribution routing plan at different times of the year to reflect seasonal variation in the pattern of demand requirements or supply availabilities. If commodity items available in one month cannot be inventoried to satify the requirements of subsequent months, then the firm only need solve 12 separate transportation problems, one for each month. Most companies facing serious seasonal variations, however, do have the opportunity to hold inventories in anticipation of demand. Considerations of optimal seasonal inventory buildups can be accommodated by a straightforward reinterpretation of the symbols in the transportation model.

To illustrate, suppose a firm with two plants and three demand points desires to establish an inventory distribution plan for January, February, . . . , December. Assume that company policy is to have no seasonal inventory on hand at the beginning of the year. Then let S_i, for $i = 1, 2, \ldots, 12$, denote the availability of the product for the first plant for the 12 months, and similarly, S_i, for $i = 13, 14, \ldots, 24$, refer to the second plant. By an analogous convention, let D_j, for $j = 1, 2, \ldots, 12$, refer to the first destination's requirements; for $j = 13, 14, \ldots, 24$, to the second's; and for $j = 25, 26, \ldots, 36$ to the third's. Assume $\sum_{i=1}^{24} S_i = \sum_{j=1}^{36} D_j$. (This restriction can be weakened, if necessary.)

Certain x_{ij} must be eliminated to prevent the supply in midyear being used to meet the requirements at the start of the year. For example, you must remove $x_{6,25}$, which would represent shipping items available at the first plant in June to meet the January requirements at the third destination. In determining c_{ij} for the remaining x_{ij}, you may want to include an inventory holding cost. This figure would reflect expenses directly associated with an inventory buildup, such as warehouse rental or interest charged on short-term borrowings if bank financing is used.

Capacity limitations. Occasionally you must add capacity restrictions on the x_{ij}. The simplest class of restrictions is

(i) $$x_{ij} \leq u_{ij}.$$

When (i) is appended to (7) through (10), the model is often referred to as the **capacitated** (or **bounded variables**) **transportation problem.** More general capacity constraints include bounding sums of the x_{ij}, such as for several plants and all demand points, or for several demand points and one plant. Frequently, adding these capacity constraints entails only a minor increase in the computational effort required to find an optimal solution; but, of course, they can be so restrictive that a feasible solution is not possible.

Variable supply. In certain situations, S_i may have to be treated as one of the *variables* in the optimization. When this happens, the transportation model is imbedded in a larger linear programming problem. With advanced algorithmic techniques, such as the decomposition algorithm described in Sec. 15.11, it still is possible to exploit the structural properties of the transportation network model in the computations.

Another important extension of the classical transportation model is the facility to route an item available at Plant i to Demand Point j through an intermediate *transshipment* point. This consideration is discussed in detail in the next section.   ◀

6.3 TRANSSHIPMENT MODEL

It is important to extend the classical transportation model to include cases in which a location can act as a point of transshipment. For example, transshipment often occurs in the distribution system of national department store chains. Such companies typically have regional warehouses that ship to smaller district warehouses, which in turn ship to the retail stores. In this illustration, the district warehouses are the transshipment points. The transshipment model is a useful tool for a company deciding on the optimal number and location of its warehouses, since the network analysis yields a minimum-cost routing plan for any specific configuration of warehouses. An additional reason for studying the model is that other operations research models which turn out to be mathematically equivalent to network problems have the transshipment form.

The model is illustrated here by means of a commercial example which, although hypothetical, is suggested by a real application arising out of the operations of military logistics systems. In the preceding section the problem was introduced by a mathematical representation and was subsequently characterized by verbal, graphical network, and tabular descriptions. Now the process will be reversed in order to give you practice in a variety of initial formulations.

The Rock-Bottom Discount Store Problem. This company has eight large major appliance discount stores located in several states. The Sales Department has decided to substantially reduce the price of a certain costly item in order to close out the stock now on hand. Before launching the advertising campaign, management wants to position its current inventory among the eight stores according to its sales expectations at each location. To do this, it is necessary to redistribute some of the stock.

Figure 6.3 is a diagrammatic map; the numbered nodes, or points, represent the eight stores. A positive value next to a node signifies the amount of inventory to be redistributed to the rest of the system. A negative value indicates the additional amount of stock required for the sale. Thus Stores 1 and 4 have excess stock of ten and two items, respectively. Stores 3, 6, and 8 require three, one, and eight more items, respectively. The inventory positions of Stores 2, 5, and 7 are to remain unchanged.

Observe that an appliance may be shipped through Stores 2, 4, 5, 6, and 7. Consequently, these locations are termed **transshipment** (or **intermediate**) **points.** Each *remaining* store is termed a **source** if it has excess inventory, and a **sink** if it needs stock. Consequently Store 1 is a source, and Stores 3 and 8 are sinks.

The value $c_{ij} \geq 0$ refers to the cost of shipping each of these items along the indi-

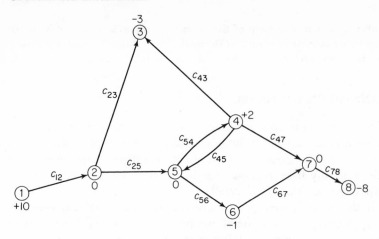

FIGURE 6.3. Map of Rock-Bottom Discount Stores.

cated route. To transport an appliance from Store 1 to Store 6, the total shipping cost is $c_{12} + c_{25} + c_{56}$. The shipping route from Store 1 to Store 6 uses 2 and 5 as transshipment points. The model allows for a shipment between 4 and 5 in either direction. Assume in this situation that $c_{45} \neq c_{54}$, for the following reason. At the time the shipment must be made the company has space available in its own truck only on the route from 4 to 5. It has to incur a higher cost in the reverse direction because it must hire a common carrier. After carefully inspecting the figure, you will realize that you cannot rule out either one of the routes between 4 and 5 until the entire problem has been analyzed. In this example, the company's objective is to redistribute its inventory at the lowest total transportation cost.

Equivalence to a transportation problem. Before translating the preceding paragraphs into formal mathematical terms, we describe two ways to convert the transshipment problem to a standard transportation problem. Such conversions are of practical significance because they permit you to use readily available computer programs written to solve standard transportation problems. You need only supply the computer the data for the transshipment model in one of the formats below. Another reason for interest in the equivalence is that it ensures there is no difficulty in finding an optimal solution with integer-valued variables.

In the first approach, you start by finding the *least-cost* ways to send one item each from Store 1, which has an excess supply, to Stores 3, 6, and 8, which require more items. Denote the associated minimum costs by the symbols c_{13}, c_{16}, and c_{18}. Turning to Store 4, which has an excess supply, you continue similarly by finding c_{43}, c_{46}, and c_{48}. Then you can proceed by using a standard transportation problem table, as illustrated by the trial solution in Fig. 6.4. Note that in this condensed table there is one row for each store with an excess supply, and one column for each store with a demand requirement. The transshipment points are not shown explicitly. But if, say, a least-cost way to ship a unit from Store 4 to Store 8 is via Store 7, then the trial level of $x_{48} = 2$ indicates that two units are transshipped from Store 4 through Store 7 destined for Store 8.

The alternative approach, presented next, often has certain advantages over the first method in actual large-scale applications. Specifically, the alternative does not entail what might be a considerable computational effort to calculate all the least-cost routes required by the first approach. In addition, it may have

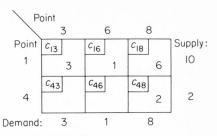

Note: c_{ij} is the least cost of shipping a unit from Point i to Point j.

FIGURE 6.4. Condensed Transshipment Table.

fewer variables in the resultant standard transportation problem. And, finally, it can more easily handle capacity constraints on each route.

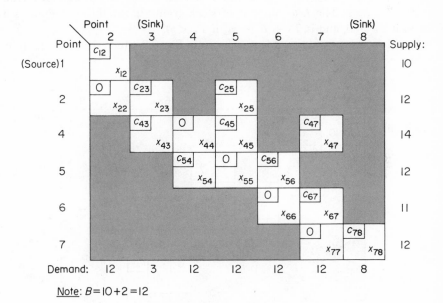

FIGURE 6.5. Expanded Transshipment Table.

To see the idea of the second alternative, study Fig. 6.5, which is constructed from the network in Fig. 6.3. The rules to be followed in making up such a table are

(i) Designate a row for each *source*. Its S_i value is the stock supplied.

(ii) Designate a column for each *sink*. Its D_j value is the amount of stock demanded.

(iii) Designate a row *and* a column for each *transshipment point*. Let T_k be the point's net stock position. If stock is supplied, T_k is a positive number. If stock is demanded, T_k is a negative number. Then for Point k, let $S_k = T_k + B$ and $D_k = B$, where B is the sum of the stock available at *all* points.

(iv) Permit x_{ij}, for $i \neq j$, only for arcs existing in the original network. For a transshipment Point k, also permit x_{kk} with $c_{kk} = 0$.

Thus Rule (i) pertains to Store 1 and Rule (ii) to Stores 3 and 8. With $B = 12$, Rule (iii) states, for example, that $D_4 = 12$ and $S_4 = 2 + 12 = 14$; $D_5 = 12$ and $S_5 = 0 + 12 = 12$; and $D_6 = 12$ and $S_6 = -1 + 12 = 11$.

To achieve the second conversion to a standard transportation model, B has been introduced in the role of a fictitious **buffer stock** at each transshipment point. If k is such a point, B has been included in both S_k and D_k. Therefore the sum of *all* the S_i remains equal to the sum of *all* the D_j. The value of S_k must be sufficiently large to accommodate any transshipment amount that is optimal. One simple way to achieve this condition is to let B be the sum of the stock available at *all* points. The *total* amount of stock transshipped through Point k is $B - x_{kk}$ if $T_k \geq 0$, and is $T_k + B - x_{kk}$ if $T_k < 0$.

A feasible routing for the problem is shown in Fig. 6.6. Study the table carefully.

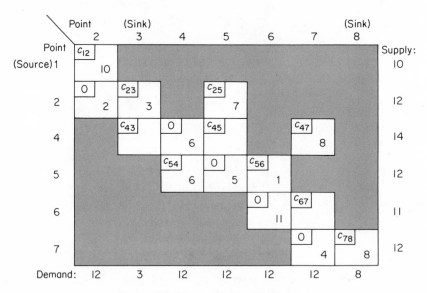

FIGURE 6.6. Illustrative Feasible Routing.

Begin with the first row of the table, representing the supply available at Source Point 1. Note that the 10 units available are shipped to Point 2. Next look at the row and column for Point 2. Observe that $S_2 = D_2 = B = 12$, because Point 2 is a transshipment point without any supply or demand. Since the solution already has $x_{12} = 10$, you must have $x_{22} = 2$ in order that the demand requirement $D_2 = 12$ be satisfied. This in turn means that the other 10 units of S_2 can be shipped out, and are shown going to Point 3, which is a sink, and Point 5, which is a transshipment point. In other words, the ten units from Point 1 are transshipped through Point 2 to Points 3 and 5.

Skipping down to the fifth row, you can see that the 7 units entering are then shipped out to Points 4 and 6. In particular, 1 unit enters Point 6 from Point 5.

Now look at the row and column for Point 6. Observe that $S_6 = 11$ whereas $D_6 = 12$, in keeping with the requirement for one unit at Point 6. Since $x_{56} = 1$ and $D_6 = 12$, you must have $x_{66} = 11$; so the unit entering Point 6 is not shipped out.

Complete your investigation, and verify that Store 1 ships three units to Store 3 via Point 2, one unit to Store 6 via Points 2 and 5, and six units to Store 8 via Points 2, 5, 4, and 7. Store 4 ships its two units to Store 8 via Point 7.

Mathematical model. To complete your understanding of the transshipment model, you should now turn to a precise mathematical description of the problem. This formal characterization is conveniently shown by the technology in Fig. 6.7. Observe there is one equation for each store, or node, of the

Shipping Activities

Points	x_{12}	x_{23}	x_{25}	x_{43}	x_{45}	x_{47}	x_{54}	x_{56}	x_{67}	x_{78}	
1	1										= 10
2	−1	1	1								= 0
3		−1		−1							= −3
4				1	1	1	−1				= 2
5			−1		−1		1	1			= 0
6								−1	1		= −1
7						−1			−1	1	= 0
8										−1	= −8
	c_{12}	c_{23}	c_{25}	c_{43}	c_{45}	c_{47}	c_{54}	c_{56}	c_{67}	c_{78}	Minimize

FIGURE 6.7. Transshipment Example.

network. There is also one variable x_{ij} for each arc to represent the amount to be shipped from Point i to Point j. A positive value on the right of the equality sign designates stock available for redistribution. A negative value indicates a requirement at that store. In summary, the linear programming technology in Fig. 6.7 is an immediate translation of the network diagram in Fig. 6.3.

Observe that whereas there are only 8 equations and 10 variables in the technology table of Fig. 6.7, there are 13 row and column restrictions and 15 variables shown in the expanded transshipment table of Fig. 6.5. The increase of five in each of these dimensions of the problem is due to the presence of the five transshipment points. But this increase in size has a negligible computational impact because the transshipment variables x_{kk} are always in a solution.

▶ It is not immediately evident that the optimization problem in the technology table of Fig. 6.7 is equivalent to that in the transportation table of Fig. 6.5. The correspondence can be argued as follows. By a quick inspection you can see in Fig. 6.5 that the row for Store 1 (a source) and the columns for Stores 3 and 8 (each a sink) agree with the constraints for these stores in Fig. 6.7. Thus the only analytic difficulties are for the rows and columns of the transshipment points.

Consider one of these points, say 4. In Fig. 6.5 the row and column restrictions of the transportation table are

(i) $$x_{43} + x_{44} + x_{45} + x_{47} \qquad = 2 + B \quad \text{(supply)}$$

(ii) $$x_{44} \qquad\qquad + x_{54} = B \qquad \text{(demand)}.$$

Subtracting (ii) from (i) yields

(iii) $$x_{43} + x_{45} + x_{47} - x_{54} = 2,$$

which is the restriction for Point 4 in Fig. 6.7. The same manipulation applies to the other transshipment points. Therefore, any feasible solution to the system in Fig. 6.5 is also feasible for the system in Fig. 6.7.

Provided B is sufficiently large, any solution to the system given by the technology table in Fig. 6.7 is also feasible in Fig. 6.5. To test this assertion, consider Point 4 again. The assumption is that (iii) is satisfied. Leave the values of x_{ij} unchanged and let $x_{44} = B - x_{54}$, so that both (i) and (ii) hold. Then $x_{44} \geq 0$ if B is large enough.

Finally, to demonstrate equivalence, note that since all $c_{kk} = 0$, any feasible solution for one formulation is also attainable in the other system at the same value of the objective function.   ◀

6.4 ASSIGNMENT MODEL

The assignment problem can be posed succinctly as follows: each of n tasks can be performed by any one of n agents. The cost of Task i being accomplished by Agent j is c_{ij}. Assign one agent to each task to minimize the total cost.

Why should this problem interest you? As usual, one reason is that the model can be applied—admittedly not very often in this case—to consequential business situations. An example is provided in the next paragraph. A more compelling reason is that this problem provides a vital link between linear programming problems and so-called combinatorial problems. The latter include those situations in which the unknown activity levels *must* be integer-valued. Such problems are studied in more detail in Chaps. 8, 10, and 13.

The Blip-Bleep Company Problem. This manufacturer of complex electronic equipment has an order for several thousand units of a newly designed product, which is assembled from component modules. The company's management has decided to subcontract for n of the components, and has selected n

outside subcontractors who have demonstrated high-quality performance capability on previous occasions. Each job is sizable enough to prevent a subcontractor
from accepting more than one task. Every subcontractor is required to submit a
bid on each of the modules, and thereby specify the total cost for which it would
bill the electronics company for producing the separate components. A few
individual bids are far out of line, indicating that some of the subcontractors
really do not want to accept a particular job assignment. With this information,
the electronic equipment firm lets out the n contracts for the n components so that
the total cost incurred is minimal.

Mathematical model. To formulate the **assignment problem**
in mathematical programming terms, define the activity variables as

(1)
$$x_{ij} = \begin{cases} 1 & \text{if Task i is performed by Agent j} \\ 0 & \text{otherwise} \end{cases}$$

$$\text{for } i = 1, 2, \ldots, n \quad \text{and} \quad j = 1, 2, \ldots, n,$$

and let c_{ij} be the corresponding cost. In the Blip-Bleep Company illustration, the
index i refers to the component number and the index j to the subcontractor.
Then the optimization model is

(2)
$$\text{minimize} \sum_{i=1}^{n} \sum_{j=1}^{n} c_{ij} x_{ij}$$

subject to

(3)
$$\sum_{j=1}^{n} x_{ij} = 1 \quad \text{for } i = 1, 2, \ldots, n$$

(4)
$$\sum_{i=1}^{n} x_{ij} = 1 \quad \text{for } j = 1, 2, \ldots, n$$

(5)
$$x_{ij} = 0 \text{ or } 1 \quad \text{for all } i \text{ and } j.$$

Notice that the assignment model (2) through (5) is a special case of the standard
transportation model, where $m = n$ and $S_i = D_j = 1$ [in (7) through (10) of
Sec. 6.2]. It is now accepted terminology to refer to any standard transportation
problem where $m = n$ and $S_i = D_j = 1$ as an assignment problem. Observe,
however, that the above illustration as well as most applications of the assignment
model do not pertain to the optimization of transportation or shipping activities.

6.5 SHORTEST-ROUTE MODEL

Like the assignment model, the **shortest-route problem** can be explained
simply: given a network in which each arc has an associated length, find
a shortest path to a specified node from any of the other nodes. This problem
actually encompasses a broad range of important operations research applications,
including replacing equipment and scheduling complex projects. Because these
specific illustrations are so diverse, it is helpful at the start to fix in mind the basic
ideas of the model in general terms.

General description. Consider a network comprised of a set of **nodes**, certain pairs of which are connected by **directed** (that is, direction-oriented) **arcs**. For example, look at the network in Fig. 6.8. Usually, one node is distin-

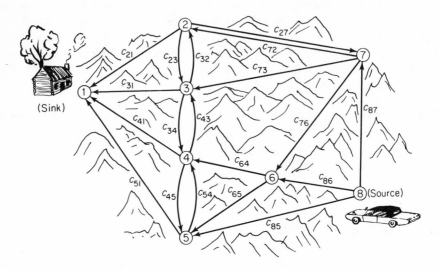

FIGURE 6.8. Example of Shortest-Route Model.

guished as the **terminal**. Then the problem is to find a shortest path to the terminal from at least one other designated point, and sometimes from every other point. The amount c_{ij} represents the length associated with traversing the arc that starts at Node i and ends at Node j.

In applications of the model, the c_{ij} actually may be measured in units other than distance. To illustrate, c_{ij} may denote the cost of going from Node i to Node j. In that case, the problem is to find a **least-cost** path. Or c_{ij} may represent the time to travel between the nodes. Then the objective is to find a **minimum-duration** path.

Frequently in these applications, c_{ij} does not equal c_{ji}. Further, some nodes may not be connected directly, which can be indicated by letting the corresponding $c_{ij} = \infty$, and usually the so-called **triangle inequality** $c_{ij} \le c_{ik} + c_{kj}$ does not hold for all possible i, j, and k.

A network like the one in Fig. 6.8 may contain paths that are **cycles**. This means that for two or more nodes it is possible to find a path leading out of a node and eventually back again. In Fig. 6.8, there are many cycles, one such being from Node 2 to Node 7 to Node 3 and back again to Node 2. If the total length of a path around a cycle is negative, then by repeatedly traversing this cycle, the objective function can be made arbitrarily small. Therefore, without imposing any further restrictions on the problem as stated, an unbounded solution can occur. Such a possibility will now be ruled out by assuming that *if a network contains cycles, the total length of every cycle path is nonnegative.* This condition is innocuous for the typical operations research application, where often all $c_{ij} \ge 0$.

From source to sink. Suppose the problem is to find a best path to the terminal from a single origin point. The model is easily shown to be *mathematically* equivalent to an assignment problem. To demonstrate this equivalence for the network in Fig. 6.8, designate Node 1 as the terminal and Node 8 as the origin. Then consider the ordinary transshipment problem in which a unit of stock is available at Node 8 (a source) and is required at Node 1 (a sink). All other nodes of the network are treated as transshipment points.

This view leads to the formulation in Fig. 6.9, which corresponds to an assign-

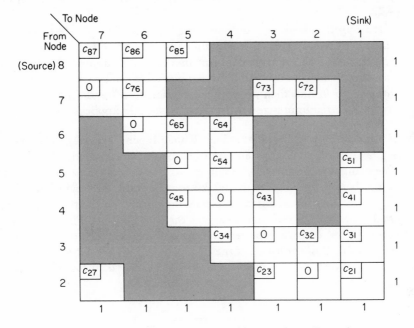

FIGURE 6.9. Tabular Representation of Shortest-Route Example.

ment model with the buffer stock $B = 1$. Notice that the shortest-route problem is a special case of the assignment model in which the objective coefficients $c_{kk} = 0$ appear in the so-called subdiagonal of the table.

A mathematical description of the shortest-route problem is

(1) $$\text{minimize} \sum_{\substack{(i,j) \text{ in} \\ \text{network}}} c_{ij} x_{ij}$$

subject to

(2) $$\sum_{\substack{(k,j) \text{ in} \\ \text{network}}} x_{kj} - \sum_{\substack{(i,k) \text{ in} \\ \text{network}}} x_{ik} = \begin{cases} 1 & \text{for } k = s \text{ (source)} \\ 0 & \text{for all other } k \\ -1 & \text{for } k = r \text{ (sink)} \end{cases}$$

(3) $$x_{ij} \geq 0 \quad \text{for all } (i,j) \text{ in network.}$$

Write out the technology table corresponding to (1), (2), and (3) for the example in Fig. 6.8—there will be one equation for each node and one variable for each arc. To illustrate, for $k = s = 8$, (2) indicates

(4) $\qquad\qquad x_{85} + x_{86} + x_{87} = 1 \qquad\qquad$ (Source Node 8)

and for $k = 7$, (2) states

(5) $\qquad\qquad x_{72} + x_{73} + x_{76} - x_{27} - x_{87} = 0 \qquad$ (Node 7).

It is much easier to solve a shortest-route problem than to solve a general assignment model. Chapter 7 presents an efficient algorithm for the shortest-route problem.

There are countless seemingly different applications of the shortest-route problem. Remember the one in the Rock-Bottom Discount Store Problem in Sec. 6.3? There you learned that the transshipment model can be approached by finding first a least-cost route from each node having available stock to every node requiring additional stock, and then an optimal solution to a standard transportation model using these minimum-cost paths. Here is another application.

Equipment replacement. The Rhode-Bloch Trucking Company is preparing a leasing plan for transportation equipment extending over $n - 1$ years. The company can meet its requirements by leasing a new piece of equipment at the beginning of Year 1 and keeping it until the beginning of Year $j \leq n$. If $j < n$, then the company replaces the equipment at the beginning of Year j and keeps it until the beginning of Year k ($\leq n$), etc. The cost figure c_{ij} (for $1 \leq i < j \leq n$) embodies the rental fee plus the expected running and maintenance costs of equipment leased at the start of Year i and replaced at the start of Year j. The network for the problem is shown in Fig. 6.10 for $n = 6$. In this

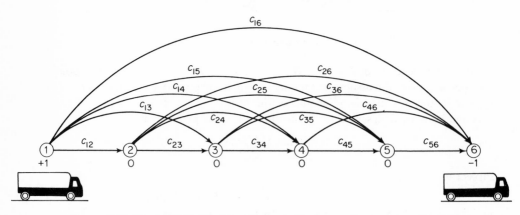

FIGURE 6.10. Rhode-Bloch Trucking Company Equipment Replacement Network.

characterization, a unit of stock is made available at Node 1 and routed to Node 6. Each transshipment node appearing in an optimal solution indicates the year a replacement is to occur.

Notice there are no cycles in the network in Fig. 6.10; consequently it is called **acyclic**. (Represent the network in terms of an assignment model table, like that of Fig. 6.9. Order the nodes in the rows as $1, 2, \ldots, 5$, and in the columns $2, 3, \ldots, 6$. Because the network is acyclic, you will find no permissible entries below the subdiagonal.) In Chap. 7, you will find that a very simple algorithm is available for determining the shortest route in an acyclic network.

▶**Grand Land Development Company Problem.** This example is included to demonstrate the versatility of the shortest-route problem. As in the preceding case, the network turns out to be acyclic. Both these illustrations fall in the category of deterministic, dynamic, and multistage optimization models. Therefore the discussion here previews what will be treated in greater detail in Chap. 10.

This land development company is about to draw up an investment plan for the current year. The concern has a total capital of C hundred thousand dollars available for allocation. There are n development opportunities under consideration. The firm may invest in any number of these ventures, and is limited only by the amount of capital it has available. The minimum investment required to buy into Alternative i is p_i, and the company assesses the associated present value to be v_{i0}. If an *additional* k hundred thousand dollars are invested, however, the resultant present value is estimated as v_{ik}. Assume $v_{i,k+1} \geq v_{i,k}$. The company wants to allocate C among the investment alternatives so as to maximize the total present value.

To set up the model in concrete terms, suppose $C = 10, n = 4$, and the minimal amounts are $p_1 = 6, p_2 = 4, p_3 = 3$, and $p_4 = 1$. Let the additional investment amounts be in increments of one hundred thousand dollars, so $k = 1, 2, \ldots$. (In this example, Alternative 4 could be thought of as an investment in securities instead of a land development project.) The network for the illustration appears in Fig. 6.11 and the corresponding transshipment tabular form in Fig. 6.12.

The network is constructed as follows. There is one column of nodes for each investment alternative. In the node designation (i, c), i refers to the alternative. The value c signifies an amount of capital available for possible investment in Alternative i, given that certain other investment decisions are made about the previous alternatives. Each arc leading out of Node (i, c) represents a specific decision about Alternative i. The arc ends at Node $(i + 1, c')$, where c' is calculated as the capital available for possible investment in Alternative $i + 1$, given the specific decision made about Alternative i.

For instance, examine Node $(3, 4)$. If the company decides either to make the minimal investment in Alternative 1 and no investment in Alternative 2, *or* to make no investment in Alternative 1 and allocate $p_2 + 2 = 4 + 2 = 6$ hundred thousand dollars to Alternative 2, then 4 hundred thousand dollars are available for possible investment in Alternative 3. These are the two decisions represented by the arcs *entering* Node $(3, 4)$. With the 4 hundred thousand dollars, the firm may decide either not to invest in Alternative 3; *or* to invest at the minimal level $p_3 = 3$; *or* to invest at the level $p_3 + 1 = 4$, which would exhaust the available capital. These three decisions are represented by the arcs *leaving* Node $(3, 4)$.

Thus every feasible pattern of investments can be represented as a path through the network starting at Node $(1, 10)$ and ending at Node $(5, 0)$, the latter signifying that the total capital is to be fully expended among the four alternatives. To test your understanding of the network, formulate several possible investment plans and find their paths in the network. Then select a few different paths and state the implied investments.

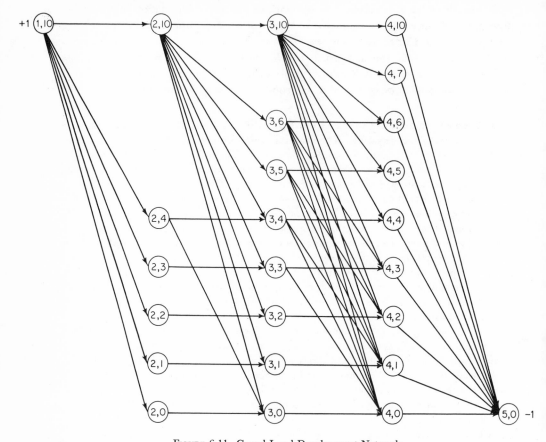

FIGURE 6.11. Grand Land Development Network.

In this problem the length of the arc is the associated present value v_{ik} of the decision involved. Since the objective function is to maximize total present value, the problem really is to find the *longest* path in the network. As you know from earlier chapters, by changing the sign of the objective function, a longest-path problem may be trivially converted to a shortest-path problem, so the two models have essentially identical structures. Since the network is acyclic, the optimal value of the objective function is finite.

The above model is summarized in mathematical terms as follows. Let

$$x_i = \text{amount of capital invested in Alternative i,}$$

and define the increasing function

$$h_i(x_i) = \begin{cases} 0 & \text{for } x_i < p_i \\ v_{ik} & \text{for } x_i = p_i + k \quad \text{where} \quad k = 0, 1, 2, \ldots. \end{cases}$$

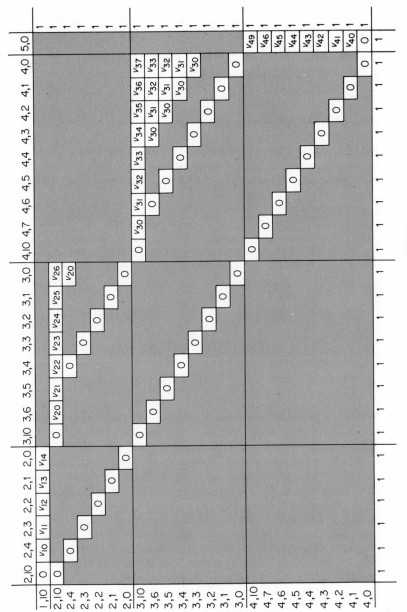

FIGURE 6.12. Table for Grand Land Development Example.

Then the model is

(i) $$\text{maximize} \sum_{i=1}^{n} h_i(x_i)$$

subject to

(ii) $$\sum_{i=1}^{n} x_i \leq C$$

(iii) $x_i = 0, 1, 2, \ldots$ for each i.

Thus the example has illustrated how network analysis can be applied to a problem of optimizing a nonlinear objective function where the variables are restricted to integer values and subject to a single constraint.

Traveling Salesman Problem. This rather facetiously named problem refers to the following situation: a traveling salesman, named Pierre plans to visit each of n cities, starting and ending at City 1. The distance between City i and City j is c_{ij}. What is the shortest tour Pierre can take?

This optimization problem and variants of it actually are faced by numerous companies that need to draw up routes for delivery trucks and the like. The mathematical model also fits situations that are entirely different. For example, the model is pertinent for an ice cream manufacturer who must optimally schedule the order of flavors to be run on his equipment. Let c_{ij} be the amount of time spent cleaning and preparing the machinery when Flavor j is scheduled to follow Flavor i. The c_{ij} vary widely, since flavors that are near-variants (vanilla and vanilla plus chocolate chips) can be run in quick succession, whereas other pairs require significant cleanup time (chocolate followed by coconut). The manufacturer wants to schedule his production to minimize the total amount of set-up time on the machine.

Returning to the salesman's problem, let

$$x_{ij} = \begin{cases} 1 & \text{if a tour includes traveling from City i to City j} \quad (\text{for } i \neq j) \\ 0 & \text{otherwise.} \end{cases}$$

Now suppose you apply the assignment model (2) through (5) in the preceding section, with all the x_{ii} omitted, to produce a minimum-distance routing through each city. The constraints in the assignment problem ensure that the route includes a departure from each city, and similarly an arrival at each city.

Will an optimal solution to the assignment problem provide a tour the salesman can use? Unfortunately, it may not. The resulting solution may include two or more *disconnected* cycles. For instance, $x_{12} = x_{23} = x_{31} = 1$ and $x_{45} = x_{56} = \cdots = x_{n4} = 1$ can occur. Thus one route is through Cities 1, 2, and 3, and an entirely separate route is through Cities $4, 5, \ldots, n$. Therefore what seems to be a modest extra requirement that the solution is a bona fide tour—that is, it contains only one cycle—in fact makes this combinatorial problem considerably harder to solve. You will return to the problem in Chap. 13.   ◄

*6.6 CRITICAL PATH SCHEDULING

This version of the **longest-path problem** is frequently applied to schedule major projects, such as the construction of a multistory office building, a maintenance overhaul of large-scale equipment, a research and development program for a new weapon system, and the market introduction of a new product. Critical path scheduling is also designated by a variety of acronyms and other names, such as CPS, CPM, and PERT. The approach has been developed to such an extent that adequate coverage of all its nuances would require an entire chapter and take you too far afield from the topic of the present chapter. However, you will find it instructive to see how the longest-route model can be applied to this sort of scheduling. The description to follow contains a number of simplifications, but the structural essentials are retained.

The Swift Building Company Problem. This firm must complete a construction project comprised of n tasks. Management has estimated the time needed for completing each task, and has established a precedence-ordering among the tasks to indicate which must be finished before each particular task can commence. As you will see in the illustration below, it is necessary to specify only the jobs that *immediately* precede a task to determine such an ordering. The company wants to calculate the earliest possible completion date for the entire project.

Suppose the project consists of five jobs, A, B, C, D, and E. It is convenient terminology to add a fictitious Job F that is to start when the entire project is finished. The precedence-ordering among the tasks is exhibited in Fig. 6.13 along with the completion times for each task. Thus Job C cannot start until Job A is finished, and Job E cannot begin until *both* Jobs B and D are finished. The entire project is finished as soon as both Jobs C and E have ended.

Job	Immediate Predecessors	Completion Time
A	– –	t_A
B	– –	t_B
C	A	t_C
D	A	t_D
E	B,D	t_E
"F"	C,E	– –

FIGURE 6.13. Swift Building Company Example: Precedence Ordering.

To formulate the corresponding mathematical optimization model, let the variables represent the starting time for each of the projects. Introduce *only* those variables essential to the analysis. Note that Jobs A and B can be considered as beginning at time 0, because they have no predecessors. Similarly Job C can be considered as starting at the same time as Job D, since both have the same immediate predecessor, namely Job A. Therefore, you need to include only the variables

$$y_{CD} = \text{starting time of Jobs C and D}$$

$$y_E = \text{starting time of Job E}$$

$$y_F = \text{starting time of Job F.}$$

Recall that y_F in fact is the time at which the entire project is finished.

The appropriate linear programming model is

(1)   minimize y_F

subject to

(2) $$y_{CD} \geq t_A$$
(3) $$y_E \geq t_B$$
(4) $$y_E \geq t_D + y_{CD}$$
(5) $$y_F \geq t_C + y_{CD}$$
(6) $$y_F \geq t_E + y_E.$$

Relations (2) through (6) are mathematical translations of the precedence relations in Fig. 6.13, and use the completion times given there. To illustrate, (3) and (4) require that Job E does not start until both Jobs B and D are completed. The completion time of Job B is merely t_B, and of Job D is its own starting time plus completion time. Notice restrictions (2) through (6) make it *unnecessary* to impose an *explicit* constraint that the variables be nonnegative. Consequently, from a formal point of view, the variables are unconstrained in sign.

y_{CD}	y_E	y_F	
1			$\geq t_A$
	1		$\geq t_B$
−1	1		$\geq t_D$
−1		1	$\geq t_C$
	−1	1	$\geq t_E$
		1	Minimize

FIGURE 6.14. Critical Path Tableau of Swift Building Company.

The technology of the model is summarized in Fig. 6.14. At first glance it does not seem to have a network structure, but further study reveals that its dual comes close to the desired format. With the few simple manipulations, given in the special material below, you can show the dual is a longest-path problem. The longest route itself is termed the **critical path**, since if the completion time of any job on this route increases, the finish date is delayed accordingly. (A critical path is not necessarily unique.)

In actual applications of critical path scheduling, which often encompass several hundred jobs, the analyst uses information such as that given in Fig. 6.13 and immediately draws a corresponding network. However, the algorithm that finds the longest path in the constructed acyclic network really solves the problem expressed in terms comparable to (1) through (6).

x_{01}	x_{02}	x_{12}	x_{13}	x_{23}	
1	1				= 1
−1		1	1		= 0
	−1	−1		1	= 0
			−1	−1	= −1
t_A	t_B	t_D	t_C	t_E	Maximize

Restriction: $x_{ij} \geq 0$

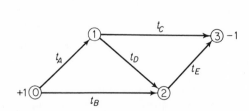

FIGURE 6.15. Swift Building Company: Tableau of Dual Problem.

FIGURE 6.16. Swift Building Company: Network of Dual Problem.

More sophisticated versions of critical path scheduling treat the job completion times as variables subject to a constrained optimization. In such cases, the analysis determines the tradeoff possibilities for reducing total project duration by increasing expedite costs.

▶ Take the three dual relations implied by Fig. 6.14 and sum them to form a redundant fourth equation. Recall that the dual relations are equalities, since the three variables in Fig. 6.14 are unconstrained in sign. Second, take each of the same three relations and multiply both sides by (-1) to change the signs of the coefficients.

The resultant model is shown in Fig. 6.15, with the redundant equation appearing in the top row. The associated network is drawn in Fig. 6.16. The problem is to find the longest route in an acyclic network; the problem is structurally equivalent to a shortest-path model.   ◀

*6.7 EMPLOYMENT SCHEDULING

The next application of network analysis demonstrates how it is sometimes necessary to manipulate the original formulation of a model in order to discover that the problem has a network equivalent.

The Spitzen-Pollish Company is a contract maintenance firm that provides and supervises semiskilled manpower for major overhauls of chemical processing equipment. A standard job frequently requires a thousand or more men and may extend from one or two weeks to a few months. Since the client's plant often is not located in a major metropolitan area, the maintenance company may have to transport workmen for several hundred miles. The firm's operating expenses include the costs of transportation, food, and on-site housing, as well as the men's wages.

For a routine assignment, the firm can estimate fairly accurately the number of crews required on a day-to-day basis for the duration of the job. The daily requirements fluctuate enough to impel the company to vary the number of crews on site during the overhaul period, in an effort to keep operating costs at a minimum. However, there are costs that do not depend on how long a crew remains on site: costs associated with recruiting, transporting, and then briefing a new crew. The firm sometimes finds it economical, therefore, to retain crews in excess of requirements if the men will be needed a few days later. Thus for each contract, the firm seeks a work force schedule that minimizes total labor expenses.

To construct the mathematical model that produces an optimal schedule, assume that the overhaul begins at the start of Period 1 and ends at the *start* of Period n. Let

x_{ij} = number of crews beginning work at the start of Period i and terminating at the start of Period j (for $1 \leq i < j \leq n$),

and let $c_{ij} \geq 0$ be the associated total operating cost of such a crew. Assume c_{ij} increases if the interval of employment increases; that is,

(1) $c_{ij} \leq c_{hk}$ for $h \leq i < j \leq k$.

Finally, let R_k be the number of crews actually needed during Period k, for $k = 1, 2, \ldots, n - 1$.

Then the constraints of the problem are

(2)
$$\sum_{j=2}^{n} x_{1j} = R_1$$

(3)
$$\sum_{i=1}^{k} \sum_{j=k+1}^{n} x_{ij} \geq R_k \quad \text{for } k = 2, 3, \ldots, n - 2$$

(4)
$$\sum_{i=1}^{n-1} x_{in} = R_{n-1}$$

(5)
$$\text{every } x_{ij} = 0, 1, 2, \ldots,$$

and the objective function is

(6)
$$\text{minimize} \sum_{i=1}^{n-1} \sum_{j=i+1}^{n} c_{ij} x_{ij}.$$

Relation (2) states that the total number of crews starting work in Period 1 equals that period's requirements. Because of (1), it is not economical to have excess crews at the start. By the same token, relation (4) specifies that there are no excess crews in the final work period, $(n - 1)$. At intermediate periods, Spitzen-Pollish may find it desirable to have more crews on site than are essential, which is permitted by the inequality in (3).

The model is displayed in its entirety in Fig. 6.17, where $n = 6$. Nonnegative

x_{12} x_{13} x_{14} x_{15} x_{16}	x_{23} x_{24} x_{25} x_{26}	x_{34} x_{35} x_{36}	x_{45} x_{46}	x_{56}	s_2 s_3 s_4		Row
1 1 1 1 1						$= R_1$	1
1 1 1 1	1 1 1 1				-1	$= R_2$	2
1 1 1	1 1 1	1 1 1			-1	$= R_3$	3
1 1	1 1	1 1	1 1		-1	$= R_4$	4
1	1	1	1	1		$= R_5$	5
c_{12} c_{13} c_{14} c_{15} c_{16}	c_{23} c_{24} c_{25} c_{26}	c_{34} c_{35} c_{36}	c_{45} c_{46}	c_{56}	0 0 0		Minimize

FIGURE 6.17. Spitzen-Pollish Company Employment-Scheduling Model.

surplus variables s_k, $k = 2, 3, 4$, have been added to convert (3) to equalities. Any connection between the technology in Fig. 6.17 and that of a network model is not obvious; but educated intuition suggests that further insight might be developed by transforming the technology into another equivalent format. The triangular appearance of the coefficients in successive sets of columns provides the clue for the transformations on the rows of Fig. 6.17.

Take Row 4 and subtract it from Row 5. Similarly, subtract Row 3 from Row 4, Row 2 from Row 3, and Row 1 from Row 2. The results are shown in Rows 5', 4', 3', and 2' of Fig. 6.18. Then multiply Row 5 by (-1), thereby changing the signs of the coefficients on the right-hand side, and add this redundant relation as Row 6' in Fig. 6.18.

x_{12}	x_{13}	x_{14}	x_{15}	x_{16}	x_{23}	x_{24}	x_{25}	x_{26}	x_{34}	x_{35}	x_{36}	x_{45}	x_{46}	x_{56}	s_2	s_3	s_4			Row
1	1	1	1	1															$= R_1$	$1' = 1$
-1					1	1	1	1							-1				$= R_2 - R_1$	$2' = 2 - 1$
	-1				-1				1	1	1				1	-1			$= R_3 - R_2$	$3' = 3 - 2$
		-1				-1			-1			1	1			1	-1		$= R_4 - R_3$	$4' = 4 - 3$
			-1				-1			-1		-1		1			1		$= R_5 - R_4$	$5' = 5 - 4$
				-1				-1			-1		-1	-1					$= -R_5$	$6' = -5$
c_{12}	c_{13}	c_{14}	c_{15}	c_{16}	c_{23}	c_{24}	c_{25}	c_{26}	c_{34}	c_{35}	c_{36}	c_{45}	c_{46}	c_{56}	0	0	0			Minimize

FIGURE 6.18. Spitzen-Pollish Equivalent Network Formulation.

Now the problem has the form of a transshipment model. As a consequence, the integrality stipulation in (5) causes no added difficulty in finding a solution. The network for the model is given in Fig. 6.19, where Node 1 is the source and Node 6

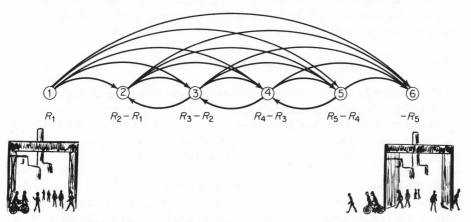

FIGURE 6.19. Network Representation of Spitzen-Pollish Employment-Scheduling Model.

is the sink. The other nodes are transshipment points. The corresponding transshipment array appears in Fig. 6.20. The buffer stock quantity can be set at

$$(7) \qquad B = .5 \left[R_1 + \sum_{k=2}^{5} |R_k - R_{k-1}| + R_5 \right].$$

Notice that without any further assumptions about the R_k, the model is *not* a shortest-route problem, and the activities s_k appear below the subdiagonal of the transportation table in Fig. 6.20. However, if $R_k = 1$, for $k = 1, 2, \ldots, 5$, then you can eliminate the s_k because no cost would be saved in routing a unit from Node j to Node k if $k < j$. Furthermore, $B = 1$ in (7). Thus, in this case, the model does simplify to a shortest-route problem in an acyclic network. What is more, the

Node → Node ↓	2	3	4	5	6	
1	c_{12} / x_{12}	c_{13} / x_{13}	c_{14} / x_{14}	c_{15} / x_{15}	c_{16} / x_{16}	R_1
2	0 / x_{22}	c_{23} / x_{23}	c_{24} / x_{24}	c_{25} / x_{25}	c_{26} / x_{26}	$R_2 - R_1 + B$
3	0 / s_1	0 / x_{33}	c_{34} / x_{34}	c_{35} / x_{35}	c_{36} / x_{36}	$R_3 - R_2 + B$
4		0 / s_2	0 / x_{44}	c_{45} / x_{45}	c_{46} / x_{46}	$R_4 - R_3 + B$
5			0 / s_3	0 / x_{55}	c_{56} / x_{56}	$R_5 - R_4 + B$
	B	B	B	B	R_5	

FIGURE 6.20. Tabular Form of Spitzen-Pollish Employment-Scheduling Model.

network is identical to that for the equipment replacement problem considered in Sec. 6.5 and illustrated by the network diagram in Fig. 6.10. In Chap. 10, you will see other special applications of the model (2) through (6).

*6.8 OVERVIEW OF NETWORK MODELS

This chapter has demonstrated how certain operations research problems can be couched in terms of optimizing within a network. The present section puts in focus the concepts you have learned so far, and describes in broader terms the entities and concepts encompassed in network models. The exposition will also introduce you to the standard vocabulary of these models.

Definitions. A **network** (or **linear graph**) consists of a set of **nodes** (or **points**, **vertices**) and a set of **arcs** (or **edges**, **links**) connecting various pairs of the nodes. Each arc has specified orientation (or direction). Consequently, the network is said to be **directed**.

A simple notation serves to describe a directed network: number the points $1, 2, \ldots, p$, and designate an arc starting at Node i and ending at Node j by (i, j). Assume there is only one arc (i, j), and call an item traversing (i, j) a **unit of flow** along that arc. The network is **bipartite** if the nodes can be partitioned into two groups G_1 and G_2 such that for every arc (i, j), Node i is in G_1 and Node j in G_2. The network for a transportation problem, shown in Fig. 6.1, is bipartite.

In all the preceding examples of this chapter, a unit of flow originating at any Node i and coursing (i, j) remains a unit on arrival at Node j. That is, no loss or gain occurs in the flow along any arc. (The impact of this assumption is explored in an illustration in the next section.) Consequently, a complete statement of a network structure is apparent from a table of structural coefficients (like Figs. 6.2, 6.7, 6.15, and 6.18). Such a table is referred to as a **node-arc incidence matrix**. Each node is represented by a row in the table, and each arc by a column. The direction of flow on the arc (i, j) is indicated by a coefficient 1 in the row for Node i and -1 in the row for Node j.

A sequence of arcs (*ignoring* their direction) that connects Node i to Node j is termed a **path** between the two nodes. When $i = j$, the path is a **loop**. A network is **connected** provided there is a path between *every* pair of points. In most applications of network models, the linear graph is connected. When the arcs in a path from Node i to Node j are all oriented so that it is actually possible for a unit of flow to traverse the path, the more restrictive term **directed chain** is often applied. (Consequently, throughout this chapter, wherever the word "path" has appeared, you may substitute "directed chain.") For example, the first approach suggested for reducing a transshipment model to a standard transportation problem, illustrated in the condensed transshipment table of Fig. 6.4, requires finding all the directed chains from nodes having available stock to nodes requiring additional supply. A directed chain beginning and ending at the same node is a **directed cycle**. An **acyclic** network is one without any directed cycles.

A tree. One special network of importance arises when there are p nodes, exactly $p - 1$ arcs, and the network is connected. This structure is called a **tree**, and does not contain any loops. (Draw a picture with $p = 6$ nodes placed randomly on the page. Then construct a connected network using only five arcs. Rotating the page and using a little imagination, you will see that your graph looks like one or more branches of a tree. What happens when you try to include a loop while constructing the network?) For example, consider the problem of finding shortest routes to a particular node (the terminal) from *every* other node in a general network. Assume the shortest routes are unique. A solution will be a set of directed chains ending at the terminal. If each arc not used by at least one of these chains is deleted from the network, the arcs remaining will form a tree. (Why will the result be a connected network? Why will it have no loops? Why will it have $p - 1$ arcs?)

General formulation. In defining a network, it is also useful to specify for the time period under consideration a capacity $u_{ij} \geq 0$ on the total flow starting at Node i and ending at Node j. For the examples in the preceding sections, the value of each u_{ij} was given *implicitly* as either infinite, implying no effective flow capacity restriction on an arc, or zero, signifying that flow was not permitted from Node i directly to Node j.

Two more kinds of quantities are needed to characterize a network in optimization applications. The first is the net flow values T_k at each Node k. If T_k is positive, then T_k more units of flow must leave the node than enter it, and vice versa if T_k is negative. If T_k is zero, all flow entering the node must also leave. It is convenient and innocuous to postulate

(1) $$\sum_{k=1}^{p} T_k = 0.$$

The second kind of data required is the cost data c_{ij} of each unit of flow traversing arc (i, j). Here it has been assumed that for every directed cycle in a network the corresponding sum of the c_{ij} is nonnegative.

Let

$$x_{ij} = \text{amount of flow over arc } (i, j) \text{ during the planning horizon.}$$

Then a network optimization problem of considerable generality and applicability is

(2) $$\text{minimize} \sum_{i=1}^{p} \sum_{j=1}^{p} c_{ij} x_{ij}$$

subject to

(3) $$\sum_{j=1}^{p} x_{kj} - \sum_{i=1}^{p} x_{ik} = T_k \quad \text{for } k = 1, 2, \ldots, p$$

(4) $$0 \le x_{ij} \le u_{ij} \quad \text{for all } i \text{ and } j.$$

The constraints (3) are frequently called **flow conservation** or **material balance equations.** By the methods you learned in this chapter, the model (1) through (4) can always be viewed as a capacitated transportation problem. The following result will be demonstrated in Chap. 7:

Integrality Theorem: If all T_k and u_{ij} are integers, then the value of (2) will not be increased by further stipulating that each x_{ij} must be an integer.

Whenever a linear programming problem is of the form (1) through (4), then it has a network equivalent. Sometimes a problem's original statement must be manipulated, such as by combining equations, changing signs of coefficients, and adding a redundant relation, or by considering the dual in order for it to appear as (1) through (4). Once the model is in this form, however, each relation in (3) corresponds to a node in the network, each variable x_{ij} to an amount of flow along a permissible arc (i, j), and each c_{ij} to the cost of a unit of flow through the arc.

▶The model (1) through (4) is occasionally stated somewhat differently, and the technique of conversion is of sufficient interest to be noted here. The modification arises when there is more than one T_k that is strictly positive or more than one T_k that is strictly negative. For the sake of generality, assume there are more than one positive and more than one negative T_k.

Add two fictitious nodes, 0 and $p + 1$. For each positive T_k, add the arc $(0, k)$ with $u_{0k} = T_k$. For each negative T_k, add the arc $(k, p + 1)$ with $u_{k, p+1} = -T_k$. Let F be the sum of the positive T_k. Then modify the model (1) through (4) by replacing (3) with

(i) $$\sum_{j=1}^{n} x_{0j} = F$$

(ii)
$$\sum_{j=1}^{p+1} x_{kj} - \sum_{i=0}^{p} x_{ik} = 0 \quad \text{for } k = 1, 2, \ldots, p$$

(iii)
$$-\sum_{i=1}^{p} x_{i, p+1} = -F.$$

As a result, there is now a single source (Node 0) and a single sink (Node p + 1), all other nodes being transshipment points. ◀

*6.9 GENERALIZED NETWORK PROBLEM

You would expect that the Integrality Theorem in the preceding section would fail to hold if the underlying structure of the network were altered. Indeed, this is true when a unit of flow originating at Node i becomes $a_{ij} \geq 0$ units on arrival at Node j. For $a_{ij} > 1$, there is a **gain**, and for $a_{ij} < 1$, a **loss**. The node-arc incidence matrix for the model is revised by substituting the appropriate $-a_{ij}$ for each -1.

One illustrative application of the generalized network model occurs for a steel fabricator with several manufacturing plants. On a monthly basis, the Vice-President for Production, with his staff, determines the allocation of customer orders to each of the plants. The manufacturing capacity of Plant i is S_i tons per month. There are n distinct products, and for the current month the total customer demand for Product j is D_j, also measured in tons. Because the plants differ in their fabricating facilities, a ton of capacity at Plant i allocated to making Product j yields a_{ij} tons of that commodity. In other words a "ton of capacity" at a plant is really a standard unit of measurement, and the differing a_{ij} indicate corresponding relative production efficiencies. A ton of Product j manufactured at Plant i costs c_{ij}, and if the plants are geographically dispersed, the c_{ij} may also include differential shipping charges. Let

x_{ij} = tons of capacity at Plant i allocated to fabricating Product j during the month.

The mathematical model is

(1)
$$\text{minimize} \sum_{i=1}^{m} \sum_{j=1}^{n} c_{ij} x_{ij}$$

subject to

(2)
$$\sum_{j=1}^{n} x_{ij} \leq S_i \quad \text{for } i = 1, 2, \ldots, m$$

(3)
$$\sum_{i=1}^{m} a_{ij} x_{ij} \geq D_j \quad \text{for } j = 1, 2, \ldots, n$$

(4)
$$x_{ij} \geq 0 \quad \text{for all } i \text{ and } j.$$

If a certain product cannot be produced at a plant, remove the x_{ij} in (1) through (4). The technology is displayed in Fig. 6.21. Notice how it closely resembles the technology for a standard transportation problem, shown in Fig. 6.2. For this reason, the linear programming model (1) through (4) is often called the **generalized transportation** (or **weighted distribution**) **problem**.

	x_{11} x_{12} x_{13} $\cdots$ x_{1n}	x_{21} x_{22} x_{23} $\cdots$ x_{2n}	$\cdots$	x_{m1} x_{m2} x_{m3} $\cdots$ x_{mn}	
Plants 1	1 1 1 $\cdots$ 1				$\leq S_1$
2		1 1 1 $\cdots$ 1			$\leq S_2$
$\vdots$			$\cdots$		$\vdots$
m				1 1 1 $\cdots$ 1	$\leq S_m$
Demands 1	$-a_{11}$	$-a_{21}$		$-a_{m1}$	$\leq -D_1$
2	$-a_{12}$	$-a_{22}$		$-a_{m2}$	$\leq -D_2$
3	$-a_{13}$	$-a_{23}$		$-a_{m3}$	$\leq -D_3$
$\vdots$	$\ddots$	$\ddots$	$\cdots$	$\ddots$	$\vdots$
n	$-a_{1n}$	$-a_{2n}$		$-a_{mn}$	$\leq -D_n$
	c_{11} c_{12} c_{13} $\cdots$ c_{1n}	c_{21} c_{22} c_{23} $\cdots$ c_{2n}	$\cdots$	c_{m1} c_{m2} c_{m3} $\cdots$ c_{mn}	Minimize

FIGURE 6.21. Generalized Transportation Problem.

*6.10 MULTICOMMODITY NETWORK

The discussion of the classical transportation problem in Sec. 6.2 made it clear that the formal mathematical statement assumed shipping only a single commodity. The text indicated a way in which a true multicommodity situation might be well enough approximated in the classical problem. But when the application involves p products to be routed through a *capacitated* transshipment network, and the pattern of stocks and requirements differs significantly from product to product, the problem may be too complex to handle by a one-commodity approximation. In this context a capacity constraint u_{ij} means that the *total* flow of *all* commodities from Node i to Node j must not exceed the given bound. (Suggest an example or two in which an aggregate constraint of this type applies.)

For an inkling of the complications that arise in a multicommodity model, consider the situation exhibited in Fig. 6.22. The network consists of three nodes. No cost is associated with traversing arcs $(1, 2)$, $(2, 3)$, and $(3, 1)$; however, a cost c per unit flow is charged on arcs $(1, 3)$, $(3, 2)$, and $(2, 1)$. One unit of Commodity A is available at Node 1 and required at Node 3. Similarly, a unit of Commodity B is available at Node 2 and needed at Node 1, and a unit of Commodity C is available at Node 3 and wanted at Node 2. If there are no arc capacity restrictions, the optimal solution, with zero total cost, is to route each item from its origin through a transshipment point to its destination.

Now suppose there is a one-unit maximum flow constraint on each arc. If the bound is imposed separately on each commodity, the previous solution remains optimal. But suppose instead that the restriction is on the *total* flow of *all* com-

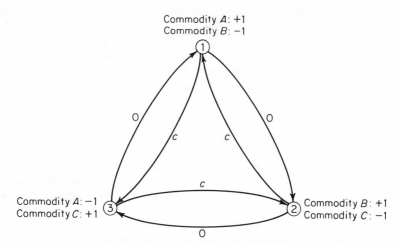

Commodity A: +1
Commodity B: −1

Commodity A: −1
Commodity C: +1

Commodity B: +1
Commodity C: −1

FIGURE 6.22. Multicommodity Network.

modities on an arc. (Test your skill by writing out a full tableau description of the model, given this assumption. In what way does the tableau structure differ significantly from that in Fig. 6.7?) The previous routings are ruled out, because together they imply a flow of 2 on the arcs $(1, 2)$, $(2, 3)$, and $(3, 1)$. The only optimal routing is to send *half* a unit of each commodity along the previous routings and the remaining *half* unit directly from its origin to its destination. The associated minimal cost now is $\frac{3}{2}c$. Thus connecting three separate flow problems, merely by imposing common capacity constraints, is sufficient to destroy the integrality result cited at the end of Sec. 6.8. The computational task of finding optimal flows in such networks is likewise more difficult.

REVIEW EXERCISES

1 Consider the transportation problem (1) through (4) in Sec. 6.2. Let the number of supply points $m = 4$ and the number of demand points $n = 5$.

(a) Write the model in full detail (that is, display the objective function and the constraints without using the summation symbol).

(b) Draw the corresponding network in Fig. 6.1, and construct the two tables in Fig. 6.2.

2 *Excess Supply*. Consider a transportation problem in which

$$S_1 = 5 \quad S_2 = 6 \quad S_3 = 7 \quad \text{and} \quad D_1 = 2 \quad D_2 = 3 \quad D_3 = 4.$$

Create a fictitious destination and construct a table like that in Fig. 6.2a in which total supply equals total demand. Be sure you indicate the cost coefficients c_{ij} for the fictitious destination and its D_j.

*3 *Seasonal Variation.* Suppose a firm having two plants and three demand points is planning a production schedule for four periods. Assume over Periods 1, 2, 3, and 4 that Plant 1 has available supplies of 4, 5, 6, and 7, respectively, and similarly Plant 2 has available supplies of 8, 9, 10, and 11, respectively. Assume over Periods 1, 2, 3, and 4 that Demand Point 1 has demands 3, 3, 10, and 10, respectively; similarly, Demand Point 2 has demands 4, 2, 6, and 6, respectively; and Demand Point 3 has demands 2, 6, 4, and 4, respectively. Let c_{ij} be the cost of shipping a unit from Plant i to Demand Point j in any period.

(a) Display the optimization problem in a table like that in Fig. 6.2a. Be sure you indicate which x_{ij} must be eliminated.

(b) Is there a feasible solution to this numerical example? Justify your conclusion. Give a general rule for discerning whether such a problem has a feasible solution.

(c) Explain how to modify the formulation when the total supply exceeds total demand.

(d) Suppose each unit of inventory held at the end of a period incurs the cost h. Will adding this cost change the optimal solution in part (a)? In part (c)?

Exercises 4 through 9 refer to the case of the Rock-Bottom Discount Store, displayed in Fig. 6.3.

4 In each part below, state which stores are transshipment (or intermediate) points, which are sources, and which are sinks. Also state whether the resulting map has a feasible shipping pattern that meets the demand requirements. Assume the removal of the route from

(a) Store 4 to Store 5.
(b) Store 5 to Store 4.
(c) Store 6 to Store 7.
(d) Store 2 to Store 5.
(e) Store 4 to Store 7.
(f) Store 4 to Store 3.

5 In each part below, state which stores are transshipment (or intermediate) points, which are sources, and which are sinks. Assume a route is added from

(a) Store 7 to Store 4.
(b) Store 6 to Store 8.
(c) Store 8 to Store 6.
(d) Store 3 to Store 4.
(e) Store 1 to Store 3.
(f) Store 3 to Store 1.

6 In each part below, construct a condensed transshipment table like that in Fig. 6.4. Show a feasible solution, and indicate whether or not your solution implies a unique routing from the supply point to the demand point. Construct an expanded transshipment table like that in Fig. 6.5; indicate the sources and sinks.

(a) Stock of 10 available at Store 1, and stocks of 2 and 8 required at Stores 3 and 8, respectively. No stock available or required at any other store.

(b) Stocks of 10 and 4 available at Stores 1 and 5, respectively, and stocks of 3, 2, 1, and 8 required at Stores 3, 4, 6, and 8, respectively. No stock available or required at any other store.

(c) Stocks of 10, 1, 2, and 5 available at Stores 1, 2, 6, and 7, respectively, and stocks of 3, 1, 6, and 8 required at Stores 3, 4, 5, and 8, respectively.

(d) Answer the above parts when the route from Store 6 to Store 7 is removed. Also state whether there is a feasible solution.

7 (a) Consider the routing in Fig. 6.6. Explain in detail how this routing implies that Store 1 ships three units to Store 3 via Point 2; one unit to Store 6 via Points 2 and 5; and six units to Store 8 via Points 2, 5, 4, and 7; and that Store 4 ships its two units to Store 8 via Point 7. Display this routing on a map like that in Fig. 6.3.

(b) Show how Fig. 6.6 is altered if Store 1 ships six units to Store 8 via Points 2, 5, 6, and 7.

(c) Show how Fig. 6.6 is altered if Store 1 ships eight, instead of six, units to Store 8, and Store 4 ships two units to Store 3, instead of to Store 8.

(d) Explain in detail the routing implied in Fig. 6.6 by letting

$$x_{12} = 10 \quad x_{22} = 2 \quad x_{25} = 10 \quad x_{43} = 3 \quad x_{44} = 11$$

$$x_{54} = 1 \quad x_{55} = 2 \quad x_{56} = 9 \quad x_{66} = 3 \quad x_{67} = 8 \quad x_{77} = 4 \quad x_{78} = 8.$$

Display this routing on a map like that in Fig. 6.3.

8 Add routes from Store 3 to Store 2; Store 3 to Store 4; Store 5 to Store 3; Store 7 to Store 6; and Store 3 to Store 8. Construct a technological table like that in Fig. 6.7 for the stocks available and required in the specified part of exercise 6.

(a) Part (a).

(b) Part (b).

(c) Part (c).

9 Suppose there is one unit of stock available at Stores 1, 4, and 5, and a requirement of one unit of stock at Stores 3, 7, and 8. No stock is available or required at Stores 2 and 6.

(a) Construct a condensed transshipment table like that in Fig. 6.4. Indicate whether the table yields an assignment problem.

(b) Construct an expanded transshipment table like that in Fig. 6.5. Indicate whether the table yields an assignment problem.

10 Explain how a standard transportation problem can be converted into a (large) assignment problem. Illustrate your technique using an example with two supply points having stocks $S_1 = 2$ and $S_2 = 3$, and two demand points having requirements $D_1 = 1$ and $D_2 = 4$.

11 (a) Display the technology table corresponding to (1), (2), and (3) in Sec. 6.5 for the shortest-route example in Fig. 6.8.

(b) Assume every $c_{ij} \geq 0$. Verify that the constraints in (2) can just as well be written as "greater-than-or-equal" inequalities. Then display the associated dual maximization problem.

12 Consider the shortest-route example in Fig. 6.8. Add arcs from Node 4 to Node 7 and from Node 6 to Nodes 3 and 7; delete arcs from Node 4 to Node 3, from Node 6 to Node 5, and from Node 7 to Node 2.

   (a) Draw the revised network, and construct the corresponding tabular representation like that in Fig. 6.9.

   (b) For part (a), display the technology table corresponding to (1), (2), and (3) in Sec. 6.5.

 *(c) Assume every $c_{ij} \geq 0$. Verify that the constraints in (2) can just as well be written as "greater-than-or-equal" inequalities. Then display the associated dual maximization problem.

13 Consider the shortest-route example in Fig. 6.8. Add arcs from Node 1 to Nodes 3 and 4, and from Nodes 5 and 6 to Node 8.

   (a) Construct a tabular representation like that in Fig. 6.9 where the sink is Node 2 and the source is Node 7.

   (b) For part (a), display the technology table corresponding to (1), (2), and (3) in Sec. 6.5.

 *(c) Assume every $c_{ij} \geq 0$. Verify that the constraints in (2) can just as well be written as "greater-than-or-equal" inequalities. Then display the associated dual maximization problem.

14 *Shortest-Route Problem.* Consider the Rock-Bottom Discount Store Problem displayed in Fig. 6.3. For each part below, draw a network representing the associated shortest-route problem, construct a tabular representation like that in Fig. 6.9, and describe a technology table corresponding to (1), (2), and (3) in Sec. 6.5. Find a shortest route from

   (a) Store 1 to Store 3.
   (b) Store 1 to Store 8.
   (c) Store 4 to Store 8.

15 *Equipment Replacement.* Consider the example of the Rhode-Bloch Trucking Company, displayed in Fig. 6.10.

   (a) Show a routing through the network corresponding to replacing equipment in Years 3 and 5. In Years 2 and 5. In Years 3 and 4. In Year 3 only. In Year 4 only. Indicate the corresponding costs incurred over the horizon.

   (b) Construct a tabular representation of the problem like that in Fig. 6.9.

   (c) Describe a technology table corresponding to (1), (2), and (3) in Sec. 6.5.

   (d) Suppose that the cost of running and maintaining the equipment for one, two, three, four, and five consecutive periods is 1, 3, 6, 10, and 15, respectively. Suppose that if a rental at the start of Period 1 extends over one, two, three, four, or five consecutive periods, the rental cost is 5, 9, 13, 16, or 19, respectively. These rental costs increase by one each period; for example, if a rental at the start of

Period 3 extends over one, two, or three consecutive periods, the costs are 7, 11, or 15, respectively. Calculate each c_{ij} from these data.

(e) Assume every $c_{ij} \geq 0$. Verify that the constraints in (2) can just as well be written as "greater-than-or-equal" inequalities. Then display the associated dual maximization problem.

16 *Equipment Replacement.* Consider the example of the Rhode-Bloch Trucking Company, displayed in Fig. 6.10. Revise the network for the case where $n = 8$, and each piece of equipment must be kept at least three years.

*17 *Critical Path Scheduling.* Consider the case of the Swift Building Company, as shown in Fig. 6.13. Suppose the immediate predecessors for Job C are Jobs A and D; for Job D is Job B, instead of Job A; and for Job E is only Job B.

(a) Reformulate the linear programming model appropriate to the new restrictions.
(b) Display the corresponding critical path tableau, as in Fig. 6.14.
*(c) Display the corresponding dual problem, as in Fig. 6.15, and construct the associated network, as in Fig. 6.16.

*18 *Critical Path Scheduling.* A network representation for the Swift Building Company case is shown in Fig. 6.13. An alternative network representation can be constructed as follows. Let Node S represent the starting point; all arcs out of Node S have 0 length. Let Node T represent the terminating point. In addition, there is a node for each job. There is an arc from Node i to Node j if Job i is an immediate predecessor of Job j; the length of the arc is t_i, the time to complete Job i. Any jobs that can start immediately have S as an immediate predecessor. Any job not followed by other jobs has an arc into Node T. Node T serves the same purpose as Job F in Fig. 6.13, and so Job F can be replaced by T.

(a) Draw this alternative network for the case in Fig. 6.13.
(b) Compare Fig. 6.13 with the above network representation.
(c) Draw the network for the case in exercise 17.

*19 *Employment Scheduling.* Consider the case of the Spitzen-Pollish Company discussed in Sec. 6.7. Let $n = 8$, and assume that a crew must be kept for at least two periods.

(a) Display the technology as in Figs. 6.17 and 6.18.
(b) Draw the associated network as in Fig. 6.19.
(c) Construct the associated tabular form as in Fig. 6.20.

*20 *Employment Scheduling.* Consider the case of the Spitzen-Pollish Company discussed in Sec. 6.7. Let $n = 9$, and assume that a crew must be kept for at least one period but not longer than four periods. Answer the questions in exercise 19.

*21 *Employment Scheduling.* Suppose $n = 6$ in the model of Sec. 6.7. Let the wage cost per crew in Period k be designated as w_k, where

$$w_1 = 100 \quad w_2 = 150 \quad w_3 = 180 \quad w_4 = 200 \quad w_5 = 120.$$

A crew hired to start in Period k incurs the hiring cost g_k, where

$$g_1 = 1 \quad g_2 = 2 \quad g_3 = 3 \quad g_4 = 2 \quad g_5 = 1.$$

A crew released at the end of Period k incurs the severence cost f_k, where

$$f_1 = .3 \quad f_2 = .5 \quad f_3 = .7 \quad f_4 = .4 \quad f_5 = .1.$$

If a crew works t consecutive periods, the resultant transportation, housing, recreation, and related expenses are h_t, where

$$h_1 = 12 \quad h_2 = 13 \quad h_3 = 14 \quad h_4 = 18 \quad h_5 = 25.$$

Calculate the appropriate values for all the objective-function coefficients c_{ij}.

*22 (a) Randomly place six nodes on a page. Construct a connected network using only five arcs. What happens if you try to include a loop when constructing the network? What happens if you add one more arc?

(b) Repeat part (a) with seven nodes and six arcs.

*23 Consider the problem of finding shortest routes to a terminal from every other node in a general network with p nodes. Assume the shortest routes are unique. Then a solution will be a set of directed chains ending at the terminal. Reduce the network by deleting each arc not used by at least one of these chains. Explain why the result will be a connected network, why it will have no loops, and why it will have $p - 1$ arcs.

*24 *Multicommodity Network.* Consider the example in Fig. 6.22. Write a full tableau description of this model including the restriction that the *total* flow of *all* commodities on an arc cannot exceed one unit. How does the tableau structure differ significantly from that in Fig. 6.7?

25 Explain your understanding of the following terms:

transportation (or distribution)   buffer stock
   problem   assignment problem
*capacitated (or bounded-variables)   shortest-route problem
   transportation problem   node
transshipment (or intermediate) point   directed arc
source point   terminal
sink point   cycle.

*26 Explain your understanding of the following terms:

longest-path problem   directed chain
critical path   directed cycle
network (or linear graph)   acylic network
node, point, or vertex   tree
arc, link, or edge   flow conservation (or material balance)
bipartite network   equations
node-arc incidence matrix   flow gain (or loss)
path   generalized transportation (or
loop   weighted-distribution) problem
connected network   multicommodity network.

FORMULATION EXERCISES

27 The Nick U. Moore Razor Blade Company has announced a revolutionary product development, and the sales response to the company's advertising program has been gratifying. The company has two manufacturing plants and three distributing warehouses located in different parts of the United States. The company ships its razor blades to the warehouses by rail in carload lots.

This month's supply at Plants 1 and 2 are $S_1 = 100$ and $S_2 = 200$, respectively. The sales potentials at Warehouses 1, 2, and 3 are $D_1 = 150$, $D_2 = 200$, and $D_3 = 250$, respectively. As you can see, potential demand vastly exceeds available supply, and consequently some demand will go unsatisfied.

Assume the cost of shipping a carload from Plant i to Warehouse j is t_{ij}, and that the sales revenue per carload at Warehouse j is p_j. (The company is able to charge different prices for its razor blades in different parts of the country.)

(a) Formulate a transportation model to obtain a profit-maximizing solution. Be sure to indicate how you would compute each objective-function coefficient c_{ij}.

(b) Construct the associated table like that in Fig. 6.2a. Be sure to indicate the values for each S_i and D_j, as well as each c_{ij}.

28 The Longview Manufacturing Company must meet demand commitments for $D_1, D_2, \ldots, D_N$ units of its product in Periods 1, 2, . . . , N, respectively. The company's production capacity in Period t is m_t units, assuming that its work force is employed for one shift a day. The associated direct cost of each unit is p_t. By using overtime, the company also can produce e_t more units at a direct unit cost of q_t, where $q_t > p_t$. Because the demand commitments fluctuate considerably, the company expects that it may have to build inventory in some periods to meet demand in subsequent periods. Each unit of inventory at the end of Period t incurs a holding charge h_t.

(a) Assuming D_t, m_t, and e_t are integer-valued, formulate a transportation model that will find a cost-minimizing production and inventory plan. Be sure to indicate how to compute each objective-function coefficient.

(b) Using your answer in part (a), construct a table like that in Fig. 6.2a for the data $(N = 4)$

$$D_1 = 12 \quad D_2 = 9 \quad D_3 = 18 \quad D_4 = 22$$
$$m_1 = 10 \quad m_2 = 8 \quad m_3 = 10 \quad m_4 = 12$$
$$e_1 = 8 \quad e_2 = 6 \quad e_3 = 5 \quad e_4 = 4$$
$$p_t = 10 \quad q_t = 15 \quad \text{and} \quad h_t = 1 \quad \text{for all } t.$$

*(c) Suggest an easy-to-apply rule for finding an optimal plan for such a model, in which p_t, q_t, and h_t may differ from period to period. Then employ your suggestion to solve part (b).

29 The Sinbad Steamship Company operates a freighter schedule between Ports X and Y and Ports A, B, and C. The schedule for the next 15 days is shown in the first table.

Dates	Port of Origin	Port of Destination
3	X	A
4	Y	A
6	X	C
6	Y	A
9	X	B
9	Y	A
10	X	A
10	X	C
10	Y	B
13	Y	B
15	Y	B
15	Y	C

After a freighter goes from a port of origin to a port of destination, it may return to either port of origin. The *total* time (in days) to sail from port to port, in either direction, is shown in the second table.

	A	B	C
X	2	3	2
Y	1	2	1

Suppose three freighters are at Port X and three at Port Y on Day 1. Let the expense of returning a freighter to Port X from Ports A, B, and C be p_A, p_B, and p_C, respectively, and similarly let the cost of returning a freighter to Port Y be q_A, q_B, and q_C, respectively.

The Sinbad Company wants to find a routing for ships from Ports A, B, and C back to Ports X and Y that minimizes total cost. Show how this problem can be solved by a transportation model.

Let a supply point correspond to (Date t, Port of Destination i), which specifies that at Date t, one or more freighters (depending on the schedule requirements above) arrive at the Port of Destination i (either Port A, B, or C), and are ready to be returned to a port of origin (either Port X or Y). For example, since on Date 6 a freighter must leave Port X and go to Port C, taking two days of travel time, there is at least one freighter available at Supply Point (6 + 2, C).

Let a demand point correspond to (Date t, Port of Origin j), which specifies that on Date t one or more freighters (depending on the schedule requirements above) sail from Port of Origin j (either Port X or Y). For example, a demand point is (9, X).

Note that the shipping times make it impossible to send a freighter from some of the supply points in sufficient time to meet the requirements at some of the demand points. For example, Supply Point (6 + 2, C) cannot meet the requirement at Demand Point (9, X), because it takes two days to go from Port C to Port X.

Construct a transportation table that indicates the structure of the model. Be sure to indicate the appropriate S_i, D_j, and every c_{ij}. Display a feasible solution in the table, and interpret your solution in terms of an actual schedule for the six freighters.

30 Consider the case of the Sinbad Steamship Company in exercise 29. Suppose the company wants to find the *minimum* number of freighters required to meet the schedule, regardless of shipping costs. Show how to solve this problem by a transportation model. Construct a transportation table that indicates the structure of the model. Be sure to indicate the appropriate S_i, D_j, and every c_{ij}.

Try to determine a feasible solution in the table for five freighters, and interpret your solution in terms of an actual schedule. Try to do the same for four freighters.

(*Hint:* add a fictitious supply point having a large number of freighters available that can be used to meet *any* requirement, and a fictitious demand point for any excess supply of freighters. Verify that the objective is to minimize the number of freighters that meet requirements from the fictitious supply point.)

31 The Marcus Metal Company mines ore at Locations 1 and 2, transports it to processing mills at Locations 3 and 4, and ships the final product to Locations 5, 6, and 7, where it is sold. A schematic map of the locations and product flow is given in Fig. 6.23.

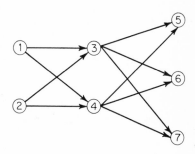

Let S_1 and S_2 represent the maximum supply available at Locations 1 and 2, respectively, and D_5, D_6, and D_7 the demand requirements that must be met at Locations 5, 6, and 7, respectively. The total maximum supply exceeds the total demand requirements.

FIGURE 6.23

Assume m_i is the cost of a unit of supply at Mine i $(i = 1, 2)$, p_j is the processing cost of unit of supply at Mill j $(j = 3, 4)$, s_{ij} is the shipping cost of a unit of supply from Mine i to Mill j $(i = 1, 2$ and $j = 3, 4)$, and t_{jk} is the shipping cost of a unit of supply from Mill j to Location k $(j = 3, 4,$ and $k = 5, 6, 7)$.

(a) Construct a condensed transshipment table like that in Fig. 6.4. Be sure to indicate in detail how to calculate each objective-function coefficient c_{ij}.

(b) Construct an expanded transshipment table like that in Fig. 6.5. Be sure to indicate how to calculate each objective-function coefficient.

(c) Construct a technology representation like that in Fig. 6.7. Use inequalities where appropriate to indicate that total supply exceeds total demand.

32 Consider the transshipment network in Fig. 6.24, where a positive number at a node indicates a supply and a negative number a requirement. Note there are two arcs, one in each direction, between every pair of nodes. The unit cost of shipping each item from Node i to Node j is c_{ij}; c_{ij} need not equal c_{ji}.

(a) Construct a condensed transshipment table like that in Fig. 6.4.

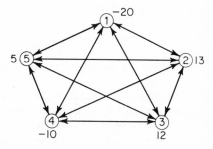

FIGURE 6.24

(b) Construct an expanded transshipment table like that in Fig. 6.5. Be sure to indicate the values for the supplies and demands.

(c) In the table of part (b), indicate the following shipment plan: five units from Node 5 to Node 4 via Node 3; five units from Node 2 to Node 4 via Nodes 5 and 3; eight units from Node 2 to Node 1 via Node 5; and 12 units from Node 3 directly to Node 1.

(d) Give another routing having the same cost as that in part (c).

(e) Construct a technology representation like that in Fig. 6.7.

*(f) Formulate the technology in part (e) so that the supply constraints are "less-than-or-equal" inequalities, and the demand constraints are "greater-than-or-equal" inequalities. Then write the associated dual *maximizing* problem.

33 Consider the transshipment network in Fig. 6.25, where a positive number at a node indicates a supply and a negative number a requirement; nodes with 0 indicate there

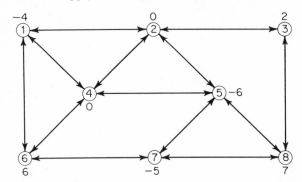

FIGURE 6.25

is neither a supply nor a demand. Note there are two arcs, one in each direction, between connected nodes. The unit cost of shipping each item from Node i to Node j is c_{ij}; c_{ij} need not equal c_{ji}.

(a) Construct a condensed transshipment table like that in Fig. 6.4. Show a feasible solution, and indicate whether your solution implies a unique routing.

(b) Construct an expanded transshipment table like that in Fig. 6.5. Are there any sources or sinks? Be sure to indicate in your table the values for the supplies and demands.

(c) In the table of part (b) indicate the following shipment plan: two units from Node 3 to Node 1 via Nodes 2 and 4; two units from Node 6 to Node 1 via Node 4; four units from Node 6 to Node 5 via Node 4; two units from Node 8 to Node 5 via Nodes 3, 2, and 4; and five units from Node 8 to Node 7 via Nodes 3, 2, 4, and 5.

(d) Construct a technology representation like that in Fig. 6.7.

34 The McReady Company operates a machine shop. Today's order file consists of n jobs, each of which can be manufactured on any of n different machines. Let t_{ij} be the amount of time (make-ready or setup plus manufacturing) to complete Job i on Machine j. Formulate an optimization model to get all the orders completed with a minimum total expenditure of time.

35 Joe Friendly, the Associate Dean of a large business school, must make a class assign-ment schedule for the faculty. Specifically, he must assign n professors to teach n classes. In the past, the students have filled out teacher-effectiveness rating question-naires, so the Associate Dean has information as to how well the students liked the professors when they have taught these several classes. (In some cases, a professor has never taught a particular class, so the Associate Dean must guess at a rating. In other cases, the professor does not wish, or is not prepared, to teach a particular class, and so the Associate Dean must rule out this assignment.)

(a) Explain how the Associate Dean might use a mathematical model to maximize student happiness.

(b) In your opinion, is this any way to run a business school?

36 Mrs. Flo Updegraph, the room scheduling clerk in a liberal arts college, has n classes to assign to n available rooms. Certain assignments are ruled out for reasons such as the class size exceeds the room size, the classroom is unavailable for use at the required time, or the classroom is too long a walk from the professor's office. Suggest a mathe-matical model that might assist the room scheduler.

37 The Lieberman Supply Company stocks an item that deteriorates with time as mea-sured in weekly periods. Suppose that Lieberman has on hand four such items, indexed $i = 1, 2, 3$, and 4, the present age of each being denoted by A_i. He has contracted to sell his stock as follows: he must deliver one item t_1 weeks from now, one item t_2 weeks from now, one item t_3 weeks from now, and one item t_4 weeks from now. The revenue he receives for each item is a function of its age at the time of delivery; this function is denoted as $R(A)$, A being the relevant age.

Formulate an optimization model that can enable Lieberman to determine which item he should supply at each delivery date so that he can maximize his total reve-nue.

38 The Overland Airlines has many scheduled flights between New York and Los Angeles; some are direct flights and others make intermediate stops. Assume there are an equal number of flights, N, each day in both directions. Let those daily flights initiating in New York be indexed $i = 1, 2, \ldots, N$, and those in Los Angeles be indexed $j = 1, 2, \ldots, N$. If a jet aircraft is *repeatedly* assigned to Flight i out of New York and Flight j out of Los Angeles, then the airline can calculate the resultant number of nonflight hours per week for planes assigned to this round-trip route. Such downtime is due not only to the delay in Los Angeles between the arrival of Flight i and the departure of Flight j, and in New York between the arrival of Flight j and the depar-ture of Flight i, but is due also to the maintenance time required by the particular pairing. Explain how you can apply a mathematical optimization model to find pairings for flights between New York and Los Angeles that minimize total downtime per week of all the aircraft.

How does the formulation change if an aircraft need not be assigned to the same flight out of New York and Los Angeles on each trip?

39 Consider the network in Fig. 6.26. The problem is to find a shortest route from Node 11 to Node 1. Let c_{ij} be the length of arc (i, j).

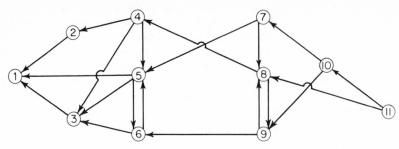

FIGURE 6.26

(a) Construct a tabular representation like that in Fig. 6.9.

(b) For part (a), display the technology table corresponding to (1), (2), and (3) in Sec. 6.5.

40 Consider the network in exercise 39. Add an arc from Node 1 to Node 11. Suppose the problem is to find a shortest route from Node 9 to Node 3. Answer the questions posed in exercise 39.

41 *Equipment Replacement.* The Goode-O'Toole Company runs a machine shop containing an expensive drill press that must be replaced periodically as it wears out. The Vice-President of Manufacturing has just authorized installing a new model, but has asked the foreman to devise an optimal replacement plan for the next seven years, after which the drill press will no longer be needed.

Let p_t be the cost of a new model in Period t, where

$$p_1 = 100 \quad p_2 = 105 \quad p_3 = 110 \quad p_4 = 115 \quad p_5 = 120 \quad p_6 = 125 \quad p_7 = 130,$$

so that the currently authorized installation incurs the cost 100. Let v_k be the salvage value of a press that is sold at the end of k periods of use, where

$$v_1 = 50 \quad v_2 = 25 \quad v_3 = 10 \quad v_4 = 5 \quad v_5 = 2 \quad v_6 = 1 \quad v_7 = 0.$$

Thus, if the new press is sold at the end of the first period, Goode-O'Toole realizes a revenue of 50; if it is sold at the end of Period 2, the revenue is 25; if it is sold at the end of Period 7, the revenue is 0.

Let r_k be the operating cost of a piece of equipment during its kth consecutive period of use, where

$$r_1 = 30 \quad r_2 = 40 \quad r_3 = r_4 = 50 \quad r_5 = 60 \quad r_6 = 70 \quad r_7 = 100.$$

(a) Formulate a shortest-route problem to find an optimal replacement policy.

(b) Construct a tabular representation of the problem like that in Fig. 6.9. Be sure to calculate every c_{ij}.

(c) Display a technology table corresponding to (1), (2), and (3).

*42 Utopian Construction Company wants to apply critical path scheduling to two projects. For each, formulate the appropriate linear programming model. Display the corresponding critical path tableau, as done in Fig. 6.14. Construct a network like that in Fig. 6.16. Throughout, let t_j denote the completion time for Job j.

(a)

Job	Immediate Predecessors
A	–
B	–
C	A
D	A
E	B, C
F	B, C
G	D, E
H	F

(b)

Job	Immediate Predecessors
A	–
B	–
C	A
D	A
E	B
F	B
G	D
H	C, F

*43 In exercise 18, an alternative technique was outlined for constructing a network representation for a critical path project. Apply this method to the designated part of exercise 42.

(a) Part (a).
(b) Part (b).

*44 After finding the critical path in the project in part (a) of exercise 42, the Utopian Company realizes that it *must* schedule overtime labor in order to fulfill its contractual obligation to complete the project by time T.

The network representation of the project has six nodes, indexed $i = 1, 2, \ldots, 6$, where Node 1 denotes the start of the project and Node 6 designates that all the tasks are complete. Let

$$d_{ij} = \text{shortest possible interval of time required to complete}$$
$$\text{the task associated with arc } (i,j);$$

each d_{ij} is a known constant, and typically involves utilizing overtime to the fullest extent possible.

Let the decision variables be

$$y_{ij} = \text{the interval of time } exceeding\ d_{ij} \text{ to complete the task}$$
$$\text{associated with arc } (i,j),$$
$$t_i = \text{the } earliest \text{ point in time to start any task leading out}$$
$$\text{from Node } i.$$

The y_{ij} and t_i are the unknowns in the optimization problem. These values must satisfy the constraints

$$t_i + d_{ij} + y_{ij} \leq t_j \quad \text{for every arc } (i,j).$$

In addition, $t_6 \leq T$ to meet the contractual commitment.

If full overtime is not used on the task associated with arc (i,j), then $y_{ij} > 0$; assume the associated cost *savings* is $s_{ij}y_{ij}$.

(a) Write a linear programming formulation of the optimizing problem. Show all the constraints and the entire objective function.

*(b) Write the corresponding dual problem. Is it a network problem? If so, explain its structural components.

*45 In each part below, draw the network corresponding to the following node-arc incidence matrix:

(a)

x_{12}	x_{14}	x_{23}	x_{24}	x_{52}	x_{53}	x_{54}
1	1					
−1		1	1	−1		
		−1			−1	
	−1		−1			−1
				1	1	1

(b)

x_{12}	x_{13}	x_{14}	x_{23}	x_{24}	x_{25}	x_{32}	x_{35}	x_{43}	x_{45}
1	1	1							
−1			1	1	1	−1			
	−1		−1			1	1	−1	
		−1		−1				1	1
					−1		−1		−1

*46 Consider the constraints

$$x_{12} + x_{13} + x_{14} - x_{41} \le 6$$
$$x_{12} + x_{32} \ge 5$$
$$x_{41} + x_{42} + x_{43} - x_{14} \le 4$$
$$x_{14} + x_{34} \ge 2$$
$$\text{every } x_{ij} \ge 0.$$

Draw a network corresponding to these restrictions. (*Hint:* convert the inequalities to equalities by adding slack variables; then add a redundant restriction corresponding to a fictitious node.)

*47 Explain how to convert a transshipment network with capacity restrictions on flow through nodes into an equivalent (enlarged) transshipment problem with capacity restrictions on the flow through arcs. (*Hint:* convert a transshipment node into two nodes connected by an arc.)

*48 *Caterer Problem.* The Cole Food Company, a catering firm, requires r_j fresh napkins at the start of Day j, where $j = 1, 2, \ldots, T$. Normal laundering takes one full day at

B cents a napkin; rapid laundering takes overnight at C cents a napkin. New napkins may be purchased at A cents a napkin. The caterer wants a plan for purchasing and laundering napkins to minimize total costs, subject to meeting all his fresh-napkin requirements.

Let x_j be the number of napkins purchased for use on the jth day; v_j the number of clean napkins left over (at the end of the day); y_j the number sent for normal laundry service (at the end of the day); z_j the number sent for rapid laundry service (at the end of the day); and s_j the number of soiled napkins on hand and not sent to the laundry (at the end of the day). The technology matrix can be summarized by the table.

	x_j	v_j	y_j	z_j	s_j
Allocation of clean napkins in Day j	-1	1			
Allocation of soiled napkins in Day j			1	1	1
Allocation of clean napkins in Day j + 1		-1		-1	
Allocation of soiled napkins in Day j + 1					-1
Allocation of clean napkins in Day j + 2			-1		
Allocation of soiled napkins in Day j + 2					
Costs	A	0	B	C	0

(a) Write in full the model for $T = 5$.
(b) Draw the associated network. (*Hint:* add a redundant restriction corresponding to a fictitious node.)

*49 *Multicommodity Network.* Figure 6.27 depicts a transshipment network over which two kinds of resources, Commodity 1 and Commodity 2, can flow. Each commodity may flow along any arc in either direction.

An unlimited supply of Commodity 1 is available at Nodes N_1 and N_2; the final destination for this commodity is Node N_3. An unlimited supply of Commodity 2 is available at Node N_4; the final destination for this commodity is Node N_1. On the arc between Node N_i and Node N_j, there is an upper capacity limit b_{ij} on the *total* amount of flow, that is, on the flow of *both commodities* in *both directions*.

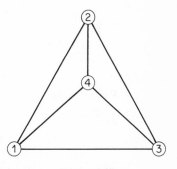

FIGURE 6.27

Each unit of Commodity 1 which reaches its final destination is worth v_1, and each unit of Commodity 2 which reaches its final destination is worth v_2. The problem is to find a feasible flow of commodities through the network having maximum total value. This problem can be viewed in two ways, as explained in each part below.

(a) Let

$x_{ijk} =$ the amount of flow of Commodity k from Node N_i to Node N_j,
$s_{ik} =$ the amount of Commodity k originating at Node N_i,

where in this example you need only s_{11}, s_{21}, s_{42}. Write the flow constraints for each commodity at each node, the flow capacity restrictions along each arc, and the objective function.

(b) An alternative way to analyze the network is to enumerate for both commodities every chain from each source node to each destination node through any possible intermediate node.

Let y_t be the amount of flow along Chain t. Each chain at unit flow level uses up a unit of capacity along the specific arcs comprising the chain; consequently there is a total flow constraint for each arc. Write the flow constraints along each arc and the objective function.

(c) Compare the two formulations.

*50 Construct a small generalized network problem having a unique optimal solution that is not integer-valued.

MIND-EXPANDING EXERCISES

51 A branch of the armed services is considering a long-range manpower training program. To keep the exposition simple, suppose at the beginning of the horizon, there are M_i men in each Skill-Class i, where $i = 1, 2, 3$. The requirements for men of Skill-Class i in Period t are designated as r_{it}. It takes one period to retrain a man from one skill-class to another. The military service may also recruit new men; a new recruit takes two periods to train. There are limits on the number of men that can be taught a particular skill in a period, and on the number of recruits. Discuss how you might formulate a network optimization model to provide an effective recruiting, training, and retraining program.

52 Consider a classical transportation problem. In each part below, further constraints are added. Suggest a way to reformulate the model to yield an enlarged transportation problem in standard format (like that in Fig. 6.2a).

(a) Each activity has a capacity restriction $x_{ij} \leq c_{ij}$.

(b) $\sum_{i=1}^{2} \sum_{j=1}^{n} x_{ij} \leq c.$

(c) $x_{11} + x_{12} + x_{13} \leq c$ where $n > 3$.

53 Consider a capacitated transshipment problem where each $x_{ij} \leq c_{ij}$. Suggest a way to reformulate the model to yield an enlarged transportation problem in a standard format (like that in Fig. 6.2a).

54 Review the case of the Kleen City Police Department in exercise 30 of Chap. 2 and the general formulation in exercise 27 of Chap. 5.

(a) Show that when the number of periods, T, is an even number, the model is equivalent to a network problem. Display the network for the Kleen City case.

(b) Explain why the model is not equivalent to a network problem when the number of periods, T, is an odd number.

55 *Bottleneck Production Line Assignment Problem.* Suppose each of n men is to be assigned to performing one of n jobs on a single production line. Man i assigned to Job j can produce a_{ij} items per unit of time, where $a_{ij} \geq 0$. The problem is to assign the men to maximize the *rate* of production for the *entire* line. The bottleneck is whatever man in the assignment produces at the slowest rate. Hence, the optimization problem is to pick an assignment that makes the bottleneck rate as large as possible.

(a) Verify that a solution to such a problem does not depend on the actual magnitudes of the a_{ij}, but only on their ordering (or ranking).

(b) Given the validity of part (a), rank the a_{ij}, and calculate the associated amount $b_{ij} = 1 - 2^{-m}$, where m is the rank order of a_{ij}. For simplicity of exposition, assume all the a_{ij} are distinct. Thus, the smallest a_{ij} yields a corresponding $b_{ij} = 1 - 2^{-1}$; the next smallest a_{ij} yields a corresponding $b_{ij} = 1 - 2^{-2}$; and the largest a_{ij} yields a corresponding $b_{ij} = 1 - 2^{-n^2}$.

   Show that an optimal solution to the assignment problem using the b_{ij} also solves the bottleneck problem.

*56 Consider the general network optimization formulation in Sec. 6.8. Assume that (1) and (3) are stated as "greater-than-or-equal" inequalities. Show how such a problem can be reformulated as an enlarged network problem in which once again the sum of the T_k equals 0 and the flow conservation constraints are properly stated as equalities.

CONTENTS

CHAPTER 7

Network
Algorithms

7.1 TOPICS IN FOCUS

By now you are familiar with many applications of linear programming, including important examples of optimization within a network. You were advised in Chap. 4 that rarely, if ever, would you solve a linear programming model by hand computations. Nevertheless, it was explained that you need to understand the *fundamental* mathematical ideas in an optimizing algorithm to become a skillful user of the technique. For this reason, you mastered the key concepts of the simplex method. Chapter 5 illustrated the prime significance of the notion of duality in linear models with numerous examples of sensitivity testing. By the end of that chapter you had been introduced to many of the insights provided by linear programming.

Chapter 6 indicated that the size of network models is so large in practice that a naive application of the simplex method would be grossly inefficient and in some instances not even possible, given the capabilities of available computer programs. The examples of Chap. 6 supported this statement, for they demonstrated how a large number of variables can occur in even small-scale network problems. But you were informed that it is possible to exploit the special structure of a network technology so that the required computational effort becomes reasonable.

At this point you may question the rationale for further explaining such linear programming algorithms, rather than proceeding swiftly to other introductory topics in operations research. Do any worthwhile insights remain? If so, why not leave them to the technical specialists? We offer two principal reasons for studying the particular techniques here.

To appreciate the first reason, you must recognize that the future direction of operations research is toward applications of staggering dimensions. High-speed electronic computing machinery, combined with successful operations research experience, has generated a steady growth in corporatewide centralized planning, information, and control systems. A company need not abrogate a policy of decentralized *operating* responsibilities to engage in total enterprise *planning*. To the contrary, such a comprehensive approach provides the very data needed to ensure that a divisionalized management scheme is truly efficient. Integrated planning leads to consistent targets that reflect corporate objectives and at the same time recognize the operating limitations of the component divisions.

To make such large-scale applications a practical reality, the design of efficient methods of solution will receive increasing emphasis. Consequently, you will need a proper perspective on these developments, and therefore you should understand what is meant by *exploiting special structure*. To do so, you must see the concept illustrated, and this chapter serves the purpose by discussing network algorithms.

A second reason for focusing on these techniques relates to their connection with dynamic and multistage models having deterministic linkage, which will be covered in Chaps. 8 through 12. The shortest-route algorithms you study here in general terms can be viewed as the basis for solving such models. Thus the chapter sets the stage for various dynamic applications that you will learn subsequently.

Four notions comprise the foundations from which network optimization algorithms are constructed. One is duality, which is reviewed in the next section. Another is called the *triangularity property* (or tree structure) *of a basis*. This idea is explained in Sec. 7.3. The third concept is the determination of shortest routes, covered in Secs. 7.6 and 7.7. The fourth notion relates to maximizing the total flow in a capacitated transshipment network model with a single source and a single sink. Because the maximum flow model is needed primarily for the more sophisticated algorithms, it is discussed in Appendix I.

7.2 SUMMARY OF THE FUNDAMENTALS

We begin with a discussion of the standard transportation model that you studied in Chap. 6, namely, the linear program:

(1)
$$\text{minimize} \sum_{i=1}^{m} \sum_{j=1}^{n} c_{ij} x_{ij}$$

subject to

(2)
$$\sum_{j=1}^{n} x_{ij} = S_i \quad \text{for } i = 1, 2, \ldots, m \quad \text{(supply)}$$

(3)
$$\sum_{i=1}^{m} x_{ij} = D_j \quad \text{for } j = 1, 2, \ldots, n \quad \text{(demand)}$$

(4)
$$x_{ij} \geq 0 \quad \text{for all } i \text{ and } j,$$

where all the S_i and D_j are nonnegative integers satisfying

(5)
$$\sum_{i=1}^{m} S_i = \sum_{j=1}^{n} D_j \quad \text{(total supply = total demand)}.$$

As you learned in Chap. 6, with some ingenuity you can transform many a network optimization problem into an equivalent transportation model.

Because of the equality between total supply and total demand in (5), and the structure of the supply and demand equations (2) and (3), the model contains a redundancy, in that if any $m + n - 1$ of the restrictions in (2) and (3) are satisfied, then the remaining restriction is satisfied too. [This fact can be demonstrated mathematically by multiplying each restriction in (3) by -1; by then adding any selection of $m + n - 1$ of the restrictions, and by using (5) to simplify the constant on the right-hand side. The resulting composite equation will be identical to the remaining restriction.] Consequently, any one of the supply and demand equations in (2) and (3) can be dropped without harm. The resultant model then consists of $m + n - 1$ *independent* restrictions, and so any basic solution contains this number of variables.

It is straightforward to show that the corresponding dual linear programming problem can be written as

$$(6) \qquad\qquad \text{maximize} \sum_{i=1}^{m} S_i v_i + \sum_{j=1}^{n} D_j w_j$$

subject to

$$(7) \qquad\qquad v_i + w_j \le c_{ij} \quad \text{for all } (i, j),$$

where the v_i and w_j are unrestricted in sign.

▶A consequence of the Dual Theorem and the Theorem of Complementary Slackness in Chap. 5 is that if x_{ij}^* for all (i, j) satisfy (2), (3), and (4), and if v_i^* and w_j^* satisfy (7), and also if

(CS) $x_{ij}^* (v_i^* + w_j^* - c_{ij}) = 0$ for all (i, j) (complementary slackness),

then x_{ij}^* is an optimal solution to the transportation model (1) through (4).

Based on this observation, a variety of network algorithms have been devised. They share the idea that at each iteration the trial values for x_{ij}, v_i, and w_j always satisfy two out of the following three conditions: (i) primal feasibility (2), (3), and (4); (ii) dual feasibility (7), and (iii) complementary slackness (CS). They differ principally in which two of the three conditions are maintained. In these algorithms, the iterations terminate when all three conditions are simultaneously satisfied. For example, the simplex method in Secs. 7.3 and 7.4 maintains (i) and (iii) at every iteration, and stops as soon as (ii) holds.   ◀

7.3 SIMPLEX TECHNIQUE FOR TRANSPORTATION PROBLEMS

Here we apply the simplex method to solve the transportation model. We demonstrate that the special structure of the transportation model substantially reduces the computational burden of the algorithm. This section motivates the method with a brief review of certain essentials from Chaps. 4 and 5, formulates the computational rules, and illustrates them with an example. Then Sec. 7.4 fills in several of the missing details on how to apply the method.

Simplex steps. The standard simplex method instructions are paraphrased below as a starting point of the discussion:

Step 1. Select a set of $m + n - 1$ routes that provides an initial basic feasible solution.

Step 2. Check whether the solution is improved by introducing a nonbasic variable. If so, go to *Step 3*; otherwise stop.

Step 3. Determine which route leaves the basis when the variable that you selected in *Step 2* enters.

Step 4. Adjust the flows of the other basic routes. Return to *Step 2*.

As you will see in the illustration below, all four steps are very easily performed for a transportation problem. Assume the model has been put in a classical transportation problem format and is arrayed in a standard $m \times n$ table, such as Fig. 7.1. The ensuing discussion refers to this table. We begin with a verbal de-

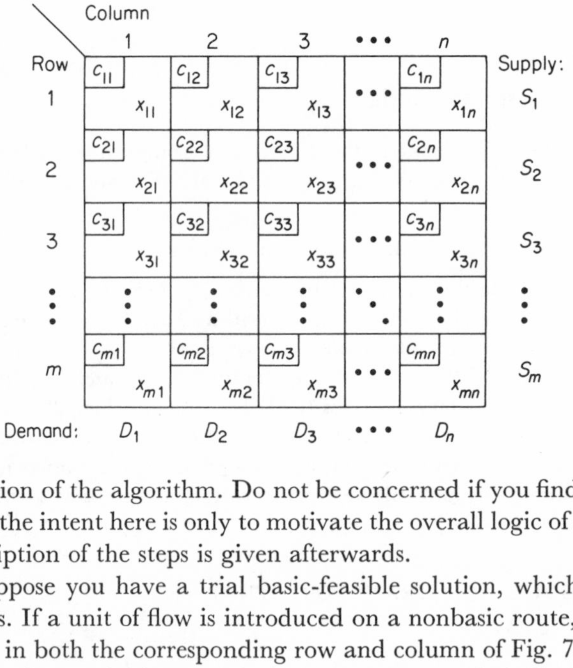

FIGURE 7.1.   Transportation Tableau.

scription of the algorithm. Do not be concerned if you find certain details unclear, since the intent here is only to motivate the overall logic of the approach. A careful description of the steps is given afterwards.

Suppose you have a trial basic-feasible solution, which consists of $m + n - 1$ routes. If a unit of flow is introduced on a nonbasic route, then to maintain feasibility in both the corresponding row and column of Fig. 7.1, a unit must be withdrawn from a basic route in the same row, and similarly in the same column. But these two alterations in turn lead to *unit* changes in the flows of other basic variables. For reasons that will be apparent shortly, each nonbasic variable gives rise to a unique *pattern* of alterations of the basic variables.

Therefore you can evaluate the resultant change as follows: take the total increase in cost from adding a unit of flow to both the new route and the appropriate basic routes, and deduct the total decrease in cost from removing a unit of flow on the other basic routes in the associated unique pattern of alterations. If the net amount shows an improvement and the new route is selected to enter the solution, then the pattern of alterations also indicates how many units of flow can be placed on the new route. Specifically, the various flows are increased and decreased according to the pattern until that level is reached where a basic variable is reduced to zero and thereby dropped from the basis.

If the procedure for testing whether a nonbasic route should enter a trial solution were really as tedious as the above description suggests, this approach would be a marginal improvement at best on the way the simplex algorithm was applied in Chap. 4. You can evaluate a nonbasic route much more simply, however, by employing an insight from duality and exploiting the structure of the network.

You learned in Sec. 5.5, which discussed the solution of the dual problem, that for a given basic solution, the value from introducing a unit of a nonbasic variable is the difference between the left- and right-hand sides of the dual restriction for this variable. Thus the key idea is to solve the $m + n - 1$ dual restrictions corresponding to the current basis:

(1) $$v_i + w_j = c_{ij} \quad \text{for each basic variable } x_{ij},$$

and then with these values to evaluate

(2) $$v_i + w_j - c_{ij} \quad \text{for } x_{ij}, \text{ a nonbasic variable.}$$

The quantities in (2) correspond to the coefficients in Row 0 of the simplex method. When (2) is positive, the nonbasic variable x_{ij} is a candidate to enter the next basis. If all such quantities are nonpositive, implying dual as well as primal feasibility, the current basic solution is optimal.

Algorithm illustrated. Consider the transportation problem shown in Fig. 7.2. (Jot down on a piece of paper your guess of an optimal solution; calculate its objective-function value.)

Row \ Column	1	2	3	4	Supply:
1	2	3	11	7	6
2	1	0	6	1	1
3	5	8	15	9	10
Demand:	7	5	3	2	

FIGURE 7.2. Transportation Example.

Step 1 of the algorithm asks for a starting trial basic solution, which contains $m + n - 1 = 3 + 4 - 1 = 6$ active routes. Suppose you allocate the supply of

6 units available in Row 1 to the cheapest route (1, 1). This exhausts the supply and leaves one more unit of demand to be filled in Column 1. Similarly, allocate the supply of 1 unit in Row 2 to the cheapest route (2, 2). The supply of 10 in Row 3 is then routed to meet all the remaining unfilled demand. The result, displayed in Fig. 7.3, has an objective-function value of 112. (Was your guessed solu-

Row \ Column	1	2	3	4	Supply:
1	[2] 6	[3]	[11]	[7]	6
2	[1]	[0] 1	[6]	[1]	1
3	[5] 1	[8] 4	[15] 3	[9] 2	10
Demand:	7	5	3	2	

Total Cost = 2 x 6 + 0 x 1 + 5 x 1 + 8 x 4 + 15 x 3 + 9 x 2 = 112

FIGURE 7.3. Initial Basic Solution.

tion any better? The advanced material below discusses a method for selecting a good initial solution.)

Step 2 calls for an evaluation of each unused route to see whether a unit of flow on the route improves the objective function. Consider route (1, 2). As you can see from Fig. 7.3, one unit allocated to this route *must* be withdrawn from the flow on route (1, 1). Then to meet the demand requirement in Column 1, another unit must be shipped on route (3, 1), and this unit may be removed from route (3, 2). The pattern of alterations is shown in Fig. 7.4.

Row \ Column	1	2	3	4	Supply:
1	[2] 6−1	[3] +1	[11]	[7]	6
2	[1]	[0] 1	[6]	[1]	1
3	[5] 1+1	[8] 4−1	[15] 3	[9] 2	10
Demand:	7	5	3	2	

Improvement Potential = Total Decrease − Total Increase
= (2 + 8) − (3 + 5) = 2 per unit

FIGURE 7.4. Pattern of Alterations for One Unit of Flow on Route (1, 2).

Will introducing a unit of flow on (1, 2) reduce the value of the objective function? A saving of 10 (= 2 + 8) results from reducing a unit of flow on routes (1, 1) and (3, 2). However, there is a partially offsetting increase in cost of 8 (= 3 + 5) due to adding a unit of flow on routes (1, 2) and (3, 1). The net improvement is 2 (= 10 − 8).

By a similar analysis, you can obtain the improvement potentials for the other nonbasic routes, as summarized in Fig. 7.5. Each of these is the value that would

Row \ Column	1	2	3	4
1	2 / O	3 / 2	11 / 1	7 / −1
2	1 / −4	0 / O	6 / 1	1 / O
3	5 / O	8 / O	15 / O	9 / O

FIGURE 7.5. Improvement Potentials for Nonbasic Routes—Initial Solution.

Note: The symbol O appears for current basic routes.

appear as the coefficient of the associated x_{ij} in Row 0 of the simplex method. To check your understanding of how these potentials might be calculated, determine the pattern of alterations for a unit of flow added to routes (1, 3) and (2, 1), and determine the cost of the implied change in the objective function.

Now you will see it is unnecessary to obtain the specific pattern of alterations for each nonbasic route in order to find its improvement potential. You can arrive quickly at the same result by evaluating the dual variables, and then by looking at the difference between the left- and right-hand sides of the dual constraints associated with the nonbasic routes. The network structure makes this process easy. A short-cut method that uses *only* an $m \times n$ table containing c_{ij} (such as Fig. 7.5) will be described. But in order to clarify what is actually going on, the mathematical relations involved in the short-cut will be explained first.

The system of linear equalities that yields trial values for the dual variables was shown in (1) above. Applied to the initial solution, Fig. 7.3, the six dual equalities for the basic routes are

$$
(3)\qquad
\begin{array}{lllllll}
v_1 & & & + w_1 & & & = 2 \quad \text{route } (1, 1)\\
& v_2 & & & + w_2 & & = 0 \quad \text{route } (2, 2)\\
& & v_3 & + w_1 & & & = 5 \quad \text{route } (3, 1)\\
& & v_3 & & + w_2 & & = 8 \quad \text{route } (3, 2)\\
& & v_3 & & & + w_3 & = 15 \quad \text{route } (3, 3)\\
& & v_3 & & & + w_4 & = 9 \quad \text{route } (3, 4).
\end{array}
$$

Observe that in (3) there are six equations and seven unknowns. To obtain a solution, one of the variables must be selected and given an arbitrary value.

You are at liberty to choose any variable and assign it any convenient value. Choose v_3 since it appears in four of the relations, and let $v_3 = 0$ for convenience. The reason (3) has an "extra" variable is the redundancy in the $m + n = 7$ supply-and-demand restrictions. Giving an arbitrary value to v_3 is equivalent to dropping the Row 3 supply equation in order to remove the redundancy in the $m + n$ relations.

With $v_3 = 0$, notice how remarkably simple it is to solve for the remaining variables. You can proceed as follows:

$$
\begin{aligned}
v_3 &= 0 \quad \text{(arbitrary)} \\
w_4 &= 9 - v_3 = 9 \\
w_3 &= 15 - v_3 = 15 \\
w_2 &= 8 - v_3 = 8 \\
w_1 &= 5 - v_3 = 5 \\
v_2 &= 0 - w_2 = 0 - (8 - v_3) = -8 \\
v_1 &= 2 - w_1 = 2 - (5 - v_3) = -3.
\end{aligned}
$$

(4)

Thus, by knowing only the values of the previously found variables, you can obtain each dual variable one by one. *In a network technology, you will always be able to proceed in such a sequential fashion.*

The mathematical term **triangularity** is used to describe a structure that admits this sequential approach of finding solution values. You can appreciate the appropriateness of the term by looking at the structure of (3). When v_3 vanishes (that is, equals 0), the array has a triangular appearance. We say that a system of m linear equations in m unknowns has a **triangular structure** if, possibly after rearranging the order of the variables and the equations, the variable that appears first in equation k is also the kth unknown, and it does not appear in any equation beyond the kth.

The triangularity property holds for the system of dual equations (3) after you select *any* dual variable and assign it an arbitrary value. However, to *see at a glance* that the system is triangular, you would have to rearrange the sequence of variables and equations. For example, if you choose to let v_1 vanish, then the variables can be arranged in the sequence $v_2, w_2, w_3, w_4, v_3, w_1$, and the routes in the sequence (2, 2), (3, 2), (3, 3), (3, 4), (3, 1), and (1, 1) to *exhibit* the triangular structure. Write the system in this form to verify its triangular appearance.

Also note in (4) that if v_3 is set at a value other than 0, then each v_i increases and each w_j decreases by this amount. Thus any sum $(v_i + w_j)$ remains unchanged, as does the test quantity $v_i + w_j - c_{ij}$.

You would suspect from your knowledge about duality that a similar triangularity property also holds for the equations that determine values of the basic x_{ij}. To see this, write the conservation of flow constraints, omitting all nonbasic routes and dropping the redundant supply equation for Row 3 (corresponding to the selection of v_3):

$$
(5)\quad
\begin{aligned}
x_{11} &&&&&&& = 6 \quad \text{Row 1}\\
&& x_{22} &&&&& = 1 \quad \text{Row 2}\\
x_{11} && &+\, x_{31} &&&& = 7 \quad \text{Column 1}\\
&& x_{22} && +\, x_{32} &&& = 5 \quad \text{Column 2}\\
&&&&& x_{33} && = 3 \quad \text{Column 3}\\
&&&&&& x_{34} & = 2 \quad \text{Column 4.}
\end{aligned}
$$

Notice that the row of coefficients in the kth equation of (5) are the column of coefficients for the kth variable in (3) (not counting v_3). Whereas (3) is *upper* triangular in shape, the system (5) is *lower* triangular and can be solved quickly starting with variable x_{11}. [How can you rearrange the variables and restrictions in (5) so that the system has the **triangular property** as defined above?]

You are now ready to determine the improvement potential for each nonbasic route from the formula

$$
(6)\qquad\qquad v_i + w_j - c_{ij}.
$$

Using the values for the dual variables that you found in (4), you can obtain

$$
(7)\quad
\begin{aligned}
-3 + 8 - 3 &= 2 & \text{route } (1,2)\\
-3 + 15 - 11 &= 1 & \text{route } (1,3)\\
-3 + 9 - 7 &= -1 & \text{route } (1,4)\\
-8 + 5 - 1 &= -4 & \text{route } (2,1)\\
-8 + 15 - 6 &= 1 & \text{route } (2,3)\\
-8 + 9 - 1 &= 0 & \text{route } (2,4).
\end{aligned}
$$

Each positive number signifies a possibility for reducing the value of the objective function. Thus three routes offer an improvement, and you should select route $(1,2)$ because it is the one with the greatest potential. This is the same rule as *Simplex Criterion I* (Minimization).

Step 3 involves the determination of how much flow to allocate to route $(1,2)$. The pattern of alterations of the basic variables in the initial solution was already

Row \ Column	1	2	3	4	Supply:
1	2	4			6
2		1			1
3	5		3	2	10
Demand:	7	5	3	2	

FIGURE 7.6. Second Basic Solution.

Total Cost = Previous Total Cost − Total Improvement
= 112 − 2(4) = 104

established for this route in Fig. 7.4. Recall that the flows on routes (1, 1) and (3, 2) decrease, and these amounts are presently 6 and 4. Consequently, the largest possible increase of flow on route (1, 2) is 4, causing route (3, 2) to be dropped from the new basis. This calculation is the same as *Simplex Criterion II*.

Step 4 performs the implied rerouting of flow, giving the second-trial basic solution in Fig. 7.6, with an objective-function value of 104.

Iteration 2. Next return to *Step 2* to check whether this solution is optimal or whether a further improvement is possible. The dual equalities for the new basis are

(8)
$$
\begin{aligned}
v_2 + w_2 &= 0 \quad \text{route } (2, 2) \\
w_2 + v_1 &= 3 \quad \text{route } (1, 2) \\
v_1 + w_1 &= 2 \quad \text{route } (1, 1) \\
w_1 + v_3 &= 5 \quad \text{route } (3, 1) \\
w_3 + v_3 &= 15 \quad \text{route } (3, 3) \\
w_4 + v_3 &= 9 \quad \text{route } (3, 4).
\end{aligned}
$$

The variables and equations in (8) have been sequenced so that the triangularity of the system is apparent when you let $v_3 = 0$. Check that the solution values are

(9)
$$
\begin{aligned}
v_3 &= 0 \\
w_4 &= 9 \\
w_3 &= 15 \\
w_1 &= 5 \\
v_1 &= 2 - w_1 = -3 \\
w_2 &= 3 - v_1 = 6 \\
v_2 &= 0 - w_2 = -6,
\end{aligned}
$$

and the improvement potentials are

(10)
$$
\begin{aligned}
-3 + 15 - 11 &= 1 \quad \text{route } (1, 3) \\
-3 + 9 - 7 &= -1 \quad \text{route } (1, 4) \\
-6 + 5 - 1 &= -2 \quad \text{route } (2, 1) \\
-6 + 15 - 6 &= 3 \quad \text{route } (2, 3) \\
-6 + 9 - 1 &= 2 \quad \text{route } (2, 4) \\
0 + 6 - 8 &= -2 \quad \text{route } (3, 2).
\end{aligned}
$$

Consequently, route (2, 3) enters the next solution. The corresponding pattern of alterations is shown in Fig. 7.7. Notice that all but one of the previous basic routes are altered. (It is possible to have a case in which every basic route is revised.) Flow decreases on routes (2, 2), (1, 1), and (3, 3). Route (2, 2) drops from the basis first, when the total change is one unit of flow. In this instance,

Row \ Column	1	2	3	4	Supply:
1	2 − 1	4 + 1			6
2		1 − 1	+ 1		1
3	5 + 1		3 − 1	2	10
Demand:	7	5	3	2	

Total Cost = 104 − 1(3) = 101

FIGURE 7.7. Pattern of Alterations for One Unit of Flow on Route (2, 3)—Third Solution.

therefore, the quantities in Fig. 7.7 also represent the flows for the third-trial basis.

Iteration 3. A simplified procedure. Now that you have seen the method to develop the improvement potentials in *Step 2* of the algorithm, it is no longer necessary to write the full dual equations for the basic variables. A shortcut is to fill in an $m \times n$ table with the potentials. Start by drawing a table with the structure appearing in Fig. 7.8. Insert all the c_{ij} in the small upper left boxes and

Row \ Column	1	2	3	4	v_i
1	[2] $\underline{0}$	[3] $\underline{0}$	[11] 1	[7] −1	−3
2	[1] −5	[0] −3	[6] $\underline{0}$	[1] −1	−9
3	[5] $\underline{0}$	[8] −2	[15] $\underline{0}$	[9] $\underline{0}$	0
w_j	5	6	15	9	

FIGURE 7.8. Improvement Potentials for Nonbasic Routes—Third Solution.

the symbol $\underline{0}$ for each basic route in the current solution. Leave blank all the other table entries, including the v_i and w_j.

Next select any v_i or w_j and give it an arbitrary value. Suppose, as previously, you let $v_3 = 0$. Then enter the selected value at the edge of the corresponding row or column (Row 3 in the example). Look across the row or column for basic routes. In Row 3, the routes (3, 4), (3, 3), and (3, 1) qualify. The dual equation for each of these routes permits you to determine another dual variable. For the example, $w_4 = 9$, $w_3 = 15$, and $w_1 = 5$. Write these values along the edge of the table.

Continue until all dual variables are evaluated. For the illustration, you can proceed in the sequence $v_2 = -9$, $v_1 = -3$, and $w_2 = 6$.

Lastly, for each nonbasic route calculate $(v_i + w_j - c_{ij})$ and enter the result in the table. The final array appears as Fig. 7.8, where you can see that only route (1, 3) shows a potential improvement.

To test your understanding of the steps, develop the pattern of alterations when route $(1, 3)$ is introduced. Verify that the largest amount of possible flow on route $(1, 3)$ is one unit, and the new flows are those in Fig. 7.9.

Column	1	2	3	4	Supply:
Row 1		5	1		6
2			1		1
3	7		1	2	10
Demand:	7	5	3	2	

Total Cost $= 101 - 1(1) = 100$

FIGURE 7.9. Fourth and Optimal Basic Solution.

Iteration 4. Perform the calculations to test for optimality of the solution, and check your answers with the results in Fig. 7.10. How close to optimal was the solution you guessed at the beginning of the illustration?

Column	1	2	3	4	v_i
Row 1	−1	$\underline{0}$	$\underline{0}$	−2	−4
2	−5	−2	$\underline{0}$	−1	−9
3	$\underline{0}$	−1	$\underline{0}$	$\underline{0}$	0
w_j	5	7	15	9	

FIGURE 7.10. Improvement Potentials for Optimal Solution.

▶ If the original problem in fact is a transshipment model, then the resultant expanded transshipment tables have both a Row i_k and Column j_k for each transshipment Node k. Accordingly, there will be two dual variables v_{i_k} and w_{j_k}. Since the buffer amount B is sufficiently large, each $x_{i_k j_k}$ is in every trial basis. Consequently $v_{i_k} + w_{j_k} = 0$, so that v_{i_k} and w_{j_k} will differ only in sign for these rows and columns. ◀

7.4 FURTHER COMMENTS ON THE SIMPLEX METHOD

A few supplementary remarks are appropriate to conclude the description of the simplex method as applied to transportation problems.

Although we have referred to the algorithm as "the simplex method applied to transportation problems" and have used terminology that is accordingly consistent, we really have not explicitly demonstrated the equivalence. We suggest that you take our word for it, unless you have a burning interest in this technical question. In that case, you can read the discussion in the advanced material below.

Special structure. The text has mentioned repeatedly that transportation problems have a special structure to be exploited. The important proposition is the theorem below.

TRIANGULARITY THEOREM: After dropping any one of the equations in the redundant system of restrictions for the transportation problem, every basis has the triangularity property. Hence, since all the coefficients in the constraints are 1, no multiplication or division is needed to sequentially determine the values of any set of basic variables; only addition and subtraction are required.

Thus when the simplex method is applied to a transportation problem, no division or multiplication is required for *Steps 3* and *4*. The technique was explained in a way that recognized and consequently exploited this fact.

Optimality. The following line of reasoning demonstrates that when the algorithm terminates, an optimal solution in fact has been obtained.

First, observe that since a solution for a transportation model must allocate the *entire* supply S_i among the routes in Row i, you can subtract the *same* constant from each c_{ij} in that row without affecting which solutions are optimal. Similarly, you can diminish each c_{ij} in Column j. In this subtraction process, let the final value of v_i be the constant used for Row i and the final value of w_j the constant for Column j. Then suppose you replace the original objective-function values c_{ij} by the *new* values $[c_{ij} - (v_i + w_j)]$. As we have reasoned, the model with the original c_{ij} and the model with the *new* coefficients have the very same optimal solutions.

Second, recall that, at termination of the simplex algorithm,

$$(1) \qquad 0 \leq c_{ij} - (v_i + w_j) \quad \text{for all } (i,j) \text{ in network,}$$

since the quantities in (1) are merely the negative of the entries in the final improvement potential table. Therefore, the minimum value of the *new* objective function cannot be smaller than 0, because the new objective-function coefficients are all nonnegative.

Finally, notice that since *equality* holds in (1) for the basic routes, the terminating solution uses only routes where the *new* cost coefficients are 0. Consequently no better solution can exist.

If the improvement potential for a nonbasic route has zero value, then an alternative optimal solution can be found by introducing the route into the basis according to *Steps 3* and *4*.

Integrality. Several times previously, we emphasized that if the transportation model is further restricted by the condition that the variables must be integers,

$$(2) \qquad \text{every } x_{ij} = 0, 1, 2, \ldots,$$

the optimal value of objective function is not increased. The following terse argument demonstrates the assertion: the simplex algorithm always finds an optimal solution to a linear programming model, and when the technique is applied to a *transportation* problem, the method looks *only* at solutions satisfying (2).

The underpinnings of the above argument are

(i) There exists an optimal basic solution, since the transportation model has a finite optimal solution.

(ii) Every basis is triangular.

(iii) Each technological coefficient is either 1 or -1.

The combined effect of these three points is that only additions and subtractions of integers occur in the sequential determination of each basic x_{ij}.

Completeness. In *Step 2*, if more than one route shows the greatest potential improvement, you can select one arbitrarily. In *Step 3*, if the flow on more than one basic route becomes zero when the new route enters, then the new basis will be degenerate. Only one route should be dropped, and the others should remain in the new basis at zero level. For practical purposes, a particular "tie-breaking" rule to select the route that drops is of no consequence. However, as you already saw in Chap. 4, the degeneracy condition must be dealt with to prove that the method always terminates in a finite number of trials.

Domain of applicability. The method applies to all network problems that can be converted to a transportation model format. Notice that the c_{ij} do not have to be nonnegative to perform the steps.

▶ **Convergence.** By the very nature of the transportation problem, an optimal solution must have a finite objective-function value. If the trial solutions make a strict improvement at each iteration, then the method must converge, since the objective function is reduced by at least one unit each time. But when degeneracy occurs, the objective function can stall for several iterations, and the possibility of cycling arises.

It is always possible to rescale the units and slightly perturb the supplies and demands, so that degeneracy never arises during the calculations. The following scheme can be shown to achieve this result. Let the new available supplies be nS_i, for $i = 1, 2, \ldots, m - 1$, and $nS_m + n$, and the new requirements be $nD_j + 1$, for $j = 1, 2, \ldots, n$. Then the objective function will improve at every iteration. The final answer is scaled back to the original units by dividing each x_{ij} by n and rounding so as to preserve the supply and demand restrictions, which always can be done. Since the rounded answer is feasible and uses the same basic routes, it remains optimal.

Relation to the standard simplex method. Figure 7.11 depicts a simplex tableau tracing the iterations. It employs the condensed format introduced in Fig. 4.11 on p. 120. The redundancy has been removed.

Notice at every iteration that each coefficient in Rows 1 through 6 is either $+1$ or -1, a condition that arises because of the network structure. The pattern of coefficients in each column corresponds to the pattern of alterations occurring when the nonbasic

Iteration	Basis	Values	x_{12}	x_{13}	x_{14}	x_{21}	x_{23}	x_{24}	Row
1	x_0	112	2	1	−1	−4	1		0
	x_{11}	6	1	1	1				1
	x_{22}	1				1	1	1	2
	x_{31}	1	−1	−1	−1	1			3
	x_{32}	4	[1]			−1	−1	−1	4
	x_{33}	3		1			1		5
	x_{34}	2			1			1	6

Iteration	Basis	Values	x_{32}	x_{13}	x_{14}	x_{21}	x_{23}	x_{24}	Row
2	x_0	104	−2	1	−1	−2	3	2	0
	x_{11}	2	−1	1	1	1	1	1	1
	x_{22}	1				1	[1]	1	2
	x_{31}	5	1	−1	−1		−1	−1	3
	x_{12}	4	1			−1	−1	−1	4
	x_{33}	3		1			1		5
	x_{34}	2			1			1	6

Iteration	Basis	Values	x_{32}	x_{13}	x_{14}	x_{21}	x_{22}	x_{24}	Row
3	x_0	101	−2	1	−1	−5	−3	−1	0
	x_{11}	1	−1	[1]	1		−1		1
	x_{23}	1				1	1	1	2
	x_{31}	6	1	−1	−1	1	1		3
	x_{12}	5	1				1		4
	x_{33}	2		1		−1	−1	−1	5
	x_{34}	2			1			1	6

Iteration	Basis	Values	x_{32}	x_{11}	x_{14}	x_{21}	x_{22}	x_{24}	Row
4	x_0	100	−1	−1	−2	−5	−2	−1	0
	x_{13}	1	−1	1	1		−1		1
	x_{23}	1				1	1	1	2
	x_{31}	7		1		1			3
	x_{12}	5	1				1		4
	x_{33}	1	1	−1	−1	−1		−1	5
	x_{34}	2			1			1	6

FIGURE 7.11. Simplex Tableau.

route is introduced. You can see that pivoting requires only additions and subtractions for this structure.

Capacitated transportation problem. When capacity constraints $x_{ij} \leq u_{ij}$ are also imposed, the upper-bounded-variables technique of Sec. 5.10 is easily specialized to a network structure. Assume each u_{ij} is an integer.

In *Step 3*, suppose flow on a nonbasic route is to be increased. Then to determine the largest amount of flow possible, take into consideration the capacity constraints on the new route and those current basic routes with *increased* flow. If any one of these bounds is reached *before* the flow on some other basic route becomes zero, then put the associated flow at its capacity level and let it be the variable left out of the basis in the next trial solution.

In *Step 2*, also consider each nonbasic route with flow at its capacity level. If the improvement potential is negative, then the route is a candidate for *reduced* flow. If it is selected, the procedure in *Step 3* is reversed to reflect a diminution of flow. A trial solution is optimal when every nonbasic route is at zero flow if it has a nonpositive improvement potential and at capacity flow if it has a positive improvement potential.

The bounded-variables network algorithm yields optimal values for x_{ij} that are also integers. We caution that the values of u_{ij} may be such that there is no feasible solution, even though the total supply equals total demand. Further, some care must be exercised in selecting an initial trial solution, in order that it contain a basic set of routes with flow not exceeding the stated capacity constraints. This is not really hard to do, but the details go beyond the intended coverage of this text.

Initial basic solution. In selecting a starting solution for *Step 1*, you must be careful to pick a basis, that is, $m + n - 1$ routes with flows *uniquely* determined by the S_i and D_j. It is usually worthwhile to perform a preliminary analysis of the c_{ij} to assist in selecting a good initial basis.

In the discussion of optimality, you learned that a constant may be subtracted from every c_{ij} in a row or in a column without affecting the selection of an optimal solution. Furthermore, when the optimal dual variables v_i and w_j are the constants for Row i and Column j, the revised costs are nonnegative and flow occurs only on zero-cost routes. These observations motivate the suggestion:

(i) Subtract the smallest c_{ij} in Row i from every cost coefficient in that row so as to form a new array.

(ii) Subtract the smallest of the numbers in Column j of the new array from every other entry in that column so as to yield a **relative cost** table.

(iii) Select an initial basis with reference to the relative costs.

The procedure is illustrated for the example in Figs. 7.12 and 7.13. To ensure that you pick a basis, follow the procedure:

(i) Select route (i, j) from those permitted and let the flow x_{ij} be the smaller of the amounts available, $a_i \geq 0$, and required, $r_j \geq 0$. For the first route chosen, $a_i = S_i$ and $r_j = D_j$.

(ii) If $a_i < r_j$, check off Row i and permit no more routes to be selected in Row i. Decrease by x_{ij} the amount required in Column j, and let r_j now be this new amount. Return to *Instruction (i)*.

(iii) If $a_i > r_j$, check off Column j and permit no more routes to be selected in

Row \ Column	1	2	3	4	Subtract
1	0	1	9	5	$2 (= c_{11})$
2	1	0	6	1	$0 (= c_{22})$
3	0	3	10	4	$5 (= c_{31})$

FIGURE 7.12. Row Reduction Calculation.

Row \ Column	1	2	3	4
1	0	1	3	4
2	1	0	0	0
3	0	3	4	3
Subtract	0	0	6	1

FIGURE 7.13. Column Reduction Calculation and Relative Costs.

Column j. Decrease by x_{ij} the amount available in Row i, and let a_i now be this new amount. Return to *Instruction* (i).

(iv) If $a_i = r_j$, stop if $m + n - 1$ routes have been selected. Otherwise, perform either *Instruction* (ii) or (iii), but not both. However, if *only* Row i remains, perform *Instruction* (iii), or if *only* Column j remains, perform *Instruction* (ii). The initial solution will be degenerate.

The procedure is illustrated in Figs. 7.14 and 7.15 by an example having a degenerate initial solution. To check your understanding, perform the operations indicated in Fig. 7.14 on the table in Fig. 7.15.

Instruction	Calculation
i	Pick $x_{11} = r_1 = S_1 = 1$
iii	Check Column 1. Set $a_1 = 7 - 1 = 6$
i	Pick $x_{12} = a_1 = r_1 = 6$
iv (ii)	Check Row 1. Set $r_2 = 6 - 6 = 0$
i	Pick $x_{23} = a_2 = r_3 = 2$
iv (ii)	Check Row 2. Set $r_3 = 2 - 2 = 0$
i	Pick $x_{32} = r_2 = 0$
iv (iii)	Check Column 2. Set $a_3 = 3 - 0 = 3$
i	Pick $x_{34} = a_3 = r_4 = 3$
iv (iii)	Check Column 4. Set $a_3 = 3 - 3 = 0$
i	Pick $x_{33} = a_3 = 0$
iv	Stop ($p - 1 = 3 + 4 - 1 = 6$ routes)

FIGURE 7.14. Selection of an Initial Basis.

Row \ Column	1	2	3	4	Supply:
1	1	6			7
2			2		2
3		0	0	3	3
Demand:	1	6	2	3	

FIGURE 7.15. Initial Basis.

General network. The two important theoretical properties of the triangularity of all basic solutions and the existence of an optimal solution that is also integer-valued are valid for a fairly general network model:

$$(i) \qquad\qquad \text{minimize} \sum_{\substack{(i,j) \text{ in} \\ \text{network}}} c_{ij} x_{ij}$$

subject to

$$(ii) \qquad \sum_{\substack{(k,j) \text{ in} \\ \text{network}}} x_{kj} - \sum_{\substack{(i,k) \text{ in} \\ \text{network}}} x_{ik} = T_k \quad \text{for } k = 1, 2, \ldots, p \quad \text{(node balance equations)}$$

$$(iii) \qquad\qquad x_{ij} \geq 0 \quad \text{for all } (i,j) \text{ in network,}$$

where

$$(iv) \qquad\qquad \sum_{k=1}^{p} T_k = 0 \quad \text{and each } T_k \text{ is integer-valued.}$$

Given (iv), there is a redundancy in restrictions (ii), but by dropping any one of the balance equations in (ii) you obtain a set of $p - 1$ independent restrictions. It can be shown that every basis for such a set of $p - 1$ restrictions has the triangularity property. Hence, since all the coefficients in (ii) are either $+1$ or -1, the corresponding solution is integer-valued.

The associated dual problem is

$$(v) \qquad\qquad \text{maximize} \sum_{k=1}^{p} T_k y_k$$

subject to

$$(vi) \qquad\qquad y_i - y_j \leq c_{ij} \quad \text{for all } (i,j) \text{ in network} \qquad \text{(arc constraints),}$$

where each y_k is unrestricted in sign. Again because of triangularity, given any basic solution, the associated values for the dual variables can be found sequentially (after selecting a variable arbitrarily and assigning it a value).

Finally, we point out that given $p - 1$ independent restrictions from (ii), a set of $p - 1$ *basic* variables corresponds to a tree (Sec. 6.8) in the network representation of (ii). The simplex method applied to this network can be interpreted as follows. Select a beneficial arc to add to a trial solution, which destroys the associated tree structure by creating a loop. Subsequently, allocate as much flow as possible to the new arc by rerouting flow on the other arcs of the loop. This maximal allocation in turn causes one of the other arcs on the loop to drop, thereby restoring the tree structure. ◀

7.5 SENSITIVITY TESTING

You found in Chap. 5 that the notion of duality is central in examining how a change in model formulation affects an optimal solution. We review a few of these ideas here in the context of the transportation problem.

Objective function. Given the value for v_i and w_j at the final iteration, the test quantities $(v_i + w_j - c_{ij})$ are all nonpositive. This implies that each c_{ij} can be as small as $(v_i + w_j)$ and the current solution remains optimal. In the numerical example of Sec. 7.3, we had at the final iteration that $v_1 = -4$ and $w_4 = 9$, as you can see in Fig. 7.10. Therefore the coefficient c_{14}, which currently is 7, can be as small as 5 $(= -4 + 9)$, and the present solution remains optimal; in other words, the test quantity -2 $(= -4 + 9 - 7)$ represents the largest decrease in c_{14} that leaves the current solution optimal.

Supplies and demands. Assume you have a nondegenerate optimal solution, that is, assume every basic route has at least one unit of flow. Suppose S_p is increased by a unit, so that an oversupply is created. It can be shown that the new optimal allocation will assign the *excess* to that source k that has maximum (v_i), and that $[v_p - \text{maximum } (v_i)] \leq 0$ will be added to the objective function.

For example, in Fig. 7.10, maximum $(v_i) = v_3 = 0$. So if $S_1 = 7$, then the flow on route $(1, 3)$ will increase by a unit and the flow on route $(3, 3)$ will decrease a unit, leaving the oversupply in Row 3. The net reduction in cost is -4 $(= 11 - 15 = v_1)$, assuming the oversupply is costless. Verify that if, instead, $S_2 = 2$, the flows can be altered so that the net reduction in cost is $v_2 = -9$.

Still assuming the optimal solution is nondegenerate, suppose next that there is a unit increase in both S_i and D_j. It can be shown that $v_i + w_j$ will be added to the objective function, as would be suggested by the dual objective function.

For example, suppose $S_2 = 2$ and $D_1 = 8$. Then the objective function becomes $[100 + (-9 + 5) = 96]$. At first it seems surprising that *adding* one more unit of flow to a transportation schedule can actually *reduce* total cost; but this happens because the cost of a unit increase in flow on routes $(3, 1)$ and $(2, 3)$ is offset by the cost of a unit decrease in flow on route $(3, 3)$. The net reduction in cost is -4 $(= 5 + 6 - 15)$. The pattern of alterations for the basic variables is established by considering what would happen if a unit of flow were to be *removed* from route (i, j). Verify that if, instead, $S_1 = 7$ and $D_4 = 3$, the flows can be altered so that 5 $(= v_1 + w_4)$ is the net increase in the objective function.

7.6 SHORTEST ROUTE FOR A GENERAL NETWORK

In Sec. 6.5 you saw several examples of optimization models that proved equivalent to finding a shortest route in a network. Review the general discussion on pp. 177–180 so that you recall the context and assumptions of the problem.

Here you will study a method of solution which, like the simplex algorithm, relies heavily on duality.

Suppose a network contains several routes from the Source Node s to the Sink Node r, and you want to obtain a shortest one. The mathematical model for the problem was given in Sec. 6.5. What we need now is a statement of the dual problem:

(1) $$\text{maximize} \quad -y_r + y_s$$

subject to

(2) $$y_i - y_j \leq c_{ij} \quad \text{for all } (i, j) \text{ in network},$$

where each y_k is unrestricted in sign.

Method. The algorithm proceeds to solve for the dual variables:

(i) Start by letting $y_r = 0$, and all other $y_k = \infty$.
(ii) If there continues to be any arc (i, j) such that $y_i > c_{ij} + y_j$, then change the corresponding value of y_i to $c_{ij} + y_j$. Otherwise stop.

Thus the values of y_k are successively decreased until (2) holds for *all* arcs. The technique will converge in a finite number of calculations, provided that the sum of c_{ij} around every loop of the network is nonnegative. [The speed of convergence can be accelerated by using a systematic approach in applying Instruction (ii). But this topic is too technical to be discussed here.]

The method actually obtains a shortest route to the Terminal Node r from every other node. Specifically, to find the path for *any* Node s, determine the arc (s, t) for which $y_s - y_t = c_{st}$. The algorithm guarantees there is at least one such arc. Similarly, at Node t find the arc (t, u) such that $y_t - y_u = c_{tu}$. Continue in the same fashion to trace a route that eventually leads to Node r. Notice that the value of y_k is the length of a shortest route from Node k to Node r. Although each y_k is unique, there can be more than one shortest path from Node k.

Example. The technique is illustrated for the example in Fig. 7.16, which is the same network structure as Fig. 6.8. You seek the shortest paths to Node 1 from every other node. The procedure is best followed by making the calculations directly on the network diagram. Copy Fig. 7.16 on a piece of paper, or write lightly with pencil on the page.

Start by putting a 0 adjacent to Node 1 and the symbol ∞ next to all the other nodes. There are many ways to proceed—here is one:

$$c_{41} + y_1 = 2 + 0 < \infty = y_4, \quad \text{therefore let } y_4 = 2$$
$$c_{34} + y_4 = 1 + 2 < \infty = y_3, \quad \text{therefore let } y_3 = 3$$
$$c_{64} + y_4 = 5 + 2 < \infty = y_6, \quad \text{therefore let } y_6 = 7$$
$$c_{54} + y_4 = 1 + 2 < \infty = y_5, \quad \text{therefore let } y_5 = 3$$
(3) $$c_{65} + y_5 = 3 + 3 < 7 = y_6, \quad \text{therefore let } y_6 = 6$$

$$c_{85} + y_5 = 6 + 3 < \infty = y_8, \quad \text{therefore let } y_8 = 9$$

$$c_{23} + y_3 = 3 + 3 < \infty = y_2, \quad \text{therefore let } y_2 = 6$$

$$c_{73} + y_3 = 5 + 3 < \infty = y_7, \quad \text{therefore let } y_7 = 8$$

$$c_{72} + y_2 = 1 + 6 < 8 = y_7, \quad \text{therefore let } y_7 = 7$$

$$c_{87} + y_7 = 1 + 7 < 9 = y_8, \quad \text{therefore let } y_8 = 8.$$

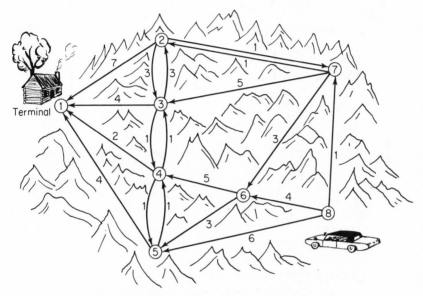

FIGURE 7.16. Shortest-Route Example.

As soon as the new value is calculated in (3) for each y_k, be sure to put it next to Node k in your diagram. At this point

(4)
$$
\begin{array}{llll}
y_1 = 0 & y_2 = 6 & y_3 = 3 & y_4 = 2 \\
y_5 = 3 & y_6 = 6 & y_7 = 7 & y_8 = 8.
\end{array}
$$

Check that the values in (4) now satisfy (2) for *all* the arcs in the figure, so the calculations terminate. In Fig. 7.17, the values for y_k appear next to each node, and the arcs in the shortest paths have been drawn with heavier lines.

▶If every optimal path is unique, then the set of all arcs on the shortest paths forms a tree, defined in Sec. 6.8.

A proof that the final y_s is indeed the length of a *shortest* path from Node s to Node r is practically immediate. By construction, all the dual constraints (2) have been satisfied. The associated value of the dual objective function is

(i)
$$y_r T_r + y_s T_s = 0(-1) + y_s(1) = y_s,$$

which is the value of the length of an *attainable* path from Node s to Node r. Therefore,

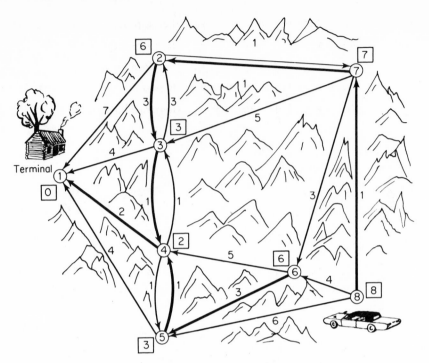

FIGURE 7.17. Shortest Routes to Node 1.

feasible solutions to both the primal and dual problems have been found. Since the two solutions have the same objective-function value, the path must be optimal.

A succinct mathematical statement of the conditions the y_i must satisfy is

(ii)
$$y_i = \underset{\substack{(i,\,j)\ \text{in} \\ \text{network}}}{\text{minimum}}\ (c_{ij} + y_j) \quad \text{for all } i \neq r,$$

where $y_r \equiv 0$.

Sometimes you may want to calculate the shortest routes between *every* pair of nodes. The following approach is an efficient way of doing so. Define

(iii)
$$c_{ij} = \begin{cases} \text{length of arc } (i,j) \text{ if } (i,j) \text{ is in network,} \\ \infty \text{ if } (i,j) \text{ is not in network and } i \neq j, \\ 0 \text{ if } i = j. \end{cases}$$

Consider the network comprised of only Nodes $1, 2, \ldots, q - 1$ ($< p$) and for this abbreviated network, let

(iv)
$$d_{ij} = \text{shortest distance between Nodes i and j, when}$$
$$\text{only Nodes } 1, 2, \ldots, q - 1 \text{ are in the network.}$$

Similarly, let

(v)
$$d_{ij}^* = \text{shortest distance between Nodes i and j, when}$$
$$\text{Nodes } 1, 2, \ldots, q \text{ are in the network.}$$

Then

(vi) $\qquad d_{qj}^* = \underset{k=1,2,\dots,q-1}{\text{minimum}} (c_{qk} + d_{kj})$ for $j = 1, 2, \dots, q-1$

(vii) $\qquad d_{iq}^* = \underset{k=1,2,\dots,q-1}{\text{minimum}} (d_{ik} + c_{kq})$ for $i = 1, 2, \dots, q-1$

(viii) $\qquad d_{qq}^* = 0$

(ix) $\qquad d_{ij}^* = \text{minimum} (d_{ij}, d_{iq}^* + d_{qj}^*)$ for $i, j = 1, 2, \dots, q-1$.

Therefore, starting with $q = 2$, and proceeding to successively larger values of q up to $q = p$, you apply, in turn, (vi) through (ix). (For $q = 2$, $d_{ij}^* = c_{ij}$ for $i, j, = 1, 2$.) The algorithm involves a total of $p(p-1)(p-2)$ additions.   ◀

7.7 SHORTEST ROUTE IN AN ACYCLIC NETWORK

The shortest-route algorithm can be made even simpler when the network is acyclic, for then the dual variables y_k can be determined recursively, that is, sequentially.

As a preliminary step, number the nodes from 1 to p such that if the network contains an arc (i, j), then $i > j$. To do this, designate the sink or terminal as Node 1, which has only inward-pointing arcs. Check off this node *and* all its arcs, and consider them no further in the labeling process. Look for *any* other node that has *only inward*-pointing arcs. Designate it as Node 2. Check off this node *and* all its arcs, and consider them no further in the labeling process. Continue in the same manner until all nodes have been numbered. The y_i will be determined in the same order as the nodes are numbered.

The algorithm is

(1) $\qquad y_1 = 0$ (terminal)

(2) $\qquad y_i = \underset{\substack{(i,\ j)\ \text{in} \\ \text{network}}}{\text{minimum}} (c_{ij} + y_j)$ for $i = 2, 3, \dots, p$.

To see how the recursion (2) works, consider the network in Fig. 7.18, where the c_{ij} are indicated next to each arc. (Carry out the node-numbering process to

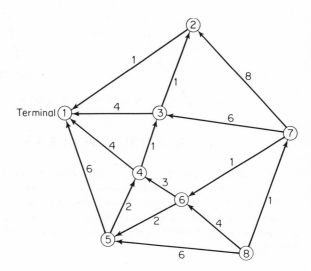

FIGURE 7.18. Acyclic Network Example.

verify that the labels have been correctly assigned.) The algorithm proceeds as follows:

$$y_1 = 0$$
$$y_2 = \text{minimum } (c_{21} + y_1) = (1 + 0) = 1$$
$$y_3 = \text{minimum } (c_{31} + y_1, c_{32} + y_2) = \text{minimum } (4 + 0, 1 + 1) = 2$$
$$y_4 = \text{minimum } (c_{41} + y_1, c_{43} + y_3) = \text{minimum } (4 + 0, 1 + 2) = 3$$
$$y_5 = \text{minimum } (c_{51} + y_1, c_{54} + y_4) = \text{minimum } (6 + 0, 2 + 3) = 5$$
$$y_6 = \text{minimum } (c_{64} + y_4, c_{65} + y_5) = \text{minimum } (3 + 3, 2 + 5) = 6$$
$$y_7 = \text{minimum } (c_{72} + y_2, c_{73} + y_3, c_{76} + y_6)$$
$$\quad = \text{minimum } (8 + 1, 6 + 2, 1 + 6) = 7$$
$$y_8 = \text{minimum } (c_{85} + y_5, c_{86} + y_6, c_{87} + y_7)$$
$$\quad = \text{minimum } (6 + 5, 4 + 6, 1 + 7) = 8.$$

(3)

As in the preceding section, the calculations may be done on the diagram itself. The routes are determined as before, and the solution here is shown in Fig. 7.19.

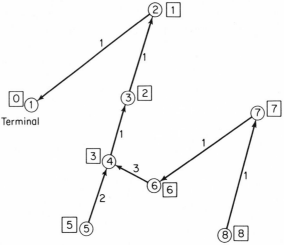

FIGURE 7.19.   Shortest Routes in Acyclic Network.

REVIEW EXERCISES

1 Write the full equations for a standard transportation model with $m = 2$ and $n = 3$, where total supply equals total demand [use the notation in (2), (3), and (5) of Sec. 7.2]. Show that if you add the supply constraints in (2) for $i = 1, 2$, and from this sum subtract the demand constraints in (3) for $j = 1, 2$, you obtain the demand constraint for $j = 3$. Indicate where you use the assumption that total supply equals total demand.

2 Write the full equations for a standard transportation model with $m = 4$ and $n = 3$. Also write the full corresponding dual linear programming problem; use the notation in (6) and (7) of Sec. 7.2.

*3 Given the primal model for the transportation problem stated as (1) through (5) in Sec. 7.2, verify that the associated dual problem is as stated in (6) and (7).

4 Arrange the dual variables and dual equalities (3) in Sec. 7.3 to display at a glance the triangularity property when you set equal to zero the dual variable indicated in each part below.

(a) w_4.

(b) w_1.

(c) v_2.

5 (a) Arrange the shipment variables and equalities (5) in Sec. 7.3 to display at a glance the upper triangularity property.

(b) Do the same where the equality for Row 3 is made explicit and the equality for Column 4 is dropped as the redundant relation.

(c) Do the same where the equality for Row 3 is made explicit and the equality for Column 1 is dropped as the redundant relation.

(d) Do the same where the equality in Row 3 is made explicit and the equality for Row 2 is dropped as the redundant relation.

6 In each part below, find the pattern of alterations, like that in Fig. 7.4, when the indicated nonbasic route is selected in Fig. 7.3. Also calculate the associated improvement potential and verify your answer in Fig. 7.5. Finally, show the values for the new basic solution if the route indicated is selected.

(a) Route $(1, 3)$.   (d) Route $(2, 3)$.

(b) Route $(1, 4)$.   (e) Route $(2, 4)$.

(c) Route $(2, 1)$.

7 In each part below, solve the dual equalities (3) in Sec. 7.3 using the indicated value for the selected dual variable.

(a) $v_3 = 1$.   (d) $w_4 = 1$.

(b) $v_3 = -1$.   (e) $w_1 = 0$.

(c) $w_4 = 0$.   (f) $w_1 = -1$.

(g) Verify that $v_i + w_j$, for every i and j, has the same value in each part above. Explain why.

8 *Northwest Corner Rule.* In Sec. 2.7, the following rule was described for finding an initial solution to a transportation model: start at the upper-left corner, or, as it is sometimes called, the *northwest corner*. Allocate the available supply S_1 to each demand requirement, beginning with D_1, until the supply is exhausted. Then continue the process with S_2 and the remaining unfilled demand requirements. Etc.

(a) Consider the example in Fig. 7.2. Let $S_2 = 2$ and $D_2 = 6$. Apply the northwest corner rule to obtain an initial solution. Calculate the associated trial value for the objective function.

(b) Revise the trial solution in part (a) for the case $S_2 = 1$ and $D_2 = 5$, which are the values in Fig. 7.2. Be sure to maintain a basic solution having $m + n - 1$ routes.

(c) Indicate how to amend the above statement of the northwest corner rule to ensure that the process yields a basic solution containing $m + n - 1$ routes.

(d) In Fig. 7.2, let $S_1 = 7$, $S_2 = 5$, and $D_4 = 7$. Is a feasible solution using routes $x_{11}, x_{13}, x_{22}, x_{31}, x_{33}$, and x_{34} a basic solution? If not, explain why, and apply your answer to part (c). (*Hint:* ascertain whether feasible values for the x_{ij} are *uniquely* determined.)

9 In each part below, find the pattern of alterations, like that in Fig. 7.7, when the indicated nonbasic route in Fig. 7.6 is selected. Also, calculate the associated improvement potential and compare your answer to (10) in Sec. 7.3. Finally, show the values for the new basic solution when the route indicated is actually selected.

(a) Route $(3, 2)$.
(b) Route $(1, 4)$.
(c) Route $(2, 4)$.

*10 Construct a basic solution for an example with $m > 2$ and $n > 2$ such that *every* basic route is revised when a particular nonbasic route is introduced. (*Hint:* let $m = n$, and let the basic solution be found by using the northwest corner rule in exercise 8.)

11 In each part below, assume that the indicated nonbasic route is selected in Fig. 7.6 at iteration 3. Continue the transportation simplex process to find the optimal solution. Use the tabular method, like that in Fig. 7.8, to calculate the improvement potentials.

(a) Route $(1, 3)$.
(b) Route $(2, 4)$.

12 (a) Explain why subtracting the same constant from each c_{ij} in a specified Row i yields a new problem that has the same optimal solutions as the original problem.

(b) Consider the transportation model applied to the distribution of an item that is manufactured at m plants. Let p_i be the production cost of each item at Plant i and t_{ij} the cost of transporting each item from Plant i to Warehouse j. Suppose total potential production at all the plants equals total demand at all the warehouses. Given your answer in part (a), explain why the actual values for the p_i do not influence an optimal distribution plan. Would your explanation be modified if total potential production exceeded total demand? If so, how?

13 In each part below, determine whether an alternative optimal solution would be indicated in Fig. 7.10, and if it would, find such a basic solution.

(a) $c_{11} = 3$.   (d) $c_{32} = 9$.
(b) $c_{11} = 1$.   (e) $c_{32} = 7$.
(c) $c_{32} = 8$.

*14 *Degeneracy*. In each part below, apply the transportation simplex method to find an optimal solution and use the starting solution given in exercise 8.

(a) Part (a).

(b) Part (b).
(c) Part (d).

*15 *Degeneracy.* In each part below, apply the rescaling procedure suggested in the special material of Sec. 7.4 for removing degeneracy. Solve the perturbed model by the transportation simplex method, and indicate how to find the optimal solution in the original problem. Use the data and starting solution in exercise 8.

(a) Part (a).
(b) Part (b).
(c) Part (d).

16 Consider the example in Fig. 7.2. Apply the transportation simplex method to find the optimal solution starting with the basis:

$$x_{11} = 2 \quad x_{12} = 4 \quad x_{22} = 1 \quad x_{31} = 5 \quad x_{33} = 3 \quad x_{34} = 2.$$

*17 Solve the problem in exercise 16 using the ordinary simplex method as presented in Chap. 4. (If you prefer, use either of the tabular formats presented in Sec. 4.9.) Check that at every iteration each variable corresponds to the pattern of alterations occurring when the associated nonbasic route is introduced. (*Suggestion:* to get the calculations started, eliminate any one of the equations as the redundant relation, and solve for the basic x_{ij} indicated in exercise 16.)

18 Let the initial basic solution in Fig. 7.3 employ the route $(2, 3)$, instead of $(2, 2)$. Find the optimal solution using the transportation simplex method. (Note that this initial starting basis is suggested by an analysis of the relative costs in Fig. 7.13.)

*19 (a) Consider the technique in Sec. 7.4 for deriving the relative costs displayed in Fig. 7.13. Apply the technique where you first perform the column calculations (ii) and then the row calculations (i). Are your answers the same as those in Fig. 7.13?

(b) Show that the solution in Fig. 7.9 is optimal for a problem having c_{ij} as indicated in Fig. 7.13. Show the relation between the value of the optimal solution in Fig. 7.9 and the process generating the c_{ij} in Fig. 7.13.

(c) Show that the solution in Fig. 7.9 is optimal for a problem having c_{ij} as indicated in your answer to part (a).

*20 *Initial Basic Solution*

(a) Perform the operations indicated in Fig. 7.14 on the table in Fig. 7.15.

(b) Use the same selection sequence of x_{ij} shown in Fig. 7.14 to find an initial basis for the supplies and demands:

$$S_1 = 3 \quad S_2 = 4 \quad S_3 = 5 \quad D_1 = 3 \quad D_2 = 1 \quad D_3 = 4 \quad D_4 = 4.$$

21 Consider the problem in Fig. 7.2. In each part below, calculate how small the indicated objective-function coefficient can be (leave the other costs unchanged) such that the solution in Fig. 7.9 remains optimal.

(a) c_{12}.   (d) c_{31}.
(b) c_{13}.   (e) c_{33}.
(c) c_{23}.   (f) c_{34}.

*22 Suppose you have an optimal solution in which every basic route has at least one unit of flow, as in Fig. 7.9. Suppose S_p is increased by a unit, so that an oversupply is created. Show that the new optimal allocation will assign the *excess* to that source k with maximum v_i, and that $[v_p - \text{maximum } (v_i)]$ will be added to the objective function.

23 Consider the example in Sec. 7.3. Suppose $S_2 = 2$. Find a new optimal solution (using sensitivity analysis on the previous optimal solution), and verify that total cost is reduced by $v_2 = -9$.

24 Consider the optimal solution shown in Fig. 7.9. In each part below, use sensitivity analysis to find a revised optimal solution and the associated value of the objective function.

(a) $S_1 = 7,\ D_1 = 8.$ (d) $S_2 = 2,\ D_4 = 3.$
(b) $S_1 = 7,\ D_4 = 3.$ (e) $S_3 = 10,\ D_2 = 6.$
(c) $S_2 = 2,\ D_2 = 6.$

25 Consider the solution in Fig. 7.9. In each part below, suppose the supply at Point i is $S_i - \delta$ and the demand at Point j is $D_j - \delta$. State how large δ can be such that the basis in Fig. 7.9 remains optimal. Also, indicate an optimal solution for this value of δ.

(a) $S_1 - \delta$ and $D_2 - \delta.$ (d) $S_3 - \delta$ and $D_1 - \delta.$
(b) $S_1 - \delta$ and $D_3 - \delta.$ (e) $S_3 - \delta$ and $D_3 - \delta.$
(c) $S_2 - \delta$ and $D_3 - \delta.$ (f) $S_3 - \delta$ and $D_4 - \delta.$

26 Answer questions in exercise 25 for each part below. [*Hint:* the pattern of alterations for the basic variables is the same as if you were going to add a unit of flow on route (i,j).]

(a) $S_1 - \delta$ and $D_1 - \delta.$ (c) $S_2 - \delta$ and $D_1 - \delta.$
(b) $S_1 - \delta$ and $D_4 - \delta.$ (d) $S_3 - \delta$ and $D_2 - \delta.$

27 Consider the network in Fig. 7.16. Delete the arcs from Node 4 to Node 3, from Node 6 to Node 5, and from Node 7 to Node 2. Add arcs corresponding to $c_{47} = 1$, $c_{63} = 3$, and $c_{67} = 1$.

(a) Apply the algorithm in Sec. 7.6 to find the shortest routes to Node 1 from every other node, and indicate their corresponding lengths.
(b) How small can c_{64} be such that your answer in part (a) remains optimal?
(c) How large can c_{34} be such that your answer in part (a) remains optimal?
(d) How large can c_{41} be such that your answer in part (a) remains optimal?

28 Consider the network in Fig. 7.16. Delete the arc from Node 5 to Node 4. Add arcs corresponding to $c_{13} = 1$, $c_{14} = 2$, $c_{56} = 3$, and let $c_{72} = 4$.

(a) Apply the algorithm in Sec. 7.6 to find the shortest routes to Node 2 from every other node, and indicate their corresponding lengths. If there are several optimal solutions, indicate the alternatives.

(b) Suppose you add an arc from Node 8 to Node 3. What is the smallest value of c_{83} that will allow your answer in part (a) to remain optimal?

(c) Suppose you add an arc from Node 8 to Node 1. What is the smallest value of c_{81} that will allow your answer in part (a) to remain optimal?

(d) Suppose you add an arc from Node 5 to Node 2. What is the smallest value of c_{52} that will allow your answer in part (a) to remain optimal?

29 Carry out the node-numbering process given at the beginning of Sec. 7.7 to verify that the labels for the network shown in Fig. 7.18 have been correctly assigned.

30 Consider the network in Fig. 7.18. Delete arcs c_{32} and c_{76}. Add an arc corresponding to $c_{74} = 5$.

(a) Apply the algorithm in Sec. 7.7 to find the shortest routes, and their respective lengths, from each node to Node 1. If there are several optimal solutions, indicate the alternatives.

(b) What is the smallest value of c_{86} that will allow your answer in part (a) to remain optimal?

(c) Suppose you add an arc from Node 8 to Node 3. What is the smallest value of c_{83} that will allow your answer in part (a) to remain optimal?

(d) Suppose you add an arc from Node 8 to Node 2. What is the smallest value of c_{82} that will allow your answer in part (a) to remain optimal?

31 Explain your understanding of the terms triangularity (or triangular structure, or triangular property) and relative cost.

Exercises 32 through 42 refer to material contained in Appendix I.

*32 In each part apply the algorithm in Sec. I.1 to find the maximum flow in Fig. I.1. Start the process with the initial flow indicated below.

(a) A unit of flow from Node 0 through Nodes 4, 5, and 6.

(b) A unit of flow from Node 0 through Nodes 1, 2, 3, 5, and 6.

*33 Consider the example in Fig. I.1. In each part below, determine whether the maximum flow can be increased if

(a) You permit flow in any direction between every pair of nodes already connected by an arc.

(b) You add an arc from Node 1 to Node 6.

(c) You make the changes in both parts (a) and (b).

*34 Consider the example in Fig. I.1. Suppose the capacity limit u_{ij} on arc (i, j) is $i + j$. (Thus, $u_{04} = 4$, $u_{36} = 9$, $u_{23} = 5$, etc.) Find the maximum flow, and indicate an optimal flow pattern.

*35 *Cut.* Consider the example in Fig. I.1. Let C_0 be all the spanned nodes associated with Fig. I.3, and let C_{p+1} be the remaining nodes.

(a) What nodes are in C_0?

(b) What is the associated cut capacity?

*36 Answer the questions in exercise 35 for the maximum flow solution in exercise 34.

*37 Apply the transportation simplex method to solve the assignment problem in Fig. I.4, where you let the initial basic solution consist of $x_{14} = x_{23} = x_{32} = x_{41} = 1$ and $x_{24} = x_{34} = x_{44} = 0$. (Let $v_1 = 0$ for the initial solution.)

*38 Apply the maximal flow approach given in Sec. I.2 to solve the assignment problem in Fig. I.4, where you let the initial values for v_i and w_j correspond to those values associated with the initial basic solution given in exercise 37 (with $v_1 = 0$ initially). At each iteration, show the scanning process, as in Fig. I.16, and the resultant network solution, as in Fig. I.17.

*39 Consider the assignment problem in Fig. I.4, and revise the costs to be $c_{ij} - v_i - w_j$, where v_i and w_j correspond to those values associated with the initial basic solution given in exercise 37 (with $v_1 = 0$ initially). Then apply the minimal cost/maximal flow approach described in Sec. I.2 with $v_i = w_j = 0$ and zero flow at the initial iteration. At each iteration draw the relevant network, like that in Fig. I.19, and a shortest route, like that in Fig. I.20.

*40 Consider the assignment problem in Fig. I.4. In each part, apply the shortest-route approach in Sec. I.2, where you consider the rows and columns in the order indicated below. At each iteration, draw the network and associated shortest route, as in Figs. I.24 and I.25.

(a) Row 1 and Column 1; Row 2 and Column 2; Row 3 and Column 3; Row 4 and Column 4.

(b) Row 4 and Column 4; Row 3 and Column 3; Row 2 and Column 2; Row 1 and Column 1.

(c) Row 1 and Column 2; Row 2 and Column 3; Row 3 and Column 4; Row 4 and Column 1.

*41 Solve the transportation problem in Sec. 7.3 using the maximal flow approach as outlined in Sec. I.3.

*42 Explain your understanding of the following terms:

maximum flow	flow-augmenting path
labeled node	cut
spanned node	cut capacity.
breakthrough	

COMPUTATIONAL EXERCISES

43 Consider a transportation problem with $m = 3$ and $n = 3$, where

$$c_{11} = 1 \qquad c_{12} = 3 \qquad c_{13} = 8$$
$$c_{21} = 10 \qquad c_{22} = 4 \qquad c_{23} = 5$$
$$c_{31} = 2 \qquad c_{32} = 4 \qquad c_{33} = 10.$$

(a) Suppose $S_1 = 4$, $S_2 = 4$, and $S_3 = 8$; and $D_1 = 2$, $D_2 = 4$, and $D_3 = 10$. Apply the transportation simplex method to find an optimal solution.

(b) Use sensitivity analysis to determine how your solution in part (a) changes if $S_1 = 5$ and $D_1 = 3$. What is the new value of the objective function?

(c) Answer the questions in part (b) for $S_2 = 5$ and $D_2 = 5$.

(d) What is the smallest value of c_{22} that will allow your solution in part (a) to remain optimal? Similarly, how small can c_{12} be?

(e) Give a range of values for c_{23} that allows the solution in part (a) to remain optimal. Do the same for c_{33}. Do the same for c_{32}.

44 Consider a transportation problem with $m = 4$ and $n = 4$, where

$$c_{11} = 7 \qquad c_{12} = 9 \qquad c_{13} = 1 \qquad c_{14} = 9$$
$$c_{21} = 22 \qquad c_{22} = 25 \qquad c_{23} = 16 \qquad c_{24} = 25$$
$$c_{31} = 25 \qquad c_{32} = 29 \qquad c_{33} = 21 \qquad c_{34} = 28$$
$$c_{41} = 12 \qquad c_{42} = 14 \qquad c_{43} = 6 \qquad c_{44} = 15.$$

(a) Suppose $S_1 = 7$, $S_2 = 3$, $S_3 = 7$, and $S_4 = 8$; and $D_1 = 5$, $D_2 = 5$, $D_3 = 7$, and $D_4 = 8$. Apply the transportation simplex method to find an optimal solution.

(b) Use sensitivity analysis to determine how your solution in part (a) changes if $S_2 = 4$ and $D_4 = 9$. What is the new value of the objective function?

(c) Rework part (b) for $S_3 = 8$ and $D_3 = 8$.

(d) What is the smallest value of c_{11} that will allow the solution in part (a) to remain optimal? Similarly, what is the smallest value of c_{21}? Similarly, how small can c_{31} be?

(e) Give a range of values for c_{23} such that the solution in part (a) remains optimal. Do the same for c_{43}. Do the same for c_{42}.

45 Consider a transportation problem with $m = 4$ and $n = 4$, where

$$c_{11} = 5 \qquad c_{12} = 7 \qquad c_{13} = 7 \qquad c_{14} = 10$$
$$c_{21} = 4 \qquad c_{22} = 5 \qquad c_{23} = 8 \qquad c_{24} = 13$$
$$c_{31} = 13 \qquad c_{32} = 15 \qquad c_{33} = 14 \qquad c_{34} = 21$$
$$c_{41} = 18 \qquad c_{42} = 20 \qquad c_{43} = 24 \qquad c_{44} = 31.$$

(a) Suppose $S_1 = 3$, $S_2 = 4$, $S_3 = 9$, and $S_4 = 18$; and $D_1 = 15$, $D_2 = 5$, $D_3 = 7$, and $D_4 = 7$. Apply the transportation simplex method to find an optimal solution.

(b) Use sensitivity analysis to determine how your solution in part (a) changes if $S_1 = 4$ and $D_1 = 16$. What is the new value of the objective function?

(c) Rework part (b) for $S_2 = 5$ and $D_1 = 16$.

(d) Rework part (b) for $S_1 = 4$ and $D_2 = 6$.

(e) What is the smallest value of c_{44} that will allow the solution in part (a) to remain optimal?

(f) Give a range of values for c_{33} such that the solution in part (a) remains optimal. Do the same for c_{23}. Do the same for c_{34}.

46 *Fly-by-Night Airlines*

(a) Solve the case given in exercise 28 of Chap. 2.

(b) What is the optimal value of the objective function and what are the revisions to the purchase plan in part (a) if one more gallon is required at Airport 1? At Airport 2? At Airport 3? At Airport 4?

(c) What is the optimal value of the objective function and what are the revisions to the purchase plan in part (a) if one more gallon is offered by Oil Company 1? By Oil Company 2? By Oil Company 3?

(d) What is the optimal value of the objective function and what are the revisions to the purchase plan in part (a) if one more gallon is offered by Company 1 and required at Airport 1? At Airport 2? At Airport 3? At Airport 4?

47 *Hayes Manufacturing Company*

(a) Solve the case given in exercise 29 of Chap. 2.

(b) What is the value of an extra unit of capacity at each plant?

(c) What is the cost associated with an extra unit of demand by each wholesaler?

(d) Give a range for the direct cost of production at each plant such that the solution in part (a) remains optimal.

48 *Longview Manufacturing Company*

(a) Apply the transportation simplex algorithm to solve the case in exercise 28 of Chap. 6. Be sure to indicate the amount produced in each period and the level of inventory at the end of each period.

*(b) Did you obtain the same solution as you did in exercise 28, part (c), of Chap. 6? If not, do the two solutions have the same total cost?

49 *Sinbad Steamship Company.* Apply the transportation simplex method to solve the case in exercise 29 of Chap. 6, where

$$p_A = 1 \quad p_B = 2 \quad p_C = 4$$

$$q_A = 4 \quad q_B = 2 \quad q_C = 1.$$

Be sure to indicate an optimal routing for each ship.

50 *Sinbad Steamship Company.* Apply the transportation simplex method to solve the case in exercise 30 of Chap. 6. Be sure to indicate an optimal routing for each ship.

51 Consider the network in exercise 32 of Chap. 6, where $c_{ij} = c_{ji}$ and

$$c_{12} = 14 \quad c_{13} = 4 \quad c_{14} = 1 \quad c_{15} = 6$$

$$c_{23} = 10 \quad c_{24} = 13 \quad c_{25} = 5$$

$$c_{34} = 3 \quad c_{35} = 2$$

$$c_{45} = 8.$$

(a) Find an optimal solution by applying the transportation simplex method to the appropriate condensed transshipment table, like that in Fig. 6.4. Be sure to indicate an optimal routing and state whether it is unique.

(b) Answer part (a) using an expanded transshipment table, like that in Fig. 6.5.

(c) What is the smallest value for c_{45} such that the current solution remains optimal? For c_{24}? For c_{34}? For c_{35}?

52 *Rock-Bottom Discount Store Example.* Consider the network in Fig. 6.3. Assume that

$$c_{12} = 1 \quad c_{23} = 7 \quad c_{25} = 3 \quad c_{43} = 1 \quad c_{45} = 3 \quad c_{47} = 4$$
$$c_{54} = 2 \quad c_{56} = 5 \quad c_{67} = 3 \quad c_{78} = 1.$$

(a) Apply the transportation simplex method to a condensed transshipment table, like that in Fig. 6.4. Be sure to indicate the implied optimal routing.

(b) Apply the transportation simplex method to an expanded transshipment table, like that in Fig. 6.5. Be sure to indicate the implied optimal routing.

(c) Does your solution change if the route from Store 6 to Store 7 is removed? If so, how?

(d) Suppose you add a route from Node 1 directly to Node 3. How small can the associated value c_{13} be such that the solution in part (a) remains optimal? Similarly, for a direct route from Node 2 to Node 7, what is the smallest possible value of c_{27}?

53 Rework exercise 52 using the supply and demand data given in exercise 6, part (a), of Chap. 6.

54 Rework exercise 52 using the supply and demand data given in exercise 6, part (b), of Chap. 6.

55 Rework exercise 52 using the supply and demand data given in exercise 6, part (c), of Chap. 6.

56 *Marcus Metal Company.* Consider the case in exercise 31 of Chap. 6, where

$$S_1 = 10 \quad S_2 = 15 \quad D_5 = 8 \quad D_6 = 10 \quad D_7 = 2$$
$$m_1 = 1 \quad m_2 = 2 \quad p_3 = 3 \quad p_4 = 5$$
$$s_{13} = 1 \quad s_{14} = 1 \quad s_{23} = 6 \quad s_{24} = 3$$
$$t_{35} = 1 \quad t_{36} = 2 \quad t_{37} = 3 \quad t_{45} = 3 \quad t_{46} = 2 \quad t_{47} = 1.$$

(a) Find an optimal solution by applying the transportation simplex method to the appropriate condensed transshipment table, like that in Fig. 6.4. Be sure to indicate the optimal routing and flow of goods.

(b) Rework part (a) using an expanded transshipment table, like that in Fig. 6.5.

(c) What is the optimal value of the objective function and what are the revisions in the solution if $S_1 = 11$? If $S_1 = 9$? If $S_2 = 16$? If $S_2 = 14$? If $D_5 = 9$? If $D_6 = 11$? If $D_7 = 3$? If $S_1 = 11$ and $D_7 = 3$? If $S_2 = 16$ and $D_5 = 9$?

(d) How large can m_1 be such that the solution in part (a) remains optimal? Similarly, how large can m_2 be? Similarly, how large can p_3 be? Similarly, how large can p_4 be?

(e) Suppose it is possible to transship the product through any of the Locations 5, 6, and 7 to any other of these locations at the cost c_{kh}. How small can each value of c_{kh} be (where k and h equal 5, 6, and 7, and $k \neq h$), such that the solution in part (a) remains optimal?

57 Consider the network in exercise 33 of Chap. 6, where $c_{ij} = c_{ji}$ and

$$c_{12} = 15 \quad c_{14} = 8 \quad c_{16} = 55 \quad c_{23} = 28 \quad c_{24} = 5 \quad c_{25} = 12$$

$$c_{38} = 6 \quad c_{45} = 20 \quad c_{46} = 48 \quad c_{57} = 20 \quad c_{58} = 7 \quad c_{67} = 12 \quad c_{78} = 10.$$

(a) Find an optimal solution by applying the transportation simplex method to the appropriate condensed transshipment table, like that in Fig. 6.4. Be sure to indicate the optimal routings.

(b) Rework part (a) using an expanded transshipment table, like that in Fig. 6.5.

(c) What is the smallest cost for the arc between Nodes 1 and 6 such that the solution in part (a) remains optimal? For the arc between Nodes 4 and 6?

(d) Suppose you add a direct route between Nodes 1 and 3. How small can the value be for $c_{13} = c_{31}$ such that the solution in part (a) remains optimal? Similarly, for a route between Nodes 4 and 7, what is the smallest possible value for $c_{47} = c_{74}$?

*58 *Employment Scheduling.* Consider the example in Fig. 6.19, with the cost data as given in exercise 21 of Chap. 6. Let

$$R_1 = 10 \quad R_2 = 15 \quad R_3 = 9 \quad R_4 = 20 \quad R_5 = 12.$$

(a) Apply the transportation simplex method to the tabular form in Fig. 6.20. Be sure to indicate how many crews start each period in an optimal plan.

(b) What is the optimal value of the objective function, and what are the revisions in the plan from part (a) if $R_1 = 11$? If $R_2 = 14$? If $R_1 = 11$ and $R_2 = 14$? If $R_3 = 8$? If $R_4 = 21$? If $R_3 = 8$ and $R_4 = 21$?

59 (a) Show that if every objective-function coefficient c_{ij} is integer-valued in a transportation model, then there are optimal values for the dual variables that are also integer-valued.

*(b) Prove the same proposition for the general network problem given by (i) through (iv) in Sec. 7.4.

60 Consider the network in Fig. 7.20. The number on each arc represents the distance between the nodes, and $c_{ij} = c_{ji}$.

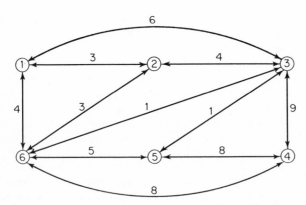

FIGURE 7.20

(a) Find the shortest routes, and their lengths, from each node to Node 1.

(b) Find the shortest routes, and their lengths, from each node to Node 2.

61 Consider the network in Fig. 7.21. The number on each arc represents the distance between the nodes, and $c_{ij} = c_{ji}$.

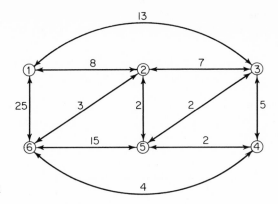

FIGURE 7.21

(a) Find the shortest routes, and their lengths, from each node to Node 1.
(b) Find the shortest routes, and their lengths, from each node to Node 3.

62 Consider the network in Fig. 7.22. The number on each arc represents the distance between the nodes, and $c_{ij} = c_{ji}$.

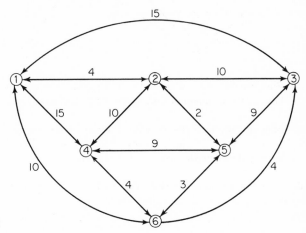

FIGURE 7.22

(a) Find the shortest routes, and their lengths, from each node to Node 1.
(b) Find the shortest routes, and their lengths, from each node to Node 3.

63 Consider a network consisting of six nodes. Assume $c_{ij} = c_{ji}$ and that there are arcs in each direction corresponding to

$$c_{12} = 15 \quad c_{13} = 5 \quad c_{14} = 8 \quad c_{15} = 3$$
$$c_{16} = 10 \quad c_{26} = 3 \quad c_{36} = 5 \quad c_{46} = 2$$
$$c_{23} = 9 \quad c_{34} = 3 \quad c_{45} = 4 \quad c_{56} = 7.$$

(a) Find the shortest routes, and their lengths, from each node to Node 1.
(b) Find the shortest routes, and their lengths, from each node to Node 2.

*64 In each part below, use the algorithm in the advanced material of Sec. 7.6 to find the shortest routes from every node to every other node and indicate the corresponding distances.

(a) Network in exercise 60.   (c) Network in exercise 62.
(b) Network in exercise 61.   (d) Network in exercise 63.

65 Consider the network in Fig. 7.23. The number on each arc represents the associated length c_{ij}. Where an arrow head appears on both ends of an arc, the length shown applies to each of the two directions.

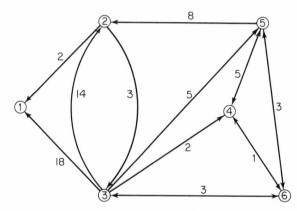

FIGURE 7.23

(a) Find the shortest routes, and their lengths, from each node to Node 1.
*(b) Discuss the problem of finding the longest routes.

66 Consider an acyclic network with five nodes and an arc from each Node i $(i = 2, 3, 4, 5)$ to every Node j, where $j < i$. Let $c_{ij} = i + (i - j)^2$. Find the shortest routes, and their lengths, from each Node i to Node 1.

67 Consider the acyclic network in Fig. 7.24. The number on each arc is the associated length c_{ij}.

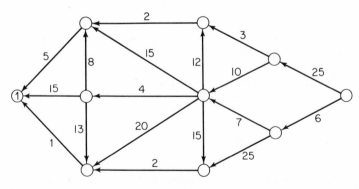

FIGURE 7.24

(a) Label the nodes by the technique given at the beginning of Sec. 7.7.

(b) Find the shortest routes from each node to Node 1 and indicate their lengths.

(c) Find the longest routes from each node to Node 1 and indicate their lengths.

68 *Equipment Replacement.* Apply the shortest-route algorithm in Sec. 7.7 to solve the Rhode-Bloch Trucking Company case in exercise 15, part (d), of Chap. 6.

69 *Equipment Replacement.* Consider the Goode-O'Toole Company case in exercise 41 of Chap. 6.

(a) Apply the shortest-route algorithm in Sec. 7.7 to find an optimal replacement policy.

(b) Determine a range for p_2, the cost of a new model in Period 2, such that the policy in part (a) remains optimal. Do the same for p_3. For p_4. For p_5.

(c) Determine a range for r_2, the cost of operating a piece of equipment during its second consecutive period of use, such that the policy in part (a) remains optimal. Do the same for r_3. For r_4. For r_5.

*70 *Equipment Replacement.* Consider the network in Fig. 6.10. Interpret the amounts that are sequentially calculated by the shortest-route algorithm (1) and (2) in Sec. 7.7 in the context of this network.

*71 Consider the problem in exercise 43, but let $S_i = D_j = 1$ for all i and j.

(a) Solve by the transportation simplex method.

(b) Solve by the maximal flow approach in Sec. I.2.

(c) Solve by the minimal cost/maximal flow approach in Sec. I.2.

(d) Solve by the shortest-route approach in Sec. I.2.

*72 Consider the problem in exercise 44, but let $S_i = D_j = 1$ for all i and j.

(a) Solve by the transportation simplex method.

(b) Solve by the maximal flow approach in Sec. I.2.

(c) Solve by the minimal cost/maximal flow approach in Sec. I.2.

(d) Solve by the shortest-route approach in Sec. I.2.

*73 Consider the problem in exercise 45, but let $S_i = D_j = 1$ for all i and j.

(a) Solve by the transportation simplex method.

(b) Solve by the maximal flow approach in Sec. I.2.

(c) Solve by the minimal cost/maximal flow approach in Sec. I.2.

(d) Solve by the shortest-route approach in Sec. I.2.

*74 Solve the transportation problem in exercise 43 using the maximal flow approach outlined in Sec. I.3.

*75 Solve the transportation problem in exercise 44 using the maximal flow approach outlined in Sec. I.3.

*76 Solve the transportation problem in exercise 45 using the maximal flow approach outlined in Sec. I.3.

MIND-EXPANDING AND
PENCIL-PUSHING EXERCISES

Exercises 77 through 81 refer to transshipment problems. Consider each example formulated as a general network, according to (i) through (iv) at the end of Sec. 7.4, and draw the network representation. [In some problems, you may have to add a fictitious node so that equality in (iv) holds.] You can carry out the simplex method directly on the network diagram without having to resort to either a condensed or an expanded table.

To start, obtain an initial feasible solution; be sure you use $p - 1$ arcs, where p is the number of nodes in the network, and that you permit no loops among the selected arcs. (In other words, select a tree, corresponding to a basic feasible solution. Some of the selected arcs may have zero flow in the trial solution.)

Then calculate the associated values of the dual variables y_k, $k = 1, 2, \ldots, p$, by the $p - 1$ equations $y_i - y_j = c_{ij}$, one equality for each route (i, j) in the trial basic solution. (Let $y_1 = 0$.) Test for dual feasibility, that is, check (iv) in Sec. 7.4. Stop if all the dual restrictions are satisfied; your solution is optimal. Otherwise, introduce a new route corresponding to a dual restriction that is violated most. Reroute the flow along this new route until a route in the previous trial solution has no more flow and hence drops. Repeat the test for optimality. Continue if necessary.

77 Solve the problem in exercise 51.

78 Solve the problem in exercise 52.

79 Solve the problem in exercise 56.

80 Solve the problem in exercise 57.

81 Solve the problem in exercise 58.

82 Explain how you would modify the above algorithm to take account of arc capacity constraints $x_{ij} \leq u_{ij}$, where u_{ij} is a positive integer.

Solve each exercise below using the simplex algorithm for a capacitated transportation problem, as outlined in Sec. 7.4.

83 The problem in exercise 43 with $u_{ij} = 2$ for all i and j.

84 The problem in exercise 44 with $u_{ij} = 3$ for all i and j.

85 The problem in exercise 45 with $u_{ij} = 5$ for all i and j.

CONTENTS

CHAPTER 8

Introduction to Dynamic
Optimization Models

8.1 ANALYSIS OF DYNAMIC PHENOMENA

Dynamic elements—time considerations—were foremost in several of the operations research applications you examined in previous chapters, such as the integrated production planning example in Sec. 2.6. But the emphasis so far has been on presenting algorithmic techniques for coming to grips with a host of simultaneous constraints. You saw, for example, the way the simplex method provides a feasible solution to all the restrictions at each iteration. You undertook sensitivity analysis of linear programming solutions in the same context. Chapters 6 and 7 explored the special structure of network models, and focused on efficient methods for obtaining numerical solutions to large-scale problems. One important departure from this orientation is the solution method for the shortest-route problem in an acyclic network, Sec. 7.7. In that method you took advantage of the "one-way" characteristic of the network. You should carefully review that material, pp. 235–236, before starting the next section.

In Chaps. 8 through 12, the simultaneity aspect still remains crucial, but the stress will now shift to dynamic structural relationships in optimization models. These chapters provide only deterministic examples, in that each decision leads to a *uniquely* determined outcome. Models with probabilistic outcomes are left for Chaps. 17 and 18. You will find, however, that the analytic solution to most of the probabilistic problems are direct generalizations of the concepts you will learn in Chaps. 8 through 12. Consequently studying the deterministic methods is also very useful in preparation for the chapters dealing with probabilistic models.

Here you will concentrate on the form and properties of optimal solutions. You will study the conditions that must be satisfied by an optimal time-staged decision process, and discover how to exploit these conditions to determine the best action. Frequently, the term *dynamic programming* is applied to this sort of analysis.

253

The main topic explored in Chap. 8 is sensitivity analysis on time as a variable. For example, you will see how lengthening the span of a planning horizon can profoundly affect your choice of a correct immediate decision. A related subject studied is the influence of starting conditions, such as the level of resources on hand, and of constraints, such as capacity limitations.

All the models treated in Chaps. 8 through 10 have a finite planning horizon, such as a year or a decade. Chapters 11 and 12 discuss the special considerations peculiar to optimization over an unbounded time horizon. (The concept of time discounting and the approach of present-value analysis are also postponed until Chap. 11.)

A price must be paid to garner these insights about dynamic phenomena. Most important, the size of an optimization model, in terms of separate constraints, must be reduced drastically as compared to typical linear programming models. There are practical advantages to the approach, however, in addition to the value of the new results. One already mentioned is that the span of the planning horizon can be made unbounded. Another is that dynamic programming opens the way toward solving certain small-scale, yet important, cases of nonlinear programming models. These include problems having nonlinear objective functions and a few nonlinear constraints, as well as integer-value restrictions on the variables. In Chap. 10, you will find specific examples demonstrating how such problems, though simple in appearance, can be intricate and subtle. Finally, the numerical techniques exhibited are applicable to a number of decision problems that are not essentially dynamic, but nevertheless can be viewed as dynamic or staged for algorithmic purposes.

So that you keep the proper perspective, we emphasize that numerical solutions to all the models in Chaps. 8 through 10 can be obtained by applying algorithms you have previously studied (in particular, the method of obtaining a shortest route in an acyclic network). The salient goal is learning how to characterize the models in such a way as to clarify their dynamic properties. Part of this task is accomplished merely by augmenting your operations research vocabulary with new terms, and introducing you to a helpful mathematical notation. But, as you will come to appreciate, there are no simple rules that can be applied mechanically to all problems so as to expose their dynamic properties. Experience *is* the best teacher, and therefore the text contains a wide variety of examples. Many specific optimization problems can be formulated in several apparently different ways, with each formulation highlighting a certain structural relationship, as you will see.

Importance of dynamic programming. These introductory comments are meant to help you make a transition from the point of view of the previous chapters. But nothing has been said about the practical importance of the models you are to study next. Are such problems of major economic consequence?

Whereas most industrial applications of the linear programming models you have seen are oriented to planning decisions in the face of large-scale complex situations, dynamic programming models are typically applied to much smaller-scale phenomena. The following illustrations typify dynamic programming decision models:

- Inventory reordering rules indicating when to replenish an item and by what amount

- Production-scheduling and employment-smoothing doctrines applicable to an environment with fluctuating demand requirements

- Spare-parts level determination to guarantee high-efficiency utilization of expensive equipment

- Capital-budgeting procedures for allocating scarce resources to new ventures

- Selection of advertising media to promote wide public exposure to a company's product

- Systematic plan or search to discover the whereabouts of a valuable resource

- Scheduling methods for routine and major overhauls on complex machinery

- Long-range strategy for replacing depreciating assets.

Most of these applications are treated in detail in this chapter and the chapters to follow, and so no further explanation is supplied here.

Frequently, the decision processes embraced by several of the above models may themselves be *micro*. But many real operating systems call for thousands of such decisions each week. These models are valuable, then, because they make it possible to take a myriad of actions through a routine (often computerized) approach with a modicum of human intervention. Needless to say, even if these decisions are inconsequential taken singly, in aggregate they can exert a major effect on a business's profits. A reduction of 25% or more in maintenance costs or in aggregate dollar inventory levels, with no degradation of service, has been the solid reward for many companies employing dynamic programming models.

A word of guidance. The common characteristic of all dynamic programming models is expressing the decision problem by means of a recursive formulation. If you have never applied this type of formal reasoning to solve a problem, then you will probably find the associated mathematical notation strange, and perhaps even puzzling. The advice below is aimed at helping you overcome these difficulties.

Plan to read the sections at least twice. First concentrate on getting a feeling for the decision problem and on becoming familiar with the symbols. Then, on the second reading, pay more attention to the details of the presentation, including the nature of the mathematical expressions. Carefully follow the numerical examples, and check the calculations wherever the text advises you to do so. Finally, be patient and give yourself plenty of time to study the sections. Reading about dynamic programming can be slow going, even if you have previously studied recursive relations. Rest assured, if you proceed as suggested, that after mastering a few examples you will suddenly find it much easier to understand subsequent recursive formulations—this threshold effect in learning is what psychologists refer to as the "aha!" phenomenon.

8.2 STAGECOACH PROBLEM: AN ALLEGORY

An allegorical example will explain several important concepts in dynamic programming and establish a symbolic way to view time-oriented models. There will be nothing new to you in the nature of the problem—you are simply to find a shortest route through an acyclic network. However, the particular illustration will contain more contextual structure than that appearing in Sec. 7.7, where you learned the shortest-route algorithm.

The scenario. Once upon a time there lived a Mr. Mark Off who decided to seek his fortune in San Francisco. In his day, the stagecoach was the only means of public transportation from the East, where he lived, to the West. His travel agent showed him a United States map, Fig. 8.1, depicting the various stagecoach

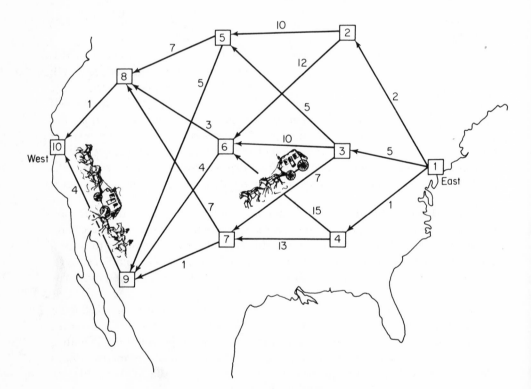

FIGURE 8.1. Stagecoach Problem.

routes then available. Each block on the map represents a state; each state is numbered for convenience. Notice that the entire trip from East to West requires Mark Off to take four stages, regardless of the particular routing.

Since the traveler knew the trip presented serious hazards to life and limb, he decided to take out an insurance policy before leaving. The cost of the policy depended on which routes he selected, since the greater the danger, the higher the cost. Let c_{ij} denote the policy cost of traveling from State i to State j. Illustrative values of c_{ij} appear in Fig. 8.1. Mark Off's objective was to pick a route from East to West that minimized the total policy cost. (See if you can find an optimal route.)

Mark Off analyzed the problem as follows. He perceived as significant the following principle.

PRINCIPLE OF OPTIMALITY: An optimal policy must have the property that regardless of the route taken to enter a particular state, the remaining decisions must constitute an optimal policy for leaving that state.

Thus he knew that an optimal routing out of State 6, say, did not depend on the particular routing that resulted in his entering State 6. (How would you calculate an optimal routing from State 6?) Pressing his logic further, he reasoned that if he knew optimal routings out of States 5, 6, and 7, then he could fairly easily determine an optimal route out of State 3, in case he decided to enter there. Why? Because he need only compare the immediate cost when he leaves State 3—either c_{35}, c_{36}, or c_{37}—*plus* the known costs of optimal routes out of States 5, 6, and 7, respectively, and then pick a state giving the minimum combined cost. By the same token, as soon as he has found optimal policies for States 2, 3, and 4, he could find an optimal routing from State 1. Explain how.

With the principle of optimality and its computational implications in mind, he defined the symbols

$f_n(s)$ = minimum policy cost when he is in State s with n more stages to go
          to his final destination,

$j_n(s)$ = a decision yielding $f_n(s)$.

Most beginning students are driven up the wall by this sort of notation, which is always used in specifying dynamic programming models. It looks even more complicated than the formulas employed in statistics texts, and those are bad enough. But like it or not, each of the letters is essential to the meaning. The letter f signals to you that the number being represented is a value for the objective function. The letter s tells you that the objective-function value actually depends on the state of the system. And the subscript n gives you the dynamic information that there are n stages left to go when the system is in State s. By the same token, the Decision j also depends on both the Stage n and the State s and signifies his journey.

As you read this and other dynamic programming examples, you may find it helpful to repeat to yourself the definition of the symbols, just as if you were learning a new language. The reason we did not need such horrendous notation to explain linear programming models is that those problems are solved in one fell swoop. But here we creep up on a solution by stages. Hopefully, we have managed at least to *ease* your anxiety by this justification.

Returning to Mark Off's problem, he realized that he knew

(1) $f_0(10) = 0$ for $j_0(10) = $ stop,

since when he was in State 10 with no more stages to go, his journey had indeed ended. But then he saw that with hardly any effort he could also calculate $f_1(8)$ and $f_1(9)$, because they were simply $f_0(10)$ plus $c_{8,10}$, and $c_{9,10}$, respectively. Heady with success, he examined how he could compute $f_2(6)$, the minimum policy cost when he is in State 6 with two more stages to go to his final destination. He noticed that he had only two ways to leave State 6, should he decide to enter there. One way is to go to State 8; the associated policy cost is $c_{6,8}$ plus $f_1(8)$, which he already has computed. The other is to go to State 9; the associated policy cost is $c_{6,9}$ plus $f_1(9)$, which he also has computed. Aha! The value of $f_2(6)$ must be the smaller of these two sums. (Is this how you calculated an optimal routing from State 6?)

Mark Off suspected that there must be a method in his madness, and, of course, he was right. The method—or madness—can be succinctly stated by a so-called dynamic recursive relationship:

(2) $f_n(s) = \underset{\substack{(s,\ j)\ \text{in} \\ \text{network}}}{\text{minimum}} [c_{sj} + f_{n-1}(j)]$ for $n = 1, 2, 3, 4.$

This formula, expressed in words, states the fact that Mark Off should compare each possible sum of the policy cost for the immediate stage, going from State s to State j, and the *optimal* policy cost when he arrives at State j with only $n - 1$ more stages to go to his final destination. He should decide on a j that gives the smallest value of these sums. Mark Off's reasoning was to apply (2) by calculating first all the values for $f_1(s)$, namely, $f_1(8)$ and $f_1(9)$; then, in turn, for $n = 2$, he would calculate the values for $f_2(5), f_2(6), f_2(7)$, followed by the values for $f_3(2)$, $f_3(3)$, and $f_3(4)$. His entire problem was solved once he found the value of $f_4(1)$, because this put him at the beginning of his journey, starting at the initial State 1 with four stages to go.

The above approach for solving the problem might almost be termed a method of lifting yourself by your own bootstraps. First you perform a small, even trivial, computation. You use that result to perform a subsequent computation, and you continue in the same fashion. In symbolic terms, the computation in (2) states that you can find the values of $f_1(s)$ when you know the values of $f_0(s)$. You then can find the values of $f_2(s)$, having calculated the values of $f_1(s)$, and so on. This sort of procedure is referred to as a **recursive algorithm**, and the formula is known as a **recursion**.

Computational process. We review the idea of employing a recursive algorithm by doing the actual calculations for the numerical values of c_{ij} appearing in Fig. 8.1.

For $n = 1$, the calculations implied by (2) and (1) are trivial:

$$(3) \qquad \begin{aligned} f_1(8) &= c_{8,10} + 0 = 1 \quad \text{for} \quad j_1(8) = 10 \quad (s = 8) \\ f_1(9) &= c_{9,10} + 0 = 4 \quad \text{for} \quad j_1(9) = 10 \quad (s = 9). \end{aligned}$$

To keep the rest of the calculations straight, use the tables shown in Figs. 8.2 through 8.5.

There is one table for each possible Stage n, namely, $n = 1, 2, 3,$ and 4. The format for a table is to have a row for each possible entering state, given that there are n stages to go, and a column for each possible state at the next stage. Thus for $n = 1$, shown in Fig. 8.2, there are two rows for States 8 and 9, because Mark

n = 1

$c_{sj} + f_0(j)$

Decision:

Entering State: $s \backslash j$	10	$j_1(s)$	$f_1(s)$
8	$1 + 0$	10	1
9	$4 + 0$	10	4

FIGURE 8.2. Stagecoach Problem.

n = 2

$c_{sj} + f_1(j)$

Decision:

Entering State: $s \backslash j$	8	9	$j_2(s)$	$f_2(s)$
5	$7 + 1$	$5 + 4$	8	8
6	$3 + 1$	$4 + 4$	8	4
7	$7 + 1$	$1 + 4$	9	5

FIGURE 8.3. Stagecoach Problem.

Off may choose to enter either of these states. But there is only one column for State 10, since that is the only destination from both States 8 and 9. For $n = 2$, shown in Fig. 8.3, Mark Off may choose to enter either State 5, 6, or 7, and so three rows are needed; he then may travel to either State 8 or 9, and so two columns are required.

The entries in a table are the sum of the immediate cost c_{sj} to go from State s to State j and the subsequent policy cost $f_{n-1}(j)$ associated with an optimal route out of State j. In each row, you examine these sums to find the smallest. That minimum is labeled $f_n(s)$ and an associated optimal decision is designated as $j_n(s)$; both are shown on the right of each table.

The computations for $n = 1$ are repeated in Fig. 8.2. In this particular example, when $n = 1$, the only feasible action is $j = 10$. Therefore, $j_1(8) = j_1(9) = 10$, as you already saw in (3).

When $n = 2$, recall j can be either 8 or 9. To complete the calculations when there are two more stages to go, it is necessary to have the c_{sj} and *only* the values $f_1(j)$. The computations are shown in Fig. 8.3. Observe that $f_1(8) = 1$ is added to each c_{s8} in the $j = 8$ column and $f_1(9) = 4$ is added to each c_{s9} in the $j = 9$ column.

The table shows that with two stages left it is optimal to go to State 8 from States 5 and 6, and to State 9 from State 7.

The analysis for $n = 3$ appears in Fig. 8.4. Notice here that two entries are

$$n = 3$$
$$c_{sj} + f_2(j)$$

Decision:

s \ j	5	6	7	$j_3(s)$	$f_3(s)$
2	10 + 8	12 + 4		6	16
Entering State: 3	5 + 8	10 + 4	7 + 5	7	12
4		15 + 4	13 + 5	7	18

FIGURE 8.4. Stagecoach Problem.

blanked out, since it is not possible to go from State 2 to State 7 or from State 4 to State 5. Once again observe that the *only* data required from the previous Fig. 8.3 are the values of $f_2(j)$. This is a key point in all dynamic programming applications: *the value of an optimal policy with* n *stages left to go depends on the economic consequence of the immediate action and the corresponding* value *of an optimal policy with* n − 1 *stages remaining.*

$$n = 4$$
$$c_{sj} + f_3(j)$$

Decision:

s \ j	2	3	4	$j_4(s)$	$f_4(s)$
Entering State: 1	2 + 16	5 + 12	1 + 18	3	17

FIGURE 8.5. Stagecoach Problem.

The computations terminate in Fig. 8.5 with $n = 4$. There you see that the minimum policy cost is

(4) $f_4(1) = 17$ for $j_4(1) = 3.$

What is the corresponding optimal policy? To answer this question, you must trace through the tables in the following fashion. Starting with the table for $n = 4$, shown in Fig. 8.5, you find that an optimal decision is to go from State 1 to State 3. Progressing to the table for $n = 3$, shown in Fig. 8.4, you see that when Mark Off enters State 3 (third row of table), an optimal decision is to go to State 7. Continuing to the table for $n = 2$, shown in Fig. 8.3, you find that when he enters State 7, an optimal decision is to go to State 9. And from State 9 he ends up at State 10. In summary, an optimal policy is the route from State 1 to 3 to 7 to 9 to 10, which as $f_4(1)$ indicates, has a policy cost of $5 + 7 + 1 + 4 = 17.$

You should understand that the dynamic programming method is more efficient than enumerating and evaluating every possible policy. In this particular problem, there are 14 distinct routes from East to West. To evaluate the policy cost of any route, it is necessary to add the four (one for each stage) appropriate c_{ij}. Therefore, a naive enumeration approach would have required 42 ($= 14 \times 3$) additions, as compared to a total of 16 additions in Figs. 8.3 through 8.5. The relative advantage of the recursive method is overwhelming in typical applications, where complete enumeration is usually out of the question.

A study questionnaire. The stagecoach allegory contains several concepts and approaches that recur in subsequent applications. To master these ideas, when you study each new model ask yourself:

(i) What are the policy or decision variables?
(ii) What is the criterion or objective function for determining an optimal policy?
(iii) How is the problem characterized and then analyzed in terms of stages?
(iv) What characterizes the state of the problem at each stage?
(v) How do the constraints influence the states of the problem and the feasible values of the policy variables?

Once you are able to formulate a model in multistage terms, you have taken the first step toward analyzing the problem's dynamic characteristics.

8.3 ELEMENTARY INVENTORY MODEL

Inventory decisions included in previous planning models—for example, the integrated production planning model in Sec. 2.6—were imbedded in a large and complex system of constraints. Now the scope is narrowed considerably so as to concentrate on several essentials of dynamic inventory decision processes. The model you are about to study plays the same role in the field of operations research as do Newton's elementary laws in the field of physics—well, *nearly* the same role. Even though the situation considered by the model is idealized, it encompasses many of the important considerations for choosing an inventory policy.

Keep in mind that the primary purpose of the discussion below is to examine the dynamic phenomena of inventory processes. For this reason, the description of the model does not comment on the severity or realism of the assumptions; these are taken up in Sec. 8.5. For the same reason, the economic concepts introduced are only described in brief. They will be elaborated in Chap. 19 and Appendix II, which are devoted entirely to inventory models.

By way of encouragement and motivation, however, let it be said that manufacturing firms have implemented versions of this model with demonstrable economic benefits. As you would imagine, in such instances all the calculations involved have been computerized.

Dependable Manufacturing Company Example. This firm wishes to establish a production schedule for an item during the next N time periods.

Assume the company has an accurate forecast of the amount it requires to meet demand for each of the N periods.

The manufacturing time to produce a batch of these items is negligible, so that production in Period t can be used to fill, entirely or partially, the demand in that period. Since the demand requirements do vary from one period to another and there are certain economies of batch production, it is often economical for the firm to produce more than is needed in one period and store the excess until it is required later. However, there is a cost of holding the resultant inventory. Depending on the circumstances, this expense is attributable to such factors as interest on capital borrowed for financing the inventory buildup, storage rental fees, insurance, and maintenance. Such inventory holding cost must be taken into account in determining a production schedule.

The objective of the Dependable Manufacturing Company is to devise a schedule that minimizes the total production and inventory holding costs subject to the restriction that it meets all the demand requirements on time. (Would you believe that the company uses the slogan "Dependable is dependable"?) We begin the analysis by translating this qualitative statement of the problem into a mathematical model.

Model formulation. Define the policy variables

$$x_t = \text{production quantity in Period t}$$

$$i_t = \text{inventory at the } end \text{ of Period t.}$$

Assume that D_t is the demand requirement in Period t, where each D_t is a nonnegative integer known at the beginning of the planning horizon.

Suppose that in each Period t the cost incurred depends only on the production quantity x_t and the ending inventory level i_t, and possibly on Period t itself. Let the function $C_t(x_t, i_t)$ denote the appropriate cost relationship for Period t. Then the objective function can be written as

$$(1) \qquad\qquad \text{minimize} \sum_{t=1}^{N} C_t(x_t, i_t).$$

Several constraints are imposed on the policy variables x_t and i_t. We restrict production to be integer-valued

(2) $x_t = 0, 1, 2, 3, \ldots$ for each Period t   (integer-valued production levels).

We assume that the management desires a policy in which the inventory level is zero at the end of Period N:

(3) $\qquad\qquad\qquad i_N = 0$ (no ending inventory).

Finally, we stipulate that each period's demand must be entirely satisfied on time. This condition can be imposed by means of two constraints. The first might be called an "accounting identity" since it states that

inventory at the end
of Period t $\equiv$

inventory entering Period t
plus
production in Period t
less
demand in Period t,

or, symbolically,

$$i_t = i_{t-1} + x_t - D_t.$$

We find it more convenient to rearrange the terms in this relationship, and express the constraint as

(4) $\qquad i_{t-1} + x_t - i_t = D_t \quad$ at each Period t, for $t = 1, 2, \ldots, N$,

where i_0 is a specified level of initial inventory at the beginning of the planning horizon.

The second constraint we impose to ensure that Dependable meets its requirements on time is that each period's entering inventory and production must always be large enough to make ending inventory a nonnegative quantity. Actually, we also want to restrict inventory levels to be integer-valued (which is a harmless assumption given that demands and production levels are integer-valued). Thus, we require

(5) $\qquad i_t = 0, 1, 2, 3, \ldots \quad$ at each Period t, for $t = 1, 2, \ldots, N - 1$.

Observe that (4) is a linear restriction. If each cost function $C_t(x_t, i_t)$ is linear, then (as shown in the advanced material below) the model is equivalent to a network problem and is easily solved by the methods in the preceding chapter. But in most actual applications of production models, the cost functions are nonlinear. For example, a costly setup may be required to produce a batch of items, so that the cost of producing the first unit is greater than the *incremental* cost of producing subsequent units. And when production exceeds the normal capacity level during a period, then the incremental cost may again increase due to the use of overtime.

To cope with such nonlinearities in each $C_t(x_t, i_t)$, we turn to a dynamic programming version of the problem.

▶Let $N = 4$, and write out the equations (4) for $t = 1, 2, 3,$ and 4. You should get the inventory constraints technology table shown in Fig. 8.6. Now on scratch paper, add

		x_1	i_1	x_2	i_2	x_3	i_3	x_4	
	1	1	-1						$= D_1 - i_0$
Periods	2		1	1	-1				$= D_2$
	3				1	1	-1		$= D_3$
	4						1	1	$= D_4$

FIGURE 8.6. Inventory Constraints.

these four equations to form a fifth equation, and then rewrite each equation in Fig. 8.6 after multiplying through by -1. Verify that the resulting system of five equations yields a network structure, as shown in Fig. 8.7.   ◀

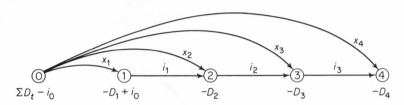

FIGURE 8.7. Inventory and Production Network.

Dynamic characterization. Recall in the stagecoach problem that the computational idea was to start at the end (no more stages to go) and work back to the beginning. We use the same approach for this problem. Here, the end is when there is only one period left in the planning horizon, and the beginning is when there are N periods to go.

In writing the mathematical formulas, we will find it convenient to use an indexing system in which the subscript 1 denotes the *end* of the horizon and the subscript N the *beginning*. Specifically, we define

d_n = the demand requirement in that period when there are n more periods to go,

$c_n(x, j)$ = cost of producing x and having j items of *ending* inventory in that period when there are n more periods to go.

In this notation, $d_1 \equiv D_N$ and $d_N \equiv D_1$. Similarly, $c_1(x, j) \equiv C_N(x, j)$.

For example, if the periods are months, $N = 4$, and the beginning of the horizon is January, then D_1 is January's demand and D_4 is April's. In the formulas, we want to use the reverse numbering system so that d_4 is January's demand and d_1 is April's. Thus d_2, the demand when there are two months to go until the end of the horizon, refers to March's requirements.

Can you guess what determines the state of the production system at the start of any period? The answer is entering inventory. Knowing *how* you arrived at this inventory level has no relevance to your current production decision. With this in mind, we define

$f_n(i)$ = minimum policy cost when entering inventory is at level i with n more periods to go,

$x_n(i)$ = a production level yielding $f_n(i)$.

Since inventory at the end of the horizon is 0, according to (3), you can write

(6) $f_0(0) = 0 \quad (n = 0)$.

Next look at $n = 1$. Entering inventory, i, can be any integer amount between the limits of 0 and d_1; but regardless of the specific level, the production amount must be $d_1 - i$ so that all of the final period's demand is met. It follows then that

(7)　　　　　　$f_1(i) = c_1(d_1 - i, 0)$　for $i = 0, 1, \ldots, d_1$.

Going on to $n = 2$, observe that if entering inventory is designated by i and the production level by x, then the associated cost is

$$c_2(x, i + x - d_2) + f_1(i + x - d_2),$$

assuming that you act optimally for $n = 1$. Note that the quantity $i + x - d_2$ is simply inventory at the *end* of the period. The value for i can be any integer amount between 0 and $d_1 + d_2$. Explain why. Given i, the integer value of x must be at least as large as $d_2 - i$ in order to meet the period's demand requirement, but no larger than $d_1 + d_2 - i$ because ending inventory must be 0. An optimal x is one that minimizes the above sum. This analysis of $n = 2$ can be summarized by the computation

$$f_2(i) = \text{minimum}_x \left[c_2(x, i + x - d_2) + f_1(i + x - d_2) \right],$$

where $i = 0, 1, \ldots, d_1 + d_2$ and the minimization is over only nonnegative integer values of x in the range $d_2 - i \leq x \leq d_1 + d_2 - i$.

As in the stagecoach problem, once you know the values for $f_2(i)$, you can find the values for $f_3(i)$, and so on, until you eventually calculate $f_N(i_0)$, where i_0 is initial inventory, as before. The general recursion is written as

(8)　　　　$f_n(i) = \text{minimum}_x \left[c_n(x, i + x - d_n) + f_{n-1}(i + x - d_n) \right]$

　　　　　　　　　　　　　　　　　　for $n = 1, 2, \ldots, N$,

where $i = 0, 1, \ldots, d_1 + \ldots + d_n$ and the minimization is over only nonnegative integer values of x in the range $d_n - i \leq x \leq d_1 + d_2 + \cdots + d_n - i$.

Observe that by letting entering inventory, i, be the state variable, the only independent decision variable in the recursion (8) is x, for ending inventory is merely $(i + x - d_n)$. Note that since $f_0(0)$ and $f_1(i)$ are easily computed in (6) and (7), it is straightforward to calculate, in turn, $f_2(0), f_2(1), \ldots, f_2(d_1 + d_2)$, then $f_3(0), f_3(1), \ldots, f_3(d_1 + d_2 + d_3)$, continuing, for successively larger values of n, eventually to $f_{N-1}(0), f_{N-1}(1), \ldots, f_{N-1}(d_1 + d_2 + \ldots + d_{N-1})$, and finally to $f_N(i_0)$.

To find an optimal schedule, you then check what production level $x_N(i_0)$ yielded the value for $f_N(i_0)$; this is an optimal decision at the start of the horizon. At the next stage, the entering inventory level will be $i_0 + x_N(i_0) - d_N$. Find a production level that yields the value for $f_{N-1}(i_0 + x_N(i_0) - d_N)$, and so on. The process will be clear when you study the example in the next section.

You should pause here to make certain you understand what has been done to characterize the model in dynamic programming terms. The problem is being viewed in stages, where n denotes the number of stages (here periods) until the end of the final period. To illustrate, suppose again that $N = 4$ and the periods are January, February, March, and April, so that $n = 1$ refers to April and $n = 4$ to January. The January requirements are denoted by d_4 in the dynamic programming recursion (8). Similar notation is used for the cost functions. There is nothing really subtle so far.

What *is* novel is letting the level of entering inventory describe the state when there are n periods left to go. Continuing with the four-month illustration, observe that given the amount of inventory at the beginning of April and that month's demand requirement, you must produce exactly the difference between these two amounts. This fact is recognized in (7). Thus the optimization in April is trivial, given entering inventory.

By the same token, given the amount of inventory at the beginning of March and that month's demand requirement, you must produce *at least* the difference between these two amounts.

Your production decision x in March, in turn, affects the amount of entering inventory in April. Specifically, what enters April is $(i + x - d_2)$. Given this amount, you act optimally in April. But you already completed April's optimization analysis at the previous stage. Therefore, in deciding the optimal March production, you need compare only March costs plus the corresponding costs of acting *optimally* after March. The entirety of these considerations is expressed by the right-hand side of the dynamic programming recursion (8). The same line of reasoning can then be repeated for February, and finally for January.

▶The recursion (8) is equivalent to the method of finding a shortest route in an acyclic network. You might wonder, "What does such a network look like for this model?" Because of the nonlinear cost functions, it is *not* one like Fig. 8.7. A diagrammatic network equivalent of (8) for an actual problem can be dense with nodes and arcs. The underlying structure can be illustrated adequately, however, by the following simple case:

(i) $d_n = 1$ for $n = 1, 2, 3, 4$ (stationary demand)

(ii) $x = 0, 1, 2$ (restricted production levels).

The network is pictured in Fig. 8.8. Each node, designated by the symbol (i, n), corresponds to a possible level of the state variable i when there are n periods remaining. The five nodes on the left designate the different possibilities for initial inventory $i_0 = 0, 1, 2, 3, 4$. The single node on the right reflects the restriction that ending inventory is 0.

Consider an arc between (i, n) and $(j, n - 1)$. Since $j = i + x - d_n$, then $x = j - i + d_n$ at the period when there are n periods to go. One arc appears for each feasible action. The associated cost $c_n(x, j)$ appears with the abbreviated symbol "nxj"; for example, $c_4(0, 1)$ is indicated by 401.

The diagram certainly appears more complicated than Fig. 8.7. This is because the problem *is* more complicated when the $C_t(x_t, i_t)$ are nonlinear.

The recursion (8) is **backward in time**, in that it commences calculations with the last period of the horizon and moves toward the first period. In the illustration for $N = 4$, the computation of $f_1(i)$ refers to April. It is also possible to construct a *forward* algorithm that starts with the first period and moves toward the last period of the horizon. Here, an assumption about initial inventory i_0 is needed. Suppose $i_0 = 0$. The approach is to let

(iii) $g_n(i)$ = minimum policy cost for Periods $1, 2, \ldots, n$ when inventory

         at the *end* of Period n is at level i.

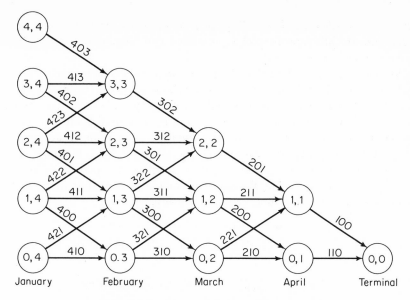

FIGURE 8.8. Inventory and Production Network.
Node Designation: (i, n).
Arc Cost Designation: $c_n(x, j) = nxj$.

Then

(iv)
$$g_0(0) = 0$$
$$g_1(i) = C_1(D_1 + i, i) \quad \text{for } i = 0, 1, \ldots, D_2 + D_3 + \cdots + D_N + i_N$$

and

(v) $$g_n(i) = \underset{x}{\text{minimum}} \, [g_{n-1}(i - x + D_n) + C_n(x, i)] \quad \text{for } n = 1, 2, \ldots, N,$$

where $i = 0, 1, \ldots, D_{n+1} + \cdots + D_N + i_N$ and the minimization is over the values of $x = 0, 1, \ldots, D_n + i$. What is being sought is the value of $g_N(i_N)$, where i_N is a specified level for inventory at the end of the horizon.

Observe in (v) that $i - x + D_n$ is the amount of inventory entering Period n. Whereas an optimal value of x giving rise to $f_n(i)$ in (8) referred to production in Period 1, with n periods left to go, an optimal value of x giving rise to $g_n(i)$ in (v) refers to production in Period n. Thus, once the values of $g_n(i)$ are tabulated, a solution is found by starting in Period N with the value of i_N, determining a corresponding best x_N, noting what the resulting entering inventory must be, finding a corresponding optimal x_{N-1}, etc. ◀

8.4 NUMERICAL SOLUTION

Now that you have a formulation of the inventory model, you are ready to solve the Dependable Manufacturing Company's specific problem. We perform the numerical calculations in this section. In subsequent sections, we analyze the effect on an optimal policy of lengthening the time horizon N, and show how an optimal policy can be drastically influenced by the imposition of a constraint. This example will demonstrate just how perplexing so-called combinatorial problems can be, even when they are small scale.

In fairness we must explain that the particular numbers below have been carefully chosen to produce the dynamic phenomena we wanted to exhibit; you should not conclude that the dynamic behavior illustrated is typical of inventory processes. You also should realize, however, that it would have been difficult to forecast the exact nature of the results *prior* to the dynamic programming analysis. This means that in a real situation you may not be able to judge beforehand whether an optimal policy is extremely sensitive to the length of the planning horizon.

To keep the analysis simple, we assume stationarity over time in the demand requirements and the cost functions. Specifically, let

$$(1) \qquad\qquad D_t = 3 \quad \text{for all periods} \quad \text{(stationary demand)}.$$

Assume that the cost function is simply the sum of a term due to production and a linear inventory holding cost:

$$(2) \qquad\qquad C_t(x_t, i_t) = C(x_t) + hi_t \quad \text{for all periods, where}$$

$$(3) \quad C(0) = 0 \quad C(1) = 15 \quad C(2) = 17 \quad C(3) = 19 \quad C(4) = 21 \quad C(5) = 23$$

$$(4) \qquad\qquad\qquad\qquad h = 1.$$

Thus production cost can be viewed as consisting of a setup cost of 13 plus a variable unit cost of 2 per item produced. Holding cost is just 1 times the level of ending inventory.

An added complication is that the Dependable Manufacturing Company has limited production capacity and storage space. In particular, it cannot produce more than five units in a period and hold more than four units at the end of the period:

$$(5) \qquad x_t = 0, 1, \ldots, 5 \quad \text{and} \quad i_t = 0, 1, \ldots, 4 \quad \text{for all periods}.$$

Notice that because the setup cost is high relative to the other costs, an optimal schedule will attempt to avoid frequent production. But since production x_t cannot exceed 5 and demand is 3, a schedule cannot increase inventory by more than 2 each period. Thus if initial inventory is 0, two setups are required in the first two periods. It is not at all obvious what is the best schedule of setups and production for longer time horizons. The dynamic programming analysis will provide the answers.

Dynamic formulation. Given the above data for the Dependable Manufacturing Company, you can write the appropriate dynamic recursion to reflect the specifics of the problem. Remember that

$f_n(i) =$ minimum policy cost when entering inventory is at level i with n more periods to go,

$x_n(i) =$ a production level yielding $f_n(i)$.

For $n = 1$,

(6)
$$\left.\begin{array}{l} f_1(i) = C(3 - i) \\ x_1(i) = 3 - i \end{array}\right\} \text{ for } i = 0, 1, 2, 3,$$

since the level of inventory at the end of the horizon is 0. The general recursion is

(7)
$$f_n(i) = \underset{x}{\text{minimum}}\, [C(x) + 1(i + x - 3) + f_{n-1}(i + x - 3)]$$
$$\text{for } n = 2, 3, \dots,$$

where $i = 0, 1, 2, 3, 4$ and the minimization is over only nonnegative integer values in the range $3 - i \leq x \leq \text{minimum}\,(5, 7 - i)$. The production constraint in (5) keeps x from exceeding 5; and the *end* of period inventory constraint in (5) keeps x from exceeding $7 - i$.

In order to perform the analyses of interest, it is necessary to have the values of $f_n(i)$ available; therefore this task is completed next. The format of the numerical solution tables is very similar to that used in the stagecoach problem. There is one table for each Stage n. A row in a table corresponds to a value of entering inventory i, and a column to a production level x. Because demand has to be met each period and the inventory at the end of a period cannot exceed 4, certain entries in the tables are eliminated from consideration—they represent infeasible combinations. The entries appearing in the body of a table are the sum of costs for the immediate period and cost of an optimal policy in the subsequent periods. For each row, the minimum of these sums is shown at the right under the column designated by $f_n(i)$ along with an associated optimal production level $x_n(i)$.

The $f_1(i)$, given by (6), are tabled in Fig. 8.9. The function $f_2(i)$ is computed in Fig. 8.10. Note the detailed construction of the table. There are five rows, one for each feasible value of i. Several of the possibilities are blocked out. For example, if $i = 1$, then $x \geq 2$ in order that all demand be met. If $i = 4$, then $x \leq 2$ in order that inventory at the end of the horizon is zero. The first entry in each column x is the value $C(x)$ from (3). The second entry is the holding cost $h = 1$ times the level of ending inventory. For example, if $i = 3$ and $x = 0$, then ending inventory is 0, and 0 appears as the second term in the sum for this case. If $i = 3$ and $x = 1$, then ending inventory is 1, so 1 appears as the second

$f_1(i) = C(3 - i)$

i	$x_1(i)$	$f_1(i)$
0	3	19
1	2	17
2	1	15
3	0	0

Entering Inventory:

FIGURE 8.9. The Dependable Manufacturing Company Model ($n = 1$).

term in the sum for this case. And so forth along the $i = 3$ row. Finally, the third term is the value of $f_1(i + x - 3)$ calculated previously in Fig. 8.9.

Given a level i, $f_2(i)$ is the minimum sum in the body of the table for that row, and $x_2(i)$ is, a corresponding production level. Thus if $i = 1$ with two periods left to go, the best production level is 5, which yields a cost of 26 for these two periods. Any other value for x is more costly.

$$C(x) + 1(i + x - 3) + f_1(i + x - 3)$$

Production:

i \ x	0	1	2	3	4	5	$x_2(i)$	$f_2(i)$
0				19 + 0 + 19	21 + 1 + 17	23 + 2 + 15	3	38
1			17 + 0 + 19	19 + 1 + 17	21 + 2 + 15	23 + 3 + 0	5	26
2		15 + 0 + 19	17 + 1 + 17	19 + 2 + 15	21 + 3 + 0		4	24
3	0 + 0 + 19	15 + 1 + 17	17 + 2 + 15	19 + 3 + 0			0	19
4	0 + 1 + 17	15 + 2 + 15	17 + 3 + 0				0	18

Entering Inventory: i

FIGURE 8.10. Dependable Manufacturing Company Model $(n = 2)$.

$$[C(x) + 1(i + x - 3)] + f_2(i + x - 3)$$

Production:

i \ x	0	1	2	3	4	5	$x_3(i)$	$f_3(i)$
0				19 + 38	22 + 26	25 + 24	4	48
1			17 + 38	20 + 26	23 + 24	26 + 19	5	45
2		15 + 38	18 + 26	21 + 24	24 + 19	27 + 18	4	43
3	0 + 38	16 + 26	19 + 24	22 + 19	25 + 18		0	38
4	1 + 26	17 + 24	20 + 19	23 + 18			0	27

Entering Inventory: i

FIGURE 8.11. Dependable Manufacturing Company Model $(n = 3)$.

Entering Inventory i	$n = 1$		$n = 2$		$n = 3$		$n = 4$		$n = 5$		$n = 6$	
	$x_1(i)$	$f_1(i)$	$x_2(i)$	$f_2(i)$	$x_3(i)$	$f_3(i)$	$x_4(i)$	$f_4(i)$	$x_5(i)$	$f_5(i)$	$x_6(i)$	$f_6(i)$
0	3	19	3	38	4	48	3, 4	67	5	79	4	96
1	2	17	5	26	5	45	5	64	5	74	5	93
2	1	15	4	24	4	43	5	54	4	72	4	91
3	0	0	0	19	0	38	0	48	0	67	0	79
4			0	18	0	27	0	46	0	65	0	75

FIGURE 8.12. Dependable Manufacturing Company Model.

The calculations yielding $f_3(i)$ are shown in Fig. 8.11. Here $C(x) + 1(i + x - 3)$ is the first term, and $f_2(i + x - 3)$ from Fig. 8.10 is the second. The remaining values of $f_n(i)$, for $n = 4, 5, 6$, are summarized in Fig. 8.12. You should test your understanding of the dynamic programming recursive calculations by constructing a complete table, laid out like Fig. 8.11, to produce $f_4(i)$. Compare your results with those in Fig. 8.12. Observe that the production levels, 3 and 4, are optimal when $n = 4$.

8.5 SENSITIVITY ANALYSIS

The tabulated numerical results needed to obtain an optimal production policy also provide considerable information about the sensitivity of the solution to assumed values of the model's parameters, such as the length of the planning horizon and the level of entering inventory. We examine sensitivity questions of this sort using the data for the Dependable Manufacturing Company contained in Figs. 8.9 through 8.12.

Length of the planning horizon. For the sake of definiteness, suppose each period in the model represents a month and that the first period is January. We want to know how the optimal monthly figures change as the horizon N increases, and, in particular, what happens to January production. The results, based on Fig. 8.12, are shown in Fig. 8.13, under the assumption that the inventory level at the beginning of January is 0.

Planning Horizon N	Jan	Feb	Mar	Apr	May	Jun	Cost	Cost/Period
1	3						19	19
2	3	3					38	19
3	4	5	0				48	16
4	3 4	4 5	5 0	0 3			67	$16\frac{3}{4}$
5	5	5	0	5	0		79	$15\frac{4}{5}$
6	4	5	0	4	5	0	96	16

FIGURE 8.13. Dependable Manufacturing Company Production Schedule When $i_0 = 0$.

Figure 8.13 is constructed as follows. When $N = 1$, January production, 3, is found from the first row of Fig. 8.12 under $n = 1$. When $N = 2$, January production, 3, is found from the first row of Fig. 8.12 under $n = 2$. And so on. When $N = 6$, January production is 4 and inventory entering February will then be 1 $(= i + x - d = 0 + 4 - 3)$. Consequently, the February production level, 5, is found in Fig. 8.12 for $n = 5$ with the new entering $i = 1$. This in turn means that inventory entering March will be 3 ($= i + x - d = 1 + 5 - 3$), so that March production is 0, as shown in Fig. 8.12 for $n = 4$ with the new entering $i = 3$. The same line of reasoning establishes that April production is 4, since $n = 3$ with entering inventory of 0 ($= i + x - d = 3 + 0 - 3$). Given the April decision, inventory entering May is $0 + 4 - 3 = 1$, so that May production is 5 ($n = 2$). Therefore June production 0 is optimal, since entering inventory is $1 + 5 - 3 = 3$ with $n = 1$. Verify that minimum total cost when $N = 6$ is $(21 + 1) + (23 + 3) + (0 + 0) + (21 + 1) + (23 + 3) + (0 + 0) = 96$, which appears as $f_6(0)$ in Fig. 8.12.

The policies in Fig. 8.13 show how the best production amount for January depends on the length of the planning horizon. As the horizon length N increases from 1 to 5, there exist optimal policies such that January production increases. For $N = 6$, however, the best policy calls for January production of 4 as compared to the amount 5 when $N = 5$. Thus initial production can either increase or decrease as the planning horizon lengthens. For $N = 4$, there are two alternative optimal policies. Figure 8.13 also exhibits how the cost per period depends on N. Note that the cost per period does not steadily decrease, but fluctuates as N increases from 2 to 6.

The policy for $N = 5$ deserves special attention. In this case, inventory is increased in January, February, and April. The May demand is thus filled by two units of April production as well as a unit produced in February. In this situation, it turns out to be optimal to bring in inventory to *both* February and April even though a setup cost is incurred in these two months.

Initial inventory. Here we study how an optimal policy depends on the amount of starting inventory. Examine Fig. 8.14 to see how the January production figure varies with different levels of initial inventory. When the horizon

Planning Horizon N	January Production			Incremental Value of Inventory	
	$i_0 = 0$	$i_0 = 1$	$i_0 = 2$	$i_0 = 1$	$i_0 = 2$
1	3	2	1	2	2
2	3	5	4	12	2
3	4	5	4	3	2
4	3,4	5	5	3	10
5	5	5	4	5	2
6	4	5	4	3	2

Figure 8.14. Dependable Manufacturing Company Inventory Valuation.

length $N = 1$, each additional unit of initial inventory brings about a unit reduction in January production. When $N = 2, 3, 4$, and 6, however, the first unit of initial inventory actually causes January production to increase. Depending on the horizon length N, the second unit may cause January production to fall (when $N = 2$, production does not fall to the previous level) or remain the same ($N = 4$).

The final two columns of Fig. 8.14 tabulate the reduction in total cost when initial inventory increases. For example, consider the horizon $N = 2$. If initial inventory is 0, the total cost is 38, shown in Fig. 8.12. One unit of initial inventory brings the total cost down to 26 and another unit to 24. Thus the value of the first unit of inventory is 12 and the next 2, as exhibited in Fig. 8.14. Notice that the value of initial inventory depends considerably on the length of the time horizon, and whether the item is the first or second unit. Using the information in Fig. 8.12, trace the optimal policies for horizons $N = 4$ and 6 and initial inventory levels $i_0 = 1$ and 2 to see why the incremental values of inventory differ as they do. (Incidentally, you will find, when $N = 4$ and $i = 2$, that four units of inventory enter February, so that if inventory at the end of each period, i_t, were constrained to be strictly less than four, this solution would be ruled out, and total cost would increase.)

*Long-run analysis of short-term policies. So far you have investigated what happens when the planning horizon N is the same as the total span over which the item is demanded. That is, the policies in Figs. 8.12 and 8.13 refer to the situation in which demand $D_t = 0$ for $t > N$.

Now suppose $D_t = 3$ *beyond* the planning horizon N, but the *current* monthly production amount is determined by looking only N periods ahead. For example, if $N = 4$, then January production is determined by taking into account inventory at the beginning of January and selecting the corresponding optimal policy *as if* the total span were merely January through April. Then, in February, the process is repeated. Given entering inventory, February production is determined *as if* the horizon were $N = 4$ (February through May). This procedure, sometimes called a **rolling schedule**, is often employed in industrial situations. The question examined is how well the procedure performs for the example here.

To begin, suppose that the true span for which $D_t = 3$ is 10 periods, and $D_t = 0$ for $t > 10$. For each planning horizon N, Fig. 8.15 shows the resulting schedule and cost, assuming initial inventory in January is 0. The truly optimal policy ($N = 10$) is to repeat twice the policy for $N = 5$ in Fig. 8.13. However, *no rolling schedule produces this optimal schedule*. When $N = 4$, several possible rolling schedules arise, since if entering inventory is 0, production of either 3 or 4 is indicated. Only two schedules are shown, and they produce different total costs. Finally, note that lengthening the planning horizon for a rolling schedule can actually be harmful. The schedule for $N = 3$ is less costly than that for $N = 5$, although neither is optimal.

Suppose that in fact D_t has the same value of 3, and a rolling schedule procedure

Planning Horizon N	Jan	Feb	Mar	Apr	May	Jun	Jul	Aug	Sept	Oct	Cost
1	3	3	3	3	3	3	3	3	3	3	190
2	3	3	3	3	3	3	3	3	3	3	190
3	4	5	0	4	5	0	4	5	0	3	163
4	3	3	3	3	3	3	3	4	5	0	181
	4	5	0	4	5	0	4	5	0	3	163
5	5	4	0	5	4	0	3	4	5	0	165
	5	4	0	5	4	0	4	5	0	3	
6	4	5	0	4	5	0	3	4	5	0	163
	4	5	0	4	5	0	4	5	0	3	
Optimal	5	5	0	5	0	5	5	0	5	0	158

Figure 8.15. Dependable Manufacturing Company Rolling Schedule Operating Over a 10-Period Span ($i_0 = 0$).

is perpetually employed. Then assuming that initial inventory i_0 is equal to 0, the resulting production patterns are the ever-repeating cycles exhibited in Fig. 8.16. Given that $i_0 = 0$, the cost functions and various constraints imply that ending

Planning Horizon N^a	$x_N(0)$	$x_N(1)$	$x_N(2)$	Repeating Production Cycle					Cost/Period
1	3	2	1						
2	3	5	4	3					19
4,7	3	5	5						
5,8,11, 14,17	5	5	4	5	4	0			$16\frac{1}{3}$
3,6,8, 11,14,17	4	5	4	4	5	0			16
4,7,9,12, 13,14,16	4	5	5						
10,13,14, 15,16,18,... Optimal	5	5	5	5	5	0	5	0	$15\frac{4}{5}$

[a] Policies for $N \leq 6$ are found in Figure 8.12, and for $N > 6$ are found by extending that analysis. For all N, $x_N(i) = 0$ when $i \geq 3$.

Figure 8.16. Dependable Manufacturing Company Rolling Schedule Operating Over an Unbounded Horizon ($i_0 = 0$).

inventory will never exceed the level 2. Therefore, if for two different planning horizons the optimal production policies are identical for entering inventory levels $i = 0, 1, 2$, they will lead to the same repeating production cycle. As a consequence, we tabulate only these three policy values in Fig. 8.16. You can see that only seven distinct optimal policies occur for $N = 1, 2, \ldots$, and these lead to only four different repeating production cycles. (For certain horizons, there are several optimal policies, so these values of N are repeated accordingly.)

Notice that not until $N = 10$ does a rolling schedule yield an optimal solution, which is defined as a policy giving minimum cost per period. Even at $N = 17$ the resultant repeating production cycles are not optimal, and it can be shown that one alternative policy for $N = 22$ incurs a cost of 16 per period. However, provided the planning horizon is large enough—namely, $N \geq 18$—the optimal policy for the unbounded horizon is also optimal for the finite horizon situation. This illustration demonstrates that without careful analysis there is ample opportunity to make an error in judging the required horizon for planning.

In Chaps. 11 and 12 you will study how to determine optimal policies when the time span of operation actually is unbounded.

Commentary. Although the particular *numerical* values for the example have been selected with some care, the general description of the situation is reasonable: production expense consists of a setup cost plus a unit cost; inventory holding cost is linear (1 per unit of ending inventory); and simple upper bounds are imposed on production and inventory. Nevertheless, an optimal policy changes drastically with various alterations in the planning horizon. It is impossible to suggest how often you will encounter such extreme planning horizon sensitivity, and how economically serious it is to mistakenly adopt a nonoptimal policy. But you ought to realize from the example that it is difficult to recognize the degree and significance of the sensitivity analysis without undertaking a precise dynamic analysis of the particular application. The operations research approach you have just learned is a fundamental tool for this type of study.

As you know, a mathematical model often is general enough to cover a multitude of real situations; a meaningful evaluation of the model in this chapter must therefore be carried out in terms of what is being assumed rather than in terms of the one particular environment described for the Dependable Manufacturing Company. The crucial assumptions are listed below.

1. *The demand forecast is accurate.* Although a company can rarely forecast several months' demand without error, the margin of error is often small enough for the deterministic model to yield a good approximation. (In such circumstances, a rolling schedule discussed in the advanced material above is usually followed; but sometimes several periods are allowed to elapse before making a schedule revision.) When the forecasting errors are substantial, models of the type described in Chap. 19 and Appendix II must be used.

2. *The manufacturing time is negligible.* The assumption actually required is that manufacturing time can be predetermined with negligible error. To illustrate, suppose it always takes two weeks to produce a batch of items. Then if a schedule found by the recursion formulas in this chapter indicates that February production is to meet February's demand, the batch really would be started two weeks earlier, in the second half of January.

Another facet of this assumption is that manufacturing time can be determined independently of other orders being processed. If several items are each produced on a single piece of equipment having limited capacity, then an agglomeration of schedules, each found independently by a dynamic programming model, may not be feasible.

The models in this chapter are often useful when an item is simply ordered from an outside vendor, who keeps an inventory on hand. The time delay then becomes the delivery lag, and the cost function includes the purchase cost, instead of the production expense.

3. *Each period's cost depends on the amount produced and on the ending inventory; each period's demand is entirely satisfied.* Without much trouble these two assumptions can be altered to cover a much wider variety of situations. We discuss how in the advanced material below.

▶Without introducing any essentially new complications, the dynamic programming recursion (8) in Sec. 8.3 can be written as

(i) $$f_n(i) = \text{minimum } [c_n(x, i, i + x - d_n) + f_{n-1}(i + x - d_n)].$$

This formulation then is able to encompass the situation in which inventory holding cost is levied against average inventory:

(ii) $$\frac{i + (i + x - d_n)}{2}.$$

It is also possible to let demand be fully backlogged until later periods. To do that,

(iii) $$i_t = i_{t-1} + x_t - D_t$$

as before, but now i_t is permitted to take on negative values to represent the amount backlogged. Or, as another alternative, it is possible to let unfilled demand be fully lost by defining

(iv) $$i_t = \text{maximum } (i_{t-1} + x_t - D_t, 0).$$

Then

(v) $$f_n(i) = \underset{x=0,1,\ldots}{\text{minimum}} \{c_n(x, i, i + x - d_n) + f_{n-1}[\text{maximum } (i + x - d_n, 0)]\}.$$

For both (iii) and (iv) the cost function $c_n(x, i, i + x - d_n)$ would include a penalty for the backlogging or lost demand condition. For example, one such cost function is

(vi) $$c_n(x, i, i + x - d_n) = c(x) + h[\text{maximum } (i + x - d_n, 0)] \\ - p[\text{minimum } (i + x - d_n, 0)],$$

where $p > 0$ represents the cost per unit of demand not met in a period. In the lost-sales case, presumably p would include the drop in sales revenue. These possibilities are examined in greater detail in Chap. 19 and Appendix II.

In some instances, a firm may incur a cost due to changing production from one period to the next. This situation can also be handled by a dynamic programming recursion, but is more complex; it is discussed in Sec. 9.7.

In truth, if demand can be forecast with sufficient accuracy so that a deterministic inventory model is useful, then the models in this chapter usually turn out to be *too* general. Typically, there is enough particular information about $c_n(x, i, i + x - d_n)$ that much stronger results concerning planning horizons and the form of optimal policies can be derived. As a result, the computational burden of finding such policies is considerably simpler than that indicated by the example in Sec. 8.4. Two important special cases are considered in the next chapter to illustrate this point.   ◀

*8.6 STRATEGIC PLANNING

If you were the Vice-President in charge of production in the Dependable Manufacturing Company, you might well be disturbed by the results of the preceding analysis. In trying to pin down the causes for the peculiar sensitivity of optimal production policies, you might turn attention, on one hand, to the incentive for avoiding a high setup cost, and, on the other hand, to the restriction of staying below the maximum production level 5. You might consider what would happen if the production and inventory restrictions were dropped completely, and

$$(1) \qquad\qquad C(x_t) = \begin{cases} 0 & \text{for } x_t = 0 \\ 13 + 2x_t & \text{for } x_t > 0, \end{cases}$$

which gives the same cost-function values as before for $x_t = 0, 1, \ldots, 5$. Then if initial inventory is 0 and demand D_t has the same value of 3, the optimal January production can be shown to be 9, and this batch size should be manufactured repeatedly whenever entering inventory is 0. The corresponding minimal cost per period is $13\frac{1}{3}$, as compared to $15\frac{4}{5}$ in Fig. 8.16.

In an effort to relieve the cost impact of the production constraint, suppose you discover there is a way to produce up to six units each period. However, the corresponding cost of six units is

$$(2) \qquad\qquad\qquad C(6) = 28.5,$$

which is incrementally large ($5.5 = 28.5 - 23$). Obviously, adding another possible production level cannot worsen the situation, because all the previous policies are still feasible. But does this new alternative make much of a difference?

The revised values of $f_n(i)$ and the corresponding $x_n(i)$ appear in Fig. 8.17. You should check your understanding of the recursive calculation process by performing the computations for finding $f_2(i)$ and $f_3(i)$. Figure 8.18 exhibits the production schedules implied by the new values, assuming that initial inventory in January is 0. Comparing these figures with the corresponding amounts in Fig. 8.13, you see that the schedules for horizons $N = 2, 4$, and 6 are revised and utilize the sixth unit of production. As a consequence, now the lowest cost per

Entering Inventory	$n=1$		$n=2$		$n=3$		$n=4$		$n=5$		$n=6$	
i	$x_1(i)$	$f_1(i)$	$x_2(i)$	$f_2(i)$	$x_3(i)$	$f_3(i)$	$x_4(i)$	$f_4(i)$	$x_5(i)$	$f_5(i)$	$x_6(i)$	$f_6(i)$
0	3	19	6	31.5	4	48	6	63	5	79	6	94.5
1	2	17	5	26	5	45	5	57.5	5	74	5	89
2	1	15	4	24	4	43	5	54	4	72	5	85.5
3	0	0	0	19	0	31.5	0	48	0	63	0	79
4			0	18	0	27	0	46	0	58.5	0	75

FIGURE 8.17. Expanded Production Capability of Dependable Manufacturing Company.

Planning Horizon N	Jan	Feb	Mar	Apr	May	Jun	Cost	Cost/Period
1	3						19	19
2	6	0					31.5	$15\frac{3}{4}$
3	4	5	0				48	16
4	6	0	6	0			63	$15\frac{3}{4}$
5	5	5	0	5	0		79	$15\frac{4}{5}$
6	6	0	6	0	6	0	94.5	$15\frac{3}{4}$

FIGURE 8.18. Dependable Manufacturing Company Production Schedule When $i_0 = 0$.

period is for horizons $N = 2, 4$, and 6. For $N = 1, 3$, and 5, the optimal January production is less than 6. Observe that for horizon $N = 5$ the previous solution is still optimal.

The influence of initial inventory in January is shown in Fig. 8.19. If initial inventory is either one or two units, the optimal January production is the same as it was in Fig. 8.14. The incremental values of initial inventory have changed, however.

If demand $D_t = 3$ for every t and a rolling schedule procedure is perpetually employed, then assuming that initial inventory is equal to 0, the patterns appear as in Fig. 8.20. Now if the planning horizon N is an even number, an optimal schedule occurs. Otherwise the previous nonoptimal pattern in Fig. 8.16 results.

Planning Horizon N	January Production			Incremental Value of Inventory	
	$i_0 = 0$	$i_0 = 1$	$i_0 = 2$	$i_0 = 1$	$i_0 = 2$
1	3	2	1	2	2
2	6	5	4	5.5	2
3	4	5	4	3	2
4	6	5	5	5.5	3.5
5	5	5	4	5	2
6	6	5	5	5.5	3.5

FIGURE 8.19. Dependable Manufacturing Company Inventory Valuation.

Planning Horizon N	Repeating Production Cycle			Cost/Period
1	3			19
5	5	4	0	$16\frac{1}{3}$
3	4	5	0	16
2,4,6 Optimal	6	0		$15\frac{3}{4}$

FIGURE 8.20. Dependable Manufacturing Company Revised Rolling Schedule Operating Over an Unbounded Horizon ($i_0 = 0$).

Take a closer look at the difference between the optimal repeating schedule for the new situation and the previous one in Fig. 8.16. In the previous situation, there are six setups in a ten-period span, maximum inventory is 4, and inventory exists at the end of eight of the ten periods. Here a batch of 6 is produced every other period, and inventory fluctuates between 3 and 0. Thus in a ten-period span, there are only five setups, maximum inventory is 3, and inventory is positive at the end of only five of the periods. By easing the constraint on production, not only has cost per period improved, but the new optimal policy itself appears qualitatively more appealing.

REVIEW EXERCISES

Exercises 1 through 6 refer to the Stagecoach Problem in Sec. 8.2.

1 (a) Enumerate the 14 distinct routes from the East to the West in Fig. 8.1.
 (b) Explain why it is not necessary to evaluate all of these routes when you employ the principle of optimality.

2 (a) Suppose the stagecoach from State 7 to State 9 does not operate. What is the best routing from the East to the West?

(b) Suppose a stagecoach service is inaugurated from State 3 to State 8. What is the smallest policy cost for this link such that Mark Off would still prefer the current routing?

(c) Determine a range for the policy cost of the stagecoach from State 1 to State 3 such that Mark Off prefers the current routing. Do the same for the policy cost from State 3 to State 7. Do the same for the policy cost from State 2 to State 6.

3 Mark Off suspects that it is the *relative* costs at each stage that determine an optimal routing. For example, he suspects that he should select the same routing if the policy costs are $c_{12} = 2 + \delta$, $c_{13} = 5 + \delta$, and $c_{14} = 4 + \delta$, where δ can be any constant value. Is Mark Off correct? If not, state why. If so, discuss how his observation may be helpful.

4 Mark Off's father, Pop Off, lives in State 8. Find an optimal routing from the East to the West that goes through State 8.

5 Mark Off's brother, Buzz, lives in San Francisco and wants to travel East. Assume that the policy cost for each stagecoach remains the same in the easterly direction.

(a) Explain why an optimal routing for Buzz is the reverse of the one Mark used.

(b) Carry out the recursive calculations implied by (2) in Sec. 8.2, starting the computations at State 1. (Note here that if $n = 1$ more stage to go, then Buzz is either in State 2, 3, or 4; similarly, if $n = 4$ stages to go, then Buzz is in State 10.)

6 *Stagecoach Problem.* In each part, find an optimal route from the East to the West, where the policy cost from State i to State j equals the c_{ij} shown in Fig. 8.1 plus the modifications specified.

(a) $c_{ij} + i$ (thus, the cost from State 1 to State 2 is 3, to State 3 is 6, and to State 4 is 2, etc.).

(b) $c_{ij} + j$ (thus, the cost from State 1 to State 2 is 4, to State 3 is 8, and to State 4 is 5, etc.).

(c) $c_{ij} + j - i$ (thus, the cost from State 1 to State 2 is 3, to State 3 is 7, and to State 4 is 4, etc.).

(d) $c_{ij} + i + j$ (thus, the cost from State 1 to State 2 is 5, to State 3 is 9, and to State 4 is 6, etc.).

*7 Compare the algorithm (2) in Sec. 8.2 with the shortest-route algorithm (2) in Sec. 7.7.

Exercises 8 through 20 refer to the production and inventory model in Sec. 8.3.

8 Each part below shows either the production quantity x_t in Period t or the inventory level i_t at the end of Period t; you are to determine the implied levels of the unspecified policy variable, either i_t or x_t. Assume that there are $N = 6$ periods, and that the demand requirements are

$$D_1 = 10 \quad D_2 = 15 \quad D_3 = 8 \quad D_4 = 25 \quad D_5 = 12 \quad D_6 = 30.$$

State whether the implied policy is feasible, that is, whether $x_t \geq 0$ and $i_t \geq 0$ for every t. The symbol i_0 denotes initial inventory available at the *start* of Period 1.

(a) $i_0 = 10$, and $x_t = 15$ every period.
(b) $i_0 = 5$, $x_1 = 20$, and $x_t = 15$ for $t = 2, 3, \ldots, 6$.
(c) $i_0 = 5$, $x_t = 15$ for $t = 1, 2, \ldots, 5$, and $x_6 = 20$.
(d) $i_0 = 1$, $x_t = 10$ for $t = 1, 2, 3$, and $x_t = 23$ for $t = 4, 5, 6$.
(e) $i_0 = 0$, $i_1 = 15$, $i_2 = 20$, $i_3 = 25$, $i_4 = 15$, $i_5 = 5$, $i_6 = 0$.
(f) $i_0 = 10$, $i_1 = 15$, $i_2 = 20$, $i_3 = 25$, $i_4 = 15$, $i_5 = 5$, $i_6 = 0$.
(g) $i_0 = 30$, $i_1 = 15$, $i_2 = 20$, $i_3 = 25$, $i_4 = 15$, $i_5 = 5$, $i_6 = 0$.
(h) $i_0 = 0$, $i_1 = 10$, $i_2 = 10$, $i_3 = 10$, $i_4 = 10$, $i_5 = 10$, $i_6 = 0$.
(i) $i_0 = 35$, $i_1 = 35$, $i_2 = 35$, $i_3 = 35$, $i_4 = 35$, $i_5 = 35$, $i_6 = 0$.
(j) $i_0 = 35$, $i_1 = 35$, $i_2 = 35$, $i_3 = 35$, $i_4 = 35$, $i_5 = 10$, $i_6 = 0$.
(k) How would you revise the plan if $i_6 = 10$ in parts (e), (g), (h), (i), and (j)?

9 Suppose the cost function $C_t(x_t, i_t)$ is described as

$$C_t(x_t, i_t) = C(x_t) + hi_t,$$

where

$$C(x_t) = \begin{cases} 0 & \text{for } x_t = 0 \\ 6 + 10x_t & \text{for } x_t > 0, \end{cases}$$

and $h = 2$. Calculate the total production and inventory cost associated with the plans in exercise 8,

(a) Part (a).   (e) Part (f).
(b) Part (b).   (f) Part (h).
(c) Part (c).   (g) Part (j).
(d) Part (e).

10 Assume you have values for production x_t and inventory i_t that satisfy all the constraints (2) through (5) in Sec. 8.3. Recall that $C_t(x_t, i_t)$ is the production and holding cost function, and that ending inventory $i_N = 0$.

(a) Consider increasing the level of x_2 by 1, decreasing the level of x_3 by 1, and revising inventory levels accordingly. Explain why the new plan is still feasible. Indicate the resultant incremental change in total cost.

(b) Consider increasing the level of x_3 by 1, decreasing the level of x_2 by 1, and revising inventory levels accordingly. Explain why the new plan may not be feasible. Give a condition involving the demand requirements that must be satisfied in order for the new plan to be feasible. Give an equivalent condition involving inventory. Assuming the new plan is feasible, indicate the resultant incremental change in total cost.

(c) Consider increasing the level of x_2 by 1, decreasing the level of x_4 by 1, and revising inventory levels accordingly. Explain why the new plan is still feasible. Indicate the resultant incremental change in total cost.

(d) Consider increasing the level of inventory i_2 by 1, and revising production levels accordingly. Explain why the new plan may not be feasible. Give a condition involving the demand requirements that must be satisfied in order for the new plan to be feasible. Assuming the new plan is feasible, indicate the resultant incremental change in total cost.

(e) Consider decreasing the level of inventory i_2 by 1, and revising production levels accordingly. Explain why the new plan may not be feasible. Give a condition that must be satisfied in order for the new plan to be feasible. Assuming the new plan is feasible, indicate the resultant incremental change in total cost.

*11 Let $N = 6$, and write equations (4) in Sec. 8.3 for $t = 1, 2, \ldots, 6$.

(a) Display the constraints of the model in a technology table, like that in Fig. 8.6.
(b) Derive an associated network structure, like that in Fig. 8.7. [*Hint:* add the six equations in part (a) to form a seventh equation; then rewrite each equation in part (a) after multiplying through by -1.]
(c) Suppose the cost function is linear,

$$C_t(x_t, i_t) = C_t x_t + h i_t,$$

where

$$C_1 = 1 \quad C_2 = 4 \quad C_3 = 3 \quad C_4 = 5 \quad C_5 = 7 \quad C_6 = 4.$$

Let initial inventory $i_0 = 0$, and let the demand requirements be those in exercise 8. Find optimal policies for $h = 0$, $h = \frac{1}{2}$, $h = 1\frac{1}{2}$, and $h = 4$. Indicate alternative optimal policies when they occur.

12 Give a verbal explanation of why the state of the system is completely summarized by the level of entering inventory each period. What are the assumptions about costs and production lags that permit this simple characterization of the state?

13 The recursive calculation process in dynamic programming has been termed a bootstrap approach in Sec. 8.2. Give a verbal explanation of the way the bootstrap approach is applied to obtain a solution to the inventory model in Sec. 8.3.

14 Suppose $N = 6$ and January is Period 1. Let d_n refer to the demand requirement in that period when there are n more periods to go. To what month does d_1 refer? Similarly, d_6? d_5? d_2?

15 Consider the recursion (8) in Sec. 8.3. Suppose that $i = 0$ when n periods remain. What is the smallest feasible value for production, x, in that period? Suppose, instead, that $i = d_1 + d_2 + \cdots + d_n$. What is the value for production in each of the n remaining periods?

16 Consider the recursion (8) in Sec. 8.3. Suppose $c_3(x, j) = 5x + 2j$. Assume that starting inventory $i = 4$ with $n = 3$ more periods to go, and that ending inventory must not exceed 4. Let $d_3 = 10$. Find an optimal level of production and the associated ending inventory level given the following.

(a) $f_2(0) = 100 \quad f_2(1) = 90 \quad f_2(2) = 82 \quad f_2(3) = 76 \quad f_2(4) = 75.$
(b) $f_2(0) = 110 \quad f_2(1) = 100 \quad f_2(2) = 92 \quad f_2(3) = 86 \quad f_2(4) = 85.$
(c) $f_2(j) = 100 - 6j.$
(d) $f_2(j) = 100 - 9j.$
(e) $f_2(0) = 100 \quad f_2(1) = 99 \quad f_2(2) = 93 \quad f_2(3) = 85 \quad f_2(4) = 75.$

17 Recall that $x_n(i)$ is an optimal production level when entering inventory is at level i with n more periods to go. Suppose $d_n = 2$ for every n and that the values for $x_n(i)$ are

$$x_3(0) = 5 \qquad x_2(0) = 4 \qquad x_1(0) = 2$$
$$x_3(1) = 4 \qquad x_2(1) = 3 \qquad x_1(1) = 1$$
$$x_3(2) = 0 \qquad x_2(2) = 0 \qquad x_1(2) = 0.$$
$$x_3(3) = 0 \qquad x_2(3) = 0$$

In parts (a) through (d), indicate an optimal production plan and the associated inventory levels when there are $n = 3$ more periods to go, and entering inventory level i equals

(a) 0.   (c) 2.
(b) 1.   (d) 3.
(e) At $n = 3$ what is the incremental value of $i = 1$ versus $i = 2$? Of $i = 4$ versus $i = 3$? [Use the symbol $c_k(x, j)$ to denote the cost function in the period when there are k more periods to go.]

*18 (a) Modify Fig. 8.8 to treat the case in which demand $d_n = 2$ for $n = 1, 2, 3, 4$.
   (b) Modify Fig. 8.8 to treat the case in which the permissible production values are $x = 0, 2, 4$.
   (c) Explain how Fig. 8.8 is modified when you impose the constraint that inventory at the end of each period cannot exceed the level 1.
   (d) Explain how Fig. 8.8 can be simplified if you know for certain that inventory entering January equals 1.

*19 Explain the connection between finding a shortest route in Fig. 8.8 and the recursive calculations indicated by (8) in Sec. 8.3.

*20 In the network displayed in Fig. 8.8, reorient each arc in the opposite direction. Assume that inventory entering January equals 1. Explain how finding a shortest route from the node labeled "Terminal" to the node for January with inventory level 1 is the same process as applying recursion (iv) in the special material at the end of Sec. 8.3, and yields the value $g_4(0)$.

Exercises 21 through 34 refer to the case of the Dependable Manufacturing Company described in Sec. 8.4.

21 In each part below, construct a complete table, laid out like Fig. 8.11, showing $f_n(i)$ and $x_n(i)$ for the indicated value of n. Use the values of $f_{n-1}(i)$ that are given in Fig. 8.12.

(a) $n = 4$.
(b) $n = 5$.
(c) $n = 6$.

22 (a) Verify that the cost function $C(x)$ given as (3) in Sec. 8.4 represents a setup cost of 13 plus a variable unit cost of 2 per item produced.
   (b) Explain why the production level x in a period must be at least $3 - i$, where i is the level of entering inventory.

(c) Explain why the production level x in a period cannot exceed $7 - i$, given the restriction that ending inventory must be less than or equal to 4.

(d) Suppose initial inventory is zero. Calculate the average cost per period if the production pattern is to produce three units every period. If the pattern is to produce five units and then one unit. If the pattern is to produce five units, five units, two units, and zero units. If the pattern is to produce five units, five units, zero units, and two units. If the pattern is to produce five units, two units, five units, and zero units. If the pattern is to produce four units and then two units. If the pattern is to produce four units, four units, four units, and zero units. Explain the cost tradeoffs among these different patterns.

23 Construct a table like that in Fig. 8.13, and assume that initial inventory entering January is

(a) $i_0 = 1$.   (c) $i_0 = 3$.
(b) $i_0 = 2$.   (d) $i_0 = 4$.

(e) Given your answers above, verify the incremental values of inventory shown in Fig. 8.14, and extend the table for $i_0 = 3$ and $i_0 = 4$.

24 Construct a table like that in Fig. 8.12 given the constraint on ending inventory as indicated below. (*Hint:* you do not have to repeat all the computations in Fig. 8.12 if you make judicious use of the information contained in Figs. 8.9 through 8.12.)

(a) $i \leq 5$.
(b) $i \leq 3$.

(c) Given your answers above, what is the smallest limiting value (3, 4, or 5) such that the restriction on the inventory level is *not* binding?

25 Construct tables like those in Figs. 8.12 and 8.13, where the constraint on the production capacity limitation is specified as

(a) Production x in each period cannot exceed four units.
(b) Production x in each period cannot exceed six units and $C(6) = 25$.

(c) Given your answers above, compare the impact of varying the production capacity limit.

(d) What is the form of an optimal policy for this company if it imposes the production level restriction that $x \geq 1$ every period?

26 Construct a table like that in Fig. 8.12 given the constraint that inventory at the end of the horizon equals

(a) One unit.   (c) Three units.
(b) Two units.   (d) Four units.

(e) For each of your answers above, construct a table like that in Fig. 8.13.

27 Construct tables like those in Figs. 8.12, 8.13, and 8.14, given the assumption that demand D_t each period equals

(a) Two units.
(b) Four units.

(c) Explain how the optimal policies differ when stationary demand equals two or four, instead of three.

28 Construct tables like those in Figs. 8.12, 8.13, and 8.14, given the assumption that

  (a) The setup cost component in $C(x)$, shown in (3) of Sec. 8.4, is 10, instead of 13.
  (b) The holding cost $h = 5$, instead of $h = 1$.
  (c) Explain how the optimal policies are affected by a decrease in setup cost or an increase in holding cost.

29 Construct tables like those in Figs. 8.12 and 8.13, given the assumption that demand in the *final* period of the horizon is as specified below, instead of three units. (For example, if $N = 4$, then demand is altered in April.) Compare your results with the policies in Figs. 8.12 and 8.13 and comment on the impact of incorrectly assuming in January that demand at the end of the horizon is three units, instead of the amount indicated below.

  (a) Two units.
  (b) Four units.

*30 Verify that using a rolling schedule over 10 periods, with the horizon length N as indicated below, yields the policies shown in Fig. 8.15.

  (a) $N = 3.$ (c) $N = 5.$
  (b) $N = 4.$ (d) $N = 6.$

*31 Verify that using a rolling schedule over an unbounded horizon, with the horizon length N as indicated below, yields the policies and associated cost per period shown in Fig. 8.16.

  (a) $N = 3.$ (c) $N = 5.$
  (b) $N = 4.$ (d) $N = 6.$

*32 Suppose the holding cost function in Sec. 8.5 is modified such that the holding cost $h = 1$ is applied to average inventory, given by (ii) at the end of Sec. 8.5. Construct tables like those in Figs. 8.12 and 8.13, and compare the effect of this alteration in costing.

*33 Suppose that the Dependable Company abandons its policy of meeting all demand requirements on time. Let the cost function, which now includes a penalty for not meeting demand, be (vi) at the end of Sec. 8.5, where the penalty cost $p = 10$. In each part below, construct tables like those in Figs. 8.12 and 8.13, and compare the effect of this alteration in operating policy.

  (a) Assume that unfilled demand is lost forever, so that ending inventory is given by (iv) at the end of Sec. 8.5.
  (b) Assume that any demand not filled in a period is backlogged and must be filled at the next period. No backlog, however, is permitted to exist at the end of the final period, so that all demand during the horizon is eventually filled. Assume the penalty cost is charged every period demand remains backlogged.

*34 In each part below, construct a complete table, laid out like Fig. 8.11, showing $f_n(i)$ and $x_n(i)$ for the indicated values of n. Use the values for $f_{n-1}(i)$ as given in Fig. 8.17.

  (a) $n = 2.$ (d) $n = 5.$
  (b) $n = 3.$ (e) $n = 6.$
  (c) $n = 4.$

35 Explain your understanding of the following terms:

dynamic programming   optimal policy
principle of optimality   stage
recursion   state
recursive algorithm   *backward in time
bootstrap process (or approach) *rolling schedule.

COMPUTATIONAL EXERCISES

36 Mark Off's fame spread world wide. He received an urgent request from the Russian Tsar Kazim to find a route to Rostov from Vladivostok. In this case, the Tsar's wife made the trip, and the expense associated with each leg of the journey is for protection against attacks by Cossacks and local tribesmen. The numbers shown on each arc in Fig. 8.21 are the rubles that must be paid for protection on that route. Find an optimal routing. Display your calculations in tables like those in Figs. 8.2 through 8.5.

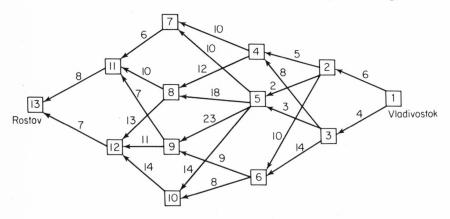

FIGURE 8.21

37 Consider Tsar Kazim's problem in exercise 36. Assume that the same number of rubles must be paid for a journey in the opposite direction. Find an optimal routing starting in Rostov and ending in Vladivostok. Display your calculations in tables like those in Figs. 8.2 through 8.5.

38 Consider Tsar Kazim's problem in exercise 36. The Tsar's wife insists on visiting Territory 5, because she has learned that they have perfected a recipe for caviar pancakes. Find an optimal routing from Vladivostok to Rostov through Territory 5.

Exercises 39 through 44 refer to specific cases of the inventory model described in Sec. 8.3, and characterized by the recursion (8). In each exercise, the production and holding cost function for Period t has the form

$$C_t(x_t, i_t) = C_t(x_t) + h_t i_t.$$

(Note if January is the beginning of the horizon, then Period 1 refers to January.)

Construct tables like those in Figs. 8.12 and 8.13 for the indicated value of the horizon length N. (*Remark:* more efficient algorithms for solving these problems are discussed in Chap. 9.)

39 Let $N = 4$, demand $D_t = 1$, and holding cost $h_t = .1$ for all periods. Assume that

$$C_1(0) = 0 \quad C_1(1) = 5 \quad C_1(2) = 10 \quad C_1(3) = 15 \quad C_1(4) = 16$$
$$C_2(0) = 0 \quad C_2(1) = 6 \quad C_2(2) = 9 \quad C_2(3) = 12$$
$$C_3(0) = 0 \quad C_3(1) = 5 \quad C_3(2) = 7$$
$$C_4(0) = 0 \quad C_4(1) = 3.$$

40 Let $N = 5$. Assume

$$D_1 = 1 \quad D_2 = 1 \quad D_3 = 2 \quad D_4 = 3 \quad D_5 = 4,$$

and that holding cost $h_t = 1$ for all periods. Suppose the production cost function is

$$C_t(x_t) = \begin{cases} 0 & \text{for } x_t = 0 \\ s_t + c_t x_t & \text{for } x_t = 1, 2, 3, \ldots, \end{cases}$$

where $c_t = 10$ for all periods, and

$$s_1 = 1 \quad s_2 = 2 \quad s_3 = 4 \quad s_4 = 8 \quad s_5 = 7.$$

41 Let $N = 4$. Assume

$$D_1 = 1 \quad D_2 = 4 \quad D_3 = 2 \quad D_4 = 2,$$

and that $h_t = 0$ for all periods. Suppose the production cost function is the same form as in exercise 40, where

$$s_1 = 1 \quad s_2 = 12 \quad s_3 = 1 \quad s_4 = 2$$
$$c_1 = 3 \quad c_2 = 1 \quad c_3 = 2 \quad c_4 = 1.$$

42 Solve the Longview Manufacturing case considered in exercise 28 of Chap. 6 and exercise 48 of Chap. 7.

43 Suppose a firm can produce a limited number of units using its work force at regular-

		Jan.	Feb.	Mar.	Apr.	May	June
Regular Time	cost/unit	2	4	2	5	2	6
	capacity	3	1	4	3	1	3
Overtime	cost/unit	5	6	6	6	3	7
	capacity	6	3	3	2	0	1
Demand Requirements D_t		1	2	7	6	0	2

FIGURE 8.22

time wage rates and an additional, but limited, number of units using its work force at overtime wage rates. The data are given in Fig. 8.22. Thus, for example,

$$C_1(x_1) = \begin{cases} 2x_1 & \text{for } x_1 = 0, 1, 2, 3 \\ 2 \cdot 3 + 5(x_1 - 3) = 5x_1 - 9 & \text{for } x_1 = 4, 5, \dots, 9. \end{cases}$$

The fluctuation in costs from period to period is due to special conditions in the company's labor market as well as to varying prices for the product's raw materials. Assume that each unit of inventory stored at the end of a period has a holding cost $h_t = 1$ for all periods.

44 Assume that the horizon length $N = 3$, that the demand requirements are

$$D_1 = 3 \quad D_2 = 6 \quad D_3 = 3,$$

and that there are no holding costs. The production costs are described by

January	February	March
setup cost = 3	setup cost = 6	setup cost = 20
cost/unit for 1 up to 5 units = 1	cost/unit for 1·to 5 units = 1	cost/unit for first item = 1
cost/unit for each item beyond 5 units and up to 10 units = 5	cost/unit for each item beyond 5 units = 25	cost/unit for each item beyond the first = 30
cost/unit for each item beyond 10 units = 30		

Construct tables like those in Figs. 8.12 and 8.13.

MIND-EXPANDING EXERCISES

45 Consider the inventory model described in Sec. 8.3. Suppose that $\bar{x}$ represents a "target" production level each period, and that if actual production x deviates from $\bar{x}$, then you must pay the "smoothing cost" $v \cdot |x - \bar{x}|$. Assume $\bar{x}$ is a prespecified constant.

 (a) Show how to reformulate the recursion (8) to take this smoothing cost into account.

*(b) Let $v = 1$, $\bar{x} = 3$, and use the data in Sec. 8.4. Construct tables like those in Figs. 8.12 and 8.13 and indicate the impact of adding a smoothing cost.

*(c) Answer part (b) for $\bar{x} = 2$.

*(d) Discuss the difficulties that arise in the dynamic programming formulation if the smoothing cost is $v \cdot |x_t - x_{t-1}|$. (This case is treated in Chap. 9.)

46 Indicate how you would modify the inventory model in Sec. 8.3 and the recursion (8) to accommodate

 (a) Deterioration, that is, inventory at the start of Period t is smaller than inventory at the end of Period t − 1.

 (b) Spoilage, that is, the production level x yields less than x usable items.

(c) Demand D_t can also be negative, indicating the return of items.

(d) Production x can also be negative, indicating the disposal of items.

*(e) Production cost in Period t also depends on the production level in the previous period.

47 Indicate how to modify the inventory model in Sec. 8.3 and the recursion (8) when $R_t(y_t)$ represents the total revenue from selling y_t units in Period t and y_t is a decision variable. (Assume you cannot sell a unit in Period t unless it actually is available by the end of the period.)

Exercises 48 and 49 ask you to formulate a model in terms of a dynamic programming recursion. Be sure to define all the symbols you use, and answer the five questions at the end of Sec. 8.2. Give the appropriate optimization function when there is a single period remaining, as well as the recursion for Stage n. Explain how to initiate and terminate the calculations.

48 Consider the Feedem-Speedem Airline Company case described in exercise 32 of Chap. 2. Formulate (but do not solve) the model in terms of a dynamic programming recursion.

49 *Warehouse Problem.* Consider the case of Byer, Long, Celler, Short described in exercise 36 of Chap. 5.

(a) Formulate the model in terms of a dynamic programming recursion.

(b) Show how you would modify your answer in part (a) if there also is a fixed transaction cost s_t of selling and a fixed transaction cost b_t of buying.

(c) Show how you would modify your answer in part (a) if gallonage at the end of Period t is charged an inventory holding cost of h_t per gallon.

(d) Show how you would modify your formulation in part (a) if the warehouse capacity is not constant throughout the horizon but equals C_t in Period t. (*Hint:* do not forget that if capacity is smaller than entering inventory in Period t, the firm must sell.)

*(e) Show how to modify your formulation in part (a) if there are liquidity constraints that limit the cash amount of a purchase in each period to be no larger than the accumulated cash available from the preceding periods (assume K is the initial amount of cash available at the start of Period 1).

CONTENTS

CHAPTER 9

Dynamic Optimization of Inventory Scheduling[†]

9.1 EXPLOITING SPECIAL STRUCTURE

The analysis of the deterministic inventory model described in Sec. 8.3 is continued here. You will see that when the cost functions are assumed to have certain shapes, considerably more can be said about the optimal schedules. In particular, you can determine the *form* of an optimal policy, and with such knowledge devise simplified computational procedures to actually find the best policy.

Throughout this chapter we assume the cost functions are

$$(1) \qquad C_t(x_t, i_t) = C_t(x_t) + h_t(i_t) \quad \text{for each period,}$$

where

$$(2) \qquad C_t(x_t) \geq 0 \qquad C_t(0) = 0 \quad \text{and} \quad h_t(i_t) \geq 0 \qquad h_t(0) = 0.$$

Thus the total cost in each period is the sum of $C_t(x_t)$, which is the cost due to producing x_t, and $h_t(i_t)$, the cost due to having i_t at the end of a period. The inventory balance equations are

$$(3) \qquad i_t = i_{t-1} + x_t - D_t \quad \text{for each period,}$$

where we postulate $i_0 = 0$ and each D_t is a nonnegative integer. An equivalent way of writing (3) is

$$(4) \qquad i_t = i_0 + \sum_{k=1}^{t} x_k - \sum_{k=1}^{t} D_k.$$

[†]The focus of this chapter is primarily inventory analysis and secondarily dynamic analysis. Without loss of continuity, you can skip this chapter now if you wish, and return to it when studying Chap. 19 and Appendix II.

Finally, we require

(5) x_t and i_t nonnegative integers,

so that all demand is satisfied on time.

9.2 CONVEX AND CONCAVE COST FUNCTIONS

The following sections will make some additional assumptions about the shape of $C_t(x_t)$ and $h_t(i_t)$. Specifically, we distinguish two important shapes.

A function $g(x)$ defined for integer values of x is said to be **convex** *if*

(1) $g(x + 1) - g(x) \geq g(x) - g(x - 1)$ for all x convex

and **concave** *if*

(2) $g(x + 1) - g(x) \leq g(x) - g(x - 1)$ for all x concave.

Several graphical illustrations of convex and concave functions are shown in Fig. 9.1.

Convex Cost Functions

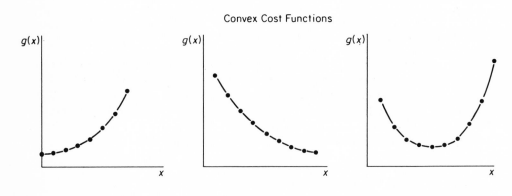

Concave Cost Functions

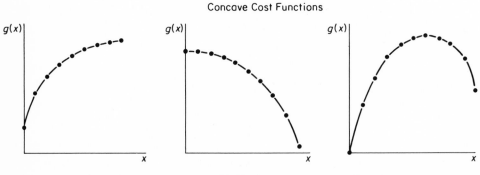

FIGURE 9.1

If you view $g(x)$ as a total cost function, then convex costs occur when each *additional* unit costs at least as much as the previous unit. Analogously, concave

costs occur when each *additional* unit costs no more than the previous unit. Sometimes the permissible values of x are constrained to be within a range, such as
$x = a, a + 1, \ldots, b - 1, b$ (where $a + 1 \leq b - 1$). Then the definitions are
to be applied to $a + 1 \leq x \leq b - 1$.

To examine the forms of particular functions, it is convenient to have the terms
in the definitions (1) and (2) rearranged as

(3) $$\frac{g(x + 1) + g(x - 1)}{2} \geq g(x) \quad \underline{\text{convex}}$$

(4) $$\frac{g(x + 1) + g(x - 1)}{2} \leq g(x) \quad \underline{\text{concave.}}$$

Consider the following six examples of $g(x)$. You will find it helpful to draw
a sketch of each function on scratch paper, and are urged to do so. For this
purpose, put $a = 2$, $b = 1$, and $c = 3$ in the first four examples.

Case i. Let $g(x) = ax + b$. Then

(5) $$\frac{[a(x + 1) + b] + [a(x - 1) + b]}{2} = ax + b,$$

so that a linear function $g(x)$ is *both* convex and concave for any values of a and
b and all x.

Case ii. Let $g(x) = ax^2 + b$. Then

(6) $$\frac{[a(x + 1)^2 + b] + [a(x - 1)^2 + b]}{2} = ax^2 + a + b \begin{cases} \geq ax^2 + b & \text{if } a \geq 0 \\ \leq ax^2 + b & \text{if } a \leq 0. \end{cases}$$

Thus for all x, $g(x)$ is convex when a is nonnegative, and concave when a is
nonpositive.

Case iii. Let $g(x) = \begin{cases} ax + b & \text{for } x \geq 0 \\ -cx + b & \text{for } x \leq 0 \end{cases}$

with $a \geq 0$ and $c \geq 0$. The test for *Case i* shows that $g(x)$ is convex (3) for
$x < 0$ and $x > 0$. At $x = 0$,

(7) $$\frac{[a + b] + [c + b]}{2} = \frac{(a + c)}{2} + b \geq b,$$

so that $g(x)$ is convex for all x.

Case iv. Let $g(x) = \begin{cases} 0 & \text{for } x = 0 \\ ax + b & \text{for } x \geq 1 \end{cases}$

with $b \geq 0$. The test for *Case i* shows that $g(x)$ is concave (4) for $x > 1$. At
$x = 1$,

(8) $$\frac{[2a + b] + [0]}{2} \leq a + b,$$

so that $g(x)$ is concave (for nonnegative x).

Case v. Let $g(x) = \begin{cases} 0 & \text{for } x = 0 \\ 13 + 2x & \text{for } x = 1, 2, 3, 4, 5 \\ 28.5 & \text{for } x = 6. \end{cases}$

The analysis for *Case iv* shows that (4) is satisfied for $x \le 4$. At $x = 5$,

(9)
$$\frac{[28.5] + [21]}{2} = 24.75 > 23,$$

so that (3) is satisfied. Consequently, $g(x)$ is neither convex nor concave.

Case vi. Check your understanding of the above process by showing that the piecewise linear function

(10)
$$g(x) = \begin{cases} a_1 x + b_1 & \text{for } 0 \le x \le w_1 \\ a_1 w_1 + a_2(x - w_1) + b_1 & \text{for } w_1 \le x \le w_2 \\ a_1 w_1 + a_2(w_2 - w_1) + a_3(x - w_2) + b_1 & \text{for } w_2 \le x \end{cases}$$

is convex if $a_1 \le a_2 \le a_3$ and concave if $a_1 \ge a_2 \ge a_3$. (Make the tests for $x = w_1$ and w_2. Draw the function by letting $a_1 = 2$, $b_1 = 1$, $w_1 = 4$, $a_2 = 3$, $w_2 = 6$, $a_3 = 4$.)

Several of the above examples are of special interest. For instance, *Case iii* includes

(11)
$$h_t(i_t) = \begin{cases} h_t i_t & \text{if } i_t \ge 0 \\ -p_t i_t & \text{if } i_t \le 0, \end{cases}$$

where $h_t \ge 0$ represents a per-unit inventory holding cost and $p_t \ge 0$ a per-unit backlog penalty charge. *Case v* encompasses the example in Sec. 8.6. Finally, *Case vi* contains

(12)
$$C_t(x_t) = \begin{cases} r_t x_t & \text{for } 0 \le x_t \le u_t \\ r_t u_t + 1.5r_t(x_t - u_t) & \text{for } u_t \le x_t \le v_t \\ r_t u_t + 1.5r_t(v_t - u_t) + 2r_t(x_t - v_t) & \text{for } v_t \le x_t, \end{cases}$$

where x_t is the total man-hours scheduled in Period t, r_t is the regular-time wage per man-hour, u_t is a given total amount of regular-time man-hours available in Period t, $1.5r_t$ is the "time and a half" wage rate per overtime hour, v_t is a given total amount of overtime hours available in Period t, and $2r_t$ is the "double-time" wage rate per man-hour.

9.3 INVENTORY MODEL WITH CONVEX COSTS

In addition to the cost, inventory, and production assumptions already made in Sec. 9.1, assume that

(1) $C_t(x_t)$ is convex   (production cost).

(2) $h_t(i_t)$ is convex   (holding cost).

A convexity assumption is sometimes called a situation of **decreasing incremental returns to scale**. It is also possible to impose, in each period, an upper-bound constraint u_t on x_t as well as a maximum amount b_t on inventory. To keep the explanation simple, suppose you handle these constraints by letting the corresponding values of $C_t(x_t)$ for $x_t > u_t$, and $h_t(i_t)$, for $i_t > b_t$, be infinitely large. This convention preserves the convexity in (1) and (2). Finally, we mention that the analysis can be extended to permit backlogging of demand requirements from a period to later periods.

In brief, the algorithm starting in Period 1 proceeds period by period to fill each unit of demand requirement as cheaply as possible, given the production already scheduled and the resultant pattern of inventory. The fact that such a simple algorithm leads to an optimal solution, of course, rests heavily on the convexity assumptions (1) and (2).

The details of the algorithm for this model are as follows.

Step 1. Let p be the earliest period in which the current demand requirement value is $D_p > 0$. For each of the Periods $1, 2, \ldots, p$ consider increasing production by one unit in the current trial schedule in order that one unit of D_p is filled.

Step 2. For each of the possible p revisions, calculate the entire incremental cost from the increased production *and* inventory holding. Select an alternative with minimum incremental cost and revise the trial schedule accordingly. If there is more than one such alternative, schedule production in as late a period as possible.

Step 3. Reduce the current value of D_p by one unit. Examine whether the current values of *all* D_t have now been reduced to 0. If so, stop; otherwise return to *Step 1.*

The example to follow illustrates the method.

The Highway Rubber Company Problem. This firm is planning its production schedule of tires for six months, January through June. The fluctuating monthly demands D_t are shown on the bottom of Fig. 9.2. Notice they accumulate to 18, so that the *total* demand for the span $N = 6$ is the same as that in the Dependable Manufacturing Company Example of Sec. 8.4.

In each period, there is a capability of producing a given number of tires at regular cost and an additional number at a premium cost. To demonstrate the flexibility of the algorithm, the regular and premium costs, and maximum amounts achievable at these costs, vary from period to period in the illustration. In Fig. 9.2, these costs appear in the pair of boxes on the diagonal, the upper figure being the regular cost. The corresponding maximum capacities are in the next to last column on the right. The far right column accumulates the monthly production capabilities.

	Jan	Feb	Mar	Apr	May	Jun	Production Capacity	Cumulative Capacity
Jan	2	3	4	5	6	7	3	9
	5	6	7	8	9	10	6	
Feb		4	5	6	7	8	1	13
		6	7	8	9	10	3	
Mar			2	3	4	5	4	20
			6	7	8	9	3	
Apr				5	6	7	3	25
				6	7	8	2	
May					2	3	1	26
					3	4	0	
Jun						6	3	30
						7	1	
Demand D_t	1	2	7	6	0	2		
Cumulative Demand	1	3	10	16	16	18		

FIGURE 9.2. Highway Rubber Company Convex Cost Model.

For example, in January as many as three units can be produced at a cost of 2 each, and as many as an additional six at a cost of 5 each. In February, one unit can be produced at a cost of 4, and as many as an additional three at a cost of 6. In March, as many as four units can be produced at a cost of 2 each, and as many as an additional three at 6 each, etc. Thus in each period the production cost function is of the form

$$(3) \qquad C_t(x_t) = r_t x_t \qquad\qquad \text{for } 0 \le x_t \le u_t \quad \text{(regular time)}$$

(4)
$$C_t(x_t) = r_t u_t + s_t(x_t - u_t)$$
$$= s_t x_t + (r_t - s_t)u_t \quad \text{for } u_t \leq x_t \leq v_t \quad \text{(overtime)}$$

with $r_t < s_t$, so that $C_t(x_t)$ is convex. In (3) and (4), r_t represents the regular cost and s_t the premium cost. The u_t and v_t are the corresponding production capacities. (So for $t = 1$, the values are $r_1 = 2$, $s_1 = 5$, $u_1 = 3$, and $v_1 = 3 + 6 = 9$.)

The rows of Fig. 9.2 refer to production scheduled in each month. The columns refer to the monthly demands. Since no backlogging is allowed, the boxes below the diagonal can be eliminated. Thus the first two rows of the figure indicate that January's *production* can be allocated to the demand in any of the six months, the second two rows indicate that February's *production* can be allocated to demand in February or a subsequent month, etc. Likewise, June's *demand* can be filled by production from any month. In order for a feasible schedule to exist, it is necessary that the cumulative monthly production capability be at least as large as the accumulated demand. Check the right-hand column and the bottom row of Fig. 9.2 to verify that this condition is satisfied in the example.

The computational method about to be described is a slight simplification of the algorithm above and is made possible because of (3), (4), and

(5)
$$h_t(i_t) = h_t i_t \quad \text{(linear holding cost)}.$$

To keep the numerical example simple, assume that $h_t = 1$ for all periods. Therefore the cost figures across each row of Fig. 9.2 increase by 1 to indicate the holding cost per item per period. For example, if an item is produced in January at the regular cost of 2 and held until February, the total unit cost becomes $3(= 2 + 1)$, which appears in the first row of the February column. If it is held another month, an additional unit is added, for a total of $4(= 3 + 1)$, which appears in the first row of the March column. Incidentally, we do not need to *assume* that ending inventory $i_N = 0$, because the cost assumptions (3), (4), and (5) ensure this condition holds in an optimal policy.

To follow the details of the algorithm, copy Fig. 9.2 on a sheet of paper. Notice that the format resembles that of a transportation problem. This is no coincidence, because the linearities in (3), (4), and (5) do yield such a model.

Computation of an optimal policy. Using transportation problem terminology, think of each permissible box in Fig. 9.2 as a route, with the associated unit cost displayed as usual. The idea simply is to fill successive units of demand, starting with January, then February, and so on, by an *available* route having the least cost. Whenever there are ties, production is scheduled as late as possible.

To help you perform the process on your copy of Fig. 9.2, here is a summary of what happens.

 (i) Fill January's demand of 1 at a unit cost of 2.
 (ii) Fill February's demand of 2 at a unit cost of 3.
 (iii) Fill the first four items of March's demand at a unit cost of 2, the next item at a unit cost of 5, and the last two items at a unit cost of 6.

(iv) Fill the first three items of April's demand at a unit cost of 5, the next two items at a unit cost of 6, and the last item at a unit cost of 7.

(v) Since there is no demand in May, make no entries in the May column.

(vi) Fill the first item of June's demand at a unit cost of 3, and the second item at a unit cost of 6.

As you progress from (i) to (vi), reduce the Production Capacity figures in the next to last column of Fig. 9.2. As soon as any such figure becomes 0, do not

	Jan	Feb	Mar	Apr	May	Jun	Production Capacity	Cumulative Capacity
Jan	2 / 1	3 / 2	4	5	6	7	~~320~~	9
	5	6	7	8	9	10	6	
Feb		4 / 1	5	6	7	8	~~10~~	13
		6	7	8	9	10	3	
Mar			2 / 4	3	4	5	~~40~~	20
			6 / 2	7 / 1	8	9	~~310~~	
Apr				5 / 3	6	7	~~30~~	25
				6 / 2	7	8	~~20~~	
May					2	3 / 1	~~10~~	26
					3	4	0	
Jun						6 / 1	~~3~~2	30
						7	1	
Demand D_t	~~10~~	~~20~~	~~7320~~	~~6310~~	0	~~210~~		
Cumulative Demand	1	3	10	16	16	18		

FIGURE 9.3. Highway Rubber Company Convex Cost Schedule.

permit the other routes in that row to be available for the rest of the schedule. Compare your schedule with that shown in Fig. 9.3.

An optimal schedule is then

(6)
$$x_1 = 3 \quad x_2 = 1 \quad x_3 = 7 \quad x_4 = 5 \quad x_5 = 1 \quad x_6 = 1$$
$$i_1 = 2 \quad i_2 = 1 \quad i_3 = 1 \quad i_4 = 0 \quad i_5 = 1 \quad i_6 = 0,$$

which can be obtained by looking at the capacities used (shown in the next to last column of Fig. 9.3) to find x_t, and by summing the amounts in the boxes above and to the right of the diagonal pair in Period $t + 1$ to find i_t.

Obviously, this procedure is much simpler than computing $f_n(i)$, as was done in Chap. 8. It also contains a couple of simplifications in the three-step algorithm above. Specifically, the tabular form makes apparent in *Step 2* the minimum incremental cost alternative with available capacity. And in *Step 3* the current values of demand are reduced as much as possible, given the currently available production capacity for the best alternative.

*Additional constraints. The earlier discussion of the convex cost assumptions (1) and (2) mentioned that the three-step algorithm for this model can encompass upper bounds u_t on x_t and upper limits b_t on the amounts inventoried. In the example, the upper bounds on x_t were honored simply by never even considering values of x_t that were too large. (No restrictions on inventory level were imposed.) You saw in the Dependable Manufacturing Company Example of Sec. 8.4 that the imposition of such constraints can have unanticipated effects. But when convex costs are assumed, the following proposition is true.

EFFECT OF CONSTRAINT VARIATIONS. (a) The optimal value of x_p will *not* decrease if the capacity limit u_p increases, or if any of the inventory limits b_t increase for $t \geq p$. (b) The optimal value of x_p will *not* increase if any capacity limit u_t increases for $t \neq p$, or if any of the inventory bounds b_t increase for $t \leq p$.

To see that the above proposition is not trivial, merely examine what happened in the Dependable Manufacturing Company illustration of Sec. 8.4. When the bound $x_t \leq 5$ was in force, $i_0 = 2$, and $N = 6$, an optimal schedule was

(7) $$x_1 = 4 \quad x_2 = 0 \quad x_3 = 3 \quad x_4 = 4 \quad x_5 = 5 \quad x_6 = 0,$$

which can be seen by tracing the solution in Fig. 8.12. Suppose that the limit on *only* x_3 is increased to 6. Then the following solution, found in Fig. 8.17, becomes optimal:

(8) $$x_1 = 5 \quad x_2 = 0 \quad x_3 = 6 \quad x_4 = 0 \quad x_5 = 5 \quad x_6 = 0.$$

Thus x_1 *increases* when the capacity limit u_3 increases, contrary to part (b). (Note that the assumption $i_0 = 2$ is of no importance, since the same result would occur if $i_0 = 0$ and $D_1 = 1$.)

▶You can encompass the possibility of backlogging by making only a few minor changes in the wording of the three-step algorithm, but the increased computational burden is considerable. Let a backlog be denoted by a negative value for i_t. Now assume that $h_t(i)$ is convex for all values of i, that is, for . . . , $-2, -1, 0, 1, 2, \ldots$. Alter *Step 1* so that you consider increasing production by one unit for each of the Periods $1, 2, \ldots, N$. Alter *Step 2* to include the incremental cost from backlogging. The bulk of added computation arises in *Step 2* in calculating the entire incremental cost for each possible revision. Given the production amounts in a revised schedule, you must allocate them to the demands already considered so that the corresponding inventory and backlogging costs are minimal. Leave *Step 3* unaltered.   ◀

*9.4 PLANNING HORIZON ANALYSIS FOR
CONVEX COST MODEL

It is clear in the application of the algorithm for the special example above that production in each period may increase, but will never decrease as the planning horizon N lengthens. The conclusion also holds for the general convex cost model of the previous section.

Preparatory to the statement of such a proposition, let cumulative demand and cumulative production for Periods $1, 2, \ldots, p$ be denoted as

$$(1) \qquad\qquad R_p = \sum_{t=1}^{p} D_t \quad \text{and} \quad X_p = \sum_{t=1}^{p} x_t.$$

Suppose you are not entirely certain about the actual demand amounts, but you can state that R_p lies within a specified range

$$(2) \qquad\qquad S_p \le R_p \le T_p \quad \text{for } p = 1, 2, \ldots, N.$$

Let $X_p(S)$ be an optimal production schedule *assuming* that $R_p = S_p$, the minimal forecast, and similarly let $X_p(T)$ be an optimal production schedule *assuming* that $R_p = T_p$, the maximal forecast, for $p = 1, 2, \ldots, N$. Then the following can be said about an optimal schedule.

CONVEX COST HORIZON THEOREM: (a) An optimal value of x_p will not decrease if any D_t increases. (b) An optimal schedule satisfies $X_p(S) \le X_p \le X_p(T)$ for $p = 1, 2, \ldots, N$.

Part (b) of the theorem is illustrated graphically in Fig. 9.4.

The preceding result is properly called a planning horizon theorem, because you can regard lengthening N to $N + 1$ as being the same as revising the value of D_{N+1} upward from its zero level in the analysis of the N-period horizon problem. Part (a) of the proposition states that you are never required to reduce a previously scheduled amount of production when more demand is encompassed in the plan.

In the Dependable Manufacturing Company Example of Sec. 8.4, both parts (a) and (b) failed to hold. As you can see in Fig. 8.13, when June demand was added into consideration, so that N increased from 5 to 6, January production decreased

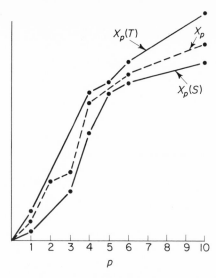

p

Note: $X_p(S)$ optimal schedule for minimal forecast

Figure 9.4. Bounds on Optimal Schedule for Convex Costs.

$X_p(T)$ optimal schedule for maximal forecast

X_p optimal schedule

from 5 to 4, and the combined January and February production decreased from 10 to 9.

An important implication of part (b) is that in particular circumstances it may be possible to select an optimal production amount x_1 with no more than rough information about demands in later periods. The idea is to find $X_1(S)$ and $X_1(T)$, and see if these differ only a little, if at all. A narrow range implies that x_1 can be set within this interval without much possible loss of optimality. Then in the following period, when more information about demand emerges, the process can be repeated. If the range is large, an examination of the two schedules $X_p(S)$ and $X_p(T)$ will help pinpoint the location where a better demand estimate is required.

▶One case of a convex cost model is of special interest, since it occurs frequently and provides extremely powerful and useful planning horizon results. Suppose there are no production and inventory constraints, the production cost relation is the same in every period, and the inventory holding costs are so negligible that they can be ignored, giving

(i) $$C_t(x_t, i_t) \equiv C(x_t).$$

For this situation, drop the assumption that x_t *must* be integer-valued, and allow x_t to be any nonnegative number. Therefore you require a definition for convexity that extends the stipulation (1) in Sec. 9.2. The *direct* generalization is to say that $g(x)$ is convex if for every w and z, $w \leq z$, and if for all p such that $0 \leq p \leq 1$,

(ii) $$p[g(z) - g(x)] \geq (1 - p)[g(x) - g(w)],$$

where

(iii) $$x = pz + (1 - p)w.$$

Rearranging the terms in (ii), and using (iii), yields

(iv) $$pg(z) + (1 - p)g(w) \geq g[pz + (1 - p)w] \quad \underline{\text{convex.}}$$

[By letting $p = \frac{1}{2}$, $w = x - 1$, and $z = x + 1$, (iv) above implies (3) in Sec. 9.2.]

Let A_p be the average demand per period for the first p periods

(v) $$A_p = \frac{R_p}{p} \quad \text{for} \quad p = 1, 2, \ldots, N,$$

and let A_n be the maximum of these. If the maximum value occurs for more than one value of p, let n be the latest period. Then it can be proved that it is optimal to schedule

(vi) $$x_t = A_n \quad \text{for} \quad t = 1, 2, \ldots, n,$$

so that $i_n = 0$. It also can be shown that the remaining optimal values for x_t satisfy

(vii) $$x_t < A_n \quad \text{for} \quad t > n.$$

A further implication is that Periods $1, 2, \ldots,$ n comprise a planning horizon, and the remaining schedule can be found by looking at Periods n $+ 1, \ldots,$ N by themselves, assuming only that inventory entering Period n $+ 1$ is zero. This means that the calculation in (v) can be repeated, now using

(viii) $$B_p = \frac{R_p - R_n}{p - n} \quad \text{for} \quad p = n + 1, \ldots, N.$$

Then the next planning interval starts in Period n $+ 1$ and ends in Period q, which occurs at the latest p yielding the maximum B_p. Once again B_q represents the actual production amount for each of the periods in the second horizon. Of course, this line of reasoning can be repeated until x_N is scheduled. One consequence of this result is that if $D_{t+1} \geq D_t$ for every t, then (v) yields $n = N$. In the opposite case, if $D_{t+1} \leq D_t$, then, for every t, $x_t = D_t$ is optimal.

The above construction can also be characterized in terms of a "graphical" procedure: insert pegs at the points (p, R_p) for $p = 1, 2, \ldots, N$, indicated on ordinary rectangular coordinate paper. Place a piece of string such that it lies above each peg, and tie one end of the string to the point $(0, 0)$. Holding the string against the peg at (N, R_N), pull the string until it is taut everywhere. The resultant graph indicated by the taut string represents an optimal cumulative schedule X_p.

If the assumption (iv) is applied to a case with the demands in Fig. 9.2, calculating (v) would yield

(ix) $$A_1 = \tfrac{1}{1} \quad A_2 = \tfrac{3}{2} \quad A_3 = \tfrac{10}{3} \quad A_4 = \tfrac{16}{4} \quad A_5 = \tfrac{16}{5} \quad A_6 = \tfrac{18}{6},$$

so that $n = 4$, and $x_t = \frac{16}{4}$ for $t = 1, 2, 3, 4$. Then (viii) would, in turn, yield

(x) $$B_5 = \frac{16 - 16}{5 - 4} = \frac{0}{1} \quad B_6 = \frac{18 - 16}{6 - 4} = \frac{2}{2},$$

so that $q = 6$ and $x_t = \frac{2}{2}$ for $t = 5, 6$.

Notice that if several values of D_t change but A_n remains the largest value of A_p, the first horizon does not change. For example, a downward alteration of any D_t, $t = n + 1, \ldots, N$, does not alter the length of the first horizon.

Finally, observe the significant and surprising fact that to establish an optimal schedule and determine the planning horizons, the *numerical* values of $C(x_t)$ are *not* required. All you need to know is that the *same* production cost function applies in every period, that its shape is convex, and that inventory holding costs are negligible.   ◄

9.5 LOT-SIZE INVENTORY MODEL WITH CONCAVE COSTS

The model to be presented here is another special case of the elementary inventory model in Sec. 8.3. It is sometimes referred to as a **dynamic lot-size model** and is noteworthy because it represents a situation of frequent practical importance. Furthermore, it provides a case of complexity intermediate to that of the general model in Sec. 8.3 and the convex cost model in Sec. 9.3.

In addition to the cost, inventory, and production assumptions already made in Sec. 9.1, assume that

(1) $C_t(x_t)$ is concave   (production cost),

(2) $h_t(i_t)$ is concave   (holding cost).

A concave cost assumption is sometimes referred to as a situation of **increasing incremental returns to scale**. Although backlogging is *not* permitted, the analysis can be easily modified to handle such a possibility, as we discuss in the advanced material of Sec. 9.6. In sharp contrast to the convex cost model, upper limits on x_t and i_t are not permitted. Recall that an upper bound on production can be viewed as letting $C_t(x_t)$ be infinitely large for x_t beyond the critical value. In such terms, $C_t(x_t)$ would no longer remain concave.

One frequent example of concave production costs occurs when production involves an initial **setup** and then each item incurs a standard unit cost:

(3)
$$C_t(x_t) = \begin{cases} 0 & \text{for } x_t = 0 \\ s_t + c_t x_t & \text{for } x_t \geq 1. \end{cases}$$

Recall that this was the cost function of the Dependable Manufacturing Company Example in Sec. 8.4, with setup cost $s_t = 13$, unit cost $c_t = 2$, for $x_t \leq 5$. Although $C_t(x_t)$ was concave over the range $x_t = 0, 1, \ldots, 5$, that example does *not* fit the assumptions of this section, since upper bounds on x_t are not allowed here.

Another example of concave costs often arises when the model is applied to a situation in which inventory is replenished by purchasing the item from an outside vendor. In these instances, the seller may offer so-called **quantity discounts** for large orders. To illustrate, the schedule of **price breaks** may be given as

(4)
$10 per item for any amount ordered up to a dozen
$ 8 per *additional* item above a dozen and up to a gross
$ 5 per *additional* item beyond a gross.

The mathematical expression corresponding to this schedule is

(5)
$$C_t(x_t) = \begin{cases} 10x_t & \text{for } \quad 0 \leq x_t \leq 12 \\ 120 + 8(x_t - 12) & \text{for } \quad 13 \leq x_t \leq 144 \\ 120 + 1056 + 5(x_t - 144) & \text{for } 145 \leq x_t. \end{cases}$$

The example is of the same form as (10) in Sec. 9.2. Thus $C_t(x_t)$ is concave, since the coefficients of x_t, namely 10, 8, and 5, are progressively smaller. If a setup cost is added to (5), the function remains concave. Hence, in finding an optimal inventory policy for this situation, a firm can add a lump-sum cost attributable to its own paper work and handling associated with its placing and receiving the order.

Structural result. The fundamental insight for the analysis of this model is given in the following proposition.

FORM OF AN OPTIMAL POLICY. There always exists a minimal cost policy with the property that x_t has one of the following values: 0, D_t, $D_t + D_{t+1}, \ldots, D_t + D_{t+1} + \cdots + D_N$.

The statement implies that in seeking an optimal policy, you need only consider $[1 + N - (t - 1) = N - t + 2]$ possible values for x_t. Compare this with the general model in Sec. 8.3, where x_t could take on *any* value between 0 and $D_t + D_{t+1} + \cdots + D_N$. An important algorithmic implication of the proposition is that to compute an optimal policy you need consider only approximately $.5N^2$ different possibilities.

A further result of the proposition is that there always exists an optimal policy with the property that, in each period, if entering inventory is positive, then no production is scheduled. (State why this follows from the form of an optimal policy.) Symbolically, the implication is that there exists an optimal policy for which

(6) $$i_{t-1}x_t = 0 \quad \text{for all } t.$$

Therefore, if D_t is satisfied from inventory $i_{t-1} > 0$, all these items were manufactured in the latest period in which production occurred. This was certainly not true for optimal policies in the convex cost case.

Whenever an optimal $x_t > 0$, the situation can be referred to as a **regeneration event**. The term reflects the notion that, at such a period, entering inventory is zero, so a production cycle starts afresh.

What now remains to be discussed is how a dynamic programming recursion can be used to efficiently find an optimum among the schedules satisfying the stated form. In preparation, we illustrate the main ideas with a verbal description.

Suppose January is the first month in the horizon. Then you begin by calculating the cost of producing in January for January's demand requirement. You then lengthen the horizon month by month, using the calculations for the previous months. For example, suppose you have found optimal policies for the planning horizons January; January and February; January, February, and March; and so on, up to January, February, March, April, May, and June. Assume each of these policies has the form stated above. You next want to add July to the horizon.

The form of an optimal policy implies that *all* of July's demand requirement will be produced in either January, February, . . . , or July—altogether seven possibilities to consider. Further, if it is produced in April, say, then April's production quantity consists of the demand requirements for April, May, June, and July (state why), and an optimal policy for January, February, and March is the three-month horizon policy that you already know. Consequently, an optimal seven-month horizon policy is one that has the smallest total cost of the seven possibilities.

▶We can easily establish the validity of the form of an optimal policy for an inventory model with concave costs. Whereas (6) was stated as a consequence of the form of an optimal policy, the approach taken here is *first* to demonstrate (6), and then show why it follows that the stated form *is* optimal.

Consider any feasible schedule in which $i_{t-1}x_t > 0$ for at least one Period t. Assume Period p is the first such instance. Examine the earlier period in which the items comprising i_{p-1} were produced, and calculate the additional cost of producing one more unit and storing it until Period p. Compare this figure with the additional cost of producing one more unit in Period p.

If the incremental cost of an additional unit of production in Period p is the smaller amount, alter the schedule by adding i_{p-1} to x_p and correspondingly reducing production in the earlier period. Because of the concave cost assumptions (1) and (2), the full cost increase in Period p will not be larger than the total decrease in cost achieved by eliminating the earlier production and inventory. By the same token, if the incremental cost of an additional unit in Period p is the greater amount, then total costs do not increase if you add x_p to the earlier period's production and eliminate production in Period p. In either event, you have constructed a feasible schedule such that (6) now holds for $t = 1, 2, \ldots, p$. If there are later periods violating the condition, apply the same line of reasoning to them. The resultant schedule, where (6) holds for all periods, costs no more than the starting schedule.

The proposition itself then follows since to assert otherwise means there would be a period, in which $0 < i_{t-1} < D_t$, requiring for feasibility that $x_t \geq D_t - i_{t-1} > 0$, contrary to (6).   ◀

9.6 ALGORITHM FOR CONCAVE COST MODEL

Let

c_{kj} = total cost of producing in Period $k + 1$ to meet the demand requirements of Period $k + 1, \ldots, j$, where $k = 0, 1, \ldots, N - 1$ and $k + 1 \leq j \leq N$.

Thus

$$(1) \qquad c_{kj} = \begin{cases} C_{k+1}(D_{k+1}) & \text{for } j = k + 1 \\ C_{k+1}(D_{k+1} + \cdots + D_j) + h_{k+1}(D_{k+2} + \cdots + D_j) \\ \qquad + \cdots + h_{j-1}(D_j) & \text{for } j > k + 1. \end{cases}$$

To illustrate, if $k + 1$ is January and j is March, then c_{kj} is the sum of the production cost for all of January, February, and March demand, the holding cost levied at the end of January on the inventory to meet February and March demand, and the holding cost levied at the end of February on the inventory to meet March demand.

The Selmore Company Problem. The numerical data for this company appear in Fig. 9.5, where the horizon $N = 4$. In addition to the $C_t(x_t)$ displayed, assume that

(2) $$D_t = 1 \quad \text{and} \quad h_t(i_t) = \frac{i_t}{10} \quad \text{for all periods.}$$

(Try to guess the optimal schedules for $N = 1, 2, 3, 4$.)

The following are a few illustrations of (1) using the data in Fig. 9.5:

(3)
$$c_{01} = C_1(1) = 5$$
$$c_{02} = C_1(1 + 1) + h_1(1) = 10 + .1 = 10.1$$
$$c_{03} = C_1(1 + 1 + 1) + h_1(1 + 1) + h_2(1) = 15 + .2 + .1 = 15.3$$
$$c_{04} = C_1(1 + 1 + 1 + 1) + h_1(1 + 1 + 1) + h_2(1 + 1) + h_3(1)$$
$$\quad = 16 + .3 + .2 + .1 = 16.6$$
$$c_{12} = C_2(1) = 6$$
$$c_{13} = C_2(1 + 1) + h_2(1) = 9 + .1 = 9.1$$
$$c_{14} = C_2(1 + 1 + 1) + h_2(1 + 1) + h_3(1) = 12 + .2 + .1 = 12.3.$$

Calculate the remaining values c_{23}, c_{24}, and c_{34}, and compare your answers with the amounts shown in Fig. 9.6.

$C_t(X_t)$ Production:				
X_t t	1	2	3	4
1	5	10	15	16
2	6	9	12	
3	5	7		
4	3			

Period:

$C_t(0) = 0$

FIGURE 9.5. Selmore Company. Concave Production Cost.

c_{kj}				
k \ j	1	2	3	4
0	5	10.1	15.3	16.6
1			6	9.1	12.3
2			5	7.1
3				3

c_{kj} = cost of producing in period $k+1$ to meet demands in periods $k+1, \ldots, j$

FIGURE 9.6. Selmore Company. Concave Cost Model.

Define

f_n = minimum policy cost for Periods $1, 2, \ldots, n$, given that the inventory level is zero at the end of Period n.

Then the appropriate dynamic programming recursion is

(4) $$f_n = \underset{k=0,1,\ldots,n-1}{\text{minimum}} [f_k + c_{kn}] \quad \text{for } n = 1, 2, \ldots, N,$$

where $f_0 \equiv 0$. Let k_n designate a value of k that yields f_n in (4). What is being sought is the value of f_N.

The bracketed expression on the right of (4) is the sum of two costs. The first cost, f_k, represents all the costs during Periods 1, . . . , k, incurred by an optimal policy for this horizon. Such a policy leaves no inventory at the end of Period k. The second cost, c_{kn}, represents the additional costs in Periods k + 1, . . . , n of starting in Period k + 1 with no inventory, and producing for all the remaining demand. A value k_n that minimizes these sums provides an optimal policy for a horizon of n periods by specifying Period k_n + 1 as the period (in the interval 1, 2, . . . , n) at which the last regeneration event occurs. The algorithm can therefore be viewed as a way to determine an optimal sequence of regeneration points. [Because entering inventory is always zero at a regeneration point, we are able to suppress the state variable i ($\equiv 0$) in expression (4).] Observe that the algorithm has been formulated so as to proceed forward in time.

The method is illustrated below for the example appearing in Fig. 9.5:

$$f_0 = 0$$
$$f_1 = \text{minimum } [f_0 + c_{01}] = [0 + 5] = 5 \quad \text{and} \quad k_1 = 0$$
$$f_2 = \text{minimum } [f_0 + c_{02}, f_1 + c_{12}]$$
$$= \text{minimum } [0 + 10.1, 5 + 6] = 10.1 \quad \text{and} \quad k_2 = 0$$

(5) $\quad f_3 = \text{minimum } [f_0 + c_{03}, f_1 + c_{13}, f_2 + c_{23}]$
$$= \text{minimum } [0 + 15.3, 5 + 9.1, 10.1 + 5] = 14.1 \quad \text{and} \quad k_3 = 1$$
$$f_4 = \text{minimum } [f_0 + c_{04}, f_1 + c_{14}, f_2 + c_{24}, f_3 + c_{34}]$$
$$= \text{minimum } [0 + 16.6, 5 + 12.3, 10.1 + 7.1, 14.1 + 3]$$
$$= 16.6 \quad \text{and} \quad k_4 = 0.$$

These calculations show that the optimal schedule for a planning horizon of length N is

(6)

$x_1 = 1$			for $N = 1$
$x_1 = 2$	$x_2 = 0$		for $N = 2$
$x_1 = 1$	$x_2 = 2$	$x_3 = 0$	for $N = 3$
$x_1 = 4$	$x_2 = 0$	$x_3 = 0 \quad x_4 = 0$	for $N = 4$.

To illustrate how these were found, suppose $N = 3$. Then $k_3 = 1$ in (5) signifies that an optimal policy for Periods 1, 2, 3 is determined by considering Period 1 by itself, and ordering in Period 2 for both Periods 2 and 3. The value $x_2 = 2$ represents the total demand in these periods. The solution to Period 1 considered by itself is given by the schedule for $N = 1$, which indicates that production $x_1 = D_1 = 1$.

Observe that the optimal value of x_1 (January production) fluctuates up and down as the horizon lengthens. As you saw in the horizon theorem of the previous section, this dynamic phenomenon does not occur if the costs are *convex* functions. But in the *concave* cost model, such fluctuations do arise, even in very simple cases, as you can see in Sec. 9.7. Thus, although the algorithm is not much more complicated than that for the convex cost case, the dynamic properties of the model do exhibit more complex behavior.

▶It is instructive to draw a network corresponding to the dynamic programming recursion (4). Let the nodes be $1, 2, \ldots, 5$ and c_{kj} be the unit cost of traversing arc $(5 - j, 6 - k)$. The diagram is given by Fig. 9.7. (Notice it is identical in struc-

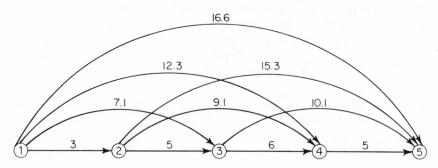

FIGURE 9.7. Selmore Company Concave Cost Model.

ture to Fig. 6.10.) The computations in (5) can be viewed as finding a shortest route to Node 5 from each of the other nodes, where f_n is the length of the shortest route to Node 5 from Node $(5 - n)$. Following the calculations in (5), trace this process on the diagram.

You will find it instructive to compare (4) with the forward dynamic programming relation (v) given in the advanced material in Sec. 8.3. Observe the connection

$$f_n \equiv g_n(0).$$

Thus by knowing the *form* of an optimal policy, you are able to eliminate completely the effort of calculating $g_n(i)$ for all $i > 0$.

Without much trouble, you can find an optimal policy under which backlogging *is* permitted; that is, i_t is allowed to be negative. Now assume that $h_t(i)$ is concave for both $i = 0, 1, 2, \ldots$, and for $i = 0, -1, -2, \ldots$; however, $h_t(i)$ need *not* be concave for $\ldots, -2, -1, 0, 1, 2, \ldots$. What continues to hold true is that x_t is either zero or the sum of demands in consecutive periods containing Period t; but here the sum can include demands prior to, as well as beyond, Period t. The key observation is that you still seek an optimal sequence of regeneration points at which entering inventory is zero. Production occurs only once between these periods. The definition of c_{kj} is generalized to mean

c_{kj} = minimum total cost of producing once during the
Periods $k + 1, \ldots, j$, to meet all demand in this interval.

Thus an intermediate optimization is required to find these costs:

$$c_{kj} = \begin{cases} C_{k+1}(D_{k+1}) \quad \text{for } j = k + 1 \\ \underset{k+1 \leqslant t \leqslant j}{\text{minimum}} \, [C_t(D_{k+1} + \cdots + D_j) + h_{k+1}(i_{k+1}) \\ \qquad\qquad\qquad\qquad + \cdots + h_{j-1}(i_{j-1})] \quad \text{for } j > k + 1. \end{cases}$$

The resultant values are used in the recursion (4).   ◀

*9.7 PLANNING HORIZON ANALYSIS FOR CONCAVE COST MODEL

As you already noted, an essential difference between the convex and concave cost models is that for the concave model the optimal value for x_t may decrease as the horizon lengthens. This can happen for the simplest examples.

To illustrate, suppose

(1) $C_t(x_t) = s_t + c_t x_t$ for $x_t > 0$ (setup cost plus linear production cost),

where $s_t \geq 0$ and $c_t \geq 0$. Specifically, let

(2)
$$s_1 = 1 \quad s_2 = 2 \quad s_3 = 4 \quad s_4 = 8 \quad s_5 = 7$$
$$c_t = 0 \quad \text{and} \quad h_t(i_t) = h_t i_t = i_t \quad (h_t = 1)$$

and assume

(3) $$D_1 = 1 \quad D_2 = 1 \quad D_3 = 2 \quad D_4 = 3 \quad D_5 = 4.$$

Employ the algorithm to verify that

(4)
$$f_1 = 1 \quad f_2 = 2 \quad f_3 = 5 \quad f_4 = 9 \quad f_5 = 16$$
$$k_1 = 0 \quad k_2 = 0 \quad k_3 = 1 \quad k_4 = 2 \quad k_5 = 4,$$

from which it follows that

(5)
$$
\begin{array}{llllll}
x_1 = 1 & & & & & \text{for } N = 1 \\
x_1 = 2 & x_2 = 0 & & & & \text{for } N = 2 \\
x_1 = 1 & x_2 = 3 & x_3 = 0 & & & \text{for } N = 3 \\
x_1 = 2 & x_2 = 0 & x_3 = 5 & x_4 = 0 & & \text{for } N = 4 \\
x_1 = 2 & x_2 = 0 & x_3 = 5 & x_4 = 0 & x_5 = 4 & \text{for } N = 5.
\end{array}
$$

Once again, to show how (5) follows from (4), consider $N = 4$. Remember $k_n + 1$ represents the latest period in which production occurs when Periods $1, 2, \ldots, n$ constitute the entire span of the schedule. Since $k_4 = 2$, Periods 1 and 2 form a horizon, and production is scheduled in Period 3 for Periods 3 and 4. Thus $x_3 = D_3 + D_4 = 2 + 3 = 5$. To determine production in the first two periods, examine the case of $N = 2$. You find $k_2 = 0$, which implies that production occurs in Period 1, and equals the first two periods' demands, namely $x_1 = D_1 + D_2 = 1 + 1 = 2$.

Notice that as the planning horizon increases, both x_1 and x_2 fluctuate up and down; however, the following planning proposition is true.

SETUP COST HORIZON THEOREM: Assume (1) holds and $c_t \geq c_{t+1}$ for $t = 1, 2, \ldots, N - 1$. (a) If $k_n = n - 1$, for $n \geq 2$, then it always is optimal to schedule Periods $1, 2, \ldots, n - 1$ as a span by itself. (b) If $t \geq n$, then $k_t \geq k_n$.

To illustrate part (a), suppose when you apply the algorithm to the periods January, February, March, and April, you find $k_4 = 3$. This signifies that for

$N \geq 4$, April demand should be met from April production. Then part (a) states that it is correct to adopt the optimal production plan for the three-month span of January, February, and March, irrespective of what demand is beyond April. Of course, if you lengthen the horizon further, you will obtain more information about the correct value x_4 of April production. But in any case, you know $x_4 > 0$, that is, the April production level is positive in an optimal schedule for $N \geq 4$. Notice that part (a) is satisfied for $N = 5$ in the example (4). Thus the values in (5) of x_t, $t = 1, 2, 3, 4$, which are optimal for $N = 4$, are also optimal for $N \geq 5$, regardless of the values of D_t, $t > 5$.

To illustrate the rest of the above proposition, suppose when you apply the algorithm to periods January through April, you find that $k_4 = 2$. This signifies that when $N = 4$, April demand should be satisfied from March production, and the schedule for January and February should be the schedule derived for $N = 2$. Part (b) states that the demand in any month after April will be filled by production *after* February, that is, in March or a subsequent month. Observe that the example (2) satisfies the hypothesis of the theorem, and accordingly the results in (4) agree with part (b).

The theorem reduces the amount of computation required by the algorithm. When the hypotheses of the proposition apply, the recursion can be written as

$$(6) \qquad f_n = \operatorname*{minimum}_{k = k_{n-1}, \ldots, n-1} [f_k + c_{kn}] \quad \text{for } n = 1, 2, \ldots, N,$$

which cuts down on the search for the minimum. To illustrate, in the example (2), f_5 can be found by considering in (6) only $k = 2, 3, 4$, since $k_4 = 2$ in (4). With this approach, not *all* c_{kj}, for $k = 0, 1, \ldots, N - 1$, and $k + 1 \leq j \leq N$, will be needed in executing (6). Therefore it is advantageous to calculate each c_{kj} only if it is required. A helpful recursion for this purpose is

$$(7) \quad c_{kn} = c_{k, n-1} + c_{k+1} D_n + h_{k+1}(D_n) + \cdots + h_{n-1}(D_n) \quad \text{for } n > k + 1,$$

where we assume the holding cost function is linear $h_t(i_t) = h_t i_t$.

In contrast with the Convex Cost Horizon Theorem, part (a) here gives a sharper result (it establishes a definite production schedule within a planning horizon), but part (b) is weaker [since as N increases, x_t may fluctuate, as you saw in (5)]. Further analytic results about this model can be obtained if you assume that the production cost (1), the holding cost, and D_t remain the same each period, and the horizon becomes unbounded. This case will be taken up later in Sec. 12.5.

▶ Observe that the theorem assumes both the production cost function (1) and $c_t \geq c_{t+1}$. The example in (5) of Sec. 9.6 shows that part (b) is false for the general concave model. The following two examples show further that the theorem does *not* hold if the inequality condition on c_t is dropped, or if all $C_t(x_t)$ are the same but do not satisfy (1).

Consider a case where the restriction $c_t \geq c_{t+1}$ in (1) is not satisfied:

(i)

$$
\begin{array}{cccc}
s_1 = 1 & s_2 = 12 & s_3 = 1 & s_4 = 2 \\
c_1 = 3 & c_2 = 1 & c_3 = 2 & c_4 = 1 \\
D_1 = 1 & D_2 = 4 & D_3 = 2 & D_4 = 2,
\end{array}
$$

and assume $h_t(i_t) = 0$. (See if you can guess the optimal schedules for $N = 1, 2, 3, 4$.)
You should apply the algorithm to check that

(ii)
$$f_1 = 4 \quad f_2 = 16 \quad f_3 = 21 \quad f_4 = 24$$
$$k_1 = 0 \quad k_2 = 0 \quad k_3 = 2 \quad k_4 = 1,$$

which violates part (b). What are the optimal schedules for $N = 1, 2, 3, 4$? (How accurate were your guesses?) Do any of the production levels increase and later decrease as the horizon lengthens?

Next consider a case in which $C_t(x)$ and $h_t(i_t)$ are the same in every period:

(iii)
$$C_t(1) = 5 \quad C_t(2) = 10 \quad C_t(3) = 11 \quad \text{and} \quad h_t(i_t) = i_t,$$

and $D_t = 1, t = 1, 2, 3$. Note that $C_t(x)$ does not satisfy the form given in (1). Verify that

(iv)
$$f_1 = 5 \quad f_2 = 10 \quad f_3 = 14$$
$$k_1 = 0 \quad k_2 = 1 \quad k_3 = 0,$$

in a disagreement with part (b).   ◄

*9.8 INVENTORY MODEL WITH
PRODUCTION SMOOTHING

The economic optimization embodied in the inventory models you have studied up to now strike a balance between the costs of production on the one hand and the costs of inventory on the other. As a result, within a specified planning horizon, production is allowed to fluctuate considerably. The very form of an optimal policy for the concave cost model of Sec. 9.5 is **batch ordering**. This sort of policy is often most appropriate when a firm produces many different items. By the same token, when a company purchases items for inventory from outside vendors, it is usually sensible to order in lot sizes large enough to cover the requirements of several periods' demand. If the situation under analysis pertains to scheduling one of a firm's main product lines, however, one should take account of an important economic consideration that has been ignored so far. This factor is the cost of *varying* production levels from one period to the next.

Conceptually, it is simple enough to add this consideration to the general model in Chap. 8. Keeping the same symbols x_t for production and i_t for ending inventory at Period t, the objective function is revised to

(1)
$$\text{minimize} \sum_{t=1}^{N} C_t(x_t, i_t, x_{t-1}).$$

For example,

(2)
$$C_t(x_t, i_t, x_{t-1}) = C_t(x_t, i_t) + v_t(x_t, x_{t-1}),$$

where the function on the right represents the cost of a variation in production between Periods t and $t - 1$.

Two simple illustrations of a **smoothing cost** function are

(3)
$$v_t(x_t, x_{t-1}) \equiv v_t \cdot (x_t - x_{t-1})^2, \quad \text{where } v_t > 0,$$

and

(4)
$$v_t(x_t, x_{t-1}) \equiv \begin{cases} a_t \cdot (x_t - x_{t-1}) & \text{for } x_t - x_{t-1} \geq 0 \quad (a_t \geq 0) \\ b_t \cdot (x_{t-1} - x_t) & \text{for } x_t - x_{t-1} \leq 0 \quad (b_t \geq 0). \end{cases}$$

When production smoothing is of consequence in planning, the analysis is often undertaken by measuring demand, production, and inventory in labor units, such as man-weeks. Then, if the representation (4) is appropriate, the value of a_t relates to the cost of increasing the labor force, whereas b_t relates to the cost of reducing it. (Assume $a_t + b_t > 0$.)

What changes are requires in the dynamic programming recursion to accommodate this new factor? Recall that the relation previously used in Chap. 8 was written as

(5)
$$f_n(i) = \underset{x}{\text{minimum}} \ [c_n(x, i + x - d_n) + f_{n-1}(i + x - d_n)]$$

$$\text{for} \quad n = 1, 2, \ldots, N,$$

where $i = 0, 1, \ldots, d_1 + \cdots + d_n$ and the minimization is over only nonnegative integer values of x in the range $d_n - i \leq x \leq d_1 + \cdots + d_n - i$, assuming inventory is 0 at the end of the horizon. Now, knowledge of entering inventory is not sufficient to characterize the state of the system at the beginning of a period. You also need to know the production level in the previous period. Therefore, the state variable for this model must contain both these dimensions. The rest of the alterations are straightforward.

Let

$f_n(i, y) = $ minimum policy cost when entering inventory is at level i and previous production at level y with n more periods to go

$x_n(i, y) = $ a production level yielding $f_n(i, y)$.

The new recursion in place of (5) is

(6)
$$f_n(i, y) = \underset{x}{\text{minimum}} \ [c_n(x, i + x - d_n, y) + f_{n-1}(i + x - d_n, x)]$$

$$\text{for} \quad n = 1, 2, \ldots, N.$$

What is sought is the value of $f_N(i_0, y_0)$, where y_0 is the level of production prior to Period 1. The calculations are initiated with the values of

(7)
$$f_1(i, y) = c_1(d_1 - i, 0, y) \quad \text{for } i = 0, 1, \ldots, d_1 \text{ and}$$

$$y = 0, 1, \ldots, d_1 + d_2.$$

Do you see any important differences between (5) and (6)? There is one. Whereas previously you needed to obtain $f_n(i)$ for all possible values of i, here you must calculate $f_n(i, y)$ for all possible *pairs* of i and y. Although the dynamic programming approach is still vastly superior to complete enumeration, the added dimension to the state variable implies a significant increase in the burden of calculations, as is demonstrated in an example below. Thus it is conceptually possible to generalize the recursive technique to take into account even more considerations—such as the production level two periods earlier, or the change in the level of inventory; but the resultant increase in computations quickly makes the approach impractical for real situations. If the application demands that you consider a multitude of interrelationships, you will need to use other solution techniques, such as linear and nonlinear programming, or you will have to exploit the form of an optimal policy.

The Surety Manufacturing Company Example. Assume the demand, production and inventory constraints, and cost data for this firm are

(8) $$D_t = 3 \quad \text{(stationary demand)},$$

(9) $$x_t = 0, 1, \ldots, 5 \quad i_t = 0, 1, \ldots, 4 \quad \text{and} \quad \text{no ending inventory},$$

(10) $$C_t(x_t, i_t, x_{t-1}) = C(x_t) + hi_t + v \cdot (x_t - x_{t-1})^2 \quad \text{(stationary cost)},$$

where

(11) $$C(0) = 0 \quad C(1) = 15 \quad C(2) = 17 \quad C(3) = 19 \quad C(4) = 21 \quad C(5) = 23,$$

(12) $$h = 1 \quad \text{and} \quad v = 1,$$

for all periods. [These data are identical with the example analyzed in Sec. 8.4 except for the third smoothing cost function on the right of (10).] The recursion (6) can be written as

(13) $$f_n(i, y) = \underset{x}{\text{minimum}} \ [C(x) + 1(i + x - 3) + (x - y)^2$$
$$+ f_{n-1}(i + x - 3, x)] \quad \text{for } n = 1, 2, \ldots, N,$$

where $i = 0, 1, \ldots, 4, y = 0, 1, \ldots, 5$, and the minimization is over only nonnegative integer values in the range $3 - i \leq x \leq \text{minimum} \ (5, 7 - i)$.

The calculations for $n = 1$ in (7) are displayed in Fig. 9.8. There must be six pairs of columns, one for each possible $y = 0, 1, \ldots, 5$. The shaded parts of the

$$f_1(i, y) = C(3 - i) + \left[(3 - i) - y\right]^2$$

Previous Production:

Entering Inventory	$y = 0$		$y = 1$		$y = 2$		$y = 3$		$y = 4$		$y = 5$	
i	$x_1(i,0)$	$f_1(i,0)$	$x_1(i,1)$	$f_1(i,1)$	$x_1(i,2)$	$f_1(i,2)$	$x_1(i,3)$	$f_1(i,3)$	$x_1(i,4)$	$f_1(i,4)$	$x_1(i,5)$	$f_1(i,5)$
0	3	28	3	23	3	20	3	19				
1	2	21	2	18	2	17	2	18	2	21		
2			1	15	1	16	1	19	1	24	1	31
3					0	4	0	9	0	16	0	25

FIGURE 9.8. Surety Manufacturing Company Production Smoothing Model ($n = 1$).

table indicate impossible combinations of i and y due to the production and inventory constraints in (9). For example, if $y = 0$, then entering inventory cannot be greater than 1, for at most 4 units of inventory could have entered the *previous* period and the previous demand would have reduced the amount by 3. Analogously, if $y = 5$, then entering inventory must be at least 2, again because demand would have reduced the amount by 3. Since ending inventory is 0 by assumption, the optimal production $x_1(i, y)$ depends only on i and is independent of y. As you will observe next, $x_n(i, y)$ does depend on y for $n > 1$.

The computations for $n = 2$ and $y = 2$ are exhibited in Fig. 9.9. Study the

$$\left[C(x) + 1(i + x - 3) \right] + (x - y)^2 + f_1(i + x - 3, x)$$

Previous Production:

i \ x	0	1	2	3	4	5	$x_2(i,2)$	$f_2(i,2)$
0				19+1 + 19	22+4 + 21	25+9 + 31	3	39
1			17 + 0 + 20	20+1 + 18	23+4 + 24	26+9+25	2	37
2		15 + 1+23	18+ 0 + 17	21 +1 + 19	24+4+ 16		2	35
3	0+4 +28	16 + 1+ 18	19 + 0+ 16	22+1 + 9			0,3	32
4								

(Entering Inventory — vertical axis label)

FIGURE 9.9. Surety Manufacturing Company Production Smoothing Model ($n = 2, y = 2$).

entries in the table to see how they are derived from the dynamic programming recursion (13). In particular, notice that the third entry in each box of the main part of the table comes from Fig. 9.8. For example, if $i = 0$ and $x = 3$, then the amount 19 is the value of $f_1(i + x - 3, x) = f_1(0, 3)$ contained in the $i = 0$ row and $y = 3$ right column of Fig. 9.8. Observe also that the row for $i = 4$ is shaded out in Fig. 9.9, because entering inventory in the *previous* period could at most be 4 units. Given that production $y = 2$ and demand is 3, then at most 3 units could enter the present period.

It should now be evident that the computational burden here is *roughly* six times as great as that for the general model in Chap. 8, since the calculations such as are shown in Fig. 9.9 are performed for each possible value of $y = 0, 1, \ldots, 5$.

The complete set of $f_2(i, y)$ and corresponding $x_2(i, y)$ are given in Fig. 9.10. Test your understanding of the recursion (13) by verifying the values of $f_2(i, 5)$. For convenience, the final column of Fig. 9.10 shows the optimum production levels from the earlier analysis in Sec. 8.4 that did not contain a production smoothing cost. Study the difference between the two sets of solutions. Notice that when $n = 2$, it is no longer optimal to let production be 5 when entering inventory is

Previous Production:

Entering Inventory	$y=0$		$y=1$		$y=2$		$y=3$		$y=4$		$y=5$		Fig. 8.10
i	$x_2(i,0)$	$f_2(i,0)$	$x_2(i,1)$	$f_2(i,1)$	$x_2(i,2)$	$f_2(i,2)$	$x_2(i,3)$	$f_2(i,3)$	$x_2(i,4)$	$f_2(i,4)$	$x_2(i,5)$	$f_2(i,5)$	$x_2(i)$
0	3	47	3	42	3	39	3	38	3	39	3	42	3
1	2	41	2	38	2	37	2,3	38	3	39	3	42	5
2			2	36	2	35	2	36	2	39	4	41	4
3					0,3	32	3	31	3	32	3	35	0
4					2	25	2	28	2	33			0

FIGURE 9.10. Surety Manufacturing Company Production Smoothing Model ($n = 2$).

1. Now it is preferable to schedule 3 if the previous production level is 3 or more, and otherwise to schedule 2. In contrast, it is no longer optimal to let production be 0 when entering inventory is 4. Now it is preferable to produce 2.

The dynamic impact of imposing a smoothing cost can be seen in Fig. 9.11.

Initial Inventory i_0	Surety Company With Smoothing		Dependable Company Without Smoothing	
	Jan	Feb	Jan	Feb
0	3	3	3	3
1	3	2	5	0
2	2	2	4	0
3	3	0	0	3
4	2	0	0	2

FIGURE 9.11. Optimal Production Schedules for Planning Horizon $N = 2$ and Previous Production $x_0 = 4$.

Observe that when initial inventory, i_0, is 1 or 2, the smoothing schedule calls for production in both January and February, whereas the previous schedule produced in only January. When i_0 is 3 or 4, the smoothing schedule calls for production in January, whereas the previous schedule produced the same amount in February. The preference toward January production arises because, in the present model, it is expensive to let production fall to zero and then increase it again later.

▶Review Sec. 6.7, which contains a description of an employment scheduling smoothing problem closely related to the preceding model. The decision variable x_{ij} of that situation was the number of crews beginning work at the start of Period i and terminating at the start of Period j. The constraint to be met was to have at least R_k crews available in Period k, where $k = 1, 2, \ldots, n - 1$. The cost associated with x_{ij} included wages, as well as recruiting, transporting, and briefing. The nonwage expenses occasionally made it desirable to have a work force above the minimal requirements. Thus the objective was to establish a feasible work force schedule that minimized total labor expenses.

The following connection can be drawn between that situation and the smoothing model above. Let

(i)
$$x_t = \sum_{j=t+1}^{n-1} x_{tj} \quad \text{and} \quad D_t = R_t,$$

so that the total number of crews hired at the beginning of Period t is aggregated. In this application, the services of a crew cannot be inventoried from one period to the next. Therefore, if a schedule has crews in excess of the requirements R_k in Period k, the surplus of labor cannot be stored until Period $k + 1$. Hence, the dimension of the state variable in the recursion (6) can be reduced by eliminating i. The resulting dynamic programming relation is

(ii)
$$g_n(y) = \underset{x \geqslant d_n}{\text{minimum}} \left[g_{n-1}(x) + c_n(x, 0, y) \right] \quad \text{for} \quad n > 1$$

(iii)
$$g_1(y) = \underset{x \geqslant d_1}{\text{minimum}} \, c_1(x, 0, y) \qquad \text{for} \quad n = 1.$$

The value of $g_N(y_0)$ is sought.

Observe the differences between (ii) and the problem in Sec. 6.7. The earlier model has the flexibility of assessing a smoothing cost that depended on both the beginning and the length of the interval (from the start of Period i to the start of Period j). The cost c_{ij} was charged for *each* crew, however, so that the cost was a linear function of the number of crews hired for the interval.

The present model with cost functions $C_t(x_t, 0, x_{t-1})$ has the opposite flexibility. It assesses a smoothing cost only against the change in employment level between two successive periods, independent of how long new crews remain engaged or how long the released crews were employed. But this model does permit the employment costs within a period to change nonlinearly with the total number of crews utilized. In addition, it allows the variation in total smoothing cost to depend nonlinearly on the actual employment levels in two successive periods.

If all the costs are linear,

(iv)
$$c_{ij} = c_i + c_{i+1} + \cdots + c_{j-1} + a_i + b_j,$$

where in Period t, for each crew, c_t is the wage cost, a_t the hiring cost, and b_t the firing cost, then an optimal schedule can be found by either approach. However, in such a situation further analysis of (ii) leads to a very simple algorithm that is related to the approach used in the convex cost inventory model of Sec. 9.3.   ◀

REVIEW EXERCISES

1 Verify the claims in Sec. 9.1 that

   (a) Formulas (3) and (4) are equivalent. Give a verbal interpretation of (4).

   (b) Requiring $i_t \geq 0$, where i_t is given by (4), implies that demand is satisfied on time.

2 (a) Give a verbal interpretation of the definitions (3) and (4) in Sec. 9.2.

   (b) Draw a sketch of the functions described in *Cases i* through *vi* in Sec. 9.2 (let $a = 2$, $b = 1$, and $c = 3$ in the first four cases, and use the parameters given in the text for the last two cases).

   (c) Draw a sketch of the function described in *Case vi*, letting the parameters be $a_1 = 4$, $b_1 = 1$, $w_1 = 4$, $a_2 = 3$, $w_2 = 6$, and $a_3 = 2$.

3 Write the cost functions $C_t(x_t)$ as given by (3) and (4) in Sec. 9.3 for each of the six periods using the data in Fig. 9.2.

Exercises 4 through 7 refer to the case of the Highway Rubber Company shown in Fig. 9.2. Reapply the algorithm to the new data and calculate the incremental effect on total cost. Be sure to indicate total production x_t and ending inventory i_t in each Period t.

4 (a) Assume January demand is 2 instead of 1.

   (b) Assume May demand is 1 instead of 0.

   (c) Suppose demand in every period remains the same, except in Period t. How large can D_t be such that there still exists a feasible schedule? (Answer this question for $t = 1, 2, \ldots, 6$.)

5 (a) Assume regular-time production capacity in January is 4, instead of 3.

   (b) Assume regular-time production capacity in January is 5, instead of 3.

   (c) Assume overtime production is unavailable in March and April.

6 In each part, explain the impact on the solution in Fig. 9.3 if the cost parameters are changed as indicated below.

   (a) Production costs in each period are identical. (For example, two per item at regular time, and five per item at overtime.)

   (b) Overtime costs equal regular-time costs. (For example, two per item in Period 1, with a total capacity of 9 items; 4 per item in period 2, with a total capacity of four items, etc.)

   (c) Holding cost is $h = 6$ per item.

   (d) Holding cost is $h = .1$ per item.

*7 Suppose the cumulative demands R_p, defined in (1) of Sec. 9.4, satisfy

$$1 \leq R_1 \leq 1 \quad\quad 1 \leq R_2 \leq 7 \quad\quad 6 \leq R_3 \leq 14$$
$$10 \leq R_4 \leq 20 \quad 10 \leq R_5 \leq 25 \quad 12 \leq R_6 \leq 27.$$

Find the associated values for $X_p(S)$ and $X_p(T)$, specified in the Convex Cost Horizon Theorem. Draw a diagram like that in Fig. 9.4. Can you give an optimal value for production in Period 1? Explain why.

*8 Consider the special convex cost model given in the advanced material at the end of Sec. 9.4. Find an optimal schedule when demand requirements are

(a) $D_1 = 1$, $D_2 = 2$, $D_3 = 7$, $D_5 = 0$, and $D_6 = 2$. Let $D_4 = 5$. Let $D_4 = 4$. Let $D_4 = 3$. Let $D_4 = 2$.

(b) $D_1 = 1$, $D_2 = 2$, $D_4 = 6$, $D_5 = 0$, and $D_6 = 2$. Let $D_3 = 11$. Let $D_3 = 12$.

(c) $D_1 = 1$, $D_2 = 2$, $D_3 = 7$, $D_4 = 6$, and $D_6 = 2$. Let $D_5 = 1$. Let $D_5 = 2$. Let $D_5 = 4$.

(d) $D_3 = 7$, $D_4 = 6$, $D_5 = 0$, and $D_6 = 2$. Let $D_1 = 2$ and $D_2 = 1$. Let $D_1 = 3$ and $D_2 = 0$.

9 Suppose a vendor offers the following price-break (quantity-discount) structure: $10 per item for any amount ordered up to a dozen units; $8 per item (that is, for *every* item) for a total amount ordered above a dozen and up to a gross; $5 per item for a total amount ordered beyond a gross. Plot the total purchase cost as a function of the number of items ordered. Is this a concave cost function? Why? Is the cost function concave if a setup cost is added? Why?

10 (a) Explain why the form of an optimal policy given for the lot-size model with concave costs in Sec. 9.5 implies that there always exists an optimal policy with the property that, in each period, if entering inventory is positive, then no production is scheduled.

(b) Given this form of an optimal policy, calculate exactly how many distinct production schedules need to be considered. For the sake of definiteness, assume that every $D_t > 0$ (recall initial inventory $i_0 = 0$).

(c) Calculate how many different c_{kj}, given by (1) in Sec. 9.6, have to be calculated in order to apply the algorithm for the general concave cost model.

*11 The validity of the form of an optimal policy for the lot-size model with concave costs is established in the special material at the end of Sec. 9.5. The argument involves either adding the amount i_{p-1} to x_p, or adding the amount x_p to an earlier period's production level. Given a schedule in which $i_{t-1}x_t > 0$ for one or more periods, is the alternative policy suggested by the argument optimal? Justify your answer.

12 *Selmore Company* (Sec. 9.6). Consider the example in Fig. 9.5. Find an optimal policy if the holding cost function is $h_t(i_t) = h_t i_t$, where, in all periods,

(a) $h_t = 1$.

(b) $h_t = 2$.

13 In the concave cost model of Secs. 9.5 and 9.6 suppose that demand $D_t = 1$,

$$C_t(x_t) = \begin{cases} 5x_t & \text{for } x_t = 0, 1, 2, 3 \\ 12 + x_t & \text{for } x_t \geq 4, \end{cases}$$

and $h_t(i_t) = h_t i_t$ in all periods. (Note the example resembles the Selmore Company Problem, where the production cost function is the same as that for $t = 1$ in Fig. 9.5.) Find an optimal policy for $h_t = .1$ in all periods, when the horizon length is

(a) $N = 4$.   (e) $N = 8$.
(b) $N = 5$.   (f) $N = 9$.
(c) $N = 6$.   (g) Do the same for all $h_t = 1$ and $N = 9$.
(d) $N = 7$.   (h) Do the same for all $h_t = 2$ and $N = 9$.

14 Answer the questions in exercise 13 where

$$C_t(x_t) = \begin{cases} 0 & \text{for } x_t = 0 \\ 3 + 2x_t & \text{for } x_t \geq 1. \end{cases}$$

15 Answer the questions in exercise 13 where demand $D_t = 2$ in every period.

16 Answer the questions in exercise 13, except assume demand alternates over the entire horizon as follows:

(a) $D_1 = 1, D_2 = 2, D_3 = 1, D_4 = 2, \ldots$.
(b) $D_1 = 2, D_2 = 1, D_3 = 2, D_4 = 1, \ldots$.

17 Answer the questions in exercise 13, except assume that the holding costs alternate as follows:

(a) $h_1 = 1, h_2 = 2, h_3 = 1, h_4 = 2, \ldots$.
(b) $h_1 = 2, h_2 = 1, h_3 = 2, h_4 = 1, \ldots$.

*18 The advanced material at the end of Sec. 9.6 asserts that the dynamic programming recursion (4) can be viewed as finding a shortest route in an acyclic network. Follow the calculations in (5) and trace the process in Fig. 9.7; show the connection with a shortest-route algorithm for an acyclic network.

*19 Suppose you can backlog demand and fill it at a later period; thus i_t is allowed to be negative (for $t < N$). (All demand must be met by the end of the horizon.) Answer the questions in exercise 13, parts (a) through (f), where the inventory holding and backlog penalty cost function is $h_t(i_t) = |h_t| \cdot i_t$ for

(a) $h_t = .1$.
(b) $h_t = 1$.
(c) $h_t = 2$.

*20 Consider the example (1) through (3) in Sec. 9.7. Verify the results in (4) and (5).

*21 Compare the planning information given by the Convex Cost Horizon Theorem in Sec. 9.4 and by the Setup Cost Horizon Theorem in Sec. 9.7.

*22 Consider the Setup Cost Horizon Theorem in Sec. 9.7, and assume the first month in the planning horizon is January.

(a) What does $k_6 = 5$ imply about an optimal schedule, according to part (a) of the theorem?

(b) What does $k_6 = 3$ imply about an optimal schedule, according to part (b) of the theorem?

*23 (a) Verify the validity of the recursion (7) in Sec. 9.7 for the case where the holding cost function is linear.

(b) Modify (7) for the case where the holding cost is a general concave function.

*24 Verify the results given in the advanced material at the end of Sec. 9.7, and explain why part (b) of the Setup Cost Planning Horizon Theorem is not satisfied.

(a) (ii).

(b) (iv).

*25 *Surety Manufacturing Company* (Sec. 9.8). The dynamic programming recursion (13) shows how to incorporate a quadratic smoothing cost function.

(a) Rewrite (13) to incorporate a piecewise linear smoothing cost function (4), with $a_t = b_t = 1$ for every period.

(b) Using your answer in part (a), calculate tables like those in Figs. 9.8, 9.10, and 9.11.

*26 Suggest at least two smoothing cost functions that are reasonable alternatives to (3) and (4) in Sec. 9.8.

*27 Explain how to modify the recursion (6) in Sec. 9.8 for the case where the cost function in Period t depends on x_{t-2}, as well as on x_t, i_t, and x_{t-1}. Assuming this dependency is added to the case of Surety Manufacturing Company, indicate how the number of computations will increase as compared to those required in Figs. 9.8, 9.9, and 9.10.

28 Explain your understanding of the following terms:

convex function   setup cost (or lump-sum cost)
concave function   quantity discounts (or price breaks)
decreasing (increasing) incremental   regeneration event (point)
   returns to scale   *batch ordering
*planning horizon analysis   *smoothing cost.
dynamic lot-size model

COMPUTATIONAL EXERCISES

Exercises 29 through 37 refer to the inventory model with convex costs, as described in Sec. 9.3. (Recall that initial inventory $i_0 = 0$.)

29 Assume the production cost functions are given by Fig. 9.12. For example, the total cost in Period 1 associated with $x_1 = 12$ is 32 ($= 1 \cdot 5 + 3 \cdot 5 + 2 \cdot 6$). Assume the holding cost functions are $h_t(i_t) = h_t i_t$, where $h_1 = 1$, $h_2 = 2$, and $h_3 = 1$. Suppose the demand requirements are

$$D_1 = 10 \quad D_2 = 3 \quad D_3 = 17 \quad D_4 = 23.$$

Production Cost of Unit k

Production of Unit k	Period 1	Period 2	Period 3	Period 4
$1 \leq k \leq 5$	1	2	1	4
$6 \leq k \leq 10$	3	3	6	4
$11 \leq k \leq 15$	6	5	7	8
$16 \leq k \leq 20$	10	8	12	9

FIGURE 9.12

(a) Find an optimal production schedule. Be sure to indicate total production x_t and ending inventory i_t in each Period t.

*(b) Find an optimal production schedule if you impose the constraint $i_t \leq 5$ in every period.

(c) Indicate the impact of requiring an additional unit in Period 1 (that is, let $D_1 = 11$). In Period 2. In Period 3. In Period 4.

(d) Find an optimal production schedule where all $h_t = 0$. Where all $h_t = 5$.

(e) Find an optimal production schedule where the demand requirements are revised such that $D_1 = 3$ and $D_2 = 10$. Such that $D_3 = 23$ and $D_4 = 17$. Such that $D_2 = 17$ and $D_3 = 3$.

*30 Consider the data in exercise 29, part (a). Suppose the cumulative demands R_p, defined in (1) of Sec. 9.4, satisfy

$$\sum_{t=1}^{p} D_t - k \leq R_p \leq \sum_{t=1}^{p} D_t + k.$$

In each part below, find the associated values for $X_p(S)$ and $X_p(T)$, specified in the Convex Cost Horizon Theorem, indicate the associated production levels and ending inventories, and draw a diagram like that in Fig. 9.4. Explain whether or not you can give an optimal value for production in Period 1. Let

(a) $k = 1$.

(b) $k = 2$.

(c) $k = 3$.

*31 Consider the data in exercise 29, part (a). Suppose the cumulative demands R_p, defined in (1) of Sec. 9.4, satisfy

$$\sum_{t=1}^{p} D_t - pk \leq R_p \leq \sum_{t=1}^{p} D_t + pk.$$

In each part below, find the associated values for $X_p(S)$ and $X_p(T)$, specified in the Convex Cost Horizon Theorem, indicate the associated production levels and ending inventories, and draw a diagram like that in Fig. 9.4. Explain whether you can give an optimal value for production in Period 1. Let

(a) $k = 1$.

(b) $k = 2$.

(c) $k = 3$.

32 Assume the planning horizon $N = 3$ periods and that the production and inventory

cost functions are $C_t(x_t) = x_t^2$ and $h_t(i_t) = h_t i_t$ for every Period t. In each part below, find an optimal schedule for production and indicate ending inventory for each period.

(a) Assume $h_t = 0$ and the demand requirement is $D_t = 6$ for every Period t.

(b) Assume $h_t = 0$ for every Period t, and $D_1 = 11$, $D_2 = 5$, and $D_3 = 2$.

(c) Assume $h_t = 0$ for every Period t, and $D_1 = 2$, $D_2 = 5$, and $D_3 = 11$.

*(d) Assume the data in part (c), and impose the constraint that production $x_t \le 5$ in every Period t.

*(e) Assume the data in part (c), and impose the constraint that ending inventory $i_t \le 3$ in every Period t.

(f) Assume $h_t = 3$ in every Period t and the same demand data as in part (c). Next, assume $h_t = 11$ in every Period t. Compare the results for $h_t = 0, 3, 11$.

(g) Assume $h_t = 0$ in every Period t, the same demand data as in part (c), and $C_3(x_3) = 1.5x_3^2$. Next assume $h_t = 3$. Finally assume $h_t = 11$. Compare your results with those in part (f).

*33 Assume the production and inventory holding cost functions in exercise 32. Suppose the cumulative demands R_p, defined in (1) of Sec. 9.4, satisfy

$$1 \le R_1 \le 3 \qquad 6 \le R_2 \le 8 \qquad 23 \le R_3 \le 29.$$

Let $h_t = 0$. Find the associated values for $X_p(S)$ and $X_p(T)$, specified in the Convex Cost Horizon Theorem, indicate the associated production levels and ending inventories, and draw a diagram like that in Fig. 9.4. Explain whether or not you can give an optimal value for production in Period 1. Do the same for $h_t = 3$ and for $h_t = 11$.

*34 Assume that backlogging is permitted, and that the production cost and the inventory holding and backlog penalty cost functions are

$$C_t(x_t) = x_t^2 \quad h_t(i_t) = \begin{cases} h_t i_t & \text{if } i_t \ge 0 \\ -p_t i_t & \text{if } i_t \le 0 \end{cases} \quad \text{for every Period t.}$$

In each part below, find an optimal schedule for production, and indicate ending inventory or backlog for each period. (All demand must be met by the end of the horizon.)

(a) Assume $h_t = p_t = 0$ for every Period t, and demand requirements are $D_1 = 2$, $D_2 = 5$, and $D_3 = 11$.

(b) Assume $h_t = p_t = 0$ for every Period t, and demand requirements are $D_1 = 11$, $D_2 = 5$, and $D_3 = 2$.

(c) Assume the same demand data as in part (b), and $h_t = 0$ and $p_t = 3$ for every Period t. Next, assume $h_t = 0$ and $p_t = 11$ for every Period t.

(d) Assume $h_t = p_t = 0$ for every Period t, and $D_1 = 2$, $D_2 = 11$, and $D_3 = 5$.

(e) Assume the same demand data as in part (d), and $h_t = p_t = 3$ for every Period t. Next assume $h_t = p_t = 11$ for every Period t. Finally assume $h_t = 2$ and $p_t = 4$ for every Period t.

35 Assume the planning horizon $N = 8$, and that the production and inventory cost functions are $C_t(x_t) = x_t^2$ and $h_t(i_t) = h_t i_t$ for every Period t. Assume the demand requirements are

$$D_1 = 4 \quad D_2 = 20 \quad D_3 = 2 \quad D_4 = 0 \quad D_5 = 6 \quad D_6 = 4 \quad D_7 = 1 \quad D_8 = 3.$$

In each part below, find an optimal schedule for production and indicate ending inventory for each period.

(a) Assume $h_t = 0$ for every Period t.
(b) Assume $h_t = 1$ for every Period t. Next assume $h_t = 3$ for every Period t.
(c) Assume $h_t(i_t) = i_t^2$ for every Period t.
(d) Assume $h_t = 0$ for every Period t. Also assume $C_t(x_t) = 1.5x_t^2$ for $t = 2$; then for $t = 4$, instead; then for $t = 7$, instead.
*(e) Assume $h_t = 0$ for every Period t, and the planning horizon $N = 9$. What is the largest value for the demand requirement D_9 such that the optimal production level for x_7 found in part (a) remains unchanged? Answer the same question for x_3? Answer the same question for x_1?
*(f) Assume $h_t = 1$ for every Period t. Answer the same questions as those in part (e).
*(g) Assume $h_t = 3$ for every Period t. Answer the same questions as those in part (e).

*36 Assume the production and inventory holding cost functions in exercise 35. Assume $h_t = 0$ for every Period t. Suppose the cumulative demands R_p, defined in (1) of Sec. 9.4, are as specified in each part below. Find the associated values for $X_p(S)$ and $X_p(T)$, specified in the Convex Cost Horizon Theorem, indicate the associated production levels and ending inventories, and draw a diagram like that in Fig. 9.4. Explain whether you can give an optimal value for production in Period 1.

(a) $\sum_{t=1}^{p} D_t - k \le R_p \le \sum_{t=1}^{p} D_t + k$. Do for $k = 1$ and $k = 2$.

(b) $\sum_{t=1}^{p} D_t - pk \le R_p \le \sum_{t=1}^{p} D_t + pk$. Do for $k = 1$ and $k = 2$.

(c) Perform the same analysis with $h_t = 1$ for every Period t.

*37 Assume that backlogging is permitted, and that the demand requirements and production cost function are the same as in exercise 35, and that the inventory holding and backlog penalty cost function is

$$h_t(i_t) = \begin{cases} h_t i_t & \text{if } i_t \ge 0 \\ -p_t i_t & \text{if } i_t \le 0. \end{cases}$$

(All demand must be met by the end of the horizon.) In each part below, find an optimal schedule for production, and indicate ending inventory or backlog for each period. Let all

(a) $h_t = p_t = 0$.   (d) $h_t = 1$ and $p_t = 3$.
(b) $h_t = p_t = 1$.   (e) $h_t = 3$ and $p_t = 1$.
(c) $h_t = p_t = 3$.

Exercises 38 through 43 refer to the inventory model with concave costs, as described in Sec. 9.5. (Recall that initial inventory $i_0 = 0$.)

38 Assume the planning horizon $N = 3$, and the production and inventory cost functions are

$$\begin{aligned} C_1(x_1) &= 12 + 8x_1 \quad \text{for} \quad x_1 \ge 1 \\ C_2(x_2) &= 2 + 9x_2 \quad \text{for} \quad x_2 \ge 1 \\ C_3(x_3) &= 5 + 10x_3 \quad \text{for} \quad x_3 \ge 1 \end{aligned} \right\} \quad \text{and} \quad h_t(i_t) = h_t i_t.$$

Assume the demand requirements are $D_1 = 0$, $D_2 = 3$, and $D_3 = 20$. In each part, find an optimal production schedule, and indicate ending inventory in each period. Assume all

(a) $h_t = 0$.
(b) $h_t = 1$.
(c) $h_t = 2$.

39 Assume the planning horizon $N = 4$, and the production cost functions are given by Fig. 9.13. For example, the total cost associated with $x_1 = 12$ is 86 ($= 10 \cdot 5 + 6 \cdot 5 + 2 \cdot 3$). Assume the holding cost functions are $h_t(i_t) = h_t i_t$, where $h_1 = 1$, $h_2 = 2$,

Production of Unit k	Production Cost of Unit k			
	Period 1	Period 2	Period 3	Period 4
$1 \leq k \leq 5$	10	8	12	9
$6 \leq k \leq 10$	6	5	7	8
$11 \leq k \leq 15$	3	3	6	4
$16 \leq k \leq 20$	1	2	1	4

FIGURE 9.13

and $h_3 = 1$. Suppose the demand requirements are

$$D_1 = 10 \quad D_2 = 3 \quad D_3 = 17 \quad D_4 = 23.$$

(a) Find an optimal production schedule. Be sure to indicate total production x_t and ending inventory i_t in each Period t.
(b) Indicate the impact of requiring an additional unit in Period 1 (that is, let $D_1 = 11$). In Period 2. In Period 3. In Period 4.
(c) Find an optimal schedule where all $h_t = 0$. Where all $h_t = 5$.
(d) Find an optimal production schedule where the demand requirements are revised such that $D_1 = 3$ and $D_2 = 10$. Such that $D_3 = 23$ and $D_4 = 17$. Such that $D_2 = 17$ and $D_3 = 3$.
(e) Find an optimal production schedule where the holding cost function is $h_t(i_t) = \sqrt{i_t}$ for every Period t.

*40 Consider the data in exercise 39, and assume that backlogging is permitted; let the inventory holding and backlog penalty cost function be

$$h_t(i_t) = \begin{cases} h_t i_t & \text{if } i_t \geq 0 \\ -p_t i_t & \text{if } i_t \leq 0 \end{cases} \quad \text{for every Period t.}$$

(All demand must be met by the end of the horizon.) In each part, find an optimal schedule for production, and indicate ending inventory or backlog in each period. Assume all

(a) $h_t = p_t = 0$.
(b) $h_t = p_t = 1$.
(c) Suppose instead that the inventory holding and backlog penalty cost function is $h_t(i_t) = \sqrt{|i_t|}$ for every Period t.

41 Assume the planning horizon $N = 8$, and the production cost function is $C_t(x_t) = \sqrt{x_t}$ for every Period t, and the demand requirements are

$$D_1 = 4 \quad D_2 = 20 \quad D_3 = 2 \quad D_4 = 0 \quad D_5 = 6 \quad D_6 = 4 \quad D_7 = 1 \quad D_8 = 3.$$

In each part below, find an optimal schedule for production and indicate ending inventory in each period. Assume for every Period t that the holding cost function is

(a) $h_t(i_t) = 0$ for every Period t.
(b) $h_t(i_t) = i_t$ for every Period t.
(c) $h_t(i_t) = \sqrt{i_t}$ for every Period t.

*42 Consider the same data as in exercise 41, and assume that backlogging is permitted; let the inventory holding and backlog penalty cost function be

$$h_t(i_t) = \begin{cases} h_t i_t & \text{if } i_t \geq 0 \\ -p_t i_t & \text{if } i_t \leq 0 \end{cases} \quad \text{for every Period t.}$$

(All demand must be met by the end of the horizon.) In each part, find an optimal schedule for production, and indicate ending inventory or backlog in each period. Assume all

(a) $h_t = p_t = 0$.
(b) $h_t = p_t = 1$.
(c) Suppose instead that the inventory holding and backlog penalty cost function is $h_t(i_t) = \sqrt{|i_t|}$ for every Period t.

43 In each part, indicate an optimal production schedule and the associated ending inventory level in every Period t for horizon lengths $1, 2, \ldots, N$, where N is specified in each part below. Assume that the production and holding cost functions are of the form

$$C_t(x_t) = \begin{cases} 0 & \text{for } x_t = 0 \\ s_t + c_t x_t & \text{for } x_t \geq 1 \end{cases} \quad \text{and } h_t(i_t) = h_t i_t \text{ for every Period t.}$$

(a) Let $N = 10$, $s_t = 36$, $c_t = 5$, $h_t = 1$, and the demand requirements $D_t = 8$ for every Period t.
(b) Assume the data in part (a), except that the demand requirements are $D_t = 20$ for Periods 3, 6, and 9 and $D_t = 2$ for all other periods.
(c) Assume the data in part (a), except that the demand requirements are $D_t = 20$ for Periods 2, 5, and 8 and $D_t = 2$ for all other periods.
(d) Assume the data in part (a), except that the demand requirements are $D_t = 20$ for Periods 1, 4, 7, and 10 and $D_t = 2$ for all other periods.
(e) Let $N = 12$, $c_t = 5$, $h_t = 1$, the demand requirements $D_t = 8$ for every Period t, and $s_t = 100$ for Periods 4, 5, 6, 10, 11, 12 and $s_t = 36$ for all other periods.
*(f) Assume the data in part (a), except that the holding cost function is $h_t(i_t) = \sqrt{i_t}$ for every Period t.
*(g) Assume the data in part (a), and that backlogging is permitted; let the inventory holding and backlog penalty cost function be $h_t(i_t) = |i_t|$ for every Period t.
*(h) In parts (a) through (e), indicate how the computations in the algorithm simplify by employing the Setup Cost Horizon Theorem in Sec. 9.7. Also show how you can use recursion (7).

44 Consider the problem in exercise 44 in Chap. 8. Determine whether you get an optimal schedule if you apply

(a) The algorithm in Sec. 9.3 for the inventory model with convex costs.
(b) The algorithm in Sec. 9.6 for the inventory model with concave costs.
(c) Interpret your results in parts (a) and (b).

MIND-EXPANDING EXERCISES

45 Consider the inventory model described in Sec. 9.1. Suppose that production cost in Period t consists of two components: labor cost $L_t(x_t)$ and raw materials cost. The latter arises as follows. In each Period r, the company can purchase an unlimited quantity of raw material at the price p_r per unit (where the units have been selected so that each item of production requires one unit of raw material). Every price p_r is known at the beginning of the planning horizon. If raw materials are purchased in early periods to be stored for use in later periods, then the company incurs a storage cost. Specifically, the charge is H_r per unit of raw material held at the end of Period r. Suggest an efficient way to incorporate the raw materials purchasing decision into the models of Sec. 9.3 and 9.5.

46 In each part below, state how you would modify the specified algorithm to account for a positive level of initial inventory $i_0 > 0$. First state the modifications assuming that all holding cost functions are of the form $h_t(i_t) = h_t i_t$. Then indicate how to revise your approach when the holding cost functions are not all linear.

(a) Inventory model with convex costs in Sec. 9.3.
(b) Inventory model with concave costs in Sec. 9.6.

47 (a) Suggest a rewording of the algorithm in Sec. 9.3 to take account of an upper bound u_t on production x_t and an upper limit b_t on the amount inventoried at the end of Period t.
(b) Consider the concave cost model in Sec. 9.5 and assume that items become obsolete (unusable) after being held in storage for K periods. Give a valid restatement of the form of an optimal policy and the resultant algorithm.

48 Consider the inventory model described in Sec. 9.1, and assume initial inventory $i_0 = 0$. Ignoring integer-value restrictions on the variables, the constraints (4) and (5) can be written as

$$\sum_{k=1}^{t} x_k \geq \sum_{k=1}^{t} D_k \quad \text{for} \quad t = 1, 2, \ldots, N \quad \text{with equality holding for } t = N,$$

and all $x_k \geq 0$. Suppose the cost function to be minimized is $C(x_1, x_2, \ldots, x_N; D_1, D_2, \ldots, D_N)$. Assume that this function is concave in all the decision variables x_k, which means that given any two feasible solutions, the cost associated with another solution that is a positive-weighted average of these two solutions is no greater than the same positive-weighted average of the costs of the two solutions. It can be shown (Sec. 14.9) that an optimal solution occurs at an extreme point of the constraint set.

(Recall a solution is an extreme point if it cannot be expressed as a positive-weighted average of other feasible solutions.)

(a) Verify that an extreme-point solution has the following property. If there are Periods p and q, where $p < q$, such that

$$x_p > 0, x_{p+1} = x_{p+2} = \cdots = x_{q-1} = 0, x_q > 0,$$

then

$$x_p = \sum_{t=p}^{q-1} D_t.$$

(b) Show that part (a) is equivalent to asserting the form of an optimal policy given in Sec. 9.5. Explain why there exists an optimal solution with integer values for the decision variables provided that each D_t is integer-valued.

(c) Show that there are 2^{N-1} feasible extreme-point solutions. Indicate how you can use this result to calculate an optimal policy. (Assume $D_1 > 0$.)

In exercises 49 through 58, you are to formulate a model in terms of a dynamic programming recursion. Be sure to define all the symbols you use. Give the appropriate optimization function where there is a single period remaining, as well as the recursion for Stage n. Explain how to initiate and when to terminate the calculations.

49 Consider the inventory model described in Sec. 9.1.

(a) Add the restriction that $(i_{t-1} + i_t)/2 \le B_t$ for $t = 1, 2, \ldots, N$, where each B_t is a nonnegative integer.

(b) Add the restriction that $x_{t-1} + x_t \le v_t$ for $t = 1, 2, \ldots, N$, where $x_0 = 0$ and each v_t is a nonnegative integer.

(c) Add the restriction that $x_{t-1} + x_t \ge 1$ for $t = 1, 2, \ldots, N$, where $x_0 = 0$.

50 *Batch Service Problem.* Several food companies send shipments for the Mom-and-Pop Grocery Store to a local public warehouse. Mom-and-Pop pays c dollars per day per hundred cubic feet of storage it utilizes in this warehouse. Suppose Mom-and-Pop forecasts, for each of the next N days, that shipments amounting to D_t hundred cubic feet will arrive on Day t. Suppose each day Mom-and-Pop can arrange to have a truck pick up all the goods stored at the warehouse. Since the cost of this trucking service is s, Mom-and-Pop does not usually order a pickup every day. However, it never lets a shipment remain in the warehouse longer than n days. (Assume that shipments arrive at the start of a day, and that the trucking service picks up the goods at the end of a day; assume that warehousing costs are assessed on the maximum space utilized during a day.) Show how Mom-and-Pop can obtain an optimal schedule for picking up goods at the warehouse.

51 *Site Location Problem.* The Crack Oil Company has a substantial share of the gasoline market in a major population center that is located along a peninsula. The area consists of N cities that are connected by a six-lane highway. Assume the cities are indexed $1, 2, \ldots, N$, and to travel from City j to City k, where $j < k$, you must proceed along the highway passing by Cities $j + 1, j + 2, \ldots, k - 1$. The Crack Oil Company wants to locate distributors in one or more of these cities. The annual

fixed cost of operating a distributorship in City j is s_j. The forecasted annual gallonage that must be supplied to City j is D_j. The distance between adjacent Cities j and $j + 1$ is $L_{j, j+1}$. If a distributor in City j serves the requirements in City k, then the annual cost associated with transportation is $h \cdot D_k \cdot$ (distance between City j and City k). The company wants an optimal pattern of locations for its distributors. Formulate a dynamic programming model for this decision problem.

(a) Assume that City k can only be served by a distributor in City j, where $j < k$.

*(b) Assume that City k is served by the closest distributor.

52 *Assortment Problem.* A Japanese industrial firm, Itsa Steel Company, manufactures structural beams of a standard length. The strength of a beam depends on its weight, and Itsa Steel indexes the various strengths it can make as $j = 1, 2, \ldots, N$, where $j = 1$ is the heaviest beam and $j = N$ the lightest. Assume that if a customer requests Strength k, then Itsa Steel may, if it chooses, supply the demand by a beam of possibly greater Strength j, where $j < k$. Itsa Steel must solve the following assortment problem. The demand requirement for Strength j is D_j beams; all demand must be satisfied. If Itsa Steel decides to manufacture Strength j, then it incurs an expensive setup cost s_j. If the company meets the demand requirement D_j by shipping beams of Strength k, where $k \le j$, then the company incurs a loss of $h \cdot (w_k - w_j) \cdot D_j$, where w_k and w_j are the respective weights of the beams and h is the cost per unit of weight. Formulate a dynamic programming model that will enable Itsa Steel to decide an optimal assortment of strengths to manufacture and the corresponding amounts of each.

53 Consider the inventory model described in Sec. 9.1. Suppose there is a cost of starting up production whenever production in the previous period is 0. Specifically, assume the cost function for Period t is

$$C_t(x_t, i_t, x_{t-1}) = C_t(x_t) + h_t(i_t) + v_t(x_{t-1}, x_t),$$

where

$$v_t(x_{t-1}, x_t) = \begin{cases} K_t & \text{if } x_t \ge 1 \quad \text{and} \quad x_{t-1} = 0 \\ 0 & \text{otherwise.} \end{cases}$$

(a) Formulate the problem as a dynamic programming model. Compare the computational difficulty of solving the recursion with that of the model in Sec. 9.1 (making no further assumptions about the shape of the cost functions).

(b) Suppose

$$C_t(x_t) = \begin{cases} 0 & \text{for } x_t = 0 \\ s_t + c_t x_t & \text{for } x_t \ge 1, \end{cases}$$

and $h_t(i_t)$ is concave. Assume all $s_t \ge 0$, $c_t \ge c_{t+1}$, demand requirements $D_t > 0$, and initial inventory $i_0 = 0$. Suppose there exists an optimal policy in which $i_{t-1} x_t = 0$ for every Period t. Suggest an appropriate modification to the algorithm in Sec. 9.6. Draw a shortest-route diagram illustrating your idea.

*(c) Prove that assumptions in part (b) imply the existence of an optimal policy with $i_{t-1} x_t = 0$.

54 Consider the inventory model described in Sec. 9.1. Suppose that production is permitted in at most K periods during the horizon of N periods (that is, no more than K of the x_t, for $t = 1, 2, \ldots, N$, can be positive). Formulate the problem as a dynamic programming model. Compare the computational difficulty of solving the recursion

with that of the model in Sec. 9.1 (making no further assumptions about the shape of the cost functions). State how you would modify your answer if production must occur in exactly K periods during the horizon.

In exercises 55 through 58 the single-item inventory model as described in Sec. 9.1 is generalized to a problem having two items (the further generalization to more items involves straightforward extensions of the results below). Accordingly, let D_{1t} and D_{2t} denote the demand requirements in Period t for Products 1 and 2, respectively, and similarly let x_{1t} and x_{2t} denote the production levels, and i_{1t} and i_{2t} the ending inventory levels. (Any assumptions left implicit are the appropriate generalization of those made for the model in Sec. 9.1.)

55 Assume the objective function is

$$\text{minimize} \sum_{t=1}^{N} C_t(x_{1t}, x_{2t}, i_{1t}, i_{2t}),$$

where

$$C_t(x_{1t}, x_{2t}, i_{1t}, i_{2t}) = C_t(x_{1t}, x_{2t}) + h_{1t}(i_{1t}) + h_{2t}(i_{2t}).$$

Formulate a dynamic programming model, and compare the computational difficulty of solving the recursion with that of the model in Sec. 9.1 (making no further assumptions about the shape of the cost functions).

56 Suppose the cost functions in exercise 55 are

$$C_t(x_{1t}, x_{2t}) = \begin{cases} 0 & \text{for } x_{1t} = x_{2t} = 0 \\ s_t + C_{1t}x_{1t} + C_{2t}x_{2t} & \text{otherwise,} \end{cases}$$

where $s_t \geq 0$, $C_{1t} \geq C_{1,t+1}$ and $C_{2t} \geq C_{2,t+1}$, and that the holding cost functions $h_{1t}(i_{1t})$ and $h_{2t}(i_{2t})$ are concave.

(a) Assume initial inventories $i_{10} = i_{20} = 0$. Suppose that there exists an optimal policy for which $(i_{1,t-1} + i_{2,t-1}) \cdot (x_{1t} + x_{2t}) = 0$ for every Period t. Explain how you would modify the algorithm in Sec. 9.6 to find an optimal production policy for both items.

*(b) Prove the existence of an optimal policy having the form stated in part (a).

57 Suppose the cost functions in exercise 55 are

$$C_t(x_{1t}, x_{2t}) = \begin{cases} 0 & \text{for } x_{1t} = x_{2t} = 0 \\ s_t + C_{1t}(x_{1t}) + C_{2t}(x_{2t}) & \text{otherwise,} \end{cases}$$

where $s_t \geq 0$, $C_{1t}(x_{1t})$ and $C_{2t}(x_{2t})$ are concave, and that the holding cost functions $h_{1t}(i_{1t})$ and $h_{2t}(i_{2t})$ are concave.

(a) Assume that the form of an optimal policy in Sec. 9.5 remains valid for each item. Explain how you would simplify the calculations in the recursion for exercise 55 by exploiting this information.

*(b) Prove that the assumption in part (a) is valid.

58 Suppose the production cost functions in exercise 55 are $C_t(x_{1t}, x_{2t}) = C_{1t}(x_{1t}) + C_{2t}(x_{2t})$, and that the production levels are constrained in each period by $a_{1t} x_{1t} + a_{2t}x_{2t} \leq b_t$, where a_{1t}, a_{2t}, b_t are nonnegative integers. Show how you would modify your formulation in exercise 55 accordingly.

CONTENTS

CHAPTER 10

Other Examples of
Dynamic Programming

10.1 REMINDER

Formulating a model in terms of a dynamic programming recurrence relation is partially an art. Hence a variety of examples are illustrated in Secs. 10.2 through 10.6 so that you can acquire a better feeling for such formulations. Since you have seen the numerical solution for two examples worked out in gory detail in Chap. 8, we do not emphasize here the computational aspects of solving the models.

At the end of this chapter, in Secs. 10.7 through 10.10, we give an overall assessment of dynamic programming. Specifically, we discuss the ingredients that are common to all dynamic programming model formulations, and summarize how this kind of analysis yields insightful information for managerial decision-making. Some perspective is given on what makes the difference between a theoretical exercise and a practical application of dynamic analysis. Finally, we point out in brief the kinds of industrial applications that have proved profitable, and the reasons for their success.

In presenting the models below, we start slowly and provide a number of the minor details; as the chapter progresses, the pace picks up, and you are asked to *carefully* study the models and provide some of this detail yourself. Our words of guidance from Chap. 8 still apply—be patient and give yourself plenty of time to study the sections. Plan to read each section at least twice. And to keep check on your understanding, for each of the models answer the questions:

1. What are the policy or decision variables?
2. What is the criterion or objective function for determining an optimal policy?
3. How is the problem characterized and then analyzed in terms of stages?

4. What characterizes the state of the problem at each stage?
5. How do the constraints influence the states of the problem and the feasible values of the policy variables?

10.2 DISTRIBUTION OF EFFORT—ONE CONSTRAINT

The following is a hypothetical, but suggestive, example of the so-called *distribution of effort model*. The owner of Shopping Basket Markets has a week's supply N of eggs to distribute among his s stores. From past experience he knows that if he allocates y_j eggs to Store j, his profit will be $R_j(y_j)$. He suspects that in order to maximize his overall profit, he should not put all his eggs in one Shopping Basket! He wants to find an optimal distribution of eggs.

This decision problem can be formulated as

$$(1) \qquad \text{maximize} \sum_{j=1}^{s} R_j(y_j)$$

subject to

$$(2) \qquad \sum_{j=1}^{s} y_j = N \quad \text{(available number of eggs)}$$

$$(3) \qquad y_j = 0, 1, 2, \ldots \text{ for each } j \quad \text{(distribute only whole eggs)}.$$

To convert the problem statement (1) through (3) into a dynamic programming version, define

$$(4) \qquad \begin{aligned} g_j(n) &= \text{profit when } n \text{ eggs are distributed optimally to Store 1, Store 2,} \\ &\qquad \ldots, \text{Store j,} \end{aligned}$$

$$y_j(n) = \text{a distribution amount for Store j that yields } g_j(n).$$

Watch the notation here. The letter g indicates a value for the company's goal, namely profit. The letter n refers to the *n*umber of eggs to be distributed. And the index j denotes *j*ust a store.

Observe that this example is not dynamic in the sense of a time-staged decision. Rather, the multistage property of the problem relates to the optimizing *technique* of considering one additional store at a time.

The dynamic programming recursion can be written as

$$(5) \qquad g_j(n) = \underset{y_j}{\text{maximum}} \; [R_j(y_j) + g_{j-1}(n - y_j)] \quad \text{for } j = 1, 2, \ldots, s$$

$$(6) \qquad g_0(n) \equiv 0 \quad \text{for } j = 0,$$

where $n = 0, 1, \ldots, N$ and the maximization is over only nonnegative integer values of y_j that satisfy $y_j \leq n$.

Given numerical data for the profit functions $R_j(y_j)$ and a value of N, you solve the problem by beginning the computations for $j = 1$ and finding $g_1(0)$, $g_1(1)$, $\ldots, g_1(N)$. Then continue by finding $g_2(0), g_2(1), \ldots, g_2(N)$. You proceed in this fashion for successively larger values of j until you finally find $g_s(N)$. You obtain the actual optimal allocation by tracing back to see the values of y_j that together yielded $g_s(N)$.

General model. The Shopping Basket Example is a special case of what is called a **distribution of effort problem**; the example is special because the single constraint (2) is linear. The same dynamic approach is equally valid when the single constraint is nonlinear. Specifically, suppose the model is

$$(7) \qquad\qquad \text{maximize} \sum_{j=1}^{s} R_j(y_j)$$

subject to

$$(8) \qquad\qquad \sum_{j=1}^{s} H_j(y_j) = N$$

$$(9) \qquad\qquad y_j = 0, 1, 2, \ldots \quad \text{for each } j.$$

Assume that each $H_j(y_j)$ is a nondecreasing function, integer-valued for each $y_j = 0, 1, 2, \ldots$, and, for simplicity, satisfies $H_j(0) = 0$. To simplify the discussion, assume that $H_1(y_1) = y_1$ so a feasible solution exists for any value of N. Each y_j can also be restricted by an upper bound, as will be illustrated in a numerical example below.

A dynamic programming recursion appropriate for (7) through (9) is

$$(10) \qquad g_j(n) = \underset{y_j}{\text{maximum}} \{ R_j(y_j) + g_{j-1}[n - H_j(y_j)] \} \quad \text{for } j = 1, 2, \ldots, s$$

$$(11) \qquad\qquad g_0(n) \equiv 0 \quad \text{for } j = 0,$$

where $n = 0, 1, \ldots, N$, and the maximization is over only nonnegative integer values of y_j that satisfy $H_j(y_j) \leq n$. The value of $g_s(N)$ is sought. To perform the computations, find each $g_j(n)$, for $n = 0, 1, \ldots, N$ in (10), beginning with $j = 1$, and terminating with $j = s$.

Numerical example. We illustrate the computational process of solving a distribution of effort problem by assuming data for the model in (7), (8), and (9). Specifically, we let $s = 3$ and $N = 8$; the values for the functions $R_j(y_j)$ and $H_j(y_j)$ are displayed in Fig. 10.1. Observe that

$$(12) \qquad \begin{aligned} R_1(y_1) &= 2y_1 & R_2(y_2) &= 3y_2 \\ H_1(y_1) &= y_1 & H_2(y_2) &= 2y_2 & H_3(y_3) &= 3y_3, \end{aligned}$$

y_j	$R_1(y_1)$	$H_1(y_1)$	$R_2(y_2)$	$H_2(y_2)$	$R_3(y_3)$	$H_3(y_3)$
0	0	0	0	0	0	0
1	2	1	3	2	4.5	3
2	4	2	6	4	4.5	6

FIGURE 10.1.   Distribution of Effort Example.

which are linear functions, but $R_3(y_3)$ is *not* linear. In addition, we impose an upper bound

(13) $y_j \leq 2$ for each j.

(In the context of this problem, we equally well could have imposed the bound $y_3 \leq 1$, since letting $y_3 = 2$ does not increase the objective function.)

The values of $g_j(n)$ and the associated optimal decisions $y_j(n)$ are tabled in Fig. 10.2. Let us review how these numbers are computed.

n	$y_1(n)$	$g_1(n)$	$y_2(n)$	$g_2(n)$	$y_3(n)$	$g_3(n)$
	j = 1		j = 2		j = 3	
0	0	0	0	0	0	0
1	1	2	0	2	0	2
2	2	4	0	4	0	4
3			1	5	0	5
4			1	7	0	7
5			2	8	1	8.5
6			2	10	0	10
7					1	11.5
8					1	12.5

FIGURE 10.2. Optimal Policies for Distribution of Effort Example $(N = 8)$.

The calculations of $y_1(n)$ and $g_1(n)$ are trivial. For example, if $n = 2$, then you can see in Fig. 10.1 that $H_1(2) = 2$, so that $y_1(2) = 2$ and, correspondingly, $g_1(2) = R_1(2) = 4$.

Similarly, the calculations of $y_2(n)$ and $g_2(n)$ for $n = 0, 1$ are almost trivial since, for these values of n, the restriction $H_2(y_2) \leq n$ can only be satisfied by $y_2 = 0$. Therefore

(14) $g_2(0) = 0$ and $y_2(0) = 0$

(15) $g_2(1) = R_2(0) + g_1(1) = 0 + 2 = 2$ and $y_2(1) = 0$.

A more typical calculation occurs in finding $y_2(2)$ and $g_2(2)$, since, when $n = 2$, the values $y_2 = 0$ and $y_2 = 1$ are both feasible, according to Fig. 10.1. Then (10) indicates

(16) $g_2(2) = \text{maximum } [R_2(0) + g_1(2),\ R_2(1) + g_1(0)]$
$$= \text{maximum } (0 + 4,\ 3 + 0) = 4 \quad \text{and} \quad y_2(2) = 0.$$

To test your understanding of this process, verify the remaining entries in Fig. 10.2. (Notice in Fig. 10.2 that as n increases from 0 to 8, the optimal amount of y_3 fluctuates.)

The optimal policy for $N = 8$ is found as follows: starting with $j = 3$, you see that $y_3(8) = 1$. Consequently, to find an optimal y_2, you must calculate $n = 8 - 3y_3(8) = 5$. Thus $y_2(5) = 2$. Then the new $n = 5 - 2y_2(5) = 1$, and thus $y_1(1) = 1$. So an optimal policy is $y_1 = 1$, $y_2 = 2$, and $y_3 = 1$. The associated optimal value of the objective function is $g_3(8) = 12.5$.

▶ For the special case in which the objective function (7) and constraint (8) are linear,

(i) $R_j(y_j) = R_j y_j$ and $H_j(y_j) = H_j y_j$ for $j = 1, 2, \ldots, s$,

further simplifications in the analysis are possible. Continue to assume that $H_1 = 1$, and for $j \neq 1$, H_j is an integer larger than 1. The following recurrence relation can be employed instead of (10) and (11):

(ii) $F(n) = \underset{j}{\text{maximum}} \, [R_j + F(n - H_j)]$ for $n = 1, 2, \ldots, N$

and

(iii) $$F(0) \equiv 0 \quad \text{for} \quad n = 0,$$

where the maximization is over values of $j = 1, 2, \ldots, s$ that also satisfy $H_j \leq n$. The computational process is to determine $F(1), F(2), \ldots, F(N-1)$, and finally $F(N)$, which is the optimal value of the objective function. Here the notions of stage and state variables coalesce, so a subscript is not needed.

Comparison of (10) and (ii) shows immediately that whereas you must determine $g_j(n)$ for $n = 0, 1, \ldots, N$ *and* $j = 1, 2, \ldots, s$, you need find $F(n)$ only for $n = 0, 1, \ldots, N$. Thus $g_s(n) \equiv F(n)$.

The difference between the two approaches (10) and (ii) is nicely demonstrated by the inventory model with concave costs treated in Sec. 9.5. Suppose demands and cost functions are unchanging over time, that is, suppose they are stationary:

(iv) $D_t = D$ $C_t(x_t) = C(x_t)$ and $h_t(i_t) = h(i_t)$ for all periods.

Then the total cost c_{kj} of producing in Period $k + 1$ to meet the demand requirements of Periods $k + 1, \ldots, j$ depends only on the *length* of the interval. Therefore for $j - k = p$, let $c_{kj} \equiv R_p = C(pD) + \sum_{m=1}^{p-1} h(mD)$. To illustrate, if $N = 4$,

(v)
$$c_{kj} = c_{01} = c_{12} = c_{23} = c_{34} \equiv R_1 \quad \text{for} \quad j - k = 1$$
$$c_{kj} = c_{02} = c_{13} = c_{24} \equiv R_2 \quad\quad \text{for} \quad j - k = 2$$
$$c_{kj} = c_{03} = c_{14} \equiv R_3 \quad\quad\quad \text{for} \quad j - k = 3$$
$$c_{kj} = c_{04} \equiv R_4 \quad\quad\quad\quad\quad \text{for} \quad j - k = 4.$$

In this situation the proposition on the form of the optimal policy implies that each production amount will be an integer multiple of D, such as $1D, 2D, \ldots, ND$. Let y_j be the number of times the production amount $j \cdot D$ is scheduled, where $j = 1, 2, \ldots, N$. Then the y_j must be determined so that total production $\sum_{j=1}^{N} (j \cdot D)y_j$ equals total demand $N \cdot D$. The associated optimization model for an N-period horizon can be stated as

(vi) $$\text{minimize} \sum_{j=1}^{N} R_j y_j$$

subject to

(vii) $$\sum_{j=1}^{N} j \cdot y_j = N \quad \text{and} \quad y_j = 0, 1, \ldots \quad \text{for all } j,$$

where D has been divided out of both sides of (vii). [Thus the summation on the left of (vii) is merely the total span of the schedule, and has to equal the length of the planning horizon.]

Observe that the objective in (vi) is minimization. Rather than convert (vi) to a maximization problem by changing the signs of R_j, you can simply change the sense of optimization in (10). The formulation (vi) and (vii) views the problem in terms of how many batches y_j of demand requirements for j periods are to be scheduled. Here $s = N$, since one possibility is to schedule the amount $N \cdot D$ in Period 1 to satisfy all demand requirements.

For examples (vi) and (vii), you can simplify (10) and (11) to

(viii) $$g_j(n) = \underset{y_j}{\text{minimum}} \, [R_j y_j + g_{j-1}(n - j \cdot y_j)] \quad \text{for} \quad j = 1, 2, \ldots, N, \quad \text{and}$$

(ix) $$g_0(n) \equiv 0 \quad \text{for} \quad j = 0,$$

where $n = 0, 1, \ldots, N$ and the minimization is over only nonnegative integer values of y_j that satisfy $j \cdot y_j \leq n$.

The recursion (ii) becomes, for $n = 1, 2, \ldots, N$,

(x) $$F(n) = \underset{j=1,\ldots,n}{\text{minimum}} \, [R_j + F(n - j)] \quad \text{and} \quad F(0) \equiv 0.$$

Letting $f_n \equiv F(n)$ and $k \equiv n - j$, an equivalent expression for (x) is

(xi) $$f_n = \underset{k=0,1,\ldots,n-1}{\text{minimum}} \, [f_k + R_{n-k}] \quad \text{and} \quad f_0 \equiv 0,$$

which is the same as the recursion (4) in Sec. 9.6, given the cost assumption in (v).

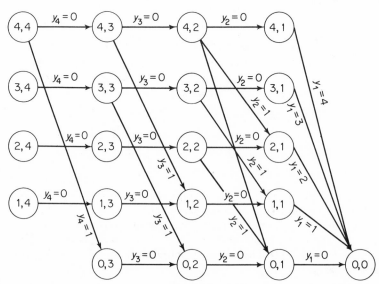

FIGURE 10.3. Concave Cost Inventory Model—Node Description: (n, j).

To compare the relative merits of (viii) and (x), let $N = 4$. Then the recursion (x) corresponds to finding the shortest route in an acyclic network structure that has the appearance of Fig. 9.7, p. 308. The recursion (viii) corresponds to a shortest-route problem in the network exhibited in Fig. 10.3. Here each node label (n, j) refers to a pair of values for n and j in (viii). Each arc out of Node (n, j) represents a value of y_j such that $j \cdot y_j \leq n$. Clearly (viii) involves more effort than (x). [Both recursive approaches can be further streamlined, but even after these additional efficiencies are exploited, (x) remains better.]　　　　　　　　　　　　　　　　　　　　　　　　　◄

10.3 DISTRIBUTION OF EFFORT—TWO CONSTRAINTS

The Genghis Motor Company is planning a radio advertising campaign for its automobiles in a large metropolitan area. The spot commercials will introduce the firm's new models, and will be aired over a two-week period. The area has s radio stations. For Radio Station j, the company's market research organization has *estimated* a sales response relation indicating the net return (sales less advertising costs) $R_j(y_j)$ due to allocating y_j dollars to commercials played on that station. The total promotional budget is N dollars. The company's advertising manager also wants only a limited number M of announcements during the daytime hours. Radio Station j has indicated that $K_j(y_j)$ is the number of daytime spots it would schedule, given that the company purchased a total of y_j dollars of advertising.

The manager's optimization model can be written as

$$(1) \qquad\qquad \text{maximize} \sum_{j=1}^{s} R_j(y_j)$$

subject to

$$(2) \qquad\qquad \sum_{j=1}^{s} y_j \leq N \quad \text{(promotional budget)}$$

$$(3) \qquad\qquad \sum_{j=1}^{s} K_j(y_j) \leq M \quad \text{(daytime announcements)}$$

$$(4) \qquad\qquad y_j = 0, 1, 2, \ldots \quad \text{for each } j.$$

Assume that N, M, and $K_j(y_j)$ are all nonnegative integers.

Since previously you needed a one-dimensional state variable in a dynamic recursion to represent one constraint, such as (2), now you might reasonably, and correctly, guess that a two-dimensional state variable is required. An appropriate recursive relation is

$$(5) \qquad g_j(n, m) = \underset{y_j}{\text{maximum}} \{R_j(y_j) + g_{j-1}[n - y_j, m - K_j(y_j)]\}$$
$$\text{for } j = 1, 2, \ldots, s,$$

where $n = 0, 1, \ldots, N$, and $m = 0, 1, \ldots, M$, and the maximization is over only nonnegative integer values of y_j such that $y_j \leq n$ and $K_j(y_j) \leq m$. Give a definition for $g_j(n, m)$ in the context of the radio advertising campaign. What is the essential difference between (5) and the earlier relation (10) in Sec. 10.2? How would the recursion appear if you added a third summation constraint to (2) and (3)?

▶Another illustration of the model arises in the process of capital budgeting. Each year the Giant Electric Company, which manufactures heavy equipment, considers a large number s of independent proposals for major plant and machinery investments. Proposal j requires a total outlay of K_j dollars, and the funds M for all such capital investments are fixed. The expected return on the investment is R_j dollars, and the company seeks to maximize its overall return. The corporate directors have also realized that due to the limited availability of supervisory management, the total number of projects undertaken in any one year should be restricted to N. Each proposal is unique, and the firm must decide to either accept or reject the proposal for the year. To represent this decision, let the variable associated with Proposal j be restricted to be $y_j = 0$ (reject) or 1 (accept). All these conditions can then be expressed by the problem

(i) $$\text{maximize} \sum_{j=1}^{s} R_j y_j$$

subject to

(ii) $$\sum_{j=1}^{s} y_j \leq N \qquad \text{(project limit)}$$

(iii) $$\sum_{j=1}^{s} K_j y_j \leq M \qquad \text{(budget limit)}$$

(iv) $$y_j = 0 \text{ or } 1 \quad \text{for each } j \quad \text{(reject or accept)}.$$

In this context

(v) $g_j(n, m)$ = return when m dollars are available to invest optimally in n projects selected from Proposal 1, Proposal 2, ..., Proposal j. ◀

10.4 DISTRIBUTION OF EFFORT—NESTED PROBLEM

The Amazing Products Chemical Company, which is divisionally organized, annually allocates funds for research and development (R & D) projects. Each of the s divisions submits information in three categories. The first pertains to research activities of an exploratory and highly speculative nature. If v_j thousand dollars are allocated to such projects in Division j, the long-term expected return is $P_j(v_j)$ million dollars. The second category refers to products that have been researched and are ready for development and field testing. In these cases, an outlay of w_j thousand dollars is expected to return $Q_j(w_j)$ million dollars over the long run. The final category is development work to improve existing manufactured products. An expenditure of x_j thousand dollars is forecasted to yield a total of $R_j(x_j)$ million dollars additional revenue.

The board of directors authorizes a total budget of N thousand dollars for all R & D projects, and the chief executive places an upper limit L_j on the amount that Division j can receive. The vice-president responsible for R & D management is to allocate the funds so as to maximize the company's total return subject to the several budget restrictions.

The mathematical model of the vice-president's problem is

$$(1) \qquad \text{maximize} \sum_{j=1}^{s} [P_j(v_j) + Q_j(w_j) + R_j(x_j)]$$

subject to

$$(2) \qquad \sum_{j=1}^{s} (v_j + w_j + x_j) \leq N \qquad \text{(company R \& D budget)}$$

$$(3) \qquad v_j + w_j + x_j \leq L_j \quad \text{for } j = 1, 2, \ldots, s \quad \text{(division budget limit)}$$

$$(4) \qquad v_j, w_j, x_j \text{ nonnegative integers for each } j.$$

Since there is only one budget constraint (2) imposed on all the policy variables, and the other budget and integer-value constraints (3) and (4) pertain to Division j, you can expect the distribution of effort problem for one constraint to apply here. Pursuing this line of reasoning, you obtain the recursion

$$(5) \quad g_j(n) = \text{maximum } [P_j(v_j) + Q_j(w_j) + R_j(x_j) + g_{j-1}(n - v_j - w_j - x_j)]$$
$$\text{for } j = 1, 2, \ldots, s,$$

where $n = 0, 1, \ldots, N$ and the maximization is over only nonnegative integer values of v_j, w_j, and x_j that satisfy $v_j + w_j + x_j \leq \text{minimum } (L_j, n)$.

Notice a new difficulty appears in (5). Whereas in the previous distribution of effort examples you had only one variable y_j to vary in the search for a maximum at each stage, now you must solve an optimization problem involving three variables. Of course, you could try to enumerate all possibilities, but that is not necessary. In this particular illustration, *at each stage* you are able to use the distribution of effort technique to solve the maximum problem, which can be stated as

$$(6) \qquad \text{maximize } P_j(v_j) + Q_j(w_j) + R_j(x_j)$$

subject to

$$(7) \qquad v_j + w_j + x_j \leq y,$$

where v_j, w_j, and x_j must be nonnegative integers. You need the solution for each value $y = 0, 1, \ldots, L_j$.

The recursive approach for (6) and (7) is to let

$$(8) \qquad p_j(y) = P_j(y) \quad \text{for } y = 0, 1, \ldots, L_j,$$

$$(9) \qquad q_j(y) = \text{maximum } [Q_j(w_j) + p_j(y - w_j)] \quad \text{for } y = 0, 1, \ldots, L_j,$$

where the maximization is over only nonnegative integer values of $w_j \leq y$, and

$$(10) \qquad r_j(y) = \text{maximum } [R_j(x_j) + q_j(y - x_j)] \quad \text{for } y = 0, 1, \ldots, L_j,$$

where the maximization is over only nonnegative integer values of $x_j \leq y$.

In summary, for each j you use $p_j(y)$ from (8) and (9) to find $q_j(y)$, and use $q_j(y)$ and (10) to find $r_j(y)$, for $y = 0, 1, \ldots, L_j$. Then you restate and solve (5) by the relation

(11) $$g_j(n) = \underset{y}{\text{maximum}} \, [r_j(y) + g_{j-1}(n - y)] \quad \text{for } j = 1, 2, \ldots, s,$$

where $n = 0, 1, \ldots, N$ and the maximization is over only nonnegative integer values of y that satisfy $y \leq \text{minimum} \, (L_j, n)$. Thus this problem requires **nesting** s distribution of effort calculations within an overall distribution of effort model.

*10.5 LINEAR PROGRAMMING WITH INTEGER VARIABLES

The approaches illustrated for the distribution of effort models extend immediately to the model

(1) $$\text{maximize} \sum_{j=1}^{s} c_j y_j$$

subject to

(2) $$\sum_{j=1}^{s} a_{ij} y_j = b_i \quad \text{for } i = 1, 2, \ldots, k$$

(3) $$y_j = 0, 1, 2, \ldots \quad \text{for each } j,$$

where each a_{ij} and b_i is a nonnegative integer. A recursion applicable to this model is

(4) $$F(n_1, n_2, \ldots, n_k) = \underset{j}{\text{maximum}} \, [c_j + F(n_1 - a_{1j}, n_2 - a_{2j}, \ldots, n_k - a_{kj})],$$

where, for each $i = 1, 2, \ldots, k$, we consider $n_i = 0, 1, \ldots, b_i$, and the maximization is over each value $j = 1, 2, \ldots, s$ that satisfies $a_{ij} \leq n_i$ for every $i = 1, 2, \ldots, k$.

This approach is completely impractical for problems of ordinary size, however, since the recursion requires finding (4) for every possible state $(n_1, n_2, \ldots, n_k)$. To illustrate, if each a_{ij} equals either 0 or 1, and every $b_i = 1$, then each n_i can equal 0 or 1. Consequently, $(n_1, n_2, \ldots, n_k)$ are enumerated by letting each n_i be 0 and 1—altogether 2^k possibilities. If k is 100, which is not a very large linear programming application, more than 10^{30} possible $(n_1, n_2, \ldots, n_k)$ exist, which implies a number of calculations far beyond the capability of electronic computers. Therefore the multistage approach (4) is not feasible unless k is very small. We will return to this model in Chap. 13.

10.6 EQUIPMENT REPLACEMENT MODEL

In Sec. 6.5, pp. 180–181, you learned how an acyclic network can be employed to represent a problem of determining a minimum-cost equipment replacement policy over an $(N - 1)$-year horizon. Review that material before proceeding.

In that section, c_{ij} represented the entire cost associated with using the machinery from the beginning of Period i until the beginning of Period j, when it is replaced. Although the example in Sec. 6.5 referred to the leasing of equipment, the model is equally applicable to the situation in which a company purchases the unit. In this case, c_{ij} is the sum of the purchase price and operating costs of the new equipment, less the salvage value of the old machine at the beginning of Period j. The problem is of the regeneration type, in that a replacement policy is tantamount to a list of periods in which new equipment is purchased. Let

(1) f_n = the minimum replacement-policy cost for Periods n, n + 1, . . . , N − 1,
         assuming that a new machine is purchased at the start of Period n.

Then we seek the value of f_1, and the dynamic recursion appropriate to such a point of view is

(2) $f_n = \underset{k=n+1,\ldots,N}{\text{minimum}} [c_{nk} + f_k]$ for $n = N − 1, N − 2, \ldots, 1$

(3) $f_N \equiv 0$.

Give a verbal description of (2). The associated acyclic network is represented for $N − 1 = 5$ in Fig. 10.4.

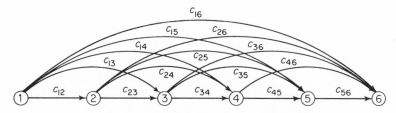

FIGURE 10.4. Equipment Replacement Network.

▶The same problem can be approached from a somewhat different dynamic view. Assume that the costs incurred by any replacement policy are comprised of the quantities

(i)
       p_{in} = net cost of selling (salvaging) an i-year-old machine in Period n and replacing it with a new machine

       k_{nt} = cost in Period n of operating a machine that at the end of the period is t years old.

Let

(ii) $f_n(i)$ = minimum replacement-policy cost for Periods n, n + 1, . . . , N − 1 when Period n is entered with an i-year-old machine.

Observe that the subscript notation in (ii) differs in this example from previous examples. Here n refers actually to Period n and beyond, until the end of the horizon. (In the inventory examples, n indicated the stage at which n periods remained before the end of the horizon.)

If it is optimal to keep the machine entering Period n, then

(iii) $f_n(i) = k_{n,i+1} + f_{n+1}(i + 1)$ (keep),

but if it is optimal to replace it, then

(iv) $f_n(i) = p_{in} + k_{n1} + f_{n+1}(1)$ (purchase).

Thus

(v) $f_n(i) = \text{minimum} \, [k_{n, i+1} + f_{n+1}(i+1), \quad p_{in} + k_{n1} + f_{n+1}(1)]$

$$\text{for} \quad n = 1, 2, \ldots, N - 1,$$

where

(vi) $f_N(i) \equiv 0.$

The value of $f_1(i_0)$ is sought, where i_0 is the age of the machine at the start of the planning horizon. If no machine exists at that time, then p_{i_01} is merely the cost of purchasing a new machine, and the *keep* decision is not applicable for $n = 1$.

Figure 10.5 is a pictorial representation of (v). The exhibit assumes that no machine

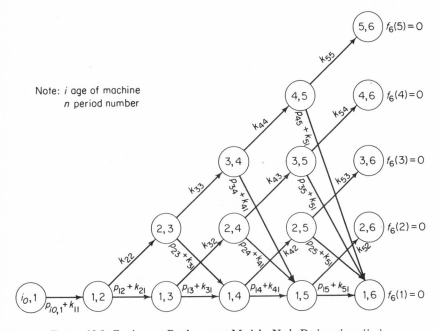

FIGURE 10.5. Equipment Replacement Model—Node Designation: (i, n).

exists prior to $n = 1$, and $N - 1 = 5$. The nodes are labeled (i, n) corresponding to the notation in (v). What arcs represent the purchase decision? Compare the relative merits of (2) and (v), using Figs. 10.4 and 10.5 to justify your opinions.   ◄

10.7 STRUCTURE OF MULTISTAGE ANALYSIS

Having seen a variety of dynamic programming applications and explored a few in depth, you may find it helpful to summarize the essential features in the approach. The remaining sections provide an overview of dynamic programming models.

The constrained optimization problems encompassed by dynamic programming are really no different *conceptually* from those you already saw prior to Chap. 8, as well as those you will study later on. Only the point of view for analyzing the model is decidedly novel. The dynamic programming approach attacks an optimization problem with multifold constraints and many variables by splitting the problem into a sequence of stages in which lower-dimension optimization takes place. In contrast, most linear and other nonlinear programming approaches attempt to solve such problems by considering all the constraints simultaneously.

The dynamic programming approach casts a problem into the following structure:

(i) The decision variables with their associated constraints are grouped according to stages, and the stages are considered sequentially.

(ii) The only information about previous stages relevant to selecting optimal values for the current decision variables is summarized by a so-called state variable, which may be *n*-dimensional.

(iii) The current decision, given the present state of the system, has a forecastable influence on the state at the next stage.

(iv) The optimality of the current decision is judged in terms of its forecasted economic impact on the present stage and on all subsequent stages.

▶Unlike linear programming, which refers to a specific mathematical model that can be solved by a variety of techniques (the most notable being the simplex method), dynamic programming deals with a particular analytic approach, which can be applied to a variety of mathematical models. There is a canonical form that conveniently illustrates the structure of points (i) through (iv) above.

Let the symbol s stand for a state of the system and S_n the collection or set of all possible states at Stage n. Define d_n as the decision made at Stage n, and let $D_n(s)$ designate all the *feasible* values for d_n given that the system is in State s. Finally, given that the system is in State s, let $R_n(s, d_n)$ denote the immediate economic return of decision d_n, and $T_n(s, d_n)$ the transformed state of the system at Stage n $-$ 1. Then a common form for a dynamic programming recursion is

(DPR) $$f_n(s) = \operatorname*{optimum}_{d_n \text{ in } D_n(s)} \{R_n(s, d_n) + f_{n-1}[T_n(s, d_n)]\} \quad \text{for every } s \text{ in } S_n,$$

where *optimum* means maximum or minimum, depending on the particular context. All the recurrence relations in Chaps. 8 through 10 were of this form. Take each point from (i) through (iv) and show exactly how it affects the appearance of (DPR). Point (ii) is sometimes referred to as the *Markov property*. State which point contains the *principle of optimality*, given in Chap. 8: an optimal policy must have the property that regardless of the route taken to enter a particular state, the remaining decisions must constitute an optimal policy for leaving that state.

You should keep in mind an important feature of (DPR). The optimization at Stage n does *not* require the values of the *decision* variables which bring about the return $f_{n-1}[T_n(s, d_n)]$. The "bootstrapping" nature of the recursion means that at each stage you only optimize with respect to a limited number of decision variables, and you retain for further calculation only the *objective-function* values. This essential simplicity is what makes the method attractive. Employing linear programming terminology, you can think of the dynamic programming process as sequentially obtaining values for the dual variables. Such an analogy is exact in the examples of this chapter for the reasons to follow.

In all of the illustrations, the stage, state, and decision variables were represented by integer numbers. (The term **discrete variable problem** is applied to such situations.) In addition, the decision processes extended over a finite time span or number of stages. Finally, no probabilistic elements influenced the outcomes and transitions from state to state.

All these assumptions made it possible to analyze (DPR) in terms of finding a best route in an acyclic network, such as you studied in Chap. 7. To construct the network, you establish a Node [s, n] for every possible value of s and n in the dynamic programming recursion (DPR). Each d_n in $D_n(s)$ results in an arc from Node [s, n] to Node $[T_n(s, d_n), n - 1]$ with arc cost $R_n(s, d_n)$. The State s at the final stage is specified (for example, as "ending inventory must equal zero"). Therefore, this node is taken as the terminal of the network, and $f_n(s)$ represents the length of a best route to the terminal from Node [s, n].

In the linear programming characterization of the network problem, $f_n(s)$ represents the value of the dual variable for the conservation of flow equation at Node [s, n]. Of course, to solve (DPR) you never need to *draw* the acyclic network, but you should note two implications of the network equivalence. First you were facilitated in comparing the relative computational merits of alternative dynamic programming formulations by analyzing the complexity of the implied acyclic networks. A rough but usually adequate rule is that the network with the fewest arcs is to be preferred. (This guide is qualified because some formulations require substantial "side calculations" to determine the arc traversal costs *prior* to applying the best-route algorithm.)

Second, once you characterized a model by a particular recursion, nothing truly innovative appeared in the technique of solution. New considerations do arise, however, in dynamic programming problems that are not discrete, finite, and deterministic. You will study several of these in Chaps. 11, 12, 17, and 18.   ◀

10.8 INSIGHTS TO DYNAMIC PHENOMENA

The dynamic programming approach by its very nature is conducive to studying questions of time horizon sensitivity. The various inventory models in Chaps. 8 and 9 demonstrated that an optimal policy can depend essentially on the length of the planning horizon. Several important ideas emerged from the analysis.

One is the notion of a **strategy**. By solving a dynamic programming recursion, you are in effect determining an optimal policy for every possible value of the state variable at each stage. Thus you obtain a prescription of what to do in every eventuality. To observe the consequences of this, consider a production scheduling model as an example. Suppose you act *as if* demand and the cost functions do not change over time, and you repeatedly consider your horizon to be N periods ahead. Then all you need is the optimal production schedule for each State s when N periods are left to the end of the horizon. Each period you ascertain State s and schedule accordingly. Another impact is that the only thing that matters, when n periods remain, is the current State s and not how you arrived there. So if your decision does not turn out the way you expect, you can let bygones be bygones in your *next* decision. In Chaps. 11 and 12 the notion of a strategy will play a central role, except there you will learn how to find an optimal policy when an unbounded time horizon assumption is built right into the analysis.

Another concept of significance is determining the *form* of an optimal policy. By an auspicious characterization of a dynamic process into a sequence of stages, you sometimes can exploit the special properties of the constraints and economic functions to discover an optimal type of policy. One illustration is regeneration type processes, such as the equipment replacement example in Sec. 10.6. Whenever a regeneration point occurred, you effectively could split the span of optimization into "before" and "after," and handle each part separately.

The preceding two notions of finding a strategy and the form of an optimal policy are closely related to the next. A planning horizon theorem, when available, can provide key information on the way an optimal policy is influenced by dynamic considerations.

▶You observed two instances, in Secs. 9.4 and 9.7, of the way particular economic structures can be helpful for discovering horizon properties. In the convex cost case, you saw an illustration in which the only possible effect of lengthening the planning span was to increase the value of the production decision variables. In the concave cost case, you noted that it was possible to ascertain when a horizon occurred without recourse to information beyond the regeneration event.   ◀

10.9 COMPUTATIONAL FEASIBILITY

For the problems illustrated in Chaps. 8 through 10, dynamic programming offers a vast improvement over complete enumeration of all possibilities. The feasibility of the technique depends critically on the dimension of the state variable, and this is one reason why skill in formulation is necessary. The difference between a clumsy and a clever characterization can be the deciding factor in whether the approach is workable.

As the examples of this chapter show, the approach can be applied to small-scale nonlinear and integer-value problems. Because no satisfactory canonical form exists for all of these (not even for finite, discrete, deterministic models), there is no single *efficient* computer program to handle *all* dynamic programming problems. But the form of the dynamic programming recursion is usually simple enough so that it is not much trouble to write a computer program for the particular model to be solved. A number of technical difficulties must be overcome in such programs, but they mainly concern the specialist and will not be discussed here. It suffices to say that in most practical problems with a state variable of one or two dimensions, designing a computer program offers no insurmountable obstacles. Except in rare cases (such as the convex cost inventory model of Sec. 9.3, where the algorithm is quite simple), a computer approach is required—if for no other reason than to eliminate the tedium of the calculations.

Questions of convergence have not arisen in Chaps. 8 through 10, since every model essentially involved only a shortest-route problem. But these considerations will reappear in the next two chapters, when you study models with unbounded horizons and solution techniques based on successive approximations.

Again due to the variation in types of models solved by dynamic programming, it has not been possible to provide any universally applicable technique of sensitivity analysis. Most sensitivity questions that are raised in dynamic programming models tend to affect several costs or constraints simultaneously. Then the formulas required for the analysis need to be worked out for the specific problem.

10.10 APPLICABILITY OF DYNAMIC PROGRAMMING

The results of Chaps. 8 through 10 can be put into two categories. Much of the analysis deepened your understanding of phenomena in dynamic optimization models. The remainder concerned applications of dynamic programming to important industrial problems. By far the most frequent applications of the technique deal with inventory replenishment, production scheduling, and certain regeneration type processes, including equipment replacement. Because a number of dynamic programming problems involve probabilistic elements and unbounded horizons, you should consider the examples you have seen as just an introduction to the subject. There are many more illustrations in the chapters to come.

The statement made at the beginning of the chapter warrants repeating in these closing remarks. The practical limitation on the dimension of the state variable in dynamic programming tends to narrow the focus of problems solved by the technique. Only infrequently can all the salient factors in an economic problem of any magnitude be boiled down in such a way as to make feasible the numerical solution to a dynamic programming formulation. This realization does not detract from the value of dynamic programming; rather, it puts into focus certain features that distinguish typical applications of dynamic programming from those of linear programming.

Specifically, many real applications of dynamic programming deal with operating decisions—when to reorder, when to make a machine setup, when to replace a piece of equipment, etc. Many of these decisions are ordinarily delegated by top management to lower echelons. Therefore, implementation of a dynamic programming model involves either using a computer to assist in routine decision-making or providing lower echelons with rules or tables based on an optimal strategy calculation. The limited impact of a single decision found by the usual dynamic programming applications, and the ease with which this decision can be determined, are the very reasons for the technique's success. The approach relieves top management of the burden of reviewing a multitude of individual actions, each having minor import. However, the senior executive is able to exercise his policy-making responsibilities effectively by selecting an appropriate model containing what he feels are the significant economic and technological considerations.

REVIEW EXERCISES

1 Suppose the restriction (2) in Sec. 10.2 is generalized to the linear constraint $\sum_{j=1}^{s} H_j y_j = N$ (where $H_1 = 1$). Revise (5) accordingly, and indicate the largest value of y_j that needs to be considered in the maximization process at Stage j.

2 Suppose you have a solution to the problem (1) through (3) in Sec. 10.2 for a specified value of N, and now you want to find the solution for the value $N + 1$. Indicate the additional computation required, assuming you use recursion (5) to obtain the answer.

3 *Shopping Basket Markets Problem* (Sec. 10.2). Suppose when eggs are shipped to Store j that a fraction f_j ($0 < f_j < 1$) breaks in transit. Revise recursion (5) accordingly.

4 *Shopping Basket Markets Problem* (Sec. 10.2). Suppose the owner has found from past experience that the profit function $R_j(y_j)$ increases as y_j increases up to a point, and then decreases for larger values of y_j (too many eggs in a store create costly handling and storage problems). Indicate how (if at all) you would modify the formulation and resultant dynamic programming recursion to permit shipping less than N eggs to all the stores.

5 In describing the distribution of effort problem in Sec. 10.2, we assumed, for simplicity, that each $H_j(y_j)$ is a nondecreasing function, is integer-valued for $y_j = 0, 1, 2, \ldots$, and satisfies $H_j(0) = 0$; in addition, we postulated that $H_1(y_1) = y_1$. Explain what complications arise when each of these four assumptions is dropped, and how the recursion (10) must be modified (if at all).

Exercises 6 through 12 refer to the numerical example (12) and (13) in Sec. 10.2, and the solution in Fig. 10.2.

6 (a) Verify the calculations in Fig. 10.2 for $j = 2$ and $n = 3, 4, 5, 6$, and for $j = 3$ and $n = 0, 1, \ldots, 8$.
  (b) Indicate all optimal solutions for $N = 4, 5, 6, 7$.

7 Assume the upper-bound restrictions are changed to $y_1 \leq 3$, $y_2 \leq 3$, and $y_3 \leq 2$. Determine all optimal solutions for

  (a) $N = 4, 5, 6, 7, 8$.
  (b) $N = 9, 10$.

8 For expositional simplicity, the three stores were arbitrarily indexed 1, 2, 3, and the recursion (10) was applied to the specified indexing. If the stores are relabeled, the computations then will be carried out in a different order, but the end results will be identical. Let the first two columns in Fig. 10.1 denote Store A, the next two columns Store B, and the last two columns Store C. The recursion (10) and the results in Fig. 10.2 correspond to letting $j = 1$ refer to Store A; $j = 2$ to Store B; and $j = 3$ to Store C. Apply the algorithm (10) to the following alternative assignments of the stores to the indexes:

(a) $j = 1$ to Store A, $j = 2$ to Store C, and $j = 3$ to Store B.
(b) $j = 1$ to Store C, $j = 2$ to Store B, and $j = 3$ to Store A.
(c) $j = 1$ to Store B, $j = 2$ to Store A, and $j = 3$ to Store C.
(d) $j = 1$ to Store C, $j = 2$ to Store A, and $j = 3$ to Store B.
(e) $j = 1$ to Store B, $j = 2$ to Store C, and $j = 3$ to Store A.

9 Suppose the return function for $j = 3$ is changed to $R_3(y_3) = 5y_3$. Use recursion (10) to determine all optimal solutions for

(a) $N = 4, 5, 6, 7, 8$.
(b) $N = 9, 10$.
(c) Answer parts (a) and (b) when all the bound restrictions on y_j are dropped.

*10 Solve exercise 9, part (c), using recursion (ii) in the special material at the end of Sec. 10.2. Compare the computational effort of using recursion (10) versus that of using recursion (ii).

*11 In each part below, formulate the lot-size inventory model as (vi) and (vii) in the advanced material at the end of Sec. 10.2; indicate the appropriate value for each R_j. Solve the problem using recursion (viii). Also solve the problem using recursion (x), and indicate the correspondence between recursions (x) and (xi). Use the data in the following exercises in Chap. 9.

(a) Exercise 13.　　(d) Exercise 43, part (a).
(b) Exercise 14.　　*(e) Exercise 43, part (f).
(c) Exercise 15.

12 Suppose the restriction $y_1 + 3y_2 + y_3 \leq 4$ is added to the example (12) and (13) in Sec. 10.2, and the restriction (8) is written as an inequality ($\leq$). Determine all optimal solutions for $N = 4, 5, 6, 7, 8$.

13 In describing the distribution of effort problem with two constraints in Sec. 10.3, we assumed, for simplicity, that the constraints (2) and (3) are inequalities, and that each $K_j(y_j)$ is nonnegative and integer-valued. Explain what complications arise if each of these assumptions is dropped, and what is the resultant impact on computing a solution with recursion (5).

14 (a) Suppose the restriction (2) in Sec. 10.3 is replaced by $\sum_{j=1}^{s} H_j(y_j) \leq N$, where the value of $H_j(y_j)$ is a nonnegative integer for $y_j = 0, 1, \ldots$. Indicate how the recursion (5) and the computational process must be modified.
   (b) Suppose the restriction $\sum_{j=1}^{s} H_j(y_j) \leq P$ is added to (1) through (4) in Sec. 10.3, where the value of $H_j(y_j)$ is a nonnegative integer for $y_j = 0, 1, \ldots$, and P is a positive integer. Indicate how the recursion (5) must be modified. Discuss the resultant increase in computational effort.

15 *Amazing Products Chemical Company Example* (Sec. 10.4). Imagine that the board of directors has elected a new president who feels it is important to encourage the pursuit of *basic* research. Let y_j thousand dollars denote an allocation of Division j for such basic research, and $T_j(y_j)$ million dollars be the best estimate the division has on the ultimate return to the company from this expenditure on basic research. The

total allocation to basic research is drawn from the company's overall R & D budget, and the amount y_j is drawn from the division's budget. Show how the formulation (1) through (4) must be modified to include the allocations for basic research. Indicate the necessary changes in the recursion (5), and the maximization process (6) and (7). Show how to appropriately modify the approach given by (8) through (11). (Be sure to define your notation and symbols.)

16 *Amazing Products Chemical Company Example* (Sec. 10.4). Imagine that there is a conservative member of the board of directors who insists that the total amount of money the company allocates to exploratory and speculative projects does not exceed V thousand dollars. Show how the formulation (1) through (4) must be modified. Indicate the appropriate recursion, the corresponding minimization process in (6) and (7), and how to modify the approach given by (8) through (11). (Be sure to define your notation and symbols.)

*17 Explain how the linearity of the objective function and the constraints are exploited in the recursion (4) of Sec. 10.5. [For example, comment on why (4) would be inappropriate if the objective function were $\sum_{j=1}^{s} c_j(y_j)$, and at least one of the functions $c_j(y_j)$ were nonlinear.]

*18 (a) Use the recursion (4) in Sec. 10.5 to solve the problem

$$\text{maximize } 3y_1 + 4y_2 + 6y_3 + 8y_4 + 6y_5$$

subject to

$$1y_1 + 2y_2 + 2y_3 + 3y_4 + 1y_5 \leq 3$$
$$2y_1 + 1y_2 + 2y_3 + 1y_4 + 3y_5 \leq 4$$

every y_j a nonnegative integer.

(b) By how much does the objective function decrease when the right-hand-side constant in the first constraint is 2, instead of 3? When the right-hand-side constant in the second constraint is 3, instead of 4? When the right-hand-side constants in both the first and second constraints are decreased by 1?

(c) By how much does the objective function increase when the right-hand-side constant in the first constraint is 4, instead of 3? When the right-hand-side constant in the second constraint is 5, instead of 4? When the right-hand-side constants in both the first and second constraints are increased by 1?

*19 *Equipment Replacement Problem.* In each part below, find an optimal replacement policy using recursion (v) in the special material at the end of Sec. 10.6. (Be sure to indicate the values for each p_{in} and k_{nt}.) Assume that a replacement must be made at the start of Period 1. Compare the algorithmic process with recursion (2).

(a) The case of the Rhode-Bloch Trucking Company, given in exercise 15, part (d), Chap. 6, and exercise 68 of Chap. 7.

(b) The case of the Goode-O'Toole Company, given in exercise 41 of Chap. 6 and exercise 69 of Chap. 7.

*20 Consider the recursion (DPR) in the special material of Sec. 10.7.

(a) Indicate how each of the points (i) through (iv) affects the appearance of (DPR).

(b) Show the correspondence between each symbol in (DPR) and the appropriate symbol in the recursion (5) of Sec. 10.2. In the recursion (10) of Sec. 10.2. In the recursion (5) of Sec. 10.3. In the recursion (5) of Sec. 10.4.

(c) Draw an acyclic network associated with the application of recursion (10) in Sec. 10.2 to the data in Figs. 10.1 and 10.2. [Label the nodes and arc costs appropriately; indicate the contents of each $D_n(s)$, and display each $T_n(s, d_n)$.]

21 Explain your understanding of the following terms:

distribution of effort problem   *discrete variable problem

nested problem   strategy.

multistage analysis

FORMULATION AND COMPUTATIONAL EXERCISES

In many of the exercises below, you are asked to formulate a model in terms of a dynamic programming recursion. Be sure to define all the symbols you use, and answer the five questions at the end of Sec. 10.1. Give the appropriate optimization function when there is a single period remaining as well as the recursion for Stage n. Explain how to initiate and when to terminate the calculations.

22 *Knapsack Problem.* Ben Dover, an exuberant mountain climber, is preparing for a lengthy hike up a dangerous slope. He can manage up to W pounds in his knapsack, which he carries on his back. He has N different types of items that he can include in his pack, and each unit of Item j weighs w_j pounds. For every Item j, he calculates a numerical value E_j representing the essentiality of each unit of the item. For example, if he packs five items of type 3 and seven items of type 9, the "value" to him of this knapsack selection is $5 \cdot E_3 + 7 \cdot E_9$. How many items of each type should he include in his knapsack?

(a) Formulate the problem as a dynamic programming model. Explain why the decision problem would be trivial if it were possible to load fractional amounts of the items; indicate what would be an optimal selection in such a case.

(b) Alter your answer in part (a) assuming that Dover places an upper limit L_j on the number of units of each Item j that he packs. Explain why the decision problem is trivial if it is possible to load fractional amounts of the items; indicate an algorithm for finding an optimal selection in such a case.

(c) Suppose Dover wants to select the lightest knapsack that has a value to him of at least E. Show how to revise the formulations in parts (a) and (b).

23 Howie Kramms is a graduating senior and needs to do as well as possible on the final examinations in order to receive his degree. He divides his available weekend study time into 10 periods of equal length. He is taking four courses, two of which he judges are easy and two difficult. He estimates that for each "gut" course, he will earn no grade points if he does not study at all, two grade points if he studies either one or two periods, three grade points if he studies three periods, and four grade points if he studies four periods. Similarly, he estimates that for each difficult course, he will earn no grade

points if he does not study, only one grade point if he studies either one or two periods, two grade points for studying three periods, three grade points for studying four periods, and four grade points if he studies five periods. Disregarding the consideration of whether he is overoptimistic in his assessments, how would you advise him to allocate his time to maximize the total grade points he receives? Formulate an appropriate dynamic programming model and find an optimal solution. How much would an extra study period be worth? What harm will be done if he goofs off for one study period?

24 Libby Doe, a girl friend of Howie Kramms, whom you advised in exercise 23, has just arrived in town and has called Howie for a date. He reassesses his situation and decides that all he really needs are nine grade points to graduate. Now he wants to allocate his time so that he spends the fewest number of study periods necessary to guarantee his receiving at least nine grade points. Formulate this decision problem as a dynamic programming model, and find an optimal solution. (If there is more than one optimal allocation, indicate the alternative solutions.)

25 The United Fund wants to assign 10 of its volunteers to solicit contributions from the companies having offices in three large downtown buildings. The executive director estimates that if y_j men are assigned to Building j, then total contribution pledges will be $R_j(y_j)$ hundred dollars, where $R_j(0) = 0$ and

$R_1(1) = 5$ $R_1(2) = 10$ $R_1(3) = 15$ $R_1(4) = 25$ $R_1(5) = 35$ $R_1(6) = 50$

$R_2(1) = 3$ $R_2(2) = 6$ $R_2(3) = 12$ $R_2(4) = 18$ $R_2(5) = 30$ $R_1(7) = 55$

$R_3(1) = 20$ $R_3(2) = 35$ $R_3(3) = 45$ $R_3(4) = 55$ $R_3(5) = 60$ $R_3(6) = 65.$

(No additional pledges would be received by sending more than seven men to Building 1, more than five to Building 2, and six to Building 3.) How many volunteers should be allocated to each of the buildings? Formulate an appropriate dynamic programming model and find an optimal solution. Show how the solution changes if there are eight volunteers. How does it change with 9, 11, or 12 volunteers?

26 Consider the case of the United Fund described in exercise 25. Suppose the executive director is in short supply of volunteers and restates his allocation problem as follows. He wants to use as few men as possible provided that they raise at least R hundred dollars in the three buildings. Formulate this problem in terms of a dynamic programming model, and find an optimal solution for

(a) $R = 80.$
(b) $R = 90.$
(c) $R = 100.$

27 Consider the case of the United Fund described in exercise 25. Suppose the executive director wants to allocate no more than M man-days to the solicitation in the three buildings. He knows that if he assigns from one to three men to any building, they require *in toto* 1 man-day to complete solicitation; if he assigns more than three men, they will require 2 man-days. How many of the 10 volunteers should he allocate to each of the buildings if

(a) $M = 3$?
(b) $M = 4$?

28 Consider the problem

$$\text{maximize } R_1(y_1) + R_2(y_2) + R_3(y_3)$$

subject to

$$2y_1 + 3y_2 + 4y_3 \leq W$$
$$\text{each } y_j = 0, 1, 2, 3,$$

where each $R_j(0) = 0$ and

$$R_1(1) = 3 \quad R_1(2) = 2 \quad R_1(3) = 8$$
$$R_2(1) = 5 \quad R_2(2) = 11 \quad R_2(3) = 9$$
$$R_3(1) = 9 \quad R_3(2) = 14 \quad R_3(3) = 15.$$

(a) Find an optimal solution for $W = 8$. Also, indicate solutions for $W = 6$ and $W = 7$. Indicate any alternative optimal solutions.

*(b) Draw an acyclic network associated with the recursion that you employ. Label the nodes and arc values appropriately.

29 Consider the Economic Order Quantity Problem for the case of a single item, as described in Sec. 1.6. Suppose that the firm has N items, and is going to replenish each one by means of a lot-size rule. Specifically, for each Item j, let M_j be the number of units the company consumes per week, K_j the fixed setup cost of placing an order, c_j the purchase cost per unit ordered, and h_j the holding cost per unit per week. Similarly, let Q_j be the replenishment lot size for Item j. The average cost per week for *all* the items is the summation of N expressions, each of the form (12) in Sec. 1.6. Suppose the company places an upper limit L on the average value of *all* inventory on hand, where each Item j contributes $c_j Q_j/2$ to this average. Show how a dynamic programming formulation can be used to find optimal values for each lot size Q_j.

*30 Consider the case of the Giant Electric Company, described in the special material at the end of Sec. 10.3. Suppose $s = 8$, $K_j = j$, for $j = 1, 2, \ldots, 8$, and

$$R_1 = 16 \quad R_2 = 28 \quad R_3 = 45 \quad R_4 = 48 \quad R_5 = 65 \quad R_6 = 66 \quad R_7 = 79 \quad R_8 = 80.$$

Find an optimal selection of projects for

(a) The project number limit $N = 4$ and the budget limit $M = 10$. Indicate a solution for $N = 2$ and for $N = 3$. Also indicate a solution for $N = 3$ and $M = 9$.

(b) $N = 3$ and $M = 11$.

31 Consider the case of the Amazing Products Chemical Company described in Sec. 10.4. Let $s = 4$, each $L_j = 5$, $N = 10$, and

$$P_j(v_j) = a_j P(v_j) \quad \text{where } P(0) = P(1) = P(2) = 0 \quad P(3) = 1 \quad P(4) = 8 \quad P(5) = 17$$
$$Q_j(w_j) = b_j Q(w_j) \quad \text{where } Q(0) = 0 \quad Q(w) = 3 + w \quad \text{for } w \geq 1$$
$$R_j(x_j) = c_j R(x_j) \quad \text{where } R(0) = 0 \quad R(1) = 8 \quad R(2) = 9$$
$$R(3) = 9.5 \quad R(4) = 9.75 \quad R(5) = 10.$$

Find an optimal budget allocation when

(a) All $a_j = b_j = c_j = 1$.

(b) $a_1 = b_1 = c_1 = 1$, $a_2 = b_2 = c_2 = 2$, $a_3 = b_3 = c_3 = 3$.

(c) $a_1 = b_2 = c_3 = 1$, $b_1 = c_2 = a_3 = 2$, $c_1 = a_2 = b_3 = 3$.

(d) Indicate the effect from letting $N = 7, 8, 9$ in each of the above parts.

(e) Indicate the effect from letting $N = 11$ in part (a).

(f) Indicate the effect from letting each $L_j = 4$ in part (a). In part (b). In part (c).

32 Three brothers operate their father's cattle ranch in Arizona called "Where the Sun's Rays Meet." At the beginning of a planning horizon of N years, the ranchers own S hundred cattle. The expense of caring and feeding for s head of cattle during Year n is $c_n(s)$. If the ranchers decide to send y_n cattle to market at the end of Year n, they receive $R_n(y_n)$ dollars of revenue. The herd not sent to market increases in size by 1.6-fold in the following year. (Thus, if none of the S cattle are sent to market at the end of Year 1, then the herd size is $1.6S$ in Year 2.) Formulate a dynamic programming recursion to determine how many cattle to send to market in each of the N periods.

33 *Capacity Expansion Problem.* The Bill Deplant Company is planning an expansion program over the next N years. At the beginning of Period 1, the firm has a capacity of c_0 units. The company estimates that it should have at least a capacity of R_t units in Period t, for $t = 1, 2, \ldots, N$. If it expands its capacity by x_t units in Period t, the associated cost is $K_t(c, x_t)$, where c represents the capacity at the *start* of the period, and x_t is integer-valued. [If certain levels of x_t are impossible to build, then the corresponding value for $K_t(c, x_t)$ can be defined as arbitrarily large.] Assume that new capacity becomes available early enough in a period that it can be used to meet the requirement R_t. Suppose the company also incurs the cost $H_t(C, R)$ in Period t of operating a plant at the level R, when capacity at the *end* of the period is C units, where $R \leq C$. Finally, assume that if C units of capacity are available by the *end* of a period, then only $D(C)$ units are available in the beginning of the next period, due to depreciation of the equipment in the plant. Formulate the expansion model in terms of a dynamic programming recursion.

34 The ARKA Mutual Fund is unmatched in its ability to perform well on the stock exchange, because the fund is able to perfectly forecast the price of a given security. Despite this uncanny talent, ARKA must still resort to operations research to derive an optimal strategy for buying and selling. Specifically, assume that p_t is the price of the security in Period t, and that ARKA knows these prices over a horizon of T periods. Let x_t be the number of shares held by ARKA at the end of Period t, where $x_t \geq 0$. Assume that at the start of Period 1, ARKA does not own any shares of the stock. ARKA must pay a transaction cost $C(x_t - x_{t-1})$ for purchases and sales, where $C(0) = 0$. The fund is also prohibited from speculating in that it cannot make a purchase of shares that exceeds its cash on hand (where M is the cash on hand at the start of Period 1), and it cannot sell short (that is, it cannot sell any shares it does not own at the start of a period).

Formulate the problem in terms of a dynamic programming recursion, assuming that

(a) ARKA wants to maximize the total amount of cash it can accumulate by the end of the horizon.

(b) ARKA places a value $v_t(d_t)$ on withdrawing the amount of cash d_t in Period t for distribution as dividend payments, and wants to maximize the sum of the $v_t(d_t)$ over the entire span of the horizon.

35 Van Fuller, the local dispatcher for a moving and storage firm, must arrange to pick up x_1 different shipments that require s_1 units of space each, and x_2 different shipments that require s_2 units of space each. (Thus the total space requirements for the day are $s_1 x_1 + s_2 x_2$.) He has available N different trucks. Truck i has a capacity of C_i units of space, and incurs an operating cost of E_i. (Assume that $C_1 + \cdots + C_n > s_1 x_1 + s_2 x_2$ and that there is a feasible solution.) Fuller wants a minimum cost selection of trucks for picking up all the loads. Formulate the decision problem as a dynamic programming model, and indicate how the recursion optimally selects truck sizes and allocates shipments to the trucks.

36 *Great Auto Works Company* (Sec. 2.6). Formulate the optimization problem in terms of a dynamic programming recursion.

37 Consider the case of the Spartan army, described in exercise 31 of Chap. 2. Formulate the optimization problem in terms of a dynamic programming recursion.

38 Consider the case of the Expando Manufacturing Company, described in exercise 36 of Chap. 2. Formulate the optimization problem in terms of a dynamic programming recursion.

MIND-EXPANDING EXERCISES

In many of the exercises below, you are asked to formulate a model in terms of a dynamic programming recursion. Be sure to define all the symbols you use, and answer the five questions at the end of Sec. 10.1. Give the appropriate optimization function when there is a single period remaining and the recursion for Stage n. Explain how to initiate and when to terminate the calculations.

39 *Where-or-When Production Problem* (Sec. 1.6). Consider the model discussed in Sec. 1.6:

$$\text{minimize} \sum_{j=1}^{N} \frac{x_j^2}{c_j}$$

subject to

$$\sum_{j=1}^{N} x_j = D \quad \text{and} \quad \text{each } x_j \geq 0,$$

where each $c_j > 0$. Use a dynamic programming formulation to establish the result (11), namely, that given the values for $x_1, x_2, \ldots, x_{t-1}$, the corresponding optimal value for $x_t = c_t(D - x_1 - \cdots - x_{t-1})/(c_t + \cdots + c_N)$.

40 Consider the problem

$$\text{maximize} \frac{x_1}{c_1} \cdot \frac{x_2}{c_2} \cdot \ldots \cdot \frac{x_N}{c_N}$$

subject to

$$\sum_{j=1}^{N} x_j = D \quad \text{and} \quad \text{each } x_j \geq 0,$$

where each $c_j > 0$. Use a dynamic programming formulation to derive the form of an optimal solution. Indicate how the optimal value of the objective function depends on D.

41 Consider the problem

$$\text{maximize} \sum_{j=1}^{s} R(x_j)$$

subject to

$$\sum_{j=1}^{s} x_j = N \quad \text{and} \quad \text{each } x_j \text{ nonnegative integer.}$$

Notice that all the functions in the objective function are identical.

(a) Suppose s is a power of 2 (such as 4, 8, 16, 32, . . .). Devise a way to compute an optimal solution using dynamic programming that does *not* require you to calculate $g_j(n)$ for *all* $j = 1, 2, \ldots , s$.

*(b) How would you modify your approach in part (a) to accommodate *any* value for s?

42 Suppose a state's legislature has R representatives. The state is sectioned into s districts, where District j has a population p_j and $s < R$. Under strictly proportional representation, District j would receive $R/p_j \equiv r_j$ representatives; this allocation is not feasible, however, because r_j may not be integer-valued. The objective is to allocate y_j representatives to District j, for $j = 1, 2, \ldots , s$, so as to minimize, over all of the districts, the maximum difference between y_j and r_j, that is, minimize [maximum $(y_1 - r_1, \ldots , y_s - r_s)$].

(a) Formulate the model in terms of a dynamic programming recursion.
(b) Apply your method to the data $R = 4$, $s = 3$ and $r_1 = .4$, $r_2 = 2.4$, and $r_3 = 1.2$. Discuss whether the solution seems reasonable, given the context of the problem.

43 Consider the problem of selecting y_j, for $j = 1, 2, \ldots , s$, so as to

$$\text{maximize } \{\text{minimum } [R_1(y_1), R_2(y_2), \ldots , R_s(y_s)]\}$$

subject to

$$\sum_{j=1}^{s} H_j(y_j) \leq N$$

$$y_j = 0, 1, 2, \ldots \quad \text{for each } j,$$

where each $H_j(y_j)$ is a nondecreasing function, integer-valued for each $y_j = 0, 1, \ldots ,$ and satisfies $H_j(0) = 0$. Develop a dynamic programming recursion to solve the problem.

44 *Minimax Route in a Network.* An exchange student from England, Red Bricker, has purchased a not-so-new automobile and plans to spend his summer motoring from New York to San Francisco. To keep the exposition simple, suppose he can choose a route from the same map as did Mark Off, in Fig. 8.1. Red is concerned that if he travels along a route between two cities where the temperature is very hot, the engine in his automobile may explode. He estimates that c_{ij} is the highest temperature he will encounter enroute from State i to State j. He wants a routing that minimizes the maximum temperature along the way. *(See (a) and (b) on p. 356.)*

(a) Formulate a dynamic programming approach, and apply it to the c_{ij} given in Fig. 8.1.

(b) State the recursion in sufficient generality to apply to acyclic networks like those considered in Sec. 7.7 [that is, express the recursion in a form analogous to (1) and (2) in Sec. 7.7].

45 *Second-Best Route in Network.* Consider the problem of finding a shortest route from a source node to the terminal node, as discussed in Secs. 7.6 and 7.7. Devise a dynamic programming formulation to find the second shortest route from the source to the terminal. To keep the task unencumbered with details, assume that the network is acyclic and the shortest route is unique. If you can think of more than one approach, then indicate the alternatives. (*Hints:* a second shortest route must differ from the shortest route in at least one arc. Alternatively, establish the validity and implication of the observation that the second shortest route from Node j to the terminal must consist of traveling along some arc (j, k) and then along either the shortest or second shortest route from Node k to the terminal.) What complications arise in a cyclic network?

46 Consider the problem of finding a shortest route from a source node to the terminal node, as discussed in Secs. 7.6 and 7.7. Devise a dynamic programming formulation to find a shortest route from the source to the terminal that involves exactly K arcs, assuming that at least one such route exists. (Might such a route involve traveling around a loop of arcs?)

47 *Knapsack Problem.* Consider the optimization problem described in exercise 22. Suppose the largest ratio E_j/w_j is E_k/w_k for Item k. Prove that there is a value W^*, such that if the weight limit $W \geq W^*$, then there is an optimal solution that includes at least one unit of Item k.

48 *Equipment Replacement and Overhaul.* Consider the model in Sec. 10.6. Suppose you have the decision opportunities of overhauling as well as replacing the equipment each period after the initial procurement in Period 1 and prior to the salvage of the machine at the beginning of Period N. Assume that the length of time required to overhaul the machine is negligible in comparison with the length of the period; hence, a machine that is overhauled at the beginning of a period is still available for use during the period. Consider a machine is bought at the beginning of Period n, overhauled at the beginning of Periods $t_1 < t_2 < \cdots < t_p$ where $n < t_1$, and is replaced at the beginning of Period k, where $k > t_p$. Assume the associated cost is

$$a_n(n, t_1) + a_n(t_1, t_2) + \cdots + a_n(t_{p-1}, t_p) + b_{nk}(t_p).$$

The quantity $a_n(h, j)$, where $n \leq h < j$, represents the cost of operating a machine during the Periods h through j, plus the expense of overhauling it at the beginning of Period j, given that the machine was initially purchased in Period n and was last overhauled in Period h (or was bought if $h = n$). The quantity $b_{nk}(t_p)$ represents the net total cost resulting from acquiring the machine in Period n, from salvaging it in Period k, and from operating it during Periods t_p through k between final overhaul and sale. The quantity $b_{nk}(n)$ represents the cost of providing the machine during Periods n through k when there are no overhauls.

Show how to use a dynamic programming recursion to calculate values for c_{nk} that then can be appropriately employed in the recursion (2) of Sec. 10.6.

49 Consider a classical transportation problem like that in Sec. 6.2, where there are $m = 2$ supply points, and total supply equals total demand (6). Suppose that the shipping cost of sending x_{ij} units from Supply Point i to Demand Point j is given by a nonlinear function $c_{ij}(x_{ij})$. Assume all S_i and D_j are integer-valued and restrict each x_{ij} to be integer-valued.

    (a) Formulate the optimization problem in terms of a dynamic programming recursion. (*Hint:* you can use the property that total supply equals total demand to yield a one-dimensional state variable.)

  *(b) Show how to modify your formulation in part (a) for $m = 3$.

*50 *Caterer Problem.* Consider the case of the Cole Food Company, described in exercise 48 of Chap. 6. Formulate the optimization problem in terms of a dynamic programming recursion.

*51 *Trim Problem.* Consider the case of the Fine-Webb Paper Company, described in exercise 25 of Chap. 2. Recall that a combination was defined as a way to slit a jumbo reel of width 70 inches into smaller reels of widths 22 inches, 20 inches, and 12 inches. Suppose in solving the linear programming model of part (b) that you include only a subset of all the possible combinations. Let $y_1, y_2,$ and y_3 be the resultant optimal values of the dual variables for the restrictions associated with the reels of widths 22 inches, 20 inches, and 12 inches, respectively. Use the Dual Theorem and a dynamic programming recursion involving the y_i to devise a test for whether the linear programming solution obtained is truly optimal, or whether one of the combinations omitted from the subset would improve the current linear programming solution.

CONTENTS

CHAPTER 11

Decision-Making Over
an Unbounded Horizon

11.1 MODELS WITH A LIMITLESS VISTA

Unquestionably most, if not all, decision-making is part of an unending history of actions. Earlier choices have affected the present, current decisions will influence the future, and so on. In this light, *all* models must be viewed as imbedded in an **unbounded horizon**. Several of the dynamic models you have studied so far simply ignored the future beyond a designated horizon period, and sometimes (as in Chap. 9) a planning horizon theorem could be established to demonstrate that such a procedure might yield an optimal current decision. Other models attempted to account for the future by selecting certain "terminal" conditions (such as a specified minimum level of work force or productive capacity). In contrast to these models, the illustrations in this chapter assume that the planning horizon is limitless.

In order to derive any definite answers for models with an unbounded horizon, it is necessary to add a restrictive assumption: broadly, the hypothesis is termed an **assumption of stationarity**. In the simplest cases, you assume that all economic return functions, decision possibilities, and external phenomena (like demand requirements) are identical in every period. Each application below is of this type, and you should keep in mind that the results are based on these stationarity assumptions. Chapters 11 and 12 consider only deterministic outcomes. Probabilistically determined outcomes will be treated in Chaps. 17 and 18, and there stationarity of the probability laws is postulated. With advanced analysis you can also solve situations with less stringent stationarity assumptions, including cyclic phenomena such as seasonal demand (an example is given at the very end of Chap. 12).

Since in reality stationarity rarely exists for an extended period of time, you well may wonder whether models assuming stationarity over an unbounded horizon have much practical significance. They do. We will distinguish two types of application to show their importance.

The first type pertains to situations in which dynamic optimization models are used to improve day-to-day operating decisions, such as replenishing inventory and scheduling production. For example, consider a firm that monitors its inventory levels daily and reorders an item every few weeks when the stock level reaches a critical point. Suppose, as is frequently true, that for at least twelve months the item's demand rate and the ordering and holding cost functions are stable. Then it is reasonable for the firm to use the same inventory replenishment rule during three to six months, and at the end of that time to revise its inventory policy based on a new twelve-month forecast. (Another important consideration also justifies this mode of operation. If the firm stocks hundreds of different items, it would be too time-consuming and disruptive to recompute a new replenishment rule at frequent intervals for every item—the costs of doing so would far outweigh any efficiency savings from the improved decisions.)

How, then, should the company set each specific replenishment rule? One possibility is to use the methods of Chaps. 8 and 9: determine, for a horizon length $N = 365$ days, the minimum cost $f_N(i)$ and optimal policy when entering inventory is i, and for the first few months employ the replenishment policy associated with $N = 365$. But given the stationarity assumptions, an unbounded horizon model can provide equally excellent answers, and typically requires much less calculation.

Accordingly, one justification for employing a stationary, unbounded horizon model is that in the context of daily operations, the approach is both an effective and relatively easy way to derive optimal decisions for the initial interval of time.

The second type of application pertains to situations in which dynamic optimization models are used to make recurring strategic investment decisions, as in the replacement of expensive equipment. Large pieces of machinery may be replaced as seldom as every 15 or 20 years. Consequently, when the next replacement is necessary, completely new types of machinery are likely to be available. How, then, should the current investment decision be made? One possibility, of course, is simply to ignore the fact that the equipment eventually must be replaced. This can be misleading and hazardous, as witness the following illustration, based on an actual case.

A food processing company facing production bottlenecks realized it could alleviate its problem by either prestocking inventory during the slack season for sales during the peak season, or by purchasing new equipment to expand its production capacity. When the ever-recurring cost associated with increased early-season inventory was compared with the *initial* cost of the added equipment, it seemed preferable to purchase the machinery. However, as soon as the equipment decision was analyzed to take account of ever-recurring future replacements, it turned out to be far the less attractive alternative, even with optimistic projections of subsequent replacement costs.

Therefore, a second justification for employing a stationary, unbounded horizon model is that in situations of repeated investment it can lead to better current decisions than those arrived at by ignoring the future.

Optimal stationary policies. Assuming stationarity, you can safely intuit the meaning of "making a current decision in the face of an unbounded horizon." What may surprise you is that your intuition is of limited help in fathoming *how* to make an *optimal* decision.

To illustrate, consider first a finite horizon dynamic programming model. At any period you need to know only the state of the system and the number of stages remaining. Optimality of any strategy is judged according to the sum of a finite stream of returns. Now let the horizon be unbounded, so by definition the "number of periods remaining" is always the same, and any strategy employed over the horizon results in an unending stream of returns. Since for every strategy this stream may grow without bound as the horizon lengthens, you need a way to *compare* the strategies. Of course, if one strategy accumulates more returns than another for *every* horizon length, no problem of comparison occurs. But typically one strategy looks better for certain finite horizons and worse for others, so the resolution is by no means obvious. Thus a limitless vista raises two pertinent questions about determining an optimal solution.

(i) What criterion is appropriate for judging the relative desirability of different infinite streams of returns?

(ii) Is it optimal in a limitless vista to consider only stationary strategies, that is, ones depending solely on the current state of the system?

This chapter focuses on answering (i). You will critically examine several frequently used criteria for evaluating infinite streams. You also will see how to apply these criteria to a simple but important regeneration model. In studying the solution of this model, you will discover several numerical methods of successive approximation that can be applied to more general problems of optimization in an unbounded horizon.

Chapter 12 will consider a large class of models in which the answer to (ii) is affirmative, that is, where you can always find a stationary strategy that is optimal. Such policies require that you know only the *current* state of the system and not the historical sequence of events leading to this state. Thus you make the same decision each time you return to the same state. Specifically, in Chap. 12 you will study the techniques for obtaining optimal stationary strategies. Such policies that can be made available in the form of rules or tables provide the key to a workable dynamic programming application for operating decisions.

11.2 SUBTLETIES OF INFINITE STREAMS

You may be surprised to learn that businessmen, economists, and mathematicians have argued for centuries over how to assess **infinite streams of returns**. You will easily see why in the examples below, and you should try to articulate the economic insights and managerial significance of these illustrations.

Experience has shown that most decision-makers can not intuitively make consistent judgments about the relative desirability of different infinite streams of returns. As a consequence, most businessmen turn to formulas for providing at least a preliminary screening or ranking of decision alternatives. We too will apply formulas that convert an infinite stream of returns into a single number so as to indicate the relative merit of the associated alternative. But before doing so, we want to make sure that you see some of the substantive issues involved in different methods for choosing among infinite streams. Only with this knowledge in mind can you appreciate both the strengths and limitations of the simple-to-apply formulas.

The discussion to follow is not intended to provide an exhaustive survey, along with suggested solutions, of the conundrums of infinite streams. Hopefully, the examples will make you cautious about accepting uncritically what seem to be alluringly simple-sounding solutions.

This section investigates two questions that are central to optimization in a dynamic setting:

(i) When is an evaluation formula appropriate for comparing different strategies?

(ii) Does such a formula *always* reduce an infinite stream to a single number that can be used as the basis for comparison?

These points are treated in considerable detail below, since the associated problems can be quite subtle.

We investigate three criteria of merit. The first is *average return per period*. Actually, this criterion arises most often when the economic measure is cost. Then the selection rule recommended is to choose an alternative having the least average cost per period. The second criterion is *present discounted value*. As you will soon see, these two criteria do not always select the same alternatives, and occasionally give rise to some nasty technical problems.

The third criterion is called *equivalent average return*. The idea is probably new to you, and is important in operations research models because it provides the mathematical connection between the other two criteria. Often you can derive the *form* of an optimal policy using this criterion; and then with this result you can calculate specific numerical solutions for either the average return per period or the present value criterion.

The "internal rate of return" is another criterion that, unfortunately, is used often in business practice. It is not discussed in this text because the approach frequently leads to incorrect decisions.

As you study the numerical examples below, you will find that most of the algebraic manipulations have been performed for you. At first reading, take it for granted that the formulas are correct—the important insights have nothing to do with the underlying algebra. Afterwards, you may want to go back to see whether you can derive the formulas.

Utility of money. You often hear it said that a dollar today is worth more than a dollar a year from today. Why? This maxim is based on several considerations. The decision-maker may find the sheer utility or personal worth of a current dollar is greater now than later. For example, consider a company that has paid its stockholders a regular quarterly dividend for 25 years. The firm may be very reluctant to forgo paying out a current dividend, even if it can promise to pay it eventually, perhaps with interest added. This difference in the utility of money at distinct points in time is the heart of the problem of making commensurate several unending streams of returns.

Actually, the same comparability problem exists in finite horizon models. In the dynamic programming examples of the previous chapters, the different policies certainly led to different time streams of profits or costs. But the previous discussion simply *ignored* the difficulty of comparability. Since it was always possible to *sum* the profits or costs over the bounded horizon, the resultant criterion function attached a unique finite number to each policy and made optimization straightforward. Here you can no longer ignore the comparability difficulty, even if you want to. Since the sum is now over an unbounded horizon, the total returns are infinite for most strategies. As you might imagine, any naive approach for comparing several infinite streams of returns can succeed in only the simplest of cases. To illustrate, comparing policies in one way or another for each and every finite horizon length does not always work. The following example shows why.

Suppose you must choose one of the profitable alternatives that are described in Fig. 11.1 by the sequence of returns (= profits) for each period, starting with the

| | | Period | | | | | |
Policy	1	2	3	4	5	6	• • •
A	3	2	1	3	2	1	• • •
B	3	1	3	1	3	1	• • •
C	1	6	−1	1	6	−1	• • •
D	$2\frac{2}{3}$	2	2	2	2	2	• • •
E	1	3	1	3	1	3	• • •
F	1	1	1	1	1	1	• • •
G	4	0	0	4	0	0	• • •

FIGURE 11.1. Illustration of Infinite Streams of Returns.

present. At the current period you receive a profit of 3 from A and B, 4 from G, etc. In the next period, you obtain a profit of 2 from A, a profit of only 1 from B, etc.

It is reasonable that you would rule out F right away, since you can do strictly better each period with A. In other words, A dominates F. It is also plausible to argue you could just as well eliminate E, since D returns a greater *cumulative* profit at any period.

But you cannot eliminate G. Although its cumulative return after Period 2 is not as good as that of A and B, its profit in Period 1 is strictly the best among all policies. If you require as large a return as possible in the current period, then G is the optimal choice.

How would you select among A, B, C, and D? In the second period, C looks most attractive. For every even-numbered period, D gives a better *cumulative* return than B. In the third period, B provides a *cumulative* return of 7 as against 6 for A and C, and $6\frac{2}{3}$ for D. What is more, B is "ahead" of A, C, and D at *every* Period $3 + 6n$, for $n = 0, 1, 2, \ldots$. Choosing among streams such as these is more the rule than the exception when models with unbounded horizons are considered.

Average return. You *must* make further assumptions in order to state that either A, B, C, D, or G is best. For example, you could make the *additional* postulate that a unit of return received in any period *is* just as good as a unit received in any other period. "Just as good" means there is no benefit of any sort in having the return earlier instead of later. How would this assumption resolve the problem?

It is reasonable now to look at the **average return per period**, letting the number of periods grow without limit, and prefer the alternative with the largest average. For A, you would compute $3/1$, $(3 + 2)/2$, $(3 + 2 + 1)/3, \ldots$; for B, you would similarly calculate $3/1$, $(3 + 1)/2$, $(3 + 1 + 3)/3, \ldots$. These calculations are summarized in Fig. 11.2. As we show in the advanced material

Period

Policy	1	2	3	4	5	6	7	8	9	• • •
A	3	$2\frac{1}{2}$	2	$2\frac{1}{4}$	$2\frac{1}{5}$	2	$2\frac{1}{7}$	$2\frac{1}{8}$	2	• • •
B	3	2	$2\frac{1}{3}$	2	$2\frac{1}{5}$	2	$2\frac{1}{7}$	2	$2\frac{1}{9}$	• • •
C	1	$3\frac{1}{2}$	2	$1\frac{3}{4}$	$2\frac{3}{5}$	2	$1\frac{6}{7}$	$2\frac{3}{8}$	2	• • •
D	$2\frac{2}{3}$	$2\frac{1}{3}$	$2\frac{2}{9}$	$2\frac{1}{6}$	$2\frac{2}{15}$	$2\frac{1}{9}$	$2\frac{2}{21}$	$2\frac{1}{12}$	$2\frac{2}{27}$	• • •
G	4	2	$1\frac{1}{3}$	2	$1\frac{3}{5}$	$1\frac{1}{3}$	$1\frac{5}{7}$	$1\frac{1}{2}$	$1\frac{1}{3}$	• • •

FIGURE 11.2. Average Return per Period.

below, the average profit per period tends toward 2 for A, B, C, and D, and toward $1\frac{1}{3}$ for G. In other words, if you let the number of periods be large enough, the average will be arbitrarily close to 2 for A, B, C, and D, and to $1\frac{1}{3}$ for G. Therefore *if* you make the special added assumption that you have no time preference for returns, the policies A, B, C, and D look equally attractive, even though they are not equally good for each and every finite horizon, and Policy G looks inferior.

▶As you can verify, the general terms in the sequences for the average return per period are

(i)   A: $\dfrac{3 + 6n}{1 + 3n}, \dfrac{5 + 6n}{2 + 3n}, \dfrac{6 + 6n}{3 + 3n}$ for $n = 0, 1, 2, \ldots$

(ii) B: $\dfrac{3 + 4n}{1 + 2n}, \dfrac{4 + 4n}{2 + 2n}$ for $n = 0, 1, 2, \ldots$

(iii) C: $\dfrac{1 + 6n}{1 + 3n}, \dfrac{7 + 6n}{2 + 3n}, \dfrac{6 + 6n}{3 + 3n}$ for $n = 0, 1, 2, \ldots$

(iv) D: $2 + \dfrac{2}{3n}$ for $n = 1, 2, 3, \ldots$

(v)   G: $\dfrac{4 + 4n}{1 + 3n}, \dfrac{4 + 4n}{2 + 3n}, \dfrac{4 + 4n}{3 + 3n}$ for $n = 0, 1, 2, \ldots$.

Thus when $n \to \infty$, each term approaches 2 for A, B, C, and D, and $1\frac{1}{3}$ for G.   ◀

The most obvious drawback of using average return per period as a selection criterion is its complete insensitivity to the level of returns over a *finite* number of periods. To illustrate, suppose you can select a policy that has returns identical to those in Policy A except that in Period 1 the return from the alternative policy is 100. Using solely the criterion of average return per period, you would judge that Policy A and the alternative policy are equally desirable, since over an unbounded horizon, the first-period advantage of the alternative policy is rendered inconsequential. There are other limitations to this criterion as well, which we explore next.

Assuming that you *do* want to employ the criterion, can you always be sure that a given stream will have a well-defined average return per period, as the number of periods grows without limit? For example, suppose the two streams for A and B are modified to have a multiplicative trend:

(1)   Policy A*:   3, 2, 1, 3, 2, 1   6, 4, 2, 6, 4, 2   9, 6, 3, 9, 6, 3, . . .
        Policy B*:   3, 1, 3, 1, 3, 1   6, 2, 6, 2, 6, 2   9, 3, 9, 3, 9, 3, ...

Although you may reason by analogy that the two streams should remain equally desirable, the *rule* of looking at average profit per period falters, since the averages grow beyond bound as the number of periods grows without limit.

Therefore, if you want to rely on an average-per-period criterion for a measure of optimality, you must also assume that there exists a unique *finite* limiting average for the particular return streams you are comparing. In many applications this assumption is reasonable.

Discounted return. An alternative approach for making different infinite streams commensurate is to deal with the so-called **present dis-counted value** (or **present worth**) of the returns.

If the stream of returns is

(2) $R_1, R_2, R_3, \ldots, R_n, \ldots,$

its merit should be judged, according to the present discounted value criterion, in terms of the sum:

(3)   Present Value $= R_1 + \alpha R_2 + \alpha^2 R_3 + \cdots + \alpha^{n-1} R_n + \cdots = \sum\limits_{t=1}^{\infty} \alpha^{t-1} R_t,$

where $i\%$ is the interest rate per period and $\alpha = [1 + (i/100)]^{-1}$ is the single-period **discount factor**. The higher the interest rate i, the smaller the value of α. The interest rate relevant for a firm's decision making is an important subject in its own right and is a lively topic of concern among scholars and practitioners in finance. We assume here that a firm can specify the appropriate value of i.

There is an environmental assumption you can make to justify the approach. Suppose you can borrow or lend as much money as you desire and whenever you want at a fixed **compound rate of interest** $i\%$ per period. (Of course, you are eventually required to pay any debts you incur.) For example, let the annual rate be 5%. Then if you borrow a dollar today, you must pay back either $(1 + .05)$ dollars a year from today, or $(1 + .05)^2$ dollars two years from today, or $(1 + .05)^n$ dollars n years from today. By the same token, a dollar received n years from today is really only worth $(1 + .05)^{-n}$ dollars right now. If you presently had $(1 + .05)^{-n}$ and lent it at 5% interest compounded, you would be paid back a dollar n years from today.

Here is why this environmental assumption justifies employing present value. Consider the choice between two policies with different present values. For the moment, suppose you selected the policy with the smaller present value. Because your utility for money may differ from period to period, you may want to borrow and lend in various periods to redistribute the returns.

For example, you may wish to have the benefit of R_2 right now rather than wait a period. Consequently you can borrow αR_2 at present, and then pay back R_2 when it becomes available. Similarly, you may want to lend for several periods, and later receive the payment with compound interest earned. As you think about it, you will see that the value of the entire stream really *is* summarized by the number representing how much you could obtain *at present* by committing the entire proceeds of the stream for repayment.

Now suppose instead you selected the policy with the larger present value. By assumption, you can borrow and lend, committing the resources of this stream, so as to attain the *same* benefits you desired with the other alternative, and in so doing you would have some additional value left over. In other words, any pattern you can obtain with the smaller present-value policy you can also obtain with the larger. The difference between the two values is a net benefit. To sum up, you do best by selecting a strategy that gives maximum present value, *regardless* of your personal time preference for money.

Of course, rarely if ever is the environmental assumption about borrowing and lending exactly satisfied, but it is often a fair enough approximation to provide adequate answers. Other kinds of arguments can be advanced in support of a present-value criterion. For example, in practical applications, a feature commending formula (3) is that returns in the distant future are weighted by a small factor, and consequently have less impact on the decision. You can see in Fig. 11.3 how the values of α^n drop rapidly as the interest rate and n increase. But remember, present value or any other formula can be justified only by making particular assumptions regarding the decision-maker's time value of money.

Now you must examine the present-value formula to see whether any additional assumptions have to be imposed for it to be a workable criterion. Start by checking whether the sum of an infinite number of terms in (3) always yields a finite value. To begin, suppose all the returns are identical:

(4)   Present Value $= R + \alpha R + \alpha^2 R$
$$+ \alpha^3 R + \cdots$$

(5) $$= \frac{R}{1 - \alpha} \quad \text{for } 0 \le \alpha < 1.$$

n ⟍ $i\%$	5	10	20
1	.952	.909	.833
5	.783	.621	.402
10	.614	.385	.161
15	.481	.239	.065
20	.377	.149	.026
40	.142	.022	.001

FIGURE 11.3. Discount Factors. $\alpha^n = \left(1 + \frac{i}{100}\right)^{-n}$.

The coefficients in (4) are simply a geometric series giving the value in (5). Notice the restriction $\alpha < 1$. If α is close to 1, then the present value is a large number, but it *is* finite. If $\alpha = 1$, then the sum in (4) is unbounded for $R \ne 0$, and (5) is ill defined. This case will be discussed later on.

Next evaluate Policies A, B, C, D, and G in Fig. 11.1: for $0 \le \alpha < 1$,

(6)   Policy A: $3 + 2\alpha + 1\alpha^2 + 3\alpha^3 + 2\alpha^4 + 1\alpha^5 + \cdots$

(7) $= (3 + 2\alpha + 1\alpha^2)(1 + \alpha^3 + \alpha^6 + \cdots) = \dfrac{3 + 2\alpha + 1\alpha^2}{1 - \alpha^3}$

(8)   Policy B: $3 + 1\alpha + 3\alpha^2 + 1\alpha^3 + 3\alpha^4 + 1\alpha^5 + \cdots$

(9) $= (3 + 1\alpha)(1 + \alpha^2 + \alpha^4 + \cdots) = \dfrac{3 + 1\alpha}{1 - \alpha^2}$

(10)   Policy C: $1 + 6\alpha - 1\alpha^2 + 1\alpha^3 + 6\alpha^4 - 1\alpha^5 + \cdots$

$= (1 + 6\alpha - 1\alpha^2)(1 + \alpha^3 + \alpha^6 + \cdots) = \dfrac{1 + 6\alpha - 1\alpha^2}{1 - \alpha^3}$

(11)   Policy D: $2\frac{2}{3} + 2\alpha + 2\alpha^2 + \cdots = 2\frac{2}{3} + 2 \cdot \dfrac{\alpha}{1 - \alpha}$

(12)   Policy G: $4 + 4\alpha^3 + 4\alpha^6 + \cdots = \dfrac{4}{1 - \alpha^3}.$

To compare A and B you can look at the difference between their present values:

(13)   P.V.[A] $-$ P.V.[B] $= \dfrac{3 + 2\alpha + \alpha^2}{1 - \alpha^3} - \dfrac{3 + 1\alpha}{1 - \alpha^2} = \dfrac{\alpha}{(1 + \alpha)(1 + \alpha + \alpha^2)} > 0$
$$\text{for } 0 < \alpha < 1.$$

Thus, even though B has a greater cumulative return than A in Period $3 + 6n$, for $n = 0, 1, 2, \ldots$, the discounted value of A is larger for *all* $0 < \alpha < 1$. Consequently, the present-worth criterion rules out B. Use the same procedure to verify that

(14) $$\text{P.V.}[A] - \text{P.V.}[C] = \frac{2(1-\alpha)}{1+\alpha+\alpha^2}$$

(15) $$\text{P.V.}[A] - \text{P.V.}[D] = \frac{(1-\alpha)(1+2\alpha)}{3(1+\alpha+\alpha^2)}.$$

What do you conclude about the relative merit of A versus C and D?

If you compare B and D, you obtain

(16) $$\text{P.V.}[B] - \text{P.V.}[D] = -2\tfrac{2}{3} + \frac{2\alpha+3}{1+\alpha}.$$

Verify that B is more advantageous when $\alpha < \tfrac{1}{2}$ and D is better when $\alpha > \tfrac{1}{2}$. Consider the situation when $\alpha = \tfrac{1}{2}$. Then check that according to (16), the two policies are equally good. As we show in the advanced material below, for any *finite* horizon n, the present value of Policy B is strictly better than that for Policy D if n is odd $(1, 3, 5, \ldots)$, and the reverse is true if n is even $(2, 4, 6, \ldots)$. Therefore you would be indifferent to these policies *only* when the horizon *is* unbounded.

▶Let $n = 2t$, where $t = 0, 1, 2, \ldots$. Then the present value of Policies B and D for the finite horizons n (even) and $n + 1$ (odd) are

(i) $\text{P.V.}[B|2t] = (3 + 1\alpha)\left(\dfrac{1-\alpha^{2t}}{1-\alpha^2}\right)$ $\text{P.V.}[D|2t] = 2\tfrac{2}{3} + 2\alpha\left(\dfrac{1-\alpha^{2t-1}}{1-\alpha}\right)$

$$\text{for } t = 1, 2, 3, \ldots,$$

(ii) $\text{P.V.}[B|2t+1] = \text{P.V.}[B|2t] + 3\alpha^t$ $\text{P.V.}[D|2t+1] = \text{P.V.}[D|2t] + 2\alpha^{2t}$

$$\text{for } t = 0, 1, 2, \ldots.$$

Consequently, for $\alpha = \tfrac{1}{2}$ the comparison is

(iii) $\text{P.V.}[B|2t] - \text{P.V.}[D|2t] = -\tfrac{2}{3}(\tfrac{1}{2})^{2t} < 0$

(iv) $\text{P.V.}[B|2t+1] - \text{P.V.}[D|2t+1] = \tfrac{1}{3}(\tfrac{1}{2})^{2t} > 0.$ ◀

When you compare A and G you find

(17) $\text{P.V.}[A] - \text{P.V.}[G] = \dfrac{3+2\alpha+\alpha^2}{1-\alpha^3} - \dfrac{4}{1-\alpha^3} = \dfrac{\alpha^2+2\alpha-1}{1-\alpha^3} > 0$

$$\text{for } \alpha > \sqrt{2} - 1 \approx .414.$$

Thus A is better only if $\alpha > \sqrt{2} - 1$, otherwise G is preferred. If the interest rate is very high, so that α is correspondingly small, then receiving a return of 4 in the first period of Policy G outweighs the later gains available from Policy A. In general, as you let α become small, the early returns are the most important, and when $\alpha = 0$ in the limit, all that matters is the first-period return R_1.

So far you have seen that using a present-value criterion may occasionally distinguish two streams in a surprising way. But the approach has always given a definite answer, because all the summations in the present-value formula (3) yielded a finite number. Was this merely the result of a felicitous selection of return streams? The answer is yes.

The kinds of difficulties occurring with the average-return criterion have their counterparts for present worth. You can see such examples in the advanced material below. On the other hand, troublesome cases for the average-return criterion may not cause difficulties for a discounted stream. Consider the example of the upward trending return stream Policy B* in (1), which did not have a finite average return per period. The present-value calculation can be shown to give

(18)   Policy B*: $(3 + 1\alpha + 3\alpha^2 + 1\alpha^3 + 3\alpha^4 + 1\alpha^5)[1 + 2(\alpha^6) + 3(\alpha^6)^2 + \cdots]$

(19) $= (3 + 1\alpha)(1 + \alpha^2 + \alpha^4)\dfrac{1}{(1 - \alpha^6)^2}$,

which is finite for $0 \leq \alpha < 1$. Verify that the present value for Policy A* in (1) is also finite.

Equivalent average return. Before concluding the discussion on how to attach a value to an infinite stream of returns, you need to study one other approach that relates the two notions of average and discounted values.

The idea is to construct an infinite stream of returns that has the same present value as the original stream. The return (before discounting) in each period will be identical, so that this constant value can be interpreted as the *equivalent average return* of the stream. Specifically, suppose $P(\alpha)$ is the present value of Policy X for a specified value of α. Then consider a new stream of returns

(20) $R_n = (1 - \alpha)P(\alpha)$ for all n.

For this stream

(21) $R_1 + R_2\alpha + R_3\alpha^2 + \cdots = (1 - \alpha)P(\alpha)(1 + \alpha + \alpha^2 + \cdots) = P(\alpha).$

The stream in (20) has the same present value as Policy X, then, and $(1 - \alpha)P(\alpha)$ is the equivalent average return. For a fixed value of α, $0 \leq \alpha < 1$, a criterion of best equivalent average return always leads to the same decision as does best present value because the equivalent average returns are simply the present values of all the alternatives multiplied by the same constant, $(1 - \alpha)$.

Applying the idea to the earlier examples, you obtain the equivalent average returns:

$$\text{Policy A:} \quad \frac{(1 - \alpha)(3 + 2\alpha + 1\alpha^2)}{1 - \alpha^3} = \frac{3 + 2\alpha + 1\alpha^2}{1 + \alpha + \alpha^2}$$

$$\text{Policy B:} \quad \frac{(1 - \alpha)(3 + 1\alpha)}{1 - \alpha^2} = \frac{3 + 1\alpha}{1 + \alpha}$$

(22) $$\text{Policy C:} \quad \frac{(1 - \alpha)(1 + 6\alpha - 1\alpha^2)}{1 - \alpha^3} = \frac{1 + 6\alpha - 1\alpha^2}{1 + \alpha + \alpha^2}$$

$$\text{Policy D:} \quad 2\tfrac{2}{3}(1 - \alpha) + 2\alpha$$

$$\text{Policy G:} \quad \frac{4(1 - \alpha)}{1 - \alpha^3} = \frac{4}{1 + \alpha + \alpha^2}.$$

The significant point is that *whenever average return per period is well defined, you always obtain it by letting α converge from below to 1 in the formula for equivalent average return.*

Thus letting $\alpha = 1$ in (22) yields

(23)
$$\text{Policy A: 2} \quad \text{Policy B: 2} \quad \text{Policy C: 2}$$
$$\text{Policy D: 2} \quad \text{Policy G: } \tfrac{4}{3},$$

which are the average values for A, B, C, D, and G obtained previously. Sometimes equivalent average return is well defined for $\alpha = 1$ when average return per period is *not* well defined. (You can see such an example for Policy H in the advanced material below.) Unfortunately, equivalent average return is not *always* well defined for $\alpha = 1$; an example is Policy B*.

The criterion of equivalent average return ranks A, B, C, and D as being equally desirable when $\alpha = 1$. Are they? This is a question of personal opinion and not scientific fact; the decision-maker alone must provide the answer. A strong case can be made, however, for saying that for $\alpha = 1$, A is **optimal**, C and D are **nearly optimal**, and B should be eliminated. From (13), (14), and (15), you can conclude that for α close to 1, the present value of A is greater than that for B, C, and D. For $\alpha = 1$ in (14) and (15), the difference between the present values is zero, so you might say that C and D are almost as good. But for B, when $\alpha = 1$ in (13), the difference is $\tfrac{1}{6}$. Thus, even though A and B have the same equivalent average return, their present values differ by $\tfrac{1}{6}$ as α approaches 1. For this reason, you may want to discard B.

In summary, the criterion of equivalent average return gives the same average return per period when the latter is well defined. Equivalent average return frequently will be adopted as a criterion function in the models of this and later chapters; but do not forget that its relevance for selecting an optimal policy in an unbounded horizon is *assumed*. (In the above examples, Policy B does offer a greater cumulative return every sixth period, starting with the third. The equivalent average return completely discounts this advantage.) Furthermore, keep in mind that additional postulates are required to ensure that the present value of each policy is always a unique finite number. And, finally, remember that if several policies have the same equivalent average return when $\alpha = 1$, there still may be good reason for preferring one of these policies to the others.

▶The above examples were straightforward, and only Policies A* and B* in (1) were really troublesome. But it is easy to devise other illustrations to show why the subject of infinite streams is full of booby traps. We give a few of these pathological examples here.

Suppose the revenue stream appears as

Policy H: $4, -4, 12, -12, 20, -20, 28, -28, \ldots, 4n, -4n, \ldots$ (n odd integers).

What would you guess to be a reasonable average return per period for this oscillating stream? To see what is happening more clearly, look at the *cumulative* returns

$$4, 0, 12, 0, 20, 0, 28, 0, \ldots, 4n, 0, \ldots \quad (n \text{ odd integers}),$$

and the corresponding sequence of *average* return per period

$$4, 0, 4, 0, 4, 0, 4, 0, \ldots, 4, 0, \ldots.$$

Here the problem is that even though the finite horizon averages are all bounded, they oscillate without converging. Therefore, in contrast with the behavior in Fig. 11.2, you cannot say for the Policy H that the average is arbitrarily close to a fixed value when the number of periods is large enough. The average at any fixed horizon is either 4 *or* 0. It is possible to modify the average return per period criterion to encompass such an oscillating sequence. For example, you could seek a policy that has the largest (or smallest) limit point of a sequence. For Policy H, 4 and 0 are the largest and smallest limit points in the sequence of average return per period.

Next consider the present-value calculation for Policy H

(i) $\qquad 4 - 4\alpha + 12\alpha^2 - 12\alpha^3 + 20\alpha^4 - 20\alpha^5 + \cdots = \dfrac{4(1 + \alpha^2)}{(1 - \alpha)(1 + \alpha)^2}.$

The present value is a well-defined finite number for $0 \le \alpha < 1$. The corresponding equivalent average return is

(ii) $\qquad\qquad\qquad\qquad\qquad \dfrac{4(1 + \alpha^2)}{(1 + \alpha)^2},$

giving the well-defined value 2 at $\alpha = 1$. Do you think this is a reasonable average value for the stream?

Consider the stream

$$R_n = R^{n-1} \quad \text{for} \quad n = 1, 2, 3, \ldots,$$

where $R > 1$, and where the present value of this stream is

(iii) $\qquad\qquad\qquad\qquad 1 + \alpha R + (\alpha R)^2 + (\alpha R)^3 + \cdots,$

which grows beyond bound as soon as $R \ge 1/\alpha$. To rely on a present-value approach, you must assume that the revenue stream does not grow fast enough to outweigh the discounting.

Finally, suppose $\alpha = a$ is specified, and that the stream is

(iv) $\qquad\qquad\qquad\qquad R_n = \left(\dfrac{-1}{a}\right)^{n-1} \quad \text{for} \quad n = 1, 2, 3, \ldots.$

Then the present-value formula (3) yields

(v) $\qquad\qquad\qquad\qquad 1 - 1 + 1 - 1 + 1 - 1 + \cdots.$

Clearly (v) seems finite, but what does it equal?

In answering, you must be wary of plausible looking arguments that really lead to absurdities. To illustrate, you might consider the present value of (v) for $\alpha < a$, and see what happens in such a formula when you let $\alpha = a$. This approach yields

(vi) $\qquad 1 - \dfrac{\alpha}{a} + \left(\dfrac{\alpha}{a}\right)^2 - \left(\dfrac{\alpha}{a}\right)^3 + \cdots = \dfrac{1}{1 + (\alpha/a)} \quad \text{for } \alpha < a.$

Thus you would be tempted to state that (v) sums to $\frac{1}{2}$, since this is the value on the right of (vi) when $\alpha = a$. The flaw in this "approach by analogy" can be seen by looking at the series:

(vii) $\quad 1 - \left(\dfrac{\alpha}{a}\right)^2 + \left(\dfrac{\alpha}{a}\right)^3 - \left(\dfrac{\alpha}{a}\right)^5 + \left(\dfrac{\alpha}{a}\right)^6 - \cdots = \dfrac{1 + (\alpha/a)}{1 + (\alpha/a) + (\alpha/a)^2} \quad \text{for } \alpha < a.$

Although (vi) and (vii) are different when $0 < \alpha < a$, both series on the left are identical when $\alpha = a$. But in (vii) the value on the right is $\frac{2}{3}$ if $\alpha = a$.

There is a variety of ways to solve the puzzle of attaching a unique value to (v), but by necessity they require you to make an explicit assumption about how you intend to treat such series. [Incidentally, most of the commonly made assumptions lead to the value $\frac{1}{2}$ for (v).]   ◀

Conclusions. The discussion in this section reached the following conclusions about selecting an optimization criterion for dynamic models:

(i)   A method of comparing streams of returns must include an assumption about the time value of money.

(ii) A technique that attempts to reduce any infinite stream to a unique finite number may not work for all such streams.

(iii) Even when a technique does reduce two different streams to the same number, the two policies may not be equally desirable if other economic considerations are examined.

At this point, you may wonder how realistic the preceding specific numerical examples really were. Of course, they were contrived, but you should not discredit them on that account. As tax experts and professional investment analysts can assure you, every corporation does face critical policy decisions that in effect are choices among alternative infinite streams exhibiting *behavior* similar to that in the examples. Such situations give rise to full-blown versions of the perplexities you studied, and commonly occur in firms undergoing rapid growth or facing steadily rising costs.

To illustrate, consider some issues that arise in the mere accounting treatment of cash flows and corporate assets. A company has several choices of how it depreciates its equipment, evaluates its current inventory, and takes a tax allowance for natural resource depletion. In each case, the strategy chosen can sharply affect the firm's reported earnings year after year.

Or consider a company deciding on a major equipment replacement expenditure. Sometimes it can postpone such an expense by temporary, but sizeable, maintenance outlays. If the investment is large, the firm may also want to assess strategies that involve leasing the equipment. The financing itself may be undertaken by several possible combinations of retaining earnings, incurring debt, and raising equity capital. To make the choice, the management must compare these strategies in terms of their impact on the company's cash flow and earnings streams.

For the remainder of this chapter and in the next, the infinite stream paradoxes are put aside (except for an occasional brief reminder). From here on, you will concentrate on applying the selection criteria and on learning the techniques for finding policies that are optimal according to the *given* criterion.

11.3 TIMBER HARVESTING MODEL

The next illustration serves a two-fold purpose. You will use the ideas in the previous section to solve a particular optimization problem. At the same time you will analyze a model structure that possesses wide applicability; it is discussed in the subsequent sections of this chapter.

The Tiny Timber Company is planning the forestation of a new area of land. The firm has estimated that a tree felled at the start of the kth period of growth yields a net return $N_k > 0$. To keep the discussion simple, assume that all expenditures on planting and maintaining a forest are negligible as compared with the cost of harvesting and transporting trees at the beginning of Period k. Further suppose that all the trees are to be cut in the same period. Consequently, N_k represents the revenue received less the costs of cutting all the trees. Assume N_k is available at the *start* of Period k, and $k = 1$ refers to the current period when the forestation commences.

Single decision. The discount factor α^{k-1} is applied to obtain the present value of the return, so the optimization problem is

(1) $$\underset{k=1,2,3,\ldots}{\text{maximize }} \alpha^{k-1}N_k.$$

The formulation (1) assumes that after the forest is harvested, replanting does *not* take place. In other words, the problem as stated so far involves a single decision: when to cut down the trees.

Suppose K is a value of k that solves (1), and assume that the sequence $\alpha^0 N_1$, $\alpha^1 N_2$, $\alpha^2 N_3$, . . . , has the property

(2) $\quad \alpha^0 N_1 \leq \alpha^1 N_2 \leq \cdots \leq \alpha^{K-2}N_{K-1} < \alpha^{K-1}N_K \geq \alpha^K N_{K+1} \geq \alpha^{K+1}N_{K+2} \geq \cdots,$

so that the present value is increasing as k goes from 1 to K and then is decreasing for larger k. Then the inequalities $(\alpha^{K-2}N_{K-1} < \alpha^{K-1}N_K)$ and $(\alpha^{K-1}N_K \geq \alpha^K N_{K+1})$ simplify to the conditions

(3) $$\frac{N_{K-1}}{N_K} < \alpha \leq \frac{N_K}{N_{K+1}}.$$

Therefore the value K can be found by calculating the ratios N_k/N_{k+1}, starting with $k = 1$, and terminating as soon as a ratio is at least as large as α. [Interpret (2) and the stopping criterion (3) for $\alpha = 1$.]

Illustration. Consider the case in which

(4) $$N_k = a - b^k \quad \text{where } 0 < b < 1 \quad \text{and} \quad a \geq b.$$

(Draw a graph of N_k for $a = .75$ and $b = .5$.) Then, as you can verify after a small amount of algebraic manipulation, (3) can be simplified to

(5) $$b^{K-1} > \frac{a(1 - \alpha)}{1 - \alpha b} \geq b^K.$$

This case points up a new difficulty. Let $\alpha = 1$, so that the middle term in (5) equals 0. Then there is no *finite* value for K satisfying (5), since $b^k > 0$ for *all* k. However, b^k is arbitrarily close to 0 for k sufficiently large. Thus when $\alpha = 1$, it is not meaningful to write "maximize" in (1) if N_k is specified by (4). Explain why a finite maximum does not exist in this circumstance (you will find it helpful to refer to the graph of N_k).

To illustrate (5) by a numerical example, suppose

(6) $N_k = .85 - (.78)^k$ and $\alpha = .8$.

Verify that $K = 4$ satisfies (5). Let P.V. $[k]$ denote the present value $\alpha^{k-1}N_k$; then, as you may want to verify for at least $k = 1$ and 2,

(7)   P.V.$[1] = .070$ P.V.$[2] = .193$ P.V.$[3] = .240$
            P.V.$[4] = .246$ P.V.$[5] = .230$.

These values will be used later.

Unbounded horizon. Now consider what happens when the forest *is* replanted in the period following the harvest, and thereafter the process is repeated infinitely often. If, each time, the forest is cut at the beginning of k periods growth, the present discounted value of the return stream over an unbounded horizon is

$$\begin{aligned}
F(k) &\equiv \text{P.V.}[k](1 + \alpha^k + \alpha^{2k} + \cdots) \\
&= \text{P.V.}[k] + \text{P.V.}[k](\alpha^k + \alpha^{2k} + \cdots) \\
&= \text{P.V.}[k] + \alpha^k \, \text{P.V.}[k](1 + \alpha^k + \cdots) \\
&= \text{P.V.}[k] + \alpha^k F(k)
\end{aligned}$$

(8)

so that

(9) $$F(k) = \frac{\text{P.V.}[k]}{1 - \alpha^k}.$$

An optimal policy over the unbounded horizon is one that maximizes $F(k)$. Let the maximal value of $F(k)$ be denoted by F, which you can find according to

(10) $$F = \underset{k=1,2,3,\ldots}{\text{maximum}} \frac{\text{P.V.}[k]}{1 - \alpha^k}$$

given the formula for $F(k)$ in (9). An immediate implication of (10) is

(11) $F \geq \dfrac{\text{P.V.}[k]}{1 - \alpha^k}$ for every k,   or,   equivalently,

(12) $F \geq \alpha^k F + \text{P.V.}[k]$ for every k,

where the equality holds in (11) and (12) for an optimal policy. This in turn implies that the value for F must satisfy

(13) $$F = \underset{k=1,2,3,\ldots}{\text{maximum}} (\alpha^k F + \text{P.V.}[k]).$$

Suppose (10) yields $k = k'$ as an optimal policy and assume that the sequence P.V. $[1]/(1 - \alpha)$, P.V. $[2]/(1 - \alpha^2)$, $\ldots$, has the property

(14) $$\frac{\text{P.V.}[1]}{1 - \alpha} \leq \cdots < \frac{\text{P.V.}[k']}{1 - \alpha^{k'}} \geq \frac{\text{P.V.}[k'+1]}{1 - \alpha^{k'+1}} \geq \cdots .$$

Then the inequalities for $k' - 1$, k', and $k' + 1$ in (14) lead to conditions analogous to (3), namely

(15) $$\frac{(1 + \alpha + \cdots + \alpha^{k'-1})N_{k'-1}}{(1 + \alpha + \cdots + \alpha^{k'-2})N_{k'}} < \alpha \leq \frac{(1 + \alpha + \cdots + \alpha^{k'})N_{k'}}{(1 + \alpha + \cdots + \alpha^{k'-1})N_{k'+1}}.$$

The value k' can be found by calculating the right-hand side of (15), starting with $k = 1$, until the ratio is at least as large as α. For each k, the ratio will be larger than N_k/N_{k+1}, which was calculated to obtain K in (3). Hence

(16) $$k' \leq K,$$

which means that the forest is usually harvested more often in the unbounded horizon case (and never less often).

Verify that when $\alpha = 1$ in (15), the inequalities can be written as

(17) $$\frac{N_{k'-1}}{k'-1} \bigg/ \frac{N_{k'}}{k'} < 1 \leq \frac{N_{k'}}{k'} \bigg/ \frac{N_{k'+1}}{k'+1},$$

implying that k' is a policy yielding the maximum average return per period.

For the numerical example in (6), an optimal policy is $k' = 2$ and

(18) $F(1) = .350$ $F(2) = .536$ $F(3) = .492$ $F(4) = .417$ $F(5) = .342,$

where $F(k)$ is the value of (9). Thus in the unbounded horizon situation, if you erroneously employed the solution $K = 4$ from the single-decision case, you would receive only $\frac{417}{536} = .78$ of the truly optimal present value.

11.4 INFINITE STAGE REGENERATION MODEL

You have already seen a few applications of so-called **regeneration models**. One such example is the timber harvesting and replanting problem in the previous section. Each time the forest is cut, the process regenerates itself in the sense that the Tiny Timber Company must again decide how long to wait until the next harvest period. Another illustration is the problem of equipment replacement discussed in Sec. 10.6. There a regeneration period occurred each time a machine was replaced. Consequently, the decision variables are really the successive intervals between replacements. Instead of pursuing any particular example in further detail, we will now treat them all in the context of a general model.

Suppose each time the decision process regenerates itself, the decision-maker can choose among N alternatives, which are indexed $k = 1, 2, \ldots, N$. Assume that if Alternative k is selected at a regeneration Period t, then the next regeneration occurs at Period $t + k$, and let

(1) $R_k = cost$ of Alternative k valued at the start of its regeneration period.

Note that (1) embodies a stationarity assumption: R_k does *not* depend on the particular period when the regeneration occurs. Also observe that since R_k is to be interpreted as a *cost*, the sense of optimization will be to *minimize*.

Finite horizon. Define

(2) f_n = present value of an optimal regeneration policy in which an alternative must be chosen when n periods remain until the end of the planning horizon.

Suppose that you choose Alternative k. Then you immediately incur the cost R_k, and assuming that you act optimally at the next regeneration point, $n - k$, you subsequently incur the cost $\alpha^k f_{n-k}$, where the factor α^k properly discounts the future cost to the present. Hence, an optimal choice when there are n periods remaining until the end of the horizon is a policy that minimizes the sum $\alpha^k f_{n-k} + R_k$, and the corresponding minimum value is f_n. Assuming that $n \geq N$, you can characterize f_n recursively by the relation

(3) $$f_n = \underset{k=1,2,\ldots,N}{\text{minimum}} \left[\alpha^k f_{n-k} + R_k \right] \quad f_0 \equiv 0 \quad \text{for } 0 \leq \alpha \leq 1.$$

(If $n < N$, then the minimum is restricted to $k = 1, 2, \ldots, n$.) Actually, if the costs of Alternative k occur throughout k periods, then each R_k would also depend on α; but we let this fact remain *implicit* and use the abbreviated symbol R_k instead of $R_k(\alpha)$. Figure 11.4 illustrates a network representation of recursion (3) for $\alpha = 1$.

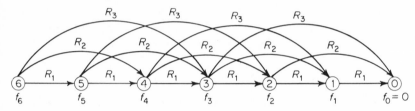

FIGURE 11.4. Finite Regeneration Model ($n = 6$, $N = 3$, $\alpha = 1$).

To see how (3) works, suppose $k = 1$ *is* optimal for *all* horizon lengths n. Then (3) yields

$$\begin{aligned}
f_n &= \alpha f_{n-1} + R_1 = \alpha[\alpha f_{n-2} + R_1] + R_1 \\
&= \alpha[\alpha(\alpha f_{n-3} + R_1) + R_1] + R_1 \\
&= \cdots = R_1 + \alpha R_1 + \cdots + \alpha^{n-1} R_1.
\end{aligned}$$

(4)

Unbounded horizon. Now suppose the planning horizon for the regeneration process is unbounded. Each time a regeneration occurs, the decision-maker continues to face an unlimited horizon. It can be proved by rigorous argument that there exists an optimal strategy (or policy) that is stationary: choose the *same* Alternative k at each regeneration point. Then if $\alpha \neq 1$, the appropriate generalization of (3) is

(5) $$f = \underset{k=1,2,\ldots,N}{\text{minimum}} \left[\alpha^k f + R_k \right] \quad \text{for } 0 \leq \alpha < 1.$$

[Recall that in (13) of the previous section, you studied an example of a similar optimization relation, the only important difference being the sense of the optimization. There P.V.[k], being a present value, *did* depend on α. Note also that here the largest value possible for k is assumed a priori to be N.]

The relation (5) is an example of what is called a **functional** or **extremal equation**. It is the value of f that is unknown, and (5) states the optimization relation that f must satisfy, given that a stationary strategy is used. When dealing with extremal equations, you must always determine:

- (i) Does the equation possess a finite solution?
- (ii) If so, is the solution unique?
- (iii) If so, is f the maximal discounted return among *all* (not necessarily stationary) policies?

To see the relevance of these questions, suppose $\alpha = 1$, contrary to the restriction on the right in (5). If you assume all $R_k > 0$, then *no* finite value for f satisfies (5). Explain why. But if instead you assume that all $R_k = 0$, then *any* finite value for f satisfies (5). Explain why. Therefore, the functional equation (5) is not appropriate for $\alpha = 1$.

You can view (5) as stating that f must satisfy

$$(6) \qquad f \leq \alpha^k f + R_k \quad \text{or} \quad f \leq \frac{R_k}{1 - \alpha^k} \quad \text{for all } k$$

and equality in (6) must hold for at least one value of k. It follows that a unique finite solution to the extremal equation (5) does exist and equals

$$(7) \qquad f = \underset{k=1,2,\ldots,N}{\text{minimum}} \left[\frac{R_k}{1 - \alpha^k} \right].$$

An optimal stationary policy corresponds to any Alternative k that yields the optimal value for f.

You can also derive (7) on the basis of stationarity. Since it is optimal to employ the same Alternative k every time a regeneration occurs, the present value of the policy is

$$(8) \qquad R_k + \alpha^k R_k + \alpha^{2k} R_k + \alpha^{3k} R_k + \cdots = \frac{R_k}{1 - \alpha^k}.$$

Thus an optimal policy is one that minimizes this quantity, as indicated in (7).

So far, the infinite stage problem has been solved assuming $\alpha \neq 1$, and you discovered that (5) is not appropriate for $\alpha = 1$. However, you can extend the analysis to $\alpha = 1$ by employing the criterion of equivalent average return suggested in Sec. 11.2. Specifically, use $g = (1 - \alpha)f$ in place of f. Verify that after some algebraic manipulation (7) then becomes

$$(9) \qquad g = \underset{k=1,2,\ldots,N}{\text{minimum}} \left[\frac{R_k}{1 + \alpha + \cdots + \alpha^{k-1}} \right].$$

Given $0 \leq \alpha < 1$, an optimal policy in (7) is an optimal policy in (9), and vice versa. By letting $\alpha = 1$ in (9), you can check that the solution corresponds to

$$(10) \qquad g = \underset{k=1,2,\ldots,N}{\text{minimum}} \left[\frac{R_k}{k} \right] \quad \text{for } \alpha = 1.$$

As we would expect, an Alternative k is optimal if it minimizes average cost per period.

To test your understanding, state how you would alter (6), (7), (9), and (10) if the optimization indicates "maximum" in (5).

Because the structure of this regeneration model is so simple, you can easily obtain an optimal stationary policy by the calculation in (7) or (10). For all practical purposes, then, the solution technique is trivial. Since problems of a more general structure do not solve so readily, however, more sophisticated approaches are required. In the context of dynamic programming, these are usually referred to as techniques of successive approximation. To help you grasp the fundamental ideas underlying each of these alternative approaches, the methods will be illustrated in the next three sections with the simple regeneration model. You will then find that only revised notation is required to extend them to more general problems.

▶One application of (10) is an important special case of the "inventory model with concave costs" that you studied in Sec. 9.5. Assume the production and inventory cost functions are stationary and of the form

(i)
$$C_t(x_t) = \begin{cases} s + cx_t & \text{for } x_t > 0 \quad (\text{setup} + \text{unit production cost}) \\ 0 & \text{for } x_t = 0 \end{cases}$$

$$h_t(i_t) = h \cdot i_t \qquad \text{for all } t \qquad (\text{linear holding cost}),$$

where $s \geq 0$, $c \geq 0$, and $h > 0$; x_t is the amount produced or ordered at the beginning of Period t, and i_t the ending inventory for Period t. Further assume demand is stationary, so that $D_t = D$ for all t, and that demand requirements must be met on time.

Let Q be the amount produced at a regeneration point, when entering inventory is zero. When the horizon is finite, you know from the form of an optimal policy given in Sec. 9.5 that

(ii)
$$Q = kD \quad (k \text{ a positive integer}).$$

Assume this form of policy for the unbounded horizon solution. The optimization problem is to find a multiple k that minimizes average cost per period.

Observe that

(iii) $R_k = s + ckD + hD[(k-1) + \cdots + 2 + 1]$ (setup + production + holding costs over k periods)

(iv) $= s + ckD + hD \dfrac{(k-1)k}{2}.$

Consequently,

(v)
$$\frac{R_k}{k} = \frac{s}{k} + cD + \frac{hD(k-1)}{2} \qquad (\text{average cost per period}).$$

An approximately optimal k can be found by differentiating (R_k/k) with respect to k and setting the quantity equal to 0. Verify that the result is

(vi)
$$k = \sqrt{\frac{2s}{hD}},$$

so that

(vii)
$$Q = kD = \sqrt{\frac{2sD}{h}}.$$

This expression for Q is often called the *economic lot-size formula*. Notice that (vi) and (vii) are approximate because in general the values are not integers. However, when (vi) is not an integer, an optimal policy can be found by calculating (v) for the next smallest and largest integers and selecting the better answer.   ◄

11.5 SUCCESSIVE APPROXIMATIONS

In this section, we initiate the discussion of numerical techniques for solving extremal equations that arise in dynamic programming models having an unbounded horizon. We use for a prototype the functional equation in the preceding section

$$(1) \qquad f = \underset{k=1,2,\dots,N}{\text{minimum}} \, [\alpha^k f + R_k] \quad \text{for } 0 \le \alpha < 1.$$

Remember, saying that you want a solution to (1) really means that you want a value for the unknown f that satisfies the equation; in addition, you would like to have an Alternative k that yields this value of f. Three solution approaches are frequently suggested.

The first emanates from the dynamic context of the underlying model. The idea is to see whether a policy that is optimal for a very long, but finite, horizon yields a solution value for f when used over an unbounded horizon. The second idea is to guess a *value* for f. Then compute the quantity on the right-hand side of (1) using this guess, and see whether the equation is satisfied. If not, let the result of the computation be a revised guess, and repeat the process. The third idea is to guess a *policy* that may be optimal over an unbounded horizon. Then solve for the corresponding present value, and use it as a trial value for f. See whether the equation is satisfied. If not, let the new guess be the policy that gives a minimum on the right-hand side of (1) and repeat the process. We consider the first approach in this section and the other two in the sections to follow.

In all of these methods, each guess can be viewed as an approximation to the solution. If the guess satisfies the extremal equation, you are done. If not, you must guess again. This iterative process is given the label **successive approximation**.

Finite horizon in the limit. Perhaps the most obvious approach for finding a policy that yields a solution to the functional equation (1) is to solve the finite horizon model

$$(2) \qquad f_n = \underset{k=1,2,\dots,N}{\text{minimum}} \, [\alpha^k f_{n-k} + R_k] \quad \text{for } 0 \le \alpha < 1$$

for a very large value of n. The examples you analyzed in Chaps. 8 and 9 should have made you cautious in your forecast of whether such an approach can be relied on to work. Can you be sure that for *any* n large enough, a k_n that results from (2) will also satisfy (1)? As you try each successively larger n, does a single k remain optimal? If the horizon n is long enough, is an optimal unbounded horizon policy also optimal as the initial decision? It is significant that for the regeneration model these questions have affirmative answers.

Regeneration Model Horizon Theorem. There exists a finite value n^* such that for any finite horizon $n > n^*$, if

(3) $f_n = \alpha^{k_n} f_{n-k_n} + R_{k_n}$ then $f = \alpha^{k_n} f + R_{k_n}$

(4) $f = \alpha^K f + R_K$ then $f_n = \alpha^K f_{n-K} + R_K$.

Thus (3) asserts that any strategy k_n that is optimal for the current decision when the horizon n is large enough (greater than n^*) is also an optimal stationary strategy for an unbounded horizon. And (4) asserts the reverse proposition. By performing the calculations of (2) according to a certain computation format, you can ascertain n^*. The details of the approach are extraneous to the purpose of this discussion, and therefore are omitted here.

11.6 SUCCESSIVE APPROXIMATIONS IN FUNCTION SPACE (VALUE ITERATION)

The guiding idea of the preceding method was to find an optimal stationary policy, K, for an unbounded horizon by examining an increasing sequence of values of n. In contrast, the notion below is to successively approximate the *function value f* in the extremal equation. Accordingly, the process is termed **value iteration**.

Let f^0 be an initial guess for f. Then the technique is to compute a sequence of approximations $f^1, f^2, f^3, \ldots$, according to the recursion

(1) $f^{n+1} = \underset{k=1,2,\ldots,N}{\text{minimum}} [\alpha^k f^n + R_k]$ for $0 \le \alpha < 1$ (value iteration),

where f^n is the *trial value* for f from iteration n. [If the optimization in the extremal equation indicates "maximum," then the corresponding change is made in (1).] An example of the method is given below.

Although the algorithm (1) is well specified, three questions arise about its application:

(i) Does the value of f^n always approach the value of f that satisfies the extremal equation?

(ii) If so, is there a *finite n* such that f^n equals f?

(iii) If Alternative k is chosen in (1) for two successive approximations, is it optimal?

To answer these, suppose for the moment all $R_k > 0$. If you let $f^0 = 0$, then it can be proved that $f^{n+1} > f^n$, so that the f^n are a **monotonically increasing sequence** of approximations. And for n sufficiently large, f^n *is* arbitrarily close to the optimal value f. In general, however, there is *no finite n* such that f^n equals f, and further, an alternative may be chosen on the right-hand side of (1) for two or more successive approximations but need not be optimal in an unbounded horizon. (For the regeneration model, you never return to a policy once it has been discarded in a function space iteration.)

Example. The following illustrates how the approximation method works when $R_k > 0$. Let $N = 5$ and

(2) $R_1 = 8.7 \quad R_2 = 12.7 \quad R_3 = 14.7 \quad R_4 = 19.7 \quad R_5 = 28.7 \quad \alpha = .8.$

Then you can determine that the solution is

(3) $f = \underset{k=1,\dots,5}{\text{minimum}} \left[\dfrac{R_k}{1 - .8^k} \right] = \text{minimum } [43.50, 35.28, 30.00, 33.39, 42.84]$

$$= 30.00$$

so that $k = 3$ is optimal.

The function space calculations in recursion (1) yield, for $n = 1, 2, 3$ and $f^0 = 0$:

$$f^1 = \underset{k=1,\dots,5}{\text{minimum}} [\alpha^k 0 + R_k] = 8.7 \quad \text{for } k = 1$$

$$f^2 = \text{minimum } [.8(8.7) + 8.7, .64(8.7) + 12.7, .51(8.7) + 14.7,$$
$$.41(8.7) + 19.7, .33(8.7) + 28.7]$$

(4)

$$= 15.66 \quad \text{for } k = 1$$

$$f^3 = \text{minimum } [.8(15.66) + 8.7, .64(15.66) + 12.7, .51(15.66) + 14.7,$$
$$.41(15.66) + 19.7, .33(15.66) + 28.7]$$

$$= 21.23 \quad \text{for } k = 1.$$

Check the individual terms in (4) to make sure you understand the computational process. For iterations $n > 3$,

(5)
$$f^4 = 25.53 \quad f^5 = 27.57 \quad f^6 = 28.76 \quad f^7 = 29.37 \quad f^8 = 29.68 \quad f^9 = 29.84$$
$$f^{10} = 29.91 \quad f^{11} = 29.95 \quad f^{12} = 29.97 \quad f^{13} = 29.98 \quad f^{14} = 29.99 \quad f^{15} = 29.99,$$

all for $k = 3$. (Calculate f^{16} and verify $k = 3$.)

Commentary. The example shows in (4) that a policy ($k = 1$) can be selected for several successive approximations but not be an optimal solution for the unbounded horizon. You can alter the example so that $k = 1$ is selected for an arbitrarily large number of approximations by reducing R_1 close enough to 6. The calculations in (5) indicate that there is a fast rate of convergence of f^n to f, but that f^n does not *equal* f for any finite n.

Observe that for $\alpha = 1$, the process breaks down. For *every* n, a k is selected if it produces the minimum R_k, and such a k does not usually agree with the solution that minimizes the average cost per period R_k/k.

The value iteration method given in (1) actually works for *any* values of R_k and initial guess f^0. But then the sequence of f^n values is not always monotonic. An alternative approach for selecting f^0 *does* always result in a **monotonically decreasing sequence** of approximations, that is, $f^{n+1} \leq f^n$. The idea is to guess an optimal *policy*, and let f^0 be the corresponding present value for this policy.

If the policy you guessed proves optimal in calculating f^1, then $f^0 = f^1 = f$. But if a new policy is strictly better in calculating f^1, then the recursion (1) proceeds as before and $f^{n+1} < f^n$. The method is illustrated next.

Convergence from above. Consider the example in (2) and assume your initial guess is $k = 1$. Then

$$(6) \qquad\qquad f^0 = \frac{R_1}{1 - \alpha^1} = 43.50,$$

and for $n = 1$,

$$(7) \qquad f^1 = \text{minimum } [.8(43.50) + 8.7, .64(43.50) + 12.7, .51(43.50) + 14.7,$$
$$.41(43.50) + 19.7, .33(43.50) + 28.7] = 36.88 \quad \text{for } k = 3.$$

For iterations $n > 1$,

$$(8) \qquad \begin{array}{llll} f^2 = 33.50 & f^3 = 31.78 & f^4 = 30.90 & f^5 = 30.45 \quad f^6 = 30.22 \\ f^7 = 30.11 & f^8 = 30.05 & f^9 = 30.02 & f^{10} = 30.01, \end{array}$$

all for $k = 3$. You can alter the example, by reducing R_4 close to 17.7, so that $k = 4$ is selected for an arbitrarily large number of approximations. Verify that had you started the process by guessing $k = 3$, then $f^1 = 30.00$ for $k = 3$.

The motivation for letting $f^0 = 0$ in the application of recursion (1) was mainly numerical convenience. You would not gain much insight from a verbal description of the approximation process with this starting point. However, letting f^0 be the present value of an initially guessed *policy* does lead to a key idea. The amount f^0 in (6) represents the present value of adopting the policy $k = 1$ over an unbounded horizon. Suppose that instead of $k = 1$, your immediate decision is $k = 3$, and thereafter you always let $k = 1$. The present value of this strategy is f^1 in (7). Analogously, f^2 in (8) actually represents the present value of letting $k = 3$ for the first two regeneration decisions, and letting $k = 1$ subsequently. This observation suggests another mode of approximation, discussed in the next section.

▶ What does it mean to say that the value iteration recursion (1) always works? Three points must be demonstrated. Two of them have already been mentioned, namely, that the extremal equation has a finite solution and that it is unique. Because the regeneration model has such a simple structure, the existence and uniqueness argument embodied in Sec. 11.4 suffices. More general models require additional care to establish these two points.

The third proposition is that the sequence of f^n converges to the solution value, for *any* R_k and initial guess f^0. The argument here is as follows. Let K be an optimal stationary policy for an unbounded horizon and let k be selected for a *given* iteration n according to the recursion (1). Then

$$(i) \qquad\qquad f = \alpha^K f + R_K,$$

since K is optimal in the unbounded horizon, and

(ii) $$f^n \leq \alpha^K f^{n-1} + R_K,$$

since k gives rise to f^n. Thus

(iii) $$f^n - f \leq \alpha^K(f^{n-1} - f) \leq \alpha|f^{n-1} - f|,$$

because $0 \leq \alpha < 1$.

Similarly,

(iv) $$f^n = \alpha^k f^{n-1} + R_k$$

(v) $$f \leq \alpha^k f + R_k,$$

so that

(vi) $$f - f^n \leq \alpha^k(f - f^{n-1}) \leq \alpha|f^{n-1} - f|.$$

Combining (iii) and (vi) gives

(vii) $$|f^n - f| \leq \alpha|f^{n-1} - f| \leq \alpha^n|f^0 - f|.$$

Since $\alpha < 1$, the right-hand side of (vii) is arbitrarily small for sufficiently large n. Therefore f^n approaches f in the limit. Notice that the convergence is at least at an exponential rate. ◄

11.7 SUCCESSIVE APPROXIMATIONS IN POLICY SPACE (POLICY ITERATION)

Suppose, in calculating the right-hand side of the recursion (1) in the previous section, you find a policy that makes a strict improvement over the one associated with f^n. This means that using this policy is an improvement over using the previous policy *for the immediate decision*. It is plausible, and correct, that using the new policy throughout the entire unbounded horizon would be even better than employing it only for the immediate decision. Then f^{n+1} can be calculated as the present value of repeatedly choosing the new policy. This process is known as **approximation in policy space**, or simply as **policy iteration**, since each iteration considers a new trial stationary policy for the unbounded horizon.

The resultant sequence of f^n is monotonically decreasing, and a strict improvement occurs at every iteration; therefore you never return to a policy once it has been discarded. Since there is a finite number N of distinct stationary policies, the approach must terminate in a *finite* number of iterations. As soon as a policy remains optimal for two successive approximations, you may stop the calculations, and f^n equals the optimal value f satisfying the extremal equation. As you will see, the price you pay to obtain a finite algorithm is the effort involved in calculating f^{n+1} for a new policy at each iteration.

The algorithm is

Step 1. Select an arbitrary initial policy, and let $n = 0$.

Step 2. Given the trial policy, calculate the associated

(1) $f^n = \dfrac{R_k}{1 - \alpha^k}$ (present value of trial k over an unbounded horizon).

Step 3. Test for an improvement by calculating

(2) $\underset{k=1,2,\ldots,N}{\text{minimum}} \, [\alpha^k f^n + R_k] = \alpha^{k'} f^n + R_{k'}$ (select k').

Step 4. Terminate the iterations if $\alpha^{k'} f^n + R_{k'} = f^n$. Otherwise, revise the policy to k'. Increase n to $n + 1$, and return to *Step 2* with the new trial policy.

Observe that whereas the very process of approximation in function space leads immediately to successive trial values for f, now these must be computed separately from (1). Notice also that the test for termination in *Step 4* is satisfied if k' is the same as the trial policy used in *Step 2*. That is, the calculations cease whenever k' is the same for two successive iterations. [How would you modify (2) if the optimization in the extremal equation indicates "maximum"?]

Example. To illustrate the approach, consider

(3) $R_1 = 8.7$ $R_2 = 12.7$ $R_3 = 14.7$ $R_4 = 19.7$ $R_5 = 28.7,$

which is example (2) of the previous section.

As before, take your initial policy guess to be $k = 1$, so that $f^0 = 43.50$. The test calculation in (2) is the same as (7) in the previous section. Thus in the value formula (1) you now find $f^1 = 30.00$ for $k = 3$. The second application of the test quantity (2) yields

(4) $\begin{aligned} \text{minimum } [&.8(30.00) + 8.7, 6.4(30.00) + 12.7, .51(30.00) + 14.7, \\ &.41(30.00) + 19.7, .33(30.00) + 28.7] = 30.00 \quad \text{for } k' = 3, \end{aligned}$

so that the process terminates.

Average return per period. As usual, to obtain the corresponding method for $\alpha = 1$, it is helpful to recast the procedure in terms of equivalent average return. The analogy to the value formula (1) is simply

(5) $g^n = \dfrac{R_{k'}}{1 + \alpha + \cdots + \alpha^{k'-1}} = \dfrac{R_{k'}}{k'} \quad \text{for } \alpha = 1.$

Note that if R_k depends on α, then the value of R_k at $\alpha = 1$ is used in calculating the ratio on the right-hand side of (5).

The expression on the left in the test quantity (2) becomes

(6) $\underset{k=1,2,\ldots,N}{\text{minimum}} \, [\alpha^k g^n + (1 - \alpha)R_k],$

but when you let $\alpha = 1$, the bracketed expression is independent of k. To rectify the situation, observe the following. If k' minimizes a function $g(k)$, then k' also minimizes $ag(k) + b$, for $a > 0$. Let $g(k)$ be the expression in the brackets of (6), $a = (1 - \alpha)^{-1}$, and $b = -g^n(1 - \alpha)^{-1}$. Make this transformation in (6), and verify that the following optimization, analogous to the test in (2), is appropriate:

(7)
$$\text{minimum}_{k=1,2,\ldots,N} \left[-(1 + \alpha + \cdots + \alpha^{k-1}) g^n + R_k \right]$$
$$= \text{minimum}_{k=1,2,\ldots,N} \left[-kg^n + R_k \right] = -k'g^n + R_{k'} \quad \text{for } \alpha = 1.$$

Once again, you must use the value of R_k appropriate for $\alpha = 1$, if in fact R_k depends on α. Give a verbal interpretation of the criterion in (7) for $\alpha = 1$.

To summarize, the technique is

Step 1. Select an arbitrary initial policy, and let $n = 0$.

Step 2. Given the trial policy, calculate the associated

(8)
$$g^n = \frac{R_k}{k} \quad \text{(average cost per period of k)}.$$

Step 3. Test for an improvement by calculating

(9)
$$\text{minimum}_{k=1,2,\ldots,N} \left[-kg^n + R_k \right] = -k'g^n + R_{k'} \quad \text{(select k')}.$$

Step 4. Terminate the iterations if $-k'g^n + R_{k'} = 0$. Otherwise, revise the trial policy to k'. Increase n to $n + 1$, and return to *Step 2* with the new trial policy.

To see how the method works, apply the algorithm to the example (3). The sequence of calculations is

(i) $g^0 = R_1/1 = 8.7$ for $k = 1$ as the initial policy,

(ii) $\text{minimum} \left[-1(8.7) + 8.7, -2(8.7) + 12.7, -3(8.7) + 14.7, \right.$
$$\left. -4(8.7) + 19.7, -5(8.7) + 28.7 \right] = -15.1 \text{ for } k' = 4,$$

(iii) $g^1 = R_4/4 = 4.925$,

(iv) $\text{minimum}_{k=1,\ldots,5} \left[-k(4.925) + R_k \right] = -.025$ for $k' = 3$,

(v) $g^2 = R_3/3 = 4.9$,

(vi) $\text{minimum}_{k=1,\ldots,5} \left[-k(4.9) + R_k \right] = 0$ for $k' = 3$.

Notice the same policy $k' = 3$ is indicated for two successive iterations, thereby causing termination at *Step 4*, and $k' = 3$ is optimal.

▶ You may not really be indifferent between two policies that look equally good according to the test in (9). For example, if you add another decision $k = 6$ with return $R_6 = 2R_3 = 29.4$, this policy has the same value of g when $\alpha = 1$ as does policy $k = 3$. But for $\alpha < 1$,

$$\frac{R_6}{1 - \alpha^6} - \frac{R_3}{1 - \alpha^3} = \frac{R_3}{1 - \alpha^3} > \frac{R_3}{2}.$$

So for $0 \leq \alpha < 1$ the present value from $k = 6$ always exceeds the present value for $k = 3$. Thus, although $k = 3$ is optimal according to the test in (9), you may really prefer $k = 6$. ◀

*11.8 A LINEAR PROGRAMMING EQUIVALENT

In Sec. 10.7 you studied the connection between dynamic recursive relations and linear programming. In brief, the dynamic programming values corresponded to the lengths of the shortest routes to the terminal from the nodes of an acyclic network. In unbounded horizon models, the network analogy remains valid, except that an optimal stationary policy implies traversing an associated cycle an infinite number of times. The network interpretation will be described in Chap. 12, but as a preview, the primal and dual linear programming problems for the simple infinite stage regeneration model are developed here.

The functional equation

$$(1) \qquad f = \operatorname*{minimum}_{k=1,2,\ldots,N} [\alpha^k f + R_k] \quad \text{for } 0 \le \alpha < 1,$$

can be expressed as

$$(2) \qquad \text{maximize} f$$

subject to

$$(3) \qquad f \le \alpha^k f + R_k \quad \text{for } k = 1, 2, \ldots, N,$$

where f is unconstrained in sign. Rearranging terms in (3) gives the constraints

$$(4) \qquad f \le \frac{R_k}{1 - \alpha^k} \quad \text{for } k = 1, 2, \ldots, N.$$

It is convenient to transform the problem into one involving equivalent average return. To do so, as usual, let $g = (1 - \alpha)f$. Equivalent to (2) and (4) is the optimization

$$(5) \qquad \text{maximize } g \qquad \text{(dual objective)}$$

subject to

$$(6) \qquad g \le \frac{R_k}{1 + \alpha + \cdots + \alpha^{k-1}} \quad \text{for } k = 1, 2, \ldots, N \quad \text{(dual constraints)},$$

where g is unconstrained in sign.

If you call (5) and (6) the dual problem, verify that the primal problem is

$$(7) \qquad \text{minimize} \sum_{k=1}^{N} \left(\frac{R_k}{1 + \alpha + \cdots + \alpha^{k-1}} \right) x_k \quad \text{(primal objective)}$$

subject to

$$(8) \qquad \sum_{k=1}^{N} x_k = 1, \qquad \text{(primal constraint)},$$

where $x_k \ge 0$. Note that when $\alpha = 1$, the objective function is

$$(9) \qquad \text{minimize} \sum_{k=1}^{N} \left(\frac{R_k}{k} \right) x_k.$$

Since the primal model has only one constraint (8), an optimal basic solution consists of a single $x_K = 1$, corresponding to a best regeneration policy, K, and all other $x_k = 0$.

11.9 SHORTEST-ROUTE PROBLEM REVISITED

In the next chapter you will study much more general dynamic models than the regeneration problem in the preceding sections. And to find policies that are optimal over an unbounded horizon, you will employ the techniques of successive approximation discussed in Secs. 11.6 and 11.7, so this material has served to prepare you for what is ahead. As further preparation, it will be helpful for you to consider once again the problem of finding a shortest route in a general network. Here we will generalize the statement of this problem so as to encompass discounting, and take a second look at algorithmic techniques, now emphasizing the ideas of successive approximation that you have learned.

As usual, the network structure consists of p nodes and a collection of arcs. As before, let (i,j) denote the arc from Node i to Node j, and c_{ij} denote the associated expense of traversing (i,j). You can let the amount c_{ij} be a present value that depends on the discount factor α, but such dependence will not be shown explicitly in the notation. The terminal is denoted by Node r.

For an example, consider the network in Fig. 11.5, which is the same as that in

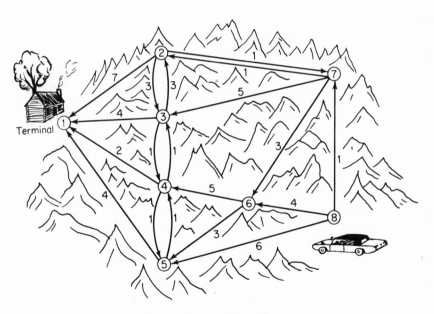

FIGURE 11.5. Shortest-Route Example.

Fig. 7.16, p. 233. The terminal is Node 1. Assume the following time orientation of a path between the terminal and Node k: let Node k be the current state and Node 1 the state at the end of the final stage. To illustrate, a path along the arcs

$(7, 2)$, $(2, 3)$, $(3, 4)$, $(4, 1)$ represents the current decision to go from Node 7 to Node 2, the subsequent decision to go from Node 2 to Node 3, etc.

Suppose that it takes only one period to traverse each arc. (A more general case where it can take more than one period to traverse certain arcs is discussed in the advanced material below.) Let the one-period discount factor be α, where $0 \leq \alpha \leq 1$. We generalize the definition of y_i, which in Sec. 7.6 denoted the length of a shortest route from Node i to the Terminal Node r. Here we let

(1) y_i = present value of an optimal path from Node i
                 to the Terminal Node r,

where optimal means a path having *minimum* present value. Thus, if a best route from Node i to Node r starts by going to Node j, then

(2) $y_i = \alpha y_j + c_{ij}$,

and

(3) $y_i \leq \alpha y_k + c_{ik}$ for all k.

[Give a verbal interpretation of (2) and (3).] Since (2) and (3) must hold for every Node $i \neq$ Terminal Node r, the y_i must satisfy a set of extremal equations,

(4) $y_i = \underset{\substack{(i, j) \text{ in} \\ \text{network}}}{\text{minimum}} (\alpha y_j + c_{ij})$ for all $i \neq r$ and $y_r \equiv 0$.

In other words, for each Node i, the minimization is taken over every arc (i, j) that exists in the network. [When $\alpha = 1$, (4), of course, represents the same relations as in Sec. 7.6.]

In one way this is a conceptually more difficult extremal-equation problem than that for the regeneration model in the preceding sections. In the regeneration model there was only a single unknown f; here there are $p - 1$ unknowns $y_i(i \neq r)$. But in another way, the shortest-route model is simpler because there is a terminal point, and hence $y_r = 0$. That is, although the actual time span to go from any Node k to Node r varies with the particular route taken, this span is always finite. You will see next how to use the methods of successive approximation to calculate all the y_i.

Value iteration. The same approaches you studied in the analysis of the regeneration model can be applied to successively approximate the y_i. The *function space* or *value iteration algorithm* is

(5) $y_i^{n+1} = \underset{\substack{(i, j) \text{ in} \\ \text{network}}}{\text{minimum}} (\alpha y_j^n + c_{ij})$ for all $i \neq r$ and $y_r^{n+1} \equiv 0$ (value iteration).

Terminate the calculations at iteration $n + 1$ if $y_i^{n+1} = y_i^n$ for every Node i. Alternatively, stop the iterations when for every Node i

(6) $y_i^n \leq \alpha y_j^n + c_{ij}$ for all (i, j) in network,

and equality holds for at least one arc (i, j). A convenient initial guess for the y_i is

(7) $y_i^0 = 0$ for every Node i.

If all the $c_{ij} > 0$, then by starting with (7) the y_i^n increase monotonically. Using (7), you can interpret the amount y_i^n as the minimal present value of any path from Node i that contains exactly n arcs, unless the terminal is on the path, in which case the path terminates at Node r. (Some arcs on a path may be traversed more than once.)

Does the value iteration algorithm (5) and (7) always work? If $\alpha = 1$ and the cost around every loop of the network is positive, then there exists an n^* such that for all $n \geq n^*, y_i^n = y_i^{n^*}$ and finite termination does occur. The reason is that as n increases, eventually every path of n arcs reaches the terminal. If $\alpha < 1$, however, then also assume that for each Node k the present value of traversing every loop that starts and ends at Node k is larger than the present value of the best loopless path from Node k to the terminal. With this assumption, the convergence is finite.

Example. The value iteration algorithm (5) and (7) is illustrated in Fig. 11.6 for the example shown in Fig. 11.5, where $\alpha = 1$. To test your understanding,

$n =$	0	1	2	3	4	5	6	7	8	9
y_1^n	0	0	0	0	0	0	0	0	0	0
y_2^n	0	1	2	3	4	5	6	6	6	6
y_3^n	0	1	2	3	3	3	3	3	3	3
y_4^n	0	1	2	2	2	2	2	2	2	2
y_5^n	0	1	2	3	3	3	3	3	3	3
y_6^n	0	3	4	5	6	6	6	6	6	6
y_7^n	0	1	2	3	4	5	6	7	7	7
y_8^n	0	1	2	3	4	5	6	7	8	8

FIGURE 11.6. Approximation from Below in Function Space (Value Iteration).

be sure to perform the detailed calculations on Fig. 11.5 (copy the figure on a piece of paper or write lightly with pencil on the page); verify the results for each n. Notice that at iteration 9 all $y_i^9 = y_i^8$, so the computations stop.

Observe

(8) $\qquad y_2^{n+1} = y_7^n + c_{27}$ and $y_7^{n+1} = y_2^n + c_{72}$ for $n = 0, 1, \ldots, 5$.

Thus for $n \leq 6$, the best path of n arcs from Node 2 involves a loop with Node 7.

Similarly, the best path of n arcs from Node 7 involves a loop with Node 2. Note also that the set of arcs at iteration $N = 7$ is optimal, but y_8^7 is not the correct value for y_8, so the procedure does not terminate at this iteration.

You can also employ the function space approximation (5) to converge monotonically on the y_i from above. For your initial guess, select an arc for each node so that every node is connected by a path to the terminal. Let y_i^0 be the corresponding present value of the path from Node i to the terminal. As before, there exists an n^* such that $y_i^n = y_i^{n^*}$ for all $n \geq n^*$ so that finite convergence occurs. This approach is most closely related to the shortest-route algorithm in Sec. 7.6. There, no special attention was given to the specific order in which the y_i were approximated. Here, a *literal* interpretation of (5) requires you to calculate a new approximation y_i^{n+1} for *every* node before returning to any previous node. Hence (5) may not converge as quickly as other possible techniques.

$n =$	0	1	2	3
y_1^n	0	0	0	0
y_2^n	6	6	6	6
y_3^n	3	3	3	3
y_4^n	2	2	2	2
y_5^n	3	3	3	3
y_6^n	7	6	6	6
y_7^n	8	7	7	7
y_8^n	9	9	8	8

FIGURE 11.7. Approximation from Above in Function Space (Value Iteration).

The procedure (5) converging from above is demonstrated by the illustration in Fig. 11.5, with $\alpha = 1$. Let the starting arcs be $(8, 7)$, $(7, 3)$, $(6, 4)$, $(5, 4)$, $(4, 1)$, $(3, 4)$, $(2, 3)$. Verify that the corresponding values for y_i^0 are those given for $n = 0$ in Fig. 11.7. Carry out the approximation process (5) on Fig. 11.5 and verify the other values of y_i^n appearing in Fig. 11.7. Notice that the set of arcs for $n = 1$ is optimal, but the iterations do not terminate at the next iteration $n = 2$, because $y_8^2 \neq y_8^1$. The calculations terminate at $n = 3$ for then all $y_i^3 = y_i^2$.

As the illustration shows, the approximation in function space procedure may determine an optimal policy at iteration n, but the associated values for y_i^n may not be optimal. When the function space approximation is from below, the y_i^n need not correspond to any realizable path from Node i to the terminal.

Policy iteration. Turning to the *approximation in policy space* approach, at every iteration n you must evaluate the *actual* y_i associated with the policy being tested. Specifically, perform the following:

Step 1. Select an arbitrary initial set of $p - 1$ arcs such that each node is connected by a path to the terminal, and let $n = 0$.

Step 2. Given the trial set, calculate the associated y_i^n, where $y_r^n \equiv 0$.

Step 3. Test for an improvement by calculating

$$(9) \qquad \underset{\substack{(i, j) \text{ in} \\ \text{network}}}{\text{minimum}} (\alpha y_j^n + c_{ij}) \equiv Y_i^n \quad \text{for each } i \neq r.$$

Step 4. Terminate the iterations if $Y_i^n = y_i^n$ for every Node i, as the set of arcs is optimal. Otherwise, using an arc yielding Y_k^n in (9), revise the set at each Node k where $Y_k^n < y_k^n$. Increase n to $n + 1$, and return to *Step 2* with the new trial set of arcs.

To test your understanding, apply the algorithm to the example of Fig. 11.5. Start with the same set of arcs that was used in Fig. 11.7 at $n = 0$, and consequently the same values for y_i^0. Check that at $n = 1$, all $Y_i^1 = y_i^1$, which are the correct values for y_i. Hence the iterations terminate at $n = 1$, as the optimal policy has been identified.

In comparing the function space and policy space approaches, observe that the same type of calculations are indicated by the right-hand side of (5) and by the left-hand side of (9). But in the function space approach, the resultant value in (5) is then used as the new approximation to y_i at the next iteration, whereas, in the policy space approach, a separate and distinct calculation for the next approximation to y_i is indicated in *Step 2*. It is this additional calculation that ensures the iterations terminate as soon as the correct policy has been found. See exercise 58 for more detail about *Step 2*.

Summary. The methods of successive approximation in both function space and policy space are applicable to solving the extremal equation for the problem of finding a best route from each Node k to the terminal. You should note two points of difference in the application of value iteration to the regeneration model and to the network model. In the regeneration model there was only one unknown, and therefore only one extremal relation, whereas in the network model there are $p - 1$ unknowns and extremal equations. In contrast, the horizon in the regeneration model was unbounded, and value iteration does not necessarily converge in a finite number of iterations, whereas finite convergence does occur for a shortest route in the network model. Chapter 12 will combine the network formulation above with the process of optimization over a limitless vista.

▶The preceding discussion assumed that only one period elapses in traversing any single arc. But sometimes you want to permit several periods to elapse in traversing an arc. For example, in the regeneration model, illustrated in Fig. 11.4, an arc (i, j) implies $i - j$ periods elapse. The solution techniques above are easily modified to permit this generalization.

Let

(i) h_{ij} = number of periods required to go from Node i to Node j along arc (i, j).

Then associated with each arc (i, j) is a discount factor

(ii) $\alpha_{ij} \equiv (\alpha)^{h_{ij}}$ for $0 \leq \alpha \leq 1$.

Instead of (4), the extremal equations for the present values y_i are

(iii) $y_i = \underset{\substack{(i, j) \text{ in} \\ \text{network}}}{\text{minimum}} (\alpha_{ij} y_j + c_{ij})$ for all $i \neq r$ and $y_r \equiv 0$, and in the same fashion, all the other formulas in this section are modified by writing α_{ij} wherever α appears.   ◄

REVIEW EXERCISES

1 Discuss the sense in which the numerical illustrations in Fig. 11.1, the timber harvesting model for an unbounded horizon as described in Sec. 11.3, and the infinite stage regeneration model as described in Sec. 11.4, assume stationarity.

2 Section 11.1 states that in comparing two strategies that operate over an unbounded horizon, there is no problem in determining their relative merit if one accumulates more returns than the other for *every* horizon length. Do you agree? Why? (Are there any implicit assumptions in the text's assertion?)

3 Verify in Fig. 11.1 that

   (a) D gives a better cumulative return than B for every even-numbered period.
   (b) B is "ahead" of A, C, and D at every Period $3 + 6n$, for $n = 0, 1, 2, \ldots$.
   *(c) The general terms in the sequences for the average return per period are those given by (i) through (v) in the advanced material at the beginning of Sec. 11.2.
   *(d) Find a value n^* such that for every Period n, where $n \geq n^*$, the average return per period is within $2 \pm .01$ for Policy A. Do the same for Policy B. For Policy C. For Policy D. Similarly find a value for n^* associated with ensuring that the average return per period is within $1\frac{1}{3} \pm .01$ for Policy G. How does the value of n^* change if the tolerance is .001 instead of .01 for Policy A?

4 Consider a choice between Policy A in Fig. 11.1 and a policy with returns identical to those in Policy A except that in Period 1 the return from the alternative policy is 100. Suggest one or more *general rules* you might apply to a choice between policies where both alternatives give the same average return per period over an unbounded horizon. Would your rules always select a unique policy from among alternatives having the same average return per period over an unbounded horizon? Justify your answer.

5 Calculate the average return per period for Policy E in Fig. 11.1. Do you agree with the argument in the text that it is plausible to eliminate Policy E from further consideration, given that you can select Policy D? Suppose Policy D were not available for selection. Would you still eliminate Policy E? Explain the reasoning behind your answers.

6 In each part below, assume that the specified policy is added to Fig. 11.1. State whether the policy dominates or is dominated by any policies now listed in the table, and compute the policy's average return per period.

   (a) $3, 4, -1,\quad 3, 4, -1, \ldots$.
   (b) $6, -1, 1,\quad 6, -1, 1, \ldots$.
   (c) $0, 0, 8, 0,\quad 0, 0, 8, 0, \ldots$.

(d) $0, 8, 0, 0,\quad 0, 8, 0, 0, \ldots$.

(e) $4, 0, 4, 0, 4, 0, \ldots$.

(f) $0, 4, 0, 4, 0, 4, \ldots$.

(g) $2, 2\frac{2}{3}, 2, 2, 2, \ldots, 2, \ldots$.

(h) $2 + e, 2 + e^2, 2 + e^3, 2 + e^4, 2 + e^5, 2 + e^6, \ldots$, where e is a constant in the interval $0 < e < 1$. (*Hint:* your answer should depend on the specific value for e.)

*7 For each part in exercise 6, derive general terms in the sequence for the average return per period, analogous to those given by (i) through (v) in the advanced material at the beginning of Sec. 11.2.

8 Consider the finite stream of returns $R_1 = 4$, $R_2 = 12$, $R_3 = 24$, $R_4 = 40$; suppose that the discount factor $\alpha = \frac{1}{2}$, and assume that you can borrow or lend as much money as you desire at the associated compound rate of interest.

(a) What is the present value of this stream? What is the associated compound rate of interest?

(b) If you wanted to redistribute the returns so as to have all the returns in Period 1 and none in other periods, how large an amount could you obtain? (Indicate how much you borrow or lend in each period, when these amounts must be repaid, and the associated amount of interest.)

(c) Answer the question in part (b), but assume you want to have all the returns in Period 2. In Period 3. In Period 4.

(d) Explain in detail why the stream $S_1 = 2$, $S_2 = 16$, $S_3 = 20$, $S_4 = 56$ is better than the stream R_j.

(e) Explain in detail why the stream $T_1 = 4$, $T_2 = 8$, $T_3 = 24$, $T_4 = 48$ is worse.

*9 Consider the return streams in exercise 8. At what value of α is the stream containing R_j as good as the stream containing S_j? At what value of α is the stream containing R_j as good as the stream containing T_j? At what value of α are the streams containing S_j and T_j equally good?

10 Derive the present-value formula (5) in Sec. 11.2, and perform all the intermediate algebraic steps to obtain the results shown in (6) through (12).

11 Determine expressions [analogous to those shown in (6) through (12) of Sec. 11.2] for the present value of the streams in exercise 6.

12 (a) Perform the intermediate algebraic steps to obtain the results shown in (13) through (17) of Sec. 11.2.

(b) What do you conclude about the relative merit of Policy A versus Policies C and D? Verify that Policy B is more advantageous than Policy D when $\alpha < \frac{1}{2}$, and is less advantageous when $\alpha > \frac{1}{2}$.

13 In each part below, determine expressions analogous to those shown in (13) through (17) of Sec. 11.2 for the indicated streams in Fig. 11.1 and the indicated part in exercise 6. State a range of values for α over which each of the policies is preferable.

(a) Policy B and Policy E.

(b) Policy B and Policy C. *Exercise continued on p. 394.*

  (c) Policy C and Policy D.
  (d) Policy A and the policy in part (a).
  (e) Policy B and the policy in part (a).
  (f) Policy C and the policy in part (a).
  (g) Policy C and the policy in part (b).
  (h) Policy A and the policy in part (c).
  (i) Policy D and the policy in part (h).

*14 Verify the results (i) through (iv) in the advanced material following (16) in Sec. 11.2.

15 (a) Perform the intermediate algebraic steps to obtain the results for Policy B* shown in (18) and (19) of Sec. 11.2.
  (b) Derive the corresponding result for Policy A*, and verify that this present value is finite for $0 \leq \alpha < 1$.
  (c) Determine an expression analogous to those shown in (13) through (17) of Sec. 11.2 for Policies A and B*. State a range of values for α over which each of these policies is preferable to the other.
  (d) Derive the present value for Policy C, defined as

$$1, 6, -1, 1, 6, -1, \quad 2, 12, -2, 2, 12, -2, \quad 3, 18, -3, 3, 18, -3, \ldots.$$

  Answer the question in part (c) but for Policies B* and C*.
  (e) Derive the present value for Policy D, defined as

$$2\tfrac{2}{3}, 2, 2, 2, 2, 2, \quad 4, 4, 4, 4, 4, 4, \quad 12, 12, 12, 12, 12, 12, \ldots.$$

  Answer the question in part (c) but for Policies B* and D*.

16 Verify the results in (22) of Sec. 11.2. Show why equivalent average return is not well defined for $\alpha = 1$ for Policy B*.

17 Determine the equivalent average return for each of the streams in exercise 6. Calculate the value for $\alpha = 1$.

18 The text states in Sec. 11.2 that although the criterion of equivalent average return ranks Policies A, B, C, and D in Fig. 11.1 as being equally desirable for $\alpha = 1$, a resolution must rest on the decision-maker's personal opinion and not on scientific fact. The text then goes on to argue that a case can be made for saying that, for $\alpha = 1$, Policy A is optimal, Policies C and D are nearly optimal, and Policy B should be eliminated. Discuss the issues involved and whether you agree with the argument offered. Give reasons for your position.

19 (a) In Sec. 11.3, the text assumes that the sequence of $\alpha^{k-1} N_k$ satisfies the inequalities in (2). Discuss what complications arise if this simplifying assumption is dropped.
  (b) Show that the inequalities in (2) imply that an optimal value for K can be determined from (3). When there are alternative optimal policies, does (3) always lead to a unique value for K? Justify your answer.
  (c) Interpret (2) and the stopping criterion (3) for $\alpha = 1$.

20 (a) Draw a graph for (4) in Sec. 11.3, where $a = .75$ and $b = .5$.
  (b) Perform the intermediate algebraic steps to verify that when N_k is given by (4), the stopping criterion (3) simplifies to (5).

*(c) Construct an example of a sequence for N_k such that, given a value for the discount factor α, where $0 < \alpha < 1$, there is no *finite* value for K that is optimal.

(d) Given the numerical example (6) in Sec. 11.3, verify that $K = 4$ satisfies (5).

(e) Verify the present values in (7) for $k = 1$ and 2.

21 Consider the timber harvesting model in Sec. 11.3. Suppose

$$N_k = a + kb \quad \text{where} \quad a + b \geq 0 \quad \text{and} \quad b > 0.$$

(a) Determine a stopping criterion analogous to that implied by (5).

(b) Let $\alpha = \frac{2}{3}$, $a = 3$, and $b = 9$. What is an optimal value for K? Calculate the present value $\alpha^{k-1} N_k$ for $k = 1, 2, 3, 4$.

22 Consider the timber harvesting model in Sec. 11.3. Suppose

$$N_k = a + k^2 b \quad \text{where} \quad a + b \geq 0 \quad \text{and} \quad b > 0.$$

(a) Determine a stopping criterion analogous to that implied by (5).

(b) Let $\alpha = \frac{2}{3}$, $a = 3$, and $b = 9$. What is an optimal value for K?

(c) Calculate the present value $\alpha^{k-1} N_k$ for $k = 1, 2, \ldots, K + 1$, where K is the optimal value you found in part (b).

23 (a) In Sec. 11.3, the text assumes that the sequence of P.V. $[k]/(1 - \alpha^k)$ satisfies the inequalities in (14). Discuss what complications arise if this simplifying assumption is dropped.

(b) Show how the inequalities in (14) imply that an optimal value for k' can be determined from (15). If there are alternative optimal policies, does (15) always lead to a unique value for k'? Justify your answer.

(c) Explain why the ratio on the right-hand side of (15) is larger than N_k/N_{k+1} for each k.

(d) Verify that when $\alpha = 1$ in (15), the inequalities can be written as (17).

24 Consider the numerical example (6) in Sec. 11.3.

(a) Use (15) to verify that $k' = 2$ is an optimal policy for an unbounded horizon.

(b) Verify the values of $F(1)$ and $F(2)$ in (18).

25 Consider the data in exercise 21. Find an optimal policy, k', for an unbounded horizon. Calculate $F(k' - 1)$, $F(k')$, and $F(k' + 1)$. What is the loss in present value from using the optimal single decision policy, K, instead of k'?

26 Consider the data in exercise 22. Find an optimal policy, k', for an unbounded horizon. Calculate $F(k' - 1)$, $F(k')$, and $F(k' + 1)$. What is the loss in present value from using the optimal single decision policy, K, instead of k'?

27 Consider the infinite stage regeneration model in Sec. 11.4.

(a) Assume all $R_k > 0$. Explain why there is no finite value for f that satisfies (5) for $\alpha = 1$.

(b) Assume all $R_k = 0$. Explain why any finite value for f satisfies (5) for $\alpha = 1$.

(c) Explain why (5) implies the inequalities in (6), and why they in turn imply (7).

(d) Show the intermediate algebraic steps to obtain the equality on the right-hand side of (8). *Exercise 27 continued on p. 396.*

(e) Show the intermediate algebraic steps to derive (9), and verify that (9) becomes (10) for $\alpha = 1$.

(f) Show how to alter (6), (7), (9), and (10) if the optimization indicates "maximum" in (5).

*28 Consider the inventory model with concave costs, discussed in the special material at the end of Sec. 11.4.

(a) Show that k in (vi) minimizes the cost expression in (v).

(b) Derive the formula for $R_k(\alpha)$, when there is a discount factor α, where $0 < \alpha < 1$, and each period's costs are discounted. How will the optimal lot-size quantity depend on the value of α? How, if at all, will this quantity depend on the value of the purchase cost c? Explain in detail.

29 Consider the Regeneration Model Horizon Theorem in Sec. 11.5. Assuming that $K = 5$ and $n^* = 8$, give a verbal interpretation of

(a) (3) for $k_{10} = 4$. For $k_{20} = 4$. For $k_{20} = 6$.

(b) (4) for $n = 10$. For $n = 20$.

(c) If Policy 12 is optimal for all $n > 22$, does $k_{30} = 12$? Is Policy 12 optimal over an unbounded horizon? [Justify your answers with reference to (3) and (4).]

*(d) If Policy 9 is optimal over an unbounded horizon and $k_3 = 9$, is Policy 9 optimal for all $n > 3$?

30 In each part below, apply the method of "finite horizon in the limit," and find the, smallest n such that the policy that is optimal for an unbounded horizon is also optimal for finite horizons of length n, $n + 1$, and $n + 2$. (Remember, the objective is to "maximize.")

(a) Timber harvesting illustration (6) and (18) in Sec. 11.3, where $R_k \equiv$ P.V. $[k]$.

(b) Problem in exercises 21 and 25.

(c) Problem in exercises 22 and 26.

31 Consider the numerical example (2) used to illustrate the value iteration algorithm (1) in Sec. 11.6.

(a) Check the individual terms in (4), and calculate the values inside the brackets to verify that $k = 1$ yields a minimum.

(b) Calculate f^{16}, given the value for f^{15} in (5), and verify that $k = 3$.

(c) Let $f^0 = 20$ and perform the value iteration algorithm. Stop the iterations at $n = 3$.

(d) Let $f^0 = 35$ and perform the value iteration algorithm. Stop the iterations at $n = 3$.

*(e) Let $R_1 = 7$. Perform the value iteration algorithm with $f^0 = 0$. At what value of n does $k = 3$ for the first time? What is the corresponding value f^n? How does it compare with f^4 in (5)?

*(f) Let $R_1 = 10$. Perform the value iteration algorithm with $f^0 = 0$. At what value of n does $k = 3$ for the first time? What is the corresponding value f^n? How does it compare with f^4 in (5)?

*(g) Let $R_4 = 17.9$. Perform the value iteration algorithm with $f^0 = 43.50$. At what value of n does $k = 3$ for the first time? What is the corresponding value f^n? How does it compare with f^1 in (7)?

*(h) Suppose at every iteration $n \geq n'$, the same optimal infinite horizon policy is selected. Derive a formula for f^n, given the value of $f^{n'}$.

32 *Graphical Representation of Value Iteration.* For each k, graph the line $y = \alpha^k f + R_k$, where y is the ordinate value and f the abscissa value. For each value of f, one (or more) of these lines is "lowest." Mark in red pencil (for example) the piecewise linear function consisting of all these "lowest" segments. Next graph the line $y = f$. The intersection of this line and the piecewise linear function gives the solution value for f. The value iteration technique starts with f^0. Draw a vertical line at f^0, and select a k corresponding to the piecewise linear function. The associated value on this function is the next trial f^1 and can be indicated by drawing a horizontal line from the point on the piecewise linear function to the line $y = f$. As the process repeats itself, the trial points move ever closer to the intersection of the line $y = f$ and the piecewise linear function.

In each part below, draw the line for each k, mark the piecewise linear function, draw the line $y = f$, show the solution, and display how the value iteration technique progresses when $f^0 = 0$ and when $f^0 = R_1/(1 - \alpha)$. [Only show the iterative technique graphically and do not perform any of the underlying computations. Remember in parts (b), (c), and (d), the objective is to "maximize."]

(a) Numerical example (2) in Sec. 11.6.
(b) Timber harvesting illustration (6) and (8) in Sec. 11.3.
(c) Problem in exercises 21 and 25.
(d) Problem in exercises 22 and 26.

33 In each part below, perform the value iteration technique in Sec. 11.7. Letting n' denote the first iteration at which the corresponding k is optimal for the unbounded horizon, terminate the calculations at $n' + 2$. First use $f^0 = 0$ as a starting value. Then use $f^0 = R_1/(1 - \alpha)$. (Remember the objective is to "maximize.")

(a) Timber harvesting illustration (6) and (8) in Sec. 11.3, where $R_k \equiv$ P.V. $[k]$.
(b) Problem in exercises 21 and 25.
(c) Problem in exercises 22 and 26.
(d) In each part, describe a strategy that actually yields the value $f^{n'+2}$. Is this policy stationary? (*Note:* such a strategy may not exist.)
*(e) In each part, verify that $|f^n - f| \leq \alpha^n |f^0 - f|$ for $n = 1, 2, \ldots, n' + 2$.

34 In each part below, perform the policy iteration algorithm of Sec. 11.7. First use $k = 1$ as the initial policy at $n = 0$. Then use $K + 1$ as the initial policy, where K is an optimal policy for an unbounded horizon.

(a) Timber harvesting illustration (6) and (8) in Sec. 11.3, where $R_k \equiv$ P.V. $[k]$.
(b) Problem in exercises 21 and 25.
(c) Problem in exercises 22 and 26.

35 Consider employing the criterion of average return per period in the policy iteration algorithm of Sec. 11.7. [*Parts (c) and (d) on p. 398.*]

(a) Demonstrate that (5) corresponds to (1) when expressed in terms of equivalent average return.
(b) Similarly, demonstrate that (6) corresponds to the test quantity (2).

(c) Let $g(k)$ be the expression in the brackets of (6). Let $a = (1 - \alpha)^{-1}$, $b = -g^n(1 - \alpha)^{-1}$. Form the expression $ag(k) + b$ and show the algebraic manipulations yielding the simplified quantity on the left-hand side of (7).

(d) Give a verbal interpretation of the test criterion in (7) for $\alpha = 1$.

36 Use the policy iteration algorithm of Sec. 11.7 to find an optimal solution to the timber harvesting illustration (6) in Sec. 11.3, for $\alpha = 1$. Let $k = 1$ be the initial policy. (Remember the objective is to "maximize.")

37 Consider the shortest-route problem in Sec. 11.9 and give a verbal interpretation of (2) and (3).

38 Apply the value iteration algorithm in Sec. 11.9 to the example shown in Fig. 11.5 with $\alpha = 1$ and $y_i^0 = 0$.

(a) Show all the detailed computations, and verify the results in Fig. 11.6.

(b) Show the best path of n arcs from Node 2 to the terminal for $n \leq 6$. Do the same from Node 7.

39 Apply the value iteration algorithm in Sec. 11.9 to the example shown in Fig. 11.5 with $\alpha = 1$ and y_i^0 corresponding to the arcs $(8, 7)$, $(7, 3)$, $(6, 4)$, $(5, 4)$, $(4, 1)$, $(3, 4)$, and $(2, 3)$.

(a) Verify the values for y_i^0 are those shown in Fig. 11.7.

(b) Show all the detailed computations, and verify the results given in Fig. 11.7. [Carry out the successive approximation process (5) on Fig. 11.5.]

40 Apply the value iteration algorithm in Sec. 11.9 to the example shown in Fig. 11.5 with $\alpha = 1$ and $y_i^0 = 10$ for every i $(i \neq r)$.

41 Apply the value iteration algorithm in Sec. 11.9 to the example shown in Fig. 11.5 with $\alpha = 1$, and y_i^0 corresponding to the arcs $(8, 5)$, $(7, 3)$, $(6, 4)$, $(5, 1)$, $(4, 1)$, $(3, 1)$, and $(2, 1)$.

*42 In each part below, apply the value iteration algorithm in Sec. 11.9 to the example shown in Fig. 11.5 with $\alpha = .8$. Stop the iterations at $n = 9$. Let

(a) $y_i^0 = 0$.

(b) y_i^0 be calculated from the policy in exercise 39.

(c) y_i^0 be calculated from the policy in exercise 41.

43 Apply the policy iteration algorithm in Sec. 11.9 using the data in exercise 41.

*44 Apply the policy iteration algorithm in Sec. 11.9 using the data in exercise 42,

(a) Part (b).

(b) Part (c).

45 Explain your understanding of the following terms:

unbounded horizon (limitless vista)   regeneration model
stationarity   regeneration period (or point)

stationary policy (or strategy)

infinite stream of returns

utility of money

average return per period

interest rate and compound interest

discount factor

present discounted value (or present worth)

equivalent average return

nearly optimal

functional (or extremal) equation

successive approximation

value iteration (successive approximation in function space)

policy iteration (successive approximation in policy space)

monotonically increasing (decreasing) sequence

convergence from above (below).

COMPUTATIONAL EXERCISES

46 *Equipment Replacement Problem.* Consider the case of the Goode-O'Toole Company, described in exercise 41 of Chap. 6. Suppose a replacement policy is desired for an unbounded horizon. Assume the cost of a new model in any period is p, the number of policies $N = 7$, and the salvage values and operating costs are as given in exercise 41 of Chap. 6. In parts (a) and (b) below, find an optimal replacement policy for $\alpha = 1$.

(a) $p = 100$.

(b) $p = 90$.

(c) Find the largest and smallest value of p such that $k = 3$ is optimal for $\alpha = 1$.

(d) Suppose $\alpha < 1$ and that purchase and operating costs occur at the "beginning" of a period and salvage value is obtained at the "end" of a period. Hence, if a drill press is purchased at the beginning of the current period and kept for three periods, the resultant present value over these three periods is $p + r_1 + \alpha r_2 + \alpha^2 r_3 + \alpha^3 v_3$. For parts (a) and (b) above, determine the smallest value of α such that the policy for $\alpha = 1$ remains optimal, and calculate the corresponding interest rate.

(e) Does increasing both the purchase cost to $p + d$ and each salvage value to $v_k + d$ yield the same optimal policy? Explain and be sure to make explicit all your assumptions.

47 A commonly employed method of numerically obtaining the square root of a positive number A is the following technique of successive approximations (suggested by Newton): $f^n = .5\,[f^{n-1} + (A/f^{n-1})]$. Give a graphical description of this technique. Indicate how the sequence of f^n approaches the correct value $f \equiv \sqrt{A}$, starting with any initial $f^0 > 0$. Also show that f^n converges to f from above (for $n \geq 1$).

48 Consider the infinite stage regeneration model in Sec. 11.4 with $N = 5$ and $R_1 = 5$, $R_2 = 8$, $R_3 = 10$, $R_4 = 12$, and $R_5 = 18$.

(a) Determine an optimal policy for *every* value of α in the interval $0 \leq \alpha \leq 1$.

(b) Let $\alpha = .9$. Apply the "finite horizon in the limit" approach in Sec. 11.5. Terminate the iterations after you select the same policy for five iterations.

(c) Let $\alpha = .9$. Apply the value iteration algorithm in Sec. 11.6 with $f^0 = 0$. Do the same with $f^0 = R_1/(1 - \alpha)$. Letting n' denote the first iteration at which the corresponding k is optimal for the unbounded horizon, terminate the calculations at $n' + 2$.

*(d) Using the graphical representation described in exercise 32, plot the iterations in part (c).

(e) Let $\alpha = .9$. Apply the policy iteration algorithm in Sec. 11.7 with $k = 1$ as the initial guess.

(f) Let $\alpha = 1$. Apply the policy iteration algorithm in Sec. 11.7 with $k = 1$ as the initial guess.

49 For each exercise in Chap. 7 listed below, apply the value iteration algorithm for a shortest-route problem as given in Sec. 11.9, with $\alpha = 1$ and $y_i^0 = 0$.

(a) Exercise 27, part (a).   (g) Exercise 62, part (a).
(b) Exercise 28, part (a).   (h) Exercise 62, part (b).
(c) Exercise 60, part (a).   (i) Exercise 63, part (a).
(d) Exercise 60, part (b).   (j) Exercise 63, part (b).
(e) Exercise 61, part (a).   (k) Exercise 65, part (a).
(f) Exercise 61, part (b).

50 For each exercise in Chap. 7 listed below, first apply the value iteration algorithm for a shortest-route problem, as given in Sec. 11.9, with $\alpha = 1$ and y_i^0 calculated from the indicated initial set of arcs. Then apply the policy iteration algorithm, as given in Sec. 11.9, starting with the same initial set of arcs.

(a) Exercise 27, part (a), with arcs $(2, 1)$, $(3, 1)$, $(4, 1)$, $(5, 1)$, $(6, 4)$, $(7, 6)$, and $(8, 5)$.
(b) Exercise 28, part (a), with arcs $(1, 4)$, $(3, 2)$, $(4, 3)$, $(5, 1)$, $(6, 5)$, $(7, 3)$, and $(8, 6)$.
(c) Exercise 60, part (a), with arcs $(2, 1)$, $(3, 2)$, $(4, 3)$, $(5, 4)$, and $(6, 5)$.
(d) Exercise 60, part (b), with arcs $(1, 2)$, $(3, 2)$, $(4, 3)$, $(5, 4)$, and $(6, 5)$.
(e) Exercise 61, part (a), with arcs $(2, 1)$, $(3, 2)$, $(4, 3)$, $(5, 4)$, and $(6, 5)$.
(f) Exercise 61, part (b), with arcs $(1, 2)$, $(3, 2)$, $(4, 3)$, $(5, 4)$, and $(6, 5)$.
(g) Exercise 62, part (a), with arcs $(2, 1)$, $(3, 2)$, $(4, 1)$, $(5, 4)$, and $(6, 5)$.
(h) Exercise 62, part (b), with arcs $(1, 2)$, $(2, 3)$, $(4, 1)$, $(5, 4)$, and $(6, 5)$.
(i) Exercise 63, part (a), with arcs $(2, 1)$, $(3, 2)$, $(4, 3)$, $(5, 4)$, and $(6, 5)$.
(j) Exercise 63, part (b), with arcs $(1, 2)$, $(3, 2)$, $(4, 3)$, $(5, 4)$, and $(6, 5)$.
(k) Exercise 65, part (a), with arcs $(2, 1)$, $(3, 2)$, $(4, 5)$, $(5, 6)$, and $(6, 3)$.

MIND-EXPANDING EXERCISES

Exercises 51 through 56 refer to the regeneration model in Sec. 11.4.

51 (a) Show that f determined by (5) is the minimal discounted return among all (not necessarily stationary) policies.

(b) Show that a stationary policy is optimal among all policies. (*Hint:* you may wish to prove and use the result in exercise 55.)

52 Prove the Regeneration Model Horizon Theorem in Sec. 11.5.

*53 *Knapsack Problem.* Show the connection between the Regeneration Model Horizon Theorem in Sec. 11.5 and the proposition about the Knapsack Problem described in exercise 47 of Chap. 10.

54 Consider the value iteration algorithm in Sec. 11.6.

(a) Show that if all $R_k > 0$, then $f^{n+1} > f^n$ at every iteration n if $f^0 = 0$.
(b) Show that if $f^0 = R_k/(1 - \alpha^k)$ for a selected k, then $f^{n+1} \leq f^n$ at every iteration n.
(c) Show that if $f^{n-1} < f^n$, then $f^n < f^{n+1}$. (Do the same for both inequalities in the reverse direction.)
(d) Show that if Policy k is selected at iteration $n - 1$ but is discarded at iteration n, Policy k it will never be selected again.

55 Consider the policy iteration algorithm in Sec. 11.7. Suppose you have any strategy (not necessarily a stationary one) and an associated trial value f^n. Show that if Policy k′ satisfies the test $\alpha^{k'} f^n + R_{k'} < f^n$, then using Policy k′ as a stationary strategy over an unbounded horizon yields an associated value $f^{n+1} < f^n$. Give a verbal interpretation of this computational test.

56 *Graphical Representation of Policy Iteration.* Devise a graphical approach, analogous to that described in exercise 32, to display the computational process of policy iteration. Apply your approach to the numerical example (3) in Sec. 11.7. Would any other starting policy ($k \neq 1$) have required more iterations?

57 Consider the shortest-route problem as characterized by the extremal equations (4) in Sec. 11.9.

(a) Suggest a direct algorithm (that is, a method that computes the correct value for each y_i once and for all) when the network is acyclic. (*Hint:* modify the approach in Sec. 7.7.)
(b) Apply your method to Mark Off's routing problem in Fig. 8.1, letting $\alpha = \frac{1}{2}$ (for simplicity).

58 Consider the policy iteration algorithm for solving the shortest-route problem in Sec. 11.9.

(a) Show that when $\alpha = 1$, at every iteration the trial set of arcs in *Step 2* has the property that each node is connected by a path to the terminal.
(b) Construct an example that shows the property in part (a) need not hold when $\alpha < 1$. Suggest a way to calculate y_i^n when the trial set of arcs contains loops; give a verbal interpretation to the values for y_i^n that are determined by your method. (Be certain your approach ensures that the algorithm eventually finds shortest routes.)

CONTENTS

CHAPTER 12

Optimization Methods for An Unbounded Horizon

12.1 DISCRETE DYNAMIC PROGRAMMING

You are now ready to integrate the various ideas you have learned about optimization in an unbounded horizon and solution by successive approximations. You should study this chapter with two purposes in mind:

(i) To discover how to characterize mathematically an optimal solution to a model with an unbounded horizon.

(ii) To see how such a solution can be obtained by techniques of successive approximation.

It is less important that you master the details of the numerical techniques. Furthermore, in real applications you would not manually calculate answers but would rely on electronic computers. To make effective managerial use of these answers, however, you must be aware of the models' underpinnings so as to realize the true applicability of any particular numerical solution.

Inventory model. We begin with a concrete example that will illustrate the appearance of a dynamic programming optimization recursion appropriate to an unbounded horizon. Specifically, we consider a stationary inventory model that closely resembles the one you previously studied in Sec. 8.3. We use notation here to reflect the assumption of stationarity. The decision variable is

$$x \equiv \text{production quantity},$$

which we require to be a nonnegative integer. Let the associated production cost function in each period be $C(x)$, and the holding cost function be $h(j)$, where j is the inventory level at the end of the period. Assume that the demand requirement is the same every period, namely d (a positive integer), and that all demand must be met on time. As usual, let α be the one-period discount factor, where $0 \le \alpha < 1$.

Define

$$f_n(i) = \text{present value of an optimum production policy when entering inventory is } i \text{ and } n \text{ periods remain.}$$

Then the appropriate dynamic programming recursion for a finite horizon model is

$$(1) \qquad f_n(i) = \operatorname*{minimum}_{x} \; [C(x) + h(i + x - d) + \alpha f_{n-1}(i + x - d)],$$

where the minimization is taken over nonnegative integer values of $x \ge d - i$.

A plausible infinite stage analogue of (1) is

$$(2) \quad f(i) = \operatorname*{minimum}_{x} \; [C(x) + h(i + x - d) + \alpha f(i + x - d)] \quad (0 \le \alpha < 1).$$

Here $f(i)$ is interpreted as the present value of an optimal policy over an unbounded horizon, given the inventory entering the current period is i.

Notice several points of difference between (1) and (2). The most important is that the *same* function $f(i)$ appears on both sides of the relation (2). For this reason (2) is called a **functional** or **extremal equation**—actually, a *set* of equations, one for each possible value of the state variable, entering inventory i. Hence (2) deals with an entire *function* $f(i)$ of the state variable. As you should recall from the discussion of the simple functional equation for the regeneration model in Sec. 11.4, you must determine whether the equations in (2) have a unique finite solution.

But rather than analyzing in depth this specific model (2), you will make further headway by analyzing the extremal equations of a more general model for which the inventory example is merely a special case (after imposing a few additional mild restrictions). In preparation for this general model, observe how (2) can be characterized in terms of a network optimization problem.

Assume the number of possible levels for entering inventory is finite, and let each node of the network correspond to one of these levels. Given a Node i, the decision to produce x can be indicated by drawing an arc from Node i to Node i + x − d. The associated arc cost is $C(x) + h(i + x - d)$. Substitute the symbol y_i for $f(i)$ in (2), and so y_i is a present value associated with Node i. The network now closely resembles that in Sec. 11.9, except here there is no terminal, so the entire path implied by the value of y_i is really endless.

Network characterization. Consider a network comprised of a set of p nodes and a set of directed arcs connecting some of the nodes. Assume that every node has at least one arc leading out. In other words, assume it is possible to go from any node to at least one other node. Each arc (i, j) has an associated return or cost c_{ij} and a traversal time of one period. The discount factor is designated α as before.

Imagine starting a path at any arbitrarily selected Node i. Suppose you travel from Node i to Node j and thereby incur a cost c_{ij}. When you get to Node j, suppose you then go on to Node k, which adds to the discounted cost αc_{jk}. If you continue the process indefinitely, the path never ends. More and more costs are added, but with higher and higher powers of the discount factor $\alpha < 1$. Let y_i denote the present value of an *optimal* unending path starting at Node i.

If you adopt a stationary policy, then every time you come back to a node, you take the same arc out that you did on the previous visit. If a stationary policy exists that is optimal, then the corresponding y_i satisfy the functional equations

$$(3) \qquad y_i = \underset{\substack{(i,\,j)\ \text{in} \\ \text{network}}}{\text{minimum}} (\alpha y_j + c_{ij}) \quad \text{for each Node i} \quad (0 \leq \alpha < 1).$$

(The problem of finding a path that minimizes average return per period is treated in Sec. 12.2.) Notice that no node is distinguished as a terminal. In this model, it is convenient to allow arcs (i, i), because an optimal path in an unbounded horizon may lead from Node i back to itself repeatedly. (For example, the network corresponding to the *infinite* stage regeneration model of Sec. 11.4 has only a single node and N arcs leading out of and back into this node.)

In stating the extremal equations (3), we assumed the existence of an optimal stationary policy and the corresponding y_i. To be able to use (3) for all actual applications, however, you must know the answers to the questions:

(i) Can the extremal equations (3) always be solved by unique finite values for every y_i?

(ii) If so, is a corresponding stationary strategy truly optimal?

In other words, before applying numerical techniques, you must ascertain whether the functional equations in (3) invariably have a solution. When they do, an arc (i, j) giving the minimum for Node i is a component of a **stationary policy** or **strategy**: traverse (i, j) *whenever* you are at Node i. Since there is only a finite number of nodes, eventually you will be repeatedly coursing a loop of arcs. The particular **cycle** or **circulation** can depend on where you are at the initial period. The second question, then, is whether it is impossible to do better by another stationary strategy or by a nonstationary strategy—that is, one that keeps track of the previous events that lead you to Node i.

Both (i) and (ii) have affirmative answers. It can be rigorously demonstrated that:

STATIONARY POLICY THEOREM. There always exist unique finite y_i that satisfy the extremal equations (3), and a corresponding stationary policy is optimal among all possible policies.

The existence of a stationary policy that is truly optimal is also demonstrable if the optimality criterion is minimum equivalent average return per period for $\alpha = 1$. However, (3) is not the appropriate set of functional equations; this case is taken up in Sec. 12.3.

With almost trivial modifications, the model can be generalized to include the situation in which more than a single period is needed to traverse an arc. The necessary modification in the notation makes the formulas look complicated (an α_{ij} would appear instead of α in almost all the formulas). Rather than clutter the expressions with extra subscripts, we treat this more general case only in the advanced material.

▶At the end of Sec. 10.7, we gave a fairly general canonical form for a finite horizon model. If we now include a discount factor α, the recursion is

(i) $f_n(s) = \underset{d_n \text{ in } D_n(s)}{\text{optimum}} \{R_n(s, d_n) + \alpha f_{n-1}[T_n(s, d_n)]\}$ for every s in S_n and $f_0(s) \equiv 0$,

where s is the state of the system, S_n is the set of all possible states at Stage n, d_n is the decision at Stage n, $D_n(s)$ is the set of all the feasible values for d_n, $R_n(s, d_n)$ is the immediate economic return of decision d_n given that the system is in State s, and $T_n(s, d_n)$ is the transformed state of the system at the next stage.

Assume that the structure of the model is stationary, so that the terms in (i) can be simplified to S, $D(s)$, $R(s, d)$, and $T(s, d)$ for every n. Further suppose there is an optimal strategy that is stationary. Then a natural infinite stage analogue of (i) is

(ii) $f(s) = \underset{d \text{ in } D(s)}{\text{optimum}} \{R(s, d) + \alpha f[T(s, d)]\}$ for every s in S $(0 \le \alpha < 1)$.

We also postulate that the system can be in only one of a finite number of states, which for convenience can be numbered $s = 1, 2, \ldots, p$, and similarly, that $D(s)$ contains only a finite number of decisions. Given these two structural assumptions, we refer to the model (ii) as a **discrete dynamic programming problem.**

There is a unique correspondence between the network extremal equations (2) and formulation (ii) provided that $T(s, d) = T(s, d')$ only if $d = d'$. Each State s corresponds to a Node s, and $f(s) = y_s$. The decision d represents an arc from Node s to Node $T(s, d)$, and $R(s, d)$ is the associated arc cost.

Consider a network in which each arc (i, j) has an associated traversal time of h_{ij} periods, and all h_{ij} do not necessarily equal 1. Let the corresponding discount factor be defined as

(iii) $\alpha_{ij} \equiv \alpha^{h_{ij}}.$

Then instead of (3), the extremal equations for this more general problem are written as

(iv) $y_i = \underset{\substack{(i, j) \text{ in} \\ \text{network}}}{\text{minimum}} (\alpha_{ij} y_j + c_{ij})$ for each Node i $(0 \le \alpha < 1)$.   ◀

12.2 SUCCESSIVE APPROXIMATIONS

We discussed many of the important ideas motivating the several techniques of successive approximations in Sec. 11.5, where we dealt with the regeneration model. These comments are equally applicable here, and you may want to quickly review them before getting into the details below.

In brief, we examine two approaches. In the first, we guess at the unknown function values y_i and at each iteration improve on the current guess or approximation. In the second, we guess at an optimal policy. If our guess leads to a solution of the extremal equations, we stop; if not, we investigate an improved trial policy. The second method as compared to the first requires more computation at each iteration, but always converges in a finite number of steps.

Value iteration. A solution to the functional equations can be sought by **successive approximations in function space**. Following the fashion in Chap. 11, let y_i^0 be arbitrarily chosen guesses for y_i and apply the so-called value iteration algorithm

(1) $\qquad y_i^{n+1} = \underset{\substack{(i,j) \text{ in} \\ \text{network}}}{\text{minimum}} (\alpha y_j^n + c_{ij}) \quad$ for each $i \quad$ (value iteration).

Then each y_i^n tends to a limit, but as you already saw in the elementary regeneration model of Sec. 11.4, convergence of the y_i^n need *not* occur in a finite number of iterations. Furthermore, that a strategy is the same for several iterations of (1) does *not* indicate that it is truly optimal for an unbounded horizon. In fact, even as the number of iterations n gets arbitrarily large, there need not be convergence in policy, that is, there need not be a single policy that is optimal for *all* finite $n \geq N$, no matter how large the value for N.

By starting with every $y_i^0 = 0$, the process is the same as looking at a certain finite horizon model. Specifically, y_i^n represents the present value of an optimal path starting from Node i and traversing n arcs. Analogous to the Regeneration Model Horizon Theorem of Sec. 11.5, there is an n^* such that for each $n > n^*$, *any* optimal strategy for the current decision in the n-period finite horizon model is also an optimal stationary strategy for the unbounded horizon model. Further, it is possible to calculate n^* given the data c_{ij} and α, so that the approach can be applied.

If all $c_{ij} \geq 0$ and all $y_i^0 = 0$, the y_i^n increase monotonically. Convergence from above is obtained for *any* c_{ij} if you initially select a trial strategy and calculate y_i^0 accordingly, using the formula (2) below. Then if you arbitrarily stop at iteration m and use the immediate optimal policy from the value iteration (1) as a stationary strategy in the unbounded horizon model, the corresponding present values will be no larger than the y_i^m in (1).

▶ The proof that the y_i^n converge to y_i for arbitrary y_i^0 is analogous to the argument given in Sec. 11.6 for the infinite stage regeneration model. We present the proof for the more general network in which the discount factor for arc (i,j) is α_{ij}.

For each Node i, let arc (i,j^*) be optimal for the unbounded horizon case and arc (i,j) be optimal at iteration n of (1). Then

(i) $\qquad\qquad\qquad y_i = \alpha_{ij^*} y_{j^*} + c_{ij^*} \quad$ for each i

(ii) $\qquad\qquad\qquad y_i^n \leq \alpha_{ij^*} y_{j^*}^{n-1} + c_{ij^*} \quad$ for each i,

so that

(iii) $\qquad\qquad\qquad y_i^n - y_i \leq \alpha_{ij^*}(y_{j^*}^{n-1} - y_{j^*}) \leq \alpha d_{n-1}$,

where $d_{n-1} \equiv \underset{k}{\text{maximum}} |y_k^{n-1} - y_k|$.

Similarly,

(iv) $\qquad\qquad\qquad y_i^n = \alpha_{ij} y_j^{n-1} + c_{ij}$

(v) $\qquad\qquad\qquad y_i \leq \alpha_{ij} y_j + c_{ij}$,

so that

(vi) $$y_i - y_i^n \leq \alpha_{ij}(y_j - y_j^{n-1}) \leq \alpha d_{n-1}.$$

Therefore,

(vii) $$|y_i^n - y_i| \leq \alpha d_{n-1} \leq \alpha^n d_0.$$

Convergence follows since $0 \leq \alpha < 1$.

Suppose all $c_{ij} \geq 0$ and all $y_i^0 = 0$. Then you can establish that the y_i^n are monotonically increasing by the following *inductive* argument. For $n = 1$ and each i,

(viii) $$y_i^1 = \underset{\substack{(i,j) \text{ in} \\ \text{network}}}{\text{minimum}} (\alpha_{ij} \cdot 0 + c_{ij}) \geq 0 = y_i^0,$$

so $y_i^1 \geq y_i^0$. Assume $y_i^n \geq y_i^{n-1}$ for $n = 1, 2, \ldots, m$, and each i. Let arc (i,j) be optimal at iteration m + 1. Then

(ix) $$y_i^{m+1} = \alpha_{ij} y_j^m + c_{ij} \geq \alpha_{ij} y_j^{m-1} + c_{ij} \geq \underset{\substack{(i,j) \text{ in} \\ \text{network}}}{\text{minimum}} (\alpha_{ij} y_j^{m-1} + c_{ij}) = y_i^m,$$

and therefore $y_i^n \geq y_i^{n-1}$ for $n = m + 1$.

Similarly, if the y_i^0 are calculated by an initial strategy, you can prove inductively that convergence is from above. For $n = 1$ and each i,

(x) $$y_i^1 = \underset{\substack{(i,j) \text{ in} \\ \text{network}}}{\text{minimum}} (\alpha_{ij} y_j^0 + c_{ij}) \leq \alpha_{ik} y_k^0 + c_{ik} = y_i^0,$$

where (i, k) is the arc in the initial strategy, and so $y_i^1 \leq y_i^0$. Assume $y_i^n \leq y_i^{n-1}$ for $n = 1, 2, \ldots, m$ and each i. Let arc (i,j) be optimal at iteration m. Then

(xi) $$y_i^{m+1} \leq \alpha_{ij} y_j^m + c_{ij} \leq \alpha_{ij} y_j^{m-1} + c_{ij} = y_i^m$$

and therefore $y_i^n \leq y_i^{n-1}$ for $n = m + 1$.

The following example, based on a network representation of a choice between Policies B and D in Fig. 11.1, p. 363, for $\alpha = .5$, shows how the y_i^n converge without a corresponding convergence in policy. Assume the network consists of four nodes, but that there is a nontrivial decision only at Node 1:

(I)

| Node 1: | $c_{12} = 2\frac{2}{3}$ | $c_{13} = 3$ | Node 2: | $c_{22} = 2$ |

Node 1: $c_{12} = 2\frac{2}{3}$ $c_{13} = 3$ Node 2: $c_{22} = 2$

Node 3: $c_{34} = 1$ Node 4: $c_{43} = 3$,

and let $\alpha = .5$. Draw the network corresponding to (I). Also verify that

(II) $$y_1 = 4\frac{2}{3} \quad y_2 = 4 \quad y_3 = 3\frac{1}{3} \quad y_4 = 4\frac{2}{3}$$

satisfy the functional equations and that arcs $(1, 2)$ and $(1, 3)$ are *both* optimal.

Begin the function space algorithm with all $y_i^0 = 0$. Then the iterations yield, for $n = 1, 2, 3$,

(III)
$$y_1^1 = \text{minimum } [.5(0) + 2\tfrac{2}{3}, .5(0) + 3] = 2\tfrac{2}{3} \quad \text{for arc } (1, 2)$$
$$y_2^1 = .5(0) + 2 = 2 \quad y_3^1 = .5(0) + 1 = 1 \quad y_4^1 = .5(0) + 3 = 3$$

(IV)
$$y_1^2 = \text{minimum } [.5(2) + 2\tfrac{2}{3}, .5(1) + 3] = 3\tfrac{1}{2} \quad \text{for arc } (1, 3)$$
$$y_2^2 = .5(2) + 2 = 3 \quad y_3^2 = .5(3) + 1 = 2\tfrac{1}{2} \quad y_4^2 = .5(1) + 3 = 3\tfrac{1}{2}$$

(V)
$$y_1^3 = \text{minimum } [.5(3) + 2\tfrac{2}{3}, .5(2\tfrac{1}{2}) + 3] = 4\tfrac{1}{6} \quad \text{for arc } (1, 2)$$
$$y_2^3 = .5(3) + 2 = 3\tfrac{1}{2} \quad y_3^3 = .5(3\tfrac{1}{2}) + 1 = 2\tfrac{3}{4} \quad y_4^3 = .5(2\tfrac{1}{2}) + 3 = 4\tfrac{1}{4}.$$

As n increases, the values of y_i^n approach the values for y_i in (II), but arc $(1, 2)$ always gives the minimum for n odd, and arc $(1, 3)$ always gives the minimum for n even. Hence there is never convergence in policy. ◀

Policy iteration. You can solve the extremal equations (1) by the **successive approximations in policy space** algorithm:

Step 1. Select an arbitrary initial policy, and let $n = 0$.

Step 2. Given the trial policy, calculate the y_i^n according to the value determination equations

(2) $$y_i^n = \alpha y_j^n + c_{ij} \quad \text{or} \quad y_i^n - \alpha y_j^n = c_{ij}$$
$$\text{for each Node i} \quad \text{(value determination routine),}$$

where arc (i, j) is the decision at Node i indicated by the specific policy being evaluated.

Step 3. Test for a policy improvement by calculating

(3) $$\underset{\substack{(i, j) \text{ in} \\ \text{network}}}{\text{minimum}} (\alpha y_j^n + c_{ij}) \equiv Y_i^n \quad \text{for each } i \quad \text{(test quantity).}$$

Step 4. Terminate the iterations if $Y_i^n = y_i^n$ for all i. Otherwise, revise the policy at each Node k, where $Y_k^n < y_k^n$, by using an arc yielding Y_k^n in (3). Increase n to $n + 1$, and return to *Step 2* with the new trial policy.

Mechanics and logic of policy iteration. Observe that the value determination routine (2) requires the solution of a set of simultaneous linear equations. Since there is one equation and one variable y_i^n for each Node i and $0 \le \alpha < 1$, (2) always has a unique solution. In applying (2) you will find it helpful to solve first for the y_i^n included in a cycle and then for the remaining variables in terms of the previously found quantities. The method terminates when $Y_i^n = y_i^n$ for all i, because then the y_i^n satisfy the extremal equations.

For $i = k$ in (3), you can interpret the quantity $(\alpha y_j^n + c_{kj})$ as the present value of going from Node k to Node j, and *afterwards* using the complete strategy being tested at iteration n—including the arc *previously* specified for Node k by the trial strategy at iteration n. Now if for some k you find $Y_k^n < y_k^n$, using arc (k, j), then it is plausible that you can do better yet by *always* using that arc whenever you are at Node k. The new value for y_k^{n+1} reflects such a revised policy.

The important conclusion then, is that you can test whether a strategy that *consistently* uses arc (k, j) gives an improvement by employing a criterion that assumes (k, j) is used only for the *current* decision! (Reread the conclusion because this insightful result is not at all obvious.)

The policy space approximation has the properties:

(i) $y_i^{n+1} \le y_i^n$ for each Node i, and $y_k^{n+1} < y_k^n$ if $Y_k^n < y_k^n$.

(ii) The algorithm terminates in a finite number of iterations.

(iii) At termination, a strategy yielding Y_i^n is optimal.

As you will see more clearly in Sec. 12.6, the policy space approximation method has these properties because it is closely analogous to the simplex method. At each iteration the current *policy* is feasible; however, the corresponding values of the variables y_i^n might not be feasible in that they might not satisfy the extremal equations. The stopping rule represents a feasibility check. A proof of finite convergence to an optimal solution by policy iteration closely parallels a proof that the simplex method stops in a finite number of iterations. The crux of the argument is that because of (i), you never return to a policy once tested. Since there is only a finite number of possible policies, eventually the iterations end.

In comparing successive approximation in function space and in policy space, note that the same type of calculation appears on the right-hand side of (1) and the left-hand side of (3). In the value iteration method, the resultant values become the new approximations for y_i at the next iteration. In contrast, the new approximations for y_i in the policy iteration method are found by the additional calculations involved in solving the value determination equations (2) at the next iteration. This added computational burden is the price paid to ensure convergence in a finite number of iterations.

The method of policy iteration will be illustrated by numerical examples in Sec. 12.4.

▶ In a network where the discount factor is α_{ij} for arc (i, j), you need only substitute α_{ij} for α in formulas (1), (2), and (3). ◀

12.3 MINIMIZING AVERAGE RETURN PER PERIOD

The extremal equations for y_i in Sec. 12.1 cannot be expected to work when $\alpha = 1$, since then a summation of returns over an unbounded horizon may be infinite (for example, when all $c_{ij} > 0$). To derive the functional equation required, we re-express the formulas in terms of equivalent average return per period, and then let $\alpha = 1$.

To begin, consider calculating mentally the equivalent average return per period for each possible cycle in the network, and let the symbol $\bar{c}$ denote the smallest such value for $\alpha = 1$. Of course, in an actual problem you would not want to calculate all of these averages, and therefore, typically, you would not know the actual value of $\bar{c}$ until you performed the optimization. But for the algebraic development to follow, merely view $\bar{c}$ as a symbol representing this constant, which does in fact exist.

To avoid treating a host of special cases, assume the network satisfies one additional property: *suppose there exists a path—more precisely, a directed chain—from every Node i to at least one of the nodes associated with a cycle yielding $\bar{c}$.* (For example, this condition is satisfied if there is a directed chain from every Node i to every Node j.) The approach explained below can be modified to treat networks in which this property does not hold.

We will develop functional equations involving $\bar{c}$. As you will see, the equations will also involve other quantities, w_i, which are required for the computations. We caution that our line of argument below really does not stand up to the scrutiny of rigorous mathematical analysis. We only intend for it to provide a means of motivating the end result, which by itself may look strange. So if you are impatient, you can skip the heuristic development and go directly to the extremal equations (5).

It is convenient to relate the equivalent average return $(1 - \alpha)y_i$ at each Node i to $\bar{c}$ by the following definitive relation for w_i:

$$(1) \qquad (1 - \alpha)y_i \equiv (1 - \alpha)w_i + \bar{c} \quad (0 \leq \alpha < 1).$$

(Give a verbal interpretation of w_i.) Thus

$$(2) \qquad y_i \equiv w_i + \frac{\bar{c}}{1 - \alpha} \quad (0 \leq \alpha < 1).$$

You can interpret w_i as the difference between y_i and $\bar{c}/(1 - \alpha)$, which is the present value of receiving $\bar{c}$ every period over an unbounded horizon. [Already the notation is inexact because both y_i and w_i depend on α; a precise notation is $y_i(\alpha)$ and $w_i(\alpha)$.]

Then the extremal equations in Sec. 12.1 can be rewritten as:

$$(3) \qquad w_i + \frac{\bar{c}}{1 - \alpha} = \underset{\substack{(i, j) \text{ in} \\ \text{network}}}{\text{minimum}} \left[\alpha\left(w_j + \frac{\bar{c}}{1 - \alpha}\right) + c_{ij} \right] \quad \text{for each Node i.}$$

Since $\bar{c}$ is a constant, we can either take the expression involving $\bar{c}$ on the left of (3) and move it to the right, or take the expression involving $\bar{c}$ on the right of (3) and move it to the left. We choose the former approach because it generalizes to the case where each arc (i, j) may have a different discount factor α_{ij}. Thus, as you should verify, (3) can be stated as

$$(4) \qquad w_i = \underset{\substack{(i, j) \text{ in} \\ \text{network}}}{\text{minimum}} \ (\alpha w_j + c_{ij} - \bar{c}).$$

When $\alpha = 1$, (4) simplifies to

$$(5) \qquad w_i = \underset{\substack{(i, j) \text{ in} \\ \text{network}}}{\text{minimum}} \ (w_j + c_{ij} - \bar{c}) \quad \text{for each Node i,}$$

or equivalently after moving the constant $\bar{c}$ to the left-hand side

$$(6) \qquad w_i + \bar{c} = \underset{\substack{(i, j) \text{ in} \\ \text{network}}}{\text{minimum}} \ (w_j + c_{ij}) \quad \text{for each Node i.}$$

[Using precise notation, we let w_i in (5) and (6) be the limiting value of $w_i(\alpha)$ as α approaches 1 from below.]

So far we have assumed that it is meaningful to transform the previous extremal equations for $\alpha < 1$ into extremal equations (5) for $\alpha = 1$. This manipulation presupposes the existence of a stationary strategy that is optimal in terms of containing a cycle having minimum equivalent average return per period. The assumption *is* justified, because by rigorous argument the following theorem can be established:

STATIONARY POLICY THEOREM. There always exist a unique finite $\bar{c}$ and finite w_j that satisfy the extremal equations (5), and a corresponding stationary policy contains a cycle with an equivalent return per period that is minimal among all possible policies.

As in the case $\alpha < 1$, an arc where the minimum occurs in (5) or (6) indicates an action to take if you are at Node i. Such a strategy must contain at least one cycle. Consequently, the strategy specifies a path leaving the current Node i and leading to a loop having minimum equivalent average return per period. (Of course, Node i may be included in the cycle.) If an optimal stationary strategy contains more than one cycle, then the equivalent average return per period must be the same for all cycles. This follows from our earlier assumption that you can always find a path from any Node i to a node associated with a cycle yielding $\bar{c}$. Since $\bar{c}$ is associated with a cycle and the c_{ij} are stationary, the value $\bar{c}$ is also the minimum average return per period among all possible cycles. That is, the "equivalent average return per period" approach yields a strategy that is optimal for the criterion "average return per period."

As we mentioned, the main interest in the w_i is computational—you have to find values for the w_i in order to calculate $\bar{c}$ and an optimal policy. But there are several interpretations of the economic significance of w_i. Here is one. You can see from (2) that for any two i and j,

$$y_i - y_j \equiv w_i - w_j \quad (0 \leq \alpha < 1).$$

So as α approaches the value 1, the limiting value of the *difference* between the present values for Node i and Node j is given by $w_i - w_j$. Therefore, $w_i - w_j$ can be thought of as the *incremental* cost from being in Node i rather than Node j when $\alpha = 1$.

Policy iteration. In the case $\alpha = 1$, you would use the technique of **successive approximations in policy space** to solve (5) or (6). For expository convenience, assume that *at every iteration the trial policy has a single cycle*. The added computational details needed to encompass the possibility of having more than one cycle at an iteration are given in the special material at the end of this section.

When you find values for w_i that satisfy the extremal equations (5) or (6), then adding any constant to these values yields new amounts for w_i that also satisfy the equations. Thus the w_i are not unique, and in the algorithm below it is convenient to set one of the values to zero. For the sake of definiteness, we make the normalization $w_1 = 0$.

The procedure is:

Step 1. Select an arbitrary initial policy, and let $n = 0$.

Step 2. Given the trial policy, calculate w_i^n and $\bar{c}^n$ according to the value determination equations:

(7)
$$w_i^n - w_j^n + \bar{c}^n = c_{ij} \quad \text{for each Node i} \quad \text{(value determination routine)}$$
$$w_1^n = 0,$$

where arc (i, j) is the decision indicated at Node i by the specific policy being evaluated.

Step 3. Test for a policy improvement by calculating

(8)
$$\underset{\substack{(i, j) \text{ in} \\ \text{network}}}{\text{minimum}} (w_j^n + c_{ij} - \bar{c}^n) \equiv W_i^n \quad \text{for each } i \quad \text{(test quantity).}$$

Step 4. Terminate the iterations if $W_i^n = w_i^n$ for all i. Otherwise, revise the policy at each Node k where $W_k^n < w_k^n$, using an arc yielding W_k^n in (8). Increase n to $n + 1$, and return to *Step 2* with the new trial policy.

Mechanics. Observe that (7) requires the solution of a set of simultaneous linear equations. Given that the trial policy has a single cycle, there is always a unique solution to (7). Notice if you sum the equations (7) for the nodes contained in the cycle, the w_i^n cancel each other and yield as a result

(9)
$$\bar{c}^n = \sum_{\substack{(i, j) \\ \text{in cycle}}} c_{ij}/\text{number of arcs in cycle.}$$

We exhibited the test quantity (8) that came from the extremal equations (5). Note that the term $\bar{c}^n$ in (8) has no influence on the minimization. Therefore you do not *have* to subtract when finding the minimum, but only when calculating the resultant value of W_i^n. We find it convenient to express the test as (8) because this form generalizes to the case where there are different traversal times for the arcs.

With proper precautions to avoid cycling phenomena, such as can occur in the simplex method, the algorithm has the properties:

(i) At every iteration $\bar{c}^n \leq \bar{c}^{n-1}$.
(ii) The algorithm terminates in a finite number of iterations.
(iii) At termination, a strategy yielding W_i^n is optimal.

▶Suppose h_{ij} is the number of time periods to traverse arc (i, j), and $\alpha_{ij} \equiv \alpha^{h_{ij}}$. Then (3), (4), and (5) would be written as

(I)
$$w_i + \frac{\bar{c}}{1 - \alpha} - \underset{\substack{(i, j) \text{ in} \\ \text{network}}}{\text{minimum}} \left[\alpha_{ij}\left(w_j + \frac{\bar{c}}{1 - \alpha}\right) + c_{ij} \right]$$

(II)
$$w_i = \underset{\substack{(i, j) \text{ in} \\ \text{network}}}{\text{minimum}} [\alpha_{ij}w_j + c_{ij} - (1 + \alpha + \cdots + \alpha^{h_{ij}-1})\bar{c}]$$

(III)
$$w_i = \underset{\substack{(i, j) \text{ in} \\ \text{network}}}{\text{minimum}} (w_j + c_{ij} - h_{ij}\bar{c}).$$

Accordingly, the coefficient h_{ij} modifies $\bar{c}^n$ in (7) and (8). And the denominator in (9) is the sum of the h_{ij} for arcs (i, j) in the cycle.

Even though the initial strategy may contain a single cycle, a trial strategy at a later iteration can have two or more cycles. In this event the algorithm must be modified slightly. Since any trial strategy indicates that each Node i is either in one cycle or on a path to one cycle, all the nodes can be partitioned into disjoint groups, one group for each cycle. Let $\bar{c}_i^n$ denote the average return per period for the cycle to which Node i is associated. We continue to use the notation for the general network in which h_{ij} is the number of periods to traverse arc (i, j).

Then given a trial strategy, you solve

(i) $$w_i^n - w_j^n + h_{ij}\bar{c}_i^n = c_{ij} \quad \text{for each Node i,}$$

where you also let all the $\bar{c}_i^n$ associated with the same cycle be equal, and you arbitrarily select one i in each cycle to let $w_i^n = 0$. [For example, if Nodes 1, 2, and 3 are all the nodes associated with one of the cycles, you have in addition to (i) the equations $\bar{c}_1^n = \bar{c}_2^n = \bar{c}_3^n$ and, say, $w_1^n = 0$.]

After (i), calculate

(ii) $$\operatorname*{minimum}_{\substack{(i,\,j)\text{ in}\\ \text{network}}} (\bar{c}_j^n) \equiv \bar{C}_i^n \quad \text{for each } i.$$

If $\bar{C}_k^n < \bar{c}_k^n$ for any k, then revise the strategy accordingly from (ii). If $\bar{C}_k^n = \bar{c}_k^n$ for any k, then apply (8), using $\bar{c}_k^n$ instead of $\bar{c}^n$, and revise the strategy if $W_k^n < w_k^n$. If the policy has been revised and still has more than one cycle, return to calculation (i); otherwise return to (7). If $\bar{C}_k^n = \bar{c}_k^n$ for every k, then $\bar{c}_k^n$ will be equal for all k; and letting $\bar{c}^n$ be the common value, apply (8) as before.

You can gain further insight into (5) by relating it to the shortest-route model for a general network. Let

(iii) $$\bar{c}_{ij} \equiv c_{ij} - h_{ij}\bar{c}.$$

Then (5) can be viewed as

(iv) $$w_i = \operatorname*{minimum}_{\substack{(i,\,j)\text{ in}\\ \text{network}}} (w_j + \bar{c}_{ij}) \quad \text{for every } i \text{ and } w_1 = 0.$$

There is one difference between (iv) and the usual shortest-route problem, such as that in Sec. 11.9. Although $w_1 = 0$, Node 1 really is not a terminal. Now a strategy may well include an arc that goes from Node 1 *to* Node j.

Suppose you have guessed a strategy for which $\bar{c}$ is the associated minimal equivalent average return per period along any cycle. Then the sum of the corresponding $\bar{c}_{ij}$ along the same cycle is 0. If all other possible cycles in the network have a nonnegative sum of $\bar{c}_{ij}$, the proposed strategy is optimal. In such an instance, a shortest-route technique of successive approximations in function space leads to a solution of (iv). If, however, a cycle exists whose average return is negative in terms of the current $\bar{c}_{ij}$, an improvement exists, and the shortest-route algorithm in Secs. 7.6 and 11.9 breaks down. In performing the steps, you eventually find that you are repeatedly revising those w_i that are a part of a cycle that represents an improvement.

Thus the following hybrid algorithm emerges. Select a stationary strategy and calculate the resultant trial $\bar{c}$. Use the value iteration algorithm (5) in Sec. 11.9, with $\bar{c}_{ij}$ from (iii). Let $w_i^0 = \infty$ for $i \neq 1$. If the calculations discover a loop such that the corresponding sum of the $\bar{c}_{ij}$ is negative, revise the stationary strategy accordingly, recalculate $\bar{c}$ for this improved cycle, revise the $\bar{c}_{ij}$, and repeat the process. When the shortest-route algorithm terminates with values for the w_i, the corresponding $\bar{c}$ is optimal. ◀

12.4 NUMERICAL EXAMPLES OF POLICY ITERATION

The models in this chapter are complex, and studying a few examples will help you master the optimization problem. The illustrations below and in Sec. 12.5 are for this purpose.

Examples 1 and 2 exhibit the detailed calculations performed in the policy iteration technique, where $0 \leq \alpha < 1$. In Example 3 there is more than one optimal strategy for $\alpha = 1$, and the iterations terminate *without* selecting one of these policies that *also* is optimal for $0 \leq \alpha \leq 1$. It is possible to add further instructions to the policy iteration algorithm so that it always selects a policy that is optimal not only for $\alpha = 1$ but for all α close to 1.

In Examples 4, 5, and 6, when $\alpha = 1$ the optimal strategy for *any* finite horizon n depends on whether n is odd or even. Nevertheless, Examples 4 and 5 demonstrate that the policy iteration algorithm can indicate a unique determination of an optimal strategy. Example 6, like Example 3, shows that when there are several optimal strategies, the technique may not distinguish between one that is correct only for $\alpha = 1$ and one that is optimal for $0 \leq \alpha \leq 1$. [In Example 7, at the first iteration a policy with two cycles is indicated, even though the initial strategy contained only one cycle; thus (i) and (ii) of the previous section are applied.]

From these illustrations you will see why you must understand the broad economic implications of formulas and algorithms. Blindly applying them can lead you to numerically correct but patently unsuitable answers.

You will find it helpful to copy on paper the formulas for value determination (2) and the test quantity (3) from Sec. 12.2, where $\alpha < 1$, and the corresponding formulas (7) and (8) from Sec. 12.3, where $\alpha = 1$.

Example 1. Consider the network in Fig. 12.1. The numbers on each arc indicate the corresponding c_{ij}. To initiate the policy iteration procedure, you must select a starting strategy consisting of an outward arc for each node. Let this policy be

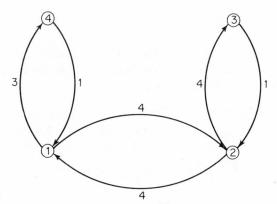

FIGURE 12.1. Example 1.

(1)
$$
\begin{array}{llll}
\text{Node 1:} & \text{arc } (1, 4) & \text{Node 2:} & \text{arc } (2, 1) \\
\text{Node 3:} & \text{arc } (3, 2) & \text{Node 4:} & \text{arc } (4, 1).
\end{array}
$$

Thus the strategy contains, as its only cycle, arcs $(1, 4)$ and $(4, 1)$.

Using the value determination formula (2) of Sec. 12.2, solve the following set of simultaneous linear equations for y_i^0:

(2)
$$
\begin{aligned}
y_1^0 &= \alpha y_4^0 + c_{14} \\
y_2^0 &= \alpha y_1^0 + c_{21} \\
y_3^0 &= \alpha y_2^0 + c_{32} \\
y_4^0 &= \alpha y_1^0 + c_{41},
\end{aligned}
$$

which can be written as

(3)
$$
\begin{aligned}
y_1^0 \qquad\qquad - \alpha y_4^0 &= 3 \\
-\alpha y_1^0 + \quad y_2^0 \qquad\qquad &= 4 \\
- \alpha y_2^0 + y_3^0 \qquad &= 1 \\
-\alpha y_1^0 \qquad\qquad + \quad y_4^0 &= 1.
\end{aligned}
$$

In a specific application, the value for α would be given. But here it will be useful to perform the calculations leaving α unspecified and showing how it affects the answers. You can solve the first and fourth relations in (3) for y_1^0 and y_4^0, these being the equations for the nodes in the cycle, and then the remaining relations can be solved. Verify that the answers are

(4)
$$
y_1^0 = \frac{3 + 1\alpha}{1 - \alpha^2}
$$

$$
y_2^0 = \alpha y_1^0 + 4 = \frac{4 + 3\alpha - 3\alpha^2}{1 - \alpha^2}
$$

$$
y_3^0 = \alpha y_2^0 + 1 = \frac{1 + 4\alpha + 2\alpha^2 - 3\alpha^3}{1 - \alpha^2}
$$

$$
y_4^0 = \frac{1 + 3\alpha}{1 - \alpha^2}.
$$

A glance at Fig. 12.1 shows that only the decisions for Nodes 1 and 2 are in question, because there is only a single arc out of Nodes 3 and 4. The test calculation (3) of Sec. 12.2 yields, for Node 1,

(5)
$$
\begin{aligned}
&\text{minimum } (\alpha y_2^0 + c_{12},\ \alpha y_4^0 + c_{14}) \\
&= \text{minimum} \left(\frac{4 + 4\alpha - \alpha^2 - 3\alpha^3}{1 - \alpha^2},\ \frac{3 + 1\alpha}{1 - \alpha^2} \right) \\
&= \frac{3 + 1\alpha}{1 - \alpha^2} \equiv Y_1^0 \quad \text{for arc } (1, 4)
\end{aligned}
$$

if $0 \leq \alpha < 1$. Similarly, for Node 2,

minimum $(\alpha y_1^0 + c_{21}, \ \alpha y_3^0 + c_{23})$

(6)
$$= \text{minimum} \left(\frac{4 + 3\alpha - 3\alpha^2}{1 - \alpha^2}, \frac{4 + \alpha + 2\alpha^3 - 3\alpha^4}{1 - \alpha^2} \right)$$

$$= \frac{4 + 3\alpha - 3\alpha^2}{1 - \alpha^2} \equiv Y_2^0 \quad \text{for arc } (2, 1)$$

if $\frac{2}{3} \leq \alpha < 1$.

Since $Y_i^0 = y_i^0$ for each Node i, the initial policy is optimal provided $\frac{2}{3} \leq \alpha < 1$. If $\alpha < \frac{2}{3}$, then the minimum in (6) would be for arc $(2, 3)$, and this decision would replace arc $(2, 1)$ at the next iteration. Explain why arc $(2, 3)$ is a better decision for values of α below $\frac{2}{3}$.

Verify that the test quantity for arc $(2, 3)$ in (6) really represents the present value of going from Node 2 to Node 3, back to Node 2, then to Node 1, and thereafter around the loop between Nodes 1 and 4. However, if $(2, 3)$ is actually used instead of $(2, 1)$, then the present value is calculated by going from Node 2 to Node 3 and back again in an endless loop. Thus you can determine if a repeated cycle between Nodes 2 and 3 is desirable by testing whether there is an improvement in making the loop only once.

From Fig. 12.1 you can also see that the strategy (1) is uniquely optimal for $\alpha = 1$. The minimum average cost cycle consists of arcs $(1, 4)$ and $(4, 1)$, so that $\bar{c} = (3 + 1)/2 = 2$.

Example 2. Consider the network and data in the previous illustration, but let $c_{23} = 3$. Since the starting strategy in (1) does not involve this arc, the trial values for y_i^0 are those in (4). Similarly, the test in (5) gives the same result. However,

(7)
$$\alpha y_3^0 + c_{23} = \frac{3 + \alpha + \alpha^2 + 2\alpha^3 - 3\alpha^4}{1 - \alpha^2},$$

and as a result,

(8)
$$\alpha y_3^0 + c_{23} \equiv Y_2^0 \quad \text{for arc } (2, 3),$$

when $0 \leq \alpha < 1$. Thus arc $(2, 3)$ replaces arc $(2, 1)$ in the strategy. This in turn means that for $n = 1$ the second equation in (3) is replaced by

(9)
$$-\alpha y_3^1 + y_2^1 = 3,$$

and the new solution is

(10)
$$y_1^1 = y_2^1 = \frac{3 + 1\alpha}{1 - \alpha^2}$$

$$y_3^1 = y_4^1 = \frac{1 + 3\alpha}{1 - \alpha^2}.$$

Now the test quantities for Nodes 1 and 2 are identical:

(11)
$$\text{minimum} \left(\frac{4 + 3\alpha - 3\alpha^2}{1 - \alpha^2}, \frac{3 + 1\alpha}{1 - \alpha^2} \right) = \frac{3 + 1\alpha}{1 - \alpha^2} \equiv Y_1^1 = Y_2^1$$

(Nodes 1 and 2)

for $0 \leq \alpha < 1$. The calculations stop, since $Y_i^1 = y_i^1$ for all i.

Example 3. Continue with the previous example, but let $\alpha = 1$. Looking at Fig. 12.1, where again $c_{23} = 3$, you see that the cycles between Nodes 1 and 4 and between Nodes 2 and 3 are equally good and optimal. If you use the same starting policy as (1), and apply the value determination routine (7) in Sec. 12.3, you obtain the system of simultaneous equations:

$$w_1^0 - w_4^0 = c_{14} - \bar{c}^0$$
$$w_2^0 - w_1^0 = c_{21} - \bar{c}^0$$
(12) $$w_3^0 - w_2^0 = c_{32} - \bar{c}^0$$
$$w_4^0 - w_1^0 = c_{41} - \bar{c}^0$$
$$w_1^0 = 0.$$

Check that the solution of (12) is

(13) $\bar{c}^0 = 2 \quad w_1^0 = 0 \quad w_2^0 = 2 \quad w_3^0 = 1 \quad w_4^0 = -1.$

The test calculations in (8) of Sec. 12.3 give

(14)   minimum $(w_2^0 + c_{12} - \bar{c}^0, \ w_4^0 + c_{14} - \bar{c}^0)$ (Node 1)
    $= $ minimum $(2 + 4 - 2, -1 + 3 - 2) = 0 \equiv W_1^0$ for arc $(1, 4)$

and

(15)   minimum $(w_1^0 + c_{21} - \bar{c}^0, \ w_3^0 + c_{23} - \bar{c}^0)$ (Node 2)
    $= $ minimum $(0 + 4 - 2, 1 + 3 - 2) = 2 \equiv W_2^0$ for both arcs.

The calculations terminate, since $W_i^0 = w_i^0$ for all i.

Notice that although the initial policy (1), which has a single cycle between Nodes 1 and 4, tests optimally, you probably would prefer to use the alternative optimal strategy, which includes the cycle between Nodes 2 and 3. The reason is that arc $(2, 3)$ is optimal not only when $\alpha = 1$, but this arc is *uniquely* optimal for $0 \le \alpha < 1$, as you found in (8).

▶Letting

(i) $\bar{c}_{ij} = c_{ij} - \bar{c} = c_{ij} - 2,$

Fig. 12.2 shows the network for

(ii) $w_i = \underset{\substack{(i, j) \text{ in} \\ \text{network}}}{\text{minimum}} (w_j + \bar{c}_{ij})$ and $w_1 = 0.$

Notice that the total length around an optimal cycle is 0, whereas the length around any other cycle is strictly positive.   ◀

Example 4. Consider the network in Fig. 12.3. To begin, suppose $c_{12} = 1.5$. Then if you examine the network, you quickly find that, for $\alpha = 1$, arc $(2, 3)$ is a better decision than arc $(2, 1)$. Period by period, starting at Node 2, a cycle between Nodes 2 and 3 accumulates less cost than between Nodes 2 and 1.

It is not so clear, however, whether for $\alpha = 1$ arc $(1, 3)$ is better than arc $(1, 2)$. To see why, calculate period by period the cumulative costs for a path

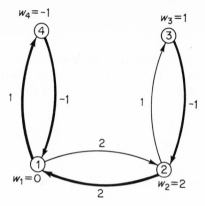

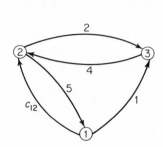

FIGURE 12.2. Example 3 ($\bar{c}_{ij}$).   FIGURE 12.3. Example 4.

starting at Node 1, going to Node 2, and looping between Nodes 2 and 3 thereafter. Compare those sums with the corresponding costs of going to Node 3 first.
You will find that arc $(1, 3)$ is better when the horizon is an odd number of periods
$(1, 3, 5, \ldots)$, and arc $(1, 2)$ is better when it is an even number.

What happens when you use the policy space algorithm? Let the starting
strategy be

(16)   Node 1:   arc $(1, 3)$ Node 2:   arc $(2, 3)$ Node 3:   arc $(3, 2)$.

Then the y_i^0 are found by solving

$$y_1^0 = \alpha y_3^0 + c_{13}$$

(17)
$$y_2^0 = \alpha y_3^0 + c_{23}$$

$$y_3^0 = \alpha y_2^0 + c_{32}.$$

Verify that the results are

$$y_1^0 = \frac{1 + 4\alpha + \alpha^2}{1 - \alpha^2}$$

(18)
$$y_2^0 = \frac{2 + 4\alpha}{1 - \alpha^2}$$

$$y_3^0 = \frac{4 + 2\alpha}{1 - \alpha^2}.$$

The test computation for Node 1 yields

minimum $(\alpha y_2^0 + c_{12}, \alpha y_3^0 + c_{13})$ (Node 1)

(19)
$$= \text{minimum} \left(\frac{1.5 + 2\alpha + 2.5\alpha^2}{1 - \alpha^2}, \frac{1 + 4\alpha + \alpha^2}{1 - \alpha^2} \right) \equiv Y_1^0 \quad \text{for arc } (1, 2)$$

if $\frac{1}{3} \leq \alpha < 1$. Thus for large α, arc $(1, 2)$ is better than arc $(1, 3)$, so the policy
in (16) must be altered. The revised optimal strategy gives

(20) $y_1^1 = Y_1^0 \quad y_2^1 = y_2^0 \quad y_3^1 = y_3^0.$

Next perform the policy iteration algorithm for $\alpha = 1$, and check that the above solution with arc $(1, 2)$ is uniquely optimal.

Example 5. Continue with the previous illustration, but here let $c_{12} = 2$. Once again, if the horizon is finite, arc $(1, 3)$ is strictly better for an odd number of periods and strictly worse for an even number. If you choose (16) as the starting strategy, (17) and (18) remain valid.

The test calculation for Node 1 is

$$(21) \qquad \underset{(1,2),\,(1.3)}{\text{minimum}} \left(\frac{2 + 2\alpha + 2\alpha^2}{1 - \alpha^2}, \frac{1 + 4\alpha + \alpha^2}{1 - \alpha^2} \right) \equiv Y_1^0 \quad \text{for arc } (1, 3),$$

when $0 \le \alpha < 1$. Therefore arc $(1, 3)$ is now optimal for all values of α below 1.

Example 6. Continue with the previous illustration, but let $\alpha = 1$. As you would suppose, arc $(1, 3)$ remains optimal. But if you test arc $(1, 2)$, it too is optimal according to the algorithm's criterion. The equations to be solved are

$$(22) \qquad \begin{aligned} w_1^0 - w_2^0 &= c_{12} - \bar{c}^0 \\ w_2^0 - w_3^0 &= c_{23} - \bar{c}^0 \\ w_3^0 - w_2^0 &= c_{32} - \bar{c}^0 \\ w_1^0 &= 0, \end{aligned}$$

with the results

$$(23) \qquad\qquad \bar{c}^0 = 3 \quad w_1^0 = 0 \quad w_2^0 = 1 \quad w_3^0 = 2.$$

Verify that you obtain the same answers using arc $(1, 3)$ instead.

The computation for Node 1 is

$$\begin{aligned} &\text{minimum } (w_2^0 + c_{12} - \bar{c}^0, \, w_3^0 + c_{13} - \bar{c}^0) \qquad\qquad &\text{(Node 1)} \\ (24) \quad &= \text{minimum } (1 + 2 - 3, 2 + 1 - 3) = 0 \equiv W_1^0 \\ &\qquad\qquad\qquad\qquad\qquad\qquad \text{for arcs } (1, 2) \text{ and } (1, 3), \end{aligned}$$

so the trial solution with $(1, 2)$ tests optimally.

▶**Example 7.** Consider the network in Fig. 12.4, where $\alpha = 1$. Let the starting strategy be

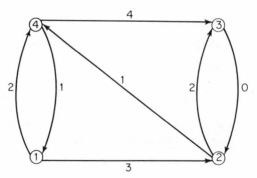

FIGURE 12.4. Example 7.

(iii)   Node 1: arc $(1, 4)$ Node 2: arc $(2, 4)$
         Node 3: arc $(3, 2)$ Node 4: arc $(4, 1)$.

Thus the only cycle is between Nodes 1 and 4. Verify that the corresponding solution is

(iv) $$\bar{c}^0 = \frac{3}{2} \quad w_1^0 = 0 \quad w_2^0 = -1 \quad w_3^0 = -\frac{5}{2} \quad w_4^0 = -\frac{1}{2}.$$

Then check that

$$W_1^0 = 0 = w_1^0 \quad \text{for arc } (1, 4)$$

$$W_2^0 = -2 < w_2^0 \quad \text{for arc } (2, 3)$$

(v)

$$W_3^0 = -\frac{5}{2} = w_3^0 \quad \text{for arc } (3, 2)$$

$$W_4^0 = -\frac{1}{2} = w_4^0 \quad \text{for arc } (4, 1).$$

The policy in (v) therefore represents an improvement. Notice that the new strategy has two cycles, and so (i) and (ii) of Sec. 12.3 must be used at the next iteration.

Accordingly, the value equations to be solved are

(vi)

$$w_1^1 - w_4^1 + \bar{c}_4^1 = 2 \quad \bar{c}_1^1 = \bar{c}_4^1 \quad w_1^1 = 0$$

$$w_2^1 - w_3^1 + \bar{c}_3^1 = 2 \quad \bar{c}_2^1 = \bar{c}_3^1 \quad w_2^1 = 0.$$

$$w_3^1 - w_2^1 + \bar{c}_2^1 = 0$$

$$w_4^1 - w_1^1 + \bar{c}_1^1 = 1$$

Verify that

(vii) $$\bar{c}_1^1 = \bar{c}_4^1 = \frac{3}{2} \quad \bar{c}_2^1 = \bar{c}_3^1 = 1,$$

and

(viii)

$$\bar{C}_1^1 = 1 < \bar{c}_1^1 \quad \text{for arc } (1, 2)$$

$$\bar{C}_2^1 = 1 = \bar{c}_2^1 \quad \text{for arc } (2, 3)$$

$$\bar{C}_3^1 = 1 = \bar{c}_3^1 \quad \text{for arc } (3, 2)$$

$$\bar{C}_4^1 = 1 < \bar{c}_4^1 \quad \text{for arc } (4, 3).$$

The new strategy in (viii) has a single cycle. Perform the next iteration and check that the strategy in (viii) is optimal.   ◀

Summary. This section applied the successive approximation in policy space algorithms to several illustrations. For the case $0 \leq \alpha < 1$, you saw how the optimality test criterion Y_i^n indicates whether a policy improvement is possible, and the way in which this quantity can depend on the specific value of α. For the case $\alpha = 1$, you observed that the method determines at least one optimal cycle, but the test criterion is not strong enough to distinguish between alternative optimal strategies that yield distinctly different present values for α near 1. As we mentioned above, it is possible to modify the algorithm to eliminate this annoying feature. Because the necessary modifications go beyond the scope of this text, they are not given here.

12.5 ELEMENTARY INVENTORY MODEL

The preceding examples were simple networks that allowed you to focus on the mechanics of successive approximation techniques. Here, the application is oriented to a dynamic problem of practical significance, namely, the elementary deterministic inventory model you first studied in Sec. 8.3, which was summarized in Sec. 12.1. We will employ the data for the Dependable Manufacturing Company illustration in Sec. 8.4:

(1) demand $D = 3$ production $x \leq 5$
ending inventory $j \leq 4$

(2) production and inventory costs
$$C(x,j) = C(x) + h \cdot j,$$

where x and j are nonnegative integers and

(3) $C(0) = 0$ $C(1) = 15$ $C(2) = 17$
$C(3) = 19$ $C(4) = 21$ $C(5) = 23$
$$h = 1$$

for all periods in an unbounded horizon.

The state variable is the level of *entering* inventory, designated by the symbol i, where $i = 0$, $1, \ldots, 4$. Therefore, a stationary strategy consists of a rule for the amount to produce given i. You already saw (Fig. 8.16) that the optimal strategy $x_\infty(i)$ for an unbounded horizon was given as

(4) $x_\infty(0) = x_\infty(1) = x_\infty(2) = 5$
$x_\infty(3) = x_\infty(4) = 0.$

You now will validate (4) using the technique of policy iteration.

The network appropriate to the example appears in Fig. 12.5. There is a node for each value of entering inventory i and an arc for each feasible production level x, given i. Specifically, if entering inventory is i, production is x, and demand is 3, then inventory entering the next period is $j \equiv i + x - 3 \geq 0$. Thus arc (i,j) represents producing an amount $j - i + 3$. Because of the production and inventory constraints in (1), certain combinations of i and j are not allowed. For example, if $i = 0$, then $j \leq 2$, since $x \leq 5$. The arc costs, given in Fig. 12.6, are

(5) $$c_{ij} = C(j - i + 3) + h \cdot j.$$

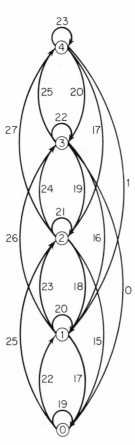

Note: node $i \equiv$ inventory level i
arc $(i, j) \equiv$ produce $j - i + 3$

FIGURE 12.5. Dependable Manufacturing Company Inventory Model (Unbounded Horizon).

Arc Costs
$$c_{ij} = C(j - i + 3) + hj$$

i \ j	0	1	2	3	4
0	19 + 0	21 + 1	23 + 2		
1	17 + 0	19 + 1	21 + 2	23 + 3	
2	15 + 0	17 + 1	19 + 2	21 + 3	23 + 4
3	0 + 0	15 + 1	17 + 2	19 + 3	21 + 4
4		0 + 1	15 + 2	17 + 3	19 + 4

FIGURE 12.6. Dependable Manufacturing Company Inventory Model.

Assume the optimality criterion is minimum average cost per period. Then the functional equation to be solved is

(6) $$w_i = \underset{\substack{(i, j) \text{ in} \\ \text{network}}}{\text{minimum}} (w_j + c_{ij} - \bar{c}) \quad \text{for each } i.$$

Suppose the starting strategy is to produce just enough when $i \leq 3$ so that ending inventory j is zero, and not to produce at all if $i = 4$ so that $j = 1$. In network terms, the policy is

(7)

Node 0: (0, 0)   Node 1: (1, 0)   Node 2: (2, 0)
  $x = 3$ $x = 2$ $x = 1$

Node 3: (3, 0)   Node 4: (4, 1).
  $x = 0$ $x = 0$

For example, at Node 1 ($i = 1$) you produce 2, so that at the end of the period the demand 3 reduces inventory to 0. Draw the network containing only these arcs, and observe that the strategy eventually leads to producing 3 every period.

Employing the policy iteration algorithm, you solve for w_i^0 and $\bar{c}^0$ in the value determination equations,

(8)
$$w_0^0 - w_0^0 + \bar{c}^0 = 19$$
$$w_1^0 - w_0^0 + \bar{c}^0 = 17$$
$$w_2^0 - w_0^0 + \bar{c}^0 = 15$$
$$w_3^0 - w_0^0 + \bar{c}^0 = 0$$
$$w_4^0 - w_1^0 + \bar{c}^0 = 1$$
$$w_0^0 = 0,$$

which yield

(9) $\bar{c}^0 = 19$ $w_0^0 = 0$ $w_1^0 = -2$ $w_2^0 = -4$ $w_3^0 = -19$ $w_4^0 = -20.$

Verify that the step

(10)
$$\underset{\substack{(i,j)\ \text{in}\\ \text{network}}}{\text{minimum}}\ (w_j^n + c_{ij} - \bar{c}^n) \equiv W_i^n$$

for $n = 0$ gives

$$
\begin{aligned}
W_0^0 &= 0 &&\text{for arc } (0, 0)\\
W_1^0 &= -12 &&\text{for arc } (1, 3)\\
W_2^0 &= -14 &&\text{for arc } (2, 3)\\
W_3^0 &= -19 &&\text{for arc } (3, 0)\\
W_4^0 &= -20 &&\text{for arc } (4, 1).
\end{aligned}
$$

(11)

Since $W_i^0 < w_i^0$ for $i = 1, 2$, the iterations are continued. Draw the network corresponding to the revised strategy in (11).

The results of the successive iterations are exhibited in Fig. 12.7. You will find it instructive to trace through the calculations yourself, using Fig. 12.7 as a check on your calculations. You should also draw the network corresponding to each trial policy. Also determine the implied production cycle, that is, the repeating quantities that would be produced over time by following the trial policy. Note the following in Fig. 12.7:

(i) There is no improvement in $\bar{c}^n$ between $n = 0$ and 1.

(ii) Although at $n = 2$ the average cost per period improves $\bar{c}^2 < \bar{c}^1$, the relative values increase $w_i^2 > W_i^1$ for all i, and $w_i^2 > w_i^1$ for all $i \neq 0$.

(iii) The implied production strategy at each iteration is:

(12) $x = 5$ for $i = 1, 2$ $x = 4$ for $i = 0, 3$ $x = 0$ for $i = 4$,
production cycle $(5, 4, 0)$ at $n = 2$;

(13) $x = 4$ for $i = 1$ $x = 5$ for $i = 0, 2$ $x = 0$ for $i = 3, 4$,
production cycle $(4, 5, 0)$ at $n = 3$;

(14) $x = 5$ for $i = 0, 1$ $x = 4$ for $i = 2$ $x = 0$ for $i = 3, 4$,
production cycle $(5, 4, 0)$ at $n = 4$;

(15) $x = 4$ for $i = 0$ $x = 5$ for $i = 1, 2$ $x = 0$ for $i = 3, 4$,
production cycle $(4, 5, 0)$ at $n = 5$;

(16) $x = 5$ for $i = 0, 1, 2$ $x = 0$ for $i = 3, 4$,
production cycle $(5, 5, 0, 5, 0)$ at $n = 6$.

Thus the iterations examine two cycles $(5, 4, 0)$ and $(4, 5, 0)$ at successively lower levels of inventory, until convergence to the optimal policy is obtained in (16), thereby verifying (4).

▶ To test your understanding, relax the assumption on production to permit $x = 6$ at a cost $C(6) = 28.5$. Perform one iteration of the policy space algorithm to *verify* that an optimal policy is

Node i	arc (i,j)	w_i^0	arc (i,j)	w_i^0	arc (i,j)	w_i^1	W_i^1	arc (i,j)	w_i^2	W_i^2	arc (i,j)	w_i^3	W_i^3	arc (i,j)	w_i^4	W_i^4	arc (i,j)	w_i^5	W_i^5	arc (i,j)	w_i^6	W_i^6
0	(0,0)	0	(0,0)	0	(0,1)	0	-9	(0,2)	0	$-3\frac{2}{3}$	(0,2)	0	0	(0,1)	0	-1	(0,1)	0	-1	(0,2)	0	0
1	(1,0)	-2	(1,3)	-12	(1,3)	-12	-12	(1,2)	$-4\frac{2}{3}$	$-5\frac{2}{3}$	(1,3)	-2	-8	(1,3)	$-6\frac{2}{3}$	$-6\frac{2}{3}$	(1,3)	-6	-6	(1,3)	$-5\frac{3}{5}$	$-5\frac{3}{5}$
2	(2,0)	-4	(2,3)	-14	(2,4)	-14	-22	(2,4)	$-11\frac{1}{3}$	$-11\frac{1}{3}$	(2,3)	-8	-10	(2,4)	$-8\frac{2}{3}$	$-11\frac{1}{3}$	(2,4)	-10	-10	(2,4)	$-9\frac{1}{5}$	$-9\frac{1}{5}$
3	(3,0)	-19	(3,0)	-19	(3,4)	-19	-24	(3,0)	$-13\frac{1}{3}$	$-17\frac{1}{3}$	(3,0)	-17	-17	(3,0)	$-16\frac{1}{3}$	$-16\frac{1}{3}$	(3,0)	-16	-16	(3,0)	$-15\frac{4}{5}$	$-15\frac{4}{5}$
4	(4,1)	-20	(4,1)	-20	(4,1)	-30	-30	(4,1)	-21	-21	(4,1)	-18	-18	(4,1)	-22	-22	(4,1)	-21	-21	(4,1)	$-20\frac{2}{5}$	$-20\frac{2}{5}$
$\bar{c}^n$		19				19			$17\frac{1}{3}$			17			$16\frac{1}{3}$			16			$15\frac{4}{5}$	

FIGURE 12.7. Dependable Manufacturing Company Inventory Model.

(i)
Node 0: $(0, 3)$ Node 1: $(1, 3)$ Node 2: $(2, 3)$
Node 3: $(3, 0)$ Node 4: $(4, 1)$,

implying

(ii)
$$x = 6 \quad \text{for } i = 0 \qquad x = 5 \quad \text{for } i = 1$$
$$x = 4 \quad \text{for } i = 2 \qquad x = 0 \quad \text{for } i = 3, 4,$$

production cycle $(6, 0)$,

and $\bar{c} = 15.75$.   ◀

12.6 LINEAR PROGRAMMING APPROACH

You will now see how to formulate a discrete dynamic programming problem in an unbounded horizon as a linear programming model. This connection will help you understand why the policy iteration algorithm converges in a finite number of trials, since it is closely related to the simplex method. Furthermore, you consequently will know how to convert such a dynamic programming problem to a format that permits the application of standard linear programming computer codes. The conversion has practical significance in actual situations, since highly sophisticated linear programming algorithms are readily available for all large-scale electronic computers. A corollary advantage is that you can then employ the well-developed techniques for sensitivity analysis.

Minimum present value. Consider the case $0 \leq \alpha < 1$ and the appropriate functional equations

$$(1) \qquad y_i = \underset{\substack{(i, j) \text{ in} \\ \text{network}}}{\text{minimum}} (\alpha y_j + c_{ij}) \quad \text{for each } i.$$

These equations imply that every y_i must satisfy the linear constraints

$$(2) \qquad \left. \begin{array}{c} y_i \leq \alpha y_j + c_{ij} \quad \text{or} \quad y_i - \alpha y_j \leq c_{ij} \\ \text{for each arc } (i, j) \text{ in network} \end{array} \right\} \quad \text{(dual arc constraints)}.$$

The y_i are unrestricted in sign; however, the set of inequalities (2) does not fully characterize extremal equations (1), because values of y_i that meet (2) may not also satisfy (1). For example, if all $c_{ij} > 0$, then $y_i = 0$ is consistent with (2) but not (1). For each i, (2) must hold with *equality* for at least one arc (i, j). Surprisingly, the correct optimal values for *all* y_i can be achieved by applying the linear objective function

$$(3) \qquad \text{maximize} \sum_{k=1}^{p} r_k y_k \qquad \text{(dual objective)},$$

where each $r_k > 0$ but otherwise is arbitrary, and p is the largest node number in the network.

Denote the restrictions (2) and the objective function (3) as the dual problem, so the primal model becomes

(4) $$\text{minimize} \sum_{\substack{(i,j) \text{ in} \\ \text{network}}} c_{ij} x_{ij} \qquad \text{(primal objective)}$$

subject to

(5) $$\sum_{\substack{(k,j) \text{ in} \\ \text{network}}} x_{kj} - \sum_{\substack{(i,k) \text{ in} \\ \text{network}}} \alpha x_{ik} = r_k \quad \text{for each Node k} \quad \text{(primal node constraints)}$$

(6) $$x_{ij} \geq 0 \quad \text{for each } (i,j) \text{ in network.}$$

As usual, the double summation sign in (4) indicates the sum is over all arcs (i,j) in the network. For each Node k in the network, the single summation signs in (5) indicate the sums are over arcs (k,j) and (i,k) with the particular value of k as given. The dual and primal linear programming technologies for the network of Example 1 in Sec. 12.4 (illustrated in Fig. 12.1, p. 415) are shown in Figs. 12.8 and 12.9. (The primal technology is closely related to that of the generalized network problem in Sec. 6.9.)

Arcs	y_1	y_2	y_3	y_4	
(1,2)	1	$-\alpha$			$\leq c_{12}$
(1,4)	1			$-\alpha$	$\leq c_{14}$
(2,1)	$-\alpha$	1			$\leq c_{21}$
(2,3)		1	$-\alpha$		$\leq c_{23}$
(3,2)		$-\alpha$	1		$\leq c_{32}$
(4,1)	$-\alpha$			1	$\leq c_{41}$
	r_1	r_2	r_3	r_4	Maximize

y_k: unrestricted in sign

FIGURE 12.8. Dual Linear Programming Model for Example 1 in Fig. 12.1.

Nodes	x_{12}	x_{14}	x_{21}	x_{23}	x_{32}	x_{41}	
1	1	1	$-\alpha$			$-\alpha$	$= r_1$
2	$-\alpha$		1	1	$-\alpha$		$= r_2$
3				$-\alpha$	1		$= r_3$
4		$-\alpha$				1	$= r_4$
	c_{12}	c_{14}	c_{21}	c_{23}	c_{32}	c_{41}	Minimize

$x_{ij} \geq 0$

FIGURE 12.9. Primal Linear Programming Model for Example 1 in Fig. 12.1.

Simplex method and policy iteration. Suppose you apply the simplex method to the primal problem (4) through (6). Since $r_k > 0$ for each Node k, at least one $x_{kj} > 0$. A trial solution at each iteration of the simplex method consists of a basic solution with p variables, where p is the number of nodes. Such a solution must therefore contain exactly *one* x_{kj} for each Node k. In other words, a basic solution in the primal model corresponds to a trial strategy in the dual model.

When a new $x_{kj'}$ is introduced in the basis, the old x_{kj} *must* leave to preserve feasibility. Thus at each iteration of the simplex method, a new arc enters the solution and an old one leaves for a particular Node k. After the change, the new solution is tested for optimality by a calculation tantamount to checking whether all the inequalities in (2) are satisfied for the current set of dual variables. The latter values are the same as y_k^n for the current policy, so the usual optimality criterion in the simplex method agrees with the policy improvement rule in the policy space algorithm.

You can now discern the only real difference between the simplex approach applied to the primal problem and the policy iteration technique applied to the dual problem. At every iteration, the latter algorithm looks at *all* nodes and makes a change for *every* potential improvement. Consequently, the policy space algorithm may alter the trial solution basis by introducing several new variables (arcs) at one iteration. In contrast, the simplex method brings into the basis only one new variable at a time, and retests for optimality. Whether such multiple basis changes between optimality checks are computationally more efficient has not been determined on theoretical grounds. The relative merit of the two approaches largely depends on the technicalities involved in designing a computer program for a particular electronic calculator.

The connection between the two approaches also provides a means of proving that the policy space successive approximation algorithm converges to an optimal solution in a finite number of iterations. Only slight modifications of the arguments showing optimality and finiteness of the simplex algorithm are required.

▶The following line of reasoning can be made rigorous to demonstrate that you can *arbitrarily* select positive r_k in the dual objective function (3) and the primal constraints (5). Assume you have solved the dual model for a particular set of r_k, and let x_{ij} have values corresponding to this strategy. According to the Dual Theorem in Chap. 5, the x_{ij} exist and are finite. Specifically, let x_B be the associated optimal basis vector. The values of x_B can be found from the primal node constraints (5):

(i) $$(I - A)x_B = r,$$

where I is a $p \times p$ identity matrix, A is the matrix of appropriate coefficients α, and r is the column vector of r_k. You can rewrite (i) as

(ii) $$x_B = r + Ax_B,$$

which by repeated substitution of x_B on the right yields

(iii) $$x_B = r + A(r + Ax_B) = (I + A + A^2 + \cdots)r.$$

Since x_B is finite and $r > 0$, the sum $(I + A + A^2 + \cdots)$ must converge to a matrix that you may denote as $(I - A)^{-1}$. The individual elements of each matrix in the sum are nonnegative, and consequently $(I - A)^{-1}$ is a nonnegative matrix, with diagonal elements having a value of at least 1.

Therefore, if $r^* > 0$ is used instead of r, then

(iv) $$x_B^* = (I + A + A^2 + \cdots)r^* \geq r^* > 0,$$

so the previous basis remains feasible (and nondegenerate). This substitution of a different right-hand side leaves the optimality indication (values for the dual variables) of the basis B unaltered, giving the desired conclusion that the optimality of the strategy x_B is preserved.   ◀

Minimum equivalent average return per period. When $\alpha = 1$, the dynamic programming functional equation is

(7) $$w_i = \underset{\substack{(i,\,j) \text{ in} \\ \text{network}}}{\text{minimum}} (w_j + c_{ij} - \bar{c}) \quad \text{for each } i,$$

where, as before, we assume that there exists a path from every Node i to at least one of the nodes associated with a cycle yielding $\bar{c}$. By appropriately modifying the extremal equations, this assumption can be dropped.

As you saw in the numerical examples of Sec. 12.4, the w_i are not unique. What is more, although the policy iteration algorithm finds a strategy containing a cycle with a minimal equivalent average return per period, the method does not distinguish among alternative optimal policies so as to select one that is also optimal for α close to 1. The corresponding linear programming approach has this same limitation. There are practical procedures, however, for finding a policy that is also optimal for α near 1.

You can find the optimal value of $\bar{c}$, and an associated policy, by solving the dual model

$$(8) \qquad\qquad \text{maximize } \bar{c} \qquad\qquad \text{(dual objective)}$$

subject to

$$(9) \qquad w_i - w_j + \bar{c} \leq c_{ij} \quad \text{for each arc } (i,j) \text{ in network} \quad \text{(dual arc constraints)},$$

where w_i and $\bar{c}$ are unrestricted in sign. The corresponding primal model is

$$(10) \qquad\qquad \text{minimize } \sum_{\substack{(i,j) \text{ in} \\ \text{network}}} c_{ij} v_{ij} \qquad\qquad \text{(primal objective)}$$

subject to

$$(11) \qquad \sum_{\substack{(k,j) \text{ in} \\ \text{network}}} v_{kj} - \sum_{\substack{(i,k) \text{ in} \\ \text{network}}} v_{ik} = 0 \quad \text{for each Node k} \qquad \text{(primal node constraints)}$$

$$(12) \qquad\qquad \sum_{\substack{(i,j) \text{ in} \\ \text{network}}} v_{ij} = 1 \quad \text{(time normalization constraint)}$$

$$(13) \qquad\qquad v_{ij} \geq 0 \quad \text{for each } (i,j) \text{ in network.}$$

The constraint (12) is imposed as a **normalizing equation** to rule out the solution $v_{ij} = 0$. As a result, the v_{ij} ordinarily will *not* be integer-valued, and the positive v_{ij} in an optimal solution will be associated with a cycle having minimum equivalent average return. The amount v_{ij} represents the fraction of periods the system spends in traversing the arc (i,j) when there is a single cycle in an optimal policy.

When you add (11) for all nodes, the terms on the left-hand side cancel each other, so there is a redundancy in the set of relations, and any one equation can be dropped in the computational process. This phenomenon occurred in the network models of Chaps. 6 and 7, and corresponds to the fact that the w_i are not unique in (9)—if the w_i satisfy (9), so do ($w_i +$ constant).

Example. The dual and primal models are illustrated in Figs. 12.10 and 12.11 for the network given in Fig. 12.1. Compare the technologies with those in Figs. 12.8 and 12.9, where $0 \leq \alpha < 1$. Verify for Example 3 on p. 418 that

$$(14) \qquad w_1 = 0 \quad w_2 = 2 \quad w_3 = 1 \quad w_4 = -1 \quad \bar{c} = 2$$

is feasible in Fig. 12.10, and that as a result the feasible solutions

Arcs	w_1	w_2	w_3	w_4	$\bar{c}$	
(1,2)	1	−1			1	$\leq c_{12}$
(1,4)	1			−1	1	$\leq c_{14}$
(2,1)	−1	1			1	$\leq c_{21}$
(2,3)			1	−1	1	$\leq c_{23}$
(3,2)			−1	1	1	$\leq c_{32}$
(4,1)	−1			1	1	$\leq c_{41}$
					1	Maximize

w_k: unrestricted in sign

FIGURE 12.10. Dual Linear Programming Model for Example 1 in Fig. 12.1.

		v_{12}	v_{14}	v_{21}	v_{23}	v_{32}	v_{41}	
	1	1	1	−1			−1	= 0
Nodes	2	−1		1	1	−1		= 0
	3				−1	1		= 0
	4		−1				1	= 0
Cycle Average		1	1	1	1	1	1	= 1
		c_{12}	c_{14}	c_{21}	c_{23}	c_{32}	c_{41}	Minimize

$v_{ij} \geq 0$

FIGURE 12.11. Primal Linear Programming Model for Example 1 in Fig. 12.1.

$$(15) \qquad v_{14} = v_{41} = \frac{1}{2} \qquad \text{all other } v_{ij} = 0$$

and

$$(16) \qquad v_{14} = v_{41} = v_{23} = v_{32} = \frac{1}{4} \qquad \text{all other } v_{ij} = 0$$

are both optimal in Fig. 12.11. [If the equation for Node 1 is eliminated as redundant, then $v_{21} = v_{32} = 0$ are also in the basis for the solution (15).]

▶ Only straightforward modifications in the above formulations are needed to encompass the situation in which h_{ij} is the number of periods to traverse arc (i, j), and $\alpha_{ij} \equiv \alpha^{h_{ij}}$. In the minimum present-value case, you merely substitute α_{ij} for α wherever it appears in the formulas. In the minimum equivalent average return per period case, you need only place the coefficient h_{ij} in front of $\bar{c}$ in the extremal equations (7) and the associated dual arc constraints (9). Likewise, place the coefficient h_{ij} in front of v_{ij} in the time normalization constraint (12). In this version, $h_{ij}v_{ij}$ is the fraction of periods the system spends in traversing arc (i, j) when there is a single cycle in an optimal policy. ◀

12.7 CONCLUDING REMARKS

In this chapter, the successive approximation methods have been applied to extremal equations for dynamic programming models with unbounded horizons that satisfy the assumptions

(i) The decision outcomes are deterministic.

(ii) The state of the system is *examined* at discrete points in time.

(iii) Both the decision and state variables are discrete and have a finite number of possible values.

(iv) The system parameters are stationary.

In Chaps. 16, 17, and 18 you will study models where assumption (i) is weakened to include probabilistic outcomes. Random events introduce a new type of behavior to be encompassed by the optimization process. However, these models are not solved much differently from those in Chaps. 8 through 12.

As you will see in the waiting line models of Chap. 20 and Appendix III, it is helpful to view certain real situations as if decisions can be made *any* moment, not only at discrete points in time given in assumption (ii). For example, during "rush hours" a supermarket manager may decide to open an additional customer checkout stand whenever he sees the waiting lines getting too long. Obviously, he is not restricted to making this decision only at periodic intervals, such as every five minutes. In these situations the various successive approximation approaches you have studied can be adapted to provide workable optimization techniques.

Assumption (iii), relating to the variables being discrete and finite-valued, is often imposed for either analytic or computational convenience. Frequently, however, a real system can be modeled just as well by letting the decision and state variables be continuous, and even unbounded. To illustrate, consider the elementary inventory model summarized in Sec. 12.1. There we assumed that the production quantity x must be integer-valued. Since the demand quantity is integer-valued, the production assumption implied that inventory would be integer-valued. Suppose, instead, that we think of the production level as a rate (quantity per period), and drop the postulate that it must be integer-valued. Then the recursion for an unbounded horizon is

(1) $$f(i) = \underset{x}{\text{minimum}} \, [C(x) + h(i + x - d) + \alpha f(i + x - d)],$$

where now $-\infty \le i \le +\infty$ and x is any nonnegative real number at least as large as $i - d$.

Analyzing such a model involves several technical details you have not yet encountered. For example, assuming $f(i)$ exists and is unique, you would want to discover when $f(i)$ also is a continuous function. Similarly, you would want to determine whether the function $x_\infty(i)$ giving an optimal policy is single-valued and continuous.

When continuous variables are used in a representation like (1), you can sometimes, by applying the calculus, derive a simple explicit formula for the solution $f(i)$ and the decision function $x_\infty(i)$. The advantages to such results are significant. Not only is the computation of specific answers simplified, but the structure of an optimal policy and its dependency on the economic parameters are rendered more apparent. The solution techniques for these continuous problems are of principal interest to the operations research specialist, and consequently will not be explored further here.

*Weaker stationarity assumption. Notice how assumption (iv) has been utilized in the network model of Sec. 12.1. The hypothesis was the set of available arcs (i, j) and the associated costs c_{ij} remain unchanged period after period. By auspiciously defining the state variables, you actually can encompass a wider variety of models than might appear at first sight. The following example suggests how the case of cyclic variation can be handled.

Consider the elementary inventory model studied in Sec. 12.5. There you assumed that $D_t = 3$ at every period. Suppose, instead, that demand alternates between 3 and 2. Then you no longer have only five nodes for the state variable $i = 0, 1, \ldots, 4$ representing the level of entering inventory. Instead you denote the level of entering inventory as $i' = 0, 1, \ldots, 4$ when the period's demand is 3, and $i'' = 0, 1, \ldots, 4$ when demand is 2. Thus the new network consists of two sets of five nodes. A feasible decision to produce x in a $D_t = 3$ period corresponds to an arc from Node i' to Node $i'' = i' + x - 3$. Likewise, a decision x when $D_t = 2$ corresponds to an arc from Node i'' to Node $i' = i'' + x - 2$. With this device you can also let production and inventory holding costs alternate between periods.

*Exploiting structure. The regeneration model in Sec. 11.4 demonstrated how the numerical solution of a functional equation can be simplified if you have information about the form of an optimal policy. You will see other examples in Chap. 18 and Appendix II. As a preview, consider the value iteration operation

$$
(2) \qquad \underset{\substack{(i, j) \text{ in} \\ \text{network}}}{\operatorname{minimum}} (\alpha y_j^n + c_{ij}).
$$

In some problems, information about the economic parameters and decision possibilities may show that if arc (i, j^*) is optimal when $i = 0$, then (i, j^*) also is optimal for all $i \le j^*$. Knowledge of the $i = 0$ solution may thus eliminate your having to solve for many other values of i.

▶ For another illustration, let

$$
(i) \qquad g_i^n(j) \equiv \alpha y_j^n + c_{ij} \quad \text{for each } i,
$$

and suppose $j = 1, 2, \ldots, N_i$. Then if the model allows you to establish $g_i^n(j)$ is concave in j, the solution in (2) is simply $j = 1$ or $j = N_i$. Thus only two values of j need to be tested in (2) for each i. If $g_i^n(j)$ is convex, a different simplification is possible. Although usually more than two values of j must be tested, not all N_i need be examined.

An efficient procedure for searching the minimum of a convex function is based on the so-called **Fibonacci numbers.** Actually, the method works for any function $g(j)$ such that $g(j)$ is strictly decreasing for $1 \le j \le j^*$, and strictly increasing for $j > j^*$. These functions are called **ditonic.** [If $g(j)$ is ditonic, $-g(j)$ is called **unimodal.**]

The sequence of Fibonacci numbers is

$$
(ii) \qquad 1, 2, 3, 5, 8, 13, 21, 34, 55, 89, 144, \ldots,
$$

in which each successive number in the sequence is the sum of the previous two numbers.

Let F_n be the nth number in (ii). Then, by a so-called Fibonacci search, the minimum of $g(j)$, for $j = 1, 2, \ldots, (F_n - 1)$, can be determined in $(n - 1)$ tests.

For example, suppose $F_n - 1 = 20$, that is, $n = 7$. Then only $n - 1 = 6$ tries are required. Start with the Fibonacci number F_{n-1} and the next smaller number F_{n-2}. In the example, $F_6 = 13$ and $F_5 = 8$. Calculate and compare $g(13)$ and $g(8)$. On the basis of the comparison, you will make the subsequent test employing the next smaller Fibonacci number, 5. Specifically, if $g(8) \leq g(13)$, you have reduced the interval of search for the minimum $g(j)$ to $j = 1, 2, \ldots, 12$. As a result, test $g(j)$ with $j = 5$ and $j = 8$. If, instead, $g(8) > g(13)$, you have reduced the interval of search to $j = 9, 10, \ldots, 20$. As a result, test with $j - 8 = 5$ $(j = 13)$ and $j - 8 = 8$ $(j = 16)$. In either case, for the subsequent test you need to calculate $g(j)$ for only one new value of j. The procedure continues in this fashion and terminates with the minimum $g(j)$ after six values of j are tested.   ◀

REVIEW EXERCISES

1 Consider the inventory model in Sec. 12.1. Suppose the only possible levels for entering inventory i are $i = 0, 1, \ldots, 7$. Assume that demand $d = 4$.

   (a) How many different values for $f(i)$ in (2) must be determined? Write the extremal equation for each of these values, and indicate the values of x to be considered in the minimization.
   (b) Suppose the optimal production policy is produce $11 - i$ for $i \leq 5$, and produce 0 otherwise. Explain how you would determine the values for $f(i)$ (write the mathematical equations).
   (c) Draw a network representation of the entire optimization problem, and indicate the path implied by the optimal policy in part (b).

2 Consider the network characterization in Sec. 12.1.

   (a) Explain why the corresponding value y_i, denoting the present value of an optimal unending path starting at Node i, is finite.
   (b) Explain why all y_i necessarily satisfy the extremal equations (3).

3 Consider the network characterization in Sec. 12.1. Suppose that there are six nodes, and there are arcs in each direction between every pair of nodes.

   (a) How many extremal equations in (3) must be satisfied? Write each of these, showing all terms that must be considered in the minimization.
   (b) Suppose an optimal set of arcs is $(1, 2)$, $(2, 3)$, $(3, 4)$, $(4, 5)$, $(5, 6)$, and $(6, 1)$. Indicate how you can solve a set of simultaneous linear equations to find the associated values for y_i.

4 In the value iteration algorithm, in Sec. 12.2, there need not be only one policy that is optimal at the current decision for *all* finite $n \geq N$—no matter how large the value for N. The text states that there is an n^* such that, for each $n > n^*$, *any* optimal strategy for the current decision in the n-period finite horizon model is also an optimal stationary strategy for the unbounded horizon model. Are these two assertions contradictory? Explain why.

5 Consider the value iteration algorithm in Sec. 12.2, and suppose you calculate y_i^0 using an initially selected trial strategy. Suppose further that you stop the process at iteration m. Describe a strategy that yields the associated values y_i^m. Is this strategy necessarily stationary?

*6 Consider the numerical illustration (I) in the advanced material following the description of the value iteration algorithm in Sec. 12.2.

    (a) Draw the network corresponding to (I).

    (b) Verify that the values in (II) satisfy the functional equations for the network, and that arcs (1, 2) and (1, 3) are both optimal.

    (c) Given the values for y_i^3 in (V), calculate y_i^4 and y_i^5, and check that arc (1, 3) is strictly better at $n = 4$ and arc (1, 2) is strictly better at $n = 5$.

7 In each part below, first find the values for y_i given the analysis in Sec. 12.4. Then apply the value iteration algorithm in Sec. 12.2, starting with $y_i^0 = 0$. Letting n' denote the first iteration at which the entire policy agrees with the optimal policy, terminate the calculations at $n' + 3$. Plot the values for y_1^n and y_2^n.

    (a) Example 1 in Fig. 12.1, with $\alpha = .8$.

    (b) Example 1 in Fig. 12.1, with $\alpha = \frac{1}{2}$.

    (c) Example 4 in Fig. 12.3 $(c_{12} = 1.5)$, with $\alpha = \frac{1}{2}$.

    (d) Example 4 in Fig. 12.3 $(c_{12} = 1.5)$, with $\alpha = \frac{1}{4}$.

  *(e) In each part, verify that for every i,

$$|y_i^n - y_i| \le \alpha d_{n-1} \quad \text{where} \quad d_{n-1} \equiv \underset{k}{\text{maximum}} |y_k^{n-1} - y_k|.$$

8 In each part, apply the value iteration algorithm in Sec. 12.2, computing y_i^0 from the initial set of arcs indicated below. Letting n' denote the first iteration at which the entire policy agrees with the optimal policy, terminate the calculations at $n' + 3$. Plot the values for y_1^n and y_2^n.

    (a) Example 1 in Fig. 12.1, with $\alpha = .8$, and starting with arcs (1, 4), (4, 1), (2, 3), and (3, 2).

    (b) Example 1 in Fig. 12.1, with $\alpha = \frac{1}{2}$, and starting with arcs (1, 4), (4, 1), (2, 1), and (3, 2).

    (c) Example 4 in Fig. 12.3 $(c_{12} = 1.5)$, with $\alpha = \frac{1}{2}$, and starting with arcs (1, 3), (3, 2), and (2, 3).

    (d) Example 4 in Fig. 12.3 $(c_{12} = 1.5)$, with $\alpha = \frac{1}{4}$, and starting with arcs (1, 2), (2, 3), and (3, 2).

  *(e) In each part, verify that for every i,

$$|y_i^n - y_i| \le \alpha d_{n-1} \quad \text{where} \quad d_{n-1} \equiv \underset{k}{\text{maximum}} |y_k^{n-1} - y_k|.$$

9 Consider a network with Nodes 1 and 2, and arcs corresponding to $c_{11} = c_{22} = 50$, $c_{12} = c_{21} = 10$. Let $\alpha = \frac{1}{2}$. Inspect the diagram and compute y_1 and y_2. Apply the value iteration algorithm in Sec. 12.2, with $y_1^0 = 0$ and $y_2^0 = 40$, up to $n = 5$. Plot y_1^n and y_2^n. Are the y_i^n monotonic?

10 Consider the network characterization in Sec. 12.1. Suppose for each Node i you select an arc (i, j).

(a) Explain why your selection of arcs includes at least one cycle. If there are two cycles, indicate why the nodes in each cycle are disjoint (that is, why a node is not included in more than one cycle).

(b) Consider the value determination routine (2) in Sec. 12.2, and suppose that your selection of arcs includes only one cycle, namely, the cycle between arcs $(1, 2)$, $(2, 3)$, and $(3, 1)$. Write the associated equations in (2). Show that the solution to these simultaneous linear equations yields the values

$$y_1^0 = c_{12} + \alpha c_{23} + \alpha^2 c_{31} + \alpha^3 c_{12} + \alpha^4 c_{23} + \alpha^5 c_{31} + \cdots$$

$$y_2^0 = c_{23} + \alpha c_{31} + \alpha^2 c_{12} + \alpha^3 c_{23} + \alpha^4 c_{31} + \alpha^5 c_{12} + \cdots$$

$$y_3^0 = c_{31} + \alpha c_{12} + \alpha^2 c_{23} + \alpha^3 c_{31} + \alpha^4 c_{12} + \alpha^5 c_{23} + \cdots.$$

*(c) Suppose you apply policy iteration, where the y_i^0 are as given in part (b). Further, suppose that you find at *Steps 3* and *4* that $Y_1^0 = \alpha y_3^0 + c_{13}$ and $Y_1^0 < y_1^0$, and $Y_i^0 = y_i^0$ for all other i. Show that $y_1^1 < y_1^0$, and, as a consequence, that $y_i^1 \le y_i^0$ for every Node i.

11 In Sec. 12.3, the text assumes for simplicity that there exists a path from every Node i to at least one of the nodes associated with a cycle yielding the minimum equivalent average return per period $(\alpha = 1)$.

(a) What complication arises if this assumption is dropped? (*Hint:* consider the network associated with the arc costs $c_{12} = c_{21} = c_{13} = 1, c_{34} = c_{43} = 2$.)

(b) Explain why there is no need to make such an assumption in the case $0 \le \alpha < 1$.

12 (a) Give a verbal interpretation of w_i in the definitions (1) and (2) of Sec. 12.3.

(b) Show the intermediate algebraic steps that allow (3) to be written as (4).

(c) Take the expression on the right of (3) and move it to the left; then show that for $\alpha = 1$, the result is (6).

(d) Suppose you interpret $w_i - w_j$ as the incremental cost associated with being in Node i rather than Node j, given an optimal policy. Present a verbal description of the extremal equations (6) using this interpretation.

(e) Suppose you are given values for w_i that satisfy the extremal equations (5) or (6). Explain why adding a constant to these values yields new amounts for the w_i that also satisfy the equations. (Illustrate your argument with a network having three nodes and arcs in each direction between every pair of nodes.)

13 Consider the policy iteration algorithm for $\alpha = 1$ described in Sec. 12.3.

(a) Suppose the network contains Nodes $1, 2, \ldots, p$. How many equations and how many unknowns are in the linear system (7)?

(b) Suppose the trial policy has the cycle $(1, 2)$, $(2, 3)$, and $(3, 1)$. Write the associated equations (7), and show that $\bar{c}^n = (c_{12} + c_{23} + c_{31})/3$, as claimed in (9).

(c) Suppose the arc (i, j) is in an optimal policy. What is the value of $w_i - w_j$? Suppose the arc (j, k) is also in this same optimal policy. What is the value of $w_i - w_k$?

(d) Rewrite the steps of the policy iteration algorithm appropriate to the extremal equations as expressed by (6).

(e) Rewrite the steps of the policy iteration algorithm if the objective is to "maximize" average return per period.

*14 Consider a network model in which h_{ij} time periods are required to traverse arc (i, j), and not all h_{ij} are equal to 1. This case is discussed in the advanced material at the end of Sec. 12.3.

   (a) Verify that (3), (4), and (5) become (I), (II), and (III).
   (b) Verify that $w_i - w_j$ can still be interpreted as the incremental cost associated with being in Node i rather than Node j for $\alpha = 1$. Present a verbal description of the extremal equations (III) using this interpretation.

15 (a) In Sec. 12.4 verify that the solution to (3) is (4).
   (b) Verify the algebraic steps in (5) and (6), that arc $(1, 4)$ gives the minimum in (5) for $0 \leq \alpha < 1$, and that arc $(2, 1)$ gives the minimum in (6) for $\frac{2}{3} \leq \alpha < 1$. Explain why arc $(2, 3)$ is a better decision for values of α below $\frac{2}{3}$.
   (c) Show the changes in (2) through (6) if arc $(2, 3)$ is used initially instead of arc $(2, 1)$. Do you arrive at the same conclusions as in part (b)?
   (d) Verify that the test quantity for $(2, 3)$ in (6) represents the present value of going from Node 2 to Node 3, back to Node 2, then to Node 1, and thereafter around the loop between Nodes 1 and 4. Compare this test value with y_2^0 in part (c).

16 (a) In Sec. 12.4, verify the algebraic steps in (7) through (11), and that the minimum is as indicated in (11) for $0 \leq \alpha < 1$.
   (b) Verify that, for $\alpha = 1$, the value determination routine yields equations (12), and that the solution is (13). Also verify the computations in (14) and (15). Discuss the assertion in the text that you probably would prefer to use the cycle between Nodes 2 and 3.
   (c) Assume that you employ the policy in (1), giving the present values in (4) for $0 \leq \alpha < 1$. Consider the quantities $y_2 - y_1$, $y_3 - y_1$, $y_4 - y_1$, and set $\alpha = 1$. Show that the resulting amounts are the same as $w_2 - w_1$, $w_3 - w_1$, $w_4 - w_1$ in (13).

17 Consider the illustration in Fig. 12.3 with $c_{12} = 1.5$ (Example 4).

   (a) Demonstrate that when you use arcs $(2, 3)$ and $(3, 2)$, selecting arc $(1, 3)$ is better than choosing arc $(1, 2)$ over a finite horizon if the number of periods is odd, but worse if the number of periods is even.
   (b) Verify in Sec. 12.4 that (18) is the solution to the equations (17). Check the algebraic steps in (19), and verify that arc $(1, 2)$ gives a minimum for $\frac{1}{3} \leq \alpha < 1$.
   (c) Show the changes in (17) through (19) when arc $(1, 2)$ is used instead of arc $(1, 3)$. Verify the statement in (20).
   (d) Perform the policy iteration algorithm for $\alpha = 1$. Check that the solution with arc $(1, 2)$ is uniquely optimal.
   (e) Consider the policy associated with arcs $(1, 2)$, $(2, 3)$, and $(3, 2)$. Assume that $0 \leq \alpha < 1$, and find the associated values for $y_1, y_2,$ and y_3 [expressed analogously to the formulas in (18)]. Consider the quantities $y_2 - y_1, y_3 - y_1$, and set $\alpha = 1$. Show that the resulting amounts are the same as $w_2 - w_1, w_3 - w_1$ in (23).

18 Consider the illustration in Fig. 12.3 with $c_{12} = 2$ (Example 5). Verify the expressions in (21), and that arc $(1, 3)$ is optimal when $0 \leq \alpha < 1$.

19 Consider the illustration in Fig. 12.3 with $c_{12} = 2$ and $\alpha = 1$ (Example 6).

(a) Verify that the value determination equations associated with using arc $(1, 2)$ are those in (22) and have the solution in (23).

(b) Write and solve the corresponding value determination equations associated with using arc $(1, 3)$.

(c) Verify that both arcs $(1, 2)$ and $(1, 3)$ test optimally in the policy iteration technique.

*20 Consider the illustration in Fig. 12.4 for $\alpha = 1$. (Example 7), discussed in the advanced material at the end of Sec. 12.4.

(a) Write the value determination equations for the policy in (iii) and verify that the solution is as indicated in (iv). Also check the test quantities in (v).

(b) Indicate how the policy in (v) contains two cycles. Verify that equations (vi) are solved as shown in (vii). Also check the test quantities in (viii).

(c) Complete the policy iteration algorithm, and determine that the strategy in (viii) is optimal.

Exercises 21 through 26 refer to the case of the Dependable Manufacturing Company case described in Sec. 12.5. All equation numbers refer to Sec. 12.5.

21 (a) Assume $0 \leq \alpha < 1$. Employing the notation corresponding to (2) in Sec. 12.1, write in full detail all the functional equations to be satisfied.

(b) Assume $\alpha = 1$. Let $g(i) \equiv w_i$ and $\bar{g} \equiv \bar{c}$ in functional equations (6) of Sec. 12.5. Rewrite the functional equations in this notation and thereby display extremal equations analogous to those in (2) of Sec. 12.1.

22 In each part below, draw the network containing only the arcs implied by the policy in

(a) (7) and (11).

(b) (12) through (16).

23 (a) Verify that (8) contains the value equations appropriate to the policy in (7), and that (9) contains the solution to (8). Show the detailed computations in (10), and verify that the results are those contained in (11).

(b) Work out in detail the rest of the computations of the policy iteration algorithm, and verify the results in Fig. 12.7. Specifically, write and solve the value equations and show the comparisons in the test quantity.

(c) Given the optimal policy in (4), assume that $\alpha < 1$, and find the corresponding values for $y_0, y_1, \ldots, y_4$. Consider the quantities $y_1 - y_0, y_2 - y_0, y_3 - y_0, y_4 - y_0$, and set $\alpha = 1$. Show that resulting amounts are the same as $w_1 - w_0$, $w_2 - w_0$, $w_3 - w_0$, $w_4 - w_0$ for the optimal policy.

24 Apply the policy iteration algorithm ($\alpha = 1$), starting initially with arcs $(0, 1)$, $(1, 0)$, $(2, 1)$, $(3, 2)$, and $(4, 3)$.

25 Apply the policy iteration algorithm, letting y_i^0 be determined according to the policy in (7). At each iteration, indicate the production cycle implied by the trial policy. Assume that

(a) $\alpha = .9$.

(b) $\alpha = \frac{1}{2}$.

(c) $\alpha = 0$.

(d) Describe the effect α has on an optimal policy.

*(e) What is the smallest value of α, and the corresponding interest rate, such that the policy in (4) remains optimal?

26 Apply the value iteration algorithm, first by letting $y_i^0 = 0$, and second by letting y_i^0 be determined according to the policy in (7). Letting n' denote the first iteration at which the entire policy agrees with the optimal policy (exercise 25), terminate the calculations at $n' + 3$. Assume that

(a) $\alpha = .9$.

(b) $\alpha = \frac{1}{2}$.

(c) $\alpha = 0$.

*27 Consider the numerical illustration described in the special material at the end of Sec. 12.5.

(a) Assume $\alpha = 1$. Verify that the policy in (i) is optimal if production $x = 6$ is permitted, with $C(6) = 28.5$. Also verify that the policy in (i) implies the production schedule shown in (ii).

*(b) Determine an optimal policy for $\alpha = \frac{1}{2}$, and compare it with that in (i).

28 Consider the numerical example in Sec. 12.5. In each part below, make the indicated modification, redraw Fig. 12.5, and find an optimal policy using the policy iteration algorithm for $\alpha = 1$.

(a) Demand in each period is 2, instead of 3.

(b) Demand in each period is 4, instead of 3.

(c) Ending inventory cannot exceed 3, instead of 4.

(d) Production in each period cannot exceed 4, instead of 5.

(e) Permissible production values are only $x = 0, 2, 4$.

(f) Production must be at least one unit $(x \geq 1)$ in every period.

(g) The setup cost component in (3) is 10, instead of 13.

(h) The holding cost h is 5, instead of 1.

*(i) The holding cost h is applied to average inventory within a period, instead of ending inventory.

*29 Consider the illustration of the inventory model in Fig. 12.5. Suppose demand can be left unfilled in a period and is then backlogged, but that the backlog level is never permitted to exceed 3.

(a) Redraw Fig. 12.5 accordingly.

(b) Suppose the penalty per unit of backlogged demand per period is 10. Show the appropriate arc costs in your diagram of part (a).

30 In each part below, write the dual and primal linear programming technologies described in Sec. 12.6. First assume $0 \leq \alpha < 1$, so that the tables are analogous to those in Figs. 12.8 and 12.9. Then assume $\alpha = 1$, so that the tables are analogous to those in Figs. 12.10 and 12.11.

(a) Figure 12.3 with $c_{12} = 1.5$ (Example 4 in Sec. 12.4). Indicate optimal solutions to the primal and dual problems for $\alpha = 1$.

*(b) Figure 12.4 (Example 7 in Sec. 12.4).

(c) Inventory model in Sec. 12.5 (illustrated in Fig. 12.5).

*(d) Indicate optimal solutions to the primal and dual problems in part (c) for $\alpha = .9$. For $\alpha = \frac{1}{2}$. For $\alpha = 0$. (See exercise 25.)

*31 The special material on "weaker stationarity" in Sec. 12.7 described a network characterizing an inventory model with alternating demands.

  (a) Draw this network. Assuming the cost functions in Sec. 12.5, guess an optimal strategy, calculate the corresponding average cost ($\alpha = 1$), and check the test quantities in the policy iteration algorithm to determine whether your suggested policy is truly optimal. (*Hint:* think carefully about the alternating demand structure and cost functions in picking your policy.)

  (b) Assume, instead, that demand alternates between 3 and 1 (instead of 3 and 2). Answer the questions in part (a).

*(c) If your guesses in parts (a) and (b) were not optimal, use the policy iteration algorithm to determine optimal policies.

*32 *Fibonacci Search.* An efficient method for finding the minimum of a ditonic function was described in the special material at the end of Sec. 12.7. Apply the method to find the minimum of the functions below.

  (a) $g(j) = (j - 7)^2$ for $j = 0, 1, \ldots, 50$.

  (b) $g(j) = 2j + (j - 7)^2$ for $j = 0, 1, \ldots, 50$.

  (c) $g(j) = -2j + (j - 7)^2$ for $j = 0, 1, \ldots, 50$.

  (d) $g(j) = \begin{cases} 100 - j & \text{for } j = 0, 1, \ldots, 10 \\ 90 - 3j & \text{for } j = 11, \ldots, 20 \\ 30 + 5j & \text{for } j = 21, \ldots, 30 \\ 180 + j & \text{for } j = 31, \ldots, 40. \end{cases}$

33 Explain your understanding of the following terms:

functional, or extremal, equations

stationary policy (strategy)

cycle (or circulation)

*discrete dynamic programming problem

successive approximations

value iteration (successive approximations in function space)

policy iteration (successive approximations in policy space)

monotonically increasing (decreasing)

convergence from above (below)

value determination routine

normalizing equation

*Fibonacci numbers

*ditonic function

*unimodal function.

FORMULATION AND COMPUTATIONAL EXERCISES

34 Consider the network in Fig. 12.12, where arrowheads at both ends of an arc signify that it is permissible to travel in either direction at the cost indicated.

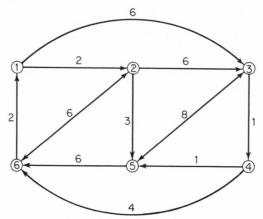

Figure 12.12

(a) Let $\alpha = 1$. Solve the associated extremal equations (5) in Sec. 12.3 using policy iteration.
(b) Apply policy iteration to find y_i and the associated strategy for $\alpha = .9$. For $\alpha = \frac{1}{2}$. For $\alpha = 0$. Use the optimal solution in part (a) as the initial policy.
(c) Let $\alpha = .9$. Apply the value iteration algorithm, starting with $y_i^0 = 0$. Letting n' denote the first iteration at which the entire policy agrees with the optimal policy, terminate the calculations at $n' + 3$.

35 Consider the network in Fig. 12.13 where arrowheads at both ends of an arc signify

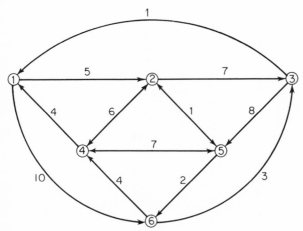

Figure 12.13

that it is permissible to travel in either direction at the cost indicated. Answer the questions in exercise 34.

Exercises 36 through 40 require modifying the formulations of problems in the exercises of earlier chapters. As before, be sure to define all the symbols you use.

36 In each part below, assume that costs and returns are to be discounted to the current period, and α is the one-period discount factor, where $0 \leq \alpha < 1$. Indicate an appropriate finite horizon dynamic programming recursion, analogous to that in (1) of Sec. 12.1.

(a) The capacity expansion problem in exercise 33 of Chap. 10.
(b) The ARKA Mutual Fund Problem in exercise 34 of Chap. 10.
(c) The GAW Company Employment Smoothing Problem in exercise 36 of Chap. 10.
(d) The Expando Manufacturing Company Problem in exercise 36 of Chap. 2 and 38 of Chap. 10.
(e) The production scheduling problem in exercise 39 of Chap. 10, assuming that the amount x_j is produced in Period j. Also show the optimal value for x_t, given values for $x_1, x_2, \ldots, x_{t-1}$.

37 In each part below, assume that all the data are stationary, the horizon is unbounded, costs and returns are discounted to the current period, and α is the one-period discount factor, where $0 \leq \alpha < 1$. Indicate an appropriate set of extremal equations, analogous to those in (2) of Sec. 12.1.

(a) Production smoothing model in exercise 45 of Chap. 8.
*(b) Production smoothing model in Sec. 9.8.
(c) Production scheduling model in exercise 53 of Chap. 9.
(d) Cattle raising problem in exercise 32 of Chap. 10.

38 Consider the production smoothing model in exercise 45 of Chap. 8. Use the data for the illustration in Sec. 12.5; let the target production level $\bar{x} = 3$ and the smoothing parameter $v = 1$.

(a) Apply the policy iteration algorithm to find an optimal strategy for $\alpha = 1$.
(b) Apply the policy iteration algorithm to find an optimal strategy for $\alpha = .9$. For $\alpha = \frac{1}{2}$. For $\alpha = 0$. Let the initial trial policy be the optimal policy in part (a). Describe the effect α has on an optimal policy.
(c) Let $\alpha = .9$. Apply the value iteration algorithm, starting with $y_i^0 = 0$. Letting n' denote the first iteration at which the entire policy agrees with the optimal policy, terminate the calculations at $n' + 3$.

39 Consider an inventory model analogous to that in Sec. 12.5. Continue to assume that demand $D = 3$, production $x \leq 5$, and ending inventory $j \leq 4$. Let production and inventory costs be $C(x) + h \cdot j$, where

$$C(x) = \begin{cases} 5x & \text{for } x = 0, 1, 2, 3 \\ 12 + x & \text{for } x \geq 4, \end{cases} \quad \text{and } h = 1.$$

(a) Apply policy iteration to find an optimal strategy for $\alpha = 1$.
(b) Apply policy iteration to find an optimal strategy for $\alpha = .9$. For $\alpha = \frac{1}{2}$. For

$\alpha = 0$. Use the optimal solution in part (a) as the initial policy. Describe the effect α has on an optimal policy.

(c) Let $\alpha = .9$. Apply the value iteration algorithm, starting with $y_i^0 = 0$. Letting n' denote the first iteration at which the entire policy agrees with the optimal policy, terminate the calculations at $n' + 3$.

(d) Repeat parts (a), (b), and (c) for $h = 2$.

(e) Repeat parts (a), (b), and (c) for demand $D = 2$. (*Note:* finite horizon versions of these questions are contained in exercises 13 and 15 of Chap. 9.)

40 Answer the questions in exercise 39, assuming that the production cost function is

$$C(x) = \begin{cases} 0 & \text{for } x = 0 \\ 3 + 2x & \text{for } x \geq 1. \end{cases}$$

(*Note:* a finite horizon version of this question is contained in exercise 14 of Chap. 9.)

MIND-EXPANDING EXERCISES

41 Consider a network such as that characterized in Sec. 12.1, and assume that the discount factor α satisfies $0 \leq \alpha < 1$.

*(a) Assume you are given a trial strategy (not necessarily stationary) and the associated present values y_i^n. Suppose that there is at least one Node k (and perhaps several) for which

$$\underset{\substack{(k, j) \text{ in} \\ \text{network}}}{\text{minimum}} (\alpha y_j^n + c_{kj}) < y_k^n.$$

Consider a *stationary* strategy which uses arcs giving minimum $(\alpha y_j^n + c_{ij})$ for each Node i. Show that this new trial strategy yields y_j^{n+1} such that $y_j^{n+1} \leq y_j^n$ for every Node j, with strict inequality holding for Node k.

(b) Given that the proposition in part (a) is true, show that there exists a stationary policy that is optimal among all possible policies.

42 Consider a network such as that characterized in Sec. 12.1, and assume that the discount factor α satisfies $0 \leq \alpha < 1$. Assume you have available a lower estimate L_i and an upper estimate U_i on each unknown y_i, that is, $L_i \leq y_i \leq U_i$. Show that it is never optimal to use arc (i, k) when

$$\alpha L_k + c_{ik} > \underset{\substack{(i, j) \text{ in} \\ \text{network}}}{\text{minimum}} (\alpha U_j + c_{ij}).$$

Suggest in detail how you might use this inequality to speed convergence in successive approximation algorithms.

*43 Consider the proof of convergence of the value iteration algorithm for $0 \leq \alpha < 1$, as given in the advanced material of Sec. 12.2. Modify the argument to show that there is at least geometric convergence (vii) for the policy iteration technique.

44 Consider the dual linear programming model for $\alpha = 1$, namely, (8) and (9) in Sec. 12.6, and the corresponding primal model (10) through (13).

(a) Show that there is no loss in assuming that each $w_i \geq 0$.

(b) Show that there is no loss in assuming that the primal model constraints are $(\geq)$ inequalities.

(c) Show that if all $c_{ij} \geq 0$, then there is no loss in assuming that $\bar{c} \geq 0$ and that the normalization constraint (12) is a $(\geq)$ inequality.

45 Suppose you drop the assumption in Sec. 12.3 that there is a path from every Node i to at least one of the nodes associated with a cycle yielding $\bar{c}$. Let $\bar{c}_i$ be the minimum average return per period attainable starting at Node i. Then analogous to the extremal equations (5), the following extremal equations must be satisfied:

$$w_i = \underset{\substack{(i, j) \text{ in} \\ \text{network}}}{\text{minimum}} (w_j + c_{ij} - \bar{c}_i) \quad \text{for each Node i}$$

$$\bar{c}_i = \underset{\substack{(i, j) \text{ in} \\ \text{network}}}{\text{minimum}} (\bar{c}_j) \qquad\qquad \text{for each Node i.}$$

*(a) Devise (heuristic) arguments establishing these extremal equations.

*(b) Indicate how these equations lead to the algorithmic steps in (i) and (ii) of the special material at the end of Sec. 12.3.

(c) Write the associated dual and primal linear programming models, analogous to (8) through (13) in Sec. 12.6. The appropriate dual objective is to maximize $\sum_{k=1}^{p} r_k \bar{c}_k$, where each $r_k > 0$ but is otherwise arbitrary.

(d) Explain why these extremal equations simplify to (5) when the special assumption in Sec. 12.3 is made.

46 Review the Kleen City Police Department case in exercise 30 of Chap. 2 and the general formulation in exercise 27 of Chap. 5. Also review the results in exercise 54 of Chap. 6, which state that if the number of periods T is odd, then the model is not equivalent to a network problem (hence, applying linear programming may not yield an integer-valued solution). Explore how to characterize the problem for any value of T in terms of a set of extremal equations, analogous to those in (5) or (6) of Sec. 12.3 for the network model. Specifically,

(a) Indicate how the underlying network is drawn. Be sure you label the nodes, and state how they characterize the state of the system at each period. Also label the arcs to make clear the associated decision, and show how the problem's constraints are taken into account.

(b) Write the extremal equations associated with your answer in part (a), and indicate why their solution gives an optimal strategy for the original model.

(c) Modify your answers in parts (a) and (b) for the situation in which a person starting work in Period t remains in the system in Periods $t + 1$ and $t + 2$; thus, the constraints are of the form $y_{t-2} + y_{t-1} + y_t \geq r_t$.

47 Consider the following composite successive approximations algorithm. Apply value iteration for N successive iterations. Use the trial policy at the Nth iteration and apply *Step 2* of policy iteration. Stop if the extremal equations are satisfied. Otherwise repeat the procedure, letting y_i^{N+1} be the values found in the value determination routine of policy iteration. Explain why this hybrid approach converges in a finite number of iterations.

CONTENTS

CHAPTER 13

Integer Programming and Combinatorial Models

13.1 QUEST FOR A PHILOSOPHER'S STONE

This chapter, as well as the next two, investigates programming models in which the two assumptions called *divisibility* and *additivity* (Sec. 2.2) are weakened. Recall that these postulates in combination implied linearity in both the objective function and the constraints, and also allowed the variables to take on fractional values, such as 2.5 or $\frac{10}{3}$. Here we drop the **divisibility assumption** and treat problems in which some, or all, of the variables are permitted to take on only integer values (or whole numbers). Later, in Chaps. 14 and 15, we remove the additivity assumption.

Consider the model

$$
\text{(1)} \qquad\qquad \text{optimize } \sum_{j=1}^{n} c_j x_j,
$$

subject to

$$
\text{(2)} \qquad\qquad \sum_{j=1}^{n} a_{ij} x_j \leq b_i \quad \text{for } i = 1, 2, \ldots, m
$$

$$
\text{(3)} \qquad\qquad x_j \geq 0 \qquad \text{for } j = 1, 2, \ldots, n
$$

$$
\text{(4)} \qquad x_j \text{ integer-valued} \qquad \text{for } j = 1, 2, \ldots, p \ (\leq n).
$$

This type of optimization model is referred to as an **integer** (or **diophantine**, or **discrete**) **programming problem**. When $p = n$, so that every variable must be integer-valued, the model is called a **pure** integer programming problem; otherwise, it is called a **mixed** integer programming problem.

Depending on the particular application, the sense of optimization in the objective function (1) may be either maximization or minimization. (We will indicate the appropriate sense for each illustration and algorithm below.) Further, an integer programming problem may include ($\geq$) inequalities and equalities. [You can view the linear constraints (2) as a canonical form, however, by applying the procedures given in Chap. 3 whenever the constraints in their original version do not appear as in (2).]

The discreteness stipulations (4) are what distinguish an integer from a linear programming problem. In case the linear constraints (2) happen to represent a network model, there exists an optimal solution to (1), (2), and (3) that also satisfies the integer-value constraints (4), as you already know from the Integrality Theorem for networks (p. 192). But, in general, imposing (4) is restrictive, so that the maximum value of an objective function for an integer programming problem is smaller than for the corresponding linear programming problem.

Importance of integer programming problems. We indicated earlier that most industrial applications of large-scale programming models are oriented toward planning decisions in the face of complex situations. There are several, frequently occurring circumstances that lead to planning models containing integer-valued variables.

1. *Equipment Utilization.* You may define a variable x_j to be the pieces of equipment that are to operate during the model's planning horizon. If each piece of equipment provides a large capacity and is expensive—for example, an automatic screw machine, an oceangoing oil tanker, or a 150-inch double-knife paper corrugator machine—then a fractional value for x_j, like $\frac{10}{3}$, may be meaningless (nonrealizable) in the context of the actual decision problem. In this event, you would have to restrict x_j to be integer-valued.

2. *Setup Costs.* You may want to consider an activity that incurs a so-called fixed cost (or *setup cost*) C_j whenever the corresponding level $x_j > 0$, where C_j is independent of the actual level of x_j. For example, if x_j represents the hourly utilization of a blast furnace in a steel plant, then C_j represents the cost of starting up the furnace and heating it to the required temperature. You will see in Sec. 13.2 how to encompass setup costs in a programming model by introducing integer-valued variables.

3. *Batch Sizes.* In some production planning situations, you may want to restrict the level of x_j to be either $x_j = 0$ or $x_j \geq L_j$. For example, x_j may be the amount of a special product to be manufactured during Period t, and L_j may represent the minimum possible production batch size for the item. This stipulation is an example of an "either-or" restriction and can be formulated by introducing integer variables, as you will learn in Sec. 13.2.

4. *"Go-No-Go" Decisions.* You may wish to specify other types of "either-or" situations. To do this you can restrict the levels of x_j to either $x_j = 1$ or $x_j = 0$, representing the decisions "go" or "no go," and "yes" or "no." To illustrate, you

may let $x_j = 1$ correspond to building a new factory, or to opening up a sales territory, or to acquiring another business, or to selling a currently owned asset. Frequently, these sorts of alternatives are categorized as *capital budgeting* decisions, because they require large expenditures of capital and resources. This is the main reason why integer programming is so important for managerial decisions. An optimal solution to a capital budgeting problem may yield considerably more profit to a firm than will an approximate or guessed-at solution. For example, a cement manufacturing firm with 25 plants may be able to substantially increase profits by cutting back to 20 plants or less, *provided* this reduction is planned optimally. The decreased overhead with fewer plants can easily outweigh any consequent increase in transportation costs, if the new plant configuration is optimal.

Many other decision problems can necessitate integer programming models. One group of problems deal with sequencing, scheduling, and routing decisions. An example is the *traveling salesman problem*. It aims at finding a least-distance route for a salesman who must visit each of n cities, starting and ending his journey at City 1. Another example is the *machine scheduling problem*. A simple illustration is when n items to be manufactured must be sequenced through each of k machines. Suppose an item cannot proceed to Machine j until it finishes being processed on Machine j $-$ 1. Assume the processing time of each item on each machine is determinate. An optimal sequence of items is then defined as a schedule that minimizes total elapsed time to complete all jobs on all machines. Further examples of scheduling, sequencing, and routing problems include *line-balancing, critical path scheduling* (see Sec. 6.6) *with resource constraints, preventive maintenance scheduling with constraints on labor availability,* and *truck dispatching.*

Despite the considerable attention given in operations research journals to such integer programming models for sequencing, scheduling, and routing problems, so far these models have been of only limited practical importance. One reason why is that the integer programming models frequently ignore some of the critical considerations that arise in actual scheduling environments. Another reason is that the computational burden of solving these models has been so great that the cost of obtaining a solution exceeds any improvements resulting from the approach.

Sequencing, scheduling, and routing problems are special cases of what are called *combinatorial* models. A **combinatorial optimization problem** consists of finding, from among a finite set of alternatives, one that optimizes the value of an objective function. For example, the finite set for the traveling salesman problem with n cities consists of $(n - 1)!$ different possible tours starting and ending in City 1. In the simple illustration of the machine scheduling problem, the finite set consists of $(n!)^k$ possible sequences of the n items on the k machines.

With sufficient ingenuity, you can always devise a nontrivial integer programming representation of a combinatorial optimization problem; some of the mathematical devices for doing so are explained in Sec. 13.2. Frequently, such integer programming problems are very large (that is, there are an enormous number of constraints and variables), and therefore the formulation is of negligible computational interest. But, as you will discover, several of the algorithmic techniques for integer programming problems can be applied directly to combinatorial models without first having to transform them into integer programming models.

The search of a lifetime. Would your guess be that integer programming problems are harder or easier to solve than linear programming models of the same size? Most students would answer that integer programming problems are probably easier. To support this opinion, they observe that a dichotomy, say, such as $x_j = 0$ or $x_j = 1$ contains considerably fewer alternatives than does the continuum $0 \leq x_j \leq 1$. And from this comparison they reason that the search for an optimum ought to be simpler. Regrettably, just the opposite is true—in a programming model, computation is easier with a continuum than with discrete alternatives. The following illustration shows why.

Consider the model

$$(5) \qquad\qquad \text{maximize } 21x_1 + 11x_2$$

subject to

$$(6) \qquad\qquad 7x_1 + 4x_2 \leq 13$$

$$(7) \qquad\qquad x_1 \text{ and } x_2 \text{ nonnegative integers.}$$

After a few moments inspection, you will find that the unique optimal solution is $x_1 = 0$ and $x_2 = 3$. Of course, since this problem is so small, you can think of many ways to discover and verify the solution (including the dynamic programming technique given for the Distribution of Effort Problem in Sec. 10.2). But since our goal here is to understand the relative difficulty of solving medium- to large-scale integer programming problems, let us rule out any solution schemes that are ad hoc to a particular problem as well as those systematic algorithms that are practical only for small-scale problems.

There is one approach for finding an integer-valued solution that is frequently suggested by beginners. The procedure is, first, ignore the integer stipulations, and solve for an optimal linear programming solution. If this answer satisfies the integer restrictions, then you have in fact found an optimal solution for the original problem. (State why?) Otherwise, obtain an integer solution by rounding the linear programming answer to whole numbers.

Now suppose you try this approach on the example in (5), (6) and (7). The optimal fractional solution is $x_1 = \frac{13}{7}$ and $x_2 = 0$. The obvious rounded solution is $x_1 = 2$ and $x_2 = 0$, which is infeasible. A "rounded-down" solution $x_1 = 1$ and $x_2 = 0$ is feasible, but far from optimal. It is hard to think of any general, systematic procedure that is practical for rounding a nonintegral solution for a medium- to large-scale model, and that yields the optimal integer solution when applied to this toy problem.

If some of the coefficients a_{ij} in the linear constraints (2) are negative for a particular model, the problem of rounding a linear programming answer to a *feasible* integer-valued solution can be a difficult task in itself. Hence, although rounding may succeed for some applications, you cannot expect such an approach to succeed in general.

An even more serious difficulty inherent in integer programming problems is that there is no easy way to verify whether a given feasible solution is actually optimal. This represents an important distinguishing difference between integer and linear programming problems. To illustrate, suppose in the above problem (5), (6), and (7) you want to test whether $x_1 = x_2 = 1$ is optimal. To do this, you might examine whether the solution represents a local optimum, in that the objective function does not improve at any neighboring feasible integer (or **lattice**) point $x_1 = 1 + d$ and $x_2 = 1 + e$, where $d, e = -1, 0, 1$. Verify that the feasible neighboring points in this case are ($x_1 = x_2 = 0$; $x_1 = 0$ and $x_2 = 1$; $x_1 = 0$ and $x_2 = 2$; $x_1 = 1$ and $x_2 = 0$). Check that the solution $x_1 = x_2 = 1$ is indeed better than *all* of these, and yet is *not* optimal. Thus a point can be locally optimal among neighboring lattice points and still not be globally optimal. (Incidentally, this enumerative test for a local optimum is really not practical for large-scale problems, since there can be a vast number of neighboring points. In fact, if the model is a pure integer programming problem and each x_j is restricted to be either 0 or 1, then searching all the neighboring points of a feasible solution is equivalent to enumerating all the solutions to the original problem.)

By now you may be sufficiently exasperated to wonder whether the best general approach is merely to enumerate all the feasible solutions, and then pick the best. Actually, if there are only a few possible solutions, such an exhaustive procedure may well be easier to implement than any of the algorithms explained later in the chapter. In some real applications, this has been the very approach used (frequently, a number of possible solutions are ruled out immediately as "obviously" nonoptimal). Most often, however, an exhaustive approach proves unworkable, and the reason, simply, is that the number of feasible solutions is not always finite, and even when it is, the magnitude is usually stupendous. For example, consider finding an optimal solution to an integer programming problem consisting of 100 variables, each restricted to equal either 0 or 1. Then the time to enumerate all 2^{100} possibilities on the fastest computer in existence far exceeds a lifetime.

Practical algorithms. It is apparent from the foregoing discussion that in order for an algorithm to be of general use in solving integer programming problems, it must avoid *explicitly* enumerating all possibilities. What we want are techniques that *partially* enumerate a manageable number of possibilities and *implicitly* enumerate all the rest. Recall that the simplex method is just such a technique for solving ordinary linear programming problems—it systematically examines only a small number of all the possible basic solutions. (Incidentally, mathematicians still do not have a good theory for *why* the simplex method, in practice, does examine so few bases.) By the same token, dynamic programming recursions exploit the *principle of optimality* to circumvent enumerating all feasible solutions. The success of these partially enumerative optimization methods motivates the quest for finding similar approaches to solve integer programming problems.

Devising such integer programming algorithms is currently a lively area of research among technical specialists. It is too early to single out a few algorithms and claim they are as effective for integer problems as the simplex method is for linear programming problems. In fact, given any of these algorithms, it is easy to devise specific integer programming examples that require computational effort equivalent to complete enumeration. Hence, the usefulness of any one of the techniques must ultimately be established by empirical findings indicating the types of problems it is likely to solve well.

Several general concepts are emerging as clearly fundamental to the various approaches that now look promising. You will study these ideas starting in Sec. 13.3. Importantly, most of the algorithms employ linear programming models and dynamic programming notions as elemental building blocks. Encouraging evidence of progress in solving real integer programming problems is rapidly accumulating. When such algorithms become perfected, operations research analysts, equipped with high-speed computers, should indeed be credited with having created a philosopher's stone.

13.2 INTEGER PROGRAMMING FORMULATIONS

If you review the various planning models in Chap. 2, you can easily envisage situations in which certain of the variables must be integer-valued. There are a myriad of other examples, primarily dealing with the allocation of resources over a short horizon (a day, week, or month), that also can be idealized by an integer programming formulation. To illustrate, these include assigning transportation vehicles of various sizes to satisfy certain pickup and delivery requirements; scheduling several assortment mixes for a paper-making or steel-rolling machine to meet a variety of customer demand commitments; and allocating a number of large orders to a company's several manufacturing plants that differ in capacities, efficiencies, and costs. Being familiar with the techniques of constructing linear programming models, you will find it a straightforward matter to formulate these resource allocation problems as integer programming models; therefore we will provide no further elaboration in this chapter. It would be misleading, however, to give you the impression that these situations constitute the main focus of interest in managerial decision-oriented applications.

By far, the most significant applications deal with setup costs, dichotomous choices, and complex capital budgeting decisions. Constructing integer programming formulations to handle such considerations is partly an art; hence, we explain below some of the standard devices that are useful. To further enhance your understanding, we also provide an illustration of how to formulate a combinatorial problem as an integer programming model. The example we have selected is the traveling salesman problem. The important point of this illustration is your seeing there is a connection between combinatorial and integer programming problems. Although such integer formulations themselves are frequently of little immediate practical consequence—even a small combinatorial problem usually becomes an enormous integer model—the connection does provide the bridge spanning several fundamental algorithmic concepts.

Plant location—an example with setup costs. In Chap. 6 you studied the classical transportation problem:

$$(1) \qquad\qquad \text{minimize} \sum_{i=1}^{m} \sum_{j=1}^{n} c_{ij} x_{ij}$$

subject to

$$(2) \qquad\qquad \sum_{j=1}^{n} x_{ij} \leq S_i \quad \text{for } i = 1, 2, \ldots, m \quad \text{(supply)}$$

$$(3) \qquad\qquad \sum_{i=1}^{m} x_{ij} \geq D_j \quad \text{for } j = 1, 2, \ldots, n \quad \text{(demand)}$$

$$(4) \qquad\qquad x_{ij} \geq 0 \quad \text{for all } i \text{ and } j.$$

Recall that one interpretation of the problem is that there are m supply points with items available to be shipped to the n demand points. Supply Point i can ship at most S_i items, and Demand Point j requires at least D_j items. The cost of shipping a unit from Supply Point i to Demand Point j is c_{ij}. The objective is to select a routing plan that minimizes total transportation costs.

In some transportation planning applications, part of the problem is to establish which of m possible supply points should actually be in operation. The supply points usually represent plants or warehouses, and incur overhead expenses that must be combined with the transportation costs in determining company profit. The typical cost tradeoff is between reduced overhead cost from fewer plants and warehouses, and increased transportation costs.

For example, consider the Goforth Manufacturing Company which is going to expand its business by serving customers in states west of the Rocky Mountains. To accommodate this extension of its marketing area, Goforth plans to open several new assembly plants. Suppose that Plant Site i represents a potential location. Assume the plant will have capacity S_i and incur a fixed overhead cost $F_i \geq 0$, independent of the amount it produces. There are m possible sites for these new plants, but the overhead expenses are so significant that it is too costly to open plants on all the sites. Let $c_{ij} \geq 0$ be manufacturing and transportation expenses for shipping an item from Plant Site i to Marketing Area j. Assume, in addition, that there is a setup cost $F_{ij} \geq 0$ associated with maintaining a shipping route from Plant Site i to Marketing Area j; this amount F_{ij} is independent of the magnitude of $x_{ij} > 0$, but is not incurred when $x_{ij} = 0$.

Accordingly, to formulate the problem as a mathematical model introduce the integer-valued decision variables

$$y_i = \begin{cases} 1 & \text{if Plant Site i is selected} \\ 0 & \text{otherwise} \end{cases} \qquad \text{for } i = 1, 2, \ldots, m,$$

and

$$z_{ij} = \begin{cases} 1 & \text{if route from Plant Site i to Area j is used} \\ 0 & \text{otherwise} \end{cases} \qquad \text{for all } i \text{ and } j.$$

Then, instead of the usual objective function (1), the objective function becomes

$$\text{(5)} \qquad \text{minimize} \sum_{i=1}^{m} F_i y_i + \sum_{i=1}^{m} \sum_{j=1}^{n} c_{ij} x_{ij} + \sum_{i=1}^{m} \sum_{j=1}^{n} F_{ij} z_{ij}.$$

Instead of imposing the supply constraints (2), you state the capacity restrictions as

$$\text{(6)} \qquad \sum_{j=1}^{n} x_{ij} - S_i y_i \leq 0 \quad \text{for } i = 1, 2, \ldots, m \quad \text{(supply)}.$$

If Plant Site i is not opened, so that $y_i = 0$, then (6) ensures that $x_{ij} > 0$ is not allowed. The demand constraints (3) and nonnegativity constraints (4) remain unchanged. For certain integer programming algorithms, it is sufficient to state in addition that the y_i and z_{ij} must be either 0 or 1. But for other algorithms, these same restrictions must be expressed in the expanded form

$$\text{(7)} \qquad y_i \leq 1 \text{ and } z_{ij} \leq 1 \quad \text{for all } i \text{ and } j$$

$$\text{(8)} \qquad y_i \text{ and } z_{ij} \text{ nonnegative integers} \quad \text{for all } i \text{ and } j.$$

[State why (7) and (8) together ensure that each y_i and z_{ij} is either 0 or 1.]

The model formulation is not yet complete, because we have not related the value of z_{ij} to the the value of x_{ij}. We want to ensure that $x_{ij} > 0$ only if $z_{ij} = 1$; this can be achieved by including the linear restrictions

$$\text{(9)} \qquad x_{ij} - U_{ij} z_{ij} \leq 0 \quad \text{for all } i \text{ and } j,$$

where U_{ij} is a sufficiently large coefficient—for example, let $U_{ij} = \text{minimum}$ (S_i, D_j). Verify that if $z_{ij} = 0$, then the nonnegativity condition (4) and (9) imply that x_{ij} must be equal to zero; and if $z_{ij} = 1$, then (9) is superfluous, given the new supply constraint (6) and the demand restriction (3). (Also check that it is never essential for optimality to have $z_{ij} = 1$ and $x_{ij} = 0$.)

It is easy to construct examples in which an ordinary linear programming problem given by (5), (6), (7), and (9) has an optimal solution with fractional values for the variables. Hence the restriction (8), requiring that the y_i and z_{ij} be integer-valued, is essential. As in the ordinary transportation problem, it is only necessary to stipulate that each x_{ij} must be nonnegative, since the integrality property of the usual transportation model continues to hold provided that y_i and z_{ij} are integer-valued.

The formulation in (9) generalizes to other situations. Whenever there is a setup cost $C_j \geq 0$ associated with an ordinary variable x_j in a programming model, then a valid integer programming formulation is to introduce a zero-one variable

($z_j = 0$ or 1) and a constraint ($x_j - Uz_j \leq 0$), where U is chosen to be appropriately large. Notice that this device complicates the model in that it adds both an integer-valued variable and a linear constraint for each variable incurring a setup cost.

Batch sizes—an example with alternative constraints. Suppose x_j is the amount of an item to be manufactured, but that either $x_j \geq L_j$, where L_j represents the smallest feasible lot size, or that $x_j = 0$ during the horizon. Assume that you can specify a large enough number U_j, such that the constraint ($x_j \leq U_j$) is certainly satisfied by an optimal solution. Then the dichotomy ($x_j = 0$ or $x_j \geq L_j$) can be formulated by adding a zero-one variable ($y_j = 0$ or 1) and two linear constraints:

$$(10) \qquad\qquad x_j - U_j y_j \leq 0$$

$$(11) \qquad\qquad x_j - L_j y_j \geq 0.$$

For $y_j = 0$, the constraints (10) and (11) imply that there is no production ($x_j = 0$). For $y_j = 1$, the constraint (10) becomes ineffective, and the constraint (11) imposes the required lot-size restriction.

The preceding idea can be generalized to handle situations in which a solution must satisfy at least k out of the p constraints

$$(12) \qquad\qquad \sum_{j=1}^{n} a_{ij} x_j \leq b_i \quad \text{for } i = 1, 2, \ldots, p.$$

Introduce the p zero-one variables ($y_i = 0$ or 1), for $i = 1, 2, \ldots, p$, and impose the $1 + p$ linear constraints

$$(13) \qquad\qquad \sum_{i=1}^{p} y_i \geq k$$

$$(14) \qquad \sum_{j=1}^{n} a_{ij} x_j \leq b_i y_i + U_i(1 - y_i) \quad \text{or}$$
$$\sum_{j=1}^{n} a_{ij} x_j - (b_i - U_i) y_i \leq U_i \quad \text{for } i = 1, 2, \ldots, p$$

where U_i is chosen so large that ($\sum_{j=1}^{n} a_{ij} x_j \leq U_i$) is certainly satisfied by an optimal solution. Explain how (13), (14), and the stipulation that each y_i be either 0 or 1 is a valid formulation of the problem. [Actually, (13) can just as well be stated as an equality. Why?]

Capital budgeting—an example with interdependent alternatives. "Go-no-go" alternatives are probably the most important managerial decisions that lead to integer programming problems. These choices frequently arise in the context of a multiperiod strategic planning model. Typically, the variable x_j indicates whether or not a particular project (or an activity, or an investment alternative, etc.) is to be undertaken, where

$$x_j = \begin{cases} 1 & \text{if Project j is accepted} \\ 0 & \text{otherwise.} \end{cases}$$

An associated coefficient a_{ij} in a constraint often represents the amount of a scarce resource, such as cash, that is required for the project at Period i, where the total amount of the resource utilized in each period is limited. These types of constraints are identical to those you would find in an ordinary linear programming model designed to aid in long-term strategic planning. Hence we go no further in developing specific examples.

But the fact that x_j is a zero-one variable can be exploited to represent combinatorial kinds of restrictions that are often present in capital budgeting problems. For example, suppose that you want to restrict the solution to accept no more than k of the first p projects. (Perhaps each project requires the full-time supervision of a senior engineer, and only k engineers are available for new assignments.) Then you can achieve this limitation by imposing the linear constraint

$$(15) \qquad \sum_{j=1}^{p} x_j \leq k.$$

If you write (15) as an equality, then exactly k alternatives will be accepted. The special case of p mutually exclusive projects can be treated by letting $k = 1$ in (15). This case can occur, for example, if the first p projects actually refer to the same alternative, and x_j indicates whether or not this activity is to commence at Period j.

If, say, alternative x_2 can be undertaken only if alternative x_1 *is* accepted, then the linear constraint

$$(16) \qquad -x_1 + x_2 \leq 0$$

on the two zero-one variables achieves this stipulation, as you should verify. Suppose, instead, that alternatives x_1 and x_2 are mutually exclusive, and x_3 can be undertaken only if either x_1 or x_2 is accepted; check that this dependency can be achieved by imposing the linear constraints

$$(17) \qquad x_1 + x_2 \leq 1$$

$$(18) \qquad -x_1 - x_2 + x_3 \leq 0.$$

By now you can see that, with sufficient ingenuity, a host of combinatorial interdependences among the projects can be represented by means of linear stipulations on zero-one variables.

Traveling salesman problem. A traveling salesman wants to visit each of n cities, starting and ending at City 1. He visits no other city twice. Let $c_{ij} \geq 0$ designate the distance between City i and City j, where we use the symbol $c_{ij} = \infty$ when there is no direct connection from City i to City j; in some applications, c_{ij} does not equal c_{ji}. The optimization problem is to find a shortest **tour**. (A production scheduling application of this model was outlined in an earlier discussion in Sec. 6.5.)

There are several valid mathematical formulations of the problem. The one to follow uses relatively few variables. Define the zero-one variables:

$$x_{ij} = \begin{cases} 1 & \text{if a tour includes traveling from City i to City j} \\ 0 & \text{otherwise} \end{cases}$$

for all i and j. The objective function is

(19)   minimize $\sum_{i=1}^{n} \sum_{j=1}^{n} c_{ij} x_{ij}$ where $c_{ii} = \infty$ for $i = 1, 2, \ldots, n$.

The variables must satisfy the constraints

(20) $\sum_{j=1}^{n} x_{ij} = 1$ for $i = 1, 2, \ldots, n$ (departure)

(21) $\sum_{j=1}^{n} x_{ij} = 1$ for $j = 1, 2, \ldots, n$ (arrival)

(22) x_{ij} nonnegative integers for all i and j.

(The convention $c_{ii} = \infty$ is adopted to rule out the meaningless possibility that $x_{ii} = 1$ occurs in an optimal solution. Alternatively, you can simply omit the variables x_{ii} from the problem specification.) Restrictions (20), (21), and (22) in concert ensure that each x_{ij} is either zero or one. Relations (20) require that a tour includes one departure from each city, and, similarly, relations (21) guarantee one arrival at each city. The model would be an assignment problem, treated in Sec. 6.4, if (19) through (22) were the complete characterization.

Unfortunately, although the x_{ij} for any tour must satisfy the above constraints, a feasible solution to these constraints need not be a tour. In particular, a feasible solution to (20), (21), and (22) may include two or more disconnected cycles or **subtours**, such as $x_{12} = x_{23} = x_{31} = 1$ and $x_{45} = x_{56} = \cdots = x_{n4} = 1$. (State why such a feasible solution is *not* a tour for the traveling salesman.) Therefore, further restrictions on the x_{ij} have to be added in order to guarantee that the result is a tour.

There are various ways to formulate linear constraints on the integer variables in order to rule out cycles. For example, the restriction $x_{23} + x_{32} \leq 1$ eliminates the subtour between Cities 2 and 3, and similarly, the restriction $x_{23} + x_{34} + x_{42} \leq 2$ rules out one of the subtours between Cities 2, 3, and 4. But the following is an elegant specification of linear restrictions that exclude *all* subtours.

Introduce the variables u_i, for $i = 2, 3, \ldots, n$, and constrain them by the $(n-1)^2 - (n-1)$ relations

(23) $u_i - u_j + n x_{ij} \leq n - 1$ for $\begin{array}{l} i = 2, 3, \ldots, n \\ j = 2, 3, \ldots, n \end{array}$ $(i \neq j)$.

The u_i need not be further constrained to rule out subtours, but no harm is done if the u_i are also restricted to be nonnegative integers. The complete formulation (20) through (23) consists of $n^2 - n + 2$ linear constraints and $n^2 + n - 1$ integer-valued variables, n of these being the x_{ii} that must equal 0. Certainly, it is not obvious why (23) works; we provide the justification in the advanced material below.

▶To validate the constraints (23), we must establish two propositions: (a) all subtours are indeed eliminated, and (b) no tour is excluded. These two statements are argued in turn.

First, the constraints (20) through (23) rule out all subtours among Cities 2, 3, . . . , n. To see why, consider any cycle among k of these cities, which would be represented by $x_{ij} = 1$ for k variables. Add the k constraints in (23) associated with the variables in the cycle. Such a composite constraint must also be satisfied by any solution that is feasible in (23). As you should verify, both u_i and $(-u_i)$ for each of the k cities appear in the resultant sum; thus, no u_i appears in the composite constraint. But it is not feasible for *all* $x_{ij} = 1$ in this constraint, for then the sum on the left of the inequality is nk, which is larger than the sum on the right of the inequality, $(n-1)k$. Hence (23) excludes such a subtour.

To illustrate the foregoing argument, consider the subtour City 2 to City 3 to City 4 to City 2, which would be represented by $x_{23} = x_{34} = x_{42} = 1$. The $k = 3$ associated constraints in (23) are

(i)
$$u_2 - u_3 + nx_{23} \leq n - 1$$
$$u_3 - u_4 + nx_{34} \leq n - 1$$
$$u_4 - u_2 + nx_{42} \leq n - 1;$$

adding these inequalities, you obtain the composite constraint

(ii) $$(u_2 - u_3 + u_3 - u_4 + u_4 - u_2) + n(x_{23} + x_{34} + x_{42}) \leq (n - 1)3.$$

Check that (ii) rules out the possibility $x_{23} = x_{34} = x_{42} = 1$.

Second, the constraints (20) through (23) do not exclude any tour. To show this, we must demonstrate that there are values for u_i that satisfy (23) for any given tour. Consider such a tour, which, by definition, visits each of the Cities 2, 3, . . . , n, once and only once. Let t_i be the position in that tour at which City i is visited, where we designate $t_1 = 1$ for City 1. For example, in the tour City 1 to City 3 to City 5 . . . , the values of t_i are $t_1 = 1$, $t_3 = 2$, $t_5 = 3$, ... Then $u_i = t_i$, for $i = 2, 3, . . . , n$, is a feasible set of values. To see why, suppose $x_{ij} = 1$ in the given tour, so that $t_j = t_i + 1$. Then the constraint for this x_{ij} in (23) is satisfied, since

(iii) $$t_i - (t_i + 1) + n(1) \leq n - 1.$$

Suppose, instead, that $x_{ij} = 0$. Then the inequality in (23) is ($u_i - u_j \leq n - 1$), which must be satisfied because $u_i \leq n$ and $u_j > 1$.   ◀

Other formulation devices. Suppose you want to permit a variable x to equal only certain values, say, $X_1, X_2, . . . , X_p$. You can impose this stipulation by removing x and appropriately introducing p zero-one variables w_k. Specifically, replace x everywhere in the model by the expression

(24) $$X_1 w_1 + X_2 w_2 + \cdots + X_p w_p$$

and then restrict the w_k by the constraints

(25) $$w_1 + w_2 + \cdots + w_p = 1$$

(26) $$\text{all } w_k \text{ integer-valued.}$$

Further, if a nonlinear function $c(x)$ also appears in the model, then using (24), (25), and (26), you can replace $c(x)$ by the expression

(27) $$c(X_1)w_1 + c(X_2)w_2 + \cdots + c(X_p)w_p,$$

which is linear in the w_k.

The preceding approach can be generalized to accommodate a programming model that contains a continuous piecewise-linear function $c(x)$ of a nonnegative variable x. This type of model is discussed at some length in Sec. 14.7, and you may postpone reading the following explanation until you have studied the material in the next chapter.

Assume, for simplicity, that x lies in the interval $0 \leq x \leq X$ and that the values $0 \equiv X_1 < X_2 < \cdots < X_p \equiv X$ are the end points of the intervals for the linear pieces; that is, $c(x)$ is linear for $X_k \leq x \leq X_{k+1}$, where $k = 1, 2, \ldots, p - 1$. To begin, introduce p nonnegative weights w_k, replace x everywhere in the model by the expression (24), impose (25), where all $w_k \geq 0$ instead of (26), and replace $c(x)$ by (27).

As you should verify, these substitutions will be valid provided that a solution contains only one variable $w_k = 1$, or at most two *adjacent* variables w_k and w_{k+1}, where $w_k + w_{k+1} = 1$. To guarantee this so-called *property of adjacent weights*, introduce $(p - 1)$ zero-one variables z_k and impose the $(p + 1)$ constraints

$$
\begin{aligned}
w_1 - z_1 &\leq 0 \\
w_2 - z_1 - z_2 &\leq 0 \\
w_3 \quad - z_2 - z_3 &\leq 0 \\
&\ \vdots \\
w_{p-1} \quad\quad - z_{p-2} - z_{p-1} &\leq 0 \\
w_p \quad\quad\quad - z_{p-1} &\leq 0
\end{aligned}
$$

(28)

(29) $$z_1 + z_2 + z_3 + \cdots + z_{p-2} + z_{p-1} = 1,$$

along with the restrictions

(30) $$\text{all } z_k \text{ integer-valued.}$$

Check that the restrictions (29) and (30) ensure that exactly one z_k equals 1, thereby guaranteeing in (28) that no more than two of the weights w_k and w_{k+1} can be positive, and that their sum must be 1 according to (25).

Variations on the above procedures permit you to treat functions that are piecewise linear but possess jump discontinuities at the X_k values.

13.3 OVERVIEW OF INTEGER PROGRAMMING
ALGORITHMS

Currently, there are two principal approaches for finding a truly optimal solution to an integer programming problem.

1. *Cutting-Plane Algorithms.* Several variants of this approach are available. The one given in the next section is for the pure integer programming model.

It starts with an optimal linear programming solution. At each iteration, it adds a linear constraint that is satisfied by any integer solution to the original problem, but that rules out the current nonintegral solution. The method terminates as soon as an integer-valued solution is obtained. Convergence is guaranteed in a finite, albeit sometimes discouragingly large, number of iterations.

2. *Backtrack Algorithms.* Here, too, various versions are available. The first one that we present in Sec. 13.5 is for the mixed integer programming model, and is called the Branch-and-Bound Algorithm. Like the Cutting Plane Algorithm, it starts with an optimal linear programming solution; it then generates a *family* of related but separate linear programming problems. We go on in Sec. 13.6 to explain several modifications of the approach, using the traveling salesman problem for illustration. Finally, we present in Sec. 13.7 the Partial (Implicit) Enumeration Algorithm, which we will apply only to problems containing zero-one integer variables. A consequence of such special structure is that the arithmetic simplifies considerably. The term "backtrack" refers to the specific way that the sequence of problems is generated and solved. The notion will become clear when you read Sec. 13.5.

There are other approaches, although not guaranteed to find an optimal solution, often do so in particular instances, and frequently provide a near-optimal solution. One of the these methods is to take a random sample of feasible solutions, perhaps making simple-to-find improvements on each sample solution whenever possible. For example, if you applied the approach to a traveling salesman problem with n cities, you would draw a random sample of permutations of the Cities $2, 3, \ldots, n$, selected from the total $(n-1)!$ possibilities, and then compare the associated tour distances. Another approach, known generically as *heuristic programming*, employs both simple and sophisticated rules of thumb, as well as partially corrective trial-and-error procedures, to produce a feasible, and hopefully near-optimal solution. In the traveling salesman problem, a simple rule would be to travel from City j to the closest city not already visited; a partially corrective technique would be to test whether interchanging pairs of cities in the trial tour reduces the total distance.

These other methods have worked well in a number of practical applications. But since there is a negligible amount of codified knowledge about the techniques —oftentimes, they are of an ad hoc nature—we do not consider them further in this text.

The nitty-gritty. In keeping with our overall goal of emphasizing essential ideas, we present each of the methods in simplified terms—we have ignored technicalities that are relevant to the design of efficient electronic computer programs. Such details are critical in constructing successful computer codes, but are of interest primarily to specialists and consequently are omitted in this chapter. One aspect of these computational details does warrant your attention, however.

As you know, an algorithmic technique must be described unambiguously in order to be generally useful. This is because in practice, an electronic computer will do the calculations and has to be instructed in no uncertain terms on how to proceed. Naturally, this requirement applies to all the other algorithms you have studied. But we emphasize the point at this juncture because the descriptions of most integer programming algorithms are replete with possibilities for arbitrary choices to be made during the course of the iterations.

Curiously, when an individual applies any of these algorithms to a small-scale problem, he often is able to exploit the special properties of the model, and to make these choices auspiciously by exercising his intuition about the optimal solution. As a result, most of these algorithms look effective when tried on such toy problems. When the methods are programmed for an electronic calculator, however, the choices are made according to predetermined rules, without any human intervention to provide intuitive guidance. Experience has shown that the computational burden of these methods is highly sensitive to the particular way the arbitrary choices are resolved. This is in sharp contrast to experience with the simplex method. In that technique, many different versions of *Criterion I* (selection of variables to enter a nonoptimal basic solution) result in roughly the same magnitude of computational effort. As you study each algorithm below, take note of where the arbitrary choices arise.

13.4 CUTTING-PLANE ALGORITHM
(METHOD OF INTEGER FORMS)

The following simple example will motivate the guiding idea of the algorithm. Consider

(1) $$\text{maximize } 5x_1 + 1x_2$$

subject to

(2) $$2x_1 + 1x_2 = 3$$

(3) $$x_1 \text{ and } x_2 \text{ nonnegative integers.}$$

As you can quickly verify, $x_1 = \frac{3}{2}$ is the optimal linear programming solution to (1) and (2), when (3) is weakened to $x_1 \geq 0$ and $x_2 \geq 0$. The linear programming solution is not feasible in (3), since it is fractional. Note that (2) and (3) together, however, imply the linear inequality constraint

(4) $$x_1 \leq 1.$$

Explain why. Verify that the optimal linear programming solution to (1), (2), (4), and $x_1 \geq 0$ and $x_2 \geq 0$, is $x_1 = 1$ and $x_2 = 1$, which *is* integer-valued. Consequently, this linear programming solution is optimal for the model (1) through (3), because it is feasible in (3).

What we have done, in effect, is to find an optimal solution to an integer programming problem by constructing and solving an enlarged *linear* programming model containing linear constraints implied by the stipulations of the original integer problem. It was simple to discover a constraint (4) that did the trick for the small example. The algorithm below provides a systematic way of deriving such constraints for *any* integer programming problem. The central notion of the algorithm, then, is to replace an integer problem by a suitably enlarged linear programming problem.

Notice in the example that the optimal integer solution contains both variables at positive levels, even though there is only a single linear restriction (2). This illustrates a characteristic distinguishing linear and integer programming models. In a linear programming problem containing m constraints and n variables, and having a finite optimal objective function value, there is always an optimal solution containing no more than m variables at strictly positive levels. In an integer programming model of the same size, an optimal solution may require every integer-valued variable to be at a positive level. This is why it is necessary in the Cutting-Plane Algorithm to enlarge the size of the original model by adding further constraints.

There are several versions of the Cutting-Plane Algorithm. We present one that solves the pure integer programming problem, in which all variables are integer-valued; the technique can be extended without difficulty to the mixed integer case. The particular version we have chosen has the merit of being easily explained. Other versions, more intricate but also more efficient, are mainly of importance to a technical specialist—all that they contain is further refinements of the essential concepts that you will learn in the method below.

▶The idea of the Cutting-Plane Algorithm can be easily motivated by reference to solution space geometry (Sec. 3.4). Define the **convex hull** of the set of feasible integer points (solutions) as the smallest convex set containing these points (or, equivalently, as the set of points in Euclidean n-space composed of all **convex combinations** of the form $[wx_1 + (1 - w)y_1, wx_2 + (1 - w)y_2, \ldots, wx_n + (1 - w)y_n]$, where $0 \leq w \leq 1$, and $(x_1, x_2, \ldots, x_n)$ and $(y_1, y_2, \ldots, y_n)$ are feasible integer solutions). Assume that the optimal value of the linear objective function is finite. Then it is easily shown that the optimal value of the objective function occurs at a vertex of this convex hull. Such an extreme point is one of the feasible integer-valued solutions.

Significantly, the convex hull itself can be represented by a finite collection of linear constraints. The Cutting-Plane Algorithm begins with the convex set defined by the linear and nonnegativity restrictions in the original model and obtains an optimal extreme point of this set. If such a solution is not integer-valued, it adds a restriction that reduces the convex set so as to thereby cut off the current extreme point. But the new constraint does not cut off any extreme point of the convex hull of feasible integer solutions. Eventually, the method imposes enough constraints so that an optimal extreme point of the reduced convex set coincides with an optimal extreme point of the convex hull. This geometric interpretation will be illustrated by an example later in the section. ◀

Detailed approach. Suppose that the pure integer programming problem is stated in the form

(5) $$\text{maximize} \sum_{j=1}^{n} c_j x_j$$

subject to

(6) $$\sum_{j=1}^{n} a_{ij}x_j = b_i \quad \text{for } i = 1, 2, \ldots, m$$

(7)   all x_j nonnegative integers.

Assume that there exists a feasible solution to (6) and (7) and that the objective-function value is finite in an optimal solution. Before giving the specific steps of the algorithm, we show in general terms how to construct additional linear restrictions that must be satisfied by any feasible solution to (6) and (7).

Consider any linear equation that can be derived by algebraic operations on the linear constraints (6)—such as, by adding two or more of the equations, or by multiplying an equation by a nonzero constant. Then if a solution satisfies (6), it also must satisfy an equation so derived. Let

(8) $$\sum_{j=1}^{n} a_j x_j = b$$

denote such a constraint; possibly one or more of the a_j and b are fractional-valued, like 2.5 or $\frac{10}{3}$. Let the symbol $[d]$ designate the **integer part** of d, that is, the largest integer that is less than or equal to the real number d; for example,

(9)
$$[2.5] = 2 \qquad [\tfrac{10}{3}] = 3 \qquad [4] = 4$$
$$[-2.5] = -3 \quad [-\tfrac{10}{3}] = -4 \quad [-4] = -4.$$

Because the x_j are also restricted in (7) to be nonnegative integers, any values of the x_j that satisfy (6), and consequently (8), must actually satisfy the weaker inequality

(10) $$\sum_{j=1}^{n} [a_j] x_j \leq b.$$

State why. Further, since the summation on the left-hand side of (10) must be integer-valued, verify that (10) can be validly strengthened to

(11) $$\sum_{j=1}^{n} [a_j] x_j \leq [b].$$

Finally, (11) can be transformed to an equality by adding a slack variable

(12) $$\sum_{j=1}^{n} [a_j] x_j + x = [b] \quad \text{(integer parts)},$$

where x is restricted to be a nonnegative integer. [Explain why (11) implies that x must be integer-valued.] Therefore, if (6) is augmented by the linear constraint (12), the problem still remains a pure integer programming model. To summarize so far, we have derived a constraint (12)—the values of a_j and b being obtained by algebraic operations on the constraints (6)—that is satisfied by any feasible solution to (6) and (7).

To simplify the verbal explanation of the algorithm, we perform an elementary manipulation on (8) and (12). Define the values f_j and f by the identities

(13) $$[a_j] + f_j \equiv a_j \quad \text{and} \quad [b] + f \equiv b,$$

so that $0 \leq f_j < 1$ and $0 \leq f < 1$; these quantities are called the **fractional parts** of a_j and b. (To illustrate, the fractional part of 2.5 and -2.5 is .5; of $\frac{10}{3}$ is $\frac{1}{3}$; and of $-\frac{10}{3}$ is $\frac{2}{3}$.) By subtracting (8) from (12), you obtain a constraint composed of only fractional parts

(14) $$\sum_{j=1}^{n} (-f_j) x_j + x = -f \quad \text{(fractional parts)}.$$

We will employ (14) instead of (12) in the algorithm below.

The following example shows how the new constraints (12) and (14) work. In the example above, multiply both sides of (2) by $\frac{1}{2}$, yielding

(15) $$1x_1 + \tfrac{1}{2}x_2 = \tfrac{3}{2}.$$

Then verify that applying the formula in (12) gives

(16) $$1x_1 + 0x_2 + x = 1,$$

which is the same as constraint (4), and that applying (14) gives

(17) $$-\tfrac{1}{2}x_2 + x = -\tfrac{1}{2},$$

which implies that $x_2 \geq 1$.

The Cutting-Plane Algorithm proceeds in this way:

Step 1. Find an optimal linear programming solution to the objective function (5) and linear constraints (6), ignoring the integer stipulations in (7) and only requiring that all $x_j \geq 0$.

Step 2. Terminate the iterations if the current linear programming solution is integer-valued. Otherwise, select a fractional-valued basic variable. Form constraint (14) from the equation that contains this basic variable in the current optimal linear programming solution.

Step 3. Augment the linear programming problem with the new constraint, find a new optimal linear programming solution, and return to *Step 2*.

We elaborate on these steps before illustrating the algorithm by an example. Suppose that at any iteration the current optimal linear programming solution is obtained by using the simplex method, as described in Sec. 4.4. Assume that x_k is the basic variable in Row i at the final iteration:

(18) $$x_k + \sum_{j \text{ nonbasic}} t_{ij} x_j = b \qquad \underline{\text{Row i,}}$$

where b is fractional-valued; hence, $x_k = b$ does not satisfy the integer stipulation. Then at *Step 2*, constraint (14), formed from (18), is simply

(19) $$\sum_{j \text{ nonbasic}} (-f_{ij}) x_j + x = -f \quad \text{(cut)},$$

where f_{ij} is the fractional part of t_{ij} and f the fractional part of b. Note that after the first iteration, the summation of nonbasic variables in (19) may include the slack variables, symbolically denoted by x in (14), that were added at *Step 2* in previous iterations. This inclusion is warranted because each of these slack variables is restricted to be integer-valued.

Observe that the current linear programming solution does not satisfy the new constraint (19), in that $x = -f$ is strictly negative, since the summation on the left-hand side, containing only nonbasic variables, currently equals 0. When the so-called **cut** (19) is appended at *Step 3* along with the stipulation that $x \geq 0$, the current linear programming solution is thereby ruled out, or, in geometric terms, is cut off. This means that the value of the objective function cannot increase, and may decrease, after the optimization in *Step 3*. In practice, you would perform the optimization by applying the dual simplex algorithm (Sec. 5.8) to the model enlarged by (19), after adding x to the current set of basic variables.

How you select a fractional-valued basic variable in *Step 2* is somewhat arbitrary. You cannot assume that the choice is completely arbitrary, however, in devising a rigorous proof that the method always converges in a finite number of iterations. But for practical purposes, it frequently speeds convergence to pick a variable having the largest fractional part (that is, one leading to the largest value for f). You could also form several such constraints for different fractional-valued basic variables and augment them in *Step 3*, but there is no empirical evidence to suggest that doing so is computationally advantageous.

If you add an amendment to *Step 3*, you can keep the augmented linear programs from growing without bound. The procedure is that whenever the current optimal basic solution includes a slack variable x introduced at a previous iteration, you drop that equation containing x in the current solution prior to performing the optimization. This amendment implies that the size of the augmented problem never exceeds n linear equations. As soon as the problem has n equations, adding any new constraint must cause a basic solution to contain one or more of the slack variables introduced by (14). An important corollary of these observations is that the computational difficulty of an integer programming problem depends significantly on the number of variables in the problem.

The algorithm is guaranteed, in theory, to converge to an optimum in a finite number of iterations; we discuss actual computational experience at the end of the section. But note that the method does not provide a feasible integer solution until the terminal iteration—in this sense, the algorithm is a dual technique. As a consequence, if you stop the iterations prematurely, you do not have a usable solution. (There are Cutting-Plane Algorithms which are primal, in that the solution at each iteration is feasible and integer-valued, but these are not discussed in the text. The ideas are illustrated in exercise 69.)

Example. Consider the problem

(20)   maximize $21x_1 + 11x_2$

subject to

(21) $7x_1 + 4x_2 + x_3 = 13$

(22) x_1, x_2, x_3 nonnegative integers.

(You can interpret x_3 as a slack variable, since it does not appear in the objective function.) As usual, express the objective function by a definitional linear equation:

$$(23) \qquad\qquad x_0 - 21x_1 - 11x_2 = 0;$$

observe that you can restrict x_0 to be integer-valued in this example. Before continuing, find the optimal solution by inspection.

As you should verify, performing *Step 1* leads to the linear programming solution

$$(24) \qquad
\begin{aligned}
x_0 \quad + \quad x_2 + 3x_3 &= 39 & \text{Row 0} \\
x_1 + \tfrac{4}{7}x_2 + \tfrac{1}{7}x_3 &= 1\tfrac{6}{7} & \text{Row 1.}
\end{aligned}$$

According to *Step 2*, since x_1 is fractional-valued, you must add a restriction (14) formed from Row 1. Check that the constraint is

$$(25) \qquad\qquad -\tfrac{4}{7}x_2 - \tfrac{1}{7}x_3 + x_4 = -\tfrac{6}{7} \qquad\qquad \text{Row 2,}$$

where x_4 is the associated integer-valued slack variable. Continuing to *Step 3*, the linear programming model consists of (24) augmented by (25). Check that the new optimal solution is

$$(26) \qquad
\begin{aligned}
x_0 \quad\quad + 2\tfrac{3}{4}x_3 + 1\tfrac{3}{4}x_4 &= 37\tfrac{1}{2} & \text{Row 0} \\
x_1 \quad\quad + \quad x_4 &= 1 & \text{Row 1} \\
x_2 + \tfrac{1}{4}x_3 - 1\tfrac{3}{4}x_4 &= 1\tfrac{1}{2} & \text{Row 2.}
\end{aligned}$$

Returning to *Step 2*, verify that the new constraint formed from Row 2 is

$$(27) \qquad\qquad -\tfrac{1}{4}x_3 - \tfrac{1}{4}x_4 + x_5 = -\tfrac{1}{2} \qquad\qquad \text{Row 3}$$

and that in *Step 3* the optimal linear programming solution to (26) and (27) is

$$(28) \qquad
\begin{aligned}
x_0 + \quad x_1 \quad\quad\quad\quad + 11x_5 &= 33 & \text{Row 0} \\
- \quad x_1 \quad + x_3 \quad - \quad x_5 &= 1 & \text{Row 1} \\
2x_1 + x_2 \quad\quad + \quad x_5 &= 3 & \text{Row 2} \\
x_1 \quad\quad + x_4 \quad\quad &= 1 & \text{Row 3.}
\end{aligned}$$

Returning again to *Step 2*, the iterations terminate with the optimal integer-valued solution $x_1 = 0$, $x_2 = 3$, and $x_3 = 1$, yielding $x_0 = 33$. [If the solution in (28) were not integer-valued, then you would drop the relation in Row 3 before performing the next optimization at *Step 3*, because x_4 has re-entered the basis.]

▶You can gain further understanding of the method by seeing how the additional constraints (25) and (27) can be expressed as inequalities in terms of the original variables x_1 and x_2. You then can easily graph these inequalities, using the *solution space representation* in Sec. 3.4 to see how they cut off the associated noninteger-valued linear programming solution.

Constraint (21) can be written as an inequality,

$$(i) \qquad\qquad 7x_1 + 4x_2 \le 13,$$

by suppressing the slack variable x_3. Eliminating x_3 from (25) by means of (21), and suppressing the slack variable x_4 in the result, gives the inequality

(ii) $x_1 \leq 1.$

Eliminating x_3 from (27) by means of (21), x_4 from the result by means of (25), and suppressing the slack variable x_5 yields the inequality

(iii) $2x_1 + x_2 \leq 3.$

Verify that the optimal nonnegative solution to the linear programming problem consisting of (20), (i), (ii), and (iii), agrees with that in (28).

In drawing the solution space representation, begin by indicating the set of feasible integer-valued solutions implied by (i) as well as the region of feasible linear programming solutions; show that $x_1 = 1\frac{6}{7}$ is the optimal linear programming solution. Next add (ii), and notice how this constraint does not eliminate any feasible integer-valued solution, but does rule out the current linear programming solution. Show that $x_1 = 1$ and $x_3 = 1\frac{1}{2}$ is optimal when (ii) is added. Finally, append (iii) and observe again how the new constraint does not eliminate any feasible integer-valued solution, cuts off the current linear programming solution, and yields a new optimal solution that is integer-valued.   ◀

Concluding remarks. Computational experience with sophisticated versions of the cutting-plane algorithm has by no means been uniformly successful. In particular, the approach has not worked well on inherently combinatorial problems that are only "tricked" into an integer programming formulation. The method also has exhibited difficulty in solving problems containing large values of the a_{ij} and b_i. But the algorithm has succeeded in problems in which the optimal linear programming solution already yields integer values for many of the variables.

The computational problem manifests itself in the optimization process of *Step 3*. After a few iterations, there may be numerous alternative optimal solutions to the linear programming problem in *Step 3*. This causes the value of the objective function to remain constant (usually at a nonoptimal value) for many iterations until the alternatives are eventually ruled out by the constraints formed in *Step 2*. (Such stalling is sometimes referred to as **massive degeneracy**.) Unfortunately, this phenomenon arises frequently in medium- and large-scale problems. Indeed, an abundance of examples of small-scale problems (10 or less variables and equations) have required thousands of iterations to achieve convergence.

The number of iterations required to obtain a solution also seems to depend considerably on the specific way the problem is formulated. As an illustration of this so-called form sensitivity, adding seemingly redundant constraints (for example, $x_1 \leq 1$ and $x_2 \leq 1$ to a model containing the constraint $x_1 + x_2 \leq 1$) can substantially improve the speed of convergence.

▶We have skipped over one point that warrants mentioning. Perhaps you found it surprising that we derived constraint (12) so simply. Were you to think about discovering other similarly motivated cutting-plane constraints, you would find that numerous possibilities are amenable to systematic derivation. But what distinguishes (12) from many other possibilities is that the resultant algorithm can be rigorously proved to converge to an optimal solution in a finite number of iterations. (Some of the other approaches can be shown incapable of converging when applied to certain classes of problems.) Because of the sporadic computational success of the Cutting-Plane Algorithm, the theoretical property of finite convergence is an admittedly weak defense for using (12); but the other approaches have not proved to be any better even when they do converge.   ◀

13.5 BRANCH-AND-BOUND ALGORITHM

This method can be applied to mixed, as well as pure, integer programming problems. For definiteness, suppose the model is stated as

$$(1) \qquad\qquad \text{maximize} \sum_{j=1}^{n} c_j x_j$$

subject to

$$(2) \qquad\qquad \sum_{j=1}^{n} a_{ij} x_j \leq b_i \qquad \text{for } i = 1, 2, \ldots, m$$

$$(3) \qquad\qquad x_j \text{ integer-valued} \quad \text{for } j = 1, 2, \ldots, p \ (\leq n)$$

$$(4) \qquad\qquad x_j \geq 0 \qquad \text{for } j = p + 1, \ldots, n.$$

In addition, assume that, for each integer-valued variable, you can provide lower and upper bounds that surely include the optimal values

$$(5) \qquad\qquad L_j \leq x_j \leq U_j \quad \text{for } j = 1, 2, \ldots, p.$$

Usually $L_j = 0$, but it need not. (As you know from Sec. 3.3, no essential generality is lost by assuming that all $L_j = 0$. The algorithm is more simply described, however, by employing the general symbol L_j.)

The idea of the Branch-and-Bound Algorithm stems from the following elementary observation. Consider any variable x_j, and let I be some integer value, where $L_j \leq I \leq U_j - 1$. Then an optimal solution to (1) through (5) will also satisfy either the linear constraint

$$(6) \qquad\qquad x_j \geq I + 1$$

or the linear constraint

$$(7) \qquad\qquad x_j \leq I.$$

To illustrate how this dichotomy can be used, suppose you ignore the integer restriction (3) and find that an optimal linear programming solution to (1), (2), (4), and (5) indicates that $x_1 = 1\frac{2}{3}$. Then formulate and solve two more linear programs. Each of these still contains (1), (2), and (4). But (5) for $j = 1$ is modified in one problem to be $2 \leq x_1 \leq U_1$, and in the other to be $L_1 \leq x_1 \leq 1$. Suppose further that each of these two problems has an optimal solution that satisfies the integer restrictions (3). Then the solution that has the larger value for the objective function is indeed optimal for the original integer programming problem. State why. Usually, one (or both) of these problems has no optimal solution that satisfies (3); hence, additional computations may be required. The algorithm below specifies how to apply the dichotomy (6) and (7) in a systematic manner to eventually obtain an optimal solution.

Detailed approach. We present the steps of the method next, and discuss its computational merits at the end of the section. The Branch-and-Bound Algorithm solves a *set* of linear programming problems. As you saw in the preceding section, an optimal solution to an integer programming problem need not be a basic solution to the m linear constraints (2); that is, an optimal solution may contain more than m variables at strictly positive levels. The bounds (5) on each x_j serve to enlarge the linear programming models sufficiently so that all variables, if necessary, can be present in an optimal solution. The enlargement is further indication that the computational burden depends critically on the number of integer-valued variables in the problem.

The method. At any iteration t, you have available a lower bound, say, x_0^t, for the optimal value of the objective function. To keep the exposition simple, assume that at the first iteration, x_0^1 either is *strictly* less than the optimal value, or equals the value of the objective function for a feasible solution that you have recorded. If worse comes to worst, you can let $x_0^1 = -\infty$ if you have no information at all about the problem. In addition to a lower bound, you have a master list of linear programming problems that must be solved; the only differences among these comprise revisions in the bounds (5). At iteration 1, the master list contains a single problem consisting of (1), (2), (4), and (5).

The procedure at iteration t is:

Step 1. Terminate the computations if the master list is empty. Otherwise, remove a linear programming problem from the master list.

Step 2. Solve the chosen problem. If it has no feasible solution, or if the resultant optimal value of the objective function is less than or equal to x_0^t, then let $x_0^{t+1} = x_0^t$, and return to *Step 1*. Otherwise, proceed to *Step 3*.

Step 3. If the obtained optimal solution to the linear programming problem satisfies the integer constraints, then record it, let x_0^{t+1} be the associated optimal value of the objective function, and return to *Step 1*. Otherwise, proceed to *Step 4*.

Step 4. Select any variable x_j, for $j = 1, 2, \ldots, p$, that does not have an integer value in the obtained optimal solution to the chosen linear programming problem. Let b_j denote this value, and $[b_j]$ signify the largest integer less than or equal to b_j. Add two linear programming problems to the master list. These two problems are identical with the problem chosen in *Step 1*, except that in one, the lower bound on x_j is replaced by $[b_j] + 1$, and in the other, the upper bound on x_j is replaced by $[b_j]$. Let $x_0^{t+1} = x_0^t$, and return to *Step 1*.

At termination, if you have recorded a feasible solution yielding x_0^t, it is optimal; otherwise, no feasible solution exists. As the example below demonstrates, you may obtain an integer-valued solution prior to the last iteration. You do not know that it *is* optimal, however, until the final iteration. For this reason, the algorithm may be called an *almost-dual* method.

Illustration. An example will clarify the details of the procedure. Consider

(8) $$\text{maximize } 3x_1 + 3x_2 + 13x_3$$

subject to

$$-3x_1 + 6x_2 + 7x_3 \leq 8$$

(9) $$6x_1 - 3x_2 + 7x_3 \leq 8,$$

where each x_j must be a nonnegative integer. Suppose we specify the bounds on each variable as

(10) $$0 \leq x_j \leq 5 \quad \text{for } j = 1, 2, 3.$$

As usual, let x_0 denote the value of the objective function. Find the optimal solution by inspection.

At iteration 1, let the lower bound be $x_0^1 = 0$, since all $x_j = 0$ is feasible. The master list contains only the linear programming problem (8), (9), and (10), which is designated as Problem 1. Remove it in *Step 1*, and in *Step 2* find the optimal solution

(11) $$x_0 = 16 \quad x_1 = x_2 = 2\tfrac{2}{3} \quad x_3 = 0 \qquad \text{(Problem 1)}.$$

Since the solution is not integer-valued, proceed from *Step 3* to *Step 4*, and select x_1. Then place on the master list

(12)

Problem 2:   constraints (9)

$$3 \leq x_1 \leq 5 \quad 0 \leq x_2 \leq 5 \quad 0 \leq x_3 \leq 5$$

Problem 3:   constraints (9)

$$0 \leq x_1 \leq 2 \quad 0 \leq x_2 \leq 5 \quad 0 \leq x_3 \leq 5.$$

Returning to *Step 1* with $x_0^2 = x_0^1 = 0$, remove Problem 2. As you can verify, *Step 2* establishes that Problem 2 has no feasible solution. Hence, put $x_0^3 = x_0^2 = 0$, and return to *Step 1*.

Now remove Problem 3, and obtain in *Step 2* the optimal solution

(13) $$x_0 = 15\tfrac{5}{7} \quad x_1 = x_2 = 2 \quad x_3 = \tfrac{2}{7} \qquad \text{(Problem 3)},$$

which is not integer-valued. Therefore, go from *Step 3* to *Step 4*, where x_3 is selected, and place on the master list:

(14)

Problem 4:   constraints (9)

$$0 \leq x_1 \leq 2 \quad 0 \leq x_2 \leq 5 \quad 1 \leq x_3 \leq 5$$

Problem 5:   constraints (9)

$$0 \leq x_1 \leq 2 \quad 0 \leq x_2 \leq 5 \quad 0 \leq x_3 \leq 0.$$

Observe that Problems 4 and 5 differ from Problem 3 only in the bounds on x_3.

Returning to *Step 1* with $x_0^4 = 0$, remove Problem 4. The optimal solution is

(15) $$x_0 = 15 \quad x_1 = x_2 = \tfrac{1}{3} \quad x_3 = 1 \qquad \text{(Problem 4)}.$$

This leads to *Step 4*; suppose you select x_2, yielding, as a consequence,

Problem 6: constraints (9)

(16)

$$0 \leq x_1 \leq 2 \quad 1 \leq x_2 \leq 5 \quad 1 \leq x_3 \leq 5$$

Problem 7: constraints (9)

$$0 \leq x_1 \leq 2 \quad 0 \leq x_2 \leq 0 \quad 1 \leq x_3 \leq 5.$$

Note that Problems 6 and 7 differ from Problem 4 only in the bounds on x_2.

Returning to *Step 1* with $x_0^5 = 0$, remove Problem 6. Check that Problems 5 and 7 remain on the master list. You will discover in *Step 2* that Problem 6 has no feasible solution, so return to *Step 1* with $x_0^6 = 0$. Now remove Problem 7, giving the optimal solution

(17) $$x_0 = 14\tfrac{6}{7} \quad x_1 = x_2 = 0 \quad x_3 = 1\tfrac{1}{7}$$ (Problem 7).

Because x_3 is fractional, this creates, in *Step 4*,

Problem 8: constraints (9)

(18)

$$0 \leq x_1 \leq 2 \quad 0 \leq x_2 \leq 0 \quad 2 \leq x_3 \leq 5$$

Problem 9: constraints (9)

$$0 \leq x_1 \leq 2 \quad 0 \leq x_2 \leq 0 \quad 1 \leq x_3 \leq 1.$$

Verify that removing Problem 8 at iteration 7 gives an indication of no feasible solution in *Step 2*, and removing Problem 9 at iteration 8 gives

(19) $$x_0 = 13 \quad x_1 = x_2 = 0 \quad x_3 = 1$$ (Problem 9)

in *Step 2*. Therefore at *Step 3*, you record (19) and let $x_0^9 = 13$.

Returning to *Step 1*, you find that only Problem 5 remains on the master list. The optimal linear programming solution is

(20) $$x_0 = 13 \quad x_1 = 2 \quad x_2 = 2\tfrac{1}{3} \quad x_3 = 0$$ (Problem 5).

Since x_0 in (20) equals x_0^9, you return to *Step 1* and terminate the computations, as the master list is now empty. The optimal solution to the integer programming problem is (19), which was recorded at iteration 8.

Note that arbitrary choices arise in the algorithm at two places: selection of the problem to remove in *Step 1* and of the variable x_j to provide additional problems in *Step 4*. The number of iterations to solve a model can vary considerably, depending on how these selections are actually made. (For example, the choice of Problem 4 instead of Problem 5 at iteration 4 turned out to be auspicious.) Auxiliary numerical tests have been devised to assist in making these choices, but they will not be discussed here, since they are of interest mainly to technical specialists. By the same token, having a better bound x_0^t lessens the likelihood that at *Step 2* you will have to go on to *Step 3* and *Step 4*.

Recapitulation. The history of the iterations can be displayed by means of a tree-like diagram, shown in Fig. 13.1. Notice each node in the tree diagram represents a problem on the master list; each branch leads to one of the problems

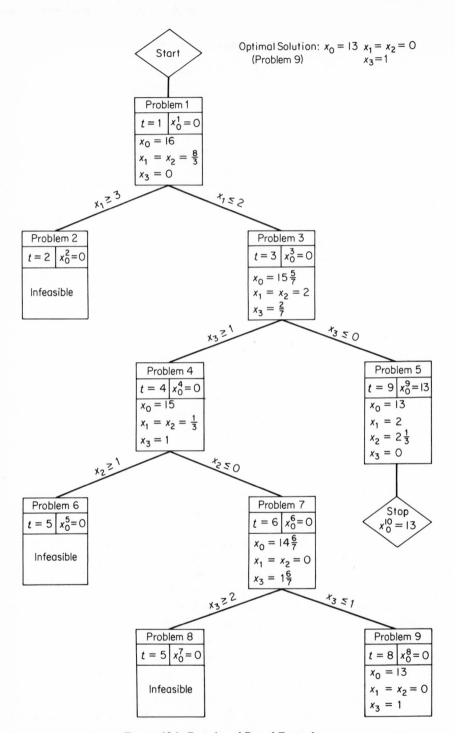

Figure 13.1. Branch-and-Bound Example.

470

added to the master list in *Step 4*. The pertinence of this graphical analogy explains why the word "branch" is used in the algorithm's name, "Branch-and-Bound." The word "bound" is suggested by the test in *Step 2*. (The technique might alternatively be designated **Branch-and-Prune**.) Note that the branch for Problem 5 is terminated, even though the optimal solution is not integer-valued. The reason is that when you reach Problem 5 at $t = 9$, you already have a feasible solution with an objective function value 13. Therefore, branching further by imposing stronger restrictions can never improve on the previously obtained feasible solution.

Now you can see why the algorithm is called a **backtracking** method. When you terminate certain branches—as at Problems 2, 6, 8, and 9 in the example—you must go back up the branch in search of any unsolved problem that remains on the tree.

▶ Several approaches aid the optimizing computations in *Step 2*. For example, by employing the transformation in Sec. 3.3, each integer variable can be redefined in *Step 2* so that its lower bound is 0 and its upper bound is $L_j + U_j$. This yields a linear programming model with m full-fledged linear constraints, corresponding to (20), and p upper-bounded nonnegative variables. You can pick the initial basis to be the optimal variables for the previous problem that generated the current one at *Step 4*. This starting basis no longer yields a nonnegative solution, because of the revised bounds; but it satisfies the conditions for initiating the Dual Simplex Algorithm, given in Sec. 5.8. (An Upper-Bounded Variables Algorithm in Sec. 5.10 can also be used.) ◀

Concluding remarks. This method shares with the Cutting-Plane Algorithm an important computational merit: it can be efficiently coded into a computer routine, and therefore run without manual intervention at any iteration. The method works well in problems containing a few integer-valued variables, but if the number of variables is large, or if the linear programming solution to the problem is far from optimal (as was the case for the example), then the number of iterations may be too large for a practical application of the algorithm.

Of course, the method is applicable to combinatorial problems containing only zero-one integer variables; then each $L_j = 0$ and $U_j = 1$. In this case, the two problems added at *Step 4* actually imply the alternatives $x_j = 0$ and $x_j = 1$. You can often improve on the efficiency of the Branch-and-Bound Algorithm, however, by adapting it to take account of a model's special structure. In the remainder of the chapter, you will see several ways to do this.

13.6 TRAVELING SALESMAN PROBLEM

We now illustrate several ways the Branch-and-Bound Algorithm of the preceding section can be modified to take advantage of the special structure of combinatorial problems. We have selected the traveling salesman problem for this purpose, and exhibit three different versions of the branch-and-bound approach. Many of the formulations in Sec. 13.2 that contain zero-one variables can be solved by one or more of these approaches, after suitable adaptation. The practical consequence of taking advantage of a model's special structure is that you then can handle moderately large problems. For example, traveling salesman problems containing up to 40 cities have been solved in a reasonable amount of computer time using the methods below.

It is convenient to characterize the traveling salesman problem by the formulation in Sec. 13.2:

(1) $\text{minimize} \sum\limits_{i=1}^{n} \sum\limits_{j=1}^{n} c_{ij} x_{ij}$ where $c_{ii} = \infty$ for $i = 1, 2, \ldots, n$

subject to

(2) $\sum\limits_{j=1}^{n} x_{ij} = 1$ for $i = 1, 2, \ldots, n$ (departure)

(3) $\sum\limits_{i=1}^{n} x_{ij} = 1$ for $j = 1, 2, \ldots, n$ (arrival)

(4) x_{ij} nonnegative integer   for all i and j

(5)   solution is a tour.

Recall $x_{ij} = 1$ implies that the salesman travels from City i directly to City j, and $c_{ij} \geq 0$ is the corresponding distance. When (5) is dropped, (1) through (4) constitute an assignment model (Sec. 6.4), which can be solved by any of the techniques explained in Appendix I (Note that the objective here is "minimization," whereas it was "maximization" in the preceding section. The methods below will differ in certain obvious details from the Branch-and-Bound Algorithm to accommodate this change.)

A particular example will be used to illustrate the three different branch-and-bound versions; the data are given in Fig. 13.2. Observe that the unique solution to the associated assignment model is $x_{15} = x_{51} = x_{23} = x_{34} = x_{42} = 1$, which does

Distances c_{ij}

From City \ To City	1	2	3	4	5
1	∞	10	25	25	10
2	1	∞	10	15	2
3	8	9	∞	20	10
4	14	10	24	∞	15
5	10	8	25	27	∞

Optimal Assignment : $c_{15} + c_{23} + c_{34} + c_{42} + c_{51} = 60$

FIGURE 13.2.   Traveling Salesman Problem.

not satisfy (5) as it contains two cycles. Therefore, the sum of the distances for this solution, namely 60, is strictly less than the length of an optimal tour. There are $(n - 1)! = 4! = 24$ possible tours; before going on, see if you can spot an optimal one.

Method of excluded subtours. Of the three methods to be discussed, this version makes the smallest modification of the Branch-and-Bound Algorithm in the preceding section. At the beginning of an iteration t, you have an *upper* bound x_0^t on the optimal value of the objective function. You can let x_0^1 be any suitably large number, such as the sum $(c_{12} + c_{23} + \cdots + c_{n1})$ corresponding to the tour City 1 to City 2 to . . . City n to City 1. In addition, you have a master list containing a number of assignment models. All of these are of the form (1) through (4), but differ from each other in that various c_{ij} values have been revised to equal ∞. At iteration 1, the master list consists of the assignment model (1) through (4), which we designate as Problem 1. Define a *subtour* as a cycle containing less than all n cities, such as $x_{15} = x_{51} = 1$, and $x_{23} = x_{34} = x_{42} = 1$.

The procedure at iteration t is

Step 1. Terminate the computations if the master list is empty. Otherwise, remove a problem from the master list.

Step 2. Solve the chosen assignment model. If the optimal value of the objective function (which may be ∞) is greater than or equal to x_0^t, then let $x_0^{t+1} = x_0^t$, and return to *Step 1.* Otherwise, proceed to *Step 3.*

Step 3. If the obtained optimal solution to the chosen assignment model is a tour, then record it, let x_0^{t+1} be the associated optimal value of the objective function, and return to *Step 1.* Otherwise, proceed to *Step 4.*

Step 4. Select in the obtained optimal solution of the chosen assignment model a subtour that contains the smallest number of cities. For each of the $x_{ij} = 1$ in the selected subtour, add a problem to the master list, and set the corresponding $c_{ij} = \infty$; leave all the other costs the same as in the problem chosen in *Step 1.* Let $x_0^{t+1} = x_0^t$, and return to *Step 1.*

The details of the method are clarified by the example shown in Fig. 13.2. At iteration 1, let $x_0^t = 65$, corresponding to the tour City 1 to City 2 to . . . City 5 to City 1. The master list contains only the assignment model with the c_{ij} given in Fig. 13.2, so you must choose this problem at *Step 1.* You find that the optimal solution in *Step 2* yields an objective-function value 60, as shown in Fig. 13.2, bringing you to *Step 3.* Since the obtained optimal solution contains two subtours, you proceed to *Step 4.* Select the subtour $x_{15} = x_{51} = 1$, because this contains one less city than does the subtour $x_{23} = x_{34} = x_{42} = 1$. Add two problems to the master list, letting one have $c_{15} = \infty$, and the other $c_{51} = \infty$; leave all the remaining c_{ij} unchanged. Let $x_0^2 = x_0^1 = 65$.

The justification for *Step 4* is elementary. Since the subtour $x_{15} = x_{51} = 1$ is infeasible, either $x_{15} = 0$ or $x_{51} = 0$ (or both) in an optimal tour. The problems added in *Step 4* allow for each of these possibilities. The reasoning applies with equal validity to any subtour. (Using subtours as the source for generating new problems at *Step 4* leads to a noteworthy difference between this version and the Branch-and-Bound Algorithm in the preceding section. Here, several problems on the master list may turn out to be identical. This occurrence is easily recognizable when performing manual computations on a small-sized example; the redundant problems can be discarded when they are discovered. If the method is computerized, it may be preferable to perform the redundant calculations rather than to check for duplications.)

Returning to *Step 1*, select the problem with $c_{15} = \infty$, which we designate as Problem 2. The optimal value of the objective function for the corresponding assignment model is 65. This represents a lower bound on any tour that excludes the route City 1 to City 5. Because you already have a *tour* with length 65, there is no need to consider this problem any further. Thus, according to *Step 2*, let $x_0^3 = x_0^2 = 65$, and return to *Step 1*. Select the remaining problem with $c_{51} = \infty$,

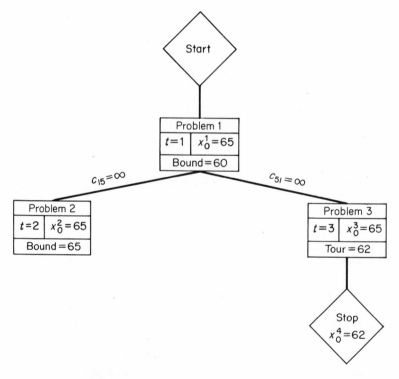

Optimal Tour: $x_0 = 62$ $x_{15} = x_{52} = x_{23} = x_{34} = x_{41} = 1$
(Problem 3)

FIGURE 13.3. Method of Excluded Subtours.

which we designate as Problem 3. Now the optimal value of the objective function for the assignment model is 62, taking you to *Step 3*. You obtain the associated optimal solution

(6)   minimum distance $= 62$ $x_{15} = x_{52} = x_{23} = x_{34} = x_{41} = 1$,

which *is* a tour. Therefore, record (6), let $x_0^4 = 62$, and return to *Step 1*, where you find the master list is empty, thereby terminating the iterations. A tree diagram for this example is given in Fig. 13.3.

Method of designated routes. The version above succeeds in limiting the number of branches to be explored by calculating an effective lower bound on the objective function for any tour emanating from each problem. But to obtain such a bound, you had to perform an assignment model optimization. Now you will see how to find more easily calculated bounds. The price you pay for this simplification, however, is that you will have to explore more branches in the associated tree for this method.

At the beginning of any iteration t, you have an upper bound x_0^t on the optimal value of the objective function; you can obtain x_0^1 as before. In addition, you have a master list of problems in which a subset of c_{ij} values have been revised to equal ∞ and a subset of $x_{ij} = 1$. There are no subtours among the $x_{ij} = 1$. At iteration 1, the master list consists of two problems; in one, a selected c_{ij} value has been revised to equal ∞ and in the other, the corresponding $x_{ij} = 1$ and $c_{ji} = \infty$. (Letting $c_{ji} = \infty$ rules out letting $x_{ji} = 1$, which would give the subtour City i to City j to City i.)

The status of each problem in the master list can be conveniently summarized as follows. Take the array of c_{ij}, as in Fig. 13.2. Cross out the kth row and hth column if $x_{kh} = 1$. The remaining c_{ij} (some of which equal ∞) correspond to x_{ij} not yet assigned. A lower bound on the optimal value of the objective function for any tour containing the specified subset of $x_{ij} = 1$ can be calculated in a variety of ways. In general, the larger the lower bound, the fewer the branches that will have to be examined.

One simple, but moderately effective, bounding technique is based on the observation that the distance must be at least equal to the sum of the c_{ij} where $x_{ij} = 1$, plus the sum of the smallest c_{ij} in each of the rows that have not been crossed out. You can (and should) raise the bound even further by subtracting the smallest c_{ij} in each row that has not been crossed out from every other c_{ij} in that row. This yields the so-called *diminished distances*. Then add to the previous sum the smallest diminished distance in each of the columns that have not been crossed out. An example is shown in Fig. 13.4. Observe that x_{23} has been designated equal to 1. The top table indicates the minimum distances for each row, excluding the second row. Each of these minima is subtracted from every element in the corresponding row to yield the bottom table.

(Actually, you can obtain a lower bound by solving an assignment model, formed from the c_{ij} in the rows and columns that have not been crossed out, and

$x_{23} = 1$ $(c_{23} = 10)$

From City	To City 1	2	3	4	5	Row Minimum
1	∞	10		25	10	10
2						
3	8	∞		20	10	8
4	14	10		∞	15	10
5	10	8		27	∞	8

Diminished Distances

From City	To City 1	2	3	4	5
1	∞	0		15	0
2					
3	0	∞		12	2
4	4	0		∞	5
5	2	0		19	∞
Column Minimum	0	0		12	0

Bound $= c_{23} + \Sigma(\text{Row Min.}) + \Sigma(\text{Col. Min.})$
$ = 10 + 10 + 8 + 10 + 8 + 0 + 0 + 12 + 0 = 58$

FIGURE 13.4. Bounding Technique for Designated Routes.

then adding the resultant optimal value of the objective function to the sum of the c_{ij} for which the specified subset of $x_{ij} = 1$. This approach is probably computationally more burdensome than the previous version of the algorithm or the simple bounding technique just described.)

The procedure at iteration t is

Step 1. Terminate the computations if the master list is empty. Otherwise, remove a problem from the master list.

Step 2. Find a lower bound on the objective function for any tour emanating from the chosen problem. If the lower bound is greater than or equal to x_0^t, then let $x_0^{t+1} = x_0^t$, and return to *Step 1.* Otherwise, proceed to *Step 3.*

Step 3. If the current solution is a tour, then record it, let x_0^{t+1} be the associated value of the objective function, and return to *Step 1.* Otherwise, proceed to *Step 4.*

Step 4. If possible, select a variable x_{hk}, not in the current solution, such that $c_{hk} < \infty$, provided that $x_{hk} = 1$ does not produce a subtour among the variables already in the solution. Given the selection, add two problems to the master list. Let each be identical with the problem chosen in *Step 1,* except that in one, make the revision $c_{hk} = \infty$, and in the other, include the stipulation $x_{hk} = 1$ and the revision $c_{kh} = \infty$. Let $x_0^{t+1} = x_0^t$, and return to *Step 1.*

Note the two principal differences between this and the previous modification of the Branch-and-Bound Algorithm. In the present version, *Step 2* calculates a lower bound for the chosen problem, but does not perform an optimization. Further, *Step 4* may add two problems to the master list, but adds no problems if there is no x_{hk} satisfying the stated stipulations. In the previous version, *Step 4* creates between 2 and $n/2$ problems.

The method, applied to the example in Fig. 13.2, gives the tree displayed in Fig. 13.5. Of course, the branches explored in this tree depend on the choice of problems from the master list in *Step 1* and on the selection of x_{hk} in *Step 4.* The rule for *Step 1* was to select the highest-numbered problem that remained on the list, where in *Step 4* we used the convention of assigning the larger number to the problem with $x_{hk} = 1$. The optimal tour was obtained at iteration t = 8 for Problem 12.

▶The number of branches can often be diminished by performing, at *Step 4,* a few more revisions of the c_{ij} in the problem added for $x_{hk} = 1$. We already indicated the revision $c_{kh} = \infty$, to rule out the subtour City h to City k to City h. But other c_{ij} values can be set equal to ∞ to rule out longer subtours. For example, if $x_{12} = x_{23} = 1$ is in the current solution and x_{34} is selected, then you can make the revisions $c_{41} = c_{42} = \infty$. If this procedure is used throughout, you need not state at *Step 4* the restriction, "$x_{hk} = 1$ does not produce a subtour . . . ," because the restriction $c_{hk} < \infty$ rules out such a possibility. ◀

Method of partial tours. The principal reason for presenting this version is to exhibit an approach that extends to many other kinds of combinatorial models, such as sequencing problems (in which $x_{ij} = 1$ corresponds to putting the ith object in the jth position of a sequence). We will need to employ the notion of a *partial tour*, which is defined as a sequence of less than n distinct cities, starting with City 1 (such as City 1 to City i to City j to City k, where $n > 4$).

At the beginning of any iteration t, you have an upper bound x_0^t on the optimal value of the objective function; you can obtain x_0^1 as usual. In addition, you have a master list of problems that contains a subset of $x_{ij} = 1$, representing a partial tour, and a subset of c_{ij} values that have been revised to equal ∞. At iteration 1, the master list contains $n - 1$ problems, one associated with each $x_{1j} = 1$ and the revision $c_{j1} = \infty$ for $j = 2, 3, \ldots, n$. You employ the same technique as in the

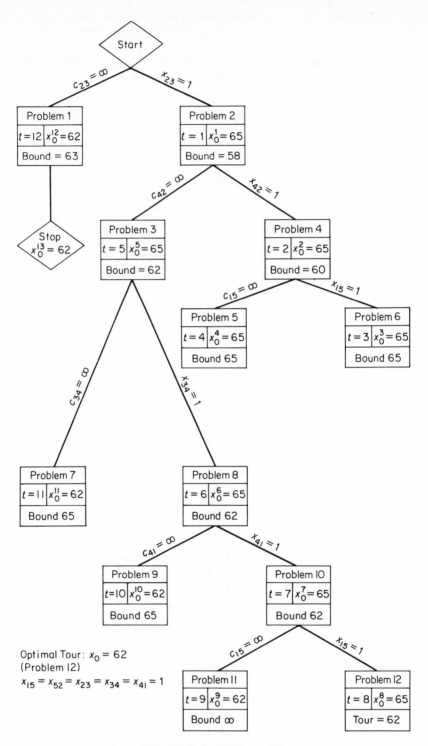

FIGURE 13.5. Method of Designated Routes.

478

method of designated routes to calculate a lower bound on the optimal value of the objective function for any tour that is a completion of the partial tour. (Alternatively, you can perform an assignment model optimization on the c_{ij} in the rows and columns not associated with the subset of $x_{ij} = 1$ in the partial tour.)

The procedure differs from the *method of designated routes* only at *Step 4*.

Step 4. For each City k not already in the partial tour of the problem chosen in *Step 1*, add a problem to the master list extending the partial tour from City j, which is the last city listed in the partial tour, to City k; also make the revision $c_{kj} = \infty$. Let $x_0^{t+1} = x_0^t$, and return to *Step 1*.

In this method, if a partial tour contains m cities (including City 1), then *Step 4*

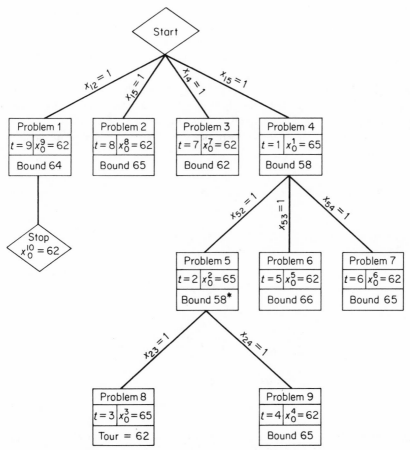

*Diminished Distances give a bound 55; but 58 is valid, since it is a bound for any tour emanating from Problem 4

Optimal Tour: $x_0 = 62$　$x_{15} = x_{52} = x_{23} = x_{34} = x_{41} = 1$
(Problem 8)

Figure 13.6. Method of Partial Tours.

adds $n - m$ problems to the master list. Notice there is no arbitrary selection to be made in *Step 4*. (Redundant calculations can occur in this method when there are several problems on the master list composed of the same m cities in their partial tours—for example, City 1 to City 2 to City 3, and City 1 to City 3 to City 2. In this event, the bounding computations in *Step 2* are duplicated.)

Applied to the example in Fig. 13.2, the algorithm produces the tree displayed in Fig. 13.6. In this case, the branches explored depend on the selection of problems from the master list in *Step 1*. (We used an auspicious procedure in solving this example.)

*Concluding remarks. As you can easily discover by making infelicitous choices in *Step 1* and *Step 4* of the three methods, the computational burden depends critically on how well you resolve the arbitrary selections. You will often find it worthwhile in branch-and-bound procedures to perform extra calculations in *Step 2* to obtain a truly good bound on the optimal value of the objective function. Your effort will be rewarded by having to explore fewer branches. Also, you can usually take advantage in *Step 2* of the calculations already done on the problem that gave rise to the current one. The practical success of applying a branch-and-bound approach to solve an actual combinatorial problem depends considerably on exploiting the special structure of your model in order to implement the foregoing suggestions.

13.7 PARTIAL (IMPLICIT) ENUMERATION
ALGORITHM

Many important integer programming models can be characterized by the problem

$$(1) \qquad\qquad \text{maximize} \sum_{j=1}^{n} c_j x_j$$

subject to

$$(2) \qquad\qquad \sum_{j=1}^{n} a_{ij} x_j \leq b_i \quad \text{for } i = 1, 2, \ldots, m,$$

where the integer-value stipulations are simply

$$(3) \qquad\qquad x_j = 0 \text{ or } 1 \quad \text{for } j = 1, 2, \ldots, n.$$

Assume each c_j is an integer (a condition that is always achievable by a proper scaling of the objective function, provided the original coefficients are rational numbers).

Capital budgeting models frequently can be put in the form (1) through (3). In addition, many pure integer programming models can be suitably transformed so that each variable satisfies (3). To illustrate, suppose a variable x has a determinable upper bound U. Then wherever x appears, you may substitute an equivalent **binary representation**

(4) $$x \equiv 1w_1 + 2w_2 + 4w_3 + \cdots + 2^{k-1}w_k,$$

where $w_j = 0$ or 1, and you choose a value of k such that $2^k - 1 \geq U$. For example, if you know a priori that $x_1 \leq 6$, and the model contains the constraint $3x_1 + x_2 \leq 25$, then let $x_1 \equiv 1w_1 + 2w_2 + 4w_3$, and write the constraint as $3w_1 + 6w_2 + 12w_3 + x_2 \leq 25$. (Observe in the example that the transformation expressed in (4) loses some information. You have formally introduced the possibility of $w_1 = w_2 = w_3 = 1$, corresponding to a maximum value of 7 for x_1, whereas you know that in fact x_1 cannot be larger than 6. This loss can easily be eliminated by using a coefficient appropriately smaller than 2^{k-1}. In the example, you can use the coefficient 3 for w_3 instead of 4. Give a general rule for the coefficient of w_k so as to keep the transformation equivalent to the initial information about the upper bound of the variable.)

Recall that if you applied the Branch-and-Bound Algorithm of Sec. 13.4 to (1) through (3), you would have to solve a sequence of linear programming problems. The alternative version below exploits the zero-one conditions (3), and thereby limits the arithmetic to additions (and subtractions). For this reason, the method is sometimes referred to as the **Additive Algorithm**.

If you take only (3) into consideration, there are 2^n possible assignments of values to $(x_1, x_2, \ldots, x_n)$. Naturally, many of these are not feasible in the linear constraints (2), and very few are optimal. Consider a subset of the x_j, where each such x_j has an assigned value (either zero or one). This subset is called a **partial solution**. The x_j not included in a partial solution are termed **free variables**. Any specific assignment of values to the free variables is denoted as a **completion** of the associated partial solution. If a partial solution contains s variables, then there are 2^{n-s} completions. In this algorithm, each problem on the master list corresponds to a *partial solution* [not necessarily feasible in (2)], and the possible completions give rise to the branches.

The following example will illustrate the terms in the preceding paragraph. Suppose $n = 5$. Then $(x_2 = 1, x_4 = 0)$ is one partial solution, and the corresponding free variables are x_1, x_3, and x_5. Letting $x_1 = 0$, $x_3 = 1$, and $x_5 = 1$ yields one completion of the partial solution. Altogether, there are $2^{5-2} = 8$ completions of $(x_2 = 1, x_4 = 0)$.

Suppose you have a lower bound on the optimal value of the objective function; assume you have recorded a feasible solution yielding this lower bound. Then given a partial solution, you need not branch further if somehow you can show that there is no feasible completion having an objective-function value greater than the current lower bound. In this case, the partial solution is said to be **fathomed**. When you fathom a partial solution containing s variables, you have implicitly enumerated 2^{n-s} possible assignments satisfying (3).

There is a close connection between the central idea of this method and the Principle of Optimality in dynamic programming. The corresponding proposition is that given a partial solution, the values of the remaining variables must be optimized accordingly in order for a completion to be optimal. If there are no values of the remaining variables that yield a feasible solution or if the resultant optimal values for these variables yield a solution that is worse than a previously found solution, then there is no optimal solution containing the given partial solution.

At any iteration t, you have a lower bound x_0^t on the optimal value of the objective function. The value of x_0^t can be chosen as in the Branch-and-Bound Algorithm, Sec. 13.4. In addition, you have a master list of problems, with each problem specifying a different partial solution. At iteration 1, the master list contains two problems formed by selecting an x_k and letting the partial solution for one be $x_k = 0$, and for the other be $x_k = 1$.

It is helpful to give a few motivating remarks before explaining the procedure. For a specified partial solution, there are several tests you can apply to find out whether there can be any feasible completion that has an objective-function value greater than the current lower bound. One simple test is suggested by the two examples below. If the model contains the constraint

$$(5) \qquad -1x_1 + 2x_2 - 6x_3 + 4x_4 - 1x_5 \leq 0,$$

then there is no completion of the partial solution $(x_1 = 1, x_3 = 0, x_4 = 1)$ that is feasible in (5). Explain why. Suppose that the objective function is

$$(6) \qquad 2x_1 + 1x_2 + 5x_3 + 3x_4 - 1x_5,$$

and $x_0^t = 7$. Then, as you should also check, a completion must satisfy the constraint

$$(7) \qquad 2x_1 + 1x_2 + 5x_3 + 3x_4 - 1x_5 \geq 8$$
$$\text{or} \quad -2x_1 - 1x_2 - 5x_3 - 3x_4 + 1x_5 \leq -8,$$

in order to make an improvement on x_0^t. No completion of the partial solution $(x_2 = 1, x_3 = 0, x_5 = 1)$ is feasible in (7). Explain why.

The logic underlying the preceding examples can be systematized as follows. Given a partial solution, view the linear constraints as

$$(8) \qquad \sum_{\substack{\text{all free} \\ \text{variables}}} a_{ij}x_j \leq b_i - \sum_{\substack{\text{partial} \\ \text{solution} \\ \text{variables}}} a_{ij}x_j \quad \text{for } i = 0, 1, 2, \ldots, m,$$

where each x_j in the partial solution has its assigned value in the summations on the right-hand side of (8), and the coefficients in the restriction for $i = 0$ are $a_{0j} = -c_j$ and $b_0 = -x_0^t - 1$. Then there is no feasible completion having an objective-function value greater than the lower bound if

$$(9) \qquad \sum_{\substack{\text{all free} \\ \text{variables}}} \text{minimum } (a_{ij}, 0) > b_i - \sum_{\substack{\text{partial} \\ \text{solution} \\ \text{variables}}} a_{ij}x_j \quad \text{for any } i.$$

The term on the left-hand side of (9) is simply the sum of all the negative coefficients of the free variables. If such a sum is larger than the right-hand side, then even letting $x_j = 1$ for every free variable where $a_{ij} < 0$ will not satisfy the ith constraint in (8). To check your understanding, apply (9) to the examples (5) and (7).

Another observation of importance is that given a partial solution, you can sometimes conclude that a free variable must have a particular value for *any* feasible completion with an objective-function value greater than the current lower bound. To illustrate, verify that if the model contains the constraint

$$(10) \qquad 1x_1 - 1x_2 + 2x_3 - 1x_4 \leq 0,$$

and the partial solution is $(x_1 = 1, x_2 = 1)$, then any completion must have $x_3 = 0$ to be feasible in (10). This example suggests a computation analogous to (9). Specifically, for any free variable x_k, if

$$(11) \qquad \sum_{\substack{\text{all free} \\ \text{variables}}} \text{minimum } (a_{ij}, 0) + |a_{ik}| > b_i - \sum_{\substack{\text{partial} \\ \text{solution} \\ \text{variables}}} a_{ij} x_j \quad \text{for any } i,$$

then $x_k = 0$ if $a_{ik} > 0$, and $x_k = 1$ if $a_{ik} < 0$.

[The tests (9) and (11) can also be applied to composite constraints formed by adding positive combinations of the constraints (2), namely,

$$\sum_{j=1}^{n} \left(\sum_{i=1}^{m} y_i a_{ij} \right) x_j \leq \sum_{i=1}^{m} y_i b_i,$$

where $y_i > 0$. To see how such **composite** or **surrogate** constraints can be useful, consider the constraints $-x_1 - x_2 - x_3 \leq -1$, $2x_2 - 2x_4 + 2x_5 \leq 0$, $2x_3 + 2x_4 - 2x_5 \leq 0$. Given the partial solution $x_1 = 0$, (9) applied to each constraint does not indicate infeasibility; but check that (9) applied to the sum of the constraints shows there is no feasible completion. Similarly, given $x_1 = 1$, (11) applied to each constraint yields no information about the values of the free variables. But (11) applied to the sum of the constraints shows that $x_2 = x_3 = 0$ in any feasible completion.]

The procedure at iteration t is

Step 1. Terminate the computations if the master list is empty. Otherwise, remove a problem from the master list.

Step 2. If you can find free variables that must have particular values for any feasible completion with an objective-function value greater than x_0^t, augment the chosen partial solution accordingly. If you can determine that there is no feasible completion having an objective-function value greater than x_0^t, then let $x_0^{t+1} = x_0^t$, and return to *Step 1*. Otherwise, continue to *Step 3*.

Step 3. If the (augmented) partial solution is complete (contains all n variables), record it, let x_0^{t+1} be the associated value of the objective function, and return to *Step 1*. Otherwise, proceed to *Step 4*.

Step 4. Select any free variable x_k not in the (augmented) partial solution. Add two problems to the master list. In one, set $x_k = 0$ in the (augmented) partial solution, and in the other, set $x_k = 1$. Let $x_0^{t+1} = x_0^t$, and return to *Step 1*.

At termination, if you have recorded a feasible solution yielding x_0^t, it is optimal;

otherwise, no feasible solution exists. The method must terminate in a finite number of iterations.

Example. Consider the problem

(12)   maximize $3x_1 + 6x_2 + 3x_3 + 6x_4 + 13x_5$

subject to

(13) $-3x_1 - 6x_2 + 6x_3 + 12x_4 + 7x_5 \leq 8 \quad (i = 1)$

(14) $6x_1 + 12x_2 - 3x_3 - 6x_4 + 7x_5 \leq 8 \quad (i = 2)$

(15) $x_j = 0 \text{ or } 1 \quad \text{for } j = 1, 2, \ldots, 5.$

This is the example in Sec. 13.5 transformed to include only zero-one variables.

Let $x_0^1 = 0$, corresponding to the feasible solution in which all $x_j = 0$. Assume that the master list contains Problem 1 with partial solution $x_5 = 1$, and Problem 2 with $x_5 = 0$.

At *Step 1*, remove Problem 1. A feasible completion having an objective-function value greater than x_0^1 must satisfy (13) through (15) as well as

(16) $-3x_1 - 6x_2 - 3x_3 - 6x_4 - 13x_5 \leq -1 \quad (i = 0).$

In the first part of *Step 2*, you try to find any free variables that must have a particular value in order to satisfy (13) through (16), given that $x_5 = 1$. Verify that applying (11) to $i = 1$ and $i = 2$ yields $x_4 = 0$ and $x_2 = 0$. Then, given that $x_5 = 1$, $x_2 = x_4 = 0$, a second application of (11) to $i = 1$ and $i = 2$ yields $x_3 = 0$ and $x_1 = 0$. Thus you have obtained an augmented solution containing all the variables. In the second part of *Step 2* you check for feasibility in $i = 0, 1, 2$, which can be formally accomplished by applying (9). [Since no free variables are left, the calculation amounts to testing whether the augmented solution is feasible in (13) through (16). Verify that it is.]

This brings you to *Step 3*, where you record the completion,

(17)   objective function = 13 $x_1 = x_2 = x_3 = x_4 = 0 \quad x_5 = 1.$

Let $x_0^2 = 13$, and return to *Step 1*.

Next remove Problem 2, where $(x_5 = 0)$. The constraint (16) is revised to

(18) $-3x_1 - 6x_2 - 3x_3 - 6x_4 - 13x_5 \leq -14 \quad (i = 0).$

Applying (11) to $i = 0, 1, 2$ does not result in augmenting the partial solution, nor does applying (9) to $i = 0, 1, 2$ rule out the possibility of a feasible completion with an objective-function value greater than 13. Hence, proceed to *Step 3* and then to *Step 4*, since the partial solution is not complete. In *Step 4*, select the variable x_1 and add to the master list Problem 3, in which $(x_5 = 0, x_1 = 1)$, and Problem 4, in which $(x_5 = 0, x_1 = 0)$.

Returning to *Step 1* with $x_0^3 = 13$, remove Problem 3. Verify that applying (11) to $i = 0, 1$ does not indicate any necessary values for the free variables. Going on to $i = 2$, check that the test in (11) indicates $x_2 = 0$ for any feasible completion. Augmenting the solution accordingly and reapplying (11) to $i = 0$, verify that there is no feasible completion. Therefore, *Step 2* is complete, and you return to *Step 1* with $x_0^4 = 13$.

Removing Problem 4, in which $(x_1 = x_5 = 0)$, the calculation (11) for $i = 0$ shows that $x_3 = 1$ for any feasible completion. Applying (11) to $i = 1, 2$, you find that $x_4 = 0$ and $x_2 = 0$. Then testing (9) for $i = 0$, you obtain that there is no feasible completion having an objective-function value greater than x_0^4. Returning to *Step 1*, you terminate the iterations as the master list is now empty. The optimal solution is (17).

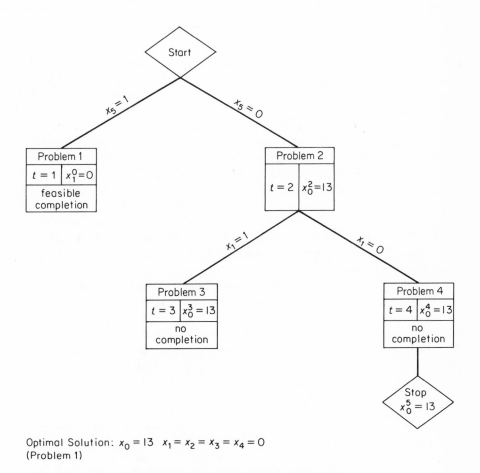

Optimal Solution: $x_0 = 13$ $x_1 = x_2 = x_3 = x_4 = 0$
(Problem 1)

FIGURE 13.7. Partial Enumeration Approach.

A diagram of the algorithm applied to the example is shown in Fig. 13.7. As you saw in Problem 3, each time the test (11) results in augmenting the partial solution, it may be auspicious to repeat the test on all the restrictions ($i = 0$, $1, \ldots, m$), employing the newly augmented partial solution.

Concluding remarks. You should note two points of difference between this method and the Branch-and-Bound Algorithm in Sec. 13.4. First, the method here requires only additions and subtractions (no multiplications or divisions). [You can guide the selections in *Steps 1* and *4* with information garnered from an optimal linear programming solution to (1), (2), and the constraints $0 \leq x_j \leq 1$.]

Second, each partial solution satisfies the integer stipulations, but may not satisfy the linear inequalities (2), in contrast to the linear programming approach. By clever selection rules in *Steps 1* and *4*, the algorithm may determine a feasible and nearly optimal solution to all the constraints at an early iteration.

If you terminate the iterations short of convergence (before the master list is empty), you can ascertain what fraction of the 2^n possibilities have been enumerated (explicitly or implicitly). To obtain this fraction, each time you return to *Step 1* from *Steps 2* or *3*, accumulate the fraction $(\frac{1}{2})^s$, where s equals the number of variables that were contained in the partial solution at *Step 1*. In the example above, after completing *Step 3* on Problem 1, you have enumerated $(\frac{1}{2})^1 = \frac{1}{2}$ of all the 2^5 possibilities. Then completing *Step 2* on Problem 3, you have enumerated an additional $[(\frac{1}{2})^2 = \frac{1}{4}]$ of the possibilities, or altogether $\frac{3}{4}$ so far. The remaining $[(\frac{1}{2})^2 = \frac{1}{4}]$ of the possibilities are enumerated when Problem 4 is terminated.

As you have observed several times already in this chapter, the computational burden is closely related to the number of integer-valued variables in the problem. In this method, the burden manifests itself primarily in terms of the number of problems placed on the master list. Note that additional constraints (especially composite or surrogate constraints) may actually be beneficial in reducing the magnitude of the computations. Although you must perform more testing at *Step 2*, you may more frequently return directly to *Step 1*, without adding new problems to the master list.

Computational experience has demonstrated that this approach (when properly modified by the addition of sophisticated surrogate constraints and programmed efficiently on a high-speed computer) can solve certain practical problems with up to 100 variables and 50 constraints. This size is modest as compared to the present-day capability for solving linear programming problems having several thousand variables and constraints. But the state of the art is in rapid flux—it is reasonable to expect that models containing several hundred integer-valued variables will be solvable in the near future.

▶Efficient computerized versions of the algorithm incorporate a number of sophisticated modifications, including a streamlined notation for designating a partial solution as well as a condensed way of representing the master list. In addition, more powerful tests than (9) and (11) in *Step 2*, as well as good selection rules in *Steps 1* and *4*, are usually employed to avoid excessive branching. In the same vein, *Step 3* is sometimes amplified to test whether you obtain a feasible solution after setting each free variable $x_j = 1$ if $c_j > 0$. If so, this is the best feasible completion, and should be recorded in the standard way.

The Partial Enumeration Algorithm can be modified as follows to solve the mixed integer programming problem in which only the variables x_j, for $j = 1, 2, \ldots, p$ ($<n$)

must be zero-one, and the remaining variables are restricted by $0 \leq x_j \leq 1$, for $j = p + 1, \ldots, n$. A partial solution is restricted to include only the integer-valued variables; but the free variables consist of all those that are not contained in a partial solution. The tests (9) and (11) remain valid, except that the test in (11) is to be applied only to the free integer-valued variables; also $b_0 = -x_0^t$ instead of $-x_0^t - 1$. Finally, the instructions are altered to read:

"*Step 3*. If the (augmented) partial solution contains all p integer-valued variables, solve the resultant linear programming problem for associated optimal values of the remaining free variables (where the constraints of the linear programming problem are stated to account for the assigned values of the integer variables in the partial solution). If there is no feasible solution, let $x_0^{t+1} = x_0^t$, and return to *Step 1*. Otherwise, record the obtained optimal solution, let x_0^{t+1} be the associated optimal value of the objective function, and return to *Step 1*. If the (augmented) partial solution contains fewer than p integer-valued variables, proceed to *Step 4*."

The algorithms in this section and Sec. 13.4 are easily adapted to solve, at least in principle, certain optimization models that contain continuous and integer-valued variables along with a nonlinear objective function and nonlinear constraints. To illustrate, consider the problem

(i) $$\text{maximize } c(x_1, x_2, \ldots, x_n)$$

subject to

(ii) $a_i(x_1, x_2, \ldots, x_n) \leq 0$ for $i = 1, 2, \ldots, m$

(iii) x_j integer-valued and $L_j \leq x_j \leq U_j$ for $j = 1, 2, \ldots, p \ (\leq n)$

(iv) $x_j \geq 0$ for $j = p + 1, \ldots, n \ (\text{if } p < n)$,

where the functions in (i) and (ii) may be nonlinear. In Chaps. 14 and 15 you will study how to solve such problems without integer stipulations. If the nonlinear functions satisfy the shape postulates given for the various methods in Chaps. 14 and 15, the integer constraints can be accommodated by a straightforward modification of the algorithm in Sec. 13.4. Specifically, you find an optimal solution to (i) through (iv) by applying the algorithms in Chaps. 14 and 15 to solve a *sequence* of nonlinear programming problems, each containing only continuous variables, and which differ as to the bounds on the integer variables.

Suppose next that (iii) and (iv) are modified to

(v) $x_j = 0 \text{ or } 1$ for $j = 1, 2, \ldots, n$

and that each function $a_i(x_1, x_2, \ldots, x_n)$ can be written in the form

(vi) $a_i(x_1, x_2, \ldots, x_n) \equiv f_i(x_1, x_2, \ldots, x_n) - g_i(x_1, x_2, \ldots, x_n)$,

where all $f_i(x_1, x_2, \ldots, x_n)$ and $g_i(x_1, x_2, \ldots, x_n)$ are nondecreasing monotone functions [that is, $f_i(x_1, x_2, \ldots, x_n) \geq f_i(y_1, y_2, \ldots, y_n)$ if $x_j \geq y_j$ for all j, and likewise for each function g_i]. Then the algorithm in this section is directly applicable. Only the tests at *Step 2* require modification.

To illustrate, let F_i be that value of $f_i(x_1, x_2, \ldots, x_n)$ where each variable in the partial solution has its assigned value, and every free variable is set equal to zero; similarly, let G_i be the value of $g_i(x_1, x_2, \ldots, x_n)$ where each variable in the partial solution has its assigned value and every free variable is set equal to one. Verify that there is no feasible completion if

(vii) $F_i - G_i > 0$ for any i,

where $i = 1, 2, \ldots, m$. This test reduces to (9) when an $a_i(x_1, x_2, \ldots, x_n)$ is linear. If the objective function $c(x_1, x_2, \ldots, x_n)$ can also be split into the difference of two nondecreasing monotone functions,

(viii) $c(x_1, x_2, \ldots, x_n) \equiv -f_0(x_1, x_2, \ldots, x_n) + g_0(x_1, x_2, \ldots, x_n)$,

then the test in (vii) can be extended to include

(ix) $F_0 - G_0 + (x_0^t + 1) > 0$ $(i = 0)$.

Let $F_{ik}(x_k)$ be the function derived from $f_i(x_1, x_2, \ldots, x_n)$ by letting each variable in the partial solution have its assigned value and letting every free variable, except x_k, equal zero. Similarly, let $G_{ik}(x_k)$ be derived from $g_i(x_1, x_2, \ldots, x_n)$ by letting each variable in the partial solution have its assigned value and every free variable, except x_k, equal one. Verify that for any free variable x_k,

(x) $\left. \begin{array}{l} \text{if } F_{ik}(0) - G_{ik}(0) > 0, \quad \text{then } x_k = 1 \\ \text{if } F_{ik}(1) - G_{ik}(1) > 0, \quad \text{then } x_k = 0 \end{array} \right\}$ for any i,

to yield a feasible completion. When (viii) is valid, then (x) can be extended to include $i = 0$, where the constant $(x_0^t + 1)$ is added to the left-hand sides, as in (ix). The test in (x) simplifies to (11) when an $a_i(x_1, x_2, \ldots, x_n)$ is linear.   ◀

REVIEW EXERCISES

1 (a) Calculate the number of tours in the traveling salesman problem for 3 cities. For 5 cities.

(b) Consider the traveling salesman problem with five cities, but assume that the salesman must return to City 1 after visiting two cities and then set out again for the remaining two cities. Calculate the number of possible sequences.

(c) Calculate the number of possible sequences in the machine scheduling problem with three items and one machine. With three items and two machines. With two items and three machines. With two items and four machines. Show how your answers change if the items must be processed in the same sequence on each machine.

(d) Consider a one-period product-mix selection model with activities x_j, $j = 1, 2, \ldots, n$, each of which incurs a setup cost K_j. Calculate how many different patterns of setups there are (assume all $x_j = 0$ is one of the possibilities).

(e) Consider the constraint $x_1 + x_2 + x_3 + \cdots + x_n = N$, where each x_j must be a nonnegative integer. Calculate the number of different feasible solutions if $n = 6$ and $N = 1$. If $n = 7$ and $N = 1$. If $n = 6$ and $N = 2$. If $n = 6$ and $N = 6$. If $n = 7$ and $N = 6$. If $n = 6$ and $N = 6$ and the restriction is stated as an inequality ($\leq$). If $n = 6$ and $N = 1$, and the restriction is stated as an inequality ($\leq$). If $n = 6$ and $N = 2$, and the restriction is stated as an inequality ($\leq$).

(f) Consider a capital budgeting problem in which there are three categories of projects. Category 1 contains eight projects, and two are to be selected. Category 2 contains ten projects, and four are to be selected. Category 3 contains seven projects and five are to be selected. Calculate the total number of distinct selection combinations that are possible. Show how this number changes if the specified number for each category is only an upper limit on the number that can be selected.

(g) A company wants to schedule three trucks to visit eight stores. Each truck can stop at one or more stores, but no store is to be visited by more than one truck. Calculate the number of different ways to assign the trucks to the stores.

(h) A firm performs preventive maintenance on four major pieces of equipment. Such work can start during any one of three weeks on Machine 1, during any one of six weeks on Machine 2, during any one of two weeks on Machine 3, and in any one of five weeks on Machine 4. Calculate the total number of distinctly different maintenance schedules (that is, "starting weeks" for each of the four machines).

(i) A corporation is working out a strategy for introducing three new products into four marketing areas. The strategy is strictly "sequential" in that the company first selects one area, then selects the sequence in which to introduce the products (one every two weeks), then afterwards selects the next area, followed by a chosen sequence, etc. Calculate the number of different strategies for introducing the new products.

(j) A company plans to build six new plants on sites that have already been selected. It wishes to accomplish this expansion over the next five years. Conceivably, it could build all the plants in Year 1 or wait to build all the plants in Year 5. More likely, it will build some plants each year. Determine the number of different patterns for building these plants. The company is also concerned with the *number* of plants it builds each year (in addition to which plants it builds each year). Determine all the possible patterns for the numbers of plants built over the five years (such as six in Year 1 and none in any other year, or six in Year 5 and none in any other year, etc.).

2 Consider the problem

$$\text{maximize } 3x_1 + 6x_2 + x_3$$

subject to

$$x_1 + 2x_2 + 2x_3 \leq 2\tfrac{2}{3}$$
$$x_1 + 2x_2 + 3x_3 \geq 2\tfrac{1}{3}$$

every x_j a nonnegative integer.

(a) What is an optimal solution if the integer-value stipulation on every x_j is dropped? Is there more than one optimal solution?

(b) Determine by inspection an optimal integer-valued solution. Does your answer in part (a) round to this solution?

(c) Draw a solution space representation of the problem, letting $x_3 = 0$ (that is, draw the implied constraints on x_1 and x_2). Indicate all the feasible integer-valued solutions.

3 Suppose a company has five manufacturing plants that ship to 100 warehouses. If the company continues to operate all of its plants and warehouses, it faces a cost minimization problem that can be characterized by a standard transportation problem, like that described in the beginning of Chap. 6.

(a) Suppose, however, that the total plant capacity is considerably more than is required at the warehouses, and each Plant i incurs a large yearly overhead cost P_i. Suggest a *practical* way to determine which plants, if any, ought to be shut down to minimize the sum of annual overhead and transportation costs.

(b) Suppose, instead, that the company wants to shut down some warehouses (the associated demand requirements would be reallocated to the warehouses that remain open). The company thereby saves overhead costs of operating some of the warehouses, but increases transportation costs as a result. Would your suggestion in part (a) be practical for this problem? Explain.

4 *Goforth Manufacturing Company* (Sec. 13.2). Consider the following data:

$$m = 3 \quad n = 4 \quad S_1 = 40 \quad S_2 = 50 \quad S_3 = 60$$
$$D_1 = 10 \quad D_2 = 15 \quad D_3 = 20 \quad D_4 = 25.$$

(a) Write in full detail all the linear constraints in the problem.

(b) Explain why (7) and (8) together ensure that y_i and z_{ij} are each either 0 or 1.

(c) Explain why it is never essential for optimality to have $z_{ij} = 1$ and $x_{ij} = 0$.

*(d) Suppose all $F_i = 100$, $c_{ij} = 1$, $F_{ij} = 0$. What is an optimal solution if the integer-value stipulations are dropped? Are there alternative optimal solutions?

(e) Explain why $U_{ij} = $ minimum (S_i, D_j) is sufficiently large in (9).

5 Consider the plant location model described in Sec. 13.2.

(a) If every $F_i = 0$, would it be optimal to let every $y_i = 1$? Explain.

(b) Assume every $y_i = 1$ and moreover that the sum of the supplies S_i equals the sum of the demands D_j. Will an optimal solution necessarily use $m + n - 1$ routes? If every $F_{ij} = F$ (a constant), is an optimal solution the same as the one for the standard transportation problem in which the F_{ij} are not present ($F = 0$)? (If you answer "yes" to a question, provide a supporting argument; if your answer is "no," provide a small example showing why.)

6 *Fixed Charge Problem.* Consider the model

$$\text{minimize} \sum_{j=1}^{n} c_j(x_j)$$

subject to

$$\sum_{j=1}^{n} a_{ij}x_j \leq b_i \quad \text{for} \quad i = 1, 2, \ldots, m$$

$$\text{every } x_j \geq 0,$$

where

$$c_j(x_j) = \begin{cases} 0 & \text{for} \quad x_j = 0 \\ K_j + c_j x_j & \text{for} \quad x_j > 0, \end{cases}$$

and each $K_j \geq 0$. The K_j are called fixed charges.

(a) Show how to formulate this problem as a mixed integer programming model.

*(b) Discuss the difficulty that can arise if the objective is to maximize instead of minimize (or if not all $K_j \geq 0$). (*Hint:* how small can x_j be, given that it is positive?)

(c) Suppose all $K_j = K > 0$. Give a sufficient condition such that an optimal solution is the same as one for the linear programming problem in which the K_j are not present (all $K_j = 0$).

(d) Show how to alter your formulation if the constraints are of the form

$$\sum_{j=1}^{n} a_{ij}(x_j) \leq b_i \quad \text{for } i = 1, 2, \ldots, m,$$

where

$$a_{ij}(x_j) = \begin{cases} 0 & \text{for } x_j = 0 \\ A_{ij} + a_{ij}x_j & \text{for } x_j > 0, \end{cases}$$

with every $A_{ij} \geq 0$.

*(e) Discuss the difficulty that can arise in part (d) if an $A_{ij} < 0$, or if an inequality for a linear constraint is ($\geq$).

7 Consider a product-mix selection problem, like that in Sec. 2.2, which is of the form

$$\text{maximize} \sum_{j=1}^{n} c_j x_j$$

subject to

$$\sum_{j=1}^{n} a_{ij}x_j \leq b_i \quad \text{for } i = 1, 2, \ldots, m$$

$$\text{every } x_j \geq 0,$$

where every $c_j > 0$ and $n \geq m$.

(a) Suppose the firm wants to produce no more than k different products. Show how to formulate this stipulation in terms of integer-valued variables.

(b) What difficulties can arise if the firm wants to produce at least k different products. (*Hint:* how small can x_j be if it is positive?)

8 *Solution Space Representation.* In each part below, graph the region of feasible solutions for the set of alternative constraints. Assume $x_1 \geq 0$ and $x_2 \geq 0$.

(a) Either $x_1 + 2x_2 \leq 1$, or $2x_1 + x_2 \leq 1$, or both.

(b) Either $x_1 + x_2 \leq 1$, or $x_1 + x_2 \geq 2$, or both.

(c) Either the pair of constraints $x_1 \leq 1$ and $x_2 \leq 1$ holds, or the pair $x_1 \geq 1$ and $x_2 \geq 1$ holds, or both pairs hold.

(d) At least one of the following constraints must be satisfied: $x_1 \leq 1$, $x_2 \leq 1$, and $x_1 + x_2 \leq 2$. At least two must hold. All three must hold.

9 Consider the approach for representing alternative constraints as described by (12), (13), and (14) in Sec. 13.2. In each part below, write in full detail the representation (13) and (14). (*Hint:* calculate a value for U_i by examining the constraints; let U_i be the smallest value that will work.)

(a) $x_1 + 2x_2 + x_3 \leq 8$
 $4x_1 + x_2 + x_3 \leq 20$
 $x_1 + x_2 + 3x_3 \leq 15$.

Show the formulation for $k = 1$ and $k = 2$.

(b) Same constraints as in part (a) augmented by $x_2 - x_4 \leq 0$. Show the formulation for $k = 3$.

(c) In parts (a) and (b) explain in detail why the representation and the stipulation that each y_i be either 0 or 1 solve the problem (that is, ensure that at least k out of the p constraints are satisfied).

(d) Explain why (13) can just as well be stated as an equality.

*(e) Discuss the difficulty in ensuring that *exactly* k out of p linear constraints (12) are satisfied.

10 In each part below, show how to formulate the problem in terms of an integer programming model.

(a) maximize $\sum_{j=1}^{n} c_j x_j$ subject to

$$\sum_{j=1}^{n} a_{ij} x_j \leq b_i \quad \text{for } i = 1, 2, \ldots, m$$

every $x_j \geq 0$

and either the three constraints $x_1 \leq 1$, $x_2 \leq 1$, and $x_1 + x_2 \leq 1.5$ hold, or the three constraints $x_1 \geq 1$, $x_2 \geq 1$, and $x_1 + x_2 \geq 2.5$ hold.

(b) maximize [maximum $(x_1 + x_2, 2x_1 + x_2, x_1 + 2x_2)$] subject to

$$\sum_{j=1}^{n} a_{ij} x_j \geq b_i \quad \text{for } i = 1, 2, \ldots, m$$

every $x_j \geq 0$

(that is, find values for x_j that satisfy the constraints and make as large as possible the maximum value for the three designated linear functions).

(c) How would you go about finding numerical solutions to the problems in parts (a) and (b)?

11 Exercise 1, part (j), describes a company that plans to start building six new plants on sites that have already been selected, and wishes to complete construction within five years.

(a) Characterize the selection problem in terms of linear constraints involving integer-valued variables. (Be sure to define your symbols and explain the meaning of each restriction.) In each part below, show how the stated stipulation can be encompassed by an integer programming formulation. Consider each of the parts separately.

(b) Plants 1, 2, and 3 must be started no later than Year 3.

(c) No more than two plants can be started in any year.

(d) No more than three plants can be started in the first two years, and no more than five plants in the first four years.

(e) Exactly three plants must be started in the first two years, and five plants in the first four years.

(f) Plant 2 cannot be started before Plant 1 (they can be started in the same year).

(g) Plants 4, 5, and 6 cannot be started before Plants 1, 2, and 3 are started (all six plants can be started in the same year).

*(h) Either Plants 1, 2, 3 must be started before Plants 4, 5, 6, or vice versa (all six plants cannot be started in the same year).

(i) Plants 1 and 2 must be started in the same year. Similarly, Plants 3, 4, and 5 must be started in the same year.

(j) If Plants 1 and 2 are started in the same year, then no other plants can be started in that year.

(k) In Year 1, the company starts either Plants 1 and 2 or Plants 3 and 4. (Assume one of these two possibilities must occur.)

(l) In the first two years, the company starts either Plants 1 and 2 or Plants 3 and 4. (Assume one of these two possibilities must occur.)

(m) Plant 1 can be started in Year 1 only if either Plant 2 or Plant 3 is started, but not if both Plants 2 and 3 are started.

(n) Suppose the company has two possible sites for Plant 1 (instead of a single site already selected). Show how to modify your previous formulations to account for this site selection problem.

(o) Suppose the company has only five sites, instead of six, and Plants 1 and 3 compete for the same site; that is, the company plans to build only Plant 1 or Plant 3 on a specified site. Show how to modify your previous formulations to account for this site selection problem. (You may find it necessary to reinterpret the assumptions in some of the parts to preserve consistency; make explicit mention when this happens.)

12 Consider a traveling salesman problem with $n = 4$ cities.

(a) Using the formulation (19) through (23) in Sec. 13.2, write all the linear constraints in full detail.

(b) Show how the tour City 1 to City 3 to City 2 to City 4 to City 1 leads to values for x_{ij} and u_i that satisfy all the restrictions in part (a).

(c) Show that a subtour City 3 to City 2 to City 3 cannot lead to values for x_{ij} and u_i that satisfy all the restrictions in part (a). Do the same for the subtour City 1 to City 2 to City 3 to City 1.

*13 Consider the problem

$$\text{maximize } 3x + 7y$$

subject to

$$2x + y \le 25$$
$$x + 2y \le 6,$$

where $y \ge 0$, and x can equal only the values 0, 1, 4, and 6.

(a) Formulate the problem in terms of an equivalent integer programming model.

(b) Suppose the objective function contained the terms $3x^2$, instead of $3x$. Revise your answer to part (a) accordingly.

*14 Consider a problem with the linear constraints in exercise 13, where $x \ge 0$ and $y \ge 0$, but assume that the objective function is to maximize $c(x) + 7y$, where

$$c(x) = \begin{cases} 4x & \text{for } 0 \le x \le 2 \\ 14 - 3x & \text{for } 2 \le x \le 3 \\ 5 & \text{for } 3 \le x \le 3.5 \\ -2 + 4x & \text{for } 3.5 \le x \le 5 \\ -22 + 8x & \text{for } 5 \le x \le 6. \end{cases}$$

(a) Plot the function $c(x)$.

(b) Formulate the problem in terms of an equivalent integer programming model, using the approach in (24) through (30) of Sec. 13.2.

(c) Explain in detail why the restrictions (29) and (30) ensure that exactly one z_k equals 1, thereby guaranteeing in (28) that no more than two of the weights w_k and w_{k+1} can be positive, and that they must sum to 1 according to (25). Use the formulation in part (b) to illustrate your reasoning.

*(d) Ignore the constraints (28), (29), and (30), and determine an optimal solution. Is this solution truly optimal for the original nonlinear problem? Explain.

(e) Show how the formulation in part (b) changes if the $c(x)$ function over the interval $0 \leq x \leq 2$ is $4x - 2$, instead of $4x$. (*Hint:* plot the function before giving an algebraic formulation.)

15 As in Sec. 13.4, let $[d]$ designate the largest integer that is less than or equal to the real number d.

(a) What are the values of

$$[12.8] \quad [12] \quad [-12.8] \quad [-12]$$
$$[0.8] \quad [0] \quad [-0.8]$$
$$[3\tfrac{3}{5}] \quad [3] \quad [\tfrac{3}{5}] \qquad [-\tfrac{3}{5}] \quad [-3] \quad [-3\tfrac{3}{5}].$$

(b) What are the fractional parts of the numbers in brackets in part (a)?

16 (a) Explain in detail what justifies, in Sec. 13.4, writing the inequalities in (10) and (11), the equality in (12), and making the stipulation that x in (12) must be integer-valued.

(b) Show the algebraic steps that justify the statement that subtracting (8) from (12) yields (14).

17 Consider the numerical illustration in Sec. 13.4. Suppose the right-hand-side constant in (2) is 5, instead of 3.

(a) What is an optimal linear programming solution (ignoring the integer-value stipulations)?

(b) Use the cutting plane idea (in an ad hoc fashion) to derive an optimal integer-valued solution.

18 Consider the problem

$$\text{maximize } x_1 + 2x_2$$

subject to

$$5x_1 + 7x_2 \leq 21$$
$$-x_1 + 3x_2 \leq 8$$

x_1 and x_2 nonnegative integers.

(a) What is an optimal linear programming solution (ignoring the integer-value stipulations)?

(b) Use the cutting-plane idea (in an ad hoc fashion) to derive an optimal integer-valued solution.

19 In solving the numerical example (20), (21), and (22) of Sec. 13.4 by the Cutting-Plane Algorithm, verify that

   (a) The restriction (14) applied to Row 1 in (24) leads to the constraint (25).
   (b) The linear programming model (24) augmented by (25) has the optimal solution displayed in (26).
   (c) A cut formed from Row 2 in (26) is that given in (27).
   (d) The optimal linear programming solution to (26) and (27) is the one displayed in (28).
   (e) Justify, verbally, that the solution in (28) is optimal for the original problem (20), (21), and (22).

20 Apply the Cutting-Plane Algorithm to the numerical example (20), (21), and (22) in Sec. 13.4, where you let

   (a) The right-hand-side constant in (21) be 15, instead of 13.
   (b) The coefficient of x_1 in (21) be 6, instead of 7.

*21 The special material at the end of Sec. 13.4 describes how to express cuts in terms of the original variables and how to show graphically the progress of the algorithm. Perform this analysis of the cuts and draw the associated graphical representation for exercise 20, part (a). Part (b).

22 Study the application of the Branch-and-Bound Algorithm to the example (8) and (9) in Sec. 13.5. Trace in detail the calculations at each iteration. Specifically, verify optimal solutions in (11), (13), (15), (17), (19), and (20). Check how the constraints in each of the nine problems are generated. Verify that Problems 2, 6, and 8 have no feasible solution. Explain in detail the rationale permitting the calculations to stop with Problem 5 and the logic behind asserting that (19) is the optimal solution.

23 Consider the example in Sec. 13.5. Suppose at iteration 4 you select Problem 5 instead of Problem 4. Complete the steps of the Branch-and-Bound Algorithm with this choice. Construct a tree analogous to that in Fig. 13.1 to show the progress of the iterations.

24 Consider the example in Sec. 13.5, where the right-hand-side constants in (9) are both 22, instead of 8. Apply the Branch-and-Bound Algorithm. Construct a tree analogous to that in Fig. 13.1 to show the progress of the iterations.

25 Consider how the traveling salesman problem example in Sec. 13.6 is solved by the *method of excluded subtours*. Suppose, at the first iteration, you add three problems associated with the subtour $x_{23} = x_{34} = x_{42} = 1$, *instead* of with the subtour $x_{15} = x_{51} = 1$. Carry out the remainder of the algorithm, and construct a tree analogous to that in Fig. 13.3 to show the progress of the iterations.

26 Consider how the traveling salesman problem example in Sec. 13.6 is solved by the *method of designated routes*. The rule that was used for *Step 1* was to select the highest-numbered problem that remained on the list. Hence, Problem 2 was selected at iteration 1. Carry out the algorithm using at *Step 1* the rule of selecting the lowest-numbered problem that remains on the list. (Hence, at iteration 1, begin with Problem

1.) Employ the same convention at *Step 4* of assigning the larger number to the problem with $x_{hk} = 1$. Construct a tree analogous to that in Fig. 13.5 to show the progress of the iterations.

27 Apply the *method of designated routes* to the traveling salesman problem example in Sec. 13.6, where you let Problem 1 designate $c_{15} = \infty$, and Problem 2 designate $x_{15} = 1$. (Use the same selection rule at *Step 1* and numbering rule at *Step 4* as in Fig. 13.5.) Construct a tree analogous to that in Fig. 13.5 to show the progress of the iterations.

28 Perform the analysis in exercise 27, where Problems 1 and 2 refer to $c_{51} = \infty$ and $x_{51} = 1$, respectively.

29 Consider how the traveling salesman problem example in Sec. 13.6 is solved by the *method of partial tours*. Given that a tour consists of a single cycle through all the cities, any one of the cities can be designated as the "starting point." Assume that the tour starts at City 2 and apply the method. Construct a tree analogous to that in Fig. 13.6 to show the progress of the iterations.

30 Suppose you know that an integer-valued variable x has an optimal solution value in the interval $0 \le x \le U$, where U is an integer. Indicate a way to represent x, analogous to that in (4) of Sec. 13.7, such that the largest possible value for this representation is exactly U.

31 Consider an integer programming model like that described at the beginning of Sec. 13.7. Suppose one of the linear constraints (2) is

$$x_1 - x_2 + 7x_3 - 10x_4 + 3x_5 - 6x_6 \le 0.$$

In each part below, apply the tests (9) and (11) to discover whether there is no feasible completion for the indicated partial solution, or whether one or more variables must take on a determinable value.

(a) $x_4 = x_6 = 0$.
(b) $x_1 = x_3 = 1$ and $x_4 = 0$.
(c) $x_1 = x_3 = 1$ and $x_6 = 0$.
(d) $x_1 = x_3 = x_5 = 1$.
(e) $x_1 = x_3 = x_5 = 1$ and $x_6 = 0$.
(f) $x_3 = 1$ and $x_2 = x_6 = 0$.

32 Consider an integer programming model like that described at the beginning of Sec. 13.7. Suppose the values of variables $x_6, x_7, \ldots, x_n$ are fixed in a partial solution and the remaining terms in the objective function to be maximized are $2x_1 - 3x_2 + 6x_3 - 7x_4 + 10x_5$; assume that $x_0^t = 7$. In each part below, apply the tests in (9) and (11) to discover whether the indicated augmentation of the partial solution can lead to a complete solution that is an improvement, and whether one or more variables must take on a determinable value in order to improve on the value $x_0^t = 7$.

(a) $x_4 = 1$.
(b) $x_5 = 0$.
(c) $x_1 = x_2 = 1$.

33 Consider the application of the Partial Enumeration Algorithm to the example (12) through (15) in Sec. 13.7. Verify all the intermediate calculations at each step. Show all the tests in detail.

34 Consider the example (12) through (15) in Sec. 13.7. Apply the Partial Enumeration Algorithm, where Problem 1 is the partial solution $x_1 = 1$ and Problem 2 is $x_1 = 0$. Let $x_0^1 = 0$, corresponding to all $x_j = 0$. Construct a tree like that in Fig. 13.7 to show the progress of the iterations.

35 Explain your understanding of the following terms:

divisibility assumption
integer (diophantine, discrete) programming problem
pure integer programming problem
mixed integer programming problem
combinatorial optimization problem
lattice point
zero-one variable
alternative constraints
"go-no-go" alternatives
traveling salesman problem
tours, subtours, and partial tours
Cutting-Plane Algorithm (Method of Integer Forms)
backtrack algorithm
*convex hull

*convex combination
integer part
fractional part
cut
*massive degeneracy
Branch-and-Bound Algorithm (Branch-and-Prune)
Partial (Implicit) Enumeration Algorithm
Additive Algorithm
binary representation
partial solution
free variables
completion
fathomed partial solution
composite (or surrogate) constraint.

COMPUTATIONAL EXERCISES

36 *Knapsack Problem.* Consider the following illustration of a knapsack problem, as described in exercises 22 and 47 of Chap. 10:

$$\text{maximize } 60x_1 + 60x_2 + 40x_3 + 10x_4 + 20x_5 + 10x_6 + 3x_7$$

subject to

$$3x_1 + 5x_2 + 4x_3 + 1x_4 + 4x_5 + 3x_6 + 1x_7 \leq 10$$

$$\text{every } x_j = 0, 1.$$

(a) Solve by the Cutting-Plane Algorithm in Sec. 13.4.
(b) Solve by the Branch-and-Bound Algorithm in Sec. 13.5.
(c) Solve by the Partial Enumeration Algorithm in Sec. 13.7.
*(d) Solve by a dynamic programming recursion.

37 Consider the argument in Sec. 13.4 establishing the validity of the cut (11) and (12), given the equation (8).

(a) Derive a cut analogous to (11) and (12) when (8) is multiplied by a constant p ($p \neq 0$).

(b) Suppose (8) is

$$2\tfrac{1}{2}x_1 + 3\tfrac{1}{4}x_2 = 6\tfrac{5}{16}.$$

What cut inequality do you obtain if $p = 1$? If $p = \tfrac{1}{2}$? If $p = 2$? If $p = 2\tfrac{1}{2}$? If $p = 3\tfrac{1}{4}$? Are all of these cuts equally strong? Explain.

(c) Let the symbol $\langle d \rangle$ designate the smallest integer greater than or equal to the real number d. Show that from (8) you can derive $\sum_{j=1}^{n} \langle a_j \rangle x_j \geq \langle b \rangle$.

38 Apply the Cutting-Plane Algorithm in Sec. 13.4 to solve each of the following problems, assuming here that all the variables must be nonnegative integers.

(a) One-Potato, Two-Potato Problem in Sec. 1.6. (*Note:* let the coefficients of the slack variables be .1, so that the slack variables are also integer-valued.)

(b) Knox Mix Company Problem, described in Sec. 2.2 and solved by the simplex method in Sec. 4.4.

*(c) Giant Electric Company, described in the special material at the end of Sec. 10.3. Use the data in exercise 30 of Chap. 10.

(d) Exercise 10, parts (b), (c), (f), and (g), of Chap. 3.

(e) Exercise 20, part (a), of Chap. 4.

(f) Example (8) and (9) in Sec. 13.5.

(g) maximize $x_1 + x_2$ subject to

$$4x_1 - x_2 \leq 10$$
$$2x_1 + 5x_2 \leq 10$$
$$4x_1 - 3x_2 \leq 6.$$

(h) maximize $10x_1 - x_2$ subject to

$$-25x_1 + 22x_2 \leq 33$$
$$20x_1 - 5x_2 \leq 24.$$

*(i) In parts (a), (d), (g), and (h), express the cuts in terms of the original variables, using the approach described in the special material at the end of Sec. 13.4. Show the progress of the algorithm on a solution space diagram.

39 Apply the Branch-and-Bound Algorithm in Sec. 13.5 to solve each of the following problems, assuming here that all the variables must be nonnegative integers. Construct a tree diagram like that in Fig. 13.1 to show the progress of the algorithm. (You may want to employ the Upper-Bounded Variables Algorithm in Sec. 5.10 on the larger problems.)

(a) One-Potato, Two-Potato Problem in Sec. 1.6.

(b) Knox Mix Company Problem, described in Sec. 2.2 and solved by the simplex method in Sec. 4.4.

(c) Exercise 18, part (a), of Chap. 10.

*(d) Exercise 18 of Chap. 10, with the right-hand-side constant in the first equation equal to 2, instead of 3.

*(e) Exercise 18 of Chap. 10, with the right-hand-side constant in the second equation equal to 3, instead of 4. Equal to 5, instead of 4.

*(f) Exercise 18 of Chap. 10, with the right-hand-side constant in the first equation equal to 2, instead of 3, and in the second equation equal to 3, instead of 4.

*(g) Giant Electric Company, described in the special material at the end of Sec. 10.3. Use the data in exercise 30 of Chap. 10.

(h) Exercise 20, part (a), of Chap. 4.

(i) Example (20), (21), and (22) in Sec. 13.4.

40 Apply the Partial Enumeration Algorithm in Sec. 13.7 to solve each of the following problems. Unless the problem already is stated in terms of zero-one variables, convert the model into an equivalent problem with all zero-one variables before applying the algorithm. Construct a tree diagram like that in Fig. 13.7 to show the progress of the algorithm.

(a) The following modified version of the Knox Mix Company Problem, described in Sec. 2.2 and solved by the simplex method in Sec. 4.4:

$$\text{maximize } 4x_1 + 28x_2 + 5x_3 + 9x_4 + 63x_5 + 11x_6$$

subject to

$$1x_1 + 7x_2 + 1x_3 + 1x_4 + 7x_5 + 1x_6 \leq 15$$
$$7x_1 + 49x_2 + 5x_3 + 3x_4 + 21x_5 + 2x_6 \leq 120$$
$$3x_1 + 21x_2 + 5x_3 + 10x_4 + 70x_5 + 15x_6 \leq 100$$

$$\text{every } x_j = 0, 1.$$

(b) Exercise 18, part (a), of Chap. 10.

(c) Exercise 18 of Chap. 10, with the right-hand-side constant in the first equation equal to 2, instead of 3.

(d) Exercise 18 of Chap. 10, with the right-hand-side constant in the second equation equal to 3, instead of 4. Equal to 5, instead of 4.

(e) Exercise 18 of Chap. 10, with the right-hand-side constant in the first equation equal to 2, instead of 3, and in the second equation equal to 3, instead of 4.

*(f) Giant Electric Company, described in the special material at the end of Sec. 10.3. Use the data in exercise 30 of Chap. 10.

(g) Exercise 20, part (a), of Chap. 4.

(h) Example (20), (21), and (22) in Sec. 13.4.

(i) Exercise 38, part (g).

(j) Exercise 38, part (h). (Assume $0 \leq x_j \leq 4$.)

(k) maximize $-4x_1 + 5x_2 + x_3 - 3x_4 + 1x_5$ subject to

$$-1x_1 + 2x_2 \qquad - 1x_4 - 1x_5 \leq -2$$
$$-4x_1 + 5x_2 + 1x_3 - 3x_4 + 1x_5 \leq -2$$
$$2x_1 - 3x_2 - 2x_3 + 6x_4 - 2x_5 \leq 1$$

$$\text{every } x_j = 0, 1.$$

41 Consider the traveling salesman problem given by the following data:

$$c_{12} = 20 \quad c_{13} = 4 \quad c_{14} = 10$$
$$c_{23} = 5 \qquad\qquad c_{25} = 10$$
$$c_{34} = 6 \quad c_{35} = 6$$
$$c_{45} = 20,$$

where $c_{ij} = c_{ji}$, and there is no route between Cities i and j if a value for c_{ij} is not shown above. Solve the problem by the

(a) Method of excluded subtours.
(b) Method of designated routes.
(c) Method of partial tours.

*42 Apply the Implicit Enumeration Algorithm to solve the following nonlinear zero-one problem. Use the approach given at the end of Sec. 13.7.

$$\text{maximize } 6x_1 - 2x_1^2 + x_1 x_2 - x_1 x_2^2 + 2x_1 x_3 - 5x_2^3 - x_2 x_3^3 + 4x_3^4 + 10x_4$$

subject to

$$3x_1^2 - 3x_1 x_2 + x_2^2 \leq 5$$
$$x_2 + 4x_3^3 + x_3^2 x_4 - 6x_4 \geq 3$$
$$7x_1^3 - x_3^2 + 3x_4 \leq 10$$
$$\text{every } x_j = 0, 1.$$

FORMULATION EXERCISES

In exercises 43 through 62, you are to formulate integer programming models. Be sure to define all the symbols you use, justify each of the constraints, and develop the objective function. When an exercise supplies numerical data, write out the model in full detail.

43 The scholarship and financial aids office at Yankee University is preparing its awards for the coming year. It has selected n students to receive awards, and wants to grant at least M_i dollars to Student i, for $i = 1, 2, \ldots, n$. The office has s different scholarships available; Scholarship j confers the amount a_j on its recipient. The office may have to award several grants to an individual student in order to provide him with at least M_i dollars, but the office cannot reduce the amount of any scholarship award below the designated level a_j. If the office does not award Scholarship j for the year, the amount a_j earns interest and is available for distribution in the following year.

(a) Devise a model for granting scholarships that maximizes the amount of undistributed money, subject to giving each student at least the minimal specified level.
(b) Show how to modify your answer in part (a) if each Student i is not permitted to receive funds from more than two different scholarships, and may not receive a total award in excess of $1.1M_i$.

44 A state government has asked for bids on n construction projects from each of n firms. No firm will be awarded more than one contract, so the decision problem can be viewed as an assignment model, as described in Sec. 6.4. For political reasons, the government officials want to award no more than N large contracts to firms that are located outside the state. Let Projects $1, 2, \ldots, s$, denote the large projects and Firms $1, 2, \ldots, t$, the companies that are located out of state. The objective is to minimize total cost given the added stipulation.

(a) Formulate this optimization problem.

(b) Show that imposing this added stipulation to the assignment model (3) and (4) in Sec. 6.4 and then finding a linear programming solution (where the integer constraints are ignored) need not produce a feasible assignment. (*Hint:* consider $n = 3$, $s = t = 2$, $N = 1$, every $c_{ii} = 0$, $c_{13} = c_{31} = 1$, and all other $c_{ij} = 2$.)

45 *Multi-Index Problem.* The governor of the state in exercise 44, Ray Gunn, is unhappy about the policy of limiting awards to out-of-state firms. He does, however, stipulate that one project must be completed in each three-month period, beginning six months from now, and ending $6 + 3n$ months from now. Accordingly, each contractor has resubmitted a bid stating the cost for each project depending on the designated period of completion. Formulate this optimization problem.

46 Consider a classical transportation model, like that described in Sec. 6.2. Impose the restriction that no supply point can serve more than M different demand points, and no demand point can be served by more than N different supply points. Assume that these stipulations permit a feasible solution. Formulate this optimization problem.

47 Fred Frosh, a first-year student at Multy University, has decided to take five courses in his first term; these courses are designated A, B, C, D, and E. Each course has four sections that meet at different times of the day; let A1, for example, denote Section 1 of Course A, and let t_{A1} be the hour at which it meets. For simplicity, assume that every course meets every day, and the starting times of courses are 8 A.M., 9 A.M., . . . , 4 P.M. Fred's preferences for when he takes courses are influenced by the time of day and the reputation of the instructor. For example, let P_{A1} denote Fred's preference for Section 1 of Course A. Unfortunately, Fred cannot select his most preferred section of each course due to time conflicts.

(a) Devise a model that selects a feasible course schedule which maximizes the sum of Fred's preference ratings.

(b) Indicate how to alter the formulation in part (a) to ensure that Fred has an hour for lunch at either noon or 1 P.M.

*(c) Indicate how to alter the formulation if Fred's objective function is to maximize the number of consecutive hours he has free either from 8 P.M. until his first class, or at the end of the afternoon.

48 Consider the problem of Van Fuller, described in exercise 35 of Chap. 10. Formulate his optimization problem in terms of an integer programming model.

49 *Multiplant Expansion Problem.* The Manne Agricultural Chemical Corporation operates three plants. At the beginning of Period 1, each plant has capacity 10. By the end of Period 3, Plant 1 must have capacity 11, Plant 2 must have capacity 12, and Plant 3 must have capacity 13; these targets are set so that after three periods each plant has enough capacity to be self-sufficient in its own marketing area. The capacity of a plant can be expanded in unit amounts in any period; for simplicity, assume that capacity that is initiated in a period is also available to meet demand requirements during that period. Also assume that capacity does not deteriorate. Thus, there are three possible ways for Plant 1 to increase its capacity from 10 at the beginning of Period 1 to 11 at the end of Period 3: (i) add 1 unit in Period 1, (ii) add 1 unit in Period 2, or (iii)

add 1 unit in Period 3. (Verify that there are six possible ways for Plant 2 to increase its capacity from 10 at the beginning of Period 1 to 12 at the end of Period 3.) Let $K_{it}(p, q)$ denote the cost in Period t of adding p units of capacity to Plant i, when its capacity at the beginning of Period t is q units.

Let D_{it} be the demand requirement during Period t in the marketing region served by Plant i. If Plant i lacks the capacity to fill requirement D_{it}, then the firm must ship items into this region from one or both of the other plants. Let c_{jit} represent the cost of shipping an item from Plant j to Plant i during Period t.

Formulate a model to determine a minimum cost policy for building capacity at each of the plants, and meeting all demands during the planning horizon.

50 The Phil T. Grimes Company must draw up a preventive maintenance schedule for five of its major pieces of equipment; the schedule extends over the next eight weeks. Assume the pieces of equipment are indexed 1, 2, 3, 4, 5. Maintenance on Piece 1 requires four units of labor (say, man-weeks) during the first week of maintenance, six units in the second week, and three units in the third week. The servicing can begin as early as Week 1 or as late as Week 4. Similar data for the other pieces of equipment are shown in Fig. 13.8.

Equipment	First Week	Second Week	Third Week	Early Start	Late Start
1	4	6	3	1	4
2	3	2	5	1	3
3	7	1	1	2	5
4	1	3	6	2	6
5	8	9	2	3	5

FIGURE 13.8

In each part below, formulate an appropriate optimization model.

(a) Assume that the maximum labor available is L_t in Week t. Find a feasible schedule (that is, determine the starting week for maintenance on each piece of equipment).

*(b) Suppose Grimes wants to minimize the sum of the weekly fluctuations in labor utilization. [If, for example, each project is started as early as possible, the weekly labor utilization is 7, 16, 20, 16, 2, 0, 0, 0, so that the sum of the week-to-week fluctuations is $(16 - 7) + (20 - 16) + (20 - 16) + (16 - 2) + (2 - 0) + (0 - 0) + (0 - 0) = 33$.]

*(c) Suppose Grimes wants to minimize the maximum labor utilized during any of the eight weeks.

*(d) Suppose Grimes wants to minimize the maximum weekly fluctuation. (If each project is started as early as possible, the resultant maximum fluctuation is $16 - 2 = 14$, between the fourth and fifth week.)

(e) Show how to modify your answer in part (a) if maintenance on Piece 3 cannot start before maintenance begins on Piece 1. If maintenance on Piece 4 has to start in the same period as maintenance on Piece 3 (hence, its "late start" week is really 5, instead of 6). If maintenance on Pieces 4 and 5 cannot start in the same week. If maintenance on Piece 5 cannot start until after maintenance on Piece 1 is complete (that is, if service on Piece 1 starts in Week 1, for example, then service on Piece 5 can start no sooner than Week 4.)

51 The Chick'n Lick'n Company operates a chain of home-delivery restaurants. Each store is franchised by the company, which tries to ensure a store owner of an adequate level of business. The company is considering n possible new sites in a major population area, and has estimated a store in Location j will result in an acceptable return R_j provided there is no other new store within a radius of 5 miles. Let $d_{ij} = 1$ if Sites i and j are within a 5-mile radius, and 0 otherwise. The company has calculated all the possible d_{ij}, and wants to choose a pattern of sites so as to maximize total return.

(a) Formulate the problem as a mathematical optimization model.
(b) Show how to modify your formulation in part (a) if the company also operates a chain of Dipp'n Donut Shops. It can use each of the n sites as either a donut shop or a Chick'n Lick'n Store. The company does not want to put two donut shops within a 10-mile radius.

52 *Covering Problem.* The Trotter Poll Company keeps a variety of data stored on magnetic tape files. It wishes to compile statistics on m different population characteristics (such as the age distribution, income distribution, size of family dwelling, etc., in eight selected metropolitan areas). Assume that all the required information is recorded within n different files. Suppose T_j, for $j = 1, 2, \ldots, n$, is the computer time required to search File j, and assume this search time is independent of the number of characteristics to be summarized from the file. Several of the m characteristics of interest are recorded in more than one of the n files, that is, the files contain duplicate information. Let $a_{ij} = 1$ if the ith characteristic is recorded in the jth file, and $a_{ij} = 0$, otherwise. Thus, for example, $a_{13} = a_{18} = a_{19} = 1$ indicates that the first characteristic is recorded in Files 3, 8, and 9.

(a) Formulate an integer programming model to determine which of the n files to search so that data on all of the characteristics are gathered in minimum searching time.
(b) Explain how to modify your formulation if the search time for File j consists of T_j if File j is searched at all, plus t_{ij} if Characteristic i is obtained during the search.

53 *Delivery Truck Problem (Covering Problem).* The Droppit Parcel Company has five customer deliveries to make today. It must unload a shipment of weight 1 at Customer A, of weight 2 at Customer B, of weight 3 at Customer C, of weight 5 at Customer D, and of weight 8 at Customer E. The company has four different delivery vans available; Truck 1 has weight capacity 2, Truck 2 has weight capacity 6, Truck 3 has weight capacity 8, and Truck 4 has weight capacity 8. The cost of operating Truck j is c_j. Assume that a single truck cannot deliver to both Customers A and C; similarly, a single truck cannot deliver to both Customers B and D.

(a) Formulate an integer programming model to determine the minimum cost allocation of delivery trucks for making all the shipments.
(b) Show how to alter your formulation if there is an additional cost c_{ij} when the truck delivers to Customer i. *Exercise continues on p. 504.*

(c) Show how to alter your formulation if a truck cannot make more than two deliveries during the day.

(d) Explain the impact on the model formulation of imposing additional constraints on the truck routes.

54 *Trim Problem.* Consider the model in exercise 25 of Chap. 2. In that description, all customer demands were met and only one size jumbo roll was used.

(a) Suppose, instead, that the Fine-Webb Paper Company can manufacture its customer orders from jumbo rolls of 50-, 60-, and 70-inch widths. There is a setup cost, however, for using each different jumbo size roll (denote these costs by K_{50}, K_{60}, and K_{70}, where the cost units have been chosen to be commensurate with the value of trim loss). Show how to alter the formulation in exercise 25, Chap. 2, to account for the possibility of using different size jumbo rolls.

(b) Suppose, instead, that the Fine-Webb Paper Company can ship each customer an amount within 20% of his order quantity; hence, the company need manufacture as few as 80 reels of 22-inch width, but may manufacture as many as 120 reels. The foreman wants a schedule that uses no more than two different combinations (ordinarily, a linear programming solution would select three different combinations, since there are three linear constraints). Show how to formulate an optimization model satisfying these restrictions.

55 The Mini Manufacturing Company produces four kinds of items. Let D_{kt} be the demand requirement in Period t for Item k, where $k = 1, 2, 3, 4$, and $t = 1, 2, \ldots, T$; assume each D_{kt} is integer-valued. Let x_{kt} denote the production level of Item k in Period t. Assume that all demand must be met each period, but it is possible to produce for inventory in one period to meet demand requirements in subsequent periods. Let $c_{kt}x_{kt}$ be the production cost associated with x_{kt}, and h_k be the inventory holding cost per unit of Item k held at the end of a period. (Assume inventory at the beginning of Period 1 is 0.) So far, the situation for each product resembles the production and inventory model in Sec. 8.3. There is an additional constraint, however, that at most only one type of item can be produced during each period.

(a) Formulate an optimization model taking account of this production limitation.

*(b) Formulate an appropriate dynamic programming recursion.

*56 Show how the variable cost structure in the inventory and production scheduling model of exercise 44, Chap. 8, can be characterized within an integer programming version of the problem.

*57 Show how the variable cost structure in the inventory model of exercise 9, Chap. 9, can be characterized within an integer programming version of the problem.

58 Consider an integer programming model containing only zero-one variables.

(a) Suppose the model contains (in the objective function or a constraint) the term $x_1^2 x_5 x_9^3$. Show how a zero-one variable y can be substituted for this term, provided that you add the constraints $x_1 + x_5 + x_9 - y \leq 2$ and $-x_1 - x_5 - x_9 + 3y \leq 0$.

(b) How does the approach in part (a) generalize to handling the product term

$(x_1)^{p_1}(x_2)^{p_2} \cdots (x_n)^{p_n}$, where each $p_j \geq 0$. [Be sure your formulation takes advantage of any $p_j = 0$, as occurred in part (a).]

(c) Verify that x_j^p, where $p > 0$, can be replaced by x_j.

*(d) Apply the observations in the above parts to exercise 42.

59 *Quadratic Assignment Problem.* The Ireson Engineering Company serves its industrial clients by advising on the layout of plants and office buildings. A typical problem of this sort involves a new plant that has been zoned into n different work areas. Each area is to be the location of one of n different production facilities. If Facility 1 is assigned, for example, to Work Area 3, and Facility 2 is assigned, for example, to Work Area 5, the arrangement gives rise to the cost $c_{13;25}$. The cost is due to the amount of "traffic" in materials and personnel flowing between Facilities 1 and 2 and the distance between Work Areas 3 and 5. (Since there are n^2 *pairings* of facilities to work areas, there are altogether n^4 cost coefficients $c_{ij;kl}$) Formulate a cost minimization model that assigns facilities to locations. (*Hint:* the objective function is quadratic.)

60 Another integer programming formulation of the traveling salesman problem is based on using zero-one variables x_{ijk}. Letting $x_{ijk} = 1$ implies that k is the position in the tour at which the salesman visits City i, and from there goes to City j. In every tour, let $k = 1$ for City 1. Write in detail all the restrictions and the objective function appropriate to this formulation for a four-city problem. (*Hint:* the salesman must depart from every city. If he visits City i at Position k and goes to City j, then he visits City j at Position k + 1.) Be sure to explain why the formulation rules out subtours.

*61 *Critical Path Scheduling.* Consider the Swift Building Company case described in Sec. 6.6 and displayed in Fig. 6.13. Suppose each job requires a specified amount of a scarce resource, such as labor time, per period the job is in process. For example, given that it takes t_A units of time to complete Job A, assume that r_A units of labor are required each week that Job A is being completed. Assume that R_p is the maximum amount of labor available in Week p for all jobs in process.

(a) Formulate the problem as a mathematical optimization model. Use the data in Fig. 6.13. The objective is still to complete the entire project as early as possible. [*Hint:* introduce zero-one variables that indicate the week a job starts. Express the time a job starts in terms of these variables, and rewrite the precedence ordering constraints (2) through (6) in Sec. 6.6 accordingly.] Explain how to modify your formulation if the labor time needed for a job differed from one week to the next while it was being completed.

(b) Show how to modify your formulation in part (a) if there also is a second resource restriction. For example, assume that s_A units of this other resource are required each week that Job A is being completed, and that S_p is the maximum amount of this resource available in Week p for all jobs in process.

*62 *Critical Path Scheduling.* Consider the Swift Building Company case described in Sec. 6.6 and displayed in Fig. 6.13. Suppose there are several alternative ways to construct the entire project. Specifically, instead of Job D, the company can use either Job G or Job H. If it uses Job G, the immediate predecessors for Job C are A and G, for Job D is B, and for Job E is B. The other data in Fig. 6.13 are unchanged. If the company uses Job H, there is no immediate predecessor for Job H, the immediate predecessor for Job E is B, and for Job F is C, E, and H. The other data in Fig. 6.13 are unchanged. Revise the formulation (1) through (6) to account for the choice possibility between Jobs D, G, and H. The objective is still to complete the entire project as early as possible.

MIND-EXPANDING EXERCISES

63 *Assembly-Line Balancing.* An assembly line consists of locations, called work stations, and one or more jobs may be performed at each station in the process of completing the manufacture of an item. Assume there are six jobs in all, that a unit must go through the assembly line from Station 1, to Station 2, . . . , to the final station. Each Job i requires t_i minutes to perform. The combined time of all jobs assigned to each work station is not permitted to exceed T, which is called the cycle time of the line; in this example, let $T = 10$. Certain jobs must be performed before others; the precedence relations and times are shown in Fig. 13.9.

Job i	Immediate Predecessor	Completion Time t_i
1	--	5
2	--	6
3	1	2
4	2,3	5
5	1,2	4
6	4	3

FIGURE 13.9

The optimization problem is to open as few work stations as possible, consistent with the cycle time restriction and the precedence relations. Formulate the problem as a mathematical optimization model. (*Hint:* let x_{ij} be a zero-one variable which equals 1 if Job i is performed at Work Station j. Each job must be performed at a station, subject to the precedence restrictions. The total time for all jobs assigned to a station must not exceed T minutes.)

64 *Machine (Job-Shop) Scheduling Problem.* Suppose that three items are to be sequenced through n machines. Each item must be processed first on Machine 1, then on Machine 2, . . . , and finally on Machine n. The sequence of jobs may be different for each machine. Let t_{ij} be the time required to perform the work on Item i by Machine j; assume each t_{ij} is an integer. The objective is to minimize the total work span to complete all the items.

(a) Formulate the problem as an integer programming model. Write the model in detail for $n = 4$. (*Hint:* One approach is to let x_{ij} represent the time at which Item i begins processing by Machine j. In this formulation, you must make sure that no two items occupy the same machine at the same time, and that an item does not start processing on Machine $j + 1$ until the work is completed on Machine j. Another approach is to let a zero-one variable x_{ijk} correspond to assigning Item i to the kth position of the sequence on Machine j.)

(b) Indicate the simplifications, if any, that are possible when you stipulate that the items are to be processed in the same sequence on each machine. (This can be shown to be an optimal policy if there are two or three machines; in the case of two machines, there is a simple algorithm for finding an optimal solution.)

65 *Machine (Job-Shop) Scheduling Problem.* In exercise 64, stipulate that the items are to be processed in the same sequence on each of the n machines. Devise a technique of solution analogous to the *method of partial tours* in Sec. 13.6. (*Hint:* given a partial assignment of items to Position $1, 2, \ldots, k$ of the sequence, a lower bound on the total time span to complete all the jobs can be found in terms of when the kth job is completed on each machine, and of the sum of the processing times on each machine required by the jobs remaining to be scheduled.)

66 *Knapsack Problem.* Consider exercise 36, and devise an algorithm for solving such problems analogous to the *method of designated routes* in Sec. 13.6. (*Hint:* given a set of variables at specified levels, an upper bound on the value of the objective function for an optimal choice of the remaining variables can be found from solving an associated linear programming problem.)

67 *Fixed Charge Problem.* Consider the model described in exercise 6. Devise an algorithm for solving such problems analogous to the *method of designated routes* in Sec. 13.6.

68 *Quadratic Assignment Problem.* Review the case of the Ireson Engineering Company, described in exercise 59. Consider each possible pair of facilities: (Facility 1, Facility 2) (Facility 1, Facility 3), $\ldots$, (Facility 1, Facility n), (Facility 2, Facility 3), (Facility 2, Facility 4), $\ldots$, (Facility n $-$ 1, Facility n). Similarly, consider each possible pair of work areas: (Area 1, Area 2), (Area 1, Area 3), $\ldots$, (Area n $-$ 1, Area n). Verify that altogether there are $n(n-1)/2$ pairs of facilities, and the same number of pairs of work areas.

Imagine a table having $n(n-1)/2$ rows, one for each pair of facilities, and the same number of columns, one for each pair of work areas. Assume that the cost structure is such that the same cost arises if, for example, Facility 1 is assigned to Work Area 3 and Facility 2 is assigned to Work Area 5, or if Facility 1 is assigned to Work Area 5 and Facility 2 is assigned to Work Area 3. In other words, only the information that the pair (Facility 1, Facility 2) is assigned to the pair (Area 3, Area 5) is needed to determine the cost. Comment on why such a cost assumption might be reasonable.

(a) Suppose that the cost associated with each pairing of facilities coupled with each pairing of work areas is inserted in this square table. Comment on whether solving an assignment problem using these costs yields an answer to the facility location problem. (*Suggestion:* let $n = 4$ and construct the square table, showing the row and column headings; then examine whether an assignment solution is always feasible for the location selection problem.)

(b) Based on your observations in part (a), suggest ways to modify the several approaches used for solving the traveling salesman problem in Sec. 13.6 so as to find a solution to the location problem.

69 *Primal Cutting-Plane Algorithm.* The cutting-plane approach in Sec. 13.4 can be characterized as a "dual" algorithm in that the dual constraints are satisfied throughout (after the simplex method has found an optimal solution ignoring the integer constraints). The successive solutions are *not* primal feasible until the final iteration, since only then are the integer constraints satisfied. A primal algorithm satisfies throughout the integer stipulations as well as the linear restrictions. The details of a primal

algorithm that is guaranteed to converge go beyond the scope of this text. But a few of the important ideas can be illustrated by an example.

Assume you have an initial nonoptimal primal feasible integer-valued solution. Apply the ordinary *Criterion I* of the simplex method to select a variable to enter the next solution. Apply *Criterion II* of the simplex method to determine the maximum level at which the selected variable can enter so as to keep all the other basic variables nonnegative. Denote this level by $r \geq 0$. If the ordinary pivot element does not equal 1, you then construct a cut to be used as the row in which the pivoting will occur. The cut must have the following two properties: (i) the pivot element for the selected variable equals 1; hence, all the coefficients and the basic variables remain integer-valued after the pivot operation. (ii) The right-hand-side constant is no larger than r, so that the basic variables remain nonnegative. Here is a way to find such a cut.

Repeat the ratio arithmetic done in *Criterion II*, now taking the integer part of each ratio. Select any row for which the integer part of the ratio is less than or equal to r. (If there are several such rows, select one having the largest integer part.) As a side calculation, divide the selected row by the coefficient of the entering variable, and then construct the cut given by (12) in Sec. 13.4. Augment the equations with this cut, pivot, and return to *Criterion I*.

(If $r < 1$, then necessarily the right-hand-side constant for the cut is 0. Therefore, the objective function does not improve at such an iteration. To guarantee convergence, the method has to be amended in such a way as to rule out the possibility of an endless sequence of cuts having 0 right-hand sides. We do not present such a procedure here.)

To see how the approach works, consider the following modified version of the Knox Mix Company Example (Secs. 2.2 and 4.4)

$$x_0 - 4x_1 - 9x_3 \qquad\qquad = 0 \qquad\qquad \text{Row 0}$$

$$1x_1 + 1x_3 + x_5 \quad = 12 \qquad\qquad \text{Row 1}$$

$$3x_1 + 10x_3 \qquad + x_7 = 85 \qquad\qquad \text{Row 2.}$$

(Verify that x_4 and x_6 have been dropped, x_2 has been set equal to 3 and then suppressed, and the second constraint has been eliminated in the original version treated in Sec. 4.4.)

On the first iteration, select x_3 to enter. Perform *Criterion II* and find that $r = \left(\frac{85}{10}\right)$ $= 8.5$. Repeat the ratio arithmetic using integer parts to obtain the values $\left[\frac{12}{1}\right]$ and $\left[\frac{85}{10}\right]$. Since only $\left[\frac{85}{10}\right] \leq r$, you must write a cut on the equation in Row 2. As a side calculation, divide Row 2 by 10 obtaining

$$\tfrac{3}{10}x_1 + x_3 + \tfrac{1}{10}x_7 = \tfrac{85}{10},$$

which results in the cut

$$x_3 + x_8 = 8 \qquad\qquad \text{Row 3,}$$

where x_8 is the slack variable for the cut. Append Row 3 to the problem and pivot on x_3.

(a) Complete the algorithm until you obtain an optimal solution. [*Hint:* the approach requires three more cuts. The value of the objective function increases from 0 to 72 (after pivoting on Row 3), then to 76, to 83, and remains 83 at the final iteration. You will introduce slack variables x_9 and x_{10}, and will eventually have to pivot on x_8 and x_9 to obtain convergence. When you pivot on x_9, use Row 1 to generate the cut. Explain why.]

(b) Apply the method to the original version of the Knox Mix Problem.

70 *Group Theoretic Algorithm.* A powerful technique for solving integer programming stems from exploiting so-called group theoretic properties of the problem. A treatment of all the details of the approach goes beyond the intended level of this text, but the gist of the idea can be explained by means of an example. Consider the case of the Knox Mix Company Problem, described in Sec. 2.2 and solved by the simplex method in Sec. 4.4. Examine the equations (7) at the final iteration. Let an algebraic representation of an equation in (7) be $\sum_{i=1}^{7} A_i x_i = B$. Then we can write

$$A_i \equiv [A_i] + f_i,$$

where $0 \leq f_i < 1$, and $B \equiv [B] + f$, where $0 \leq f < 1$. In other words, f_i is the fractional part of A_i, and f is the fractional part of B. The equation, then, is

$$\sum_{i=1}^{7} [A_i] x_i + \sum_{i=1}^{7} f_i x_i = [B] + f.$$

Explain why it is necessary that $\sum_{i=1}^{7} f_i x_i - f$ be integer-valued for every feasible integer-valued solution. Check that if x_i is a basic variable, then $f_i = 0$. Hence, explain why it is necessary that the x_i must satisfy $\sum_{i=1}^{7} f_i x_i \equiv f \pmod{1}$, that is, the left- and right-hand sides must differ by an integer for feasibility.

Verify from (7) that, as a consequence, it is necessary to satisfy

$$\tfrac{5}{7} x_2 + \tfrac{2}{7} x_4 + \tfrac{3}{7} x_5 + \tfrac{6}{7} x_7 \equiv \tfrac{1}{7} \pmod{1}$$

$$\tfrac{1}{7} x_2 + \tfrac{6}{7} x_4 + \tfrac{2}{7} x_5 + \tfrac{4}{7} x_7 \equiv \tfrac{3}{7} \pmod{1}$$

$$\tfrac{2}{7} x_2 + \tfrac{5}{7} x_4 + \tfrac{4}{7} x_5 + \tfrac{1}{7} x_7 \equiv \tfrac{6}{7} \pmod{1}.$$

Check that after multiplying through by 7, an equivalent statement is

$$5x_2 + 2x_4 + 3x_5 + 6x_7 \equiv 1 \pmod{7}$$

(M) $\qquad 1x_2 + 6x_4 + 2x_5 + 4x_7 \equiv 3 \pmod{7}$

$$2x_2 + 5x_4 + 4x_5 + 1x_7 \equiv 6 \pmod{7}.$$

Verify that a feasible solution to these equations (M), when substituted back into (7), results in integer values for the basic variables, but such integer values may not be nonnegative.

You also know from (7) that the objective-function value will equal $\tfrac{695}{7} - \tfrac{3}{7} x_2 - \tfrac{11}{7} x_4 - \tfrac{13}{7} x_5 - \tfrac{5}{7} x_7$. Therefore, you seek feasible values for these nonbasic variables that minimize $3x_2 + 11x_4 + 13x_5 + 5x_7$ (where we have multiplied through by 7 to eliminate fractions).

Verify that given the modulus arithmetic in (M), $x_2 = 2$ has the same effect as $x_5 = 1$; $x_5 = 2$ has the same effect as $x_7 = 1$; $x_5 = x_7 = 1$ has the same effect as $x_4 = 1$. The underlying principle is that there is a group of seven columns, each column containing an entry for every row, that can be associated with *any* set of integer values for the x_i in (M). In this example, you can generate these columns by picking any column of coefficients, say, that for x_2, which is $\begin{pmatrix} 5 \\ 1 \\ 2 \end{pmatrix}$ in (M), and calculate the columns $\begin{pmatrix} 5x_2 \\ 1x_2 \\ 2x_2 \end{pmatrix}$, for $x_2 = 0, 1, \ldots, 7$, using modulus 7 arithmetic. Verify this process gives

$$\begin{pmatrix} 0 \\ 0 \\ 0 \end{pmatrix} \begin{pmatrix} 5 \\ 1 \\ 2 \end{pmatrix} \begin{pmatrix} 3 \\ 2 \\ 4 \end{pmatrix} \begin{pmatrix} 1 \\ 3 \\ 6 \end{pmatrix} \begin{pmatrix} 6 \\ 4 \\ 1 \end{pmatrix} \begin{pmatrix} 4 \\ 5 \\ 3 \end{pmatrix} \begin{pmatrix} 2 \\ 6 \\ 5 \end{pmatrix}$$
①   ②   ③   ④   ⑤   ⑥   ⑦ ,

where the circled numbers underneath the columns will serve to identify them. Note that ④ is the right-hand side of (M).

You can identify minimizing the above stated objective function subject to (M) in terms of a shortest-route problem. Designate the nodes ①, ②, . . . , ⑦, corresponding to the seven columns of numbers. Associate all $x_i = 0$ on the left-hand side of (M) with Node ①. Associate each $x_i = 1$ with an arc from Node ① to another node. For example, $x_2 = 1$ yields an arc from Node ① to Node ② with a cost 3; $x_4 = 1$ yields an arc from Node ① to Node ⑦ with a cost 11; $x_5 = 1$ yields an arc from Node ① to Node ③ with a cost 13. What does $x_7 = 1$ yield?

By the same token, draw four arcs leading out of each other node, except Node ④, which is the right-hand side of (M). (Also, you do not need to draw arcs leading back to Node ①.) For example, there is an arc with cost 3 from Node ② to Node ③ corresponding to a unit of x_2; there is an arc with cost 13 from Node ② to Node ④ corresponding to a unit of x_5. The nodes and a few arcs are shown in Fig. 13.10. Complete the network diagram. The problem is to find a shortest route from Node ① to Node ④. Solve this optimization problem in the completed network.

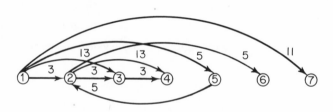

FIGURE 13.10

A route such as ① to ⑤ to ② to ④ corresponds to letting $x_7 = 2$ and $x_5 = 1$. Verify that the shortest route in the completed network corresponds to letting $x_2 = 3$. What are the values for the basic x_i in (7) when you let $x_2 = 3$? Explain why this is the optimal solution to the original problem.

(a) Perform the algorithm on the example (20), (21), and (22) in Sec. 13.4.

*(b) The problem in part (a) is an example of a *knapsack model*, described in exercises 22 and 47 of Chap. 10. Use your analysis in part (a) to characterize an optimal solution for every possible value of the right-hand-side constant of the constraint.

*(c) Suppose you add to the Knox Mix Company Problem a variable x_8, having coefficients a_1, a_2, a_3 in Rows 1, 2, 3, respectively, where each a_i is integer-valued. Show that the column of fractional parts, associated with x_8 in (7), would, after multiplication by 7, be one of the columns ①, ②, . . . , ⑦.

*(d) Establish the connection between the algorithm and the network representation given above and the algorithm and network implied by the recursion (ii) in the special material at the end of Sec. 10.2.

71 A solution to the traveling salesman problem can be characterized in terms of a dynamic programming recursion. Observe that at any point of the salesman's tour, when he is about to choose the next city, the associated state variable can be viewed as the city where he is currently located, and the *set* of cities he has visited previously (but *not* the order in which he has visited them). Develop a dynamic programming recursion on the basis of this observation. Comment on whether the approach is practical for obtaining numerical solutions.

*72 The advanced material at the end of Sec. 13.2 suggests a way to treat a piecewise-linear function $c(x)$ so that it may be incorporated into an integer programming problem. The formulation involves using (24), (25), and (27) through (30). The method is a variant of an approach discussed in Sec. 14.7. Another formulation can be based on an approach in the special material of Sec. 14.7, namely, (i) through (vii). Show how that approach can be formulated as an integer programming model so as to guarantee the *property of adjacent weights*.

CONTENTS

CHAPTER 14

Optimization with a Nonlinear Objective Function [†]

14.1 INTRODUCTION TO NONLINEAR PROGRAMMING

Recall that any linear optimization model can be viewed as

$$(1) \qquad \text{maximize} \sum_{j=1}^{n} c_j x_j$$

subject to

$$(2) \qquad \sum_{j=1}^{n} a_{ij} x_j \le b_i \quad \text{for } i = 1, 2, \ldots, m$$

$$(3) \qquad x_j \ge 0 \quad \text{for } j = 1, 2, \ldots, n.$$

You have already studied several nonlinear variations of this model, such as the dynamic programming examples in Chaps. 8, 9, and 10, as well as the combinatorial models in Chap. 13, in which several of the x_j were restricted to having integer values. The term **nonlinear programming** usually refers to problems such as

$$(4) \qquad \text{maximize } c(x_1, x_2, \ldots, x_n)$$

subject to

$$(5) \qquad a_i(x_1, x_2, \ldots, x_n) \le 0 \quad \text{for } i = 1, 2, \ldots, m,$$

where both $c(x_1, \ldots, x_n)$ and $a_i(x_1, \ldots, x_n)$ are real-valued, nonlinear, but well-behaved functions of n real variables. Actually, (4) and (5) can be viewed as a canonical form for a nonlinear programming problem, since you can employ the techniques of Chap. 3 to treat the optimization as "maximize" and the con-

[†] This chapter requires a knowledge of differential calculus.

513

straints as inequalities with the direction given in (5). A nonnegativity restriction on a variable x_j can be contained in (5), expressed as $-x_j \leq 0$. Customarily, integer-valued stipulations on the x_j are not encompassed in what are termed "nonlinear programming problems."

▶ A qualification is in order here, since you can always include in (5) a set of nonlinear constraints that will "trick" a model into allowing only integer-valued variables for feasible solutions. To illustrate, suppose x_j is restricted to be either 0 or 1. Then this discrete-valued stipulation can be ensured by imposing the constraints $-x_j \leq 0$, $x_j - 1 \leq 0$, and $x_j(1 - x_j) \leq 0$. Such tricks are *not* treated in this and the next chapter. The end of Sec. 13.6 briefly treats the solution of nonlinear programming problems containing integer-valued variables.   ◀

Need for nonlinear programming techniques. Even a quick review of the simple, yet illustrative, examples of linear programming models contained in Chap. 2 should suffice to raise your doubts that many actual situations really fit the mold of strict linearity. You may easily have gotten the impression that a linear approach simply *ignores* such phenomena as: efficiencies or inefficiencies of large-scale operations in a product-mix model; nonadditive volume relationships when chemicals are combined; the effect of sales quantity on sales price, and therefore on sales revenue. If you did get such an impression, the discussion below will clear up this misunderstanding.

There is plenty of evidence that linear programming models have been applied very successfully in nonlinear environments. Since any model, inevitably, only approximates reality, the important question is "*when* does a linearized version provide an adequate representation of a nonlinear phenomenon?" What you must learn, then, is to distinguish between circumstances that are and are not amenable to a straightforward application of linear programming.

In a particular application, if you have some knowledge about the range of values for an optimal solution, then you can usually restrict the solution to this range and employ a trustworthy linear approximation. It is only when the model has a wide region of feasible solutions, and you have very little idea about an optimal solution, that you may be unable to find a good enough linear approximation. These statements are tautological to some extent, because they relate to how you formulate the model in the first place, in terms of specifying the objective function and constraints. But for most applications, you will find that the issue of whether or not a linearized version suffices is more readily resolved than you might guess from the foregoing, admittedly vague, comments. The following two illustrations suggest when a linearized version is liable to be inadequate in a real situation.

Consider a company in the initial stages of developing a model for corporate-wide long-range planning. A management scientist usually knows that, even if he is an experienced businessman, it is difficult to give accurate, detailed forecasts of optimal production levels and market penetrations for his company for the next 10 or more years. Indeed, a major reason for an executive employing such a model is that he realizes how easily his intuition can be amiss when trying to fathom the influence of economic factors projected beyond the present. If production costs and revenues vary nonlinearly with the scale of operations, linearized guesses may not be good enough to give valid answers. (After the model has been used repeatedly, however, a linear version may prove workable, provided the model parameters do not change drastically over time.)

The second example is a firm that schedules production by employing a dynamic, multi-item model that reflects the presence of significant machine setup times, limited machine-group capacities, and fluctuating demand requirements. Typically, in such a case, the *essence* of the optimization problem is to modulate the various nonlinear effects of scheduling decisions. Unless the production planner can make a very good guess at an optimal solution, any simple linearization of the problem is likely to do violence to the fundamental nature of the optimization.

Even though a specific application may require you to build a *nonlinear model*, you may be able to use a *solution technique* that is only a slight variation of a linear model. If the nonlinearities are severe, however, because of their shape characteristics or their pervasiveness in the model description, you will have to resort to solution techniques that are truly more sophisticated than the simplex algorithm. This point will become clear below and in the next chapter.

Managerial significance of nonlinear models. Today, the preponderance of mathematical programming applications to real managerial decision-making situations employ linear approximations, rather than explicit nonlinear formulations. But the importance of nonlinear programming applications is growing. This is due to the rapidly increasing sophistication of managers and operations researchers in implementing decision-oriented mathematical models, as well as to the growing availability of computer routines capable of solving large-scale nonlinear problems.

Most nonlinearities encompassed in a programming model fall into two categories:

(i) Empirically observed relationships, such as nonproportional variations in costs, process yields, and quality characteristics.
(ii) Structurally derived relationships, which encompass postulated physical phenomena, mathematically deduced behavior, and managerially determined rules.

Obviously, no hard-and-fast line separates these two categories, since with enough data you may be able to derive a structural relationship underlying an empirically observed phenomenon.

An example of (i) occurs when over a period of years factory output does not rise proportionately with an increase in man-hours, whereas process scrap rises more than proportionately. An illustration of (ii) arises in a firm having to pay an electricity bill calculated from a nonlinear formula involving both the firm's daily average and its peak-load requirements. In this instance, the firm knows of the nonlinear cost structure from a rate schedule negotiated with the utility company.

Other situations in which nonlinearities are built into the programming models are:

1. *Gasoline Blending.* A model for blending gasoline from so-called refinery raw stocks usually contains nonlinear constraints relating to each blend's octane rating, since this quality characteristic varies nonlinearly with the amount of tetraethyl lead (TEL) added to the mix.

2. *Process Control.* In a model for a steel-processing plant, a variable representing the temperature of a blast furnace can be described by a nonlinear function of variables indicating the amount and duration of heat energy applied. Each of these variables, in turn, is contained in other constraints as well as in the objective function.

3. *Sales Revenue.* A company may face a responsive price-volume relationship for its products: the lower a product's price, the greater the sales quantity, even in the face of resultant price decreases by competitors. Therefore, sales revenue does not vary proportionately with price, and this phenomenon is reflected in the objective function of a product-mix model by a nonlinear component. To illustrate, let $x(p)$ represent the sales quantity as a function of the price p; then $p \cdot x(p)$ is the associated sales revenue. Suppose the sales quantity function is linear, $x(p) = ap + b$, over the range of interest for p. Then the sales revenue component in the objective function is quadratic $(ap^2 + bp)$ in the decision variable p.

4. *Multi-Item Order Quantities.* The inventory models in Chaps. 8 and 9 dealt with single-item situations. But frequently a wholesaler replenishes his inventory by ordering several items at one time from a single supplier, thereby taking advantage of economies in shipping costs, paper work, and quantity discounts offered by a supplier. This situation can be treated by a large-scale programming model in which the associated costs of replenishment appear as nonlinear functions of the several order quantities.

5. *Safety-Stock Inventory Levels.* In most mathematical programming models used for corporate planning, the time periods are rarely less than three months and often are a year or more. Such a multiperiod model for a manufacturing company usually includes provision for inventory levels that are to act as safety-stocks to accommodate weekly fluctuations in sales. One approach employed in these models is to let the safety-stock level for an item be a function of both its forecasted sales quantity and the fraction of capacity utilization implied by this forecast. For example, c may be the weekly capacity available to produce an item, s the item's forecasted *average* weekly sales, and $n \cdot s$ the item's safety-stock level, where n represents the number of weeks' sales depending on the capacity utilization factor s/c. To illustrate, suppose management has established the formula for n to be

$[n = m + f \cdot (s/c)]$; then the resultant safety-stock level is a quadratic function $[ms + (f/c)s^2]$ of the item's forecasted average weekly sales. This level may appear in several of the planning model's constraints as well as in the objective function.

6. *Distribution of Effort.* In Chap. 10 you saw several illustrations of the so-called Distribution of Effort Problem. The decision variables were assumed to be integer-valued, and the constraints were limited to one or two, in order to make the dynamic programming approach computationally feasible. If you eliminate the stipulation of integer-valued variables, a nonlinear model can also be employed to solve a Distribution of Effort Problem. Then you can apply nonlinear programming techniques, which are computationally practical even when considerably more than two constraints are imposed.

7. *Probabilistic Elements.* Nonlinearities frequently arise when a programming model's coefficients are viewed as random variables. The two illustrations below are described in brief.

Consider, first, an ordinary transportation model like the one in Secs. 2.7 and 6.2. Suppose, however, that the demand D_j at each Destination j is specified by a probability distribution, and that the actual values of all D_j are not known until *after* the shipments are made. If a total amount of x_j is shipped to Destination j, the amount remaining after demand occurs is $(x_j - D_j)$, where a negative value indicates the amount of unfilled demand. Suppose the cost $c_j(x_j - D_j)$ is assigned to the event $(x_j - D_j)$. Explain why this cost *function* would be nonlinear. The model's objective function, then, is to minimize the sum of transportation costs plus the sum of *expected* values for $c_j(x_j - D_j)$. Accordingly, the objective function displays a nonlinear dependence on the decision variables x_j. This model is discussed in detail in Sec. 16.6.

The preceding example can be formulated as a transportation model in which several right-hand-side coefficients of the corresponding constraints are random. Now consider any linear programming model in which the b_i coefficients in the linear inequality constraints (2) above are random. To illustrate, suppose the model has two constraints $i = 1, 2$ in (2), and that the coefficients b_i are independently distributed, where $G_i(b)$ represents the probability that the random variable b_i is at least as large as b. Suppose you want to select the x_j so that the joint probability of every constraint being satisfied is at least β:

$$(6) \qquad P\left[\sum_{j=1}^{n} a_{1j}x_j \leq b_1\right] \cdot P\left[\sum_{j=1}^{n} a_{2j}x_j \leq b_2\right] \geq \beta \quad (0 < \beta \leq 1).$$

Then, as you will see in Sec. 16.5, the programming constraints equivalent to (6) can be written as

$$(7) \qquad -y_i + \sum_{j=1}^{n} a_{ij}x_j = 0 \quad \text{for } i = 1, 2$$

$$(8) \qquad G_1(y_1) \cdot G_2(y_2) \geq \beta,$$

where the product in (8) leads to a nonlinear restriction on y_1 and y_2.

*8. *Portfolio Selection.* Financial analysts in banks and insurance companies have devoted considerable attention to mathematical models that assist in managing portfolios of common stocks, bonds, and other securities. Inherent in such models is an assessment of a proposed portfolio's expected gain and the associated risk, or probable variation, in the actual gain. A full discussion of how to build these models goes beyond the main purpose of this chapter, but the ensuing simple version suggests how nonlinear programming formulations have proved useful.

Let x_j represent the *proportion* of available funds to be allocated to Security j. Suppose that at the end of the planning horizon, a_j is the actual (random) gain per dollar invested in Security j, and α_j the associated *expected* gain. Assume further that you stipulate b to be the lowest acceptable expected gain per dollar invested in the entire portfolio. Then the constraints of the model are

$$(9) \qquad \sum_{j=1}^{n} x_j = 1 \quad \text{and} \quad x_j \geq 0 \quad \text{for } j = 1, 2, \ldots, n$$

$$(10) \qquad \sum_{j=1}^{n} \alpha_j x_j \geq b,$$

where the left-hand side of (10) represents the expected gain per dollar invested, since the expected value of a sum equals the sum of expected values.

The consideration of risk is introduced by means of the objective function. Suppose the x_j are to be selected so as to minimize the variance of the *actual* gain, subject to (9) and (10). Then the objective function involves a quadratic form:

$$(11) \qquad \text{minimize} \sum_{i=1}^{n} \sum_{j=1}^{n} \sigma_{ij} x_i x_j,$$

where

$$(12) \qquad \sigma_{ij} \equiv E[a_i - \alpha_i] \cdot [a_j - \alpha_j]$$

symbolizes the covariance of gain between Securities i and j.

In more sophisticated versions of the model, there can be additional constraints on the composition of the portfolio, several time periods, and other measures of risk. Frequently, the computations for these models include a thorough sensitivity analysis showing the tradeoffs between expected gain and risk. Needless to say, these models must be applied cautiously since the values of α_j and σ_{ij} are based largely on historical data, and hence may be subject to error when applied to future events.

Summary. As you have seen, many different circumstances lead to nonlinear formulations of the constraints or objective functions in mathematical programming models. Naturally, you pay a price for introducing nonlinearities into a programming model. If the nonlinearities are few, or minor, the additional computational burden may be insignificant. Then your only inconvenience is to find a computer routine capable of solving the nonlinear model. Otherwise, the added complexity may substantially increase the amount of computations necessary to find a solution, and you may have to curtail the number of constraints and variables comprising the model.

In any particular situation, you must gain a proper perspective on an appropriate size and complexity for the model by assessing its intended impact on decisions. For instance, you may find that you need to employ only a moderate-size nonlinear programming model to obtain useful information about the region containing an optimal solution. Then you can apply a larger and more detailed linear model, making approximations based on the previous answers. This two-step approach is especially helpful if the context of the application is strategic planning rather than day-to-day operating decisions.

14.2 DIRECTION AND FOCUS

As elsewhere in the book, this and the next chapter concentrate on the subject's fundamental concepts. Here we set the stage for the technical discussion to follow.

Selection of techniques. The underlying theory of nonlinear programming is still evolving, and computational experience with specific algorithms is limited. Hence, it would be rash to single out two or three approaches, call them eminently successful, and claim they are as important for nonlinear programming as the simplex method is for linear programming. Practice has indicated that, although it may be possible to discard some suggested techniques as inferior, there most likely will never be only two or three methods that are superior for *all* nonlinear programming problems. So you should consider the algorithms presented in these chapters to be merely a limited selection of solution techniques.

A systematic comparison between methods is complicated by the fact that a nonlinear method can be very effective for one type of problem and yet fail miserably for another. Furthermore, the success of an algorithm in a particular problem can depend significantly on the model formulation itself. For example, transforming the measurement scales of the variables can dramatically affect an algorithm's rate of convergence! (This phenomenon is sometimes called *form sensitivity*.) And lastly, a relative evaluation of algorithms must compare the computational burden of methods requiring only a few iterations, but each involving many calculations, with those taking many iterations, but each involving only a few calculations. Such comparisons also hinge, in part, on the characteristics of the specific computer to be used. For these reasons, this text does not contain relative evaluations of the techniques.

In sharp contrast with linear and dynamic programming techniques, most of the nonlinear programming algorithms that are easy to motivate and explain are so computationally inefficient as to be impractical. And, unfortunately, the algorithms that have proved most powerful in practice are too intricate to include in an introductory text. Therefore, in trying to give a presentation of nonlinear programming techniques that is honest and yet readable by beginners, we have selected methods that can be *explained* in elementary terms, and, if appropriately modified for an electronic computer, can be made efficient. But we leave such modifications, which are indeed essential for successful application to actual problems, to texts that specialize in numerical analysis. Also, we only emphasize techniques that are effective for solving medium- to large-scale problems, and give almost no attention to those procedures that might work well if the model contained merely a few variables and constraints.

Crux of the computational problems. We suggest that you take a few minutes to review the discussion of the algorithmic method given in Sec. 4.3 (pp. 99–102). Four interrelated characteristics were highlighted as being descriptive of an algorithm:

- Completeness
- Domain of applicability
- Convergence properties
- Computational requirements.

Most of these characteristics are considerably harder to ascertain for nonlinear programming techniques than with linear programming algorithms. Such considerations preoccupy mathematicians investigating the theory of nonlinear programming. But apart from the theoretical questions, there are computational problems in applying nonlinear techniques to a specific situation.

For example, suppose you employ an algorithm that *does* completely specify how to proceed, step by step. You may find that there are mathematical conditions—either necessary, or sufficient, or both—to be satisfied by a model's objective function and constraints in order to guarantee that the algorithm converges. But in a real application, these conditions may be too complex to verify. You may actually have to try the algorithm to determine whether it will solve the problem.

Further, you may know that the technique converges for an easy-to-recognize class of problems, yet you may not have a very good prediction of the number of iterations that will be required to obtain a usable answer.

What is more, you may sometimes find it advantageous to apply a method that is indeed *theoretically* shaky—the algorithm may not always converge to a correct answer. But in practice, this method may work quite well, often converging to a truly optimal solution in relatively few iterations.

▶Research in the development of nonlinear programming techniques is advancing on two fronts. At the theoretical level, research is concentrated on establishing weak, and hopefully verifiable, conditions on the objective function and constraints that are sufficient to *guarantee* that an algorithm converges to the optimal value of the objective function, regardless of the starting point. Research at the computational level is focused on how well an algorithm solves actual problems. The nub of the difficulties at both of these levels is that most nonlinear programming methods do *not* always converge in a finite number of iterations (unless the starting point happens to be optimal). A technique may ensure that the objective function strictly improves from one iteration to the next. But even if the method is known to converge, in an actual application the trial solutions may oscillate wildly as the objective function improves. Moreover, unless the technique has been shown to be theoretically sound, the objective function may converge to a value that is *not* optimal. (This fact is demonstrated in Sec. 14.4 below.)   ◀

Organization of topics. The next few sections lay the necessary groundwork by explaining how to find an optimal value for a function of a single variable, and, afterwards, for a function of several unconstrained variables. As you will discover, most of the fundamental notions for obtaining an unconstrained optimal solution need only to be suitably embellished in order to handle the imposition of constraints.

The rest of this chapter deals mainly with techniques for solving optimization models having linear constraints and special, but important, types of nonlinear objective functions. Several algorithms for more general nonlinear programming models are presented in Chap. 15. It is noteworthy that many of the methods explained in both chapters for treating constrained problems turn out to employ the solution of related linear programming problems as part of the computations. Chapter 15 also provides the mathematical theory for nonlinear programming that corresponds to the notion of duality in linear programming.

14.3 OPTIMIZING A NONLINEAR FUNCTION OF
A SINGLE VARIABLE

There are two motivating reasons for studying how to optimize a function of only a single variable. The first is that one-dimensional problems can illustrate many of the difficulties that must be handled in nonlinear optimization. There is no need to resort to multidimensional examples, which are sometimes less apparent, to explain these new problems. The second reason is that many of the techniques for solving several-variable nonlinear optimization problems actually employ single-variable optimization in one of the steps. You will have to know methods for one-dimensional optimization, therefore, in order to apply the approaches designed for more general optimization problems.

To begin, it is convenient to postulate "maximization" as the sense of optimization throughout the following discussion. [If the real problem is to minimize an objective function $f(x)$, then you can reformulate the model so as to maximize $-f(x)$.]

Consider, first, the problem of maximizing a *linear* function $c(x) \equiv (c_0 + c_1 x)$ of a single variable x. The answer to this problem is so trivial that it was not even discussed in the chapters on linear programming, but we raise it here as a point of departure for the treatment of nonlinear optimization. If x is completely unconstrained, then the objective function can be made arbitrarily large for any $c_1 \neq 0$. (State how.) If, instead, x is constrained to be in the interval $[a_1, a_2]$ (that is, $a_1 \leq x \leq a_2$), then $x = a_1$ is optimal if $c_1 \leq 0$, and $x = a_2$ is optimal if $c_1 \geq 0$. Hence an **end-point** or **extreme-point** solution is always optimal. As soon as you drop the assumption that $c(x)$ is linear, other situations can occur, and several are illustrated in Fig. 14.1.

One possibility is that $c(x)$ may reach its maximum for a finite value of x, even if x is completely unconstrained. This happens in Case 2 in Fig. 14.1, where $x = 2$ is optimal. And even if x is constrained to be in the interval $[a_1, a_2]$, an extreme-

Case 1

$$c(x) = c_0 + c_1 x$$

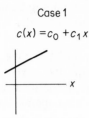

Case 2

$$c(x) = -x^2 + 4x - 3$$
$$\max c(x) = c(2) = 1$$

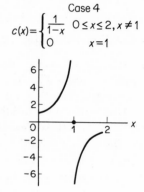

Case 3

$$c(x) = x^2 - 4x + 3$$

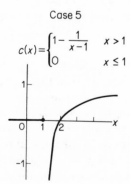

Case 4

$$c(x) = \begin{cases} \dfrac{1}{1-x} & 0 \le x \le 2, x \ne 1 \\ 0 & x = 1 \end{cases}$$

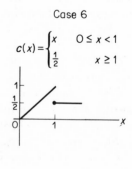

Case 5

$$c(x) = \begin{cases} 1 - \dfrac{1}{x-1} & x > 1 \\ 0 & x \le 1 \end{cases}$$

Case 6

$$c(x) = \begin{cases} x & 0 \le x < 1 \\ \tfrac{1}{2} & x \ge 1 \end{cases}$$

FIGURE 14.1. Illustrations of Nonlinear Functions.

point solution may not be optimal. To illustrate, if x must be in the interval $[0, 3]$, then the optimal x in Case 2 does *not* occur at either extreme point of the interval, $x = 0$ or $x = 3$, but inside the interval at $x = 2$, as before.

In Case 3, as in Case 1, the value of $c(x)$ grows without bound provided x is unconstrained. Unlike Case 1, an arbitrarily large value for $c(x)$ can now be achieved by letting x be *either* sufficiently large *or* small. Case 4 shows that it is also possible that $c(x)$ can be made arbitrarily large by values for x that are constrained, say, to be in the interval $[0, 1]$. Here there is a discontinuity in $c(x)$ at $x = 1$; by letting x approach 1 from below, $c(x)$ grows without bound.

Finally, $c(x)$ may be bounded from above, and yet there may be no *finite* value for x that maximizes $c(x)$. This occurs in Case 5, where x is unrestricted. Notice $c(x)$ is less than 1 for all finite x, but can be made arbitrarily close to 1 by letting x be sufficiently large. [The value 1 is called the **supremum** of $c(x)$, which is defined as the least upper bound for $c(x)$.] A second example is Case 6. How large can you make $c(x)$ here?

To summarize, it is possible that $c(x)$ grows without bound, irrespective of whether x is constrained, and that $c(x)$, although bounded from above, does not attain a maximum, also irrespective of whether x is constrained. Any exhaustive treatment of algorithmic approaches for maximizing a nonlinear function of a single variable would have to take account of all these various possibilities. But we find it convenient for the purpose of this chapter to assume:

(i) x lies within a finite interval $I \equiv [a_1, a_2]$, that is, $a_1 \leq x \leq a_2$, where $-\infty < a_1 < a_2 < \infty$.

(ii) $c(x)$ is continuous for all x in the interval I.

An important implication of these two assumptions is that $c(x)$ does attain a finite maximum value for a value of x in the interval I.

To test your understanding, explain why assumption (ii) does not permit I to include $x = 1$ in Case 4, or $x \geq 1$ in Case 5, or $x \leq 1$ in Case 6. Also observe in Fig. 14.1 how the shape of $c(x)$ and the specification of I affects the determination of an optimal x. For example, in Case 3, an optimal x is *always* one of the end points $x = a_1$ or a_2, whereas such an extreme-point solution is optimal in Case 2 *only* if $x = 2$ is not contained in the interior of I. These observations suggest that an algorithm for optimizing $c(x)$ over x in I should exploit the orientation and shape characteristics of $c(x)$.

Consider first what happens when $c(x)$ is monotonic over the interval I. Then $c(x)$ always attains its maximum over x in I at an extreme point, either $x = a_1$ or $x = a_2$. The same is also true when $c(x)$ is a **convex** function for x in I, that is, if, for any x_1 and x_2 in I, where $x_1 < x_2$, and for all p, $0 \leq p \leq 1$, $c(x)$ satisfies

$$(1) \qquad\qquad pc(x_1) + (1 - p)c(x_2) \geq c(px_1 + (1 - p)x_2) \qquad\qquad \underline{\text{Convex.}}$$

Verify that $c(x)$ in Case 3 is a convex function, and so is always maximized at an extreme point of I.

▶More generally, $c(x)$ always attains its maximum at an extreme point of I when $c(x)$ is a **quasi-convex** function over I, that is, if, for any x_1 and x_2 in I, where $x_1 < x_2$, and for all p, $0 \leq p \leq 1$, $c(x)$ satisfies

(i) $\text{maximum } [c(x_1), c(x_2)] \geq c(px_1 + (1 - p)x_2)$ Quasi-convex.

If $c(x)$ is either monotonic or convex, then (i) holds. Two examples of quasi-convex functions that are neither monotonic nor convex are the following modifications of $c(x)$ in Case 3. The first is $c(x) \equiv x^2 - 4x + 3$ for $x \leq 3$, and $c(x) \equiv 0$ for $x > 3$. The second is $c(x) \equiv x^2 - 4x + 3$ for $x \neq 2$ and $c(2) \equiv -2$. Draw these two examples, and verify that (i) holds.   ◀

If the shape of $c(x)$ does not ensure that an extreme-point solution is optimal, then you must also search the interior of the interval I for an optimal x. To do this, you can divide I into a grid of equally spaced points, and test each of these points. If $c(x)$ is "ill-behaved," the best obtained value for x may be far from an optimal x, because the search is like trying to find the proverbial "needle in a haystack." But even if the function *is* well behaved—if it does not vary wildly within small intervals of x—you can usually improve on such a grid procedure by employing a so-called *adaptive search* technique. Instead of prespecifying a sequence of values of x to be tried, you use the information from the previously tested x values to determine the next trial value for x. This means you must be able to make a valid inference about the possible values for an optimal x given the limited information about $c(x)$ furnished by previous trials. This notion is explored next.

Adaptive search. Consider the function $c(x)$ shown in Fig. 14.2. The maximum value for $c(x)$ is at $x = f$. As you might imagine, an adaptive procedure for maximizing $c(x)$ is not likely to work well, except by accident, on a function of this sort. To illustrate, suppose the first trial value of x is less than a. Then it is possible that the successsive values for x would get closer and closer to a, but never beyond a, since $c(a)$ is a **local maximum**. Suppose, instead, that the first trial value for x is in the interval $[d, e]$. Then an adaptive method is likely

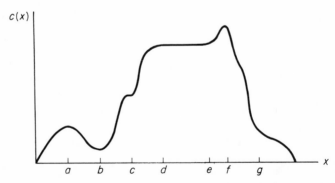

FIGURE 14.2. Example with Multiple Local Optima.

to terminate, for there would not seem to be any possible improvement in $c(x)$ by making x either a little smaller or larger. The adaptive methods to be explained below cannot be guaranteed to eventually narrow the search to a small interval around f in Fig. 14.2. But $c(x)$ taken over the interval $[0, g]$ is really a more general situation than we need to consider for the purpose at hand—namely, to provide adaptive search procedures for single-variable optimization that are to be used in multidimensional nonlinear optimization problems. Hence, we impose an additional postulate on the shape of $c(x)$.

Specifically, consider a so-called **unimodal** function with the following properties: if $\bar{x}$ is the unique optimal value of x over the interval I, then $c(x)$ *strictly* increases for $x \leq \bar{x}$ and *strictly* decreases for $x \geq \bar{x}$. If the maximum value of $c(x) = \bar{c}$ over I occurs for an interval of values for x, then $c(x)$ strictly increases to $\bar{c}$, remains at the value $\bar{c}$ over the interval of optimal x, and then strictly decreases. A formal and more precise definition is the following: a function $c(x)$ is **unimodal** over the interval I if, for any x_1 and x_2 in I, where $x_1 < x_2$ and $c(x_1) < c(\bar{x}) \equiv \bar{c}$, $c(x)$ satisfies

(2)
$$c(x_1) < c(x_2) \quad \text{for } x_1 < x_2 < \bar{x}$$
$$c(x_1) > c(x_2) \quad \text{for } \bar{x} < x_1 < x_2$$

Unimodal.

A function is unimodal whenever it is **concave**, that is, if for any x_1 and x_2 in I, where $x_1 < x_2$, and for all p, $0 \leq p \leq 1$, $c(x)$ satisfies

(3) $$pc(x_1) + (1 - p)c(x_2) \leq c(px_1 + (1 - p)x_2)$$

Concave.

If $c(x)$ possesses a well-defined second derivative d^2c/dx^2, then an equivalent condition for concavity is $d^2c/dx^2 \leq 0$ for all x. [If $d^2c/dx^2 < 0$ for all x, then $c(x)$ is **strictly concave**.] Assume from here on that, in addition to (i) and (ii),

(iii) $c(x)$ is unimodal for x in the interval I.

Check that assumption (iii) rules out $[b, g]$ as an interval I in Fig. 14.2, but allows the intervals $[b, e]$ and $[e, g]$. Now you will see how adding assumption (iii) permits an adaptive technique for finding an interval of prespecified width that contains a value of x maximizing $c(x)$.

Suppose you know that an optimal value of x lies in the interval $[A_1, A_2]$, and you have evaluated $c(x)$ at two points, x_{LFT} and x_{RT}, in that interval, where $x_{\text{LFT}} < x_{\text{RT}}$ (the first point is on the "left" and the second on the "right"). If $c(x_{\text{LFT}}) \geq c(x_{\text{RT}})$, then $c(x)$ cannot increase for $x > x_{\text{RT}}$, and so an optimal $\bar{x}$ *must* lie in the interval $[A_1, x_{\text{RT}}]$. Make a sketch and explain why. If $c(x_{\text{LFT}}) \leq c(x_{\text{RT}})$, then $c(x)$ cannot increase for $x < x_{\text{LFT}}$, and so an optimal $\bar{x}$ must lie in the interval $[x_{\text{LFT}}, A_2]$. Explain why. In either case, the comparison of $c(x_{\text{LFT}})$ and $c(x_{\text{RT}})$ has reduced the length of the interval in which you know an optimal value of x must lie. As you would imagine, there are numerous adaptive search procedures you can devise to exploit this inferential property of a unimodal function.

The following approach, sometimes termed the **Method of Golden Sections**, has the advantage of being both simple and fairly efficient. (The approach is closely related to what is named the *Fibonacci Search Method*.) Define

$$(4) \qquad\qquad r \equiv .5(\sqrt{5} - 1) \doteq .618033 \ldots .$$

The significance of this constant will be made clear after giving the algorithm for maximizing $c(x)$, where x lies in the interval $I = [a_1, a_2]$.

Step 1. Let $A_1 = a_1, A_2 = a_2, H = A_2 - A_1, x_{LFT} = A_1 + r^2 H$ and $x_{RT} = A_1 + rH$.

Step 2. Compare $c(x_{LFT})$ with $c(x_{RT})$. Go to *Step 3* or *Step 4*, whichever is appropriate.

Step 3. If $c(x_{LFT}) \geq c(x_{RT})$, let $A_2 = x_{RT}$ and $H = x_{RT} - A_1$. Stop if H is sufficiently small. Otherwise, let the new x_{RT} be the previous x_{LFT}, and let the new $x_{LFT} = A_1 + r^2 H$. Return to *Step 2*.

Step 4. If $c(x_{LFT}) < c(x_{RT})$, let $A_1 = x_{LFT}$ and $H = A_2 - x_{LFT}$. Stop if H is sufficiently small. Otherwise, let the new x_{LFT} be the previous x_{RT}, and let the new $x_{RT} = A_1 + rH$. Return to *Step 2*.

Given the value of r specified in (4), the algorithm has three important properties. First, after each iteration, the new value for H is r times the previous value for H. Hence, after n iterations, you can infer that an optimal x lies in a specified interval of width $r^n(a_2 - a_1)$. A short table of r^n is given in Fig. 14.3.

Second, at each iteration, x_{LFT} and x_{RT} are the same distance from their respective interval end points; that is, $x_{LFT} - A_1 = A_2 - x_{RT}$.

Third, in performing *Step 2* (after the first iteration), only one of the points x_{LFT} and x_{RT} is really new, so there is only a single additional value of $c(x)$ to compute.

An example of the algorithm appears in Fig. 14.4; the value $x = 6$ is the unique optimal solution. The initial interval is $[a_1, a_2] = [0, 10]$. Observe that by iteration 2, the interval has narrowed to $[A_1, A_2] = [3.82, 7.64]$. The trial value $x_{LFT} = 5.28$ is $1.46 \ (= 5.28 - 3.82)$ above A_1, and the trial value $x_{RT} = 6.18$, which was already examined at iteration 1, is $1.46 \ (= 7.64 - 6.18)$ below A_2. Verify that if you complete a fourth iteration, the new value for x_{RT} to be evaluated at *Step 2* is 6.74. Since $a_2 - a_1 = 10$, the interval $[A_1, A_2]$ at the end of the nth iteration has length $r^n 10$, where r^n is exhibited in Fig. 14.3.

n	r^n	$(.5)^{n+1}$
1	.6180	.25
2	.3820	.125
3	.2361	.0625
4	.1459	.0313
5	.0902	.0156
6	.0557	.0078
7	.0344	.0039
8	.0213	.0020
9	.0132	.0010
10	.0081	.0005

$$r \equiv .5(\sqrt{5} - 1)$$

FIGURE 14.3. Method of Golden Sections and Interval Bisection.

▶Note that the adaptive procedure only guarantees information about an interval in which an optimal $\bar{x}$ must lie. Except by accident, it does not find an optimal $\bar{x}$ in a finite number of iterations. In fact, if the calculations maintain accuracy at a finite number of decimal places, then the method may never be able to determine $\bar{x}$ *exactly*. For example, if $c(x) = -.25x^4 + 2x$ and $I = [1, 2]$, then the unique optimal $\bar{x}$ is $\bar{x} = \sqrt[3]{2} = 1.2599\ldots$, which can never be determined precisely with only a finite number of decimals.

Furthermore, the method provides no information about the maximum value of $c(x)$. [Given that you are going to terminate the search as soon as the interval H is below a specified width, you can always construct a function for which the maximum value of $c(x)$ is arbitrarily larger than the best $c(x)$ you have obtained during the search.] But suppose that you know $c(x)$ is actually concave and has well-defined derivatives at $x = A_1$ and $x = A_2$, where $A_1 < A_2$. In this case you *can* calculate an upper bound on $c(x)$:

$$\text{(ii)} \quad c(x) \le \left[\frac{1}{dc(A_1)/dx} - \frac{1}{dc(A_2)/dx} \right]^{-1} \left[A_2 - A_1 + \frac{c(A_1)}{dc(A_1)/dx} - \frac{c(A_2)}{dc(A_2)/dx} \right] \quad \underline{\underline{\text{Concave}}}$$

for any x in I. To check your understanding of (ii), verify that this bound in the example for Fig. 14.5 is $c(x) \le 6$ at every iteration.

An alternative adaptive search procedure, sometimes called the **Method of Interval Bisection**, can be devised that employs information about the value of derivatives of $c(x)$ for a nonoptimal x. The technique exploits the fact that for a unimodal function the derivative of $c(x)$ never changes sign more than once. Suppose that $c(x)$ is not simply monotonic. Hence the derivative of $c(x)$ is nonnegative at $x = a_1$ and remains so, as x increases, until $c(x)$ reaches its maximum value; then for further increases in x, the derivative is nonpositive. Therefore, an optimal $\bar{x}$ occurs where the derivative changes sign; the approach repeatedly narrows the intervals in which this sign change must occur. [The method is also valid when $c(x)$ is monotonic.]

In order to use the approach, you must determine the formula for the derivative dc/dx and *assume*, in addition, that the shape of $c(x)$ is such that dc/dx is both well defined and equal to 0 only for optimal x. (It is easy to devise unimodal functions over a finite interval I that do not satisfy these shape assumptions—such examples include functions that, for nonoptimal x, are piecewise linear, or have an inflection point, or have a point with an unbounded value for dc/dx.) Each application of the bisection method halves the length of the interval in which an optimal $\bar{x}$ must lie. After n calculations of the derivative dc/dx, the interval is $(.5)^{n+1}(a_2 - a_1)$, whereas after n evaluations of $c(x)$, the Method of Golden Sections has reduced the interval to only $r^n(a_2 - a_1)$. Thus the factor $(.5)^{n+1}$ is to be compared with r^n and is shown in Fig. 14.3. There may be an offsetting computational disadvantage, however, if dc/dx is a more complex expression than $c(x)$ [for example, when $c(x) = x^2 e^x$].

The idea of the algorithm is that if $dc/dx > 0$ at a value x_{trial}, then there is an optimal $\bar{x} > x_{\text{trial}}$. Similarly, if $dc/dx < 0$, then there is an optimal $\bar{x} < x_{\text{trial}}$. Specifically, the technique is

Step 1. Let $A_1 = a_1$, $A_2 = a_2$, and $H = A_2 - A_1$.

Step 2. Let $x_{\text{trial}} = A_1 + .5H$. Compute dc/dx at x_{trial}. Stop if $dc/dx = 0$, for x_{trial} is optimal. Otherwise, go to *Step 3* or *Step 4*, whichever is appropriate.

Step 3. If $dc/dx < 0$, let $A_2 = x_{\text{trial}}$ and $H = x_{\text{trial}} - A_1$. Stop if H is sufficiently small. Otherwise, return to *Step 2*.

Step 4. If $dc/dx > 0$, let $A_1 = x_{\text{trial}}$ and $H = A_2 - x_{\text{trial}}$. Stop if H is sufficiently small. Otherwise, return to *Step 2*.

The Method of Interval Bisection is illustrated in Fig. 14.5 for the same example as in Fig. 14.4. After the fourth evaluation of dc/dx, the interval length for an optimal $\bar{x}$ has been reduced to .625, as compared with an interval of length 2.36 after four evaluations of $c(x)$ by the Method of Golden Sections.   ◀

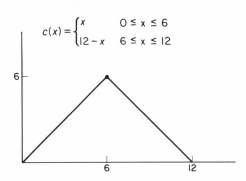

$$c(x) = \begin{cases} x & 0 \le x \le 6 \\ 12 - x & 6 \le x \le 12 \end{cases}$$

Iteration n	Step	Calculations
0	1	$A_1 = 0, A_2 = 10, H = 10, x_{LFT} = 3.82, x_{RT} = 6.18$
1	2	$c(3.82) = 3.82, c(6.18) = 5.82$
	4	$A_1 = 3.82, (A_2 = 10), H = 10 - 3.82 = 6.18, x_{LFT} = 6.18,$ $x_{RT} = 3.82 + (.618)6.18 = 7.64$
2	2	$c(6.18) = 5.82, c(7.64) = 4.36$
	3	$(A_1 = 3.82), A_2 = 7.64, H = 7.64 - 3.82 = 3.82, x_{RT} = 6.18,$ $x_{LFT} = 3.82 + (.382)3.82 = 5.28$
3	2	$c(5.28) = 5.28, c(6.18) = 5.82$
	4	$A_1 = 5.28, (A_2 = 7.64), H = 7.64 - 5.28 = 2.36$

Figure 14.4. Example of Method of Golden Sections.

Iteration n	Step	Calculations
0	1	$A_1 = 0, A_2 = 10, H = 10$
1	2	$x_{trial} = 5, dc/dx = 1 > 0$
	4	$A_1 = 5, (A_2 = 10), H = 10 - 5 = 5$
2	2	$x_{trial} = 5 + .5(5) = 7.5, dc/dx = -1 < 0$
	3	$(A_1 = 5), A_2 = 7.5, H = 2.5$
3	2	$x_{trial} = 5 + .5(2.5) = 6.25, dc/dx < 0$
	3	$(A_1 = 5), A_2 = 6.25, H = 1.25$
4	2	$x_{trial} = 5 + .5(1.25) = 5.625, dc/dx > 0$
	3	$A_1 = 5.625, (A_2 = 6.25), H = .625$

Figure 14.5. Example of Method of Interval Bisection.

14.4 MAXIMIZING A NONLINEAR FUNCTION OF
SEVERAL UNCONSTRAINED VARIABLES

This and the next section show how to maximize a real-valued function $c(x_1, x_2, \ldots, x_n)$, where each x_j is permitted to have any real value, positive or negative. (This assumption on the x_j is frequently expressed by saying that the set of values $x_1, x_2, \ldots, x_n$ lies in *Euclidean n-space*, abbreviated E^n, or equivalently, that each x_j lies on the real line, abbreviated R^1.) There are two motivating reasons for studying this problem. First, an analysis of the multidimensional, unconstrained, nonlinear maximization problem sets the stage for the analyses of constrained models. The algorithmic difficulties to be overcome here are also present in the constrained cases, and the techniques presented below can be suitably modified when constraints are imposed. Second, a constrained problem can often be solved by first converting it to an unconstrained problem. An algorithm utilizing this approach is treated in Sec. 15.9.

As in the preceding section, in order to *guarantee* that the solution techniques are valid, we have to impose certain assumptions on the objective function. Loosely put, we postulate that $c(x_1, x_2, \ldots, x_n)$ is smooth and possesses a finite maximum value, occurring at the finite values $\bar{x}_1, \bar{x}_2, \ldots, \bar{x}_n$. Abbreviating a set of values for $x_1, x_2, \ldots, x_n$ by the symbol x, and the expression $c(x_1, x_2, \ldots, x_n)$ by the symbol $c(x)$, these assumptions can be stated more precisely as:

  (i) For all values of x, $c(x)$ is uniquely defined and finite.
  (ii) For all values of x, every partial derivative $\partial c(x)/\partial x_j$ is uniquely defined, finite, and continuous, and hence $c(x)$ is continuous.
 (iii) $c(x)$ possesses a finite maximum $\bar{c}$.
  (iv) For any possible value of $c(x)$, say c, there exists an associated finite number M_c such that every $|x_j| \leq M_c$ if $c(x) \geq c$.

You will find it useful to copy these four assumptions, as we repeatedly refer to them throughout the rest of the chapter.

Given the first three assumptions, (iv) implies that $c(x)$ takes on its maximum value c for finite values of $x_1, x_2, \ldots, x_n$. Actually, assumption (iv) implies an even stronger property: given any possible value c for $c(x)$, larger values for $c(x)$ occur only when each x_j lies within a finite interval, that is, $-M_c \leq x_j \leq M_c$ for every j (where $M_c < \infty$ and depends on c).

To see the force of these assumptions, examine Case 5 in Fig. 14.1. Such a $c(x)$ is ruled out, first by assumption (ii), since dc/dx is discontinuous at $x = 1$. But even if $c(x)$ is modified so that dc/dx is continuous, keeping $c(x) < 1$ for all x, the case would still be ruled out by assumption (iii) because $c(x)$ has no maximum. [Although $c(x) \leq 1$ for all x, there is no finite x such that $c(x) = 1$.] And what is more, even if $c(x)$ is further modified to possess a finite maximum—for example, $\bar{c} = 3$ at $x = \frac{1}{2}$—the case would remain excluded by assumption (iv). To see why, suppose $c = \frac{1}{3}$ in (iv); then $c(x) \geq \frac{1}{3}$ for all $x \geq 2.5$. Hence there does not exist an M_c postulated in assumption (iv).

▶By employing mathematical terminology, we can state the four assumptions more succinctly. First, assumption (ii) can be reworded to read that $c(x)$ must be *continuously differentiable;* this implies assumption (i) and that $c(x)$ is continuous. Second, we stipulate that for any x', the set of x such that $c(x) \geq c(x')$ is *compact* (closed and bounded); this implies assumption (iv). Since a continuous function possesses a finite maximum over a compact set, the two succinct postulates imply assumption (iii).   ◀

Applying differential calculus, we can state the following.

NECESSARY CONDITION FOR A MAXIMUM. Given assumptions (i) through (iii), the function $c(x)$ has a maximum at $\bar{x}$ only if $\partial c(\bar{x})/\partial x_j = 0$, for $j = 1, 2, \ldots, n$.

The validity of the result is easy to see. Suppose there is a variable x_j such that $\partial c(\bar{x})/\partial x_j > 0$. Then $c(x)$ can be increased by increasing $\bar{x}_j$ by a small amount. Analogously, if $\partial c(\bar{x})/\partial x_j < 0$, then $c(x)$ can be increased by decreasing $\bar{x}_j$ by a small amount.

What are the computational implications of the necessary condition? You can conclude immediately that a specified set of values $\bar{x}_1, \bar{x}_2, \ldots, \bar{x}_n$ does not optimize $c(x)$ unless *all* $\partial c(\bar{x})/\partial x_j = 0$. But, unfortunately, without imposing further restrictions on the shape of $c(x)$, the necessary condition is *not* sufficient for a maximum: $\bar{x}$ may not maximize $c(x)$ when all $\partial c(\bar{x})/\partial x_j = 0$. The illustration in Fig. 14.2 shows why. The derivative $dc/dx = 0$ at Points a, b, c, d, e, as well as at f, which gives the *only* global maximum.

Suppose, for a moment, you can assert that the necessary condition is also sufficient for a specified function $c(x)$. Would knowing that an x is optimal if and only if all $\partial c(\bar{x})/\partial x_j = 0$ make it a trivial matter to solve for $\bar{x}$? Probably not, because typically the conditions $\partial c/\partial x_j = 0$, for $j = 1, 2, \ldots, n$, necessitate solving a system of n simultaneous *nonlinear* equations, which can be as difficult a computational task as maximizing $c(x)$. {In fact, a frequently used procedure for solving a set of nonlinear equations $a_i(x) = 0$, for $i = 1, 2, \ldots, m$, is to solve, instead, the associated optimization problem: minimize $\sum_{i=1}^{m} [a_i(x)]^2$.} Note, however, that when $c(x)$ is a quadratic function, the conditions $\partial c/\partial x_j = 0$, for $j = 1, 2, \ldots, n$ give rise to a system of n simultaneous *linear* equations, which usually are easily solved. In the more general case, we find an optimal $\bar{x}$ by an iterative procedure of the type explained below.

Algorithmic method. Many of the computational techniques for maximizing $c(x)$ can be expressed in a standardized format:

Step 1. Select an arbitrary initial trial point x^0.

Step 2. Terminate the iterations if $\partial c/\partial x_j = 0$, for $j = 1, 2, \ldots, n$, at the trial point x^k. Otherwise, determine values y_j^k, for $j = 1, 2, \ldots, n$, and continue to *Step 3.*

Step 3. Calculate a new trial point

$$(1) \qquad\qquad x_j^{k+1} = x_j^k + y_j^k \quad \text{for } j = 1, 2, \ldots, n.$$

Return to *Step 2*, where x^{k+1} replaces x^k.

For most nonlinear objective functions, the iterative process never obtains an x^k such that all $\partial c/\partial x_j = 0$. Hence, the algorithm never terminates according to the test specified in *Step 2*, and must be stopped when $c(x^k)$ is nearly optimal. To ensure the calculations stop in a finite number of iterations, you can, for example, impose a limit on the number of iterations, or terminate when all the values of $|\partial c/\partial x_j|$ are sufficiently small.

Various algorithms differ in the selection of y_j^k in *Step 2*. Many of these methods proceed as follows. First, pick what is called a **direction** d_j^k, for each $j = 1, 2, \ldots,$ n; this selection is usually based on information about how $c(x)$ behaves near the trial point x^k, that is, it is based on the *local* properties of $c(x)$. Second, choose a **step size** t^k, based on information about how $c(x)$ behaves beyond the local vicinity of x^k when proceeding in the selected direction $d_1^k, d_2^k, \ldots, d_n^k$. Finally, combine the direction and step size by letting

(2) $$y_j^k = t^k d_j^k \quad \text{for } j = 1, 2, \ldots, n.$$

A visual representation of the process will help you remember the meaning of these terms.

Suppose you want to maximize $c(x_1, x_2) \equiv -(x_1 - 3)^2 - 4(x_2 - 2)^2$. You can tell by inspecting $c(x)$ that the unique optimal solution is $\bar{x}_1 = 3$, $\bar{x}_2 = 2$, yielding $c(\bar{x}) = 0$. [Since $c(x)$ is a quadratic function, the optimal x can be calculated directly from the necessary conditions $\partial c/\partial x_j = 0$, for $j = 1, 2$. Nevertheless, the quadratic example serves to exhibit the main ideas of the algorithm.] The contour levels of $c(x_1, x_2)$ are ellipses, and are depicted in Fig. 14.6. Starting with *Step 1*, let $x_1^0 = x_2^0 = 0$, and hence $c(x^0) = -25$. Since

(3) $$\frac{\partial c}{\partial x_1} = -2(x_1 - 3) \quad \text{and} \quad \frac{\partial c}{\partial x_2} = -8(x_2 - 2),$$

which are both strictly positive at x^0, *Step 2* indicates that a further improvement is possible.

In preparation for choosing the directions d_1 and d_2, draw the tangent line to the contour $c(x)$ at x^0, given by the equation

(4) $$\frac{\partial c}{\partial x_1} \cdot (x_1 - x_1^0) + \frac{\partial c}{\partial x_2} \cdot (x_2 - x_2^0) = 0.$$

Verify that for $x_1^0 = x_2^0 = 0$, (4) yields

(5) $$6x_1 + 16x_2 = 0 \quad \text{or} \quad x_2 = -\tfrac{3}{8}x_1,$$

which is plotted in Fig. 14.6a. Any direction (d_1, d_2) can be indicated graphically by a vector pointing away from the origin. Several possibilities are drawn in Fig. 14.6b. The value of $c(x)$ increases beyond $c(x) = -25$ by moving along *any* direction vector (d_1, d_2) that lies above the tangent line at x^0, *provided* that the step size in this direction is not too large. No matter which direction you choose, eventually $c(x)$ decreases as the step size grows large.

If you were fortunate enough to have selected d_1^0 and d_2^0 proportional to 3 and 2—for example, $d_1^0 = 1$ and $d_2^0 = \tfrac{2}{3}$—then you can obtain the optimal solution if

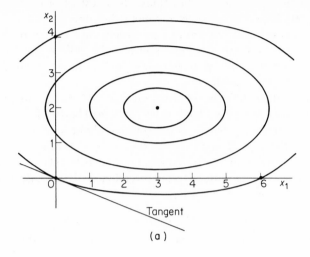

(a)

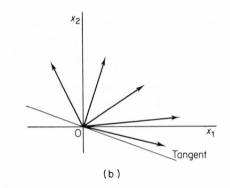

(b)

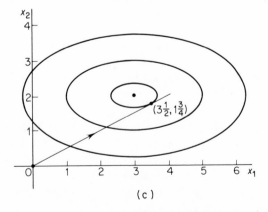

(c)

FIGURE 14.6 (a) Contours. (b) Directions. (c) Optimal Step Size.

you pick the right step size. But in maximizing an arbitrary nonlinear function $c(x)$, there generally is no way to ensure that the direction you pick leads to an optimal solution in only one iteration. Suppose, in the example, that you selected $d_1^0 = 2$ and $d_2^0 = 1$, as shown in Fig. 14.6c. If you want to make $c(x)$ as large as possible along that direction, then you should extend the vector $(d_1^0 = 2, d_2^0 = 1)$ until it is tangent to a contour of $c(x_1, x_2)$. Explain why. This tangency is exhibited in Fig. 14.6c, at point $(x_1 = 3\frac{1}{2}, x_2 = 1\frac{3}{4})$, so that (1) and (2) can be expressed as

(6)
$$x_1^1 = 0 + (1\tfrac{3}{4})(2) = 3\tfrac{1}{2}$$
$$x_2^1 = 0 + (1\tfrac{3}{4})(1) = 1\tfrac{3}{4},$$

where $t^0 = 1\frac{3}{4}$ is the optimal step size. At the new point in (6), $c(x^1) = -\frac{1}{2}$.

Given a set of directions d_j^k, for $j = 1, 2, \ldots, n$, the problem of choosing the assocated **optimal step size** is merely a one-dimensional optimization problem:

(7)
$$\text{maximize}_{t \geqslant 0} \; c(x_1^k + td_1^k, x_2^k + td_2^k, \ldots, x_n^k + td_n^k)$$
$$= c(x_1^k + t^k d_1^k, x_2^k + t^k d_2^k, \ldots, x_n^k + t^k d_n^k)$$
$$= c(x^{k+1}).$$

In other words, each argument of $c(x)$ is simply $x_j^k + td_j^k$, or in abbreviated form $c(x^k + td^k)$, and hence depends on the *single* variable t. The optimal step size t^k is that value of t that maximizes $c(x^k + td^k)$, which is expressed symbolically in (7), and the new point x^{k+1} is simply $x^k + t^k d^k$.

To illustrate in the example, let $x_1^0 = x_2^0 = 0$ and select $d_1^0 = 1$ and $d_2^0 = 2$. Then according to (7), you want to maximize

(8)
$$c(0 + t\cdot 1, \, 0 + t\cdot 2) = -(t - 3)^2 - 4(2t - 2)^2.$$

Because the expression on the right of (8) is a concave quadratic function of t, you can find the optimal t analytically by setting the derivative to 0. Verify that this procedure gives $t^0 = 1\frac{2}{9}$. For more complex functions $c(x)$, finding the *optimal step size* may not be an easy task unless the shape of $c(x)$ permits use of a technique explained in Sec. 14.3. We return to this consideration in the next section, where we discuss the case of maximizing a concave function $c(x)$.

You can now appreciate what is a distinguishing difference between linear and nonlinear optimization. In the linear case, the objective function changes by c_i for each additional unit of x_i, irrespective of the actual value of x_i or of any other x_j. In the nonlinear case, the change in the objective function for an added unit of x_i may depend on the actual values of x_i and all other x_j. It is this dependency that is the source of difficulty in choosing good directions for *Step 2*.

▶Consider a procedure that at every iteration both picks a direction yielding a strict improvement in $c(x)$ and selects the associated optimal step size. As the following example shows, although such a procedure causes $c(x)$ to tend to a limit, the limit need not be the maximum value for $c(x)$.

Let $c(x) \equiv -(x_1)^2 - (x_2)^2$, which is a strictly concave function and assumes its unique maximum value at $x_1 = x_2 = 0$. Let x^0 be a point on a circle centered at the origin and having radius 2. Then for $k = 0, 1, 2, \ldots$, let the point x^{k+1} be chosen such that the line drawn from x^k through x^{k+1} is tangent to the circle having radius $(k + 2)/(k + 1)$. For definiteness, take the tangent in the clockwise direction. Check that $c(x)$ is improved at each trial, and that the procedure employs the optimal step size, because of the tangency assumption. As k becomes large, the trial solutions x^k spiral closer and closer to the circle centered at the origin and having radius 1. Thus the successive values of $c(x)$ are strictly increasing but are approaching $- (x_1)^2 - (x_2)^2 = -2$ in the limit, whereas the maximum value of $c(x)$ is 0 at the origin. As this example demonstrates, the directions in *Step 3* must be chosen with some care, even when $c(x)$ is very well behaved.

14.5 METHOD OF STEEPEST ASCENT

As was mentioned above, most rules for selecting the directions d_j^k, for $j = 1$, $2, \ldots, n$, are **myopic** in that they use information about $c(x)$ obtained at the current trial value x^k. A well-known myopic procedure for performing *Step 2* is described below.

STEEPEST ASCENT WITH OPTIMAL STEP SIZE. (a) Let each $d_j^k = \partial c / \partial x_j$, evaluated at trial point x^k. (b) Find $t^k \geq 0$ that maximizes $c(x_1^k + td_1^k, \ldots, x_n^k + td_n^k)$. (c) Then, in *Step 2*, let each $y_j^k = t^k d_j^k$.

(This approach was first suggested in 1847 by the mathematician Cauchy.) The idea of using for directions the set of partial derivatives—usually called the **gradient** of $c(x)$ at x^k and abbreviated by the symbol $\nabla c(x)$—is intuitively appealing. Loosely put, the gradient represents the direction of fastest increase in $c(x)$ in the vicinity of x^k. Nevertheless, the approach cannot *guarantee* swift convergence of an optimal solution, because, like all myopically determined directions, the function $c(x)$ need not increase so fast once the trial point has moved along the gradient beyond the immediate vicinity of x^k.

▶ The so-called **directional-derivative** of $c(x)$ at the point x along the direction $d_1, d_2, \ldots, d_n$ is defined as the limiting value of

(i)
$$\frac{c(x_1 + hd_1, \ldots, x_n + hd_n) - c(x_1, \ldots, x_n)}{h\sqrt{\sum_{j=1}^{n} (d_j)^2}}$$

as h approaches 0 from positive values. Given the smoothness assumptions on $c(x)$ in Sec. 14.4, this limit equals

(ii)
$$\frac{\sum_{j=1}^{n} \frac{\partial c}{\partial x_j} \cdot d_j}{\sqrt{\sum_{j=1}^{n} (d_j)^2}}.$$

If the d_j are normalized so that the denominator of (ii) is 1, then the value of the directional derivative is maximized for d_j that are proportional to $\partial c / \partial x_j$. In other words, the rate of increase in $c(x)$ per unit of Euclidean distance is largest for the gradient direction. It is precisely in this sense that the gradient is said to be the direction of steepest ascent.   ◀

Examples. For the first example, consider again $c(x) \equiv -(x_1 - 3)^2 - 4(x_2 - 2)^2$. The steepest ascent rule gives $d_1^0 = 6$ and $d_2^0 = 16$ at $x_1^0 = x_2^0 = 0$, according to the partial derivatives in (3) above. Check that the optimal step size must maximize $[-(6t - 3)^2 - 4(16t - 2)^2]$, yielding $t^0 = \frac{73}{530}$. As a result,

(1)　　$x_1^1 = 0 + \left(\frac{73}{530}\right)(6) = \frac{219}{265} \doteq .83$　　$x_2^1 = 0 + \left(\frac{73}{530}\right)(16) = \frac{584}{265} \doteq 2.20,$

giving $c(x^1) \doteq -4.89$; the point is shown in Fig. 14.7. [Notice that using the

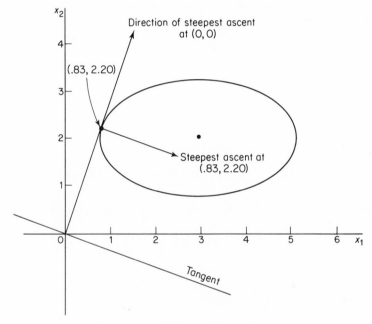

FIGURE 14.7. Method of Steepest Ascent.

gradient did not increase $c(x)$ as much as using the directions yielding (6) in Sec. 14.4.] Continuing the calculations for one more iteration, the directions at x^1 are

(2)
$$\frac{\partial c}{\partial x_1} = -2\left(\frac{219}{265} - 3\right) = \frac{1152}{265}$$

$$\frac{\partial c}{\partial x_2} = -8\left(\frac{584}{265} - 2\right) = -\frac{432}{265}.$$

Note in Fig. 14.7 that this direction is **orthogonal**, that is, perpendicular, to the previous direction. The reason is that the old gradient is also the tangent to the contour at x^1, since an optimal step size is used, and the new gradient, by its very nature, is orthogonal to the tangent of the contour at x^1. This orthogonality property holds for all pairs of successive gradients and can be expressed mathematically as

(3)
$$\sum_{j=1}^{n} \frac{\partial c(x^k)}{\partial x_j} \cdot \frac{\partial c(x^{k+1})}{\partial x_j} = 0.$$

For the second example, consider maximizing

(4) $c(x) \equiv 6x_1 + 4x_2 + 2x_3 - 3x_1^2 - 2x_2^2 - \frac{1}{3}x_3^2,$

which has the partial derivatives

(5) $\dfrac{\partial c}{\partial x_1} = 6(1 - x_1)$ $\dfrac{\partial c}{\partial x_2} = 4(1 - x_2)$ $\dfrac{\partial c}{\partial x_3} = 2(1 - \frac{1}{3}x_3).$

The Necessary Condition for a Maximum in Sec. 14.4 yields $\bar{x}_1 = 1$, $\bar{x}_2 = 1$, and $\bar{x}_3 = 3$, which indeed is globally optimal. [This example is repeated in the sections below, so copy (4), (5), and $\bar{x}$ on a sheet of paper for easy future reference.] Given *any* set of directions d_j and a step size t, the expression in (4) becomes a quadratic function of t:

(6) $6(x_1 + td_1) + 4(x_2 + td_2) + 2(x_3 + td_3)$
$$- 3(x_1 + td_1)^2 - 2(x_2 + td_2)^2 - \tfrac{1}{3}(x_3 + td_3)^2.$$

Further, in this case it can be shown that expression (6) is a concave function of t, and the optimal step size can be analytically found by setting the derivative equal to zero and solving for t. Verify that this calculation yields

(7)   optimal $t = \dfrac{6(1 - x_1)d_1 + 4(1 - x_2)d_2 + 2(1 - \frac{1}{3}x_3)d_3}{6(d_1)^2 + 4(d_2)^2 + \frac{2}{3}(d_3)^2}.$

Given that $d_j = \partial c/\partial x_j$ in the method of steepest ascent, the optimal t is never negative.

The results of applying the method of steepest ascent are shown in Fig. 14.8,

$$c(x) = 6x_1 + 4x_2 + 2x_3 - 3x_1^2 - 2x_2^2 - \tfrac{1}{3}x_3^2$$

Iteration k	$c(x_1^k, x_2^k, x_3^k)$	x_1^k	x_2^k	x_3^k	Step Size t^k
0	0	0	0	0	.1981
1	5.547	1.189	.729	.396	.4001
2	6.544	.736	1.125	1.091	.2554
5	7.646	1.088	.999	2.004	.3642
6	7.778	.895	1.000	2.246	.2551
10	7.965	.959	1.000	2.702	.2551
11	7.978	1.022	.999	2.753	.3642
18	7.999	.994	1.000	2.954	.2551
19	7.999	1.003	1.000	2.961	.3642
20	7.999	.996	1.000	2.971	--
Optimal Values	8	1	1	3	0

FIGURE 14.8. Example of Steepest Ascent with Optimal Step Size.

where the initial point is each $x_j^0 = 0$. Notice how the successive values of x_1^k and x_2^k oscillate around their optimal values. Observe how rapidly the value of the objective function rises for the first few iterations; by the fifth iteration, $c(x)$ is within nearly 5% of its maximum. In contrast, more than twice as many iterations are required to obtain all values of x_j^k that are within 5% of their optimal levels.

The special nature of this example can be used to illustrate why moving in the direction of the gradient does not *always* lead to swift convergence. Suppose you used a "move one variable at a time" approach to selecting the directions, instead of using the gradient. Since in this example there are no cross-product terms in $c(x)$, such as $x_1 x_2$, you obtain the exact optimal solution in three iterations (regardless of the order you select for considering the variables). The method of steepest ascent converges only in the limit for this example (starting with all $x_j^0 = 0$).

*Modifications of steepest ascent. The preceding algorithm is termed a *first-order* method, since it uses only the first-order partial derivatives. Unless modified, the method of steepest ascent is likely to converge slowly after the first few iterations and exhibit certain annoying characteristics. For example, the orthogonality property in (3) gives rise to a **zigzagging** phenomenon, illustrated in Fig. 14.7. There are several numerical techniques for modifying the method of steepest ascent that reduce the approach's propensity to zigzag, and thereby speed up convergence.

One such technique, named the **Newton-Raphson Method** after the scientists who proposed it, employs a direction based on a quadratic fit of the objective function. This method results in using the second-order partial derivatives to form a weighted average of the first-order partial derivatives, and falls in the category of so-called **modified gradient** techniques.

Specifically, the d_j^k are found by solving the linear system

$$(8) \qquad \sum_{j=1}^{n} \frac{\partial^2 c}{\partial x_i \partial x_j} d_j = -\frac{\partial c}{\partial x_i} \quad \text{for } i = 1, 2, \ldots, n,$$

where $c(x)$ is assumed to be such that (8) always has a well-defined solution at each trial point x^k. This second-order method applied to a quadratic function $c(x)$ yields a stationary point in a single iteration for any x^0. And if you let each $x_j^0 = 0$, then solving the system (8) is equivalent to solving the system $\partial c/\partial x_j = 0$ for $j = 1, 2, \ldots, n$.

Another acceleration approach, called **subrelaxation**, uses a smaller than optimum step size. The variety of useful modifications to the method of steepest ascent is too large and the subject itself is too special be treated any further in this text.

A notable property of gradient approaches is that their speed of convergence can depend on the way a problem is formulated. For example, in the above illustration with $c(x) = -(x_1 - 3)^2 - 4(x_2 - 2)^2$, let $z \equiv 2x_2 - 2$ so that $x_2 = .5(z + 2)$. Then verify that $c(x_1, z) = -(x_1 - 3)^2 - (z - 2)^2$, and $x_1 = 3$ and $z = 2$ are optimal. Now $\partial c/\partial x_1 = -2(x_1 - 3)$ and $\partial c/\partial z = -2(z - 2)$.

Letting $x_1^0 = z^0 = 0$ gives the steepest ascent directions $d_1^0 = 6$ and $d_2^0 = 4$; hence $t^0 = \frac{1}{2}$ and x_1^1 and z^1 are optimal. Thus this transformation of variables causes the method of steepest ascent to converge in one iteration.

Convergence of Steepest Ascent Algorithm.

The foregoing examples of $c(x)$ were general enough to exhibit the sequence of calculations in the method of steepest ascent using an optimal step size. But the specific numerical behavior exhibited may have been misleading, since the selected functions were quadratic, and satisfied the Necessary Condition for a Maximum at a unique point. You may wonder how this algorithm would behave on a function such as that in Fig. 14.2. It can be shown that if $c(x)$ satisfies assumptions (i) through (iv) in Sec. 14.4, then for an arbitrary initial trial value x^0:

  (A) The entire sequence $c(x^k)$ always increases to a limit c^*.
  (B) At least a subsequence of x^k converges to a point x^*.
  (C) At x^*, the objective function is $c(x^*) = c^*$, and the Necessary Condition for a Maximum is satisfied, that is, each $\partial c / \partial x_j = 0$.

Hence, not only is the sequence of $c(x^k)$ strictly increasing, but for k large enough, $c(x^k)$ becomes arbitrarily close to a limiting value c^*. In general, however, there is no *finite* k such that $c(x^k) = c^*$ or $x^k = x^*$; roughly stated, the **convergence is infinite**.

Regrettably, the three properties above do not mean that the entire sequence of x^k converges to a point $\bar{x}$ such that $c(\bar{x})$ is maximum. First, c^* need not be the maximum value for $c(x)$. Second, x^* may be a point in Fig. 14.2 like a, c (if $x^0 = c$), d, or e. (In a multidimensional example, x^* may be a saddle point.) Therefore, x^* may only be what is called a **stationary point**, that is, a point satisfying the Necessary Condition for a Maximum.

Property B can be clarified using two-dimensional terminology. It asserts there is a point x^* such that if you draw a circle centered at x^* and let the radius be arbitrarily small, then infinitely many x^k lie within this circle. But the fact that x^{1000}, say, is in the circle does *not* guarantee that the next point x^{1001} is also in the circle. Although the *entire* sequence x^k need not converge to x^*, it typically does in real applications.

Unless you impose further restrictions on the function $c(x)$, the above convergence properties are the best you can obtain. If you are uncertain about the shape of a particular $c(x)$, then ordinarily you would apply the algorithm several times, each time using an x^0 that is distant from the previous initial points as well as from the resultant x^*.

▶Properties A and B are demonstrated by appealing to a well-known result in mathematical analysis, namely, that every infinite sequence in a compact space has a convergent subsequence. (This proposition is frequently referred to as the Bolzano-Weierstrass Theorem.) Assumptions (i), (iii), and (iv) in Sec. 14.4 imply that the set of points $[x, c(x)]$ in E^{n+1} for which $c(x) \geq c(x^0)$ is compact; hence, there is a subsequence that converges to $[x^*, c^*]$. Since $c(x^{k+1}) \geq c(x^k)$, the entire sequence $c(x^k)$ tends to c^* in the limit. Thus Properties A and B hold for any algorithm that improves the value of $c(x)$ at each iteration. The specific characteristics of the method of steepest ascent using an *optimal* step size are employed in proving Property C.

Let X^i denote a general term in the subsequence converging to x^*. Then, by the continuity of $c(x)$,

(i) $$c(x^*) = \lim c(X^i) = c^*.$$

Abbreviating $c[X_1^i + t^i(\partial c/\partial x_1), \ldots, X_n^i + t^i(\partial c/\partial x_n)]$ by the symbol $c[X^i + t^i\nabla c(X^i)]$, we have

(ii) $$c(X^{i+1}) \geq c[X^i + t^i\nabla c(X^i)] \geq c[X^i + t\nabla c(X^i)] \quad \text{for } t \geq 0,$$

where the first inequality follows from the "steepest ascent" procedure, and the second from the "optimal step size" procedure. Taking limits on both ends of (ii), employing the continuity assumption on each $\partial c/\partial x_j$, and using (i) gives

(iii) $$c(x^*) \geq c[x^* + t\nabla c(x^*)] \quad \text{for all } t \geq 0.$$

Now (iii) in turn implies $\nabla c(x^*) = 0$, that is, each $\partial c/\partial x_j = 0$ at x^*; for if not, there is a positive value for t such that the right side of (iii) is strictly greater than $c(x^*)$, contradicting the inequality in (iii). Hence Property C is established. ◀

Concave objective functions. Suppose the function $c(x)$ is now restricted further by adding an assumption about its shape. A several-variable function $c(x)$ is defined as **concave** if for any two points $x \neq y$, and for all p, $0 \leq p \leq 1$,

(9) $$pc(x) + (1 - p)c(y) \leq c(px_1 + (1 - p)y_1, \ldots, px_n + (1 - p)y_n) \quad \underline{\text{Concave,}}$$

and as **strictly concave** if there is a strict inequality ($<$) in (9) for $0 < p < 1$. Using geometric language, a function is said to be concave if the chord connecting every pair of points on its graph lies on or below the graph, and is strictly concave if it always lies strictly below (except at end points x and y). Equivalently, a function is concave if it lies on or below every plane that is tangent to its surface. Case 2 in Fig. 14.1 shows a strictly concave function; if it were modified to include a linear segment, then it would be only concave. The case represented by Fig. 14.6 is also an example of a strictly concave function. We can state the following condition.

SUFFICIENT CONDITION FOR A MAXIMUM OF A CONCAVE FUNCTION. Given assumptions (i) through (iv) in Sec. 14.4, and that $c(x)$ is concave, if each $\partial c/\partial x_j = 0$ at a point $\bar{x}$, then $c(\bar{x})$ is the maximum value for $c(x)$. Further, if $c(x)$ is strictly concave, then $\bar{x}$ is unique.

Therefore, a *local* maximum of a concave function is also a *global* maximum. As an important consequence, if you apply the method of steepest ascent using an optimal step size, the sequence $c(x^k)$ increases in the limit to the maximum value of $c(x)$; and if the function is strictly concave, the *entire* sequence x^k converges to the unique optimal solution $\bar{x}$. A further significant computational implication is that the optimal step size procedure of the algorithm can be achieved by employing a search method explained in Sec. 14.3. The reason is that if $c(x)$ is concave, then $c(x_1 + td_1, \ldots, x_n + td_n)$ is a concave function of t. {At each iteration, you will have to supply an upper bound $\bar{t}$ on the optimal step size, and then search for the best value of t in the interval $[0, \bar{t}]$.}

▶If you terminate the algorithm at the trial value x^k, and $c(x)$ is concave, then you can obtain a bound on the maximum value for $c(x)$. The approach is based on the fact that a tangent plane to $c(x)$ at x^k overestimates $c(x)$ for any x. Specifically,

(i) $$c(x) \leq c(x^k) + \sum_{j=1}^{n} \frac{\partial c(x^k)}{\partial x_j} \cdot (x_j - x_j^k) \qquad \underline{\underline{\text{Concave}}}$$

for any x.

To illustrate the idea, suppose you can assert how far an optimal $\bar{x}$ might be from x^k. Specifically, assume that $|\bar{x}_j^k - x_j^k| \leq e$ for every j, where $e > 0$. Then the maximum value of $c(x)$ cannot be larger than $c(x^k) + e \sum_{j=1}^{n} |\partial c(x^k)/\partial x_j|$. The correction factor is small when e and the gradient at x^k are nearly zero.

In examining the method of steepest ascent as pictured in Figs. 14.6 and 14.7, you may have concluded that the shape of the level-contours ensured that a local optimum was also a global optimum. Specifically, the set of points x such that $c(x) \geq c$ was convex, which, in turn, ensured that the contours $c(x) = c$ were nested as c increased. There were no "pockets" or "traps" for x^k to be lured away from the optimum $\bar{x}$. It is easily shown that concave functions always have this nested convexity property for the level contours. But so do certain other functions. [For example, consider the function $c(x) = -x^2/(1 + x^2)$, which is bell-shaped and hence not concave. The set of points x such that $c(x) \geq c$ is convex, namely, an interval centered at $x = 0$. As c increases, the intervals shrink and are nested.]

Suppose, then, you postulate only the nested convexity property about the level sets of $c(x)$. A function with this property is termed **quasi-concave** and is mathematically defined by the condition that for any two points $x \neq y$, and for all $p, 0 \leq p \leq 1$,

(ii) $$\text{minimum } [c(x), c(y)] \leq c(px_1 + (1 - p)y_1, \ldots, px_n + (1 - p)y_n)$$
$$\underline{\underline{\text{Quasi-concave.}}}$$

(A concave function is always quasi-concave.) This assumption is not quite enough to ensure that the sequence $c(x^k)$ tends to its maximum value in the method of steepest ascent. The quasi-concavity assumption (ii) does not rule out the possibility that the limit of the subsequence of x^k, namely x^*, can be an inflection point. But if you also assume that $c(x)$ has *no* inflection points, or if you can verify that x^* is *not* an inflection point [the value of $c(x)$ does not increase in any direction from x^*], then $c(x^*)$ is indeed the maximum value.

Incidentally, if you assume quasi-concavity and that $c(x)$ has no inflection points, then you can also use the single-dimension adaptive search techniques given in Sec. 14.3 for finding an optimal step size.   ◀

14.6 QUADRATIC PROGRAMMING

This section begins the discussion of techniques for optimizing a nonlinear objective function when the variables are subject to constraints. We start with what is perhaps the simplest nonlinear extension of a linear programming model.

A **quadratic programming** problem consists of an objective function composed of linear and quadratic terms and a set of linear constraints. The specific version considered below is

$$(1) \qquad \text{maximize} \sum_{j=1}^{n} c_j x_j + \sum_{j=1}^{n} \sum_{k=1}^{n} c_{jk} x_j x_k$$

subject to

$$(2) \qquad \sum_{j=1}^{n} a_{ij} x_j + s_i = b_i \quad \text{for } i = 1, 2, \ldots, m$$

$$\text{all } x_j \geq 0 \quad \text{and} \quad \text{all } s_i \geq 0,$$

where each s_i represents a slack variable. To avoid treating all the various cases that can arise, assume each $b_i \geq 0$. Also assume that $c(x)$ reaches a finite maximum $\bar{c}$ over all feasible solutions, where $c(x)$ denotes the objective function in (1). The modifications required to handle b_i of any sign (or problems without all the slacks present) and unbounded optimal solutions are straightforward, but will not be covered in this text.

Section 14.1 included several illustrations ("sales revenue," "safety-stock inventory levels," "portfolio selection") that contained quadratic terms in the model formulation. The practical importance of such situations is one justification for devoting this entire section to solving quadratic programming problems. But, in truth, these applications are not the most frequently occurring examples of nonlinear problems. Hence, the main justification for discussing this special case is that the topic represents the next logical step in mastering the ideas and techniques of nonlinear programming. It is particularly important that you observe

(i) How the imposition of constraints influences an optimal solution.
(ii) How a gradient optimization procedure has to take account of all the constraints.
(iii) How the quadratic assumption leads to linearized algorithms. And specifically, how the simplex method is modified to provide an algorithm that converges to an exact solution in a *finite* number of iterations.

Quadratic programming techniques are also significant because they are sometimes used as subroutines in more general nonlinear programming algorithms—at a trial point, the nonlinear objective function is approximated by a quadratic function which, in turn, is optimized to provide a direction of improvement. This device falls under the heading of an advanced numerical technique for accelerating convergence, and so will not be treated in this text.

Given our assumptions about b_i and $c(x)$, three types of optimal solutions are possible, as shown in Fig. 14.9. Case 1 demonstrates that the optimal solution may be in the interior of the constraint region; for the particular example, the unique optimal solution is the **interior** point $\bar{x}_1 = 1$ and $\bar{x}_2 = 2$. Case 2 exhibits that an optimal solution may be on the **boundary** of the constraint region, but not necessarily at a vertex or an extreme point. Case 3 corresponds to the kind of solution that arises when an objective function is linear, namely, when

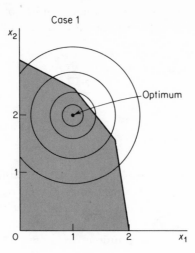

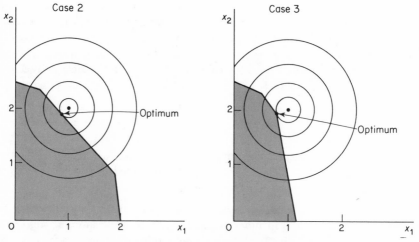

FIGURE 14.9. Constrained   Optimal   Solutions $c(x) = -(x_1 - 1)^2 -$ $(x_2 - 2)^2 + 5 = 2x_1 + 4x_2 - x_1x_2 - x_2x_2$. Case 1 Optimum in Interior. Case 2 Optimum at Boundary. Case 3 Optimum at Vertex.

there is a basic optimal solution occurring at a *vertex* of the constraint region. Since Case 3 is not the only possibility here, nonlinear programming algorithms *must* permit consideration of nonbasic solutions, in sharp contrast to linear programming techniques.

Preliminaries. Before discussing the steps of the algorithm, it is helpful to make a few remarks about the nature of a quadratic objective function. To begin, we adopt a convenient way to display the function; the approach is easily explained by an example. Suppose

(3) $$c(x) \equiv 2x_1 + 5x_2 - \tfrac{1}{4}x_1^2 + 1x_1x_2 - 3x_1x_3 - 4x_2^2.$$

Note that $c(x)$ has been written in (3) so that there is at most only one term containing any given pair of variables. For example, if the quadratic function originally contained the expressions $-5x_1x_3 + 2x_3x_1$, then these two terms, both containing the pair x_1 and x_3, would be simplified to $-3x_1x_3$. The convention is to display $c(x)$ in the format:

(4)
$$
\begin{aligned}
c(x) = \quad & (0 + 1x_1 + \tfrac{5}{2}x_2 + 0x_3)\cdot 1 \\
+ \; & (1 - \tfrac{1}{4}x_1 + \tfrac{1}{2}x_2 - \tfrac{3}{2}x_3)\cdot x_1 \\
+ \; & (\tfrac{5}{2} + \tfrac{1}{2}x_1 - 4x_2 + 0x_3)\cdot x_2 \\
+ \; & (0 - \tfrac{3}{2}x_1 + 0x_2 + 0x_3)\cdot x_3.
\end{aligned}
$$

Verify that the expression in (4) agrees with (3) when the terms are multiplied and combined. Note in (4) that the diagonal terms $(-\tfrac{1}{4}, -4, \text{ and } 0)$ are the coefficients of the squared variables in (3), and the off-diagonal terms are one-half of the corresponding coefficients in (3). Also observe that the array of coefficients in (4) is symmetric—the term in the ith row and jth column is the same as that in the jth row and ith column.

Next consider the partial derivatives of $c(x)$ in the example (3):

(5)
$$\frac{\partial c}{\partial x_1} = 2 - \tfrac{1}{2}x_1 + 1x_2 - 3x_3 \equiv 2(1 - \tfrac{1}{4}x_1 + \tfrac{1}{2}x_2 - \tfrac{3}{2}x_3)$$

$$\frac{\partial c}{\partial x_2} = 5 + 1x_1 - 8x_2 \equiv 2(\tfrac{5}{2} + \tfrac{1}{2}x_1 - 4x_2)$$

$$\frac{\partial c}{\partial x_3} = -3x_1 \equiv 2(-\tfrac{3}{2}x_1).$$

Hence, the partial derivative of $c(x)$ with respect to x_j is twice the value of the parenthetical expression multiplying x_j in (4). A positive value for a partial derivative indicates that the objective function is increased by increasing the associated variable. Note that the partial derivatives are linear functions of the x_j. It is this fact that leads to only a minor modification of the simplex algorithm presented below.

In the course of this algorithm, you will need to introduce new variables related to the parenthetical expressions in (4). For reasons that will become clear later on, these are named **free variables**. To illustrate, suppose you want to introduce a free variable—call it u—associated with the expression multiplying x_1 in (4). Then construct the following definitional relation for u:

(6) $$\tfrac{1}{4}u = 1 - \tfrac{1}{4}x_1 + \tfrac{1}{2}x_2 - \tfrac{3}{2}x_3.$$

Again by convention, the coefficient for u is the same as minus the coefficient for x_1 in (6). Rearranging terms in (6), you can express x_1 as

(7) $$x_1 = 4 - u + 2x_2 - 6x_3.$$

▶In applying the algorithm, you will also need to eliminate a variable x_j from a quadratic expression, and substitute, instead, a linear expression containing the other variables. For example, you may need to eliminate x_1 in (4) and substitute the expression on the right of (7) in its place. To do this systematically, first eliminate x_1 from the expressions in parentheses:

(i)
$$(4 - 1u + \tfrac{9}{2}x_2 - 6x_3) \cdot 1$$
$$+ (0 + \tfrac{1}{4}u + 0x_2 + 0x_3) \cdot x_1$$
$$+ (\tfrac{9}{2} - \tfrac{1}{2}u - 3x_2 - 3x_3) \cdot x_2$$
$$+ (-6 + \tfrac{3}{2}u - 3x_2 + 9x_3) \cdot x_3.$$

Second, substitute the expression (7) for x_1 in (i); then expand the resultant product, term by term for each element in (7), and combine with the other expressions in the parentheses in (i). For example, the third term in the expanded expression is $(0 + \tfrac{1}{4}u + 0x_2 + 0x_3) \cdot 2x_2$, which is to be combined with $(\tfrac{9}{2} - \tfrac{1}{2}u - 3x_2 - 3x_3) \cdot x_2$. The complete result is

(ii)
$$(4 + 0u + \tfrac{9}{2}x_2 - 6x_3) \cdot 1$$
$$(0 - \tfrac{1}{4}u + 0x_2 + 0x_3) \cdot u$$
$$(\tfrac{9}{2} + 0u - 3x_2 - 3x_3) \cdot x_2$$
$$(-6 + 0u - 3x_2 + 9x_3) \cdot x_3,$$

which once again is symmetric. To confirm your understanding, perform the calculations yielding (i) and (ii).

It is no accident that the coefficients in the row and column for u are all zero (except the diagonal term), and that the other coefficients are the same as in (i). This simplification *always* arises when you substitute an expression based on a relation for a free variable; hence, in such a case, you need not perform the arithmetic in the second step. But if, for example, you substitute $(1 + 4x_2 - 4x_3)$ for x_1, then you do need to perform the expansion indicated by the second step.   ◀

Quadratic Simplex Algorithm. The method, in outline, is:

Step 1. Let $s_i = b_i \geq 0$, for $i = 1, 2, \ldots, m$, be the initial feasible basic solution.

Step 2. Determine directions of local improvement from the current solution. Stop if there are none. Otherwise, find the optimal step size in the selected direction, and continue to *Step 3.*

Step 3. Calculate the new solution accordingly. Return to *Step 2.*

The status of the algorithm at any iteration can be summarized as follows. There is a system of linear constraints derived from (2) as well as some additional relationships that have been imposed during the course of previous iterations. At *Step 1*, only the m constraints in (2) are present, but at later iterations there can be up to $m + n$ constraints in all. Associated with this system is a set of basic variables, comprised of the x_j and the slack variables s_i. The nonbasic variables consist of the remaining x_j, s_i, as well as "free variables" that have been introduced at earlier iterations.

The detailed instruction for determining directions of improvement in *Step 2* is given by the following criterion.

QUADRATIC SIMPLEX CRITERION I. (a) Select any free variable to enter the solution if the corresponding partial derivative of the objective function is nonzero. (b) If all such derivatives for the free variables equal zero, then select a variable (an x_j or s_i) to enter for which the corresponding partial derivative of the objective function is most positive. (c) Terminate the iterations when the partial derivatives are zero for the free variables and less than or equal to zero for the other nonbasic variables.

Aside from the changes in wording necessitated by the nature of the nonlinear problem, *Quadratic Simplex Criterion I* is in the same spirit as *Simplex Criterion I*. In both cases, the direction of improvement is the result of entering a *single* nonbasic variable.

The optimal step size calculation resembles *Simplex Criterion II*. In part, it tests for the largest value of the selected nonbasic variable that will maintain feasibility in the constraints. But it also finds the value for this variable beyond which the objective function decreases. The optimal step size, then, is the smaller of these two values. The rule is stated specifically in the criterion below.

QUADRATIC SIMPLEX CRITERION II. Introduce the selected nonbasic variable at a level that yields the most favorable improvement in the objective function, consistent with the constraints.

The fine details of this criterion are shown fully in the example below.

Example. Consider the problem

$$(8) \qquad \text{maximize } 6x_1 + 4x_2 + 2x_3 - 3x_1^2 - 2x_2^2 - \tfrac{1}{3}x_3^2$$

subject to

$$(9) \qquad\qquad x_1 + 2x_2 + x_3 + s = 4 \qquad\qquad \underline{\text{Row 1}};$$

all $x_j \geq 0$ and $s \geq 0$. [You will find it helpful to copy (8) and (9) for future reference.] Recall that this same $c(x)$ was analyzed in Sec. 14.5, where you saw that the unique unconstrained optimum is $x_1 = 1$, $x_2 = 1$, and $x_3 = 3$. Verify that this point is not feasible in (9). Let $s = 4$ be the initial feasible solution for *Step 1*; since s is a slack, it does not appear in (8). Using the suggested convention for arraying the objective function, you can write (8) as

$$(10) \qquad
\begin{aligned}
&(\ \ + 3x_1 - 2x_2 + 1x_3) \cdot 1 \\
&+ (3 - 3x_1 \qquad\qquad) \cdot x_1 \\
&+ (2 \qquad - 2x_2 \qquad) \cdot x_2 \\
&+ (1 \qquad\qquad - \tfrac{1}{3}x_3) \cdot x_3,
\end{aligned}$$

where the zero-valued terms have been suppressed in the formula. Recall that the leading term in each parenthetical expression is one-half the value of the partial derivative with respect to the corresponding nonbasic variable. Therefore part (b) of *Criterion I* indicates that x_1 enters the solution. Explain why.

To find the value for x_1, first apply the approach used in *Simplex Criterion II* to calculate the maximum value of x_1 consistent with feasibility in the linear constraint. This involves taking the ratios of the current right-hand side to the coefficients of the entering variable. In the example, the result is

(11) $x_1 \leq \dfrac{4}{1} = 4$ for a step size that satisfies the constraints.

The value of x_1 giving the *maximum* improvement in the objective function, *holding all other nonbasic variables at their current level*, is the solution to

(12) $\dfrac{\partial c}{\partial x_1} = 0$ or equivalently $\dfrac{1}{2}\dfrac{\partial c}{\partial x_1} = 0,$

where the partial derivative is calculated for the value of the current trial solution. This equation yields $3 - 3x_1 = 0$, so that

(13) $x_1 \leq 1$ for a step size that improves the current value
                   of the objective function.

Since the inequality in (13) is more restrictive than that in (11), the *Quadratic Simplex Criterion II* specifies that x_1 enters at the level 1. This completes *Step 2*, and you now continue to *Step 3*.

You can achieve $x_1 = 1$ at the next trial solution by adding the definitional equation for a free variable associated with x_1:

(14) $3u_1 = 3 - 3x_1$ or equivalently $x_1 + u_1 = 1.$

At the current solution, $u_1 = 1$ since $x_1 = 0$. But by pivoting, so that u_1 becomes nonbasic and falls to level 0, you force x_1 to the value 1. In summary, impose (14) along with (9), pivot on x_1 in (14), and thereby obtain the set of constraints:

(15)
$$2x_2 + x_3 + s - u_1 = 3 \qquad \text{Row 1}$$
$$x_1 \qquad\qquad + u_1 = 1 \qquad \text{Row 2.}$$

Eliminate x_1 in the objective function (10) by substituting the relation in (14) to give

(16)
$$
\begin{aligned}
&(3 \qquad\quad + 2x_2 + 1x_3)\cdot 1 \\
+\ &(\ -3u_1 \qquad\qquad\quad)\cdot u_1 \\
+\ &(2 \qquad -2x_2 \qquad\quad)\cdot x_2 \\
+\ &(1 \qquad\qquad\quad -\tfrac{1}{3}x_3)\cdot x_3.
\end{aligned}
$$

Each parenthetical expression still represents one-half the value of the partial derivative with respect to the corresponding nonbasic variable, but takes into account that changing such a variable also affects $c(x)$ through the associated changes in the basic variables. Sometimes this value is called a **reduced par-**

tial derivative. The first iteration is complete. The value 3 in the upper-left corner of (16) equals the level of the objective function at the current trial solution.

Returning to *Step 2*, you see that the solution can be improved by introducing x_2. The feasibility restriction, according to (15), is that $x_2 \leq \frac{3}{2} = 1.5$. Verify that the value of x_2 giving the best improvement in the objective function is $x_2 = 1$. Hence to accomplish *Step 3*, you introduce another free variable:

$$(17) \qquad 2u_2 = 2 - 2x_2 \quad \text{or equivalently} \quad x_2 + u_2 = 1.$$

Combine (17) with (15), and pivot on x_2 in (17) to obtain

$$(18) \qquad
\begin{array}{llll}
x_3 + s - u_1 - 2u_2 = 1 & \qquad \text{Row 1} \\
x_1 + u_1 = 1 & \qquad \text{Row 2} \\
x_2 + u_2 = 1 & \qquad \text{Row 3.}
\end{array}$$

Then use (17) to eliminate x_2 from (16), giving the reduced objective function:

$$(19) \qquad
\begin{aligned}
&(5 &&+ 1x_3) \cdot 1 \\
+ &(-3u_1 &&) \cdot u_1 \\
+ &(- 2u_2 &&) \cdot u_2 \\
+ &(1 && - \tfrac{1}{3}x_3) \cdot x_3.
\end{aligned}$$

Observe in both (16) and (19) that the first term in the parentheses associated with the free variables u_1 and u_2 equals 0. Therefore the partial derivative of the transformed objective functions (16) and (19) for each free variable equals 0 in these trial solutions.

Now part (b) of *Criterion I* indicates that x_3 should enter. In performing the step size computation, you will find that the feasibility calculation based on (18) is restrictive. So in this case, you perform in *Step 3* an ordinary change-of-basis calculation—the variable x_3 enters the basis and s leaves. Since x_3 appears only in Row 1 of (18), no pivoting calculations are needed in the constraints. (If the original problem had contained more constraints, then pivot calculations would usually have occurred.) But x_3 must be eliminated from (19) by means of Row 1 in (18), giving

$$(20) \qquad
\begin{aligned}
&(\ 6\tfrac{2}{3} + \tfrac{2}{3}u_1 + \tfrac{4}{3}u_2 - \tfrac{2}{3}s) \cdot 1 \\
+ &(\ \tfrac{2}{3} - \tfrac{10}{3}u_1 - \tfrac{2}{3}u_2 + \tfrac{1}{3}s) \cdot u_1 \\
+ &(\ \tfrac{4}{3} - \tfrac{2}{3}u_1 - \tfrac{10}{3}u_2 + \tfrac{2}{3}s) \cdot u_2 \\
+ &(-\tfrac{2}{3} + \tfrac{1}{3}u_1 + \tfrac{2}{3}u_2 - \tfrac{1}{3}s) \cdot s.
\end{aligned}$$

The current trial solution is

$$(21) \qquad x_1 = 1 \quad x_2 = 1 \quad x_3 = 1,$$

so that all three variables are at positive levels. Is this solution optimal? Not according to part (a) of *Criterion I* above, and here is why. The relations (14) and (17) associated with u_1 and u_2 were imposed as artifices to ensure taking the optimal step size in applying *Criterion II*. There is no reason why u_1 and u_2 *have* to be zero. In fact, u_1 and u_2 are unconstrained in sign—the very reason they are called *free* variables. Consequently, if the partial derivative of the objective function for a free variable is nonzero, then the solution can be improved by moving this variable in the direction indicated by the sign of the partial derivative. As you can see in (20), the partial derivatives for u_1 and u_2 are nonzero. Therefore, select u_1 to enter the solution.

Because the partial derivative for u_1 is positive, you should increase u_1. The procedure for finding the new level for u_1 is exactly the same as that used at previous iterations. Check that for feasibility, u_1 cannot exceed 1. [If the value of the partial derivative were negative, then you would examine the constraints in (18) to ascertain how negative u_1 could be without violating the constraints. This is equivalent to testing how large $(-u_1)$ can be.] The value of u_1 that gives the maximum improvement in the objective function, *holding all other nonbasic variables at their current levels*, is $u_1 = \frac{2}{10}$, which is the solution to

$$(22) \qquad \frac{1}{2}\frac{\partial c}{\partial u_2} = \left(\frac{2}{3} - \frac{10}{3}u_1\right) = 0 \quad \text{at the current trial solution.}$$

Therefore, to ensure $u_1 = \frac{2}{10}$ at the next trial solution, you must introduce a new free variable u_3:

$$(23) \qquad \tfrac{10}{3}u_3 = \tfrac{2}{3} - \tfrac{10}{3}u_1 - \tfrac{2}{3}u_2 + \tfrac{1}{3}s$$

or

$$(24) \qquad -\tfrac{1}{10}s + 1u_1 + \tfrac{1}{5}u_2 + 1u_3 = \tfrac{1}{5}.$$

Then use (24) to eliminate u_1 from (18), yielding

$$(25) \qquad
\begin{array}{ll}
x_3 + \tfrac{9}{10}s - \tfrac{9}{5}u_2 + u_3 = \tfrac{6}{5} & \text{Row 1} \\
x_1 + \tfrac{1}{10}s - \tfrac{1}{5}u_2 - u_3 = \tfrac{4}{5} & \text{Row 2} \\
x_2 + u_2 = 1 & \text{Row 3,}
\end{array}$$

and also eliminate u_1 from (20), giving

$$(26) \qquad
\begin{aligned}
&(\ 6\tfrac{4}{5} + \tfrac{6}{5}u_2 - \tfrac{3}{5}s)\cdot 1 \\
+&(\phantom{6\tfrac{4}{5}} - \tfrac{10}{3}u_3 \phantom{+ \tfrac{6}{5}u_2})\cdot u_3 \\
+&(\ \tfrac{6}{5} - \tfrac{16}{5}u_2 + \tfrac{3}{5}s)\cdot u_2 \\
+&(-\tfrac{3}{5} + \tfrac{3}{5}u_2 - \tfrac{3}{10}s)\cdot s.
\end{aligned}$$

Since u_1 has become a basic variable in (24) and is unrestricted in sign, it can never again be made nonbasic. Thus, (24) can be dropped in subsequent iterations, and the set of constraints is merely (25).

In general, as soon as a free variable enters the solution, the corresponding relation can be dropped—that is why the total number of constraints never exceeds $m + n$. (For in the worst case, where all x_j and s_i are basic variables, so that there are $m + n$ constraints, every nonbasic variable must be a free variable. After selecting one of these to enter to basis, one of two cases occurs. Either an x_j or s_i becomes nonbasic, and you then drop the row in which the selected free variable has become basic. In this case, the total number of constraints is reduced by one. Or the free variable associated with a newly imposed definitional constraint becomes nonbasic, and you then drop this relation after pivoting on the selected free variable. In this case, the total number of constraints is unchanged.)

Returning again to *Step 2*, you must introduce u_2 since it has a positive partial derivative in (26). Verify that the step size computations indicate that you must add another free variable:

$$(27) \qquad \tfrac{16}{5}u_4 = \tfrac{6}{5} - \tfrac{16}{5}u_2 + \tfrac{3}{5}s.$$

Check that eliminating u_2 from (25) yields

$$
\begin{array}{lll}
x_3 + \tfrac{9}{16}s + u_3 + \tfrac{9}{5}u_4 = \tfrac{15}{8} & \qquad & \text{Row 1} \\
(28) \qquad x_1 \quad + \tfrac{1}{16}s - u_3 + \tfrac{1}{5}u_4 = \tfrac{7}{8} & \qquad & \text{Row 2} \\
x_2 \quad + \tfrac{3}{16}s \quad - u_4 = \tfrac{5}{8} & \qquad & \text{Row 3,}
\end{array}
$$

and eliminating u_2 from (26), gives

$$(29) \qquad
\begin{array}{l}
(\ 7\tfrac{1}{4} \qquad\qquad\qquad - \tfrac{3}{8}s) \cdot 1 \\
+ (\quad - \tfrac{10}{3}u_3 \qquad\qquad) \cdot u_3 \\
+ (\qquad - \tfrac{16}{5}u_4 \qquad) \cdot u_4 \\
+ (-\tfrac{3}{8} \qquad\qquad - \tfrac{1}{6}s) \cdot s.
\end{array}
$$

This time, you find in *Step 2* that the iterations can terminate. Explain why. The current solution

$$(30) \qquad x_1 = \frac{7}{8} = .875 \quad x_2 = \frac{5}{8} = .625 \quad x_3 = \frac{15}{8} = 1.875$$

is globally optimal, and the value of the objective function is 7.25.

Review. Look back over the approach to see the main ideas. In particular, note these properties of the algorithm:

A. As in the simplex method, the direction of improvement is characterized by changing only a single nonbasic variable at each iteration.
B. As in the simplex method, this new variable cannot exceed a level at which a current basic variable falls to zero.
C. Additional relations are added to the constraints (2) whenever the objective function reaches a maximum in the selected direction before any current basic variable falls to zero.
D. Each additional constraint is proportional to the partial derivative of the objective function with respect to the entering variable, and hence is linear because the objective function is quadratic.
E. Such constraints are added as artifices to facilitate taking the optimal step size in the selected direction. Further, they thereby enlarge the basis, and so enable an optimal solution to contain more than m variables at positive levels.

We caution that the preceding discussion did not present the method in a form best suited for coding into a computer program; such details are inappropriate for this introductory text. The practical necessity of using an electronic calculator for finding a solution is underscored by the preceding example; even though the model consisted of a single linear constraint plus the nonnegativity restrictions, a considerable number of calculations were required to find an optimal solution. (Thus you would only apply this algorithm manually when solving a toy example.)

Convergence properties. A rather simple argument (not given here) can be constructed to establish that the method terminates in a finite number of iterations for any quadratic objective function and set of linear constraints. (Actually, the algorithm must be amended to take the same precaution against cycling that was mentioned for the simplex method in Sec. 4.7.) But so far, no pronouncement has been made on whether the method ensures that the final solution is always optimal. We treat this subject next.

As you must expect from the discussion in Secs. 14.4 and 14.5, unless you make additional assumptions about the shape of the objective function, the most you can assert is that the final solution is a *relative* stationary point. By the same token, the Sufficient Condition for a Maximum in Sec. 14.5 generalizes to the constrained case: if the *quadratic function is concave, then the terminal solution is globally optimal among all feasible solutions.* (Of course, this sufficient condition for global optimality is not necessary; that is, the quadratic function may not be concave, yet the final solution may turn out to be truly optimal.) The quadratic function in (1) is concave if and only if

$$(31) \qquad \sum_{j=1}^{n} \sum_{k=1}^{n} c_{jk} x_j x_k \leq 0 \quad \text{for all } x_i, \text{ where } i = 1, 2, \ldots, n.$$

In mathematical terminology, (31) states that the **quadratic form** is **negative semidefinite.**

Most textbooks on linear algebra and matrix theory contain straightforward computational tests to determine whether a quadratic form satisfies the condition in (31). Such formulas are easy to verify if n is small, and general procedures can be programmed for an electronic calculator to make the tests when n is large. In practice, the very formulation of the model often provides the answer. To illustrate, in the portfolio selection example in Sec. 14.1, the objective is to minimize a quadratic form [expression (11)] in which the coefficients are covariances. You can find a proof in most advanced statistics texts that such a form is **positive semidefinite**, that is, the inequality sign in (31) is reversed. Hence on multiplying the form by (-1) and changing the sense of optimization to "maximize," concavity is automatically established.

Other algorithms. There are many other algorithms for solving quadratic programming problems. Of particular importance is one based on using dual variables; this technique is given in Sec. 15.8, and likewise converges in a finite number of iterations. The methods in the remainder of this and the next chapter also can be employed, but, in sharp contrast to the algorithm above, they do not always converge to a stationary point in a *finite* number of iterations. The numerical example in this section will be used to illustrate this fact.

14.7 SEPARABLE PROGRAMMING

You saw in the preceding section how only a minor modification of the simplex method is required to solve quadratic programming problems. The approach exploited the fact that the partial derivatives of a quadratic objective function are linear. Here we turn to an approach for solving nonlinear problems that involves a different modification of the simplex method. The technique applies to problems in which all the nonlinear functions are separable, a property that is described below. The idea is to construct a constrained optimization model that linearly *approximates* the original problem. The approximations enlarge the size of the model, but since a version of the simplex method can be applied as a solution technique, the method has considerable practical significance. Since the approach can be used equally well to approximate a nonlinear objective function and nonlinear constraints, both cases are treated below.

Separable objective functions. Suppose the objective function can be written as the sum of n functions, one for each variable x_j:

$$(1) \qquad c(x) \equiv \sum_{j=1}^{n} c_j(x_j);$$

such a function is termed **separable**. For the moment, we leave unspecified whether $c(x)$ is to be maximized or minimized. To keep the exposition simple, the technique is outlined only for the variable x_1 and the associated function $c_1(x_1)$; a directly analogous construction applies to each of the other variables. Also, since only variable x_1 is modified below, it is convenient to suppress the subscript in the notation, and refer merely to x.

Assume, again for simplicity, that you know x must lie in the interval $0 \leq x \leq X$ To apply the linearizing technique, choose a grid of values for x, designated as $0 \equiv X_1 < X_2 < \cdots < X_{p-1} < X_p \equiv X$, and express any value for x in terms of a weighted average of the grid values:

$$(2) \qquad x = X_1 w_1 + X_2 w_2 + \cdots + X_p w_p,$$

where the weights w_k must satisfy

$$(3) \qquad \sum_{k=1}^{p} w_k = 1 \quad \text{and} \quad w_k \geq 0 \quad \text{for } k = 1, 2, \ldots, p.$$

In selecting the grid, always observe the convention that if $c_1(x_1)$ is linear over a specified interval of values for x_1, then no more than two grid points are located in this interval.

To construct the "approximate" model, substitute the right-hand side of (2) wherever x appears in the constraints, add the restrictions in (3), and substitute the

piecewise-linear, or **polygonal**, **approximation**.

$$(4) \qquad\qquad \sum_{k=1}^{p} c_1(X_k) w_k$$

for $c_1(x_1)$ in the objective function.

To illustrate the construction, consider the convex function $c_1(x_1) = x_1^2$ and $0 \le x_1 \le 10$, as shown in Fig. 14.10.

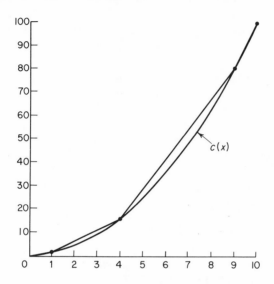

Figure 14.10. Linear Approximation $c(x) = x^2$.

For the example, let the grid points be 0, 1, 4, 9, 10. Then (2) becomes

$$(5) \qquad\qquad x \equiv 0w_1 + 1w_2 + 4w_3 + 9w_4 + 10w_5$$

and (4) becomes

$$(6) \qquad\qquad 0w_1 + 1^2 w_2 + 4^2 w_3 + 9^2 w_4 + 10^2 w_5.$$

Suppose $x = 6$. Then the weights corresponding to representation (5) are $w_3 = \frac{3}{5}$, $w_4 = \frac{2}{5}$, and all other $w_k = 0$. This gives the approximate value in (6) of $\frac{210}{5} = 42$ for the true value $c_1(6) = 36$. Suppose, further, that $x_1 \equiv x$ is constrained by

$$(7) \qquad\qquad 5x - 2x_2 \le 1.$$

Then after substituting (5) into (7), the constraint is written as

$$(8) \qquad\qquad 5w_2 + 20w_3 + 45w_4 + 50w_5 - 2x_2 \le 1.$$

The analysis of the numerical example has *assumed* that the weights used to give $x = 6$ are w_3 and w_4, since 6 lies between the grid points $X_3 = 4$ and $X_4 = 9$. But the weights $w_1 = .4$ and $w_5 = .6$ also yield the value 6 in (5), only in this case the approximate value for $c_1(6)$ in (6) is $10^2(.6) = 60$. Therefore, in order that (4) really results in the *intended* piecewise-linear approximation to $c_1(x_1)$, it is essential to ensure that a solution employs at positive values either only one w_k, or at most, two *adjacent* weights w_k and w_{k+1}. We can easily establish the following property.

PROPERTY OF ADJACENT WEIGHTS. Given that all the constraints are linear, if $c(x_1, x_2, \ldots, x_n)$ is to be maximized, and $c_1(x_1)$ is a concave function, then every optimal solution to the approximate model based on (2), (3), and (4) contains only one w_k, or at most, two adjacent weights w_k and w_{k+1} at positive levels. The same solution property holds if $c(x)$ is to be minimized and $c_1(x_1)$ is convex.

An important implication of this property is that if the hypotheses are satisfied for all $c_j(x_j)$, and given that all the constraints on x_j are linear, the transformed model is a linear programming problem and can be solved by applying the ordinary simplex method of Chap. 4. In this case, if the original model has m linear inequality constraints, the enlarged model has $m + n$ constraints, the additional n restrictions being of the form (3). Hence, it is possible that an associated optimal basic solution implies that all n of the x_j (as well as all m of the slack variables) appear at strictly positive levels. Further, the resultant solution is an approximation to a globally optimal solution of the original problem.

But if the hypotheses are not satisfied—for example, $c(x)$ is to be maximized and $c_1(x)$ is *convex*—the solution to the approximate model usually does not satisfy the Property of Adjacent Weights. This difficulty can be rectified by modifying the details of *Simplex Criterion I* so as to *force* the Property of Adjacent Weights to hold. Specifically, add the stipulation that at any iteration, if one weight w_k is in the current basis, then only the adjacent weights w_{k-1} and w_{k+1} are to be considered for entry into the solution. And if two adjacent weights w_k and w_{k+1} are in the current basis, then no other weights are considered for entry at the present iteration. This modification is referred to as a **restricted-basis-entry rule**. When the hypotheses are not satisfied and the restricted-basis-entry rule is used, *the resultant solution is only an approximation to a locally optimal solution of the original problem.* (An alternative to the restricted-basis-entry rule is to employ an integer programming model, described at the end of Sec. 13.2. Although this approach approximates a globally optimal solution of the original problem, it is usually less attractive than the restricted-basis-entry technique because it involves greater computational difficulties.)

Actually, it is possible to construct pathological examples demonstrating that the restricted-basis-entry rule can cause the simplex method to terminate at other than a local optimum of the approximate problem. Such a situation occurs when two adjacent weights w_k and w_{k+1} are in the current basis, and yet, if you introduced w_{k+2} you would cause w_k to drop from the next basis, and the value of the objective function would improve. This bizarre event rarely happens.

▶ In place of a weighted average technique, which requires that (3) be added to the set of constraints, you can employ another approach that leads to adding a set of nonnegative, upper-bounded variables. The idea can be easily explained in terms of the preceding example. Rather than (2), express a value for x as a sum:

(i) $$x \equiv y_1 + y_2 + \cdots + y_{p-1},$$

where $0 \leq y_k \leq X_{k+1} - X_k$ for $k = 1, 2, \ldots, p - 1$. Therefore in the example, instead of (5), you have

(ii) $$x \equiv y_1 + y_2 + y_3 + y_4,$$

where the nonnegative and upper-bound constraints are

(iii) $0 \le y_1 \le 1 - 0 = 1$ $0 \le y_2 \le 4 - 1 = 3$ $0 \le y_3 \le 5$ $0 \le y_4 \le 1.$

Then, instead of (4), you use

(iv) $$\sum_{k=1}^{p-1} C_k y_k,$$

where

(v) $$C_k \equiv \frac{c_1(X_{k+1}) - c_1(X_k)}{X_{k+1} - X_k}.$$

Thus C_k equals the slope of the linear approximation to $c_1(x_1)$ between the points X_k and X_{k+1}. In the example, (iv) becomes

(vi) $$\frac{(1^2 - 0)}{1 - 0} y_1 + \frac{(4^2 - 1^2)}{4 - 1} y_2 + \frac{(9^2 - 4^2)}{9 - 4} y_3 + \frac{(10^2 - 9^2)}{10 - 9} y_4$$
$$= 1y_1 + 5y_2 + 13y_3 + 19y_4.$$

If $x = 6$, a set of values for y_k corresponding to representation (ii) is $y_1 = 1, y_2 = 3$, $y_3 = 2$, and $y_4 = 0$, which in (vi) yields the value 42 as an approximation to $c_1(6) = 36$. Using (ii), the constraint (7) is

(vii) $$5y_1 + 5y_2 + 5y_3 + 5y_4 - 2x_2 \le 1.$$

If all the constraints in the model are linear, you can use the Bounded-Variables Algorithm explained in Sec. 5.10.

In this formulation, the analogous wording of the Property of Adjacent Weights is that y_{k+1} is positive only if y_k is at its upper bound $X_{k+1} - X_k$. To see why the property also holds in this version under the same hypotheses as before, consider the numerical example. Notice that all the variables y_k in (vii) have the same coefficient, so that they have an identical effect on the constraints. But the convexity of $c_1(x_1)$ causes the coefficients in (vi) to be monotone increasing. Hence, if the objective is to minimize $c(x)$, the variable y_k is always used to its fullest extent before y_{k+1} enters a trial solution.

For this version of the problem, when all the constraints are linear, the Bounded-Variables Algorithm can also be modified by a restricted-basis-entry rule forcing the Property of Adjacent Weights. At any iteration, allow y_{k+1} to enter the solution only if y_k is out of the basis and at its upper bound $X_{k+1} - X_k$. And allow y_k to leave the solution only if y_{k+1} is out of the basis and at its lower bound 0.   ◀

Separable constraint functions. Suppose the optimization problem contains a separable-type constraint

(9) $$\sum_{j=1}^{n} a_j(x_j) \le b.$$

Then the linearization techniques explained above may be applied here too. Again, consider only the variable x_1 and the associated function $a_1(x_1)$, and assume the identification in (2) and (3) is employed. The expression

(10) $$\sum_{k=1}^{p} a_1(X_k) w_k$$

is substituted for $a_1(x_1)$ in (9), and represents a polygonal approximation.

If all the constraints are separable, as in (9), and each component is a convex function, then using a transformation such as (10) leads to an optimal solution that satisfies the Property of Adjacent Weights. Such a solution approximates a globally optimal solution to the original problem. If one of the component functions is not convex, then you may have to force the Property by adding the restricted-basis-entry rule to *Simplex Criterion I* in the manner already described. The result may only approximate a locally, but not globally, optimal solution to the original problem.

　*Examples. Consider the quadratic programming illustration that was treated in Sec. 14.6:

(11)　　　　　maximize $(6x_1 - 3x_1^2) + (4x_2 - 2x_2^2) + (2x_3 - \frac{1}{3}x_3^2)$

subject to

(12)　　　　　　$x_1 + 2x_2 + x_3 \le 4$　and　all $x_j \ge 0$.

The terms in $c(x)$ have been grouped in (11) to display the function's separable character. Verify that each component function in parentheses is concave. Let the grid for x_1 and x_2 be (0, .4, .7, 1), and for x_3 be (0, 1, 1.5, 2, 3); let

$$x_1 \equiv 0u_1 + .4u_2 + .7u_3 + 1u_4$$

(13)　　　$x_2 \equiv 0v_1 + .4v_2 + .7v_3 + 1v_4$

$$x_3 \equiv 0w_1 + 1w_2 + 1.5w_3 + 2w_4 + 3w_5.$$

Then the constraints for the separable model are

$$.4u_2 + .7u_3 + 1u_4 + .8v_2 + 1.4v_3 + 2v_4 + 1w_2 + 1.5w_3 + 2w_4 + 3w_5 \le 4$$

(14)　　　　　　$\sum_{k=1}^{4} u_k = 1 \quad \sum_{k=1}^{4} v_k = 1 \quad \sum_{k=1}^{5} w_k = 1$

$$\text{all } u_k, v_k, w_k \ge 0.$$

Check that the objective function for the separable model is

(15)　maximize $1.92u_2 + \cdots + 1.28v_2 + \cdots + 1.6667w_2 + \cdots + 3w_5$.

The optimal solution is $u_4 = 1$, $v_3 = 1$, $w_3 = .8$, $w_5 = .2$ with an objective-function value 7.15. This corresponds to $x_1 = 1$, $x_2 = .7$, $x_3 = .8(1.5) + .2(2) = 1.6$ with a value 7.167 in (11). The exact optimal solution is $x_1 = .875$, $x_2 = .625$, $x_3 = 1.875$ with a value 7.25 in (11).

　Consider the "reciprocal" problem of maximizing

(16)　　　　　　　　$-x_1 - 2x_2 - x_3$

subject to

(17)　　　　　$-c(x) \le -7.25$　and　all $x_j = 0$.

The optimal point x is the same as that for (11) and (12). Explain why. Using the same grid and substitution of variables (13), the optimal solution to the separable approximation is $u_4 = 1$, $v_3 = 1$, $w_3 = .568$, $w_4 = .432$. This corresponds to

$x_1 = 1$, $x_2 = .7$, $x_3 = 1.716$ with a value of -4.116 in (16) and yields the value 7.270 for $c(x)$.

Obtaining separability. To summarize, suppose the entire optimization problem can be stated as

$$(18) \qquad\qquad \text{maximize} \sum_{j=1}^{n} c_j(x_j)$$

subject to

$$(19) \qquad\qquad \sum_{j=1}^{n} a_{ij}(x_j) \le b_i \quad \text{for } i = 1, 2, \ldots, m,$$

where (19) may also include nonnegativity constraints on the variables. Then the techniques explained above permit you to convert the model into a problem in which all the nonlinear functions have been approximated by piecewise-linear functions. If every $c_j(x_j)$ is concave, and if every $a_{ij}(x_j)$ is convex, then a solution obtained by the simplex method will be globally optimal for the approximate model and, hopefully, a good approximation to a globally optimal solution for the original problem. If these conditions are not satisfied, then by modifying the simplex method, you can obtain at least a local optimum for the approximate model.

The importance of the approach hinges on two factors. One is the ability to formulate a nonlinear problem so that the objective function and constraints contain only separable functions; this aspect is discussed next. The other is the severity of the computational burden imposed by the technique; this aspect is discussed afterwards.

Surprisingly many nonlinear expressions can be put into separable form by introducing additional variables and definitional constraints. To some extent, the techniques are ad hoc—they might even be called "tricks"—and, hence, do not lend themselves to systematic cataloguing. But a couple of illustrations will suggest the sort of approaches that work.

Suppose the model contains in the objective function or the constraints (or both) the product of two expressions:

$$(20) \qquad\qquad f(x_1, \ldots, x_n) \cdot g(x_1, \ldots, x_n).$$

A simple example would be $x_1 \cdot x_2$. As the first step in obtaining separability, substitute the single variable w wherever (20) appears. Second, introduce two more variables y and z, and relate them by adding the pair of definitional constraints

$$(21) \quad f(x_1, \ldots, x_n) - (y + z) = 0 \quad \text{and} \quad g(x_1 \ldots, x_n) - (y - z) = 0.$$

If $f(x_1, \ldots, x_n)$ and $g(x_1, \ldots, x_n)$ are themselves separable, then the restrictions in (21) are separable in *all* the variables; if not, you will have to apply further transformations to convert $f(x_1, \ldots, x_n)$ and $g(x_1, \ldots, x_n)$ into separable functions. Third, to complete the procedure, impose the separable-type constraint relating w to y and z:

(22) $$w - (y^2 - z^2) = 0.$$

This ensures that $[w \equiv f(x_1, \ldots, x_n) \cdot g(x_1, \ldots, x_n)]$. Explain why. Note that the function $-y^2$ in (22) is *not* convex. In short, the expression $f \cdot g$ in (20) is eliminated everywhere by substituting w in its place, and the constraints (21) and (22) are added to the model. Verify that if (20) is simply $x_1 \cdot x_2$, then the transformation requires three additional constraints and three additional variables.

As a second illustration, suppose the model contains the expression

(23) $$[h(x_1, \ldots, x_n)]^{f(x_1, \ldots, x_n)},$$

where $h(x_1, \ldots, x_n) > 0$ for all possible x_j. Here the function e^w is substituted for (23), and the definitional constraint

(24) $$w - f(x_1, \ldots, x_n) \cdot \ln h(x_1, \ldots, x_n) = 0$$

is added to the model. Although (24) is itself not separable, it can be treated by the approach used to separate the expression in (20) (where $g \equiv \ln h$).

Computational aspects. As you have seen, converting a nonlinear programming model into an approximate version with separable functions increases the size of the model in two ways: first, the separability transformations introduce new constraints and variables. Second, the subsequent linearization expands the number of constraints and variables even further. If the original problem contains only a few nonlinearities, this approach is quite workable. But if the model is highly nonlinear, then the technique may not be as efficient as the algorithms presented in the next chapter.

If the objective and constraint functions imply the Property of Adjacent Weights, then you can employ the ordinary simplex algorithm, which is available for all electronic computers. The modified method that forces this Property is not so widely available, but, nevertheless, is obtainable for most large computers.

In applying the method to an actual problem, you must, of course, consider the selection of the grid for each approximation. Broadly stated, the goal is to select the grids that will yield a nearly optimal solution for the original problem. Although this goal suggests a grid of finely spaced points, the countervailing factor is the resultant effect on the size of the approximate problem. Any further discussion of this aspect goes beyond the level of this text, but we point out that an alternative algorithm for exploiting a separable structure is explained in Sec. 15.10. This technique does not require that you *preselect* the grids; the method does, however, involve more computations at each iteration.

*14.8 DIRECT LINEARIZATION

Occasionally, a nonlinear objective function $c(x_1, x_2, \ldots, x_n)$ can be optimized by converting the problem into an equivalent one having a linear objective function with linear constraints, and then solving it by the simplex method. Of course, the transformed problem remains a linear programming model if the variables are further restricted by other linear constraints. Three important examples of direct linearization are given below.

Minimum sum of absolute deviations. Consider the following nonlinear objective function to be *minimized*:

$$(1) \qquad c(x) \equiv \sum_{k=1}^{p} | \sum_{j=1}^{n} c_{kj}x_j - f_k|.$$

For the conversion, impose the p linear constraints

$$(2) \qquad \sum_{j=1}^{n} c_{kj}x_j - f_k = y_k - z_k \quad \text{for } k = 1, 2, \ldots, p$$

or, on rewriting,

$$(3) \qquad \sum_{j=1}^{n} c_{kj}x_j - y_k + z_k = f_k \quad \text{for } k = 1, 2, \ldots, p,$$

where

$$(4) \qquad y_k \geq 0 \quad \text{and} \quad z_k \geq 0 \quad \text{for } k = 1, 2, \ldots, p.$$

The appropriate linear objective function to be *minimized* in the transformed model is

$$(5) \qquad \sum_{k=1}^{p} (y_k + z_k).$$

The idea of the transformation is that if the expression on the left of (2) is positive, then y_k equals this value and $z_k = 0$. Similarly, if the expression is negative, then $(-z_k)$ equals this value and $y_k = 0$. The optimization in (5) ensures that indeed either y_k or z_k, or both, will be zero in an optimal solution. The linear programming model, then, consists of (5), the constraints (3) and (4), plus any other constraints that must be satisfied by the x_j (such as nonnegativity).

Minimax objective. Next consider as the nonlinear objective function to be *minimized*:

$$(6) \qquad c(x) \equiv \text{maximum} \left(\sum_{j=1}^{n} c_{1j}x_j - f_1, \ldots, \sum_{j=1}^{n} c_{pj}x_j - f_p \right).$$

To make the transformation, impose the p linear constraints

$$(7) \qquad \sum_{j=1}^{n} c_{kj}x_j - f_k \leq y \quad \text{for } k = 1, 2, \ldots, p,$$

or, on rewriting,

$$(8) \qquad \sum_{j=1}^{n} c_{kj}x_j - y \leq f_k \quad \text{for } k = 1, 2, \ldots, p.$$

Here y is a variable unconstrained in sign. The linear objective function for the transformed model is

$$(9) \qquad \text{minimize } y.$$

Suppose $c(x)$ in (6) is modified to

(10) $c(x) \equiv \text{maximum} \left(|\sum_{j=1}^{n} c_{1j}x_j - f_1|, \ldots, |\sum_{j=1}^{n} c_{pj}x_j - f_p| \right).$

Note that

$$|\sum_{j=1}^{n} c_{ij}x_j - f_i| = \text{maximum} \left(\sum_{j=1}^{n} c_{ij}x_j - f_i, f_i - \sum_{j=1}^{n} c_{ij}x_j \right).$$

Hence, in addition to (8) and (9), the model for the objective (10) includes the constraints

(11) $-\sum_{j=1}^{n} c_{kj}x_j - y \leq -f_k \quad \text{for } k = 1, 2, \ldots, p,$

and $y \geq 0$. The objective function (10) is sometimes called a **Chebyshev criterion** (it minimizes the maximum absolute deviation).

Both (6) and (10), as well as the objective function (1), which minimizes the sum of the absolute deviations, occur in curve-fitting and regression problems. The coefficients c_{kj} are calculated for p sets of data on the n independent variables, where $p > n$, and the f_k are the associated values of the dependent variable. The x_j are the regression coefficients to be chosen for the curve-fitting expression.

Ratio of linear forms. Suppose the objective function to be *maximized* is

(12) $$c(x) \equiv \frac{c_0 + \sum_{j=1}^{n} c_j x_j}{f_0 + \sum_{j=1}^{n} f_j x_j}.$$

(Sometimes this model is referred to as **fractional programming**, and occasionally as **hyperbolic programming**.) To avoid having to consider a host of possibilities in the exposition assume that the x_j are so constrained that the denominator in (12) is strictly positive for all feasible values of x_j, and that the maximum of $c(x)$ is finite.

To convert the problem to a linear model, define the variable r as

(13) $$r \equiv (f_0 + \sum_{j=1}^{n} f_j x_j)^{-1},$$

and hence (12) can be written as

(14) $$c_0 r + \sum_{j=1}^{n} c_j x_j r.$$

By assumption, $r > 0$ for all feasible values of x_j. Next make a change of variables:

(15) $$y_j \equiv r x_j.$$

Then the transformed model becomes

(16) $$\text{maximize } c_0 r + \sum_{j=1}^{n} c_j y_j,$$

where, according to (13), the r and y_j must satisfy the linear constraint

(17)
$$f_0 r + \sum_{j=1}^{n} f_j y_j = 1,$$

and $r > 0$. Note that the change of variables (15) must also be performed in any other constraints on x_j. For example, if any additional conditions are linear

(18)
$$\sum_{j=1}^{n} a_{ij} x_j = b_i \quad \text{for } i = 1, 2, \ldots, m,$$

the transformed constraints are found by multiplying each relation in (18) by r, yielding

(19)
$$\sum_{j=1}^{n} a_{ij} y_j - b_i r = 0 \quad \text{for } i = 1, 2, \ldots, m.$$

Applications of (12) occur for certain kinds of production scheduling models in which the manufacturing processes generate scrap material. To illustrate, the denominator represents the total amount of raw material utilized by the production schedule, and the numerator the amount that is usable (nonscrap); thus, the ratio to be maximized by the schedule is the fraction of usable raw material.

*14.9 MAXIMIZING A CONVEX OBJECTIVE FUNCTION

Consider the case when all the constraints are linear and the objective function to be *maximized*, $c(x)$, is convex. Such an objective function is sometimes said to represent a situation with economies of scale. We continue to assume that $c(x)$ is well defined and possesses a finite maximum $\bar{c}$ over the feasible values of x. We need not assume, however, that each partial derivative $\partial c/\partial x_j$ is defined and continuous for all values of x satisfying the constraints. The convexity assumption itself ensures that $c(x)$ is continuous in the *interior* of the constraint region. The function $c(x)$ can have discontinuities at the *boundary* of the constraint set. For example, $c(x)$ can include a setup cost component that is charged only if a variable x_j is strictly positive. We can prove the following proposition.

FORM OF AN OPTIMAL SOLUTION. Given that all the constraints are linear and possess a basic feasible solution, if $c(x)$ is convex, well defined, and possesses a finite maximum over the feasible values of x, then there exists a *basic* solution that maximizes $c(x)$.

This result can be exploited to compute an optimal solution if the number of linear constraints is small, or if the model has a special structure. A few illustrations are given below.

Suppose the model is a Distribution of Effort Problem, discussed in Sec. 10.2; specifically, let the objective be to

(1)
$$\text{maximize } R(y_1, y_2, \ldots, y_s)$$

subject to a single linear constraint

(2) $$\sum_{j=1}^{s} H_j y_j = N,$$

where each $y_j \geq 0$ and is a continuous variable. Assume that $R(y)$ is convex and each $H_j > 0$. Then the proposition implies that there is an optimal policy containing only one y_j at a positive level. The optimal y_j can be found by comparing the values of $R(0, 0, \ldots, N/H_j, \ldots, 0)$ for $j = 1, 2, ., \ldots, s$. If there are m linear constraints, then an optimal solution can be found by comparing the objective function for each possible basic solution, of which there are no more than $\binom{n}{m}$. When m is small, or n is small relative to m, this enumeration is feasible on a large-scale computer. For example, if $m = 2$, then only $n(n-1)/2$ possibilities have to be considered.

A second illustration is the inventory model with deterministic demand and concave costs treated in Sec. 9.5. If you multiply the cost function by (-1), and thereby change the sense of the optimization, the resultant model meets the assumptions of maximizing a convex objective function subject to linear constraints.

The special structure of the linear constraints in this deterministic inventory model can be exploited to find all the basic feasible solutions. To illustrate, suppose demand in every period is positive and initial inventory is zero. Then there are only 2^{N-1} basic feasible schedules for an N-period horizon, which is smaller than $\binom{2N}{N}$. Each of these schedules corresponds to a pattern of periods in which the production variable is strictly positive (production in Period 1 must be positive), and satisfies the Form of an Optimal Policy given in Sec. 9.5. This complete enumeration is appropriate if total cost is a general concave function of all the production and inventory variables; the task can easily be done on a high-speed computer, provided that $N \leq 12$. But if the objective function is also separable in the cost functions for each period, then the algorithm in Sec. 9.6 can be applied, and the computations reduce to considering only $.5N^2$ possibilities.

▶ The Form of an Optimal Solution stated above holds for the case when $c(x)$ is linear, and hence convex. Since a linear function is also concave, a basic solution that is locally optimal must be globally optimal. These comments provide an alternative justification for the conclusion that when the simplex method terminates, the final basic solution is globally optimal. ◀

REVIEW EXERCISES

1 Suggest several managerial decision-making applications of mathematical programming models in which you would expect to find nonlinearities in the objective function or constraints. Be as specific as you can in describing the nature of the nonlinearities. State whether the relationships would be empirically observed or structurally derived (or a combination of both). Comment on whether you could use a linear approximation. Discuss what difficulties, if any, might arise in obtaining data to give a numerical representation of the nonlinearities.

2 Discuss why it is usually harder to solve a nonlinear programming problem containing n variables and m constraints than it is to solve a linear programming problem of the same dimensions.

3 Show how to modify (6) through (8) in Sec. 14.1 if there is a third constraint, $i = 3$, with a random b_i, and

(a) The joint probability that every constraint being satisfied is at least β.
(b) The joint probability that constraints $i = 1$ and $i = 2$ are satisfied is β_1, that $i = 2$ and $i = 3$ are satisfied is β_2, and that $i = 3$ and $i = 1$ are satisfied is β_3.
(c) Show how (8) can be transformed into an equivalent constraint containing the sum of two nonlinear functions (be sure to state any additional assumptions you require to write the transformation).

4 Discuss the possible decision-making implications of the following situation: you have applied an iterative algorithm to solve a nonlinear problem such as that given by (4) and (5) in Sec. 14.1, and have obtained a feasible trial solution $x_1^k, x_2^k, \ldots, x_n^k$ that yields a value $c(x_1^k, \ldots, x_n^k)$ which is close to being maximal (you conclude this from an available upper bound on the maximum value). You have good reasons to know, however, that the values of several x_j^k are far from optimal.

5 Assumptions (i) and (ii) in Sec. 14.3 imply that a function $c(x)$ of a single variable x attains its maximum for a value of x in the interval I. In each part below, determine whether $c(x)$ attains its maximum in the stated interval, and if not, whether (i) or (ii), or both, are not satisfied.

(a) $c(x) = 7x$ for $3 \leq x < 8$.
(b) $c(x) = \begin{cases} x & \text{for } 0 \leq x < \frac{1}{2} \\ x - 1 & \text{for } \frac{1}{2} \leq x \leq 1. \end{cases}$
(c) $c(x) = \left| \dfrac{1}{x - 2} \right|$ for $1 \leq x \leq 3$.
*(d) $c(x) = \begin{cases} 0 & \text{if } x \text{ is rational} \\ x & \text{otherwise} \end{cases}$ for $0 \leq x \leq 1$.

6 In each part below, state the values (if any) of the parameters a and b for which the function $c(x)$ is convex for $0 \leq x \leq 1$. Is concave. Is monotonic. Is unimodal.

(a) $c(x) = ax + b$.
(b) $c(x) = ax^b$.
(c) $c(x) = a^{bx}$.
(d) $c(x) = a \log bx$.
(e) Do the same for $-1 \leq x \leq 0$.
(f) Do the same for $-1 \leq x \leq 1$.

*7 In each part below, either prove the statement is true, or give a counterexample showing it is false. (You may assume the functions are of a single variable x.)

(a) The sum of two convex functions is convex.
(b) The sum of two concave functions is concave.
(c) The sum of two monotonic functions is monotonic.
(d) The sum of two unimodal functions is unimodal.
(e) The sum of a convex and a concave function is either convex or concave.
(f) The sum of a unimodal function and a convex function is either unimodal or convex.

(g) The difference between two convex functions can be convex, or concave, or neither, or both.

(h) If $c(x)$ possesses a well-defined second derivative, then the function is convex if $d^2c/dx^2 \geq 0$ for all x.

(i) The function $c(x)$ is concave if and only if $-c(x)$ is convex.

8 In each part below, apply the Method of Golden Sections to the example in Fig. 14.4, where

(a) $5 \leq x \leq 10$.

(b) $2 \leq x \leq 8$.

(c) $c(x) = 18 - 2x$ for $6 \leq x \leq 12$, and the initial search interval is $[0, 10]$.

9 In each part below, apply the Method of Golden Sections to search for a maximum; stop after $n = 3$.

(a) Case 2 in Fig. 14.1 over the interval $1 \leq x \leq 4$.

(b) Case 2 in Fig. 14.1 over the interval $0 \leq x \leq 3$.

(c) Case 3 in Fig. 14.1 over the interval $2 \leq x \leq 4$.

(d) Case 3 in Fig. 14.1 over the interval $0 \leq x \leq 2$.

*(e) Apply the upper bound (5) in Sec. 14.3 for parts (a) and (b). Demonstrate why (5) is inappropriate for parts (c) and (d).

*(f) Apply the Method of Interval Bisection to parts (a) and (b).

*10 After the description of the Method of Golden Sections in Sec. 14.3, the text states three properties of the algorithm, which are based on the definition of r in (4). Prove that these properties hold.

*11 Derive the bound (5) in the special material at the end of Sec. 14.3.

12 Consider the general algorithm for finding an unconstrained maximum, as described in Sec. 14.4.

(a) Explain what difficulties can arise if you use a fixed step size length, instead of an optimal step size.

(b) Use the example in Fig. 14.6 to illustrate the following approach for selecting directions. At the first iteration, let the direction be parallel to the coordinate axis for x_1, that is, let $d_1^0 = 1$ and all other $d_j^0 = 0$. At the next iteration, let the direction be parallel to the coordinate axis for x_2, that is, let $d_2^1 = 1$ and all other $d_j^1 = 0$. Continue in this way, eventually returning to the $d_1^k = 1$ again, and so on. (This is known as *coordinatewise ascent*.) Employ an optimal step size throughout. In how many iterations does the method converge? Rotate the axes of the ellipses in Fig. 14.6 by $45°$. Again illustrate the method and determine the convergence behavior.

(c) Explain in a two-dimensional diagram, like Fig. 14.6, why an optimal step size is indicated by a tangency condition on a contour. Try to draw the corresponding three-dimensional representation, where the third axis refers to values of the objective function.

13 (a) Verify that if $c(x_1, x_2, \ldots, x_n)$ is a quadratic function, then the expression that is

maximized to find an optimal step size is also a quadratic function of the step size.

(b) Assume you are given a quadratic function $c(x)$ of a single variable that is *strictly concave* for all x. Derive a formula for the unconstrained maximum of $c(x)$ and justify your derivation.

14 Consider the numerical example (4) and (5) in Sec. 14.5.

(a) Verify the formula in (6).
(b) Given (6), perform the intermediate algebra showing the optimal step size is that displayed in (7).
(c) Verify the results for $k = 0$, 1, and 2 in Fig. 14.8.

15 Consider the numerical example (4) and (5) in Sec. 14.5. Apply the method of steepest ascent with optimal step size for each of the starting points below. Terminate after completing the calculations for $k = 3$.

(a) $x_1^0 = x_2^0 = 0$ and $x_3^0 = 3$.
(b) $x_1^0 = 0$, $x_2^0 = 1$, and $x_3^0 = 3$.
(c) $x_1^0 = \frac{1}{3}$, $x_2^0 = 0$, and $x_3^0 = -\frac{5}{3}$.
(d) $x_1^0 = 2$, $x_2^0 = 2$, and $x_3^0 = 6$.

*16 Consider the Newton-Raphson Method of selecting directions, namely, (8) in the advanced material of Sec. 14.5. Demonstrate that letting each $x_j^0 = 0$ and solving the system (8) is equivalent to solving the system $\partial c/\partial x_j = 0$ for every j when $c(x)$ is quadratic.

*17 Explain what happens when the step size is, say, .9 times the optimal step size and you employ steepest ascent to determine directions. Use contours like those in Fig. 14.5 for illustration. Give a plausible explanation of why this so-called *subrelaxation approach* might converge faster than the approach using the optimal step size.

18 (a) Show that if $c(x)$ is strictly concave for all $x = (x_1, x_2, \ldots, x_n)$, where $c(\bar{x})$ is the maximum value, then there is no other $x \neq \bar{x}$ such that $c(x^*) = c(\bar{x})$ [that is, there is a unique point at which $c(x)$ reaches its maximum].
(b) Show that if $c(x)$ is a concave function, then $c(x_1 + td_1, \ldots, x_n + td_n)$ is a concave function of t.

19 Consider a function $c(x)$ of a single variable and suppose it satisfies conditions (i), (ii), and (iii) in Sec. 14.3.

(a) Is the condition $dc/dx = 0$ at a point x^* necessary or sufficient, or both, for $c(x^*)$ to be the unconstrained maximum value?
(b) Devise a condition for x^* that is both necessary and sufficient for $c(x^*)$ to be maximal. (Be careful in your answer, because $dc/dx = 0$ may hold over an interval of values for x.)

20 In each part below, write the function $c(x)$ in a format analogous to (4) in Sec. 14.6. Calculate all the first-order partial derivatives. Show a definitional relation, analogous to (7), for a free variable u associated with x_2.

(a) $3x_1 - 2x_2 + x_3 + 7x_1^2 + 3x_1x_2 - 8x_2x_1 + 20x_2^2$.

(b) $5x_1 + 9x_3 + 4x_1x_2 - 2x_1x_3 + 6x_2^2 + x_2x_3 - 3x_3^2 + x_3x_1 + 6x_3x_2$.

(c) $3(-4x_1 + 2x_2 + 3x_3 - 5)^2$.

(d) $(2x_1 + 3x_2 + 1)^2 + 2(4x_1 - x_3 + 2)^2 + 3(-5x_2 + 5x_3)^2$.

*(e) In each of the above expressions, eliminate the variable x_2 by substituting in the relation for the free variable u.

*(f) In each of the above expressions, eliminate the variable x_2 by substituting in the relation $1 - x_1 - x_3$.

21 Consider the function $c(x)$ in (3) of Sec. 14.6, and the partial derivatives in (5). Assume the trial values for each x_j are 0.

  (a) Does the objective function improve if you enter x_1? If you enter x_2? If you enter x_3? Describe the behavior of the objective function as you let x_1 increase, and leave the other x_j equal 0. Do the same for x_2.

  (b) In applying the *Quadratic Simplex Criterion II*, it is possible that the selected nonbasic variable x_j can be made arbitrarily large without violating the constraints. It is also possible that $\partial c/\partial x_j > 0$ for all nonnegative values of x_j (assuming the other nonbasic variables remain equal to 0). What would happen if these two conditions arose simultaneously? What assumption made at the beginning of Sec. 14.6 rules out these two conditions arising simultaneously?

22 Consider the example (8) and (9) in Sec. 14.6 solved by the Quadratic Simplex Algorithm.

  (a) Show all the intermediate calculations and verify the results in (10) through (30).

  (b) When you reach (20), enter u_2, instead of u_1, into the solution and continue the iterations until you obtain an optimal solution.

23 Consider the example (8) and (9) in Sec. 14.6. Apply the Quadratic Simplex Algorithm, where the problem is modified as indicated below.

  (a) Let the right-hand-side constant in (9) be 8, instead of 4.

  (b) Let the right-hand-side constant in (9) be 3, instead of 4.

  (c) Let the right-hand-side constant in (9) be 2, instead of 4.

  (d) Add the constraint $x_1 + x_2 \le 1$.

  (e) Add the constraint $x_2 + x_3 \le 2$.

  (f) Add the constraint $-2x_1 + 2x_3 \le 1$.

  (g) Let the objective function be $6x_1 + 4x_2 + 2x_3 - \frac{1}{3}x_1^2 - 2x_2^2 - 3x_3^2$.

  (h) Let the objective function be $2x_1 + 6x_2 + 4x_3 - 3x_1^2 - 2x_2^2 - \frac{1}{3}x_3^2$.

  (i) Add to the objective function the terms $-x_1x_2 - 2x_2x_3$.

24 Apply the Quadratic Simplex Algorithm in Sec. 14.6 to the example in Fig. 14.9, where the linear constraints are as indicated in the three cases below. Plot the trial solutions on a diagram like Fig. 14.9 to show the progress at each iteration.

  (a) Case 1: $x_1 + 2x_2 \le 6$
               $8x_1 + 6x_2 \le 23$
               $6x_1 + x_2 \le 12$.

  (b) Case 2: $x_1 + 2x_2 \le 5$
               $16x_1 + 12x_2 \le 37$
               $6x_1 + x_2 \le 12$.

(c) Case 3: $x_1 + 2x_2 \leq 5$
$16x_1 + 12x_2 \leq 37$
$24x_1 + 4x_2 \leq 27.$

25 Consider the example of a separable function $c_1(x_1) = x_1^2$ treated in Sec. 14.7. Modify the analysis in (5) through (8) when $0 \leq x_1 \leq 20$, and the grid points are 0, 5, 8, 10, 15, 20. What weight values in the approximation correspond to $x_1 = 6$ and how close is the approximation value? Answer these questions for $x_1 = 9$. For $x_1 = 12$. For $x_1 = 17$.

26 Suppose $c_1(x_1) = \sqrt{x_1}$. Explain how to construct a piecewise-linear approximation for $0 \leq x_1 \leq 10$, using the grid points 0, 1, 4, 9, 10. Show how the linear constraint $3x_1 + 4x_2 \geq 12$ appears after substituting the approximation. What weight values in your approximation correspond to $x_1 = 6$?

27 (a) Give a plausible argument establishing the Property of Adjacent Weights in Sec. 14.7. (*Suggestion:* use the example (5) through (8) to illustrate your reasoning; remember that x^2 is a convex function.)

(b) Suppose you want to maximize $c(x)$ in (1), where $c_1(x_1) = x_1^2$ and $c_j(x_j) = c_j x_j$ for all other j, and where you use the approximation in (5) and (6). Assume $x_1 = 8$ in a truly optimal solution. What difficulty can arise if you do not use a restricted-basis-entry rule?

(c) Give a plausible argument establishing that if all the constraints are separable, as in (9), and each component is a convex function, then using a transformation such as (10) leads to an optimal solution that satisfies the Property of Adjacent Weights.

*28 Consider the alternative technique for representing a separable function, as described and illustrated in (i) through (vii) of the special material in Sec. 14.7.

(a) Modify the analysis in (vi) and (vii) when $0 \leq x_1 \leq 20$, and the grid points are 0, 5, 8, 10, 20. What values for the y_k correspond to $x_1 = 6$ and how close is the approximation value? Answer these questions for $x_1 = 9$. For $x_1 = 12$. For $x_1 = 17$.

(b) Suppose $c_1(x_1) = \sqrt{x_1}$. Explain how to apply the method for $0 \leq x_1 \leq 10$, using the grid points 0, 1, 4, 9, 10. Show how the linear constraint $3x_1 + 4x_2 \geq 12$ appears after substituting the approximation. What values for the y_k correspond to $x_1 = 6$?

*29 Consider the example (11) and (12) in Sec. 14.7.

(a) Write the objective function (15) in full detail. Verify that the stated solution is indeed optimal.

(b) Indicate how to revise (13) through (15) if the grid for both x_1 and x_2 is (0, .3, .6, .8, 1), and for x_3 is (0, 1.2, 1.4, 1.6, 1.8, 3).

(c) Obtain an optimal solution for the approximate problem in part (b). (*Hint:* use the information you have above for the truly optimal solution.) Indicate what this answer corresponds to in the original problem.

(d) Consider the "reciprocal" problem (16) and (17). Find an optimal solution to a separable approximation, using the grids in part (b). Indicate what this answer corresponds to in the original problem.

30 Convert each problem below into a separable form.

(a) maximize $x_1x_2 + x_2x_3 + x_1x_2x_3$ subject to

$$x_1^2 + x_1 - 2x_1x_2x_3 \leq 0$$
$$2x_2^2 + 3x_2 + 6x_2x_3 \leq 12$$
$$x_3^2 + 4x_1x_3 \leq 5$$
$$\text{every } x_j \geq 0.$$

(b) maximize $(x_1 + 2x_2 + 3x_3)(x_1 + x_3)$ subject to

$$(x_1 - x_2 + 4x_3)^2 + 3(2 + x_1x_2)^{(x_1x_3 + x_2)} \leq 52$$
$$x_1x_2 \geq 1$$
$$\text{every } x_j \geq 0.$$

(c) maximize $5(2 + x_1x_2 + x_3)(x_3/x_4)^{(x_1 - x_2)}$ subject to

$$x_1x_2x_3x_4 \leq 16$$
$$x_1 \geq 0 \quad x_2 \geq 0 \quad x_3 \geq 2 \quad x_4 \geq 2$$

(d) maximize $4x_1x_2x_3$ subject to

$$(5 + 3x_1)^{x_1 + 2x_2^2}\left(\frac{2x_3}{x_3}\right) \leq 100$$
$$x_1 \geq 0 \quad x_2 \geq 0 \quad x_3 \geq 1.$$

*(e) Suppose after obtaining separability in each part, you then approximate every nonlinear separable function by a piecewise-linear function using 10 grid points (for each function). Calculate the size of the corresponding linear programming problem. Show your analysis in detail.

*31 Consider the three objective functions (1), (6), and (10) in Sec. 14.8. Suppose the context of the problem is fitting a linear regression, where c_{k1} refers to the kth value of the independent variable, c_{k2} the "coefficient" of the intercept, and f_k the observed value associated with c_{k1}. Thus, x_1 is the slope of the fitted regression line and x_2 is the intercept. Specifically, assume $c_{k1} = k$ and $c_{k2} = 1$ for $k = 1, 2, \ldots, 10$, and

$$f_1 = 87 \quad f_2 = 100 \quad f_3 = 107 \quad f_4 = 98 \quad f_5 = 99$$
$$f_6 = 108 \quad f_7 = 104 \quad f_8 = 113 \quad f_9 = 116 \quad f_{10} = 107.$$

(a) Assuming there are no restrictions on x_1 and x_2, write in full detail an equivalent linear programming model for minimizing $c(x)$ given by (1). By (6). By (10).
(b) Indicate how your formulations in part (a) change if you also impose the constraints $\frac{1}{2} \leq x_1 \leq 2$ and $x_2 \geq 2$.
*(c) Write the dual linear programming problems associated with your answers in part (a).
(d) Show how to formulate an optimization model for minimizing the sums of the squares of the differences between the linear fit and f_k. First assume x_1 and x_2 are unconstrained. Then impose the restrictions in part (b).

*32 Consider the problem

$$\text{minimize } [\text{maximum } (x - 2, -x, -\tfrac{1}{4}x - \tfrac{1}{2})].$$

(a) Plot each of the linear functions, show the piecewise-linear curve of the maximum of the three functions, and indicate where the minimum occurs.

(b) Formulate the problem using approach (8) and (9) in Sec. 14.8. Then draw the solution space representation for x and y, and show the optimal solution.

(c) Answer parts (a) and (b), also using (11), for the objective function

$$\text{minimize } [\text{maximum } (|x - 2|, |-x|, |-\tfrac{1}{4}x - \tfrac{1}{2}|)].$$

If your answers differ, explain why.

*33 In each part below, assume that $0 \le x \le 1$ and the function $c(x)$ to be maximized is as specified. Plot the function $c(x)$ for x in the feasible region. Formulate an equivalent linear problem using the approach in (13) through (19) of Sec. 14.8. Draw the solution space representation for this equivalent problem and indicate the optimal solution.

(a) $\dfrac{2 + 3x}{4 - x}.$ (c) $\dfrac{2 - 2x}{4 + x}.$

(b) $\dfrac{2 - 3x}{4 - x}.$ (d) $\dfrac{2 + 2x}{4 + x}.$

*34 Convert the following problem into an equivalent linear model:

$$\text{maximize } \frac{-3 + 2x_1 + 4x_2 - 5x_3}{6 + 3x_1 - x_2}$$

subject to

$$x_1 - x_2 \ge 0$$
$$7x_1 + 9x_2 + 10x_3 \le 30$$
$$x_1 \ge 0 \quad x_2 \ge 1 \quad x_3 \ge 0.$$

*35 Devise an argument establishing the Form of an Optimal Solution in Sec. 14.9. [*Suggestion:* illustrate your reasoning by using Fig. 14.9 where you maximize $-c(x)$.]

*36 Find an optimal solution to

$$\text{maximize } (4y_1 + 3y_2 - y_3 + 1)^2$$

subject to

$$3y_1 + 4y_2 + 2y_3 = 12$$
$$\text{every } y_j \ge 0.$$

Justify your answer.

*37 Section 14.9 discusses the computational implications of knowing that an optimum occurs at a basic or extreme-point solution. Parts (a) and (b) refer to a numerical evaluation mentioned in the text.

(a) Calculate the maximum number of basic feasible solutions to a problem having m linear constraints and n unknowns, for $m = 2, 3, 4$, and $n = 6, 7, 8$ (altogether nine pairs of m and n).

(b) Calculate 2^{N-1} and $\binom{2N}{N}$ for $N = 1, 2, 3, 4, 5, 6$.

38 Explain your understanding of the following terms:

nonlinear programming
end-point (or extreme-point) solution
interior point
boundary point
unconstrained maximization
   (minimization)
*supremum
discontinuity
continuous function
bounded function
convex function
concave function
strictly convex (concave) function
*quasi-convex (-concave) function
unimodal function
adaptive search
local maximum (minimum)
global maximum (minimum)
inflection point
Method of Golden Sections
*Method of Interval Bisection
necessary and/or sufficient condition
direction
step size (optimal step size)
contours
method of steepest ascent

myopic rule
gradient
*directional-derivative
infinite convergence
convergent sequence (subsequence)
orthogonal
*zigzagging
*Newton-Raphson Method
*modified gradient
*subrelaxation
stationary point
quadratic programming problem
Quadratic Simplex Algorithm
free variable
reduced partial derivative
quadratic form
negative (positive) semidefinite
separable function
piecewise-linear (or polygonal)
   approximation
Property of Adjacent Weights
restricted-basis-entry rule
*direct linearization
*Chebyshev criterion
*fractional (or hyperbolic) programming.

COMPUTATIONAL AND FORMULATION EXERCISES

39 Consider the Quadratic Simplex Method described in Sec. 14.6.

(a) Suggest a way to apply the algorithm where not every $b_i \geq 0$ and not every s_i is present in the constraints (2).

(b) Discuss how the algorithm operates if there are no linear and nonnegativity constraints. Illustrate your discussion with the objective function (8).

(c) Explain the way the algorithm proceeds in the terminology of Sec. 14.4, namely, in terms of selecting a set of directions and choosing a step size. Be sure you show, explicitly, what directions are taken at each iteration. Also comment on whether the step size is optimal. [*Suggestion:* illustrate your answer by using the example (8) and (9) in Sec. 14.6.]

40 Consider the objective function: maximize $6x_1 - 2x_1^2 + 2x_1x_2 - 2x_2^2$.

(a) Solve by the method of steepest ascent, starting at $x_1^0 = x_2^0 = 0$. Illustrate the progress of the iterations on a two-dimensional diagram. Stop after $k = 5$ iterations.

(b) Rework part (a), starting at $x_1^0 = x_2^0 = 10$.

(c) Impose the constraints $x_1 + x_2 \leq 2$, $x_1 \geq 0$, and $x_2 \geq 0$. Solve by the Quadratic Simplex Method. Illustrate the progress of the iterations on a solution space diagram.

(d) Rework part (c), letting $x_1 + x_2 \leq 3$.

(e) Rework part (c), letting $x_1 + x_2 \leq \frac{1}{2}$.

(f) Rework part (c), letting the linear constraint be $2x_1 + x_2 \leq 2$.

(g) Rework part (c), letting the linear constraint be $x_1 + 2x_2 \leq 2$.

*(h) Solve the unconstrained problem using the Quadratic Simplex Method.

(i) Rework part (c), adding the constraint $x_1 \leq 1$.

(j) Rework part (c), adding the constraint $x_1 \leq 1\frac{7}{12}$.

(k) Rework part (c), adding the constraint $x_2 \leq \frac{1}{6}$.

(l) Rework part (c), adding the constraint $x_2 \leq \frac{5}{12}$.

41 Consider the objective function: maximize $36x_1 + 36x_2 - 5x_1^2 - 8x_1x_2 - 5x_2^2$.

(a) Solve by the method of steepest ascent, starting at $x_1^0 = x_2^0 = 0$. Illustrate the progress of the iterations on a two-dimensional diagram. Stop after $k = 5$ iterations.

(b) Rework part (a), starting at $x_1^0 = x_2^0 = 3$.

(c) Impose the constraints $x_1 + x_2 \leq 2$, $x_1 \geq 0$ and $x_2 \geq 0$. Solve by the Quadratic Simplex Method. Illustrate the progress of the iterations on a solution space diagram.

(d) Rework part (c), but let the linear constraint be $x_1 + 3x_2 \leq 2$.

(e) Rework part (c), adding the constraint $x_1 \leq \frac{1}{2}$.

(f) Impose the constraints $x_1 - x_2 \leq 3$, $-x_1 + x_2 \leq 3$, $x_1 \geq 0$, and $x_2 \geq 0$. Solve by the Quadratic Simplex Method. Illustrate the progress of the iterations on a solution space diagram.

42 Consider the objective function:

$$\text{maximize } 16x_1 + 16x_2 + 40x_3 - 4x_1^2 + 6x_1x_2 - 6x_1x_3 - 11x_2^2 + 8x_2x_3 - 11x_3^2.$$

(a) Solve by the method of steepest ascent, starting at $x_1^0 = x_2^0 = x_3^0 = 0$. Stop after $k = 5$.

(b) Rework part (a), starting at $x_1^0 = x_2^0 = x_3^0 = 3$.

(c) Impose the constraints $x_1 + x_2 + x_3 \leq 4$, and every $x_j \geq 0$. Solve by the Quadratic Simplex Method.

*(d) Solve the unconstrained problem using the Quadratic Simplex Method.

43 Consider the objective function:

$$\text{maximize } 40x_1 + 10x_2 + 30x_3 - 6x_1^2 - 8x_1x_2 - 4x_1x_3 - 11x_2^2 + 14x_2x_3 - 9x_3^2.$$

(a) Solve by the method of steepest ascent, starting at $x_1^0 = x_2^0 = x_3^0 = 0$. Stop after $k = 5$.

(b) Rework part (a), starting at $x_1^0 = x_2^0 = x_3^0 = 5$.

(c) Rework part (a), starting at $x_1^0 = 2$, $x_2^0 = 3$, $x_3^0 = 1$.

(d) Impose the constraints $x_1 + x_2 + x_3 \leq 3$ and every $x_j \geq 0$. Solve by the Quadratic Simplex Method.

*(e) Solve the unconstrained problem using the Quadratic Simplex Method.

44 Consider a mathematical optimization model consisting of n nonnegative variables, a linear objective function, $m - 1$ linear constraints, and one quadratic constraint,

$$\sum_{j=1}^{n} a_j x_j + \sum_{j=1}^{n} \sum_{k=1}^{n} a_{jk} x_j x_k \geq b,$$

where the left-hand function is concave. Suggest a computational scheme for finding a numerical solution to a particular problem that employs linear and quadratic programming algorithms.

45 Consider the problem

$$\text{maximize } 2x_1^2 + x_2^2$$

subject to

$$2x_1 + x_2 \leq 2 \quad x_1 \geq 0 \quad \text{and} \quad x_2 \geq 0.$$

(a) Solve by inspection.
(b) Apply the Quadratic Simplex Algorithm. First, let the initial basic solution be "all slack." Next, let the initial basic solution be $x_1 = 1$. Discuss the behavior of the algorithm on this problem.
(c) Transform the model into an approximate problem using the separable programming technique in Sec. 14.7. Let the grid for x_1 be $(0, \frac{1}{2}, \frac{3}{4}, 1)$, and for x_2 be $(0, \frac{1}{2}, 1, \frac{3}{2}, 2)$. Apply the simplex method to find a solution. Discuss your result. (Do you have to use the restricted-basis-entry rule?)

46 Consider the problem

$$\text{maximize } 6x_1 + 8x_2 - x_1^2 - x_2^2$$

subject to

$$4x_1^2 + x_2^2 \leq 16$$

$$3x_1 + 5x_2 \leq 15$$

$$x_1 \geq 0 \quad \text{and} \quad x_2 \geq 0.$$

(a) Formulate the model into an approximate problem using the separable programming technique in Sec. 14.7. Let the grid for x_1 be $(0, \frac{1}{2}, 1, \frac{3}{2}, 2)$, and for x_2 be $(0, 1, 2, 3, 4)$.
(b) Find an optimal solution to the approximation in part (a). Draw a solution space diagram and indicate the progress of the iterations as well as the truly optimal solution.
*(c) Change the signs of all the coefficients in the objective function and reverse the inequality sign in the first constraint. Alter your formulation in part (a) accordingly. Apply the simplex method to find a solution. (Do you have to use the restricted-basis-entry rule?) Draw a solution space diagram and indicate the progress of the iterations as well as the truly optimal solution.

47 *One-Potato, Two-Potato Problem* (Sec. 1.6). Recall in this example that there are two sources of supply, each source yielding different fractions of the products French fries, hash browns, and flakes. Suppose that it is possible, at differing costs, to alter these yields somewhat. Let f_1, f_2, and f_3 be the fractional yield per unit of weight of Source 1 potatoes made into the three products; similarly, let g_1, g_2, and g_3 be the

yields for Source 2. Suppose that each f_i and g_i can vary within plus or minus 10% of the yields shown in Fig. 1.1. Let $c_1(f_1, f_2, f_3)$ and $c_2(g_1, g_2, g_3)$ be the *expense* associated with obtaining the corresponding yields.

(a) Formulate the appropriate optimization model.
(b) Apply the techniques in Sec. 14.7 to convert the problem into separable programming form. Discuss whether you would apply a restricted-basis-entry rule to obtain a numerical solution.

48 The Tooke Gas Company desires a scientific approach to setting equitable salaries. The company plans to base its pay structure on the following point system. The Personnel Department rates each type of job according to three different characteristics (such as skill required, responsibility exercised, seniority demanded). Suppose that the first factor is evaluated for five levels of achievement, designated by $A1$, $A2$, $A3$, $A4$, or $A5$, where $A1$ is the lowest and $A5$ the highest level of attainment. Similarly, the second factor is evaluated $B1$, $B2$, $B3$, or $B4$, where $B1$ is the lowest and $B4$ the highest level. And the third factor is scored as $C1$, $C2$, $C3$, $C4$, or $C5$, where $C1$ is the lowest and $C5$ the highest level. The company wants to assign a dollar value to each level within each characteristic, and thereby to determine the *average* salary for a type of job according to the sum of the assigned dollar values. For example, suppose a job type is rated $A2$, $B3$, and $C5$. If $A2$ has been assigned a value of $300, $B3$ a value of $400, and $C5$ a value of $250, then the resultant *average* wage for the job is ($300 + $400 + $250 = $950).

Assume the company has evaluated P job types, and thinks that a 10% increase in the present average salary for each job is fair. Let a_p, b_p, and c_p be the ratings of the three categories for the pth job, and let s_p be 110% of the present *average* salary. The company wants to assign values for $A1, A2, \ldots, A5, B1, \ldots, B4, C1, \ldots, C5$ so as to minimize the sum of squares between the resulting new *average* wage and s_p, for $p = 1, 2, \ldots, P$. Show how to formulate this problem as a nonlinear programming model. Assume each assigned value must be at least $20 greater than the next lower level (that is, the value of $A2$ must be at least $20 greater than the assigned value of $A1$), and that the assigned values for $A1, B1$, and $C1$ must each be at least $25. Illustrate the constraints for the jobs using the data that Job 1 has ratings $A3$, $B1$, and $C4$, and $s_1 = $10,000; and Job 2 has ratings $A2$, $B3$, and $C5$, and $s_2 = $12,000.

49 Consider the regression model $y = f(x) +$ error, where y is the dependent variable and x is the independent variable. Assume you have available p paired observations of the independent and dependent variables, denoted by x_k and y_k, for $k = 1, 2, \ldots, p$, and wish to estimate the function $f(x)$ from these data. Suppose you assume no specific form for $f(x)$, such as a linear or quadratic function. For simplicity, assume that the values of x_k are distinct, that is, $x_i \neq x_j$ for $i \neq j$, and the x_k are ordered such that $x_1 < x_2 < \cdots < x_p$. Let f_k represent the value of $f(x_k)$ in the estimated regression function. (Note that f_k may have any sign.)

(a) Write a set of equations, one for each k, determining the error e_k between the estimated value f_k and the observed value of the dependent variable y_k. (Note that e_k may have any sign.)
(b) If there are no further constraints on the f_k, state what their optimal values would be so as to minimize the sum of e_k^2, for $k = 1, 2, \ldots, p$.

(c) Explain how to constrain f_k such that the estimated function for $f(x)$ is monotonic increasing. Is monotonic decreasing. Is increasing only for $x \leq x_4$.

(d) Explain how to constrain f_k such that the estimated function for $f(x)$ is convex. Is concave.

(e) Explain how to constrain f_k such that estimated values of $f(x_i)$ and $f(x_{i+1})$ differ by no more than $d > 0$. Differ by at least d.

(f) Indicate how the above formulations can be altered if there are several x_k that are equal.

*(g) Discuss the type and size of model you obtain if the objective is to minimize the sum of absolute deviations $|e_k|$. If the objective is to minimize the maximum absolute deviation.

*50 (a) Consider the problem of "minimizing the sum of absolute deviations" given by (1) in Sec. 14.8. (Assume that each x_j is unrestricted in sign.) Write the dual linear programming problem. Show how the dual problem can be transformed to a problem having n linear constraints and p nonnegative upper-bounded variables.

(b) Consider the problem of "minimizing the maximum absolute deviation" given by (10) in Sec. 14.8. (Assume that each x_j is unrestricted in sign.) Write the dual linear programming problem.

51 *Trim Problem.* Consider the model described in exercise 25 of Chap. 2. For simplicity, alter the data as follows. Assume the jumbo reel is 44 inches wide, the customer orders are for four reels of 13-inch width, and four reels of 14-inch width. Suppose the company considers using only two cutting combinations, namely, (two reels each 13 inches wide, one reel of 14-inch width) and (one reel of 13-inch width, 2 reels each 14 inches wide).

(a) Formulate the associated linear programming model where the objective is to minimize total trim. Draw a solution space diagram and indicate the optimal solution.

(b) Suppose, instead, that the objective is to minimize the *fraction* of trim waste, that is, the ratio of total trim to total liner board used, inclusive of trim waste. Assume that an optimal solution is at an extreme point of the feasible region and find the best schedule. Comment on the relative merit of the solutions in parts (a) and (b).

(c) Suppose, instead, that the objective is to minimize the ratio of total trim to total liner board shipped to the customers (that is, total liner board used exclusive of trim waste). Assume that an optimal solution is at an extreme point of the feasible region and find the best schedule. Comment on the relative merit of the solutions in parts (a) and (c).

*(d) Utilize the formulation (12) through (19) in Sec. 14.8 in parts (b) and (c) to establish equivalent linear programs. Verify that the solutions you found are optimal in these equivalent linear programs.

MIND-EXPANDING EXERCISES

52 (a) Consider the function $g(c)$ which is defined as

$$g(c_1, c_2, \ldots, c_n) \equiv \text{maximize} \sum_{j=1}^{n} c_j x_j$$

subject to

$$\sum_{j=1}^{n} a_{ij} x_j \leq b_i \quad \text{for} \quad i = 1, 2, \ldots, m$$

$$\text{every } x_j \geq 0.$$

Thus $g(c)$ represents the optimal value for a linear programming problem having objective function coefficients $c \equiv (c_1, c_2, \ldots, c_n)$. Determine if $g(c)$ is a convex or a concave function.

(b) Consider the function $h(b)$ which is defined as

$$h(b_1, b_2, \ldots, b_m) \equiv \text{maximize} \sum_{j=1}^{n} c_j x_j,$$

where the x_j are subject to the constraints in part (a). Thus $h(b)$ represents the optimal value for a linear programming problem having right-hand-side constants $b \equiv (b_1, b_2, \ldots, b_m)$. Determine if $h(b)$ is a convex or a concave function. Comment on whether your result means that the optimal value for the ith dual variable overstates or understates the benefit of having an additional unit of the scarce resource for the ith constraint.

53 Prove the Sufficient Condition for a Maximum of a Concave Function that is stated in Sec. 14.5.

54 Suppose $c(x_1, x_2, \ldots, x_n)$ is a concave function. Consider two points $w \equiv (w_1, w_2, \ldots, w_n)$ and $y \equiv (y_1, y_2, \ldots, y_n)$. Show that the function $C(t) \equiv c(tw + (1 - t)y)$ is concave in t, where $0 \leq t \leq 1$. What is the corresponding result if $c(x_1, x_2, \ldots, x_n)$ is convex?

55 Section 14.4 states a Necessary Condition for a Maximum of $c(x_1, x_2, \ldots, x_n)$ in terms of the first-order partial derivatives. Assume that $c(x)$ possesses continuous second-order partial derivatives. Show that, in addition, if $c(\bar{x})$ is maximal, then the quadratic form

$$\sum_{j=1}^{n} \sum_{k=1}^{n} \frac{\partial^2 c(\bar{x})}{\partial x_j \partial x_k} x_j x_k$$

must be negative semidefinite. [In linear algebra books, this condition is sometimes stated as "the Hessian of the function $c(x)$ evaluated at $\bar{x}$ must be negative semidefinite."]

56 Consider the separable programming model in Sec. 14.7. Suppose the objective function, which is to be minimized, contains $c_1(x_1) = x_1^2$, where $0 \leq x_1 \leq 10$.

(a) Explain how the value of $c_1(x_1)$ can be approximated by a value y, where y is constrained by

$$y \geq \text{maximum } (p_1 x_1 + q_1, p_2 x_2 + q_2, \ldots, p_k x_k + q_k).$$

Using the illustration in Fig. 14.10, let $p_1 = 1$ and $q_1 = 0$, corresponding to the first linear segment. What are the other values for p_i and q_i in Fig. 14.10? Comment on the merits of this approximation as compared to the approximation in (5) through (18).

(b) Discuss what shape characteristics a function $c(x)$ of a single variable x must have in order for the approximation approach in part (a) to be valid.

(c) Assume that the sense of optimization is maximization. Will the approach in part (a) work? Explain. Give a formulation analogous to that in part (a) that will work if $c(x)$ is a concave function.

*(d) Suggest how the approach in part (a) can be generalized to handle convex functions $c(x_1, x_2, \ldots, x_n)$ of several variables.

57 Consider the function $c(x)$ of a single variable x, where $0 \leq x \leq U$. Suppose you want to approximate $c(x)$ by a continuous piecewise-linear function having n segments. Assume that the vertices of the approximation lie on $c(x)$ [that is, the approximation has the same value as $c(x)$ at each vertex], and that the vertices can occur only at values $x = 0, 1, 2, \ldots, U$, where U is integer-valued and much larger than n.

(a) Devise a dynamic programming formulation to find an approximation that minimizes the maximum absolute deviation between the approximation and $c(x)$ for $x = 0, 1, 2, \ldots, U$.

(b) Show how to alter your formulation in part (a) to minimize the sum of the absolute deviations between the approximation and $c(x)$ at $x = 0, 1, 2, \ldots, U$.

*58 Consider the fractional programming model and its equivalent linear programming formulation (12) through (19) in Sec. 14.9.

(a) Suppose you have found an optimal solution to the equivalent linear program using the simplex method. Assume x_k is a nonbasic variable in the optimal solution. Explain how you can find an interval of values for c_k over which the solution remains optimal. Do the same for f_k. Do the same for an a_{ik}. [*Suggestion:* let w_i be the dual variable corresponding to equation (19) and w_0 be the dual variable corresponding to equation (17).]

(b) Assume that $f_0 > 0$. Show how you can use (17) to eliminate the variable r so that the equivalent linear program contains only m constraints. Show how to modify your answer if $f_0 = 0$.

(c) Devise an algorithmic technique that maintains the m constraints in their original form, uses *Criterion II* of the simplex method to select the basic variable to remove, employs the usual pivoting procedure, but that calculates $\partial c(x)/\partial x_j$, evaluated at the current basic solution, for each nonbasic variable and enters that variable having the most positive value for its partial derivative. Explain how this approach differs, if at all, from applying the simplex method to the equivalent linear program (16), (17), and (19).

CONTENTS

CHAPTER 15

Advanced Techniques in Nonlinear Programming[†]

15.1 LARGE-STEP APPROACHES

In the previous chapter, you saw how to solve several important cases of nonlinear programming problems. Each technique exploited some special form of the objective function—quadratic or separable—as well as a special form of the constraints—linear or separable. Now you will study the solution of more general nonlinear programming problems.

The techniques presented below do not permit the objective function $c(x)$ to be completely arbitrary. It must possess at least the smoothness properties assumed in the case of unconstrained maximization treated in Sec. 14.4. In the initial four sections of this chapter, we assume that all the constraints are linear. Then, starting in Sec. 15.5, we treat models containing nonlinear constraints. These restrictions must also satisfy certain smoothness and shape properties.

To keep matters clear, we repeat the optimization model to be solved along with the postulates on $c(x)$. In Secs. 15.2 through 15.4, we consider the problem

$$(1) \qquad \text{maximize } c(x_1, x_2, \ldots, x_n)$$

subject to

$$(2) \qquad \sum_{j=1}^{n} a_{ij}x_j + s_i = b_i \quad \text{for } i = 1, 2, \ldots, m,$$

$$\text{all } x_j \geq 0 \quad \text{and} \quad \text{all } s_i \geq 0.$$

To avoid an elaborate discussion that would be necessary to handle "all cases,"

[†] This chapter requires a knowledge of differential calculus.

577

assume that the constraints (2) satisfy the stipulations:

(i) All $b_i \geq 0$, and hence there exists a feasible basic solution to the constraints, namely, all $x_j = 0$ and each $s_i = b_i$.
(ii) The constraints (2) are sufficiently restrictive so that the maximum of $c_1 x_1 + c_2 x_2 + \cdots + c_n x_n$ is finite over all feasible x, for *arbitrarily* chosen constants c_j.

Assumption (i) ensures that the model has a feasible solution, and trivializes the task of finding such a solution. If assumption (i) is dropped, then the algorithms must be expanded to show how to find a feasible solution when one exists.

Assumption (ii) is sometimes termed a **regularization postulate**. It serves two purposes in explaining the algorithms below. First, it eliminates having to deal with unbounded solutions arising during the intermediate steps of the methods, when $c(x)$ is approximated by a linear function. Second, when coupled with the smoothness assumptions on $c(x)$, it rules out an unbounded optimal solution to the original problem (1) and (2). [One way to ensure assumption (ii) is to include in (2) a constraint that the sum of all the variables cannot exceed a large, but finite, upper bound.] If assumption (ii) is eliminated, then the steps of the algorithms have to be amended in order to handle the possibility of an unbounded solution at an intermediate iteration.

Assume that $c(x)$ also satisfies the following smoothness and shape conditions:

(iii) $c(x)$ is single-valued and finite for each x satisfying the constraints (2).
(iv) Every partial derivative $\partial c(x)/\partial x_j$ is single-valued, finite, and continuous, and hence $c(x)$ is continuous at each x satisfying the constraints (2).
(v) $c(x)$ possesses a finite maximum $\bar{c}$ over all values of x satisfying the constraints (2).

If you compare (iii) through (v) with assumptions (i) through (iii) made in Sec. 14.4, you will find (iii) through (v) apply to only those x that are feasible in the constraints. The condition that $c(x)$ reaches its maximum for finite values of x_j is implied by assumptions (i) through (v). Assumptions (iii) through (v) can be weakened, at the expense of increasing the number of cases that have to be treated in the steps of the algorithms.

Preliminary observations. Note that formulation (1) and (2) includes, as a special case, the quadratic programming problem considered in Sec. 14.6. Therefore, the same kinds of optimal solutions that arise there can also occur here. Specifically, an optimal solution may be in the interior of the constraint region; or on the boundary but not at an extreme point; or at an extreme point. Since an optimal solution need not be at a vertex of the constraint set, more than m of the x_j variables may be strictly positive in an optimal solution. Further, all the slack variables s_i may be positive, which occurs when an optimal solution is in the interior of the constraint region. Be sure to see how each algorithm below allows for the possibility that all n of the x_j and all m of the s_i may be strictly positive in an optimal solution.

As in the case of unconstrained maximization, the algorithms may not always converge to a globally optimal solution unless $c(x)$ is specially shaped—for example, concave. And even when $c(x)$ approaches a limiting value, convergence usually does not occur in a finite number of iterations.

Many of the algorithms in the chapter can be conveniently explained by means of a format similar to that employed in Secs. 14.4 and 14.5 for the "steepest ascent with optimal step size" algorithm; you should review that material before reading further. The large-step procedure in general is

Step 1. Select an arbitrary initial feasible point x^0.

Step 2. (a) At iteration k, determine the directions d_j^k for $j = 1, 2, \ldots, n$. (b) Find a step size t^k such that $c(x)$ is maximized over all *feasible* points lying in the selected direction from x^k. Terminate the calculations if $t^k = 0$. Otherwise, continue to *Step 3*.

Step 3. Compute the new trial point

$$(3) \qquad x_j^{k+1} = x_j^k + t^k d_j^k \quad \text{for } j = 1, 2, \ldots, n.$$

Return to *Step 2*, where x^{k+1} replaces x^k.

The term **large-step approach** refers to the fact that the optimal step size is used in *Step 2*. If you look back to the "steepest ascent with optimal step size" algorithm in Secs. 14.4 and 14.5 (pp. 530 and 534), you will notice three important differences in the wording of *Step 2*. First, the condition that every $\partial c/\partial x_j = 0$ is no longer used as a criterion for termination. The reason is that the partial derivatives do *not* all have to equal zero at a stationary point of a *constrained* problem. Second, the optimal step size t^k cannot be determined with reference to $c(x)$ alone; t^k must be chosen so that the point x^{k+1} satisfies the constraints. Given the regularization assumption (ii), the feasibility stipulation means that t^k is always finite. The resultant value of t^k might be termed the **optimal feasible step size**. Third, each direction in *Step 2* is no longer specified as $\partial c/\partial x_j$, evaluated at the current trial point. The reason that values of the partial derivatives are not adequate for the directions is easily illustrated by an example.

Consider the quadratic problem previously analyzed in Sec. 14.6:

$$(4) \qquad \text{Problem P:} \begin{cases} \text{maximize } c(x) \equiv 6x_1 + 4x_2 + 2x_3 - 3x_1^2 - 2x_2^2 - \tfrac{1}{3}x_3^2 \\ \text{subject to} \\ x_1 + 2x_2 + x_3 + s = 4, \end{cases}$$

$$(5)$$

where all $x_j \geq 0$ and $s \geq 0$. Let the trial point be $x_j^k = 1$ for all j, so that (5) is satisfied with $s = 0$, and $c(x^k) = 6.67$. Suppose, as in the method of steepest ascent, you let each $d_j^k = \partial c/\partial x_j$. Then verify that $d_1^k = d_2^k = 0$ and $d_3^k = \tfrac{4}{3}$. Unfortunately, *no feasible* points lie in this direction from x^k. The trial point, nevertheless, is *not* locally optimal. Consider the direction ($d_1^k = -1$, $d_2^k = 0$, $d_3^k = 1$), which is along the constraint (5). You can check that for step size $t = .1$, the objective function improves $c(x^{k+1}) = 6.76$.

To summarize, the test for termination, the choice of step size, and the selection of direction must take account of what happens when the trial point either reaches or lies on a boundary of the constraint set.

The next three sections discuss several large-step approaches that exploit the linearity of the constraints. Be sure to note how each algorithm specifies the details for *Step 2*.

As you will quickly realize, the instructions in nonlinear algorithms have numerous details, and even small illustrative examples require a fair amount of calculation. To help you read this material, we will suggest here and there that you record certain equations or other information. If you heed these suggestions, you can avoid flipping back and forth between pages.

Problem P in (4) and (5) will be used repeatedly to illustrate the algorithms in this chapter. Consequently, copy (4) and (5) on a piece of paper for ready reference. The unique optimal solution is

(6) $\bar{x}_1 = \frac{7}{8} = .875 \quad \bar{x}_2 = \frac{5}{8} = .625 \quad \bar{x}_3 = 1\frac{7}{8} = 1.875 \quad \text{with } \bar{c} = 7.25;$

jot down this solution too.

15.2 METHOD OF CONVEX COMBINATIONS

The idea of this algorithm is to determine directions in *Step 2* by means of a linear programming optimization, using a linear approximation to $c(x)$ and the problem's linear constraints. Consider a feasible trial point x^k. Given assumption (iv) in Sec. 15.1 on the partial derivatives of $c(x)$, the value of $c(x)$ at another point z in the neighborhood of x^k can be approximated by a first-order Taylor's expansion:

(1) $$c(z) \approx c(x^k) + \sum_{j=1}^{n} \frac{\partial c(x^k)}{\partial x_j} \cdot (z_j - x_j^k).$$

Suppose, then, you find a feasible point z that maximizes the term

(2) $$\sum_{j=1}^{n} \frac{\partial c(x^k)}{\partial x_j} \cdot z_j$$

subject to the linear constraints on the variables. Let $\bar{z}$ be this point, and suppose

(3) $$\sum_{j=1}^{n} \frac{\partial c(x^k)}{\partial x_j} \cdot \bar{z}_j > \sum_{j=1}^{n} \frac{\partial c(x^k)}{\partial x_j} \cdot x_j^k.$$

Then the summation on the right of (1) is strictly positive. In all likelihood, $\bar{z}$ is *not* in the immediate neighborhood of x^k, and so the approximation (1) is poor. In fact, $c(\bar{z})$ may be smaller than $c(x^k)$. But because of the continuity of $c(x)$ and its partial derivatives, there is a **convex combination**, or **weighted average**, of x^k and $\bar{z}$ that yields an increase in $c(x)$ above the value $c(x^k)$. In other words, there is a t, where $0 < t \le 1$, such that by letting

(4) $$x_j^{k+1} = (1 - t)x_j^k + t\bar{z}_j \quad \text{for } j = 1, 2, \ldots, n,$$

you obtain

(5) $$c(x^{k+1}) > c(x^k).$$

Since all the constraints are linear, a convex combination of x^k and $\bar{z}$ is feasible for any t in the interval $0 < t \leq 1$.

Let each direction be defined as

(6) $$d_j^k \equiv \bar{z}_j - x_j^k \quad \text{for } j = 1, 2, \ldots, n;$$

then (4) can be written in the standard form

(7) $$x_j^{k+1} = x_j^k + t d_j^k \quad \text{for } j = 1, 2, \ldots, n \quad (0 < t \leq 1),$$

as you should verify. [Rearrange the summations in (3) so as to express the inequality in terms of the directions.]

To recapitulate, the detailed procedure for *Step 2* is:

(i)   Evaluate all the partial derivatives $\partial c / \partial x_j$ at the trial point x^k.
(ii) Solve the linear programming problem consisting of the objective function in (2) and the linear constraints, where the symbol z_j is substituted for x_j in all the constraints. Define the directions d_j^k according to (6).
(iii) Terminate the calculations unless the inequality in (3) holds.
(iv) Otherwise, find a step size t^k such that $c(x^k + t d^k)$ is maximized, where $0 < t \leq 1$.

If an optimal linear programming solution $\bar{z}$ yields an equality between the two summations in (3) at iteration k, the current trial x^k is a constrained stationary point. This frequently means that there is no feasible point in the immediate neighborhood of x^k at which $c(x)$ is greater than $c(x^k)$. (But it can happen that x^k is only a point of "inflection.") Usually, however, there is no iteration k where an equality occurs between the two summations in (3). Nevertheless, for an arbitrary initial trial point x^0, the method always converges in the limit, in the following sense:

(A) The entire sequence $c(x^k)$ monotonically increases to a limit.
(B) At least a subsequence of the x^k converges to a *feasible* point x.
(C) The point $\bar{x}$ is a **constrained stationary point:** either *all* the partial derivatives equal zero at x; or some partial derivatives do not equal zero but there is no possible improvement in $c(x)$ in the *feasible* neighborhood of $\bar{x}$.

Consider the important case when $c(x)$ is concave. Recall the definition: a several-variable function $c(x)$ is **concave** if, for any two points $x \neq y$, and for all p, $0 \leq p \leq 1$,

$$pc(x) + (1 - p)c(y) \leq c(px_1 + (1 - p)y_1, \ldots, px_n + (1 - p)y_n) \quad \underline{\text{Concave,}}$$

and is **strictly concave** if the inequality is strict ($<$) for $0 < p < 1$.

When $c(x)$ is concave, the point $\bar{x}$ is always a global optimum, and $c(\bar{x})$ truly is the maximum value. Further, in this case, the optimal step size t^k can be found by using a single-variable search technique given in Sec. 14.3.

The Method of Convex Combinations has several characteristics worth noting:

(i) Only by happenstance would each direction in (6) equal the corresponding partial derivatives of $c(x)$ at x^k. In general, each d_j^k does *not* equal the direction of steepest ascent at the trial point.

(ii) Since $\bar{z}$ is an optimal solution to a linear programming problem with m constraints, it has at most m strictly positive components, assuming simplex algorithm is used. Nevertheless, if $x_j^k \neq \bar{z}_j$, then x_j^{k+1} will differ from x_j^k according to (4). In other words, the trial value of *every* x_j may change at an iteration.

(iii) If the linear constraints have a special structure—for example, if they represent a network model—then you may exploit this fact in the linear programming optimization of *Step 2*.

(iv) If the objective function is only slightly nonlinear, so that most of the x_j appear only linearly with coefficient c_j, then the coefficients in (2) are also c_j for these variables. This simplifies the computations at *Step 2*.

(v) If $c(x)$ is concave, then at each iteration you may calculate an upper bound on the optimal value of $c(x)$. This property is especially helpful, since the bound can be employed to terminate the iterations when a sufficiently good solution is obtained. The calculation is based on the fact that a first-order Taylor's expansion of $c(x)$, as in (1), yields an overstatement if $c(x)$ is concave. Specifically, let $\bar{x}$ denote an optimal solution; then

$$(8) \quad c(\bar{x}) \leq c(x^k) + \sum_{j=1}^{n} \frac{\partial c(x^k)}{\partial x_j} \cdot (\bar{x}_j - x_j^k) \leq c(x^k) + \sum_{j=1}^{n} \frac{\partial c(x^k)}{\partial x_j} \cdot (\bar{z}_j - x_j^k),$$

where the first inequality follows from the concavity assumption, and the second from the optimization with objective function (2). The upper bound, then, is the expression on the right of (8). Since this bound does not always decrease at every iteration, you should keep track of the lowest bound found in all the previous iterations.

▶Convergence of the algorithm can be accelerated by using a *second-order* Taylor's expansion of $c(x)$, thereby leading to a quadratic, instead of a linear, programming problem in *Step 2*. The inequality (3) is modified accordingly by adding the terms involving second-order partial derivatives.   ◀

Example. To illustrate the technique, consider Problem P, stated at the end of the preceding section. The corresponding linearized objective function (2) is

$$(9) \qquad [6(1 - x_1^k)]z_1 + [4(1 - x_2^k)]z_2 + [2(1 - \tfrac{1}{3}x_3^k)]z_3.$$

Given the single linear constraint, the only basic feasible solutions of the linear programming problem are

$$(10)$$

Point 1:	$z_1 = 4$	$z_2 = 0$	$z_3 = 0$
Point 2:	$z_1 = 0$	$z_2 = 2$	$z_3 = 0$
Point 3:	$z_1 = 0$	$z_2 = 0$	$z_3 = 4$
Point 4:	$z_1 = 0$	$z_2 = 0$	$z_3 = 0.$

To test your understanding so far, devise a simple rule that indicates which of these points is optimal, given values for x_j^k in (9).

The step size formula (7) in Sec. 14.5 (p. 543) can also be utilized here, with a slight modification:

$$(11) \quad \text{optimal } t = \text{minimum} \left[\frac{6(1 - x_1)d_1 + 4(1 - x_2)d_2 + 2(1 - \frac{1}{3}x_3)d_3}{6(d_1)^2 + 4(d_2)^2 + \frac{2}{3}(d_3)^2}, 1 \right]$$

where, for brevity, the superscript k has been omitted in the notation.

Recall that the unique optimal solution is

$$(12) \quad \bar{x}_1 = \tfrac{7}{8} = .875 \quad \bar{x}_2 = \tfrac{5}{8} = .625 \quad \bar{x}_3 = 1\tfrac{7}{8} = 1.875 \quad c(\bar{x}) = 7.25.$$

Verify that if you let the trial x^k be $\bar{x}$, then the objective function (9) becomes $\frac{6}{8}z_1 + \frac{12}{8}z_2 + \frac{6}{8}z_3$; as a result, each of the first three points in (10) is optimal for the associated linear programming calculation, and the two quantities shown for the test in (3) have equal values, indicating that $\bar{x}$ is optimal.

Suppose you initiate the Method of Convex Combinations for this example by letting each $x_j^0 = 0$. Check that the linearized objective function (9) yields Point 1 in (10) as optimal. As a result, $d_1^1 = 1 - 0 = 1$ and $d_2^1 = d_3^1 = 0$; according to (11), the associated optimal t^1 is .25. Then the formula (7) for the next trial point yields $x_1^1 = 0 + (\frac{1}{4})4 = 1$ and $x_2^1 = x_3^1 = 0$. The subsequent iterations are summarized in Fig. 15.1.

$$c(x) \equiv 6x_1 + 4x_2 + 2x_3 - 3x_1^2 - 2x_2^2 - \tfrac{1}{3}x_3^2$$

$$x_1 + 2x_2 + x_3 \leq 4$$

Iteration k	$c(x^k)$	x_1^k	x_2^k	x_3^k	Step Size t^k	Upper Bound	Extreme Point
0	0	0	0	0	.25	24	1
1	3	1	0	0	.48	11	3
2	4.92	.52	0	1.92	.12	13.56	1
3	5.417	.920	0	1.699	.26	11.50	2
4	6.222	.677	.529	1.250	.06	10.21	1
5	6.338	.871	.498	1.177	.16	8.09	3
6	6.480	.730	.418	1.633	.04	9.32	1
10	6.717	.768	.484	1.670	.03	8.73	1
11	6.748	.868	.469	1.618	.07	7.82	2
18	6.907	.806	.532	1.725	.02	8.16	1
19	6.919	.868	.521	1.691	.04	7.59	2
20	6.934	.830	.587	1.617	--	--	--
Optimal Values	7.25	.875	.625	1.875			

FIGURE 15.1. Method of Convex Combinations.

Notice that the successive values of $c(x)$ rise rapidly at the start, and then increase quite slowly after the fifth iteration. This is typical behavior for a first-order method. Observe how the linear programming solution is Point 1 in (10) on every even-numbered iteration, and alternates between Points 2 and 3 on the odd-numbered iterations. This alternation causes a dampening oscillation in the x_j^k. Finally, note that the trial x^k are always interior to the linear inequality constraint, although the optimal solution satisfies the constraint exactly.

▶For the sake of contrast, consider how the algorithm proceeds when x^0 is one of the other extreme points in (10), or the point where each $x_j^0 = 1$, which also exactly satisfies the linear inequality constraint. The speed of convergence of the $c(x^k)$ is shown in Fig. 15.2. Notice how much faster $c(x^k)$ approaches its maximum for these initial points. By the tenth iteration, not only is $c(x^k)$ nearly equal to its optimal value, but the corresponding x_j^k differ from the optimal $\bar{x}_j$ by less than .03.

Iteration k	Point 4 $x_j^0 = 0$	Point 2	Points 1 and 3	$x_j^0 = 1$
1	3.000	4.571	6.000	7.167
2	4.920	7.020	7.143	7.219
3	5.417	7.187	7.228	7.236
4	6.222	7.224	7.244	7.244
5	6.338	7.239	7.248	7.247
10	6.717	7.249	7.249	7.249
20	6.934	7.249	7.249	7.249

Optimal Value of $c(x) = 7.25$

FIGURE 15.2. Speed of Convergence of $c(x)$.

As another point of comparison, consider what happens when the linear constraint is relaxed by letting the right-hand side be 6 or 8. In these two cases, the constraint is not really binding, in that the *unconstrained* optimal solution ($x_1 = 1, x_2 = 1, x_3 = 3$) is feasible as it has an objective function value 8. When the right-hand side is 6, and starting with each $x_j^0 = 0$, the trial solution at $k = 20$ is ($x_1^{20} = .9162, x_2^{20} = .8307,$ $x_3^{20} = 2.3585$) giving $c(x^{20}) = 7.7844$. Again, convergence is very slow after the fifth iteration. When the right-hand side is 8, the result at $k = 20$ is much better ($x_1^{20} = .9851,$ $x_2^{20} = .9485, x_3^{20} = 2.7668$) yielding $c(x^{20}) = 7.9759$. ◀

*15.3 CONCAVE SIMPLEX METHOD

As the name suggests, this algorithm obtains an optimal solution if $c(x)$ is concave, and is based on merely a few modifications of the ordinary simplex method. Actually, it combines the ideas used in the simplex method for upper-bounded variables (Sec. 5.10) and in the Quadratic Simplex Method (Sec. 14.6). Like the upper-bounded variables algorithm, the method employs a set of only m constraints. It classifies the original variables into the categories of basic and non-basic, and allows some of the nonbasic variables to be in the solution at a positive level. Like the Quadratic Simplex Method, it considers the effect of changing one nonbasic variable at a time. If the value of a selected nonbasic variable can be altered to increase the objective function, then it is so changed to maintain feasibility and bring about the maximum improvement in the objective function. The approach differs most importantly from the preceding Method of Convex Combinations in that here no more than $(m + 1)$ of the variables change their levels at any iteration, these being the current basic variables and the selected nonbasic variable. If $c(x)$ is not concave, the method yields a constrained stationary point.

Let x^k be the trial feasible point at iteration k. For ease of exposition, suppose that the variables are numbered such that $x_1, x_2, \ldots, x_m$ are basic, and $x_{m+1}, \ldots, x_N$ are nonbasic at iteration k. Note we define $N \equiv m + n$ so that the slack variables are also designated by the same letter, x. Suppose, at iteration k, the system of linear constraints is displayed as in the application of the simplex method:

(1)

$$
\begin{array}{ll}
x_1 + t_{1,m+1}x_{m+1} + \cdots + t_{1N}x_N = \bar{b}_1 & \text{Row 1} \\
 x_2 + t_{2,m+1}x_{m+1} + \cdots + t_{2N}x_N = \bar{b}_2 & \text{Row 2} \\
\qquad\qquad \vdots & \qquad \vdots \\
x_m + t_{m,m+1}x_{m+1} + \cdots + t_{mN}x_N = \bar{b}_m & \text{Row } m,
\end{array}
$$

where the superscript k has been dropped for simplicity of notation. Since in this algorithm some of the nonbasic variables may be strictly positive, a $\bar{b}_i$ may be negative. But the appropriate nonnegativity assumption can be written as

$$
(2) \qquad x_i = \bar{b}_i - \sum_{j=m+1}^{N} t_{ij}x_j \geq 0 \quad \text{for } i = 1, 2, \ldots, m
$$

at the point x^k.

The rationale establishing the relevance of the objective function in the preceding Method of Convex Combinations continues to apply here. Specifically, consider the function

$$
(3) \qquad \sum_{j=1}^{N} \frac{\partial c(x^k)}{\partial x_j} \cdot x_j,
$$

or, expressed in the fashion of the simplex method,

$$
(4) \quad x_0 - \frac{\partial c(x^k)}{\partial x_1} \cdot x_1 - \cdots - \frac{\partial c(x^k)}{\partial x_m} \cdot x_m - \frac{\partial c(x^k)}{\partial x_{m+1}} \cdot x_{m+1} - \cdots - \frac{\partial c(x^k)}{\partial x_N} \cdot x_N = 0
$$

Row 0.

If you were applying the simplex method, Row 0 would have a coefficient of zero for every variable in the current basis. To achieve this condition here, you can employ the relations in (1) to eliminate $x_1, \ldots, x_m$ from (4). Specifically, for $i = 1, 2, \ldots, m$, multiply Row i by $\partial c(x^k)/\partial x_i$ and add the result to (4), thereby obtaining

(5) $\qquad x_0 + 0x_1 + \cdots + 0x_m + t_{0,m+1}x_{m+1} + \cdots + t_{0N}x_N = \bar{b}_0 \qquad$ <u>Row 0,</u>

where, as a result of the elimination process,

(6) $\qquad t_{0j} \equiv \sum_{i=1}^{m} \frac{\partial c(x^k)}{\partial x_i} \cdot t_{ij} - \frac{\partial c(x^k)}{\partial x_j} \quad$ for $j = m+1, \ldots, N$.

[If $c(x)$ were linear, then each partial derivative under the summation sign in (6) would be the original objective-function coefficient c_i for the basic variable x_i.] The value of t_{0j} is called a **reduced** (or **relative**) **partial derivative**. As we mentioned above, the superscript k on t_{0j} has been dropped for notational convenience. Since the constant $\bar{b}_0$ on the right-hand side of (5) will play no role in the computations, we adopt the convention of indicating it by the symbol $\bar{0}$ throughout.

As in the simplex method, the value of t_{0j} can be given the following meaning:

INTERPRETATION OF COEFFICIENTS IN ROW 0. Each coefficient for a nonbasic variable represents the *rate* of increase (for negative coefficients) or decrease (for positive coefficients) in $c(x)$ with an increase in the associated nonbasic variable above its current level x_j^k.

A few comments are in order about the relevance and numerical significance of this interpretation.

Suppose that all $t_{0j} \geq 0$ at iteration k, that is, all t_{0j} are "positive coefficients." Is the solution optimal? It would be, provided all the nonbasic variables were at zero level, for then any small increase in a nonbasic x_j would decrease $c(x)$ below $c(x^k)$. Consequently, x^k would be a constrained stationary point, and therefore optimal, since $c(x)$ is concave. But if there is a nonbasic variable x_j at a positive level and $t_{0j}x_j^k > 0$, then the solution may possibly be improved by *reducing* the value of x_j^k. If both conditions

(7) $\qquad$ all $t_{0j} \geq 0 \quad$ *and* $\quad$ all $t_{0j}x_j^k = 0$

are satisfied, then x^k is truly optimal.

Suppose (7) is not satisfied, so that there is either a negative t_{0j} or a positive $t_{0j}x_j^k$, or both. Then you must select a nonbasic variable and alter its value in an effort to improve the current level of the objective function. Toward this end, first determine, as in *Criterion I* of the simplex method, the smallest t_{0j} coefficient:

(8) $\qquad$ minimum $(t_{01}, \ldots, t_{0N}) = t_{0p} \equiv t_{\min}$.

Verify that $t_{\min} \leq 0$ and may be negative if (7) is not satisfied. Second, determine the largest value for a $t_{0j}x_j^k$:

(9) $\qquad$ maximum $(t_{01}x_1^k, \ldots, t_{0N}x_N^k) = t_{0q}x_q^k \equiv t_{\max}$.

Verify that $t_{\max} \geq 0$ and may be positive if (7) is not satisfied. Given that (7) is not satisfied, either $t_{\min}$ or $t_{\max}$, or both, are nonzero. It can be shown that a valid rule for determining which nonbasic variable to alter is:

CHOICE OF A NONBASIC VARIABLE. If (7) is not satisfied, increase variable x_p if $t_{min} < -t_{max}$. Otherwise, decrease variable x_q.

Having picked a nonbasic variable to change, you must next compute the corresponding directions d_j. Actually all $d_j = 0$ *except* those for the basic variables and the selected nonbasic variable. Consider first the case when x_p is chosen. Then a straightforward modification of *Criterion II* of the simplex method will yield the following rule:

DIRECTIONS WHEN x_p INCREASES. (a) Take the ratios of x_i evaluated in (2) to the coefficients t_{ip} (ignore ratios with zero or negative numbers in the denominator). (b) Let r be the value of the minimum ratio. (c) Let $d_p = r$ and $d_i = -t_{ip}r$ for $i = 1, 2, \ldots, m$.

Second, consider the case when x_q is chosen. Then a straightforward modification of *Criterion II* of the bounded-variables simplex method (p. 149) yields the rule:

DIRECTIONS WHEN x_q DECREASES: (a) Take only the ratios of $-x_i$ evaluated in (2) to the coefficients t_{ip} (ignore ratios with zero or positive numbers in the denominator). (b) Let R be the value of the minimum ratio, and let $r = $ minimum (R, x_q^k). (c) Let $d_q = -r$ and $d_i = t_{ip}r$ for $i = 1, 2, \ldots, m$.

Note that $r \geq 0$ in both cases. (If $r = 0$, then all $d_j = 0$, but you still do not terminate the calculations.)

Finally, given the directions, you must calculate the optimal step size t, thereby completing the computations in *Step 2*. The step size procedure is exactly the same as in the Method of Convex Combinations.

The new trial point x^{k+1} is calculated as usual in *Step 3*. If the optimal step size t^k is in the interval $0 < t^k < 1$, or if both $t^k = 1$ and $r = x_q^k < R$, then return to *Step 2*, and repeat the process, revising the values of t_{0j} in (6) at the new trial point x^{k+1}. But if $t^k = 1$ is optimal (which occurs if $r = 0$), and $r \neq x_q^k$, then perform a change-of-basis calculation prior to returning to *Step 2*. Specifically, introduce the variable x_p or x_q (whichever is appropriate) into the basis, and drop a basic variable associated with the ratio giving r.

We now summarize the algorithm for any iteration k. The current trial point x^k is composed of a set of basic variables, and a set of nonbasic variables, some of which may be positive. The procedure is

(i)   Calculate the reduced partial derivatives according to (6), and test for optimality according to (7). If an improvement is possible, choose a nonbasic variable to alter.

(ii) Determine the directions of change for the current basic variables and the selected nonbasic variable; these are computed so that the solution remains feasible if the optimal step size $t^k = 1$.

(iii) Given the directions, find a step size t^k that maximizes the value of the objective function along the selected direction from x^k, that is, maximize $c(x^k + td)$ for $0 < t \leq 1$.

(iv) Shift the trial point accordingly, and, unless $r = x_q^k < R$, also perform a change-of-basis calculation to complete iteration k when the optimal step size $t^k = 1$.

The algorithm guarantees that $c(x^{k+1}) \geq c(x^k)$. But to *prove* that $c(x^k)$ tends, in the limit, to the maximum value for $c(x)$ when $c(x)$ is concave, additional care must be taken to circumvent cycling. (This phenomenon will not be discussed here, but you may want to review the problem in the context of the simplex method, as discussed in Sec. 4.7.)

This algorithm shares two desirable properties with the Method of Convex Combinations. A special structure for the linear constraints can be exploited in the change-of-basis calculations, and the computations for the objective function in (6) simplify if $c(x)$ is only slightly nonlinear. To repeat the point made at the start, the methods differ principally in that all directions may be nonzero for the Method of Convex Combinations, whereas at most only $m + 1$ directions are nonzero in the Concave Simplex Method.

Example. To illustrate the algorithm, again consider Problem P in Sec. 15.1. Since we want to exhibit several iterations of the technique, we now drop the convention on the numbering of the basic variables used to display (1). The linearized objective function (4) becomes

$$(10) \qquad x_0 - [6(1 - x_1^k)]x_1 - [4(1 - x_2^k)]x_2 - [2(1 - \tfrac{1}{3}x_3^k)]x_3 = \bar{0} \qquad \text{Row 0.}$$

Let the initial solution be all $x_j^0 = 0$ and $s = 4$, giving

$$(11) \qquad\qquad x_0 - 6x_1 - 4x_2 - 2x_3 = \bar{0} \qquad\qquad \text{Row 0.}$$

Then x_1 is chosen to be increased. Verify that $d_1 = 4$, $d_2 = d_3 = 0$, and $d_4 = -4$, where d_4 is the direction for the slack variable. The step size formula (11) in Sec. 15.2 still applies and yields $t^0 = .25$. Hence the next trial point is $(x_1^1 = 1, x_2^1 = x_3^1 = 0, s^1 = 3)$, with $c(x^1) = 3$. Since $t^0 < 1$, no change of basis is required.

At $k = 1$, the objective function (10) becomes

$$(12) \qquad\qquad x_0 - 4x_2 - 2x_3 = \bar{0} \qquad\qquad \text{Row 0.}$$

This time x_2 is chosen to be increased. Since

$$(13) \qquad\qquad s^1 = 4 - x_1^1 - 2x_2^1 - x_3^1 = 3,$$

verify that $d_1 = 0$, $d_2 = \tfrac{3}{2}$, $d_3 = 0$, and $d_4 = -3$, and the optimal t^1 is $\tfrac{2}{3}$, yielding $(x_1^2 = 1, x_2^2 = 1, x_3^2 = 0, s^2 = 1)$ with $c(x^2) = 5$.

At $k = 2$, the objective function (10) becomes

$$(14) \qquad\qquad x_0 - 2x_3 = \bar{0} \qquad\qquad \text{Row 0,}$$

so that x_3 is to be increased. Since

$$(15) \qquad\qquad s^2 = 4 - 1(1) - 2(1) - 1(0) = 1,$$

verify that $d_1 = 0$, $d_2 = 0$, $d_3 = 1$, and $d_4 = -1$. Now the optimal step size is $t^2 = 1$, so that the new trial point is $(x_1^3 = 1, x_2^3 = 1, x_3^3 = 1, s^3 = 0)$, with $c(x^3) = 6.67$. Here you must perform a change of basis: introduce x_3 and drop s.

Check that using the linear constraint to eliminate x_3 from Row 0 in (10) yields

(16)
$$x_0 + [1 \cdot 2(1 - \tfrac{1}{3}x_3^k) - 6(1 - x_1^k)]x_1 + [2 \cdot 2(1 - \tfrac{1}{3}x_3^k) - 4(1 - x_2^k)]x_2$$
$$+ [1 \cdot 2(1 - \tfrac{1}{3}x_3^k)]s = \bar{0} \qquad \underline{\text{Row 0.}}$$

Note in (16) how the attractiveness of changing x_1, x_2, or s depends on the partial derivative for x_3 and the coefficients of each x_j and s in the linear constraint. Verify that for the trial point x^3, (16) is

(17) $$x_0 + \tfrac{4}{3}x_1 + \tfrac{8}{3}x_2 + \tfrac{4}{3}s = \bar{0} \qquad \underline{\text{Row 0.}}$$

All the coefficients $t_{0j} \geq 0$; but $t_{01}x_1^3 = \tfrac{4}{3}$ and $t_{02}x_2^3 = \tfrac{8}{3}$, so the iterations do not terminate. Suppose you choose to decrease x_2. Check that $d_1 = 0$, $d_2 = -1$, $d_3 = 2$, $d_4 = 0$, and the optimal $t = .4$. This gives $(x_1^4 = 1, x_2^4 = .6, x_3^4 = 1.8, s^4 = 0)$, with $c(x^4) = 7.2$. The subsequent iterations are summarized in Fig. 15.3. The basic variable remains x_3. At $k = 5$ the value x_1 is reduced; at $k = 6$,

$$c(x) \equiv 6x_1 + 4x_2 + 2x_3 - 3x_1^2 - 2x_2^2 - \tfrac{1}{3}x_3^2$$

$$x_1 + 2x_2 + x_3 + s = 4$$

Iteration k	$c(x^k)$	x_1^k	x_2^k	x_3^k	s^k	Step Size t^k
1	3	1	0	0	3	.2500
2	5	1	1	0	1	.6667
3	6.667	1	1	1	0	.4000
4	7.2	1	.6	1.8	0	.12
5	7.248	.88	.6	1.92	0	.025
6	7.2499	.88	.624	1.872	0	.005
7	7.2499	.8752	.624	1.8768	0	.0010
8	7.2499	.8752	.6250	1.8745	0	.0002
Optimal Values	7.25	.875	.625	1.875	0	

FIGURE 15.3. Concave Simplex Method.

the value of x_2 is increased again. Thereafter, the alterations are negligible. As you can see, the method converges swiftly in this special example to the optimal value of $c(x)$ as well as to the optimal value of each x_j.

*15.4 OTHER APPROACHES

There are scores of scientific methods for optimizing a nonlinear objective function subject to linear constraints. The second part of this chapter contains several more of these approaches. Two other techniques are mentioned briefly here because of their prominence in nonlinear programming literature. They can be adapted to problems having nonlinear constraints, but the necessary modifications are not given in this text.

One technique is called the **Cutting-Plane Method**, which makes use of the linear bound (8) in Sec. 15.2, and can be applied to the case of a concave $c(x)$. At any iteration k, you have a current trial feasible point x^k along with a set of *linear* constraints consisting of the original relations as well as some bounding relations, to be described momentarily. The problem has been augmented by a variable x_0 that appears in all the bounding relations. The variable x_0 is to be maximized, so the problem at iteration k can be solved by applying linear programming techniques. The resultant optimal value of x_0 provides an upper bound on the optimal value of $c(x)$.

To find x^{k+1}, you add another bounding linear relation to the current set of constraints:

$$(1) \qquad x_0 - \sum_{j=1}^{n} \frac{\partial c(x^k)}{\partial x_j} \cdot x_j \leq c(x^k) - \sum_{j=1}^{n} \frac{\partial c(x^k)}{\partial x_j} \cdot x_j^k.$$

This restriction is *not* satisfied by x_0^k and x^k (unless these are optimal values), because x_0^k is always larger than $c(x^k)$. Consequently, by imposing (1), the current trial point is cut off from further consideration.

It follows that $x_0^{k+1} \leq x_0^k$. Further, it can be proved that the sequence of x_0^k converges to the optimal value $c(x)$, and there is a subsequence of the x^k that converges to an optimal solution. But the associated sequence of $c(x^k)$ need *not* be monotonically increasing. Hence, when you terminate the iterations short of convergence, you should accept the trial point giving the largest value of $c(x)$

$$c(x) \equiv 6x_1 + 4x_2 + 2x_3 - 3x_1^2 - 2x_2^2 - \tfrac{1}{3}x_3^2$$

$$x_1 + 2x_2 + x_3 \leq 4$$

Iteration k	$c(x^k)$	x_0^k	x_1^k	x_2^k	x_3^k
0	0	--	0	0	0
1	-24	24	4	0	0
2	2	16	2	1	0
3	5.908	12.667	1.167	0	2.833
4	6.066	11.022	.756	1.233	.778
5	5.685	8.887	.222	.511	2.756
8	5.849	7.530	1.437	.855	.853
9	6.869	7.390	1.036	.892	1.180
10	6.702	7.373	1.281	.464	1.791
15	7.249	7.264	.868	.639	1.853
Optimal Values	7.25	7.25	.875	.625	1.875

FIGURE 15.4. Cutting-Plane Method.

found so far, which need not be the x^k from the final iteration. The algorithm is illustrated for Problem P in Fig. 15.4. Notice in particular the erratic behavior of the successive trial solutions x^k.

Another algorithm is termed the **Gradient Projection Method**. Unlike any of the techniques explained so far, it does *not* apply linear programming in *Step 2*. Rather, it is more akin to the method of steepest ascent in the way it determines a direction based on the partial derivatives of $c(x)$ at the trial point x^k, and a step size that maximizes $c(x)$ over all *feasible* points lying in the selected direction from x^k. The component directions are calculated by projecting the gradient of $c(x)$ on the intersection of those constraints that are exactly satisfied at x^k (the slack variables for the constraints are at zero level). (The actual computational process is slightly more involved than this, but the details are not important for the exposition here.) The step size calculation proceeds by first finding the largest value of t, say T, such that the point $(x^k + td)$ is feasible, and then by doing a one-dimensional search for the maximum of $c(x^k + td)$ in the interval $[0, T]$, using an approach explained in Sec. 14.3.

The calculations are illustrated for Problem P. Suppose that the trial point x^k is *on* the linear constraint for x_1, x_2, and x_3 (that is, the slack variable $s = 0$). Consider *any* set of directions D_1, D_2, D_3. The technique transforms these directions to d_1, d_2, d_3 such that the resultant point x^{k+1} remains on the constraint. In order for this to happen, the d_j must satisfy

$$(2) \qquad 1d_1 + 2d_2 + 1d_3 = 0.$$

State why. The appropriate transformation, or **projection**, of the D_j to the

$$c(x) \equiv 6x_1 + 4x_2 + 2x_2 - 3x_1^2 - 2x_2^2 - \tfrac{1}{3}x_3^2$$

$$x_1 + 2x_2 + x_3 \leq 4$$

Iteration k	$c(x^k)$	x_1^k	x_2^k	x_3^k	Step Size t^k
0	0	0	0	0	.1981
1	5.547	1.189	.793	.396	.3667
2	6.537	.774	1.097	1.033	.2749
3	6.966	1.060	.817	1.306	.3075
4	7.137	.835	.813	1.539	.2749
5	7.205	.949	.701	1.648	.3075
6	7.232	.859	.700	1.741	.2749
10	7.249	.872	.637	1.854	.2749
15	7.249	.876	.626	1.873	.3075
Optimal Values	7.25	.875	.625	1.875	--

FIGURE 15.5. Gradient Projection Method.

values of d_j can be shown to be

$$d_1 = \tfrac{5}{6}D_1 - \tfrac{2}{6}D_2 - \tfrac{1}{6}D_3$$

(3)
$$d_2 = -\tfrac{2}{6}D_1 + \tfrac{2}{6}D_2 - \tfrac{2}{6}D_3$$

$$d_3 = -\tfrac{1}{6}D_1 - \tfrac{2}{6}D_2 + \tfrac{5}{6}D_3.$$

Verify that substituting the right-hand sides of (3) into the left-hand side of (2) yields 0, as required. The gradient projection approach uses the partial derivatives of $c(x)$ at x^k to provide the values of D_j. Loosely put, the method operates by taking the steepest ascent along the contours of $c(x)$ that lie on the binding constraints at x^k.

The sequence of iterations for Problem P is shown in Fig. 15.5. By the second iteration, the trial x^k is already on the constraint. A good starting point on the constraint can speed convergence. For example, if you use any of the first three extreme points in (10) in Sec. 15.2, or let each $x_j^0 = 1$, the value of $c(x^5)$ is within .04 of the optimum 7.25.

15.5 OPTIMIZATION WITH NONLINEAR
CONSTRAINTS

Starting with this section, you will learn how to solve optimization problems containing nonlinear constraints. For the sake of definiteness, suppose the model is stated as

(1) $$\text{maximize } c(x_1, x_2, \ldots, x_n)$$

subject to

(2) $$a_i(x_1, x_2, \ldots, x_n) \leq 0 \quad \text{for } i = 1, 2, \ldots, m \quad \text{and} \quad \text{each } x_j \geq 0.$$

Any of the constraints may be linear, and, in a formal sense, (1) and (2) include, as special cases, linear programming problems as well as the models in Chap. 14 and the preceding sections in this chapter. The restriction that *every* variable be nonnegative is made for expository ease; all the algorithms below are trivially modified to allow several x_j to be unconstrained in sign. Many of the formulation techniques described in Sec. 3.2 apply to nonlinear functions, and so you can view (1) and (2) as a canonical statement of a nonlinear programming problem. Copy (1) and (2) so that you can easily refer to the model as you read the rest of the chapter.

Because our purpose is to explain the fundamental ideas underlying various solution techniques, we make several simplifying assumptions about the nature of $c(x)$ and $a_i(x)$. Most of the techniques are valid, however, under weaker assumptions. We first discuss the postulates on the constraint functions $a_i(x)$, and subsequently treat those on the objective function $c(x)$.

Feasible region. The assumptions on each nonlinear function $a_i(x)$ are given in terms of its shape and smoothness characteristics. To set the stage, define a real-valued function $a(x)$ to be **convex** if, for any two points $x \neq y$, and for all p, $0 \leq p \leq 1$,

$$(3) \quad pa(x_1, \ldots, x_n) + (1 - p)a(y_1, \ldots, y_n)$$
$$\geq a(px_1 + (1 - p)y_1, \ldots, px_n + (1 - p)y_n) \quad \underline{\text{Convex,}}$$

and **strictly convex** if there is a strict inequality $(>)$ in (3) for $0 < p < 1$. [Note that if $-a(x)$ is concave, then $a(x)$ is convex.]

A related characteristic of a convex function is that for any two points x and y,

$$(4) \quad a(y) \geq a(x) + \sum_{j=1}^{n} \frac{\partial a(x)}{\partial x_j} \cdot (y_j - x_j) \quad \underline{\text{Convex.}}$$

You can interpret (4) in geometric terms as follows. Let x be any specified point such that $a(x) = 0$. Then equating the summation on the right-hand side of (4) to 0 yields a hyperplane that is tangent to the contour $a(y) = 0$. More generally, the right-hand side of (4) is a **linear support** to the function at the given point x, and the inequality (4) can be interpreted as stating that the function always lies above any of its linear supports. [Let $a(x) \equiv x_1^2 - x_2$, and specify the given point as $x_1 = 2$ and $x_2 = 4$. Draw the contour $a(y) = y_1^2 - y_2 = 0$. Verify that the line given by setting the summation on the right side of (4) equal to 0 is $4(y_1 - 2) - (y_2 - 4) = 0$, and is a linear support at the given point.]

We assume for the remainder of the chapter, unless stated otherwise, that the $a_i(x)$ in (2) satisfy the following shape and smoothness assumptions:

  (i) Each $a_i(x)$ is uniquely defined, finite, and convex for *all* values of $(x_1, x_2, \ldots, x_n)$.
  (ii) Each $\partial a_i(x)/\partial x_j$ is continuous for all x satisfying the constraints (2).

[Note that although assumption (i) implies that $a_i(x)$ is continuous, we need the stronger assumption (ii) that each first partial derivative is continuous.]

In addition, we stipulate the following.

CONSTRAINT QUALIFICATION. There exists at least one point $x^0 \geq 0$ such that each $a_i(x^0) < 0$.

Loosely put, the Constraint Qualification states that there is a feasible solution that lies strictly in the interior of the region defined by (2). (As you will see, such a point is needed to initiate several of the algorithms below.) You will find it helpful to jot down assumptions (i), (ii), and the Constraint Qualification, as we will refer to them repeatedly throughout the chapter.

An important implication of (i) is that all the points satisfying (2) form what is called a **convex set**. Specifically, if any two points $x \neq y$ are feasible in the constraints (2), then a point that is a convex combination or weighted average $[px + (1 - p)y]$, where $0 \leq p \leq 1$, is also feasible. The reason follows from (3): since $a_i(x) \leq 0$ and $a_i(y) \leq 0$ for each i, then $a_i(px_1 + (1 - p)y_1, \ldots, px_n + (1 - p)y_n) \leq 0$, where $0 \leq p \leq 1$. Verify that the same line of reasoning applies to the nonnegativity restrictions. The Constraint Qualification ensures that the convex set of feasible solutions contains a full-dimensional interior with an infinite number of points.

Two other implications of assumptions of (i), (ii), and the Constraint Qualification are not so obvious. First, if the point z is feasible for the constraints in (2), and $a_i(z) = 0$ for a particular i, then the gradient of $a_i(x)$ at z cannot be zero; that is, there is at least one j such that $\partial a_i(z)/\partial x_j \neq 0$. Second, the model does not really accommodate an equality constraint unless this constraint function is linear; in that case, it is permissible to include it in (2) by inserting a pair of inequalities, and removing the Constraint Qualification for this pair.

In many situations, you can establish that a function $a_i(x)$ is convex by analyzing whether it can be described as:

(A) A sum of convex functions—for example, $3x^2 - 6x$.

(B) The negative of a concave function—for example, $-(4y - 2y^2)$.

(C) A monotone increasing convex function of a convex function—for example, a^{x^2} for $a > 0$, since $a(z) \equiv a^z$ is monotone increasing and convex for $a > 0$, and $z \equiv x^2$ is convex.

(D) A monotone decreasing convex function of a concave function—for example, a^{y^2} for $a > 0$, since $a(z) \equiv a^{-z}$ is monotone decreasing and convex for $a > 0$, and $z \equiv -y^2$ is concave.

(E) A convex function of a linear function—for example, $a^{(x-y)^2}$ for $a > 0$, since $a(z) \equiv a^{z^2}$ is convex for $a > 0$, and $z \equiv x - y$ is linear.

According to (A), then, the function $3x^2 - 6x - 4y + 2y^2 + a^{x^2} + a^{y^2} + a^{(x-y)^2} + 10$ is convex for $a > 0$. Also, if $a(x)$ is a function of a single variable x and has a continuous second derivative, then $a(x)$ is convex if and only if $d^2a(x)/dx^2 \geq 0$ for all x. (The multidimensional analogue of this inequality is that the Hessian matrix of second-order partial derivatives must be positive semidefinite.)

Objective function. The function $c(x)$ is also hypothesized to satisfy certain shape and smoothness assumptions. We maintain assumptions (iii) through (v) in Sec. 15.1 and add one more postulate. Specifically,

(iii) $c(x)$ is single-valued and finite for each x satisfying the constraints (2).

(iv) Every partial derivative $\partial c(x)/\partial x_j$ is single-valued, finite, and continuous at each x satisfying the constraints (2).

(v) $c(x)$ possesses a finite maximum $\bar{c}$ over all values of x satisfying the constraints (2).

(vi) $c(x)$ is concave over all values of x satisfying the constraints (2).

[You also should add assumption (vi) to your previous list for easy reference as you read the rest of the chapter.]

Assumptions (i) through (vi) and the Constraint Qualification together guarantee that:

(A) There exists at least one feasible solution $\bar{x}$ such that $c(\bar{x}) = \bar{c}$.

(B) If $c(x)$ is strictly concave, then there is a unique optimal solution $\bar{x}$.

(C) If x is a constrained stationary point, then x is a constrained global optimum.

These three conclusions remain valid under somewhat weaker assumptions on the $a_i(x)$ and $c(x)$. But an essential requirement for conclusion (C) is that the feasible region be convex; for otherwise, a locally optimal point need not be globally optimal, even if $c(x)$ satisfies assumptions (iii) through (vi).

New difficulty. The algorithms for nonlinear constraints have much in common with those for linear constraints. In particular, each iteration commences with a feasible trial point x^k and tests whether x^k is optimal. If $c(x)$ can be increased further, a direction of improvement is determined and a trial point with a larger value of $c(x)$ is found. But a new difficulty arises in calculating the directions when the constraints are nonlinear. (Before continuing, you may want to reflect on how the techniques in Sec. 15.2, as well as in Secs. 15.3 and 15.4, exploited the linearity of the constraints to determine *feasible* directions of improvement.)

Suppose the trial point is at the boundary of a truly nonlinear constraint, as is shown in Fig. 15.6. The diagram suggests that the trial point be moved *along*

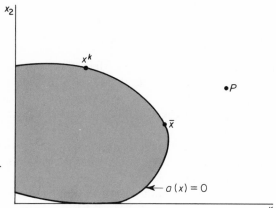

FIGURE 15.6. Problem of Feasible Directions Model: Find a Feasible Point x Closest to P.

the constraint boundary. This approach can be very awkward computationally, however, because of the nonlinearity of the boundary. There are several alternative ways to proceed in finding feasible directions of improvement, and you will see these described in the subsequent sections. The differences among the several ways can be summarized as follows.

One is to consider only directions that point into the interior of the constraint region when the trial solution is on a nonlinear boundary. Notice in Fig. 15.6 that there is *always* such a direction of improvement unless the trial point is truly optimal. This approach is used in Sec. 15.6. Another way is to prohibit a trial point from ever reaching a boundary; this approach is treated in Sec. 15.9. A third way is to use a grid of feasible points and approximate the constraint region by linearization among these points. This method is employed in Sec. 15.10. In all of these approaches, the successive values of $c(x)$ converge monotonically to the optimal value $\bar{c}$. At least a subsequence of the trial points converges to an optimal solution, and if the optimal solution is unique, then the entire sequence converges to this point.

The several algorithms will be illustrated using Problem P in Sec. 15.1 as well as

$$\text{Problem Q} \begin{cases} \text{maximize} & c(x) \equiv -x_1 - 2x_2 - x_3 \\ \text{subject to} & -6x_1 - 4x_2 - 2x_3 + 3x_1^2 + 2x_2^2 + \frac{1}{3}x_3^2 + 7.25 \le 0 \\ & \text{and} \quad \text{all } x_j \ge 0, \end{cases}$$

which has the same unique optimal solution as Problem P and $\bar{c} = -4$. Copy Problem Q for easy reference in reading the subsequent sections.

We repeat the warning from Chap. 14 that you should be very cautious in making relative evaluations of the techniques based on the particular numerical results below, since Problems P and Q are quite special—they contain a quadratic form without any cross-product terms. Furthermore, the results do not show what happens when acceleration devices are applied to improve the rate of convergence. But these examples do underscore the significant observation that nonlinear problems are typically much harder to solve than linear ones.

15.6 METHOD OF FEASIBLE DIRECTIONS

This algorithm is an extension of the Method of Convex Combinations treated in Sec. 15.2. The principal procedural difference is the formulation of the linear programming problem for obtaining the directions of improvement in *Step 2*. Like the Method of Convex Combinations, the algorithm still converges to a constrained stationary point when you drop assumption (vi) that $c(x)$ is concave.

You saw at the end of the preceding section that a fundamental difficulty in finding **feasible directions** arises when a trial solution x^k is on a nonlinear boundary of the constraint region. The formulation below attacks this difficulty by taking linear approximations to the constraint functions at x^k, and then selecting directions that point inward from those nonlinear constraints that are binding at x^k. To explain the approach, it is convenient to formulate the ideas in terms of the directions d_j, and for notational simplicity we drop the superscript k denoting the values of d_j at the current iteration.

Given the continuity assumptions on $c(x)$, the current value of $c(x)$ will improve by moving in the directions d_j from x^k provided that

$$(1) \qquad \qquad \sum_{j=1}^{n} \frac{\partial c(x^k)}{\partial x_j} \cdot d_j > 0.$$

Therefore, (1) gives a test for whether a specific set of directions can bring about an increase in the objective function.

It is also convenient to drop the distinction between the $a_i(x)$ and the nonnegativity stipulations, and therefore we designate the entire collection of constraints as

$$(2) \qquad \qquad A_i(x) \le 0 \quad \text{for } i = 1, 2, \ldots, M \ (= m + n).$$

We employ a first-order linear approximation to $A_i(x^k + d)$:

$$(3) \qquad A_i(x_1^k + d_1, x_2^k + d_2, \ldots, x_n^k + d_n) \approx A_i(x^k) + \sum_{j=1}^n \frac{\partial A_i(x^k)}{\partial x_j} \cdot d_j.$$

Recall, from the preceding section, that the assumptions on the $a_i(x)$ ensure that at least one partial derivative under the summation sign is nonzero.

Suppose x^k is interior to the ith constraint so that $A_i(x^k) < 0$. Then the right-hand side of (3) is strictly negative if all $d_j = 0$. Verify that in this case the point $(x + td)$ will satisfy the ith constraint for *any* set of directions d, provided $t > 0$ is sufficiently small.

Suppose next that x^k is on the boundary of the ith constraint, so that $A_i(x^k) = 0$. Then there is a $t > 0$ such that the point $(x^k + td)$ satisfies the ith constraint only if the directions d_j make the right-hand side of (3) *strictly* negative. The reason is that the right-hand side of (3) equated to 0 yields values for the directions that lie on the linear support (or tangent hyperplane) to the constraint $A_i(x)$ at the point x^k. Therefore, if the directions d_j produce zero or positive values for the right-hand side of (3), then these directions point on or above this support, and a new trial solution $(x^k + td)$ will not satisfy the ith constraint for any $t > 0$ if $A_i(x)$ is nonlinear. State why.

In summary, the directions d_j lead to a new *feasible* trial point $(x^k + td)$ that increases $c(x)$ if the value in (1) is strictly positive and the right-hand sides in (3) are strictly negative. If no such directions exist, then x^k is a constrained stationary point.

A linear programming model can be employed for finding feasible directions to improve $c(x)$, if such exist at the point x^k. Specifically, the formulation is to determine $x_0, d_1, \ldots, d_n$ satisfying

$$(4) \qquad\qquad\qquad \text{maximize } x_0$$

subject to

$$(5) \qquad x_0 \leq \sum_{j=1}^n \frac{\partial c(x^k)}{\partial x_j} \cdot d_j \quad \text{or equivalently} \quad x_0 - \sum_{j=1}^n \frac{\partial c(x^k)}{\partial x_j} \cdot d_j \leq 0,$$

$$A_i(x^k) + \sum_{j=1}^n \frac{\partial A_i(x^k)}{\partial x_j} \cdot d_j \leq -x_0 \quad \text{or equivalently}$$

$$(6)$$

$$x_0 + \sum_{j=1}^n \frac{\partial A_i(x^k)}{\partial x_j} \cdot d_j \leq -A_i(x^k) \quad \text{for } i = 1, 2, \ldots, M$$

$$(7) \qquad\qquad x_0 \text{ and each } d_j \text{ unconstrained in sign.}$$

Explain why (4) through (6) can be used to discover directions that satisfy the test in (1) and make the right-hand sides of (3) strictly negative when x^k is not a constrained stationary point. (Note that the optimal x_0 is never negative, since all $d_j = 0$ and $x_0 = 0$ is feasible.)

For computational purposes, the formulation (4) through (7) is not quite complete. The optimization can lead to an unbounded solution. To circumvent this nuisance, it is convenient to add linear regularization restrictions. The nonnegativity constraints included in the $A_i(x)$ guarantee in (6) that the d_j are bounded from below by $-x_j^k$ for $x_0 \geq 0$; hence, the added regularization restrictions need to protect only against large d_j. There are many stipulations that will work, a simple set being

$$(8) \qquad\qquad d_j \leq b \quad \text{for each } j,$$

where b is an arbitrarily chosen positive constant (such as 1). By using (8) and changing variables $(z_j \equiv d_j + x_j^k)$, you can transform (5) through (7) into a linear programming model with only $1 + m$ constraints and n nonnegative and upper-bounded variables. Specifically, one constraint corresponds to (5), and m constraints correspond to only the $a_i(x)$ relations contained in (6); each z_j, for $j = 1, 2, \ldots, n$, satisfies $0 \leq z_j \leq b + x_j^k$. Therefore, you can apply the upper-bounded simplex algorithm in Sec. 5.10 to solve the transformed version.

The entire procedure for *Step 2* is:

   (i) Evaluate all the partial derivatives $\partial c / \partial x_j$ at trial point x^k.
  (ii) Solve the linear programming problem consisting of (4) through (8).
 (iii) Terminate the calculations if the optimal $x_0 = 0$.
  (iv) Otherwise, find a step size t such that $c(x^k + td)$ is maximized over all *feasible* points lying in direction d from x^k.

If the optimal value of $x_0 = 0$ at (iii), then x^k is a constrained stationary point. The optimal feasible step size in (iv) is always finite, given the assumption that $c(x)$ possesses a finite maximum $\bar{c}$ for all values of x satisfying the constraints.

▶Actually, it is not necessary to obtain an optimal value for x_0 at *every* iteration. Provided an optimum is sought regularly—for example, on every 10th iteration—you need only find a feasible solution that gives a positive value for x_0 on the other iterations.

If $c(x)$ is linear, then the value for the upper bound b in (8) should be made large, since (5) is an exact representation of the incremental effect on $c(x)$. If a constraint $A_i(x)$ is linear, then the variable x_0 can be omitted from the corresponding restriction in (6). (Such a simplification applies to the nonnegativity restrictions $-x_j \leq 0$.) This modification permits the directions to be chosen so as to lie along any of the linear constraints that are binding at the current trial solution. In the limiting case when all of the $A_i(x)$ are linear, so that x_0 is thereby eliminated from all the constraints except (5), the formulation is nearly the same as that in the Method of Convex Combinations in Sec. 15.2. The principal difference is the regularization procedure. Given the assumption in Sec. 15.2 that the original linear constraints satisfy a regularization postulate, there is no need to impose any further bounding conditions. But here the additional regularization must be imposed because the formulation is in terms of the directions. It is also possible to devise a procedure to obtain an upper bound on the optimal $c(x)$ in a manner analogous to (8) in Sec. 15.2 for the Method of Convex Combinations.

The approach employs only the first-order partial derivatives of $c(x)$, and can be modified to be a second-order approach. Then a quadratic programming technique will be used to calculate the directions.   ◀

Example. Applying the technique to Problem Q, the constraint (5) is

(9) $$x_0 - d_1 - 2d_2 - d_3 \leq 0,$$

and restrictions in (6) become

(10) $$x_0 + [-6(1 - x_1^k)]d_1 + [-4(1 - x_2^k)]d_2 + [-2(1 - \tfrac{1}{3}x_3^k)]d_3$$
$$\leq 6x_1^k + 4x_2^k + 2x_3^k - 3(x_1^k)^2 - 2(x_2^k)^2 - \tfrac{1}{3}(x_3^k)^2 - 7.25$$

(11) $$x_0 - d_j \leq x_j^k \quad \text{for } j = 1, 2, 3.$$

The resultant sequence of trial points is exhibited in Fig. 15.7. The problem was solved using $b = 1$ in (8). The procedure was simplified further by imposing the

Iteration k	$c(x^k)$	x_1^k	x_2^k	x_3^k	d_1^k	d_2^k	d_3^k	Step Size t^k
0	−4	1	1	3	−1	−1	−1	.37
1	−4.51	.627	.627	2.627	1	−.67	−1	.29
2	−4.17	.918	.460	2.336	−1	.71	−1	.14
3	−4.09	.781	.557	2.199	1	−.21	−1	.12
4	−4.05	.900	.532	2.080	−1	−.83	−1	.07
5	−4.02	.826	.594	2.006	1	.10	−1	.06
9	−4.00	.869	.625	1.881	1	0	−1	.01
10	−4.00	.875	.625	1.875	——	——	——	——
Optimal Values	−4	.875	.625	1.875				

FIGURE 15.7. Method of Feasible Directions—Problem Q.

regularization constraints $(-d_j \leq 1)$ instead of (11). For $k \geq 1$, the trial point x^k lies on the quadratic constraint. The solution at $k = 10$ agrees with the optimal solution to four decimal places.

15.7 THEORETICAL PROPERTIES OF AN OPTIMAL SOLUTION

Before you go any further in studying other algorithms for the nonlinear programming problem posed at the beginning of Sec. 15.5, you will find it helpful to learn certain fundamental ideas about the problem's theoretical underpinnings. In this section you will see several closely related statements of conditions that are both necessary and sufficient for a point to be an optimal solution. Such results are useful in at least three ways; these conditions:

(i) Provide numerical approaches for testing the optimality of a proposed solution.
(ii) Give information about solution sensitivity.
(iii) Lead to algorithmic methods for obtaining an optimal solution.

Each of these uses is illustrated below. The purpose of this discussion, then, is to develop your insights into the nature of optimal solutions as well as to enhance your understanding of optimization techniques.

Recall from the preceding section that you can determine whether there are directions of improvement from a trial point x^k by solving the following linear programming model:

(1) $$\text{maximize } x_0$$

subject to

(2) $$x_0 - \sum_{j=1}^{n} \frac{\partial c(x^k)}{\partial x_j} \cdot d_j \leq 0$$

(3) $$x_0 + \sum_{j=1}^{n} \frac{\partial A_i(x^k)}{\partial x_j} \cdot d_j \leq -A_i(x^k) \quad \text{for } i = 1, 2, \ldots, M \ (=m+n)$$

(4) $$x_0 \text{ and each } d_j \text{ unrestricted in sign.}$$

For the purposes here, there is no need to add any regularization conditions on each d_j, and so conditions such as (8) in the preceding section are omitted. Given assumptions (i) through (vi) on $c(x)$ and $a_i(x)$ in Sec. 15.5, the point x^k is truly optimal if, and only if, the optimal value of x_0 is 0 in (1) through (4).

Now suppose $\bar{x}$ is an optimal point, and let $x^k = \bar{x}$ in (2) and (3), so that $x_0 = 0$ is optimal in (1) through (4). Then consider the corresponding dual linear program (see the advanced material in Sec. 5.4):

(5) $$\text{minimize } -\sum_{i=1}^{M} A_i(\bar{x}) y_i$$

subject to

(6) $$\sum_{i=0}^{M} y_i = 1$$

(7) $$-\frac{\partial c(\bar{x})}{\partial x_j} \cdot y_0 + \sum_{i=1}^{M} \frac{\partial A_i(\bar{x})}{\partial x_j} \cdot y_i = 0 \quad \text{for } j = 1, 2, \ldots, n$$

(8) $$y_i \geq 0 \quad \text{for } i = 1, 2, \ldots, M.$$

The Dual Theorem ensures that optimal values $\bar{y}_i$ exist, and also that the optimal value for the expression in (5) is 0, given that $\bar{x}$ is an optimal point. Furthermore, the assumptions in Sec. 15.5 ensure that $\bar{y}_0 > 0$. Therefore, after rearranging and simplifying terms in (7), we can state the following.

OPTIMALITY CONDITIONS. Given the Constraint Qualification and the assumptions (i) through (vi) on $a_i(x)$ and $c(x)$ in Sec. 15.5, a point $\bar{x}$ is optimal if, and only if,

(9) $$A_i(\bar{x}) \leq 0 \quad \text{for} \quad i = 1, 2, \ldots, M \ (= m+n),$$

and there exists $\bar{u}_i \geq 0$, for $i = 1, 2, \ldots, M$, such that

(10) $$A_i(\bar{x}) \cdot \bar{u}_i = 0 \quad \text{for } i = 1, 2, \ldots, M \qquad \underline{\text{Complementary slackness}}$$

(11) $$\frac{\partial c(\bar{x})}{\partial x_j} - \sum_{i=1}^{M} \frac{\partial A_i(\bar{x})}{\partial x_j} \cdot \bar{u}_i = 0 \quad \text{for } j = 1, 2, \ldots, n,$$

where $\bar{u}_i = \bar{y}_i / \bar{y}_0$, and $\bar{y}_i$ satisfy (5) through (8).

The relations (10) and (11) are often referred to as the **Kuhn-Tucker conditions**, in honor of the mathematicians who first proved their validity.

The inequalities in (9) include the nonnegativity restrictions on each variable, and hence (9) merely expresses that $\bar{x}$ must be feasible. Verify that the conditions in (10) can be derived by dividing the expression in (5) by $\bar{y}_0 > 0$, noting that the resultant sum still equals 0 at the optimum, implying that each term in the sum equals 0, since each $A_i(\bar{x}) \leq 0$ and $\bar{u}_i \geq 0$. Finally, check that the conditions in (11) can be obtained by dividing the conditions in (7) by $-\bar{y}_0$. Hence the Optimality Conditions can be deduced from the validity of using the linear programming problem (1) through (4) to verify that a point $\bar{x}$ is optimal. If you specifically designate $A_i(x) \equiv a_i(x)$, for $i = 1, 2, \ldots, m$, and $A_{m+j}(x) \equiv -x_j$, for $j \equiv 1, 2, \ldots, n$, then (10) and (11) can be shown to imply

$$(12) \qquad a_i(\bar{x}) \cdot \bar{u}_i = 0 \quad \text{for } i = 1, 2, \ldots, m$$

$$(13) \qquad \left[\frac{\partial c(\bar{x})}{\partial x_j} - \sum_{i=1}^{m} \frac{\partial a_i(\bar{x})}{\partial x_j} \cdot \bar{u}_i \right] \cdot \bar{x}_j = 0 \quad \text{for } j = 1, 2, \ldots, n$$

$$(14) \qquad \frac{\partial c(\bar{x})}{\partial x_j} - \sum_{i=1}^{m} \frac{\partial a_i(\bar{x})}{\partial x_j} \cdot \bar{u}_i \leq 0 \quad \text{for } j = 1, 2, \ldots, n.$$

Note in (12) that if $a_i(\bar{x}) < 0$, then $\bar{u}_i = 0$; and in (13), that if $\bar{x}_j > 0$, then the corresponding expression in (14) equals 0. [To check your understanding, verify that when $c(x)$ and all the $a_i(x)$ are linear, then (9), (12), (13), and (14) reduce to the results given by the Theorem of Complementary Slackness in Sec. 5.3.]

▶ The conditions (9), (10), and (11) remain *sufficient* for $\bar{x}$ to be an optimal solution under somewhat weaker shape assumptions on $c(x)$ and $a_i(x)$. Loosely put, the $A_i(x)$ must be such that they define a convex constraint region, and, together with $c(x)$, must imply that a locally optimal solution is also a globally optimal solution.

Instead of eliminating y_0, we can state the Optimality Conditions (10) and (11) as: there exists $\bar{y}_i \geq 0$ for $i = 0, 1, \ldots, M$, but not *all* $\bar{y}_i$ equal to 0, such that

$$(\text{i}) \qquad A_i(\bar{x}) \cdot \bar{y}_i = 0 \quad \text{for } i = 1, 2, \ldots, M$$

$$(\text{ii}) \qquad \frac{\partial c(\bar{x})}{\partial x_j} \cdot \bar{y}_0 - \sum_{i=1}^{M} \frac{\partial A_i(\bar{x})}{\partial x_j} \cdot \bar{y}_i = 0 \quad \text{for } j = 1, 2, \ldots, n.$$

[The relations (i) and (ii) are sometimes referred to as the **John conditions.**] The fact that not all $\bar{y}_i$ equal 0 follows from (6).

This formulation is important, because the conditions (9), (i), and (ii) remain *necessary* for $\bar{x}$ to be an optimal solution under very general assumptions. The only stipulation needed is that all the functions $a_i(x)$ and $c(x)$ have continuous first-order partial derivatives for every value of $(x_1, x_2, \ldots, x_n)$; subject to this restriction, they can have any shape. In order that (9), (10), and (11) also be *necessary* under such mild restrictions, an additional hypothesis such as the Constraint Qualification in Sec. 15.5 must be imposed to ensure that $\bar{y}_0 > 0$. ◀

The Optimality Conditions are useful in all three of the ways indicated at the start of this section. We demonstrate next how they can be employed to verify or derive an optimal solution in a small problem; subsequently, we show why they are significant for sensitivity testing and for the development of algorithms to solve large problems.

Consider Problem P in Sec. 15.1, and let the constraints be designated as

(15)
$$A_i(x) \equiv -x_i \leq 0 \quad \text{for } i = 1, 2, 3$$
$$A_4(x) \equiv x_1 + 2x_2 + x_3 - 4 \leq 0.$$

Then (10) yields, after simplification,

(16)
$$x_1 u_1 = 0 \quad x_2 u_2 = 0 \quad x_3 u_3 = 0$$
$$(x_1 + 2x_2 + x_3 - 4)u_4 = 0,$$

and (11) gives, after simplification,

(17)
$$6(1 - x_1) = -u_1 + u_4$$
$$4(1 - x_2) = -u_2 + 2u_4$$
$$2(1 - \tfrac{1}{3}x_3) = -u_3 + u_4.$$

Suppose you guess that all $x_j > 0$ in an optimal solution, and consequently, from (16), that $u_1 = u_2 = u_3 = 0$. Then you can express each x_j in terms of u_4 according to (17):

(18)
$$x_1 = 1 - \frac{u_4}{6} \quad x_2 = 1 - \frac{u_4}{2} \quad x_3 = 3 - \frac{3u_4}{2}.$$

Substituting the relations (18) into the u_4 constraint in (16) yields, after simplification,

(19)
$$(3 - 4u_4)u_4 = 0,$$

so that

(20)
$$u_4 = \frac{3}{4} \quad \text{and} \quad x_1 = \frac{7}{8} \quad x_2 = \frac{5}{8} \quad x_3 = \frac{15}{8} \quad c(x) = 7.25.$$

Accordingly, the point x in (20) is optimal, since it is feasible in the constraints (15), and there exists an associated set of $u_i \geq 0$ satisfying the conditions (16) and (17) at x. To check your understanding, show that the assumptions $x_1 > 0$ and $x_2 = x_3 = 0$ imply that there are no $u_i \geq 0$ that satisfy (16) and (17).

The dual linear program (5) through (8) provides a source of information about solution sensitivity. But instead of employing this device, we will provide in the next paragraphs an important alternative formulation of optimality conditions that directly yields the desired sensitivity analysis. What is more, the approach is convenient for explaining the algorithmic implications of the preceding Optimality Conditions; these computational aspects are developed subsequently in this chapter.

A Lagrangian function and its saddle point. Necessary and sufficient conditions for a trial solution $\bar{x}$ to be optimal can also be stated in terms of what is called a **Lagrangian function**. Specifically, let

$$(21) \qquad \qquad \mathrm{L}(x, u) \equiv c(x) - \sum_{i=1}^{M} A_i(x) \cdot u_i.$$

The Lagrangian function $\mathrm{L}(x, u)$ is said to possess a **saddle point** at the pair $(\bar{x}_1, \bar{x}_2, \ldots, \bar{x}_n)$ and $(\bar{u}_1, \bar{u}_2, \ldots, \bar{u}_M)$, where each $\bar{u}_i \geq 0$ if

$$(22) \qquad \qquad \mathrm{L}(x, \bar{u}) \leq \mathrm{L}(\bar{x}, \bar{u}) \leq \mathrm{L}(\bar{x}, u)$$

for all $(x_1, x_2, \ldots, x_n)$ and nonnegative $(u_1, u_2, \ldots, u_M)$. In this context, the variables u_i are called **Lagrange multipliers**. Loosely put, the function $\mathrm{L}(x, \bar{u})$ decreases as x moves away from $\bar{x}$, and the function $\mathrm{L}(\bar{x}, u)$ increases as u moves away from $\bar{u}$.

It can be shown that a pair $\bar{x}$ and $\bar{u} \geq 0$ satisfying the Optimality Conditions (9), (10), and (11) is also a saddle point of $\mathrm{L}(x, u)$, and vice versa. Therefore, from the Lagrangian view, we can state the following conditions.

LAGRANGE OPTIMALITY CONDITIONS. Given the Constraint Qualification and the assumptions (i) through (vi) on $a_i(x)$ and $c(x)$ in Sec. 15.5, a point $\bar{x}$ is optimal if, and only if, there is a point $\bar{u} \geq 0$ such that the pair $(\bar{x}, \bar{u})$ is a saddle point of $\mathrm{L}(x, u)$. Further, the summation term of the right of (21) equals 0 for a saddle point.

[Interestingly, the *sufficient* condition that $\bar{x}$ is optimal if the pair $(\bar{x}, \bar{u})$ is a saddle point holds when all the smoothness and shape assumptions on $a_i(x)$ and $c(x)$ in Sec. 15.5 are dropped.]

Notice that the Lagrangian $\mathrm{L}(x, u)$ is concave in x for $u \geq 0$, and linear in u. The connection between the previous and the Lagrange Optimality Conditions can be reasoned as follows. At a saddle point, the first-order partial derivative of $\mathrm{L}(x, u)$ with respect to each x_j must be nonpositive, in agreement with (14). State why. Further, in agreement with (13), either $\bar{x}_j$ or the first-order partial derivative of $\mathrm{L}(x, u)$ with respect to x_j (or both) must equal 0, for otherwise, $\mathrm{L}(x, u)$ can be increased by varying $\bar{x}_j$. Similarly, the first-order partial derivative of $\mathrm{L}(x, u)$ with respect to each u_i must be nonnegative, in agreement with (9). And either $\bar{u}_i$ or the first-order partial derivative of $\mathrm{L}(x, u)$ with respect to u_i (or both) must equal 0, in agreement with (12). State why.

Because $\mathrm{L}(x, u)$ equals the optimal value of $c(x)$ at a saddle point, the sensitivity of the optimal value of $c(x)$ can be determined by calculating the corresponding impact on $\mathrm{L}(x, u)$. For example, if the ith constraint is revised to $A_i(x) \leq e$, where e is a very small positive number, then the optimal value of $c(x)$ will increase approximately by the amount $e\bar{u}_i$ (except in cases where $\bar{x}$ and $\bar{u}$ are not continuous functions of e for infinitesimal values of e). To illustrate, you saw in (20) that $u_4 = \frac{3}{4}$ for Problem P. If the fourth constraint in (15) is changed to $A_4(x) \leq e$, then $c(x)$ increases from the value 7.25 by approximately $\frac{3}{4}e$ for infinitesimal e.

▶A Lagrangian function can also be used *directly* in the computation of an optimal solution. There are a variety of ways of doing this; one is treated in detail in Sec. 15.9, and a couple of others are sketched below.

Suppose the model has a single nonlinear constraint, say, $a_1(x)$, and all the other constraints are linear. Then revise the objective function to be $[c(x) - a_1(x)u]$, and drop $a_1(x)$ from the constraints. Starting with $u = 0$, solve the model, which consists of a nonlinear objective function and only linear constraints; thus, a technique such as one in Secs. 15.2, 15.3, and 15.4 can be employed. If $u = 0$ yields a solution such that $a_1(x) \leq 0$, then the solution is optimal. Otherwise, continue to increase the value of u until $a_1(x) = 0$. When this occurs, you have in effect obtained a saddle point of the Lagrangian expression (21), and the resultant solution is optimal.

The same approach can also be applied in solving certain dynamic programming problems, such as the Distribution of Effort Model in Sec. 10.2. A problem having two constraints, for example, can be reduced to one having only a single constraint. Consequently, a dynamic programming recursion with a single state variable can be used to solve this modified version. If the decision variables must really be integers, then the final solution found by such an approach may be only approximately optimal in the original problem.

Another computational use of a Lagrangian function is in so-called *small-step gradient* algorithms. Such methods form a set of differential equations based on the first-order partial derivatives of the Lagrangian function with respect to each x_j and u_i. Under certain assumptions, the associated time paths of the variables determined by the differential equations converge to an optimal solution.   ◄

****Duality.** Using the Lagrangian function $\mathrm{L}(x, u)$ in (21), we state the following optimization problem, which is termed the *dual problem*: find an x and $u \geq 0$ to

$$(23) \qquad\qquad \text{minimize } \mathrm{L}(x, u)$$

subject to

$$(24) \qquad \frac{\partial c(x)}{\partial x_j} - \sum_{i=1}^{M} \frac{\partial A_i(x)}{\partial x_j} \cdot u_i = 0 \quad \text{for } j = 1, 2, \ldots, n.$$

We can prove the following theorem.

DUAL THEOREM OF NONLINEAR PROGRAMMING. Given the Constraint Qualification and the assumptions (i) through (vi) on $a_i(x)$ and $c(x)$ in Sec. 15.5, (i) if $\bar{x}$ is an optimal solution to the nonlinear programming problem, then there exists a $\bar{u} \geq 0$ such that the pair $\bar{x}$ and $\bar{u}$ solves the dual problem (23) and (24). Further, if x is feasible in the original problem, and x and u are feasible for the dual problem, then $c(x) \leq \mathrm{L}(x, u)$; equality holds for an optimal pair $\bar{x}$ and $\bar{u}$. (ii) Conversely, if the pair $\bar{x}$ and $\bar{u}$ solve the dual problem, (23) and (24), if $A_i(\bar{x}) \leq 0$ for every i, and if either $c(x)$ is strictly concave, or there exists a k such that $A_k(x)$ is strictly convex and $\bar{u}_k > 0$, then $\bar{x}$ solves the original nonlinear programming problem. Further, $c(\bar{x}) = \mathrm{L}(\bar{x}, \bar{u})$.

Notice that the objective function (23) for this dual problem is not so simple as it is in the dual problem for a linear programming model. In particular, $\mathrm{L}(x, u)$ includes the *primal* objective function $c(x)$. The theorem has several applications of importance. One, which is not pursued in this text because of its advanced nature, is the use of the dual formulation of a quadratic programming problem to derive several elegant computational algorithms. Another application will be taken up in Sec. 15.9.

*15.8 QUADRATIC PROGRAMMING REVISITED

The following quadratic programming problem was considered in Sec. 14.6:

$$(1) \qquad \text{maximize } c(x) \equiv \sum_{j=1}^{n} c_j x_j + \sum_{j=1}^{n} \sum_{k=1}^{n} c_{jk} x_j x_k$$

subject to

$$(2) \qquad \sum_{j=1}^{n} a_{ij} x_j \leq b_i \quad \text{for } i = 1, 2, \ldots, m$$

$$(3) \qquad \text{all } x_j \geq 0.$$

Assume here that the c_{jk} have been defined so that $c_{jk} = c_{kj}$ for all k and j; this convention is innocuous, for any quadratic expression can be written in this fashion (to illustrate, $8x_1 x_2 - 5x_2 x_1 \equiv 1.5 x_1 x_2 + 1.5 x_2 x_1$). (Slack variables $s_i \geq 0$ were also included in the formulation of Sec. 14.6, and will be introduced again below.) Assume, for simplicity, that each $b_i \geq 0$. Also postulate that the double summation quadratic term on the right of (1) is a concave function. (Expressed mathematically, the assumption is that the quadratic form is negative semidefinite.)

Now we apply the necessary and sufficient conditions for an optimal solution, given by (10) and (11) in the preceding section. For this purpose,

$$(4) \qquad \begin{aligned} A_i(x) &\equiv \sum_{j=1}^{n} a_{ij} x_j - b_i \quad \text{for } i = 1, 2, \ldots, m \\ A_{m+j}(x) &\equiv -x_j \qquad\qquad \text{for } j = 1, 2, \ldots, n. \end{aligned}$$

As you can verify,

$$(5) \qquad \frac{\partial c(x)}{\partial x_j} = c_j + 2 \sum_{k=1}^{n} c_{jk} x_k \quad \text{for } j = 1, 2, \ldots, n.$$

Then (10) in the preceding section gives

$$(6) \qquad \left(\sum_{j=1}^{n} a_{ij} x_j - b_i \right) \cdot u_i = 0 \quad \text{for } i = 1, 2, \ldots, m$$

$$(7) \qquad (-x_j) \cdot u_{m+j} = 0 \quad \text{for } j = 1, 2, \ldots, n,$$

and (11) yields

$$(8) \qquad c_j + 2 \sum_{k=1}^{n} c_{jk} x_k - \sum_{i=1}^{m} a_{ij} u_i + u_{m+j} = 0 \quad \text{for } j = 1, 2, \ldots, n.$$

These expressions can be simplified by introducing some additional notation. Let $s_i \geq 0$ be the slack variable for the ith constraint in (2), so that

$$(9) \qquad \sum_{j=1}^{n} a_{ij} x_j + s_i = b_i \quad \text{for } i = 1, 2, \ldots, m,$$

and let $w_j \equiv u_{m+j}$ for $j = 1, 2, \ldots, n$. Then (6) and (7) become, after simplification,

$$(10) \qquad s_i u_i = 0 \quad \text{for } i = 1, 2, \ldots, m$$

(11) $$x_j w_j = 0 \quad \text{for } j = 1, 2, \ldots, n.$$

Since s_i, u_i, x_j, and w_j must be nonnegative, (10) and (11) can be expressed by a single constraint:

(12) $$\sum_{i=1}^{m} s_i u_i + \sum_{j=1}^{n} x_j w_j = 0 \qquad \text{Complementary slackness.}$$

Using the newly defined variables w_j, (8) can be written as

(13) $$2 \sum_{k=1}^{n} c_{jk} x_k - \sum_{i=1}^{m} a_{ij} u_i + w_j = -c_j \quad \text{for } j = 1, 2, \ldots, n.$$

An implication of the Optimality Conditions in Sec. 15.7 is that if you can find nonnegative values for x_j, s_i, u_i, w_j such that (9), (12), and (13) are satisfied, then such x_j are optimal for the quadratic programming problem. Observe that (9) and (13) represent $m + n$ *linear* constraints in $2(m + n)$ nonnegative variables. Of course, (12) is not a linear constraint, but it is so special that numerous techniques can be devised that are capable of fully exploiting the linearity of the other necessary and sufficient conditions for an optimal solution. One such algorithm, to be presented next, is based on fairly simple modifications of the simplex method, and converges in a finite number of iterations.

Modified Simplex Algorithm. Before stating the procedure, we first establish some helpful nomenclature. Denote x_j ·and s_i as *primal* variables and w_j and u_i as *dual* variables. Designate as *complementary* variables each pair x_j and w_j, and, likewise, each pair s_i and u_i. In this method, the linear constraints consist of (9) and (13), and at each iteration, there is a basic solution containing $m + n$ variables. Every primal variable in the basis is nonnegative, so, as a consequence, the original constraints (2) are always satisfied. As in the simplex method, the iterations do not terminate so long as any dual variable is negative.

A basic solution at any iteration is always one of two types: the first possibility is that for each j and each i, the basis contains only one complementary variable. Such a solution is called a *standard basis*, and satisfies the complementary slackness constraint (12). The other possibility is that the solution contains a *basic pair* of complementary variables, and as a result there is also a *nonbasic pair* of complementary variables. Such a solution is called a *nonstandard basis*. (Some authors use the terms *complementary basis* and *almost complementary basis* as synonyms for "standard" and "nonstandard.") The principal modification of the simplex method is that whenever a nonstandard basis occurs, the selection procedure for entering a new variable into the basis seeks to re-establish the complementary slackness condition (12).

Straightforward algebraic manipulation using the constraints (9) and (13) yields the following formula for $c(x)$ which is valid whenever the complementary slackness condition (12) holds:

(14) $$c(x) = \tfrac{1}{2} \left(\sum_{j=1}^{n} c_j x_j + \sum_{i=1}^{m} b_i u_i \right) \qquad \text{Standard basis.}$$

Letting

(15) $$x_0 \equiv 2c(x),$$

you can append the *linear* relation

(16) $$x_0 - \sum_{j=1}^{n} c_j x_j - \sum_{i=1}^{m} b_i u_i = 0$$

to the set of constraints to provide the value of $2c(x)$ at a standard basis.

In explaining the specific rules, we illustrate the process using Problem P from Sec. 15.1. The linear constraints consisting of (16), (9), and (13) are

(17)
$$
\begin{array}{llll}
x_0 - 6x_1 - 4x_2 - 2x_3 - 4u_1 & = 0 & \text{Row 0} \\
\quad x_1 + 2x_2 + x_3 + s_1 & = 4 & \text{Row 1} \\
\quad -6x_1 \qquad\qquad - u_1 + w_1 & = -6 & \text{Row 2} \\
\qquad\quad -4x_2 \qquad - 2u_1 + w_2 & = -4 & \text{Row 3} \\
\qquad\qquad -\tfrac{2}{3}x_3 - u_1 + w_3 & = -2 & \text{Row 4.}
\end{array}
$$

Let the initial solution contain the variables x_0, s_1, w_1, w_2, w_3, which is a standard basis. Then apply the following criterion.

MODIFIED SIMPLEX CRITERION I. (a) For a standard basis, terminate the iterations if all the dual variables are nonnegative. Otherwise, select the nonbasic primal variable that is complementary to the most negative basic dual variable. (b) For a nonstandard basis, select the dual variable of the nonbasic pair.

In (17), since w_1 is the most negative dual variable, select x_1 to enter the basis.

In determining the variable to drop from the basis, it is desirable to maintain a standard basic solution, or if none exists, to establish one. But since the method maintains feasibility in terms of the primal variables, it is not always possible to maintain or establish a standard basic solution. The following criterion for selecting a variable to drop from the basis takes account of these considerations.

MODIFIED SIMPLEX CRITERION II. (a) Take the ratios of the current right-hand side to the coefficients of the entering variable in those rows corresponding to a primal basic variable (ignore ratios with zero or negative numbers in the denominator). Let r be the value of the minimum ratio, which occurs for a primal basic variable in Row k. (b) For a standard basis, take the ratio of the current right-hand side to the coefficient of the entering primal variable in the row of the corresponding complementary dual variable. If this ratio is positive and does not exceed r, then drop the complementary dual variable from the basis. Otherwise, drop the basic primal variable in Row k. (c) For a nonstandard basis, take the ratio of the current right-hand side to the coefficient of the entering unknown in the row corresponding to the dual variable of the basic pair. If this ratio is positive and does not exceed r, then drop this dual variable from the basis. Otherwise, drop the primal basic variable in Row k.

Since x_1 is to enter, and the current solution (17) is a standard basis, part (a)

indicates $r = 4/1$, and part (b) indicates the ratio $-1/-1$. Therefore, the complementary dual variable w_1 leaves the basis, and the next solution is a standard basis. The pivot operation is exactly the same as in the ordinary simplex method.

Verify that the constraints, after pivoting out w_1 and entering x_1, are:

$$
\begin{array}{lll}
x_0 \quad - 4x_2 - 2x_3 - 3u_1 \quad - w_1 \qquad\qquad = 6 & \text{Row 0} \\
\qquad\quad 2x_2 + x_3 - \tfrac{1}{6}u_1 + s_1 + \tfrac{1}{6}w_1 \qquad = 3 & \text{Row 1} \\
\text{(18)} \qquad x_1 \qquad\quad + \tfrac{1}{6}u_1 \qquad - \tfrac{1}{6}w_1 \qquad = 1 & \text{Row 2} \\
\qquad\quad - 4x_2 \qquad - 2u_1 \qquad\qquad + w_2 \quad = -4 & \text{Row 3} \\
\qquad\qquad\quad -\tfrac{2}{3}x_3 - u_1 \qquad\qquad\qquad + w_3 = -2 & \text{Row 4.}
\end{array}
$$

Now *Criterion I* implies that x_2 enters the basis, since w_2 is the most negative dual variable in (18). Therefore, according to *Criterion II*, $r = 3/2$ and the ratio in part (b) is $-4/-4$, so that w_2 leaves the basis. Once again, the next solution is a complementary basis, and a so-called **complementary pivot operation** occurs, since a primal variable enters and a complementary dual variable leaves the basis.

Check that the constraints after pivoting are

$$
\begin{array}{lll}
x_0 \quad - 2x_3 - u_1 \quad - w_1 - w_2 \qquad = 10 & \text{Row 0} \\
\qquad\quad x_3 - \tfrac{7}{6}u_1 + s_1 + \tfrac{1}{6}w_1 + \tfrac{1}{2}w_2 \quad = 1 & \text{Row 1} \\
\text{(19)} \qquad x_1 \quad + \tfrac{1}{6}u_1 \qquad - \tfrac{1}{6}w_1 \qquad = 1 & \text{Row 2} \\
\qquad\quad x_2 \quad + \tfrac{1}{2}u_1 \qquad\qquad - \tfrac{1}{4}w_2 \quad = 1 & \text{Row 3} \\
\qquad\qquad - \tfrac{2}{3}x_3 - u_1 \qquad\qquad\qquad + w_3 = -2 & \text{Row 4.}
\end{array}
$$

Here *Criterion I* specifies that x_3 is to enter. Accordingly, $r = (1/1)$ from Row 1, and the ratio in part (b) of *Criterion II* is $-2/-\tfrac{2}{3}$, so s_1 leaves the basis. Consequently, the next solution is a nonstandard basis.

After pivoting, you have

$$
\begin{array}{lll}
x_0 \quad - \tfrac{10}{3}u_1 + 2s_1 - \tfrac{2}{3}w_1 \qquad\qquad = 12 & \text{Row 0} \\
\qquad\quad x_3 - \tfrac{7}{6}u_1 + s_1 + \tfrac{1}{6}w_1 + \tfrac{1}{2}w_2 \quad = 1 & \text{Row 1} \\
\text{(20)} \qquad x_1 \quad + \tfrac{1}{6}u_1 \qquad - \tfrac{1}{6}w_1 \qquad = 1 & \text{Row 2} \\
\qquad\quad x_2 + \tfrac{1}{2}u_1 \qquad\qquad - \tfrac{1}{4}w_2 \quad = 1 & \text{Row 3} \\
\qquad - \tfrac{16}{9}u_1 + \tfrac{2}{3}s_1 + \tfrac{1}{9}w_1 + \tfrac{1}{3}w_2 + w_3 = -\tfrac{4}{3} & \text{Row 4.}
\end{array}
$$

The basic variables in (20) are x_0, x_1, x_2, x_3, w_3; the nonbasic pair of complementary variables consists of s_1 and u_1. Consequently, part (b) of *Criterion I* indicates that u_1 enters. Accordingly, $r = \text{minimum } (1/\tfrac{1}{6}, 1/\tfrac{1}{2}) = 2$, and the ratio in part (c) is $(-\tfrac{4}{3}/-\tfrac{16}{9}) = \tfrac{3}{4}$; hence, w_3 leaves the basis, thereby restoring the next solution to a standard basis.

The equations, after pivoting, are

$$x_0 \qquad + \tfrac{3}{4}s_1 - \tfrac{7}{8}w_1 - \tfrac{5}{8}w_2 - \tfrac{15}{8}w_3 = 14\tfrac{1}{2} \qquad \text{Row 0}$$

$$x_3 \quad + \tfrac{9}{16}s_1 + \tfrac{3}{32}w_1 + \tfrac{9}{32}w_2 - \tfrac{21}{32}w_3 = 1\tfrac{7}{8} \qquad \text{Row 1}$$

(21) $$x_1 \qquad + \tfrac{1}{16}s_1 - \tfrac{5}{32}w_1 + \tfrac{1}{32}w_2 + \tfrac{3}{32}w_3 = \tfrac{7}{8} \qquad \text{Row 2}$$

$$x_2 \qquad + \tfrac{3}{16}s_1 + \tfrac{1}{32}w_1 - \tfrac{5}{32}w_2 + \tfrac{9}{32}w_3 = \tfrac{5}{8} \qquad \text{Row 3}$$

$$u_1 - \tfrac{3}{8}s_1 - \tfrac{1}{16}w_1 - \tfrac{3}{16}w_2 - \tfrac{9}{16}w_3 = \tfrac{3}{4} \qquad \text{Row 4.}$$

The iterations terminate, since the current solution is a standard basis with non-negative values for all the dual variables. The optimal value of $c(x)$ is $.5x_0 = 7.25$.

A full comparison of the computational merits of this algorithm and the one in Sec. 14.6 goes beyond the scope of this text, as it involves a number of technical details relating to the development of an efficient computer program. But briefly, the tradeoff seems to be that the algorithm in this section converges in fewer iterations at the expense of maintaining a system of $m + n$ equations throughout. The technique in Sec. 14.6 has the advantage of always converging to a constrained stationary point, even when the objective function is not concave; the algorithm here does not always converge for an arbitrary shaped quadratic objective function.

A number of other quadratic programming algorithms that have been devised resemble the Modified Simplex Algorithm, in that they too give special attention to complementary pivot operations and converge in a finite number of iterations.

15.9 PENALTY FUNCTION APPROACH

In Sec. 15.7, you saw that a nonlinear programming problem can be posed in terms of finding a saddle point for a Lagrangian function. The Penalty Function Approach stems from that kind of formulation. In the method, several (or all) of the constraints are incorporated into the objective function. There are several ways to do this; we selected the approach below because it has been successful in practice. We continue to assume that the nonlinear problem satisfies the assumptions (i) through (vi) and the Constraint Qualification in Sec. 15.5.

We begin the explanation by showing how to combine a single $a_i(x)$ with the objective function. This simple case will serve to motivate the general approach, which is treated afterwards. Specifically, consider as the modified function to be maximized:

$$(1) \qquad c(x \mid r) \equiv c(x) + r[1/a_i(x)],$$

where $r > 0$ is a parameter. For those x such that $a_i(x) < 0$, the function $[1/a_i(x)]$ is concave, and therefore $c(x \mid r)$ is concave for x strictly in the interior of the region defined by $a_i(x) \leq 0$. The term $r[1/a_i(x)]$ becomes a very negative number for a feasible point that is near the boundary $a_i(x) = 0$. Consequently, a point that maximizes $c(x \mid r)$ subject to all the constraints can never be *on* the boundary $a_i(x) = 0$. If the value of the parameter r is close enough to 0, however, it can be shown that such a point is nearly optimal for the original problem.

To apply the Penalty Function Approach, you combine several (or all) of the constraints with the objective function in a fashion analogous to (1). Then you obtain a feasible solution that is optimal for the modified objective function, given an initial value for r. You successively reduce the value of r (> 0)—each time finding a new solution to the modified problem. You terminate the algorithm when the expression involving r has negligible effect on $c(x|r)$, and accept the resultant solution as approximately optimal. If the original model contains the constraint $f_i(x) \leq 0$, and you suspect that an optimal solution actually does lie on the boundary $f_i(x) = 0$, then you can define $a_i(x) \equiv f_i(x) - e$, where you choose e to be a small positive number. Such an approach, however, can lead to a point where $f_i(x) > 0$, if you chose e too large.

What makes this type of approach computationally attractive? Since a trial point is never on a nonlinear boundary, at each iteration you can calculate *directions* for improvement *as if* the optimization process were for an unconstrained objective function, and for this reason, you may view the method as a *sequential unconstrained maximization technique* (the approach is sometimes referred to by the acronym *SUMT*). After computing a set of directions, you next calculate an optimal *feasible* step size. You are aided in this optimization by the fact that the modified objective function is strictly concave in the interior of the feasible region. When actually applying the approach, you find only a near optimum to $c(x|r)$ for each r, since ordinarily you cannot calculate an exact optimum in a finite number of iterations. The complete details of the method are given below.

The method, as it will be described, combines all the constraints, including the nonnegativity conditions, into a modified objective function. But note that if the constraints contain only a few nonlinear functions, the rest being linear, then the Penalty Function Approach can be coupled with any technique for optimizing a nonlinear function subject to linear constraints. Specifically, the objective function can be modified by introducing only the nonlinear constraints; then a method, such as one of those discussed in Secs. 15.2, 15.3, and 15.4, can be employed for successively smaller values of $r > 0$. Each resultant solution is feasible in the original problem, and also is approximately optimal for r sufficiently small.

SUMT Algorithm. Assume that all the constraints are to be added to the objective function, including the nonnegativity conditions $x_j \geq 0$. Accordingly, designate the constraints as $A_i(x) \leq 0$ for $i = 1, 2, \ldots, M (= m + n)$. The modified problem is to maximize

$$(2) \qquad\qquad c(x|r) \equiv c(x) + r\left[\sum_{i=1}^{M} \frac{1}{A_i(x)}\right] \quad (r > 0)$$

over all feasible x. The second summation on the right of (2) includes the terms $(1/-x_j)$ so that $c(x|r)$ is strictly concave and possesses a unique optimal solution for each r. The bracketed term on the right of (2) is negative for all feasible x, so that $c(x|r) < c(x)$.

The procedure in detail is:

Step 1. Select an initial value $r^1 > 0$, and an initial trial point x^0 such that each $A_i(x)^0 < 0$. Let $k = 0$ and $n = 1$.

Step 2. If x^k nearly maximizes $c(x \mid r^n)$, go to *Step 4*. Otherwise, determine directions d_j^k for $j = 1, 2, \ldots, n$. Choose the step size t^k that maximizes $c(x^k + td^k \mid r)$, where the point $(x^k + t^k d^k)$ must satisfy all the constraints. Continue to *Step 3*.

Step 3. Calculate the new trial point

(3) $$x_j^{k+1} = x_j^k + t^k d_j^k \quad \text{for } j = 1, 2, \ldots, n.$$

Increase k to $k + 1$, and return to *Step 2*.

Step 4. Terminate the iterations if x^k is nearly optimal. Otherwise, calculate a new r^{n+1}, where $0 < r^{n+1} < r^n$. Increase n to $n + 1$, and return to *Step 2*.

Effective ways of performing *Step 1* are mainly of interest to operations research specialists, and thus are not discussed at length in this text. But we do mention what is at issue with regard to the choice of r^1. If r^1 is too large, then an optimal solution to $c(x \mid r^1)$ is likely to be far from an optimal solution of the original problem. On the other hand, if r^1 is too small, then finding a near maximum of $c(x \mid r^1)$ usually requires a considerable number of iterations. A proper choice of r^1 strikes a balance between these two effects.

You can employ any procedure for selecting directions in *Step 2* that is effective for an unconstrained problem. Because $c(x \mid r)$ is strictly concave for feasible x, the conditions

(4) $$\frac{\partial c(x \mid r)}{\partial x_j} = \frac{\partial c(x)}{\partial x_j} - r \sum_{i=1}^{M} \left[\frac{\frac{\partial A_i(x)}{\partial x_j}}{[A_i(x)]^2} \right] = 0 \text{ for each } j$$

are necessary and sufficient for a feasible x to maximize $c(x \mid r)$. If you select the directions according to the method of steepest ascent, described in Sec. 14.5, then each $d_j = \partial c(x \mid r) / \partial x_j$. (Practitioners have found it beneficial to actually use second-order methods.)

A formula for reducing r in *Step 4* that works well is $r^{n+1} = f r^n$, where $0 < f < 1$. The particular value for f does not seem to be very critical, except that as f is made small, more iterations are required to optimize $c(x \mid r^n)$ for each n.

The method ensures that $c(x \mid r)$ increases at each new trial point, and it can be proved that the maximum value of $c(x \mid r)$ converges to the optimum value $\bar{c}$ for the original problem as r approaches 0. Furthermore, if x^k truly maximizes $c(x \mid r^n)$ when *Step 4* is reached, then $c(x^k)$ is at least as large as it was at the previous *Step 4*, and usually is strictly better. Similarly, the bracketed term on the right of (2) is never larger than it was at the previous *Step 4*, and an upper bound on $\bar{c}$ is

(5) $$\bar{c} \le c(x^k) - r^n \left[\sum_{i=1}^{M} \frac{1}{A_i(x^k)} \right].$$

As we mentioned earlier, in practice x^k will not truly maximize $c(x\,|\,r^n)$ when *Step 4* is reached. So in applying the algorithm, the foregoing properties will actually be fulfilled only if $c(x^k\,|\,r^n)$ is sufficiently close to its maximum value. Observing the same warning, you can compare the value for the expression on the right-hand side of (5) to $c(x^k)$ in deciding whether to terminate the iterations at *Step 4*. A final word of caution about applying the approach: you must perform the calculations with care, because as both r and the denominators of the bracketed terms in (2) get small, the arithmetic becomes quite delicate and sensitive to round-off errors.

▶The validity of (5) is based on the duality result in Sec. 15.7. Let x be a truly optimal solution to $c(x\,|\,r^n)$. Then, according to (4), x must satisfy

(i)
$$\frac{\partial c(x)}{\partial x_j} - r^n \left[\sum_{i=1}^{M} \frac{\frac{\partial A_i(x)}{\partial x_j}}{[A_i(x)]^2} \right] = 0 \quad \text{for each } j.$$

Let

(ii)
$$u_i \equiv \frac{r^n}{[A_i(x)]^2} \geq 0 \quad \text{for } i = 1, 2, \ldots, M,$$

and therefore, x and u satisfy (24) in Sec. 15.7. Hence, from the Dual Theorem of Nonlinear Programming:

(iii)
$$\bar{c} \leq L(x, u) = c(x) - r^n \left[\sum_{i=1}^{M} \frac{1}{A_i(x)} \right],$$

in agreement with (5).   ◀

Examples. The results for Problems P and Q from Secs. 15.1 and 15.5 are shown in Figs. 15.8 and 15.9. At each r^n, the nearly optimal value for $c(x\,|\,r^n)$ was found by using the method of steepest ascent; that is, the directions were chosen to be the first-order partial derivatives of $c(x\,|\,r^n)$ at x^k. The values of k shown in the figures correspond to those of x^k that are deemed nearly optimal

$f = .5$

n	r^n	k	$c(x^k)$	x_1^k	x_2^k	x_3^k	Upper Bound	$c(x^k\,|\,r^n)$
	$--$	0	1.147	.1	.1	.1	$--$	$--$
1	.0365	14	7.091	.854	.595	1.755	7.397	6.785
2	.0182	19	7.136	.872	.606	1.770	7.323	6.950
3	.0091	22	7.168	.877	.619	1.779	7.285	7.051
4	.0046	25	7.189	.881	.628	1.786	7.262	7.115
5	.0023	27	7.203	.883	.634	1.790	$--$	7.157
10	.0001	34	7.239	.890	.650	1.801	$--$	7.232
Optimal Values	$--$	$--$	7.25	.875	.625	1.875	$--$	7.25

FIGURE 15.8. SUMT Algorithm—Problem P.

$$f = .5$$

n	r^n	k	$c(x^k)$	x_1^k	x_2^k	x_3^k	Upper Bound	$c(x^k \mid r^n)$
	— —	0	−6	1	1	3	— —	— —
1	.3	15	−4.679	.935	.776	2.193	−3.120	−6.239
2	.15	23	−4.474	.913	.724	2.113	−3.553	−5.396
3	.075	29	−4.332	.897	.685	2.064	−3.774	−4.890
4	.0375	31	−4.240	.884	.656	2.043	−3.899	−4.581
5	.0188	33	−4.171	.874	.634	2.028	−3.955	−4.387
6	.0094	36	−4.119	.868	.618	2.015	−3.975	−4.263
7	.0047	39	−4.085	.866	.609	2.001	−3.989	−4.182
Optimal Values	— —	— —	−4.00	.875	.625	1.875	— —	−4.00

Figure 15.9. SUMT Algorithm—Problem Q.

in *Step 2*. Notice that the biggest improvement in the objective function $c(x)$ occurs in maximizing $c(x \mid r^1)$.

▶ In Problem P, using the same initial point x^0 but letting $f = .75$ slows the convergence somewhat. In this case, $r = .0027$ at $n = 10$; the corresponding nearly optimal solution to $c(x \mid r^{10})$ is $x^{33} = (.8813, .6372, 1.7873)$ with $c(x^{33}) = 7.2043$ and $c(x^{33} \mid r^{10}) = 7.1473$. The result is comparable to $n = 5$ and $k = 27$ in Fig. 15.8.

Using a better initial point $x^0 = (.5, .5, .5)$ with $c(x^0) = 4.6667$ but a larger $r^1 = .6068$ (and $f = .5$) yields surprising results. Although the initial trial point is better than that in Fig. 15.8, at $n = 5$ and $k = 44$ the trial solution is $x^{44} = (.8748, .6246, 1.6646)$ with $c(x^{44}) = 7.0767$ and $c(x^{44} \mid r^5 = .0379) = 6.7704$. The larger value for r^1 results in many more iterations to obtain a result comparable to $n = 1$ and $k = 14$ in Fig. 15.8.

Using a value of 4.1 instead of 4 in specifying the linear constraint yields, at $n = 3$ and $k = 33$, the trial solution $x^{33} = (.8869, .6584, 1.7775)$ with $c(x^{33}) = 7.2301$. This point does not differ much from the solution x^{34} in Fig. 15.8.

In Problem Q, using r^1 equal to either .1 or .2 has a negligible effect on the k required to give an answer comparable to $n = 7$ and $k = 39$ in Fig. 15.9. ◀

15.10 GENERALIZED PROGRAMMING
ALGORITHM

This method has much in common with the Separable Programming Approach in Sec. 14.7, since it employs linear approximations with a grid of points, and uses the simplex method to compute a corresponding solution. But the Generalized Programming Algorithm is more sophisticated, in that it allows the grid to be refined during the course of the iterations. This approach can be formulated in a variety of ways; hence, you should view the presentation below as merely illustrative of the general idea. We continue to postulate that the nonlinear functions satisfy assumptions (i) through (vi) and the Constraint Qualification in Sec. 15.5.

To begin, suppose we partition the entire group of nonlinear *and* nonnegativity constraints into two categories. Let the first partition contain R constraints, to be designated as

$$(1) \qquad A_i(x_1, x_2, \ldots, x_n) \leq 0 \quad \text{for } i = 1, 2, \ldots, R;$$

some of these restrictions may be the nonnegativity constraints. Possibly (1) may contain all the constraints, in which case $R = m + n$; then the second category would be vacuous. When $R < m + n$, the region satisfying the second category of constraints is convex and contains all of its boundary points, given assumption (i) imposed on the constraints in Sec. 15.5. For convenience, let the symbol

$S \equiv$ set of all points satisfying those constraints that
    are not contained in (1).

(When $R = m + n$, S is all of Euclidean n-space.) Hence, the optimization problem can be stated as

$$(2) \qquad \text{maximize } c(x_1, x_2, \ldots, x_n)$$

subject to the point x satisfying (1) and lying in S.

Consider iteration k of the algorithm. Assume that the current approximating grid is $X^0, X^1, \ldots, X^T$, where each of these points satisfies the constraints in S, and at least one of them is feasible in (1), with a strict inequality holding for each truly nonlinear $A_i(x)$. (Recall from Sec. 15.5 that we postulated the existence of such a point in the Constraint Qualification.) With this grid, you solve what is called a **restricted master program** representing a linear approximation to the original model:

$$(3) \qquad \text{maximize } \sum_{t=0}^{T} c(X^t) w_t$$

subject to

$$(4) \qquad \sum_{t=0}^{T} A_i(X^t) w_t \leq 0 \quad \text{for } i = 1, 2, \ldots, R$$

$$(5) \qquad \sum_{t=0}^{T} w_t = 1 \quad \text{and} \quad \text{each } w_t \geq 0.$$

The adjective "restricted" refers to the fact that (3), (4), and (5) do not contain every possible X^t that is feasible in S, but only the subset of $T + 1$ grid points. Each w_t represents a weight for the point X^t. The restricted master program is a linear programming problem, and has a basic feasible solution and a finite maximum value c^k. (State why.) Because the $A_i(x)$ are convex functions and the set S is convex, it is easy to show that *any* feasible solution to (4) and (5) yields a point

$$(6) \qquad x_j = \sum_{t=0}^{T} X_j^t w_t \quad \text{for each } j$$

that is itself feasible in the original problem.

Consider next the dual problem corresponding to (3), (4), and (5), namely

(7) $$\text{minimize } y_{R+1}$$

subject to

(8) $$\sum_{i=1}^{R} A_i(X^t)y_i + y_{R+1} \geq c(X^t) \quad \text{for } t = 0, 1, \dots, T$$

(9) $\quad y_i \geq 0 \quad \text{for } i = 1, 2, \dots, R$ and y_{R+1} unrestricted in sign.

As explained below, reference to the dual yields a test of whether an optimal solution to the restricted master program is also optimal for the original problem.

Assume that w^k is optimal for the restricted master program (3), (4), and (5), and that the corresponding x^k is found by calculating the weighted average (6). Let y^k be an associated optimal solution to the dual problem. It is easily shown that if

(10) $$\sum_{i=1}^{R} A_i(x)y_i^k + y_{R+1}^k \geq c(x) \quad \text{or equivalently} \quad y_{R+1}^k \geq c(x) - \sum_{i=1}^{R} A_i(x)y_i^k,$$

for *all* x in S, then x^k is truly optimal in the original problem. But if there exists an X^{T+1} in S such that

(11) $$y_{R+1}^k < c(X^{T+1}) - \sum_{i=1}^{R} A_i(X^{T+1})y_i^k,$$

then adding this new point to the restricted master program may result in an improved solution. Finding whether such an X^{T+1} exists is referred to as the **subprogram**. The effectiveness of the Generalized Programming Algorithm depends significantly on the difficulty of computing a solution to the subprogram. This aspect will be discussed in more detail later in the section.

To summarize, the procedure at iteration k is

Step 1. Find an optimal solution to the restricted master program. The associated trial point x^k can be calculated according to (6).

Step 2. Determine whether there is a point X^{T+1} in S such that the inequality in (11) holds. If not, terminate the iterations; x^k is truly optimal. Otherwise, continue to *Step 3.*

Step 3. Add the point X^{T+1} to the restricted master program by introducing a new weight w_{T+1} having the coefficients $c(X^{T+1})$ in (3), $A_i(X^{T+1})$ in (4), and 1 in (5). Increase k to $k+1$, and return to *Step 1.*

It can be proved that the optimal values c^k for the objective function of the restricted master program increase monotonically to the optimal value $\bar{c}$ for the objective function of the original problem. And since $c(x)$ is concave, the value $c(x^k)$ is at least as large as c^k.

Solution of the subprogram. Determining an X^{T+1} satisfying the inequality in (11) can itself be posed as an optimization problem: find an x in S to maximize

(12) $$c(x) - \sum_{i=1}^{R} A_i(x) \cdot y_i^k.$$

For ease of exposition, assume throughout the remainder of this section that the maximum in (12) is finite. (When this assumption is not justified, the procedure can be modified in a straightforward fashion.) Verify that (12) is a concave function, since $y_i^k \geq 0$ for all $i \leq R$. If all the original constraints have been included in the R restrictions, then (12) is to be solved as an unconstrained maximization problem.

Given that X^{T+1} is a solution to (12), you can state that

(13) $$\bar{c} \leq c^k + \left[c(X^{T+1}) - \sum_{i=1}^{R} A_i(X^{T+1}) \cdot y_i^k - y_{R+1}^k \right],$$

where, as above, c^k is the maximum value of the objective function for the restricted master program. Further, the algorithm can be terminated at iteration k + 1 if $w_{T+1} = 1$ is optimal. (Explain why.) But note that X^{T+1} will not usually be feasible for all the R constraints, and accordingly, $w_{T+1} = 1$ will not be feasible in the restricted master program. In general, then, the algorithm does not converge in a finite number of iterations; you can terminate the calculations when the current value $c(x^k)$ is sufficiently close to the lowest obtained value of the expression on the right-hand side of (13).

Observe that the expression (12) has the same form as the Lagrangian function (21) in Sec. 15.7 (p. 603). Indeed, when R contains all $m + n$ constraints, the Generalized Programming Algorithm can be viewed as a procedure that systematically searches for a saddle point of a Lagrangian function. Loosely put, it alternates between finding an improved trial solution, given trial values for the Lagrange multipliers, and revising the values of the Lagrange multipliers, consistent with the current trial solution.

Separable problem. The procedure works quite well for a model having a separable objective function and separable constraints:

(14) $$\text{maximize} \sum_{j=1}^{n} c_j(x_j)$$

subject to

(15) $$\sum_{j=1}^{n} a_{ij}(x_j) - b_i \leq 0 \quad \text{for } i = 1, 2, \ldots, m \equiv R,$$

and where now S consists of only the nonnegativity conditions. Here each $c_j(x_j)$ is concave and each $a_{ij}(x_j)$ is convex.

The subprogram (12) then breaks into n separate optimizations:

(16) $$\underset{x_j \geq 0}{\text{maximize}} \; c_j(x_j) - \sum_{i=1}^{m} a_{ij}(x_j) \cdot y_i^k \quad \text{for } j = 1, 2, \ldots, n.$$

In some applications, the form of the functions in (16) may be so simple that a computable formula for X_j^{T+1} results from setting the derivative equal to zero. At worst, a single-variable search technique, such as one given in Sec. 14.3, can be employed to find X_j^{T+1}.

t	X_1^t	X_2^t	X_3^t	$Q(X^t)$	$L(X^t)$	k	x_1^k	x_2^k	x_3^k	Optimal Weights		c^k	$c(x^k)$	Upper Bound	y_1^k
0	0	0	0	0	0	--	--	--	--	$w_0 = .33$	$w_1 = .67$	--	--	--	--
1	1	1	3	8	6	1	.667	.667	2	$w_1 = .44$	$w_2 = .56$	5.33	7.11	7.70	1.33
2	.778	.333	1	5.63	2.44	2	.875	.625	1.875	$w_2 = .125$	$w_3 = .875$	6.67	7.25	7.26	.67
3	.889	.667	2	7.41	4.22	3	.875	.625	1.875	$w_3 = .75$	$w_4 = .25$	7.19	7.25	7.34	1.00
4	.833	.5	1.5	6.67	3.33	4	.875	.625	1.875	$w_3 = .5$	$w_5 = .5$	7.22	7.25	7.26	.83
5	.861	.583	1.75	7.07	3.78	5	.875	.625	1.875	$w_6 = 1$		7.24	7.25	7.25	.75
6	.875	.625	1.875	7.25	4.00	6	.875	.625	1.875			7.25	7.25	--	--
Optimal Values	--	--	--	--	--	--	.875	.625	1.875	--		--	7.25	--	--

$Q(x) \equiv 6x_1 + 4x_2 + 2x_3 - 3x_1^2 - 2x_1^2 - \frac{1}{3}x_3^2$

$L(x) \equiv x_1 + 2x_2 + x_3$

FIGURE 15.10. Generalized Programming Algorithm—Problem P.

▶There is a more elaborate version of the algorithm for the separable case that usually speeds convergence, at the expense of a larger restricted master program. It is essentially the same formulation as that given for separable programming in Sec. 14.7. Weights are introduced for *each* x_j, and a summation analogous to (5) is included for each set of weights. The subprogram (16) is unchanged, but the test (11) is performed using the dual variable for the summation equation associated with weights that yield x_j.   ◀

Examples. Problems P and Q in Secs. 15.1 and 15.5 satisfy the separability formulation in (14) and (15). Write Problems P and Q to exhibit the specific formulas for $c_j(x_j)$ and $a_{1j}(x_j)$. Verify that the $n = 3$ separate subprograms to be solved for Problem P are

$$
\begin{aligned}
&\text{maximize } 6x_1 - 3x_1^2 - x_1 y_1^k \quad \text{for } x_1 \geq 0 \\
(17) \quad &\text{maximize } 4x_2 - 2x_2^2 - 2x_2 y_1^k \quad \text{for } x_2 \geq 0 \\
&\text{maximize } 2x_3 - \tfrac{1}{3}x_3^2 - x_3 y_1^k \quad \text{for } x_3 \geq 0.
\end{aligned}
$$

The corresponding solutions can be found by taking the derivative of each expression in (17) and setting it equal to zero, thereby yielding

$$
(18) \qquad X_1^{T+1} = 1 - \frac{y_1^k}{6} \quad X_2^{T+1} = 1 - \frac{y_1^k}{2} \quad X_3^{T+1} = 3 - \frac{3\,y_1^k}{2},
$$

provided y_1^k is small enough for these expressions to be nonnegative. If an expression in (18) is negative for a particular j, then let $X_j^{T+1} = 0$.

A similar analysis for Problem Q leads to the formulas

$$
(19) \qquad X_1^{T+1} = 1 - \frac{1}{6y_1^k} \quad X_2^{T+1} = 1 - \frac{1}{2\,y_1^k} \quad X_3^{T+1} = 3 - \frac{3}{2\,y_1^k},
$$

instead of (18).

The behavior of the algorithm is exhibited in Figs. 15.10 and 15.11. Notice in Fig. 15.10 that at $k = 2$ the trial solution x^2 is optimal, although several more

t	k	x_1^k	x_2^k	x_3^k	Optimal Weights		$Q(x^k)$	$c^k = c(x^k)$	Upper Bound	y_1^k
0	--	--	--	--	--		--	--	--	--
1	1	.906	.906	2.719	$w_0 = .91$	$w_1 = .09$	-7.93	-5.44	-3.66	.75
2	2	.933	.789	2.367	$w_1 = .68$	$w_2 = .32$	-7.76	-4.88	-3.99	1.50
3	3	.879	.637	1.911	$w_2 = .09$	$w_3 = .91$	-7.30	-4.06	-3.91	1.00
4	4	.877	.631	1.894	$w_3 = .79$	$w_4 = .21$	-7.27	-4.03	-3.99	1.20
5	5	.876	.627	1.882	$w_3 = .53$	$w_5 = .47$	-7.26	-4.01	-3.99	1.33
6	6	.875	.625	1.875	$w_6 = 1$		-7.25	-4	--	--
Optimal Values	--	.875	.625	1.875	--		-7.25	-4	--	--

$$
Q(x) \equiv -6x_1 - 4x_2 - 2x_3 + 3x_1^2 + 2x_1^2 + \tfrac{1}{3}x_3^2
$$

Figure 15.11. Generalized Programming Algorithm—Problem Q.

iterations are needed to verify this fact. Observe that the upper bound from (13) does *not* steadily decrease. Interestingly, the technique applied to Problem Q gives, for every k, a value of y_1^k that is the reciprocal of the value of y_1^k in Fig. 15.10. As a result, the algorithm produces according to (18) and (19) the very same sequence of X^t as in Problem P. (Hence, these X^t are not repeated in Fig. 15.11.) But in Problem Q, the optimal solution x^k is not obtained until $k = 6$.

*15.11 DECOMPOSITION OF LINEAR PROGRAMS

An important special case of the separable model (14) and (15) in the preceding section is an ordinary linear programming problem. In this case, categorize the m constraints into a restricted master program with $R(< m)$ linear restrictions, and a subprogram with the remaining $m - R$ linear constraints *and* the nonnegativity stipulations. There are two reasons why decomposing the problem in this way may be beneficial. First, m may be too large for the capacity of whatever electronic computer is available to you. Splitting the problem into smaller pieces may alleviate the capacity restriction. Second, the $m - R$ restrictions contained in S may have a special structure that can be computationally exploited in solving the subprogram; for example, they may represent the flow-balance equations for a network. Since there are several ways to decompose a linear programming problem, the presentation below is meant to be an illustrative rather than a comprehensive treatment of the approach.

Specifically, suppose you characterize the model as

$$(1) \qquad \text{maximize} \sum_{j=1}^{n} c_j x_j$$

subject to

$$(2) \qquad A_i(x) \equiv \sum_{j=1}^{n} a_{ij} x_j - b_i \leq 0 \quad \text{for } i = 1, 2, \ldots, R,$$

where x must also satisfy

$$(3) \qquad \sum_{j=1}^{n} a_{ij} x_j - b_i \leq 0 \quad \text{for } i = R + 1, \ldots, m \quad \text{and} \quad \text{each } x_j \geq 0.$$

The restricted master program is exactly the same as in (3), (4), and (5) of the preceding section; therefore, it contains $R + 1$ linear restrictions. The corresponding subprogram is to find values of x_j satisfying (3) that maximize

$$(4) \qquad \sum_{j=1}^{n} c_j x_j - \sum_{i=1}^{R} \left(\sum_{j=1}^{n} a_{ij} x_j \right) \cdot y_i^k = \sum_{j=1}^{n} \left(c_j - \sum_{i=1}^{R} a_{ij} y_i^k \right) \cdot x_j,$$

where the y_i^k are the dual variables associated with the solution to the restricted master program at iteration k. Observe that the expression in (4) is a linear function of x_j, and consequently, the subprogram is an ordinary linear programming problem. If there exists a solution $x_j = X_j$ such that

$$(5) \qquad y_{R+1}^k < \sum_{j=1}^{n} \left(c_j - \sum_{i=1}^{R} a_{ij} y_i^k \right) \cdot X_j + \sum_{i=1}^{R} b_i y_i^k,$$

then the iterations continue with X introduced into the restricted master program as a new grid point.

This case of the Generalized Programming Algorithm is often referred to as the **Decomposition Algorithm** for linear programs. It converges to an optimal solution in a *finite* number of trials. Further, at the end of *Step 1*, you can discard from the restricted master program those grid points corresponding to the non-basic variables. The restricted master program, therefore, never need contain more than $R + 1$ variables (weights) at the beginning of an iteration. Each grid point X^t contains at most $m - R$ variables at positive levels, if the simplex method is used to solve the subprogram. But since an optimal solution corresponding to the basic variables in the restricted master program is a weighted average of these X^t, namely $\sum_{t=0}^{T} X_j^t w_t$ for each j, this solution can contain *more* than m of the x_j at positive levels (unless the entire problem has a unique optimal solution). This is an important difference between the simplex method applied to the entire problem and the Decomposition Algorithm.

The following example illustrates the method and also exhibits a minor variation in the approach. Consider the problem

$$(6) \qquad \text{maximize } x_1 + x_2 + x_3 + x_4$$

subject to

$$(7) \qquad \begin{array}{lll} x_1 + 2x_2 + 2x_3 & \leq 3 & \text{Row 1} \\ -x_1 \qquad\quad + x_3 + 2x_4 \leq 2 & & \text{Row 2} \\ \qquad\qquad\quad x_3 + x_4 \leq 3 & & \text{Row 3} \\ \qquad\qquad\quad x_3 - x_4 \leq 1 & & \text{Row 4,} \end{array}$$

$$\text{and all } x_j \geq 0.$$

Since x_1 and x_2 appear in the first two constraints only, we will include them *explicitly* in the following restricted master program:

$$(8) \qquad \text{maximize } x_1 + x_2 + \sum_{t=0}^{T} [X_3^t + X_4^t] w_t$$

subject to

$$(9) \qquad \begin{array}{l} x_1 + 2x_2 + \sum_{t=0}^{T} [2X_3^t] w_t \leq 3 \\[2mm] -x_1 \qquad\quad + \sum_{t=0}^{T} [X_3^t + 2X_4^t] w_t \leq 2 \\[2mm] \qquad\qquad\quad \sum_{t=0}^{T} w_t = 1 \end{array}$$

$$x_1, x_2, \text{ and all } w_t \geq 0.$$

Observe that in this version the constants ($b_1 = 3$, $b_2 = 2$) have been brought to the right-hand side of (9).

Let the subprogram consist of the variables x_3 and x_4, the second two constraints, and the nonnegativity conditions. Therefore the summation in (4) is modified to include only x_3 and x_4. Specifically, the subprogram is

(10)   maximize $[1 - (2y_1^k + 1y_2^k)]x_3 + [1 - (0y_1^k + 2y_2^k)]x_4$

subject to the constraints in Rows 3 and 4 of (7) and $(x_3 \geq 0, x_4 \geq 0)$.

The region of feasible points for x_3 and x_4 in the subprogram is shown in Fig. 15.12; note that there are four vertices, labeled A, B, C, D, which represent pos-

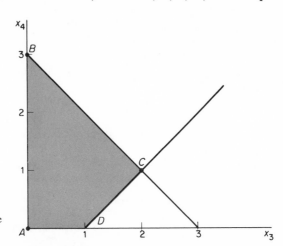

Figure 15.12. Feasible Region for Subprogram.

sible basic solutions for the subprogram at each iteration. If there exists a solution X_3 and X_4 to the subprogram such that

(11) $y_{M+1}^k < [1 - (2y_1^k + 1y_2^k)]X_3 + [1 - (0y_1^k + 2y_2^k)]X_4,$

then the iterations continue. Observe that the term $(\sum_{i=1}^{R} b_i y_i^k)$ does *not* appear on the right of (11), since the constants b_1 and b_2 have been moved to the right-hand side of the restricted master program (9).

Let the initial trial solution be $(X_3^0 = 0, X_4^0 = 0)$, which is point A in Fig. 15.12. The optimal solution to the restricted master program is $(x_1^1 = 3, w_0^1 = 1)$, and the associated dual variables are $(y_1^1 = 1, y_2^1 = 0, y_3^1 = 0)$.

The resultant objective function for the subprogram is

(12)   maximize $-x_3 + x_4.$

Verify in Fig. 15.12 that the optimal solution to this subprogram is at vertex B, giving $(X_3^1 = 0, X_4^1 = 3)$. Since this point yields a value of 3 for the objective function in (12) and $y_3^1 = 0$ at the current solution, point B must be introduced to the restricted master program. Calculate the impact of this point on (8) and (9).

The optimal solution to the next restricted master program is $(x_1^2 = 3, w_0^2 = \frac{1}{6}, w_1^2 = \frac{5}{6})$, and the corresponding dual variables are $(y_1^2 = \frac{3}{2}, y_2^2 = \frac{1}{2}, y_3^2 = 0)$.

Verify that the objective function of the subprogram becomes:

(13)   maximize $-\frac{5}{2}x_3.$

Now the optimal solution is point A, which already is in the optimal solution of the restricted master program. Hence, this point yields an equality in (11), and the present trial solution is truly optimal. The associated values for x_3 and x_4 are

(14)
$$x_3 = X_3^0 w_0^2 + X_3^1 w_1^2 = (0)\frac{1}{6} + (0)\frac{5}{6} = 0$$

$$x_4 = X_4^0 w_0^2 + X_4^1 w_1^2 = (0)\frac{1}{6} + (3)\frac{5}{6} = \frac{5}{2}.$$

Several Decomposition Algorithms for linear programs are available on large-scale electronic computers. These techniques usually involve considerably more calculations than does the simplex method applied to the same problem. Hence, such an approach is attractive only when the original problem is too large to be solved directly by the simplex method, because of computer capacity limitations, or when the subproblem has a special structure that can be exploited.

REVIEW EXERCISES

1 Consider the problem maximize $-(x_1 - 1)^2 - (x_2 - 1)^2$ subject to $x_1 + x_2 \leq 1$, $x_1 \geq 0$, and $x_2 \geq 0$.

(a) Construct a solution space diagram, show the optimal solution and the unconstrained optimal solution.

(b) Let a trial solution be the point $x_1^0 = 1$, $x_2^0 = 0$. Indicate on the diagram the direction of steepest ascent. Are there any feasible points lying in this direction from the trial solution?

(c) Show graphically how the Method of Convex Combinations in Sec. 15.2 finds an optimal solution. (For $k = 1, 2, 3, 4$, indicate x^k, $\bar{z}$, and the linear objective function.)

(d) Do the same analysis for the trial point $x_1^0 = \frac{1}{4}$, $x_2^0 = \frac{3}{4}$.

2 Consider the problem maximize $-(x_1 - 3)^2 - (x_2 - 3)^2$ subject to $0 \leq x_1 \leq 6$ and $0 \leq x_2 \leq 2$.

(a) Construct a solution space diagram, show the optimal solution and the unconstrained optimal solution.

(b) Show graphically how the Method of Convex Combinations in Sec. 15.2 finds an optimal solution, starting at the point $x_1^0 = x_2^0 = 0$ (for $k = 1, 2, 3, 4$, indicate the successive x^k and associated $\bar{z}$.) Show how $c(\bar{z})$ can be smaller than $c(x^k)$, and indicate why there is a convex combination of x^k and $\bar{z}$, namely, x^{k+1} such that $c(x^{k+1}) > c(x^k)$. Show how the actual directions used are not the directions of steepest ascent.

(c) What difference does it make if $x_1^0 = 3$, $x_2^0 = 0$? If $x_1^0 = 0$, $x_2^0 = 1$? If $x_1^0 = 0$, $x_2^0 = 2$?

3 Consider the problem in exercise 2, but let $0 \leq x_2 \leq 4$.

(a) Construct a solution space diagram and show the optimal solution.

(b) Show graphically how the Method of Convex Combinations in Sec. 15.2 finds an optimal solution, starting at the point $x_1^0 = x_2^0 = 0$ (for $k = 1, 2, 3, 4$, indicate the successive x^k and associated $\bar{z}$).

4 (a) Give an algebraic proof of the statement in Sec. 15.2 that a convex combination of two feasible solutions, x^k and $\bar{z}$, is also feasible for any t in the interval $0 < t \le 1$.
   (b) Verify that (4) can be written as (7) if you use the directions defined in (6).
   (c) Rearrange the summations in (3) so as to express the inequality in terms of directions. Give a verbal interpretation of the resulting inequality.
   (d) Explain how the Method of Convex Combinations relies on assumptions (ii), (iv), and (v) in Sec. 15.1.

5 *(a) Derive the first inequality in the bounding relation (8) shown in Sec. 15.2.
   (b) Derive the second inequality in (8).
   (c) Explain why the validity of the inequalities in (8) implies that if $\bar{z}$ yields an equality between the two summations in (3), then the associated x^k is truly optimal.

6 Consider the problem maximize $(x_1 - 3)^2 + (x_2 - 3)^2$ subject to

$$x_1 + x_2 \le 7 \quad -x_1 + 3x_2 \le 9 \quad 3x_1 - x_2 \le 9 \quad x_1 \ge 0 \quad \text{and} \quad x_2 \ge 0.$$

   (a) Construct a solution space diagram and show the optimal solution.
   (b) Suppose you apply the Method of Convex Combinations, starting at $x_1^0 = 3$, $x_2^0 = 4$. Determine how the algorithm behaves.
   (c) Rework part (b), starting at $x_1^0 = x_2^0 = 3\frac{1}{2}$.
   (d) Rework part (b), starting at $x_1^0 = x_2^0 = 3$.
   (e) Rework part (b), starting at $x_1^0 = 3$, $x_2^0 = 0$.

7 Consider the problem maximize $18x_1 + 18x_2 - 5x_1^2 - 8x_1x_2 - 5x_2^2$ subject to $x_1 + x_2 \le 1$, $x_1 \ge 0$, and $x_2 \ge 0$. Apply one iteration of the Method of Convex Combinations in each part below to find a $\bar{z}$ corresponding to the indicated x^0. Then calculate $c(x^0)$, $c(\bar{z})$ and the upper bound (8) in Sec. 15.2.

   (a) $x_1^0 = x_2^0 = 0$. (d) $x_1^0 = \frac{1}{4}$, $x_2^0 = \frac{1}{4}$.
   (b) $x_1^0 = 1$, $x_2^0 = 0$. (e) $x_1^0 = \frac{1}{3}$, $x_2^0 = \frac{2}{3}$.
   (c) $x_1^0 = \frac{1}{4}$, $x_2^0 = \frac{3}{4}$. (f) $x_1^0 = x_2^0 = \frac{1}{2}$. Is this an optimal solution? Explain.

8 Consider the application of the Method of Convex Combinations to the example (9) through (12) in Sec. 15.2. Perform the detailed calculations for $k = 0, 1, \ldots, 5$ and verify the results shown in Fig. 15.1.

*9 Consider the application of the Concave Simplex Method to the example (10) through (17) in Sec. 15.2. Perform the detailed calculations for $k = 1, 2, \ldots, 5$ and verify the results shown in Fig. 15.3.

*10 In each part below, apply the Concave Simplex Method described in Sec. 15.2 to Problem P, modified as indicated. Stop the iterations after $k = 4$ (if convergence has not yet occurred). (These modifications were also treated in exercise 23 of Chap. 4.)

   (a) Let the right-hand-side constant in (9) be 8, instead of 4.
   (b) Let the right-hand-side constant in (9) be 3, instead of 4.
   (c) Let the right-hand-side constant in (9) be 2, instead of 4.
   (d) Add the constraint $x_1 + x_2 \le 1$.
   (e) Add the constraint $x_2 + x_3 \le 2$.
   (f) Add the constraint $-2x_1 + 2x_3 \le 1$. *Parts (g) to (i) on p. 624.*

(g) Let the objective function be $6x_1 + 4x_2 + 2x_3 - \frac{1}{3}x_1^2 - 2x_2^2 - 3x_3^2$.

(h) Let the objective function be $2x_1 + 6x_2 + 4x_3 - 3x_1^2 - 2x_2^2 - \frac{1}{3}x_3^2$.

(i) Add to the objective function the terms $-x_1x_2 - 2x_2x_3$.

*11 In each part below, apply the Concave Simplex Method described in Sec. 15.2. Stop the iterations after $k = 4$ (if convergence has not yet occurred). Indicate the progress of the iterations on a solution space diagram.

(a) Exercise 1.   (c) Exercise 3.

(b) Exercise 2.   (d) Exercise 7.

(e) maximize $10x_2 - 6x_1^2 - 19x_2^2 + 16x_1x_2$ subject to

$$3x_1 + x_2 \leq 3 \quad x_1 \geq 0 \quad \text{and} \quad x_2 \geq 0.$$

(f) Change the signs of the objective-function coefficients in part (e), and let the initial basic solution be $x_1 = 3$. Do you obtain a global optimum? Justify your answer.

*12 Section 15.3 states that, in the Method of Convex Combinations, all directions may be nonzero at an iteration, whereas, in the Concave Simplex Method, at most only $m + 1$ directions are nonzero at an iteration. Give a detailed justification for this assertion.

*13 Consider the Cutting-Plane Method (as described in Sec. 15.4) applied to the following problem: maximize $-x^2 + 4x$ subject to $0 \leq x \leq 5$.

(a) Find the optimal value for x. Plot the objective function for $0 \leq x \leq 5$.

(b) Let $x^0 = 0$. Indicate the progress of the algorithm for $k = 1, 2, 3, 4$ by drawing a solution space diagram for the variables x and x_0, and showing the cutting plane added at each iteration as well as the values for x^k and x_0^k. Explain in this diagram the reason for calling the method a cutting-plane approach.

*(c) Change the signs of the coefficients in the objective function in part (a), and explain why the method does not work if the objective function to be maximized is convex.

14 Consider the function $a(x) \equiv x_1^2 - x_2$.

(a) Draw the contour $a(x) = 0$.

(b) Let $x_1 = 2$ and $x_2 = 4$, and write (4) in Sec. 15.5 in full detail. Verify that the line given by setting the summation on the right-hand side of (4) equal to 0 is $4(y_1 - 2) - (y_2 - 4) = 0$, and is a linear support to the contour in part (a) at the indicated point.

(c) Perform the same analyses for $a(x) \equiv 9x_1^2 - x_2$ and the point $x_1 = \frac{2}{3}, x_2 = 4$.

15 Determine for each part whether $a(x)$ satisfies assumptions (i), (ii), and the Constraint Qualification in Sec. 15.5. Determine the feasible values for x. Check whether $da(z)/dx \neq 0$ for a point z such that $a(z) = 0$.

(a) $x^2 - 4 \leq 0$.   (f) $(x^2 - 4)^2 \leq 0$.

(b) $x^2 + 4 \leq 0$.   (g) $-(x^2 - 4)^3 \leq 0$.

(c) $-x^2 - 4 \leq 0$.   (h) $(x^2 - 4)^3 \leq 0$.

(d) $-x^2 + 4 \leq 0$.   (i) $-(4 - x^2)^3 \leq 0$.

(e) $-(x^2 - 4)^2 \leq 0$.   (j) $(4 - x^2)^3 \leq 0$.

16 Determine for each part whether $a(x)$ satisfies assumptions (i), (ii), and the Constraint Qualification in Sec. 15.5. Determine the feasible values for x_1 and x_2. Check whether $\partial a(z)/\partial x_j \neq 0$ for at least one j at a point z such that $a(z) = 0$.

(a) $x_1 + x_2 - 1 \leq 0$.   (d) $(x_1 + x_2 - 1)^2 \leq 0$.
(b) $-x_1 - x_2 + 1 \leq 0$.   (e) $-(x_1 + x_2 - 1)^3 \leq 0$.
(c) $-(x_1 + x_2 - 1)^2 \leq 0$.   (f) $(x_1 + x_2 - 1)^3 \leq 0$.

17 In each part, construct a diagram indicating the set of feasible points. Explain in geometric terms why the set is convex. (Assume $x_1 \geq 0$ and $x_2 \geq 0$.) Check whether the Constraint Qualification is satisfied.

(a) $x_1^2 + (x_2 - 1)^2 - 1 \leq 0$ and $(x_1 - 1)^2 + x_2^2 - 1 \leq 0$.
(b) $x_1^2 + (x_2 - 1)^2 - 1 \leq 0$ and $x_1^2 + x_2^2 - 1 \leq 0$.
(c) $x_1^2 + (x_2 - 2)^2 - 1 \leq 0$ and $x_1^2 + x_2^2 - 1 \leq 0$.
(d) $x_1^2 + x_2^2 - 4 \leq 0$, $(x_1 - 3)^2 + x_2^2 - 4 \leq 0$ and $(x_1 - \frac{3}{2})^2 + (x_2 - 3)^2 - 4 \leq 0$.
(e) $x_1^2 + x_2^2 - 1 \leq 0$ and $x_1 + x_2 - \frac{1}{2} \leq 0$.
(f) $x_1^2 + x_2^2 - 1 \leq 0$ and $-x_1 - x_2 + \frac{1}{2} \leq 0$.
(g) $x_1^2 + x_2^2 - 8 \leq 0$ and $x_1 + x_2 - 3 \leq 0$.
(h) $x_1^2 + x_2^2 - 8 \leq 0$, $-x_1 - x_2 + 3 \leq 0$, and $x_1 + x_2 - 3.5 \leq 0$.
(i) $x_1^2 + x_2^2 - 8 \leq 0$ and $-x_1 - x_2 + 4 \leq 0$.
(j) $-e^{2x_1 + 3x_2} + 10 \leq 0$ and $2x_1 + 3x_2 - 10 \leq 0$.
(k) $-x_1 x_2 + 1 \leq 0$ and $x_1 + x_2 - 2 \leq 0$.
(l) Reverse the inequality of the first constraint in part (a). Show why the feasible region is no longer convex.

18 Show the intermediate algebraic steps demonstrating that if each constraint function $a_i(x)$ is convex according to (3) in Sec. 15.5, then the region of feasible solutions is convex.

*19 Section 15.5 states five ways to establish whether a particular function $a_i(x)$ is convex. Demonstrate the validity of these conclusions.

20 In each part below, establish whether or not the specified function is convex. If the function is convex, justify your conclusion by citing one of the five properties (A)–(E) given in Sec. 15.5. If the function is not convex, use a numerical illustration to show that the definition of convexity (3) is not satisfied.

(a) $e^{-\log x}$ for $x > 0$.
(b) $-x_1 - x_2 + x_1^4 + x_2^6$ for all x_1 and x_2.
(c) $x_1 x_2$ for $x_1 \geq 0$ and $x_2 \geq 0$.
(d) $-\log(2x_1 + 3x_2 + 4) + 5(x_1 - 6x_2)^2$ for $x_1 \geq 0$ and $x_2 \geq 0$.
(e) $(x_1 - 2)^3 - (x_2 - 2)^3$ for $x_1 \geq 0$ and $x_2 \geq 0$.
(f) $(2 - x_1)^3 + (2 - x_2)^3$ for $x_1 \geq 0$ and $x_2 \geq 0$.

21 Consider a nonlinear optimization problem satisfying the assumptions in Sec. 15.5. Suppose you have a trial point that is on a boundary of the constraint set but is not truly optimal. Explain why there must be a direction of improvement moving into the interior of the constraint region. (*Suggestion:* use a diagram like Fig. 15.6 to illustrate your reasoning.)

22 (a) Explain why, if x^k is interior to the ith constraint, the point $(x^k + td)$ will satisfy the ith constraint for *any* set of directions d, provided $t > 0$ is sufficiently small.

(b) Consider the point x^k in Fig. 15.6. Draw the linear support (tangent hyperplane) to the nonlinear function at x^k. Indicate those directions that make the right-hand side of (3) *strictly* negative. Must any such direction intersect the boundary of the nonlinear function? Explain why, for any such direction, there is a point near to x^k that lies in the interior of the constraint region.

23 (a) Explain why the optimization formulation (4) through (6) in Sec. 15.6 can be used to discover directions that satisfy the improvement test (1) and make the right-hand sides of (3) strictly negative when the trial point x^k is not a constrained stationary point.

(b) Show that the nonnegativity constraints included in the $A_i(x)$ guarantee in (6) that the d_j are bounded from below by $-x_j^k$ for $x_0 \geq 0$.

24 (a) Verify that the optimization formulation (4) through (6) in Sec. 15.6 when applied to Problem Q, given at the end of Sec. 15.5, yields (9) through (11).

(b) Write in detail and solve the optimization for $k = 0$, using the trial point $x_1^0 = x_2^0 = 1, x_3^0 = 3$ in Fig. 15.7. Verify that you obtain the trial point x^1.

(c) Write in detail and solve the optimization assuming that x^k is the truly optimal solution (given at the bottom of Fig. 15.7).

25 (a) Formulate Problem P, given by (4) and (5) in Sec. 15.1, in terms of the optimization problem (4) through (8) in Sec. 15.6.

*(b) Compare the formulation in part (a) to that used in the Method of Convex Combinations in Sec. 15.2. State the effect of selecting the value for b in (8).

*(c) Show how to convert your answer in part (a) to a model containing two constraints and three upper-bounded variables.

(d) Let $b = 1$ and the initial trial point be $x_1^0 = x_2^0 = x_3^0 = 0$ in your answer to part (a). Complete the optimization for $k = 0$, and derive the new trial point for $k = 1$. Do the same for $b = 5$.

(e) Write the formulation in part (a) in detail and solve the resultant optimization problem when the trial point is truly optimal.

26 Let $m = 3, n = 5$, and $A_{3+j}(x) \equiv -x_j$ for $j = 1, 2, \ldots, 5$. Write in detail the linear programming model (1) through (4) and its dual (5) through (8) in Sec. 15.7. Also write in detail the Optimality Conditions (9), (10), and (11).

27 In each part below, write in full detail the Optimality Conditions (9), (10), and (11).

(a) Problem P, given by (4) and (5) in Sec. 15.1. Verify (16) and (17).

(b) Problem Q, given at the end of Sec. 15.5. Also find values for $\bar{u}_i$ satisfying the conditions for the optimal $\bar{x}$.

(c) Show in Problems P and Q that the assumptions $x_1 > 0$ and $x_2 = x_3 = 0$ implies that no $u_i \geq 0$ satisfy the Optimality Conditions.

28 Consider the Optimality Conditions in Sec. 15.7.

(a) Verify that (10) can be derived by dividing the expression in (5) by $\bar{y}_0 > 0$. Justify the remaining steps in the argument.

(b) Derive conditions (11) from the conditions in (7). Justify your approach.

(c) Show why (10) and (11) imply (12), (13), and (14).

*(d) Assume that $c(x)$ and all the $a_i(x)$ are linear. Show that (9), (12), (13), and (14) reduce to the results given by the Theorem of Complementary Slackness in Sec. 5.3.

29 Suppose you want to test whether a trial feasible point x^k is optimal for a nonlinear programming problem. Discuss how you can apply the Optimality Conditions in Sec. 15.7, instead of the linear programming model (1) through (4). Describe the connection between the two approaches.

30 In each part below, find an optimal solution by inspection. Check whether the Optimality Conditions in Sec. 15.7 are satisfied, that is, find values for the $\bar{u}_i \geq 0$.

(a) Maximize $-(x - 4)^2$ for $1 \leq x \leq 3$. Are the Optimality Conditions satisfied at $x = 1$? At $x = 3$? Why?

(b) Maximize $(x - 4)^2$ for $1 \leq x \leq 6$. Are the Optimality Conditions satisfied at $x = 6$? At $x = 4$? Why?

(c) Maximize x subject to $(x^2 - 4)^2 - 25 \leq 0$.

(d) Maximize x subject to $(x^2 - 4)^2 \leq 0$. Explain the difference in your answers to parts (c) and (d).

(e) Show that your answers in parts (a) and (c) yield a saddle point for the Lagrangian function (21).

(f) Show that the Lagrangian function for the problems in parts (b) and (d) do not have saddle points.

(g) Maximize $(x - 4)^3$ for $1 \leq x \leq 6$. Are the Optimality Conditions satisfied at $x = 1$? At $x = 4$? At $x = 6$? Why?

31 Consider the Lagrangian function $L(x, u)$ given by (21) in Sec. 15.7. Write the expression in detail when $c(x)$ and all $a_i(x)$ are linear functions. Discuss the connection between the Lagrange Optimality Conditions for this case and the Dual Theorem for linear programs.

*32 Let $m = 2$ and $n = 3$ in a quadratic programming model given in Sec. 15.8. Write in detail the expressions (1) through (4) and provide the intermediate steps to justify the statements (5) through (14).

*33 Consider the solution to Problem P by the Modified Simplex Algorithm, as shown in Sec. 15.8. Perform the detailed numerical operations, check the steps of the algorithm, and verify the results in (18) through (21).

*34 In each part, apply the Modified Simplex Algorithm described in Sec. 15.8 to Problem P, altered as indicated below. (These alterations were also treated in exercise 23 of Chap. 14.) *Parts (f) through (i) on p. 628.*

(a) Let the right-hand-side constant in (9) be 8, instead of 4.

(b) Let the right-hand-side constant in (9) be 3, instead of 4.

(c) Let the right-hand-side constant in (9) be 2, instead of 4.

(d) Add the constraint $x_1 + x_2 \leq 1$.

(e) Add the constraint $x_2 + x_3 \leq 2$.

(f) Add the constraint $-2x_1 + 2x_3 \leq 1$.

(g) Let the objective function be $6x_1 + 4x_2 + 2x_3 - \frac{1}{3}x_1^2 - 2x_2^2 - 3x_3^2$.

(h) Let the objective function be $2x_1 + 6x_2 + 4x_3 - 3x_1^2 - 2x_2^2 - \frac{1}{3}x_3^2$.

(i) Add to the objective function the terms $-x_1 x_2 - 2x_2 x_3$.

35 (a) Assume that $a_i(x)$ is a convex function. Show that $[1/a_i(x)]$ is a concave function for those x such that $a_i(x) < 0$.

(b) Verify the first equality in (4) of Sec. 15.9.

*(c) Give the detailed reasoning establishing (iii) and (5) in Sec. 15.9.

36 Consider the problem: maximize $-x^2 + 4x$ subject to $x \leq 1$.

(a) Write the penalty function (2) in Sec. 15.9.

(b) Perform the differentiation in (4) and construct a graphical representation for the x that maximizes $c(x|r)$, given a value of r. [*Hint:* you can manipulate (4) to yield an equality between a linear and a hyperbolic function, which in turn can be represented graphically by an intersection of the two functions.] Show how the solution varies as r tends to 0. Is the limiting value for x truly optimal?

(c) Suppose the constraint is $x \leq 5$. How does this affect the behavior of the solution for a given r and the limiting solution as r approaches 0?

37 Consider the generalized programming formulation (1) through (5) in Sec. 15.10.

(a) Explain why the restricted master program has a basic feasible solution and a finite maximum value c^k.

(b) Show that any feasible solution to (4) and (5) yields a point, given in (6), that is feasible in the original problem.

(c) Let $R = 2$ and $T = 3$ in (3), (4), and (5). Write in detail the associated dual problem (7), (8), and (9).

(d) Show that if the inequality in (10) holds for all x in S, then x^k is truly optimal in the original problem, as claimed.

(e) Show that the objective function in (12) for the subprogram is concave.

(f) Justify the bound for $\bar{c}$ in (13). [*Hint:* since X^{T+1} can be any of the X^t, $t = 0, 1, \ldots, T$, the inequality ($\leq$) holds immediately in (11).]

(g) Explain why the algorithm can be terminated at the next iteration if $w_{T+1} = 1$.

38 (a) Consider solving the Problems P and Q by the Generalized Programming Algorithm, as described in Sec. 15.10. Show the intermediate steps justifying that the approach leads to (17), (18), and (19).

(b) Carry out the algorithm for Problem P to the point of deriving x^k for $k = 2$, shown in Fig. 15.10. (Note that $X_1^0 = X_2^0 = X_3^0 = 0$.)

(c) Write in detail the restricted master program for Problem P, where you include only X^3 and X^5 from Fig. 15.10 and the slack variable for the first constraint. Verify that the optimal weights are $w_3 = w_5 = .5$, as shown in Fig. 15.10, and complete the next (final) iteration.

*39 Consider the example (6) and (7) in Sec. 15.11 illustrating the application of the Decomposition Algorithm. Verify the expressions in (8) through (11), and carry out the detailed calculations to obtain the results shown in (12), (13), and (14).

40 Consider the example (6) and (7) in Sec. 15.11. Change the objective function to $x_1 + x_2 + 9x_3 + 3x_4$, and let the right-hand-side constant be 0, instead of 1, in Row 4. Solve by the Decomposition Algorithm.

*41 Consider the case of the Knox Mix Company, described in Sec. 2.2 and solved by the simplex method in Sec. 4.4. Solve by the Decomposition Algorithm, where you let the subprogram consist of the first constraint $(x_1 + x_2 + x_3 + x_4 \leq 15)$ and the nonnegativity conditions.

42 Explain your understanding of the following terms:

large-step approach
regularization postulate
optimal feasible step size
constrained stationary point
convex combination (weighted average)
concave function (strictly concave function)
convex function (strictly convex function)
first-order method (second-order method)
Method of Convex Combinations
*Concave Simplex Method
*reduced (or relative) partial derivative
*Cutting-Plane Method
*Gradient Projection Method
*projection
linear support (tangent hyperplane)

Constraint Qualification
convex set
feasible direction
Method of Feasible Directions
Kuhn-Tucker conditions
*John conditions
Lagrangian function
Lagrange multipliers
saddle point
*complementary pivot operation
penalty function approach (SUMT Algorithm)
Generalized Programming Algorithm
restricted master program
subprogram
Decomposition Algorithm.

PENCIL-PUSHING EXERCISES

43 Consider the following problem [which was also treated in exercise 24, part (a), of Chap. 14, and represents Case 3 in Fig. 14.9]

$$\text{maximize} -(x_1 - 1)^2 - (x_2 - 2)^2 + 5$$

subject to

$$x_1 + 2x_2 \leq 5$$
$$16x_1 + 12x_2 \leq 37$$
$$24x_1 + 4x_2 \leq 27$$
$$x_1 \geq 0 \quad \text{and} \quad x_2 \geq 0.$$

Solve each part below by the method indicated. Draw a solution space diagram and show the progress of the iterations. (In those approaches that do not converge in a finite number of iterations, stop the calculations after $k = 5$.)

(a) Method of Convex Combinations in Sec. 15.2.
* (b) Concave Simplex Method in Sec. 15.3.
* (c) Modified Simplex Algorithm in Sec. 15.8.
(d) Generalized Programming Algorithm for a separable problem in Sec. 15.10.
(e) Apply the Optimality Conditions in Sec. 15.7 to derive an optimal solution.

44 Answer the questions in exercise 43, except let the constraints be (Case 2 in Fig. 14.9)

$$x_1 + \ 2x_2 \le 5$$
$$16x_1 + 12x_2 \le 37$$
$$6x_1 + \ \ x_2 \le 12$$
$$x_1 \ge 0 \quad \text{and} \quad x_2 \ge 0.$$

45 Answer the questions in exercise 43, except let the constraints be (Case 1 in Fig. 14.9)

$$x_1 + 2x_2 \le 6$$
$$8x_1 + 6x_2 \le 23$$
$$6x_1 + \ x_2 \le 12$$
$$x_1 \ge 0 \quad \text{and} \quad x_2 \ge 0.$$

46 Consider a standard transportation problem, like that in Sec. 6.2, with supplies $S_1 = 4$, $S_2 = 6$, and demands $D_1 = 5$, $D_2 = 2$, and $D_3 = 3$. Assume the cost function is

$$4(x_{11}^2 + x_{12}^2 + x_{22}^2 + x_{23}^2) + 3x_{13}^2 + 2x_{21}^2.$$

In each part below, explain how the algorithm makes use of the problem's special structure. Is an optimal solution integer-valued? (Do not carry the calculations beyond $k = 5$.)
(a) Solve by the Method of Convex Combinations.
* (b) Solve by the Concave Simplex Method.

47 Consider the following problem (which was also treated in exercise 46 of Chap. 14):

$$\text{maximize } 6x_1 + 8x_2 - x_1^2 - x_2^2$$

subject to

$$4x_1^2 + \ x_2^2 \le 16$$
$$3x_1 + 5x_2 \le 15$$
$$x_1 \ge 0 \quad \text{and} \quad x_2 \ge 0.$$

Solve each part below by the method indicated. Draw a solution space diagram and show the progress of the iterations. (In those approaches that do not converge in a finite number of iterations, stop the calculations after $k = 5$.)

(a) Method of Feasible Directions in Sec. 15.6.
(b) Generalized Programming Algorithm for a separable problem in Sec. 15.10.
(c) Apply the Optimality Conditions in Sec. 15.7 to derive an optimal solution.
(d) Consider, instead, the objective function maximize $(x_1 - 1)^3 + (x_2 - 1)^3$. Apply

the Method of Feasible Directions, starting at $x_1^0 = x_2^0 = 0$ and using $b = 1$. Do you obtain an optimal solution? What would happen if you use $b = 2$? Apply the Optimality Conditions in Sec. 15.7 at the point $x_1 = x_2 = 1$, and discuss the implication of your result.

48 Consider the problem

$$\text{maximize } x_1 + x_2$$

subject to

$$x_1^2 + (x_2 - 4)^2 - 16 \leq 0$$
$$(x_1 - 4)^2 + x_2^2 - 16 \leq 0$$
$$x_1 \geq 0 \quad \text{and} \quad x_2 \geq 0.$$

Solve each part below by the method indicated. Draw a solution space diagram and show the progress of the iterations. (Stop the calculations after $k = 5$.)

(a) Method of Feasible Directions in Sec. 15.6.
(b) Generalized Programming Algorithm for a separable problem in Sec. 15.10.
(c) Apply the Optimality Conditions in Sec. 15.7 to find an optimal solution.
(d) Consider an alternative objective function: maximize $(x_1 - 1)^3 + (x_2 - 1)^3$. Apply the Method of Feasible Directions, starting at $x_1^0 = x_2^0 = 0$ and using $b = 1$. Do you obtain an optimal solution? What would happen if you used $b = 2$? Apply the Optimality Conditions in Sec. 15.7 at the point $x_1 = x_2 = 1$, and discuss the implication of your result.

49 Answer parts (a), (b), (c) in exercise 48, except let the objective function be

$$\text{maximize } -26x_1 + 50x_2 - 3x_1^2 - 9x_2^2 + 10x_1x_2.$$

50 Show how to solve the problem in exercise 2 using the Generalized Programming Algorithm in Sec. 15.10, where you let R contain all the constraints. (Do not carry the calculations beyond $k = 5$.) Show the progress of the iterations on a solution space diagram.

*51 Use the Decomposition Algorithm in Sec. 15.11 to solve the upper-bounded variables problems in exercise 28 of Chap. 5. Let the subprogram contain the upper bounds and nonnegativity conditions.

*52 Use the Decomposition Algorithm in Sec. 15.11 to solve the transportation problem example in Sec. 7.3 (see Fig. 7.2). Let R contain the supply constraints, and S the demand and nonnegativity constraints.

FORMULATION AND NUMERICAL EXERCISES

53 Consider a nonlinear optimization model like that discussed in Sec. 15.5. Show how to convert the problem into an equivalent one in which the objective function is linear. (*Hint:* introduce another variable and another constraint that involves the new variable and the original objective function.)

54 Consider a problem containing the nonlinear constraint

$$\sum_{j=1}^{n} a_j x_j - K \left[\sum_{i=1}^{n} \sum_{j=1}^{n} a_{ij} x_i x_j \right]^{1/2} - b \geq 0,$$

where $K > 0$ and the term inside the brackets is nonnegative for all x_k. Show an equivalent formulation composed of two constraints, one of which is linear and one nonlinear, and where the nonlinear $a(x)$ is a convex function.

55 Consider the problem of maximizing a nonlinear function $c(x)$ subject to linear constraints, as displayed by (1) and (2) in Sec. 15.1.

(a) Write the Optimality Conditions and their implications (9) through (14) given in Sec. 15.7. [*Suggestion:* first eliminate the slack variables s_i in (2) of Sec. 15.1.]
(b) Apply your answer in part (a) to the problem

$$\text{maximize} \; -(x_1 - 4)^2 - (x_2 - 4)^2$$

subject to

$$x_1 + 3x_2 \leq 12$$
$$3x_1 + x_2 \leq 12$$
$$-x_1 - x_2 \leq -1$$
$$-x_1 + x_2 \leq 3$$
$$x_1 \geq 0 \quad \text{and} \quad x_2 \geq 0.$$

(c) Draw a solution space diagram for the problem in part (b). Indicate the optimal solution. Interpret conditions (13) and (14) in the diagram. {*Hint:* you can represent $[\partial c(\bar{x})/\partial x_1, \partial c(\bar{x})/\partial x_2]$ as the direction of steepest ascent from $\bar{x}$. You can represent $[\partial a_i(\bar{x})/\partial x_1, \partial a_i(\bar{x})/\partial x_2]$ for each constraint i that is satisfied as an equality by a direction that is orthogonal (perpendicular) to the constraint at $\bar{x}$.}

56 Consider the problem

$$\text{maximize} \; x_1 + 2x_2$$

subject to

$$x_1^2 + (x_2 - 1)^2 - 1 \leq 0 \quad x_1^2 + x_2^2 - 1 \leq 0 \quad x_1 \geq 0 \quad \text{and} \quad x_2 \geq 0.$$

(a) Draw a solution space diagram and show the optimal solution.
(b) Write the Optimality Conditions and their implications (9) through (14) in Sec. 15.7.
(c) Give a geometrical interpretation for your answer in part (b). {*Hint:* you can represent $[\partial c(\bar{x})/\partial x_1, \partial c(\bar{x})/\partial x_2]$ as the direction of steepest ascent from $\bar{x}$. You can represent $[\partial a_i(\bar{x})/\partial x_1, \partial a_i(\bar{x})/\partial x_2]$ for each constraint i that is satisfied as an equality by a direction that is orthogonal (perpendicular) to the linear support of the constraint at $\bar{x}$.}

57 Consider the problem

$$\text{maximize} \; c_1 x_1 + x_2$$

subject to

$$x_1^2 + x_2^2 \leq 25 \quad x_1 - x_2 \leq 1 \quad x_1 \geq 0 \quad \text{and} \quad x_2 \geq 0.$$

Use the Optimality Conditions in Sec. 15.7 to derive a range of values for c_1 over which the solution $x_1 = 4$ and $x_2 = 3$ is optimal. Display your results on a solution space diagram.

58 *Where-or-When Problem* (Sec. 1.6). Find the form of an optimal solution for this case by applying the Optimality Conditions in Sec. 15.7. Do the same for the problem

$$\text{maximize } (x_1 + x_2 + \cdots + x_N)$$

subject to

$$\sum_{j=1}^{N} \frac{x_j^2}{c_j} \leq C \quad \text{and} \quad \text{every } x_j \geq 0.$$

59 Consider the problem

$$\text{maximize } \sum_{j=1}^{n} c_j(x_j)$$

subject to

$$\sum_{j=1}^{n} a_j x_j \leq b \quad \text{and} \quad \text{every } x_j \geq 0,$$

where each $c_j(x_j)$ is strictly concave for all x_j and has a continuous first derivative.

(a) Write the Optimality Conditions and their implications (9) through (14) in Sec. 15.7.

(b) Show that if b is increased to $b + e$ ($e > 0$), then the new optimal value of each x_j is at least as large as it was for b.

60 Consider the three-period production and inventory model with convex costs given in exercise 3 2 of Chap. 9. Drop the assumption that each x_t must be integer-valued.

(a) Use the Optimality Conditions in Sec. 15.7 to solve each part of that exercise. Show the cost impact of an infinitesimal change in each demand requirement D_t.

(b) Assume the production cost function in Period 1 is $C_1(x_1) = c_1 x_1^2$ (where $c_1 = 1$ in exercise 3 2 of Chap. 9). Use the Optimality Conditions to derive a range of values for c_1 over which the solutions in parts (a), (b), (c), and (f) of exercise 3 2, Chap. 9, remain optimal.

61 A company requires a work force of size D_t in Period t, where $t = 1, 2, \ldots, n$. At the beginning of Period 1, the initial work force $x_0 = 0$. Let x_t be the amount the company hires (for $x_t \geq 0$) or fires (for $x_t < 0$) at the beginning of Period t. The values of x_t must satisfy

$$\sum_{j=1}^{t} x_j \geq D_t \quad \text{for } t = 1, 2, \ldots, n,$$

where the summation on the left-hand side represents the work force available in Period t. In each Period t, let the hiring/firing cost be $c_1(x_t)$ and the *idle* work force cost be $c_2(\sum_{j=1}^{t} x_j - D_t)$. Assume that these two functions are strictly convex with continuous first derivatives, and the derivative of $c_2(x)$ is nonnegative at $x = 0$. Assume that $c_1(x)$ grows without bound as $|x|$ increases, and $c_2(x)$ grows without bound as x

increases. The objective function is

$$\text{maximize} \ - \sum_{t=1}^{n} \left[c_1(x_t) + c_2 \left(\sum_{j=1}^{t} x_j - D_t \right) \right].$$

(a) Write the Optimality Conditions (9), (10), and (11) in Sec. 15.7.

(b) Show that if there is a Period $t < n$ in which it is optimal to have some idle work force $\sum_{j=1}^{t} x_j > D_t$, then it is optimal to hire in the next period so that $x_{t+1} > x_t$.

*62 Consider the Dual Theorem of Nonlinear Programming given in Sec. 15.7. Write the dual problem (23) and (24) when in fact every constraint is linear. Show how (23) and (24) can be reduced to the usual dual problem in linear programming.

63 A constrained stationary point is obtained in the Method of Feasible Directions in Sec. 15.6 when there is no feasible direction yielding an improvement as evaluated in terms of the first-order partial derivatives; this condition is expressed by the text in (1). Show that when $c(x)$ is concave and x^k is a constrained stationary point, then x^k is globally optimal. $\left[\textit{Hint:} \ \text{you can use the property of a concave function that} \right.$

$c(x + d) \leq c(x) + \sum_{j=1}^{n} \dfrac{\partial c(x)}{\partial x_j} \cdot d_j \quad \text{for any point } x \text{ and direction } d. \Big]$

64 Suppose $A_i(x)$ is a linear constraint and x^k is a point satisfying $A_i(x^k) \leq 0$. Show that directions d_j that satisfy (6) in Sec. 15.6 with the variable x_0 omitted will be feasible.

65 Consider the problem

$$\text{maximize } c_1 x_1$$

subject to

$$a_{11} x_1 - x_2 \leq 0$$
$$a_{21} x_1 - x_3 \leq 0$$
$$- \log a_{32}(x_2 + 1) - \log a_{33}(x_3 + 1) - b_3 \leq 0$$
$$\text{every } x_j \geq 0,$$

where all $a_{ij} > 0$. Consider solving the problem using the Generalized Programming Algorithm in Sec. 15.10. Compare the difficulty of solving the restricted master program and the subprogram when the nonlinear constraint is included in S and when it is not.

66 Consider the application of the Generalized Programming Algorithm to a separable problem, as described in Sec. 15.10. Discuss the effect of including the nonnegativity constraints $x_j \geq 0$ explicitly in the restricted master program and removing them from the subprogram. (*Suggestion:* illustrate your answer using Problem P.)

67 *One-Potato, Two-Potato Problem* (Sec. 1.6). Exercise 47 of Chap. 14 generalized this case to account for the possibility of varying the yield coefficients. Show how the problem in exercise 47, Chap. 14, can be formulated and solved by the Generalized Programming Algorithm when you assume the *expense* functions $c_1(f_1, f_2, f_3)$ and $c_2(g_1, g_2, g_3)$ are linear.

MIND-EXPANDING EXERCISES

68 (a) Assume $a(x)$ is a convex function, where $x \equiv (x_1, x_2, \ldots, x_n)$. Consider points $y_1, y_2, \ldots, y_s$, and weights $w_1, w_2, \ldots, w_s$, where each $w_i \geq 0$ and $\sum_{i=1}^{s} w_i = 1$. Show that

$$\sum_{i=1}^{s} a(y_i)w_i \geq a\left(\sum_{i=1}^{s} y_i w_i\right),$$

where the summation on the right denotes the weighted average, coordinate by coordinate, of the points $y_1, \ldots, y_s$. What is the corresponding proposition for a concave function?

(b) Assume each $a_i(x)$ is a convex function, for $i = 1, 2, \ldots, s$, where $x \equiv (x_1, x_2, \ldots, x_n)$. Show that $A(x) = \text{maximum } [a_1(x), a_2(x), \ldots, a_s(x)]$ is a convex function. What is the corresponding proposition when each $a_i(x)$ is a concave function?

69 (a) Show that a continuously differentiable function $a(x)$ satisfies the inequality (4) in Sec. 15.5 if and only if it is convex.

*(b) Show that a function $a(x)$ having continuous second-order partial derivatives is convex if and only if the quadratic form

$$\sum_{i=1}^{n} \sum_{j=1}^{n} \frac{\partial^2 a(x)}{\partial x_i \, \partial x_j} d_i d_j$$

is positive semidefinite at every point x.

*(c) Show how to modify your answers when $a(x)$ is concave.

70 Suppose the inequality (1) in Sec. 15.6 is satisfied by a set of directions d_j (not necessarily feasible). Prove that there exists a point $(x^k + td)$, where $t > 0$, such that $c(x^k + td) > c(x^k)$.

71 Consider a nonlinear optimization model like that discussed in Sec. 15.5. Assume that $c(x_1, x_2, \ldots, x_n)$ is a *strictly convex* function. Prove that the optimal value $\bar{c}$ occurs at an extreme point of the constraint region. (*Recall:* x is an extreme point if it cannot be represented as the weighted average of two other feasible points.)

72 Consider the Lagrange Optimality Conditions in Sec. 15.7. Show that a point $\bar{x}$ is optimal if there is a point $\bar{u} \geq 0$ such that the pair $(\bar{x}, \bar{u})$ is a saddle point of $\mathrm{L}(x, u)$.

73 Let $c(x_1, x_2, \ldots, x_n)$ and $a_i(x_1, x_2, \ldots, x_n)$, for $i = 1, 2, \ldots, m$, be arbitrary real-valued functions defined over an arbitrary region R for $x_1, x_2, \ldots, x_n$. Let $\bar{u}_i \geq 0$, for $i = 1, 2, \ldots, m$, be specified values. Suppose that $\bar{x}_1, \bar{x}_2, \ldots, \bar{x}_n$ is an optimal solution to

$$\text{maximize } c(x) - \sum_{i=1}^{m} a_i(x)\bar{u}_i,$$

where x must be in R. Show that $\bar{x}_1, \bar{x}_2, \ldots, \bar{x}_n$ is also an optimal solution to

$$\text{maximize } c(x)$$

subject to

$$a_i(x) - a_i(\bar{x}) \leq 0 \quad \text{for} \quad i = 1, 2, \ldots, m,$$

where x must be in R.

74 Consider the problem of maximizing a nonlinear function $c(x)$ subject to linear constraints, as displayed by (1) and (2) in Sec. 15.1. Alter the formulation to include constraints that are equalities (that is, an s_i is not present) and to include variables that are unrestricted in sign. Derive the Optimality Conditions and their implications analogous to those in (9) through (14) of Sec. 15.7.

75 The Penalty Function Approach in Sec. 15.9 utilizes a particular form for the expression that multiplies the parameter r, namely, the summation of terms $[1/A_i(x)]$. Consider a more general formulation in which the expression that multiplies r is the summation of terms $G_i[A_i(x)]$.

   (a) Discuss the properties that the function G_i should have to be appropriate for a penalty function. Suggest one or more functions G_i having these properties and show the resultant expressions for $\partial c(x|r)/\partial x_j$. (*Hint:* consider, for example, the logarithm.)
   *(b) Devise a penalty function appropriate to letting r approach "minus infinity."
   *(c) Devise a penalty function that can encompass equality constraints $a_i(x) = 0$.

*76 Consider the Generalized Programming Algorithm in Sec. 15.10. Prove that the optimal values c^k for the objective function of the restricted master program increase monotonically to the optimal value c for the objective function of the original problem.

77 Consider a nonlinear optimization model like that discussed in Sec. 15.5. The Constraint Qualification postulated the existence of a point x^0 such that each $a_i(x^0) < 0$.

   (a) Suppose you want to find a point z such that every $a_i(z) \leq 0$. Discuss how to obtain z. [*Hint:* start with an arbitrary point y that may satisfy some, but not all, of the constraints. For example, suppose $a_1(y) > 0$. Suggest an optimization problem, involving $a_1(x)$ in the objective function, that eventually produces a point z such that $a_1(z) \leq 0$, and that maintains feasibility in all the constraints satisfied by y. Alternatively, suggest an approach that uses artificial variables.]
   (b) Suggest one or more ways to alter your answer in part (a) so that you obtain a point x^0 for which every $a_i(x^0) < 0$.

CONTENTS

CHAPTER 16

Introduction to Stochastic
Programming Models

16.1 IMPACT OF UNCERTAINTY

All our previous examples have assumed that the data required by a model are known exactly. This was true of the linear models in Chap. 2, which postulated that unit profits, demand requirements, and supply availabilities were specified with perfect certainty. Similarly, the illustrations of dynamic phenomena in Chaps. 8 through 11, pertaining to inventory replenishment, production scheduling, and equipment replacement, assumed there was no uncertainty about the data needed by the models. But in real life, since you never know *all* these values with perfect certainty, you may ask distrustfully, "Are the preceding deterministic models and techniques really practical?" Rest assured that they are. But the more important and harder question is, "When?" The discussion below will help you learn *when* to apply what model.

For full comprehension, you must recognize three factors:

- The true nature of uncertainty in a particular real situation.
- The way a proposed mathematical model deals with such uncertainty.
- The computational technique appropriate for solving this suggested mathematical model, given the data for the particular situation.

Therefore, in applying operations research to a real managerial decision-making problem, you always should ascertain

(i) *What uncertainties must be faced, and how they may influence the selection of an optimal decision.*

(ii) *Whether a given mathematical model takes suitable account of these uncertainties.*

Choosing the most efficient computational approach for obtaining numerical solutions is an important step in any application, but it can be left to the technical specialist. You will have ample opportunity to become acquainted with such techniques in the chapters ahead. But as you study the material, do not become so engrossed in mathematical details that you lose sight of (i) and (ii), and thus miss the more significant aspects.

Below are two simplified case studies that clarify the three factors cited above and indicate how you proceed in answering (i) and (ii) in actual situations.

New plant expansion. The Yum-Yum Company, a food processing firm, is deciding whether to expand its present plant or build a new plant. The President believes that an important factor in this decision is his firm's share of the market during the next ten years. Assume that Yum-Yum's planning staff is fairly confident about the other pertinent data, and finds that the structure of the production and marketing processes can be mathematically represented by a linear model resembling those found in Chap. 2. The President wants to be sure that the economic analysis of the decision explicitly reflects the element of uncertainty about the company's future market share.

Bear in mind that the critical management decision is *where* to add productive capacity. The values of the other variables calculated by the model, such as the sales quantities of individual products, the average and peak levels of inventory, and the required amounts of raw food supplies, are *assumed* to be of less interest, although they are used in the analysis of the major decision. Consequently, it is quite reasonable for the economic study to proceed as follows.

With a deterministic linear model, find the best expansion alternative for each of several possible and reasonable values for Yum-Yum's future market share. If the results show that the optimal decision is insensitive to the market-share parameter, the linear model has *adequately* dealt with the impact of uncertainty. If, on the contrary, the decision proves to be highly sensitive to market share, then further study is required. In particular, for each major decision, evaluate the resultant profit for several possible market shares. This may indicate that although the optimal expansion decision is sensitive to market share, the actual profit level is not. If profit also varies significantly with market share, however, then it will be necessary for the analysis to include, in one way or another, a judgment of the relative likelihood (probability) of each possible market share. The company may choose to embark on further market research to narrow the range of this uncertainty prior to making a final expansion decision.

To sum up, during an expansion analysis, the firm learns the nature and possible impact of uncertainty about market share. The problem is characterized by a linear programming model, and the influence of market share is tested through sensitivity analysis, like that explained in Chap. 5. If these analyses demonstrate that profit is significantly affected by the market-share value, the President of Yum-Yum can judge the risk of each decision by estimating the likelihoods of the possible market-share values. Further, the company can assess in economic terms the precise importance of obtaining additional market information before making a final decision.

As to *calculating* specific answers in so complex a situation, Yum-Yum's planning staff undoubtedly should employ a linear programming routine on a large-scale computer.

New computer facility. Now we turn to the second case study, which on the surface resembles the first one. The Lead-Nickel Company, a major primary-metal producer, has several dozen plants scattered throughout the United States. At its central headquarters the firm has four relatively small-scale computers that are used 70% of the time to prepare standard corporate accounting reports, and the rest of the time to perform calculations for special studies conducted by staff groups, such as the Operations Research Department. Although these special studies consume a significant fraction of time on an annual basis, their demands for computer time vary considerably from day to day and frequently occur in bunches. A number of small-scale computers are also located at the different plants; these machines produce plant accounting reports about 50% of the time, and the rest of the time service the needs of resident technical groups, such as the Industrial Engineering staff. Here, too, there is considerable day-to-day variation in work load.

The company Controller, who has corporate responsibility for all these computers, has observed that at least four or five days a month, and sometimes up to ten days, the computers seem overloaded both at headquarters and at the plants. Feeling sure this congestion results in costly and irritating delays in getting jobs processed, he wants to install, at corporate headquarters, either a medium-scale computer to replace only the four small ones, or a large-scale computer to replace, in addition, several of the plants' machines.

The Controller realizes that his decision must recognize certain intangible factors, such as the relative merits of decentralized operations, but he wants to weigh these considerations against the possible advantages of a larger and economically more efficient piece of computing equipment. Further, he wants the new configuration of computers to eliminate, or at least drastically reduce, the problem of overloading with all its ensuing delays and disruptions.

Several years ago, the Controller anticipated he would someday want to make this computer equipment decision, and started collecting data on all the jobs processed by the company's computers. Thus he knew, for example, how many hours of computer time were being spent at each location on processing payroll, keeping inventories, billing accounts receivable, etc. The computer manufacturers supplied him with the comparable amount of time required to process these same jobs on their medium- and large-scale computers.

The Controller asked the Operations Research Department whether it could help him analyze the situation. In fact, he had a rough description of a linear model. He thought the variables would be the annual frequency with which

Job Type i is placed on Computer Type j; the coefficients of these variables would show the relative speed of each computer for each job; the constraints would indicate the total annual frequency for each Job Type i and the time available of each Computer Type j; and the objective function would contain the cost of processing Job Type i on Computer Type j.

Do you think Lead-Nickel's computer capacity expansion decision can be analyzed in the same way as Yum-Yum's plant capacity question? Is the impact of uncertainty the same? To both questions, the correct answer is "no." Here are the reasons why.

In the Yum-Yum example, annualized figures appropriately measure profit, because the company's market share, by definition, indicates the overall basis for the year's entire operations. In Lead-Nickel's situation, the same annualized approach would obscure the very *essence* of the congestion problem: the day-to-day variation in requirements for computer time. After all, under the current computer configuration all jobs are processed *eventually*—the extra capacity is needed to reduce the delays due to daily fluctuations. Thus, for an analytic model to be useful in this case, it *must* indicate the impact of the random elements in the operating environment. In other words, the approach must take daily phenomena into account to show how many jobs will be seriously delayed during a year's operation.

You may wonder if a deterministic model could be devised to use annualized data and still handle the impact of daily uncertainty. Perhaps one could be put together, but you would probably find it unsatisfactory to work with. You could try to encompass the congestion factor in an ad hoc fashion by overstating the time required to perform Job Type i on Computer Type j. This approach, bolstered by considerable sensitivity analysis as well as ingenuity, might be usable if there were only a very few types of jobs and computers. But, as you will find in studying the second half of this book, there are alternative probabilistic models that are far better for analyzing a capacity problem of this sort. These models will use the historical data indicating the day-to-day variations in requirements, and thereby will put into sharp focus the elements of uncertainty contained in this kind of problem.

With regard to numerical techniques for solving such probabilistic models, this topic, of course, anticipates what is ahead, and therefore cannot be pursued here in any detail. Suffice it to say that, depending on the particular mathematical statement of the model, you actually may be able to use linear or nonlinear programming algorithms, or a dynamic programming approach, or, if these are not appropriate, what is called *computer simulation*. As you continue reading this book you will therefore find that the computational approaches in the previous chapters are also helpful techniques for solving many stochastic problems. In addition, you will discover some new techniques that are especially suited to models containing elements of uncertainty.

Introducing probabilities. The cases above referred to two approaches for dealing with uncertainty: testing solution sensitivity in deterministic models, and designing models containing probabilistic elements. The underlying theme for the rest of the book is how to introduce probability analysis into optimization models. Now uncertainties will be viewed as imperfect predictions to be characterized by probability distributions for the different possible events. Frequently, the resultant models will merely be more complicated versions of deterministic models and can be solved by the same numerical techniques. But this will not always be so. Sometimes you will be justified in substituting a single expected value in the deterministic version; but more often, in order to calculate solutions you will have to exploit the form of an *optimal* strategy, if this is not too difficult to find, or otherwise you will have to use an arbitrary, but reasonable, form.

No matter what, you will see that probabilistic models are *inherently* harder to use than deterministic versions. First, there are new conceptual difficulties, such as the interpretation of the probabilities themselves and the meaning of optimality; these are discussed in Sec. 16.2. Second, there are new technical difficulties relating to the mathematics of optimization. To illustrate, even when a stochastic model is a straightforward generalization of a deterministic version, the computational burden increases, since you must consider each possible event instead of only a single estimate. Further, in stochastic models the criterion functions are typically nonlinear, so that the task of optimization is more complex. And third, there are increased data requirements for the specification of the probability distributions. For example, a manager may see that the price of his competitor's product fluctuates, but he may find it difficult to state a meaningful probability distribution for this variation.

Thus, aside from the intellectual curiosity engendered by stochastic phenomena, there would be limited interest in these probabilistic models were it not for their practical necessity in certain real decision-making situations.

The art of management science once more. Here we return to the question, "How do you select the right model for a particular application?" Regrettably, no textbook can furnish you with an infallible set of rules—you will have to rely on experience, mature judgment, and continuing analysis.

In real applications, of course, you can often get expert advice from other people based on their own past experience and mature judgment. There is some solace in that thought. But if you have managerial responsibility, then never forget that you—not your advisors—must bear the ultimate responsibility for your decisions, good or bad. Consequently, if you want to make effective managerial use of the powerful analytic tools in this book, there is no good substitute for educating your own judgment. To assist you in this task, we have selected many of the examples in the remainder of this book to be stochastic versions of the deterministic models in earlier chapters. You should strive to see how uncertainty affects a decision-making problem by studying how this factor is reflected in each analytic model. Then, when faced with a real decision-making problem in an environment of uncertainty, you can more confidently ferret out the essentials you want reflected by an analytic model, and so choose an effective approach.

Study guide. The remainder of this chapter and the next two will show you how to generalize many of the examples in earlier chapters to include random elements. At the same time, you will see a few important general propositions about optimal solutions to stochastic models. Finally, the material will demonstrate the applicability of techniques such as linear and dynamic programming for finding numerical solutions. These three chapters, then, link the first part of the book with what is to come. It is important for you to realize, however, that many of the models in these introductory chapters are really too general. They do not sufficiently exploit a model's special structure or take advantage of the form of an optimal solution. Consequently, they often obscure the fundamental nature of an optimal solution and are computationally inefficient. For these reasons, you will want to study the models in subsequent chapters, where special structure is exploited.

One important group of probability models deals with inventory stockage problems in which you cannot assume that the demand requirements are known with certainty. Chapter 19 and Appendix II explain several of these models, including a few approaches that have proved eminently successful in practice. Another useful class of probability models treats what are sometimes called waiting line, queuing, or congestion problems. The illustration of Lead-Nickel's computer capacity expansion problem can be put in this category. If the structure of a waiting line environment is not too complex, the operating characteristics of the system—such as the average line length, the average waiting time, and the probability of the line's being empty—can be found by the analytic methods presented in Chap. 20 and Appendix III. Furthermore, the results in these chapters indicate the insights to be gained in the analysis of typical complex congestion problems. Such queuing phenomena as well as other intricate probabilistic environments may be too complicated to yield to standard mathematical analysis, and consequently may have to be studied through computer simulation. Chapter 21 surveys many of the concepts that are fundamental to an understanding of computer simulation and also presents several techniques that are effective in building such models.

As you continue your reading, you will find it helpful to answer two questions about each stochastic model:

1. What is an optimal policy for a deterministic version of the model?
2. How much information about the probability distributions is required to state an optimal solution?

By considering the first question, you will better perceive the influence of the elements of uncertainty. In a few instances the deterministic version will have a trivial optimal solution, so you can see exactly how uncertainty complicates the decision problem. In every case, the computation of an optimal solution for the deterministic version will be simpler, so you can come to appreciate the degree of additional complexity arising from introducing probabilities. The importance of keeping the second question in mind will become quite clear when you study the so-called chance-constrained approach in Sec. 16.5, for example, which requires only the fractiles of the probability distributions to calculate an optimal policy. Conscientious effort to answer these two questions for each example will greatly assist you in gaining the fundamental insights to be had from stochastic models.

16.2 DECISION-MAKING IN AN UNCERTAIN ENVIRONMENT

Before launching into an extended discussion of specific models and examples, we state in a few sentences what new complications are introduced when you seek an optimal decision in an uncertain environment. We assume that you are now fairly well acquainted with model building and optimizing techniques for deterministic problems. In particular, you understand that when you solve linear and dynamic programming problems, like the ones treated in the first half of this book, you know exactly what your decisions will be and precisely what future effect they will have. For example, in a deterministic planning model, if you decide to process 10 units of raw material, then you know exactly how many items will be produced for sale. Or, in a deterministic inventory model, if you choose to purchase five dozen units for the next six months and two dozen units for the following six months, then as a result, you can forecast precisely what the inventory levels will be for the 12-month horizon.

But suppose instead that if you decide to process 10 units of raw material, the yield may be any one of several possible numbers of items. Or if you purchase dozens of units as specified above, then the future inventory levels depend on the amounts of demand that actually materialize. In other words, consider the impact on your immediate and future decision choices if you cannot know for certain what will happen as a result of your actions.

When uncertainties do impinge on your choice, you first must resolve the question of what is an *optimal* decision. We elaborate on the question in this section.

Second, if some decisions have to be made now but others can be deferred until several of the *un*certainties disappear, you also must consider the possibility of employing a **contingency plan** or **strategy.** Returning again to the purchasing example above, you may want to decide to order five dozen units this period, and then devise a "set of ordering instructions" to be used over the remaining periods. These rules would state how much to purchase given the *observed* demands and the orders in previous periods. Thus, you do not know exactly how much will be ordered after this period, but only what you will purchase conditional on the actual ordering and demand history when the future purchase decisions must be made. In the paragraphs below, we will elaborate further on the notion of a decision strategy.

Expected value. If you have had an opportunity to apply any of the models in the first half of this book to an actual planning situation, you will have discovered that stating a single objective function to be optimized is merely a convenient way to select a solution when there are a myriad of feasible possibilities. Executives experienced in applying operations research know quite well that such a solution is rarely optimal in any absolute, "all things considered" sense. In fact, almost always such a solution is manually adjusted to provide a better fit to reality, or the model specifications themselves are altered and a new "optimal" solution is found.

In solving decision models containing uncertainties, we continue in the same spirit and state only a single objective function to be optimized. But we caution here at the outset that in an actual application, you should investigate various operating characteristics of a solution that is selected by a single optimization criterion. You may have to adjust this solution or modify the model before being able to successfully implement the result.

For most of the models you will study, uncertainty will affect the actual or realized value of the economic criterion. We will consistently employ the *expected value* of the economic criterion as the objective function to be optimized. In recent years, scholars of decision-theory have devised several ways of justifying the use of the expected value as the sole criterion for an optimal choice. Many recent texts in statistical analysis present these arguments. As fascinating as the subject is, we do not pursue the topic here, because regardless of whether or not you find these justifications convincing, we still are going to use expected value as the objective function in the optimization models. (We do, however, temper this intransigent attitude by showing in several chapters how you can calculate relevant operating characteristics of a selected policy.)

With the exception of the advanced material, we employ only elementary notions of probability theory, like the expected value and the cumulative probability function. Frequently, we use discrete probability distributions, so that you can calculate answers without resorting to the calculus. Sometimes we provide you with the end results of applying the calculus; although the formula may look complicated, you will have no trouble in computing answers when you are given specific values for the variables.

But if you are like most students—even if you have had a full-term course in probability theory—you will find some of the mathematical expressions new, and therefore strange looking. The reason is that most probability textbooks do not concentrate on decision-making or optimization problems. Consequently, the mean and variance of a probability distribution may be the most complicated expected values you have ever derived up to now.

Calculating the types of expected values that are used in this text is really not much more complicated than finding the mean of a probability distribution. To demonstrate this claim, we review the ideas below to familiarize you with the process for when you read the subsequent examples.

Suppose X is a random variable that can have any of the values $n = 0, 1, 2, \ldots, N$. Let $P[X = n]$ designate the probability that X takes the value n. Then the expected value of the random variable X is

$$(1) \qquad E[X] \equiv \sum_{n=0}^{N} n \cdot P[X = n] \quad \text{(expected value of } X\text{)}.$$

If X can equal *any* nonnegative integer with positive probability, then we will use the symbol ∞ instead of N in (1); in this case (as well as for all summations over an infinite number of terms), we postulate that the expected value is a finite number.

Next, suppose we want to compute the expected value of the random variable X^2. This is simply

$$(2) \qquad E[X^2] \equiv \sum_{n=0}^{N} n^2 \cdot P[X = n] \quad \text{(expected value of } X^2\text{)}.$$

In general, if we wish to calculate the expected value of a function of X, which we denote as $f(X)$, then we will compute

$$(3) \qquad E[f(X)] \equiv \sum_{n=0}^{N} f(n) \cdot P[X = n]. \quad \text{[expected value of } f(X)\text{]}.$$

Hopefully, you remember this much from your previous training in probability theory.

Now let us apply (3) to an example containing an economic criterion function. A simple, but instructive, illustration is the expected cost associated with an inventory stockage rule for a one-period horizon. Let D denote a random variable representing the amount of customer demand in a single period. Assume the possible values for D are $d = 0, 1, 2, \ldots, N$, and the associated probabilities are $P[D = d]$. Suppose that you purchase y items to stock for customer demand, where each item costs c dollars. If any of these items are left over at the end of the period, you incur a holding cost of h per unit. (Assume there is no salvage value for items left over.) But if demand D exceeds the amount you order y, then you incur a penalty cost p per item short. Thus, the actual cost in a period depends on not only how much you order but also what value of demand really occurs. Since you have to order y before knowing demand D, it is reasonable to assess the effect of your decision in terms of *expected* cost.

Specifically, let $f(d|y)$ represent the actual cost when demand $D = d$, given that you order y. Then

$$(4) \quad f(d|y) = \begin{cases} cy + h \cdot (y - d) & \text{if } d \leq y \quad \text{(demand is less than amount ordered)} \\ cy + p \cdot (d - y) & \text{if } d > y \quad \text{(demand exceeds amount ordered)}. \end{cases}$$

Hence the expected cost, given that you order $y(\leq N)$, is

(5) $\quad E[f(D|y)] = \sum_{d=0}^{N} f(d|y) \cdot P[D = d]$

(6) $\qquad\qquad = \sum_{d=0}^{y} f(d|y) \cdot P[D = d] + \sum_{d=y+1}^{N} f(d|y) \cdot P[D = d] \qquad$ (if $y < N$)

(7) $\qquad\qquad = \sum_{d=0}^{y} [cy + h \cdot (y - d)] \cdot P[D = d]$

$\qquad\qquad\quad + \sum_{d=y+1}^{N} [cy + p \cdot (d - y)] \cdot P[D = d].$

The equation in (5) is simply the definition of expected value; the equation (6) follows by breaking the summation in (5) into two parts, one for demand less than the amount ordered, and one for demand exceeding the amount ordered; the third equality (7) is simply a substitution of the formulas in (4) for $f(d|y)$.

You can carry the algebra further. Notice in (7) that the term cy appears inside both summations. Therefore, the amount cy is multiplied by the probability $P[D = d]$ for every possible value d; since the sum of the probabilities $P[D = d]$ over *every* d equals 1, you can write

(8) $\quad E[f(D|y)] = cy + \sum_{d=0}^{y} h \cdot (y - d) \cdot P[D = d] + \sum_{d=y+1}^{N} p \cdot (d - y) \cdot P[D = d]$

$\qquad\qquad\qquad\qquad\qquad\qquad\qquad\qquad$ (expected cost, given y).

The formula in (8) has an important direct interpretation: given that you stock y, the expected cost equals the sum of the purchase cost, the expected holding cost, and the expected penalty cost.

We have derived (8) in a straightforward fashion using only "first principles" of expectations. But in building decision-making models such as this, it is far more convenient to start immediately with the statement in (8). Consequently, we will adopt the practice of initially writing the objective function as a sum of the component expected costs (and revenues). When you are in doubt as to whether the objective function has been written correctly, then make an analysis parallel to the one above. Start with the value of the economic criterion exhibited as a function of the random variables, for given levels of the decision variables. Then take the expected value of this function over the possible values for the random variables, and simplify the results.

Now we analyze a specific decision problem using an expected value criterion to see the impact of uncertainty on making an optimal choice.

Optimal decisions. Consider once again the plant expansion problem of the Yum-Yum Company discussed in the previous section. The two alternatives are to expand the present facility or build a new plant. For either decision, the resultant profit depends on the firm's future share of the market. Suppose the President assesses the probability of his firm's maintaining its present 35% market share as $\frac{1}{2}$, and the probabilities of 30% and 40% shares as $\frac{1}{8}$ and $\frac{3}{8}$, respectively. The corresponding annual profit values are shown in Fig. 16.1.

Share of Market	President's Assessed Probability of Share	Annual Profit ($ Millions)	
		Expand Facility	Build New Plant
30%	$\frac{1}{8}$	90	50
35%	$\frac{1}{2}$	100	100
40%	$\frac{3}{8}$	130	150

FIGURE 16.1. Yum-Yum Company.

If you were this company's president, how would you decide between the two alternatives? How calamitous would it be if you built a new plant and the market share then fell to 30%, so that the company made only $50 million instead of $90 million? How embarrassing would it be if you expanded the facility and then the market share increased to 40%, so that the firm made $130 million but could otherwise have made $150 million?

In situations like this, when there are only a few alternative actions, it is feasible to calculate the probability distribution of the possible objective-function values and then examine the relative merits of each action. But in most problems we will at least initially recommend an action that optimizes the expected value of the economic criterion. For the two alternatives in Fig. 16.1, verify that:

(9)
$$\text{Expand facility:} \quad \text{expected profit} = (90)\tfrac{1}{8} + (100)\tfrac{1}{2} + (130)\tfrac{3}{8} = 110$$
$$\text{Build new plant:} \quad \text{expected profit} = (50)\tfrac{1}{8} + (100)\tfrac{1}{2} + (150)\tfrac{3}{8} = 112.5$$

In terms of expected profit, building a new plant is slightly better.

You well may conclude that the small difference between the expected values in (9) does not really convey the true qualitative difference between the probable economic effects of the two decisions. If that is your feeling, then let this example serve as a lesson. Whenever you employ an objective function that for the purpose of comparison reduces an entire probability distribution of economic outcomes to a single number, at least examine other characteristics of the solution to test the reasonableness of the recommendation.

Uncertain actions. In the various dynamic deterministic models of Chaps. 8 through 12, you can predict with perfect certainty the precise sequence of decisions that is implied by any given policy. For example, in a production scheduling model, where demands are known exactly over the horizon, you can trace the precise production levels period by period. But if, instead, the demands can be described only by means of a probability distribution, then ordinarily you cannot say for certain what the production levels are beyond the current decision.

Suppose in this production example that you employ a dynamic policy that specifies the amount to be produced for *each* level of entering inventory at any period. Then such a policy actually induces a probability distribution on the future production decisions.

To illustrate this critical observation, let $i = 0, 1, 2, 3$ be the possible levels of entering inventory at any period. Assume the horizon is unbounded and the dynamic policy is stationary. Let $x_\infty(i)$ be the current production decision given i, where

$$(10) \qquad x_\infty(0) = x_\infty(1) = x_\infty(2) = 3 \quad x_\infty(3) = 0.$$

Hence, each period you produce 3 unless entering inventory equals 3. Suppose in any period the amount demanded is described by the probability distribution

$$(11) \qquad D_t = 2 \text{ with probability } \tfrac{1}{2} \qquad D_t = 3 \text{ with probability } \tfrac{1}{2}.$$

If entering inventory in the current period is 2, then current production is 3, and production in the next period will be either 0, with probability $\tfrac{1}{2}$ (if the current demand is 2), or 3, with probability $\tfrac{1}{2}$ (if the current demand is 3). Explain why.

Continuing the analysis in the same fashion, production in the period *after* next will be either 0, with probability $\tfrac{1}{4}$ (if the current and next period's demands are 3 and 2, respectively), or 3, with probability $(1 - \tfrac{1}{4} = \tfrac{3}{4})$. Again, explain why.

This line of reasoning leads to the important insight that even though the component decisions implied by the stationary strategy (10) are deterministic, they actually will occur over time in a random fashion because of the uncertain elements (11) in the structure of the model. As a result, the associated costs over the horizon are described by a complex joint probability distribution.

In most dynamic models containing probabilistic elements, you will need to treat future decisions so as to reflect their future uncertainty. With this in mind, you should always carefully examine any such model for the specific assumptions as to what information about previous values of the random variables is available each time a decision is to be made. In constructing a mathematical model it is easy to make an error in describing what is typically an intertwined time sequence of random events and the subsequent decisions that are based, in part, on the actual outcome of the earlier events. The examples below and in Chap. 17 will show you how to approach these time-staged decision problems.

Another notion arising from induced randomness in an unfolding sequence of decisions is the idea of steady-state behavior. As an illustration, look again at the production example, (10) and (11). Let p_i denote the proportion of periods that entering inventory is at level i, when the system operates over an unbounded horizon. It can be shown for the strategy (10) and the demand distribution (11) that

$$(12) \qquad p_0 = \frac{1}{6} \quad p_1 = \frac{1}{3} \quad p_2 = \frac{1}{3} \quad p_3 = \frac{1}{6}.$$

Further, let q_x denote the proportion of periods during which production is at level x when the system operates over an unbounded horizon. Then as you should verify, from (10) and (12) it follows that

$$(13) \qquad q_0 = p_3 = \frac{1}{6} \qquad q_3 = p_0 + p_1 + p_2 = \frac{5}{6}.$$

▶Occasionally, the optimal policy for a model calls for the decision-maker himself to introduce randomness as part of his strategy. Of course, issue can be taken about the particular structural details in models giving rise to this type of solution, but there hardly is reason to object to such **randomized strategies** per se, since, as you have just seen, there already is randomness in the actions induced by the uncertain elements.

The following hypothetical example shows how a randomized strategy can be optimal. The manager of the *Toute de Suite* Bakery has found that the daily demand for one of his specialty cakes is described by the probability distribution

(i) $P[\text{no cakes}] = \dfrac{1}{6}$ $P[\text{one cake}] = \dfrac{1}{6}$ $P[\text{two cakes}] = \dfrac{2}{3}.$

Assume that the demand on any day is independent of demands on previous days. Each cake costs c to bake and must be thrown away if it is not sold at the end of the day. The manager does not want to make too many cakes as c is large; but still he wants to satisfy a reasonable level of demand. Accordingly, he formulates his decision problem as: minimize expected baking cost subject to the constraint that the probability of meeting the total daily demand is at least $\frac{1}{3}$.

It might appear that the optimal solution is to bake one cake at a cost of $1c$, for then total demand is met with probability $(\frac{1}{6} + \frac{1}{6} = \frac{1}{3})$. However, suppose the manager uses the following **randomized decision rule**: bake no cakes with probability $\frac{4}{5}$ and bake two cakes with probability $\frac{1}{5}$. He then still meets total demand with probability $[(\frac{4}{5})\frac{1}{6} + (\frac{1}{5})1 = \frac{1}{3}]$, and what is more, his expected cost is $[(\frac{4}{5})0c + (\frac{1}{5})2c = .4c]$, which is less than the cost of $1c$ for the nonrandomized strategy. This randomized rule is optimal.

Suppose that, instead of imposing a probability constraint, he formulates his decision problem as: minimize baking cost subject to satisfying, on the average, at least $\frac{1}{3}$ of expected daily demand. Verify from (i) that expected daily demand is $\frac{3}{2}$, so that the constraint is to sell at least $\frac{1}{2}$ a cake a day, on the average. Once again, if he uses a deterministic strategy of baking one cake, on the average he sells $[(\frac{1}{6})0 + (\frac{1}{6})1 + (\frac{2}{3})1 = \frac{5}{6}]$ cakes per day, which is in excess of the minimal constraint, $\frac{1}{2}$. His optimal strategy is to randomize: bake no cakes with probability $\frac{2}{5}$ and bake one cake with probability $\frac{3}{5}$. Then he sells $[(\frac{2}{5})0 + (\frac{3}{5})\frac{5}{6} = \frac{1}{2}]$ cakes per day, on the average, and the expected cost is $[(\frac{2}{5})0c + (\frac{3}{5})1c = .6c]$, which is less than $1c$.

In general, whenever an optimization model contains constraints on the probabilities of events or on their expected values, an optimal solution may indicate randomization. ◀

Multiperiod objective function. In a dynamic model, where you have to evaluate a stream of returns, each component of which is random, the objective function will be the expected value analogue to the approaches in the first half of this book.

To illustrate, let R_t designate the return in Period t of a dynamic model. As you have seen in the paragraphs above, when there are uncertain events, a decision strategy followed over the planning horizon gives rise to a joint probability distribution on the elements of the returns stream $(R_1, R_2, R_3, \ldots)$. Suppose we postulate that the objective function is the expected present value of the stream:

(14) $E[\text{present value}] \equiv E[R_1 + \alpha R_2 + \alpha^2 R_3 + \cdots],$

where α is the one-period discount factor, and $0 \le \alpha < 1$. We assume that the value in (14) is finite.

The expected value in (14) is taken over the *joint* probability distribution of $(R_1, R_2, R_3, \ldots)$. We can simplify the expression by employing a Fundamental Theorem of Random Variables: *the expected value of a sum always equals the sum of the expected values.* Consequently

$$(15) \qquad E[\text{present value}] = E[R_1] + \alpha E[R_2] + \alpha^2 E[R_3] + \cdots,$$

where we have brought each discount-factor coefficient in front of the associated expectation since the factor itself is a constant. In (15), each expectation is taken over the *marginal* probability distribution of the displayed random variable.

For a second illustration, consider again the production example in (10) and (11). In this case, suppose the objective function is the long-run expected cost per period. You saw in (12) the exact proportion of periods that entering inventory is at level i, where the system is viewed over an unbounded horizon. Similarly, you saw in (13) the exact proportion of periods during which production is at level x. Denote the stationary production and inventory costs each period as $C(x)$ and $h(i)$, respectively. Then you can compute the value of the objective function for the stationary policy in (10) as

$$(16) \quad \begin{aligned} \genfrac{}{}{0pt}{}{\text{expected cost per period}}{\text{over an unbounded horizon}} &= E[C(x)] + E[h(i)] \\ &= \{[C(0)]\tfrac{1}{6} + [C(3)]\tfrac{5}{6}\} \\ &\quad + \{[h(0)]\tfrac{1}{6} + [h(1)]\tfrac{1}{3} + [h(2)]\tfrac{1}{3} + [h(3)]\tfrac{1}{6}\}, \end{aligned}$$

as you should verify.

Specifying probability distributions. The stochastic models in this book assume that the decision-maker can state probability distributions to describe the elements of uncertainty in the model. Loosely put, the decision-maker must be able to assign nonnegative numerical weights to each possible event such that: (i) If an event is certain, its associated weight equals 1. (ii) If two events A and B are mutually exclusive, the weight of the event "either A or B" equals the sum of the weights for each of the events A and B. Since most elementary texts on probability theory discuss how to characterize a probability distribution in this way, we give no further elucidation here. What is more, for the purpose of this book, nothing else really *has* to be said, as the models to be treated merely apply the weights, employing the type of elementary probability calculations you find in an introductory text. Nevertheless, we do add a few comments on the interpretation of the weights and how a decision-maker might go about assigning specific numerical values, so that you have a better appreciation of these models' intended meaning.

Over the years, probability theory scholars have suggested a variety of interpretations for the weights. The most widespread notion is the *relative frequency* interpretation. In optimization-oriented models, a more insightful view, however, is that probability assessments reflect the decision-maker's state of mind. To illustrate what this means, recall the market-share probabilities in Fig. 16.1 that were specified by the President of the Yum-Yum Company. These weights are really a quantification of the President's current judgment about the future, and guide him in making an immediate decision (on whether to expand an existing plant or build a new one). For another illustration, consider the Lead-Nickel Controller who was evaluating whether to install a new large-scale computer. The historical data he collected, showing congestion, are of decision-making relevance only if he feels that they embody his judgments about future conditions.

Much has been written recently on the issues and techniques of deriving probability weights that reflect the decision-maker's personal prognosis. The topic is usually referred to as *statistical decision theory*, and sometimes by the more restricted term *Bayesian analysis*. Despite the subject's importance and relevance, delving into the details here would only be too distracting from the main task of analyzing optimizing models. But as a pragmatic matter, essentially, you can utilize four approaches to obtain these probability distributions:

1. *Use introspection.*
2. *Employ historical data.*
3. *Find convenient approximations.*
4. *State descriptive axioms.*

Most often, you would apply two or more of these approaches in combination.

To illustrate these, consider the Peppy Pill Company, a wholesale jobber of pharmaceutical products, that wants to install a computerized scientific inventory control system for stocking about 1500 products. In particular, once a week the computer is to update the inventory status of each item, and if the stock is too low, to indicate that Peppy Pill should send a replenishment order to a manufacturer. Since there is considerable weekly variation in customer demand for each item, the scientific replenishment rules are to be derived from probabilistic inventory models like those you will study in Chap. 19. These models require specifying the probability distributions of weekly demand for each item.

To begin, suppose Peppy Pill has little or no historical demand data. This situation sometimes arises because of insufficient records, and frequently because an item to be stocked is a new product that has no demand history. Then Peppy's inventory manager has no recourse other than to use Approach 1, applying whatever experience he can bring to bear in quantifying his judgments. As the inventory system operates for a while and demand data are accumulated, he can then apply the numerical techniques of Bayesian analysis to update his probability assessments.

Now assume, instead, that this company has customer demand data for 6 to 18 months back, depending on whether an item has a fast or slow turnover. These quantities have been manually posted on makeshift record cards. Then Peppy Pill can combine Approaches 1 and 2 by summarizing between one and two years' weekly demand data into an historical distribution for each item and by applying judgmental corrections to reflect the management's future assessment of demand. You should realize, however, that in most actual situations, using historical data to compute empirical distributions is ordinarily not feasible: usually not enough data are available, and even when they are, the expense of computing so many individual demand distributions is prohibitive.

Hence, Approach 3 is added as a modification to Approaches 1 and 2. To illustrate, the inventory manager may have calculated the empirical mean, and perhaps the variance of each item's weekly demands, making whatever judgmental corrections he deems necessary. Then in a computerized stochastic inventory control model, he may employ, as an approximation, a Normal distribution having such a mean and variance. These values would be systematically updated by the computer as new demand experience accumulates.

Approach 4 is a more sophisticated version of Approach 3. The inventory manager first chooses a model describing the *process* by which demands are generated. For example, the model may include the total number of Peppy's customers, the chance that any one of these will want an item during a week, the pattern of order sizes for a customer, etc. Obviously, this method is more complicated than Approach 3, but it can be effective when the resultant analysis provides an explicit form for the probability distribution of demand, such as a Poisson or a binomial distribution. Then the historical data and judgmental corrections are used to obtain the few parameters needed to describe the derived probability law. (For Peppy's inventory problem, Approach 3 is likely to be better than Approach 4.)

In conclusion, uncertainty influences stochastic models in two ways. The first way is the direct effect stemming from the random phenomena explicitly accounted for by the model. The second is the indirect impact coming from the process of specifying the probability weights to describe the phenomena. For the most part, the rest of this book concentrates only on the direct effect.

▶A lively area of research on stochastic models is testing the sensitivity of solutions to variations in the specification of the probability distributions. Several topics of interest are: how best to estimate the parameters of distributions used in optimization models; how to find good approximations; how to take explicit account in a model of the uncertainty about the probability distributions; and how to derive reliable models that need only a limited amount of historical data.   ◀

Where do we go from here? Having established the groundwork for analyzing probabilistic decision models in the preceding pages, we can progress in earnest to some important insights and several useful applications. In the next section, we show how, in a complex dynamic decision process, you can go astray should you try to ignore randomness by using an expected value in lieu of the random variable itself. We dub this mistake the *Fallacy of Averages*. It implies that in a linear programming planning model, for example, you usually are not justified in simply substituting expected values for the problem's coefficients when they really are random. The rest of the chapter explores what you can do in linear programming problems when some of the coefficients are characterized by probability distributions.

In Sec. 16.4 we discuss one possible way to treat a fairly simple, so-called two-stage stochastic linear programming model. The model clearly illustrates some of the nasty difficulties that have to be resolved in order to make an optimal decision when faced with uncertainty. (The generalization to a multistage problem is explained in the advanced material of Sec. 16.7.)

In Sec. 16.5 we present another possible way of solving the problem. The approach, named *chance-constrained programming*, is an alternative to the two-stage model. We compare the two approaches by means of an illustrative planning example.

The advanced material in Sec. 16.6 provides a second example of both the two-stage and chance-constrained approaches. It is an interesting problem in its own right. The model is a standard transportation problem, like the one you studied in Chap. 6, except here the demands are random variables. In the final advanced section we explain a programming model for which it *is* appropriate to substitute an expected value wherever a random variable occurs.

If you like to read suspense stories, then skip immediately to the next section—you will discover the villain soon enough. But if you like to be primed for what lies ahead, then we must prepare you for discouraging news. Only rarely in practice will you be able to easily modify a linear programming model so as to take account of uncertainty in the coefficients. True, the methods in this chapter are formally capable of solving such models. But for real problems, usually these techniques are not applicable. Actual decision problems are seldom only two-stage situations, and a full-blown treatment of these actual problems requires a programming model of staggering dimensions.

Nevertheless, don't lay down this book yet! There are some practical probability models that you *can* solve. We have saved these for the subsequent chapters, after you have come to appreciate what difficulties must be overcome.

16.3 FALLACY OF AVERAGES

The following case is a simplified example of an actual decision problem dealing with uncertain elements. It demonstrates how you can be dangerously misled by using average values in a model appropriate for a deterministic situation.

The Galactic Reaper Company, which manufactures farm machinery, is planning to construct a new plant to build its latest equipment, a combine for harvesting, threshing, and cleaning grain. Five major tasks must be completed in order to put the plant into full operation:

A. Erect plant building.
B. Complete final design of combine model.
C. Expand nucleus labor force to full-scale production size.
D. Install manufacturing equipment.
E. Debug prototype models.

Let t_A, t_B, ..., t_E be the number of periods required for Tasks A, B, ..., E. A period consists of three months. Assume that these tasks must be performed in the sequence indicated by Fig. 16.2. For example, both Tasks A and B can be started immediately. Both Tasks C and D can be started as soon as Task A is completed. Task E can start when *both* Tasks B and D are finished. The plant is in full-scale production as soon as *both* Tasks C and E are completed. (The network diagram is identical to Fig. 6.16, p. 186, used to illustrate critical path scheduling. Although the explanation of the case here is complete, you may find it helpful to review Sec. 6.6.)

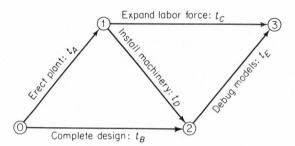

FIGURE 16.2. Galactic Reaper Company Example.

If the values of t_A, t_B, . . . , t_E were known with perfect certainty, then the total span of time required to put the plant into operation could be determined by finding the length of a longest route from Node 0 to Node 3 in the network of Fig. 16.2. Several of these values are uncertain, however. Relying in part on past experience in constructing plants, Galactic Reaper's President has estimated the probability of each possible value, as shown in Fig. 16.3. Thus, it is equally likely that t_B be either 2, 3, or 4 periods (that is, 6, 9, or 12 months); similar statements hold for t_C and t_E. The times for t_A and t_D are known exactly. The President believes that there is complete independence among the random events.

Task	Possible Number of Periods	President's Assessed Probability
A	2	perfect certainty
B	2, 3, 4	$\frac{1}{3}$ each
C	2, 3, 4	$\frac{1}{3}$ each
D	1	perfect certainty
E	1, 2, 3	$\frac{1}{3}$ each

FIGURE 16.3. Galactic Reaper Company. Possible Time Requirements (One Period = 3 Months).

Verify that when each random event takes its smallest value, the total time span is 4 periods; and when each takes its largest value, the span is 7 periods. Thus the range of completion times is between 12 and 21 months. Also check that if each random event takes its average value ($t_B = 3$, $t_C = 3$, $t_E = 2$), then the time span is 5 periods (15 months).

The President of Galactic Reaper feels there is a significant competitive advantage to having the plant in operation as soon as possible. His estimates of the in-

cremental profit impact for different completion times of less than 7 periods are
shown in Fig. 16.4. Being concerned about
the drop in profit that occurs if the completion time stretches out to 6 or 7 periods,
he considers the possibility of hiring an
experienced manager to act as special
assistant to supervise the construction
project. He believes that the extra attention
such a man could provide would reduce the
total time span by 1 period in *any* event.
That is, even if the span would have been 4
periods, the manager would cut the time

Total Time Span (Periods)	Incremental Profit ($ 1000)
3	120
4	110
5	100
6	50
7	0

FIGURE 16.4. Galactic Reaper Company. Competitive Advantage of Early Completion.

to 3 periods, and likewise for any other possible total span between 5 and 7
periods. The total cost of hiring this manager is $20,000. If the President knew for
certain that the total span would be 4 or 5 periods, then he would decide against
adding the man, since the gain of $10,000 would not offset the additional cost of
$20,000. The opposite would be true if the President knew for certain that the
span would be 6 or 7 periods. Given the factual information in Figs. 16.2 through
16.4, would you hire the new manager if you were President of Galactic Reaper?

Analysis. If you were to base your analysis on the total span of 5 periods,
calculated by using the *average* time for each task, then you would not hire the
special assistant. The reason is that a reduction from 5 to 4 periods implies
the profit gain would be $10,000 (= $110,000 − $100,000) and this is less than
the additional cost of $20,000. As you will see, this analysis is quite faulty.

Such an approach makes two mistakes: first it assumes that the total time span
calculated by looking at individual averages is a useful approximation to the
expected total time span. Second, it overlooks the fact that the relevant criterion
is expected incremental profit, and not incremental profit for the expected time
span.

By evaluating all the different possible events and their probabilities of occurrence, it can be shown that

(1) $P[T = 4] = \frac{2}{27} \quad P[T = 5] = \frac{8}{27} \quad P[T = 6] = \frac{14}{27} \quad P[T = 7] = \frac{3}{27},$

where T denotes the total time span. Therefore, verify that

(2) $E\begin{bmatrix} \text{incremental profit} \\ \text{without new manager} \end{bmatrix} = (110)\frac{2}{27} + (100)\frac{8}{27} + (50)\frac{14}{27} + (0)\frac{3}{27}$

$= 64,$

and

(3) $E\begin{bmatrix} \text{incremental profit} \\ \text{with new manager} \end{bmatrix} = (120)\frac{2}{27} + (110)\frac{8}{27} + (100)\frac{14}{27} + (50)\frac{3}{27}$

$= 99.$

To keep the arithmetic uncluttered, we have rounded the computations to the nearest thousand dollars. Thus the gain in expected incremental profit from the new manager is \$35,000 (= \$99,000 — \$64,000), which exceeds the additional cost of \$20,000. Notice that the faulty analysis using the time average went astray because it was considerably overoptimistic in assessing the *economic* outcome when the new assistant was not hired.

The faulty analysis exhibited the following fallacy.

FALLACY OF AVERAGES. Given an arbitrary nonlinear function $f(x_1, \ldots, x_n)$ of random variables $x_1, \ldots, x_n$, it is usually erroneous to assume $E[f(x_1, \ldots, x_n)] = f(E[x_1], \ldots, E[x_n])$.

Although mathematical analysis of a particular nonlinear function *may* establish that its expected value is well approximated by the same function of the expected values, you should never blindly assume that it does.

Uncertainty and information. What is the **economic impact of uncertainty** in the foregoing example? A way to give a quantified answer to this question is to evaluate the gain in expected profit that would occur if Galactic Reaper's President were able to obtain a perfect prediction of the uncertain elements. In other words, the impact of uncertainty can be measured as the maximum amount the President would be willing to pay if, *after* the payment, he were able to learn the exact values of the random elements and consequently decide without error whether to hire the new manager. This figure is easily computed.

Recall that the decision to hire the man is better only when $T = 6$ and 7, and the net profit will be \$80,000 (= \$100,000 — \$20,000) and \$30,000 (= \$50,000 — \$20,000), respectively. Then the expected net profit when the values of the random elements are known prior to the decision is

(4) $$E\begin{bmatrix} \text{net profit with} \\ \text{perfect information} \end{bmatrix} = (100)\tfrac{2}{27} + (100)\tfrac{8}{27} + (80)\tfrac{14}{27} + (30)\tfrac{3}{27}$$

$$= 83,$$

as you should check. Given the expectation in (3), the expected net profit with uncertainty is \$79,000 (= \$99,000 — \$20,000). Therefore the **gain from perfect information** is \$4,000 (= \$83,000 — \$79,000), taking account of the added cost of the new manager. This figure may be interpreted as measuring the impact or loss from uncertainty, for the President of Galactic Reaper would not pay over \$4000 to have perfect foresight.

16.4 TWO-STAGE LINEAR MODEL

In this section we begin consideration of how to account for probabilistic uncertainty in the coefficients of a linear programming problem. As you know by now, linear programming has a multitude of applications. You may easily have gotten the impression after reading Chap. 2 that linear programming is a "model for all seasons." For this reason alone, trying to extend the linear programming problem to encompass chance elements is a worthwhile goal.

Our task in the next several sections is to devise ways of formulating a so-called **stochastic linear programming model** that yields ordinary linear programming problems as a result. Because of the great diversity of applications mentioned above, we cannot hope to succeed in this task unless we add some specific postulates about the underlying structure of the decision process. In particular, we have to formalize the evolution of "which decisions have to be made when what information is known about the previous decisions and the random variables."

A fairly general structure of this sort is contained in the advanced material of Sec. 16.7. That formulation permits you to model a long and involved history of decisions and information flow. You can glean many of the principal ideas, however, by examining a scaled-down version with only two stages to the decision process. Consequently that is the problem we consider in this section.

In particular, you will learn two things from investigating the two-stage model. First, you will see how to formulate a simple stochastic programming model to yield an equivalent ordinary linear programming problem. Second, you will see that such a formulation magnifies the size of the problem. You will be justified in concluding that the more general situation modeled in Sec. 16.7 is likely to be beyond practicality for most real linear programming applications.

In Sec. 16.5, you will study a chance-constrained model, which is an alternative formulation for a stochastic programming problem. The approach avoids some of the drawbacks in the two-stage formulation below, but, as you will see, it gives rise to some limitations of its own.

An easy case. Before presenting an example of a two-stage model, we acknowledge a fundamental result for what might be termed a simple one-stage problem. To ease the exposition, suppose a deterministic version of the model can be written in the canonical form:

$$(1) \qquad \text{maximize} \sum_{j=1}^{n} c_j x_j$$

subject to

$$(2) \qquad \sum_{j=1}^{n} a_{ij} x_j = b_i \quad \text{for } i = 1, 2, \ldots, m$$

$$(3) \qquad x_j \geq 0 \quad \text{for } j = 1, 2, \ldots, n.$$

Now assume that the coefficients in the objective function really are random, and that all the levels of the variables have to be determined prior to learning the actual values for the random c_j. Such a situation might arise in a planning model where future market prices and labor costs are not known exactly at the time the plan is being developed. Since all the structural coefficients a_{ij} and the right-hand-side coefficients b_i are known with certainty, no difficulty arises in selecting feasible levels for the x_j.

Postulating that the appropriate objective function is to maximize the expected value of the summation in (1), it is easy to establish the theorem below.

LINEAR CERTAINTY-EQUIVALENCE THEOREM: Assume that all the a_{ij} and b_i in (2) are known exactly, but c_j in (1) are random variables independent of all x_j. If the levels of x_j, for $j = 1, \ldots, n$, must be set prior to knowing the exact values of c_j, then a solution to

$$(4) \qquad\qquad\qquad \text{maximize } E\left[\sum_{j=1}^{n} c_j x_j\right]$$

subject to (2) and (3), is given by levels for x_j that satisfy

$$(5) \qquad\qquad\qquad \text{maximize } \sum_{j=1}^{n} E[c_j] x_j$$

subject to (2) and (3).

Thus if the only random variables are the objective-function coefficients, and these are independent of the specific activity levels, then an optimal solution can be found from an equivalent deterministic linear program, where the corresponding expected values are used in the objective function. As you will see next, a linear problem with uncertainty is not solved so simply when there are other random elements, or when there are x_j that can be set after learning the exact values for several of the random elements.

Example. We start with a small example showing how a two-stage model can arise in a decision-making context. By studying the specifics of this illustration, you will find it easier to understand the more general explanation at the end of this section.

Each month, the Big Board Company, a wood-products manufacturer, processes a given tonnage supply of timber, T, into lumber and plywood. To keep the example simple, suppose Big Board makes only one premium quality grade of each of the two timber products. At the start of a month, the company must decide the levels of

$x_1 = $ the tons of timber supply allocated to lumber manufacturing
$x_2 = $ the tons of timber supply allocated to plywood manufacturing
$x_3 = $ the tons of timber not allocated to either manufacturing process.

Assume that by the end of the month x_1 yields $a_1 x_1$ hundred board-feet of lumber, and x_2 yields $a_2 x_2$ thousand sheets of plywood. Let D_1 denote the *maximum* amount of lumber the company can sell at the end of the month, and D_2 the *maximum* amount of plywood. For each manufactured product ($j = 1$ and 2), let r_j represent the market price Big Board receives per unit (that is, per hundred board-feet of lumber and per thousand sheets of plywood); hence, the amount $r_j(a_j x_j)$ is the total revenue from Product j. Let e_j be the production cost of processing a ton of timber into Product j; therefore, $e_j x_j$ is the total manufacturing cost associated with Product j. Consequently, defining $c_j \equiv r_j a_j - e_j$, the quantity $c_j x_j$ represents the profit from Product j, where $j = 1, 2$. In addition the company receives

c_3x_3 from selling the unused timber on the open commodity market; even if Big Board decided to sell all its timber on the commodity market, it would not affect the value of c_3.

If the values of a_j, c_j, and D_i are all known with certainty, the decision problem can be characterized as an ordinary linear programming problem:

$$(6) \qquad\qquad \text{maximize } c_1x_1 + c_2x_2 + c_3x_3$$

subject to

$$(7) \qquad\qquad x_1 + x_2 + x_3 = T \quad \text{(total supply)}$$
$$(8) \qquad\qquad a_1x_1 \qquad\qquad + s_1 = D_1 \quad \text{(lumber demand)}$$
$$(9) \qquad\qquad\qquad a_2x_2 + s_2 = D_2 \quad \text{(plywood demand)}$$
$$(10) \qquad\qquad\qquad x_j \text{ and } s_i \text{ nonnegative,}$$

where s_i represents the *unfilled* demand for Product i. Study the simple structure (6) through (10) and explain why a numerical solution is trivial once you are given values for a_j, c_j, and D_i.

In a typical situation, the market prices for the products vary from week to week, depending on the supply and demand conditions. Therefore the Big Board Company cannot know the exact values of prices r_1 and r_2 (and thus c_1 and c_2) until several weeks *after* the company decides the levels of x_1, x_2, and x_3. Furthermore, both the yields a_1 and a_2 as well as the potential demands D_1 and D_2 are subject to random variation. Therefore s_1 and s_2 are actually determined *after* the values of a_j and D_i become known. What is more, if a_jx_j exceeds the maximum demand, the company will have units left over. Thus you see that the structure (7) through (10) is not yet complete for the case where the a_j and D_i are random.

To complete the description of the optimization model, assume the Big Board Company *must* dispose of any units left over, and has to sell them at a lower profit margin to do so. Consequently, add the terms $-t_1$ to (8), $-t_2$ to (9), and $-f_1t_1 -f_2t_2$ to (6), where $t_i \geq 0$ denotes excess units of Product i and $-f_it_i$ is the profit loss due to a disposal sale of the amount t_i. The loss coefficients f_i are also random and unknown when the levels of x_j must be chosen. The actual levels of t_i are to be determined along with the s_i *after* the values of all the random variables are learned.

To summarize the approach, note that the timing sequence is:

(i) *First Stage.* The company selects the levels of x_1, x_2, and x_3 knowing only the exact value of e_1, e_2, and c_3.

(ii) *Random Event.* The specific values of the random elements c_1, c_2, f_1, f_2, a_1, a_2, D_1, and D_2 become known, and are independent of the levels of x_1, x_2, x_3.

(iii) *Second Stage.* The company establishes the levels of s_1, s_2, t_1, and t_2.

Given this information structure, Big Board selects those levels for x_1, x_2, x_3 that maximize expected profit.

Without any further simplifying assumptions, even this small-scale example would be difficult to solve. So first postulate that for each Product $j = 1$ and 2, the yield coefficient a_j and the market price r_j are independent random variables. Therefore, you can write the expected value of the profit coefficient c_j as

(11) $E[c_j] = E[r_j] \cdot E[a_j] - e_j$ for $j = 1$ and 2.

Then make one more postulate about the nature of uncertainty, which will enable you to solve the problem as a standard linear program: assume there are only a finite number Q of different possible sets of values for $(f_1, f_2, a_1, a_2, D_1, D_2)$. To illustrate with the above example, suppose $Q = 3$. That is, assume that only three sets of values can occur:

$$(f_{11}, f_{12}, a_{11}, a_{12}, D_{11}, D_{12}) \text{ with probability } p_1,$$
(12) $$(f_{21}, f_{22}, a_{21}, a_{22}, D_{21}, D_{22}) \text{ with probability } p_2,$$
$$(f_{31}, f_{32}, a_{31}, a_{32}, D_{31}, D_{32}) \text{ with probability } p_3,$$

where $p_1 + p_2 + p_3 = 1$. With this information, you can calculate

$$E[a_j] = \sum_{q=1}^{3} p_q a_{qj},$$

and given $E[r_j]$ and e_j, you can determine $E[c_j]$ from (11). Then the appropriate linear programming formulation for this two-stage model is

(13)   maximize $E[c_1]x_1 + E[c_2]x_2 + c_3 x_3$
         $- p_1[f_{11}t_{11} + f_{12}t_{12}] - p_2[f_{21}t_{21} + f_{22}t_{22}] - p_3[f_{31}t_{31} + f_{32}t_{32}]$

subject to

(14) $x_1 + x_2 + x_3 \qquad = T$ (total supply)

(15) $a_{11}x_1 \qquad + s_{11} - t_{11} = D_{11}$ (lumber demand for $q = 1$)

(16) $a_{12}x_2 + s_{12} - t_{12} = D_{12}$ (plywood demand for $q = 1$)

(17) $a_{21}x_1 \qquad + s_{21} - t_{21} = D_{21}$ (lumber demand for $q = 2$)

(18) $a_{22}x_2 + s_{22} - t_{22} = D_{22}$ (plywood demand for $q = 2$)

(19) $a_{31}x_1 \qquad + s_{31} - t_{31} = D_{31}$ (lumber demand for $q = 3$)

(20) $a_{32}x_2 + s_{32} - t_{32} = D_{32}$ (plywood demand for $q = 3$)

(21)   all $x_j \geq 0$ all $s_{qt} \geq 0$ and   all $t_{qt} \geq 0$

Examine (12) through (21) to see how the two-stage decision process has been formulated. In particular, note that:

(i) The deterministic timber supply constraint restricting the first-stage variables is included as (14).

(ii) There are $Q = 3$ groups of constraints, one group for each possible set of values for the random elements—the three groups in the example are [(15), (16)], [(17), (18)], and [(19), (20)].

(iii) The first-stage variables appear in each of the three groups of constraints given in (ii). The coefficients of these variables are the specific values of the random elements corresponding to the index q, where $q = 1, 2, 3$.

(iv) There is a set of second-stage variables (s_{q1}, t_{q1}) and (s_{q2}, t_{q2}) associated with each of the three groups of constraints given in (ii). Their levels are relevant and to be implemented if and when the corresponding values for the random elements actually do occur.

(v) The objective function contains the unconditional expected values of the profit coefficients for the first-stage variables.

(vi) The objective function weights the profit coefficients for the second-stage variables by the probability p_q that the associated set of second-stage variables will be relevant.

Solving (13) through (21) is not a trivial task, as compared to solving (6) through (10). To check your understanding, how would (13) through (21) be simplified if the values for a_1, a_2, and D_2 were not random (do not allow an excess of Product 2)?

It is very important that you perceive the true nature of the solution. You must decide right now the levels of the first-stage variables, and the model (13) through (21) provides the optimal levels. You do not need to set the levels of the second-stage variables until the uncertainties are resolved. Consequently, what you find *now* for the second-stage variables are optimal **decision rules,** that is, a strategy that indicates what levels you will choose for each and every possible outcome of the uncertain events, given the values you already selected for the first-stage variables. The fact that you *have* to determine *rules* for your future actions is what distinguishes a stochastic from a deterministic dynamic optimization model and is what makes the computational task much more difficult.

Summary. We give here a general formulation of the so-called **two-stage linear model.** Using the notation of the deterministic version (1) through (3), assume that in the stochastic version:

1. The value of each random element is independent of the levels of all x_j.

2. The levels of x_j, for $j = 1, 2, \ldots, k \leq n$, must be fixed at the first stage before any exact values of the random elements are known.

3. The constraints $i = 1, 2, \ldots, g$ contain only the first-stage variables, and the associated a_{ij} and b_i are known with certainty.

4. There always exist feasible levels for the remaining second-stage variables x_j, for $j = k + 1, \ldots, n$. These are to be established after all the random values are known.

5. There are a finite number Q of possible sets of values for the c_j, where $j = k + 1, \ldots, n$, and for a_{ij} and b_i, where $i = g + 1, \ldots, m$ and where $j = 1, \ldots, n$. Denote these sets by $(c_{qj}, a_{qij}, b_{qi})$ and the associated probability of occurrence by p_q, for $q = 1, 2, \ldots, Q$.

Then an optimal decision rule can be found by solving the linear program

(22) $$\text{maximize } \sum_{j=1}^{k} E[c_j]x_j + \sum_{q=1}^{Q} p_q \left[\sum_{j=k+1}^{n} c_{qj}x_{qj} \right]$$

subject to

(23) $$\sum_{j=1}^{k} a_{ij}x_j = b_i \quad \text{for } i = 1, 2, \ldots, g \quad \text{(first stage)}$$

(24) $$\sum_{j=1}^{k} a_{qij}x_j + \sum_{j=k+1}^{n} a_{qij}x_{qj} = b_{qj} \quad \text{(second-stage decision rules)}$$

$$\text{for } i = g + 1, \ldots, m \quad \text{and} \quad q = 1, 2, \ldots, Q$$

(25) $$\text{all } x_j \geq 0 \quad \text{and} \quad \text{all } x_{qj} \geq 0.$$

[If any c_j is known exactly, then use this value in (22). If any b_i for $i = g + 1, \ldots,$ m is known, then let b_{qi} equal this value in (24), and do the same for any a_{ij} that is known.] Notice that (24) contains $(m - g)Q$ equations. In real applications where $(m - g)$ can easily be between 25 and 50, the approach is impractical if Q is large.

You can read Sec. 16.7 if you are curious to learn how a multistage stochastic linear programming problem can be transformed by an analogous line of reasoning into a very large ordinary linear programming problem. The advanced material below discusses when you can give easily computed bounds on the optimal value of the objective function in a stochastic programming problem. In the next section, you will see another formulation for stochastic linear programming that does not expand the size of an equivalent standard linear programming model in a two-stage decision process.

▶You can exploit the special structure of (23) and (24) in computing a numerical solution by employing the Decomposition Algorithm of Sec. 15.11 on the dual problem. The dual constraints associated with variables x_j for $j = 1, 2, \ldots, k$ comprise the master program, and for each q, the dual constraints associated with the variables x_{qj}, for $j = k + 1, \ldots, n$, comprise a subprogram. To guide your understanding, write the dual to (13) through (21) and identify the master and subprograms.

The model in (22) through (25) assumes that the values of all the random elements are known by the time you have to decide the levels for the second-stage variables. With only negligible added complication you can expand the model to include the possibility that certain of the objective-function coefficients of the second-stage variables become known after the levels of these variables have been determined. Specifically, for $j = h + 1, \ldots, n$ (where $k \leq h \leq n$), let $E[c_j|q]$ denote the conditional expected value of c_j given that the random event associated with the index q occurs. Then let $c_{qj} \equiv E[c_j|q]$ for $j = h + 1, \ldots, n$, in (22).

Section 16.1 emphasized the importance of assessing the impact of uncertainty in a particular model. The development to follow will help you gain further insight into the effect of the random elements in the two-stage model. In some situations, the formulas also provide a useful way to measure whether an approximate solution is nearly optimal.

The model (22) through (25) is sometimes called the *here-and-now problem*, because the levels of several variables must be established immediately, before the exact values of all the random elements are known. A convenient alternative mathematical representation of (22) through (25) is

(i) $\displaystyle \operatorname*{maximize}_{x_1,\ldots,x_k} E_{A,b,c}\left[\sum_{j=1}^{k} c_j x_j + \operatorname*{maximize}_{x_{k+1},\ldots,x_n} \sum_{j=k+1}^{n} c_j x_j\right] \equiv E[\text{here and now}],$

where the levels $x_j \geq 0$, for $j = 1, 2, \ldots, k$ are set first and must satisfy

(ii) $\displaystyle \sum_{j=1}^{k} a_{ij} x_j = b_i \quad \text{for } i = 1, 2, \ldots, g \quad \text{(first stage)},$

and subsequently the levels $x_j \geq 0$, for $j = k + 1, \ldots, n$ are set to satisfy

(iii) $\displaystyle \sum_{j=k+1}^{n} a_{ij} x_j = b_i - \sum_{j=1}^{k} a_{ij} x_j \quad \text{for } i = g + 1, \ldots, m \quad \text{(second stage)}$

after the values of all the coefficients in (iii) are known. In (i) through (iii) and the models below, you can drop the assumption that there are only Q possible sets of values for the random elements. Assume, however, that there is always a feasible solution to (iii). A contrasting model, sometimes called the *wait-and-see problem*, arises when the value of every random variable is known before the levels of any x_j are set. Denote this model as

(iv) $\displaystyle E_{A,b,c}\left[\operatorname*{maximize}_{x_1,\ldots,x_n} \sum_{j=1}^{n} c_j x_j\right] \equiv E\,[\text{wait and see}],$

where the levels of all $x_j \geq 0$ are determined simultaneously so as to satisfy both (ii) and (iii). In the event there *are* only Q possible sets of values for the random elements, the value of (iv) can be calculated by finding an optimal solution to each of the Q linear programming problems and then weighting the objective-function value by the associated probability p_q. In this case, each linear programming problem has the same size and structure as the deterministic version (1) through (3). Since being able to wait and see gives you helpful information, the value of $E\,[\text{wait and see}]$ is an upper bound for $E\,[\text{here and now}]$.

Suppose next that only the b_i are random, and consider an optimal solution to a deterministic version of the model in which each b_i is replaced by its expectation; denote this situation as the *average-value problem*. Let $\bar{x}_j \geq 0$, for $j = 1, 2, \ldots, n$, be a solution to

(v) $\displaystyle \operatorname*{maximize} \sum_{j=1}^{n} c_j x_j \equiv C[\text{average value}]$

subject to (ii) and

(vi) $\displaystyle \sum_{j=1}^{n} a_{ij} x_j = E[b_i] \quad \text{for } i = g + 1, \ldots, m.$

Notice (v), (ii), and (vi) comprise an ordinary linear programming problem with the same size and structure as the deterministic version (1) through (3). Given the previous assumption that there is always a solution to (iii), there will always be a feasible solution to (ii) and (vi), as we establish below. Also we demonstrate that $C\,[\text{average value}]$ is an upper bound for $E\,[\text{wait and see}]$.

Finally, suppose that in the two-stage model, you set $x_j = \bar{x}_j$, for $j = 1, 2, \ldots, k$, found by (v), (ii), and (vi); this is a feasible action since these levels satisfy (ii). Set the other variables x_j, for $j = k + 1, \ldots, n$, as previously in (iii). Denote this situation as the *first-stage, average-value approximation* approach. The expected value of the objective function for this strategy can be written as

(vii) $\displaystyle E_{A,b,c}\left[\sum_{j=1}^{k} c_j \bar{x}_j + \operatorname*{maximize}_{x_{k+1},\ldots,x_n} \sum_{j=k+1}^{n} c_j x_j\right] \equiv E\,[\text{first-stage, average-value approximation}].$

If there are Q possible sets of values for the random elements, the value of (vii) can be computed by solving each of Q linear programming problems, using only the constraints (iii), and then weighting each resultant objective-function value by the associated probability p_q. In some applications, the solution to each smaller problem is trivial.

It can be proved that the objective function values for the above problems do exhibit the relations

$$E\ [\textit{first-stage, average-value approximation}] \leq E\ [\textit{here and now}]$$

(viii)
$$\leq E\ [\textit{wait and see}]$$
$$\leq C\ [\textit{average value}].$$

The validity of the first inequality can be argued by noting that the first-stage, average-value approximation is a particular one of the many feasible solutions considered in the here-and-now problem; consequently, it cannot be better than an optimal here-and-now solution.

The second inequality reflects the fact that the expected value of the objective function may be improved if all the values of the random elements are known before the levels of x_j are set. The difference $\{E[\textit{wait and see}] - E[\textit{here and now}]\}$ may be called the *cost of uncertainty*. The quantity represents the maximum amount to pay if, as a result, you then receive a perfect prediction of the random elements before setting the levels of all the x_j.

The final inequality provides an easily computed upper bound for the other three expected values. It can be established as follows. Calculate the "expected value" of the x_j, for $j = 1, 2, \ldots, n$, as determined by the optimal decision rules for the wait-and-see problem. This solution is feasible in the average-value problem. Further, from (iv) this solution gives the optimal $E[\textit{wait and see}]$ as the value of the objective function in (v), and hence the optimal $C[\textit{average value}]$ must be at least as large.

In the event that $E\ [\textit{first-stage, average-value approximation}]$ is easy to calculate and that its value does not differ much from $C\ [\textit{average value}]$, then the strategy of letting the first-stage variables be set at level $\bar{x}_j$, for $j = 1, 2, \ldots, k$, is a near-optimal solution to the here-and-now problem.

In some situations it is possible to find another approximate solution to the here-and-now problem. Assume that all c_j, for $j = k + 1, \ldots, n$, and b_i, for $i = g + 1, \ldots, m$, have smallest values, denoted by c_j^* and b_i^*, and that all a_{ij}, for $i = g + 1, \ldots, m$ and $j = 1, 2, \ldots, n$, have largest values denoted by a_{ij}^*. Finally, assume there exist levels $x_j^* \geq 0$, for $j = 1, 2, \ldots, n$, that solve what is termed the *most stringent problem*:

(ix)
$$\text{maximize} \sum_{j=1}^{k} c_j x_j + \sum_{j=k+1}^{n} c_j^* x_j \equiv C\ [\textit{most stringent problem}]$$

subject to (ii) and

(x)
$$\sum_{j=1}^{n} a_{ij}^* x_j = b_i^* \quad \text{for } i = g + 1, \ldots, m.$$

Note that (ix), (ii), and (x) is a linear programming problem with the same size and structure as the deterministic version. Further, the levels x_j^*, for $j = 1, 2, \ldots, k$, are feasible for the here-and-now problem. Note, however, that $C\ [\textit{most stringent problem}]$ understates the expected value of the objective function when x_j^*, for $j = 1, 2, \ldots, k$, are used in the here-and-now problem, since (ix) does not take into account that the x_j, for $j = k + 1, \ldots, n$, will be chosen optimally after the random elements are known. But it can be proved that

(xi)
$$C\ [\textit{most stringent problem}] \leq E\ [\textit{here and now}],$$

so if C [*most stringent problem*] and E [*average value*] are nearly the same, then the levels x_j^*, for $j = 1, 2, \ldots, k$, are nearly optimal for the here-and-now problem. ◀

16.5 CHANCE-CONSTRAINED MODEL

As you reflect on the solution technique for the two-stage stochastic linear programming model given in the preceding section, you will conclude that one of its major drawbacks is the resultant size of the equivalent standard linear program. The expanded dimensions are due to the explicit provision for complete decision rules to be applied at the second stage. If you make a few more simplifying assumptions, then you can employ another linear programming formulation that has the same number of constraints as the original stochastic model. The approach is called **chance-constrained programming** (named by Professors A. Charnes and W. W. Cooper, who have pioneered the technique). We motivate the approach by re-examining the illustration in the preceding section.

Example. Reconsider the case of the timber products manufacturer, the Big Board Company. We further simplify the problem by assuming that the two yield coefficients a_1 and a_2 are known exactly. And instead of including the explicit assumption that the company disposes of excess production, we suppose that several action alternatives are open but we do not specify the economic consequences of these. Thus the only random elements are the market prices r_j and the demand limitations D_i. Now the expected value of a profit coefficient is simply $E[c_j] = E[r_j] \cdot a_j - e_j$, for each Product $j = 1$ and 2.

The objective function can be written as

$$(1) \qquad \text{maximize } E[c_1]x_1 + E[c_2]x_2 + c_3 x_3.$$

Note that (1) contains only the first-stage variables, because we are not specifying the action alternatives in the event production exceeds demand. We also impose the previous supply and nonnegativity constraints

$$(2) \qquad x_1 + x_2 + x_3 = T \quad \text{(total supply)}$$

$$(3) \qquad \text{all } x_j \geq 0.$$

Finally, we must place restrictions to limit production, because otherwise the model, in maximizing expected profit, is likely to indicate a solution that will exceed actual demand. Suppose, then, that the President of Big Board stipulates that with a probability of at least β_i, he wants to be able to sell *all* the output produced, namely $a_i x_i$, for $i = 1, 2$. His goal can be expressed mathematically as

$$(4) \qquad P[a_1 x_1 \leq D_1] \geq \beta_1 \quad \text{(lumber demand)}$$

$$(5) \qquad P[a_2 x_2 \leq D_2] \geq \beta_2 \quad \text{(plywood demand)}.$$

Restrictions (4) and (5) are called **chance-constraints**, because they impose restrictions on probabilities. These restrictions imply an equivalent pair of ordinary linear inequalities:

(6) $\qquad a_1 x_1 \leq B_1$ (deterministic equivalent for lumber)

(7) $\qquad a_2 x_2 \leq B_2$ (deterministic equivalent for plywood).

In other words, the linear programming model comprised of the objective function (1), the supply and nonnegativity constraints (2) and (3), and the **deterministic equivalent constraints** (6) and (7) yields an optimal solution to the chance-constrained problem.

The appropriate values for each B_i in the deterministic equivalent is the largest number such that $P[D_i \geq B_i] \geq \beta_i$; the number B_i is called the $(1 - \beta_i)$ *fractile* of the probability distribution of D_i. Note that the probability distribution is the *marginal* distribution for D_i. This means that if you start with a joint probability distribution for D_1 and D_2, you must, as a side calculation, derive the two marginal distributions.

A numerical example will illustrate how to determine the B_i from a marginal distribution. Suppose the marginal probability distribution for D_1 is

(8) $P[D_1 = 1] = .2 \quad P[D_1 = 3] = .4 \quad P[D_1 = 8] = .3 \quad P[D_1 = 10] = .1,$

giving the graph of $P[D_1 \geq B_1]$ shown in Fig. 16.5. Then verify that $B_1 = 1$ if $.8 < \beta_1 \leq 1.0$, and $B_1 = 3$ if $.4 < \beta_1 \leq .8$, etc.

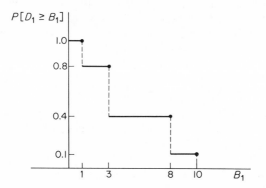

FIGURE 16.5. Big Board Company Example.

Observe that the linear programming model (1), (2), (3), (6), and (7) is as trivial to solve as the deterministic version (6) through (10) in the previous section.

The approach. With the Big Board Company Example as background, we give a general statement of the technique. Let x_j for $j = 1, 2, \ldots, k$ refer to the first-stage variables. We do not explicitly represent the second-stage variables. Assume that all the coefficients a_{ij} are known exactly. And, finally, postulate that each random element is statistically independent of the levels for the first-stage variables.

The chance-constrained model is to find levels x_j that satisfy

(9) $\qquad\qquad\qquad \text{maximize} \sum_{j=1}^{k} E[c_j] x_j$

subject to

(10) $$\sum_{j=1}^{k} a_{ij}x_j = b_i \quad \text{for } i = 1, 2, \ldots, g \quad \text{(first stage)}$$

(11) $$P\left[\sum_{j=1}^{k} a_{ij}x_j \le b_i\right] \ge \beta_i \quad \text{for } i = g + 1, \ldots, m \quad \text{(chance-constraints)}$$

(12) $$\text{all } x_j \ge 0.$$

You interpret (11) as constraining the unconditional probability to be no smaller than β_i, where $0 \le \beta_i \le 1$, that the actual value for b_i is at least as large as $\sum_{j=1}^{k} a_{ij}x_j$.

Assuming there are levels x_j satisfying (10) through (12), the above formulation can be solved as a standard linear program with objective function (9), constraints (10), (12), and instead of the chance-constraints (11), the linear constraints:

(13) $$\sum_{j=1}^{k} a_{ij}x_j \le B_i \quad \text{for } i = g + 1, \ldots, m \quad \text{(deterministic equivalents)},$$

where B_i is the largest number satisfying

(14) $$P[b_i \ge B_i] \ge \beta_i$$

or, equivalently,

(15) $$P[b_i < B_i] \le 1 - \beta_i \quad [B_i : (1 - \beta_i) \text{ fractile}].$$

Discussion. You can compare the chance-constrained approach with the earlier two-stage approach. The chance-constrained model has two desirable properties. First, it leads to an equivalent linear program that has the same size and structure as a deterministic version of the model. Consequently, the computational burden of the stochastic version is no greater after the proper right-hand-side values have been determined. Second, the only information required about each uncertain element b_i is the $(1 - \beta_i)$ fractile for the unconditional distribution of the right-hand-side coefficient. These properties compare favorably with the larger size of the linear program of the previous section and the restrictive assumption that there are only Q possible sets of values for the random elements.

The principal weakness of the chance-constrained model is that it only indirectly evaluates the economic consequence of violating a constraint. In the example of the Big Board Company, the chance-constrained approach indicates no differential penalty between a small and large amount of excess production. Put somewhat differently, in most situations, specifying the correct values for β_i should be *part* of the optimization problem. (An additional conceptual limitation is that the approach arbitrarily excludes randomized strategies that could be better, as was pointed out in the advanced material in Sec. 16.2. Also, as you will discover if you read the next section, a particular optimal solution for one formulation may never be optimal in an analogous formulation of the other. So you cannot be assured that there exist probabilities β_i that in a chance-constrained model would yield a given solution that is optimal for a two-stage formulation.)

Therefore, when faced with a choice between the two approaches for modeling a two-stage decision process, you will have to compare the serious limitation on the problem size imposed by the two-stage model of the previous section against the restricted meaning of optimality implied by the chance-constrained version. When you come to a multistage model, you will find the conceptual difficulties in a chance-constrained approach compound tremendously. The applicability of the approach in these instances is a question still being explored by theoreticians and practitioners.

The remainder of the chapter treats a special example of a two-stage model and other formulations of stochastic programming models. The material is of interest if you want to round out your understanding of how to structure stochastic programming models into equivalent deterministic models. In any event, the preceding introduction to determining optimal strategies under uncertainty has given you the necessary preparation to consider dynamic programming models with probabilistic elements, explained in Chap. 17.

▶In some applications it may be appropriate to have one or more **joint chance-constraints** instead of the individual constraints (11). Usually these versions are equivalent to nonlinear programming models and can be solved by the techniques in Chap. 15. To illustrate what is involved, suppose (11) is replaced by the single probability restriction

(i)
$$P[\sum_{j=1}^{k} a_{g+1,j}x_j \leq b_{g+1}, \ldots, \sum_{j=1}^{k} a_{mj}x_j \leq b_m] \geq \beta$$

$$\text{where} \quad 0 < \beta \leq 1 \quad \text{(joint chance-constraint).}$$

Notice that here only one β need be specified, so the resultant task of sensitivity testing is relatively easy. Let the marginal distribution functions be denoted as $F_i(b) \equiv P[b_i < b]$, and assume that each F_i is continuous. Also assume the joint distribution function for the b_i is simply $\prod_{i=g+1}^{m} F_i$, where the symbol $\prod$ denotes the "product" operation. Thus the $b_{g+1}, \ldots, b_m$ are statistically independent. Finally, let $G_i \equiv 1 - F_i$. Then an equivalent deterministic model is (9), (10), (12), and

(ii)
$$-y_i + \sum_{j=1}^{k} a_{ij}x_j = 0 \quad \text{for } i = g + 1, \ldots, m \quad \text{(fractile definition)}$$

(iii)
$$\prod_{i=g+1}^{m} G_i(y_i) \geq \beta \quad \text{(equivalent joint-constraint),}$$

where the y_i are unconstrained in sign. Note that (iii) is a nonlinear constraint. Only rarely will the G_i be such that (iii) is concave, as is required for most nonlinear algorithms. However, a transformed version

(iv)
$$\sum_{i=g+1}^{m} \ln G_i(y_i) \geq \ln \beta \quad \text{(transformed equivalent constraint)}$$

is frequently concave—for example, when the density for b_i is given by a Normal, gamma, or uniform distribution. Techniques such as those in Chap. 15 can be applied to solve (9), (10), (12), (ii), and (iv).

Consider the situation where the values of b_i are known exactly but the a_{ij} are random elements. In particular, suppose that (11) is replaced by

(v)
$$P\left[b_i \leq \sum_{j=1}^{k} a_{ij}x_j\right] \geq \beta_i \quad \text{for } i = g + 1, \ldots, m \quad \text{(random coefficients).}$$

If you can assume that for each i, the random elements a_{ij}, for $j = 1, 2, \ldots, k$, have a joint Normal distribution with means α_{ij}, for $j = 1, 2, \ldots, k$, and covariances σ_{ijh}, for j and $h = 1, 2, \ldots, k$, then a deterministic nonlinear equivalent for (v) is

$$\text{(vi)} \qquad \sum_{j=1}^{k} \alpha_{ij}x_j + B_i\left(\sum_{j=1}^{k}\sum_{h=1}^{k} \sigma_{ijh}x_jx_h\right)^{1/2} \geq b_i \quad \text{for } i = g + 1, \ldots, m$$

$$\text{(deterministic equivalent)},$$

where B_i is the $(1 - \beta_i)$ fractile of a unit Normal distribution. If $\beta_i \geq \frac{1}{2}$ so that $B_i \leq 0$, then (vi) is concave and the model (9), (10), (12), and (vi) can be solved by techniques such as those in Chap. 15. ◀

*16.6 TRANSPORTATION NETWORK EXAMPLE

Recall from Chap. 6 that the transportation (or distribution) problem is a very important network model, mathematically described as

$$\text{(1)} \qquad\qquad\qquad \text{minimize} \sum_{i=1}^{m}\sum_{j=1}^{n} c_{ij}x_{ij}$$

subject to

$$\text{(2)} \qquad\qquad \sum_{j=1}^{n} x_{ij} = S_i \quad \text{for } i = 1, 2, \ldots m \quad \text{(supply)}$$

$$\text{(3)} \qquad\qquad \sum_{i=1}^{m} x_{ij} = D_j \quad \text{for } j = 1, 2, \ldots, n \quad \text{(demand)}$$

$$\text{(4)} \qquad\qquad\qquad x_{ij} \geq 0 \quad \text{for each } i \text{ and } j,$$

where you may interpret S_i as the available amount of supply for shipment at the ith source and D_j as the required amount of demand at the jth destination, and where the model has been structured so that total supply equals total demand $(\sum S_i = \sum D_j)$. In Chap. 6, we assumed that the values for S_i and D_j were known exactly, and in Chap. 7 you saw how to apply the simplex method to obtain numerical solutions. Here we consider the problem where the demand requirements D_j are uncertain. You will see how the appropriate two-stage model is not much more complicated than the deterministic version (1) through (4).

Assume the time sequence of events is

(i) *First Stage.* All the levels of x_{ij} must be established, with knowledge of exact values for every S_i, c_{ij}, and possibly a few D_j.

(ii) *Random Event.* The particular values of the random elements D_j then become known. The values of D_j are independent of the levels of the x_{ij}.

(iii) *Second Stage.* The resultant amount of over- or underfulfillment of demand is established.

Note that (iii) really implies that the model (1) through (4) has been augmented by n second-stage variables:

(5) $$u_j \equiv D_j - \sum_{i=1}^{m} x_{ij} \quad \text{for } j = 1, 2, \dots, n,$$

where the u_j are unconstrained in sign. To make the first-stage problem nontrivial, it is also necessary to add the effect of u_j into the objective function, since otherwise, an optimal solution is to ship, for each i, the total S_i to that Destination j where c_{ij} is a minimum. Let $c_j(u_j)$ denote the cost or penalty associated with the resultant level u_j. Realize that each function $c_j(u_j)$ need not be linear; for example, you may want to use a quadratic penalty function. Then assume that the objective function is the sum of the transportation costs and the expected value of the penalty costs:

(6) $$\text{minimize} \sum_{i=1}^{m} \sum_{j=1}^{n} c_{ij}x_{ij} + \sum_{j=1}^{n} E\left[c_j\left(D_j - \sum_{i=1}^{m} x_{ij}\right)\right].$$

subject to (2) and (4). Each expectation in (6) is over the corresponding marginal probability distribution of D_j.

Note an important characteristic of this particular two-stage model: there is no *optimization* problem at the second stage. The levels of the second-stage variables u_j are uniquely determined according to (5) by the levels of the first-stage variables and the values of the random elements. This special structure can be fully exploited so that you do not have to deal with an equivalent deterministic problem of the sort suggested by the two-stage formulation given in Sec. 16.4.

By your making two further postulates, the two-stage stochastic model, (2), (4), (5), and (6), becomes mathematically equivalent to an ordinary transportation problem. First, assume that for every j, the only possible values for D_j are integers. Define, for each j,

(7) $$x_j \equiv \sum_{i=1}^{m} x_{ij} \quad \text{(total shipment to Destination j)}$$

and

(8) $$C_j(x_j) \equiv E[c_j(D_j - x_j)] \quad \text{(expected penalty at Destination j.)}$$

An illustration of how to calculate (8) is given in the example below. Second assume that for every Destination j, the expected penalty cost function $C_j(x_j)$ is convex:

(9) $$C_j(x_j + 1) - C_j(x_j) \geq C_j(x_j) - C_j(x_j - 1) \quad \text{for all integers } x_j.$$

A sufficient condition for $C_j(x_j)$ to be convex is that the penalty function $c_j(u_j)$ is itself convex. The example below will illustrate how integer-value and convexity assumptions are sufficient to permit you to view the model as an expanded transportation problem.

So that you are not misled, we caution that there are much more efficient computational techniques for obtaining numerical solutions than solving the problem in the fully expanded form. (Most of these techniques are applications of the Generalized Programming Algorithm in Sec. 15.10.) Hence, in studying the example here, you should give primary attention to understanding why the introduction of uncertain elements presents only a minor conceptual complication for this particular two-stage model. You can leave the streamlined algorithms to the technical specialists.

Example. Consider the deterministic example given in Fig. 16.6 (which is the same as Fig. 7.2, p. 217); the unique optimal solution is also shown. Suppose now

Row \ Column	1	2	3	4	Supply:
1	[2]	[3] 5	[11] 1	[7]	6
2	[1]	[0]	[6] 1	[1]	1
3	[5] 7	[8]	[15] 1	[9] 2	10
Demand:	7	5	3	2	

Minimal Total Cost = 100

FIGURE 16.6. Transportation Example (Optimal Deterministic Solution).

that the values of D_3 and D_4 are uncertain, and, specifically, assume that their probability distributions are

$$(10) \qquad P[D_3 = 1] = P[D_3 = 3] = P[D_3 = 5] = \frac{1}{3} \quad \text{so that } E[D_3] = 3$$

$$(11) \qquad P[D_4 = 0] = P[D_4 = 1] = P[D_4 = 3] = P[D_4 = 4] = \frac{1}{4} \quad \text{so that } E[D_4] = 2.$$

Thus the expected demands are the same as the previous deterministic demand; however, although $E[D_4] = 2$, an actual demand value ($D_4 = 2$) never occurs.

Assume for $j = 3, 4$, there is no economic penalty for oversupply ($u_j \leq 0$) at the jth destination, but that each unit of undersupply incurs a loss of f_j:

$$(12) \qquad c_j(D_j - x_j) = \begin{cases} 0 & \text{for } D_j \leq x_j \\ f_j \cdot (D_j - x_j) & \text{for } D_j > x_j \end{cases} \quad \text{(penalty function).}$$

Verify that $c_j(u_j)$, where $u_j \equiv D_j - x_j$, is convex. Thus the expected cost is

$$(13) \qquad C_j(x_j) = \sum_{D > x_j} f_j \cdot (D - x_j) P[D_j = D] \quad \text{(expected penalty function).}$$

To illustrate, for $x_3 = 1$,

$$(14) \qquad C_3(1) = \sum_{D=3,5} f_3 \cdot (D-1) P[D_3 = D] = f_3[(3-1)\tfrac{1}{3} + (5-1)\tfrac{1}{3}] = 2f_3,$$

and for $x_4 = 3$,

$$(15) \qquad C_4(3) = \sum_{D=4} f_4 \cdot (D-3) P[D_4 = D] = f_4(4-3)\tfrac{1}{4} = \tfrac{1}{4} f_4.$$

All the $C_j(x_j)$ are tabled in Fig. 16.7. To test your understanding, verify the values for $C_3(3)$ and $C_4(0)$. Also explain verbally why $C_j(0) = f_j E[D_j]$ and why $C_j(x_j)$ decreases to 0 as x_j increases to the largest possible value for D_j. Check that each $C_j(x_j)$ is convex according to (9); the values $C_j(x_j) - C_j(x_j + 1)$, shown in Fig. 16.7, can be used to assist you.

x_j	$C_3(x_3)$	$C_3(x_3) - C_3(x_3 + 1)$	$C_4(x_4)$	$C_4(x_4) - C_4(x_4 + 1)$
0	$3f_3$	$1f_3$	$2f_4$	$\frac{3}{4}f_4$
1	$2f_3$	$\frac{2}{3}f_3$	$\frac{5}{4}f_4$	$\frac{2}{4}f_4$
2	$\frac{4}{3}f_3$	$\frac{2}{3}f_3$	$\frac{3}{4}f_4$	$\frac{2}{4}f_4$
3	$\frac{2}{3}f_3$	$\frac{1}{3}f_3$	$\frac{1}{4}f_4$	$\frac{1}{4}f_4$
4	$\frac{1}{3}f_3$	$\frac{1}{3}f_3$	0	0
5 and larger	0	0	0	0

FIGURE 16.7. Expected Cost of Undersupply.

To transform the stochastic model into an expanded transportation problem, think of each *possible* unit of demand comprised in D_3 and D_4 as a destination all by itself. In the example, there are five destinations for D_3, since the maximum possible value for D_3 is 5; similarly, there are four destinations for D_4. Each of these destinations has a demand requirement of one unit. This transformation means that the sum of the demand requirements is now 21 ($= 7 + 5 + 5 + 4$). Since the total supply available in Fig. 16.6 is 17 ($= 6 + 1 + 10$), it also is necessary to add a fourth (fictitious) supply point with $S_4 = 4$ ($= 21 - 17$). So a unit of supply from S_4 really represents an unfilled demand. Assume that the demand requirements D_1 and D_2 must be satisfied, and S_4 consequently cannot ship to these two destinations. The resultant transportation tableau is shown in Fig. 16.8.

For $i = 1, 2, 3$, the c_{ij} in Fig. 16.8 correspond to those in Fig. 16.6, and are equal in each of the columns associated with the same D_j. The c_{ij} for $i = 4$ require some explanation. These are the *incremental* values $C_j(x_j) - C_j(x_j + 1)$ as shown in Fig. 16.7. Observe that the *sum* of the *incremental* values, starting at the bottom of Fig. 16.7 and moving upward, equals $C_j(x_j)$. Because $C_j(x_j)$ is decreasing and convex, the coefficients of f_j are successively smaller as you progress from left to right. (Notice that where two coefficients are the same, a plus sign is placed on the leftmost so that you may consider it to be "slightly" larger.) It follows that for each D_j an optimal solution will allocate S_4 to the columns starting on the right and moving progressively to the left. Therefore, in an optimal solution, the sum of the costs associated with allocating S_4 (unfilled demand) to the columns associated with each D_j will equal the value of $C_j(x_j)$.

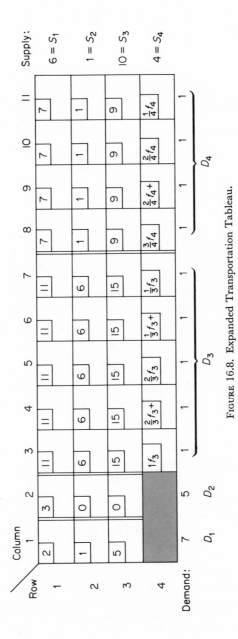

FIGURE 16.8. Expanded Transportation Tableau.

For example, suppose three units of S_4 are allocated to columns 5, 6, and 7 associated with D_3. Then $x_3 = 2$ (explain why), and

(16) $$C_3(2) = \tfrac{2}{3}f_3 + \tfrac{1}{3}f_3 + \tfrac{1}{3}f_3 = \tfrac{4}{3}f_3,$$

in agreement with Fig. 16.7. (Since $S_4 = 4$, you know that $x_3 \geq 1$ and, therefore, the first entry for D_3 in the fourth row, having a cost $1f_3$, can be eliminated from consideration. Suppose $S_1 = 7$; then $x_3 \geq 2$ and, therefore, the first two entries for D_3 in the fourth row can be eliminated. A further simplification would be to combine the corresponding columns and let the associated demand requirement for the composite column be 2.)

If the $C_j(x_j)$ were not convex, there would be no guarantee that an optimal solution would allocate units of unfilled demand, represented by S_4, starting at the highest level of possible demand and working progressively downward. In summary, the minimum total cost solution to Fig. 16.8, for given values of f_3 and f_4, will correspond to (6), and can be found by applying the transportation algorithm in Sec. 7.3.

Sensitivity analysis. Having established an enlarged transportation problem that is mathematically equivalent to the two-stage model, you are ready to assess the impact of uncertainty. In particular, you can explore the sensitivity of the solution to the values of f_3 and f_4. Since total available supply is 17 ($= S_1 + S_2 + S_3$), and demand of 12 ($= D_1 + D_2$) must be satisfied, there are 5 ($= 17 - 12$) units of supply to allocate in total to D_3 and D_4. This means that the only *possible* solutions are

(17) $$x_3 = 1, 2, \ldots, 5 \quad \text{and} \quad x_4 = 5 - x_3.$$

Given each of these values for x_3 and x_4, the corresponding optimal solutions for all the x_{ij} are shown in Fig. 16.9 (these can be found by solving each associated

| | | Optimal Allocation[a] | | | | | Ratios $f_3/f_4 =$ | | |
x_3	x_4	x_{23}	x_{24}	x_{33}	x_{34}	Total Expected Cost	3	1	$\tfrac{1}{3}$
1	4	0	1	–	3	$89 + 2f_3 + 0f_4$	$0 \leq f_3 \leq \tfrac{60}{7}$	$0 \leq f_3 \leq 12$	$0 \leq f_3$
2	3	1	–	0	3	$94 + \tfrac{4}{3}f_3 + \tfrac{1}{4}f_4$	$\tfrac{60}{7} \leq f_3 \leq 12$	$12 \leq f_3 \leq 36$	
3	2	1	–	1	2	$100 + \tfrac{2}{3}f_3 + \tfrac{3}{4}f_4$	$12 \leq f_3 \leq 36$	$36 \leq f_3$	
4	1	1	–	2	1	$106 + \tfrac{1}{3}f_3 + \tfrac{5}{4}f_4$	$36 \leq f_3 \leq 72$		
5	0	1	–	3	–	$112 + 0f_3 + 2f_4$	$72 \leq f_3$		

[a]And $x_{12} = 5$, $x_{13} = 1$, $x_{31} = 7$.

Figure 16.9. Optimal Allocations, With Given Values of (x_3, x_4) and (f_3, f_4).

deterministic problem, such as in Fig. 16.6). Of course, which of these specific allocations is truly optimal for the expected cost objective function (6) depends on the particular values of f_3 and f_4. Actually, the optimal allocation will depend on the value of f_3 relative to f_4 and the absolute magnitude of f_3. For three values of f_3/f_4, Fig. 16.9 also shows the values of f_3 for which each possible solution is optimal. Observe that:

(i) If the ratio f_3/f_4 is large, such as 3, then more units are allocated to the third destination as f_3 increases.

(ii) If the ratio f_3/f_4 is small, such as 1/3, then the minimal amount is allocated to the third destination no matter what the value for f_3.

(iii) There exist values for f_3 and f_4 that can make each of the possible allocations optimal.

▶You can measure the economic effect of uncertainty by comparing the minimal expected cost from (6) against what the expected cost would be if you could obtain a perfect forecast of D_3 and D_4 prior to making the allocation. In order to make the latter calculation, assume that f_3 is large enough so that it is always preferable to fill demands whenever possible, and that all five units are shipped to the third and fourth destinations, even when $(D_3 + D_4)$ is less than five. Then it can be shown that

(i)
$$E\begin{bmatrix}\text{total transportation} \\ \text{and penalty cost with} \\ \text{perfect information}\end{bmatrix} = \begin{cases} 100\frac{1}{3} + \frac{11}{36}f_3 & \text{for } \frac{f_3}{f_4} = 3 \\ 95 + \frac{11}{12}f_3 & \text{for } \frac{f_3}{f_4} = 1 \text{ and } \frac{1}{3}, \end{cases}$$

and, consequently,

(ii)
$$\text{expected cost of uncertainty} = \begin{cases} 11\frac{2}{3} + \frac{13}{36}f_3 & \text{for } \frac{f_3}{f_4} = 3 \\ -1 + \frac{2}{3}f_3 & \text{for } \frac{f_3}{f_4} = 1 \\ -6 + 1\frac{1}{12}f_3 & \text{for } \frac{f_3}{f_4} = \frac{1}{3}, \end{cases}$$

for f_3 sufficiently large. The quantities in (ii) represent the maximum amount you should be willing to pay if, as a result, you obtain a perfect prediction. The cost of uncertainty is linear in f_3; for sufficiently large f_3, this cost is greatest for $f_3/f_4 = \frac{1}{3}$, since at this ratio the least amount of supply is allocated to D_3. ◀

Chance-constrained approach. You will find it enlightening to compare the foregoing two-stage model with a chance-constrained version, which consists of the deterministic objective function (1), the supply constraints (2), the demand constraints (3) for $j = 1, 2$, the nonnegativity conditions (4), and the chance-constraints

(18) $P[D_3 \leq x_3] \geq \beta_3$ and $P[D_4 \leq x_4] \geq \beta_4$ (chance-constraints),

where the total shipment to Destination j is x_j, defined by (7). Thus (18) requires that for $j = 3, 4$ the probability of meeting demand D_j should be at least β_j, which is presumably large. [Note that in (18) the protection is against under fulfillment of demand, whereas in (4) and (5) of Sec. 16.5 the protection was against over fulfillment.]

Given values for β_3 and β_4, the chance-constrained model can be solved by letting the demand constraints be

$$(19) \qquad \sum_{i=1}^{m} x_{ij} \geq B_j \quad \text{for } j = 3 \text{ and } 4 \quad \text{(deterministic equivalents)},$$

where B_j is the *smallest* number satisfying

$$(20) \qquad P[D_j \leq B_j] \geq \beta_j.$$

The rest of the model consists of (1), (2), and (3) for $j = 1$ and 2.

Once again, the only possible distributions of the five units available for the third and fourth destinations are given by (17), and the associated values for $P[D_j \leq x_j]$ appear in Fig. 16.10. There are two important conclusions to draw from Fig. 16.10. First, there may not be a feasible solution if the values for β_3 and β_4 are *both* too large. For example, if $\beta_3 = \frac{2}{3}$, then there is no feasible solution for $\beta_4 > \frac{1}{2}$. Second, the allocations $(x_3 = 2, x_4 = 3)$ and $(x_3 = 4, x_4 = 1)$ are *never* optimal for any values of β_3 and β_4. The allocation $(x_3 = 1, x_4 = 4)$ strictly dominates $(x_3 = 2, x_4 = 3)$, since the corresponding probabilities of meeting D_j, for $j = 3$, 4, are at least as good and the total transportation cost is less. Explain why $(x_3 = 4, x_4 = 1)$ would never be optimal.

This divergence between the previous two-stage and the chance-constrained approaches points out that there is a fundamental difference between the two models: the set of possible optimal solutions can be distinct. Do you think it is reasonable to rule out the two above-mentioned allocations? Why?

x_3	x_4	Total Transportation Cost	$P[D_3 \leq x_3]$	$P[D_4 \leq x_4]$
1	4	89	$\frac{1}{3}$	1
2	3	94	$\frac{1}{3}$	$\frac{3}{4}$
3	2	100	$\frac{2}{3}$	$\frac{1}{2}$
4	1	106	$\frac{2}{3}$	$\frac{1}{2}$
5	0	112	1	$\frac{1}{4}$

FIGURE 16.10. Probabilities of Meeting Demand Requirements, With Given Values of (x_3, x_4).

*16.7 MULTISTAGE LINEAR MODEL

The mathematical logic that permitted you to transform a two-stage stochastic linear programming model with uncertain elements to an ordinary linear programming problem can be applied just as well to multistage models. As before, you must assume there are only a finite number Q of possible sets of values for the random elements. In a real multistage situation, Q is likely to be so large that it would be impractical to solve the resultant linear programming problem; therefore, you should study the analysis below with the idea of gaining further insight into the problems of decision-making under uncertainty. Only infrequently will you find the model of practical use, however.

Let the deterministic version of the problem be described as

$$(1) \qquad\qquad\qquad \text{maximize} \sum_{j=1}^{n} c_j x_j$$

subject to

$$(2) \qquad\qquad \sum_{j=1}^{n} a_{ij} x_j = b_i \quad \text{for } i = 1, 2, \ldots, m$$

$$(3) \qquad\qquad x_j \geq 0 \quad \text{for } j = 1, 2, \ldots, n.$$

Assume for the stochastic version that the c_j, a_{ij}, and b_i can be random. Specifically, suppose there are Q possible sets of values for these elements. Denote these sets of values by $(c_{qj}, a_{qij}, b_{qi})$, and the associated probability by p_q. We give a three-step procedure for formulating the appropriate linear programming problem. The procedure is completely general, so that it will work for any multistage model. You will often be able to take some shortcuts in applying the approach, however, when considering a particular model.

The idea is to start with a formulation that assumes you know which of the Q possible outcomes has occurred before you have to make any decisions. If such a formulation were a true representation of the problem, then you would have Q sets of values or decision rules for the variables, the composite of these representing a complete strategy. The next step is to recognize that in fact you will *not* know some of the random elements when you have to decide on the levels of particular variables. Therefore, you have to revise the initial formulation by inserting constraints to indicate that the levels for these particular variables must be identical in the appropriate sets of decision rules. To illustrate, each first-stage variable must have the same level in all Q of the decision rules. The final step is to tidy up the appearance of the model after applying the second step.

The method in detail is

Step 1. Write the problem that would be appropriate *if* you could learn the exact values of all the uncertain elements prior to deciding the levels for the x_j:

$$(4) \qquad\qquad\qquad \text{maximize} \sum_{q=1}^{Q} p_q \sum_{j=1}^{n} c_{qj} x_{qj}$$

subject to

$$(5) \qquad \sum_{j=1}^{n} a_{qij} x_{qj} = b_{qi} \quad \text{for } i = 1, 2, \ldots, m \quad \text{and } q = 1, 2, \ldots, Q,$$

$$(6) \qquad\qquad\qquad \text{all } x_{qj} \geq 0,$$

where x_{qj}, for $j = 1, 2, \ldots, n$, are levels associated with outcome $(c_{qj}, a_{qij}, b_{qi})$.

Step 2. Account for the *actual* sequence of information specified in the particular multistage model by equating the appropriate x_{qj}. For example, if the level of x_1 must be determined before any of the random elements are known, then add to the constraints (5) and (6) the restrictions $x_{11} = x_{21} = \cdots = x_{Q1}$.

Step 3. Use the restrictions in *Step 2* to simplify the form of the resultant problem. For the example in *Step 2*, put x_{11} wherever x_{q1}, for $q = 2, 3, \ldots, Q$, appears; then collect terms and eliminate any redundant equations.

It is important that you realize that the optimal values for x_{qj} in (4), (5), and (6) are precisely the decisions to be taken if and when the values $(c_{qj}, a_{qij}, b_{qi})$ for the random elements actually occur. Consequently, the analysis provides a complete prescription of the actions to be taken for every possible eventuality. Rather than elaborate further on the details of these steps so as to remove any ambiguities, we present an example that will serve as well in showing you how to apply the technique.

Production scheduling example. Consider a firm that must schedule its production level x_t for $t = 1, 2, 3$. Let D_t be demand occurring in Period t, and assume that any part of this demand not satisfied in Period t is lost forever. Let i_t be the inventory level at the end of Period t; assume that initial inventory is 0 and inventory at the end of Period 3 is worthless. Let c_t be the unit *profit* associated with producing an item in Period t and selling it at any time during the horizon; assume $c_t = r - e_t$, where r is the unit selling price and e_t the unit production cost in Period t. Let h_t be the unit cost of holding an item in inventory at the end of Period t. Then the deterministic version of this model can be stated as

$$\text{(7)} \qquad \text{maximize} \sum_{t=1}^{3} c_t x_t - \sum_{t=1}^{2} h_t i_t - (h_3 + r)i_3$$

subject to

$$\text{(8)} \qquad x_1 - i_1 \qquad\qquad\qquad + s_1 = D_1 \quad \text{(inventory balance—period 1)}$$

$$\text{(9)} \qquad\quad i_1 + x_2 - i_2 \qquad\quad + s_2 = D_2 \quad \text{(inventory balance—period 2)}$$

$$\text{(10)} \qquad\qquad\quad i_2 + x_3 - i_3 + s_3 = D_3 \quad \text{(inventory balance—period 3)}$$

$$\text{(11)} \qquad\qquad\qquad \text{all } x_t, i_t, s_t \geq 0,$$

where s_t is the level of lost sales in Period t.

The model is quite similar to that in Sec. 8.3 (see Fig. 8.6), but there are two points of difference requiring comment. First, the variables s_t allow for unfilled demand. [How would you modify (8) and (9) to permit backlogging of unfilled demand?] Second, the objective function is "maximize profit." Since the selling price r is included in c_t (the coefficient for a *production* variable), the coefficient of i_3 contains r to indicate that revenue is not in fact realized on items left over at the end of Period 3. For given values of D_t, the model is trivial to solve: assuming all $c_t > 0$, fill demand in Period t by production in that Period k, $k \leq t$, where the value of c_k minus accumulated inventory cost is maximal. You hardly need a model to obtain this common sense answer.

But now suppose that the problem contains elements of uncertainty. Specifically, let the values of D_t be random. What are optimal levels for x_t? To answer this question, you have to know more about the probability law that generates the values for D_t, and know more about the sequence in which the individual levels x_t are set and demand information becomes available. Assume that the values for D_t are independent of x_t. Further suppose that D_1 has two possible values. For each value of D_1, the demand D_2 may be either one of two values; in other words there are four possible values of D_2. Similarly, there are two possible values of D_3 for each possible value of D_1 and D_2; therefore D_3 may be any one of eight possible values. In short, the D_t are *dependent* random variables, and there are $Q = 8$ possible sets of values for (D_1, D_2, D_3), which are denoted by (D_{q1}, D_{q2}, D_{q3}), for $q = 1, 2, \ldots, 8$, and are summarized in Fig. 16.11. To see how the

D_1		D_2	D_3	P_q
$D_{11} = D_{21} = D_{31} = D_{41}$	$D_{12} = D_{22}$		D_{13}	P_1
			D_{23}	P_2
	$D_{32} = D_{42}$		D_{33}	P_3
			D_{43}	P_4
$D_{51} = D_{61} = D_{71} = D_{81}$	$D_{52} = D_{62}$		D_{53}	P_5
			D_{63}	P_6
	$D_{72} = D_{82}$		D_{73}	P_7
			D_{83}	P_8

FIGURE 16.11. Possible Demand Sequences.

sequence of information and decisions affects the formulation of the model, consider four different situations:

Perfect Information. Assume that the specific values of *all* the random elements are known prior to setting the levels of any of the decision variables. Then the model described in *Step 1* above gives the appropriate linear programming problem:

$$(12) \qquad \text{maximize} \sum_{q=1}^{8} p_q \left[\sum_{t=1}^{3} c_t x_{qt} - \sum_{t=1}^{2} h_t i_{qt} - (h_3 + r) i_{q3} \right]$$

subject to

$$(13) \quad x_{q1} - i_{q1} \qquad\qquad\qquad + s_{q1} = D_{q1} $$

$$(14) \qquad i_{q1} + x_{q2} - i_{q2} \qquad\qquad + s_{q2} = D_{q2} \left.\right\} \quad \text{for } q = 1, 2, \ldots, 8$$

$$(15) \qquad\qquad i_{q2} + x_{q3} - i_{q3} + s_{q3} = D_{q3} $$

$$(16) \qquad\qquad \text{all } x_{qt}, i_{qt}, s_{qt} \geq 0.$$

All together, there are 72 variables and 24 equality constraints. [Of course, to obtain a numerical solution to this model, you can factor (12) through (16) into $Q = 8$ separate linear programs. Each of these can be solved trivially since it has the same structure as the deterministic model (7) through (11). To calculate (12) you would weight the resultant optimal value of the objective function for each small problem by the associated p_q.]

(x_{q1}, i_{q1}, s_{q1})	(x_{q2}, i_{q2}, s_{q2})
$x_{11} = x_{21} = x_{31} = x_{41}$ $i_{11} = i_{21} = i_{31} = i_{41}$ $s_{11} = s_{21} = s_{31} = s_{41}$	$x_{12} = x_{22}$ $i_{12} = i_{22}$ $s_{12} = s_{22}$
	$x_{32} = x_{42}$ $i_{32} = i_{42}$ $s_{32} = s_{42}$
$x_{51} = x_{61} = x_{71} = x_{81}$ $i_{51} = i_{61} = i_{71} = i_{81}$ $s_{51} = s_{61} = s_{71} = s_{81}$	$x_{52} = x_{62}$ $i_{52} = i_{62}$ $s_{52} = s_{62}$
	$x_{72} = x_{82}$ $i_{72} = i_{82}$ $s_{72} = s_{82}$

FIGURE 16.12. Additional Restrictions for "Learn Demand—Then Produce."

Learn Demand—Then Produce. Suppose before setting the level of Period t production, you know the exact value of D_t and previous demands. Then in accord with Step 2 above, you must add the restrictions shown in Fig. 16.12. For example, if $D_1 = D_{11} = \cdots = D_{41}$, then the levels of first-period production, ending inventory, and lost sales will be the same for $q = 1$, 2, 3, 4. Similarly if $D_2 = D_{32} = D_{42}$, then the levels of second-period production, inventory, and lost sales will be the same for $q = 3$, 4.

To carry out Step 3, it is helpful to use a single symbol each time two or more quantities are equal. For example, use x_{11} wherever x_{21}, x_{31}, and x_{41} appear, and use i_{11}, s_{11}, and D_{11} analogously. You can see immediately that the constraints (13) for $q = 1, 2, 3, 4$ are identical, and therefore only one of these needs to be written. Thus the simplified form of the problem contains the variables

$$(17) \qquad x_{qt}, i_{qt}, s_{qt} \quad \text{for} \begin{cases} q = 1, 5 & \text{if } t = 1 \\ q = 1, 3, 5, 7 & \text{if } t = 2 \\ q = 1, 2, \ldots, 8 & \text{if } t = 3, \end{cases}$$

and consists of constraints (13) for $q = 1$, 5, (14) for $q = 1, 3, 5, 7$, (15) for $q = 1, 2, \ldots, 8$, and (16). All together, there are 42 variables and 14 equality constraints in the reduced model. Write the simplified form of the objective function, and verify, for example, that the coefficients of x_{11} and x_{51} are $(p_1 + \cdots + p_4)c_1$ and $(p_5 + \cdots + p_8)c_1$, respectively.

Produce—Then Learn Demand. Suppose before setting the level of Period t production, you know only the exact values of previous demands. The additional restrictions according to Step 2 are shown in Fig. 16.13. Notice that all the x_{q1} must be identical, since the production level in Period 1 is set prior to any exact knowledge

x_{q1}	(i_{q1}, s_{q1}, x_{q2})	(i_{q2}, s_{q2}, x_{q3})
$x_{11} = \cdots = x_{81}$	$i_{11} = \cdots = i_{41}$	$i_{12} = i_{22}$ $s_{12} = s_{22}$ $x_{13} = x_{23}$
	$s_{11} = \cdots = s_{41}$ $x_{12} = \cdots = x_{42}$	$i_{32} = i_{42}$ $s_{32} = s_{42}$ $x_{33} = x_{43}$
	$i_{51} = \cdots = i_{81}$	$i_{52} = i_{62}$ $s_{52} = s_{62}$ $x_{53} = x_{63}$
	$s_{51} = \cdots = s_{81}$ $x_{52} = \cdots = x_{82}$	$i_{72} = i_{82}$ $s_{72} = s_{82}$ $x_{73} = x_{83}$

FIGURE 16.13. Additional Restrictions for "Produce— Then Learn Demand."

of demand. Also observe that the equality restrictions on i_{q1}, s_{q1}, and x_{q2} occur for the same values of q because the levels of these variables are established with the same amount of information, namely, the exact value of D_1.

After performing *Step 3*, the simplified form of the problem contains the variables

$$x_{11}, i_{q1}, s_{q1}, x_{q2} \quad \text{for } q = 1, 5$$
(18)
$$i_{q2}, s_{q2}, x_{q3} \quad \text{for } q = 1, 3, 5, 7 \quad \text{and}$$
$$i_{q3}, s_{q3} \quad \text{for } q = 1, 2, \ldots, 8,$$

and the constraints (13) for $q = 1, 5$, (14) for $q = 1, 3, 5, 7$, (15) for $q = 1, 2, \ldots,$ 8, and (16). All together, there are 35 variables and 14 equality constraints in the reduced model. Write the appropriate objective function, and verify that the coefficient of x_{11} is just c_1.

Full Commitment. Finally, suppose all the production levels must be set before you know the exact values for any D_t. Verify that the simplified form of the model contains the variables

(19)
$$x_{11}, x_{12}, x_{13} \qquad\qquad i_{q1}, s_{q1} \quad \text{for } q = 1, 5$$
$$i_{q2}, s_{q2} \quad \text{for } q = 1, 3, 5, 7 \qquad i_{q3}, s_{q3} \quad \text{for } q = 1, 2, \ldots, 8,$$

and the same set of constraints as in the case "Produce—Then Learn Demand." Thus there are 31 variables and 14 equality constraints.

In going from the first case to the last, there is progressively less information available as the production levels are established. Consequently, the successive optimal values for the objective function will usually decrease (and will never increase). (The supporting mathematical argument is that each successive problem adds more equality constraints and therefore further restricts the possible levels of the variables.) The "Perfect Information" case represents the best you could do with a perfect predictor of the random elements. For any of the other situations, the difference between the optimal objective function value and the best you can do from the "Perfect Information" case measures the cost of uncertainty.

Other approaches. In some situations, like the above production scheduling example, you can use other techniques of model formulation for the multistage problem. One such approach is adding chance-constraints, as was done in Secs. 16.5 and 16.6. When there is a finite number Q of possible sets of values for the random elements, the chance-constrained approach may involve a smaller-size linear programming problem than does the above technique. But the complexity of keeping distinct the variables and constraints associated with the particular sets of information about values of the random elements is inherent in the problem —no correct method can avoid it. When the random variables in a period are completely independent of the variables in other periods, then a dynamic programming technique often can be applied, as will be illustrated in the next chapter.

*16.8 QUADRATIC CRITERION FUNCTION (LINEAR DECISION RULE)

The following multistage model with uncertain elements represents a situation where you *can* make optimal decisions while you only know the *expected value* of the random elements. The time sequence of decisions and emerging information about the values of the random variables can be as complex as in the preceding section. However, assume the constraints are of the form

$$(1) \qquad\qquad x_i + \sum_{j=m+1}^{n} a_{ij}x_j = b_i \quad \text{for } i = 1, 2, \ldots, m,$$

where x_j for $j = 1, 2, \ldots, n$, are *un*constrained in sign, all a_{ij} known exactly, but b_i are random with known expectation. As the example below will demonstrate, there are situations where the resultant optimal policy will yield all $x_j \geq 0$; there also are situations where the x_j represent deviations about given target values, so that negative levels for x_j are meaningful.

Further, suppose that the objective function can be written as minimizing the expected value of a quadratic form

$$(2) \qquad\qquad \sum_{j=1}^{n} \sum_{k=1}^{n} c_{jk}x_jx_k + \sum_{j=1}^{n} c_jx_j,$$

where (2) is strictly positive for *any* levels x_j, for $j = 1, 2, \ldots, n$, except all $x_j = 0$. Assume all the c_{jk} are known; the c_j may be random.

As usual, define the first-stage decisions as the levels of those variables that must be set before knowing the exact values of any of the random elements. It can be proved that the optimal levels of the *first-stage* variables are found by acting *as if* the model were deterministic:

Step 1. Insert the unconditional expectation for each c_j and b_i in (1) and (2).

Step 2. Substitute the x_i, for $i = 1, 2, \ldots, m$, from (1) into (2).

Step 3. Collect terms in x_j, for $j = m + 1, \ldots, n$.

Step 4. Set equal to 0 the partial derivatives of the quadratic form with respect to x_j, for $j = m + 1, \ldots, n$.

Step 5. Solve the resultant $(n - m)$ linear equations with respect to x_j, where $j = m + 1, \ldots, n$.

Step 6. Determine the associated values of x_i, for $i = 1, 2, \ldots, m$, in (1).

An important implication of these steps is that the optimal levels of the first-stage variables depend linearly on the $E[c_j]$ and $E[b_i]$. Consequently this problem is sometimes referred to as the **linear decision rule** model. After the levels of the first-stage variables have been set according to the above, wait until the next values of the random elements become known, and repeat the procedure. This entails renaming as first-stage variables what were previously second-stage variables, etc., and possibly recalculating the expectations for the c_j and b_i if the new information indicates that the future expectations should be revised. The following, completely hypothetical, example illustrates the approach.

Employment smoothing example. The manager of the Greasy Spoon Restaurant must determine the number of waitresses to have on duty during the rush hours each Day t, for $t = 1, 2, \ldots, T$. It is costly to change this number from day to day, because of such factors as employee morale and limited availability of experienced waitresses. Having either too many or too few waitresses is also expensive, because of the extra wages or the loss in revenue from customers who will not wait in a crowded line. However, it is not possible to know exactly how many waitresses are needed because of daily fluctuations in the number of customers and the amount of service they require. Let D_t denote the number of waitress-service hours that would be required by the restaurant's potential customers during the rush period on Day t. Let y_t denote the number of such hours scheduled ahead of time by the manager. Let f_t be the level of fluctuation in the scheduled hours between Day t − 1 and Day t, and let e_t be the level of error between the actually scheduled and the required number of hours:

$$(3) \qquad f_t = y_{t-1} - y_t \quad \text{for } t = 1, 2, \ldots, T \quad \text{(employment fluctuation)}$$

$$(4) \qquad e_t = y_t - D_t \quad \text{for } t = 1, 2, \ldots, T \quad \text{(demand fluctuation),}$$

where y_0 is the employment level right before Day 1. In this example, the variables f_t and e_t correspond to x_i, for $i = 1, 2, \ldots, m$, and the variables y_t to x_j, for $j = m + 1, \ldots, n$ in (1).

Assume the objective function is to minimize the expected value of

(5) $$\sum_{t=1}^{T} (f_t^2 + c e_t^2) \quad \text{(quadratic criterion)}$$

subject to (3) and (4), where $c \geq 0$ is a given constant. Note if $c = 0$, then an optimal solution is $y_t = y_0$ for all t; if c is arbitrarily large, then $y_t = E[D_t]$ is optimal. The first-stage decision is the level of y_1.

According to *Steps 1* and *2* in the procedure above, insert $E[D_t]$ for D_t in (4), substitute the f_t and e_t in (5), yielding

(6) $$C \equiv \sum_{t=1}^{T} \{(y_{t-1} - y_t)^2 + c(y_t - E[D_t])^2\}.$$

Then collecting terms and setting $\partial C/\partial y_t = 0$, for $t = 1, 2, \ldots, T$, you obtain T linear equations in T unknowns:

(7) $$(2 + c)y_1 - y_2 = cE[D_1] + y_0$$

(8) $$-y_{t-1} + (2 + c)y_t - 1y_{t+1} = cE[D_t] \quad \text{for } t = 2, \ldots, T - 1$$

(9) $$-y_{T-1} - (1 + c)y_T = cE[D_T].$$

You can solve (7) through (9) for given values of c, $E[D_t]$, and y_0. The resultant value of y_1 is the optimal level for the first-stage decision, and depends linearly on the $E[D_t]$.

Suppose the planning horizon really is unbounded, and the level of y_1 is to be set so that it is optimal for any arbitrarily large T. Then it can be shown that the solution of (7) through (9) for y_1, as $T \to \infty$, is

(10) $$y_1 = \alpha(y_0 + cE[D_1]) + \sum_{t=2}^{\infty} \alpha^t cE[D_t] \quad \text{(unbounded horizon)},$$

assuming the summation on the right converges, where

(11) $$\alpha = \frac{(2 + c) - \sqrt{4c + c^2}}{2}$$

so that $0 < \alpha \leq 1$ for $0 \leq c < \infty$, and $y_1 \geq 0$. Once again, note that y_1 in (10) is a linear function of the $E[D_t]$.

After observing an actual value for D_1, the manager may revise his expectations about subsequent D_t, so that on the second day, the calculation (10) would be repeated with $E[D_1]$ set equal to the new expectation of service requirements for the second day, etc. However, if $E[D_t] = D^*$, for all t, regardless of previous values for D_t, that is, if the expectation of requirements remains stationary, then the values for all future y_t are given by

(12) $$y_t = \alpha y_{t-1} + \frac{\alpha c D^*}{1 - \alpha} = \alpha^{t-1} y_0 + \frac{\alpha c D^*}{1 - \alpha}\left(\frac{1 - \alpha^{t-1}}{1 - \alpha}\right) \quad \text{(stationary demand)},$$

for $0 \leq c < \infty$, and $y_t \to D^*$ as $t \to \infty$.

REVIEW EXERCISES

1 In each case below, state what you think might be both the sources and the impact of uncertainty on the management decisions at issue. Also discuss whether performing sensitivity analysis on a deterministic model is likely to uncover the impact of uncertainty.

(a) Selecting sites for new warehouses that will serve existing retail outlets.
(b) Eliminating a product.
(c) Introducing a new product.
(d) Choosing the number of elevators to install in a new office building.
(e) Designing delivery routes for postmen.
(f) Determining the number of emergency operating rooms in a hospital.
(g) Floating a new bond issue. (Discuss the situation for a corporation and for a municipal government.)
(h) Determining the frequency of scheduling truck deliveries of gasoline to a major oil company's gas stations.
(i) Determining the size of a corporation's bank balance.
(j) Choosing the number of crews of telephone repairmen.
(k) Selecting the capacity of a dam.
(l) Determining the seating capacity of a supersonic airplane.

2 In each part below, calculate the expected value of the random variable D, the expected value of D^2, the expected value of $f(D) \equiv (-1)^D \cdot D/(D+1)$, and $E[f(D|y)]$ in (8) of Sec. 16.2, where $c = 1$, $h = 2$, $p = 5$, and $y = 0, 1, \ldots, 6$.

(a) $P[D = d] = \frac{1}{7}$ for $d = 0, 1, \ldots, 6$.
(b) $P[D = d] = \frac{1}{6}$ for $d = 1, 2, \ldots, 6$.
(c) $P[D = d] = \frac{1}{6}$ for $d = 0, 1, \ldots, 5$.
(d) $P[D = d] = \frac{1}{4}$ for $d = 0, 2, 4, 6$.
(e) $P[D = d] = \frac{1}{3}$ for $d = 1, 3, 5$.
(f) $P[D = d] = \binom{3}{d-1}(.5)^{d-1}(.5)^{3-d+1}$ for $d = 1, 2, 3, 4$.
(g) $P[D = d] = \binom{3}{d-2}(.5)^{d-2}(.5)^{3-d+2}$ for $d = 2, 3, 4, 5$.
(h) $P[D = 2j] = \binom{3}{j}(.5)^j(.5)^{3-j}$ for $j = 0, 1, 2, 3$.
(i) $P[D = 2j] = \binom{3}{j}(\frac{3}{4})^j(\frac{1}{4})^{3-j}$ for $j = 0, 1, 2, 3$.
(j) $P[D = 2j] = \binom{3}{j}(\frac{1}{4})^j(\frac{3}{4})^{3-j}$ for $j = 0, 1, 2, 3$.

3 In each of the three parts below, derive an expression analogous to (8) for the indicated function $f(D|y)$.

(a)
$$f(D|y) = \begin{cases} cy^2 + h \cdot (y-d)^2 & \text{if } d \leq y \\ cy^2 + p \cdot (d-y)^2 & \text{if } d > y. \end{cases}$$

(b)
$$f(D|y) = \begin{cases} c(y) + H - v \cdot (y-d) & \text{if } d \leq y \\ c(y) + P & \text{if } d > y, \end{cases}$$

where

$$c(y) = \begin{cases} 0 & \text{for } y = 0 \\ K + cy & \text{for } y > 0. \end{cases}$$

(c) $f(D|y) = c(y) + h(y - d) + p(y, d)$, where

$$c(y) = \begin{cases} 0 & \text{for } y = 0 \\ K + cy & \text{for } y > 0, \end{cases}$$

$$h(y - d) = \begin{cases} h_1 \cdot (y - d) & \text{if } 0 < y - d \le I \\ H + h_2 \cdot (y - d) & \text{if } y - d > I \\ 0 & \text{otherwise,} \end{cases}$$

$$p(y, d) = \begin{cases} p_1 \cdot \left(\dfrac{d - y}{d}\right) & \text{if } 0 < d - y \le S \\ P & \text{if } d - y > S \\ 0 & \text{otherwise.} \end{cases}$$

4 Yum-Yum Company (Sec. 16.2)

(a) Suppose the annual profit from expanding the present facility when the share of market equals 30% is $90 + e$, where $e > 0$. What is the largest value of e such that building a new plant remains the optimal decision? Make the same sensitivity analysis for the profit associated with a 35% market share. With a 40% market share.

(b) Suppose the annual profit from building a new plant when the share of market equals 30% is $50 - e$, where $e > 0$. What is the largest value of e such that building a new plant remains the optimal decision? Make the same sensitivity analysis for the profit associated with a 35% market share. With a 40% market share.

(c) Let p_1 be the assessed probability that the market share is 30% and p_2 that it is 35%, where $p_1 + p_2 = \frac{5}{8}$. How large can p_1 be such that building a new plant remains the optimal decision?

*(d) Let p_1, p_2, p_3 be the assessed probabilities that the market share equals 30%, 35%, and 40%, respectively. Note $p_3 = 1 - p_1 - p_2$. Construct a diagram showing all the values for p_1 and p_2 such that building a new plant is the optimal decision. (*Hint:* write an inequality between the expected profits for the two decisions that expresses building a new plant is optimal and then simplify. Draw the resultant solutions space diagram for p_1 and p_2.)

(e) Suppose the assessed probabilities are realistic but, by paying the amount K, the President can learn the actual share of market. In other words, he can find out what the share of market will be *before* having to make his decision. What is the largest value of K that still makes such perfect information worth purchasing?

5 Consider the production policy (10) and the demand distribution (11) in Sec. 16.2.

(a) Assuming entering inventory in the current period is 2, explain why production in the next period will be 0 with probability $\frac{1}{2}$. Explain why production will be 0 with probability $\frac{1}{4}$ in the period after next. What is the probability that production will be 0 three periods from now?

(b) Suppose, instead, that $D_t = 2$ with probability $\frac{1}{4}$ and $D_t = 3$ with probability $\frac{3}{4}$. Revise the probabilities in part (a) accordingly.

(c) Suppose, instead, that the policy is revised such that

$$x_\infty(i) = \begin{cases} 5 - i & \text{for } i = 0, 1, 2 \\ 0 & \text{otherwise} \end{cases}$$

and $D_t = 2$ with probability $\frac{3}{4}$ and $D_t = 3$ with probability $\frac{1}{4}$. Determine the probabilities that production will be 0 in the next period, the period after next, and three periods from now, assuming entering inventory in the current period is 2.

(d) Suppose each time production occurs there is a setup cost $K = 4$ and a production cost per item $c = 1$. There is also a holding cost $h = 2$ per item left over at the end of the period. Use the information in (12) and (13) to determine the expected cost per period over an unbounded horizon.

(e) Suppose that the policy in (10) is revised as shown below so that occasionally demand exceeds inventory on hand, in which case the excess demand is backlogged until the following period,

$$x_\infty(-2) = x_\infty(-1) = x_\infty(0) = 3 \quad x_\infty(1) = 0;$$

thus, if entering inventory is 1, no production occurs, and the demand backlogged is 1 if $D_t = 2$, or 2 if $D_t = 3$, represented by the negative inventory levels -1 and -2, respectively. Revise the steady-state probabilities in (12) and (13) accordingly. Justify your answer.

*6 Consider the *Toute de Suite* Bakery case, described in the special material in Sec. 16.2.

(a) What is an optimal solution if the manager wants the probability of meeting the total daily demand to be at least $\frac{1}{4}$? At least $\frac{1}{2}$?

(b) What is the optimal solution if he wants to sell at least $\frac{1}{3}$ a cake a day, on the average? If he wants to sell at least one cake a day, on the average?

7 Consider a three-period revenue stream (R_1, R_2, R_3), and assume that each R_t equals either 0 or 1. Let the possibility $(1, 0, 0)$ occur with probability 0, $(0, 1, 0)$ with probability $\frac{1}{4}$, $(0, 1, 1)$ with probability $\frac{3}{16}$, $(1, 1, 0)$ with probability $\frac{1}{16}$, and each other possibility with probability $\frac{1}{8}$. Let $\alpha = \frac{1}{2}$.

(a) Determine the expected present value of the stream using the joint probability distribution for (R_1, R_2, R_3), that is, calculate the value $R_1 + \alpha R_2 + \alpha^2 R_3$ for each possible (R_1, R_2, R_3), weight the value by the associated probability, and sum over all possibilities.

(b) Determine $E[R_t]$ for $t = 1, 2, 3$. Calculate (15) in Sec. 16.2 and compare your answer with that in part (a).

8 Consider each example in exercise 1. Suggest how you might obtain the required probability distributions; refer to the four approaches listed in Sec. 16.2.

9 *Galactic Reaper Company* (Sec. 16.3). Consider the data in Figs. 16.2 and 16.3.

(a) Verify the probabilities shown in (1).

(b) Check that the time span is 5 periods if each random event takes its average value. Calculate the actual expected time span.

(c) Should the new manager be hired if there is only a $\frac{3}{4}$ probability of his reducing the total time span by 1 period? Show the calculations justifying your answer. *Parts (d) through (j) follow on p. 690.*

(d) Suppose the manager has a fifty-fifty chance of either reducing the total time span by 2 periods or not reducing it at all. Assume the incremental profit from a total time span of 2 periods is 130. Should the manager be hired?

(e) Suppose the President decides not to hire the new manager, but considers the option of paying a fee F to ensure that Task B takes exactly 3 periods. What is the largest value for F that makes this option worthwhile?

(f) Perform the analysis in part (e), but assume that the fee F ensures that Task C takes 3 periods.

(g) Perform the analysis in part (e), but assume that the fee F ensures that Task E takes 2 periods.

(h) Perform the analysis in part (e), but assume that both Tasks B and C each take exactly 3 periods.

(i) What are the largest values for the fees in parts (e), (f), (g), and (h) if the President decides to hire the new manager?

*(j) Suppose Task A can take 1 or 2 periods with a fifty-fifty chance, and similarly, Task B can take 3 or 4 periods, Task C can take 3 or 4 periods, and Task E can take 2 or 3 periods; Task D still requires 1 period. Analyze whether the new manager should be hired. Given the optimal decision, calculate the gain from perfect information.

10 Devise an argument establishing the Linear Certainty–Equivalence Theorem in Sec. 16.4. (Illustrate your argument with the problem maximize $c_1 x_1 + c_2 x_2$ subject to $2x_1 + 3x_2 \leq 6$, where there is a fifty-fifty chance that c_1 equals 0 or 1, and similarly, there is an independent fifty-fifty chance that c_2 equals 0 or 1.)

11 *Big Board Company* (Sec. 16.4)

(a) Explain why the structure (6) through (10) is so simple that a numerical solution is trivial once you are given values for a_j, c_j, and D_i. (Illustrate your answer using $c_1 = 10$, $c_2 = 15$, $c_3 = 3$, $T = 10$, $a_1 = 3$, $a_2 = 5$, $D_1 = 10$, $D_2 = 50$.)

(b) Show how (13) through (21) are altered if $Q = 4$. Give a formula showing how the numbers of equations and variables depend on Q.

(c) Show how (13) through (21) are altered if there is a capacity constraint on x_3, namely, $x_3 \leq K$, where K is a given constant. How does your answer change if K is a random variable to be included in the characterization (12)? Assume that if x_3 exceeds K, there is a penalty charge $f_3(K - x_3)$.

(d) Show how (13) through (21) are simplified if the values for a_1, a_2, and D_2 are not random (do not allow an excess of Product 2).

(e) Explain how the formulation in (12) through (21) changes if r_j and a_j are correlated. (Continue to assume that there are $Q = 3$ different possible sets of values for all the random variables.)

(f) Show how (12) through (21) are altered if the production costs e_j are random variables. Assume that the e_j are not known until after the first-stage decisions are made. (Continue to assume that there are $Q = 3$ different possible sets of values for all the random variables.)

(g) Suppose that the actual values of f_1 and f_2 become known *after* the levels of the second-stage variables are fixed. Let $E[f_i|q]$ denote the expected value of f_i *given* that possibility q occurs, where $q = 1, 2, \ldots, Q$. Show how the objective function (13) is altered.

12 *Big Board Company* (Sec. 16.4). Suppose the President of Big Board can pay a fee F to learn which of the Q possible values for the random variables will actually occur.

(a) Suggest how to calculate the largest value for F that still makes it worthwhile for the President to purchase this perfect information.

*(b) Suppose the fee F purchases only perfect information about the yield a_1, and that a_1 is statistically independent of the other random variables (knowledge of a_1 is of no help in predicting the values of the other random factors). Explain how to modify your answer in part (a)?

*13 *Big Board Company* (Sec. 16.4). The special structure of this case permits an alternative formulation containing a single constraint (the total supply restriction) and a *nonlinear* objective function. Observe in (15) through (20) that there really is no optimization performed at the second stage; given $a_{qi}x_i$ and D_{qi}, feasibility dictates whether s_{qi} or t_{qi} is positive. Let $u_i(x_i | a_i, f_i, D_i)$ represent the loss of profit associated with the decision x_i, given specific values for the random variables $a_i, f_i,$ and D_i.

(a) For $i = 1, 2$, write the appropriate formula for $u_i(x_i | a_i, f_i, D_i)$. (*Hint*: the value of the function depends on whether $a_i x_i$ is "less than or equal to" or "greater than" D_i.)

(b) Let $U_i(x_i)$ be the expected value of $u_i(x_i | a_i, f_i, D_i)$. Write a formula indicating how to calculate $U_i(x_i)$ given the Q possible sets of values for the random variables.

(c) Show the complete nonlinear programming optimization model characterizing the problem.

14 Consider the general two-stage linear model in Sec. 16.4. In each part below, explain how the stated assumption is embodied in the formulation (22) through (25).

(a) The value of each random element is independent of the levels of x_j.

(b) The levels of x_j, for $j = 1, 2, \ldots, k$, must be fixed at the first stage before any exact values of the random elements are known.

(c) The levels of the second-stage variables are established after all the random values are known. Is assuming that there always exist feasible levels for the second-stage variables equivalent to assuming that (23), (24), and (25) have a feasible solution? Explain.

(d) There is a finite number Q of possible sets of values for the random variables. Does the formulation imply the assumption that the random variables are mutually independent? Explain. If not, does such an assumption simplify the formulation? Explain.

(e) State why it is permissible to use an exact value that is known for any c_j, b_i, or a_{ij} in (22) through (25). What simplifications occur if any b_i or a_{ij} is known, where $i = g + 1, \ldots, m$? (Be specific.)

*15 (a) Write the dual linear program to (13) through (21) in Sec. 16.4.

(b) Write the dual linear program to (22) through (25) in Sec. 16.4.

16 Consider the two-stage problem: maximize $6x_1 + 8x_2 - 12x_3 - 3x_4$ subject to $a_1 x_1 + a_2 x_2 + x_3 - x_4 = D$, where every $x_j \geq 0$, where the random quantities are (a_1, a_2, D) and x_3 and x_4 are the second-stage variables. Suppose the only two possible sets of values for the random variables are $(1, 2, 4)$, occurring with probability $\frac{1}{3}$, and $(2, 1, 10)$ with probability $\frac{2}{3}$.

(a) Formulate this two-stage problem in an equivalent linear programming model and find the optimal decision rule. Give an economic interpretation to your answer.

*(b) Suggest an alternative characterization that involves maximizing a *nonlinear* function subject only to the explicit constraints $x_1 \geq 0$ and $x_2 \geq 0$. (*Hint*: exploit the fact that if you are given levels for x_1 and x_2 and specific values for a_1, a_2, D, then feasibility dictates whether x_3 or x_4 is positive. Derive a nonlinear formula showing the expected value contribution to the objective function stemming from the second stage when the first-stage decisions are x_1 and x_2.)

*(c) Using the ideas developed in the advanced material at the end of Sec. 16.4, calculate E [*wait and see*], E [*average value*], E [*first-stage, average-value approximation*], C [*most stringent problem*], and the cost of uncertainty.

17 *Big Board Company* (Sec. 16.5). Consider the chance-constrained version (1) through (5). Suppose $E[c_1] = 10$, $E[c_2] = 15$, $c_3 = 3$, $T = 10$, $a_1 = 3$, $a_2 = 5$. Assume that D_1 and D_2 each have the marginal probability distribution given in (8). What is an optimal solution if

(a) $\beta_1 = \beta_2 = .9$?   (e) $\beta_1 = .5, \beta_2 = .9$?
(b) $\beta_1 = \beta_2 = .95$?   (f) $\beta_1 = \beta_2 = .3$?
(c) $\beta_1 = \beta_2 = .5$?   (g) $\beta_1 = \beta_2 = 0$?
(d) $\beta_1 = .9, \beta_2 = .5$?

18 *Big Board Company* (Sec. 16.5). Answer the questions in exercise 17, except let the marginal probability distribution for each of the products be $P[D = d] = \frac{1}{10}$ for $d = 1, 2, \ldots, 10$.

*19 (a) Let $c_j(u_j)$ be a convex function, where u_j is integer-valued. Show that $C_j(x_j) \equiv E[c_j(D_j - x_j)]$ is a convex function of x_j. (Assume that there are a finite number of possible values for the random variable D_j.)

(b) Explain why the objective function (6) in Sec. 16.6 is appropriate even when demands D_j are correlated.

Exercises 20 through 24 refer to the transportation model and the example in Sec. 16.6.

*20 (a) Verify the values for $C_3(x_3)$ and $C_4(x_4)$ in Fig. 16.7. Also verify the column $C_3(x_3) - C_3(x_3 + 1)$. Check that each $C_j(x_j)$ is convex according to (9).

(b) Explain why $C_j(0) = f_j E[D_j]$, and why $C_j(x_j)$ decreases to 0 as x_j increases to the largest possible value for D_j.

(c) Find an optimal solution for $f_3 = 15$ and $f_4 = 5$; check your answer with that given in Fig. 16.9.

*21 Assume, instead of (11), that $P[D_4 = d] = \frac{1}{5}$ for $d = 0, 1, 2, 3, 4$. Accordingly, revise $C_4(x_4)$ in Fig. 16.7, rewrite the Expanded Transportation Tableau in Fig. 16.8 and find an optimal solution for $f_3 = 15$ and $f_4 = 5$.

*22 (a) Verify the solution $x_3 = 2$ and $x_4 = 3$ is optimal for the associated values of f_3 and f_4 stated in Fig. 16.9.

(b) Do the same for the solution $x_3 = 3$ and $x_4 = 2$.

*23 (a) Verify (i) and (ii) in the special material.

(b) Derive expressions analogous to (i) and (ii) in terms of f_4.

*24 Consider the chance-constrained version.

(a) Verify the total transportation cost given in Fig. 16.10 for the allocation $x_3 = 2$ and $x_4 = 3$. Do the same for $x_3 = 3$ and $x_4 = 2$.

(b) Explain why $x_3 = 4$ and $x_4 = 1$ is never an optimal allocation in this approach.

(c) Discuss the fundamental difference between this approach and the two-stage approach to the stochastic transportation problem. Do you think it reasonable in the example to rule out the allocation $(x_3 = 2, x_4 = 3)$ and $(x_3 = 4, x_4 = 1)$? Explain your reasoning.

*25 Consider the production scheduling example in Sec. 16.7.

(a) Explain why (12) through (16) characterizes the case of *Perfect Information.* Justify the statement that there are 72 variables and 24 equality constraints. Explain why (12) through (16) can be factored into Q separate linear programs.

(b) Verify in the case of *Learn Demand—Then Produce* that the simplified form contains only the variables in (17), and justify the statement that there are 42 variables and 14 equality constraints. Exhibit in detail the simplified form of the objective function.

(c) Verify in the case of *Produce—Then Learn Demand* that the simplified form contains only the variables in (18), and justify the statement that there are 35 variables and 14 equality constraints. Exhibit in detail the appropriate objective function.

(d) Verify in the case of *Full Commitment* that the simplified form contains only the variables in (19), and justify the statement that there are 31 variables and 14 equality constraints.

(e) Suppose the horizon extends one more period, so that $t = 1, 2, 3, 4$; assume D_4 is generated analogous to the other D_t so that, all in all, $Q = 16$. Determine the number of variables and equations in each of the four cases.

*26 Consider the production scheduling example in Sec. 16.7.

(a) Explain how, if at all, the four cases are altered when the demands D_t are mutually independent. (Be sure to determine whether there are fewer variables and equations in each formulation.)

(b) Explain in detail the equivalent linear programming model appropriate to the following case. In Period t you know both D_t and D_{t+1} before deciding production x_t. (Be sure to state the number of variables and equations in the model and exhibit the objective function.)

*27 Consider the production scheduling example in Sec. 16.7.

(a) Suppose each profit coefficient c_t in (7) is a random variable, and you learn its value at the same time you learn D_t. Also assume that there are $Q = 8$ possible sets of values for $(D_1, D_2, D_3; c_1, c_2, c_3)$, and that the D_t are generated as in Fig. 16.11. Explain how each of the four cases are appropriately altered.

(b) Suppose demand left unfilled in Period 1 is backlogged to Period 2, and demand left unfilled in Period 2 is backlogged to Period 3. Let d_t be the penalty cost per unit of unfilled demand at the end of Period t. Any demand left unfilled at the end of Period 3 is lost. All the other stipulations in the model remain unchanged. Explain how each of the four cases are appropriately altered. (Be sure to state the number of variables and equations in each model, and exhibit the objective function.)

*28 Consider the employment smoothing example in Sec. 16.8.

(a) Verify that setting $\partial C/\partial y_t = 0$ for $t = 1, 2, \ldots, T$ in (6) yields the equations in (7), (8), and (9).

(b) Verify that $0 < \alpha \leq 1$ for $0 \leq c < \infty$, where α is given by (11).

(c) Verify that $y_t \rightarrow D^*$ as $t \rightarrow \infty$ in (12).

*29 Consider the employment smoothing example in Sec. 16.8. Let $y_0 = 0$ and $c = \frac{1}{2}$. In each case below, find the optimal y_1.

(a) Suppose $T = 4$ and $E[D_t] = 16$ for every t.

(b) Suppose $T = 4$ and $E[D_t] = 4t$ for $t = 1, 2, 3, 4$.

(c) Suppose $T = 4$ and $E[D_t] = 20 - 4t$ for $t = 1, 2, 3, 4$.

(d) Suppose $T = 4$ and $E[D_1] = E[D_3] = 4$ and $E[D_2] = E[D_4] = 16$.

(e) Suppose $T = 4$ and $E[D_1] = E[D_3] = 16$ and $E[D_2] = E[D_4] = 4$.

(f) Suppose the horizon is unbounded and $E[D_t] = D^* = 16$ for all t. Also show the optimal y_t for $t = 2, 3, 4$.

*30 Answer the questions in exercise 29, assuming that

(a) $c = \frac{1}{2}$.

(b) $c = \frac{9}{4}$.

31 Explain your understanding of the following terms:

impact of uncertainty

contingency plan, strategy, decision rule

expected value

uncertain actions

induced randomness

*randomized strategies (or decision rules)

Fallacy of Averages

gain from (or value of) perfect information, cost of uncertainty

stochastic linear programming model

two-stage linear model

Linear Certainty–Equivalence Theorem

*here-and-now problem

*wait-and-see problem

*average-value problem

*first-stage, average-value approximation

*most stringent problem

chance-constrained programming

deterministic equivalent constraint

*joint chance-constraint

*multistage linear model

*quadratic criterion function

*linear decision rule.

FORMULATION AND COMPUTATIONAL EXERCISES

32 *Galactic Reaper Company* (Sec. 16.3). Suppose in Fig. 16.2 that the arc between Nodes 1 and 2 is drawn in the opposite direction. Analyze the same decision problem, assuming that the incremental profit is equal to 0 from a total time span of seven or more

periods. (Be sure to indicate the optimal decision and also compute the gain from perfect information, as defined at the end of the section.)

*33 *Critical Path Scheduling.* Consider the example in Sec. 6.6 and its linear programming characterization (1) through (6). Assume that several of the completion times are random, as given by the data in Fig. 16.3. Suppose you want to determine job starting-time values y_{CD}, y_E, and y_F such that the probability is at least .5 that each of the inequalities (2) through (6) is satisfied (for example, you want $P[y_F \geq t_C + y_{CD}] \geq .5$). These starting-time values are to be determined prior to knowing the exact values of any of the random completion times. Give a verbal interpretation of the chance-constraints.

(a) Formulate an equivalent linear programming model. Also exhibit the corresponding dual problem.

(b) Solve the primal and dual problems in part (a). Indicate how the solution varies if the stated probability is .25, instead of .5. Is .75, instead of .5.

34 *One-Potato, Two-Potato Problem* (Sec. 1.6). Typically the actual yields of agricultural raw materials are subject to random variation. Assume that the yields for Source 1 are either (.2, .2, .3), as shown in Fig. 1.1, or (.25, .25, .35), or (.18, .15, .29), where each of these possibilities occurs with equal likelihood. Also assume that the yields for Source 2 are either (.3, .1, .3), as shown in Fig. 1.1, or (.35, .1, .25), where the first possibility occurs with probabilitiy $\frac{2}{3}$ and the second with probability $\frac{1}{3}$. Assume that French fries manufactured in excess of the stated purchase limitation can be sold directly to institutional buyers at the relative profit of F per unit weight, and similarly, excess hash browns at H and flakes at L per unit weight.

(a) Write a two-stage linear model that selects purchase quantities to maximize expected profit.

*(b) Write the corresponding dual linear program.

35 *Knox Mix Company* (Sec. 2.2)

(a) Suppose the unit profit of each activity is composed of a revenue factor less a cost component, where cost is partly random. Specifically, let the unit revenue for Processes 1 and 2 be 15, and for Processes 3 and 4 be 20. Assume that the cost components are

Process 1: $8 + c$ Process 2: $8 + 2c$ where $P[c = 0] = \frac{1}{3}$ $P[c = 1] = \frac{2}{3}$
Process 3: $6 + d$ Process 4: $6 + 3d$
$$\text{where } P[d = 0] = \tfrac{1}{6} \quad P[d = 1] = \tfrac{1}{2} \quad P[d = 2] = \tfrac{1}{3}.$$

Display a model for selecting the production levels to maximize expected profit.

(b) Suppose the availability of labor W is random, where

$$P[W = 10] = \frac{1}{8} \quad P[W = 12] = \frac{1}{2} \quad P[W = 15] = \frac{3}{8}.$$

Assume that if the production schedule requires more man-weeks than are available, then the additional requirement is met by scheduling overtime, which costs c per man-week required. (The production levels are established at the start of the week and any overtime is incurred at the end of the week.) Display a model for selecting production levels to maximize expected profit. *Part (c) on p. 696.*

(c) Consider the situation in part (b), except suppose that the company seeks a schedule that stays within the available amount of labor with probability of at least .8. (The dollar cost of overtime is not *explicitly* taken into account.) Display an appropriate linear optimization model. Show how to alter the formulation if the probability is .9, instead of .8.

36 *Hion Hog Farm Problem* (Sec. 2.3). After reading a recent research report issued by the Department of Agriculture, the production manager feels that the minimal amount r of Nutritional Ingredient B is either 225, with probability $\frac{1}{5}$, or 250, with probability $\frac{3}{10}$, or 300, with probability $\frac{1}{2}$. Formulate the appropriate linear optimization model that ensures his hogs receive at least the minimal required amount of B with probability of at least .25. With probability of at least .50. With probability of at least .75.

37 *Trim Problem* (exercise 25 of Chap. 2). Suppose that Fine-Webb produces in anticipation of customer orders for 22-inch width rolls. Assume that such demand turns out to be $90 + D$, where D has the probability distribution $P[D = d] = d/190$ for $d = 1, 2, \ldots, 19$. Formulate a linear programming model that minimizes trim costs subject to the previous demand constraints on the rolls of 20-inch and 12-inch widths, and the restriction that all demand for 22-inch width rolls be satisfied with probability of at least .5. At least .8. At least .9.

38 *Blip-Bleep Problem* (Sec. 6.4). Suppose the manufacturer is concerned about the ability of certain subcontractors to meet the required specifications for the electronic components. Let p_{ij} be the manufacturer's probability estimate that each Component i produced by Subcontractor j will meet standards, and let K_i be the loss incurred by the manufacturer when any units of Component i are produced below standard. Formulate an optimization model that minimizes expected total cost. Indicate whether the formulation is still a standard assignment problem.

39 *Shortest-Route Model* (Sec. 6.5). Consider the example in Fig. 6.8. Suppose that the arc costs are random and that traversing each arc requires one period. Assume that during each of the first three periods of the horizon the arc cost from Node i to Node j is either c_{ij}, with probability p_{ij}, or d_{ij}, with probability $1 - p_{ij}$. After the third period, the arc cost is either e_{ij}, with probability q_{ij}, or f_{ij}, with probability $1 - q_{ij}$. Assume that each arc cost for each period is completely independent of every other arc cost. (Thus, for example, one possible sequence of arc costs from Node 3 to Node 4 over seven periods is $c_{34}, d_{34}, c_{34}, f_{34}, f_{34}, e_{34}, f_{34}$.) A complete route must be selected prior to knowing the exact values of any of the arc costs, and the objective is to minimize expected cost in going from Node 8 (source) to Node 1 (sink). Show how to formulate the problem as an equivalent deterministic shortest-route model. (Draw the network diagram and indicate the arc costs.)

40 Consider a linear programming model containing the constraint

$$P\left[\sum_{j=1}^{n} a_{1j}x_j \le b\right] \ge .25,$$

where a_{11} is the random variable and has the probability distribution $P[a_{11} = a] = .1$ for $a = 1, 2, \ldots, 10$.

(a) Show how to convert this chance-constraint into an ordinary linear inequality.

(b) Answer part (a), except let the probability limit be .75, instead of .25. Be .8, instead of .25.

(c) Rework part (a), letting $P[a_{11} = a] = .1$ for $a = 6, 7, \ldots, 15$. For $a = -4, -3, \ldots, 5$.

41 *Great Auto Works Problem* (Sec. 2.6). Let $T = 3$, and assume that the sales requirements S_t each period is random, where

$$P[S_1 = 10] = \frac{1}{4} \quad P[S_2 = 20] = \frac{1}{2} \quad P[S_3 = 16] = \frac{4}{5}$$

$$P[S_1 = 15] = \frac{3}{4} \quad P[S_2 = 25] = \frac{1}{2} \quad P[S_3 = 18] = \frac{1}{5},$$

and the requirements are completely independent of each other. If the actual requirement exceeds the available supply (at the end of the period), the unfilled demand is lost at a cost of r_t per unit in Period t.

(a) Assume there is "perfect information" at the beginning of the horizon, analogous to the case of *Perfect Information* in Sec. 16.7. Write the appropriate linear model in full, and indicate the total number of variables and equations.

(b) Analyze how the formulation in part (a) is altered if the exact values of S_t and the previous sales requirements are known before setting the levels of the Period t decision variables, analogous to the case of *Learn Demand—Then Produce* in Sec. 16.7.

(c) Analyze how the formulation in part (a) is altered if only the exact values of the previous sales requirements are known before setting the levels of the Period t decision variables, analogous to the case of *Produce—Then Learn Demand* in Sec. 16.7.

(d) Analyze how the formulation in part (a) is altered if the levels of all the decision variables must be set before knowing any of the exact values for the sales requirements, analogous to the case of *Full Commitment* in Sec. 16.7.

MIND-EXPANDING EXERCISES

42 *Neyman-Pearson Lemma*. Consider a random variable V that can assume a value of either $1, 2, \ldots, n$. Suppose you wish to find out which of two possible probability distributions is giving rise to V by taking a single sample observation. Let one of the possible distributions be denoted by P, containing the probabilities $p_j > 0$, and the other by Q, containing the probabilities $q_j > 0$. Explain why it is always possible to assign index values $j = 1, 2, \ldots, n$ to the observation values $1, 2, \ldots, n$, in such a way that

$$\frac{p_1}{q_1} \leq \frac{p_2}{q_2} \leq \cdots \leq \frac{p_n}{q_n}$$

so that the index $j = 1$ refers to the observation value having the smallest ratio and the index $j = n$ to the observation having the largest ratio. Given that the sample yields the observation indexed as j, let x_j be the probability that you decide the distribution is P (and $1 - x_j$ that it is Q).

(a) Formulate a linear programming model that maximizes the probability of deciding the distribution is P when indeed it is P, subject to the constraint that the probability of deciding it is P when in fact it is Q does not exceed β, where $0 < \beta < 1$. Also write the dual problem.

(b) Show that an *optimal* solution has the form that $x_j = 0$ for $j < J$, $x_j = 1$, for $j > J$, and $0 \leq x_j \leq 1$ for some critical J.

*43 Consider the transportation example in Sec. 16. 6. Suppose in addition that the S_i are also random, and that their exact values are not known until after the x_{ij} are determined. Let $P[S_i = S]$ denote the probability that the value of S_i is S. (The level of x_{ij} is to be viewed as a commitment to ship x_{ij} units from the ith source to the jth destination.) If $x_{i1} + x_{i2} + \cdots + x_{im}$ exceeds the actual value of S_i, the difference must be supplied by another means at a cost C_i per unit. Discuss in detail how you can alter the formulation in Sec. 16.6 to obtain an equivalent enlarged deterministic transportation problem.

*44 *Warehouse Problem* (exercise 36 of Chap. 5). Suppose the selling price and purchase cost are random variables. Specifically, consider the random variable r, which has probability distribution $q_t(r)$ in Period t, where $r = 1, 2, \ldots, 10$. Then assume that the selling price and purchase cost in Period t are related to r by the functions $p_t(r)$ and $c_t(r)$, and that these values are known at the start of Period t, prior to deciding the number of gallons to be sold or purchased. Formulate an equivalent multistage linear programming problem that yields a strategy maximizing expected profit. (Be sure to define your variables in such a way as to exhibit their dependence on r.) State the numbers of variables and constraints in the linear model.

*45 *Caterer Problem* (exercise 48 of Chap. 6). Suppose that p is the probability of losing a bundle of napkins sent for normal laundering. The catering firm learns about a loss at the beginning of the period when the laundry is to be returned, and when there is time to purchase new napkins if necessary. Formulate an equivalent linear programming model. State the numbers of variables and constraints in the linear model.

*46 *Expando Manufacturing Company* (exercise 36 of Chap. 2). Suppose the company anticipates the possibility of a strike in the construction industry. Let p_j, $j = 0, 1, \ldots, 6$, denote that a strike occurs during the jth period, where p_0 represents the probability of no strike at all. Assume that if a strike occurs during Period j, then any expansion by Method 2 undertaken in the previous period or any expansion undertaken in Period j extends for an additional period. In case of a strike, the company is willing to alter its objective function to include production capacity that would have become available by the end of the sixth period were it not for the strike.

(a) Formulate an equivalent linear programming model assuming that the entire expansion plan must be made at the beginning of Period 1, prior to knowing when a strike occurs (if at all). State the numbers of variables and constraints in the model.

(b) Formulate an equivalent linear programming model assuming that the company knows prior to each period whether a strike will occur in that period. (Assume that if a strike occurs in Period k, it does not recur in any subsequent period.) State the numbers of variables and constraints in the model.

*47 *Employment Scheduling.* Consider the example of the Spitzen-Pollish Company in Sec. 6.7. Suppose the number of required crews R_k in Period k is a random variable. Specifically, let $P[R_k = R] \equiv p_k(R)$, where $R = 1, 2, \ldots, 10$, and assume that the R_k are mutually independent. In each part below, show how to formulate an equivalent linear programming model, given the specified assumption about when the actual values of R_k become known. Be sure to define all the symbols you use and indicate the numbers of equations and variables.

   (a) Assume that R_k becomes known at the start of Period k, prior to making decisions $x_{k,k+1}, \ldots, x_{kn}$.
   (b) Assume that R_k becomes known at the start of Period $k - 1$, prior to making the decisions $x_{k-1,k}, \ldots, x_{k-1,n}$. (Hence, R_1 and R_2 are known at the start of the horizon, R_2 and R_3 at the start of Period 2, etc.)

*48 (a) Consider a nonlinear programming problem that can be solved by an algorithm of the sort described in Chaps. 14 and 15. Suppose that the underlying application lends itself to a two-stage description, analogous to that given in Sec. 16.4. Discuss whether the approach used in Sec. 16.4 generalizes to the nonlinear problem. State whether you can construct an enlarged equivalent nonlinear problem solvable by the same sort of algorithm that was applicable in the deterministic case.
   (b) Do the same for a multistage stochastic nonlinear problem and the approach used in Sec. 16.7.
   (c) Do the same for two-stage and multistage stochastic integer programming problems of the sort described in Chap. 13 and the approaches used in Secs. 16.4 and 16.7.

CONTENTS

CHAPTER 17

Probabilistic Dynamic Programming Models

17.1 INTRODUCTION

In the preceding chapter you studied the impact of uncertainty on optimal decision processes. Proper structuring of a model containing random elements was emphasized, especially taking into account the intermingled sequence of decisions and emergent information about the exact values of the random elements. Most of the analysis was in the context of linear models, and you saw that the stochastic generalizations frequently lead to expanded linear models that are too large to solve in practice.

This chapter partially reverses the emphasis. Each model below is a specific application of probabilistic dynamic programming. The examples will show that stochastic versions of many dynamic programming models are *not* much more difficult to solve than their deterministic counterparts.

Except for the advanced material in Sec. 17.7, each illustration in this chapter is for a finite horizon or finite stage dynamic programming problem. (Optimization over an unbounded horizon is treated in Chap. 18.) This chapter focuses on how to include random phenomena in multistage problems. We assume that you are already familiar with formulating deterministic dynamic programming problems, and suggest that you take a few minutes to review Chaps. 8 and 10 to refresh your memory on the concepts used in dynamic programming, and in particular, on the notions of state and stage variables, the appearance of a recursion formula, and the numerical procedures for computing solutions from such recursions.

We explain probabilistic dynamic programming in a manner similar to the approach in Chaps. 8 and 10, namely, by presenting several illustrative examples. The models get progressively more complicated looking, and a few represent

701

stochastic versions of deterministic models that you previously studied in Chaps. 8 and 10. We do not dwell in this chapter on the details of computing answers to specific problems, because in practice, the computational task is so lengthy that you would use an electronic computer and a program written by a technical expert. Instead, we concentrate on problem formulation and on certain insights into what happens when you introduce probabilistic elements.

To keep perspective on assessing the impact of uncertainty while reading the material below, be sure you answer these questions:

1. What is an optimal policy for a deterministic version of the model?
2. How much information about the probability distribution does an optimal solution require?
3. How does the dynamic programming algorithm for the stochastic model differ from that for the deterministic version?

17.2 DISTRIBUTION OF EFFORT EXAMPLE

We begin with an example in which the introduction of probabilistic elements has an almost trivial impact on the way the appropriate dynamic recursion is formulated. The model is a stochastic version of what was called the Distribution of Effort Problem in Chap. 10. To save you from flipping back to Sec. 10.2 where the particular example was first discussed, we repeat the statement of the deterministic problem here.

The owner of Shopping Basket Markets has one week's supply, N, of eggs to distribute among his s stores. From past experience he knows that if he allocates y_j eggs to Store j, his profit will be $R_j(y_j)$. He wants to find a distribution of eggs among his Shopping Basket stores that maximizes overall profit.

The mathematical characterization of the problem is given as

$$(1) \qquad\qquad \text{maximize} \sum_{j=1}^{s} R_j(y_j)$$

subject to

$$(2) \qquad\qquad \sum_{j=1}^{s} y_j = N \quad \text{(available number of eggs)}$$

$$(3) \qquad\qquad y_j = 0, 1, \ldots \quad \text{for each } j \quad \text{(distribute only whole eggs)}.$$

In Sec. 10.2, we let

(4) $g_j(n)$ = profit when n eggs are distributed optimally to Store 1, Store 2, . . . , Store j.

You saw that (1) through (3) could be solved as a multistage problem by employing the dynamic programming recursion

$$(5) \qquad g_j(n) = \underset{y_j}{\text{maximum}} \ [R_j(y_j) + g_{j-1}(n - y_j)] \quad \text{for } j = 1, 2, \ldots, s$$

$$(6) \qquad\qquad\qquad g_0(n) \equiv 0 \quad \text{for } j = 0,$$

where $n = 0, 1, \ldots, N$ and the maximization is over only nonnegative integer values of y_j that satisfy $y_j \leq n$. The optimal value of (1) is given by $g_s(N)$.

The above formulation proceeded under the assumption that the profit from distributing y_j eggs to Store j is known with certainty. Suppose, however, that profit depends not only on y_j, but also on the actual demand at Store j, which can be described as a random variable independent of the levels of all y_j, and known exactly only *after* y_j are all set. Specifically, let

(7) $r_j(d|y)$ = profit at Store j when demand actually equals d, given that Store j has been allocated y eggs

(8) $p_j(d)$ = probability that demand actually equals d at Store j.

For example, the profit function in (7) might be described by

$$(9) \qquad r_j(d|y) = \begin{cases} r_j d & \text{for } d \leq y \quad \text{(supply satisfies demand)} \\ r_j y & \text{for } d > y \quad \text{(demand exceeds supply).} \end{cases}$$

In this case, the number r_j represents the profit at Store j for each egg sold. When the supply y is large enough to satisfy all demand d, the total profit is $r_j d$; but when actual demand exceeds supply, then only the y eggs are sold, so total profit is $r_j y$.

The *expected profit* from distributing y_j eggs to Store j is

$$(10) \qquad\qquad R_j(y_j) \equiv \sum_d r_j(d|y_j)p_j(d),$$

where the letter d underneath the summation sign designates that the sum is to be taken over every possible value of demand. Using the above definition for $R_j(y_j)$, a solution to (1) through (3) represents an optimal allocation given the criterion of maximizing *expected* total profit, and an optimal solution can still be obtained by employing (4) through (6). Therefore, once the expected profit functions in (10) have been calculated, the stochastic model is no more complicated to solve than the deterministic version.

17.3 new product introduction—a decision tree

Hopefully, the preceding section has restored your self-confidence in working with dynamic programming recursions and you are ready to go on to a more challenging problem. In Chap. 16, you learned a fundamental proposition about finding optimal solutions to a dynamic decision-making problem with stochastic elements: you can only find specific optimal values for the first-stage decisions, and must determine optimal **decision rules** that are to be applied in future periods. Such rules indicate what decision is optimal based on the *actual* history of the system at the time the particular choice is made.

The "Cool It" Baby Air Conditioner Company is developing a major design improvement for its window-installation models. The design is far enough along for the change to be made right away. The company prefers to wait, however, until additional research and testing have been completed, because some minor difficulties still beset the manufacturing process. On the other hand, the President of Cool It knows that if he delays too long, one or more of his competitors will surely announce a similar product improvement and his share of sales will consequently be smaller. What he must do, then, is balance the profit improvement from waiting until the "bugs" in his production process are worked out against the possible loss of sales to his competitors.

Consider the following mathematical representation of this situation. Suppose the manufacturer wants to decide the optimal month in which to announce the new improvement. Assume that he considers the latest possible month to be T, and that he definitely will introduce the change at any time his competition advertises a similar improvement. Let

r_t = profit when, in Month t, Cool It announces the improvement in advance of competition

g_t = profit when, in Month t, Cool It and any competitor simultaneously introduce the change

h_t = profit when, in Month t, Cool It announces the improvement after competition has already done so,

where it is plausible (although not really essential) to postulate that $r_t > g_t > h_t$, and r_t, g_t, and h_t increase as time goes on, that is, with larger values of t.

Assume that if no improvement is announced before Month t, then Cool It and its competitors make their Month t decisions independently, without knowledge of each other's current decisions. Accordingly, suppose that the President of Cool It believes p_t represents the probability that his competition will announce an improvement in Month t, *given* that no one of his competitors has introduced the change up to that time, where he feels that $p_T = 1$. By assumption, then, the manufacturer postulates that these values for the conditional probabilities p_t do *not* depend on the particular strategy he decides to use. The President predicts, however, that if Cool It introduces the improvement in Month t in advance of competition, then the competitors assuredly will make a similar introduction in the next period. Consequently, he calculates the values for r_t to reflect such competitive reaction.

The underlying decision process can be described by a **decision tree** as shown in Fig. 17.1, where we let $T = 3$. The labels M and C at each node refer to the action taken by the manufacturer and his competitors. The tree terminates at Month t unless *both* the manufacturer and his competitors decide to delay the introduction.

Study the tree to see how it graphically displays the multiperiod decision process. The bottom of the tree represents the first-stage or immediate decision the manufacturer must make. If he chooses to introduce the improvement, his decision process terminates. But if he decides to delay, then he may or may not have an opportunity to delay again at Period 2, depending on the outcome of the probabilistic

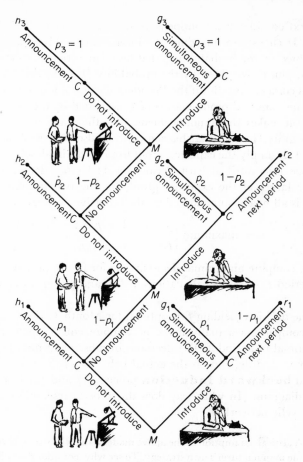

FIGURE 17.1. Cool It Com-
pany's Decision Tree for
New Product Introduction
($T = 3$).

Note: M = manufacturer's decision (Cool It Company)
      C = competitors' decisions

element representing the competitors' behavior. Similar remarks hold for his other decision points on the tree.

Assume that the President wants a strategy that maximizes expected profit. As usual in a dynamic programming problem, you can easily find the optimal decision in case the process continues to the final period, Period T. At that time, you need only compare the expected profit of his introducing the improvement with the expected profit of a further delay. Explain why these two quantities are $p_T g_T$ and $p_T h_T$, respectively. Since by assumption $p_T = 1$ and $g_T > h_T$, the better decision is to introduce the improvement if the decision process lasts until the final period. The foregoing computations can be written as

$$(1) \qquad f_T = \text{maximum} \begin{Bmatrix} p_T g_T: & \text{introduce} \\ p_T h_T: & \text{do not introduce} \end{Bmatrix} = g_T,$$

where we have let f_T denote the expected profit of an optimal decision at Period T.

Next consider what happens at an earlier period, Period t. If the President of Cool It chooses to introduce the improvement, his expected profit consists of g_t, weighted by the probability p_t that his competition also makes the same announcement, plus r_t, weighted by the probability $(1 - p_t)$ that Cool It "jumps the gun" on its competition. But if the President chooses not to introduce the improvement, then his expected profit consists of h_t, weighted by the probability p_t that his competition makes the announcement, plus the value of delaying, weighted by the probability $(1 - p_t)$ that his competition also delays. What is the value of delaying? It is simply the expected profit from an optimal policy given that the decision process lasts until at least Period $t + 1$; let f_{t+1} denote this quantity. Then f_t is the larger of the expected profits for the two possible decisions at Period t. This is all nicely summarized by the recursive calculation, for $t = T - 1, \ldots, 1$,

$$(2) \qquad f_t = \text{maximum} \begin{cases} p_t g_t + (1 - p_t) r_t: & \text{introduce} \\ p_t h_t + (1 - p_t) f_{t+1}: & \text{do not introduce} \end{cases}.$$

To compute an optimal decision rule for future periods and the optimal action at Period 1, start the calculations at (1), and perform the arithmetic indicated in (2).

The decision yielding f_1 is optimal for Month 1. If it is "do not introduce" *and* the competitors actually make no announcement, then the decision yielding f_2 is optimal in Period 2. The decisions in subsequent months are found in a similar manner, and depend on the actual behavior of the competition. Explain the so-called **backward induction** process (1) and (2) in relation to the decision tree diagram. (In what way does this process resemble finding the best route in an acyclic network?)

▶A critical assumption in the above model is that the values of p_t are indeed independent of the manufacturer's own strategy. To see why, consider the following situation. Suppose there is a single competitor whose profit figures are identical to the manufacturer's. Then if the competitor could learn that the manufacturer planned to introduce the improvement in Period s, the competitor would thus announce his own change in Period $s - 1$ (if $r_{s-1} > g_s$). But if the manufacturer suspected this action by his competitor, he would then let $p_{s-1} = 1$, and would change his initial decision accordingly. As you quickly recognize, this line of reasoning can lead to a sequence of revisions on the part of the manufacturer and his competitor. The question arises whether strategies exist for the manufacturer and the competitor that are in equilibrium, that is, which would not be revised if either one learned the decision of the other. And even if there are such equilibrium strategies, are they optimal in any sense? Such topics fall in the realm of game theory, and are treated in texts on that subject.   ◀

17.4 ELEMENTARY INVENTORY MODEL

The Cool It Company example was fairly simple because the state of the system at any Period t was really an indication of whether the decision process had lasted that long, in other words, whether either the manufacturer or his competitors had announced the improvement in prior periods. The state variable in this next illustration accords with what you have seen in previously presented deterministic problems.

The illustration is a probabilistic version of the Dependable Manufacturing Company production and inventory example contained in Sec. 8.4. (An extensive treatment of inventory models with stochastic demands will be given in Chap. 19 and Appendix II. The emphasis there will be on deriving the *form* of an optimal policy, and then exploiting this knowledge to calculate numerical answers.)

In the previous deterministic case, we made the following assumptions about the data for Dependable Manufacturing Company's problem:

(1)   demand $D = 3$ production $x \leq 5$ ending inventory $j \leq 4$

(2)   production and inventory costs $C(x, j) = C(x) + hj$,

where x and j are nonnegative integers and

(3)
$$C(0) = 0 \quad C(1) = 15 \quad C(2) = 17$$
$$C(3) = 19 \quad C(4) = 21 \quad C(5) = 23 \quad \text{and} \quad h = 1,$$

for all periods. Thus the model's parameters are stationary over time.

The state variable is *entering* inventory, designated by the symbol i, where $i = 0, 1, \ldots, 4$. The appropriate recursion is

(4) $f_n(i) = \underset{x}{\text{minimum}} \, [C(x) + 1(i + x - 3) + f_{n-1}(i + x - 3)]$

for $n = 2, 3, \ldots,$

with

(5) $f_1(i) = C(3 - i) \quad \text{for } i = 0, 1, 2, 3,$

where in (4), $i = 0, 1, \ldots, 4$, and the minimization is over only nonnegative integer values in the range $3 - i \leq x \leq \text{minimum} \, (5, 7 - i)$.

Suppose now that the demands are independently and identically distributed random variables, where

(6) $P[D = 2] = \dfrac{1}{2} \quad P[D = 4] = \dfrac{1}{2} \quad$ so that $E[D] = 3$ for all periods.

To make the analysis of this stochastic version comparable to the deterministic model, a few additional assumptions need to be specified. First, assume that inventory at the end of the horizon has no salvage value and incurs no holding cost (in the deterministic case the final inventory level equalled 0). Second, assume that production x is made large enough so that a stockout never occurs, implying the restriction

(7)   entering inventory + production ≥ 4.

Since demand may be as small as 2 and ending inventory cannot be larger than 4, the constraint

(8)   entering inventory + production ≤ 6

must also be satisfied.

The most important observation is that the state variable in this stochastic version continues to be the level of entering inventory. Think about why. Since the random demands are completely independent, the only thing that matters about the previous history when there are n periods remaining is the level of inventory currently available. Assuming that the objective function is to minimize expected cost over the horizon, the symbol $f_n(i)$ can now be interpreted as the *expected* cost of operating an optimal policy when entering inventory is at level i and there are n periods remaining in the horizon.

The case of $n = 1$ is easy to compute:

$$(9) \qquad f_1(i) = C(4 - i) \quad \text{for } i = 0, 1, \ldots, 4.$$

Explain why the assumptions justify that the optimal production level x is $4 - i$ when $n = 1$.

For larger values of n, the expected cost of an optimal policy, given the level i, can be reasoned as follows. First, you have to add in the production cost $C(x)$ for producing x. Second, you have to include the *expected* holding cost on inventory at the end of the period, which is the quantity $(i + x - D)$. And finally, you have to account for the cost that will be incurred in later periods. But this last amount is simply the expected value $E[f_{n-1}(i + x - D)]$, where D has the probability distribution in (6). State why. Thus the appropriate dynamic programming recursion for the stochastic model is, for $n = 2, 3, \ldots,$

$$
\begin{aligned}
(10) \quad f_n(i) = \underset{x}{\text{minimum}}\, &\{C(x) + 1\,[\tfrac{1}{2}(i + x - 2) + \tfrac{1}{2}(i + x - 4)] \\
&+ \tfrac{1}{2}f_{n-1}(i + x - 2) + \tfrac{1}{2}f_{n-1}(i + x - 4)\} \\
= \underset{x}{\text{minimum}}\, &\{C(x) + 1\,[i + x - 3] \\
&+ \tfrac{1}{2}[f_{n-1}(i + x - 2) + f_{n-1}(i + x - 4)]\}
\end{aligned}
$$

where $i = 0, 1, \ldots, 4$, and the minimization is over only nonnegative integer values in the range $4 - i \le x \le$ minimum $(5, 6 - i)$.

Note that the major difference between the recursion for the deterministic problem (4) and for the stochastic problem (10) is that in the latter an extra amount of arithmetic must be performed to compute $E[f_{n-1}(i + x - D)]$.

In Fig. 17.2 optimal production decisions $x_n(i)$ for $n = 1, 2, \ldots, 5$ are shown along with $f_n(i)$. It can be proved that the optimal policy for $n = 3$ is also optimal for all $n \ge 3$.

A comparison of the results in Fig. 17.2 with those for the deterministic version in Fig. 8.12 (p. 270) indicates:

1. For any initial inventory, i, and horizon, n, the expected cost from an optimal policy is higher when demands are stochastic.
2. Given i, the optimal decision $x_n(i)$ never decreases as n gets larger when demands are stochastic.
3. The optimal policy for an extended horizon is obtained as soon as $n = 3$ when demands are stochastic, as compared to $n = 18$ in the deterministic version.

Of course, these conclusions arise from the numerical values of the specific example, but the illustration is evidence of the general observation that the **solution characteristics** for deterministic and stochastic versions of a model can be quite disparate.

Entering Inventory	$n = 1$		$n = 2$		$n = 3$		$n = 4$		$n = 5$		Unbounded Horizon
i	$x_1(i)$	$f_1(i)$	$x_2(i)$	$f_2(i)$	$x_3(i)$	$f_3(i)$	$x_4(i)$	$f_4(i)$	$x_5(i)$	$f_5(i)$	$x_\infty(i)$
0	4	21	4	41	5	57.5	5	75.25	5	93	5
1	3	19	5	34.5	5	52.25	5	70.00	5	87.43	5
2	2	17	4	32.5	4	50.25	4	68.00	4	85.43	4
3	1	15	3	30.5	3	48.25	3	66.00	3	83.43	3
4	0	0	0	20	0	37.75	0	54.87	0	72.62	0

FIGURE 17.2. Dependable Manufacturing Company Example. Stochastic Version of Inventory Model.

17.5 OPTIMAL BATCH SIZE MODEL

The Voltex Company, a manufacturer of industrial tape recorders, purchases from a supplier some very expensive and specially made electronic components. The company does not maintain an inventory of these components, since Voltex produces only to customer order and the specifications vary widely from customer to customer. Because of the exceptionally high quality standards required for the tape recording equipment, components often fail from a short circuit during the performance inspection phase. In this event, Voltex can return the components to the supplier for a full refund. In order to avoid the expense and inconvenience of having to delay production until more components arrive from the supplier, Voltex initially orders a larger batch than it actually needs. But if Voltex orders too large a batch and consequently has excess components, it has to pay a cost penalty. (In some instances, the supplier will repurchase the excess items at a lower price than Voltex paid. But in other instances, the supplier will not buy back the component because it is so special that it is worthless to anyone else.)

The manufacturer's decision problem is to choose an optimum batch size. If the production manager at Voltex knew *exactly* how many components would fail for each batch size, his decision problem would be simple. But he does not—and that makes the analysis nontrivial.

Let

c = cost per electronic component purchased from the supplier

v = salvage value per component in excess of required amount (where $0 \leq v \leq c$)

K = expense of *reordering* if additional components are required

$p_x(j)$ = probability that j out of a batch of x components fail during the inspection process [where $p_x(x) < 1$].

As you think about the way an actual decision process of this sort would evolve over time, you will discover how to formulate the problem as a multistage optimization model. Suppose N undamaged components are required, and you place an order for $x \geq N$. If j turn out to be defective, but $j \leq x - N$, then you have met your requirement, and $x - N - j$ good components are left over as salvage. But if $j > x - N$, then you still need $N - x + j$ more. [For example, if to receive 10 good components, you order 15 and there are 6 defectives, then you still need $1 (= 10 - 15 + 6)$ more component.]

So when $j > x - N$, you have to reorder. Your decision problem at this point will be of the same character as before, except now you need fewer components (unless all that you ordered before turned out to be defective). In any event, the only information you need to have about the outcome of the previous batch is how many good components you still require. Thus, the appropriate state variable is the number of undamaged components required.

Assume that an optimal policy is one that minimizes the expected total cost to meet the requirements. Let n denote the amount required, and consider what the total expected cost is if you order x. First, you must add in the actual purchase cost less the *expected* cost of defective components from the batch, since these are returned for credit. Second, in case there were so few defectives that you have met your requirements and have some good ones left over, you must reduce the overall expected cost by the expected salvage value. Third, in case there were so many defectives that you have to reorder, you must also add in the reorder cost K, weighted by the probability of having to reorder, and likewise the expected cost because you need more components.

Consequently, letting $f(n)$ denote the minimum expected cost when n working components are required, verify that the values for $f(n)$ must satisfy

(1)
$$f(n) = \operatorname*{minimum}_{x \geq n} \left\{ c\left[x - \sum_{j=0}^{x} j p_x(j)\right] - v \sum_{j=0}^{x-n} (x - n - j) p_x(j) \right.$$
$$\left. + \sum_{j=x-n+1}^{x} [K + f(n - x + j)] p_x(j) \right\} \quad \text{for } n = 1, 2, 3, \ldots.$$

An $x(n)$ that yields $f(n)$ is an optimal batch size. The set of $x(n)$, for $n = 1, 2, 3$, ... is an optimal decision rule. (Explain how you would employ the rule.)

If N components are required, then $f(n)$ is successively computed for $n = 1, 2, \ldots, N$. But note that (1) has to be manipulated slightly because the term $f(n)$ also appears on the right-hand side of (1) for $j = x$ in the third summation. [Explain what random event causes $f(n)$ to appear on both sides of (1).] Accordingly, (1) must be simplified to yield a form suited for computational solution.

The algebra is straightforward, and leads to the formula

$$
\text{(2)} \quad f(n) = \underset{x \geq n}{\text{minimum}} \, [1 - p_x(x)]^{-1} \left\{ c \left[x - \sum_{j=0}^{x} j p_x(j) \right] - v \sum_{j=0}^{x-n} (x - n - j) p_x(j) \right.
$$
$$
\left. + K \sum_{j=x-n+1}^{x} p_x(j) + \sum_{j=x-n+1}^{x-1} f(n - x + j) \, p_x(j) \right\},
$$

where you ignore the final summation on the right for $n = 1$.

Numerical example. To illustrate (2), suppose

$$
\text{(3)} \qquad\qquad c = 10 \qquad v = 0
$$

and $p_x(j)$ is described by a binomial probability law

$$
\text{(4)} \qquad p_x(j) = \frac{x!}{j!(x-j)!} p^j (1-p)^{x-j} \quad \text{for } j = 0, 1, \ldots, x,
$$

where p is the probability of a single component failing. Then Fig. 17.3 shows the optimal batch size amounts $x(n)$, when n components are required, and when the

$$
(c = 10, v = 0)
$$

K	n	$p = \frac{1}{4}$			$p = \frac{1}{2}$			$p = \frac{3}{4}$		
		x(n)	f(n)	f(n)−cn	x(n)	f(n)	f(n)−cn	x(n)	f(n)	f(n)−cn
50	1	2	19.3	9.3	3	24.3	14.3	8	27.8	17.8
	2	3	33.5	13.5	6	38.3	18.3	13	42.7	22.7
	3	5	44.9	14.9	8	51.3	21.3	17	56.1	26.1
	5	8	68.3	18.3	12	75.7	25.7	26	80.9	30.9
	10	15	123.8	23.8	23	132.4	32.4	46	138.8	38.8
1000	1	4	34.0	24.0	7	43.1	33.1	17	50.4	40.4
	2	6	49.8	29.8	11	61.1	41.1	24	69.5	49.5
	3	8	64.4	34.4	13	76.7	46.7	30	86.2	56.2
	5	11	90.3	40.3	19	105.1	55.1	41	116.5	66.5
	10	19	151.7	51.7	31	170.5	70.5	67	184.5	84.5

Note: K = reorder cost
      c = purchase cost
      v = salvage value
      p = failure probability
      n = number required

FIGURE 17.3. Voltex Company Batch Ordering Example.

$$(c = 10, v = 0, p = \tfrac{1}{2})$$

n	\multicolumn{4}{c}{K}
	50	500	5000	50,000
1	3	6	9	13
2	6	9	13	17
3	8	12	16	20
5	12	17	22	27
10	23	30	36	41

Note: K = reorder cost
   c = purchase cost
   v = salvage value
   p = failure probability
   n = number required

FIGURE 17.4. Voltex Company Optimal Batch Size $x(n)$.

failure probability $p = \tfrac{1}{4}, \tfrac{1}{2}$, and $\tfrac{3}{4}$, and the reorder cost $K = 50$ and 1000. Of course, $x(n)$ increases as the values of n, p, and K increase. Additional information on the way $x(n)$ varies with n and K is given in Fig. 17.4, where $p = \tfrac{1}{2}$.

If the batch order size is $\bar{x}$, then the expected number of usable components is $(1 - p)\bar{x}$. Therefore when $\bar{x} = n/(1 - p)$, the expected number of usable components equals the requirement n. In the example, the value $x(n)$ is always larger than $\bar{x}$. The difference between these two values, which can be termed the **safety component**, is tabulated in Fig. 17.5. Notice that the difference increases with n; however, the *ratio* of the difference to $\bar{x}$ decreases with n. (Explain why such behavior is plausible.)

One way to assess the economic impact of uncertainty is to compare the value of $f(n)$ with cn, which is the minimum cost (to Voltex) of obtaining n usable components. The difference $[f(n) - cn]$ can be interpreted as the most the manufacturer should be willing to pay if the

$$(c = 10, v = 0)$$

K	n	\multicolumn{2}{c}{$p = \tfrac{1}{4}$}	\multicolumn{2}{c}{$p = \tfrac{1}{2}$}	\multicolumn{2}{c}{$p = \tfrac{3}{4}$}
		$\bar{x}$	$x(n) - \bar{x}$	$\bar{x}$	$x(n) - \bar{x}$	$\bar{x}$	$x(n) - \bar{x}$
50	1	1.33	.66	2	1	4	4
	5	6.66	1.33	10	2	20	6
	10	13.33	1.66	20	3	40	6
1000	1	1.33	2.66	2	5	4	13
	5	6.66	4.33	10	9	20	21
	10	13.33	5.66	20	11	40	27

Note: $\bar{x} = \dfrac{n}{1-p}$

   K = reorder cost
   c = purchase cost
   v = salvage value
   p = failure probability
   n = number required

FIGURE 17.5. Voltex Company Safety Component of Optimal Batch Size.

supplier can provide components that always work. This quantity is evaluated in Fig. 17.3 for the numerical example. Note that $[f(n) - cn]$ increases with larger values for n, the reorder cost K, and the failure probability p, but as you can verify, the value $[f(n) - cn]/n$ decreases with n. (Explain why this behavior is reasonable.)

*17.6 SALES FORECASTING PROBLEM

Each example so far had a one-dimensional state variable, and the random elements were completely independent. In the illustration below, we show how correlated random variables can be introduced at the expense of enlarging the dimension of the state variable.

Consider the following simplified version of an actual situation. During the first N weeks of a season, the Buss-Stout Company, a manufacturer of lady's sweaters, has some flexibility in adjusting the level of total production for each item in its line. In the fashion-wear industry, as in many another, a manufacturer cannot predict with certainty the total amount of orders it will receive for each item. Since the company's salesmen call on the retail trade throughout the N weeks, new bookings arrive continually during the season.

The manufacturing expenses include not only labor and materials costs but also costs due to adjusting the level of total production. The latter expense arises from the disruptions associated with substantially varying the size of the production line at the factory; it is particularly costly to increase the total production level late in the season. If the Buss-Stout Company sets the level for an item too high, it accordingly has goods left over at the end of the season, and must dispose of them at a loss. If the company schedules the level too low, it may lose potential sales revenue. And the company incurs a penalty cost if it tries to adjust the production schedule upward too much as it receives better information each week about the amount of total orders. In addition to the impact of the penalty cost, the variation in production level is also constrained to be within certain bounds, depending on the production level in the previous period as well as on how many periods in the season have elapsed.

The manufacturer's own season runs several months ahead of its customers' season. Buss-Stout produces the fall line early in the year, for example. In general, the company completes its production before the retailers' season begins, and sales revenue depends only on how many orders *in total* the company is able to fill by the time it ceases production. Consequently, Buss-Stout's scheduling problem is essentially due to the *uncertain* elements, because if it could know the amount of total orders exactly, the company would produce at an even rate throughout its season.

This scheduling problem for each item can be formulated by an optimization model. Let

D_t = *accumulated* bookings of the item at the beginning of Week t.

Since there are cancellations as well as new orders each week, D_{t+1} may be smaller than D_t. Assume that D_{t+1} depends only on D_t and is independent of earlier book-ings and the production level. Let

$p_t(D\,|\,d)$ = conditional probability that accumulated bookings D_{t+1} will equal D, *given* that accumulated bookings D_t equal d, for $t = 1, 2, \ldots$, $N - 1$

$p_N(D\,|\,d)$ = conditional probability that *total bookings* for the season will be D, given that accumulated bookings D_N equal d.

The manufacturer bases the values of these probabilities on booking statistics from previous seasons. (Suggest how you might use past data to obtain such prob-abilities.)

Also let

r = dollar return from an item sold during the season
s = dollar return from an item disposed after the end of the season
$c_t(X\,|\,x)$ = cost of setting the *total* production level at X in Week t, given that the level was set at x in the previous week,

where r and s *include* the direct labor and materials cost of manufacturing a unit, and $s < 0$. Assume that $L_t(x)$ and $U_t(x)$ are the lower and upper limits on X, representing the range of feasible levels given that x is the scheduled level just prior to Week t.

A decision rule then consists of a strategy indicating a level for current produc-tion X given values for previous production x and D_t; assume an optimal rule is one that maximizes expected return. An optimal strategy may be found by solving the dynamic programming recursion:

(1)
$$f_N(x, d) = \underset{L_N(x) \leq X \leq U_N(x)}{\text{maximum}} \left\{ \sum_{D=0}^{X} [rD + s(X - D)]\, p_N(D\,|\,d) \right.$$
$$\left. + rX \sum_{D>X} p_N(D\,|\,d) - c_N(X\,|\,x) \right\}$$

(2)
$$f_t(x, d) = \underset{L_t(x) \leq X \leq U_t(x)}{\text{maximum}} \left\{ -c_t(X\,|\,x) + \sum_D f_{t+1}(X, D)\, p_t(D\,|\,d) \right\}$$
$$\text{for } t = N - 1, \ldots, 1,$$

where the inequality $D > X$ under the second summation sign in (1) indicates that the sum is over every possible value of end-of-the-season accumulated bookings that is greater than X, and the D under the summation sign in (2) indicates that the sum is over every possible value for accumulated bookings D_{t+1}.

The value of $f_1(X^*, D^*)$ represents the maximum expected return, assuming that the preseason production level is set at X^* and bookings-to-date at the start of Week 1 are D^*. Notice that the state variable in (2) is two-dimensional; the first component reflects the previous decision and the second indicates the realized value of a random event.

To test your understanding of the formulation, write a definition for $f_N(x, d)$

and $f_t(x, d)$. Explain why the terms on the right of (1) represent the sum of expected returns, depending on whether production exceeds total bookings or vice versa, and the penalty cost of changing the production level. State how this model actually uses sales forecast data. Indicate how the formulation (1) and (2) would differ if D_{t+1} depended on both D_t and D_{t-1}.

17.7 STOCHASTIC REGENERATION MODEL—
EQUIPMENT REPLACEMENT

In this final illustration, we discuss both a finite and an unbounded horizon optimization problem. You should carefully review Sec. 11.4 before going further, as we build directly on the previous analysis and do not start afresh.

In Sec. 11.4, you studied the following deterministic problem: each time a decision process regenerates itself, the decision-maker must choose among N alternatives, which are indexed $k = 1, 2, \ldots, N$. If Alternative k is selected at a Period t, the next regeneration occurs at Period t + k. Let

(1) R_k = cost of Alternative k valued at the start of a regeneration period.

Then for the finite horizon problem, we defined

(2) f_n = present value of an optimal regeneration policy in which an alternative must be chosen when n periods remain until the end of the planning horizon,

and these values must satisfy the recursion

(3) $f_n = \underset{k=1,2,\ldots,N}{\text{minimum}} \left[\alpha^k f_{n-k} + R_k \right]$ $f_0 \equiv 0$ for $0 \leq \alpha \leq 1$,

where $n \geq N$. (For $n < N$, the minimum is taken over $k = 1, 2, \ldots, n$.)

In the infinite horizon problem the appropriate extremal equation is

(4) $f = \underset{k=1,2,\ldots,N}{\text{minimum}} \left[\alpha^k f + R_k \right]$ for $0 \leq \alpha < 1$,

yielding

(5) $f = \underset{k=1,2,\ldots,N}{\text{minimum}} \left[\frac{R_k}{1 - \alpha^k} \right]$ (present value).

Re-expressing (5) in terms of equivalent average return as

(6) $g = \underset{k=1,2,\ldots,N}{\text{minimum}} \left[\frac{R_k}{1 + \alpha + \cdots + \alpha^{k-1}} \right]$

gives

(7) $g = \underset{k=1,2,\ldots,N}{\text{minimum}} \left[\frac{R_k}{k} \right]$ for $\alpha = 1$ (average return per period).

Equipment replacement. An important example of a regeneration problem is equipment replacement. In the deterministic version, the value of k represents the length of time that a new piece of equipment is actually used.

For a stochastic version of this problem, suppose that the equipment may break down *before* the planned replacement in Period $t + k$. That is, if at Period t the planned replacement decision is k but the machine breaks down during Period $t + j$, for $j < k$, then assume the equipment must be replaced at the start of Period $t + j + 1$. Let

k = planned replacement interval

p_j = probability that the equipment breaks down for the first time during the jth period of usage

$r_j \equiv$ cost of operating the equipment during the jth period of usage if the equipment does not break down

$r_j + s_j \equiv$ cost of operating the equipment if it does break down during the jth period of usage when $j < k$ (where $s_j > 0$),

and where $\sum p_j = 1$, r_1 includes the initial purchase cost of the equipment, and for expositional simplicity, the equipment is assumed to have no salvage value. You can interpret s_j as a penalty cost for early breakdown.

Assume that an optimal policy is one that minimizes expected discounted cost. If you are at a regeneration period and your planned-replacement decision is k, then expected discounted cost is comprised of the following. First, you must add in the expected discounted cost incurred at the next regeneration point and beyond in the event that the equipment breaks down before the planned replacement period. Second, you must include the expected discounted cost at the next regeneration point and beyond in the event that the equipment does not break down before the planned replacement period. And finally, you must add the expected operating cost between this and the next regeneration point.

Accordingly, for a finite horizon, the appropriate generalization of (3) for $n \geq N$ and $0 \leq \alpha \leq 1$ is

$$(8) \qquad f_n = \operatorname*{minimum}_{k=1, 2, \ldots, N} \left[\sum_{j=1}^{k-1} \alpha^j f_{n-j} p_j + \alpha^k f_{n-k} \left(1 - \sum_{j=1}^{k-1} p_j \right) + R_k \right] \qquad f_0 \equiv 0$$

and where now

$$(9) \qquad \begin{aligned} R_k = r_1 &+ \alpha r_2 (1 - p_1) + \alpha^2 r_3 (1 - p_1 - p_2) + \cdots \\ &+ \alpha^{k-1} r_k \left(1 - \sum_{j=1}^{k-1} p_j \right) + \sum_{j=1}^{k-1} \alpha^{j-1} s_j p_j. \end{aligned}$$

Here and in the formulas below, ignore the summations whenever $k = 1$. [As before, for $n < N$, the minimum in (8) is taken over $k = 1, 2, \ldots, n$.] Verify that (8) reduces to (3) when $p_j = 0$, for $j = 1, 2, \ldots, N$. Also note that R_k in (9) depends on α, and has been omitted from the notation only for simplicity.

Unbounded horizon. For an infinite horizon, drop all the subscripts where f appears in (8). This gives the stochastic analogue of (4):

$$(10) \qquad f = \operatorname*{minimum}_{k=1, 2, \ldots, N} (E[\alpha^j | k] f + R_k) \qquad \text{for } 0 \leq \alpha < 1,$$

where

(11) $E[\alpha^j | k] \equiv \sum_{j=1}^{k-1} \alpha^j p_j + \alpha^k \left(1 - \sum_{j=1}^{k-1} p_j\right)$ (expected discount factor),

and R_k is given by (9). Analogous to (5), you can rewrite (10) as

(12) $f = \underset{k=1,2,\ldots,N}{\text{minimum}} \left(\dfrac{R_k}{1 - E[\alpha^j | k]}\right)$ for $0 \le \alpha < 1$ (expected present value).

Here f represents the expected value of discounted cost over an unbounded horizon when an optimal policy is followed.

The formulations (10) and (12) take for granted that it is optimal to use a *stationary* strategy (always select k as the planned replacement interval each time a new piece of equipment is purchased). It can be proved rigorously that such an assumption is warranted (actually the proposition can be shown to follow from the Stationary Strategy Policy Theorem in Sec. 18.3). Thus, once the expected discount factors in (11) have been calculated, the optimization in (12) is no more complex than that in (5).

For the case $\alpha = 1$, it is necessary to re-express (12) in terms of expected equivalent average return $[g = (1 - \alpha)f]$:

(13) $$g = \underset{k=1,2,\ldots,N}{\text{minimum}} \left\{\frac{(1 - \alpha)R_k}{1 - E[\alpha^j | k]}\right\},$$

which can be shown to yield

(14) $g = \underset{k=1,2,\ldots,N}{\text{minimum}} \left(\dfrac{R_k}{E[j | k]}\right)$ for $\alpha = 1$ (expected cost per period),

where R_k is calculated in (9) with $\alpha = 1$, and

(15) $E[j | k] = \sum_{j=1}^{k-1} j p_j + k \left(1 - \sum_{j=1}^{k-1} p_j\right)$ (expected replacement interval).

Observe that (15) represents the expected number of periods that each piece of equipment is used, given that the *planned* replacement interval is k. Thus the

k	p_k	r_k	s_k	R_k	$E[j \vert k]$	$\dfrac{R_k}{E[j \vert k]}$
1	$\frac{1}{4}$	100	20	100	1	100
2	0	$6\frac{2}{3}$	0^*	110	$1\frac{3}{4}$	$62\frac{6}{7}$
3	$\frac{1}{4}$	20	180	125	$2\frac{1}{2}$	50
4	0	20	0^*	180	3	60
5	0^*	56	0^*	208	$3\frac{1}{2}$	$59\frac{3}{7}$

FIGURE 17.6. Stochastic Replacement Model Example.

*The policy $k = 3$ remains optimal even if these entries are made positive

value g in (14) can be interpreted as the *minimum ratio* of *expected cost during the interval between successive replacements* to *expected interval length*. Or, loosely speaking, you can say that g is the minimum expected cost per period over an unbounded horizon. Here, too, using a stationary strategy can be justified as optimal.

An illustration of the case $\alpha = 1$ is shown in Fig. 17.6. Notice that $k = 3$ is optimal. In this illustration, costly mistakes occur if you do not correctly account for uncertainty. For example, verify that if the erroneous criterion (R_k/k) were used, then the decision would be $k = 5$; and if $(\sum_{j=1}^{k} r_j/k)$ were used, the decision would be $k = 4$. In these instances, expected cost per period would increase nearly 20% above the optimal value.

▶ It is straightforward to justify the mathematical manipulations that yield (14) and (15) as the limit of (13) when α approaches 1. For example, you can make a substitution $\epsilon \equiv 1 - \alpha$ in (13), use the binomial expansion in the denominator, and let ϵ approach 0. Or more directly, you can simply apply L'Hospital's rule. [Use these approaches to verify (14) and (15).] However, it is not trivial to give a rigorous justification of the interpretation that g is an expected cost per period over an unbounded horizon for the policy selected by (14). The reason is that there are several ways to define the meaning of "expected cost per period over an unbounded horizon."

For example, one way is to define such a quantity as the *limit* of the *ratio* of *expected costs during n periods* to *n*, as *n* gets arbitrarily large. Another way is to define the quantity as the *limit* of the *ratio* of *expected costs during T replacement intervals* to the *total number of periods in the combined intervals*, as *T* gets arbitrarily large. The questions to be answered are, "Do these limits exist?" "If so, are they equal?" It can be demonstrated that the answers are both "yes" (assuming that the corresponding R_k is finite).   ◀

17.8 APPLICABILITY AND COMPUTATIONAL FEASIBILITY OF STOCHASTIC DYNAMIC PROGRAMMING MODELS

You will find it helpful to review the summary remarks about dynamic programming in Secs. 10.9 and 10.10, since they are equally pertinent to models with stochastic elements. In brief, the most important applications of these models are in special contexts, such as finding optimal inventory replenishment rules, minimal cost maintenance and replacement policies, efficient waiting line disciplines, etc. Beyond Chap. 18, this book focuses on obtaining deeper understanding of these particular types of phenomena, and, when possible, on finding special solution techniques that exploit the structure of the phenomenon considered.

In sharp contrast to the situation pertaining to the application of linear programming, no general purpose dynamic programming computer codes are widely available. This does not represent any real drawback to the use of the technique, however, since the computational formulas for any specific problem are simple enough to be coded for computer solution on an ad hoc basis with only a modest effort.

Using advanced analytic methods, it is possible to solve stochastic dynamic programming models with less restrictive assumptions than those made in this chapter. For example, you sometimes can analyze situations in which time is treated as a continuous variable, and where the states and decisions are not necessarily discrete or finite. And in many of these cases, the approaches in this chapter are generalized in a straightforward fashion. But such extensions will not be pursued in this text.

Chapter 18 treats models in which the time horizon is unbounded. Rather than deal with a host of special examples, the results are given in terms of a network formulation; thus the approach in many ways parallels the exposition in Chap. 12. The most significant results cited are the theorems establishing the optimality of stationary policies. Whenever a specific model has a structure meeting the assumptions in the next chapter, then you can restrict your search to stationary strategies without any loss of optimality. The chapter also presents numerical techniques for solving such general network models. But as we pointed out above, you can improve on these general techniques in most applications by exploiting the special structure of the particular model. You will learn how to do this in Chap. 19 and beyond.

REVIEW EXERCISES

1 Consider the Distribution of Effort Model in Sec. 17.2. Assume the demand distribution at Store j is $p_j(d) = \frac{1}{5}$, for $d = 0, 1, \ldots, 4$. In each part below, calculate the expected profit $R_j(y_j)$, for $y_j = 0, 1, \ldots, 5$, given by (10), employing the specified profit function $r_j(d \mid y)$, as defined by (7).

(a)
$$r_j(d \mid y) = \begin{cases} 10d & \text{for } d \leq y \\ 10y & \text{for } d > y. \end{cases}$$

(b)
$$r_j(d \mid y) = \begin{cases} 10d & \text{for } d \leq y \\ 10y + 8(d - y) & \text{for } d > y. \end{cases}$$

(c) Rework part (b), using the coefficient 6, instead of 8.

(d)
$$r_j(d \mid y) = \begin{cases} 10d & \text{for } d \leq y \\ 10d - 2 & \text{for } d > y. \end{cases}$$

(e) Rework part (d), using the constant 4, instead of 2.

*(f) Suggest situations that might give rise to the profit functions in parts (b) and (d). (*Hint:* consider the possibilities of the customer purchasing another brand or the store manager expediting a resupply.)

2 Answer the questions in exercise 1, parts (a) through (e), except let the demand distributions be

(a) $p_j(d) = \dfrac{d + 1}{15}$ for $d = 0, 1, \ldots, 4$.

(b) $p_j(d) = \dfrac{5-d}{15}$ for $d = 0, 1, \ldots, 4$.

(c) $p_j(0) = p_j(4) = \frac{1}{9}, p_j(1) = p_j(3) = \frac{2}{9}, p_j(2) = \frac{3}{9}$.

(d) $p_j(0) = p_j(4) = \frac{3}{11}, p_j(1) = p_j(3) = \frac{2}{11}, p_j(2) = \frac{1}{11}$.

*3 *Shopping Basket Markets* (Sec. 17.2). Suppose the demand at the s stores are correlated. In particular, assume there are Q possible sets of values for the demands $(D_1, D_2, \ldots, D_s)$ at Stores $1, 2, \ldots, s$, and p_q is the probability of the qth set of values. Show how to determine the cost of uncertainty. (That is, indicate how to calculate the maximum value to the owner of having a perfect prediction of demand before he allocates the eggs.)

4 *Cool It Company* (Sec. 17.3). Suppose the data pertinent to the decision tree in Fig. 17.1 are

$$h_1 = 40 \quad g_1 = 50 \quad r_1 = 60 \quad p_1 = \frac{1}{5}$$

$$h_2 = 60 \quad g_2 = 70 \quad r_2 = 100 \quad p_2 = \frac{1}{2}$$

$$h_3 = 70 \quad g_3 = 80 \quad \underline{\qquad} \quad p_3 = 1.$$

(a) Calculate f_3, f_2, f_1 and exhibit the optimal strategy.

(b) Give the probability distribution for the decision process terminating in Period t, for $t = 1, 2, 3$.

(c) Explain why the expected profit is different at the beginning of Period 1 from what it is at the beginning of Period 2, *given* that the decision process continues beyond the first period.

(d) What is the largest value for r_1 such that the Period 1 decision remains optimal? Similarly, what is the smallest value for h_1? Similarly, what is the smallest value for r_2?

(e) Assuming that the decision process lasts beyond the first period, what is the smallest value for r_2 such that the Period 2 decision remains optimal? Similarly, what is the largest value for h_2? Similarly, what is the largest value for g_3?

(f) What is the largest value for p_1 such that the Period 1 decision remains optimal? Similarly, what is the largest value for p_2?

(g) Assuming that the decision process lasts beyond the first period, what is the smallest value for p_2 such that the Period 2 decision remains optimal?

*(h) Suppose that the p_t are accurate probabilities for the competitors' decisions, but that the President can purchase information indicating whether the competitors will introduce before he has to make his own decision. If the decision process lasts beyond the first period, the President can again find out whether the competitors will introduce in Period 2, etc. How much is such perfect information worth?

*5 *Cool It Company* (Sec. 17.3). Show how the value of f_1 in (2) can be obtained from a linear programming formulation. (Show all the constraints for $t = 1, 2, \ldots, T$ and each decision; display the objective function). Exhibit the model in detail for $T = 3$. Write the dual problem and interpret the variables and constraints. (*Hint:* the variables in the dual problem can be viewed as probabilities.)

Exercises 6 through 12 refer to the stochastic inventory model described in Sec. 17.4.

6 (a) Justify in detail the constraints (7) and (8).
   (b) Explain why the optimal production level x is $4 - i$ when $n = 1$.
   (c) Justify in detail each term after the first equality in (10).
   (d) Suppose the holding cost function is $h \cdot (i + x - D)^2$ for $i + x > D$, and 0 otherwise. How is (10) modified?
   (e) Verify the entries in Fig. 17.2 for $n = 2$. For $n = 3$.
   (f) Suppose there are three periods remaining in the horizon and entering inventory is 1. What is the probability distribution for the optimal production quantity in the next period? In the final period?

7 Suppose the demand distribution is $P[D = 1] = \frac{1}{3}$ and $P[D = 4] = \frac{2}{3}$.

   (a) Write the appropriate recursion analogous to (10).
   (b) Calculate $f_n(i)$ and $x_n(i)$, analogous to the entries in Fig. 17.2, for $n = 1$ and 2. For $n = 3$.

8 Suppose the demand distribution is $P[D = d] = \frac{1}{3}$ for $d = 2, 3, 4$.

   (a) Write the appropriate recursion analogous to (10).
   (b) Calculate $f_n(i)$, and $x_n(i)$, analogous to the entries in Fig. 17.2, for $n = 1$ and 2. For $n = 3$.

9 Give a plausible argument explaining why the optimal policy "settles down" so much faster (at $n = 3$) than it did in the deterministic version (at $n = 18$).

10 Suppose you drop the assumption that a stockout never occurs, so that the restriction in (7) is eliminated; whenever demand exceeds entering inventory plus production, the excess is lost. Suppose, however, the company earns revenue r per item of demand filled. Let the symbol $p(q)$ denote the probability that demand is q, where $q = 0, 1, 2, \ldots$. Show how to alter the recursion (10) accordingly. (*Note:* the objective is to maximize expected profit.)

11 (a) Suppose the minimization criterion is expected *discounted* cost, where the one-period discount factor is $\alpha, 0 \leq \alpha \leq 1$. Show how to alter the recursion (10) accordingly.
   (b) Suppose there is a probability $q, 0 \leq q \leq 1$, representing at each period the chance that the items will not be needed anymore in future periods. In other words, q is the probability that the horizon does not last beyond the current period; if, however, the items *are* demanded in the next period, then again probability q is the chance that the horizon does not extend beyond the second period, etc. Show how to alter the recursion (10) accordingly.

12 Suppose the company can obtain a perfect forecast of each period's demand. That is, prior to choosing production x, suppose the company can learn the actual level of demand. [This amount still varies from period to period according to the probability distribution in (6).]

(a) Formulate a dynamic programming recursion to find an optimal policy. (*Hint:* you can let the state variable be entering inventory minus current demand.)

(b) Calculate optimal policies for $n = 1, 2, 3, 4$.

(c) What is the maximum worth to the company of having such a perfect forecast if the horizon $n = 1$? If $n = 2$? If $n = 3$? Assume initial inventory at the start of the horizon equals 0.

13 *Voltex Company* (Sec. 17.5)

(a) Give a verbal interpretation of each term in the recursion (1).

*(b) Give the detailed algebraic justification for transforming (1) into (2).

(c) Consider the data in Fig. 17.3. Suppose you require three items, $K = 50$, and $p = \frac{1}{4}$. Explain the optimal strategy in detail. What is the maximum number of items that may be ordered? (Be careful!) Is it possible that you would ever place an order for three items more than once?

*(d) What is the expected number of items ordered in part (c)?

(e) How do your answers to the questions in part (c) change if $p = \frac{1}{2}$?

14 *Voltex Company* (Sec. 17.5). Consider the policies in Fig. 17.3. Verify the values of $x(n)$ and $f(n)$ for

(a) $K = 50$, $n = 1, 2, 3$, and $p = \frac{1}{4}$.

(b) $K = 50$, $n = 1$, $p = \frac{1}{2}$.

(c) $K = 1000$, $n = 1$, $p = \frac{1}{4}$.

15 *Voltex Company* (Sec. 17.5). Suppose the salvage value $v > 0$. How are $x(n)$ and $f(n)$ in Fig. 17.3 affected? Corroborate your economic intuition by letting $v = 5$, $K = 50$, $p = \frac{1}{4}$, and finding $x(n)$ and $f(n)$ for $n = 1, 2, 3$.

16 *Voltex Company* (Sec. 17.5)

(a) Consider the tabulation of the safety components in Fig. 17.5. Give a plausible explanation of why the ratio of the safety component to $\bar{x} = n/(1 - p)$ decreases with n.

(b) Give a plausible explanation of why the ratio $[f(n) - cn]/n$ decreases with n, where the bracketed quantity is tabulated in Fig. 17.3.

17 Consider the Optimal Batch Size Model in Sec. 17.5. Suppose N working items are required. Show how the value of $f(N)$ can be obtained from a linear programming formulation. (Show all the constraints for $n = 1, 2, \ldots, N$, and each x; assume that you have an upper bound X_n on x when n items are required.) Write the entire problem in detail for $N = 3$, $X_1 = 3$, $X_2 = 4$, and $X_3 = 5$. Also write the dual problem and interpret the variables and constraints. (*Hint:* the variables in the dual problem can be viewed as probabilities.)

*18 *Buss-Stout Company* (Sec. 17.6)

(a) Explain each term in the dynamic programming recursions (1) and (2). (Specifically, state how the formulation includes the expenses of labor and materials, as well as the costs of adjusting the level of total production. Indicate how disposal loss is accounted for, and how the formulation implies that there is a revenue loss if the production level is too low.) Write a definition for $f_N(x, d)$ and $f_t(x, d)$.

(b) Explain what factors influence the values for the lower and upper limits on accumulated production in Week t, namely, $L_t(x)$ and $U_t(x)$. (Explain why these limits ordinarily depend both on the scheduled level x in the previous week and on the week itself.) Do the same for the cost function $c_t(X | x)$.

(c) Explain what decision rules emerge from the solution of the recursions. Does the analysis yield a production quantity for each week? If not, suggest how to determine the weekly production level from the analysis.

*(d) How does the formulation (1) and (2) differ if D_{t+1} depends on both D_t and D_{t-1}? (Be sure to define any new symbols you introduce.)

(e) Suppose that the disposal value $s > 0$. How, if at all, does this affect the recursion (1) and an optimal policy?

(f) Many companies like this one use statistical demand forecasting techniques. Is the information conveyed by the probability distributions $p_t(D | d)$ and $p_N(D | d)$ the same as a demand forecast? Explain. Why would you expect these probabilities to depend on both the accumulated bookings in Week t as well as Week t itself?

Exercises 19 through 25 refer to the Stochastic Replacement Model described in Sec. 17.7.

19 Consider the finite horizon problem.

(a) Explain each term in the recursion (8).

(b) Derive the formula (9) for R_k. (Start with the conceptualization that the equipment may break down in either the first, second, third, ..., kth period of usage, or not at all during the planned replacement interval.)

*20 Consider the finite horizon problem. Let the horizon length be 6 and $N = 3$. Show how f_6 also can be found by a linear programming formulation. Write the dual problem and interpret the variables and restrictions.

21 Consider the infinite horizon problem.

(a) Perform the algebra justifying the statement that dropping the subscripts on f_j in (8) yields (10).

(b) Why is the expression in (11) termed the *expected discount factor*? Give a verbal interpretation of the formula. Answer the corresponding questions for the expression in (15).

*(c) Show that (14) and (15) result from letting α approach 1 as a limiting value in (13).

22 (a) Verify all the entries in the examples shown in Fig. 17.6.

(b) Show why the policy $k = 3$ remains optimal even if the entries marked 0* are made positive.

23 Consider the example in Fig. 17.6, where $\alpha = 1$. Suppose the horizon is finite and let $N = 5$.

(a) Apply the recursion (8) to find an optimal policy for $n = 1, 2, \ldots, 6$.

(b) Do the same, but let $\alpha = \frac{1}{2}$.

24 (a) Suppose there is a probability q, where $0 \leq q \leq 1$, that the equipment will not have to be *replaced* again (because it will not be needed). Show how to alter the formulations for both the finite and infinite horizon models.

(b) Given that the equipment *is* needed in any Period t, suppose there is a probability q, where $0 \leq q \leq 1$, that the equipment will *not* be required in any future periods. Show how to alter the formulations for both the finite and infinite horizon models.

*25 Suppose that when a new piece of equipment is purchased, the probability that the equipment breaks down during the jth period of usage is still p_j, but that you can know with certainty in which period a failure actually occurs. Hence you may decide to keep the equipment anywhere from 1 to j periods.

(a) Formulate a dynamic programming recursion for the finite horizon problem.

(b) Formulate a dynamic programming recursion for the infinite horizon problem and discuss how to calculate an optimal policy. (Assume the discount factor satisfies $0 \leq \alpha < 1$.)

(c) Given your answer to part (a), apply the recursion to the data in Fig. 17.6, where $\alpha = 1$; let $N = 5$. Find an optimal policy for $n = 1, 2, \ldots, 6$.

(d) Rework part (c), letting $\alpha = \frac{1}{2}$.

26 Explain your understanding of the following terms:

decision rules
decision tree
backward induction
solution characteristics
safety component (in the Batch Size Model).

FORMULATION AND COMPUTATIONAL EXERCISES

In the exercises below, you are asked to formulate models in terms of dynamic programming recursions. Be sure to define all the symbols you use, and give the appropriate optimization function when there is a single period (stage) remaining. Explain how to initiate and when to terminate the calculations.

27 The Ball Sapphire Company is planning its annual budget for the exploration of sites at which to mine rare gems. The company has N potential locations. The President and Chief Geologist, Mr. Ball, estimates that if d_j dollars are spent in digging at Location j, then there is a probability $p_j(d_j)$ of finding gem stones, and *if* there is a successful finding, the return or value of the site will be v_j, where v_j is a random variable with probability distribution $q_j(v_j)$. Formulate a dynamic programming model to determine an exploration budget not to exceed D dollars that maximizes expected total return.

28 *Ghengis Motor Company* (Sec. 10.3). The previous objective function for this example was to maximize net return from a radio advertising budget. Suppose, instead, that the company wants most to reach a certain type of customer with its ads. It estimates that each daytime spot announcement on Station j has a probability p_j of reaching the

desired type of customer, where p_j is assumed independent of the total number of spots on that station; recall $K_j(y_j)$ is the number of daytime spots aired on Station j from an allocation of y_j dollars. Similarly, let q_j denote the probability of reaching this type of customer in a prime time, and let $H_j(y_j)$ denote the number of such prime-time spots obtained on Station j with an allocation of y_j dollars. Define an optimal allocation to be one that minimizes the probability that the desired type of customer misses all of the commercials.

(a) Formulate the problem as a mathematical model, and show how a dynamic programming approach, analogous to that in Sec. 10.3, can be used to find an optimal solution.

(b) Show how to alter the formulation in part (a) if the objective is to maximize the expected number of times such a customer hears the company's ads.

29 The Saki Tumi Company is a Japanese manufacturer of portable television sets. It is designing a high-priced model and wants to ensure maximum reliability. The set contains N circuits in series, so that a failure in any one of the circuits causes the set to malfunction. Therefore, the design will include redundant parallel circuitry. Specifically, let x_n denote the number of parallel elements placed in the nth circuit, let $p_n(x)$ denote the probability that the nth circuit operates properly during the first year of usage, given a redundancy level x, and let $c_n(x)$ be the corresponding manufacturing cost.

(a) Formulate an optimization model that maximizes the first-year reliability of the set, subject to the constraint that total manufacturing cost cannot exceed C.

(b) Show how the model can be solved by dynamic programming.

(c) Use your answer to part (b) to find an optimal solution for $N = 3$, where $c_n(x) = nx^2$, $C = 15$, and $p_n(x) \equiv 1 - p_n^x$, where $p_1 = .08$, $p_2 = .05$, $p_3 = .1$.

(d) Formulate an optimization model that minimizes cost subject to the constraint that first-year reliability of the set be at least R. Show the model can be solved by dynamic programming.

30 Rock Kitt and his crew are planning a space mission to a distant planet. They must carry N different types of electronic gear, which, even in this day and age, are prone to failure. Each unit of Equipment i weighs w_i pounds, and there is a total weight restriction W. The value of W is large enough to permit taking along a limited number of spares to be put into operation when a piece of equipment fails. Let $p_i(t)$ be the probability distribution of the number of periods t that a unit of Equipment i operates before it breaks down (and must be discarded), and let x_i be the number of spares of Equipment i that Kitt takes along. When the supply of any of the types of equipment is exhausted (that is, when, for any Equipment i, all x_i have broken down) the mission has to return to Earth.

(a) Devise a dynamic programming model for selecting the quantities x_i to maximize the expected time the mission stays on the planet. (*Note:* all N types of equipment are operated continuously on the mission.)

(b) Devise a dynamic programming model for selecting the quantities x_i to maximize the probability that the mission stays on the planet at least T periods.

(c) Explain how to revise the answers to parts (a) and (b) if each piece of Equipment i costs c_i and there is a total cost restriction C.

31 Newton Dewing has to solve a difficult homework problem for his operations research course. He knows from past experience that if he works too long on a problem, he goes "stale." Hence, he realizes that he may have to make several tries. Let $p_q(t)$ denote the probability that he solves the problem if he allocates t hours on the qth trial. He wants to minimize the probability of his failing to solve the problem.

(a) Formulate a dynamic programming model to give him an optimal strategy assuming that he will spend no more than T hours in total trying to solve the problem. (*Note:* he may take as many as T trials, each one lasting one hour. Also, at the qth trial he can not have more than $T - q + 1$ hours left, since each trial must take at least one hour.)

(b) Show how the formulation simplifies if $p_q(t)$ does *not* depend on q, that is, if the probability of solution at each trial depends only on the number of hours t that is spent and not on how many previous trials there have been.

*(c) Show how the formulation becomes more complicated if the probability of success at the qth trial also depends on the total number of hours previously allocated to solving the problem.

32 Professor Frank N. Stein is notorious for his monstrous examinations. This term he is offering his students the opportunity to take a treacherously planned oral exam. He will ask a series of questions, each question being progressively more difficult. If the student correctly answers Question k, where $k = 1, 2, \ldots, K$, he can exercise the option of going on to the next (more difficult) question or terminating the exam and receiving the grade G_k, where $G_k < G_{k+1}$. If he misses Question k, Professor Stein flunks him. Suppose you are a student in this class, and you estimate p_k to be the probability of your correctly answering Question k.

(a) Formulate a dynamic programming model that gives you a rule for when to voluntarily terminate the examination if you have not already flunked—your objective is to maximize the expected grade you receive.

(b) Alter your formulation in part (a) if Professor Stein looks kindly upon you and allows you to make one error before flunking. (*Note:* if you decline Question k and missed Question k-1, your grade is G_{k-2}.)

33 The Chuckles Ice Cream Company operates a fleet of small trucks that cruise through residential districts and sell products directly to consumers. Assume that there are I products, where $i = 1, 2, \ldots, I$, and each unit of Product i requires c_i cubic inches of space in a truck. The total cubic space available on a truck is C. Consider the route of a particular truck and assume that the demand q_i for Product i is described by a continuous uniform distribution, having the density function

$$p_i(q_i) = \begin{cases} \dfrac{1}{b_i} & \text{for } 0 \leq q_i \leq b_i \\ 0 & \text{otherwise.} \end{cases}$$

Let x_i be the number of units of Product i loaded into the truck; for simplicity, assume x_i is a continuous nonnegative variable. Since all the products sell for the same price, the company sets as its objective to minimize the expected number of unsatisfied demands per trip.

(a) Formulate the optimization problem for loading the truck. Explain how it can be solved by dynamic programming.

*(b) Discuss alternative approaches of solution that exploit the fact that the problem consists of a special type of nonlinear objective function subject to a single linear constraint in nonnegative variables.

*(c) Apply your proposed method in part (b) to the data $I = 4$ and

$$c_1 = 1 \qquad c_2 = \frac{5}{3} \qquad c_3 = \frac{9}{3} \qquad c_4 = \frac{10}{3}$$

$$b_1 = 20 \qquad b_2 = 24 \qquad b_3 = 25 \qquad b_4 = 27$$

and $C = 5$, 15, and 75.

34 Ivan Tew is a salesman for the Suburban Life Insurance Company. This week he will make as many as T telephone calls during the evening hours in trying to reach n potential clients. He estimates that Individual j may buy a policy worth v_j. To keep matters simple, suppose that he decides to allocate up to x_j calls in order to reach Individual j, where the sum of the x_j cannot exceed T. If he reaches Individual j before making x_j calls, assume he does *not* reallocate the unused calls to other potential clients. Let the probability that he can reach Individual j be p_j for each call he makes to j, and assume this probability is independent of the previous (unsuccessful) calls he has made. He wants to select the x_j to minimize the expectation of the estimated policy values for all those individuals he fails to reach during the week.

(a) Formulate the problem as a mathematical optimization model. Show how a solution can be found using dynamic programming.

*(b) Show how to formulate the problem if Tew does not select the x_j at the beginning of the week, but makes his calling decisions one by one (depending on which potential clients he has not yet reached). Will this formulation yield a lower expected value than that in part (a)? Explain.

35 The Dolittle Washing Machine Company has been approached by Slips, a large chain of retail department stores, to manufacture a specially branded line of washing machines for sole distribution by Slips. Dolittle's annual profit is currently $1 million, and Slips' proposition will bring about an annual contribution to profit of $250 thousand. But the promotion of these machines by Slips will cut into Dolittle's own sales in such a way that the profit on its current business will drop by 25% with probability .1, 30% with probability .6, and 35% with probability .3.

If Dolittle turns Slips down, then there is a .4 chance that a competitor will accept Slips' offer. In that case, Dolittle stands to lose profit, as already described, unless it undertakes a costly advertising campaign or lowers its price. The advertising budget will reduce profit by $100 thousand; as a result, the profit on current business will only decline by 10% with probability .2, 15% with probability .7, and 20% with probability .1. The price cut has the combined effect of keeping the profit-reduction to 10% with probability .1, 15% with probability .8, and 20% with probability .1, *provided* that competition does not also reduce price. But there is a probability .5 that competition meets the price cut, in which case profit will decline by 10% with probability .1, 15% with probability .6, and 20% with probability .3. Construct a decision tree showing the structure of the problem, and determine an optimal strategy.

36 The Trans-Send Television Network has an elaborate approach for developing and selecting programs to be viewed over its affiliate TV stations. Each possible program

goes through one or more stages of idea review, script development, pilot testing, and audience preview. (Actually some of these stages are subdivided into component stages.) Suppose there are at most T stages, and let c_t denote the cost of making the tth review. A program is judged a hit if the audience reaction is high, as determined by the Neil Downe TV Rating Service; the network stands to gain r dollars in revenue from a hit. The probability of a hit is p. But if a program turns out to be a bomb, the network earns only s dollars, where $s < r$. Since Trans-Send can always show old movies which earn v dollars, where $s < v < r$, it does not want to air a bomb.

If the program *is* going to be a hit, then p_t is the probability that the tth stage of review judges it so; *if* the program *is* going to bomb, then q_t is the probability that the tth review judges it so. Assume that after the tth review, you can safely ignore the review test information from the previous stages. Thus, given the tth review outcome, you can calculate the probability of a hit using p_t or q_t along with p. After each review, Trans-Send can choose to drop the program from further development (and show a movie in the time slot), or to go on to the next review stage, or to air the show without any further reviewing stages.

(a) Let $T = 4$, and draw a decision tree for the review process.

(b) Devise a dynamic programming formulation for determining a review strategy that maximizes expected net return (that is, earnings less total reviewing costs).

(c) Compute an optimal strategy for $s = 50$, $v = 100$, $r = 200$, $p = \frac{1}{4}$, and

$$p_1 = \frac{1}{3} \quad p_2 = \frac{1}{2} \quad p_3 = \frac{2}{3} \quad p_4 = \frac{3}{4}$$

$$q_1 = \frac{9}{10} \quad q_2 = \frac{3}{4} \quad q_3 = \frac{1}{2} \quad q_4 = \frac{5}{6}$$

$$c_1 = 1 \quad c_2 = 10 \quad c_3 = 30 \quad c_4 = 5.$$

37 The Eurohne Bag Company has made considerable profits on the sale of its major product due to a lack of any direct competition. The President of the company believes that in all likelihood the Micks Bag Company will announce a highly competitive product. To ward off a significant drop in his share of market, the President is going to allocate D dollars for advertising during the next T months. He estimates that the probability is p_t that Micks Bag will enter the market in Month t, if it has not already done so by then (assume $p_T = 1$ and that each p_t is unaffected by Eurohne's advertising strategy). If the President allocates d dollars in Period t to advertising, he can purchase $m_t(d)$ "messages." He feels that if his competitor enters the market at the end of Period t and if he has accumulated M advertising messages over the first t periods, then his company has a probability $q_t(M)$ of maintaining most of its present share. Formulate an advertising expenditure strategy that maximizes the probability of the Eurohne Bag Company retaining its market position.

38 Consider the *deterministic* inventory model, summarized by (1) through (3) in Sec. 17.4. Suppose that the production cost function is random

$$C(x) = \begin{cases} 0 & \text{for } x = 0 \\ 13 + cx & \text{for } x = 1, 2, \ldots, 5, \end{cases}$$

where $P[c = 1] = P[c = 3] = \frac{1}{2}$.

(a) Assume that the production quantity x must be decided each period *prior* to knowing the value of c. Formulate the appropriate dynamic programming recursion, and indicate how it differs from (4) and (5).

(b) Assume that the production quantity x is decided after learning the value of c. Formulate the appropriate dynamic programming recursion.

(c) Find optimal policies in part (b) for $n = 1, 2, \ldots, 5$.

39 Consider the stochastic inventory model in Sec. 17.4, characterized by the recursion (10). Suppose that when one or more units of inventory exist at the end of a period, there is a probability $\frac{1}{5}$ that one of these units is damaged beyond use.

(a) Show how to alter the recursion (10) accordingly.

*(b) Find an optimal policy for $n = 1, 2, 3$.

40 Consider the stochastic inventory model described in Sec. 17.4. Suppose that $\bar{x}$ represents a "target" production level each period, and that if actual production x deviates from $\bar{x}$, a "smoothing cost" $v \cdot |x - \bar{x}|$ is incurred, where $\bar{x}$ is a prespecified constant.

(a) Show how to reformulate (10) to take account of this smoothing cost.

*(b) Let $v = 1$ and $\bar{x} = 3$. Find an optimal solution for $n = 1, 2, \ldots, 5$.

41 Consider the example of the Elementary Inventory Model with stochastic demands in Sec. 17.4. Suppose that the value of demand in Period t influences the value in Period t + 1. Specifically, assume that

$$P[D_{t+1} = 2 \,|\, D_t = 2] = \frac{4}{5} \quad P[D_{t+1} = 4 \,|\, D_t = 2] = \frac{1}{5}$$

$$P[D_{t+1} = 2 \,|\, D_t = 4] = \frac{1}{5} \quad P[D_{t+1} = 4 \,|\, D_t = 4] = \frac{4}{5}.$$

(a) Write a dynamic programming recursion analogous to (10).

(b) Find an optimal policy for $n = 1, 2, \ldots, 5$, and compare the results to those in Fig. 17.2. Assume $D_0 = 2$.

(c) Rework part (b), assuming that

$$P[D_{t+1} = 2 \,|\, D_t = 2] = \frac{1}{5} \quad P[D_{t+1} = 4 \,|\, D_t = 2] = \frac{4}{5}$$

$$P[D_{t+1} = 2 \,|\, D_t = 4] = \frac{4}{5} \quad P[D_{t+1} = 4 \,|\, D_t = 4] = \frac{1}{5}.$$

Also compare the results with those in part (b).

(d) What is the average demand per period over an unbounded horizon in part (b)? In part (c)?

42 *Equipment Replacement with Uncertain Costs.* Consider the example of the Rhode-Bloch Trucking Company in Sec. 6.5. Suppose the cost of a new piece of equipment leased at the start of Year i and replaced at the start of Year j is a random variable. Specifically, let r be a random variable having probability distribution $p_i(r)$ in Year i, and assume that the cost of initiating rental in Year i and replacing in Year j is given by a function $c_{ij}(r)$. Also assume that when a replacement occurs in Year i, the value of r in Year i is known before the decision is made to next replace at Year j. *See parts (a) and (b) on p. 730.*

(a) Formulate an appropriate dynamic programming model.

(b) Suppose that the probability distribution of r in Year i depends on the value of r in the previous year; let $p_i(r|r_{i-1})$ designate this probability distribution, where at $i = 1$, the value of r_0 is known exactly. Show how to alter the formulation in part (a) accordingly.

43 *Shortest-Route Model* (Sec. 6.5). Consider the example in Fig. 6.8. Suppose that the arc costs are random and that traversing each arc requires one period. Assume that during Period t, the arc cost c_{ij}, where $c_{ij} = 0, 1, 2, \ldots$, occurs with probability $p_{ij,t}(c_{ij})$. Assume that each arc cost each period is completely independent of all the other random events. Suppose you can learn the actual value of c_{ij} only when the system arrives at Node i. The objective is to select a route from Node 8 (source) to Node 1 (sink) that minimizes expected total cost; the route must end no later than Period T. (*Note:* the *entire* route is *not* selected at the beginning of the horizon; each period, you select an arc, depending on the current node and the arc costs.)

(a) Formulate a dynamic programming model to find an optimal strategy.

*(b) Suppose the number of periods to traverse arc (i, j) is random. Specifically, assume that during Period t, the arc time d_{ij}, where $d_{ij} = 1, 2, \ldots$, occurs with probability $q_{ij,t}(d_{ij})$. Suppose you can learn the actual value of d_{ij} only after you have selected arc (i, j). Show how to alter your formulation in part (a) accordingly.

44 *Stagecoach Problem* (Sec. 8.2). Consider the data in Fig. 8.1 and let $c_{ij}/20$ represent the probability that Mark Off does not survive the journey from State i to State j; for example, the probability of mortal danger in traveling from State 2 to State 6 is $c_{26}/20 = \frac{3}{5}$. Find a route that maximizes Mark Off's probability of survival. If you were Mark Off, would you take the trip? Explain.

*45 *Assortment Problem* (exercise 52 of Chap. 9). Suppose Itsa Steel does not know the exact amounts for the demand requirements D_j when it has to select the assortment of strengths. The company does, however, learn the demand quantities prior to the actual manufacturing of the beams. Let $P[D_j = D] \equiv p_j(D)$ be the demand distribution for Beam j. Show how to formulate the problem as a dynamic programming model.

46 Consider the study-time allocation problem of Howie Kramms, described in exercises 23 and 24 of Chap. 10. Suppose the grade point assessments given in those exercises occur only with probability $\frac{3}{4}$, and that the actual outcomes are one grade point lower with probability $\frac{1}{4}$. For example, if Howie studies three periods, he receives three grade points with probability $\frac{3}{4}$ and two grade points with probability $\frac{1}{4}$. Assume each random event is completely independent of the others.

(a) Formulate a dynamic programming model and find a solution; assume that Howie's objective is to maximize the expected number of grade points he receives.

(b) Assume instead, that Howie's objective is to maximize the probability that he receives at least nine grade points. Revise your formulation in part (a) accordingly.

47 Consider the cattle ranching problem in exercise 32 of Chap. 10. Suppose that the revenue received in Year n is $R_n(y_n|p)$, where p is a random variable representing a general price level, and $q_n(p)$ designates the probability distribution of p in Year n.

Also assume that the herd not sent to market increases in size by f-fold by the beginning of the following year, where $q(f)$ denotes the associated probability distribution for f. Formulate a dynamic programming recursion to determine how many cattle to send to market in each of the N periods; assume that

(a) The value of p is *not* known until after y_n is chosen.
(b) The value of p *is* known prior to choosing y_n.

48 *Capacity Expansion Problem* (exercise 33 of Chap. 10). Suppose each capacity requirement R_t is random, with probability distribution $p_t(R)$. Assume that $H_t(C, R)$ is also defined for $R > C$, and in that case includes a penalty cost for having too little capacity. Formulate the expansion model in terms of a dynamic programming recursion; assume that

(a) The value of R_t is *not* known until after x_t is chosen.
(b) The value of R_t *is* known before x_t is chosen.

49 *ARKA Mutual Fund Problem* (exercise 34 of Chap. 10). Suppose ARKA's gift of perfect prophecy is nullified, and instead, ARKA knows only the probability distribution $q_t(p)$ for the security price in a future Period t. Assume that when Period t occurs, the actual value of p_t becomes known before x_t is chosen.

(a) Formulate the problem in terms of a dynamic programming recursion, and assume that ARKA wants to maximize the expected total amount of cash it can accumulate by the end of the horizon.
*(b) Show how to alter the formulation in part (a) if the price in Period t depends on the price in the previous period, and the associated probability distribution is denoted by $q_t(p \mid p_{t-1})$.

50 Consider the case of the Feedem-Speedem Airline Company, described in exercise 32 of Chap. 2. Let the flight service requirement in Month t be D_t, where D_t has a probability distribution $p_t(D_t)$. Assume that D_t becomes known at the beginning of each month, and that the company must pay a penalty cost C for each stewardess-flight-hour that is required in excess of the time actually available for flight service during that month. Show how to find an optimal hiring and training schedule by means of dynamic programming.

51 Ina Rush is a busy lawyer with a passion for peanut brittle. Each day she passes a crowded candy store and faces the "moment of truth" as to whether to enter. Addicted to rationality as well as sweets, she estimates that each minute of her time is worth c; so if she waits w minutes in line, the associated waiting cost is cw. The candy, however, is worth r (measured in the same units as cw). She has carefully observed that if there are n customers in the store ahead of her, then there is a probability $p_n(s)$ that s of them will be served each minute (for the sake of simplicity, assume the random events take place in intervals of a minute and are independent in successive minutes). She limits the time she is willing to wait until being served to T minutes, and is psychologically prepared to leave the store if she finds the service is too slow.

(a) Formulate a dynamic programming model to find an optimal policy for entering or leaving the store that maximizes Miss Rush's expected value.
(b) Explain whether the formulation changes if Miss Rush only leaves the store after she is served or when the T minutes have elapsed.

52 Each year Willie B. Poore allocates funds between personal consumption and investment in either common stocks or bonds. Let $U_t(c)$ represent the value, or utility, to
Poore in Year t of spending c dollars on consumption. Let r_s denote the return per
dollar invested in stocks (that is, a dollar put into stocks at the beginning of the
year yields r_s dollars at the beginning of the next year). Similarly, let r_b denote the
return per dollar invested in bonds. Let $p_t(r_s)$ and $q_t(r_b)$ be the associated probability
distributions of the returns in Period t. (Assume these distributions are discrete, and
$r_s \geq 0$ and $r_b \geq 0$.) Suppose Poore's horizon is T years and he starts with M dollars.
He wants to maximize the expected sum of his consumption utilities over the entire
planning horizon; assume cash after Period T is of no value to him.

(a) Exhibit a dynamic programming model that finds an optimal consumption and
investment policy.
(b) Discuss how the formulation is changed if he revises his probability estimates each
year on the basis of the previous year's return performance in stocks and bonds.
(c) Show how to alter the formulation if Poore does not have a fixed horizon T,
but instead estimates that if he is still living in Year t, he will survive another year
with probability l_t, where $l_t = 0$ for $t > T$. [Make the beneficent assumption
that if Poore dies during Period t, he will have already enjoyed $U_t(c)$.]

53 James Stock, Agent 0007, is assigned to make photocopies of documents in the secret
files of The Unfriendly Country. There are two such files, situated in separate locations.
File X has M documents to be copied and File Y has N documents. Agent 0007
figures that he can make at most T tries at photographing the documents. For each
picture-taking session, he believes the probability is p_X that he will be caught when
rifling through File X, and similarly p_Y for File Y. Assume that if Stock gets caught,
it means the demise of his life and camera. If he selects File X on his tth trial and it
contains m documents remaining to be copied, he estimates that he can photograph
$g(m)$; similarly, if he selects File Y and it has n documents remaining, he can photograph $h(n)$.

(a) Construct a dynamic programming model to devise a strategy that maximizes the
expected number of documents photographed.
*(b) Suppose the probability is q_X for File X and q_Y for File Y that he hears a guard
approaching while he is rifling a file. When this happens, he is able to slip away
but must forego taking photographs during this attempt. Show how to revise your
formulation in part (a) accordingly. (Assume that hearing a guard and being
caught are mutually exclusive events and $p_X + q_X < 1$, and $p_Y + q_Y < 1$.)

54 Hedda Gambler is a bettin' woman and unlucky only in love. On each of the next N
days, she has the opportunity to wager money on probabilistic outcomes. Assume she
begins with I dollars and each day can bet any sum up to the amount she has at the
start of the day. If she bets y_n dollars on Day n, the probability is p_n of increasing her
capital by the same amount and the probability is $1 - p_n$ of losing that amount. She
wants to maximize the probability that she has S dollars at the end of the N days.

(a) Formulate a dynamic programming recursion to find an optimal betting level
each day, given the amount of cash at the start of the day.
(b) Suppose the situation is altered so that if she bets y_n dollars on Day n, she has
probability $\frac{1}{4}$ of increasing her capital by $(8p_n - 1)y_n$, where p_n is the same

quantity as above, and probability $\frac{3}{4}$ of losing y_n. Show how to revise the formulation in part (a) accordingly.

(c) Assume $N = 3$, $I = 1$, $p_1 = \frac{3}{8}$, $p_2 = \frac{5}{8}$, and $p_3 = \frac{1}{2}$. Find optimal policies in parts (a) and (b) for $S = 3$. For $S = 6$. Draw the corresponding decision trees.

(d) Given the probabilistic assumptions in parts (a) and (b), show formulations appropriate to the objective of maximizing the expected amount of cash at the end of Day N.

(e) Apply the formulations in part (d) to the data in part (c) and find optimal policies.

55 *Cash Management Problem.* New York bankers always look forward to meeting their friends at the Bankers Tryst, a long established annual convention in the Poconos. This year members of the Chaste National Bank have proposed the following service-charge structure for corporate bank accounts. Each time a corporation makes a direct deposit or withdrawal of cash from its account, the bank will charge D or W, respectively. These cash transactions must occur at the start of the day. During the day, the balance of the corporation's account fluctuates due to deposited checks from creditors and due to other companies cashing the checks the corporation has written. If the balance falls below 0, the bank will automatically lend the customer the additional amount at the interest charge of r per dollar per day.

Suppose you are a Chaste customer and assess that your "opportunity cost" is s per dollar per day (that is, you can earn s on each dollar invested elsewhere). Assume that s, like r, is assessed on the bank balance at the end of the day. Let q be the amount by which the level of your account fluctuates during a day, and let $p_t(q)$ be the probability distribution of q on the tth day. Note that q may be either positive or negative.

(a) Formulate a finite horizon dynamic programming model to determine the optimal amount of cash to deposit or withdraw at the start of each day.

(b) Show how your formulation changes if the transaction service and interest charges are deducted from your account.

56 An end-of-the-year sale on late model automobiles is being held by the Wheeler Dealer Agency. The firm has N autos it wants to sell in the next T days. The agency owner estimates that if he has n autos on Day t and sets the price at r, he can sell s autos that day with probability $p_t(s|r, n)$, where $s = 0, 1, \ldots, n$. If he has any cars left at the end of Day T, he realizes a value v on each. Formulate a dynamic programming model that sets price each day so as to maximize Wheeler's expected return on the N autos.

57 The Plutocratic Party, a national political organization, is trying to gain support for its Presidential candidate. It intends to spend as much as S dollars in newspaper advertisements over the next T weeks to raise campaign funds. If it has raised r dollars by the beginning of Week t, then $p_t(r_t|r, s_t)$ is the probability that it will raise r_t dollars during the tth week, given that it spends s_t on advertising. The Party wants to advertise in such a way as to maximize the expected number of dollars raised (inclusive of unspent advertising funds).

(a) Show how an optimal strategy for the amount of advertising to be done each week can be found using dynamic programming.

(b) Show how to alter the formulation in part (a) if S dollars are available at the beginning of Week 1 and the Party is willing to spend any additional funds it raises during the ensuing weeks to finance further advertising.

58 The Buy-and-Bye Food Store gives its customers excellent service by keeping open sufficient checkout stands to take care of the afternoon rush hour surge of customers. The manager has gathered data on the number of customers that enter the store in each period (15 minutes) as well as on the number of customers m served during a period, which depends on both the number of customers in the store and the number of checkers s. Let $p_t(e)$ denote the probability that e customers enter the store at Period t (for simplicity, assume they enter at the start of the period). Let $q_t(m \mid n, s)$ be the probability that m customers are served during Period t, given that n are in the store at the beginning of the period and s checkout stands are open. Let w be the cost per period per checkout stand open. The manager makes a rough estimate of a commensurate cost due to customers waiting for checkout. Assume that this cost is h_t per customer remaining in the store at the end of Period t.

(a) Formulate a dynamic programming model to determine an optimal policy during the rush hours, which consist of T periods.

(b) Show how to alter your formulation in part (a) if there is an added cost K each time a checkout stand is opened up (hence, the cost is pK if p stands are opened up in a period).

MIND-EXPANDING EXERCISES

59 A beverage manufacturer is planning to introduce a new instant drink called Nicetea. He estimates that if the product is successful, then the company will make a profit of R (this figure actually represents a present value over a horizon of several years). He currently assesses the likelihood of this event to be p. If the product fails, the company stands to *lose* L, due to expenditures on equipment, packaging, and initial advertising. The manufacturer can do some preliminary market testing before spending L, and thereby get a better idea as to whether to introduce the product. Assume, for simplicity, that there are at most two market areas in which to test Nicetea, and that he does not have to decide to make a test in the second market area until he sees the outcome in the first. If Nicetea is going to be successful, the probability is p_1 that the first market deems it such, and q_1 that the first market deems it a failure. Similarly, if the product is going to be successful, the probability is p_{s2} that both the first and second markets deem it such, and p_{f2} that only the second market deems it such. If the product is going to fail, the probability is q_{f2} that the first and second markets deem it such, and q_{s2} that only the second market deems it such. Let the first market test cost C_1 and the second market test cost C_2 (assume these amounts do not depend on the test outcomes).

(a) Draw a decision tree for this problem. (*Note:* the manufacturer can decide to introduce or drop Nicetea at any point, and he only incurs L when he introduces the product.)

(b) Explain how to find an optimal strategy. Use the following data to illustrate your procedure: $R = 100$, $L = 50$, $C_1 = 5$, $C_2 = 10$, $p_1 = .5$, $q_1 = .75$, $p_{s2} = .8$, $p_{f2} = .5$, $q_{f2} = .9$, $q_{s2} = .6$.

(c) How does the procedure in part (b) simplify (if at all) when $p_{s2} = p_{f2}$ and $q_{f2} = q_{s2}$? Give a verbal interpretation of this assumption. Illustrate your answers using the data in part (b), except let $p_{f2} = .8$, and $q_{s2} = .9$.

60 *Secretary Problem* (Sec. 1.6)

(a) Formulate this example in terms of a dynamic programming recursion. Assume that the executive wishes to see no more than n girls (in Sec. 1.6, we let $n = 3$). Show how to alter the formulation if there is a cost c per interview.

(b) Assume the executive does not limit the number of girls he is willing to interview. What strategy would you suggest that he follow if $c = 0$?

(c) Assume the executive does not limit the number of girls he is willing to interview and $c > 0$. Also assume he applies a one-period discount factor α, where $0 \le \alpha \le 1$. Write a set of extremal equations to determine an optimal strategy. (*Hint:* let the states represent his having interviewed a terrific, a fair, or a good girl, and let the decisions be to hire or to make another interview.)

(d) Write primal and dual linear programming characterizations of the formulation in part (c).

(e) Use your answer in part (d) to find an optimal solution with the data in the example of Sec. 1.6, $c = .15$, and $\alpha = 1$.

(f) Suppose that the executive has the option of "postponing" his decision about a girl so that he can make additional interviews and subsequently decide to hire a girl whom he saw earlier in the interviewing process. Under what circumstances might he want to exercise this option? Show how to alter the formulation in part (c) to allow for the added option. Answer parts (d) and (e) given this revised formulation.

61 *Parking-Place Problem.* You are driving with your date to a movie and want to decide on an optimal strategy for parking your car (prior to seeing the movie). You can always put your car in a parking lot that charges B, which represents a lot of "bread" to you. Or you can try to park on the street. But if you park too far away from the movie, your date will think you are a piker, and probably inept in solving other parking problems. Suppose there are N parking slots on the street on each side of the movie house; for purposes of analysis, assume these are numbered $-N, -N + 1$, $-N + 2, \ldots, -1, 0, 1, \ldots, N - 2, N - 1, N$. (Place 0 is in front of the movie and not available for parking.) You estimate that the "piker factor" loss is $|n|$, where n is the number of the slot where you decide to park. Let p_n, for $n = -N, \ldots, -1, 1, \ldots, N$, be the probability that slot n is vacant.

(a) Formulate a dynamic programming model that yields an optimal strategy. For simplicity, assume you only see one place at a time. (*Hint:* let the states of the system refer to the parking slot number and whether or not it is empty.)

(b) Write in detail primal and dual linear programming characterizations of your answer in part (a). Assume $N = 3$.

*62 Consider the inventory model with perfect forecasts of fluctuating demand that is described in exercise 12. Suppose that the forecasting procedure yields perfect knowledge of the amounts for both the present and following periods' demands. What is the most the company would be willing to pay for such a perfect forecast if the horizon $n = 2$? If $n = 3$? Assume initial inventory at the start of the horizon equals 0.

63 *Warehouse Problem* (exercises 36 of Chap. 5 and 49 of Chap. 8). Suppose the selling price and purchase cost are random variables. Specifically, consider the random variable r that has probability distribution $q_t(r)$ in Period t, where $r = 1, 2, \ldots, 10$. Then assume that the selling price and purchase cost in Period t are related to r by the functions $p_t(r)$ and $c_t(r)$, and that these values are known at the start of Period t, prior to deciding on the number of gallons to be sold or purchased. Formulate a dynamic programming model that yields a strategy maximizing expected profit.

64 *Astronaut Problem.* Not wanting to make mercurial decisions, an astronaut, C. U. Rowan, has turned to operations research for guidance. His mission plan calls for N orbits around the Earth. At the beginning of each orbit, he must judge his spacecraft to be in States 1, 2, or 3, corresponding to AOK (all systems "go"), minor malfunctioning, and major malfunctioning. In State 1, Rowan always elects to make another orbit if he has not completed his mission, and in State 3, Rowan must terminate the mission. In State 2, he can elect to go another orbit or to terminate. Let $P_n(j\,|\,i)$ denote the probability that if the astronaut makes the nth orbit and the state of his craft is i, where $i = 1, 2$, then the state of his craft at the next orbit is j, where $j \geq i$. Let $j = 4$ refer to the disasterous event that the mission has to be terminated immediately due to an emergency condition, and let $P_n(4\,|\,i)$, for $i = 1, 2$, be the associated probability. If the astronaut terminates the mission after completing n orbits successfully, the value of the mission is v_n, where $v_n > v_{n-1}$. But if he must terminate during the nth orbit because of an emergency condition, the value is only w_n, where $w_n < v_n$.

(a) Formulate a dynamic programming model that yields an optimal strategy.
(b) Write in detail primal and dual linear programming characterizations of your answer in part (a). Assume $N = 4$.

65 Each month the Bank of Hong Kong determines the amounts of funds it needs to borrow on the world money markets in order to finance the loan demands of its own customers. For simplicity, assume that the total requirements for Month t are D_t. Let the actual value for D_t be given according to a probability distribution $p_t(D_t)$, but suppose that the value of D_t is known at the start of Period t, prior to making any decisions in that period. Each month the Bank may decide to borrow funds for one, two, or three months, and denote these quantities as x_1, x_2, x_3. Since D_t is to be interpreted as a "capacity" requirement, the amount $x_1 + x_2 + x_3$ can be used, in part, to meet the requirement for D_t, and similarly, $x_2 + x_3$ for D_{t+1}, and x_3 for D_{t+2}. Suppose that the cost of borrowing x_j in Period t depends on a parameter r and is given by the function $c_{tj}(x_j\,|\,r)$, where r has a probability distribution $q_t(r)$, and the exact value of r is known at the start of Period t, prior to making any decisions in that period. Assume that all the random elements are completely independent of each other.

(a) Formulate a dynamic programming model that yields a minimum total expected discounted cost subject to the stipulation that all loan requirements are met. (Write a dynamic programming recursion for a general Period t, letting α denote the one-month discount factor.)
(b) Show how the formulation in part (a) simplifies (if at all) when the requirement D_t is known after making the Period t decisions; assume that if D_t exceeds the supply of available funds, there is a loss of c per unit.

66 The Big Cheese Corporation wants to hire a vice-president to head its newly organized Limburger Division, and has contracted the service of the Dupry Company, an

executive placement firm. This company conducts a series of tests and interviews of each applicant who seems promising. Dupry will charge Big Cheese a cost c_j for administering Test (or Interview) j; past experience has shown that there is a probability p_j that an applicant passes the test. (Assume, for simplicity, that Dupry has cleverly designed its testing procedures so that an individual's performances on the various tests are completely independent.) Big Cheese will accept only an applicant that has passed all J tests; therefore, if the candidate fails a test, he is immediately disqualified. Formulate an approach for finding a sequence of tests to minimize expected total cost per applicant considered.

67 Cary Silver, the President of a multibranch bank, sent a confidential letter by mistake to one of the bank's vice-presidents, of which there are N. To Silver's embarrassment, he does not know which VP has received the letter, and wants to find out by telephone. He assigns probability p_j to having sent the letter to Vice-President j; the probability is q_j that Vice-President j will be away from his desk when Silver calls, and so Silver will not know whether that VP received the letter. Devise a dynamic programming formulation to indicate the telephone calling strategy that minimizes the expected number of calls Silver must make to find the letter. (*Hint:* let the state at the nth call represent his probabilities that each VP has the letter, given the knowledge obtained from the previous telephone calls.)

68 *Optimal Batch Size Problem.* The example of the Voltex Company in Sec. 17.5 can be described as a single-stage production process. Batch size problems frequently arise in multistage processes. Consider, for example, a manufacturing sequence composed of four stages. The first stage is like that in Sec. 17.5, namely, a decision must be made to select the initial batch size x in an attempt to produce n good items by the end of the final stage. Some items that are produced at this stage do not meet standards and are scrapped. Assume every good item is then transmitted to the second stage. Here the production quantity cannot exceed the number of good items entering, but it can be less and the resultant excess can be sold. (If the number of good items entering is less than n, all of them are processed at this stage.) Again, some of the items processed at the second stage may not meet standards and are scrapped; the rest are transmitted to the third stage. A similar decision structure exists at the third and fourth stages. If fewer than n good items have been manufactured at the end of the fourth stage, the process starts all over again in an effort to fill the remaining requirement (which typically is smaller than n).

For Stage t, where $t = 1, 2, 3, 4$, let $c_t(x)$ denote the cost of processing x units, let $p_{tx}(j)$ denote the probability that j out of a batch of x components fail to meet standards, let s_t be the scrap value of an item below standard, and v_t the disposal value of an item sold.

(a) Write a dynamic programming formulation of the model. (*Hint:* let the state variable at the first stage be the number of good items required, and at subsequent stages be the number of good items required along with the number of items that met the standards from the previous stage.)

(b) Let the requirement $n = 2$ and assume that a batch size at Stage 1 cannot exceed 3. Write in detail the formulation in part (a). Then exhibit equivalent primal and dual linear programming models for finding an optimal policy. Also state the numbers of equations and variables in these models when the limit at Stage 1 is 4. When the requirement $n = 3$ and the limit at Stage 1 is 4.

CONTENTS

CHAPTER 18

Dynamic Programming in Markov Chains

18.1 INTRODUCTION

All the examples in the preceding chapter can be viewed as special cases of a more general model, sometimes referred to as a **Markovian decision process**. Taking such a general point of view is insightful, for it helps you establish several important dynamic properties that all these models share. For example, you will discover sufficient conditions ensuring the existence of a **stationary strategy** that is optimal over an unbounded horizon. You will also learn when you can advantageously employ methods of successive approximation and linear programming to find numerical solutions to those problems for which the optimal policy has no special form that can be exploited.

This chapter builds on many of the ideas you learned in Chaps. 11, 12, and 17. In particular, we use the concepts of

- *present value* explained in Sec. 11.2
- *equivalent average return* explained in Sec. 11.2
- *extremal equations* developed in Secs. 12.1 and 12.3
- *value iteration algorithm* contained in Sec. 12.2
- *policy iteration algorithm* contained in Secs. 12.2 and 12.3
- *decision rule* or *strategy* illustrated in Chap. 17.

Although the explanations to follow are self-contained, we do not repeat all the motivational discussion for the above ideas that we provided when they were first introduced in earlier chapters. Consequently, we recommend your spending a few minutes reviewing these notions before going on. The emphasis in this chapter is on showing how the previously explained dynamic programming formulations and solution techniques are modified to account for probabilistic elements.

Therefore most of the motivational discussion here focuses on the impact of uncertainty.

Throughout the chapter we maintain the convention that the objective function is to *minimize* an expected value. Depending on the context of the illustration, we will refer to the objective function as representing cost, present value, or economic return. But to repeat, in every dynamic programming formulation below, the sense of the optimization is minimization. Only simple modifications in the formulas are needed to treat maximization problems. (Of course, by changing the sign of the objective function in a maximizing problem, you can find an optimal solution using a minimization algorithm.)

18.2 STOCHASTIC SHORTEST-ROUTE MODEL

While studying deterministic dynamic programming models, you saw in Chaps. 10 and 12 that it is convenient to view such problems in terms of a network. Recall that the network for a general finite horizon problem consists of nodes representing the system's being in State s and Stage n, and arcs indicating the results of decisions. The network is acyclic, with the terminal node representing the initial state of the system. The network for a general unbounded horizon is similarly constructed, except that the node designation no longer includes a stage number and only refers to a state.

For the finite horizon case, the recursive relations expressing the appropriate optimization problem are

$$(1) \quad y_i = \underset{\substack{(i, j) \text{ in} \\ \text{network}}}{\text{minimum}} (\alpha y_j + c_{ij}) \quad \text{for all } i \neq r \text{ and } y_r \equiv 0 \quad \text{(finite horizon)},$$

where r is the terminal node and α is the one-period discount factor. For a finite horizon, you can let α have any value in the interval $0 \leq \alpha \leq 1$.

You can similarly view finite horizon (or finite stage) and finite state stochastic dynamic programming models—like those in Chap. 17—in terms of a probabilistic shortest-route model. To do so, three straightforward generalizations of the previous deterministic shortest-route models are required. The first accounts for the fact that now a decision d at Node i can result in the system moving to one of *several* possible nodes. Let

$$(2) \quad p(j \,|\, i, d) = \text{conditional probability that the state of the system becomes}$$
$$\text{Node } j \text{ given that, at Node } i, \text{ you make decision } d,$$

where, for a given i and d, the sum of the $p(j \,|\, i, d)$ over all possible j equals 1.

Actually, (2) embodies a so-called **Markov property** assumption. Specifically, we postulate that each transition probability in (2) is influenced *only* by the values of i and d and *not* by the specific history of the system (previous states and decisions) *prior* to arriving at Node i.

The second generalization recognizes that the return or cost associated with making the current decision d at Node i can also be a random variable. Let

$$(3) \quad c_{id} = \textit{expected} \text{ return in the current period from making decision } d \text{ at Node i.}$$

If you let $c(j|i, d)$ denote the actual return in the current period from making decision d at Node i, when, as a consequence, the state of the system at the next period is Node j, then

$$(4) \qquad\qquad c_{id} = \sum_j c(j|i, d) p(j|i, d),$$

where the sum is over all possible j.

The third modification postulates a generalized acyclic property. Assume that the nodes can be ordered such that the terminal node is $r = 0$, and for all i, j, and d,

$$(5) \qquad\qquad p(j|i, d) = 0 \quad \text{if } j \geq i \quad \text{(acyclic assumption).}$$

In other words, it is impossible to go from Node i to a higher-numbered Node j. A consequence of (5) is that no node will be visited more than once, if at' all, in any realized history of the system. As you will see in the inventory model example below, property (5) often follows immediately from the underlying structure of the specific problem being analyzed.

Then the stochastic generalization of the recursion (1) is

$$(6) \qquad y_i = \underset{d \text{ in } D(i)}{\text{minimum}} \left[\sum_{j=0}^{i-1} p(j|i, d) \alpha y_j + c_{id} \right] \quad \text{for all } i \neq 0 \quad \text{and} \quad y_0 \equiv 0$$

$$\text{(stochastic shortest route),}$$

where $D(i)$ is the set of possible decisions at Node i. Thus y_i now represents the minimum expected present value of reaching the terminal Node 0 when starting at Node i. Compare (6) with (1). What is the most important difference?

Observe that you can calculate the values in (6) in the order $y_1, y_2, y_3, \ldots$. It is because of the acyclic assumption in (5) that it is always possible to solve (6), starting the computations with the lowest-numbered node and progressing to successively higher-numbered nodes. The procedure is almost identical with that for finding a shortest route in a deterministic acyclic network (discussed in Sec. 7.7), the only difference here being the necessity to compute the summation indicated on the right of (6).

Inventory model. To see how the above model (6) is applied consider once again the Dependable Manufacturing Company's problem. The data for the stochastic version of this problem (introduced in Chap. 17) are

$$\text{demand: } P[D = 2] = \frac{1}{2} \qquad P[D = 4] = \frac{1}{2}$$

$$\text{constraints: production } x \leq 5 \quad \text{and} \quad \text{ending inventory } j \leq 4$$

$$\text{production and inventory costs: } C(x) + h \cdot j,$$

where production x and ending inventory j are nonnegative integers and

$$C(0) = 0 \quad C(1) = 15 \quad C(2) = 17$$
$$C(3) = 19 \quad C(4) = 21 \quad C(5) = 23 \quad \text{and} \quad h = 1$$

for all periods.

These data led to the recursion (in Sec. 17.4) for $n = 2, 3, \ldots,$

(7)
$$f_n(i) = \operatorname*{minimum}_{x} \{C(x) + 1[i + x - 3]$$
$$+ \tfrac{1}{2}[f_{n-1}(i + x - 2) + f_{n-1}(i + x - 4)]\},$$

where $i = 0, 1, \ldots, 4$, and the minimization is over only nonnegative integer values in the range $4 - i \leq x \leq$ minimum $(5, 6 - i)$.

You can establish the correspondence between (7) and a network of the type assumed for (6) as follows. Let Node $5n + i$ designate the state of the system when there are n periods remaining, for $n = 1, 2, \ldots,$ and entering inventory is at level i, for $i = 0, 1, \ldots, 4$; let Node 0 be the terminal state. (Observe that each node number corresponds to a *unique* pair of values for n and i; for example, Node 36 corresponds to $n = 7$ and $i = 1$.)

Suppose entering inventory is at level i when there are n periods remaining and the production decision is x. Then when there are $n - 1$ periods remaining, entering inventory will be either $(i + x - 2)$ for demand $D = 2$, or $(i + x - 4)$ for demand $D = 4$, each possibility occurring with probability $\tfrac{1}{2}$. Consequently, verify that the only positive transition probabilities are

(8) $p[5(n-1) + i + x - 2 \,|\, 5n + i, x] = p[5(n-1) + i + x - 4 \,|\, 5n + i, x] = \dfrac{1}{2}$

for $n \geq 2$. When $n = 1$, the optimal decision is

(9) $x = 4 - i$ for $n = 1$,

so that

(10) $p[0 \,|\, 5 + i, 4 - i] = 1$ for all $i \leq 4$ and for $n = 1$.

Verify that (8) and (10) satisfy the acyclic assumption (5).

For the inventory problem, assume that $\alpha = 1$. As you saw in (7), the expected value for the decision to produce x when entering inventory is i and there are n periods remaining is

(11) $c_{5n+i, x} = C(x) + 1[i + x - 3]$.

As a consequence, the correspondence between (7) through (11) and the solution to the recursion (6) is simply

(12) $y_{5n+i} \equiv f_n(i)$ for $n \geq 1$ and $0 \leq i \leq 4$

(and $y_0 = 0$). Thus the y_j, for $j = 1, 2, \ldots,$ can be determined in the very same fashion as the calculations yielding $f_n(i)$, shown in Fig. 17.2.

In Fig. 18.1 you see a diagram associated with the policy in (9) for $n = 1$ and the stationary production policy:

(13)   produce $x = \begin{cases} 5 & \text{if } i = 0 \\ 6 - i & \text{if } i = 1, 2, 3, 4 \end{cases}$ for $n \geq 2$.

Notice the production *decision* at any node for $n \geq 2$ has two arcs associated with it, one for each possible probabilistic occurrence.

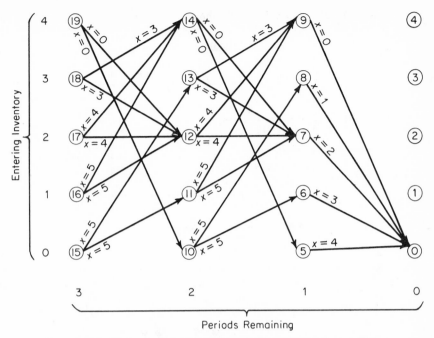

FIGURE 18.1. Stochastic Network—Inventory Example (Stationary Policy).

▶**Linear programming version.** From a computational point of view, there is little to be gained by converting the recursion (6) to an equivalent linear programming model. The only possible advantages in this regard are the widespread availability of computer algorithms for linear programming, and the accompanying facility for performing sensitivity testing. However, such a conversion will further prepare you for the analysis of the unbounded horizon model in the next three sections, and what is more, it will show you how to impose chance-constraints on this type of model.

Suppose the nodes are numbered $0, 1, 2, \ldots, T$. The value for y_T can be found by solving

(i)   maximize y_T

subject to

(ii) $y_i - \sum_{j=1}^{i-1} p(j \mid i, d) \alpha y_j \leq c_{id}$ for each possible i and d,

where all the y_i are unconstrained in sign, and y_0 has been suppressed since $y_0 = 0$.

The corresponding dual problem is

(iii)   minimize $\sum_{i=1}^{T} \sum_{d \text{ in } D(i)} c_{id} x_{id}$

subject to

(iv) $\sum_{d \text{ in } D(j)} x_{jd} - \sum_{i=j+1}^{T} \sum_{d \text{ in } D(i)} p(j \mid i, d) \alpha x_{id} = 0$ for $j = 1, 2, \ldots, T-1$

(v) $\sum_{d \text{ in } D(T)} x_{Td} = 1$

(vi)   all $x_{id} \geq 0$.

An illustration for $T = 3$ and $d = 1, 2$ is shown in Fig. 18.2.

Primal

i	d	y_1	y_2	y_3	
1	1	1			$\leq c_{11}$
	2	1			$\leq c_{12}$
2	1	$-p(1\|2,1)\alpha$	1		$\leq c_{21}$
	2	$-p(1\|2,2)\alpha$	1		$\leq c_{22}$
3	1	$-p(1\|3,1)\alpha$	$-p(2\|3,1)\alpha$	1	$\leq c_{31}$
	2	$-p(1\|3,2)\alpha$	$-p(2\|3,2)\alpha$	1	$\leq c_{32}$
				1	Maximize

y_i unrestricted in sign

Dual

j	x_{11}	x_{12}	x_{21}	x_{22}	x_{31}	x_{32}	
1	1	1	$-p(1\|2,1)\alpha$	$-p(1\|2,2)\alpha$	$-p(1\|3,1)\alpha$	$-p(1\|3,2)\alpha$	$= 0$
2			1	1	$-p(2\|3,1)\alpha$	$-p(2\|3,2)\alpha$	$= 0$
3					1	1	$= 1$
	c_{11}	c_{12}	c_{21}	c_{22}	c_{31}	c_{32}	Minimize

$x_{id} \geq 0$

FIGURE 18.2. Linear Programming Versions of Stochastic Shortest Route Model (Acyclic).

It can be proved that there always exists an optimal solution to (iii) through (vi) such that at most only one x_{id} is positive for each i; such a solution corresponds to an optimal policy determined by (6). The summation in (iii) is the associated expected discounted cost over the finite horizon when you start at Node T and use an optimal policy.

When $\alpha = 1$, then x_{id} can be interpreted as the unconditional probability that in an actual realization of the decision process, the system will arrive at Node i and decision d will be taken. In this case the dual model therefore views the decision optimization problem in terms of determining system probabilities. The value of $(\sum_{d \text{ in } D(i)} x_{id})$ represents the probability that in an actual realization of the process the system reaches Node i.

When $\alpha = 1$, it is simple to add chance-constraints to (iii) through (vi). For example, if Node i* is in some way undesirable and this cannot be adequately indicated by the values for c_{i*d}, then you can impose the chance-constraint

(vii)
$$\sum_{d \text{ in } D(i^*)} x_{i^*d} \leq p,$$

where p is a suitably small probability. If chance-constraints are added, it is not always true that there is an optimal solution in which only one x_{id} is positive for each i. In fact the solution will usually indicate a randomized strategy, where $(x_{id'}/\sum_{d \text{ in } D(i)} x_{id})$ represents the conditional probability that decision d' is taken, *given* that the system arrives in Node i (assuming $\sum_d x_{id} > 0$).

Variable transition times. In Sec. 12.1 we mentioned that without much further complication the deterministic model can be generalized to encompass the situation where the transition times vary from arc to arc. The same approach can be applied in the stochastic model. Let $\alpha_{ij}(d)$ be the appropriate discount factor associated with the system's arriving at Node j, given that decision d is taken at Node i. Actually, $\alpha_{ij}(d)$ could itself be an expected value, that is, an expected discount factor, if the length of the transition is itself a random variable. The only required alteration in (6) is to substitute $\alpha_{ij}(d)$ for α. Similar modifications are appropriate in the formulas below. ◀

18.3 UNBOUNDED HORIZON WITH DISCOUNTING $(\alpha < 1)$

The stochastic shortest-route model in the previous section deals with an acyclic structure and provides a convenient way to view probabilistic dynamic programming models with a finite number of stages, states, and decisions. Here the analysis is extended to situations with an unbounded horizon and with a finite number of states and decisions.

The mathematical description of the model to be treated is simply enough stated: solve the **extremal equations**

$$(1) \qquad y_i = \underset{d \text{ in } D(i)}{\text{minimum}} \left[\sum_{\substack{j \text{ in} \\ \text{network}}} p(j \mid i, d)\alpha y_j + c_{id} \right] \quad \text{for each } i,$$

where we assume $0 \le \alpha < 1$. Note that we do *not* postulate any acyclic property here [such as (5) in the preceding section], and now there is *no* terminal node. The value of y_i represents the minimal expected present value of starting at Node i and using an optimal strategy over an unbounded time horizon. Notice again the Markov property assumption about the transition probabilities, namely, that they are *conditional* only on i and d; they do *not* depend on the system's history of previous states and decisions.

The description (1) is sufficiently flexible to encompass most dynamic programming models where the number of states and decisions is finite, the horizon is unbounded, and the transition probabilities are stationary.

▶We can establish the stochastic version of the canonical form for describing discrete dynamic programming models, namely, expression (i) of Sec. 12.1 (p. 406). Let S represent the set of all possible states; $D(s)$ the set of all feasible values for the decision d when the system is in State s; $R(s, d)$ the immediate *expected* economic return of decision d, given that the system is in State s; and $T(s, d)$ the transformed state of the system at the next stage, where $p[T(s, d)]$ denotes the probability that the system reaches State T(s, d) at the next period, given that you make decision d at State s in the current period.

Then the functional equation for the stochastic version can be written as

(i) $f(s) = \underset{d \text{ in } D(s)}{\text{optimum}} \{R(s, d) + \alpha \sum_T f[T(s, d)]p[T(s, d)]\}$

for every s in S $(0 \le \alpha < 1)$,

where $f(s)$ represents the expected present value of following an optimal policy over an unbounded horizon, given that the current state is s.   ◄

Inventory example. Consider once again the structure of the stochastic inventory model in the preceding section, where here we assume there is a discount factor α. You saw in the preceding section how to construct the network equivalent when the horizon is finite. For the unbounded horizon case, the period number is no longer relevant, and the states of the system can therefore be denoted merely by the value for entering inventory i, for $i = 0, 1, \ldots, 4$. (You may recall this simplification was also possible for the deterministic case in an unbounded horizon, analyzed in Sec. 12.5.)

The appropriate dynamic programming functional equation is simply

(2) $f(i) = \underset{x}{\text{minimum}} \{C(x) + 1[i + x - 3] + \alpha \cdot \tfrac{1}{2}[f(i + x - 2)$
$+ f(i + x - 4)]\}$ for $i = 0, 1, \ldots, 4$ $(0 < \alpha < 1)$,

where the minimization is over only nonnegative integer values in the range $4 - i \le x \le \text{minimum } (5, 6 - i)$.

The notational correspondences for the network version in (1) are

(3) $y_i \equiv f(i)$

(4) $c_{ix} \equiv C(x) + 1[i + x - 3]$

(5) $p[i + x - 2 | i, x] = p[i + x - 4 | i, x] = \dfrac{1}{2}$,

where a decision $d \equiv x$, the production quantity. These data are summarized in Fig. 18.3.

Suppose the stationary production policy

(6)   produce $x = \begin{cases} 5 & \text{if } i = 0 \\ 6 - i & \text{if } i = 1, 2, 3 \\ 0 & \text{if } i = 4 \end{cases}$

is used. Then the behavior of the system can be described in terms of a Markov chain array or matrix of transition probabilities:

Next period's
entering inventory

$j = 0 \quad 1 \quad 2 \quad 3 \quad 4$

(7)   Current period's entering inventory

$\begin{array}{c} i = 0 \\ 1 \\ 2 \\ 3 \\ 4 \end{array} \begin{bmatrix} 0 & \frac{1}{2} & 0 & \frac{1}{2} & 0 \\ 0 & 0 & \frac{1}{2} & 0 & \frac{1}{2} \\ 0 & 0 & \frac{1}{2} & 0 & \frac{1}{2} \\ 0 & 0 & \frac{1}{2} & 0 & \frac{1}{2} \\ \frac{1}{2} & 0 & \frac{1}{2} & 0 & 0 \end{bmatrix}.$

i	d in $D(i)$	$p(j\|i,d)$ 0	1	2	3	4	c_{id}
0	4	$\frac{1}{2}$		$\frac{1}{2}$			22
	5		$\frac{1}{2}$		$\frac{1}{2}$		25
1	3	$\frac{1}{2}$		$\frac{1}{2}$			20
	4		$\frac{1}{2}$		$\frac{1}{2}$		23
	5			$\frac{1}{2}$		$\frac{1}{2}$	26
2	2	$\frac{1}{2}$		$\frac{1}{2}$			18
	3		$\frac{1}{2}$		$\frac{1}{2}$		21
	4			$\frac{1}{2}$		$\frac{1}{2}$	24
3	1	$\frac{1}{2}$		$\frac{1}{2}$			16
	2		$\frac{1}{2}$		$\frac{1}{2}$		19
	3			$\frac{1}{2}$		$\frac{1}{2}$	22
4	0	$\frac{1}{2}$		$\frac{1}{2}$			1
	1		$\frac{1}{2}$		$\frac{1}{2}$		17
	2			$\frac{1}{2}$		$\frac{1}{2}$	20

Figure 18.3. The Data for a Stochastic Inventory Model.

Note: i = entering inventory this period
j = entering inventory next period
d = production quantity

[Use Fig. 18.3 to verify the entries in (7).] Likewise, *any* stationary production strategy will give rise to a Markov chain array of conditional probabilities.

Justification of extremal equations. Define a *policy* over an unbounded horizon as a complete description of the decisions to be made, period by period and state by state. Such a policy need not be stationary in that the decision rule may differ from period to period. This definition is the concept discussed in Chaps. 16 and 17. Define an *optimal policy* as one that gives the minimum obtainable expected present value for *every* possible initial state of the system. Again such a strategy need not be stationary. However, the extremal equations in (1) implicitly assume: there *is* an optimal **deterministic stationary strategy** (the same decision d is to be made each time the system arrives at Node i), and there *are* unique values y_i satisfying (1) corresponding to such an optimal strategy. The validity of these two assumptions must be proved, and indeed we can show the following theorem.

Stationary Policy Theorem for $0 \leq \alpha < 1$. There always exist unique finite y_i that satisfy the extremal equations (1), and a stationary policy corresponding to these y_i is optimal among all possible policies.

This is the same important theorem as in Sec. 12.1 for the deterministic case and, in fact, most of the analysis there remains applicable here. For convenience, the discussion in Sec. 12.1 is repeated below in a somewhat abbreviated form and with special attention given to the minor modifications required to encompass transition probabilities.

▶Without going into a detailed algebraic proof of the Stationary Policy Theorem, we can state the line of reasoning used to establish the result.

Denote a general policy (not necessarily stationary) by the symbol π that indicates what action to take in the current period, given the actual state of the system; and what action to take in each future Period n, where $n = 2, 3, 4, \ldots$, for the state of the system at that particular time. Given π, consider a *composite policy* consisting of a decision rule at each state for the initial period—denote these by f—and followed thereafter by π (that is, the policy π moved ahead by one period). Let $(f\pi)$ symbolize this composite policy. Thus, the action for the current period is given by the rule f. The action *rule* you would have used in the current period under π, you now use at Period 2 under the composite policy $(f\pi)$. And similarly, the rule you would have used at Period n under π, you use at Period n + 1 under $(f\pi)$.

Then it can be proved that

(i) Given a general policy π, if *every* composite policy $(f\pi)$ results in an expected present value for each state that is at least as large as the associated expected present value for π, then π *is* optimal.

(ii) If a general policy π has an expected present value for every state that is at least as large as the corresponding expected present value for a compositite policy $(f\pi)$, but is strictly larger for at least one state, then a *stationary* policy using only f will result in an associated expected present value for every state that is no larger than the corresponding expected present value for policy π, and has an expected present value that is strictly less for at least one state.

Given (i) and (ii), an algorithmic type of argument demonstrates there is an optimal policy that is stationary: consider any trial policy that *is* stationary. Then by (i), it is optimal unless there are decision rules for the initial period that make a strict improvement for at least one state. If there are such decisions, then by (ii), using these decisions as a new trial *stationary* policy yields an improvement. Therefore the sequence of improved trial policies can be restricted to include only stationary policies. Since the number of states and decisions is finite, there is only a finite number of stationary policies. Consequently, the process of obtaining improved trial solutions is finite; that is, in a finite number of trials, we obtain a stationary policy that is optimal.

We can then show that the expected present values, which do exist, must satisfy the extremal equations (1), thus establishing the existence of a solution to (1). The uniqueness of these values follows from an examination of the algebraic structure of (1). ◀

Successive approximations. A solution to the extremal equations (1) can be obtained by the process of **successive approximations in function space**. Let y_i^0 be arbitrarily chosen and apply the **value iteration algorithm**

(8) $\quad y_i^{n+1} = \underset{d \text{ in } D(i)}{\text{minimum}} \left[\sum_{\substack{j \text{ in} \\ \text{network}}} p(j \mid i, d) \alpha y_j^n + c_{id} \right]$ for each i (value iteration).

Each y_i^n always will converge to a limit that satisfies the extremal equations in (1), but the convergence generally is *not* finite. If all $c_{id} \geq 0$ and all $y_i^0 = 0$, the y_i^n increase monotonically. By starting with every $y_i^0 = 0$, the process is the same as looking at a certain finite horizon model. Specifically, y_i^n represents the expected present value of an optimal path starting from Node i and traversing n arcs.

For *any* c_{id}, you can obtain convergence from above as follows. Select a trial stationary policy; for brevity of notation, denote each of these decisions by the symbol d'. Then solve the set of simultaneous linear equations

(9) $\quad y_i - \sum_{\substack{j \text{ in} \\ \text{network}}} p(j \mid i, d') \alpha y_j = c_{id'}$ for each i (value determination)

for the initial values $y_i^0 \equiv y_i$ to be used in the algorithm (8). If you arbitrarily stop at iteration m and employ the immediate optimal policy from (8) as a stationary policy in the unbounded horizon model, the corresponding expected present values will be no larger than the y_i^m in (8).

$(\alpha = .9)$

Entering Inventory	$n = 1$		$n = 2$		$n = 3$					Unbounded Horizon	
i	$x^1(i)$	y_i^1	$x^2(i)$	y_i^2	$x^3(i)$	y_i^3	y_i^{10}	y_i^{20}	y_i^{30}	$x_\infty(i)$	y_i
0	4	22	4	40	5	54.29	122.89	163.82	178.09	5	185.73
1	3	20	5	34.55	5	49.19	117.75	158.68	172.95	5	180.59
2	2	18	4	32.55	4	47.19	115.75	156.68	170.95	4	178.59
3	1	16	3	30.55	3	45.19	113.75	154.68	168.95	3	176.59
4	0	1	0	19	0	33.64	102.11	143.03	157.30	0	164.94

*Initial iteration: $y_i^0 = 0$ for each i

FIGURE 18.4. Stochastic Inventory Example—Value Iteration (From Below*).

An application of *value iteration* is shown in Figs. 18.4 and 18.5 for the stochastic inventory model in Fig. 18.3. Notice convergence to the optimal stationary policy is rapid—at iteration $n = 3$ in Fig. 18.4 and iteration $n = 2$ in Fig. 18.5. (At iteration $n = 40$, the values of y_i^n starting with $y_i^0 = 0$ are within 1% of the minimal y_i.) The initial y_i^0 in Fig. 18.5 are found by solving the value determination equations (9), which in this case are

$$(\alpha = .9)$$

Entering Inventory	$n = 0$		$n = 1$		$n = 2$					Unbounded Horizon
i	$x^0(i)$	y_i^0	$x^1(i)$	y_i^1	$x^2(i)$	y_i^2	y_i^{10}	y_i^{20}	y_i^{30}	y_i
0	4	202	4	202	5	200.09	191.94	187.89	186.48	185.73
1	3	200	5	196.55	5	195	186.80	182.75	181.34	180.59
2	2	189	4	194.55	4	193	184.80	180.75	179.34	178.59
3	1	196	3	192.55	3	191	182.80	178.75	177.34	176.59
4	0	181	0	181	0	179.44	171.15	167.11	165.70	164.94

*Values of y_i^0 are calculated from the value determination equation (9) using the policy shown in $x^0(i)$ column above.

FIGURE 18.5. Stochastic Inventory Example—Value Iteration Approximations in Function Space (From Above*).

$$(10) \quad \begin{aligned} + (1 - .5\alpha)\,y_0 && - .5\alpha\,y_2 && = 22 \\ - .5\alpha\,y_0 + 1y_1 && - .5\alpha\,y_2 && = 20 \\ - .5\alpha\,y_0 && + (1 - .5\alpha)\,y_2 && = 18 \\ - .5\alpha\,y_0 && - .5\alpha\,y_2 + 1y_3 && = 16 \\ - .5\alpha\,y_0 && - .5\alpha\,y_2 \quad + 1y_4 = 1, \end{aligned}$$

where $\alpha = .9$, yielding

$$(11) \qquad y_0 = 202 \quad y_1 = 200 \quad y_2 = 189 \quad y_3 = 196 \quad y_4 = 181.$$

[Write the equations (9) for the optimal policy and verify the minimal values y_i in Fig. 18.4.] Notice that convergence to y_i occurs more rapidly by starting with y_i^0 for the stationary policy in (6) rather than by letting $(y_i^0 = 0)$. Explain why, for $i = 1, 2, 3$, the values of y_i^n and y_i differ by the amount 2 in Figs. 18.4 and 18.5. In Fig. 18.6 observe how the optimal policy and the values for y_i change with different α values. Explain why the decision amounts $x_\infty(i)$ decrease as α gets smaller.

You also can solve (1) by **successive approximation in policy space**, that is, by the **policy iteration** algorithm:

Step 1. Select an arbitrary initial policy, and let $n = 0$.

Step 2. Given the trial policy, calculate the y_i^n according to the value determination equations:

$$(12) \quad y_i^n - \sum_{\substack{j \text{ in} \\ \text{network}}} p(j\,|\,i, d')\alpha y_j^n = c_{id'} \quad \text{for each } i \quad \text{(value determination routine)},$$

Entering Inventory	$\alpha = .9$		$\alpha = .8$		$\alpha = .5$	
i	$x_\infty(i)$	y_i	$x_\infty(i)$	y_i	$x_\infty(i)$	y_i
0	5	185.73	4	97.2	4	42
1	5	180.59	5	92.8	3	40
2	4	178.59	4	90.8	2	38
3	3	176.59	3	88.8	1	36
4	0	164.94	0	76.2	0	21

FIGURE 18.6. Stochastic Inventory Example—Optimal Solutions for Unbounded Horizon.

where d' represents the decision at Node i indicated by the specific policy being evaluated.

Step 3. Test for a policy improvement by calculating

$$(13) \quad \underset{d \text{ in } D(i)}{\text{minimum}} \left[\sum_{\substack{j \text{ in} \\ \text{network}}} p(j|i, d)\alpha y_j^n + c_{id} \right] \equiv Y_i^n \quad \text{for each } i \quad \text{(test quantity).}$$

Step 4. Terminate the iterations if $Y_i^n = y_i^n$, for all i. Otherwise, revise the policy at each Node k where $Y_k^n < y_k^n$, using a decision yielding Y_k^n in (13). Increase n to $n + 1$, and return to *Step 2* with the new trial policy.

The policy iteration algorithm has the properties

(i) $y_i^{n+1} \leq y_i^n$ for each Node i. and $y_k^{n+1} < y_k^n$ if $Y_k^n < y_k^n$.
(ii) The algorithm terminates in a *finite* number of iterations.
(iii) At termination, a policy yielding Y_i^n is optimal.

When the policy iteration algorithm is applied to the stochastic inventory example in Fig. 18.3, the sequence of stationary policies is the same as that shown in Fig. 18.5. However, the values for y_i^2, calculated from the linear equations (12), are the minimal y_i and so the iterations terminate at $n = 2$. [Check to see that when y_i^2 given by y_i in Fig. 18.4 are used in the test (13), the iterations stop.]

A linear programming approach for finding an optimal policy is explained in Sec. 18.5.

18.4 EQUIVALENT AVERAGE RETURN $(\alpha = 1)$

You will recall from the discussion of deterministic models in Chap. 12 that the case where $\alpha = 1$ gives rise to certain conceptual as well as computational difficulties. In particular, it is *not* legitimate merely to set $\alpha = 1$ in the extremal equations (1) in the preceding section; doing so produces a set of functional equations that has either no solution or only an indeterminate solution.

We approach the analysis of this situation in three steps. First, we define the criterion for an optimal policy when $\alpha = 1$. Then we assert there always exists a *stationary* policy that is optimal. Finally, we give appropriate extremal equations and a successive approximation technique for finding a stationary policy that optimizes the objective function. In the first two steps, we make no further assumptions about the structure of the model beyond those given in the preceding section. For the third step dealing with the algorithm, however, we will impose some mild restrictions to make the exposition easier.

Consider a *given* policy (not necessarily stationary), denoted by the symbol π^*. We also permit the possibility that the policy π^* includes randomized rules, such as, "when at Node i, pick decision d_1 with probability p and decision d_2 with probability $1 - p$." For any specified value of α, $0 < \alpha < 1$, let $y_i^*(\alpha)$ signify the expected present value if the system starts at Node i and the given policy π^* is followed. [For a fixed α, if π^* is stationary and nonrandomized, then you can compute the numerical values of $y_i^*(\alpha)$ by using the value determination routine indicated in (12) of the preceding section. Otherwise, $y_i^*(\alpha)$ can be computed by a straightforward but lengthy series of calculations.] As before, denote the *minimal* expected present value if the system starts in Node i by $y_i(\alpha)$. Observe here we have *explicitly* included the symbol α, and, for a fixed α, the $y_i(\alpha)$ are just the solution values to the extremal equation (1) in Sec. 18.3.

The policy π^* is defined as optimal for $\alpha = 1$ if

(1) $$y_i^*(\alpha) = y_i(\alpha) \quad \text{for each } i \quad \text{(optimal policy)}$$

for *all* α sufficiently close to 1. That is, policy π^* is optimal if there exists a number $\alpha^* < 1$ such that for *all* α in the interval $\alpha^* \leq \alpha < 1$, the expected present values for π^* equal the minimal possible expected present values. A significant result that can be proved is the following theorem.

STATIONARY POLICY THEOREM FOR $\alpha = 1$. There always exists a stationary policy that is optimal. Furthermore, there always exists such a policy that does not randomize.

As plausible as these conclusions seem, their proof is not trivial. Indeed, the result is *not* true if the number of states is unbounded, because then there may be no optimal policy that is *both* stationary and deterministic. (See exercise 46.)

Markov chain structure. Prior to establishing the appropriate extremal equations and solution algorithm, we elaborate on the probabilistic structure of the model when a stationary policy is employed. We will impose an assumption in (3) below that serves to eliminate some special cases that are of importance primarily to technical specialists. This postulate eases the exposition considerably without much loss of practical applicability. Afterwards we present a thumbnail sketch of Markov chain behavior. If you are already familiar with the details of Markov theory, then skim over, or skip, these examples.

For simplicity, assume from here on that the states are numbered $0, 1, \ldots, T$. Consider any stationary policy, and, for brevity of notation, denote each of the indicated decisions by the symbol d'. Then the **law of motion** for the system is completely specified by the corresponding square matrix of transition probabilities for moving from State i in one period to State j in the next period:

$$(2) \quad \begin{bmatrix} p(0\,|\,0, d') & p(1\,|\,0, d') & \cdots & p(j\,|\,0, d') & \cdots & p(T\,|\,0, d') \\ p(0\,|\,1, d') & p(1\,|\,1, d') & \cdots & p(j\,|\,1, d') & \cdots & p(T\,|\,1, d') \\ \cdot & \cdot & & \cdot & & \cdot \\ \cdot & \cdot & & \cdot & & \cdot \\ \cdot & \cdot & & \cdot & & \cdot \\ p(0\,|\,i, d') & p(1\,|\,i, d') & \cdots & p(j\,|\,i, d') & \cdots & p(T\,|\,i, d') \\ \cdot & \cdot & & \cdot & & \cdot \\ \cdot & \cdot & & \cdot & & \cdot \\ \cdot & \cdot & & \cdot & & \cdot \\ p(0\,|\,T, d') & p(1\,|\,T, d') & \cdots & p(j\,|\,T, d') & \cdots & p(T\,|\,T, d') \end{bmatrix}.$$

Such a system that is *completely* characterized by its one-period transition probabilities is known as a **Markov chain**. [You already saw an example of such an array for the inventory model in (7) of Sec. 18.3.] In keeping with tradition, we will treat Markov Chains in terms of *states* rather than *nodes*. We will resume the network language when we return to discussing algorithmic techniques.

Before stating the extremal equations for $\alpha = 1$, we now *assume* there is an optimal stationary policy with decisions d^* having **stationary probabilities** q_j, for $j = 0, 1, \ldots, T$, that are *uniquely* characterized by the $T + 1$ linear equations

$$(3) \quad q_j = \sum_{i=0}^{T} q_i p(j\,|\,i, d^*) \quad \text{for } j = 0, 1, \ldots, T \quad \begin{matrix}\text{(unique stationary} \\ \text{probability postulate)}\end{matrix}$$

and the restriction $(\Sigma\, q_j = 1)$. This assumption does not hold for *all* Markov chain models, but it is valid for many cases of practical interest. The theory and techniques below can be suitably modified to treat cases where the assumption in (3) is not justified.

One interpretation of (3) is the following: suppose each q_j is the probability that in a given period the system is at State j. Then the right-hand side of (3) is just the probability that the system is at State j in the next period. According to (3), the values of q_j are such that these two probabilities are the same. Thus, repeating the same line of argument, if the q_j satisfy (3) and in fact are the probabilities of the system being at State j in the initial period, then the q_j are also the probabilities that the system is at State j in *any* future period.

A second interpretation of q_j that holds for most practical cases is that the values represent the **limiting probabilities** of the system being at State j far in the future, when the system approaches **statistical equilibrium**. A third interpretation, imprecise but intuitive, is that each q_j represents the long-run relative frequency of the system being at State j.

The stationary probabilities are important, because they provide most of the information needed to calculate the system's **operating characteristics**. For example, you will see below [in (5)] how to use the q_j to compute the system's expected return per period. In subsequent chapters you will learn how to exploit the special structure of certain Markov models in order to write explicit expressions for q_j.

*__Examples of stationary probabilities.__ The following examples illustrate the notion of stationary probabilities.

Case 1. Let the array of transition probabilities be

(i)
$$\begin{pmatrix} \frac{1}{3} & \frac{2}{3} \\ \frac{1}{2} & \frac{1}{2} \end{pmatrix}.$$

Since $q_0 + q_1 = 1$, the equation for $j = 0$ from (3) is

(ii)
$$q_0 = q_0(\tfrac{1}{3}) + (1 - q_0)(\tfrac{1}{2}),$$

so that

(iii)
$$q_0 = \frac{3}{7} \quad q_1 = \frac{4}{7}.$$

Let $q_j(n)$ denote the probability that the system is at State j in the beginning of Period n, where $q_j(1) = \bar{q}_j$ is *any given* probability for the initial period. Then analogous to (3), it is easy to verify that

(iv)
$$q_j(n + 1) = \sum_{i=0}^{T} q_i(n) p(j \mid i, d^*).$$

When $T = 1$, it can be proved that (iv) may be written in the form

(v) $\quad q_j(n + 1) = q_j + [\bar{q}_j - q_j][1 - p(1 \mid 0, d^*) - p(0 \mid 1, d^*)]^n \quad$ for $j = 0, 1$.

The term following the plus sign on the right-hand side of (v) is called the **transient correction**, since it represents the difference $[q_j(n + 1) - q_j]$ attributable to the system's operating only over a finite horizon. What is the range of possible values for $[1 - p(1 \mid 0, d^*) - p(0 \mid 1, d^*)]$?

In the case of (i), since $(1 - \frac{2}{3} - \frac{1}{2})^n = (-\frac{1}{6})^n$ approaches 0 as n gets arbitrarily large, the values of $q_j(n + 1)$ approach q_j in the limit. Thus the values in (iii) can be interpreted as limiting state probabilities as well as long-run relative frequencies.

Case 2. Given the chain matrix

(vi)
$$\begin{pmatrix} \frac{1}{3} & \frac{2}{3} \\ \frac{1}{3} & \frac{2}{3} \end{pmatrix},$$

then

(vii)
$$q_0 = \frac{1}{3} \quad q_1 = \frac{2}{3}.$$

Whenever all the rows of a Markov array are identical, the stationary probabilities equal these row elements. Calculate $q_j(n + 1)$ from (v).

Case 3. Given the transition law

(viii)
$$\begin{pmatrix} \frac{1}{3} & \frac{2}{3} \\ \frac{2}{3} & \frac{1}{3} \end{pmatrix},$$

check that the stationary probabilities are

(ix)
$$q_0 = \frac{1}{2} \quad q_1 = \frac{1}{2}.$$

Whenever the entries in every *column* of a Markov array add to 1, all the q_j are equal (that is, $q_j = 1/T + 1$). Such an array is called **doubly stochastic**.

Case 4. Show that for

(x)
$$\begin{pmatrix} \frac{1}{3} & \frac{2}{3} \\ 1 & 0 \end{pmatrix},$$

the stationary probabilities are

(xi)
$$q_0 = \frac{3}{5} \quad q_1 = \frac{2}{5}.$$

Case 5. Suppose the chain matrix is

(xii)
$$\begin{pmatrix} \frac{1}{3} & \frac{2}{3} \\ 0 & 1 \end{pmatrix}.$$

Notice that once this system reaches State 1, it remains there forever. State 0 is referred to as a **transient state**. The associated stationary probabilities are

(xiii)
$$q_0 = 0 \quad q_1 = 1.$$

If the system is at State 0 in the initial Period 1, use (v) to verify that it is still at State 0 in the beginning of Period n with probability $(\frac{1}{3})^n$. Thus as n gets arbitrarily large, the probability of being at State 0 becomes negligible, and equals 0 in the limit. Thus (xiii) is in accord with the limiting probability and long-run frequency interpretations.

Case 6. Suppose the transition probabilities are

(xiv)
$$\begin{pmatrix} 0 & 1 \\ 1 & 0 \end{pmatrix},$$

so that the system alternates between States 0 and 1. Then check that

(xv)
$$q_0 = \frac{1}{2} \quad q_1 = \frac{1}{2}.$$

Although the long-run relative frequency interpretation for the values in (xv) are intuitive, observe from (v) that

(xvi)
$$q_j(n + 1) = \frac{1}{2} + \left(\bar{q}_j - \frac{1}{2}\right)(-1)^n = \begin{cases} \bar{q}_j & \text{for } n \text{ even} \\ 1 - \bar{q}_j & \text{for } n \text{ odd.} \end{cases}$$

Thus (if $\bar{q}_j \neq \frac{1}{2}$) the value of $q_j(n+1)$ depends on whether n is odd or even and does *not* approach a limit as n gets arbitrarily large. For this illustration, it is therefore inappropriate to interpret the values in (xv) as limiting probabilities of the system being at State j. This case represents an example of a so-called **cyclic chain**.

Case 7. Finally, consider the system described by

(xvii)
$$\begin{pmatrix} 1 & 0 \\ 0 & 1 \end{pmatrix}.$$

Notice if the system begins at any State j, it remains there forever. In this case (3) does not have a *unique* solution; *any* probabilities q_j satisfy (3). The system (xvii) is an illustration of what is sometimes called a **multiple chain**: the system can be split into separable subsystems, each of which can be analyzed independently.

Thus by assuming the equations in (3) are uniquely solvable for an optimal stationary policy, we are ruling out systems with optimal multiple chain policies. It is not really difficult to obtain optimal policies for multiple chains, but this situation is better left to more advanced texts.

Extremal equations. Suppose a deterministic stationary policy π^* *is* optimal. Then by definition, for α sufficiently close to 1,

(4) $y_i = \underset{d \text{ in } D(i)}{\text{minimum}} \left[\sum_{j=0}^{T} p(j \mid i, d) \alpha y_j + c_{id} \right] = \sum_{j=0}^{T} p(j \mid i, d^*) \alpha y_j + c_{id^*}$ for each i,

where d^* denotes the decision at Node i indicated by π^*. Further let

(5)
$$c^* \equiv \sum_{i=0}^{T} q_i^* c_{id^*},$$

where q_i^* are the stationary probabilities calculated from the equations in (3) for policy π^*. An intuitive interpretation for c^* is the system's long-run expected return (or cost) per period. Although this description is somewhat imprecise, we shall use it below in referring to c^*.

We employed a heuristic argument in Sec. 12.3 to derive the appropriate extremal equations for the case $\alpha = 1$, and will apply the same approach here. But we repeat the warning that the reasoning is meant mainly to motivate the resulting extremal equations, which may look strange to you; the derivation is not a mathematically rigorous approach to the development of the functional equations. A different heuristic approach is explained in the special material below.

Consider the expected equivalent return $(1 - \alpha)y_i$ and define w_i by means of the identity

(6)
$$(1 - \alpha)y_i \equiv (1 - \alpha)w_i + c^* \quad \text{for each } i.$$

Then you can rewrite the functional equations (4) as

(7) $w_i + \dfrac{c^*}{1 - \alpha} = \underset{d \text{ in } D(i)}{\text{minimum}} \left[\sum_{j=0}^{T} p(j \mid i, d) \alpha \left(w_j + \dfrac{c^*}{1 - \alpha} \right) + c_{id} \right]$ for each i.

Since $\sum_{j=0}^{T} p(j|i, d) = 1$, and c^* is a constant, the term involving c^* on the right of (7) can be brought to the left. Check that after doing so and letting $\alpha = 1$, you have the extremal equations

$$(8) \qquad w_i + c^* = \underset{d \text{ In } D(i)}{\text{minimum}} \left[\sum_{j=0}^{T} p(j|i, d)w_j + c_{id} \right] \quad \text{for each } i$$

$$\text{(extremal equations for } \alpha = 1).$$

You can interpret the quantity $w_i - w_j$ as the incremental expected return of starting at Node i instead of at Node j. (In formal terms, $w_i - w_j$ is the limiting value of $y_i - y_j$ as α approaches 1.)

[As we pointed out in Chap. 12, in order to make the above derivation precise, you should use the notation $y_i(\alpha)$ and $w_i(\alpha)$ in (6) and (7) and define w_i in (8) as the limiting value of $w_i(\alpha)$ as α approaches 1 from below.]

Verify that if a set of w_i satisfies (8), then so do $(w_i + K)$ for an arbitrary constant K. Therefore, it is necessary to add a normalizing restriction. A convenient one is

$$(9) \qquad\qquad\qquad w_0 = 0 \quad \text{(normalization)}.$$

Applying the same reasoning to the second equality in (4) yields the *value determination equations* for policy π^*:

$$(10) \quad w_i + c^* = \sum_{j=0}^{T} p(j|i, d^*)w_j + c_{id^*} \quad \text{for each } i \quad \text{(value determination routine)}.$$

The system (9) and (10) consists of $T + 2$ linear equations in $T + 2$ unknowns $w_0, w_1, \ldots, w_T$ and c^*. An implication of the postulate in (3) that unique stationary probabilities exist is that the equations in (9) and (10) have a unique solution. Further, the resultant value for c^* is indeed the same value as given in (5). To see this, first multiply each relation in (10) by q_i^* and sum over i, thereby giving

$$(11) \qquad \sum_{i=0}^{T} q_i^*(w_i + c^*) = \sum_{i=0}^{T} q_i^* \sum_{j=0}^{T} p(j|i, d^*)w_j + \sum_{i=0}^{T} q_i^* c_{id^*}.$$

Then use (3) to verify that the equation in (11) simplifies to (5).

We now summarize the principal implication of the extremal equations.

NECESSARY CONDITION FOR OPTIMALITY. (a) Given a deterministic stationary policy π^*, if π^* is optimal, then the solution to (9) and (10) satisfies the extremal equations (8) and (9). (b) Equivalently, if the solution (9) and (10) does not satisfy the extremal equations (8) and (9), then π^* is not optimal.

Since there always exists a stationary policy that is optimal, it follows that there always exists a solution to (8) and (9).

The Necessary Condition asserts that an optimal stationary policy yields a solution to the extremal equations. Now we ascertain whether a stationary policy that yields a solution to the extremal equations is optimal.

Consider a stationary strategy π' having decision elements d'. Let w_i' and c' be the associated solution to

(12) $$w_0' = 0$$

(13) $$w_i' + c' = \sum_{j=0}^{T} p(j \mid i, d') w_j' + c_{id'} \quad \text{for each } i.$$

The following proposition can be proved.

SUFFICIENT CONDITION FOR MINIMUM EXPECTED RETURN PER PERIOD. (a) Given a deterministic stationary policy π', if the corresponding w_j', and c' from (12) and (13) satisfy the extremal equations (8) and (9), then c' is minimal among all policies. (b) Equivalently, if c' is not minimal, then the solution (12) and (13) does not satisfy the extremal equations (8) and (9).

Consequently, a stationary policy leads to a solution of the extremal equations, only if the associated c' has the same value as an optimal policy. Note, however, that such a policy π' may not be optimal according to the particular definition of an optimal policy in (1), that is, π' may not be optimal for *every* Node i when α is *near* to 1. But in many practical situations, obtaining a policy having the minimum obtainable expected return per period is adequate. What is more, you can expand the formulation in a way that leads to computational techniques for finding an optimal policy as defined in (1). These topics are more appropriate for advanced texts and are not pursued here.

▶The Sufficient Condition can be demonstrated as follows. As before, let $d*$ refer to a decision in an optimal stationary policy $\pi*$. Since the strategy π' yields a solution in (12) and (13) to the extremal equations, it follows that

(i) $$w_i' + c' \leq \sum_{j=0}^{T} p(j \mid i, d*) w_j' + c_{id*} \quad \text{for each } i.$$

Using (10), you can write (i) as

(ii) $$w_i' + c' - \sum_{j=0}^{T} p(j \mid i, d*) w_j' \leq w_i + c* - \sum_{j=0}^{T} p(j \mid i, d*) w_j.$$

Multiply (ii) by the stationary probabilities q_i* for policy $\pi*$, sum over i, and thereby obtain

(iii) $$c' \leq c*.$$

Since $c*$ is minimal by hypothesis, $c' = c*$, as was to be shown.

When the model is in fact deterministic, the extremal equations (8) reduce to those given in Chap. 12, namely, (6) in Sec. 12.3. Examples 3 and 6 in Sec. 12.4 demonstrate how a stationary policy can yield a solution to the extremal equations but not be optimal according to the definition (1) above.   ◀

Policy iteration. A straightforward extension of the policy space algorithm in Sec. 12.3 can be used to obtain a policy π' having minimal c'. To simplify the exposition of the technique, we make one further postulate that is satisfied in most practical situations: *assume that unique stationary probabilities exist for each trial policy*

π' *tested in Step 2 below.* (The algorithm can be easily modified to handle the situation where this assumption is not satisfied.)

The policy space algorithm is

Step 1. Select an arbitrary initial stationary policy, and let $n = 0$.

Step 2. Given the trial policy π' at iteration n, solve the value determination equations

(14)
$$w_0^n = 0 \qquad \text{(value determination routine)}$$
$$w_i^n + c^n = \sum_{j=0}^{T} p(j\,|\,i, d')w_j^n + c_{id'} \quad \text{for each } i,$$

where d' represents the decision at Node i indicated by the specific policy being evaluated.

Step 3. Calculate

(15)
$$\underset{d \text{ in } D(i)}{\text{minimum}} \left[\sum_{j=0}^{T} p(j\,|\,i, d)w_j^n + c_{id} \right] \equiv W_i^n \quad \text{for each } i \quad \text{(test quantity)}.$$

Step 4. Terminate the iterations if $W_i^n = w_i^n + c^n$ for all i; then c^n is minimal. Otherwise, revise the policy at every Node k, where $W_k^n < w_k^n + c^n$, using a decision yielding W_k^n in (15). Increase n to $n + 1$, and return to *Step 2* with the new trial policy.

The policy iteration algorithm converges in a finite number of iterations.

In Fig. 18.7 the policy space algorithm is applied to the stochastic inventory example in Fig. 18.3. Using in *Step 1* the policy of the smallest feasible value for production, the algorithm converges at $n = 2$.

$(\alpha = 1)$

Entering Inventory	$n = 0$			$n = 1$			$n = 2$		
i	$x^0(i)$	w_i^0	W_i^0	$x^1(i)$	w_i^1	W_i^1	$x^2(i)$	w_i^2	W_i^2
0	4	0	20	4	0	$16\frac{1}{2}$	5	0	$17\frac{4}{7}$
1	3	-2	$13\frac{1}{2}$	5	$-6\frac{1}{2}$	$11\frac{1}{4}$	5	$-5\frac{3}{7}$	$12\frac{1}{7}$
2	2	-4	$11\frac{1}{2}$	4	$-8\frac{1}{2}$	$9\frac{1}{4}$	4	$-7\frac{3}{7}$	$10\frac{1}{7}$
3	1	-6	$9\frac{1}{2}$	3	$-10\frac{1}{2}$	$7\frac{1}{4}$	3	$-9\frac{3}{7}$	$8\frac{1}{7}$
4	0	-21	-1	0	-21	$-3\frac{1}{4}$	0	$-20\frac{2}{7}$	$-2\frac{5}{7}$
c^n	20			$17\frac{3}{4}$			$17\frac{4}{7}$		

FIGURE 18.7. Stochastic Inventory Example—Policy Iteration.

▶Consider again the case of the Dependable Manufacturing Company. The recursion when $0 \leq \alpha < 1$ was exhibited as (2) in Sec. 18.3. If you apply to this recursion the heuristic derivation used to obtain the extremal equations (8) above, you obtain the corresponding functional equations

(i) $$w_i + c^* = \underset{x}{\text{minimum}} \{C(x) + 1[i + x - 3] + \tfrac{1}{2}[w_{i+x-2} + w_{i+x-4}]\}.$$

This recursion can also be developed by another heuristic argument that sheds further insight into the meaning of the w_i values. Before presenting this line of reasoning, we record from Fig. 18.7 that the solution to the extremal equations (i) is

(ii) $c^* = 17\tfrac{4}{7}$ $w_1 = -5\tfrac{3}{7} = -5.43$ $w_3 = -9\tfrac{3}{7} = -9.43$

$w_0 \equiv 0$ $w_2 = -7\tfrac{3}{7} = -7.43$ $w_4 = -20\tfrac{2}{7} = -20.29.$

Consider the finite horizon recursion (7) in Sec. 18.1. You would expect that as n gets sufficiently large, the value for $f_n(i)$ would nearly equal n times the expected cost per period c^* plus a correction to account for the initial condition that entering inventory is i:

(iii) $$f_n(i) \approx nc^* + w_i,$$

where here w_i denotes the "correction" factor. Verify that substituting the right-hand side of (iii) into the recursion (7) in Sec. 18.1, and simplifying terms, also yields the set of extremal equations (i) above.

Using the normalization $w_0 = 0$, you have from (iii) that

(iv) $$f_n(i) - f_n(0) \approx w_i - w_0 = w_i.$$

For $n = 5$, the values found in Fig. 17.2 give

(v) $f_n(1) - f_n(0) = -5.57$ $f_n(3) - f_n(0) = -9.57$

$f_n(2) - f_n(0) = -7.57$ $f_n(4) - f_n(0) = -20.38,$

which already agree closely with (ii).   ◀

18.5 LINEAR PROGRAMMING APPROACH

Numerical solutions to the extremal equations in the preceding two sections can also be obtained by means of linear programming formulations. The approach is analogous to that used in Sec. 12.6 for the deterministic shortest-route model.

Consider first the case where $0 \leq \alpha < 1$. Then the extremal equations (1) in Sec. 18.3 imply the linear inequalities

(1) $$y_i - \sum_{\substack{j \text{ in} \\ \text{network}}} p(j|i, d)\alpha y_j \leq c_{id}   \text{ for each } i \text{ and } d,$$

where the y_i are unconstrained in sign. You can obtain *all* the minimal values for y_i by using the objective function

(2) $$\text{maximize} \sum_{\substack{j \text{ in} \\ \text{network}}} r_j y_j,$$

where each r_j is an arbitrary but strictly positive number. [When $\sum r_j = 1$, you can interpret r_j as the probability that the system is at Node j in the initial period, and the value of (2) can be interpreted as the associated expected present value.]

The corresponding dual problem is

$$(3) \qquad \text{minimize} \sum_{\substack{i \text{ in} \\ \text{network}}} \sum_{d \text{ in } D(i)} c_{id} x_{id}$$

subject to

$$(4) \qquad \sum_{d \text{ in } D(j)} x_{jd} - \sum_{\substack{i \text{ in} \\ \text{network}}} \sum_{d \text{ in } D(i)} p(j \mid i, d) \alpha x_{id} = r_j \quad \text{for each } j \text{ in network}$$

$$(5) \qquad \text{all } x_{id} \geq 0.$$

It can be shown that an optimal basic solution contains one $x_{id} > 0$, for each i corresponding to an optimal strategy.

Now consider the case $\alpha = 1$, where we impose the same assumptions as we did for the *policy iteration* algorithm in Sec. 18.4. (It is possible to formulate modified linear programming models, which are larger, for cases where these assumptions are not justified.)

The appropriate primal linear programming model is

$$(6) \qquad \text{maximize } c$$

subject to

$$(7) \qquad w_i - \sum_{j=0}^{T} p(j \mid i, d) w_j + c \leq c_{id} \quad \text{for each } i \text{ and } d,$$

where w_i and c are unconstrained in sign.

The corresponding dual problem is

$$(8) \qquad \text{minimize} \sum_{\substack{i \text{ in} \\ \text{network}}} \sum_{d \text{ in } D(i)} c_{id} v_{id} \quad \text{(expected cost per period)}$$

subject to

$$(9) \qquad \sum_{d \text{ in } D(j)} v_{jd} - \sum_{\substack{i \text{ in} \\ \text{network}}} \sum_{d \text{ in } D(i)} p(j \mid i, d) v_{id} = 0 \quad \begin{array}{l} \text{for each } j \text{ in network} \\ \text{(conservation of probability)} \end{array}$$

$$(10) \qquad \sum_{\substack{i \text{ in} \\ \text{network}}} \sum_{d \text{ in } D(i)} v_{id} = 1 \quad \text{(normalization restriction)}$$

$$(11) \qquad \text{all } v_{id} \geq 0.$$

The v_{id} can be interpreted as the joint probability that the system is at Node i *and* the decision d is taken. Thus the dual model views the optimization as determining system probabilities for every possible pair (i, d). The restrictions (9) can be interpreted as conservation of probability equations: the total probability of leaving Node j equals the total probability of entering Node j. The restriction (10) states that the sum of the joint probabilities must be unity. It can be proved that there always exists an optimal solution to (8) through (11) such that at most only one $v_{id} > 0$ for each i; such a solution corresponds to a policy that yields a minimum value for c in (6) and (7).

Since the dual model is expressed in terms of probabilities, it provides a convenient formulation for those situations where you wish to impose chance-constraints. If such restrictions are added, however, then in general an optimal policy will indicate a randomized strategy; that is, there may be more than one v_{id} that is strictly positive in any optimal policy. In such an event, $(v_{id'}/\sum_{d \text{ in } D(i)} v_{id})$ represents the optimal probability for choosing decision d' when the system is at Node i.

Inventory example. The dual model for the stochastic inventory example (Dependable Manufacturing Company) is shown in Fig. 18.8 The optimal solution is

$$(12) \qquad v_{05} = \frac{2}{14} \quad v_{15} = \frac{1}{14} \quad v_{24} = \frac{6}{14} \quad v_{33} = \frac{1}{14} \quad v_{40} = \frac{4}{14}.$$

The associated expected cost per period is

$$(13) \qquad \tfrac{2}{14}(25) + \tfrac{1}{14}(26) + \tfrac{6}{14}(24) + \tfrac{1}{14}(22) + \tfrac{4}{14}(1) = 17\tfrac{4}{7}$$

as compared to $15\tfrac{4}{5}$ when demands are deterministic $(D = 3)$ for every period.

j	v_{04}	v_{05}	v_{13}	v_{14}	v_{15}	v_{22}	v_{23}	v_{24}	v_{31}	v_{32}	v_{33}	v_{40}	v_{41}	v_{42}	
0	$\frac{1}{2}$	1	$-\frac{1}{2}$			$-\frac{1}{2}$			$-\frac{1}{2}$			$-\frac{1}{2}$			$=0$
1		$-\frac{1}{2}$	1	$\frac{1}{2}$	1		$-\frac{1}{2}$			$-\frac{1}{2}$			$-\frac{1}{2}$		$=0$
2	$-\frac{1}{2}$		$-\frac{1}{2}$		$-\frac{1}{2}$	$\frac{1}{2}$	1	$\frac{1}{2}$	$-\frac{1}{2}$		$-\frac{1}{2}$	$-\frac{1}{2}$		$-\frac{1}{2}$	$=0$
3		$-\frac{1}{2}$		$-\frac{1}{2}$			$-\frac{1}{2}$		1	$\frac{1}{2}$	1		$-\frac{1}{2}$		$=0$
4					$-\frac{1}{2}$			$-\frac{1}{2}$			$-\frac{1}{2}$	1	1	$\frac{1}{2}$	$=0$

$v_{ix} \geq 0$

Normalization constraint: $\sum \sum_{(\text{all } i, x)} v_{ix} = 1$

Minimize: $\sum \sum_{(\text{all } i, x)} \left\{ C(x) + 1[i + x - 3] \right\} v_{ix}$

FIGURE 18.8. Dual Linear Program for Stochastic Inventory Example.

Also in the deterministic case, production is 0 in $\frac{2}{5}$ of the periods, and is 5 in $\frac{3}{5}$ of the periods. For the stochastic version, the probabilities in (12) indicate that the production quantity is 0 in $\frac{4}{14}$ of the periods, and is 3, 4, and 5 in $\frac{1}{14}$, $\frac{6}{14}$, and $\frac{3}{14}$ of the periods, respectively. Thus expected production per period is

$$(14) \qquad \tfrac{4}{14}(0) + \tfrac{1}{14}(3) + \tfrac{6}{14}(4) + \tfrac{3}{14}(5) = 3,$$

in agreement with the assumption that all requirements are filled.

*18.6 COMPUTATIONAL CONSIDERATIONS

Two points must be made in assessing the computational burden associated with obtaining numerical solutions to Markov chain dynamic programming models. The first pertains to overall computational feasibility, and the second to the relative merit of each algorithmic approach given in Secs. 18.2 through 18.5.

Letting N_i denote the number of distinct decisions that can be made at Node i, where $i = 0, 1, \ldots, T$, the structure of the network model can be viewed roughly in terms of a rectangular array with dimensions $(\sum N_i)$ by $(T + 1)$. Figure 18.3 represents such an array for the inventory model considered in this chapter. Note these are approximately the dimensions of the linear programming versions in the preceding section. For even a simple problem, the values $(\sum N_i)$ and $(T + 1)$ can be quite large. For this reason, it is important to find techniques that exploit the specific form of an optimal policy in particular situations. The example in the next section clearly illustrates this conclusion. Sometimes you can specify the Markov chain model to reflect the form of an optimal policy. Often such formulations slightly increase the number of states but drastically decrease the number of possible decisions at most states. (See exercises 50 and 51.)

With regard to the relative merit of each algorithmic approach, the remarks in Chap. 12 are equally applicable here. Specifically, when $\alpha < 1$, value iteration has the advantage of numerical simplicity, but the disadvantage of nonfinite convergence. The advantage of policy iteration is its finite convergence, but the associated computational burden at each iteration is greater since you must solve a complete system of simultaneous linear equations. (It is a simple matter to combine the two approaches into a composite algorithm.) A merit of the linear programming approach is that you can draw on the widespread availability of sophisticated computer programs. What is more, the simplex method applied to the dual problems given in Sec. 18.5 is closely related to the method of policy iteration. Specifically, each iteration of the simplex method corresponds to making a policy improvement at only a *single* state rather than at every state where an improvement is possible.

*18.7 MARKOV CHAIN VERSION OF THE EQUIPMENT REPLACEMENT MODEL

Recall the stochastic equipment replacement model of Sec. 17.7, where

$k =$ planned replacement interval

$p_j =$ probability that the equipment breaks down for the first time during the jth period of usage

$r_j \equiv$ cost of operating the equipment during the jth period of usage if the equipment does not break down

$r_j + s_j \equiv$ penalty cost of operating the equipment if it does break down during the jth period of usage when $j < k$.

If at a regeneration Period t the planned replacement is k but the machine breaks down at the end of Period t + j, for $j < k$, then the equipment is replaced at the start of Period t + j + 1.

For the discount factor $\alpha = 1$, an optimal k was characterized as the solution to

$$(1) \qquad\qquad g = \operatorname*{minimum}_{k=1, 2, \ldots, N} \left(\frac{R_k}{E[j|k]} \right),$$

where R_k is the expected return and $E[j|k]$ is the expected number of periods each piece of equipment is used, given that the *planned* replacement interval is k. The development of this simple solution exploits the fact that an optimal policy is of the regeneration type.

Now you will see how this same problem can be formulated and solved by means of Markov chain analysis. The discussion serves a twofold purpose. First, it demonstrates how the stochastic equipment model is a special case of the model in Sec. 18.4. Second, it makes apparent that a naive Markov formulation is cumbersome as compared to an analysis that exploits the form of an optimal solution. [See exercise 50, part (f), for an alternative Markov formulation.]

Let Node j of the system denote the age of the equipment at the beginning of the period, immediately *after* the decision to keep or replace the old equipment has been made. Thus $j = 0$ designates that a new piece of equipment was purchased, and $j = 1, 2, \ldots,$ indicates that the old equipment has been retained.

Let

$d_1 =$ decision to replace equipment at the beginning of the next period
$d_2 =$ decision not to replace the equipment at the beginning of the next period unless it breaks down in the current period.

Then, for all i,

$$(2) \qquad\qquad\qquad p(0|i, d_1) = 1$$

and

$$(3) \qquad\qquad p(0|i, d_2) = \frac{p_i}{\sum\limits_{k=i}^{\infty} p_k} \qquad p(i+1|i, d_2) = 1 - p(0|i, d_2);$$

also,

$$(4) \qquad\qquad c_{id_1} = r_i \quad \text{and} \quad c_{id_2} = r_i + p(0|i, d_2)s_i.$$

Notice the value $p(0|i, d_2)$ represents the probability that a new piece of equipment is purchased because the old piece fails before the planned replacement period.

The Markov chain formulation for the example in Fig. 17.6 (p. 717) is displayed in Fig. 18.9. The optimal policy is

$$(5) \qquad\qquad d_1 \text{ for } i \geq 2 \quad \text{and} \quad d_2 \text{ otherwise.}$$

Verify that the extremal equations (8) and (9) in Sec. 18.4 are satisfied by

		$p(j\|i,d)$					
i	d	0	1	2	3	4	c_{id}
0	d_1	1					100
	d_2	$\frac{1}{4}$	$\frac{3}{4}$				$100 + \frac{1}{4}(20)$
1	d_1	1					$6\frac{2}{3}$
	d_2	0		1			$6\frac{2}{3} + 0(0)$
2	d_1	1					20
	d_2	$\frac{1}{3}$			$\frac{2}{3}$		$20 + \frac{1}{3}(180)$
3	d_1	1					20
	d_2	0				1	$20 + 0(0)$
4	d_1	1					56

FIGURE 18.9. Markov Formulation of Replacement Model.

(6) $w_0 = 0 \quad w_1 = \dfrac{-220}{3} \quad w_2 = -30 \quad w_3 = -30 \quad w_4 = 6 \quad c^* = 50$

in accordance with the policy in (5), and the associated stationary probabilities are

(7) $$q_0 = \frac{4}{10} \qquad q_1 = q_2 = \frac{3}{10}.$$

Since $\frac{4}{10}$ of the time the system is at Node 0, that is, a new piece of equipment has just been purchased, the expected interval between successive purchases is $[1/\frac{4}{10} = 2\frac{1}{2}]$ periods, in agreement with $E[j|3]$ in Fig. 17.6 (p. 717).

A linear programming or policy space approximation approach to the solution of this example involves computations with a system of size (9×5), as indicated by Fig. 18.9. Such techniques applied to this "naive" formulation are inefficient as compared to the use of the simple optimization in (1).

REVIEW EXERCISES

1 Consider the stochastic shortest-route model in Sec. 18.2.

(a) Suppose $c(j|i, d)$ denotes the actual return in the current period from making decision d at Node i, when as a consequence, the state of the system at the next period is Node j. Perform the intermediate algebra justifying the recursion (6), where c_{id} is calculated as in (4).

(b) Justify the validity of the recursion (6), and compare (6) with the deterministic version (1). Show where the acyclic assumption is exploited in writing the recursion (6).

(c) Explain how finding a numerical solution to (6) provides an optimal decision rule. State how to implement such a rule.

2 Consider the production and inventory example in Sec. 18.2.

(a) Suppose the production constraint is a maximum of 6 items, instead of 5. How does this alteration affect the network characterization of the model?

(b) Suppose the ending inventory constraint is a maximum of 5 items, instead of 4. How would you number the nodes in the equivalent network formulation?

(c) Verify that the only positive transition probabilities are those given in (8). Also verify that (8) and (10) satisfy the acyclic assumption (5).

(d) Explain the equality in (11). Is $c_{5n+i,\,x}$ an expected value? Explain.

(e) Draw a network characterization, analogous to Fig. 18.1, for the policy: produce 3 if $i = 0, 1, 2, 3$, and produce 0 otherwise, for $n \geq 2$.

*3 Consider the linear programming version of the stochastic shortest-route model, as described in the special material at the end of Sec. 18.2.

(a) Perform the intermediate algebraic steps leading from the recursion (6) to the constraints (ii).

(b) Verify that (iii) through (vi) is the dual problem to (i) and (ii).

(c) Write the primal and dual linear programs for $T = 4$ and $d = 1, 2, 3$, analogous to the tables in Fig. 18.2.

(d) What effect does the acyclic assumption have on the appearance of the primal and dual problems, such as shown in Fig. 18.2?

(e) Suppose $\alpha = 1$. Interpret all the linear constraints in the dual problem.

(f) How many variables and constraints are in the primal and dual problems for the inventory and production example? Assume the horizon is three periods, as in Fig. 18.1.

(g) Answer the question in part (f) assuming that the production constraint is a maximum of six items, instead of five.

(h) Answer the question in part (f) assuming that the ending inventory constraint is a maximum of five items, instead of four.

(i) Consider the illustration in Fig. 18.2 and let $\alpha = 1$. Show in the dual problem how to constrain the probability that the system enters Node 2 to be at least $\frac{1}{4}$ but no more than $\frac{3}{5}$. Show in the dual problem how to ensure that *if* the system enters Node 2, then $d = 1$ is chosen with no greater than a $\frac{1}{3}$ probability.

4 *Optimal Batch Size Model* (Sec. 17.5). Assume you require three working items, and that no more than five items can be ordered at a time from the vendor.

(a) Describe how this problem can be characterized as a stochastic shortest-route problem. Be sure you indicate the definition and number of nodes in the network. Explain the connections between this characterization and the recursion (2) in Sec. 17.5.

(b) Draw the network illustrating the policy of always ordering two more items than are required. (*Hint:* use a "dummy" node to represent the event that there are enough working items in the order received to fill the requirement.)

(c) Write explicitly the formula for each expected return c_{id}.

(d) Write explicitly the conditional probabilities $p(j\,|\,i, d)$. {*Hint:* consider and interpret the probabilities $p_x(j)/[1 - p_x(x)]$, for $j = 0, 1, \ldots, x - 1$.}

(e) What difficulty arises in formulating a stochastic shortest-route model based on the recursion (1) in Sec. 18.2?

5 Show that if, in fact, the model characterized by the extremal equations (1) in Sec. 18.3 is really deterministic, then (1) simplifies to the corresponding recursion in Chap. 12.

6 Each part below indicates a change in assumption for the stochastic inventory model in Sec. 18.3. For each change, explain in detail the alterations in Fig. 18.3.

   (a) The holding cost function is $1 \cdot (i + x - D)^2$, where D designates the demand level.
   (b) The probability that demand is 2, 3, or 4 is $\frac{1}{3}$ for each value.
   (c) Maximum production is 6, where $C(6) = 25$.
   (d) Maximum entering inventory is 5, instead of 4.
   (e) Assume maximum entering inventory is 5, instead of 4, and that the policy in (6) is used with $x = 0$ if $i = 5$. Write the array of transition probabilities analogous to (7). Do the same for the policy of producing 3 if $i = 0, 1, 2, 3$ and producing 0 otherwise.

7 Consider the stochastic inventory model, as described in Sec. 18.3.

   (a) Perform the value iteration algorithm and verify the entries in Fig. 18.4 for $n = 1$ and $n = 2$. Do the same for $n = 3$.
   (b) Write the equations (9) for the optimal policy over an unbounded horizon with $\alpha = .9$, and verify the minimal values y_i given in Fig. 18.4.
   (c) Explain why, for $i = 1, 2, 3$, the values of y_i^n and of y_i differ by the amount 2 in Figs. 18.4 and 18.5.
   (d) Calculate the present values associated with using the policy shown for $n = 1$ in Fig. 18.5 over an unbounded horizon.
   (e) Give a plausible explanation for why the amounts $x_0(i)$ decrease as α gets smaller, as shown in Fig. 18.6.
   (f) Write the equations (9) for the optimal policy over an unbounded horizon with $\alpha = .5$, and verify the minimal values y_i given in Fig. 18.6.
   (g) Suppose you have applied the policy iteration algorithm and at $n = 2$, the values of y_i^2 equal the optimal y_i in Fig. 18.4. Perform the test in (13) to verify that the iterations terminate.

*8 Consider employing the value iteration algorithm, as described by (8) in Sec. 18.3. Suppose you let the initial values y_i^0 be obtained by selecting a trial stationary policy and solving (9). The text states that if you stop at iteration m and employ the immediate optimal policy from (8) as a stationary policy for the unbounded horizon model, the corresponding expected values will be no larger than the y_i^m in (8). Show how this conclusion follows from the argument sketched in the advanced material justifying the Stationary Policy Theorem.

9 (a) Compare the value iteration algorithm for the stochastic shortest-route problem in Sec. 18.3 with that for the deterministic problem in Chap. 12. In what ways are the algorithms alike? In what ways are they different? Compare the computational burdens and convergence properties.
   (b) Answer part (a) for the policy iteration algorithm.

10 Give a verbal interpretation of the definition of an optimal policy for $\alpha = 1$ expressed

by the equality in (1) of Sec. 18.4. (*Hint:* remember that $y_i^*(\alpha)$ is calculated for a *specified* policy π^*.) Recall from Chap. 12 that when $\alpha = 1$, several policies may give the same average return per period over an unbounded horizon, but may differ in their behavior "en route." (For example, the two streams 100, 1, 1, 1, ... and 10, 1, 1, 1, ... both have an average return of 1 per period.) How does the definition in (1) treat such transient effects?

11 In each part below, determine whether there exist stationary probabilities, and if so, calculate them.

*(a) *Cases 2* and *3* in Sec. 18.4.

*(b) *Case 4* in Sec. 18.4.

*(c) *Case 6* in Sec. 18.4.

(d) $\begin{pmatrix} \frac{1}{4} & \frac{3}{4} \\ \frac{1}{2} & \frac{1}{2} \end{pmatrix}$.

(e) $\begin{pmatrix} \frac{1}{4} & \frac{3}{4} \\ \frac{3}{4} & \frac{1}{4} \end{pmatrix}$.

(f) $\begin{pmatrix} \frac{1}{4} & \frac{3}{4} & 0 \\ 0 & \frac{1}{4} & \frac{3}{4} \\ \frac{3}{4} & 0 & \frac{1}{4} \end{pmatrix}$.

(g) $\begin{pmatrix} \frac{1}{4} & \frac{3}{4} & 0 \\ 0 & \frac{1}{4} & \frac{3}{4} \\ \frac{1}{4} & 0 & \frac{3}{4} \end{pmatrix}$.

(h) $\begin{pmatrix} \frac{1}{4} & \frac{3}{4} & 0 \\ 0 & \frac{1}{4} & \frac{3}{4} \\ 0 & \frac{1}{4} & \frac{3}{4} \end{pmatrix}$.

(i) $\begin{pmatrix} \frac{1}{4} & \frac{3}{4} & 0 \\ 0 & \frac{1}{4} & \frac{3}{4} \\ 0 & \frac{3}{4} & \frac{1}{4} \end{pmatrix}$.

(j) $\begin{pmatrix} \frac{1}{4} & 0 & \frac{3}{4} \\ \frac{3}{4} & 0 & \frac{1}{4} \\ 1 & 0 & 0 \end{pmatrix}$.

(k) $\begin{pmatrix} \frac{1}{4} & 0 & \frac{3}{4} \\ \frac{3}{4} & 0 & \frac{1}{4} \\ 0 & 1 & 0 \end{pmatrix}$.

(l) $\begin{pmatrix} \frac{1}{4} & 0 & \frac{3}{4} \\ \frac{3}{4} & 0 & \frac{1}{4} \\ 0 & 0 & 1 \end{pmatrix}$.

(m) $\begin{pmatrix} 0 & \frac{1}{4} & \frac{3}{4} \\ \frac{3}{4} & \frac{1}{4} & 0 \\ 0 & 0 & 1 \end{pmatrix}$.

(n) $\begin{pmatrix} 0 & 1 & 0 \\ 0 & 0 & 1 \\ 1 & 0 & 0 \end{pmatrix}$.

(o) $\begin{pmatrix} 0 & 0 & 1 \\ 1 & 0 & 0 \\ 0 & 1 & 0 \end{pmatrix}$.

(p) $\begin{pmatrix} \frac{1}{2} & \frac{1}{2} & 0 & 0 \\ \frac{1}{2} & \frac{1}{2} & 0 & 0 \\ 0 & 0 & \frac{1}{2} & \frac{1}{2} \\ 0 & 0 & \frac{1}{2} & \frac{1}{2} \end{pmatrix}$.

(q) $\begin{pmatrix} 0 & 0 & \frac{1}{2} & \frac{1}{2} \\ 0 & 0 & \frac{1}{2} & \frac{1}{2} \\ \frac{1}{2} & \frac{1}{2} & 0 & 0 \\ \frac{1}{2} & \frac{1}{2} & 0 & 0 \end{pmatrix}$.

(r) $\begin{pmatrix} \frac{2}{5} & \frac{3}{5} \\ \frac{3}{4} & \frac{1}{4} \end{pmatrix}$.

(s) $\begin{pmatrix} \frac{2}{5} & \frac{3}{5} \\ \frac{1}{4} & \frac{3}{4} \end{pmatrix}$.

(t) $\begin{pmatrix} \frac{2}{5} & \frac{3}{5} & 0 \\ 0 & \frac{3}{4} & \frac{1}{4} \\ 1 & 0 & 0 \end{pmatrix}$.

(u) $\begin{pmatrix} \frac{2}{5} & \frac{3}{5} & 0 & 0 \\ 0 & \frac{3}{4} & \frac{1}{4} & 0 \\ 0 & 0 & 0 & 1 \\ 1 & 0 & 0 & 0 \end{pmatrix}$.

*12 Formulas (iv) and (v) in Sec. 18.4 show how to calculate the probability $q_j(n)$ that the system is in State j at Period n, given probabilities $\bar{q}_j$ for the state of the system at the initial period. In each part below, calculate the $q_j(n)$ for $n = 2, 3, 4$, assuming that the initial probability $\bar{q}_0 = 1$ (the system starts in the first state). Consider the problems in exercise 11,

(a) Part (a).   (h) Part (n).
(b) Part (b).   (i) Part (q).
(c) Part (d).   (j) Part (r).
(d) Part (e).   (k) Part (s).
(e) Part (j).   (l) Part (t).
(f) Part (l).   (m) Part (u).
(g) Part (m).
(n) Answer questions (a)-(m) assuming $\bar{q}_1 = 1$.
(o) Name the problems above where $q_j(n)$ does *not* approach a limit as n becomes arbitrarily large?

13 (a) Consider the extremal equations (8) in Sec. 18.4. Show the intermediate algebraic steps that justify going from (7) to (8).
   (b) Consider the heuristic argument establishing (8). Explain where the reasoning uses the assumption that there exists an optimal stationary strategy having stationary probabilities uniquely characterized by (3).
   (c) Verify that if the w_i satisfy (8), then so do $(w_i + K)$ for an arbitrary constant K.
   (d) Verify the algebraic steps in (11) and use (3) to verify that (11) simplifies to (5).

14 (a) Consider the Necessary Condition for Optimality, given in Sec. 18.4. Explain why parts (a) and (b) are equivalent. Why is the condition termed "Necessary"?
   (b) Consider the Sufficient Condition for Minimum Expected Return, given in Sec. 18.4. Explain why parts (a) and (b) are equivalent. Why is the condition termed "Sufficient"?

15 Compare the policy iteration algorithm for $\alpha = 1$ in Sec. 18.4 with that for the deterministic problem in Chap. 12. In what ways are the algorithms alike? In what ways are they different? Compare the computational burdens and convergence properties.

16 (a) In Fig. 18.7 the policy space algorithm is applied to the stochastic inventory example in Fig. 18.3. Verify the entries.
   (b) Apply the algorithm starting in *Step 1* with the policy of producing 3 if $i = 0, 1, 2, 3$ and producing 0 otherwise.

*17 Consider the case of the Dependable Manufacturing Company in the special material at the end of Sec. 18.5.

(a) Show how to derive (i) from the recursion (2) in Sec. 18.3.
(b) Verify that the values in (ii) satisfy the extremal equations (i).
(c) Verify that substituting the right-hand side of (iii) into the recursion (7) in Sec. 18.1, and simplifying terms, also yields the set of extremal equations (i).

*18 Consider the canonical form for discrete dynamic programming models given by (i) in the special material at the start of Sec. 18.3. *See parts (a) and (b), p. 770.*

(a) Apply the same heuristic reasoning given in Sec. 18.5 to derive a functional equation for $\alpha = 1$. Use the notation $w(s)$ and c^*.

(b) Similarly, write the finite horizon version, using the notation $f_n(s)$. Then let $f_n(s) \approx nc^* + w(s)$ and derive a functional equation for $\alpha = 1$ analogous to the approach suggested at the end of Sec. 18.4.

19 Consider the primal and dual linear programming models in Sec. 18.5.

(a) Write (1) through (5) in detail for a network containing Nodes 0, 1, 2, 3 and having two decisions $d = 1$ and $d = 2$ at each node.

*(b) Given that each r_j is a strictly positive number, devise an argument for why a basic solution to the dual model (3), (4), and (5) contains one $x_{id} > 0$ for each Node i.

(c) Repeat part (a) for (6) through (11).

(d) In the dual problem of part (c), show how to constrain the probability that the system enters Node 2 to be at least $\frac{1}{4}$ but no more than $\frac{3}{5}$. Also show how to ensure that when the system enters Node 2, then $d = 1$ is chosen with no greater than $\frac{1}{3}$ probability.

20 (a) Verify that the solution (12) for the inventory example in Sec. 18.5 is feasible and optimal in the dual linear program shown in Fig. 18.8. Translate the solution in (12) into a decision rule.

(b) What are the coefficients in Fig. 18.8 if the probability that demand is 2, 3, or 4 is $\frac{1}{3}$ for each value?

*(c) Find an optimal policy for the demand assumptions in part (b).

21 Consider the primal problem (1) and (2) in Sec. 18.3. Suppose there are two nodes $(i = 0, 1)$ and three decisions $(d = 1, 2, 3)$ at each node. Assume the probabilities $p(j \mid i, d)$ are

$$p(0 \mid 0, 1) = \frac{1}{4} \quad p(0 \mid 0, 2) = \frac{3}{4} \quad p(0 \mid 0, 3) = \frac{1}{2}$$

$$p(1 \mid 0, 1) = \frac{3}{4} \quad p(1 \mid 0, 2) = \frac{1}{4} \quad p(1 \mid 0, 3) = \frac{1}{2}$$

$$p(0 \mid 1, 1) = \frac{1}{3} \quad p(0 \mid 1, 2) = \frac{1}{2} \quad p(0 \mid 1, 3) = \frac{2}{3}$$

$$p(1 \mid 1, 1) = \frac{2}{3} \quad p(1 \mid 1, 2) = \frac{1}{2} \quad p(1 \mid 1, 3) = \frac{1}{3},$$

and the costs are

$$c_{01} = 24 \quad c_{02} = 60 \quad c_{03} = 48$$
$$c_{11} = 36 \quad c_{12} = 24 \quad c_{13} = 45.$$

Also assume $\alpha = \frac{1}{2}$. Write the equations in detail. Construct a solution space diagram and show that the optimal solution is obtained for *any* positive r_0 and r_1 used in the objective function, which is maximize $r_0 y_0 + r_1 y_1$.

*22 Consider the stochastic equipment replacement model in Sec. 18.7.

(a) Justify the transition probabilities given by (2) and (3), and the expected costs given by (4).

(b) Verify that the optimal policy is that stated in (5). Use the extremal equations in (8) and (9) of Sec. 18.4 and the values given in (6).

23 Explain your understanding of the following terms:

Markovian decision process
stationary strategy (policy)
deterministic policy
stochastic shortest-route model
Markov property
extremal equations
value iteration algorithm (successive
    approximations in function space)
value determination routine
policy iteration algorithm (successive
    approximations in policy space)
law of motion for a system

Markov chain
stationary probabilities
limiting probabilities
statistical equilibrium
operating characteristics
*transient correction
*doubly stochastic
*transient state
*cyclic chain
*multiple chain
conservation of probability restrictions
normalization restriction.

FORMULATION AND COMPUTATIONAL EXERCISES

In many of the following exercises, you are asked to formulate models in terms of dynamic programming recursions. Be sure to define all the symbols you use.

24 For the exercises in Chap. 17 listed below, show how to formulate the problem as a stochastic shortest-route model, analogous to the formulation used for the inventory model at the end of Sec. 18.2.

(a) Exercise 23.
(b) Exercise 38, part (b).
(c) Exercise 39.
(d) Exercise 41, part (a).
(e) Exercise 42, part (a).
(f) Exercise 42, part (b).
(g) Exercise 47, part (a).

(h) Exercise 47, part (b).
(i) Exercise 49, part (a).
(j) Exercise 51, part (a).
(k) Exercise 52, part (a).
(l) Exercise 53, part (a).
(m) Exercise 56.

25 Consider the extremal equations (1) in Sec. 18.3. Assume you have available a lower estimate L_i and an upper estimate U_i on each unknown y_i, that is, $L_i \leq y_i \leq U_i$. Show that it is *never* optimal to use decision d' in $D(i)$ if

$$\sum_{\substack{j \text{ in} \\ \text{network}}} p(j \mid i, d') \alpha L_j + c_{id'} > \underset{d \text{ in } D(i)}{\text{minimum}} \left[\sum_{\substack{j \text{ in} \\ \text{network}}} p(j \mid i, d) U_j + c_{id} \right].$$

Suggest how you might use the above inequality to speed convergence in successive approximation algorithms.

26 Consider the inventory model with uncertain production costs in exercise 38, part (b), of Chap. 17. Let $\alpha = 1$ and find an optimal policy over an unbounded horizon.

27 Consider the stochastic inventory example in Fig. 18.3. Suppose that the production limit is raised to 6 and that $C(6) = 28.5$; assume $\alpha = 1$.

(a) Use the policy space algorithm to find an optimal policy. (*Hint:* examine Figs. 8.17 and 8.18 to select an initial trial policy.)

*(b) As was shown in the special material at the end of Sec. 18.4, $f_n(i) - f_n(0) \approx w_i$. Examine how close this approximation is for each i and $n = 3, 4, 5$, using the values of w_i from part (a) and $f_n(i)$ from Fig. 8.17.

28 Consider the stochastic inventory model with smoothing costs in exercise 40, part (b), of Chap. 17. Let $\alpha = 1$ and find an optimal policy over an unbounded horizon; use the policy iteration algorithm.

29 Consider the inventory example in Sec. 18.3. Suppose the demand distribution alternates from period to period:

$$P[D = 2] = \frac{1}{2} \quad P[D = 4] = \frac{1}{2} \quad \text{(in Period t)}$$

$$P[D = 1] = \frac{1}{3} \quad P[D = 4] = \frac{2}{3} \quad \text{(in Period t + 1)}.$$

(a) Show how to alter the recursion (2) accordingly.

*(b) Let $\alpha = 1$ and determine the appropriate extremal equations.

*(c) Find an optimal policy using the formulation in part (b).

30 In each part below, find an optimal inventory stockage policy over an unbounded horizon with $\alpha = 1$; use the policy iteration algorithm.

(a) Exercise 41, part (a), of Chap. 17.

(b) Exercise 41, part (b), of Chap. 17.

31 Consider the stochastic inventory model described in Sec. 18.2. Suppose that a demand need not occur in every period. Specifically, assume that if demand occurs in Period t, the next demand occurs in Period t + s, where $s = 1, 2, 3$, and the associated probability is $q_s = \frac{1}{3}$.

(a) Alter the recursion (7) accordingly. (Note that if inventory at the end of Period t is j and the next demand occurs in Period t + s, then the holding cost on the j items is incurred s times.)

(b) Suppose the horizon is unbounded and that the one-period discount factor is α, where $0 \leq \alpha < 1$. Show how to alter the extremal equations (2) in Sec. 18.3 accordingly.

*(c) Suppose the horizon is unbounded. Derive the appropriate extremal equations for $\alpha = 1$.

*(d) Using your answer in part (c), find an optimal policy.

32 Sally Forth, a campus politico, enjoys spending her Saturday nights attending a Cause meeting in The Big City. Feeling the need for a male escort, she asks, each week, one of her three regular dates, whom she affectionately refers to as The Beard, The Haircut, and The Square. To keep the scenario simple, assume she asks only one each week, and if he turns her down, then she goes unescorted. Suppose the following

conditional probabilities represent the chance that each of her dates accepts the invitation, given the person she dated on the previous week:

Last Week's Date	Probability of Acceptance by		
	The Beard	The Haircut	The Square
No Escort	$\frac{1}{2}$	$\frac{1}{2}$	$\frac{3}{4}$
The Beard	$\frac{1}{2}$	$\frac{1}{3}$	$\frac{1}{4}$
The Haircut	$\frac{1}{4}$	$\frac{2}{3}$	$\frac{1}{3}$
The Square	$\frac{3}{5}$	$\frac{2}{5}$	$\frac{1}{5}$

(a) Suppose there are n more weeks until summer vacation. Formulate a dynamic programming model to provide an asking policy that maximizes her expected number of escorts.

(b) Suppose Sally's horizon is unlimited, but she has a discount factor $\alpha = \frac{1}{2}$. Write the appropriate extremal equations. Given the data and these assumptions, find an optimal policy.

*(c) As in part (b), suppose Sally has an unending future, but wants to maximize the "expected number of escorts per week." Derive the appropriate extremal equations and find an optimal solution.

33 The manager of Maisie's Department Store has to decide how much advertising copy to place in the local Sunday newspaper; in particular, he can choose either light (L) or heavy (H) coverage. He classifies weekly sales into three categories: average (A), above average (AA), and below average (BA), and believes that the current week's sales depend probabilistically on both the previous week's sales and the advertising level. Specifically, his data are

Last Week's Sales	Light Coverage (L)			Heavy Coverage (H)		
	This Week's Sales:			This Week's Sales:		
	AA	A	BA	AA	A	BA
AA	.2	.5	.3	.6	.3	.1
A	0	.6	.4	.4	.5	.1
BA	0	.3	.7	.2	.7	.1

Thus, for example, if last week's sales were A and his advertising is H, then there is a .4 probability that this week's sales are AA, .5 probability that they are A, and .1 probability that they are BA. Assume that advertising coverage L costs 100 and H costs 300, and suppose that the weekly return (excluding advertising costs) from sales AA is 1200, A is 1000, and BA is 800.

(a) Use the policy iteration algorithm to find an advertising strategy that *maximizes* weekly net return (including advertising costs) over an unbounded horizon.

(b) Over what range of cost for coverage L does the policy in part (a) remain optimal? For coverage H?

(c) Over what range of weekly return from sales AA does the policy in part (a) remain optimal? From sales A? From sales BA? *Parts (d) and (e) on p. 774.*

*(d) Let p_1 denote the probability that this week's sales are AA and p_2 that they are A, given that last week's sales are A and that there is heavy coverage, where $p_1 + p_2$ = .9. What is the range for p_1 such that the policy in part (a) remains optimal?

(e) Formulate the primal and dual linear programming models, and find an optimal solution to the dual problem. Interpret your solution.

34 A large soap company, renowned for successful research and advertising promotions of its products, has introduced a new wonder detergent called "LYE." The product manager, in conjunction with the advertising department, is investigating a special sales campaign built on the slogan "Come LYE with us." Like all of the company's products, the first six months sales will start at a high level. The manager thinks there is a .8 chance that the sales will remain at a high level at the beginning of the next six months if he uses this LYE campaign. He feels that if he does not use the special advertising, the probability is only .5 that the sales will remain high at the start of the next six months. If the sales drop to an average level, then the product manager has two options. He can initiate research to improve the product. This has a .7 chance of returning sales to a high level by the beginning of the subsequent six months. Alternatively, he can keep the product "as is." Then there is a .6 chance that it remains at the average sales level at the beginning of the subsequent six months; but consumers being changeable, the probability is .4 that sales will pick up again to the high level.

When the sales start out high and ordinary advertising is used, the six-month returns are 19 if sales stay at a high level and are 13 if they don't; if a special advertising campaign is used, then the analogous returns are 4.5 and 2. When starting sales are average and research is initiated, then the returns are 11 if the sales rise to high level and are −9 if they don't; if the product remains "as is," the analogous returns are 13 and 3. Assume the same decision problem concerning the marketing of LYE repeats itself every six months over an unbounded horizon.

(a) Formulate the appropriate dynamic programming extremal equations for the cases $0 \leq \alpha < 1$ and $\alpha = 1$. (*Note:* the sense of optimization is to maximize.)

(b) Write the associated primal and dual linear programming models given your formulation in part (a).

(c) Solve the case $\alpha = 1$ by the value iteration algorithm.

35 *Cash Management Problem.* Suppose in the example in exercise 55, Chap. 17, that the horizon is unbounded and that the probability distribution of the daily fluctuation is stationary. Write the appropriate extremal equations for the cases $0 \leq \alpha < 1$ and $\alpha = 1$.

36 *Tiny Timber Company* (Sec. 11.3). Suppose the probability is $1 - p$ that at the end of each period the entire forest burns down.

(a) Derive the appropriate optimizing formulation for the single decision problem. Assume a burned-down forest has no value, and that a forest fire cannot destroy harvested trees.

(b) Repeat the analysis for the unbounded horizon problem, where you assume that if the forest burns down prior to the planned harvest period, then the forest is replanted in the next period. Exhibit formulas that determine the optimal planned harvest interval k for the cases $0 \leq \alpha < 1$ and $\alpha = 1$.

37 The Kitch-Kitchy Water System consists of a dam and a subsidiary reservoir. The dam has capacity K. Each period the inflow to the dam is S, where the actual amount S in Period t has an associated probability distribution $p_t(S)$. If the water in the dam plus S exceeds K, the excess is spillover. Let D_t be the demand for water in Period t; this demand can be satisfied from either the dam or the reservoir, but not from any spillover. (For simplicity, assume that we refer to the supply of water in the dam before the demand for water must be filled.) Denote the cost of a unit of water from the dam as c_{1t} and from the reservoir as c_{2t} in Period t, where $c_{1t} < c_{2t}$. For all practical purposes, you can consider the reservoir to have an "unlimited" supply of water so that there always exists a feasible policy for meeting demands.

(a) Formulate a dynamic programming model to find a strategy for determining the amounts of water to draw from the dam and from the reservoir in order to minimize expected discounted cost over a T-period horizon. (Let α denote the one-period discount factor, where $0 \le \alpha < 1$.)

(b) Show how to alter the formulation in part (a) if the demand level D_t is characterized by a probability distribution $q_t(D_t)$.

(c) Show how to alter the formulation in parts (a) and (b) if the probability distribution for S_t depends on S_{t-1}, denoted by $p_t(S \mid S_{t-1})$. If the probability distribution for S_t depends on $S_1 + S_2 + \cdots + S_{t-1}$, denoted by $p_t(S \mid \sum_{j=1}^{t-1} S_j)$.

(d) Discuss whether the decision problem is made simpler or more complex if, in parts (a) and (b), all the probability distributions and costs are stationary over time and the horizon is unbounded.

(e) Suppose that any excess water spilling over the dam is worth v_t per unit in Period t. (For example, spillover may be used for irrigation, or routed to another reservoir.) Show how to alter the formulation in part (a) accordingly.

38 *Kleen City Police Problem* (exercises 30, Chap. 2, and 27, Chap. 5). Let $p_t(r_t)$ be the probability distribution of the minimal requirement in Period t; assume that the exact value of r_t is known before making the decision x_t of the number of men to start on duty.

(a) Assume there is a one-period discount factor α, where $0 \le \alpha < 1$, and the horizon is unbounded. Formulate an appropriate dynamic programming model.

(b) Show how the formulation in part (a) simplifies (if at all) when all the probability distributions are identical $p_t(r) \equiv p(r)$.

*(c) Derive the extremal equations to be satisfied in parts (a) and (b) when $\alpha = 1$.

39 The Kleen City Hospital has a well-designed procedure for the regular staffing of its emergency ward with a sufficient number of interns. But occasionally, there is a greater than normal influx of patients so that the regularly assigned staff has to be augmented with additional interns. The hospital wants a rational policy for determining when to call in supplemental staff and for deciding how many additional interns to call. Assume that each additional intern is assigned a cost factor c per period (15 minutes). Let w denote the assigned cost factor of a patient waiting to be treated (assessed at the beginning of each period). The state of the system is the number of patients waiting to be treated; given this state, the hospital decides the number of extra interns s it needs. Assume that $p(j \mid i, s)$ is the probability that there are j patients waiting at the beginning of the next period, given that i patients are waiting at the

beginning of the current period and s extra interns are placed on duty. Past experience has shown that there are never more than 10 patients waiting.

(a) Formulate a set of extremal equations to yield a policy that minimizes the expected cost per period.

(b) Comment on the difficulties attendant with estimating the model's parameters.

(c) Explain how the formulation in part (a) must be altered if there is a cost $k(s_{t-1}, s_t)$ due to changing the number of extra interns from Period $t-1$ to Period t.

40 Captain Ron, operator of the Crocker Ship Company, runs a charter tanker between two ports, A and B. Assume that it takes the tanker a day to sail between these ports. Each morning the Captain must decide whether to load the tanker with the freight available and sail to the other port, or to wait in port another day hoping that the freight to be moved will be more profitable. Let the daily cost of sailing the ship be c_1 and the daily cost of leaving the ship at anchor be c_2, where $c_1 > c_2$. Assume there are two types of cargo shipments that are loaded at Port A, having values a_1 and a_2. Suppose $a_1 > a_2$ and that p_a is the probability that a_1 is available (so that $1 - p_a$ is the probability that only a_2 is available). Also suppose that the cargo available each day is independent of the availabilities on previous days (hence if the Captain does not sail on one day, he still has probability p_a of obtaining a_1 on the next day). Analogously, let the values of the cargos at Port B be b_1 and b_2, where $b_1 > b_2$, and p_b be the probability of b_1.

(a) Formulate a dynamic programming model for an unbounded horizon. Treat both cases of $0 \le \alpha < 1$ and $\alpha = 1$.

(b) Write the primal and dual linear programs corresponding to your formulations in part (a).

*(c) Discuss how to alter your formulations in part (a) if the sailing times between the ports are three days. If the sailing time from Port A to Port B is three days and from Port B to Port A is two days.

*(d) Discuss how to alter your formulation in part (a) if each sailing time t is a random variable having probability distribution $p(t)$.

41 At the start of each day, an expensive piece of machinery is examined to determine whether it is in good working order, in need of minor maintenance, or requiring a major repair. Denote these states as $0, 1, 2$, respectively. If the machine is in good working order, the probability that it remains so at the beginning of the next day is $p(0|0)$, that it needs maintenance is $p(1|0)$, and that it needs repair is $p(2|0)$. If the machine is not in good working order, the company can utilize either of two maintenance-and-repair services. The We-Fix-It Service Company charges M for minor maintenance and R for a major repair. The We-Try-to-Fix-It Service charges m and r, where $m < M$ and $r < R$. As you might suppose, We-Fix-It does better quality work, and this is reflected in the probabilities that at the beginning of the next day, the equipment is in good working order. Let $d = 1$ refer to using We-Fix-It and $d = 2$ to using We-Try-to-Fix-It; let $p(j|i, d)$ denote the transition probability of the machine being in State j next period $(j = 0, 1, 2)$ if it is in State i this period $(i = 1, 2)$ and decision d is made $(d = 1, 2)$.

(a) Formulate dynamic programming extremal equations for $0 \le \alpha < 1$ and $\alpha = 1$ that determine an optimal policy over an unbounded horizon for deciding which service to use, given the state of the equipment.

(b) Write the corresponding primal and dual linear programs, as described in Sec. 18.5.

(c) Let $\alpha = 1$ and assume that

$$
\begin{array}{lllll}
p(0\,|\,0) & = .6 & p(1\,|\,0) & = .3 & p(2\,|\,0) & = .1 \\
p(0\,|\,1,1) = .9 & p(1\,|\,1,1) = .1 & p(2\,|\,1,1) = 0 & M = 14 \\
p(0\,|\,1,2) = .7 & p(1\,|\,1,2) = .2 & p(2\,|\,1,2) = .1 & m = 12 \\
p(0\,|\,2,1) = .6 & p(1\,|\,2,1) = .3 & p(2\,|\,2,1) = .1 & R = 21 \\
p(0\,|\,2,2) = .5 & p(1\,|\,2,2) = .4 & p(2\,|\,2,2) = .1 & r = 19.
\end{array}
$$

Find an optimal policy and the minimum expected cost per period. (Use the policy iteration algorithm.) Show the corresponding optimal solution to the dual linear programming problem in part (b).

*(d) Suppose that We-Fix-It requires a full day to perform a major repair, and We-Try-to-Fix-It requires two full days. Assume that the company loses c for each day the machine is inoperative. Show how to alter the formulations in part (a). (*Hint:* define two new states, "first day inoperative" and "second day inoperative.")

*(e) Find an optimal policy in part (d) using the data in part (c) and $c = 2$.

42 *Optimal Replacement Problem.* The Hard Core Computer Company, manufacturers of solid-state memory devices, serves several installations at Cape Kennedy. In one such installation an expensive device is service tested every morning and then rated as being in Working Condition j, where $j = 1, 2, \ldots, J$. Condition $j = J$ means that the device is inoperative and must be replaced. The testing procedure is calibrated such that Condition j is deemed better than Condition $j + 1$. If the condition is i, where $i < J$, the company has the option of letting the device operate for the day; denote this decision $d = 1$ and the consequent probability that the machine is in Condition j tomorrow morning as $p(j\,|\,i, 1)$. The company can instead install a new device; denote this decision $d = 2$. The associated transition probability is simply $p(j\,|\,2)$, and does not depend on the current Condition i. The value of using a machine in Condition j during a period is c_j. If the device is replaced, a cost c_0 is incurred. And if the device deteriorates to Condition J by the beginning of the next period, an additional cost c_J is incurred.

(a) Formulate the appropriate unbounded horizon extremal equations for $0 \le \alpha < 1$ and for $\alpha = 1$ to determine the conditions at which a new device should be installed.

(b) Show how to alter the formulation in part (a) if it takes a day to install a new device. If it takes two days. Let v represent the cost per day of having the equipment out of order due to installation of a new device. (*Hint:* consider adding the states "first day of installation" and "second day of installation.")

(c) Consider a problem having the data $J = 3$, $c_0 = 100$, $c_1 = 5$, $c_2 = 10$, $c_3 = 75$, and

$$
\begin{array}{lll}
p(1\,|\,1,1) = .7 & p(2\,|\,1,1) = .2 & p(3\,|\,1,1) = .1 \\
p(1\,|\,2,1) = .1 & p(2\,|\,2,1) = .7 & p(3\,|\,2,1) = .2 \\
p(1\,|\,2) = .8 & p(2\,|\,2) = .1 & p(3\,|\,2) = .1.
\end{array}
$$

Write the formulations in part (a) in detail. Let $\alpha = 1$ and find an optimal solution using the policy iteration algorithm. *Parts (d) through (f) on p. 778.*

(d) Write the primal and dual linear programs, as described in Sec. 18.5, for the example in part (c) for both $0 \leq \alpha < 1$ and $\alpha = 1$. Exhibit the optimal solution to the dual problem for $\alpha = 1$.

(e) Determine the number of variables and equations in the primal and dual linear programming versions for your formulation in part (a) with $\alpha < 1$.

*(f) Suppose the device is specially made for the Cape Kennedy installation and that $c(x)$ is the cost of manufacturing x units of the device, where $c(x)$ is nonlinear. Hard Core wants an optimal policy that combines both the production decision and the replacement decisions. Explain why these two decisions have an interactive cost effect. Formulate a dynamic programming model that jointly optimizes the two types of decisions. Assume that h is the holding cost per period for each device held in reserve at the end of a period. (Assume for simplicity that $0 \leq \alpha < 1$.) Suppose that the maximum production quantity is X. Determine the number of variables and equations in the associated primal and dual linear programming versions of your formulation.

43 The Coast Guard operates a navigation guidance and weather ship in the North Atlantic. The ship utilizes two pieces of expensive electronic gear that are subject to failure. The ship can continue performing its mission, at a degraded level, if one piece has failed. But if both pieces are not in working order, the Coast Guard must perform an emergency airdrop with replacements. The Coast Guard has the option, however, of sending a replacement by supply ship when only one of the pieces fails.

Assume each time period is a week. Let State 0 refer to the condition that both pieces are working, State 1 to the condition that only Piece 1 has failed, State 2 to the condition that only Piece 2 has failed, and State 12 to the condition that both pieces have failed. The cost of being in States 1, 2, and 12 are F_1, F_2, and F_{12}, respectively; State 0 is costless. Let the decision $d = 0$ denote there is no replacement action; $d = 1$ that only Piece 1 is replaced by sending a supply ship, at the cost k_1; $d = 2$ that only Piece 2 is replaced by sending a supply ship, at the cost k_2; and $d = 12$ that an emergency airdrop is required at the cost k_{12}. Note that $d = 0$ is relevant for States 0, 1, 2; $d = 1$ is relevant only for State 1; $d = 2$ is relevant only for State 2; and $d = 12$ is relevant only for State 12. Accordingly, let $p(j \mid i, d)$ designate the probability that the system is in State j next week, given that it is in State i this week and the decision is d.

(a) Enumerate every possible policy and give a verbal description of each. Explain why the probabilistic and economic assumptions do not make it worthwhile to replace a piece that is in working condition. Explain why $p(12 \mid 1, 0)$ might not equal $p(12 \mid 2, 0)$, and why $p(12 \mid 0, 0)$ might not equal $p(12 \mid 1, 0) \cdot p(12 \mid 2, 0)$.

(b) Formulate a dynamic programming model for an unbounded horizon using the criterion of minimum expected cost per week and show the extremal equations to be satisfied.

(c) Write the corresponding primal and dual linear programs, as described in Sec. 18.5. Be sure to indicate explicitly those $p(j \mid i, d)$ that equal 0.

MIND-EXPANDING EXERCISES

44 Consider the stochastic shortest-route model in Sec. 18.2. Suppose that if you make decision d in Period t when the system is at Node i, then the system arrives at Node j in Period $t + h_{ij}(d)$ with probability $p(j \mid i, d)$, where $h_{ij}(d)$ is a nonnegative integer. Let α be the one-period discount factor, where $0 \le \alpha < 1$.

   (a) Show how to alter (6) in Sec. 18.2 accordingly.

   (b) Consider the extension to the case of an unbounded horizon, where $0 \le \alpha < 1$. Show how to alter (1) in Sec. 18.3 accordingly.

 *(c) Consider the extension to the case of an unbounded horizon, where $\alpha = 1$. Show how to alter (8) in Sec. 18.3 accordingly. (*Hint:* review the deterministic case in the special material at the end of Sec. 12.3.)

   (d) Suppose that $h_{ij}(d)$ is a random variable. Let $q(h \mid i, j, d)$ denote the probability that $h_{ij}(d)$ equals h. Show how to alter the formulation in part (b). [*Note:* in an application of this model, the value of c_{id} has to be calculated so as to reflect the random variation in $h_{ij}(d)$.]

 *(e) Given the assumptions in part (d), show how to alter the formulation in part (c).

45 Show that the value iteration algorithm (8) in Sec. 18.3 ensures at least geometric convergence, that is, $|y_i^n - y_i| \le \alpha^n K$ for every i and a suitably chosen constant K.

46 Section 18.4 states that the Stationary Policy Theorem is not true when the number of states is unbounded. Each part below illustrates this statement.

   (a) Consider a network containing the Nodes $1, 2, 3, \ldots$, as shown in Fig. 18.10. Notice that there are two decisions (arcs) at each of the odd-numbered nodes, both having an associated cost 1, and one decision at each of the even-numbered nodes, having an associated cost $1/n$. Assume the process starts at Node 1 and the criterion is minimum cost per period over an unbounded horizon. Show that there is *no* strategy of any sort that yields a cost per period of 0 over an unbounded horizon. Then show that given any strategy, there exists another strategy having a strictly smaller (but positive) cost per period. Hence, there is no optimal strategy. (*Hint:* given an arbitrarily small, but positive, number e, show how to find a strategy yielding a cost per period that is less than or equal to e.)

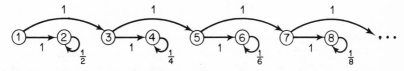

FIGURE 18.10

   (b) Consider the network containing Nodes $1, 2, 3, \ldots$, as shown in Fig. 18.11. Let Action 1 denote going from Node i to Node $i + 1$ and Action 2 denote going from Node i back to Node i. Assume that the process starts at Node 1 and the criterion is minimum expected cost per period over an unbounded horizon. Show

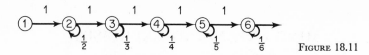

FIGURE 18.11

that any stationary policy that does not randomize has cost per period that is strictly positive. Show that there is a nonstationary policy that does not randomize and has a cost per period of 0. (*Hint:* consider what happens if, when the system first arrives at each State i, you take Action 2 for i consecutive periods and then take Action 1.) Also show that there is a stationary policy that randomizes and has expected cost per period of 0. (*Hint:* consider what happens if at each Node i you select Action 1 with probability $1/i$. Write the Markov chain for this strategy and examine whether stationary probabilities exist.)

47 Consider the Stationary Policy Theorem for $\alpha = 1$ in Sec. 18.4. Prove the proposition that there always exists an optimal policy that does not randomize.

48 Consider the extremal equations (10) for the case $\alpha = 1$ in Sec. 18.4. Assume the policy d^* is used; to keep the notation uncluttered, we suppress the symbol d^* in M_{i0} and C_{i0}, which are defined next. Let M_{i0} denote the expected number of periods (sometimes called the *mean first passage time*) for the system to next arrive at State 0 when it starts at State i; M_{00} can be called the *expected cycle time* for State 0. Similarly, let C_{i0} denote the expected cost (return) during the same periods; C_{00} can be called the *expected cycle cost* for State 0.

*(a) Show that M_{i0} and C_{i0} can be calculated from the linear equations

$$M_{i0} = 1 + \sum_{j=1}^{T} p(j \mid i, d^*) M_{j0} \quad \text{for } i = 0, 1, \ldots, T$$

$$C_{i0} = c_{id^*} + \sum_{j=1}^{T} p(j \mid i, d^*) C_{j0} \quad \text{for } i = 0, 1, \ldots, T.$$

(*Hint:* at least 1 period has to elapse in going from State i to State 0; if the first transition is to State j, where $j \neq 0$, then the *additional* expected number of periods is the same as if the system started in State j. Similarly, c_{id^*} is the expected cost incurred at the first period; if the first transition is to State j, where $j \neq 0$, then the *additional* expected cost is the same as if the system started in State j.)

(b) Consider using the following quantities as a solution to the extremal equations in (10):

$$c^* = \frac{C_{00}}{M_{00}} \qquad w_i = C_{i0} - c^* M_{i0}.$$

Give an interpretation of these quantities. Check that the associated value $w_0 = 0$. Use the formulas in part (a) to show that these quantities actually satisfy (10).

(c) Calculate M_{i0} and C_{i0}, for $i = 0, 1, \ldots, 4$, for the inventory example in Fig. 18.3, using the optimal policy shown in Fig. 18.7 ($n = 2$).

(d) Calculate each M_{i0} and C_{i0} for the optimal policy in exercise 26. Also compute c^* and w_i according to part (b).

(e) Same as part (d) for exercise 28.

(f) Same as part (d) for exercise 34.

(g) Same as part (d) for exercise 41, part (c).

(h) Same as part (d) for exercise 42, part (c).

49 The Onagen Ophagen Company operates a delicate machine that sometimes works properly and sometimes doesn't. Let $j = 0$ denote the state in which the machine is operating properly, and $j = 1$ indicate that the machine is in need of repair. If the machine is used when it is in good order, the daily production cost is c_0. If the machine is used when it is not in good order, the daily production cost is c_1 where $c_1 > c_0$. Unfortunately, it is only possible to tell the actual state of the machine by making an expensive test on the items produced during the day. Let I be the associated inspection cost. A repair action ensures that the machine is in good operating condition immediately and incurs the cost R.

Let p denote the probability that the machine is still in good operating condition at the beginning of the next period, given that it is in good operating condition this period, where a period is one day. Assume that once the machine is in the need-of-repair state, it remains there.

Let P denote the probability that the machine is in good operating condition at the beginning of a period. Explain why the value of P can be used to represent the state of the production system. Exhibit a dynamic programming recursion for an unbounded horizon (assume $0 \leq \alpha < 1$) that determines whether to operate the machine for a day without inspection, to perform the inspection, or to take the repair action, given the current value of P. (*Hint:* check that the probability that the machine is in good operating condition at the beginning of next period when no inspection or repair occurs is Pp.)

Many important examples of the models in this chapter have a special structure that can be exploited to simplify the Markovian formulation and the calculation of an optimal solution. The next exercises illustrate several techniques for exploiting special structure.

50 *Separable Markovian Decision Problems.* Consider an infinite horizon stochastic shortest-route model, like that discussed in Sec. 18.3. Assume, initially, that the nodes (or states) are $i = 1, 2, \ldots, T$, and that there are K distinguished decisions available at every state. The special nature of these K decisions is indicated by the extremal equations that are to be satisfied:

$$y_i = \text{minimum} \left\{ \sum_{j=1}^{T} p(j \mid 1)\alpha y_j + a_i + b_1, \ldots, \sum_{j=1}^{T} p(j \mid K)\alpha y_j + a_i + b_K, \right.$$

$$\left. \underset{d \text{ in } D(i)}{\text{minimum}} \left[\sum_{j=1}^{T} p(j \mid i, d)\alpha y_j + c_{id} \right] \right\} \quad \text{for } i = 1, 2, \ldots, T,$$

where $0 \leq \alpha < 1$.

(a) Give a verbal interpretation of the economic and structural assumptions made about the K distinguished decisions. Let N_i be the number of decisions in the set $D(i)$. Determine the numbers of constraints and variables in the associated primal linear programming model, analogous to that in (1) and (2) of Sec. 18.5.

(b) Show that by introducing an additional Node 0, a solution to the above extremal equations can be obtained by solving, instead, the extremal equations

$$y_0 = \text{minimum} \left[\sum_{j=1}^{T} p(j \mid 1) \alpha y_j + b_1, \ldots, \sum_{j=1}^{T} p(j \mid K) \alpha y_j + b_K \right]$$

$$y_i = \text{minimum} \left\{ y_0 + a_i, \underset{d \text{ in } D(i)}{\text{minimum}} \left[\sum_{j=1}^{T} p(j \mid i, d) \alpha y_j + c_{id} \right] \right\} \text{ for } i = 1, 2, \ldots, T.$$

(c) Write the primal linear programming model, analogous to that in (1) and (2) of Sec. 18.5, for the extremal equations in part (b). Determine the numbers of constraints and variables.

(d) Let $z_i \equiv a_i + y_0 - y_i$, for $i = 1, 2, \ldots, T$, and show how to eliminate T of the linear constraints in part (c) by this change of variables. (*Hint:* recall that the y_i are unconstrained in sign.) Explain how to modify the formulation if the K distinguished decisions are available only in Nodes i $= 1, 2, \ldots, $ t, where $t < T$.

*(e) Derive the appropriate extremal equations for $\alpha = 1$, analogous to those in part (b), and exhibit a *streamlined* primal linear programming problem analogous to that in part (d).

*(f) Apply the analysis above to formulate the equipment replacement model in Secs. 17.7 and 18.7. (*Hint:* you can let the Node i represent the age of a piece of equipment entering a period, prior to the decision of whether or not to replace.) Exhibit in detail a *streamlined* linear programming model corresponding to part (d).

*(g) Continuing with the analysis in part (f), exhibit in detail the linear programming model corresponding to part (e), using the data for the example in Figs. 17.6 and 18.9. Determine the associated optimal solution.

(h) Apply the analysis above to formulate the quality control model in exercise 42, part (a). Exhibit in detail the *streamlined* linear programming model corresponding to part (d).

51 *Separable Markovian Decision Problems* (*continued*). Consider an infinite horizon stochastic shortest-route model, like that discussed in Sec. 18.3. Assume, initially, that the nodes (or states) are $i = 1, 2, \ldots, T$, and that there are K distinguished decisions available in every state. The special structure of these K decisions is indicated by the extremal equations that are to be satisfied:

$$y_i = \text{minimum} \left\{ y_{i+1} + a_i + b_1, \ldots, y_{i+K} + a_i + b_K, \right.$$

$$\left. \underset{d \text{ in } D(i)}{\text{minimum}} \left[\sum_{j=1}^{T} p(j \mid i, d) \alpha y_i + c_{id} \right] \right\} \text{ for } i = 1, 2, \ldots, t$$

$$y_i = \underset{d \text{ in } D(i)}{\text{minimum}} \left[\sum_{j=1}^{T} p(j \mid i, d) \alpha y_j + c_{id} \right] \text{ for } i = t + 1, \ldots, T,$$

where $0 \leq \alpha < 1$, and $K \leq t \leq T - K$. (Assume that the values for all the a_i, b_k, and c_{id} guarantee that the extremal equations possess a unique finite solution.)

(a) Give a verbal interpretation of the economic and structural assumptions made about the K distinguished decisions. Let N_i be the number of decisions in the set $D(i)$. Determine the numbers of constraints and variables in the associated primal linear programming model, analogous to that in (1) and (2) of Sec. 18.5.

(b) Show that by introducing an additional Node 0, a solution to the above extremal equations can be obtained by solving, instead, the extremal equations

$$y_0 = \text{minimum } [y_{t+1} + b_1, \ldots, y_{t+K} + b_K]$$

$$y_i = \text{minimum} \left\{ y_0 + a_i, \underset{d \text{ in } D(i)}{\text{minimum}} \left[\sum_{j=1}^{T} p(j\,|\,i, d)\alpha y_j + c_{id} \right] \right\} \quad \text{for } i = 1, 2, \ldots, t$$

$$y_i = \underset{d \text{ in } D(i)}{\text{minimum}} \left[\sum_{j=1}^{T} p(j\,|\,i, d)\alpha y_j + c_{id} \right] \quad \text{for } i = t + 1, \ldots, T.$$

(c) Write the primal linear programming model, analogous to that in (1) and (2) of Sec. 18.5, for the extremal equations in part (b). Determine the numbers of constraints and variables.

(d) Show how to eliminate T of the linear constraints in part (c) by changing variables

$$z_i \equiv a_i + y_0 - y_i, \quad \text{for } i = 1, 2, \ldots, t.$$

Show how to eliminate K more of the linear constraints by making a second change of variables

$$Z_{t+k} \equiv a_{t+k} + b_k - z_{t+k} \quad \text{for } k = 1, 2, \ldots, K.$$

*(e) Derive the appropriate extremal equations for $\alpha = 1$, analogous to those in part (b), and exhibit a *streamlined* primal linear programming problem analogous to that in part (d).

(f) Consider a stochastic inventory model in which $p(q)$ denotes the probability that demand is q (demand is independently and identically distributed from period to period), the purchase cost is $S + cx$ for $x = 1, 2, \ldots$, where $S > 0$, and the inventory-holding-and-penalty-cost function is $H(l - q)$, where l is the level of inventory *after* an order is placed (assume delivery is immediate) and *before* demand occurs. Assume that when demand q exceeds l, the excess demand is lost.

Suppose you want to find a policy of the following type. If entering inventory exceeds 10, no replenishment order is placed. If entering inventory is 10 or less, then a replenishment order can (but need not) be placed; inventory after an order but before demand is not permitted to exceed 15. (Assume that inventory at the start of the horizon is 0).

Formulate the model to give a set of extremal equations analogous to those in part (a). Determine the numbers of constraints and variables in the associated primal linear programming model. Show how to reduce the problem to the version given in part (b); again determine the numbers of constraints and variables in the associated primal linear programming model. Apply the analysis in part (d) and exhibit in full the associated linear programming model. [*Hint:* let $a_i = -ci$ and $b_k = S + (k + 10)c + \sum_q H(k + 10 - q)p(q).$]

(g) Consider the example in part (f). Show how the problem can also be characterized by the extremal equations in exercise 50, parts (a) and (b). Determine the number of constraints and variables in the corresponding primal linear programming models. Exhibit in full the associated *streamlined* linear programming model in part (d). Is this alternative formulation preferable to that in part (f) above? Explain.

CONTENTS

CHAPTER 19

Probabilistic
Inventory Models

19.1 NEW ORIENTATION

Previous chapters have focused on the development of widely applicable mathematical models and algorithms. For example, Chaps. 2, 6, 8, 10 and 11 dealt with linear programming, network, and multistage models; Chaps. 4, 7, and 12 presented numerical techniques for solving these models. Throughout, the mathematical models and the algorithms were illustrated by specific examples suggestive of real managerial applications of operations research. You may even have been surprised that these examples covered such a broad range of decision-making situations.

In Chaps. 19 and 20, and Appendices II and III, the orientation of "models first, applications later" is reversed. These chapters deal with particular decision areas in which operations research has proved beneficial, namely the management of inventories and the design of waiting line systems. The resulting mathematical models and algorithms are designed to fit the particular context of the problem. The solutions commonly yield optimal decision rules to be applied in an operating environment, and not merely guidelines to be used for planning purposes.

Of course, in a strictly formal sense, each model and algorithm can be classified as a special case of the models and algorithms you have already studied. But the new insights you will experience come from analyzing the particular nature of the models, *not* from recognizing that the models can be viewed as linear, non-linear, or dynamic programming problems. Now you will fully exploit the specific structure of these models.

The change in emphasis requires that you make a corresponding change in *your* study orientation. You should seek the fundamental concepts that are critical to the analysis of most problems in the particular area of application. Since there are infinite variations in the circumstances describing a particular application, it is impossible for any book, let alone an introductory text, to provide enough models to cover every eventuality. You can, however, learn the ideas that make up the basic building blocks of such models, and these fundamentals are contained in the next two chapters and the last two appendices.

In studying the material, remember to answer the following questions:

1. What decisions are to be made? What managerial problem is being solved?
2. What causes the real decision environment to be so complex as to require the use of operations research models? What elements of this complexity are embodied in the models? How do these elements affect the solution? What elements are ignored?
3. What distinguishes a good decision from a poor one?
4. If you were a manager, how would you employ the results of the analysis? In what ways might you want, or need, to temper the results because of factors not explicitly considered in the models?

Keep in mind that the answers should reflect the day-to-day nature of the decision problems in these areas.

19.2 SCIENTIFIC APPROACH TO INVENTORY
MANAGEMENT

Seeing inventories everywhere, every day, may have dulled your awareness that they are the direct result of managerial decisions. Your awareness is likely to be sharpened only when you find some item you want is out of stock in a grocery store, a hi-fi shop, or a bookstore. Irritated, you may say, "Somebody slipped up!" If the item is a Valentine's Day greeting card and the date is February 13, that "somebody" may be *you*. A shopkeeper can hardly be expected to have a large inventory of stock when his forecast of future demand is negligible.

Of course, the sheer pervasiveness of inventory decisions in business enterprises is not enough to justify an operations research approach. At least one additional condition must be present to warrant a company's applying this point of view: both the likelihood and economic impact of incorrect inventory decisions must be substantial enough to outweigh the cost of scientific analysis. To illustrate, a large stationery store may well find it profitable to derive an optimal inventory policy for stocking its supply of pencils, whereas you would find it silly to derive such a policy for the supply of pencils in your desk drawer. Why?

So that you are not misled by the frequent reference to retail firms we mention that applications of inventory models are more widespread in manufacturing and wholesale companies, although this historical pattern is rapidly changing. For example, you will commonly find scientifically based inventory replenishment rules employed in large manufacturing plants to control hundreds, and often thousands, of items of raw materials, intermediate goods, and finished products. Typically, in these situations, only a very few men are responsible for all the inventory replenishment decisions. You may wonder how mathematically derived rules can be an improvement over the experienced judgment of these men. The answer is given below.

Systemwide economics. Often a manager *does* outperform a mathematical formula in the replenishment of any given item. But to do so, he must carefully forecast the demand for the item and keep tab on the exact length of time required to obtain a resupply. If the item is important to the firm—because of its high cost or essentiality to the production process—then continual managerial review may well be the best policy. But there is a limit to the number of items that an individual can closely scrutinize. Since most companies inventory a myriad of items, it is inevitable that many of them will be stocked according to some routine or rule-of-thumb approach. Operations research can provide a cost-saving means of management for this large segment of the inventory system.

By establishing methodical procedures for replenishing most inventoried items, the scientific approach frees the decision-maker to concentrate his talents on discretionary and exceptional situations, where his experience is of greatest benefit. Thus an effective scientific inventory system really requires a harmonious combination of human judgment and mathematical formulas.

Operational simplicity. Inventory models are among the few instances in which the resultant optimal solutions of operations research models are implementable on a day-to-day basis. The reason is that in most inventory situations, the essence of the solution is simply

   (i) A rule indicating *when* to replenish.
   (ii) A rule indicating the *amount* to replenish.

In other words, an inventory policy signals the timing and magnitude of the resupply decision. No matter how complex the mathematical model or algorithm underlying the replenishment rules, the description of the policy in terms of (i) and (ii) is always easy to understand. Sometimes the rules are given by tables and only require the manager to state data, such as the item's price and average demand. But frequently the entire system is computerized, in which case the computer keeps an up-to-date record of the inventory level, and at the appropriate time prints out a replenishment order showing the correct amount.

Even though inventory models are widely accepted, there are still many environments in which replenishment decisions are made according to arbitrary rules and judgment, despite the substantial losses that mistakes can inflict. A major contributing factor for the persistence of such rules-of-thumb is that these situations have not yet been studied intensively by operations research specialists. Further, the few solutions derived so far are much more complicated than (i) and (ii), so that implementation is correspondingly more difficult. Typically, these highly complex environments include situations in which there are significant interrelationships between the demands for the different items (for example, when several of the items can be substituted for each other) and when a firm stocks an item at more than one location (for example, at a regional warehouse as well as at several retail outlets). In time, operations research will deal successfully with these difficult problems.

Study objective. In the remainder of this chapter and in Appendix II, you will see several formulations of inventory models. Each is a prototype of a class of models that has been studied by operations research theorists. By understanding these basic approaches, you will become familiar with the main principles of inventory theory. Consequently, you will have the mastery required of a manager to comprehend the objectives, strengths, and limitations of a scientific inventory system. What is more, you will be equipped to study an in-depth text devoted to operations research inventory models, if you wish to learn more within this area.

19.3 GROUND WORK FOR INVENTORY ANALYSIS

What considerations are important for a firm's decision of when and how much to inventory of an item? The significant elements fall into three major categories. These factors are discussed below in general terms, and in the subsequent sections, they are made precise by the particular mathematical formulations of the models. For clarity of exposition, consider the case of the Les Luster Company, a wholesaler of fabricated metal supplies, such as aluminum wire, rods, coils, sheets and plates, etc., which it buys from a vendor aluminum company. You should have no trouble in relating this wholesaler's decision considerations to those of other firms carrying inventory.

Demand and supply. Certainly the wholesaler needs to forecast, in one way or another, its own local customers' future demand for the item. Such a forecast directly influences the order quantity, and most frequently is represented by a probability distribution. This chapter assumes throughout that different item-demands are independent of each other. Even when this assumption does not strictly hold, it is often an adequate approximation on which to base an inventory rule. Further, the demand distribution is assumed to be independent of the selection of a replenishment rule or any other managerial action. By using advanced mathematical analysis, one can find optimal policies in which these approximating assumptions are omitted.

Employing a probability distribution to describe future demand is a useful way of combining partial knowledge with partial ignorance. By stating the *form* and *parameters* of the distribution—such as the mean of a Poisson distribution, or the mean and variance of a negative binomial distribution—you can express what you know about the relative *likelihoods* of demand values. Thus the probabilities summarize your uncertainty about the precise demand value that will occur.

The wholesaler also needs to know the so-called **lead time** or **delivery lag** between the moment the replenishment action is initiated and the moment the items ordered are available to meet its customers' demands. The interval obviously encompasses all the time required by the vendor to process the wholesaler's order, including shipping time; but it also encompasses any delays on Les Luster's own premises due to placing the order as well as receiving and unpacking it on arrival. The lead time may be specified deterministically or stochastically, depending on the situation.

Occasionally, there may be variations between the amounts ordered and actually received—for example, scrap losses are significant in some manufacturing process, and the vendor may have some leeway in the amount he ships. Such situations will not be considered in this chapter; however, they can be treated by using more advanced analysis.

Replenishment economics. If you examine most large-scale inventory systems, you will quickly find that for items frequently demanded, the replenishment quantity is usually sizeable, and certainly greater than 1. There are several reasons why. The most important is that very small orders would result in frequent reordering and thereby incur a considerable expense associated with processing and receiving the order; this expense is referred to as the **setup** or **reorder cost.** A second and less obvious reason is that a large order protects the company against running out too often. Other reasons that are sometimes significant (but not treated by the models in this chapter) include quantity discounts or minimal order sizes stipulated by the vendor, or the firm's forecast of rising vendor prices.

What limits the order quantity? The principal factor is the **inventory holding cost.** Keeping items in stock is costly because inventories tie up capital that might otherwise be profitably employed, and also they incur the expenses of storage, maintenance, insurance, etc. Other limiting reasons that arise in real situations (but will not be embodied in the models of subsequent sections) include spoilage, obsolescence, budgetary and space restrictions, etc.

So far we have not discussed *which* items the wholesaler should try to keep in inventory. After all, even a supermarket or department store does not stock *everything* that its customers might want. Presumably there is a **penalty cost** or **profit loss** whenever the wholesaler is out of stock of an item a customer requests. Obviously, a lost sale means less revenue. But there is a penalty even if the customer is willing to have his order backlogged, for then the wholesaler must incur some extra expense from keeping backlog records and filling the order in a later shipment. As a consequence, the firm will inventory an item if the out-of-stock cost is high; this qualitative statement is made precise for each of the inventory models in this chapter.

The optimality criterion for inventory models is stated traditionally in terms of expected cost rather than expected profit. Since most models consider the item's selling price to be fixed, this cost convention is legitimate, provided sufficient care is exercised in defining the penalty cost to include lost or delayed revenue when a sale is lost or backlogged. Another reason for this cost convention is that frequently such inventory models are applied to items used by a firm's own personnel; consequently, the items are not really being "sold" at a profit.

Assuming an item is to be stocked, an optimal inventory policy is one that strikes the proper balance among the reorder, holding, and penalty costs. As you will see, all *three* cost elements influence how much and when to reorder. The timing decision usually amounts to a specification of a reorder point: whenever the inventory position falls below the reorder level, a replenishment action is taken. The higher the reorder point, the more protection there is against stockouts. Thus in changing the reorder level, there is a direct tradeoff between stockout and holding costs. Incidentally, if the order quantity is so large as to give considerable protection against stockouts, and if customers are willing to have their demands backlogged, the company may find it is optimal to allow a backlog to build up before placing a replenishment order. You will see how this happens in Sec. 19.5.

As you know from the analysis in previous chapters, if the firm's criterion function is in terms of expected present value, then the tradeoff between present and future returns must also be accounted for in the optimization process. To illustrate, as the interest rate increases, the optimal policy will order less in the current period, because postponement becomes less costly when reckoned in terms of present value.

It is important for you to realize that in real applications of inventory models, the task of estimating reordering, holding, and penalty costs can be quite difficult. Nevertheless, the problem is not insurmountable, as demonstrated by the widespread adoption of these models. What you seek are approximate and reasonable cost estimates. More will be said about such matters of implementation in Sec. 19.7.

Systems specifications. The third category of elements influencing the selection of an inventory policy deals with a disparate variety of environmental factors, only some of which are under the control of the decision-maker.

One such specification relates to whether the inventory level is continuously or only periodically reviewed. In the continuous case, a replenishment order is initiated as soon as the inventory level drops below the reorder point. In the periodic or discrete review case, the inventory status is checked only at specified intervals—for example, each Monday. In this system, replenishment occurs only at the interval point—even when inventory drops below the reorder point at an early moment in the interval. Section 19.6 analyzes a continuous review model with probabilistic demand; Appendix II treats the periodic review case.

Like all mathematical models, these inventory models are only approximations to reality. In an actual situation, then, the choice between a continuous and a periodic review model depends on which is the better representation of reality. A detailed discussion of how to make this choice is best left to specialized texts on inventory control. If you read Appendix II, however, you should carefully compare the two types of models and their underlying assumptions so that you learn in what ways they are essentially different.

A related specification concerns restrictions on the order quantity. Sometimes it is required or convenient to order only in multiples of a standard amount, such as a dozen. (Note that, in this case, it is not generally permissible merely to change the scale of measurement—to dozens, say—since *customer* demand may not occur in the same transformed units.) Sometimes the order quantity is limited because the company has limited warehouse space available for inventory. These kinds of restrictions have been successfully treated in the operations research literature, but they will not be considered in this book.

Finally, the replenishment rule may be affected by interactive factors. For example, Les Luster Company, the metals-supply wholesaler, may be constrained to ordering a freight-car load at a time from the fabricating mill. Therefore, its order quantities for individual items must reflect this overall constraint. Or an item may be stocked at several different warehouse locations, so that more than one inventory level must be examined in determining a replenishment action. Again, for the sake of simplicity, this text will not treat inventory optimization models with interactive constraints, although such models have been solved by operations research technicians.

Summary and a look ahead. In brief, the models in this chapter and Appendix II separately consider each different type of item inventoried. They take as given the environmental factors of continuous or periodic review, the planning horizon, the lead time, future demand, purchase cost, setup cost, holding cost, penalty cost, and the discount factor. Then each model finds an optimal rule for when and how much to order. No additional system constraints are imposed. In studying these models, be sure to ask yourself how each of the environmental factors affects the optimal policy.

Although the goal of this chapter is to analyze models in which demand is treated as being probabilistic and the inventory decision problem is recurring, that is, dynamic, you will find it helpful to consider each of these two elements in isolation. Specifically, Sec. 19.4 discusses finding an optimal inventory policy when demand is probabilistic but the ordering decision is made only once. Section 19.5 treats the situation where the decision problem is dynamic but demands are perfectly forecastable (in terms of an average rate). Section 19.6 and Appendix II, then, will combine the two elements so as to highlight the interaction between them.

In each case analyzed, the aim is to completely characterize an *optimal* policy in terms of merely two numbers: the reorder point and the order quantity. The resultant algorithmic problem of calculating the optimal values becomes one of optimizing a nonlinear objective function of only two variables. As you will see, knowing the form of an optimal solution and having so few decision variables make the algorithmic task fairly easy and also allow you to use simple, yet very effective, numerical approximations.

19.4 STATIC (SINGLE DECISION) MODEL

This section treats the so-called static, or one-period, model in which only a single inventory decision is made in anticipation of demand, which is viewed as a random variable.

The model is important for two reasons. First, occasionally the model does fit a real situation, as exemplified by the example in the next paragraph. Second, the optimization analysis provides a useful starting point for considering the subsequent dynamic models.

The following illustration, based on an actual application, suggests how a static model can be employed. (The discussion overlooks several details that influenced the exact policy implemented, but that are unimportant here.) The *Daily Defender*, a large newspaper in a major metropolitan area, has been concerned with controlling the number of papers to be distributed to individual newsstands. Unsold papers are returned to the publisher, and as a result the total out-of-pocket costs attributable to these returns amounts to over $1 million annually. Better stockage rules would therefore promise sizeable savings.

Although the daily decision as to the total number of papers to put on each stand is a recurring one, the *decision problem* can be treated by a static model. Each day's newspaper is unsalable by the following day, so there is only one inventory decision to be made about these papers. The daily demand for newspapers can be viewed as a random process that is only partly predictable by such factors as the day of the week and the importance of the headline story. Also, the unit cost of the papers differs daily; for example, the Sunday edition, being larger, costs more to print than the other daily editions. Consequently, the *Daily Defender* applied an operations research model such as that given below by the *linear holding and penalty cost* case. (For the obvious reason, this model is sometimes referred to as the **newsboy problem**.) On any particular day, the appropriate costs are used in the model and the probability distribution for demand employed depends on the predictable factors for that day.

Can you think of any other commercial situations in which a one-period inventory model is applicable? Under what circumstances would it be profitable to use an operations research approach for these situations?

Form of replenishment policy. To begin the discussion, we define the symbols

i = level of inventory *prior* to the ordering decision
x = amount ordered $(x \geq 0)$
$y = i + x$ = total inventory available to meet future demand
q = actual demand quantity (a random variable, where $q \geq 0$)
$p(q)$ = probability that demand equals q.

For expository convenience, we assume i, x, y, and q are integer-valued. (The continuous variable case will be treated in the advanced material at an appropriate juncture in the discussion.) Typically, optimal values for x and y will depend on the level of starting inventory i, and so the symbols $x(i)$ and $y(i)$ will be used to denote an optimal policy.

It is easy to construct plausible-looking examples that have surprising-looking optimal policies. If you are curious to see such an illustration, you can read the special material in a later part of this section. Most often, managers use the following simple type of replenishment rule:

(1)
$$y(i) = i \quad \text{and} \quad x(i) = 0 \qquad \text{for } i \geq s \quad \text{(do not order)}$$
$$y(i) = S \quad \text{and} \quad x(i) = S - i \quad \text{for } i < s \quad \text{(place an order)}.$$

According to (1), no order is placed if initial inventory $i \geq s$; but if i is small enough ($i < s$), then an order is placed so that the *total* inventory available for future demand is S. The rule in (1) is referred to as an **(s, S) policy**, where s denotes the **reorder point** and S the **reorder level**.

In the special material in the second part of this section, we also give sufficient conditions on the underlying cost structure to ensure that an (s, S) rule is the *optimal* form of policy. But prior to considering a general one-period model, we treat in detail the most important special case of the model.

Linear holding and penalty cost. Suppose that the expected cost for the entire period is the sum of the purchase cost and the expected holding and penalty cost. Specifically, let the cost of ordering the amount x be

(2)
$$c(x) = \begin{cases} 0 & \text{for } x = 0 \\ K + cx & \text{for } x > 0, \end{cases}$$

where $K \geq 0$ represents the setup cost and $c \geq 0$ the unit purchasing cost.

Assume that the expected holding and penalty cost during the period depends only on the *total* amount of inventory available to meet demand, namely, the level y, which equals initial inventory i plus the order amount x. Let $L(y)$ denote this expected cost function, and in particular, assume that $L(y)$ is calculated from the formula

(3)
$$L(y) = \sum_{q=0}^{y} h \cdot (y - q) p(q) + \sum_{q > y} \pi \cdot (q - y) p(q) \quad \text{for } y \geq 0,$$

where $h \geq 0$ is the unit holding cost per item left over at the end of the period, and $\pi \geq 0$ is the unit penalty cost per item short at the end of the period. Thus the first summation is the *expected* holding cost and the second summation is the *expected* penalty cost. We also make the reasonable assumptions that $c + h > 0$ and $\pi > c$, implying that $h + \pi > 0$.

To illustrate, let

(4)
$$p(q) = \frac{1}{5} \quad \text{for } q = 0, 1, \ldots, 4 \quad \text{so that } E[q] = 2.$$

Verify that

(5)
$$L(y) = \begin{cases} h \cdot (y - 2) & \text{for } y \geq 4 \\ \dfrac{h}{5} \sum_{q=0}^{y} (y - q) + \dfrac{\pi}{5} \sum_{q=y+1}^{4} (q - y) & \text{for } 0 \leq y \leq 3. \end{cases}$$

The values of $L(y)$ for holding cost $h = 5$ and penalty cost $\pi = 0, 5, 10, 20, 25$ are shown in Fig. 19.1. [To test your understanding, calculate (5) for $h = 5$ and $\pi = 10$; check your answers with the values in Fig. 19.1, and plot $L(y)$ to see its convex shape.] Note that the value of y that minimizes $L(y)$ increases as the penalty cost π increases.

y	Penalty Cost π				
	0	5	10	20	25
0	0	10	20	40	50
1	1	7	13	25	31
2	3	6	9	15	18
3	6	7	8	10	11
4	10	10	10	10	10
5	15	15	15	15	15
y ≥ 6	5(y−2)	5(y−2)	5(y−2)	5(y−2)	5(y−2)

FIGURE 19.1 $L(y)$ for $h = 5$.

When there is a salvage value v (where $0 < v \leq c$) for each item remaining at the end of the horizon, this value can be subtracted from the unit holding cost. Consequently, h in (3) really represents the *net* holding cost ($h = h' - v$), and can be negative. By the same token, if the item is being stocked for sale, and demand in excess of inventory on hand is lost, then π includes the sales price r ($\pi = \pi' + r$).

It is easy to show that an (s, S) rule is the optimal form of policy for this special case. We now explain how to find optimal values for s and S. Let

(6)
$$R \equiv \frac{\pi - c}{\pi + h},$$

and denote the value of R as the **critical ratio**. Observe that $0 < R < 1$ because we assumed that $\pi > c$ and $\pi + h > 0$. Then it can be shown that an optimal reorder level $S \geq 0$ is the *smallest* integer such that

(7) $P(S) \equiv \sum_{q=0}^{S} p(q) \geq R$ (determination of reorder level S).

Since $P(S)$ is simply the *cumulative* distribution function at $q = S$, an optimal reorder level S is set such that there is at least a probability R of satisfying all demand.

Observe from (6) that

(i) R increases as π increases, so that the reorder level S is a nondecreasing function of the penalty cost π.

(ii) R decreases either as the holding cost h or purchase cost c increases, so that the reorder level S is a nonincreasing function of h and c.

(iii) If $\pi \geq 2c + h$, then $R \geq \frac{1}{2}$ and S is at least as large as the median of the demand distribution.

To illustrate, consider the example in (4) and (5). The graph of the cumulative distribution

$$(8) \qquad\qquad P(y) = \sum_{q=0}^{y} p(q) = \frac{y+1}{5} \quad \text{for } y = 0, 1, \ldots, 4$$

appears in Fig. 19.2. The graph is drawn as a staircase to assist in the exposition.

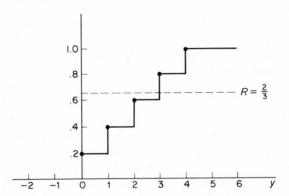

FIGURE 19.2 Cumulative
Distribution $P(y)$.

Suppose the holding cost $h = 5$, the penalty cost $\pi = 10$, and the purchase cost $c = 0$ so that $R = \frac{2}{3}$. Then according to (7) and (8), S is the smallest integer such that

$$(9) \qquad\qquad \frac{S+1}{5} \geq \frac{2}{3},$$

and therefore,

$$(10) \qquad\qquad \text{reorder level } S = 3.$$

An optimal S can always be read off immediately from a graph of the cumulative distribution function such as Fig. 19.2. You merely locate the value of the ratio R on the vertical axis, extend a horizontal line over until it intersects the cumulative function $P(y)$, and the reorder level S is the associated value of y. [If R coincides with a horizontal segment of $P(y)$, then S is the smallest value of y associated with that segment.] What is the optimal S if the holding cost $h = 5$, the penalty cost $\pi = 10$, and the purchase cost $c = 5$?

To summarize, an optimal reorder level S can be found by first calculating the critical ratio R in (6) and then using the cumulative function $P(y)$. Note it is not necessary to calculate the expected holding and penalty cost function $L(y)$ to obtain S.

Suppose the setup cost $K = 0$. Then, as we demonstrate later in this section, it is optimal to let $s = S$. This means that if initial inventory i is *any* amount less than S, you order the quantity $x = S - i$. And if initial inventory is larger than S, you order nothing.

Consider the more challenging case where the setup cost $K > 0$. Now an optimal value for the reorder point s may be strictly less than S. The reason is that if the setup cost K is relatively large and initial inventory i ($\leq S$) is sufficiently close to S, then the additional expense of the setup and purchase costs may not be offset by the reduction in expected holding and penalty costs. For simplicity of exposition we will assume that an optimal $s \geq 0$.

The (s, S) rule states that you do *not* order when initial inventory *equals* s. Hence, the expected holding and penalty cost of letting $y = s$ (that is, amount ordered $x = 0$), which is $L(s)$, must be no greater than the ordering cost plus expected holding and penalty cost of letting $y = S$ (that is, amount ordered $x = S - s$), which is $K + c(S - s) + L(S)$. But since you *do* order when initial inventory is less than s, the preceding cost advantage must go the other way for $y = s - 1$.

We can summarize the reasoning so far by stating that you choose s to be the smallest number such that

(11) $L(s) \leq K + c(S - s) + L(S)$ (determination of reorder point s).

Thus, when $K > 0$, you calculate the reorder point s by computing and comparing the expected holding and penalty cost function $L(y)$ with the sum $[K + c(S - y) + L(S)]$, for successively smaller trial values of y, starting at $y = S$, and then continuing until $y = s$ is the smallest trial value for which (11) holds. [In performing the calculations, you may find it easier to make the equivalent comparison between $L(y) + cy$ and $K + cS + L(S)$, since then the latter value is a constant.]

In the example (8) with $h = 5$, $\pi = 10$ and $c = .1$, the inequality (11) yields

(12) $L(s) \leq K + .1(3 - s) + 8 = 8.3 + K - .1s.$

Suppose $K = 4$. Then $s = 2$, since

(13)
$$L(2) =\ \ 9 \leq 8.3 + 4 - .1(2) = 12.1$$
$$L(1) = 13 > 8.3 + 4 - .1(3) = 12,$$

where the values of $L(s)$ are found in Fig. 19.1. What is the optimal s if $K = 12$? When is an order placed in this case?

You have just seen how to find an optimal (s, S) policy in the important special case of linear holding and penalty costs. The remainder of this section treats the static model from a more general point of view. The discussion shows how to formulate and solve the problem for other cost functions and discusses sufficient conditions on the cost functions that imply an (s, S) policy is optimal.

*General description. We continue to use the definitions for i, x, y, q, and $p(q)$ given above. Also define

$g(y|i) \equiv$ *expected* cost when y is the inventory available to meet demand *after* ordering, given that initial inventory is i.

In most actual applications of the static model, you start with initial inventory $i = 0$. But this is not always so. Indeed, we will even permit the value of i to be negative so as to indicate the presence of **backlogged demand** from previous periods. (Thus i might be termed the **net inventory position** prior to the ordering decision.)

Note that y instead of x has been used in the description of the expected cost function $g(y|i)$. Since $(x \equiv y - i)$, employing either x or y is valid, but using y is mathematically more convenient. Also observe that $g(y|i)$ represents an expected cost. Given specific values for y and i, the actual cost during the horizon must be viewed as a random variable because the demand quantity q is described as random.

Reminiscent of dynamic programming analysis, the optimization problem can be indicated as finding

$$(14) \qquad\qquad f(i) \equiv \operatorname*{minimum}_{y} g(y|i),$$

so that $f(i)$ represents the minimum expected cost when initial inventory is i. In the discussion below, we will always restrict the minimization to values of y at least as large as i, but there is no conceptual difficulty in permitting y to be smaller than i, thereby denoting a disposal decision. Given an associated optimal value $y(i)$, you have that the optimal order quantity is

$$(15) \qquad\qquad\qquad x(i) \equiv y(i) - i.$$

Typically, the function $g(y|i)$ is easy to compute and eventually increases without bound as y increases. Explain why. So even if $g(y|i)$ has no special mathematical properties to be exploited by the minimization in (14), the computational task of finding an optimal $y(i)$ is straightforward—if worse comes to worst, you can enumerate $y = i,\ i + 1, \ldots$, until you find the minimum $g(y|i)$. (In the computational process, you must take care not to be fooled by a *local* minimum that is not also a *global* minimum.)

But you would think that knowing $y(i)$ for one or more values of i should help you infer the values of $y(i)$ for other values of i. Here is a test of your intuition.

Assume initial inventory can be any of the values $i = 0, 1, \ldots, 8$, and that maximum demand is 8. Then you can suppose that $y(i) \le 8$ for every i, if the cost function is reasonable. In solving the minimization (14) suppose you find

Case 1. For $i = 7, y(i) = 8$ so that $x(i) = 8 - i = 1$. Then what do you think are the values of $y(i)$ and $x(i)$ for $i = 0, 3, 4$?

Case 2. For $i = 3, y(i) = 4$ so that $x(i) = 4 - i = 1$. Then what do you think are the values of $y(i)$ and $x(i)$ for $i = 0, 4, 7$?

Write your answers to *Cases 1* and *2* on a piece of scratch paper and jot down a sentence or two recording your justification. You will want to refer to your answers after reading the example below.

   *Lump-sum penalty cost. This illustration is intended to show how a model that contains seemingly straightforward assumptions can have a surprising-looking optimal solution. Assume that there are only two possible values, 4 and 8, for demand, having the probabilities

(16) $$p(4) = p(8) = \frac{1}{2} \quad \text{and} \quad p(q) = 0 \quad \text{for} \quad q \neq 4, 8.$$

   Let the ordering cost function be

(17) $$c(y - i) \equiv \begin{cases} 0 & \text{for } y = i \quad (x = 0) \\ K + c \cdot (y - i) & \text{for } y > i \quad (x = y - i > 0), \end{cases}$$

so that a setup cost $K \geq 0$ is incurred if an order is placed, and to this is added a unit purchase cost $c \geq 0$ times the amount ordered.

   Assume there is no holding or inventory cost, nor is there any salvage value for items left over at the end of the horizon. But there is a **lump-sum penalty cost** $\pi > 0$ that occurs if demand exceeds y. Given these assumptions, the *expected* penalty cost function can be written as

(18) $$L(y) \equiv \pi \sum_{q>y} p(q) = \begin{cases} \pi & \text{for } y = 0, 1, 2, 3 \\ \dfrac{\pi}{2} & \text{for } y = 4, 5, 6, 7 \\ 0 & \text{for } y = 8. \end{cases}$$

Using (16), explain how (18) indicates that the actual loss is the same (π), no matter by how much the actual demand q exceeds the available supply y, and then verify the numerical expressions on the right of (18).

   The following is a frivolous but indicative illustration of when a lump-sum penalty, such as that in (18), is applicable. Suppose you go shopping downtown and must park your automobile on a street having parking meters. Let q be the quantity of time you need to conduct your business and y be the amount of time you "purchase" by putting nickles in the parking meter. The street is well policed, so that if you spend more time on your errand than you paid for $(q > y)$, you are certain to get a parking ticket costing π. Since you cannot predict q perfectly, your decision problem in selecting y is a matter of balancing the cost of nickles in the meter against the expected cost of a parking ticket.

   (A commercial example of a lumpy penalty cost arises in the scheduling of what is known as the "air-shuttle" service between New York and Washington, D.C. A passenger does not need to have reservations for a flight on the air-shuttle; if he arrives at the airport on time, the airline *guarantees* him a seat. The airline's decision problem is to select the size of aircraft to schedule for a given flight. If the scheduled aircraft fills up, the airline *must* make ready and fly a second plane, even if only *one* additional passenger is waiting to board!)

To summarize, the expected cost function $g(y|i)$ is the sum of the ordering cost (17) and the expected penalty cost (18):

(19) $$g(y|i) \equiv c(y - i) + L(y).$$

After a few moments reflection about (16), (17), and (18), you will conclude that for *any* i, the only policies that need be considered in the optimization process are

(20) $$y = i, 4, \text{ or } 8 \quad \text{and} \quad x = 0, 4 - i, \text{ or } 8 - i.$$

Why is this so?

Now look at two numerical examples. First let the unit purchase cost $c = 1$, the setup cost $K = 4.5$, and the lump-sum penalty cost $\pi = 12$. For initial inventory $i = 7$, the optimization in (14) indicates

$$f(7) = \underset{y \geq 7}{\text{minimum}} \, g(y|7) = \text{minimum} \, [g(7|7), g(8|7)]$$

(21) $$= \text{minimum} \left[0 + \frac{12}{2}, 4.5 + 1 \cdot 1 + 0 \right]$$

$$= 5.5 \quad \text{for } y(7) = 8.$$

Therefore, when initial inventory $i = 7$, it is optimal to order $x(7) = 8 - 7 = 1$. Consider next $i = 0$:

$$f(0) = \underset{y \geq 0}{\text{minimum}} \, g(y|0) = \text{minimum} \, [g(0|0), g(4|0), g(8|0)]$$

(22) $$= \text{minimum} \left[0 + 12, 4.5 + 1.4 + \frac{12}{2}, 4.5 + 1.8 + 0 \right]$$

$$= 12 \quad \text{for } y(0) = 0.$$

Verify that for $i = 3$ and 4

(23) $$y(3) = 8 \quad \text{and} \quad y(4) = 4,$$

and in summary,

(24) $$y(i) = i \quad \text{and} \quad x(i) = 0 \qquad \text{for } i = 0, 4, 5, 6, 8$$
$$y(i) = 8 \quad \text{and} \quad x(i) = 8 - i \quad \text{for } i = 1, 2, 3, 7.$$

Translate (24) into a verbal description of the inventory policy. Do your answers in *Case 1* above agree with (24)? If not, explain why.

For the second example, let the unit purchase cost $c = 1$, the setup cost $K = 1$, and the lump-sum penalty cost $\pi = 5$. Check that

(25) $$y(i) = i \quad \text{and} \quad x(i) = 0 \quad \text{for } i \neq 3, 7$$
$$y(3) = 4 \quad \text{and} \quad x(3) = 1 \quad \text{for } i = 3$$
$$y(7) = 8 \quad \text{and} \quad x(7) = 1 \quad \text{for } i = 7.$$

Translate (25) into a verbal description of the inventory policy. Again, do your answers in *Case 2* above agree with (25)? If not, explain why.

Although the policies in (24) and (25) *are* optimal, you may have difficulty in explaining to an "experienced manager" that he should not order when initial inventory $i = 0$, even though it is to his benefit to place an order (and incur a setup cost) when initial inventory $i = 3$. We now specify sufficient conditions on the cost functions to ensure that an "easy-to-explain" (s, S) policy is optimal.

*Optimal (s, S) policy. First, we need to review the notion of a convex function from Chap. 9. A function $L(y)$ defined for integer values of y is said to be convex if

(26) $L(y + 1) - L(y) \geq L(y) - L(y - 1)$ for all y Convex.

(You will find a number of convex functions illustrated on pp. 292-294.)

Suppose that the expected cost function is the sum of an ordering cost and a term representing expected holding and penalty costs:

(27) $g(y|i) \equiv c(y - i) + L(y)$.

Let the ordering cost $c(y - i)$ consist of a setup cost $K \geq 0$ and a unit purchase cost $c \geq 0$:

(28) $c(y - i) = \begin{cases} 0 & \text{for } y = i \quad (x = 0) \\ K + c \cdot (y - i) & \text{for } y > i \quad (x = y - i > 0) \end{cases}$ Ordering cost.

Assume that $cy + L(y)$ grows without bound as $|y| \to \infty$, and that the expected holding and penalty cost function $L(y)$ is convex.

Suppose that holding cost is expressed as an increasing function $h(y - q)$ of inventory left over $(y - q)$ provided actual demand $q \leq y$; in formal terms, assume

$$h(j) \begin{cases} \geq 0 & \text{for } j \geq 0 \\ = 0 & \text{for } j < 0, \end{cases}$$

and $h(j)$ is increasing for $j \geq 0$. Similarly, suppose the penalty cost is an increasing function $\pi(q - y)$ of unfilled demand $(q - y)$ provided $q > y$; again, in formal terms, assume

$$\pi(j) \begin{cases} \geq 0 & \text{for } j > 0 \\ = 0 & \text{for } j \leq 0, \end{cases}$$

and $\pi(j)$ is increasing for $j \geq 0$. Then the expected holding and penalty cost function is

(29) $L(y) \equiv \begin{cases} \sum\limits_{q=0}^{y} h(y - q)p(q) + \sum\limits_{q > y} \pi(q - y)p(q) & \text{for } y \geq 0 \\ \sum\limits_{q \geq 0} \pi(q - y)p(q) & \text{for } y < 0 \end{cases}$ (expected holding and penalty cost function).

It can be proved that: *if the sum of the actual holding and penalty cost functions $h(j) + \pi(-j)$ is convex for every integer j, then the expected holding and penalty cost function $L(y)$ in (29) is convex.* [When holding cost is to be assessed on the level of inventory before demand occurs, the function $h(y)$ replaces the first summation in (29).]

The following result is easy to demonstrate.

OPTIMALITY OF (s, S) POLICY FOR STATIC MODEL. Given the cost functions in (27) and (28), and that $L(y)$ is convex, then the form of an optimal policy is (s, S), defined in (1). Further, the value for the reorder level S does not depend on the setup cost K in (28), and if $K = 0$, then the reorder point $s = S$.

Knowing the form of an optimal policy makes the computation of the rule much simpler, for you only need to find the values of the reorder point s and the reorder level S. You already saw how simple the computations can be when you considered the case of linear holding and penalty cost functions. (The above optimal policy theorem remains true under more general hypotheses about the expected cost function, but we do not explore these variations here.)

▶A proof of the optimal policy theorem as well as a general computational technique can be established by the following line of argument. Observe first that

(i) $\qquad f(i) = \underset{y \geq i}{\text{minimum}}\, g(y|i) = \text{minimum} \begin{cases} \underset{y > i}{\text{minimum}}\, g(y|i) \\ g(i|i) \end{cases}$

(ii) $\qquad = \text{minimum} \begin{cases} K - ci + \underset{y > i}{\text{minimum}}\, [cy + L(y)] \\ L(i). \end{cases}$

Since both cy and $L(y)$ are convex, their sum is convex and by assumption increases without bound as $|y|$ gets very large. Consequently, there exists an S such that

(iii) $\qquad\qquad \underset{y}{\text{minimum}}\, [cy + L(y)] = cS + L(S).$

Further, a locally optimal value S is also globally optimal.

Suppose $i \geq S$; then according to (iii),

(iv) $\qquad\qquad \underset{y > i}{\text{minimum}}\, [cy + L(y)] \geq ci + L(i) \quad (i \geq S)$

so that

$$K - ci + \underset{y > i}{\text{minimum}}\, [cy + L(y)] \geq L(i) \quad (i \geq S).$$

Therefore from (ii), you have for $i \geq S$

(v) $\qquad\qquad f(i) = L(i) \qquad y(i) = i \ \text{ and } \ x(i) = 0 \quad (i \geq S).$

Now suppose $i \leq S$; then according to (ii) and (iii),

(vi) $\qquad f(i) = \text{minimum} \begin{cases} K - ci + cS + L(S) & \text{for } y = S \\ L(i) & \text{for } y = i \end{cases} \quad (i < S).$

Consider the case $K = 0$; (iii) implies that

(vii) $\qquad\qquad\qquad L(i) \geq -ci + cS + L(S),$

so that the minimum in (vi) is given by

(viii) $f(i) = c(S - i) + L(S) \quad y(i) = S \ \text{ and } \ x(i) = S - i \ \text{ for } i \leq S \ \text{ and } \ K = 0.$

Next consider the case $K > 0$; now $L(i)$ may be the smaller-valued term in (vi) for i near S. Let s be the smallest number such that

(ix) $$L(s) \leq K - cs + cS + L(S),$$

or, equivalently,

(x) $$L(s) + cs \leq K + cS + L(S).$$

Then (v) also holds for $i \geq s$. But for $i < s$,

(xi) $$f(i) = K + c(S - i) + L(S) \qquad y(i) = S \quad \text{and} \quad x(i) = S - i.$$

In summary, the values for the reorder level S and the reorder point s in (12) are found according to (iii) and (x), and

(xii) $$f(i) = \begin{cases} K + c(S - i) + L(S) & \text{for } i < s \\ L(i) & \text{for } i \geq s. \end{cases}$$

We gave simple formulas (6) and (7) for finding an optimal value of S in the case of the linear holding and penalty cost model. The result can be derived as follows.

A consequence of (iii) is that S must satisfy

(xiii) $$[c(S + 1) + L(S + 1)] \geq [cS + L(S)],$$

or

(xiv) $$L(S + 1) - L(S) \geq -c.$$

The holding cost component on the left of (xiv) is

(xv) $$h\left[\sum_{q=0}^{S+1} (S + 1 - q)p(q) - \sum_{q=0}^{S} (S - q)p(q)\right] = h\sum_{q=0}^{S} p(q) = hP(S).$$

Similarly, the penalty cost component on the left of (xiv) is

(xvi) $$\pi\left[\sum_{q=S+2}^{\infty} (q - S - 1)p(q) - \sum_{q=S+1}^{\infty} (q - S)p(q)\right] = \pi\left[-\sum_{y>S}^{\infty} p(q)\right] = -\pi[1 - P(S)].$$

Adding the rightmost terms in (xv) and (xvi), the inequality in (xiv) becomes

(xvii) $$(h + \pi)P(S) - \pi \geq -c,$$

which simplifies to (7).

Consider the linear holding and penalty cost case in which $p(q)$ is a probability density function, the variable y is continuous, and

$$L(y) = \begin{cases} \int_0^y h\cdot(y - q)p(q)\, dq + \int_y^\infty \pi\cdot(q - y)p(q)\, dq & \text{for } y \geq 0 \\ \int_0^\infty \pi\cdot(q - y)p(q)\, dq & \text{for } y < 0. \end{cases}$$

Then if $dL(y)/dy \equiv L'(y)$ exists, the $y = S$ that minimizes $[cy + L(y)]$ must satisfy

(xviii) $$c + L'(y) = 0.$$

It can be shown by advanced calculus that, for $y \geq 0$,

(xix) $$\begin{aligned} L'(y) &= h(y - y)p(y) + \int_0^y hp(q)\, dq - \pi(y - y)p(y) - \int_y^\infty \pi p(q)\, dq \\ &= (h + \pi)\int_0^y p(q)\, dq - \pi. \end{aligned}$$

Therefore from (xviii) and (xix), S satisfies

(xx)
$$P(S) \equiv \int_0^S p(q)\, dq = \frac{\pi - c}{\pi + h}.$$

The value of s is found by solving (11) expressed as an equality.

Throughout this section the holding cost formulas have been based on the value of inventory at the end of the horizon. If the holding cost is linear and assessed on the value of y, then

$$R = \frac{\pi - (c + h)}{\pi}.$$

If the holding cost is linear and assessed on the expected average value of inventory, namely $[.5y + .5(y - q)]$, then

$$R = \frac{\pi - (c + .5h)}{\pi + .5h}. \qquad \blacktriangleleft$$

19.5 ECONOMIC ORDER QUANTITY MODELS

The assumptions to be made here depart substantially from those employed in the models of the preceding section. Now consider the situation in which the horizon is unbounded so that an infinite number of replenishments will occur. Having complicated the analysis by introducing a dynamic factor, let us make an offsetting simplifying assumption that demand is perfectly forecastable at a stationary *rate*:

$$M = \text{number of items demanded per unit of time.}$$

The particulars of any actual application will dictate a convenient unit of time to use; but for the sake of definiteness in the discussion to follow, let the unit be a week. Then if $M = 30$, the demand assumption is that exactly 30 units are demanded in one week, 60 in two weeks, 15 in a half a week, etc.

We pause momentarily to mention that most textbooks treat the model below in chapters on deterministic inventory models, like Chap. 9. But we have waited until now to discuss this model in detail because *in practice* it almost always is modified to take account of uncertainties in demand. So you should look upon this section as establishing the groundwork for the modified versions that are presented in the next section.

In the lot-size models below, both time itself and the inventory level are treated as continuous variables. Note that this approach is in sharp contrast to most of the dynamic models you have studied in previous chapters. The impact of the continuity postulates is easily conveyed by a diagram. Suppose again that $M = 30$ items a week and the replenishment rule is to order 45 whenever the inventory reaches the 0 level. Assume for this illustration that there is no lead time, so that the items arrive immediately after an order is placed. Then the pattern showing inventory on hand at any moment in time appears in Fig. 19.3. Notice three features of this sawtooth pattern:

(i) The inventory repeatedly drops from the level 45 continuously to the level 0 as time moves forward continuously.

$$S = Q = 45 \quad s = 0 \quad M = 30$$

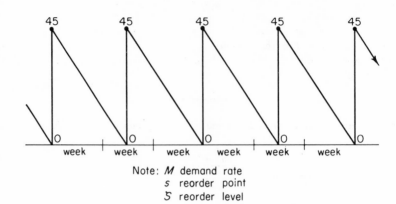

Note: M demand rate
s reorder point
S reorder level
$Q \equiv S - s$ reorder quantity

FIGURE 19.3. Sawtooth Pattern of Inventory.

(ii) The downward slope of the sawtooth is -30, representing the rate of withdrawal due to demand M.

(iii) A replenishment occurs every $\frac{45}{30} = 1.5$ weeks.

Clearly, you can rarely be certain that demand behaves in so precise a manner. Both the stationarity and perfect predictability of demand are severe postulates. Nevertheless, many industrial firms have been able to employ these models and have thereby realized substantial inventory cost savings. To do so, however, the models below are usually modified so that demand is treated probabilistically. The generalization required to handle uncertain demand is explained in the next section. You will find it helpful in preparing for that section to first study how an optimal inventory policy can be obtained when demand is perfectly predictable.

Let the ordering cost for items consist of a setup cost $K \geq 0$ plus a unit purchase cost $c \geq 0$ times the amount ordered x:

(1)
$$c(x) = \begin{cases} 0 & \text{for } x = 0 \\ K + cx & \text{for } x > 0, \end{cases}$$

and let the holding cost be linear, where

(2) $h = $ cost for each item per unit of time (a week),

and $h \geq 0$. Observe that the costs in (1) and (2) are stationary (unchanging over time). Also note that (2) implies it is equally costly to hold five items in inventory for one week, or one item for five weeks, or 2.5 items for two weeks, or two items for 2.5 weeks, etc. Ordinarily, h is a function of the purchase cost c, such as $(h = h' \cdot c)$, but to keep the notation simple, only the symbol h will be used. As you study the formulas, remember that a change in c will typically imply a corresponding change in the value of h. Without much difficulty, you can analyze models with more complicated cost assumptions—for example, the ordering cost function can exhibit quantity discounts. But such cases will not be treated in this chapter. (See exercise 52.)

Assuming repeated replenishments *are* to occur, suppose next that all demand must be met. (The formulas to follow actually indicate when it is preferable not to stock an item.) You can allow a backlog to build up, however, before placing a replenishment order; in such a case, the entering inventory would be immediately allocated to the backlogged demand, and the remainder then used for future demand. A backlog condition is represented by a negative value for i. For many reasonable stationary functions representing the penalty cost of a backlog, an optimal policy will be of the (s, S) form:

(3)   when inventory level $i = s$,   order $Q \equiv S - s$.

The form in (3) has been written more succinctly than the description of an (s, S) policy in the preceding section. The reason is that if, at any instant, the inventory level equals the reorder level S, then Q/M weeks later, it will *exactly* equal the reorder point s, because of the continuity and demand rate assumptions.

After a few moments thought, you can see that a *strictly* positive value of s is not optimal, for then there would always be at least $s > 0$ units of inventory on hand that incur a holding cost and serve no function in meeting demand. By the same token, given that repeated replenishments *are* to occur, you can conclude that, for a reasonable penalty cost function, a strictly negative value of S is not optimal. Why? Consequently, the search for optimal values of s and S can usually be restricted to $s \leq 0$ and $S \geq 0$.

Assuming that lead time is 0, so that a replenishment occurs as soon as the reorder decision is made, the resultant **sawtooth cyclic pattern** for a general (s, S) policy is shown in Fig. 19.4. (Actually, the essential lead-time assumption

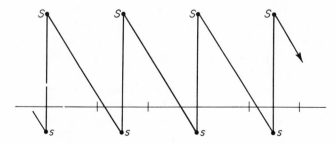

FIGURE 19.4. General Sawtooth Pattern.

underlying the pattern in Fig. 19.4 is that lead time is a known constant value. If you know that lead time is L, and you want the order to arrive at the moment when inventory equals s, then you would place the order L weeks earlier. So if $LM < Q$, the reorder point is simply LM plus the value of s as determined for $L = 0$.) Note that when the reorder point $s < 0$, demand continues at the rate M

per unit of time, so that the slope of the inventory function in Fig. 19.4 remains $-M$ throughout each cycle.

Finally, assume that the optimality criterion is minimum cost per unit of time. Provided the item is to be stocked, the purchasing and holding cost contribution to the average cost per unit of time is

(4)
$$\frac{KM}{Q} + cM + \frac{hS^2}{2Q}.$$

Each term in (4) can be derived as follows:

(i) Since M/Q is the average number of setups per unit of time, KM/Q is the average setup cost per unit of time.

(ii) Since all demand must be met, cM is the average purchase cost per unit of time.

(iii) Given the sawtooth pattern in Fig. 19.4, inventory is positive for a fraction of time equal to S/Q. The *average* level of inventory, during the interval when inventory *is* positive, is $S/2$. Consequently, $(S/Q) \cdot (S/2)$ represents the average level of inventory per unit of time, and $hS^2/2Q$ is the corresponding holding cost.

If the reorder point $s < 0$ so that a backlog builds up before a replenishment occurs, then an average penalty cost should be added to (4) to give the overall average cost per unit of time. Since in this model any backlogged demand is filled by the next replenishment, no sales are lost and the penalty cost will not include a factor representing lost profit. But a backlog condition frequently does require extra paper work to maintain the records of which customers are awaiting delivery. Further, there may be a loss in good will if a customer has to wait at all for delivery. In these situations you would expect that the penalty cost contains a factor proportional to the size of the backlog right before a replenishment, namely, the amount $(-s)$. In contrast, if the item is being used by personnel within the company, then frequently the penalty cost includes a component that is not only proportional to the size of the backlog but also to the length of time the backlog condition is present. The implications of each of these two types of penalty costs are explored below. In order not to obscure their effect on the selection of an optimal policy and also to keep the mathematical manipulations simple, the two types of penalty costs will be handled separately. They can, of course, be combined into a single model, but we will not do so in this text.

Size-of-backlog penalty cost. Suppose here that each time a backlog occurs the associated cost is π times the maximum amount short $(-s)$, where $\pi > 0$ and $s \leq 0$. Then the cost $\pi(-s)$ is incurred once during each cycle, and so the average shortage cost per unit of time is

(5)
$$\pi(-s)\frac{M}{Q}.$$

Since $Q = S - s$, you can substitute $(Q - S)$ for $(-s)$ in (5); verify that doing so and adding the result to (4) yields

(6)   average cost per unit of time $\equiv \text{AC} = \dfrac{KM}{Q} + cM + \dfrac{hS^2}{2Q} + \pi M - \dfrac{\pi MS}{Q}.$

The discussion below is considerably simplified if you assume further that the backlog cost factor $\pi > \sqrt{2Kh/M}$; this postulate is not very restrictive, since a backlog cost factor is usually large.

Given that the item is to be stocked, it is shown in the special material below that the optimal value for S is Q, and therefore $s = 0$. But it may not be optimal to keep the item in inventory at all.

To begin, suppose $S = Q$ *is* optimal. Then (6) simplifies to

(7) $\text{AC} = \dfrac{KM}{Q} + cM + \dfrac{hQ}{2}.$

The optimal Q is found by differentiating AC with respect to Q, setting the derivative equal to 0, and solving for Q, giving

(8)   optimal $Q = \sqrt{\dfrac{2KM}{h}}$ minimal $\text{AC} = cM + \sqrt{2KhM}.$

The formula for the optimal Q is frequently called the **economic order quantity**, or **EOQ**. (Sometimes you will find it referred to as the **lot-size formula**, or the **Wilson lot size**.)

If the item is not stocked, then there is a cost associated with *not* meeting the demand of M per unit of time. For simplicity, suppose that cost is represented by $\bar{\pi} M$. In this instance, you would ordinarily include in $\bar{\pi}$ a factor indicating lost profit, so that $\bar{\pi}$ need not equal π. The economic test is

(9)   if $\bar{\pi} M \leq cM + \sqrt{2KhM}$, do not stock,

and otherwise order according to (8).

▶ The following abbreviated argument underlies a proof that the optimal S is either Q or 0, given that $\pi > \sqrt{2Kh/M}$. Define f such that

(i) $S \equiv fQ$

and, consequently, $0 \leq f \leq 1$, since $s \leq 0$ and $S \geq 0$. Further let $C(f) = cM$ if $f > 0$, and 0 if $f = 0$. Then substituting (i) into (6), the optimization problem can be stated as minimizing

(ii) $\text{AC}(Q,f) \equiv \dfrac{KM}{Q} + C(f) + \dfrac{hf^2 Q}{2} + \pi M - \pi Mf.$

A necessary condition for the optimal Q is that it satisfy

(iii) $\dfrac{\partial \text{AC}\,(Q,f)}{\partial Q} = 0$ for $f > 0$,

yielding the condition

(iv)   optimal $Q = \dfrac{1}{f}\sqrt{\dfrac{2KM}{h}}.$

Substituting (iv) into (ii) gives $\text{AC}[Q\,(f),f]$, which is a linear function of f.

Calculating $dAC\,[Q\,(f),f]/df$ for $f > 0$ results in

(v) $$\frac{dAC}{df} = \sqrt{2KhM} - \pi M \quad \text{for } f > 0,$$

so that $dAC/df < 0$ since $\pi > \sqrt{2Kh/M}$ by assumption. Then $f = 1$ is optimal *provided* AC $[Q\,(1), 1]$ is no greater than the cost of not stocking, which is the comparison in (9).

We also mention that this model is closely related to the case in which demand is lost when there is no inventory on hand. Assuming that each unit of demand lost reduces profit by π, the optimal policy again is to either let $S = Q$ (no demand is lost), or $S = 0$ (all demand is lost). ◄

Sensitivity analysis of EOQ. Notice that the EOQ increases *less* than proportionately with increases in the setup cost K and the demand rate M, and decreases in the holding cost h. For example, if the rate M quadruples, then the EOQ only doubles. Analogously, if the value of h quadruples, then the EOQ only decreases by a half. Observe that the time interval between orders is

(10) $$\text{optimal } T = \frac{\text{EOQ}}{M} = \sqrt{\frac{2K}{hM}}.$$

Thus as the demand rate M gets larger, not only does the optimal Q get larger but the optimal time interval between orders T gets smaller so that ordering occurs more frequently.

In many situations the vendor requires that the amount ordered be a "convenient" number. To illustrate, if the optimal $Q = 53$, you may have to place an order for either 50 or 60. You should note that there is very little impact on average cost when only a *near*-optimal Q is employed. Let

(11) $$\text{actual } Q = r \cdot \text{optimal } Q = r \cdot \sqrt{\frac{2KM}{h}},$$

where $r > 0$, and let the *variable* cost be written as

(12) $$VC(r) = \frac{KM}{\text{actual } Q} + \frac{h \cdot \text{actual } Q}{2} = \frac{KM}{r\sqrt{2KM/h}} + \frac{h \cdot r\sqrt{2KM/h}}{2},$$

so that the *fixed* purchase cost component cM is omitted. Verify from (12) that

(13) $$\frac{VC(r)}{VC(1)} = \frac{1}{2}\left(\frac{1}{r} + r\right).$$

As you can see by calculating (13) for trial values of r, the increase in variable cost from a near-optimal Q is slight. For example

(14) $$\frac{VC(r)}{VC(1)} \leq 1.1 \quad \text{for } .64 \leq r \leq 1.56.$$

[Also note in (13) that the ratio has the same value for a given r and its reciprocal $r' = 1/r$.]

▶The analogous model in which both time and the items are in discrete units was previously analyzed by means of a regeneration approach, and is contained in the advanced material of Sec. 11.4. For ease of comparison, the model is briefly summarized here, employing the notation used in this chapter.

For the sake of definiteness, let M (an integer) be the amount of demand per week and

$C_T = $ *total* cost associated with ordering MT units of the item,

where $T = 1, 2, \ldots$. Therefore C_T represents the entire cost over T weeks, and

(i) $$C_T = K + cMT + \frac{hM(T-1)T}{2}.$$

The objective is

(ii) $$\operatorname*{minimize}_{T=1,2,\ldots} \left(\frac{C_T}{T}\right) = \operatorname*{minimize}_{T} \left[\frac{K}{T} + cM + \frac{hM(T-1)}{2}\right].$$

Ignore the integer-value constraint on T momentarily, differentiate the expression on the right of (ii), and set the result equal to zero, obtaining

(iii) $$T^* = \sqrt{\frac{2K}{hM}},$$

which is the same value as (10). Accordingly

(iv) $$Q^* = MT^* = \sqrt{\frac{2KM}{h}}.$$

Since T^* is usually not an integer, calculate the expression on the right of (ii) for the next smallest and largest integers and select the better value.

To check your understanding of the derivation of the average cost formula in (6), find C_T for the continuous model and calculate C_T/T. You should get an expression equivalent to (6) after MT has been substituted for Q. ◄

Average-backlog penalty cost. Now suppose the penalty cost is assessed against the average level of backlog per unit of time, analogous to the inventory holding charges. Looking again at Fig. 19.4, you will see that a backlog condition exists for a fraction of time $-s/Q$, where the reorder point $s \le 0$. The average level of backlog, during the interval when inventory is negative, is $-s/2$. Consequently, the average level of backlog per unit of time is $s^2/2Q$, which must be multiplied by the corresponding penalty cost. It is convenient for the purpose of comparison to again let the penalty cost be denoted by the symbol $\pi > 0$. But you should realize that the cost measurement units are different in the previous case than they are here. Specifically, now π represents the cost per item per unit of time the backlog is present, whereas previously π was simply the cost per item backlogged. Using the identity $(S - s \equiv Q)$ to eliminate s, you obtain after simplification,

(15) $$\begin{array}{c}\text{average cost per}\\ \text{unit of time}\end{array} \equiv \mathrm{AC} = \frac{KM}{Q} + cM + \frac{(h+\pi)S^2}{2Q} - \pi S + \frac{\pi}{2}Q.$$

(Here it is not necessary to explicitly assume that π is large relative to the other costs.)

Taking the partial derivative of AC in (15) with respect to S, setting the result equal to 0, and simplifying yields

(16) $$S = \left(\frac{\pi}{h+\pi}\right)Q.$$

Doing the same with respect to Q and using (16) to eliminate S gives

$$\text{optimal } Q = \sqrt{2KM} \cdot \sqrt{\frac{1}{h} + \frac{1}{\pi}} \qquad \text{optimal } S = \sqrt{\frac{2KM}{h}} \cdot \sqrt{\frac{\pi}{h + \pi}}$$

(17)

$$\text{optimal } s = -\sqrt{\frac{2KM}{\pi}} \cdot \sqrt{\frac{h}{h + \pi}} \qquad \text{minimal AC} = cM + \frac{\sqrt{2KM}}{\sqrt{\frac{1}{h} + \frac{1}{\pi}}}.$$

What is the optimal time interval between successive orders? As in the previous case, the decision of whether to stock at all depends on a comparison of the minimal AC in (17) with the cost of not meeting demand.

As you were already cautioned, the measurement unit for the penalty cost in (17) is not the same as in (8), since here π represents the cost per item per unit of time a backlog is present, whereas previously π represented the cost per item backlogged. Nevertheless, it is instructive to compare the solutions in (17) and (8) assuming that π has the same numerical value in both sets of formulas. Specifically notice in (17) that for a finite value of the penalty cost π, the optimal order quantity Q is larger, the optimal reorder level S is smaller, the optimal reorder point s is smaller (actually negative), and the minimal average cost is smaller. Only when π is infinite do the values in (17) equal the corresponding solution in (8). Also, only when the holding cost factor h is infinite is the optimal $S = 0$; but even then, Q and s are finite.

Study (17) to see how each optimal quantity varies with changes in the values of K, h, π, and M. In particular, note that the optimal order quantity Q decreases as the penalty cost π increases, and the optimal reorder point s decreases as either the setup cost K or the demand rate M increases. Observe from (16) that if $h = \pi$, then there is a backlog condition during the second half of the interval between successive orders.

*Production lot sizes. So far the discussion of economic order quantity models has been in the context of a company replenishing its inventory by ordering an item from a vendor. Accordingly, the inventory policies indicated *when* and *how much* to reorder. Let us now turn to a related problem of a company that manufactures certain of its items in lot-size quantities. Many of the economic considerations encompassed in the preceding models are just as relevant in this situation: a setup cost, the direct manufacturing costs, and holding and shortage costs. Assuming the stationarity and demand assumptions remain reasonable, can the (s, S) policies derived in (8) and (17) be used here as optimal lot sizes and production trigger points? Sometimes, but not usually.

The significant difference between ordering an item from a vendor and producing it in your own plant is that a production activity requires the use of other limited resources, namely, men, equipment, and component materials. Most manufacturing plants carefully schedule ahead, taking into account available manpower and equipment capacity limitations, and ensuring that sufficient materials are on hand. Consequently, if an economic lot-size approach is used for all the manufactured items and is based on the above models—or those in the next section—the result may not yield a feasible overall schedule for a production plant. In short, a single-item EOQ model applied to a multitude of internally manufactured items is typically a poor approximation to reality, for it ignores the operating constraints on scarce resources.

What is required in a production setting is a dynamic planning model that combines the cost elements in EOQ models with the constrained multi-item considerations. The component time periods in the model must be short enough so that the plan can be implemented by production decisions. Several breakthroughs have occurred in operations research models capable of handling these situations, but the complexity of the analyses goes beyond the scope of this text.

*Raw materials inventories. A related area of inventory decisions is the stockage of raw materials to support a manufacturing firm's production activities. Here too the economic considerations encompassed in the EOQ models are relevant to storing raw materials. But analogous to the production lot-size situation, the manufacturing activity itself, through a production schedule, also exerts an influence on the inventory policy. Only in the case of continuous and nearly level production would you expect an EOQ approach to be useful. A more widely applicable operations research approach for the stockage of raw materials is a dynamic programming model like one of those in Chap. 9. Such a model employs the production schedule requirements as "demand" data, and while minimizing costs, at the same time ensures that the required raw materials are on hand when needed.

19.6 STOCHASTIC DYNAMIC CONTINUOUS
REVIEW MODEL

This section extends the preceding economic lot-size model analysis to include probabilistically described demand. Continue to assume that time is a continuous variable; the ordering and holding costs are stationary

(1)
$$c(x) = \begin{cases} 0 & \text{for } x = 0 \\ K + cx & \text{for } x > 0 \end{cases} \quad \text{(ordering cost)}$$

(2) h = holding cost for each item per unit of time,

where $K \geq 0$, $c \geq 0$, and $h \geq 0$. Suppose that any demand occurring when the inventory level is 0 is backlogged and eventually filled. Assume here that the penalty cost $\pi > 0$ is stationary and proportional to the size of a backlog just before a replenishment order arrives. Now the objective is to minimize *expected* average cost per unit of time. Let

(3)

M = *expected* number of items demanded per unit of time

L = lead time, the length of the interval between placing and receiving an order

M_L = *expected* number of items demanded during an interval of L units of time, where L is fixed and known. Since "the expected value of a sum is always equal to the sum of the expected values,"

(4) $$M_L = ML.$$

If the lead time $L = 0$—an order arrives immediately after it is placed—then the analysis of the average cost formula (6) in the preceding section needs to be modified only slightly. Provided the items should be stocked, and the optimal reorder point $s = 0$, the optimal order quantity and minimal cost formulas in (8) above apply, where the cost expression now represents an expected value. The reason is that when $L = 0$, there is never an opportunity for a backlog condition to arise.

If the lead time $L > 0$, however, the situation is quite different. Let

q_L = actual demand during an interval between placing and receiving an order.

Here the random variable q_L may exceed s, which is the level of inventory at the start of the interval, so that a backlog condition occurs. How then should Q and s be chosen optimally?

A naive approach is to calculate Q according to the economic order quantity formula (8) above, and to pick s using the static model analysis in Sec. 19.4, in which the demand probability distribution relates to demand during lead time and the expected holding and penalty cost function $L(y)$ is given by (3) in that section. Then $S = s + Q$.

For example, suppose

(5)
purchase cost: $c = 1$ setup cost: $K = 31.25$ holding cost: $h = 5$
penalty cost: $\pi = 20$ demand rate: $M = 2$ lead time: $L = 1$.

Verify that

(6) $$Q = \sqrt{\frac{2KM}{h}} = 5.$$

Suppose further that the probability distribution of **demand during a lead time** is

(7) $$p_L(q_L) = \frac{1}{5} \quad \text{for } q = 0, 1, \ldots, 4 \qquad E[q_L] = M_L = 2.$$

The distribution in (7) is the same as that in (4) of Sec. 19.4, and as the entries in Fig. 19.1 show for penalty cost factor $\pi = 20$,

(8)   reorder point $s = 3$ so that   reorder level $S = s + Q = 8$.

Therefore this naive analysis leads to the policy $(s, S) = (3, 8)$.

The logical error in the above approach is that the analysis ignores the cost interaction between the reorder point s and the order quantity Q. Specifically, if you keep s fixed and let Q get larger, then the actual penalty cost component of average cost will decrease. The reason is there are fewer replenishments and corresponding exposures to stockouts per unit of time. Consequently, you can reduce average cost by letting the order quantity Q be larger than indicated by the economic lot-size formula. By the same token, you may obtain further cost savings from an even lower value for the reorder point s.

Having recognized that optimal values for s and Q are interdependent, you are ready to explore a way to calculate them. As usual, the first step is to develop the appropriate expression for the criterion function, and afterwards to optimize the value of the expression with respect to s and Q. Before taking the first step, we will impose a few additional assumptions. Of course, all assumptions, in one way or another, represent approximations to a real situation. But the ones to follow are imposed primarily to keep the exposition simple and the mathematical manipulations tractable. Nevertheless, the model below (and minor variants of it) have proved in practice to be very effective in establishing workable inventory policies.

Assume for the mathematical development of the criterion function that

(i) The probability distribution of demand during a lead time $p_L(q_L)$ does not depend on when the inventory reaches the reorder point s.

(ii) The inventory level i can be treated as a continuous variable.

(iii) After a replenishment order arrives, there exists a future moment in time when the inventory level $i = s$, and a reorder action occurs as a consequence.

(iv) In an optimal policy, the reorder point $s > 0$ and during any lead time, actual demand does not exceed the order quantity ($q_L \leq Q$).

The meaning of these assumptions is clear, but you should observe where each is used in developing the criterion function. The postulate that the optimal $Q \geq q_L$ deserves further comment. Note that just before a replenishment order arrives the inventory level is $s - q_L$, and just after it is $s - q_L + Q$, which is at least s given postulate (iv). As a result, there is never more than one replenishment order outstanding at any instant. Explain why.

▶Observe that the discussion stressed that the above assumptions are made for the purpose of writing a mathematical expression for the average cost function. Here is why they were *not* introduced as assumptions about reality.

After giving a precise mathematical description of (i) and (iii), you can prove they logically imply that for any interval of time T, the probability distribution for demand during T *must* be a Poisson distribution with a single parameter MT that equals both the mean and variance. This is much too restrictive a conclusion about *reality*. Rarely in practice will you find that the mean and variance of a demand distribution are equal —most often, the variance is several times greater than the mean. Assuming (i) and (iii) only for mathematical convenience permits you to use an arbitrary distribution form for $p_L(q_L)$ in all the computations. In summary, the model is often an excellent approximation despite its containing a few internal inconsistencies.   ◀

Expected cost. The purchase cost component of the objective function is just like the lot-size models:

(9) $$\frac{KM}{Q} + cM \quad \text{(average ordering cost)}.$$

We next obtain the expected holding and penalty cost. You can, if you want, skip this derivation and go directly to the end result in (16) below.

Consider the time interval between two successive reorder actions; two examples of what can happen are shown in Fig. 19.5, one for actual demand during lead time less than the reorder point, $q_L < s$, and one for $q_L > s$. In the case $q_L > s$, taking into account that the inventory level is 0 *before* the replenishment arrives makes the holding cost formulas complicated. Therefore, as a mathematical approximation, assume that when $q_L > s$, inventory becomes 0 just before the replenishment arrives. Then, as you can verify,

(10) $$\begin{aligned}\text{expected average inventory level during lead time} &= \sum_{q_L=0}^{s} \tfrac{1}{2}[s + (s - q_L)]p_L(q_L) + \sum_{q_L>s} \tfrac{1}{2}[s + 0]p_L(q_L) \\ &= \tfrac{1}{2}\left[s + \sum_{q_L=0}^{s} (s - q_L)p_L(q_L)\right],\end{aligned}$$

Case $q_L < s$

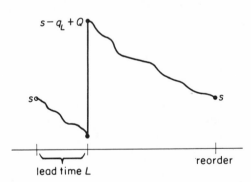

Case $q_L > s$

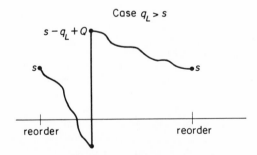

Note: q_L demand during lead time L
Q reorder quantity
s reorder point

Figure 19.5. Sawtooth Patterns for Probabilistic Demands.

(11)　expected average inventory
level after replenishment $= \frac{1}{2}[(s - M_L + Q) + s] = \frac{1}{2}(2s - M_L + Q).$
until next reorder

The expression in (10) must be weighted by M_L/Q, the fraction of time the system is waiting for a replenishment, and correspondingly, the expression in (11) must be weighted by $(1 - M_L/Q)$. You can verify that after applying these weights, adding the results, and rearranging terms, you get

(12)　expected average
inventory per
unit of time
$$= \frac{M_L}{2Q}\left[-2s + M_L - Q + s + \sum_{q_L=0}^{s}(s - q_L)p_L(q_L)\right]$$
$$+ \frac{1}{2}(2s - M_L + Q).$$

As you may want to check for yourself,

(13)
$$\sum_{q_L=0}^{s}(s - q_L)p_L(q_L) = s - M_L - \sum_{q_L>s}(s - q_L)p_L(q_L),$$

so that the expression in (12) can be written as

(14)
$$\frac{Q}{2} - M_L + s + \frac{M_L}{2Q}\sum_{q_L>s}(q_L - s)p_L(q_L).$$

Finally,

(15)　expected shortage
during a lead time $= \sum_{q_L>s}(q_L - s)p_L(q_L),$

which must be weighted by M/Q to obtain the expected shortage per unit of time, just as in the economic lot-size model of the previous section.

Combining (9), (14) multiplied by the holding cost h, and (15) multiplied by M/Q times the penalty cost π gives

(16)　expected average
cost per unit
of time
$$\equiv E[AC] = \frac{KM}{Q} + cM + h\left(\frac{Q}{2} - M_L + s\right)$$
$$+ \left(\frac{hM_L}{2Q} + \frac{M\pi}{Q}\right)\sum_{q_L>s}(q_L - s)p_L(q_L).$$

To see the relation between (16) and the formulas derived in the preceding section, observe that if demand is deterministic, then the optimal reorder point $s = M_L$ and the summation on the right of (16) would be 0, since each of the probabilities would be 0; the resulting expression agrees with the average cost formula (7) in Sec. 19.5.

Partially differentiating $E[AC]$ with respect to Q, setting the derivative equal to 0, and solving for Q, gives the formula

(17)　optimal $Q = \sqrt{\dfrac{2KM}{h} + \left(M_L + \dfrac{2M\pi}{h}\right)\sum_{q_L>s}(q_L - s)p_L(q_L)}$

(determination of order quantity).

Define the cumulative demand distribution as

(18)
$$P_L(y) \equiv \sum_{q_L=0}^{y}p_L(q_L).$$

Then it can be shown that the optimal $s \geq 0$ is the *smallest* integer such that

(19) $P_L(s) \geq R$ (determination of reorder point),

where here the critical ratio is

(20) $$R \equiv 1 - \frac{hQ}{\dfrac{hM_L}{2} + M\pi}.$$

More precisely, the order quantity Q and reorder point s are optimal values if they *simultaneously* satisfy (17) and (19). Substituting (17) into (16) yields

(21) $$\text{minimal } E[\text{AC}] = cM + \sqrt{2h\left[KM + \left(\frac{hM_L}{2} + M\pi\right)\sum_{q_L > s}(q_L - s)p_L(q_L)\right]}$$
$$+ h(s - M_L),$$

assuming that s is found according to (19). What terms in (21) indicate the impact of uncertainty? [To decide whether the item is to be inventoried at all, the value in (21) must be compared to the cost of not stocking.]

Notice the second term under the radical sign in (17) causes the optimal value for Q to be larger than the economic lot size for the case of deterministic demand. Also the smaller the value of s, the larger the value of Q. By the same token, the larger the value of Q in (20), the smaller the value of R and the smaller the value of s satisfying (19). The value of $P_L(s)$ is sometimes referred to as the **service level** and the amount $s - E[q_L]$ as the **buffer** or **safety stock.**

Unless you make additional assumptions about the form of the probability distribution $p_L(q_L)$, you are not able to state much about the sensitivity of the optimal policy to the economic parameters, the mean demand M, and the lead time L. To see why, consider an increase in the penalty cost π. On the one hand, it tends to directly increase the second term under the radical in (17); on the other, it tends to indirectly decrease that term due to its direct effect on R and s in (19) and (20). Several illustrative examples showing policy sensitivity will be given in the discussion of a Normal distribution approximation below.

▶ The formulas developed in (17) and (19) have a wider applicability than simply the model specified by the various assumptions so far. To illustrate, suppose lead time L is random but the assumption that demand during lead time $q_L \leq Q$ still holds. Then $p_L(q_L)$ is defined accordingly to be the probability distribution of demand during a lead time.

As another illustration, suppose the value of s is determined by (19) but R is a probability *prespecified* by the decision-maker; that is, R represents the minimum allowable probability of filling all demand during a lead time. (The value $1 - R$ is the maximum allowable probability of having any shortages.) Postulating that only a policy of the (s, S) form is to be considered, and that expected average purchase and holding cost per unit of time is to be minimized, then the optimal Q is given by (17) with $\pi = 0$. Recall from Chap. 16, however, that given the *chance-constraint* $P(s) \geq R$, a randomized strategy might yield an even lower expected purchase and holding cost.

Finally, with only minor modifications, the approach can be applied to the situation where unfilled demand is not backlogged but is lost. (See exercise 56.)   ◀

Algorithmic solution. The following simple procedure can be used to yield values for Q and s that simultaneously solve (17) and (19):

Step 1. Let the initial trial value of Q be $\sqrt{2KM/h}$.

Step 2. Compute R in (20) using the current trial value for Q, and find a corresponding trial value for s in (19).

Step 3. Stop if the new trial s is the same as the previous trial value. Otherwise calculate a new trial value for Q according to (17), and return to *Step 2.*

Notice, as the iterations progress, the trial values of s get smaller and of Q get larger. The method will always converge in a finite number of iterations provided the optimal s *is* positive. A sufficient condition ensuring convergence is that

$$(22) \qquad Q_{\max} < \frac{\dfrac{hM_L}{2} + M\pi}{h},$$

where $Q_{\max}$ is the expression on the right of (17) evaluated for $s = 0$ (so that the summation term is simply M_L). Once again, because no assumptions have been made about the form of $p_L(q_L)$ other than that it is a discrete distribution, the terminating value for s may not be globally optimal; at worst, a neighboring value of s and the associated optimal Q may have a lower expected cost.

Consider the following example, which contains the same data as (5) and (7):

$$(23) \qquad \begin{array}{cccc} c = 1 & K = 31.25 & h = 5 & \pi = 20 \\ L = 1 & p_L(q_L) = \dfrac{1}{5} \ \text{for } q = 0, 1, \ldots, 4 & E[q_L] \equiv M_L = M = 2. \end{array}$$

According to *Step 1,*

$$(24) \qquad\qquad\qquad \text{initial trial } Q = 5.$$

Then for *Step 2,*

$$(25) \qquad\qquad R = 1 - \frac{25}{5 + 40} = .44 \quad \text{and} \quad P(2) \geq .44.$$

Using the trial value $s = 2$, the computation in *Step 3* is

$$(26) \qquad\qquad \text{trial } Q = \sqrt{25 + (18)(.6)} = 5.98.$$

Repeating *Steps 2* and *3* gives

$$(27) \qquad R = .34 \quad \text{and} \quad P(1) \geq .34 \qquad \text{trial } Q = \sqrt{25 + (18)(1.2)} = 6.83.$$

The final iteration is

$$(28) \qquad \begin{array}{ll} R = .24 \ \text{and} \ P(1) \geq .24 \ \text{optimal } s = 1 \\ \text{optimal } Q = 6.83 \qquad\qquad \text{optimal } S = s + Q = 7.83 \end{array}$$

and as a consequence,

$$(29) \quad \text{minimal } E[AC] = 2 + \sqrt{10[62.5 + (45)(1.2)]} + 5(1 - 2) = 31.13.$$

Observe how the optimal solution differs from the policy in (6) and (8) obtained by the naive analysis. That approach led to a policy $(s, S) = (3, 8)$; the associated expected cost according to (16) is 33.9, which is 9% larger than the optimal value in (29).

To test your understanding of the algorithm, apply it to the case in (23) with $\pi = 30$. (You should find that $s = 2$ is optimal.)

*Normal approximation. When applying the model in this section to an inventory system containing a multitude of items, you typically would assume as an approximation that the distribution $p_L(q_L)$ is of a particular type, such as Poisson, negative binomial, uniform, etc. Then you would only need to specify the parameters of the selected distribution. A very convenient approach is to use a Normal distribution (which is continuous), letting the mean and variance be

$$(30) \qquad E[q_L] = M_L \qquad \text{Var}[q_L] = \sum_{q_L \ge 0} (q_L - M_L)^2 p_L(q_L) \equiv V_L.$$

From a practical point of view, the approximation method turns out to be very effective, even though the theoretical properties of the Normal distribution (such as symmetry, and the possibility of arbitrarily small and large values of the random variable) may depart considerably from the distribution $p_L(q_L)$. Of course, you should not apply this or any other approximation unless you investigate how well it holds for the range of parameters in which you are interested.

Define

$$(31) \qquad u_s = \frac{s - M_L}{\sqrt{V_L}},$$

so that

$$(32) \qquad s = M_L + u_s \sqrt{V_L}.$$

Accordingly, as before, let

$$(33) \qquad R = 1 - \frac{hQ}{\frac{hM_L}{2} + M\pi}.$$

Denote the *cumulative standardized Normal distribution* as

$$(34) \qquad P_N(u) = \int_{-\infty}^{u} \frac{1}{\sqrt{2\pi}} e^{-.5t^2} \, dt,$$

and the so-called **standardized Normal loss integral** as

$$(35) \qquad I_N(u) = \int_{u}^{\infty} (t - u) \frac{1}{\sqrt{2\pi}} e^{-.5t^2} \, dt.$$

The loss integral is used for the approximation

$$(36) \qquad \sum_{q_L > s} (q_L - s) p_L(q_L) \approx \sqrt{V_L} \cdot I_N(u_s).$$

The functions $P_N(u)$ and $I_N(u)$ are tabled in Fig. 19.6.

u	$P_N(u)$	$I_N(u)$	$P_N(-u)$	$I_N(-u)$
0	.5000	.3989	.5000	.3989
.1	.5399	.3509	.4601	.4509
.2	.5793	.3068	.4207	.5068
.3	.6180	.2667	.3820	.5667
.4	.6555	.2304	.3445	.6304
.5	.6915	.1977	.3085	.6977
.6	.7258	.1686	.2742	.7686
.7	.7581	.1428	.2419	.8428
.8	.7882	.1202	.2118	.9202
.9	.8160	.1004	.1840	1.0004
1.0	.8414	.0833	.1586	1.0833
1.1	.8644	.0686	.1356	1.1686
1.2	.8850	.0561	.1150	1.2561
1.3	.9032	.0455	.0968	1.3455
1.4	.9193	.0366	.0807	1.4366
1.5	.9332	.0293	.0668	1.5293
1.6	.9453	.0232	.0547	1.6232
1.7	.9555	.0182	.0445	1.7182
1.8	.9641	.0142	.0359	1.8142
1.9	.9713	.0110	.0287	1.9110
2.0	.9773	.0084	.0227	2.0084
2.1	.9822	.0064	.0178	2.1064
2.2	.9861	.0048	.0139	2.2048
2.3	.9893	.0036	.0107	2.3036
2.4	.9919	.0027	.0081	2.4027
2.5	.9938	.0020	.0062	2.5020
2.6	.9954	.0014	.0046	2.6014
2.7	.9966	.0010	.0034	2.7010
2.8	.9975	.0007	.0025	2.8007
2.9	.9982	.0005	.0018	2.9005
3.0	.9987	.0003	.0013	3.0003

FIGURE 19.6. Tables of Cumulative and Loss Integral for a Standardized Normal Distribution.

Then, instead of (19), the value u_s is determined by

$$(37) \qquad\qquad P_N(u_s) = R,$$

and, instead of (17), the value of Q is found by

$$(38) \qquad \text{optimal } Q = \sqrt{\frac{2KM}{h} + \left(M_L + \frac{2M\pi}{h}\right)\sqrt{V_L} \cdot I_N(u_s)}.$$

Write down the expression corresponding to (21) for the minimal $E[AC]$.

The algorithm is

Step 1. Let the initial trial value of Q be $\sqrt{2KM/h}$.

Step 2. Compute R in (33) using the current trial value for Q, and find a corresponding trial value for u_s from (37) and s from (32).

Step 3. Stop if the new trial s is approximately the same as the previous trial value. Otherwise calculate a new trial value for Q according to (38) and return to *Step 2*.

Notice in *Step 3* you must specify a numerical tolerance defining when two trial values for s are approximately the same.

To illustrate the method, consider the example

$$(39) \qquad \begin{aligned} K = 32 \quad & h = 1 \quad \pi = 9 \\ L = 1 \quad & M = M_L = 16 \quad V_L = 48. \end{aligned}$$

From *Step 1*,

$$(40) \qquad \text{initial } Q = 32,$$

and for *Step 2*,

$$(41) \qquad R = \left(1 - \frac{32}{\frac{16}{2} + 144}\right) = \frac{120}{152} = .789,$$

so that from Fig. 19.6 you have

$$(42) \qquad \text{trial } u_s = .8 \quad \text{and} \quad \text{trial } s = 16 + (.8)\sqrt{48} = 21.6.$$

Then in *Step 3*,

$$(43) \qquad \text{trial } Q = \sqrt{(32)(32) + (16 + 144)\sqrt{48}(.12)} = 35.71.$$

Returning to *Step 2*,

$$(44) \qquad R = \left(1 - \frac{35.71}{\frac{16}{2} + 144}\right) = .765,$$

so that

$$(45) \qquad \text{trial } u_s = .72 \quad \text{and} \quad \text{trial } s = 16 + (.72)\sqrt{48} = 21.01.$$

Then in *Step 3*

$$(46) \qquad \text{trial } Q = \sqrt{(32)(32) + (16 + 144)\sqrt{48}(.14)} = 36.24.$$

Further iterations will affect only the decimal parts of s and Q in (45) and (46). The associated expected cost is

$$(47) \qquad E[AC] = c16 + 41.3.$$

Check your understanding of the method by finding an optimal policy for $M = 16$, $L = 5$, $M_L = 80$, $V_L = 240$, and the other parameter values as given in (39). (The optimal s is about 91.)

Several optimal policies found by the approximation method are shown in Fig. 19.7. Note that an increase in each parameter π, K, M, L, and V_L tends to

Case	Varied Parameters	s	Q	$E[AC]$	EOQ
	None	11	26	28.0	24
	$\pi = 99$	15	25	31.2	24
	$K = 64$	10	36	37.2	33.9
1	$\pi = 99$ $K = 64$	14	35	40.2	33.9
	$M = 16$	19	34	37.4	32
	$L = 5$	49	28	32.5	24
	$V_L = 27$	11	28	29.6	24
	None	109	52	80.7	45.3
	$\pi = 9$	88	56	64.2	45.3
	$K = 32$	111	38	69.3	32
2	$\pi = 9$ $K = 32$	91	42	53.2	32
	$M = 9$	65	39	59.0	33.9
	$L = 1$	29	48	61.0	45.3
	$V_L = 80$	97	49	65.9	45.3

Nonvaried Parameter Values:
Case 1: $h = 1$ $\pi = 9$ $K = 32$ $c = 0$ $M = 9$ $L = 1$ $(M_L = 9)$ $V_L = 9$
Case 2: $h = 1$ $\pi = 99$ $K = 64$ $c = 0$ $M = 16$ $L = 5$ $(M_L = 80)$ $V_L = 240$

(The values for s and Q have been rounded to the nearest integer.)

FIGURE 19.7. Sensitivity Analysis for Normal Approximation.

increase both the optimal s and Q, *except* that an increase in π decreases Q and an increase in K decreases s. This sensitivity pattern holds provided that the probability that q_L is negative is negligible in the Normal approximation to $p_L(q_L)$, as is true when $M_L/\sqrt{V_L}$ is larger than 2. Also observe that the optimal Q can be significantly larger than the deterministic EOQ formula value, but even when this occurs, the values are found in only three or four iterations.

19.7 CONCLUDING REMARKS ON IMPLEMENTATION

Any detailed discussion of the steps required to implement a scientific inventory management system would go far beyond the intended scope of this chapter. But because the text mentioned that a model as simple as the one in the preceding section has proved effective, the paragraphs below briefly indicate how in reality you would handle the approximating assumptions. Remember throughout that the context of the discussion is the employment of a mathematical approach to stocking those items that are to be managed on a *routine* basis.

Stationarity. The foregoing dynamic continuous review model postulated that the economic parameters as well as the demand distribution are unchanging over time. In an application, each time the policy is calculated for an item, you would use the current economic parameters and a probability distribution estimated by giving greatest weight to the most recent demand data. In many inventory systems, each policy is updated at most every three months, and often not until six months or a year elapses. If the economic parameters and demand distribution are shifting so rapidly as to invalidate the approximations made in the above model, you then will have to resort to a dynamic programming approach, such as that given in Appendix II.

Form of the economic functions. Ordering and holding cost functions as simple as those exhibited in this chapter are obviously approximations. Nevertheless, as such they are still capable of being estimated within an acceptable degree of accuracy. Ordinarily you would arrive at the setup cost element by looking at the cost of the total annual manpower and associated costs required to support the reordering function (consisting mainly of placing and receiving replenishment orders) and averaging this cost over the corresponding reorder activity level. Often the principal component of the inventory carrying charge is the firm's cost of working capital. The additional holding costs due to warehousing and insurance are easily calculated in aggregate, and typically are prorated among the different items stocked.

The shortage or penalty cost is the hardest economic factor to estimate. Typically, you would first make a rough guess and then perform a sensitivity analysis to refine your estimate. A little more will be said about this aspect under the topic of "Validation" below.

Form of the demand distribution. In an inventory system with a multitude of items, you necessarily have to develop a routine procedure for estimating the demand distributions using historical data. Standard statistical approaches for estimating means and variances are usually employed. You must apply a certain amount of caution, however, in the data processing step. For example, you must be careful not to use data so old as to be irrelevant for future demand prediction. Similarly, you must be careful to cull out of the data so-called extreme values, which can exert a strong upward bias in the value of a sample mean, and which in fact represent occasions when a demand is so large that it *has* to be treated on a nonroutine basis.

You will ordinarily assume a standard form for the probability distributions. For example, if you use the Normal approximation approach in the preceding section, then you need to estimate only the mean and variance of demand during lead time. Often, by examining a sample of items, you will find through statistical regression analysis that you can employ an approximating relationship between the mean and variance. To illustrate, you may find there is a reasonably constant ratio between the mean and variance. In such a case, you would estimate the variance indirectly from an estimate of the mean.

Calculation of optimal policies. There is a variety of techniques for computing the specific optimal policies. The primary factor determining the appropriate method is whether an electronic computer is employed to maintain current inventory records. When a company utilizes a computer to keep an up-to-date record of stock on hand, then ordinarily it also has the computer calculate the policies according to formulas such as those in the preceding section. The electronic calculator uses recent demand data to update the policies, and as already mentioned, the policies are revised from one to four times a year. In the most sophisticated computer applications, as soon as the inventory level reaches the reorder point, the electronic calculator prints out a reorder slip to be mailed to the vendor.

The scientific approach to inventory decisions has also been implemented in companies making only minor use of a computer for stock control. In such situations, tables (or nomographs) are constructed so that an inventory manager is not required to perform any complex computations, but only needs to enter a modest amount of economic and demand data to find the optimal policy. The tables themselves are usually calculated by means of an electronic computer.

Validation. By now, having seen a succession of simplifying assumptions piled one on top of another, you must be wondering how it is possible to tell whether the resultant recommended policies will *really* bring about an improvement in an actual inventory system. The real test is how well all of the policies will operate in the aggregate.

The most commonly employed technique for performing this test is computer simulation, and several standard computer programs are available for just this purpose. Since the topic of simulation is taken up in detail in Chap. 21, only a few comments are given here. A simple, yet effective, approach to the validation phase is the following. You take a sample of items, use early historical data to estimate the statistical parameters, and thereby determine the recommended policies. Then, employing these policies, you simulate how the inventory system would have operated using more recent data. All of the calculations are done by an electronic computer, so little manual effort is involved in the simulation.

The simulated results are then compared against data showing the historical performance, looking at, for example, average inventory levels, frequency of orders, size of backlogs, etc. Usually you would perform a sensitivity analysis, especially with respect to the stockout parameters. The higher the penalty cost, the higher the average inventory.

In evaluating the simulation sensitivity results, the exercise of managerial judgment is far more important than technical expertise. The reason is that it is operating management who must accept the final responsibility for balancing low purchase and holding costs against maintaining customer service at a competitive level.

REVIEW EXERCISES

1 In each part below, discuss the elements of the situation that may make the inventory decisions nontrivial. Specifically, describe what you think might represent the appropriate considerations relating to supply and demand, the replenishment economics, and the systems specifications, as illustrated in Sec. 19.3.

(a) Refilling an auto's gasoline tank.

(b) Refilling a gasoline station's storage tank.

(c) Maintaining an adequate balance in a personal checking account.

(d) Maintaining an adequate balance in a corporation's checking account.

(e) Determining an adequate level of cash reserves and liquid assets for a bank. For a savings and loan company. For a life insurance company. For a fire insurance company.

(f) Determining the number of cans of tomato juice to keep in your kitchen cupboard. In a restaurant's store room. On a grocer's shelf.

(g) Determining the numbers of new and used automobiles to be stocked by a car dealer.

(h) Determining the number of buses and their replacement dates by a local transit authority.

(i) Determining the number of spare flashlight batteries to keep at home.

(j) Determining the number and size of auxiliary power generators to install in a hospital.

(k) Determining the number of paper clips an executive should keep in his home and office desks.

(l) Determining the number of spare jet engines an airline should keep at its different maintenance bases.

(m) Determining the number of different size scratch pads to stock in a busy office.

(n) Determining the number of different size boards of lumber to stock in a lumber yard. In a lumber mill.

(o) Determining the number of towels a department store should stock at its annual white sale. Determining the number of bathing suits the store should stock at the beginning of the summer season.

(p) Determining the total number of seats in a new movie theater. The number of loge seats.

(q) Determining the number of first-class seats in a new supersonic jet aircraft.

(r) Determining the number of prizes to award in a state-run lottery.

(s) Determining the number of men to enlist monthly into the armed services.

(t) Determining the amount of ammunition to keep in a field-supply area. In a continental U.S. depot.

(u) Determining the amount of funds to allocate each year to aid so-called *disaster areas.* Determining the amount of funds to put in a Community Chest contingency fund.

(v) Determining the amount of water to let spill over a dam.

(w) Determining the number of life jackets and life boats on an ocean liner. Determining the number of bottles of champagne to have in store for passengers.

2 Suggest some commercial situations in which a one-period inventory model is applicable. Discuss the circumstances under which it would be profitable to use an operations research approach to derive an inventory policy for these situations.

3 (a) Consider the inventory policy $(s, S) \equiv (3, 10)$. What is the order quantity if entering inventory equals 0? Equals 2? Equals 3? Equals 5? Equals 10? Equals 15? In each of these cases, what is the amount of inventory available to meet demand *after* the order is placed? Assume no delivery lag.

(b) Let $c(x)$ have the form given by (2) in Sec. 19.4, and let $K = 5$ and $c = 2$. Draw a graph of $c(x)$ for $x = 0, 1, 2, \ldots, 5$.

(c) Consider the expected cost function (3) in Sec. 19.4. Explain why it is reasonable to assume that $c + h > 0$ and $\pi > c$. Show that these two inequalities imply $h + \pi > 0$.

(d) Verify that the probability distribution in (4) yields the expression $L(y)$ given in (5) of Sec. 19.4.

(e) Let $h = 5$ and $\pi = 10$ in (5) of Sec. 19.4. Calculate $L(y)$ and check your answers with the values in Fig. 19.1. Also plot $L(y)$.

(f) Rework part (e), except let $\pi = 20$.

(g) Rework part (e), except let $\pi = 5$.

(h) Rework part (e), except let $h = 10$. [*Hint:* make use of your answer in part (f).]

(i) Explain in detail why the holding cost h in (3) of Sec. 19.4 can be interpreted as a *net* cost, where the salvage value has been subtracted out. What would be an optimal policy if the salvage value v were greater than the unit purchasing cost c?

(j) Suppose entering inventory is 0, and optimal $s > 0$. Derive a formula for the "cost of uncertainty" appropriate to (2) and (3) in Sec. 19.4.

4 Consider the critical ratio R, given by (6) in Sec. 19.4.

(a) Assume $c = 0$ and $h = 1$. What value of π yields $R = \frac{1}{2}$? $R = \frac{2}{3}$? $R = \frac{3}{4}$? $R = \frac{9}{10}$? $R = \frac{99}{100}$?

(b) Assume $c = 1$ and $h = 1$, and answer part (a).

(c) Assume $c = 10$ and $h = 1$, and answer part (a).

(d) Assume $c = 10$ and $h = 10$, and answer part (a).

(e) Assume $c = 100$ and $h = 10$, and answer part (a).

(f) Describe the optimal policy when $c = h = 0$.

(g) Describe the optimal policy when $\pi \le c$. Justify your answer.

5 Consider the critical ratio R, given by (6) in Sec. 19.4.

(a) Plot the region of values for π/c and h/c that yields R in the interval $.8 \le R \le .9$.

(b) Plot a region of values for π/h and c/h that yields R in this interval.

(c) Plot a region of values for c/π and h/π that yields R in this interval.

6 Consider the critical ratio R, given by (6) in Sec. 19.4. Suppose $.8 \leq R \leq .9$, and find the corresponding interval for π, given that

(a) $c = 0$ and $h = 1$.
(b) $c = 1$ and $h = 1$.
(c) $c = 10$ and $h = 1$.
(d) $c = 10$ and $h = 10$.
(e) $c = 100$ and $h = 10$.
(f) Answer parts (a) through (e) for the interval $.7 \leq R \leq .8$.
(g) Answer parts (a) through (e) for the interval $.85 \leq R \leq .95$.

7 (a) Consider the cumulative distribution in Fig. 19.2. Determine an optimal S from (7) in Sec. 19.4 for $h = 5$, $\pi = 10$, and $c = 5$. For $R = .8$. For $R = .6$.
   (b) Plot $cy + L(y)$, where $h = 5$, $\pi = 10$, and $c = 5$, and indicate the optimal S.

8 Consider the critical ratio R, given by (6) in Sec. 19.4. In each part below, find an optimal S for values of R equal to $\frac{1}{2}$, $\frac{3}{4}$, and $\frac{9}{10}$.

(a) $p(q) = (q + 1)/15$, for $q = 0, 1, \ldots, 4$.
(b) $p(0) = p(4) = \frac{1}{9}, p(1) = p(3) = \frac{2}{9}, p(2) = \frac{3}{9}$.
(c) $p(q) = (5 - q)/15$, for $q = 0, 1, \ldots, 4$.
(d) $p(0) = p(4) = \frac{3}{11}, p(1) = p(3) = \frac{2}{11}, p(2) = \frac{1}{11}$.

9 Consider the probability distribution (8) in Sec. 19.4 and assume that $h = 5$, $\pi = 10$, and $c = .1$ in (2) and (3).

(a) Verify that the optimal $S = 3$.
(b) Plot $L(y)$ for $y = 0, 1, \ldots, 5$.
(c) Let $K = 4$ and plot $K + c(S - y) + L(S)$, where $S = 3$. Show graphically that the optimal $s = 2$.
(d) Let $K = 12$ and answer part (c).
(e) Find a range of values for K such that $s = 1$ is optimal.

10 Assume $p(q) = \frac{1}{10}$ for $q = 1, 2, \ldots, 10$. Let $h = 5$, $\pi = 10$, and $c = .1$ in the one-period model (2) and (3) of Sec. 19.4.

(a) Find an optimal S.
(b) Find an optimal s for $K = 1$. For $K = 2$. For $K = 5$. For $K = 10$.
(c) Find a range of values for K such that $s = 2$ is optimal.
(d) Let $c = 5$ and answer parts (a) and (b).

*11 Consider the general description of the static model in Sec. 19.4. Assume $p(q) = \frac{1}{10}$, for $q = 1, 2, \ldots, 10$. Let the expected cost be

$$g(y|i) = c \cdot (y - i) + \sum_{q=0}^{y} h \cdot (y - q)^2 p(q) + \sum_{q>y} \pi \cdot (q - y)^2 p(q) \quad \text{for } y \geq 0,$$

when y is the inventory available to meet demand after ordering, given that initial inventory is i.

(a) Assume $i = 0$, $h = 5$, $\pi = 10$, and $c = .1$. Find an optimal y.
(b) Rework part (a), except let $c = 5$.

*12 Consider the example (16), (17) and (18) in the special material of Sec. 19.4.

(a) Using (16), explain how (18) indicates that the actual loss is the same π, no matter by how much the actual demand q exceeds the available supply y.

(b) Verify the numerical expressions on the right of (18).

(c) Why does (20) contain the only policies that need to be considered in the optimization process?

(d) Justify the calculations in (21) through (23).

(e) Translate (24) into a verbal description of the inventory policy.

(f) Check the results shown in (25), and translate (25) into a verbal description of the inventory policy.

*13 (a) Consider the example in exercise 11, part (a). Find an optimal (s, S) policy where the purchase cost function includes a setup cost $K = 1$.

(b) Do the same for $K = 5$.

*14 Justify in detail the derivation (i) through (xii) in the advanced material at the end of Sec. 19.4.

*15 Justify in detail the derivation (xiii) through (xvii) in the advanced material at the end of Sec. 19.4.

16 Consider the economic order quantity examples displayed in Figs. 19.3 and 19.4. Assume $Q = 45$, $s = -10$, $M = 30$.

(a) Calculate S, the average number of setups per week, the average level of inventory during the interval when inventory *is* positive, and the average level of inventory per week.

(b) Suppose lead time $L = 1$ week. When should a replenishment be initiated?

(c) Suppose lead time $L = 2$ weeks. When should a replenishment be initiated?

(d) Answer parts (a), (b), and (c) for $Q = 60$.

(e) Answer parts (a), (b), and (c) for $M = 15$.

(f) Answer parts (a), (b), and (c) for $s = -5$.

17 (a) Verify the algebra leading to the formula for average cost per unit of time as given by (6) in Sec. 19.5.

(b) Show that if $S = Q$, then (6) simplifies to (7).

(c) Show that if the square root formula for Q as given in (8) is used, then the minimal average cost is that also given in (8).

*(d) Differentiate AC in (7) with respect to Q, set the derivative equal to 0, and solve for Q; verify that the result is the formula in (8).

18 (a) Consider the lot-size formula (8) in Sec. 19.5. Determine the value for the ratio K/h such that an order is for one week's demand. For two weeks'. For four weeks'. For 12 weeks'. For 26 weeks'.

(b) Define the *turnover ratio* as the average inventory level divided by the rate of demand per unit of time. Assume that you employ (8), and derive a formula for the turnover ratio. Explain how the ratio varies with the demand rate. With the ratio K/h.

19 (a) Verify from (12) in Sec. 19.5 the sensitivity analysis formula (13).
   (b) Find a range for r in (13) such that $VC(r)/VC(1) \leq 1.15$.
   (c) Explain why the ratio in (13) is the same for a given r and its reciprocal $r' = 1/r$.
   (d) Draw a graph of the ratio in (13) for r in the range $.1 \leq r \leq 10$.

20 Consider the economic order quantity formula given by (8) in Sec. 19.5. Suppose M is the true demand rate, but that you mis-estimate the rate to be $r \cdot M$, where $r > 0$. Let $VC(r)$ be the variable cost, analogous to (12), assuming that $r \cdot M$ is used in (8). instead of M.

   (a) Derive a formula for $VC(r)/VC(1)$.
   (b) Find the interval of values for r such that $VC(r)/VC(1) \leq 1.1$.
   (c) Plot $VC(r)/VC(1)$ for r in the range $.1 \leq r \leq 10$.

21 Perform the analysis in exercise 20, except suppose that the setup cost K is mis-estimated to be $r \cdot K$.

22 Perform the analysis in exercise 20, except suppose that the holding cost is mis-estimated to be $r \cdot h$.

23 Consider the average-backlog penalty cost model expressed by the cost function (15) in Sec. 19.5.

   (a) Verify the formula in (15).
   *(b) Take the partial derivative of AC in (15) with respect to S, set the result equal to 0, and solve for S; verify the formula in (16).
   *(c) Verify the results in (17).
   (d) What is the optimal time interval between successive orders?
   (e) Simplify and interpret the results in (17) for the case $h = \pi$.
   (f) Simplify and interpret the results in (17) for the case $3h = \pi$.

24 Assume $h = 1$, $\pi = 9$, $K = 32$, $c = 0$, $M = 9$.

   (a) Evaluate the formulas in (17) of Sec. 19.5.
   (b) Let $h = 4$ and rework part (a).
   (c) Let $\pi = 36$ and rework part (a).
   (d) Let $M = 36$ and rework part (a).

25 Consider the formulas for an optimal policy, as given by (17) in Sec. 19.5. Suppose that you actually use an order quantity that equals r times the order quantity in (17), where $r > 0$. Let $VC(r)$ be the associated variable cost (exclusive of cM).

   (a) Derive a formula for $VC(r)/VC(1)$.
   (b) Assume $h = 1$, $\pi = 9$, $K = 32$, $M = 9$, and plot $VC(r)/VC(1)$ for r in the range $.1 \leq r \leq 10$.

26 Consider the formulas for an optimal policy, as given by (17) in Sec. 19.5. Suppose M is the true demand rate, but that you mis-estimate the rate to be $r \cdot M$, where $r > 0$. Let $VC(r)$ be the corresponding variable cost (exclusive of cM), assuming that $r \cdot M$ is used in (17) instead of M.

   (a) Derive a formula for $VC(r)/VC(1)$.

(b) Assume $h = 1$, $\pi = 9$, $K = 32$, $M = 9$, and find the interval of values for r such that $VC(r)/VC(1) \leq 1.1$.

(c) Plot $VC(r)/VC(1)$ for r in the range $.1 \leq r \leq 10$.

27 Perform the analysis in exercise 26, except suppose that the setup cost K is mis-estimated to be $r \cdot K$.

28 Perform the analysis in exercise 26, except suppose that the holding cost h is mis-estimated to be $r \cdot h$.

29 Perform the analysis in exercise 26, except suppose that the penalty cost π is mis-estimated to be $r \cdot \pi$.

30 Consider the formulas for an optimal policy, as given by (17) in Sec. 19.5. Assume $h = 1$, $\pi = 9$, $K = 32$, $M = 9$, unless stated otherwise below. Plot each of the optimal quantities in (17), as a function of

(a) The holding cost h.   (c) The setup cost K.
(b) The penalty cost π.   (d) The demand rate M.

*31 (a) Exhibit all the intermediate algebraic steps to justify the derivations in (9) through (15), leading to the formula for the expected average cost per unit time, given by (16) in Sec. 19.6.

(b) Partially differentiate $E[AC]$ with respect to Q, set the derivative equal to 0, and solve for Q; verify that the result is that given by (17).

*(c) Derive the formula (19) that determines an optimal s.

(d) Substitute the optimal Q formula given in (17) into the $E[AC]$ formula in (16), and verify that the result is (21). What terms in (21) indicate the impact of uncertainty?

32 (a) Verify the calculations in the numerical example (23) through (29) of Sec. 19.6.

(b) Find an optimal policy using the data in (23), except let $\pi = 30$.

33 Assume $p_L(q_L) = \frac{1}{10}$ for $q = 1, 2, \ldots, 10$, where $L = 1$. Let $h = 5$, $\pi = 10$, and $c = .1$. In each part below, find an optimal inventory policy using the algorithm in Sec. 19.6.

(a) Let $K = 1$.   (d) Let $\pi = 20$ and $K = 10$.
(b) Let $K = 5$.   (e) Let $\pi = 50$ and $K = 10$.
(c) Let $K = 10$.

34 Assume $p_L(q_L) = \frac{1}{20}$, for $q = 0, 1, \ldots, 19$, where $L = 1$. In each part below, apply the algorithm in Sec. 19.6 to graph the optimal Q, s, S, and expected cost, as functions of the indicated parameter. (Only consider cases where optimal $s > 0$. *Suggestion:* select a few sample points for the indicated parameter, and, by eye, fit the curves through the optimal policies for these sample points.)

(a) Let $h = 1$, $\pi = 50$, and let the parameter be K, where $0 < K \leq 30$.

(b) Let $h = 1$, $K = 20$, and let the parameter be π, where $0 < \pi \leq 100$.

(c) Rework parts (a) and (b), assuming that $L = 2$.

*35 Consider the Normal approximation approach described at the end of Sec. 19.6. In each part below, find the approximately optimal Q, s, S, and the associated approximate value for the expected cost.

(a) $M = 16$, $L = 5$, $M_L = 80$, $V_L = 240$, and all the other parameters are those given by (39).
(b) Case 1 in Fig. 19.7.
(c) Case 2 in Fig. 19.7.

*36 Study the sensitivity analysis in Fig. 19.7. Give a plausible explanation of why an increase in each parameter π, K, M, L, and V_L tends to increase both the optimal s and Q, *except* that an increase in π decreases Q and an increase in K decreases s. (Trace the direct impact of the economic parameters on the policy variables and the consequent indirect impact due to the interactive effect among the policy variables.)

37 Explain your understanding of the following terms:

lead time (delivery lag)   *net inventory position
setup (reorder) cost   *lump-sum penalty cost
inventory holding cost   economic order quantity (lot-size) models
penalty cost (profit loss)   sawtooth pattern of inventory
static (single decision) model   size-of-backlog penalty cost
newsboy problem   EOQ (lot-size formula, Wilson lot size)
(s, S) policy   average-backlog penalty cost
reorder point   demand during lead time
reorder level   service level
linear holding and penalty cost   safety (buffer) stock
critical ratio   *standardized Normal loss integral.
backlogged demand

FORMULATION AND COMPUTATIONAL EXERCISES

38 The Sayure Prairie Airlines is ordering a fleet of new jet aircraft. Provisioning engine spare parts in advance is less expensive than waiting until they are needed. Specifically, suppose c_1 is the unit purchase price now, and c_2 the price if ordered subsequently, where $c_1 < c_2$. Assume that any parts left over when the fleet becomes obsolete have a salvage value v per unit. Let $p(d)$ be the probability that d parts will be needed by SPA over the lifetime of the fleet.

(a) Exhibit a formula for the expected total cost associated with purchasing Q spares now.
*(b) Derive a formula for determining an optimal Q. (State any assumptions you are making about the value of v.)

39 The Sayure Prairie Airlines must also decide how many first-class and tourist seats to install in the airplanes. Assume that the total number of rows of seats is R. Let r_1 be the number of rows of first-class seats, and r_2 the number of rows of tourist seats. There are four seats in each first-class row and six seats in each tourist row. Assume

that $p_1(d_1)$ is the probability that d_1 customers desire first-class seats on each flight. For simplicity, assume that if all the first-class seats are filled, these customers call another airline. Let v_1 be the profit value from selling a first-class seat. Similarly, let $p_2(d_2)$ be the probability distribution for tourist-class seats and v_2 the profit value per seat. Write the appropriate expression for expected profit, and explain how you would find an optimal seat allocation.

40 (k, Q) *Inventory Replenishment Policy.* Consider the one-period model with costs given by (2) and (3) in Sec. 19.4. Suppose that an order quantity must be an integer multiple of Q, where Q is a prespecified number. (For example, Q may be a dozen.)

  *(a) Show that the form of an optimal policy is the following: if entering inventory is less than some number k, the smallest integral multiple of Q is ordered such that inventory after ordering is at least k; if entering inventory is k or greater, no order is placed. For example, suppose the policy is $(k, Q) \equiv (8, 5)$; if entering inventory is 8 or more, then no items are ordered; if entering inventory is 3, 4, ..., 7, then 5 units are ordered; if entering inventory is $-2, -1, ..., 2$, then 10 units are ordered, etc.

  (b) Given the validity of the policy in part (a), describe how to calculate an optimal k.

  (c) Apply your method in part (b) to the numerical example (4) and (5), with $h = 5$, $\pi = 10$, and $c = .1$. Find optimal policies for $Q = 2$ and $Q = 4$.

  (d) Assume $p(q) = \frac{1}{10}$ for $q = 1, 2, ..., 10$. Let $h = 5$, $\pi = 10$, and $c = .1$. Apply your method in part (b) to find optimal policies for $Q = 2$ and $Q = 4$.

*41 Consider a one-period inventory model with linear holding and penalty costs and demand described by a probability density function, as discussed in the special material at the end of Sec. 19.4. Suppose $p(q) = me^{-mq}$ for $q \geq 0$, where $m > 0$ and $E[q] = 1/m$.

  (a) Derive an analytic expression for the optimal S.

  (b) Derive an expression for the determining optimal s. [*Hint:* the optimal s is the solution of the equation $L(s) + cs = K + cS + L(S)$.] Let $D \equiv S - s$, and use part (a) to express your answer in terms of D.

  (c) Derive an approximation to the optimal D from the formula in part (b) by using a series expansion $e^x \approx 1 + x + .5x^2$.

42 In each part below, assume that $h = H \cdot c$ and $\pi = \Pi \cdot c$, where c is the unit purchasing cost. Discuss how the optimal policy depends on the value of c.

  (a) The lot-size model given by (7) and (8) in Sec. 19.5.

  (b) The lot-size model given by (17) in Sec. 19.5.

  (c) The stochastic demand model given by (17) through (20) in Sec. 19.6.

43 Consider the lot-size models in Sec. 19.5 yielding the average cost formulas (6) and (15).

  (a) Show how to modify (6) and (15) if the purchase cost of Q is cQ^2, instead of cQ.

  *(b) Derive the associated optimal lot-size formulas.

44 Consider the lot-size model yielding formula (7) in Sec. 19.5 for the average cost per unit of time (where optimal $s = 0$). Suppose that the firm can request a fraction f

of the order quantity to be delivered right away, and the remainder to be delivered after the quantity fQ is exhausted.

(a) Suppose f is a given fraction. Derive the optimal Q analogous to (8). (*Note:* inventory holding cost is assessed against only the inventory on hand.)

*(b) Suppose both f and Q can be determined by the firm. Find formulas for the optimal values of f and Q. What is the optimal time interval between the arrival of fQ and the remainder of the order?

45 *Optimal Production Lot-Size Model.* Consider a lot-size model like that giving rise to the sawtooth pattern shown in Fig. 19.3. Suppose, however, that the order must be manufactured by the firm itself, and the production rate is N per unit of time, where $N > M$. Hence, the level of inventory no longer exhibits a vertical jump at the arrival of the lot of Q items. Rather, the inventory level increases at a slope of $N - M$ until the lot Q has been produced, and then decreases at a slope $-M$ (as before).

(a) Suppose $N = 75$ and the rest of the data are as given in Fig. 19.3. Draw the resultant diagram for the inventory level.

(b) Assuming $s = 0$ so that $S = Q$, derive the formula for the average cost per unit of time, analogous to (4) in Sec. 19.5, and determine the corresponding EOQ. Also determine the corresponding minimal average cost and the optimal time interval between successive production startups.

(c) Show how to modify your answer in part (b) where you permit s to be negative and you assume an "average-backlog penalty cost." Derive the formula for the average cost per unit of time, analogous to (15) in Sec. 19.5, and determine the corresponding EOQ, optimal s and S, minimal average cost, and the optimal time interval between successive production startups.

(d) Apply your answers in parts (b) and (c) to the data $h = 1, K = 32, c = 0, M = 9$, $N = 36, \pi = 9$.

46 Assume $p_L(q_L) = \frac{1}{10}$, for $q_L = 1, 2, \ldots, 10$, where $L = 1$. Let $h = 5$, $\pi = 10$, and $c = .1$. In each case below, apply the algorithm in Sec. 19.6 to find an optimal policy. (Compare the results with those in exercise 10.)

(a) Let $K = 5$.

(b) Let $K = 10$.

47 Assume $p_L(q_L) = \frac{1}{20}$, for $q = 0, 1, \ldots, 19$, where $L = 1$. Let $h = 1$ and $K = 20$.

(a) Find the values of s corresponding to $P_L(s) = .75, .8, .85, .9, .95$, according to (18), (19), and (20) in Sec. 19.6.

(b) Calculate the corresponding values for Q using (17) and letting $\pi = 0$. Calculate the associated expected average inventory per unit of time using (12).

(c) Summarize the results of the above parts by plotting a graph of expected average inventory as a function of the service level $P_L(s)$. Give an economic interpretation of your results.

48 Assume $p_L(q_L) = \frac{1}{20}$, for $q = 0, 1, \ldots, 19$, where $L = 1$. Let $h = 1$ and $K = 20$.

(a) Find the values of s corresponding to $P_L(s) = .75, .8, .85, .9, .95$, according to (18), (19), and (20) in Sec. 19.6.

(b) For each s in part (a), find a value of π such that using this value and s in (17), the resultant value of R in (20) equals $P_L(s)$.

(c) Employing your answers in part (b), calculate the associated expected average inventory per unit of time using (12).

(d) Summarize the results of the above parts by graphing expected average inventory as a function of the service level $P_L(s)$. Also plot a graph of the service level as a function of π. Give an economic interpretation of your results.

49 Let $p(q)$ represent the probability of demand in a week, where $q = 0, 1, \ldots, D$. Let $t(w)$ represent the probability that lead time is w weeks, where $w = 1, 2, \ldots, W$. Assume weekly demands and lead times are completely independent random variables.

(a) Derive a computational method for finding $p_L(q_L)$, which represents the probability that demand during lead time is q_L.

(b) Illustrate your method for $p(q) = \frac{1}{4}$, $q = 0, 1, 2, 3$, and $t(w) = \frac{1}{3}$, $w = 1, 2, 3$.

(c) Using the data in part (b), calculate the probability of stockout if the reorder point is 5. Is 8. Is 10.

*50 Consider Case 1 in Fig. 19.7.

(a) Suppose you estimate the demand rate to be 6 and use the corresponding policy, but in fact the actual demand rate is 9. What is the expected average cost increase due to mis-estimation? Answer the same question if you incorrectly assume the demand rate is 12 when in fact it is 9. (*Suggestion:* calculate the actual expected average cost, the expected average cost if you had correctly estimated the parameter, and the expected average cost if the mis-estimated value of the parameter were truly correct.)

(b) Suppose you estimate the variance of demand during lead time to be 6 and use the corresponding policy, but in fact the actual variance is 9. What is the expected average cost increase due to mis-estimation? Answer the same question if you incorrectly assume the variance is 12, but in fact it is 9.

(c) Answer parts (a) and (b) where you mis-estimate *both* the demand rate and variance to be 6. To be 12.

*51 Consider Case 2 in Fig. 19.7. Suppose you estimate the lead time to be 4 and use the corresponding policy, but in fact the actual lead time is 5. What is the expected average cost increase due to mis-estimation? Answer the same question if you incorrectly assume the lead time is 6, but in fact it is 5. (*Suggestion:* calculate the actual expected average cost, the expected average cost if you had correctly estimated the parameter, and the expected average cost if the mis-estimated value of the parameter were truly correct.)

MIND-EXPANDING EXERCISES

52 Consider the lot-size model yielding formula (7) in Sec. 19.5 for the average cost per unit of time (where optimal $s = 0$). In each part below, devise a computational technique for finding an optimal order quantity, given that the vendor offers quantity discounts for purchasing large-size lots.

(a) Assume that c_j is the price per item if the order quantity Q satisfies $q_j \leq Q < q_{j+1}$, where $c_j > c_{j-1} \geq 0$. Also assume that $h = H \cdot c_j$, where c_j is the unit cost incurred. Illustrate your procedure with the data $K = 32$, $M = 9$, $H = 1$, and $c_1 = 16$, for $0 \leq Q < 7$; $c_2 = 9$, for $7 \leq Q < 75$; and $c_3 = 1$, for $75 \leq Q$. Determine whether the solution differs if $c_2 = 9$, for $7 \leq Q < 50$; and $c_3 = 1$, for $50 \leq Q$. (*Suggestion:* explain your approach using a graph that contains for each c_j the average cost per unit of time as a function of Q.)

(b) Assume that $C(Q)$ is the total purchase cost and

$$C(Q) = C(q_j) + c_j \cdot (Q - q_j) \quad \text{for } q_j \leq Q < q_{j+1},$$

where $c_j > c_{j-1} \geq 0$, and $C(0) = 0$. Thus the discount is offered on an incremental basis. Illustrate your procedure using the data in part (a) and $h = H \cdot C(Q)/Q$. (*Suggestion:* explain your approach using a graph that contains for each c_j the average cost per unit of time as a function of Q.)

*(c) Determine in parts (a) and (b) whether an optimal Q can ever occur at a price break q_j.

53 Consider a firm that purchases n different kinds of items from a single vendor and wants to determine the optimal time interval T between successive orders of all n kinds of items. For each kind of item j, let M_j be the demand rate, c_j the unit purchasing cost, h_j the unit holding cost. Assume that if $n = 1$, the appropriate average cost per unit of time would be given by (7) in Sec. 19.5 (where $s = 0$). For $n > 1$, continue to assume that the setup cost is K for the *entire* order, which now consists of n different kinds of items.

(a) Find the optimal T and the associated order quantities Q_j for each kind of item j.

(b) Apply your answer in part (a) to the data $n = 2$, each $h_j = 1$, $c_j = 0$, $K = 32$, and $M_1 = 9$ and $M_2 = 36$.

(c) Suppose the firm has the option of separately ordering both items in part (b), except that the individual setup cost $K_j = 32r$, where $r > 0$. Find the value for r such that the firm would be indifferent between separate and joint ordering policies.

54 Consider the example (23) in Sec. 19.6. Suppose there are two locations in the firm. Assume these data are applicable at each location, and that the demands at the two locations are completely independent. Suppose the firm has the option of either stocking the item at each location, thereby leading to the policy in (28) and twice the cost in (9), or combining the two sources of demand, and stocking in a single location.

(a) Derive an optimal policy for the combined operation. What is the cost differential between this combined stocking and the independent stocking at two separate locations? [*Hint:* calculate the probability distribution of the sum of two independent random demands during a lead time, where the probability distribution for each demand is given by (23).]

*(b) Perform the same analysis as in part (b) except use the data in (39) and the Normal approximation technique. (*Hint:* the variance of the sum of two *independent* random variables is the sum of the variances.)

55 You can develop as follows a cruder approximate expected average cost per unit of time analogous to (16) in Sec. 19.6. Assume that, on the average, the lowest level of

inventory is $s - E[q_L]$ so, as an approximation, the average inventory level is the sum $(Q/2) + s - E[q_L]$.

(a) Derive the cost function analogous to (16).

(b) Find formulas for the optimal order quantity and reorder point, analogous to (17) through (20), and compare the results.

56 (a) Show how to modify the derivation in (9) through (16) in Sec. 19.6 if excess demand during a lead time is lost. (Hence, the level of inventory never falls below 0, as it does in Fig. 19.5.) Specifically, find the appropriate expected average cost per unit of time, analogous to (16), and derive formulas for the optimal order quantity and reorder point. Compare your results with those in (16) through (20).

*(b) Derive a formula for the expected average cost per unit of time in part (a) by taking the ratio of the expected cost between successive reorders and the expected time between successive reorders. (Assume that lead time is constant and that there is never more than one order outstanding at any moment in time.)

CONTENTS

CHAPTER 20

Waiting Line
Models †

20.1 INTRODUCTION

Waiting lines, like stocks of inventory, are omnipresent. Think back for a moment on the times you waited for service during the past few days—perhaps at a cafeteria, bookstore, library, bank, gasoline station, dean's office, and the like. Less apparent examples occur when you wait for a telephone operator to answer, for a traffic light to change, for the morning mail to be delivered, and for a midterm examination to be corrected and returned. Common to all of these cases are the arrivals of people or objects requiring service and the attendant delays when the service mechanism is busy.

Operations research can very effectively analyze such queuing or congestion phenomena. But, as is true of all practical applications of operations research, the relevant decision problems must be of sufficient economic significance to warrant whatever expenditure of effort is needed to perform the scientific analysis. There are two important situations in which it has proved to be economically advantageous to use waiting line models; as you will quickly recognize, there is no clear line of demarcation between these two situations, and any particular application may fall somewhere in between.

The first relates to a company that must design and operate many similar service facilities. Examples include deciding the number of

- Checkout stands in each store of a large grocery chain.
- Tellers' windows in each local branch of a statewide bank.
- Gasoline pumps and attendants in each station of a major oil company.
- Trunk lines in each local telephone exchange.
- Maintenance men to service leased photocopy equipment in each city.

†This chapter requires a knowledge of elementary differential and integral calculus.

Although the environmental data vary from store to store, branch to branch, station to station, and so forth, the same *procedure* can be used to analyze each service facility decision. Consequently, once a company develops the methodology for an operations research approach, the technique can be used repeatedly; for each separate application, the company need only apply the relevant data.

The second category relates to a company that must make a facility decision involving the purchases of very expensive equipment, such as deciding on the number and capacity of automatic elevators to be installed in a large office building, or furnaces in a steel processing plant, or runways at an airport.

To round out the discussion of applications, we mention two examples that combine the characteristics of both categories above: determining the number of check-in counters at an airport, and of fire engines at each local fire station of a metropolitan area.

Once again, reflect on your activities during the past few days, and this time pick out those queuing situations that you think might actually warrant a scientific study. In which of the two categories above do they fall? What are the decisions that might be made as a result of such a study? How would you distinguish a good decision from a poor one? Try to answer these questions for several of the examples you picked.

Perspective. What is said about birds is also true of waiting line models: their variety and number seem infinite. Even a treatise of several hundred pages would be too small for a complete survey of all the mathematical results of queuing models. And then it would have to be significantly enlarged within a year or so to encompass the continual growth in new research findings. Consequently, this chapter and Appendix III cannot possibly provide a survey of all waiting line models; instead this chapter highlights typical and critical insights to be garnered from queuing model analysis, and presents several models that are now fundamental in the literature of waiting line theory.

This chapter and Appendix III deal with many waiting line models that are amenable to *mathematical* analysis. As you will see, the underlying waiting line systems in these models appear considerably simpler than most of the queuing situations you encounter in reality. What we demonstrate in this chapter is that you can sometimes employ these *relatively* simple models to provide qualitative and approximate quantitative information about the behavior of more complex structures. Then later in Chap. 21 you can learn how to apply computer simulation techniques to analyze intricate waiting line situations.

In previous chapters, we have offered at least heuristic proofs of the most fundamental results. When the underlying mathematical intricacies were beyond the intended level of the text, we tried to present verbal arguments that could be made rigorous. Our rationale was that you would reach a better understanding of the results by having a "feel" for the way they are derived. There are some places below where we continue to follow this expository practice. But many mathematical derivations of waiting line results are not, in our opinion, very enlightening to a person intent on applying the theory. (The proofs are important, of course, to technical specialists who may want to apply similar approaches to solving new waiting line models.) Consequently, some of the formulas in this chapter are presented in "cookbook" fashion.

We will mostly stress the insights to be gained from performing sensitivity analysis in waiting line models. In reading the material, you should pay special attention to the differing assumptions in the various models, and observe the qualitative effect these differences have on the results. You also should notice the impact of varying the numerical values for the parameters in models. As you will see, the scientific analysis of queuing phenomena can be complex; you will not be able to rely solely on unaided intuition to determine the impact of varying arrival rates, service rates, the number and arrangement of service facilities, etc.

In sharp contrast to the rest of this text, the emphasis in this chapter and Appendix III is on a model's **operating characteristics**, such as the average number of customers in a system, their average waiting time, the probability that all service facilities are busy, and similar measures of operating effectiveness. Once these characteristics have been obtained, you can proceed to construct an appropriate economic framework that encompasses them, and subsequently find optimal decisions.

The optimizing task may be either easy or hard, depending on the complexity of the queuing system and the range of alternatives you wish to consider. For example, if you want to choose between having four versus five checkout stands at a grocery store, you can find the optimal decision by examining the effects of each separate alternative. But if you wish to design an air traffic control system at a busy airport, you may need a more sophisticated optimization technique than "examine each separate alternative"; the number of such alternatives may be unlimited.

At present, there is no unified body of optimization theory for waiting line models. In most applications, the optimizing technique employed is ad hoc. But advanced research is underway in extending dynamic programming techniques analogous to those presented in Chap. 18 to assist in optimizing queuing system design.

20.2 TAXONOMY OF WAITING LINE MODELS

Before examining the solution of specific queuing models, you will find it useful to have an overview of such systems. This section provides a general framework, and also serves the purpose of building your vocabulary of the terms frequently employed in the description of waiting line models. An outline for the rest of the chapter appears at the end of this section.

You can describe a queuing system by its input or arrival process, its queue discipline, and its service mechanism. Several possibilities for each of these are discussed in general terms below. In subsequent sections, more precise mathematical assumptions are specified in treating particular cases.

Input process. The usual description of the pattern of arrivals into the system is given by the probability distribution of time between successive arrival events, and the number of individuals or units that appear at each of these events. For example, an arrival event at, say, a barber shop or a restaurant may occur on the average of once in any 10-minute interval. For the barber shop, each arrival event consists of a *single* customer entering; for the restaurant, a party of *one or more* customers. (When more than one customer can enter the system at an arrival event, the situation is termed **bulk arrivals**.) Often, successive interarrival times are in fact statistically independent and stationary over long intervals of time, but, of course, they need not be in any particular situation. The two extreme assumptions about interarrival times are that they are predetermined or completely random, a notion to be made precise in the next section.

Usually the source population from which the arrivals are drawn is considered as unlimited. To illustrate, such an assumption seems warranted in the case of train passengers seeking help in New York's Grand Central Station.

But in other situations, the source population is more appropriately modeled as being finite. One such example might be the number of drill presses breaking down and requiring service from a factory's regular staff of repairmen.

In some situations, a customer seeing a long line may **balk**, that is, not join the line. Depending on the circumstance, he may return later for service. Sometimes a customer cannot join the queue because there is no room left for him to wait in. Thus the input or arrival process may depend in part on the status of the queuing system.

Queue discipline. This characteristic describes the order in which customers entering the *system* are eventually served. Frequently, the discipline is **first come, first served**. Certainly it is the easiest ordering to handle in mathematical models; it is also the ordering applied to customers who have entered a particular *line*. If you reflect on most of the waiting line situations you are familiar with, however, you will realize that many other disciplines are possible. Sometimes it is **last come, first served**. For example, consider what happens when you enter an empty elevator near the top floor of a multistory building, and as the elevator descends, it becomes crowded with additional passengers. The discipline in this situation may well be viewed as last come, first served, if you define "service" to be your exiting from the elevator when it reaches the ground floor.

Sometimes the service order is virtually **random**. For example, teachers often try to use this discipline in calling upon students for recitation. And sometimes the discipline is governed by a priority system, such as "women and children first," when waiting for a seat in a lifeboat on a sinking ship, or "age before beauty," when waiting your turn in a revolving door. Finally, a customer may become **impatient** and decide to leave the system before being served; this behavior is termed **reneging.**

Service mechanism. In common with the arrival process, a specification of the service mechanism includes a description of time to complete a service, and of the number of individuals whose requirements are satisfied at each service event. Referring again to the barber shop and restaurant, a service event is the departure of a single customer or of a party having several patrons. The time needed for service partly depends on the nature of the customer's or patron's requirements. But it may also depend on the state of the system—for example, the servers may hurry if many customers are waiting. Likewise, for each service facility, successive service times may, but need not, be described as independently and identically distributed random variables. Occasionally, it is appropriate to add a probabilistic contingency of a server breaking down over a limited period of time.

The service mechanism also prescribes the number and configuration of **servers** or **channels**. When you arrive at a British airport, for example, you must go through Passport Control. There all passengers wait in a *single* line. When your turn comes, you will be directed to whichever official has just finished processing a passenger. In contrast, when you enter a bank during rush hours, you will find lines in front of each window. There you must select a single line to wait in. If you make a poor choice, you may wait longer to be served than someone who arrived after you did. (If the lines are not too crowded, you may be able to **jockey** into a line that is getting shorter than the one you are in.)

Both the Passport Control and bank counter illustrations are examples of **servers** (or **channels**) **in parallel**. There are also numerous queuing systems in which the servers are arranged **in series** (**tandem**), and the customer must proceed from one server to the next, possibly waiting in line in front of each channel. One example is a job-shop, in which an order to be manufactured may be delayed at each of several machine facilities. Another example arises in driving an automobile from one end of the main downtown shopping street to the other, if the car has to wait at several stoplights.

Waiting line analysis. Even with as sketchy a description of possibilities as the above, you can quickly appreciate that the number of conceivable waiting line models is enormous. Although it is easy to give precise mathematical formulations for these possibilities, they often do not yield usable mathematical results about the system's characteristics. Consequently, in order to analyze most waiting line systems, you will find it standard practice to combine two approaches. The first is to use simple models, such as those given in this chapter, as rough approximations to the real system. Then, with these results for insight and guidance, you may go on to develop a computer simulation model that takes account of those facets that are important but hard to deal with by mathematical analysis. Since simulation is treated in Chap. 21, no more will be said about this approach here.

Of course, the context of an application determines the particular system characteristics that are most important for design decisions. But usually you are interested in the probability distributions of the number of customers in the system and their waiting times, or at least in the long-run average values for these random variables. In addition, you sometimes want to know the probability of all the servers being idle or busy, the probability distribution for the length of the idle and busy periods for each server, the probability that the line length will exceed a specified number, and the probability distribution between successive departures. If the queuing model is not too complicated, then explicit and easy-to-compute formulas can be derived for most of the above-mentioned quantities; the results in the present chapter are of this sort. But as soon as more complex assumptions are made, you may only be able to determine these quantities by so-called *transforms*, which are implicit formulas. A few such examples are given in Appendix III for the sake of illustration.

The preceding section emphasized that an operations research approach to studying congestion systems is used to aid managerial decisions. Review the several examples in this and the previous section, and suggest a variety of managerial options that can be selected for the design of a system. You should find that in practically every instance, the decision-maker can affect all three aspects of the queuing system: the input process, the queue discipline, and the service mechanism. What is more, there are some intricate tradeoffs among the various decision alternatives. For example, the average time a customer spends in the system may be decreased by changing the arrival rate, adding servers, using faster servers, or reducing the variation in service time. The sections below will illustrate the relative effectiveness of each of these possibilities.

A time to be born and a time to die. You can view the rest of this chapter as illustrating **systems synthesis**. We begin in the next section with a description of the **birth** or **arrival process** for customers entering a system. We examine the probabilistic characteristics of perhaps the most important birth process (in waiting line models, that is), namely, *Poisson input*. In Sec. 20.4, we perform a similar study of service times, or as it sometimes is gravely termed, a **death process**. A classic synthesis occurs in Sec. 20.5, which treats a system having a single server. The extension to a multiple-server situation is examined in Sec. 20.6. The advanced material at the end of the chapter presents a fairly general birth-and-death model which can be used to derive many of the earlier results as special cases. Appendix III is devoted to advanced mathematical techniques for systems synthesis.

20.3 PROBABILITY DISTRIBUTIONS OF INTERARRIVAL TIMES

From here on we assume that an arrival event is synonymous with a *single individual* coming to the system. (Bulk arrivals will only be treated in exercise 34.) The most convenient way to describe the arrival mechanism is to specify the probability distribution of interarrival times.

Assume that the lengths of the intervals between arrivals are independently and identically distributed, and described by a continuous density function. This sort of input is an example of what is called a **renewal process**, and the succession of arrivals demonstrates what is termed a sequence of **recurrent events**. Let

$f(t) \equiv$ density function for the time interval t between any two successive arrivals,

where $t \geq 0$, and also *define*

$$\frac{1}{\lambda} \equiv \text{mean time between arrivals,}$$

so that

$$\lambda = \text{arrival rate per unit of time.}$$

Jot down the verbal description of $1/\lambda$ and λ (lambda). You can determine λ from $f(t)$ by taking the mathematical expectation of t:

(1) $$\int_0^\infty tf(t)\, dt \equiv \frac{1}{\lambda} \quad \text{(mean time between arrivals).}$$

For example, if the unit of time is an hour and ($\lambda = 4$) is the average number of arrivals per hour, then $1/\lambda$ equals one-fourth (.25) of an hour between arrivals (that is, one arrival on the average in any quarter of an hour). Similarly, if one arrival occurs on the average in any 10-minute interval, then the arrival rate λ is one-tenth (.1) per minute.

Random arrivals. The most important example of an interarrival time distribution is that associated with **completely random arrivals**. Complete randomness means that the probability of an arrival occurring in *any* small interval of time $(T, T + h)$ depends only on the length of the interval h and *not* on the interval's starting point T or on the specific history of arrivals prior to T. In other words, the arrival process is both **stationary**, or as it is often called, **homogeneous**, and **memoryless**. In the special material below, we indicate how the assumption of **completely random arrivals** corresponds to postulating

(2) $$f(t) = \lambda e^{-\lambda t}, \quad t \geq 0 \quad \text{negative exponential distribution,}$$
$$(\text{mean} = 1/\lambda, \text{ variance} = 1/\lambda^2),$$

where $e = 2.71818\ldots$. Several examples of the (negative) exponential distributions for different values of λ are given in Fig. 20.1.

To check the *memoryless property* of the exponential distribution, suppose $t = 0$ represents the system's starting point in time. Then the probability that no arrival occurs in the interval $(0, T)$ is the same as the probability that the first arrival occurs after T:

(3) $$P[t \geq T] = \int_T^\infty \lambda e^{-\lambda t}\, dt = e^{-\lambda T}.$$

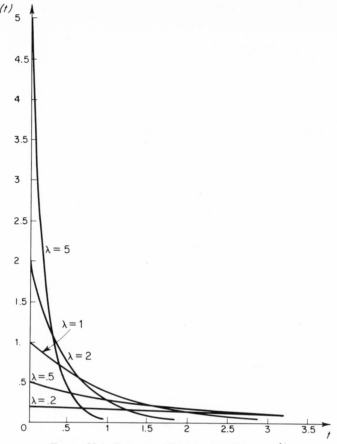

FIGURE 20.1. Exponental Distribution $f(t) = \lambda e^{-\lambda t}$.

Now, the conditional probability that no arrival occurs in the interval $(0, \ T + h)$ *given* that no arrival occurs in the interval $(0, \ T)$ is, by definition,

$$(4) \qquad \frac{\int_{T+h}^{\infty} \lambda e^{-\lambda t}\, dt}{\int_{T}^{\infty} \lambda e^{-\lambda t}\, dt} = \frac{e^{-\lambda(T+h)}}{e^{-\lambda T}} = e^{-\lambda h} = P[t \geq h],$$

which depends *only* on h. According to (4), the probability of no arrival in the interval $(T, \ T + h)$ is the same regardless of whether there is no arrival in $(0, \ T)$ or whether an arrival occurs at T and thereby "renews" the arrival process.

There is another way of describing the completely random nature of the exponential input process. The idea is given here in rough terms, but can easily be made exact. Suppose there are n arrivals in the interval $(0, \ T)$. Then if the **interarrival times** are exponentially distributed, the n arrival times are independently and uniformly distributed over the interval $(0, \ T)$. This observation provides the basis for several statistical tests to determine whether an exponential distribution adequately describes an actual input process.

A complementary insight into the assumption of exponential interarrival times is gained by expressing $e^{-\lambda h}$ in its Taylor series expansion

$$(5) \qquad P\begin{bmatrix} \text{no arrival in} \\ \text{any interval} \\ \text{of length } h \end{bmatrix} = e^{-\lambda h} = 1 - \lambda h + \frac{(-\lambda h)^2}{2!} + \frac{(-\lambda h)^3}{3!} + \cdots.$$

For a very small, but positive, value of h, the term $1 - \lambda h$ in (5) is *relatively* large as compared to the remaining terms in the summation. Therefore, this value can be used to approximate the probability in (5) when h is *very* small. We use the symbol ($\doteq$) to denote such an approximation. So we have, for *very* small $h > 0$,

$$(6) \qquad P\begin{bmatrix} \text{no arrival in} \\ \text{any interval} \\ \text{of length } h \end{bmatrix} \doteq 1 - \lambda h \quad (h \text{ small}).$$

A verbally inexact, but nevertheless helpful, way to explain the mathematical manipulation below is to state that at most only one arrival occurs for a time interval $h \geq 0$ sufficiently small. Since the approximate probability of no arrival occurring in the interval of length h is given by (6), the corresponding approximate probability of one arrival occurring is

$$(7) \qquad P\begin{bmatrix} \text{single arrival} \\ \text{in any interval} \\ \text{of length } h \end{bmatrix} \doteq \lambda h \quad (h \text{ small}).$$

A more precise way of expressing the reasoning would be to display the exact probability of a single arrival, in a manner similar to (5), and then show that for *very* small h, the term λh is *relatively* large as compared to the remaining terms. Throughout this chapter you should always interpret the symbol ($\doteq$) as meaning that a quantity of *relatively* negligible magnitude is being ignored in the approximation.

To illustrate, suppose λ equals four arrivals per hour. Then the probability of no arrival occurring in an interval of .01 hour is exactly .96079 from (5), and approximately $1 - .04 = .96$ from (6); the probability of an arrival is approximately .04 from (7).

Given that the density function for interarrival times is exponential (2), an immediate consequence is that the density function of the *total* arrival time y for any n consecutive arrivals is

$$(8) \qquad g(y) = \frac{\lambda(\lambda y)^{n-1} e^{-\lambda y}}{(n-1)!}, \quad y \geq 0 \quad (\text{gamma distribution}),$$

where n is a positive integer. You may interpret y as the sum of n independent values drawn from the same exponential density (2). Then

$$(9) \qquad P\begin{bmatrix} \text{total interval for} \\ \text{any } n \text{ consecutive} \\ \text{arrivals} \leq T \end{bmatrix} = \int_0^T g(y)\, dy = 1 - \sum_{j=0}^{n-1} \frac{(\lambda T)^j e^{-\lambda T}}{j!},$$

as can be verified by repeatedly applying integration by parts.

Finally, you should note that assuming exponential interarrivals is tantamount to postulating that the probability distribution of the number of arrivals n in *any* interval of length T is Poisson:

(10) $P\begin{bmatrix} n \text{ arrivals in} \\ \text{any interval} \\ \text{of length } T \end{bmatrix} = \dfrac{(\lambda T)^n e^{-\lambda T}}{n!}$ for $n = 0, 1, 2, \ldots$ (Poisson distribution),

with

(11) $E[n|T] = \lambda T$ and $\text{Var}\,[n|T] = \lambda T$ (Poisson—interval of length T).

For this reason, a synonym for the term **exponential arrivals** is **Poisson input**. (Sometimes the term **Markovian** is also used, and abbreviated by the symbol M.)

From (9) and (10), you should verify that

(12) $P\begin{bmatrix} \text{total interval for any } n \\ \text{consecutive arrivals} \le T \end{bmatrix} = P\begin{bmatrix} \text{number of arrivals in} \\ \text{any interval } T \ge n \end{bmatrix}.$

Actually, (12) is valid for any recurrent input process, not merely the Poisson, if the interval starts right after an arrival.

It is straightforward to apply the foregoing results to a **pure-birth model**. Consider a system that starts at Time 0 with no customers. Assume that customer arrivals obey a Poisson process, and that customers never depart from the system after they have arrived. Then at Time T, the Poisson distribution in (10) gives the probability of n customers in the system. Similarly, (9) gives the density function for the total arrival time of the first n customers.

▶The following discussion outlines how assuming certain properties of the arrival process leads to the derivation of exponentially distributed interarrival times and Poisson input. We postulate that

  (A) The time intervals between successive arrivals are independently and identically distributed; further, the probability of an arrival occurring in the time interval between T and $T + h$ depends only on the length h of the interval and not on T. The corresponding interarrival density function is designated as $f(t)$.
  (B) In any interval of time $h > 0$, there is a positive probability of an arrival.
  (C) In any sufficiently small interval of time, at most only one arrival can occur.

Suppose for simplicity that the system starts at Time 0 and the first arrival occurs at Time t, where $t > 0$. Therefore $f(t)$ represents the density function for both the length of the arrival intervals as well as the actual time for the first arrival.
  Define

(i) $r(T) \equiv 1 - \displaystyle\int_0^T f(t)\, dt,$

so that

(ii) $r(T) = P[\text{first arrival occurs after Time T}].$

Then given postulates (A) and (B),

(iii) $r(T + h) = r(T)r(h)$ for all $T, h > 0,$

and it can be proved that the only function that satisfies (iii) is

(iv) $$r(T) = e^{-\lambda T}$$

where λ is a positive constant. Therefore,

(v) $$e^{-\lambda T} = 1 - \int_0^T f(t)\, dt,$$

so that

(vi) $$f(t) = \lambda e^{-\lambda t},$$

as was to be shown.

Define

(vii) $$P_n(T) \equiv P[n \text{ arrivals occur in the interval } (0, T)].$$

Let $t = x$ be the time of the first arrival event, and according to postulate (C), only one customer enters at x. By postulate (A), we can write

(viii) $$P_n(T) = \int_0^T P_{n-1}(T - x) f(x)\, dx = \int_0^T P_{n-1}(y) f(T - y)\, dy \quad \text{for } n = 1, 2, \ldots,$$

where $y = T - x$. Using (vi),

(ix) $$P_n(T) = \int_0^T P_{n-1}(y) \lambda e^{-\lambda(T-y)}\, dy.$$

Differentiating with respect to T yields

(x) $$\frac{dP_n}{dT} = -\lambda P_n(T) + \lambda P_{n-1}(T) \quad \text{for } n = 1, 2, \ldots.$$

Since $P_0(T) = g(T) = e^{-\lambda T}$, the equations in (x) can be solved recursively, starting with $n = 1$, as each is a linear first-order differential equation with constant coefficients. The complete solution is simply the Poisson distribution,

(xi) $$P_n(T) = \frac{(\lambda T)^n e^{-\lambda T}}{n!} \quad \text{for } n = 0, 1, 2, \ldots.$$

Verify that this solution does in fact satisfy (x) by differentiating $P_n(T)$ in (xi). The same line of reasoning applies to any interval T, thus yielding the result given in (10). ◀

Taxicab Example. The following illustration indicates both the memoryless property of the exponential distribution and the kind of surprising result that can occur in queuing systems. Consider the illustration of hailing a taxicab on a corner of Times Square in New York City. Assume, on the average, one empty cab goes by the corner in any 30-second interval, that is, the mean time between arrivals is $1/\lambda = 30$ seconds. Suppose you come to the corner at an arbitrary instant. On the average, how long will you wait until the first empty cab arrives? Most persons reply 15 seconds when asked this question. Did you? As you will see below, that answer is correct *only* if an empty cab arrives at intervals of *exactly* 30 seconds. If there is *any* variability in the interarrival times, the answer is *always* larger than 15 seconds.

It can be shown that if you examine the system at an arbitrary moment, then

(13) $\begin{array}{l} \text{average time} \\ \text{to first arrival} \end{array} = \dfrac{1}{2}\left[\dfrac{1}{\lambda} + \lambda \cdot (\text{variance of interarrival times})\right].$

Hence if the term "variance of interarrival times" is positive, then the average time to the first arrival is larger than $\frac{1}{2}(1/\lambda)$. Note that when the interarrival distribution is exponential, its variance is $1/\lambda^2$, so that the average time to the first arrival is $1/\lambda$. And when the variance is larger than $1/\lambda^2$, the average time to the first arrival is actually *larger* than the average interarrival time!

Erlang arrivals. Another important example of an interarrival time distribution is

(14) $f(t) = \dfrac{(\lambda n)(\lambda n t)^{n-1} e^{-\lambda n t}}{(n-1)!}, \quad t \geq 0 \quad \text{(Erlang distribution-order } n\text{)},$

where n is a positive integer; the expectation and variance are

(15) $$E[t] = \frac{1}{\lambda} \qquad \text{Var } [t] = \frac{1}{n\lambda^2} \quad \text{(Erlang)}.$$

(Frequently, this distribution is denoted by the symbol E_n.) Replacing λn in (14) by λ yields the gamma distribution, shown in (8).

By varying λ and n appropriately, you can use the Erlang distribution to provide good approximations for many different interarrival distributions; several illustrative examples are given in Fig. 20.2. Be sure you notice that when $n = 1$, the Erlang distribution is simply the exponential distribution. What is more, when you let $n \to \infty$, so that Var $[t] \to 0$ as a result, then the Erlang distribution represents the case of **periodic** or **regular** arrival times, that is, a **constant** interarrival interval of $1/\lambda$. Examples employing this distribution are given in Appendix III.

20.4 PROBABILITY DISTRIBUTIONS OF SERVICE TIMES

The considerations in specifying the probability density for each service time are very similar to those for interarrival times. We assume that each server, or channel, processes one customer at a time. (We will not consider *bulk service* in this book.) For a specified server, assume that successive serving times are independently and identically distributed, and described by a continuous density function. Let

(1) $g(t) \equiv$ density function for the length of time t to serve any customer,

where $t \geq 0$, and also let

(2) $\text{mean service time} = \displaystyle\int_0^\infty t g(t)\, dt \equiv \frac{1}{\mu}$

so that

(3) $\mu =$ service rate per unit of time that the server is busy.

Jot down the definitions in (2) and (3).

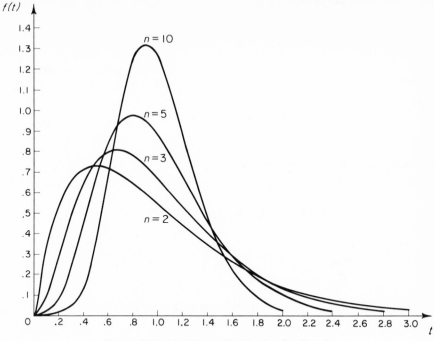

FIGURE 20.2 (a) Erlang Distribution for $\lambda = 1$.

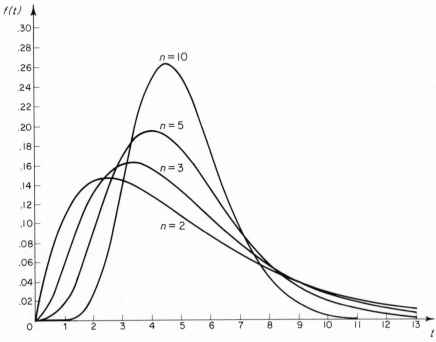

FIGURE 20.2 (b) Erlang Distribution for $\lambda = .2$.

849

To illustrate, if the unit of time is an hour and μ (mu) equals five services per hour while the server remains busy, then the average service time $1/\mu$ is one-fifth (.2) of an hour. Similarly, if a service on the average requires one-half an hour, then the service rate μ is 2 per hour, during an interval when the server remains busy.

Frequently, the service time distribution is assumed to be exponential:

$$(4) \qquad\qquad g(t) = \mu e^{-\mu t}, \; t \geq 0.$$

Mathematical convenience is the usual reason for such an assumption. But the **exponential service** assumption can also provide guiding insight into the operation of any system, since it represents the extreme case of service times that are memoryless. When the service distribution is exponential, the probability of completing a service to a customer in any subsequent interval of length h is independent of how much service time has already elapsed for that customer.

Accordingly, given assumption (4), if a customer is being served at Time t and you observe the system at Time t + h, then

$$(5) \qquad P[\text{service is not completed in interval of length } h] = e^{-\mu h}.$$

Consequently, for $h > 0$ *very* small,

$$(6) \quad P[\text{service is not completed in interval of length } h] \doteq 1 - \mu h \quad (h \text{ small})$$

and

$$(7) \qquad P[\text{service is completed in interval of length } h] \doteq \mu h \qquad (h \text{ small}).$$

Consider the following **pure-death model**. Let $t = 0$ represent the system's starting point in time. Suppose that there are M customers in the system at Time 0, and that no more customers ever arrive. Assume that there is a single server having an exponential time density (4), and let

$$(8) \quad P_n(T) = \text{probability that } n \text{ customers are in the system at Time T.}$$

[The dependence of $P_n(T)$ on the value of M has been suppressed in the notation.] The formula for $P_n(T)$ can be derived using an exact approach analogous to the derivation of (10) that we gave in the special material at the end of the preceding section. But the result can also be obtained by employing (6) and (7) above, and the approach is illustrated next because it is so useful for analyzing more complex models.

As in the preceding section, we calculate approximate probabilities by ignoring *relatively* small quantities. And in the same approximative vein, we say that at most only one departure occurs during a *very* small interval of time $h > 0$. Hence, when there are n customers in the system at Time T + h, we consider only the possibilities that at Time T either there were n customers and none have departed, or there were $n + 1$ customers and one departed during the very small interval of length h. (Actually, the other possibilities of there being more than $n + 1$ customers and accordingly more than one departure are *relatively* improbable when $h > 0$ is *very* small.) Consequently, for $1 \leq n < M$,

(9) $$P_n(T + h) \doteq (1 - \mu h)P_n(T) + (\mu h)P_{n+1}(T).$$

The first term on the right is the approximate probability that no service occurred in the interval of length h and that n customers were in the system at Time T. Interpret the second term on the right of (9). Rearranging terms yields

(10) $$\frac{P_n(T + h) - P_n(T)}{h} \doteq -\mu P_n(T) + \mu P_{n+1}(T),$$

so that on letting $h \to 0$,

(11) $$\frac{dP_n}{dT} = -\mu P_n(T) + \mu P_{n+1}(T) \quad \text{for } 1 \leq n < M.$$

The reason equation (11) holds exactly, instead of approximately, is that all the terms of *relatively* small magnitude that were ignored in (10) actually disappear in the process of letting h approach 0 in the limit.

By a similar line of reasoning, you can determine that

(12) $$\frac{dP_M}{dT} = -\mu P_M(T) \quad \text{for } n = M.$$

The unique solution to the system of linear differential equations (11) and (12) is

(13) $$P_n(T) = \frac{(\mu T)^{M-n}e^{-\mu T}}{(M - n)!} \quad \text{for } n = 1, 2, \ldots, M$$

(14) $$P_0(T) = 1 - \sum_{n=1}^{M} P_n(T) \quad \text{for } n = 0.$$

The distribution in (13) and (14) is sometimes called a *truncated Poisson*.

If the Mth person is the last to be served, then the total time y that he spends in the system, including his own service time, has the density given by the sum of M exponentially distributed variables

(15) $$h(y) = \frac{\mu(\mu y)^{M-1}e^{-\mu y}}{(M - 1)!}, \ y \geq 0 \ \text{(gamma distribution)},$$

with

(16) $$E[y] = \frac{M}{\mu} \qquad \text{Var } [y] = \frac{M}{\mu^2} \ \text{(gamma)}.$$

Although an exponential service time distribution is by far the most mathematically convenient form to assume, it is possible to derive usable mathematical results for certain simple queuing models when the service distribution is assumed to be Erlangian, as given by (14) in the previous section. An illustration appears in Appendix III.

*Self-service model. Now suppose, instead of there being only a single server, that at Time 0 each of the M customers starts self-service. Assume that the service time is the same exponential density for every customer, namely (4). This assumption is reasonable enough in a self-service situation. Consider a very small interval of time $h > 0$. Then because the servers are independent, you can apply binomial probability calculations, using the approximate expression in (6), to obtain

(17) $P[\text{none of } n \text{ customers departs}] \doteq (1 - \mu h)^n \doteq 1 - n\mu h$ (h small)

(18) $P[\text{one of } n \text{ customers departs}] \doteq n\mu h$ (h small).

Once again, the justification for (18) is that when interval $h > 0$ is *very* small, we can restrict attention to the events of no and one departure; the possibilities of more departures have *relatively* negligible probability. Consequently, when there are n customers in the system at Time $T + h$, we consider only the possibilities that at Time T there were n customers and none have departed, or there were $n + 1$ customers and one departed—giving, for $0 \leq n < M$,

(19) $P_n(T + h) \doteq (1 - h\mu n)P_n(T) + (n + 1)\mu h P_{n+1}(T)$ (h small).

Bringing $P_n(T)$ to the left-hand side of (19), dividing by h, and letting $h \to 0$ yields

(20) $\dfrac{dP_n}{dT} = -n\mu P_n(T) + (n + 1)\mu P_{n+1}(T)$ for $0 \leq n < M$.

Similar reasoning gives

(21) $\dfrac{dP_M}{dT} = -M\mu P_M(T)$ for $n = M$.

As you can verify by substitution, the complete solution to (20) and (21) is

(22) $P_n(T) = \binom{M}{n}(e^{-\mu T})^n(1 - e^{-\mu T})^{M-n}$ for $n = 0, 1, 2, \ldots, M$
                    (binomial distribution),

with

(23) $E[n \,|\, T] = Me^{-\mu T}$ $\text{Var}[n \,|\, T] = Me^{-\mu T}(1 - e^{-\mu T})$.

*Queuing model nomenclature. In reading the queuing theory literature, you will find that a standardized terminology is employed. (It is often called **Kendall's notation**.) Each model is signified by three symbols: the first designates the input process; the second, the service distribution; and the third, the number of servers. The standard symbols for the probability distributions are

$M \equiv$ exponentially distributed interarrival or service time (M is an abbreviation for Markovian)

$D \equiv$ deterministic (or constant, regular) interarrival or service time

$E_n \equiv$ Erlangian distribution of order n for interarrival or service time [some books also use the symbol K_n, and then employ the formula for a gamma distribution (15)]

$GI \equiv$ general independent distribution of interarrival time

$G \equiv$ general distribution of service time.

To illustrate, the model of Poisson input, exponential service, and single server is denoted by $M/M/1$. If the input were deterministic instead, then the notation would be $D/M/1$; further, if there were S servers, the notation would be $D/M/S$.

20.5 SINGLE-SERVER MODEL WITH POISSON INPUT AND EXPONENTIAL SERVICE

Most waiting line systems are composed of several servers, and more often than not, the queue *discipline* is quite complex. For example, a woman choosing a checkout stand at a supermarket looks at the number of women already in line and the number of items in their carts. She also considers which lines are closest to the aisle she is emerging from, as well as which checkout clerks are the fastest. Similar considerations are relevant when a man selects a line in front of a teller's window at a bank, or when a driver chooses a toll booth on a turnpike. But sometimes the discipline is on a strict first come, first served basis. One example is a bakery that gives each entering customer a number, and then serves the customers in numerical order. Other examples occur at gasoline stations, camera shops, shoeshine stands, and in a crowded but orderly cafeteria line.

As we have stated earlier, developing an operations research model for an actual situation inherently involves making approximations. This is so regardless of whether, in the case of a waiting line model, you analyze the problem using either mathematics or a computer simulation or both. Often you can obtain approximate information about a complex system's operating characteristics by examining certain extreme or limiting cases. One such approximate approach is to consider a queuing system with multiple servers as being comprised of a collection of separate and independent single-server systems. For example, suppose the system consists of five servers and the input process indicates that 20 customers arrive per hour. Then *as an approximation*, the system can be viewed as five separate single-server systems, each with an arrival rate of 4 per hour. The approach is approximate for two reasons: a customer is assumed to join each line with equal probability, regardless of the length of the several lines; and once a customer joins a line, he is assumed to stay there. The expected number of customers that are in each system, summed over all the separate systems, and the average time a customer spends in a system will usually be larger than in most actual multiple-server systems. The reason is that if this queuing system were to operate in real life, then there would be more times than you would expect when one server is idle and yet customers are waiting in line for other servers.

If you also consider the approximation that there is only a *single* line in a multiple-server system and that customers are processed on a first come, first served basis, then you may obtain smaller than actual values for the expected number of customers and the average time each spends in the system.

Fortunately, single-server systems often do yield to mathematical analysis, as do many cases of multiple servers with a single line and a first come, first served discipline. We therefore begin here with a simple single-server queuing system, and treat a simple multiple-server model in Sec. 20.6. More complex single-server models are studied in Appendix III.

Model description. The simplest single-server model having both input and service processes described probabilistically is one with exponential interarrival and service times (denoted by $M/M/1$). Specifically, assume

(1)   exponential interarrival density: $\lambda e^{-\lambda t}$

exponential service time density: $\mu e^{-\mu t}$.

Define the number of customers n in the system at any point in time as including the persons waiting in line plus those in service. Let $t = 0$ represent the system's starting point in time, and define

(2) $P_n(T) \equiv$ probability that n customers are in the system at Time T.

Actually $P_n(T)$ depends on the number of customers i in the system at Time 0, but this dependence is suppressed in the notation.

Let $h > 0$ be a *very* small interval of time. If there are $n > 0$ customers in the system at Time $T + h$, then we consider only the possibilities that there were either $n - 1$, n, or $n + 1$ customers at Time T. Any other possibilities are of relatively insignificant probability. Consequently, for $n > 0$

(3)
$$P_n(T + h) \doteq (\lambda h)(1 - \mu h)P_{n-1}(T) + (1 - \lambda h)(1 - \mu h)P_n(T)$$
$$+ (\lambda h)(\mu h)P_n(T) + (1 - \lambda h)(\mu h)P_{n+1}(T) \qquad (h \text{ small}).$$

The first term on the right corresponds to the event of one arrival and no departure when $n - 1$ customers are in the system at Time T. The second and third terms refer to the events of no arrival and no departure, and of one arrival and a departure when n customers are in the system at Time T. And the final term relates to the event of no arrival and one departure when there are $n + 1$ customers in the system at Time T. As the symbol ($\doteq$) indicates, the expression in (3) is approximate; it can be made exact by adding probability terms with coefficients h^k, where $k \geq 2$.

Bringing the term $P_n(T)$ to the left-hand side of (3), dividing by h, and letting $h \to 0$, yields

(4) $\dfrac{dP_n}{dT} = \lambda P_{n-1}(T) - (\lambda + \mu)P_n(T) + \mu P_{n+1}(T)$ for $n > 0$.

This expression is exact because the terms neglected in (3) become 0 as $h \to 0$. Similarly, you can show that

(5) $\dfrac{dP_0}{dT} = -\lambda P_0(T) + \mu P_1(T)$ for $n = 0$.

With moderately advanced analysis it is possible to solve the system of linear differential equations (4) and (5) for each $P_n(T)$. (To do so, you must also state the number of customers i in the system at Time 0.) The result is called the **transient solution**, since it depends directly on the value of T.

Suppose, however, we examine the values of $P_n(T)$ as $T \to \infty$. If $P_n(T)$ approaches a limiting value, say, P_n, and if $E[n]$ is finite for this limiting distribution, then we will say that the system reaches **statistical equilibrium.** We denote the resulting P_n values as **equilibrium** or **stationary probabilities.** The label "stationary" derives from the property that if the number of customers in the system at any Time t is given according to the probability distribution P_n, then for *any* $h > 0$, P_n is also the probability that n customers are in the system at Time t + h. The value of P_n can also be interpreted as the limiting fraction of an arbitrarily long period of time during which the queue contains n customers.

Provided

$$(6) \qquad\qquad \rho \equiv \frac{\lambda}{\mu} < 1 \quad \text{(traffic intensity assumption)},$$

the stationary probabilities P_n always exist; the symbol ρ (rho) in (6) is frequently called the **traffic intensity.** Give a verbal interpretation of the assumption in (6).

You can find the equilibrium solution $P_n(T) \equiv P_n$, for all T, by using the consequence that each dP_n/dT must equal 0, if the solution P_n is indeed independent of T. Hence to obtain P_n, all you need to do is set the time derivatives in (4) and (5) equal to 0, yielding

$$(7) \qquad\qquad 0 = \lambda P_{n-1} - (\lambda + \mu)P_n + \mu P_{n+1} \quad \text{for } n = 1, 2, 3, \ldots$$

$$(8) \qquad\qquad 0 = -\lambda P_0 + \mu P_1 \qquad\qquad\qquad \text{for } n = 0.$$

The system of **difference equations** (7) and (8) is easily solved recursively, starting with (8),

$$(9) \qquad\qquad P_1 = P_0\left(\frac{\lambda}{\mu}\right) = P_0 \rho$$

and proceeding to (7) for $n = 1, 2, \ldots$,

$$(10) \qquad\qquad P_n = P_0 \rho^n.$$

[Verify that P_n in (10) does satisfy (7).] Given (6),

$$(11) \qquad\qquad \sum_{n=0}^{\infty} P_n = P_0 \sum_{n=0}^{\infty} \rho^n = \frac{P_0}{1 - \rho} = 1,$$

and it follows that $P_0 = 1 - \rho$, so that

$$(12) \qquad P_n = (1 - \rho)\rho^n \quad \text{for } n = 0, 1, 2, \ldots \quad \text{(geometric distribution)}$$

with

$$(13) \qquad E\begin{bmatrix}\text{number of} \\ \text{customers} \\ \text{in system}\end{bmatrix} \equiv E[n] = \frac{\rho}{1 - \rho} = \frac{\lambda}{\mu - \lambda} \qquad \text{Var}[n] = \frac{\rho}{(1 - \rho)^2}$$

$$P[n \geq N] = \rho^N.$$

Notice the probability distribution in (12) depends *only* on the traffic intensity ratio $(\lambda/\mu = \rho)$. Since $\rho(= 1 - P_0)$ is also the fraction of time the server is busy, the quantity ρ is sometimes called the system's **utilization factor.** It is significant that this interpretation of ρ remains valid even when both the inter-arrival and service time distributions are general (that is, for the model $GI/G/1$).

▶Letting $P_n(T|i)$ denote the transient solution to (4) and (5) when i customers are in the queue at $t = 0$, it can be shown that

(i) $|P_n(T|i) - P_n| \leq e^{-T(\lambda + \mu - 2\sqrt{\lambda\mu})}.$

Consequently, $P_n(T|i)$ approaches P_n at least exponentially by a factor proportional to T. Note, however, that the proportionality factor, which can be written as $(\sqrt{\lambda} - \sqrt{\mu})^2$, approaches 0 as λ approaches μ. Hence T may have to be very large before $P_n(T|i)$ and P_n are nearly equal; this is especially so when ρ is large and i is small.   ◀

Operating characteristics. The expected line length can be found by noting that

(14) $\text{line length} = \begin{cases} \text{number in system} & \text{if } n = 0 \\ \text{number in system} - 1 & \text{if } n > 0, \end{cases}$

so that

$$E[\text{line length}] = 0 \cdot P_0 + \sum_{n=1}^{\infty} (n-1)P_n = \sum_{n=0}^{\infty} nP_n - \sum_{n=1}^{\infty} P_n$$

(15)

$$= E[n] - (1 - P_0) = \frac{\rho^2}{1-\rho} = \frac{\lambda^2}{\mu(\mu - \lambda)}.$$

Next consider the time intervals when the server is idle. Since these begin when a service terminates and end when a new arrival occurs, the length of the idle periods has the same distribution as the interarrival time, that is, exponential with mean $1/\lambda$. Let the period of length T be so long that we can safely utilize expected values. Then the server is idle for $[TP_0 = T(1 - \rho)]$ units of time, and $[T(1 - \rho)/(1/\lambda) = \lambda T(1 - \rho)]$ is the number of separate idle periods during T. Because idle and busy periods alternate, $\lambda T(1 - \rho)$ is also the number of separate busy periods during T, and ρT is the total duration of all busy periods. Consequently,

(16) $E[\text{length of busy period}] = \dfrac{\rho T}{\lambda T(1 - \rho)} = \dfrac{1}{\mu - \lambda}$

and

(17) $E\begin{bmatrix} \text{number of customers} \\ \text{served per busy period} \end{bmatrix} = \mu E\begin{bmatrix} \text{length of} \\ \text{busy period} \end{bmatrix} = \dfrac{1}{1 - \rho}.$

The relations (16) and (17) are actually valid for any service time distribution (that is, for the model $M/G/1$).

Now turn to the probability density for the time a customer spends in the system, which is defined as the interval a customer waits in line plus his time in service. Suppose the system is in statistical equilibrium, so that when a new customer arrives, he finds n customers in the system ahead of him with probability

P_n given by (12). Assume that the queue discipline is first come, first served. Then his total time spent in the system is composed of the sum of $n + 1$ independent and identically distributed exponential random variables, and has a gamma density

$$(18) \qquad\qquad \frac{\mu(\mu y)^n e^{-\mu y}}{n!} \quad \text{for } y \geq 0,$$

as you already saw in (15) of Sec. 20.4. Hence the density of time that a customer who arrives at an arbitrary instant spends in the system is given by

$$(19) \qquad h(w) = \sum_{n=0}^{\infty} (1 - \rho)\rho^n \left[\frac{\mu(\mu w)^n e^{-\mu w}}{n!} \right]$$

$$= \mu(1 - \rho)e^{-\mu(1-\rho)w} \qquad \text{(exponential distribution)},$$

with

$$(20) \qquad E[\text{time in system}] = E[w] = \frac{1}{\mu(1 - \rho)} = \frac{1}{\mu - \lambda},$$

$$E[\text{time in line}] = E[\text{time in system}] - E[\text{service time}]$$
$$(21) \qquad\qquad\qquad = \frac{1}{\mu}\left(\frac{\rho}{1 - \rho}\right) = \frac{\lambda}{\mu(\mu - \lambda)}.$$

For fixed ρ, the expected times in the system and in line vary inversely with the service rate μ.

▶Suppose you look at only the time that a customer waits in line, where you exclude his service time as well as that of any customers who arrive when the server is idle. Then it can be proved that the *conditional* probability density of the *time spent in line* by those customers who *do* have to wait in line is also given by (19) for any interarrival distribution, that is, for the model $GI/M/1$. Consequently, $E[w]$ in (20) is also the *conditional expected time waiting in line* given that a customer *does* have to wait in line.   ◀

Sensitivity analysis. Various operating characteristics of this simple queuing system are displayed in Fig. 20.3 for different values of traffic intensity ρ and service rate μ.

Notice that as the traffic intensity ρ increases, the expected values of the number of customers, the line length, the time in the system, and the time in line [formulas (13), (15), (20), and (21) above] all increase rapidly. Although these quantities can be made arbitrarily large for sufficiently large $\rho < 1$, the system may take an accordingly long time to reach steady-state equilibrium. For a given service rate μ, when intensity ρ is small, most of the expected time a customer spends in the system is due to the average service time $1/\mu$; but as intensity ρ increases (that is, as the arrival rate λ increases), most of the expected time spent in the system is due to waiting in line.

For the sake of illustration, suppose the unit of time in Fig. 20.3 is an hour (or 60 minutes) and that $\rho = .8$. Then on the average, the server is idle .2 hour (or

Traffic Intensity ρ	Probability of Server Idle $= 1-\rho$	Expected Number in System $= \dfrac{\rho}{1-\rho}$	Expected Line Length $= \rho^2/1-\rho$	$\mu = 10$			$\mu = 20$		
				λ	Time in System	Time in Line	λ	Time in System	Time in Line
.1	.9	.11	.01	1	.11	.01	2	.06	.01
.3	.7	.43	.13	3	.14	.04	6	.07	.02
.5	.5	1.00	.50	5	.20	.10	10	.10	.05
.7	.3	2.33	1.63	7	.33	.23	14	.17	.12
.8	.2	4.00	3.20	8	.50	.40	16	.25	.20
.9	.1	9.00	8.10	9	1.00	.90	18	.50	.45
.95	.05	19.00	18.05	9.5	2.00	1.90	19	1.00	.95
.99	.01	99.00	98.01	9.9	10.00	9.90	19.8	5.00	4.95
.999	.001	999.00	998.00	9.99	100.00	99.90	19.98	50.00	49.95

λ = arrival rate per unit of time
μ = service rate per unit of time
$\rho = \lambda/\mu$ traffic intensity

Note: E[Length of Busy Period] = E[Time in System]

FIGURE 20.3 Operating Characteristics of $M/M/1$ System.

12 minutes per hour) and there are four persons in the system. If $\mu = 10$, so that the service rate is 10 per hour (or at the rate of six minutes per customer), then the average time a customer spends in the system is .5 hour (or 30 minutes), and .4 hour (or 24 minutes) of this is due to waiting in line. If ρ remains .8 but both the arrival rate and service rate double, so that $\mu = 20$, then the average times spent in the system and in waiting are cut in half.

Secretaries example. The following hypothetical example will indicate briefly how the model's operating characteristics, such as those shown in Fig. 20.3, can be used to assist decision-making. Noah Peale, the manager of a law office, is deciding whether to employ two or four secretaries. To simplify matters, suppose he faces only two alternatives: to hire two experienced legal secretaries who can each type at the rate of 20 documents a day, or four novice secretaries who can each type at the rate of only 10 documents a day. On the average, there are 36 documents to be typed per day. Copy these data on a piece of paper for easy reference, since this example will be used again later in the chapter.

Suppose the manager uses, as an approximation, the simple model above. In the case of the two faster typists, each will be assigned documents at the rate $\lambda = \frac{36}{2} = 18$ per day, and in the case of the four slower typists, at the rate $\lambda = \frac{36}{4} = 9$ per day. Verify that in either case, traffic intensity $\rho = .9$.

Then the average number of documents on each girl's desk is 9, according to (13), so that there are an average of 18 documents in the entire system having two secretaries and 36 in the system having four secretaries. The average time for a document to be in the system is $\frac{1}{2}$ [$= 1/(20 - 18)$] day for the two faster secretaries as compared to 1 [$= 1/(10 - 9)$] day for the four slower secretaries, according to (20). By the same token, each experienced secretary will be busy over intervals that average one-half a day, whereas, each novice secretary will be busy over intervals that average a full day.

In what ways do you think this simple model approximates the real situation? Why would the average delay for a document tend to be smaller than (20) in actuality? If you were the office manager, what else would you take into account in deciding between these two alternatives?

*Finite queue. So far no limitation has been imposed on the total number of customers present in the system at any time. Now suppose that at most M customers are allowed to be in the entire system, and therefore no more than $M - 1$ persons are permitted to wait in line at any instant. (An example is a one-pump gasoline station with a small driveway leading into a busy street.) If a customer arrives when M persons are already in the system, then he is restricted from entering, and is said to be lost from the system. (Consequently, this model is sometimes termed a combined **loss-delay system**.) An important difference between the previous model and this **finite-queue model** is that here statistical equilibrium is reached for *any* value of the intensity ratio λ/μ. Give a reason why.

The steady-state difference equations (7) and (8) still apply for $n = 0, 1, \ldots, M - 1$, but the equation for $n = M$ is

$$(22) \qquad\qquad 0 = \lambda P_{M-1} - \mu P_M.$$

The corresponding solution for $n = 0, 1, \ldots, M$ is

$$(23) \qquad P_n = \begin{cases} \left(\dfrac{1 - \rho}{1 - \rho^{M+1}}\right)\rho^n & \text{for } \lambda \neq \mu \\[2ex] \dfrac{1}{M + 1} & \text{for } \lambda = \mu. \end{cases}$$

Of course, when $\lambda < \mu$ and $M \to \infty$, P_n in (23) agrees with (12). By elementary calculations it can be shown that for $\lambda \neq \mu$

$$(24) \qquad E\begin{bmatrix} \text{number of} \\ \text{customers} \\ \text{in system} \end{bmatrix} \equiv E[n] = \frac{\rho}{(1 - \rho)}\left[\frac{1 - (M + 1)\rho^M + M\rho^{M+1}}{1 - \rho^{M+1}}\right]$$

$$= \frac{\rho}{1 - \rho} - \frac{(M + 1)\rho^{M+1}}{1 - \rho^{M+1}} \quad \text{for } \lambda \neq \mu.$$

Observe when $\lambda < \mu$, the expected number of customers in this system is smaller than that for the previous case of an unlimited line length (13). Similarly, it can be proved that for $\lambda = \mu$

(25) $\qquad E\begin{bmatrix} \text{number of} \\ \text{customers} \\ \text{in system} \end{bmatrix} \equiv E[n] = \dfrac{M}{2} \quad \text{for } \lambda = \mu.$

A delicate question arises in *defining* the amount of time a customer spends in the system (and waiting in line). If a customer arrives when there are already M persons in the system, he does not enter, and consequently he literally spends no time in the system. Hence average time spent in the system can be defined so as to refer either to all customers who arrive, regardless of whether they enter, or only to those customers who are permitted to enter. We adopt the latter, since in most situations the interest in delay time is only for those who actually do enter the system. So, given that a customer arriving at an arbitrary moment *does* join the system, and that the discipline is first come, first served, it can be shown that

(26)
$$E[\text{time in system}] \equiv E[w] = \frac{\rho}{\mu(1-\rho)}\left[\frac{1 - \mu\rho^{M-1} + (M-1)\rho^{M}}{1-\rho^{M}}\right] + \frac{1}{\mu}$$
$$= \frac{1}{\mu(1-\rho)} - \frac{M\rho^{M}}{\mu(1-\rho^{M})} \quad \text{for } \lambda \neq \mu,$$

and

(27) $\quad E[\text{time in system}] \equiv E[w] = \dfrac{1}{\mu} \cdot \dfrac{M+1}{2} \quad \text{for } \lambda = \mu.$

▶By advanced analysis, it is also possible to derive dreadful-looking, but nevertheless computable, formulas for the transient solutions to the finite queue model. These are given here only so that you can see how intricate the mathematical form of the transient solution turns out to be. Let i denote the number of customers in the system at Time 0. Then for any λ and μ,

(i)
$$P_n(T|i) = P_n + \frac{2}{M+1}\sum_{j=1}^{M}\frac{e^{-(\lambda+\mu)T+2T\sqrt{\lambda\mu}\,\cos\,[j\pi/(M+1)]}\rho^{(n-i)/2}}{\left(1 - 2\rho\cos\dfrac{j\pi}{m+1} + \rho\right)}\cdot\left[\sin\frac{ij\pi}{M+1}\right.$$
$$\left.-\sqrt{\rho}\,\sin\frac{(i+1)j\pi}{M+1}\right]\left[\sin\frac{nj\pi}{M+1} - \sqrt{\rho}\,\sin\frac{(n+1)j\pi}{M+1}\right],$$

where the P_n are given by (23). As $T \to \infty$, the summation term approaches 0.

For the case of $M = 1$, in which a customer is allowed to enter only if the server is free, and no customer is in the system at Time 0, (i) simplifies to

(ii)
$$P_0(T|i=0) = \frac{\mu}{\lambda+\mu} + \frac{\lambda}{\lambda+\mu}e^{-(\lambda+\mu)T}$$
$$P_1(T|i=0) = \frac{\lambda}{\lambda+\mu} - \frac{\lambda}{\lambda+\mu}e^{-(\lambda+\mu)T}$$

for all λ and μ. Thus as $T \to \infty$, the transient corrections to the stationary probabilities die out exponentially.   ◀

Arbitrary service distribution. Other versions of single-server models in which the interarrival and service distributions are not exponentially distributed will be explained in the advanced material in Appendix III. But it is possible to state in simple terms the expected number of customers in the system and the average time spent in the system for the case in which the interarrival distribution is exponential and the service distribution is arbitrary (that is, for the model $M/G/1$).

Let

$$(28) \qquad V \equiv \text{Var [service time]} = \int_0^\infty \left(t - \frac{1}{\mu} \right)^2 g(t) \, dt,$$

where, as before, $1/\mu$ is the mean service time and $g(t)$ is the service time density function. Then

$$(29) \qquad E[\text{number of customers in system}] = \rho + \frac{\lambda^2 V + \rho^2}{2(1 - \rho)}$$

$$(30) \qquad E[\text{line length}] = \frac{\lambda^2 V + \rho^2}{2(1 - \rho)}$$

$$(31) \qquad P[\text{server is idle}] \equiv P_0 = 1 - \rho,$$

where the intensity factor $\rho \equiv \lambda/\mu < 1$, as usual.

Assuming that the system operates on a first come, first served basis, then the average time a customer spends in the system is given by

$$(32) \qquad \begin{aligned} E[\text{time in system}] &= E[\text{time in line}] + E[\text{service time}] \\ &\equiv \frac{\lambda}{\mu^2} \left[\frac{\mu^2 V + 1}{2(1 - \rho)} \right] + \frac{1}{\mu} = \frac{1}{\lambda} \left[\rho + \frac{\lambda^2 V + \rho^2}{2(1 - \rho)} \right]. \end{aligned}$$

[Frequently, (29) and (32) are referred to as **Pollaczek-Khintchine formulas**.]

Verify that when $g(t)$ is exponential, so that $V = 1/\mu^2$, then (29), (30), and (32) reduce to (13), (15), and (20), respectively. The above formulas also give the expectations when service time is constant $1/\mu$, since then $V = 0$ (the resultant model is designated as $M/D/1$). Observe that all the averages vary linearly with V, and depend only on the arrival rate λ, the traffic intensity ρ, and the service variance V, and not on any other parameters of the input and service distributions.

Note further the equilibrium relation

$$(33) \qquad E[\text{number of customers in system}] = \lambda E[\text{time in system}].$$

Actually, (33) holds under much more general conditions, including many multiple-server models. Give a verbal interpretation of (33) that makes the relation plausible.

To check your understanding of these formulas, consider once again the above example of hiring either two experienced legal secretaries or four slower novice secretaries. Recall a rapid secretary can complete an average of 20 documents a day, whereas the corresponding figure for a slower secretary is 10. Since an average of 36 documents must be typed each day, the arrival rate for each rapid secretary is 18 as compared to 9 for a slower secretary.

When both the interarrival and service time distributions were assumed to be exponential, there were on the average, 9 documents on each girl's desk. The average time for a document to be in the system was one-half day for a faster secretary as compared to one day for a slower secretary.

Now suppose instead of exponential service times, the service times are constant ($V = 0$). Then verify in (29) that there will be an average of only 4.95 documents on each girl's desk and in (32) that the average time for a document to be in the system is .275 of a day for the faster secretary and .55 of a day for the slower one. Hence, elimination of service time variations nearly cuts the averages in half as compared to the exponential case.

In contrast, suppose that the variance of service times is double that of the exponential case—($\frac{2}{400}$) for a faster typist and ($\frac{2}{100}$) for a slower typist. Check that there will be an average of 13.05 documents on each girl's desk, and that the average time for a document to be in the system is .725 of a day for a faster secretary, and 1.45 days for a slower one. Therefore, doubling the service time variability as compared to the exponential case increases these averages by only about 50%. Work out the impact of tripling the variability.

▶ We outline a proof of (29) to illustrate an application of the proposition, "the expectation of a sum of random variables is the sum of the expectations." To keep the argument simple, we assume that the system is examined at those instants in time when a service has just been completed and the associated customer has departed. If the system is in equilibrium, the formula in (29) also holds for an arbitrary moment in time, but a proof substantiating this assertion is much more difficult.

Let n be the number of persons in the system just after a departure at Time T, and n' the number of persons just after the *next* departure at Time T'. Let j be the number of arrivals during this next interval of service. Then

(i) $$n' = \begin{cases} j & \text{if } n = 0 \\ n - 1 + j & \text{if } n > 0. \end{cases}$$

The equality for $n = 0$ follows because the first person to arrive after Time T is also the one who departs at Time T'; consequently, the customers remaining are just those who arrived during the interval of his service. The equality for $n > 0$ holds because the next service interval begins immediately at Time T, and hence the departure at Time T' is one of the n customers in the system at Time T.

Relation (i) can be expressed more conveniently by introducing the so-called *Heaviside Unit Function*

(ii) $$\delta(n) = \begin{cases} 0 & \text{if } n = 0 \\ 1 & \text{if } n > 0, \end{cases}$$

for then according to (i),

(iii) $$n' = n - \delta(n) + j \quad \text{for all } n.$$

As a preliminary to finding $E[n]$, recall that for a given length of service time t, the number of arrivals j has a Poisson distribution with mean λt. Therefore

(iv) $$E[j] = \int_0^\infty E[j|t]g(t)\, dt = \int_0^\infty \lambda t g(t)\, dt = \frac{\lambda}{\mu} = \rho,$$

where $E[j|t]$ is the conditional expectation of j given t, and $g(t)$ is the service time density. Also

(v)
$$E[j^2] = \int_0^\infty E[j^2|t]g(t)\, dt = \int_0^\infty [\lambda t + (\lambda t)^2]g(t)\, dt$$
$$= \frac{\lambda}{\mu} + \lambda^2 \left\{ \text{Var [service time]} + \left(\frac{1}{\mu}\right)^2 \right\} = \rho + \lambda^2 V + \rho^2.$$

It can be shown (see Appendix III.2) that

(vi)
$$P_0 = 1 - \rho \quad \text{so that } E[\delta] = E[\delta^2] = \rho.$$

Now square both sides of (iii) and take expectations

(vii)
$$E[(n')^2] = E[n^2] + E[\delta^2] + E[j^2] - 2E[n\delta(n)] + 2E[nj] - 2E[\delta(n)j]$$
$$= E[n^2] + \rho + E[j^2] - 2E[n] + 2E[n]E[j] - 2\rho E[j],$$

due to (vi), $n\delta(n) = n$, and n and j being independent. Using the equilibrium condition $E[(n')^2] = E[n^2]$, and (iv), we can write (vii) as

(viii)
$$E[n] = \frac{E[j^2] + \rho - 2\rho^2}{2(1 - \rho)}.$$

Substituting (v) into (viii) and simplifying yields

(ix)
$$E[n] = \rho + \frac{\lambda^2 V + \rho^2}{2(1 - \rho)}.$$

Go back over the argument and indicate where we applied the proposition, "the expectation of a sum equals the sum of the expectations."

The proof of (32) is usually based on first establishing (33), and then dividing $E[n]$ by λ. ◀

*Priority discipline. In many real situations, the queuing discipline is not according to a first come, first served basis. Consider, for example, a young executive who returns to his office after being away several days on a business trip. He may find a number of telephone messages awaiting him, including one from his boss. Most likely, he will return his boss's call before any others.

Suppose the input to a queuing system can be classified into r distinct types, and priorities from 1 to r are assigned to these types in decreasing order of importance, so that Type 1 has the highest priority and Type r the lowest. As soon as the server finishes with a customer, he always goes on to serve the next customer in line who has the highest priority. (If several individuals in line have the same priority number, then they are served on a first come, first served basis.) In some situations, an additional assumption is made that the service of a customer being waited on is **preempted** whenever a customer with a higher priority enters the system. The results given below, however, are for the *nonpreemptive* discipline.

Assume that each customer Type k arrives according to a Poisson input process with mean rate λ_k. Also suppose that the service distribution for each Type k is arbitrary with density $g_k(t)$ and

(34)　　$E[\text{service time} | \text{Type k}] = \dfrac{1}{\mu_k}$　　$V_k \equiv \text{Var [service time | Type k]}.$

Define

$$\sigma_k \equiv \sum_{j=1}^{k} \frac{\lambda_j}{\mu_j} \qquad \sigma_0 \equiv 0$$

and assume $\sigma_r < 1$ to ensure the system reaches statistical equilibrium.

Consider the system at an instant in time just after a service of a customer has been completed. Then if a Type k customer just arrives, the expected time he waits in line is given by

(35)
$$E\,[\text{time in line}\,|\,\text{Type k}] = \frac{\sum_{j=1}^{r} \lambda_j \left[V_j + \left(\frac{1}{\mu_j}\right)^2 \right]}{2(1 - \sigma_{k-1})(1 - \sigma_k)}.$$

Verify that when $r = 1$, the expression in (35) reduces to that for E [time in line] in (32). Since $\lambda_k / \sum \lambda_j$ equals the probability that an entering customer *is* of Type k, you can find the expected time in line for an arbitrary customer by calculating

(36)
$$E\,[\text{time in line}] = \frac{\sum_{k=1}^{r} \lambda_k E\,[\text{time in line}\,|\,\text{Type k}]}{\sum_{k=1}^{r} \lambda_k}.$$

The following numerical example will illustrate the impact of imposing a priority discipline. Suppose the arrival rate for the system is $\lambda = 18$ and the service rate is $\mu = 20$ without a priority discipline. Then, as you saw in Fig. 20.3 and for the example of the legal office typists, the expected time in line is .45. Suppose instead that the arrivals are classified into Type 1 and Type 2, having the respective arrival rates λ_1 and λ_2, where $\lambda_1 + \lambda_2 = \lambda = 18$. Assume that the service rate μ applies to both types and that the service distribution is exponential. Then verify that according to (35) and (36),

$$E\,[\text{time in line}\,|\,\text{Type 1}] = \frac{2(9)\left[\dfrac{1}{20^2} + \dfrac{1}{20^2}\right]}{2(1)\left(1 - \dfrac{\lambda_1}{20}\right)} = \frac{.045}{\left(1 - \dfrac{\lambda_1}{20}\right)}$$

(37)
$$E\,[\text{time in line}\,|\,\text{Type 2}] = \frac{E\,[\text{time in line}\,|\,\text{Type 1}]}{\left(1 - \dfrac{\lambda_1}{20} - \dfrac{\lambda_2}{20}\right)} = \frac{E\,[\text{time in line}\,|\,\text{Type 1}]}{.1}$$

$$E\,[\text{time in line}] = .45.$$

Hence, the average time in line for an arbitrary customer is still .45, but the expected time is always less than .45 for a Type 1 customer and always greater than .45 for a Type 2 customer. Further, the smaller the value of λ_1, the smaller the expected wait in line for *both* Types 1 and 2, even though the average time in line for an arbitrary customer remains unaffected. To illustrate, suppose $\lambda_1 = \lambda_2 = 9$; check in (37) that the expected time in line for a Type 1 customer is ($\frac{9}{110} = .0818$) and for a Type 2 customer is .8181. What happens when $\lambda_1 = 3$? When $\lambda_1 = 15$?

In some instances, the several types of customers require different lengths of service. Then assigning priorities according to the mean service rates—the highest *rate* having the highest priority—will always reduce the overall average time in line. To illustrate, consider again the above example with $\lambda = 18$ and $\mu = 20$; the associated utilization factor is ($\frac{18}{20} = .9$), and the expected time in line is .45. Suppose in a two-priority-discipline scheme that $\lambda_1 = \lambda_2 = 9$, and $\mu_1 = 30$ and $\mu_2 = 15$, so that the utilization factor ($\sigma_r = \frac{9}{30} + \frac{9}{15} = .9$) remains the same. Verify from (35) and (36) that the expected time in line for a Type 1 customer is ($\frac{1}{14} = .0714$) and for a Type 2 customer is ($\frac{10}{14} = .7142$), which are smaller values than the corresponding averages for $\mu_1 = \mu_2 = \mu = 20$. Now the expected time in line for an arbitrary customer is .3928, which is *smaller* than .45 in the system without priorities or with $\mu_1 = \mu_2 = 20$.

20.6 MULTIPLE-SERVER MODEL WITH POISSON INPUT AND EXPONENTIAL SERVICE

Certainly most queuing systems are composed of several servers, and hence waiting line models with more than one server are important. In this section, we generalize the results in the preceding section. The queuing discipline for this model is relatively simple as compared to most realistic situations. Nevertheless, the results can be used at least as an initial approximation to the behavior characteristics of more complex systems.

Let

$$(1) \qquad\qquad S \equiv \text{number of servers}$$

and assume that

$$(2) \qquad \begin{aligned} &\text{interarrival density:}\quad \lambda e^{-\lambda t}\\ &\text{service time density}\\ &\text{for each server:}\qquad \mu e^{-\mu t}, \end{aligned}$$

where the individual service times are all mutually independent (that is, for each server as well as among the servers).

The appropriate difference equations [analogous to those for the single-server case (7) and (8) in the preceding section] that determine the stationary probabilities are:

$$(3) \qquad \begin{aligned} &0 = \lambda P_{n-1} - (\lambda + n\mu)P_n + (n+1)\mu P_{n+1} \quad \text{for } 1 \le n < S\\ &0 = \lambda P_{n-1} - (\lambda + S\mu)P_n + S\mu P_{n+1} \qquad\quad \text{for } n \ge S. \end{aligned}$$

(These equations are derived in the next section.) The associated solution is

$$(4) \qquad \begin{aligned} P_n &= \frac{\rho^n}{n!}\cdot P_0 \qquad \text{for } 0 \le n < S\\[2mm] P_n &= \frac{\rho^n}{S!\,S^{n-S}}\cdot P_0 \quad \text{for } n \ge S, \end{aligned}$$

where $\rho = \lambda/\mu$ and

(5)
$$P_0 = \frac{1}{\left[\sum_{j=0}^{S-1} \frac{\rho^j}{j!} + \frac{\rho^S}{S!\left(1 - \frac{\rho}{S}\right)}\right]}.$$

In order for the system to have the stationary probability distribution given in (4) and (5), you must assume that $\lambda < \mu S$ (or $\rho < S$). What do you think would happen if $\lambda > \mu S$? [Check that when $S = 1$, (4) and (5) simplify to (12) in Sec. 20.5.]

In the case of an unlimited number of servers—for example, a self-service situation—the first formula for P_n in (4) applies for *all* n. Consequently, P_n is then a Poisson distribution, with $E[n] = \rho$. (This model is designated as $M/M/\infty$. When $S = \infty$, the conclusion that P_n is Poisson actually holds for any general service distribution, that is, for the model $M/G/\infty$.)

▶ The formulas in (4) also apply to the case with a finite limit $M \geq S$ on the total number of customers in the entire system. Then $n \leq M$ and P_0 is determined from

(i)
$$\sum_{n=0}^{M} P_n = 1.$$

Further, the stationary probabilities (4) exist even if $\lambda > \mu S$.   ◀

Operating characteristics. By elementary algebraic manipulations involving P_n, you can easily derive most of the system's operating characteristics. A useful quantity for this purpose is the probability that all the servers are busy:

(6)
$$P\,[\text{busy period}] \equiv P\,[n \geq S] = \frac{\rho^S \mu S}{S!(\mu S - \lambda)} \cdot P_0 = \frac{\rho^S}{S!\left(1 - \frac{\rho}{S}\right)} \cdot P_0.$$

Some authors call the quantity in (6) the probability of a delay—actually a better term might be **virtual delay**. The value $P[n \geq S + 1]$ represents the fraction of time that customers are actually being delayed in the system.

Define the symbols

(7)
$$\text{Poisson}\,(x = s|\rho) \equiv \frac{\rho^s e^{-\rho}}{s!} \quad \text{and} \quad \text{Poisson}\,(x < s|\rho) \equiv \sum_{x=0}^{s-1} \frac{\rho^x e^{-\rho}}{x!}.$$

You can compute (6) by the formula

(8)
$$P\,[\text{busy period}] = \frac{\text{Poisson}\,(x = S|\rho)}{\text{Poisson}\,(x = S|\rho) + \left(1 - \frac{\rho}{S}\right)\text{Poisson}\,(x < S|\rho)};$$

The tables on pages A76-A78 provide values of $P[\text{busy period}]$ for selected values of $\rho \equiv \lambda/\mu$ and S.

Then

(9)
$$E\,[\text{line length}] = P\,[\text{busy period}] \cdot \frac{\rho}{S - \rho} = \frac{\rho^S \lambda \mu S}{(\mu S - \lambda)^2} \cdot P_0$$

(10) $E\begin{bmatrix}\text{number of}\\ \text{customers}\\ \text{in service}\end{bmatrix} = \sum_{n=0}^{S-1} nP_n + S\sum_{n=s}^{\infty} P_n = \rho$

(11) $E\begin{bmatrix}\text{number of}\\ \text{customers}\\ \text{in system}\end{bmatrix} \equiv E[n] = E[\text{line length}] + E\begin{bmatrix}\text{number of}\\ \text{customers}\\ \text{in service}\end{bmatrix}.$

For this model,

(12) $\lambda E[\text{time in system}] = E[\text{number of customers in system}],$

so that dividing (11) by λ yields

(13) $E[\text{time in system}] = \dfrac{P[\text{busy period}]}{\mu S - \lambda} + \dfrac{1}{\mu},$

the first term on the right of (13) being $E[\text{time in line}]$, and the second being $E[\text{time in service}]$.

A significant property about this system is that the distribution of *departures* over an interval T is Poisson with mean λT per unit of time. Consider, then, a large-scale queuing system composed of groups of servers in tandem—that is, arranged so that the output of one group becomes the input to the next. If each group can be described by a multiple-server model like that above, the system averages can be easily found by first analyzing each group in isolation, assuming the same input rate λ, and afterwards adding the results.

Sensitivity analysis. Once again, consider the example in Sec. 20.5 of the manager of the legal office, Noah Peale, who is about to hire either two experienced typists or four novice typists. Recall that the arrival rate for documents is 36 per day, and each faster secretary can type 20 documents per day as compared to 10 per day for the newer secretaries. You found in Sec. 20.5 that if each typist operates separately and independently, then there will be an average of 9 documents on each girl's desk, and a document will spend an average of half a day on the desk of a faster secretary and a full day for a slower secretary. When the service time is a constant (variance $\equiv V = 0$), the average number of documents on each girl's desk falls to 4.95 and the expected time to .275 of a day for a faster typist, and .55 of a day for a slower one.

Now suppose that the secretaries do *not* operate separately and independently. Instead let the system be composed of a "typing pool." In this system, a single stack of documents waits to be typed; when any girl completes one document, she goes to the stack and takes the next one in the pile. Accordingly, using the table on page A76, you can find that

(14) $P[\text{busy period}] = \begin{cases}.7877 & \text{for } S = 4 \text{ and } \mu = 10 \\ .8526 & \text{for } S = 2 \text{ and } \mu = 20\end{cases}\quad (\lambda = 36).$

Therefore, from (9), (10), and (11),

(15) $E\begin{bmatrix}\text{number of} \\ \text{documents} \\ \text{in system}\end{bmatrix} = \begin{cases} 7.0887 + 3.6 = 10.6887 & \text{for } S = 4 \text{ and } \mu = 10 \\ 7.6741 + 1.8 = 9.4741 & \text{for } S = 2 \text{ and } \mu = 20, \end{cases}$

and from (13),

(16) $E[\text{time in system}] = \begin{cases} .1969 + .1 = .2969 & \text{for } S = 4 \text{ and } \mu = 10 \\ .2132 + .05 = .2632 & \text{for } S = 2 \text{ and } \mu = 20. \end{cases}$

Notice that although the probability of a document being delayed before typing is smaller when there are four secretaries, the corresponding slowness of the novice typists is more than offsetting in terms of the average number of documents as well as the average time spent in the system. Pooling the secretaries into a single system substantially reduces the average number of documents in the entire system and the average time each document spends in the system. In fact, the average time is almost that for the constant-service-time case. Also there is not much difference between having two faster or four slower typists, given that their combined service rate in the system is $S\mu = 40$.

The systems you have considered so far are the cases of $S = 2$ or $S = 4$ combined with the possibilities of each secretary operating separately or all S secretaries operating in a typing pool. Turn now to an intermediate possibility having two secretarial pools, each operating independently of the other, and consisting of two novice typists. Then, for each pool, $\lambda = \frac{36}{2} = 18$, and, for $S = 2$, $\mu = 10$,

(17) $P[\text{busy period}] = .8526$

(18) $E[\text{number of documents in each pool}] = 9.4741$

(19) $E[\text{time in system}] = .4264 + .1 = .5264.$

Consequently, the probability of a busy period and the average number of documents in each pool are the same as for the case of the two faster secretaries; but the two-pools arrangement results in twice as many documents on the average being in the entire system. Further, the expected time a document spends in the system doubles as compared to the case of $S = 2$ and $\mu = 20$.

The various comparisons in the above illustration are valid for other numerical values of the arrival rate λ, the service rate μ, and the number of servers S. In particular, given values for λ *and* μS, the $P[\text{busy period}]$ increases for smaller values of S, as does the expected number waiting in line and average time spent waiting. But the expected number in the entire system as well as average time spent in the system decreases for smaller values of S.

Depending on the application, you may be able to affect the values of λ, μ, and S and therefore select them optimally. If the associated objective function is very simple, you may be able to derive an analytic formula or construct tables and nomographs to aid in the optimization search. You may also be able to apply certain advanced algorithmic techniques, similar to those in Chap. 18.

*Priority discipline. The end of Sec. 20.5 shows how imposing a priority discipline affects the average time in line for customers of different types. Recall that Type k arrives according to a Poisson process with rate λ_k, and that the priority numbers are assigned so that $k = 1$ is the highest and $k = r$ the lowest. Here we assume that the service time distribution is exponential with rate μ for *every* type of customer. Define, as before,

$$(20) \qquad \sigma_k \equiv \sum_{j=1}^{k} \frac{\lambda_j}{\mu_j} = \frac{\sum_{j=1}^{k} \lambda_j}{\mu} \qquad \sigma_0 \equiv 0.$$

Assume $\sigma_r < S$ to ensure the system reaches equilibrium. Then

$$(21) \qquad E[\text{time in line} \mid \text{Type k}] = \frac{\dfrac{S}{\mu}}{(S - \sigma_{k-1})(S - \sigma_k)} \cdot P[\text{busy period}].$$

The average time in the system for an *arbitrary* arrival remains the same as in a system without priorities having an arrival rate $\lambda = \sum \lambda_j$.

To illustrate, consider the example of $\lambda = 36$, $S = 2$, and $\mu = 20$. In a system without any priorities, you saw in (16) that the expected time in line is .2132. Suppose now that there are two priorities with $\lambda_1 = \lambda_2 = 18$. Verify from (21) that the expected time in line for Type 1 is $(.8526/22 = .0387)$ and for Type 2 is $(.8526/2.2 = .3875)$. The smaller the value of λ_1, the smaller will be the average wait for both types.

*20.7 BIRTH-AND-DEATH PROCESS

Here we present a unified treatment of the special cases you have seen so far, and, at the same time, develop a model that assists in analyzing other cases as well. This model is termed a **birth-and-death process**.

To begin, assume the probability transition laws for the system do not change over time; that is, postulate the process to be **time-homogeneous**. The system is considered to operate continuously without any specific starting point, and is characterized at Time t by the number of customers n in the system ($n = 0, 1, 2, \ldots$). We will want to designate a particular instant of time, however, to serve as a reference point. It is convenient to let $t = 0$ be this point, and to let i be the number of customers in the system at Time 0.

Define

(1) $P_{in}(T) \equiv$ probability that the system contains n customers at Time T, given that it contains i customers at Time 0.

Because the system *is* time-homogeneous, the value of $P_{in}(h)$ for $h > 0$ not only gives the probability defined in (1) at Time h, but also the probability that the system contains n customers at Time $T + h$, given that it contains i customers at Time T.

We postulate that the $P_{in}(T)$ satisfy what are known as the **Chapman-Kolmogorov equations** for a **time-homogeneous Markov process**:

$$(2) \qquad P_{in}(T + h) = \sum_m P_{im}(T) P_{mn}(h) \quad (h > 0),$$

for every i and n. You can interpret (2) as stating that the probability of the system having n customers at Time $T + h$, given that it has i customers at Time 0, can be found by adding, over all possible m, the joint probabilities that there are m customers in the system at Time T, given the system has i customers at Time 0, and the probability that there are n customers in the system at Time $T + h$, given that the system has m customers at Time T. The so-called *Markov property* relates simply to the assumption that the only relevant information about the system at Time T is the number of customers in the system, namely, m, and not the detailed history of the process leading up to Time T. In this sense, the system is memoryless, and hence (2) represents a nontrivial assumption. [Think of an example or two in which (2) does not apply.]

The birth-and-death process is a special case of (2). Assume that for a *very* small interval of time, $h > 0$, we need only consider that at most one customer enters or leaves the system, and that

(3)
$$P_{m,m+1}(h) \doteq (\lambda_m h)(1 - \mu_m h) \doteq \lambda_m h \quad \text{for } m = 0, 1, 2, \ldots$$
$$P_{m,m-1}(h) \doteq (1 - \lambda_m h)(\mu_m h) \doteq \mu_m h \quad \text{for } m = 1, 2, \ldots,$$

so that

(4)
$$P_{mm}(h) \doteq 1 - P_{m,m-1}(h) - P_{m,m+1}(h) \doteq 1 - (\lambda_m + \mu_m)h \quad \text{for } m = 1, 2, \ldots,$$
$$P_{00}(h) \doteq 1 - P_{01}(h) \doteq 1 - \lambda_0 h \qquad\qquad\qquad\qquad \text{for } m = 0,$$

where $\lambda_m \geq 0$, for all m, and $\mu_m > 0$, for $m \geq 1$; all other $P_{mk}(h) = 0$. In other words, for a very small interval of time, h, the probability that the number of customers increases from m to $m + 1$ is approximately $\lambda_m h$, and that it decreases from m to $m - 1$ is approximately $\mu_m h$. Given our approximation, the probability that the number of customers remains at m can be written as approximately 1 minus these two values. The approximations can be made exact by adding terms that have coefficients h^k, where $k \geq 2$.

The values λ_m and μ_m may be thought of as arrival and departure rates, respectively, when there are m customers in the system. It is important that you realize no assumption has been made about the number of servers or the queue discipline in the system. The postulates refer only to probabilities of an arrival and a departure.

Substituting (3) and (4) into (2) yields for $n \geq 1$

(5)
$$P_{in}(T + h) \doteq P_{i,n-1}(T)P_{n-1,n}(h) + P_{in}(T)P_{n,n}(h) + P_{i,n+1}(T)P_{n+1,n}(h)$$
$$\doteq P_{i,n-1}(T)\lambda_{n-1}h + P_{in}(T)[1 - (\lambda_n + \mu_n)h]$$
$$+ P_{i,n+1}(T)\mu_{n+1}h \quad (h \text{ small}).$$

Bringing the term $P_{in}(T)$ to the left-hand side of (5), dividing by h, and letting $h \to 0$, yields the so-called **forward system of differential equations**

(6)
$$\frac{dP_{in}}{dT} = \lambda_{n-1}P_{i,n-1}(T) - (\lambda_n + \mu_n)P_{in}(T) + \mu_{n+1}P_{i,n+1}(T).$$

The relation (6) is exact because the terms neglected in (5) drop out as $h \to 0$. You can also use (6) to represent the case of $n = 0$ by letting $\lambda_{-1} \equiv 0$ and $\mu_0 \equiv 0$;

write the equation for $n = 0$. Thus (6) represents a system of equations corresponding to $n = 0, 1, 2, \ldots$, where i is taken as a given initial condition.

▶The term "forward" refers to the fact that the equations were derived by looking at the second interval of time $(T, T + h)$ and using (3) and (4) to approximate the transition probabilities in this small interval. You can also derive *backward* equations by interchanging T and h on the right of (2), and then using (3) and (4) to approximate $P_{im}(h)$. In the resulting differential equations for dP_{in}/dT, the value of n at Time T is taken as given, and i at Time 0 is considered as the variable, so that $i = 0, 1, 2, \ldots$. ◀

Review. Let us pause here to see that (6) really does include queuing models that you have already examined. Consider the pure-birth model with Poisson input, treated in Sec. 20.3. For that situation, $\lambda_n = \lambda$ and $\mu_n = 0$, for all n. Assuming that $i = 0$ at Time 0, (6) becomes

$$(7) \qquad \frac{dP_{0n}}{dT} = \lambda P_{0, n-1}(T) - \lambda P_{0n}(T).$$

The solution for any i is

$$(8) \qquad P_{in}(T) = \frac{(\lambda T)^{(n-i)} e^{-\lambda T}}{(n - i)!} \quad \text{for } n \geq i,$$

which agrees with (10) and (xi) of Sec. 20.3 for $i = 0$.

Next, consider the pure-death model in Sec. 20.4 having a single-server with exponential service times and M customers in the system at Time 0. For that situation, $\lambda_n = 0$, for all n, and $\mu_n = \mu$, for $1 \leq n \leq M$, so that (6) becomes

$$(9) \qquad \frac{dP_{Mn}}{dT} = -\mu M_{Mn}(T) + \mu P_{M, n+1}(T) \quad \text{for } 1 \leq n < M$$

$$(10) \qquad \frac{dP_{MM}}{dT} = -\mu P_{MM}(T) \qquad\qquad \text{for } n = M,$$

which has the solution $P_{Mn}(T) = P_n(T)$ as given by (13) in Sec. 20.4. Suppose, instead of there being a single server, each of the M customers can start service at Time 0. Then $\mu_n = n\mu$ for $0 \leq n \leq M$; and check that (6) gives the same results as (20) and (21) in Sec. 20.4.

Finally, consider the single-server model with Poisson input and exponential service treated in Sec. 20.5. Verify that for $\lambda_n = \lambda$, for $n \geq 0$, and $\mu_n = \mu$, for $n \geq 1$, the system (6) is the same as (4) and (5) in Sec. 20.5. Recall that the subscript i in (6) designating the number of customers in the system at Time 0 was suppressed in (4) and (5) of Sec. 20.5, since the emphasis there was on obtaining stationary probabilities. [To obtain an explicit transient solution to (6), you must use the fact that $P_{ii}(0) = 1$, and all other $P_{in}(0) = 0$.]

Steady-state solution. The forward equations (6) depend on both i and T. Now suppose $T \to \infty$, and assume that in the limit the system reaches statistical equilibrium. For the limiting process, the influence of the value of i at Time 0 vanishes, and hence the subscript i can once again be suppressed in the probability notation. As in Sec. 20.5, you can solve for the equilibrium or stationary values of P_n by setting the time derivatives in (6) equal to 0:

(11) $0 = \lambda_{n-1}P_{n-1} - (\lambda_n + \mu_n)P_n + \mu_{n+1}P_{n+1}$ for $n \geq 1$

(12) $0 = -\lambda_0 P_0 + \mu_1 P_1$ for $n = 0$.

Starting with $n = 0$, this system of difference equations can be solved recursively, yielding the general result (assuming all $\mu_n > 0$, for $n \geq 1$)

(13) $$P_n = \frac{\lambda_{n-1}}{\mu_n} \cdot \frac{\lambda_{n-2}}{\mu_{n-1}} \cdots \frac{\lambda_0}{\mu_1} \cdot P_0 \quad \text{for } n \geq 1.$$

[If there is a number N such that $\mu_N = 0$ and $\mu_n > 0$ for $n > N$, and if $i > N$ at Time 0, then $P_n = 0$, for $n < N$, and (13) is easily modified by adding N to all the subscripts.]

The value of P_0 is determined from

(14) $$1 = P_0 + \sum_{n=1}^{\infty} P_n = P_0\left(1 + \frac{\lambda_0}{\mu_1} + \frac{\lambda_1}{\mu_2} \cdot \frac{\lambda_0}{\mu_1} + \frac{\lambda_2}{\mu_3} \cdot \frac{\lambda_1}{\mu_2} \cdot \frac{\lambda_0}{\mu_1} + \cdots\right),$$

where we postulate for all the models to be considered in this text that the infinite series on the right of (14) converges to a finite value. For example, in the single-server, Poisson input, exponential service model of Sec. 20.5,

(15) $1 + \dfrac{\lambda_0}{\mu_1} + \dfrac{\lambda_1}{\mu_2} \cdot \dfrac{\lambda_0}{\mu_1} + \cdots = 1 + \rho + \rho^2 + \cdots = \dfrac{1}{1 - \rho}$ for $\rho < 1$,

so that

(16) $P_0 = 1 - \rho$.

An easily verified sufficient condition ensuring that the series on the right of (14) converges is that for n large enough, say $n \geq N$, all $\lambda_n \leq r\mu_{n+1}$, where $0 < r < 1$.

In the case of a finite limit M on the total number of persons in the system, you can let $\lambda_n = 0$, for $n \geq M$ in (11) and (12), so that $P_n = 0$, for $n > M$ in (13). Consequently, P_0 can always be easily determined from a finite-valued summation analogous to (14).

Examples. We now illustrate the usefulness of the birth-and-death process equations.

Case i. Suppose customers arrive according to a Poisson process with input rate λ, but each customer serves himself, according to an exponential distribution with rate μ. (This situation may be conceived of as a system with an infinite number of servers, and is designated accordingly as $M/M/\infty$.) Then $\lambda_n = \lambda$ and $\mu_n = n\mu$—recall this value for μ_n was established in (17) of Sec. 20.4. Consequently,

(17) $1 + \dfrac{\lambda_0}{\mu_1} + \dfrac{\lambda_1}{\mu_2} \cdot \dfrac{\lambda_0}{\mu_1} + \dfrac{\lambda_2}{\mu_3} \cdot \dfrac{\lambda_1}{\mu_2} \cdot \dfrac{\lambda_0}{\mu_1} + \cdots = 1 + \dfrac{\rho}{1} + \dfrac{\rho^2}{2 \cdot 1} + \cdots = e^\rho$,

so that

(18) $$P_0 = e^{-\rho} \quad \text{and} \quad P_n = \frac{\rho^n e^{-\rho}}{n!} \quad \text{(Poisson distribution)}.$$

(Another system in which $\mu_n = n\mu$ consists of a single server that speeds up its service rate proportionately as the number of persons in the system gets larger.)

Case ii. Suppose there is a single exponential server so that $\mu_n = \mu$, for $n \geq 1$. But customers who are about to enter the system are discouraged by a long line in such a way that $\lambda_n = \lambda/(n + 1)$. Verify that this assumption also leads to the results given in (17) and (18).

Case iii. Consider the multiple-server model in Sec. 20.6. There

(19) $$\lambda_n = \lambda \quad \text{for } n \geq 0.$$

Applying the result (17) in Sec. 20.4, we may conclude that the departure rate is $n\mu$ when there are $n \leq S$ customers in the system, and $S\mu$ if $n > S$, so that

(20) $$\mu_n = \begin{cases} n\mu & \text{for } 1 \leq n \leq S \\ S\mu & \text{for } n > S. \end{cases}$$

You can verify that the difference equations (3) in Sec. 20.6 agree with (11) and (12) above as does the corresponding solution (4) and (5) with the formulas (13) and (14) above.

Case iv. So far, all the examples assumed, in effect, an unlimited population from which arrivals occur. Now consider a model in which the source population is finite, and therefore the rate of arrivals decreases as the number *in* the system grows. An industrial situation of some practical significance that meets this description is a factory containing a group of machines that occasionally break down and require repair. (In queuing theory literature such a problem is sometimes referred to as a **machine interference model**.)

Let

$$M = \text{number of machines} \quad \text{and} \quad R = \text{number of repairmen}.$$

Assume that if a machine is operative, then the time at which it breaks down is described by an exponential probability distribution that has rate λ and is independent of the operating behavior of the other machines. Suppose further that any nonfunctioning machine requires the attention of only a single repairman, and that the service time probability distribution is exponential with the same rate μ for every repairman and every machine.

Suppose n machines have broken down, and hence $M - n$ are operative. Then in a *very* small interval of time, $h > 0$, the approximate probability that one of the operative machines breaks down can be calculated as usual:

(21) $$P\begin{bmatrix} \text{one out of } M - n \text{ machines} \\ \text{breaks down in an interval } h \end{bmatrix} \doteq (M - n)\lambda h.$$

By the same token,

(22) $\quad P\begin{bmatrix} \text{one out of } n \text{ inoperative} \\ \text{machines completes} \\ \text{service in an interval } h \end{bmatrix} \doteq n\mu h \quad \text{for } 1 \leq n \leq R.$

State why the probability in (22) is $R\mu h$, for $R < n \leq M$. Then in terms of a birth-and-death process, you can define

(23)
$$\lambda_n = \begin{cases} (M - n)\lambda & \text{for } 0 \leq n \leq M \\ 0 & \text{for } n > M \end{cases}$$

$$\mu_n = \begin{cases} n\mu & \text{for } 1 \leq n \leq R \\ R\mu & \text{for } R < n \leq M. \end{cases}$$

Then the difference equations in (11) and (12) become

(24)
$$0 = -M\lambda P_0 + \mu P_1 \qquad\qquad\qquad\qquad\qquad \text{for } n = 0$$

$$0 = (M - n + 1)\lambda P_{n-1} - [(M - n)\lambda + n\mu]P_n + (n + 1)\mu P_{n+1}$$
$$\text{for } 1 \leq n < R$$

$$0 = (M - n + 1)\lambda P_{n-1} - [(M - n)\lambda + R\mu]P_n + R\mu P_{n+1}$$
$$\text{for } R \leq n \leq M,$$

and letting $\rho \equiv \lambda/\mu$, (13) can be written as

(25)
$$P_n = \binom{M}{n}\rho^n P_0 \qquad\qquad \text{for } 0 \leq n \leq R$$

$$P_n = \binom{M}{n}\rho^n \cdot \frac{n!}{R!R^{n-R}} \cdot P_0 \quad \text{for } R < n \leq M,$$

where $\binom{M}{n} = M!/n!(M - n)!$ is the standard *binomial coefficient* and P_0 is computed from the relation

(26)
$$\sum_{n=0}^{M} P_n = 1.$$

There are no simple expressions for the expected number of nonoperative machines, but in any specific case, the value of $E[n]$ can easily be computed directly using the values for P_n in (25).

*Model interpretation. The probabilistic structure of each queuing model in the preceding sections was described in terms of interarrival and service time distributions. For the birth-and-death process model, no ambiguity arises in interpreting the corresponding interarrival and service distribution assumptions insofar as the model is applied to situations in which the input *is* a Poisson process, and the service time for each server *is* an exponential distribution. But when λ_n is defined, for example, as in *Case ii* above, there is no simple way of providing a specified form for the interarrival distribution. The reason is that the time between successive arrivals depends on the number of customers in the system, which in turn depends on the service events. A similar remark holds with regard to defining a service time distribution. (For example, such difficulty occurs when μ_n is specified, as at the end of *Case i*, to be the service rate for a single server and dependent on the number of persons in the system.) Therefore only in special cases are you able to interpret the above birth-and-death model as being a combination of Poisson input and exponential service times.

By the same token, it is difficult to work out the probability distribution and expectations of the time a customer spends in the system, even when the discipline is first come, first served.

*20.8 OTHER QUEUING MODELS

Most of the results in this chapter have pertained to queuing models in which arrivals are described by a Poisson input process and the service times for each server are given by an exponential distribution. All of the models have assumed there is a single waiting line, and customers are processed on a first come, first served basis. (The situation of multiple waiting lines was treated approximately as several systems operating side by side and independently of each other.)

It is not too difficult to extend such results to other cases containing minor variations on the assumptions. For example, it is fairly easy to encompass the phenomenon of *balking* (a tendency for a customer not to enter the system as the line gets longer) and *impatience* or *reneging* (a tendency for a customer to leave the system before being served). (The required approach makes only minor modifications in the specification of λ_n and μ_n in the birth-and-death model of Sec. 20.7.) In Appendix III we treat several examples in which the interarrival and service times are other than exponentially distributed. (Some of the techniques that will be illustrated can also be used to analyze cases in which there are bulk arrivals or bulk service.) It is also possible to obtain usable formulas to handle different, but simple, queuing disciplines, such as random service or last come, first served. Such variations, however, are not considered in this book.

In any particular industrial application, it is the exception rather than the rule that any of these models precisely represents reality. Therefore you should use these models primarily for general insights and guidance in determining how sensitive a system's operations may be to the relevant decision alternatives. If the resultant approximate analysis shows that the economic impact of a wrong decision may be serious, you should then augment your analysis by applying computer simulation to explore in further detail the specific questions of system design.

REVIEW EXERCISES

1 Suggest two or there queuing situations that you think might warrant a scientific study. State in which of the two categories described at the beginning of Sec. 20.1 your suggested applications might fall. Explain the decisions that might be made as a result of a scientific study, and how you would distinguish a good decision from a poor one.

2 In each part below, suggest one or two queuing situations that illustrate the indicated characteristic. (Be imaginative and do not use the examples already given in the text.)

(a) Customers arriving singly.
(b) Bulk arrivals.
(c) Predetermined arrivals.
(d) Completely random arrivals.
(e) Unlimited source population.
(f) Finite source population.
(g) Customers that always join the system when they arrive.
(h) Customers that may balk when they arrive.
(i) First come, first served discipline.
(j) Last come, first served discipline.
(k) Random service discipline.
(l) Special priority service discipline.
(m) Customers that always remain in the line after joining it.
(n) Customers that may renege after joining a line.
(o) Single waiting line.
(p) Parallel waiting lines.
(q) Customers that may jockey for position.
(r) Servers in parallel.
(s) Servers in series (tandem).
(t) Service time mechanism that is independent of the line length.
(u) Service time mechanism that is influenced by the line length.

3 Consider three or four of the queuing situations that you suggested in exercise 2.

(a) State what you think are the four or five most important operating characteristics to measure in assessing the performance of these systems.
(b) Also suggest a variety of managerial options that can be selected in designing these systems to operate efficiently. (Be sure to define what you mean by "efficient.")

4 (a) Consider the negative exponential distribution given by (2) in Sec. 20.3. Show that the mean equals $1/\lambda$ and the variance $1/\lambda^2$.
(b) Verify the mathematical manipulations that establish in (3) and (4) the memoryless property of the exponential distribution.
(c) Verify that the sum of n independent values drawn from the same exponential density (2) has a gamma distribution, as given by (8).
(d) Verify the probability statement in (9) by repeatedly applying integration by parts.
(e) Use (10) to state the probability of one arrival in an interval of length $T = h$. Then apply a Taylor series expansion and verify the approximation in (7).
(f) Show that the mean and variance of a Poisson distribution are as given in (11).
(g) Verify the equality in (12) from (9) and (10). Give a verbal interpretation of (12).
(h) Show that replacing λn in the Erlang distribution (14) by λ yields the gamma distribution (8).

5 Compare Figs. 20.2a and 20.2b and discuss how the shape and concentration of probability mass shift with variations in n and λ.

6 Consider the pure-death model in Sec. 20.4.

    (a) Derive (12) by using reasoning analogous to that employed in obtaining (11).

    (b) Show that the probabilities (13) and (14) satisfy the differential equations (11) and (12).

    (c) Determine how $P_n(T)$ behaves as T grows without bound, for $n = 1, 2, \ldots, M$. For $n = 0$. [*Suggestion:* use the example $M = 2$ and $\mu = 1$, and draw a graph of each $P_n(T)$.]

*7 Consider the self-service model in Sec. 20.5.

    (a) Justify in detail the approximations in (17) and (18).

    (b) Justify in detail the approximation in (19), and show how to obtain (20).

    (c) Verify that the binomial probability distribution (22) satisfies the differential equations (20) and (21).

    (d) Determine how $P_n(T)$ behaves as T grows without bound, for $n = 0, 1, \ldots, M$. [*Suggestion:* Use the example $M = 2$ and $\mu = 1$, and draw a graph of each $P_n(T)$.]

    (e) Suppose $M = 1$. Compare the probabilities in (13) and (14) with those in (22) for $n = 0, 1$.

8 Consider the single-server model with Poisson input and exponential service, discussed in Sec. 20.5.

    (a) Perform the detailed algebraic steps to derive (4) from (3). Also show how to obtain (5).

  *(b) Devise a situation in which each $P_n(T)$ approaches a limiting value as $T \to \infty$ but $E[n]$ is not finite. Comment on why the term statistical equilibrium is not applied to such a case. [*Hint:* consider $\lambda > \mu$.]

    (c) Give a verbal interpretation of the assumption in (6).

    (d) Verify that the stationary probabilities P_n in (10) satisfy the difference equations in (7).

  *(e) Perform the detailed algebraic steps to derive the formulas $E[n]$, Var $[n]$, and $P[n \geq N]$ shown in (13) for the geometric distribution.

    (f) Provide the detailed justification and show the intermediate algebraic steps for each equality in (15) that gives $E[\text{line length}]$.

    (g) Perform the detailed algebraic steps to derive the formula for the waiting time density $h(w)$ in (19).

    (h) Perform the detailed algebraic steps to derive the formulas for $E[\text{time in line}]$ in (21).

9 Consider the secretaries example in Sec. 20.5. How does this simple model approximate the real situation? Why would the average delay for a document tend to be smaller in actuality than the delay given by (20)? If you were the office manager, what else would you take into account in deciding between the two alternatives?

10 Consider the secretaries example in Sec. 20.5. In each part below, determine the average number of documents on each girl's desk and in the entire system. Calculate the average time for a document to be in the system and the average length of the busy periods.

(a) $S = 1$ and $\mu = 40$.
(b) $S = 10$ and $\mu = 4$.

11 Suppose in the secretaries example in Sec. 20.5, there are an average of 38 documents to be typed per day. For each alternative in the text, determine the average number of documents on each girl's desk and in the entire system. Calculate the average time for a document to be in the system and the average length of the busy periods.

*12 Consider the finite-queue model discussed in Sec. 20.5.

(a) Give a plausible explanation of why statistical equilibrium is reached for *any* value of the intensity ratio λ/μ.
(b) Verify that when $\lambda < \mu$ and $M \to \infty$, P_n in (23) agrees with (12).
*(c) Derive E[number of customers in system] using the probabilities P_n, for $\lambda \neq \mu$, as given in (23). Do the same for $\lambda = \mu$.
(d) For $\rho = .7, .8, .9, .95$, find the corresponding value of M such that E[number of customers in system] in (24) is within .01 of the same operating characteristic as given by (13).
(e) Determine the limiting value of E[number of customers in system] in (24) as ρ grows arbitrarily large.
(f) Show that (23) is the limiting value of P_n for $\lambda \neq \mu$ for as ρ approaches 1.
(g) Let $M = 3$. Calculate E[number of customers in system] for $\rho = 1, 2, 5, 10$.

13 Consider the single-server model with Poisson input and arbitrary service distribution, as described in Sec. 20.5.

(a) Verify that when the service time is exponential, then (29), (30), and (32) reduce to (13), (15), and (20), respectively.
(b) Assume $\mu = 10$. Calculate the operating characteristics (29), (30), and (32), for $\rho = .7, .8, .9$, and .95 with $V = 0$.
(c) Rework part (b) with $V = .01$.
(d) Rework part (b) with $V = .1$.
(e) Rework part (b) with $V = 1$.

*14 Consider the single-server model with priority discipline, as discussed at the end of Sec. 20.5.

(a) Verify that when $r = 1$, (35) reduces to E[time in line] in (32).
(b) Verify the sample calculations in (37).
(c) Suppose $\lambda_1 = \lambda_2 = 9$ in (37). Find the expected time in line for Types 1 and 2 customers. Determine what happens when $\lambda_1 = 3$ and when $\lambda_1 = 15$ (remember $\lambda_1 + \lambda_2 = 18$).
(d) Suppose $\lambda_1 = \lambda_2 = 9$, $\mu_1 = 30$, $\mu_2 = 15$, and the service distributions are exponential. Determine the expected time in line for Types 1 and 2 customers.
(e) Suppose $\lambda_1 = \lambda_2 = 9$, $\mu_1 = \mu_2 = 20$, and let $V_1 = 0$ and $V_2 = 1/20^2$. Determine the expected time in line for Types 1 and 2 customers.

(f) Rework part (e), except let $V_1 = 1/20^2$ and $V_2 = 0$.

(g) Suppose $\lambda_1 = \lambda_2 = 9$, $\mu_1 = 30$, $\mu_2 = 15$, and let $V_1 = 0$ and $V_2 = 1/15^2$. Determine the expected time in line for Types 1 and 2 customers.

(h) Rework part (g), except let $V_1 = 1/30^2$ and $V_2 = 0$.

(i) Suppose there are three classifications, where $\lambda_1 = \lambda_2 = \lambda_3 = 6$. Assume that the service rate $\mu = 20$ applies to all three types and that the service distributions are exponential. Determine the expected time in line for each of the three types of customers.

(j) Rework part (i), except let $\mu_1 = 33\frac{1}{3}$ and $\mu_2 = \mu_3 = 16\frac{2}{3}$.

(k) Rework part (i), except let $\mu_1 = 40$, $\mu_2 = 20$, and $\mu_3 = 13\frac{1}{3}$.

15 Consider the multiple-server model in Sec. 20.6.

(a) Verify that the probabilities P_n in (4) and (5) satisfy the difference equations (3).

(b) Check that when $S = 1$, the probabilities in (4) and (5) reduce to the formula in (12) of Sec. 20.5.

(c) Give the intermediate algebraic steps to justify the statement that when the number of servers is unlimited (self-service), then P_n in (4) is a Poisson distribution. (*Hint:* use a series expansion for e^x.)

*16 Consider the multiple-server model in Sec. 20.6. In each part below, show the detailed algebraic steps justifying the formula that is cited in the text.

(a) P[busy period] in (6).   (c) E[line length] in (9).

(b) P[busy period] in (8).   (d) E[number of servers] in (10).

17 Consider the secretaries example where the girls work in a typing pool, as in Sec. 20.6. Suppose the arrival rate is $\lambda = 38$. Calculate the P[busy period], E[number of documents in system], and E[time in system], for each case below.

(a) $S = 4$ and $\mu = 10$.   (c) $S = 1$ and $\mu = 40$.

(b) $S = 2$ and $\mu = 20$.   (d) $S = 10$ and $\mu = 4$.

*18 Consider the multiple-server model with priority discipline discussed at the end of Sec. 20.6. In each part below, apply (21) to find the expected time in line for each Type k.

(a) Let $k = 2$, $\lambda_1 = \lambda_2 = 18$, $\mu = 10$, and $S = 4$.

(b) Rework part (a), except let $S = 1$ and $\mu = 40$.

(c) Rework part (a), except let $S = 10$ and $\mu = 4$.

(d) Let $k = 3$, $\lambda_1 = \lambda_2 = \lambda_3 = 6$, $\mu = 20$, and $S = 2$.

*19 Consider the birth-and-death process in Sec. 20.7.

(a) Substitute the approximate probabilities in (3) and (4) into the Chapman-Kolmogorov equations (2) and verify the result in (5). Also exhibit the intermediate steps yielding the differential equations (6).

(b) Write the equation in (6) corresponding to $n = 0$.

(c) Examine the pure-birth model for an arbitrary i, and write the exact expression for (6). [For $i = 0$, (6) is given by (7).] Show that (8) satisfies the differential equations.

(d) Show that $P_{Mn}(T) = P_n(T)$, as given by (13) in Sec. 20.4, is the solution to (9) and (10) for the pure-death model with a single server.

(e) Examine the pure-death model where all M customers start service at Time 0. Check that (6) gives the same results as (20) and (21) in Sec. 20.4.

(f) Examine the single-server model with Poisson input and exponential service in Sec. 20.5. Verify that the system (6) is the same as (4) and (5) in Sec. 20.5.

(g) Check that the stationary probabilities P_n in (13) satisfy the difference equations (11) and (12).

(h) Explain why $P_n = 0$ for $n < N$, where N is a number such that $\mu_N = 0$ and $\mu_n > 0$, for $n > N$, assuming that $i > N$ at Time 0.

(i) Verify that if there is an N such that $\lambda_n \leq r\mu_{n+1}$, where $0 < r < 1$, for $n \geq N$, then the series on the right of (14) converges.

*20 Consider the birth-and-death process discussed in Sec. 20.7.

(a) Examine *Case ii* and show that the probabilities P_n are given by (17) and (18).

(b) Examine *Case iii* and show that the difference equations (3) in Sec. 20.6 agree with (11) and (12), as does the solution (4) and (5) with the formulas (13) and (14).

(c) Examine *Case iv*, the machine interference model. Explain why the probability in (22) is $R\mu h$, for $R < n \leq M$. Verify that substituting (23) into the difference equations (11) and (12) yields (24). Also verify that (13) leads to the solution (25).

21 Explain your understanding of the following terms:

operating characteristics	periodic (regular, constant) arrivals
input process	service time
bulk arrivals	exponential service
balk	pure-death model
reneging (impatience)	service rate μ
queue discipline	*self-service model
first come, first served	*Kendall's notation
last come, first served	single-server model
random service order	multiple-server model
servers (or channels)	transient solution
jockey	statistical equilibrium
servers in parallel	equilibrium (stationary) probabilities
servers in series (tandem)	traffic intensity ρ
systems synthesis	utilization factor ρ
birth (arrival) process	difference equations
death process	*finite-queue model
renewal process	*loss-delay system
recurrent events	Pollaczek-Khintchine formulas
completely random arrivals	*priority discipline
stationary (homogeneous) time process	*preemptive priority
memoryless property	busy period
interarrival time	virtual delay
exponential arrivals (Poisson input, Markovian input)	*birth-and-death process
	*Chapman-Kolmogorov equations

pure-birth model
arrival rate λ
Erlang arrivals

*time-homogeneous Markov process
*forward system of differential equations
*machine interference model.

FORMULATION AND COMPUTATIONAL EXERCISES

22 Suppose an item held in inventory is replenished according to the rule "when the inventory level falls *below* 1, order 10 items." Assume that the current level of inventory is 3, that items are demanded one at a time, and that the time between demands is exponentially distributed with a mean rate of two per week.

   (a) What is the probability distribution of the number of items demanded in a two-week period? (Give both the form of the distribution and the values of its parameters.)

   (b) What is the probability that no replenishment will take place during the coming week? During the coming two weeks? (Write the detailed formulas for these probabilities; calculate the numerical values if you have access to the appropriate tables.)

23 Consider a production process with two machines, A and B, in tandem. The output of items from the first machine, A, is Poisson, with the rate of 10 per hour. The second machine, B, processes each item with exponential service time at the rate of 12 per hour. There is a congestion problem when more than two items are waiting to be processed on Machine B.

   (a) Calculate the fraction of time that the system is congested.

 *(b) Suppose Machine A is turned off when ever more than two items are waiting to be processed by Machine B. Explain why your answer in part (a) overestimates the fraction of time that Machine A is turned off. Calculate the correct probability. (Be sure to indicate the specific queuing model you use.)

*24 The P. Kaboo Camera Store tries to keep in stock only one unit of a very expensive lens. When the lens is sold, the store reorders a new one. Assume that, on the average, the store has one customer in four weeks who wants to buy such a lens; if the lens is out of stock, the customer goes elsewhere. What is the probability of the lens being out of stock if the average replenishment time is one week? Two weeks? Four weeks? (Assume the customer interarrival and replenishment time probability distributions are exponential.)

25 Consider a single-server model with Poisson input and a customer arrival rate of 30 per hour. Currently, service is provided by a mechanism that takes *exactly* 1.5 minutes. Suppose the system can instead be served by a mechanism that has an exponential service time distribution. What must be the mean service time for this mechanism in order to ensure the same average time a customer spends in the system? The same average number of customers in the system?

26 Let the value of M denote the "degree of service" offered by a single server. The value $M = 1$ represents a minimal degree of service, and larger values of M represent more

thorough and longer-lasting service. Suppose that the form of the service time distribution is gamma, given by (16) in Sec. 20.4, where $\mu = 1$. Note that both the mean and variance of the service time distribution depend linearly on the "degree of service" parameter M. Suppose the arrival rate is $\lambda = .8$, for $M = 1$, and assume that for $M > 1$, the arrival rate decreases; interarrival times are exponentially distributed. The reason for this effect on the arrival rate is that as the degree of service increases, such service is required less often. In each part below, determine the arrival rate such that the expected number of customers in the system is the same as for $M = 1$ and $\lambda = .8$.

(a) $M = 2$.
(b) $M = 4$.
(c) $M = 8$.

27 The Schmerz Auto Rental Company must choose between operating one of two types of service shops for maintaining its cars. It estimates that cars will arrive at the maintenance facility on the average of one every 40 minutes (assume this rate is virtually independent of which facility is chosen). In the first type of shop, there are dual facilities operating in parallel; each facility can service a car in 30 minutes on the average. In the second type, there is a single facility, but it can service a car in 15 minutes on the average. Assume that each minute a car must spend in the shop reduces contribution to profit by one monetary unit. Let C_1 and C_2 be the cost per minute of operating the first and second type facilities, respectively. Find the value of $C_2 - C_1$ such that Schmerz would be indifferent between operating the two shops.

28 Dusty Page, the Head Librarian of the Free Kowt College, is considering staffing an extra checkout desk in the main library. Up to now, two desks have been in operation. On the average, one student arrived every two minutes, and the total checkout time (that is, time in line plus in service) averaged a minute. The College has just become co-educational, and with the influx of female students, Page expects an increased birth rate in the system. Determine the value of the arrival rate such that three checkout desks still ensure an average total checkout time of a minute. Assume that the multiple-server model in Sec. 20.6 can be used to yield good approximations.

29 The Gabby Company has leased three WATS ("wide area telephone service") lines to enable its executives to make toll-free long distance calls. Let c be the cost per hour per WATS line. Suppose that the frequency of calls per hour is described by a Poisson distribution with mean 10, and the lengths of the calls are exponentially distributed with mean 15 minutes. Let w denote the cost per hour of executive waiting time (that is, time waiting until one of the lines is free). Let $c = 1$ and determine the range of values for w that will make the decision to lease *three* WATS lines optimal.

30 The manager of the Hippon Drug Store is remodeling his facility and is considering three ways of organizing his branded-items business. The first way is to employ a fast clerk to wait on all customers. Assume such a clerk serves customers exponentially at an average rate of two minutes per customer. The second way is to employ two moderately fast clerks to wait on all customers. Assume each serves customers exponentially at an average rate of four minutes per customer. The third way is to use a self-service system in which each customer waits on himself. Self-service, at an average

rate of six minutes, is slower than clerk service. The manager wants to calculate the average number of customers in the store, the average time each spends in the store, and the average time each spends waiting for service, under each way of organizing. Assume that customers arrive completely randomly, one at a time, at the rate of 15 per hour. Calculate the operating characteristics of interest to the manager. Also determine these characteristics assuming that the fast clerk could service each customer in *exactly* two minutes time.

31 The Paine N. B. Heind Infirmary of Ye Owl College has noticed that each day two students, on the average, arrive in need of hospital care. Such a student requires, on the average, a three-day confinement to bed. Assume that interarrival times and service times are both exponentially distributed.

  (a) What is the probability distribution of the number of students occupying hospital beds? What is the associated average number? (Be sure to indicate which model in the text you are applying to derive your answer.)

  (b) Suppose there are five students in the hospital at the start of a day. How many of these students, on the average, will remain in the hospital at the same time tomorrow? Three days from today? Seven days from today?

*32 In each part below, apply (13) and (14) in the birth-and-death model in Sec. 20.7 to find the equilibrium probabilities P_n.

  (a) $\lambda_0 = 1, \lambda_1 = \frac{1}{2}, \lambda_2 = \frac{1}{4}, \lambda_n = 0$, for $n \geq 3$; $\mu_n = 1$, for all $n \geq 1$.

  (b) $\lambda_0 = \frac{1}{4}, \lambda_1 = \frac{1}{2}, \lambda_2 = 1, \lambda_n = 0$, for $n \geq 3$; $\mu_n = 1$, for all $n \geq 1$.

  (c) $\lambda_n = 1$, for $n = 0, 1, 2$, and $\lambda_n = 0$, for $n \geq 3$; $\mu_1 = 1, \mu_2 = 2, \mu_3 = 4$.

  (d) $\lambda_n = 1$, for $n = 0, 1, 2$, and $\lambda_n = 0$, for $n \geq 3$; $\mu_1 = 4, \mu_2 = 2, \mu_3 = 1$.

*33 The Nockov and Weldon Machine Shop operates three delicate pieces of equipment, each of which breaks down on the average of once every 2.5 hours. A single repairman is needed to service a broken machine and requires 45 minutes, on the average, to repair the equipment. Assume the machine interference model (*Case iv*) in Sec. 20.7 applies. In each part below, calculate the equilibrium probability that all the machines are in good working order, and the expected number of machines that are inoperative.

  (a) The shop employs only one repairman.

  (b) The shop employs two repairmen.

  (c) Suggest the various costs that you would measure to determine an optimal choice between one and two repairmen. Indicate the appropriate operating characteristics you would calculate to ascertain the expected cost for each alternative, and display a formula for the expected cost.

MIND-EXPANDING EXERCISES

Exercises 34 through 39 refer to the birth-and-death model in Sec. 20.7. In each exercise, define the appropriate values for λ_n and μ_n, and exhibit the linear difference equations that yield the equilibrium probabilities. You will find it necessary in a few of these exercises to adapt the logic used to develop the difference equations in Sec. 20.7 in order to accommodate a more complex description of the states of the system.

34 Consider a single-server model with exponential interarrival times and exponential service. Suppose, however, that there are bulk arrivals, that is, when an arrival *event* occurs, r customers enter the system with probability q_r, $r = 1, 2, \ldots, R$, where R is the largest group that ever enters.

35 Consider the following single-server system with Poisson input and exponential service. When a customer arrives at the system and sees n persons present, he joins the system with probability r_n, and balks with probability $1 - r_n$. Also, when n persons are in the system, the rate of departure due to reneging is g_n (that is, in a relatively small interval of time, $h > 0$, the probability of one customer in line departing *prior* to service is $g_n h$); note $g_0 = g_1 = 0$.

36 Consider *Case iv* in Sec. 20.7 and suppose $M = R$.
   (a) Check that the formula for P_n in (25) for $0 \le n \le R = M$ is appropriate.
   (b) Show how P_n can be written as a *binomial distribution* with parameter p. Exhibit a formula for the mean number of inoperative machines that explicitly indicates the dependence on the failure and service rates.

37 Consider the following single-server preemptive priority system. Two types of customers arrive at the system: Type 1 at the rate λ_1 and Type 2 at the rate λ_2. Type 1 has complete priority over Type 2. Service will be terminated on a Type 2 customer (implying there are no Type 1 customers waiting in the system) when a Type 1 customer arrives; service will then commence immediately on the Type 1 customer. Service on the "bumped" customer resumes after the system no longer contains any Type 1 customers. Service rates for Types 1 and 2 are μ_1 and μ_2, respectively. (*Hint:* let the state of the system be indicated by both the number of Type 1 and the number of Type 2 customers in the system.)

38 Consider a two-server model with Poisson input (rate λ) and exponential output, except let the rate for the first server be μ_1 and for the second server be μ_2, where $\mu_1 \neq \mu_2$. (*Suggestion:* when the number of customers n in the system equals 0 or is greater than 2, let the probability P_n have its usual meaning; when the number of customers equals 1, let P_{01} denote the state that the first server is free but the second is busy, and let P_{10} denote the opposite condition.)

39 Consider the following system of two channels in tandem (series). Arrivals to Channel 1 are at the rate λ (Poisson input distribution). Service rates at Channels 1 and 2 are μ_1 and μ_2, respectively, and service times are exponentially distributed. When a customer finishes service in Channel 1, he then requires service at Channel 2. If Channel 2 is occupied with another customer, the customer in Channel 1 has to wait where he is, and hence blocks the service of any customer that is waiting in the line in front of Channel 1. (*Suggestion:* designate each possible state of the system as follows. Let 0 denote no customers in the entire system and let 1 denote a customer being served in Channel 2 and no other customers in the entire system. Define i, for $i =$

1, 2, . . . , as the number of customers waiting in line plus those in service at Channel 1. Let i, 0 denote the level i at Channel 1 and no one being served at Channel 2; let i, 1 denote the level i at Channel 1 and customers being served at both Channels 1 and 2; let i, 2 denote the level i at Channel 1, and a customer being blocked in Channel 1 due to a customer being served in Channel 2.)

CONTENTS

CHAPTER 21

Computer Simulation of
Management Systems

21.1 WHEN ALL ELSE FAILS...

If you have patiently proceeded from one chapter to the next, you have studied a perhaps bewildering variety of operations research models and techniques. Students often ask, in effect, "Is this arsenal of tools powerful enough to encompass all the important managerial decision problems requiring data analysis?" The answer is no, not by a long shot. To see why, reflect on the kinds of problems that you know *can* be effectively analyzed by the operations research tools presented thus far. As you become aware of gaps, you will see more clearly why so many significant types of decision-analysis problems are still not solvable by these approaches, and therefore must be attacked in other ways. In the next few paragraphs we summarize the limitations as well as the strengths of operations research tools including linear and dynamic programming, inventory and queuing theory.

You have already learned that linear programming models are most successful in aiding the planning efforts of corporate enterprises. If the planning horizon is 10 years or longer, a corresponding multiperiod linear programming model typically deals only with annualized data. The effects of the resultant plan on week-to-week and month-to-month operations are left implicit. Analogously, if the planning horizon is much shorter, say three months to a year, the corresponding model usually ignores the day-to-day and week-to week variations. Thus, for the most part, linear programming analysis falls short of prescribing rules that translate a recommended plan into operating procedures for time spans shorter than the periods in the model.

A second limitation of linear programming analysis relates to uncertainty about the future. Imprecise forecasts to some degree exist in all planning studies.

Frequently, this uncertainty is not really the *essence* of the planning problem, or it reflects a lack of knowledge about only a *few* parameters in the model. In such cases, sensitivity analysis, as discussed in Chap. 5, suffices to determine the impact of uncertainty. But on other occasions uncertainty pervades the entire model, and standard sensitivity analysis is too clumsy and computationally burdensome for analyzing the impact of uncertainty.

To illustrate, consider a chemical manufacturing company that seeks a long-range strategy for the development and marketing of new products. Substantial research and investment costs are associated with each product, and the actual size of the product's market is uncertain. Furthermore, most of the profits that are generated from a successful product will be used to finance the research and development of new products. A linear programming model that manages to capture the dynamic elements of this situation, but treats the uncertainty aspects by simply using average values, is not likely to yield a good strategy.

In contrast, dynamic programming models can analyze multiperiod planning problems containing uncertainty, and so can be used to determine optimal strategies. But, as compared with linear programming applications, these dynamic programming models in practice can treat only drastically simplified systems. As you learned in Chaps. 10 and 17, unless the underlying system is characterized by only a few state variables, the computational task of solving a dynamic programming model is horrendous.

A similar limitation holds for those dynamic probabilistic models that are amenable to mathematical analysis, such as the inventory and queuing phenomena you studied in Chaps. 19 and 20. To solve these models, you not only must restrict yourself to a small-scale system, but you also must simplify the way the system can operate. To illustrate, a *realistic* analysis of waiting lines in a job-shop is intractable using mathematical queuing theory like that presented in Chap. 20 and Appendix III. Those models serve only as rough approximations to realistic queuing phenomena.

Thus, despite the great diversity of applications of mathematical programming and probabilistic models, many important managerial decision-making problems must be analyzed by other kinds of techniques.

Challenge remaining. The expanding scientific literature on operations research bears witness that there is steady progress in finding techniques to overcome the above-mentioned limitations. But for now and the foreseeable future, the approaches given in the preceding chapters cannot be relied on to provide a complete analysis of managerial decision-making problems pertaining to:

(i) *Choice of Investment Policies for Strategic Planning.* A major corporation's investment *policy*, to be comprehensive, should include provisions relating to research and development of new products, expansion into new markets, choice of selection criteria for major projects, measurement and evaluation of risk, means of financing by debt and equity, reinvestment of earnings, disposition of liquid assets, evaluation of mergers and acquisitions, and divestment of assets. A full-fledged operations research model for the analysis of alternative *policies* must recognize the impact of the uncertain and dynamic nature of investments, as well as provide a means for screening the enormous variety of investment decisions that face an organization.

(ii) *Selection of Facilities in Operations Planning.* Several examples in this category were already discussed in Sec. 20.1. They included the determination of the number of checkout stands in a supermarket, the number of gasoline pumps at a service station, and the number of elevators in a new office building. There are numerous other examples dealing with personnel staffing, plant layout, and machine capacity decisions. Typical facilities selection questions are of the form: "How many?" "How large?" "Where located?"

(iii) *Design of Information-Feedback Scheduling and Operations Rules.* Illustrations of decision problems in this category are equally numerous, although you may not think of them right away, unless you have had some previous work experience. An important example is the design of scheduling rules for a job-shop manufacturing plant, or an equipment repair facility, or a computer center. Such rules for a manufacturing plant take account of promised due dates to customers, the requirements for, and the availabilities of, machine capacities, the deployment of skilled labor, and the provisioning for raw materials. As information on new orders arrives, and as completed orders leave the system, the shop schedule has to be updated and revised.

Another example of an information-feedback system is a scheduling procedure for routing transport facilities. To illustrate, a freighter shipping company in making a schedule of its ocean going equipment for several months ahead, must take into account cargo demands at various ports, ship capacities and speeds, uncertainties in sailing times due to vagaries in the weather, and delays due to port congestion. Many shipping lines that own a large fleet of vessels must reschedule daily as they receive more accurate information about uncertain events. Similar problems arise in the scheduling of patients into a hospital, and the timing of traffic lights on a major thoroughfare.

What makes the three types of problems described above so difficult to analyze? It is the combined effect of uncertainty, the dynamic interactions between decisions and subsequent events, the complex interdependencies among the variables in the system, and, in some instances, the need to use finely divided time intervals. Such total systems problems are too big and too intricate to handle with linear and dynamic programming models, or standard probabilistic models.

Frequently, actual decisions arising from these three types of problems involve spending at least several hundred thousand dollars, and vitally affect the future operating costs and efficiencies of a company. Thus, management is highly motivated to employ a systematic approach to improve on intuitive, or "seat-of-the-pants," analysis. So far, the best operations research approach available is **digital computer simulation.**

Simulation approach. Our main concern in this chapter will be to describe simulation and the kinds of problems you encounter in employing this technique. We do not show you in detail how to design and run simulations. Such instructions are in texts devoted to simulation and in manuals distributed by computer manufacturers to explain special simulation programming languages.

In brief, the simulation approach starts by building an experimental model of a system. Then various specific alternatives are evaluated with reference to how well they fare in test runs of the model.

If you think about it, you will recall occasions when you have been involved in a simulated environment. For example, an amusement park, like Disneyland, offers you many attractions, such as the jungle boat-ride and the Matterhorn bobsled, that try to simulate actual experience. Less frivolous examples are planetarium shows and the environments in a museum of natural history. You may have learned how to drive an automobile in a mock-up mechanism with a steering wheel and gas and brake pedals. And if you have been in the armed services, you will remember that boot camp or basic training consists mainly of simulated exercises.

It is usually too inconvenient and expensive to solve managerial decision problems by environmental analogue simulations, such as the field combat war games that are used in boot camp and basic training. Rather, it is preferable to represent a complex system by a computerized mathematical model. In a computer, the only thing that can be shot is an electronic circuit.

The uncertainties, dynamic interactions, and complex interdependencies are all characterized by formulas stored in the memory of the high-speed digital electronic computer. The system simulation begins at a specified starting state. The combined effects of decisions, and of controllable and uncontrollable events, some of which may be random, cause the system to move to another state at a future instant in time. The evolutionary process continues in this fashion until the end of the horizon. Frequently, the time intervals are finely divided and extend over a fairly long horizon. As a consequence, the simulation experiments involve a vast number of calculations, rapidly performed by the computer. This feature of years of history evolving in a few minutes on a computer is termed **time compression.**

The only game in town. Most operations research analysts look upon digital computer simulation as a "method of last resort"—hence the title of this section, "When All Else Fails. . . ." There are two reasons for this gloomy attitude.

The first reason is the nature of most simulation results. When the model includes uncertain events, the answers stemming from a particular simulation must be viewed only as estimates subject to statistical error. For example, a simulated queuing model yields only an estimate of a waiting line's average length or the associated probability of a delay. Therefore, when you draw conclusions about the relative merit of different specific trial policies as tested by a simulation model, you must be careful to assess the accompanying random variations.

The second reason for diffidence about simulation involves the nature of the applications themselves. If a system is so complicated that it is beyond the reach of such operations research tools as linear and dynamic programming or standard probability analysis, then the required model-building effort and the subsequent analysis of the simulated results are likely to be difficult. Many an unwary analyst has found, to his chagrin, that the simulated world is as unfathomable as the real world he hoped to approximate—he allowed so much to go on in the model that it hampered his finding any insightful information.

The above two reasons also suggest why electronic computers are indispensable in performing simulations. To obtain sufficient statistical accuracy for reliable decisions, a considerable number of simulation runs are usually necessary. Each experiment is so complicated that it would be virtually impossible to perform the simulation manually in a reasonable period of time. It is not surprising, then, that computer simulation is often an expensive way to study a complex system.

21.2 SIMULATION IN PERSPECTIVE

As you read in the preceding section, many important managerial decision problems are too complex and too large to be solved by mathematical programming and standard probability analysis. In such cases, real-life experimentation, even if feasible, is usually too costly a way to analyze the alternatives. These observations establish the need for other problem-solving approaches, but do not by themselves justify computer simulation. Here we discuss why computer simulation is a useful technique, as well as what its limitations are.

Unlike the situation with mathematical programming, there are as yet no underlying principles guiding the formulation of simulation models. Each application is *ad hoc* to a large extent. Computer simulation languages come the closest to providing any general guidelines. [SIMSCRIPT and the General Purpose Systems Simulator (GPSS) are the two best-known languages; we say more about these programs in Sec. 21.8.]

The absence of a unifying theory of digital simulation is both a boon and a bane. On the positive side, you can build a simulation model containing arbitrarily high-order complexities and a huge number of dynamic interdependencies, as well as nonstationarities and correlated random phenomena. On the negative side, the more complicated the model, the more you will have to rely on embryonically developed statistical theory to perform the data analyses. As mentioned above, the very intricacy of the model can make it difficult to assess the model's validity. If the model is very complicated, you may have to expend a great deal of computer time on replication to obtain trustworthy answers and nearly optimal policies. Given the considerable research interest in simulation techniques, however, many of the current deficiencies in the theory and design of simulation experiments are bound to be eliminated in the years ahead.

Objectives. You would construct a simulation model to assist in analyzing managerial decision problems with one or more of the following purposes in mind:

(i) *To Describe a Current System.* Consider a manufacturing firm that recently has witnessed an increase in its customer orders, and has noticed a consequent marked deterioration in meeting due-dates promised to its customers. This company may want to build a simulation model to study how its current procedures for estimating due-dates, scheduling production, and ordering raw material are giving rise to the observed delays.

(ii) *To Explore a Hypothetical System.* Consider a hospital that is contemplating the installation of a new computerized inventory replenishment system for its medical supplies. It may want to build a simulation model using historical data to test what the average level of inventory investment would be, and how often there would be shortages of various supplies under the proposed plan.

(iii) *To Design an Improved System.* Consider a job shop in which machine capacities are allocated by priorities assigned to each job. The company may want to build a simulation model in order to find an effective way to assign such priorities so that the jobs are completed without long delays and, at the same time, so that equipment utilization is acceptably high.

We turn next to the steps in constructing and applying a simulation model.

So you want to build a simulation. The outline to follow describes the way you would go about constructing a simulation:

Step 1. Formulate the Model. This step is much the same as that for other operations research models. There is an ever-present danger, however, of including too much detail in a simulation model and, as a result, consuming excessive amounts of computer time to perform the experiments. The best guard against this tendency is to keep your specific purpose constantly in mind. For example, if a model is to aid in the choice between two different locations for a new warehouse, it is probably not necessary to simulate activities on a hour-to-hour, or even day-to-day basis; weekly aggregates ought to suffice. If, on the other hand, a model is to aid in the choice between one or two loading docks at a new warehouse, then it may be necessary to simulate activities occurring in intervals as small as 5 to 15 minutes.

Step 2. Design the Experiment. You will reduce the chance of making mistakes and wasting time if you work out the details of the experimental procedures before running the model. This means that you need to think out carefully what operating characteristics of the simulated system you plan to measure. Further, you must consider the statistical tools you intend to apply to take account of the experimental fluctuations in the measurements.

Step 3. Develop the Computer Program. The simulation experiments will be performed entirely by a high-speed electronic calculator. That is, each historical evolution of the model, including the generation of random events, will take place within the computer. If the simulated model has a very simple structure, you may find it easiest to use a standard programming language, such as FORTRAN, PL/1, or ALGOL, to develop the computerized version. More likely, you will find it preferable to employ one of the several simulation languages, such as SIMSCRIPT or GPSS, that are available on many large-scale electronic computers.

When you undertake an actual application, you will find that the above steps are not completely separate and sequential. For example, if you have already become familiar with, say, the GPSS simulation language, then you may want to formulate the model, initially, in terms of this language. We give more detail on each of these steps in the sections below.

21.3 STOCK MARKET SIMULATION EXAMPLE

An investor, Wynn Doe, wants to evaluate a particular strategy for buying and selling common stocks. To keep the exposition straightforward, suppose he does all of his trading in a single stock. At present, he holds 100 shares of the stock, which currently has a price of $10 a share. Again for the sake of simplicity, assume that the stock price can change each day by only $1, so that some of the possible stock prices are $8, $9, $10, $11, $12, ... The investor makes, at most, one transaction each day, and pays a commission of 2% of the transaction value whenever he buys or sells; of course, he need not make a transaction every day.

Wynn Doe wants to test the profitability of the following rule for buying and selling that has been suggested by his broker Benton Cherning:

(i) If you own the stock, then sell it whenever the price falls.

(ii) If you do not own the stock, then buy it whenever the price rises.

According to this rule, if Wynn Doe owns the stock he will hold on to it while the price stays the same or rises; if he does not own the stock, he will refrain from buying it as long as the price stays the same or falls.

In order to evaluate this strategy, Wynn Doe must also postulate how he believes the stock price will fluctuate from day to day. After analyzing historical data, he formulates the price-movement model shown in Fig. 21.1. To illustrate, if the share prices on Monday and Tuesday are both $10, then he believes that the price on Wednesday will be $11 with probability $\frac{1}{4}$, $10 with probability $\frac{1}{2}$, and $9 with probability $\frac{1}{4}$, as can be seen in the second row of Fig. 21.1. If, instead, Tuesday's price is $9, then he believes that the share price on Wednesday will

Today's Stock Price:

Yesterday's Stock Price:	Increases	Stays the Same	Decreases
Increased	$\frac{1}{2}$	$\frac{1}{4}$	$\frac{1}{4}$
Stayed the Same	$\frac{1}{4}$	$\frac{1}{2}$	$\frac{1}{4}$
Decreased	$\frac{1}{4}$	$\frac{1}{4}$	$\frac{1}{2}$

FIGURE 21.1. Stock Price Movement Probabilities.

be $10 with probability $\frac{1}{4}$, $9 with probability $\frac{1}{4}$, and $8 with probability $\frac{1}{2}$, as can be seen in the third row of Fig. 12.1. Notice that as the stock price increases, the investor thinks there is probability $\frac{1}{2}$ that it will increase again, and analogous statements hold if the share price remains the same or decreases.

To begin testing Cherning's rule by **manual simulation** generate a specific history of price movements according to the probabilities given in Fig. 21.1. A simple mechanism for doing this is to toss a pair of unbiased coins, using the correspondences shown in Fig. 21.2. Verify that in Fig. 21.2 the assignments of the outcomes of a toss of two unbiased coins yield the postulated probabilities in Fig. 21.1.

Today's Stock Price:

Yesterday's Stock Price:	Increases	Stays the Same	Decreases
Increased	A Head and A Tail	Two Heads	Two Tails
Stayed the Same	Two Heads	A Head and A Tail	Two Tails
Decreased	Two Heads	Two Tails	A Head and A Tail

FIGURE 21.2. Price Movements Generated by Tosses of a Pair of Unbiased Coins.

Suppose you simulate 20 days of activity, starting on Day 1 and ending on Day 20. Then you must toss the two coins 20 times; a particular sequence of tosses is recorded in Fig. 21.3. To determine the associated sequence of stock prices, you have to specify the initial conditions, namely, the stock price on Day 0 and whether it represents a fluctuation from the preceding day. In Fig. 21.3, the price on Day 0 is $10, which presents no change from the preceding day. Given these initial conditions and a toss having a head and a tail on Day 1, the stock price for Day 1 is $10, according to the second row of Fig. 21.2. Then on Day 2, since yesterday's price remained the same, the toss of two tails implies that the share price falls to $9, again according to the second row of Fig. 21.2. Proceeding to Day 3, since yesterday's price decreased, the toss of two heads causes the share price to be $10, according to the third row of Fig. 21.2. Check the entries in Fig. 21.3 for Days 5, 10, 15, and 20.

You can now determine how well Cherning's suggested rule for buying and selling has performed on this particular simulated 20-day history of price movements. The details are shown in Fig. 21.4; notice that the history of prices from Fig. 21.3 has been copied for easy reference. The entries in the column labeled "Decision" are a direct consequence of the price history and the suggested rule. The entries in the last three columns are determined after some auxiliary calculations.

To illustrate, on Day 2, the investor sells his 100 shares at a price $9; but he must pay a 2% commission, which amounts to ($.02 \times \$9 \times 100 = \$18$); thus he receives only $882(= \$900 - \$18$) from the sale. On Day 3, he repurchases the stock. Once again he must pay a 2% commission, so effectively the stock price is $10.20 a share. Since he has $882 cash, he can purchase only 86 shares, leaving him $4.80 (= \$882 - 86 \times \$10.20$) cash. Notice that at the end of the 20th day, the investor's cash position—$931.90—is worse following the rule than it would have been if he had sold his 100 shares on Day 0 and thereby received $980 cash, after paying the commission.

Given all the model's assumptions, is Cherning's rule profitable? Probably your immediate reaction is, "No." But wait a minute. Suppose instead of arbitrarily selecting 20 days as the length of the simulation, you had picked either 6 or 16 days instead. What would your answer have been then? Or suppose you rerun the simulation with a new history of 20 tosses. Will the rule still look poor at termination? The issue of whether the rule is any good really depends in part on the statistical variability in the result obtained on Day 20, and on the significance of looking at a horizon of 20 versus 200, versus 2000, versus any other number of simulated days.

As you think further about the model, you will realize that the evaluation issue is complicated by the fact that as the horizon lengthens, there is an increase in the possible range of variability in the investor's wealth position at the end of the horizon. Further, even *if* the rule implies an upward drift in the expected wealth position as the horizon lengthens, there is at least an initial increase in the probability that the investor may go broke along the way.

Day	Coin Toss	Yesterday's Price Movement	Today's Stock Price
0	--	--	10*
1	H/T	Same*	10
2	2T	Same	9
3	2H	Decreased	10
4	2H	Increased	10
5	2H	Same	11
6	H/T	Increased	12
7	2H	Increased	12
8	2T	Same	11
9	2H	Decreased	12
10	H/T	Increased	13
11	2T	Increased	12
12	H/T	Decreased	11
13	2T	Decreased	11
14	2H	Same	12
15	H/T	Increased	13
16	H/T	Increased	14
17	2T	Increased	13
18	H/T	Decreased	12
19	H/T	Decreased	11
20	2T	Decreased	11

Legend: *H/T* ≈ A Head and A Tail
  2H ≈ Two Heads
  2T ≈ Two Tails

*Initial Conditions

FIGURE 21.3. Simulated Price Movements.

Day	Stock Price	Decision	Shares Held	Value of Stock	Cash
0	10		100	1000	
1	10		100	1000	
2	9	Sell	0	· 0	882.00
3	10	Buy	86	860	4.80
4	10		86	860	4.80
5	11		86	946	4.80
6	12		86	1032	4.80
7	12		86	1032	4.80
8	11	Sell	0	0	931.88
9	12	Buy	76	912	1.64
10	13		76	988	1.64
11	12	Sell	0	0	895.40
12	11		0	0	895.40
13	11		0	0	895.40
14	12	Buy	73	876	1.88
15	13		73	949	1.88
16	14		73	1022	1.88
17	13	Sell	0	0	931.90
18	12		0	0	931.90
19	11		0	0	931.90
20	11		0	0	931.90

FIGURE 21.4. Twenty-Day Test of Wynn Doe's Trading Rule.

So as you can see, even this simple-minded simulation gives rise to some difficult questions concerning what to measure and how to design a scientific experiment to test the effectiveness of the rule. What is more, if you take the trouble to run the model by hand for another 20 periods, you will quickly appreciate the desirability of letting an electronic computer do all the coin tossing and arithmetic.

21.4 BUILDING A SIMULATION MODEL

We now return to a more general discussion of the steps involved in using computer simulation. In this section we examine three aspects of model building: specifying the model's components; testing its validity and reliability; determining its parameters and measuring its performance.

Model components. The structure of most simulation models is conveniently described in terms of its **dynamic phenomena** and its **entities**. The dynamic phenomena in the stock market simulation of the preceding section include the investor's activity of buying or selling the stock, according to the stated **decision rule**, and the factors governing the movement of stock prices. The entities on any day include the amount of stock the investor holds, his cash position, and wealth. Typically, the entities in a model have **attributes**. To illustrate, the amount of stock the investor holds has a monetary value, given the associated price of the stock. Further, there are **membership relationships**

providing connections between the entities. For example, the investor's wealth on any day includes both his cash and stock positions.

At any instant of a simulation, the model is in a particular **state**. The description of the state not only embodies the current status of the entities but frequently includes some historical information. For example, the state of the system at the beginning of a day in the stock market simulation is described by yesterday's price, how yesterday's price differed from the price on the day before, the number of shares held, and the cash position.

A model also can encompass **exogenous events**, that is, changes that are not brought about by the previous history of the simulation. To illustrate, the investor in the stock market simulation may have decided to add $1000 more cash from his savings on Day 21, regardless of how well he has done using the tested strategy.

Knowing the state of the system and the dynamic phenomena, you can then go on to determine the subsequent activities and states. Frequently, simulation models having this evolutionary structure are called **recursive** or **causal.**

Note that in building a causal model, you must resolve the way activities occur *within* a period. For example, on each day of the stock market simulation, first the price is determined, then the decision to buy or sell is exercised. Actually, the price of a stock may change several times during a day, so the model we constructed is only a rough approximation to reality. The model also assumes that if the investor sells the stock, he receives the cash at the end of the day; and analogously, if he purchases the stock, he pays the cash at the end of the day. Such financial transactions do not always occur so rapidly in practice.

Model validity and reliability. After building a simulation model, you are bound to be asked, "How realistic is it?" The more pertinent question is, "Does the model yield valid insights and reliable conclusions?" After all, since the model can only approximate reality, it must be evaluated by its power to analyze the particular managerial decisions you are studying.

Once the purpose of the simulation experiment is defined, you construct each piece of the model with a commensurate amount of detail and accuracy. A caveat is in order here. As simulation experts can attest, it is easy for a novice to build a model that, component by component, resembles reality; yet when the pieces are hooked together, the model may not behave like reality. So beware not to assume blindly that the entire simulated system is sufficiently accurate, merely because each of the component parts seems adequate when considered in isolation. This warning is especially important, because usually the objective of a simulation model is to fathom the behavior of a total system, and not that of the separate parts.

Model parameters and performance measures. It is one thing to describe the pieces of a simulation model abstractly, and it is another to collect sufficient data for a trustworthy representation of these pieces. Limited availability of data may very well influence the way you build a simulation.

You must be particularly cautious when you are dealing with extrapolated data and nonstationary performance measures. (Remember the story of the cracker barrel manufacturer who, not so very long ago, forecasted that he would be selling millions of barrels today. He assumed, unquestioningly, that his sales trend would continue as it had in the past.)

You also must watch out for cyclical or periodic phenomena. When these are present, you must be judicious in selecting the variables to measure in the experiments. If you look only at "ending values," for example, then your conclusions may be very sensitive to the exact length of the horizon that you simulated.

21.5 GENERATING RANDOM PHENOMENA

Most applications of simulation models encompass random phenomena. For example, in simulated waiting line models, the random variables include arrival and service times; in inventory models, the variables include customer demand and delivery times; and in research and development models, the variables include events of new product discoveries. Frequently, such simulations require thousands, and sometimes hundreds of thousands, of draws from the probability distributions contained in the model. How an electronic computer makes these draws is the subject of this section.

Uniform random numbers. As you will see, the basic building block for simulating complex random phenomena is the generation of random digits. The following experimental situation is an illuminating description of what we mean by generating a sequence of *uniform random numbers*.

Suppose you take ten squares of paper, number them 0, 1, 2, . . . , 9, and place them in a hat. Shake the hat and thoroughly mix the slips of paper. Without looking, select a slip; then record the number that is on it. Replace the square and, over and over, repeat this procedure. The resultant record of digits is a particular realized sequence of uniform random numbers. Assuming the squares of paper do not become creased or frayed, and that you thoroughly mix the slips before every draw, the nth digit of the sequence has an equal, or uniform, chance of being any of the digits 0, 1, 2, . . . , 9, irrespective of all the preceding digits in the recorded sequence.

In a simulation, you typically use random numbers that are pure decimals. So, for example, if you need such numbers with four decimal places, then you can take four at a time from the recorded sequence of random digits, and place a decimal point in front of each group of four. To illustrate, if the sequence of digits is 3, 5, 8, 0, 8, 3, 4, 2, 9, 2, 6, 1, . . . , then the four-decimal-place random numbers are .3580, .8342, .9261, ...

Suppose you have to devise a way for making available inside a computer a sequence of several hundred thousand random numbers. You would probably first suggest this idea: perform something like the "slips-in-a-hat experiment" described above, and then store the recorded sequence in the computer's memory. This is a good suggestion, and it is sometimes employed. The RAND Corporation, using specially designed electronic equipment to perform the experiment, actually did generate a table of a million random digits. The table can be obtained on magnetic tape, so that blocks of the numbers can be read into the high-speed memory of a computer as they are needed. Several years ago, this tabular approach looked disadvantageous, because considerable computer time was expended in the delays of reading numbers into memory from a tape drive. But with recent advances in computer technology and programming skill, these delays have been virtually eliminated.

Experts in computer science have devised mathematical processes for generating digits that yield sequences satisfying many of the statistical properties of a truly random process. To illustrate, if you examine a long sequence of digits produced by these deterministic formulas, each digit will occur with nearly the same frequency, odd numbers will be followed by even numbers about as often as by odd numbers, different pairs of numbers occur with nearly the same frequency, etc. Since such a process is not really random, it is dubbed a **pseudo-random number generator.**

Computer simulation languages, like those discussed in Sec. 21.8, invariably have a built-in pseudo-random number generator. Hence, you will rarely, if ever, need to know specific formulas for these generators. But if you want to strengthen your confidence in the process of obtaining the numbers, then you can study the example of a pseudo-random number generator given below. If not, go on to the discussion of how to generate random variables.

*Congruential method. To begin, we need to review the idea of **modulus arithmetic**. We say that two numbers x and y are **congruent, modulo** m, if the quantity $(x - y)$ is an integral multiple of m. For example, letting $m = 10$, we can write

(1)

$$3 \equiv 3 \text{ (modulo 10)} \qquad\qquad 4 \equiv 4 \text{ (modulo 10)}$$
$$13 \equiv 3 \text{ (modulo 10)} \qquad\qquad 84 \equiv 4 \text{ (modulo 10)}$$
$$513 \equiv 3 \text{ (modulo 10)} \qquad\qquad 124 \equiv 4 \text{ (modulo 10)}$$
$$48{,}653 \equiv 3 \text{ (modulo 10)} \qquad 1{,}000{,}004 \equiv 4 \text{ (modulo 10)}.$$

To find the value of, say, 857 (modulo 10), you calculate the integer *remainder* of 857 divided by 10, which is 7.

One popular approach for generating pseudo-random numbers is the so-called **Multiplicative Congruential Method**. The general formula for producing the random numbers is

(2)
$$r_n = a r_{n-1} \text{ (modulo } m\text{)},$$

where the parameters a and m, and the **seed** r_0 are specified to give desirable statistical properties of the resultant sequence. Note that because of the modulus arithmetic, each r_n must be one of the numbers $0, 1, 2, 3, \ldots, m - 1$.

Clearly, you must be careful about the choice of a and r_0. For example, if $a = 1$, then $r_n = r_0$, for all n. Or if $r_0 = 0$, then $r_n = 0$, for all n. The values of a and r_0 should be chosen to yield the largest **cycle** or **period**, that is, to give the largest value for n at which $r_n = r_0$ for the first time.

To illustrate the technique, suppose you want to generate ten-decimal-place numbers $u_1, u_2, u_3, \ldots$. It can be shown that if you use $u_n = r_n \times 10^{-10}$, where

(3)
$$r_n = 100{,}003 \, r_{n-1} \text{ (modulo } 10^{10})$$
$$r_0 = \text{any odd number not divisible by 5,}$$

then the period of the sequence will be 5×10^8; that is, $r_n = r_0$ for the first time at $n = 5 \times 10^8$, and the cycle subsequently repeats itself. Given that you want ten-decimal-place numbers, this is the maximum possible length of period using (2). (There are other values for a that also give this maximum period.) Verify that the selection of r_0 in (3) eliminates the possibility that $r_n = 0$; so u_n satisfies $0 < u_n < 1$.

Let us look at an example of (3). Suppose $r_0 = 123{,}456{,}789$. Then

(4)
$$r_1 = (100{,}003) \cdot (123{,}456{,}789) = 12{,}346{,}049{,}270{,}367$$
$$\equiv 6{,}049{,}270{,}367 \text{ (modulo } 10^{10}),$$

so that $u_1 = .6049270367$, and

(5)
$$r_2 = (100{,}003) \cdot (6{,}049{,}270{,}367) = 604{,}945{,}184{,}511{,}101$$
$$\equiv 5{,}184{,}511{,}101 \text{ (modulo } 10^{10}),$$

so that $u_2 = .5184511101$. The decimals u_n, $n = 1, 2, \ldots,$ 20, are shown in Fig. 21.5. Notice that the rightmost digits in this sequence form a short cycle 7, 1, 3, 9, 7, 1, 3, 9, $\ldots$. Thus the statistical properties of the digits near the end of the number are far from random.

While (2) works reasonably well for some types of simulation models, it has poor serial correlation properties that make it dangerous to use for dynamic systems. A simple device for rectifying this deficiency is to intermix several sequences, each being generated with a different value for the seed r_0, and possibly a different value for a. For example, you can sequentially rotate among, say, 10 of these generators.

The advantage of using a pseudo-random number generator in lieu of a recorded table of random numbers is that only a few simple computer instructions are required to generate the sequence. Therefore, the approach uses only a small amount of memory space and does not require reading magnetic tape.

n	u_n	
1	.60492	70367
2	.51845	11101
3	.66636	33303
4	.33211	99909
5	.99544	99727
6	.98361	99181
7	.94266	97543
8	.80343	92629
9	.33660	77887
10	.78869	33661
11	.70269	00983
12	.11790	02949
13	.38319	08847
14	.23804	26541
15	.97953	79623
16	.73484	38869
17	.59322	16607
18	.94573	49821
19	.33541	49463
20	.50087	48389

FIGURE 21.5. The Multiplicative Congruential Method: $a = 100{,}003$; $r_0 = 123{,}456{,}789$.

Generating random variables. We turn next to an explanation of how to employ a sequence of uniform random numbers to generate complex probabilistic phenomena. The treatment below suggests several techniques that can be used; but it is by no means exhaustive. Further, the examples that illustrate the techniques are chosen more for expository ease than computational efficiency. In an actual situation, you should seek the advice of a computer science specialist to determine the appropriate technique for your model.

Inverse Transform Method. The following is the simplest and most fundamental technique for simulating random draws from an arbitrary single-variable probability distribution. Let the distribution function for the random variable be denoted by

$F(x) \equiv$ probability that the random variable has a value less than or equal to x.

For example, suppose the random phenomenon has an exponential density function

(6) $$f(t) = \lambda e^{-\lambda t}, \qquad t \geq 0;$$

then

(7) $$F(x) = \int_0^x \lambda e^{-\lambda t}\, dt = 1 - e^{-\lambda x}.$$

Now $0 \leq F(x) \leq 1$, and suppose $F(x)$ is continuous and strictly increasing. Then given a value u, where $0 < u < 1$, there is a unique value for x such that $F(x) = u$. Symbolically, this value of x is denoted by the inverse function $F^{-1}(u)$. The technique is to generate a sequence of uniform random decimal numbers $u_n, n = 1, 2, \ldots$, and from these, determine the associated values as $x_n = F^{-1}(u_n)$.

The correctness of this approach can be seen as follows. Consider *any* two numbers u_a and u_b, where $0 < u_a < u_b < 1$. Then the probability that a *uniform* random decimal number u lies in the interval $u_a \leq u \leq u_b$ is $u_b - u_a$. Since $F(x)$ is continuous and strictly increasing, there is a number x_a such that $F(x_a) = u_a$, and a number x_b such that $F(x_b) = u_b$, where $x_a < x_b$. The Inverse Transform Method is valid provided that the *true* probability of the random variable having a value between x_a and x_b equals the generated probability $u_b - u_a$. This true probability is $F(x_b) - F(x_a) = u_b - u_a$ by construction, so that the method is indeed valid.

To see how this method works, return to the exponential distribution (6) and (7). Let v_n denote a uniform random decimal number. Set

(8) $$v_n = 1 - e^{-\lambda x_n},$$

so that

(9) $$x_n = \frac{-\log_e (1 - v_n)}{\lambda} = \frac{-\log_e u_n}{\lambda},$$

where $u_n = 1 - v_n$, and hence is itself a uniform random decimal number. Thus, you generate a sequence of uniform random decimal numbers $u_1, u_2, u_3, \ldots$, and by (9) compute $x_1, x_2, x_3, \ldots$, to obtain a random exponentially distributed variable. A diagrammatic representation of the technique is shown in Fig. 21.6.

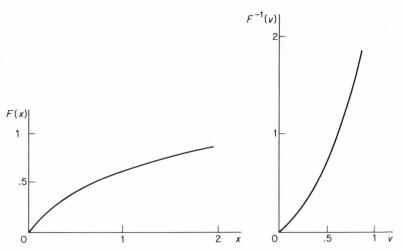

FIGURE 21.6. Inverse Transform Method for a Continuous and Strictly Increasing $F(x)$. Example: $F(x) = 1 - e^{-\lambda x}$; $F^{-1}(v) = -\log_e(1 - v)/\lambda$ for $\lambda = 1$.

The idea can also be applied to a probability mass function $P(j)$. Suppose $j = 0, 1, 2, 3, \ldots$, so that

$$(10) \qquad\qquad F(x) = \sum_{j=0}^{x} p(j).$$

Then the inverse function can be written as

$$(11) \qquad\qquad x_n = j \quad \text{for } F(j-1) < u_n \le F(j),$$

where we let $F(-1) = 0$. For example, suppose the probability mass function is the *binomial distribution*:

$$(12) \qquad\qquad p(j) = \binom{k}{j} p^j (1 - p)^{k-j} \quad \text{for } j = 0, 1, \ldots, k,$$

where $0 < p < 1$, and k is a positive integer. In particular, assume $k = 2$ and $p = .5$; then $p(0) = \frac{1}{4}$, $p(1) = \frac{1}{2}$, and $p(2) = \frac{1}{4}$, so that by (11) you have

$$(13) \qquad\qquad x_n = \begin{cases} 0 & \text{for } 0 < u_n \le .25 \\ 1 & \text{for } .25 < u_n \le .75 \\ 2 & \text{for } .75 < u_n \le 1. \end{cases}$$

Since u_n is a uniform random decimal number, there is a $\frac{1}{4}$ probability that u_n lies between 0 and .25, a $\frac{1}{2}$ probability that it lies between .25 and .75, and a $\frac{1}{4}$ probability that it lies between .75 and 1. A diagrammatic representation of the technique is shown in Fig. 21.7.

Of course, many continuous distribution functions $F(x)$ do not have analytic inverse functions as does the exponential distribution. The Inverse Transform Method can still be applied in these instances by employing a discrete approximation to the continuous function, that is, by storing the values of $F(x)$ for only a finite set of x. The accuracy of the approximation can be improved by interpolating between the stored values. In several computer simulation languages (such as

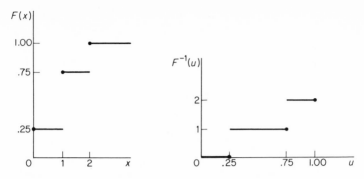

FIGURE 21.7. Inverse Transform Method for a Probability Mass Function.
Example: $p(0) = \frac{1}{4}$, $p(1) = \frac{1}{2}$, $p(2) = \frac{1}{4}$.

GPSS), you need only specify this discrete approximation, and the corresponding random phenomenon will be automatically generated.

*Tabular Method. The rule in (11) is easily implemented for an electronic computer by means of a few standard programming instructions. But if the range of possible values for j is large, then an excessive amount of time may be consumed in searching for the j that satisfies the inequalities in (11). A faster version of the Inverse Transform Method can be employed at the expense of using part of the computer's internal memory for storing a long table. We illustrate the idea with the binomial example (13).

You can store the inverse function in computer memory in the form

$$(14) \qquad G(s) = \begin{cases} 0 & \text{for } s = 1, 2, \ldots, 25, \\ 1 & \text{for } s = 26, 27, \ldots, 75, \\ 2 & \text{for } s = 76, 77, \ldots, 100. \end{cases}$$

Given a value of u_n, let d_n be the number formed from the first two digits of u_n. Set $s_n = d_n + 1$, and let $x_n = G(s_n)$. For example if $u_n = .52896\ldots$, then $s_n = 52 + 1 = 53$, and so $x_n = G(53) = 1$ in (14). Once the function $G(s)$ has been stored in memory, only a few calculations must be performed by the computer to produce x_n.

*Method of Convolutions. Sometimes you can view a random variable as the sum of other independently distributed random variables. When this is so, the probability distribution of the random variable is a convolution of probability distributions, which may be easy to generate. (Occasionally, you can obtain a workable approximation to a complex probability distribution by using a *weighted* sum of independently distributed random variables. For this reason, the approach also has been called the **Method of Composition.**)

To illustrate, consider a random variable having a *gamma density function*

$$(15) \qquad g(y) = \frac{\lambda(\lambda y)^{k-1} e^{-\lambda y}}{(k-1)!}, \qquad y \geq 0, k \text{ a positive integer.}$$

Such a variable can be considered as the sum of k independent random variables, each drawn from the same exponential density specified in (6). Consequently, adding k independent values of x_n, as given by (9), yields a random variable with the distribution in (15).

Similarly, a binomial random variable, as specified in (12), can be viewed as the sum of k draws of a variable described by

$$(16) \qquad i = \begin{cases} 1 & \text{with probability } p \\ 0 & \text{with probability } 1 - p. \end{cases}$$

You can therefore obtain a binomially distributed variable by adding k values of i. Each of these values for i is determined by the rule

$$(17) \qquad i = \begin{cases} 1 & \text{for } 0 < u \leq p \\ 0 & \text{for } p < u \leq 1, \end{cases}$$

where u is a uniform random decimal number.

*Method of Equivalent Transformations. Sometimes you can generate a random variable by exploiting a correspondence between its probability distribution and that of a related random variable.

For example, consider the Poisson distribution written in the form

$$(18) \qquad p(j) = \frac{(\lambda T)^j e^{-\lambda T}}{j!} \quad \text{for } j = 0, 1, 2, \ldots,$$

which has mean λT. In terms of the waiting line models in Chap. 20, you can interpret j as the number of customers arriving during a period of length T, where the interarrival times for the customers are independently and identically distributed exponential random variables with the density function specified in (6).

Consequently, you can generate a Poisson distributed random variable by making successive independent draws of an exponentially distributed variable— using (9) to obtain such values. You stop making draws as soon as the sum of $j + 1$ of these variables exceeds T. The distribution of the resultant j is (18). Explain why.

*Normally distributed random variables. Unfortunately, the distribution function for the Normal density with mean 0 and variance 1,

$$(19) \qquad F(x) = \int_{-\infty}^{x} \frac{1}{\sqrt{2\pi}} e^{-t^2/2} \, dt,$$

does not yield an analytic formula for the inverse function $F^{-1}(u)$. Of course the Inverse Transform Method can be used by employing a discrete approximation, and interpolating between values. But there are other methods for generating a Normally distributed random variable. Only a few are presented here.

One technique requires generating a pair of independent uniform random decimal numbers u and v, and in turn yields a pair of independently distributed Normal random variables x and y having the distribution function in (19). Specifically, compute

(20)
$$x = (-2 \log_e u)^{1/2} \cos 2\pi v$$
$$y = (-2 \log_e u)^{1/2} \sin 2\pi v.$$

Alternatively, you can apply the Method of Convolutions and invoke the *Central Limit Theorem*. This technique employs the sum of k independently and identically distributed uniform random variables. Specifically, let u_i, for $i = 1$, $2, \ldots, 12$, be independent draws of a uniform random decimal number; then compute

(21)
$$x = \sum_{i=1}^{12} u_i - 6.$$

The distribution of x will have mean 0 and variance 1, and will be approximately Normal. The approximation is poor for values beyond three standard deviations from the mean.

A third approach is to compute

(22)
$$x = \frac{[(1 - u)^{-1/6.158} - 1]^{-1/4.874} - [u^{-1/6.158} - 1]^{1/4.874}}{.323968}$$

where u is a uniform random decimal number.

*Correlated random variables. There are straightforward ways to generate variables from a multivariate Normal distribution, and from other joint probability distributions, as well as random variables having serial correlation. The techniques go beyond the scope of this book, but can be found in most texts on computer simulation.

21.6 How to Mark Time

A dynamic systems simulation model can be structured in either of two ways. One approach, which is the more obvious, views simulated time as elapsing period by period. The computer routine performs all the transactions taking place in Period t, and then proceeds to Period t + 1. If the events in Period t imply that certain other transactions are to occur in future periods, then the computer stores this information in memory, and recovers it when the future periods arrive. You already saw an illustration of this approach using **fixed-time increments** in the stock market simulation of Sec. 21.4. Another example is given below.

In some simulations, the periods have to be relatively short. But there may be many of these periods in which no transactions occur. For such models, there is a second approach that lets the simulation advance by **variable-time increments.** This idea is illustrated in the second example below.

Time-step incrementation—inventory model. Suppose you wish to evaluate the operating characteristics of a proposed inventory replenishment rule. Assume that you can specify the probability distribution for each day's demand, and that daily demand is identically and independently distributed. If demand exceeds the amount of inventory on hand, the excess represents lost

sales. Let us postulate that, during a daily time period of the simulation model, the sequence of events is: first, any replenishment order due in arrives; then demand occurs; and finally, the inventory position is reviewed, and a reorder is placed if the replenishment rule indicates it should be. An order placed at the end of Period t arrives at the start of Period t + L, where L is fixed and $L \geq 1$.

To keep the exposition simple, assume that the replenishment rule is to order Q units whenever the amount of inventory on hand plus inventory due in is less than or equal to s, where $Q > s$. Verify that the inequality $Q > s$ implies there is never more than one replenishment order outstanding. (Since our focus here is simulation and not inventory theory, we do not comment further on the reasonableness of the replenishment rule; we do point out, however, that the model is an approximation to that in Sec. 19.6.)

A simulation model of this inventory system is easily constructed by stepping time forward in the fixed increment of a day, beginning with Day 1 $(t = 1)$. To start the simulation, you must specify the initial conditions of the level of inventory on hand, the amount due in, and the associated time due in. You must also designate the number of periods that the simulation is to run; let the symbol "HORIZON" denote this value.

A flow chart of the simulation is shown in Fig. 21.8. The initializing is done in Block 1. For example, you can let the amount INVENTORY ON-HAND = Q, the AMOUNT DUE-IN = 0, the TIME DUE-IN = 0, and $t = 1$. Verify that when Block 2 is reached, the answer is "No," and you proceed at Block 4 to generate a value of demand q for Day 1. Here is where you use an approach from the preceding section.

At the end of Day 1, INVENTORY ON-HAND is diminished by q, unless q exceeds the amount available, in which case the amount of INVENTORY ON-HAND becomes 0. This calculation is performed at Block 5.

At Block 6, a test is made to determine whether a replenishment order is to be placed. If so, the AMOUNT DUE-IN becomes Q, and the TIME DUE-IN becomes $1 + L$ (since at the start $t = 1$), as indicated in Block 7. If a replenishment order is not placed, you continue directly to Block 8, where the time step is incremented by 1; that is, the simulation clock is advanced to Day 2.

If Day 2 goes beyond the HORIZON you specified, the simulation terminates. Assuming that you set the HORIZON > 1, the simulation returns from Block 9 to Block 2.

At some day, TIME DUE-IN will equal t, and then the simulation branches from Block 2 to Block 3, where the amount of INVENTORY ON-HAND is augmented by Q, and the AMOUNT DUE-IN is reset to 0.

The flow chart does not indicate where you would collect statistical data on the operating characteristics of the system. In programming the model, you would keep a tally at Block 5 of the level of INVENTORY ON-HAND at the end of a day, as well as of the amount of lost sales and the number of days when a stockout occurs. You would tabulate at Block 6 the number of days an order was placed.

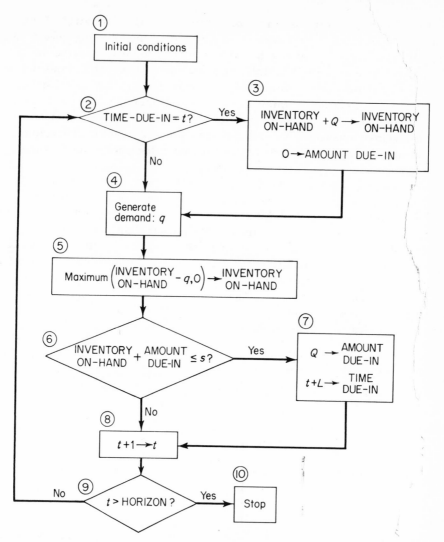

FIGURE 21.8. Inventory Model Simulation Flow Chart.

Then, before terminating the simulation at Block 10, you would summarize these tallies into frequency distributions, along with their means, standard deviations, and other statistical quantities of interest.

Suppose the item is a "slow mover," that is, there is a high probability that demand $q = 0$ on any day. Then the time-step method may be inefficient, because there will be many consecutive days when the computations in Blocks 2, 5, and 6 will be identical. Such redundancies can be eliminated by using the technique illustrated below.

*Event-step incrementation—waiting line model. Suppose you want to examine the operating characteristics of the following queuing system, which is simple to describe but proves difficult to analyze mathematically. Customers arrive at the system according to a specified probability distribution for interarrival times. The system has two clerks, A and B. When both servers are busy, arriving customers wait in a single line and are processed by a first come, first served discipline. The service times for each clerk can be viewed as independent draws from a specified probability distribution; but each clerk has a different service time distribution. Neither the interarrival nor the service time distributions are exponential.

After thinking about the way this system evolves over time, you will discover that the dynamics can be characterized by three types of events: a customer's arrival, a customer's service begins, and a customer's service ends. Each event gives rise to a subroutine in the computerized version of the system.

A simulation model using variable-time increments also contains a **master program** having an **event list,** which is repeatedly updated as the master program switches from one **event subroutine** to another. At the start of a simulation run, the event list is usually empty; but at a later instant in the run, it indicates when some of the future events are to occur. The role this event list plays will be clearer as you examine the event flow charts in Fig. 21.9.

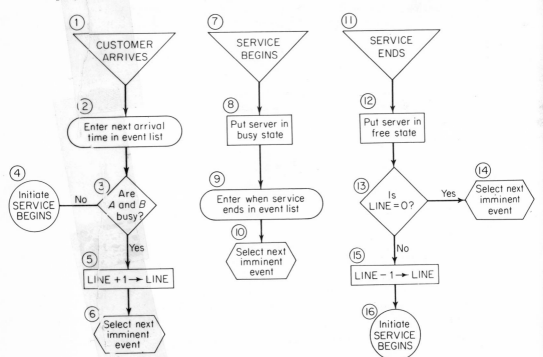

FIGURE 21.9. Waiting Line Model Chart of Events.

Assume that you specify the initial conditions of the simulation as: a customer arrives, say, at Time 0, there are no customers in line, and both the clerks are free. The master program starts with the event subroutine CUSTOMER ARRIVES, shown as Block 1 in Fig. 21.9. Using a technique from the preceding section, the computer selects a random interarrival time at Block 2. The information that this next arrival event occurs at the implied future time is entered into the event list. A determination of whether both clerks are busy is made in Block 3. Since the answer is "No" at the start, the master program switches to the event subroutine SERVICE BEGINS, as indicated in Block 4. To keep the flow diagram uncluttered, we have suppressed the details that would specify that the computer must keep track of which clerk serves the customer, an item of information that is needed when the master program switches to the subroutine SERVICE BEGINS in Block 7.

The first instruction in SERVICE BEGINS is at Block 8, which records that the selected clerk is now busy. Then the service time of the customer is determined in Block 9, using the appropriate service time probability distribution for the selected clerk. The information that a service-ends event occurs at the implied future time is entered into the event list. The subroutine then transfers back to the master program with the instruction in Block 10 to find the **next imminent event** in the event list. So far, this can be either the arrival of the next customer or the completion of service of the first customer. Suppose it is the latter, so that the master program switches to the subroutine SERVICE ENDS in Block 11.

The first instruction in SERVICE ENDS is at Block 12, which records that the server is now free again. Then a test is made at Block 13 to see whether the waiting line designated by the symbol "LINE" is empty. Verify that the answer is "Yes." Also check that when control switches back in Block 14 to the master program, the next imminent event will be the arrival of the second customer.

Later in the run, the LINE will contain customers, and then the answer is "No" at Block 13. As a result, the length of the LINE is decreased by 1 in Block 15, and control transfers in Block 16 to the subroutine SERVICE BEGINS. Explain what can happen subsequently if Block 10 leads to the CUSTOMER ARRIVES subroutine.

A simulation run progresses as each event subroutine either switches to another event subroutine or instructs the master program to increment time to the next imminent event. As you can imagine, considerable skill is required to write a simulation program that uses event-step incrementation. In particular, expertise is needed to program the updating of the event list efficiently as future events are generated by the subroutines. Many simulation languages of the type discussed in Sec. 21.8 already include a master program that maintains an updated list of events; to employ these languages, you only have to specify the separate event subroutines.

We have glossed over a number of details in describing the queuing simulation model. We briefly mention a few of these before going on to the next section, which considers the design of simulation experiments. First, note that the charts in Fig. 21.9 do not show a test for terminating a simulation run. Of course, you must include such a calculation; you might state it by means of a time horizon or limit on the number of customers arriving. Second, observe that tabulating statistics on the operating characteristics is not an easy process because of the variable-time increments between successive events. Care must be taken to measure, for example, not only the frequency with which the waiting line has n customers, but also the associated fraction of the simulated horizon. Finally, recall that the initial conditions were chosen arbitrarily. If the queuing system in fact tends to be congested, then the effect of letting LINE $= 0$ at the start will take a while to wear off. Specifying appropriate initial conditions is part of the tactics of designing a simulation experiment.

21.7 DESIGN OF SIMULATION EXPERIMENTS†

After constructing a simulation model, you face the difficult task of designing a set of runs of the model and analyzing data that emanate from these runs. For example, you must decide the

- Starting conditions of the model.
- Parameter settings to expose different system responses.
- Length of each run (the number of simulated time periods and the amount of elapsed computer time).
- Number of runs with the same parameter settings.
- Variables to measure and how to measure them.

If you are not careful, you can expend an enormous amount of computer time in validating the model to see whether it behaves like a real system, in estimating the system responses of the model to different parameter settings, and in discovering the response relationships among these parameters. Even then, and even after collecting a vast amount of data, you still may not have sufficiently accurate information to guide a managerial decision.

Surprising as it may seem, there has been relatively little development of statistical techniques aimed at constructing efficient designs of simulation experiments. By and large, professional management scientists have tried to "make do" with standard statistical tools to analyze experimental data from simulations. These techniques at best are only moderately successful, because most of them are not constructed for the analysis of multidimensional time series data. In particular, many (but not all) of the commonly used statistical tools assume that separate observations of the variables being measured are uncorrelated and drawn from a Normal distribution with the same parameters.

We cannot possibly summarize all of the standard statistical techniques that can be applied to analyze simulation data. Instead, we discuss certain design procedures that enable you to employ many techniques ordinarily found in a

†This section requires a knowledge of statistical methods.

modern text on experimental statistics. We also give a brief overview of some statistical approaches that are particularly well suited to the design of computer simulations.

In search of Normality. Suppose you have constructed a queuing model to test two different service disciplines. For example, your application may be a model of a job-shop production system, and the two disciplines for processing orders are "first come, first served" and a particular priority scheme. Assume further that the difference in the two disciplines is to be measured solely in terms of the average waiting time (exclusive of service) for orders. How might you ascertain what this difference is?

This question is more difficult than it may appear at first glance. Since your measurements will be random variables, you must consider their statistical variability and be on the watch for certain kinds of complications. In any single simulation run, the waiting times of successive orders will be **serially correlated** (sometimes called **autocorrelated**); that is, there is a greater likelihood that the $(n + 1)$st order will be delayed if the nth order waits, than if the nth order commences service immediately. The extent of variation in waiting times may itself be affected by the two different disciplines. The model may be unstable and the trend of waiting times may be ever upward. Even if the system does approach equilibrium, which may require a considerably long run, waiting times need not be Normally distributed. To ignore all these considerations and simply compare the average waiting times from a simulated run of each discipline is to court disaster.

Suppose you can demonstrate, on theoretical grounds, that the queuing model is stable, and that the effects of the starting conditions eventually fade away. Then it can be proved that even though the waiting times of successive orders are autocorrelated, the expected value of the sample average of these waiting times, taken over a sufficiently long run, is approximately that implied by the equilibrium distribution.

More precisely, let x_t, for $t = 1, 2, \ldots, q$, represent q successive data observations of the random variable in a given simulation run, and define the **time-integrated average** as

$$(1) \qquad \bar{x} = \sum_{t=1}^{q} \frac{x_t}{q}.$$

Let μ represent the so-called **ensemble mean** of this random variable, as calculated from the *equilibrium* distribution. Then for q sufficiently large, we have the approximation

$$(2) \qquad E[\bar{x}] \approx \mu.$$

Furthermore, it can be shown that the sampling distribution of $\bar{x}$ is approximately Normal. You can calculate an estimate of the variance of this distribution as follows. Assuming that the process is **covariance-stationary** (the covariance between x_t and x_{t+k} depends only on k and not on t), and that the associated autocorrelations tend to 0 as k grows large, you first estimate these autocorrelations by:

(3) $$r_k = \frac{1}{q-k}\sum_{t=1}^{q-k}(x_t - \bar{x})(x_{t+k} - \bar{x}) \quad \text{for } k = 0, 1, 2, \ldots, M,$$

where M is chosen to be much smaller than q. (Unfortunately, a discussion of how much smaller M should be is too complicated to be given here, but can be found in the statistics literature under the subject title **autocorrelation** and **spectral analysis.**) The appropriate *estimate* of the variance of $\bar{x}$ is

(4) $$V_{\bar{x}} = \frac{1}{q}\left[r_0 + 2\sum_{k=1}^{M}\left(1 - \frac{k}{M}\right)r_k\right].$$

Note that if, in fact, the time series is known to be free of autocorrelation, then the terms r_k, for $k = 1, 2, \ldots, M$, would be eliminated from (4). The presence of positive autocorrelation, however, implies greater statistical variability in $\bar{x}$ as compared with the case of uncorrelated observations.

We now can look at two commonly employed approaches to statistical analyses. For the first method, consider making one very long run of each service discipline; specifically, take T consecutive observations in each run. Then you can apply (1) through (4) with $q = T$. If T is sufficiently large, the statistic $(\bar{x} - \mu)/\sqrt{V_{\bar{x}}}$ is approximately Normally distributed with mean 0 and variance 1. This fact allows you to perform standard statistical procedures for hypothesis testing and constructing confidence intervals for μ, as well as to use modern Bayesian analysis. To compare the effect of the two service disciplines on average waiting time, you can apply standard statistical theory for discerning the difference between the means of two Normally distributed variables that have possibly unequal and estimated variances.

For the second method, consider making n independent replications, that is, n different runs. Suppose you want to have T observations *in toto* from the n replications and that you take T/n observations from each run (assume T/n is an integer). Then for each replication p, calculate a time-integrated average $\bar{x}_p$, for $p = 1, 2, \ldots, n$, using (1) with $q = T/n$. Afterwards compute the grand average

(5) $$\bar{\bar{x}} = \sum_{p=1}^{n}\frac{\bar{x}_p}{n}.$$

For any T/n, if n is large enough, the sampling distribution of $\bar{\bar{x}}$ is approximately Normal due to the *Central Limit Theorem* for the mean of independently and identically distributed random variables (namely, the $\bar{x}_p$). If you let T/n be large enough, the approximation is improved because of the near-Normality of the sampling distribution for *each* $\bar{x}_p$. What is more, it follows from (2) that when T/n is sufficiently large,

(6) $$E[\bar{\bar{x}}] \approx \mu.$$

To determine the accuracy of $\bar{\bar{x}}$, you can *estimate* the variance of the sampling distribution of $\bar{\bar{x}}$ from the variation in $\bar{x}_p$, using

(7)
$$V_{\bar{\bar{x}}} = \frac{1}{n}\left[\frac{\sum_{p=1}^{n}(\bar{x}_p - \bar{\bar{x}})^2}{n-1}\right].$$

Once again, if n and T are large, the quantity $(\bar{\bar{x}} - \mu)/\sqrt{V_{\bar{\bar{x}}}}$ is approximately Normally distributed with mean 0 and variance 1, and so the same sorts of statistical analyses can be performed as in the one-long-replication procedure.

Although the preceding discussion has related to a comparison of two different service disciplines in a job-shop model, these statistical approaches are generally applicable. In summary, assuming that the simulated system does approach an equilibrium, then under widely applicable conditions, you can legitimately average the successive observations of a simulated time series. As the number of observations grows large, this time-integrated average, in a probabilistic sense, converges to the desired ensemble mean implied by the equilibrium distribution. (You can find the subject of probabilistic convergence treated in detail in texts on stochastic processes under the heading of **ergodic theorems.**) And furthermore, under widely applicable conditions, the time-integrated average is approximately Normally distributed. (You can look up the topic of Normal approximations in advanced statistics texts under the heading of the Central Limit Theorem for correlated random variables.)

Therefore, in many situations you can apply Normal-distribution theory if you either replicate simulation runs and then take a grand average of the individual time-integrated averages, or if you take a single time-integrated average from a very long run. A comparison of the relative merits of these two approaches as well as of other methods goes beyond the scope of this text. (The issues involved concern the amount of bias introduced by the starting conditions of the simulation and the stability properties of $V_{\bar{x}}$.)

Sample size. Assume that you take a sufficient number of replications or let the simulation run long enough to justify using the Normal distribution to approximate the sampling distribution of the calculated averages. You still may need even more replications or a longer run to obtain the accuracy you require for decision analysis. The determination of an appropriate sample size for a simulation is no different from sample-size determination in ordinary statistical problems. Therefore, you can find the question discussed in detail in every text on statistical analysis.

We do emphasize, however, the influence of the number of observations on the accuracy of the statistical estimates. Whether you use the single-long-run approach, depicted in (1) through (4), with $q = T$, or the n-replication approach, depicted in (5) through (7), with $q = T/n$, the true variance of the sampling distribution for the calculated mean equals the reciprocal of the total number of observations T multiplied by another factor that is independent of T. Therefore, to reduce the standard deviation of the sampling distribution of either $\bar{x}$ or $\bar{\bar{x}}$ from a value of s, say, to $(.1)s$, you must increase the total number of observations to

$100T$. More generally, to reduce the standard deviation by a factor of $1/f$, you have to take f^2 as many observations.

Usually, you cannot know how many observations to take at the start of a simulation, because you do not know the factors that multiply $1/T$ in the expressions for the true variances of the sampling distributions of $\bar{x}$ and $\tilde{x}$. For this reason, a commonly used procedure is to sample in two stages. In the first stage, you take a relatively small number of observations, and thereby calculate an estimate of the factor that multiplies $1/T$. With this estimate, you determine the remaining number of observations to take in the second stage to give the required accuracy.

In actual applications, you may be surprised to find how many observations are needed to yield reasonable accuracy in the estimates. As pointed out above, the root of the difficulty is often the presence of positive autocorrelation. We discuss below a few approaches for coping with inherently large variation in the statistical estimates.

*Variance-reduction techniques. There are a number of ways to improve the accuracy of the estimate of the ensemble average for a given number of data observations. These techniques are explained in texts on simulation under the heading of **Monte Carlo** or **variance-reduction methods.** Their use in management-oriented simulations is not yet widespread. We give only a couple of illustrations to suggest what is involved.

To assist in the exposition, we return to the example above of simulating a job-shop production system. Suppose, for the sake of definiteness, that you are simulating under the "first come, first served" discipline, and that you want to estimate the average waiting time of an order.

The first device we examine is sometimes called the **Method of Control Variates**, or alternatively, the **Method of Concomitant Information.** We present a highly simplified example of the idea. By elementary considerations you know that the interarrival times and the waiting times of each order are negatively correlated—roughly put, the longer the time since the previous order arrived, the shorter the waiting time of the latest order. State why. Therefore, suppose in a particular simulation run that the observed average of interarrival times is greater than the true average. Then you can use this information to add a positive correction to the observed average value of the waiting times. Similarly, suppose the observed average of interarrival times is smaller than the true average. Then you can make a negative correction to the observed average value of the waiting times. The technique explained below calculates either a positive or negative correction, whichever is appropriate.

Specifically, from the input data for the simulation you have the value of the true mean interarrival time, say, $1/\lambda$. Then let x_t represent the waiting time of Order t, and y_t the interarrival time between Orders t $-$ 1 and t. Consider the measurement

(8)
$$z_t \equiv x_t + y_t - \frac{1}{\lambda},$$

and its time-integrated average

$$(9) \qquad \bar{z} = \frac{\sum\limits_{t=1}^{T} z_t}{T} = \frac{\sum\limits_{t=1}^{T} \left(x_t + y_t - \dfrac{1}{\lambda} \right)}{T} \equiv \bar{x} + \bar{y} - \frac{1}{\lambda}.$$

Note that the expectation of $\bar{z}$ is the same as that of $\bar{x}$, since $\bar{y}$ is an unbiased estimator of $1/\lambda$. So you can use $\bar{z}$ as a consistent estimate of the average waiting time. But if x_t and y_t are sufficiently negatively correlated, then the variance of $\bar{z}$ will be less than the variance of $\bar{x}$. A sample estimate of the variance of $\bar{z}$ can be calculated by assessing the variation in $\bar{z}$ from several replications, or by substituting z_t for x_t in (1), (3), and (4) above.

A more sophisticated method than (8) is to calculate $z_t \equiv x_t + a(y_t - 1/\lambda)$, where now the value of a is specifically chosen to make the variance of $\bar{z}$ small. Under ideal conditions, a can be set such that $\mathrm{Var}\,(\bar{z}) = \mathrm{Var}\,(\bar{x})(1 - \rho^2)$, where ρ is the correlation between $\bar{x}$ and $\bar{y}$.

Before going on, we caution that the preceding example is meant only to be illustrative of the control variate idea. If you actually apply the technique to a queuing model like a job-shop production system, you should select a control variate that would absorb more of the sampling variation that would be accounted for by the interarrival times of orders. In fact, you probably should use several control variates instead of only one.

The second variance-reducing device we examine is called the **Method of Antithetic Variates.** The aim here is to introduce negative correlation between two separate replications of the simulation, so that the variance of the combined averages is less than if the replications were independent. (The idea can also be extended to more than two replications.)

Suppose in the job-shop production simulation that the interarrival times are determined by the Inverse Transform Method of Sec. 21.5. Let u_t, for $t = 1$, $2, \ldots, T/2$, be the corresponding uniform random decimal numbers for generating the interarrival times y_t in the first simulation run of the model. Then in the second simulation, by using the values $1 - u_t$, which are also uniform random decimal numbers, the two time-integrated sample averages will be negatively correlated. State why.

Notice that the two simulations involve a total of T observations. Whether the mean of the two separate negatively correlated averages has less statistical variation than does the average of T autocorrelated observations from a single run depends on the extent to which the antithetic variates u_t and $1 - u_t$ induce negative correlation. Thus, the answer depends on the particular model being simulated, and the specific values of the model's parameters.

The crucial factor in deciding when to use variance-reduction techniques is whether, in fact, a given approach diminishes the variance of the estimates, and if so, whether the reduction is sufficient to warrant the extra computations required.

*Multivariate analysis. The discussion so far has been partly misleading in that we have discussed examples involving the measurement of only a single operating characteristic for a system, such as average waiting time, and the comparison of only two alternatives, such as two different service disciplines. In real applications of simulation models, there are usually several operating characteristics of relevance and a multitude of alternatives to evaluate.

Multivariate analysis is by no means a new subject in statistics literature, but techniques for the analysis and design of experiments involving multivariate time series are just emerging. The reason for this relatively late development is that only recently has the availability of electronic computers made it practical to perform such data analyses.

By employing the approaches previously described to yield measurements that are Normally distributed, you have at least partially opened the storehouse of standard multivariate statistics. But still it is no simple matter to design a simulation experiment that can legitimately apply, say, latin squares, factor analysis, or multivariate regression.

Progress in devising helpful tools for multivariate analysis and complex experimentation is being made on two fronts. One important development, known as *spectral analysis*, aims at exploring the nature of serial correlation and periodicities in time series. The other front seeks methods for finding optimal levels of the decision variables; two such developments are *response surface* and *stochastic approximation techniques*. You can find these developments explained in the technical statistics literature.

21.8 COMPUTER LANGUAGES

Unless you become both an operations research specialist and a computer programmer, you personally will not have to translate your simulation model into a workable computer program. You should, however, know the major steps involved in this translation.

If your model is fairly simple and is a common application of simulation, then a so-called **canned program** may be available in which all you need do is specify a modest amount of input information. The best examples of this type of program are inventory control simulators. There are a number of canned programs that test the effectiveness of inventory replenishment rules. To employ these routines, you must supply the specific rules, such as "when down to 4, order 10 more," or a formula to calculate the rules, given demand data. You also supply as part of the input either actual historical data on customer demand or a probability distribution for demand. The computer program then simulates the system for whatever number of time periods you designate, and calculates statistics such as the frequency of stockouts, the average inventory level, the number of orders placed, etc.

More typically, your model will require some special computer programming. If the simulation is only moderately complex, is to be used infrequently, and is to be programmed by personnel inexperienced in simulation techniques, then using a general purpose language, such as FORTRAN, PL/1, or ALGOL, is probably the easiest way to accomplish the task. This type of computer language is familiar to all programmers of scientific problems; a programmer requires only the details of your model to translate it into computer language.

There is an important drawback to employing languages like FORTRAN, PL/1, and ALGOL. The programmer has to write, from scratch, subroutines for certain kinds of calculations that are included in almost all simulations. In the vernacular, the programmer has to "reinvent the wheel." For example, most simulations require generating random variables, and so a subroutine is needed for each such variable in the model. In addition, since you want to collect statistics on the system's operating characteristics, subroutines have to be written to calculate these statistics, and a fair-sized associated programming effort must be accomplished to format the output of the simulation runs. Even a moderately complex model requires careful attention in organizing the data within the computer memory, writing a master routine for sequencing events in their proper order, and keeping track of simulated time within the computer.

Several computer languages have been developed for the specific purpose of easing the programming task of building a simulation model. These programs require that you specify only the probability distribution functions, and they automatically generate random events according to the distributions you indicate. Several of the languages collect statistics on whatever operating characteristics you want to examine, and report the results on predesigned output forms. These languages also properly sequence events and keep track of time as it elapses in the model.

With such advantages, you may wonder why all simulations are not programmed in one of these languages. At present, there are several good reasons. One is that the languages differ to some extent from FORTRAN, PL/1 or ALGOL, and hence require a programmer to become familiar with a new system.

One of the most powerful simulation languages is SIMSCRIPT; it requires a knowledge of FORTRAN and is fairly complex because of its considerable flexibility. At the other extreme of complexity is the General Purpose Systems Simulator (GPSS). It is a self-contained language that is easy to learn by beginners, but, accordingly, is restricted in its scope.

A second reason for not employing a simulation language is that it may not be available on the computer you want to use. This is rarely the determining factor today because SIMSCRIPT and GPSS programs are available for many computers, and there is widespread access to computer service bureaus that have these programs.

A third reason becomes important if the simulation is complex and is to be run frequently. A price you pay in using a simulation language is that it often runs slowly and consumes large amounts of a computer's high-speed memory. As a result, you may find it costly to perform many experiments, and your model may literally not fit into the available memory capacity of the computer.

As further technical improvements in simulation languages continue, and as management scientists gain more experience in employing computer simulation, it seems likely that such languages will be the common mode of solution.

21.9 DEUS EX MACHINA

So far we have discussed only simulation models that to some degree represent approximations to real situations. Their orientation has been to provide a simulated environment in which to test the effects of different managerial policies. A related class of simulation models tries to encompass goal-seeking or purposeful behavior. These models display what is termed **artificial intelligence.**

Some of the popular examples of artificial intelligence programs include computer routines for playing such games as chess and checkers. There also have been a few applications to managerial problems. One group of applications focuses on the behavioral patterns of individual decision-makers. A measure of such a model's success is how well it yields decisions agreeing with those of the individual whose behavior is allegedly represented.

Another group of applications deals with complex combinational problems, like those discussed in Chap. 13. They are sometimes referred to as **heuristic programming** methods. For example, several of these models have been designed to derive good schedules for intricate sequencing problems. The following illustration suggests how they work.

Suppose the goal of the model is to schedule orders through a job-shop with maximum equipment efficiency. The computer starts by tentatively scheduling a few orders. It then selects another order to schedule, and examines various feasibility restrictions, due dates, and equipment efficiency. As a consequence, the computer may have to reschedule some of the previous orders. In brief, the computer model uses a number of "look-back" and "look-ahead" rules, and proceeds by educated trial-and-error toward a feasible schedule. If the rules are sufficiently sophisticated, then usually the schedule is good. Frequently, the schedule is nearly optimal according to the specified efficiency criterion, assuming the heuristic rules are promulgated with reference to this criterion.

▶Management scientists have also employed computer models for **operational gaming.** Some of the early applications, known as **management games,** involved several teams of players, each representing a business firm. A team made decisions about pricing, production quantities, advertising, etc. The computer served the two-fold purpose of keeping the accounting records, and of calculating the net impact of the decisions made by the several teams. More recently, such applications have been used to train personnel in administrative procedures, and to explore the system dynamics of an industry in which the competing firms are employing specified strategies.   ◀

REVIEW EXERCISES

1 Suggest two or three managerial decision problems that seem to go beyond the capabilities of the mathematical models treated in earlier chapters of this text. Select situations that involve the optimization of an objective function subject, perhaps, to constraints or uncertainties. Explain what makes these problems so complex to solve.

2 Consider the stock market simulation example in Sec. 21.3. Repeat the experiment for another 20 days, starting with the same initial conditions as in Fig. 21.3. Array your calculations and results in tables like Figs. 21.3 and 21.4. Calculate Doe's cash position at the end of Day 20; if he holds stock, compute his cash position by assuming he sells out at the end of Day 20. (*Suggestion:* if you are in a class that is assigned this problem, collect the results from all the students and calculate the mean and standard deviation of Doe's cash position on Days 5, 10, 15, and 20.)

3 Consider the stock market simulation example in Sec. 21.3. Test the rule: (i) if you own the stock, then sell it whenever the price falls two days in a row, and (ii) if you do not own the stock, then buy it whenever the price rises two days in a row.

   (a) Use the same data as in Fig. 21.3, and construct a table like Fig. 21.4. Calculate Doe's cash position at the end of Day 20; if he holds stock, compute his cash position by assuming he sells out at the end of Day 20.

   (b) Extend the length of the simulation run another 20 days, and calculate Doe's cash position at the end of Day 40. (*Suggestion:* if you are in a class that is assigned this problem, collect the results from all the students and calculate the mean and standard deviation of Doe's cash position on Days 30 and 40.)

4 Suggest one or two experimental setups (analogous to the "slips-in-a-hat" approach) for generating uniform random digits. Discuss whether any of these approaches can be modified to generate other discrete probability distributions.

*5 Consider the Multiplicative Congruential Method for generating random digits in Sec. 21.5. In each part below, assume modulo 10 arithmetic and determine the length of the cycle.

   (a) Let $a = 2$ and $r_0 = 1, 3,$ and 5.
   (b) Let $a = 3$, and $r_0 = 1, 2,$ and 5.

6 In each part below, apply the Inverse Transform Method in Sec. 21.5, and devise specific formulas analogous to (9) and (13) that yield the value of the variate x_n, given a random decimal number u_n.

   (a)

$$f(t) = \begin{cases} (b - a)^{-1} & \text{for } a \leq t \leq b \\ 0 & \text{otherwise,} \end{cases}$$

where a and b are real numbers and $a < b$.

(b)

$$f(t) = \begin{cases} t & \text{for } 0 \le t \le 1 \\ 1 - t & \text{for } 1 \le t \le 2 \\ 0 & \text{otherwise.} \end{cases}$$

(c)

$$F(x) = \begin{cases} 0 & \text{for } x < 0 \\ .5x & \text{for } 0 \le x \le .4 \\ x - .2 & \text{for } .4 \le x \le .8 \\ 2x - 1 & \text{for } .8 \le x \le 1 \\ 1 & \text{for } x > 1. \end{cases}$$

(d) Binomial distribution, given by (12), where $k = 2$ and $p = .1$.
(e) Binomial distribution, given by (12), where $k = 3$ and $p = .5$.

7 Explain how the description of the Inverse Transform Method in Sec. 21.5 needs to be altered to treat the case where $F(x)$ is continuous and nondecreasing (that is, not necessarily *strictly* increasing).

*8 In each part below, explain how you would apply the Tabular Method in Sec. 21.5.

(a) Binomial distribution, given by (12), where $k = 2$ and $p = .1$.
(b) Binomial distribution, given by (12), where $k = 3$ and $p = .5$.
(c) $p(0) = .3$, $p(2) = .25$, $p(5) = .15$, and $p(60) = .3$.

*9 (a) Explain how you can apply the Method of Convolutions in Sec. 21.5 to generate the triangular distribution in exercise 6, part (b).
(b) Consider the Method of Equivalent Transformations in Sec. 21.5, and explain why the suggested procedure for generating a Poisson random variable is valid.

*10 Consider the approach (21) in Sec. 21.5 for generating Normally distributed random variables. Explain why (21), which involves a sum of 12 uniform random decimals, produces a random variable with a distribution having mean 0 and variance 1.

11 (a) Suggest one or more methods for generating a geometric distribution $p(j) = p(1 - p)^j$, for $j = 0, 1, 2, \ldots$, where $0 < p < 1$. [*Recall:* let p represent the probability of a head appearing on the toss of a possibly biased coin; then $p(j)$ represents the probability that a head appears for the first time on Toss j.]
(b) Suggest one or more methods for generating a negative binomial distribution $p(j) = \binom{k+j-1}{j} p^k (1 - p)^j$, for $j = 0, 1, 2, \ldots$, where $0 < p < 1$. [*Recall:* let p represent the probability of a head appearing on the toss of a possibly biased coin; then $p(j)$ represents the probability that the kth head appears on Toss k + j.]

12 Consider the inventory simulation in Sec. 21.6. Assume $Q = 2$, $s = 1$, $L = 2$, and the demand distribution probabilities are $p(1) = p(3) = .5$. Simulate the system for 20 days, letting INVENTORY ON-HAND = 2, AMOUNT DUE-IN = 0, TIME DUE-IN = 0, and $t = 1$ in Block 1. (*Suggestion:* flip a coin to generate the daily demand quantities.)

13 Consider the inventory model simulation in Sec. 21.6.

 (a) Explain how you would modify Fig. 21.8 if lead time L were random.

 (b) Explain what complications arise if $Q \leq s$. If demand in excess of INVENTORY ON-HAND is backlogged.

 *(c) Suppose the probability process for demands can be formulated in terms of a distribution generating interarrival times between successive customers, and a distribution generating the quantity demanded by each customer. Devise an event-step incrementation flow chart for simulating the system.

14 Construct a time-step incrementation flow chart for the stock market example in Sec. 21.3.

*15 Explain how to design an event-step incrementation simulation for the stock market example in Sec. 21.3. Try to construct an appropriate flow chart.

*16 Consider the waiting line model in Sec. 21.6. Suppose the interarrival time is either 2 or 3, each possibility occurring with probability $\frac{1}{2}$; that service time for Clerk A is either 1 or 2, each occurring with probability $\frac{1}{2}$, and for Clerk B is either 1 or 4, each occurring with probability $\frac{1}{2}$. At $t = 0$, assume that the first customer arrives and that both clerks are free. Simulate an hour's operation of the system. (*Suggestion:* determine the random events by flipping a coin. If you are in a class that is assigned this problem, collect the following statistics for all the students and calculate the associated mean and standard deviation: the number of persons waiting in line at $t = 30$, 45, and 60 minutes; the number of persons that were served during the hour and their average time in the system, in line, and in service.)

17 Consider the OR Airline telephone line simulation, discussed in Sec. 1.6. In each part below, draw a flow chart indicating how to simulate a two-line system. Also explain what statistics you would tabulate.

 (a) Use a time-step incrementation formulation.

 *(b) Use an event-step incrementation formulation.

18 Explain your understanding of the following terms:

digital computer simulation	*Method of Equivalent Transformations
manual simulation	fixed-time increments
time compression	variable-time increments
dynamic phenomena	time-step incrementation
entities	*event-step incrementation
decision rule	*master program
attributes	*event list
membership relationships	*event subroutine
state of the simulated system	*next imminent event
exogenous events	serial correlation (autocorrelation)
recursive (causal) structure	time-integrated average
validity and reliability	ensemble mean
performance measure	covariance-stationary

uniform random numbers
pseudo-random number generator
*Multiplicative Congruential Method
*modulus arithmetic
*congruent, modulo *m*
*seed
*cycle (period)
Inverse Transform Method
*Tabular Method
*Method of Convolutions (Method of Composition)

spectral analysis
ergodic convergence
*Monte Carlo (variance-reduction) methods
*Method of Control Variates (Method of Concomitant Information)
*Method of Antithetic Variates
canned program
artificial intelligence
heuristic programming
*operational gaming (management games).

FORMULATION EXERCISES

19 In each part below, describe how you would build a simulation model to represent the system. State explicitly the random phenomena and how you would obtain the probability distributions required as input. Describe the performance measures you would collect, and explain their relevance to the associated managerial decision problem. Try to develop a flow chart describing the simulation of a "toy" version of the system.

  (a) Checkout stands in a grocery store. (How would you test the effectiveness of an express counter to serve customers with five or less items?)
  (b) Tellers' windows at a bank. (How would you test the effectiveness of having an express window to serve customers requiring only a single transaction?)
  (c) Pumps at a gasoline station.
  (d) Runways at an airport.
  (e) Traffic lights in a configuration of eight city blocks.
  (f) Parking lot for a doctors' office building.
  (g) Telephone operators at a metropolitan police station.
  (h) Restaurant facilities at a World's Fair.
  (i) Layout of tables at a posh restaurant.
  (j) Layout of equipment in a job-shop.
  (k) Piers at a harbor facility.
  (l) Allocation of substitute teachers in a school district.
  (m) Layout of rooms and facilities in a new school building.
  (n) Screening methods for evaluating proposed capital investments by a corporation.
  (o) Design of an electronic computer installation at a college or university.
  (p) A decision problem that you suggested in exercise 1.

CONTENTS

CHAPTER 22

Implementation of
Operations Research

22.1 LIKE IT IS

In the past few years, many significant technical breakthroughs have been made in operations research. Even greater progress occurred, however, in implementing operations research in commercial and governmental enterprises.

In the early 1960's, a practicing operations researcher had to be both a scientific expert and a master of the "art of persuasion." Ethical, but convincing, salesmanship was needed then because relatively few companies firmly believed that operations research was a profit-yielding activity. Most executives classified the effort as blue-sky research and development, and, in fact, several major corporations placed their operations research group in an R & D department.

Since then, the picture has changed dramatically. Only rarely now is an operations researcher called upon to defend his *raison d'etre*. Today, executives show pride in employing computer models that have been designed to assist them in analyzing complex decision problems. (Many managers guard their computer models as a part of their territorial imperative.) In short, very few executives in leading corporations still ask, "Why do we need operations research?" They know *why*.

The questions that managers do raise are, "What areas of application are the most profitable?" "Is our company spending too little or too much on operations research?" "How can I best use operations research?" In other words, the present interest of businessmen is learning *how* to get the maximum benefit from operations research.

The sections below explore the practical implications of this managerial attitude and offer some insights into the implementation process. Although the sections are entitled "How to. . . ," the chapter is not really a comprehensive nuts-and-bolts manual of procedures for guaranteeing profitable implementation. Rather, the chapter provides a few guidelines for making operations research work effectually. The orientation of the discussion is toward people, not mathematical techniques.

As you will soon discover, the key to the successful conduct of operations research is the joint exercise of good judgment by executives and professional operations researchers. In particular, the managers and technicians must decide in concert what projects to pursue, what goals to sight, what level of effort to expend, and what timetable to follow. These are the subjects analyzed below.

▶ You may be curious to know why implementation is so much easier now. The reasons may not be obvious, as many of the most useful mathematical techniques have existed for more than 15 years. Part of the answer has already been given in Sec. 1.7, which explained how executives have come to appreciate the powerful analytic assistance of operations research. But this recognition is by no means the only factor contributing to a widespread acceptance of the approach.

An equally important reason is that computing equipment has become vastly more accessible, and that the number of programming specialists has increased concomitantly. The improvement in so-called *software computer programs* that assist in solving large-scale optimization and simulation problems as well as the development of *time-shared computing systems* have diminished the task of systems design and lessened the difficulties of obtaining numerical solutions. Another reason is that the population of well-trained and experienced operations researchers has expanded sufficiently to provide the required professional manpower.   ◄

22.2 HOW TO PUT OPERATIONS RESEARCH TO MANAGERIAL USE

What commonly distinguishes an executive familiar with employing operations research from a first-time user is his recognition of the need to exercise responsibility vis-a-vis the conduct of the project. For quite understandable reasons, tyro managers are usually "stand-offish" in their involvement. Such a posture is ill advised and can be expensive to the company, even when the operations research application ultimately succeeds.

In essence, line managers must take responsibility to see that the right problem is analyzed and that adequate controls are exercised to monitor the progress of the application. Experience has shown repeatedly that ignoring this responsibility is detrimental to all and may easily be the root cause of failure, despite the expertise and sincerity of the operations research technical staff. This section suggests some ways for an executive to ensure that an operations research effort is well directed and aimed at bettering the entire organization.

What benefits should a manager expect? Operations research can be employed to mount a massive analysis, when warranted, of an important and intricate decision-making problem. As you will readily observe in applying operations research, the approach *inherently* requires adhering to systematic procedures and paying careful attention to details. (No other approach for solving complex management problems even comes close in demanding so much discipline in analysis.) The combined utilization of advanced mathematical techniques and enormous computing power permits a thorough exploration of relevant alternatives. A good operations research study will leave no doubt in an executive's mind that all reasonable courses of action have been investigated, and will make crystal clear the relative merits of specific alternative actions and their possible consequences.

A central ingredient to a sound operations research investigation is extensive sensitivity testing. Careful managerial scrutiny of comparative case studies provides the principal means by which an executive can confirm his understanding of the underlying model, its assumptions, and its data. Furthermore, the benefits a manager receives from a planning-oriented model stem largely from such insightful sensitivity testing. Rarely, if ever, does an executive seek "numbers" as answers; rather, most decision-makers want a quantitative assessment of what risks are at stake with different actions, what changes in direction are likely to yield profit improvements, and what avenues are promising for further investigation (such as the development of new products, expansion into new markets, location of new plant sites, etc.). Often sensitivity testing reveals that the uncertainty of an allegedly critical factor is actually not very important in making a good decision, whereas another factor, previously thought insignificant, is truly pivotal.

To determine whether an operations research project is meeting acceptable standards of quality, some easy items to check are the ready availability of input data and model assumptions in a form understandable to nontechnicians, the summarization of results and the backup detail printed in the format of managerial reports, and reasonable turnaround times for running additional analyses having slightly modified input data or assumptions. The best way for a manager to make these checks is to ask questions and probe the answers. A competently designed model should provide a manager comprehensible answers to his spontaneous "why does. . ." and "what if. . ." questions without requiring a mammoth crash effort. (We hasten to add, however, that it is unfair to expect such rapid service at the initial stages of a study. A line executive should continue to ask questions throughout the duration of the project, and monitor whether the effort required to answer these questions eventually becomes routine and commensurate with the value of the analytic assistance provided.)

Another indicator of project quality is the extent to which the analysis results in a recommended *strategy*, as distinct from a suggested *single decision*. To illustrate, the output from a long-range capacity-expansion study should not be merely a string of recommended equipment purchases and forecasted production levels. Rather, the output should indicate the decisions to take immediately, should include recommendations of when to make the next set of decisions, given the present data, and should establish the circumstances for reviewing, and possibly revising, these future decisions. Even the immediate decision recommendations should be qualified to the point of ascertaining what other alternatives are appropriate if the data are varied within a plausible range of values and any restrictive assumptions are relaxed.

What limitations should a manager recognize? This question was partially answered in Sec. 1.3, and you may want to review that material. Three more cautions are added here.

First, when an operations research model is used to reduce costs, the percentage savings may be *relatively* small. But if this percentage is applied to a large cost base, the absolute savings can pay for the operations research study many times over. Occasionally, a planning model will uncover a costly error in current operating procedures; in such an instance, the savings may be large. Most often, profit improvements stem from executives possessing a deeper understanding of the problem area, and hence developing a keener sense for taking correct actions and maintaining control in an uncertain and competitive environment. It is impossible to assign a precise dollar improvement figure to this type of impact; nevertheless, the benefits are real and are perceived and valued by company management. In a preponderence of successful applications, the beneficial effects are truly manifest in the altered decision behavior of executives and managers at several levels of the corporation.

Second, although an operations research model often uses the mathematics of optimization, the resultant solution should not be viewed as *necessarily* yielding an optimal answer to the real problem. After all, as the text has stressed throughout, a model is *inherently* an approximation to reality, and therefore an optimal solution to this approximation need not be the "final" answer to the actual decision problem. The important issue, however, is not whether a proposed solution is *optimal*, but whether the solution yields a significant enough *improvement* over the alternatives to make it worthy of acceptance.

Third, while providing a solution to one set of problems, the operations research model may create, in turn, another set of problems. For example, the analysis may demonstrate the need for an improved information gathering system or for a restructuring of operating policies. And, ensuring the continued maintenance of an up-to-date model does, itself, pose new managerial problems.

When should a manager initiate an operations research project? It is helpful to distinguish between so-called *one-shot* or infrequent decision problems and *recurring* decision analyses (like devising an annual plan, scheduling men and equipment, and replenishing inventories).

In special studies, a decision to apply operations research depends on the economic and strategic importance of the decision, the time span available for performing the analysis, and the relevance and availability of data. It is difficult and hazardous to apply operations research under "time pressure." Consequently, a manager should consider employing the approach when the stakes are sizeable, the decision does not *have* to be made next Monday morning, data are available for the analysis, and the choice is not so governed by political and personality considerations within the company that economic analysis is of only minor import.

In planning situations, the decision to apply operations research also depends on the economic and strategic stakes of the problem and the available data. But planning applications differ from special studies most critically in the longer time horizon over which the model can be developed and tested. As we point out in later sections, controlling progress in the conduct of an operations research study is important; nevertheless, the corporation will not grind to a halt if a couple of weeks' delay postpones the completion of an operations research planning model. (And there always *is* a couple of weeks' delay!)

The decision to develop a computerized model for daily operations usually is more involved. Numerous companies have successfully constructed such models for as diverse applications as inventory control, tanker-fleet routing, and job-shop scheduling. Often the economic benefits are small percentagewise, the systems design effort is staggering, and the implementation process is painful. Hence, this type of application is usually justified in terms of producing economic benefits that will extend over a relatively long term.

Sometimes executives misjudge whether the available data are sufficiently accurate as to warrant using an operations research approach. Applications of statistical techniques to the design of industrial research experiments, to the monitoring of continuous production processes and machinery, and to the auditing of voluminous accounting transactions demonstrate that mathematical techniques can be effective in analyzing sparse data that are subject to variability and measurement errors. Inaccurate or limited data do not *per se* negate the application of a mathematical technique. Even if there are no historical data at all, managers may be able to impart their experience-based knowledge by means of probabilistic statements. Hence, it is inappropriate for an executive to reject using operations research solely on the grounds of less than perfect factual information.

Sometimes executives shy away from operations research because they feel that their company personnel are not sophisticated enough to use mathematical techniques. This fear may be well founded, but the apprehension also may be based on a limited or even erroneous understanding of the degree of sophistication that is actually required. And all too often, senior managers underestimate the capability of their experienced personnel to learn how to apply operations research.

Many successful applications have been made by personnel who are trained in accounting, engineering, economics, or business, and who have been away from school for years. Their first-hand knowledge of the company more than compensates for their initial unfamiliarity with technicalities of operations research. In addition, the widespread availability of easy-to-use canned computer programs has removed much of the burden in going from a model formulation and actual data to a numerical solution and sensitivity analysis. And, finally, although the mathematical methods employed to obtain a numerical solution may be advanced, the solution itself may be easy to interpret and to implement. (A good example of this type of application is inventory control. The computations of a reorder point and replenishment quantity can sometimes be intricate; nevertheless, the resultant ordering policy may simply be of the form "when down to 4, order more" and thus may be easily understood.)

How can a manager get what he pays for? Perhaps the most difficult responsibility that an executive faces in controlling the progress of an operations research application is to strike the right balance between conducting the effort as a "research project" and as a "task-force assignment."

Estimating how profitable or beneficial an application will be in a particular company is central to the research aspect. For example, many companies are able to reduce inventory investment by at least 25% by adopting scientific inventory control, but the level of reduction in a specific company can only be estimated *after* the operations research project is begun and some trial tests are completed. Similarly, most medium-sized oil refineries are able to cut costs by $1000 a day when using a linear programming model to make a weekly operating schedule, but an estimate of savings at any particular refinery can only be made after a preliminary model is built and run on a trial basis. Thus, an executive should view the initial phases of an operations research effort as exploratory.

It is erroneous, however, for management to view the *entire* project as research. Companies with the best record of implementing operations research plan each project from the very beginning as an effort to improve current procedures. The line managers who are involved share a sense of urgency about completing the effort and remain vigilant in keeping the study practical and pertinent to the actual decision problems.

Standard control techniques for managing include formulating a statement of goals, assigning task responsibilities, developing and updating a time schedule for completing various tasks, and planning for managerial reviews. It is the nature of operations research studies to encounter delays and unforeseen difficulties. Hence, expect that the unexpected will occur. The inevitability of these contingencies is the very reason why an operations research project needs careful managerial control.

Most operations research efforts require two to three man-years of effort and extend over a period of three to nine months. Naturally, if the project is important and complicated, these figures will be exceeded. The economic benefits of a well-conceived and controlled application should far outweigh the expense of developing and operating the system.

22.3 HOW TO SUCCESSFULLY CONDUCT AN OPERATIONS RESEARCH PROJECT

This section outlines the components of a successful operations research application and expands on several of the factors already discussed above; the context here is the conduct of a selected project.

Managerial guidance and participation. Both top management and operating management must recognize their respective roles in the evolution of a project. Since an operations research application typically cuts across different departments, the effort must have the sincere sponsorship of top management and the needed entrées into line activities. Furthermore, top management must watch that the corporation's best interests are held paramount and that the study is not diverted so as to serve the interests of individual groups at the expense of the company.

Operating management must actively participate in the project's goal formulation, administration, and evaluation. It is both difficult and foolish to impose an operations research system on an operating management that has not been a party to the system's design. Anyone with only a modicum of experience knows that the best of plans can be so cleverly sabotaged by a group of unwilling personnel that the promulgator looks like a fool. But more is at issue than just personality conflicts. When operating management has not been actively engaged in the study, there is substantial likelihood that the proposed methods of the system will not be sufficiently comprehensive and flexible to handle the inevitable exigencies. Thus, if operating management has not participated in the evaluation (and, as a result, has little confidence in the worth of the endeavor), trouble looms ahead, even with the most insistent encouragement of top management.

Project planning and control. The need for monitoring the progress of a project has been underscored. Now we highlight several factors in this process that are critical to success.

- The project team should realize at the outset where managerial judgment will be required. Specific plans should be made to obtain this counsel, and these provisions may in turn require some preparatory educational effort. People, not computers, make managerial decisions.

- The technical phase should be executed carefully, because if it is poorly done, the outcome can be disastrous. The team should recognize, however, that the mathematical side of the study will represent probably only a minor part of the total effort of developing and implementing the application.

- The data requirements should be ascertained early, and the information collection indicated soon enough to avoid long delays in the project. Often, this phase is poorly executed in an operations research study, even when the project is led by an experienced practitioner.

- Managers and operating personnel should be alerted to any transitional difficulties that may arise in testing and installing a new system. For example, when scientific inventory replenishment rules are implemented, total inventory investment usually rises for the first few months. (Can you explain why?) Top management is likely to express consternation unless properly forewarned.

• The team should be careful to document the model's components and assumptions, and to record the input data and sources. In a large-scale effort, assumptions made several months earlier are easily forgotten. Furthermore, as test results and new data are examined, the model is inevitably altered. So it is essential that the team systematically catalogues each revision.

Credibility. Just like pregnancy, there is no such thing as a little credibility. Either an executive believes that the operations research representation of his problem is valid or he dismisses the results as worthless. The following paragraphs discuss how to develop a model that legitimately earns the trust of managers.

The project team should realize from the very beginning that the economic benefits of an operations research application never prove themselves and are never self-evident. And to make matters worse, a reliable "before and after" comparison is always extremely difficult to perform. There are two reasons why.

First, sufficient data about past operations may not be available, at least not in a form convenient for tabulation and analysis with acceptable accuracy. Hence, in its enthusiasm to design and implement a new approach the operations research team should not slight the job of installing a data-gathering system to reflect the true economic impact of a change. And when past data are insufficient, the team should start collecting current data long before it institutes new procedures. The team also should recognize the need to design a controlled experiment that focuses the effects to be evaluated. Unless the team heeds these cautions, it will, itself, be unable to prove factually that an improvement has occurred.

Second, only in exceptional circumstances can a team make a completely parallel comparison between two systems operating under different sets of procedures. There is no guarantee that an approach that looks attractive in terms of last year's operations will be just as attractive during this year's activities (or vice versa). Further, because managerial decisions at one point in time may have a specific effect on business conditions later, it may be futile to attempt to show with great precision how anything but an actually operating system behaves over an extensive period of time.

Thus, it is hard to prove precisely how well an operations research approach would have performed historically, or how much better an implemented operations research approach *is* faring as compared to what the previous system *would have done*. Management and the professionals must realize at the outset that they are limited in providing irrefutable evidence that improvements actually result from an operations research approach. But it is important to remember that the same limitations exist in measuring the impact of any competing problem solution.

The above observations mean that by and large credibility ought to be established *during* the course of the project and not relegated to the end. Most executives express the following doubts about an operations research model: "How do I know that it uses the right data? . . . makes realistic assumptions? . . . computes the economic consequences correctly? . . . and encompasses the enormous number of relevant detailed considerations?" If you pause to think, it does stagger the imagination that the essence of a complex decision-making problem can be transferred to the "brain" of an inanimate electronic device. The following analogy may help to explain the psychology of establishing credibility and suggests some ways of allaying those doubts expressed by managers.

Suppose you are handed a telephone book for the first time and told that the volume contains the correct telephone numbers of *everyone* in the city. In a moment, you surely would realize that the claim is an overstatement. After all, telephones are installed and removed every day, so the telephone book is only an approximate representation of *all* the telephone numbers in the city. (In this sense, the volume of listings is a "model.") What really concerns you is whether the approximation is worth using. How would you find out?

Probably you would start by looking up a telephone number you already know (perhaps, your own). If you find that the listed number is correct, you then might select a person whose number you do not know, look up the number, and place a call to see if the book in fact gives the right listing. After several more tries of this kind, assuming you are successful each time, you would be willing to *start* using the book. And most likely you would continue to use it until you observed an increased frequency of wrong numbers. Then you would complain to the telephone company, or go back to relying upon the Information Operator.

Now consider the telephone company's objectives. It wants to provide a model or system that gives you the right numbers. There are many possible systems (or models, if you like) for providing this service. The telephone company has discovered that the most economical solution is to publish one book containing every listed number and to distribute the volume to you and all other subscribers. The company knows full well that you will use only a miniscule fraction of all the numbers; even so, you will judge the system's merit on the validity of this small fraction.

The preceding analogy is relevant to the design of an operations research system in several ways. An executive first tests the validity of an operations research model by asking questions about data and conclusions; he *knows* the right answers to some of the questions and has some intuition about others. His confidence builds if the forthcoming answers are straightforward, comprehensible, and correct. He will start to rely on the model until his confidence is shaken by some "obvious" mistakes.

The operations research project team should try to anticipate what questions managers *may* ask and what data yield answers. This task is helped by discussing the detailed designs of the data reports and numerical summaries with the executives involved. The computer analysis should include not only summary reports similar to standard management information reports but also detailed backup analyses that clearly show the "how" and "why" of the summary figures. Much of the output may be examined infrequently; but it is there "just in case."

The telephone book analogy should not be pushed too far, because it is impractical and impossible to provide *every* number that an executive might possibly request. But novice operations researchers invariably make the mistake of providing far too little backup information, documentation, and analysis. As a consequence, they are frequently put in a position that is embarassing to them and annoying to a manager, namely, having to go "back to the drawing board" to obtain the information that executives want in order to understand the model's results.

The above discussion stresses the output requirements of a well-conducted operations research analysis. Of course, the team also must employ other means of effective communication. These are familiar to professional task-force leaders and amount to maintaining an open dialogue between the managers, who ultimately have to judge the merit of the results, and the team members. To repeat, managerial guidance and participation is a *sine qua non* for establishing credibility.

Responsive and responsible implementation. Truly effecting change within a corporate organization, whether the change be installing a new computer system or reassigning managerial responsibilities, is usually a difficult job. Aside from any special aversion that personnel may have to computer-based systems analysis, there are few, if any, problems of implementing change that are peculiar to an operations research project. As is true for effecting most significant changes within a company, the support of top management is vital, adequate educational training of operating personnel is necessary, a carefully worked out plan for introducing the changes is essential, and the implementation process must be controlled and monitored to sense and then correct difficulties that may arise. Unfortunately, there is no substitute for experience in knowing how to implement change skillfully.

One problem does deserve additional discussion. The difficulty is reminiscent of that encountered in factory mechanization many years ago. Certain operations research applications, especially those involving daily operations, may drastically change the character of the decision-maker's job. For example, developing a computer scheduling model for the processing of orders in a factory, or the routing of ships between ports, or the purchasing of materials from vendors, may transform a job requiring long familiarity with the decision problem into one of routinely supplying raw data to a computer. An operations research approach may remove the fun, challenge, exercise of judgment, sense of contribution, and mystique in a job. Rarely is top management willing to forego the resultant economic benefits for these reasons. But the project team must face up to the likely reaction of individuals who will be so affected. The team should recognize that the implementation process will arouse hostility; accordingly, they should provide post-implementation procedures to control a situation that might easily deteriorate because of a hostile environment.

Systems design. If the application is to be used again after the initial testing and analysis, then the ultimate success of the project depends upon the model's long-term viability. In the early years of commercial applications of operations research, many companies achieved noteworthy success for a while; later they discovered that their efforts had dissipated with the changing of business conditions and the promotion or resignation of operations research personnel. Now experienced firms realize the necessity for building systems support to maintain and update a continuing operations research application.

This point would not merit special mention except for a commonly observed phenomenon that most executives still find paradoxical. The typical operations researcher, although having expertise in model building and analyzing complex problems, is usually ill equipped and frequently disinterested in the above-mentioned systems requirements. Consequently, experienced companies include systems-oriented personnel in an operations research project team to devise procedures for maintaining the model in good working order.

22.4 HOW TO MANAGE AN OPERATIONS RESEARCH STAFF

In keeping with the tenor of the chapter, this section highlights only a few issues that pertain directly to the profit-making impact of a corporate operations research activity.

Location and size. The proper placement of an operations research group within a large corporation is no longer a subject of much debate among professionals. No standard pattern has evolved, even within an industry, and these technical staffs have successfully operated under the guidance of controllers, chief planners, vice-presidents of manufacturing, as well as chiefs of research and development departments. Today, pragmatic considerations dominate the location decision. And divisionalized companies operating under a policy of decentralized management frequently have operations research activities at both the corporate and division levels.

The size of an operations research staff is an unreliable indicator of the group's productivity; a small staff of six talented professionals may have a much greater profit impact on a corporation than a group of 20 that contains only two or three top-notch scientists. In operations research, quantity is a *very* poor substitute for quality.

Corporate responsibilities. Top management expects the operations research staff to exercise a high degree of *intellectual integrity*. This means not only that the group must meet demanding professional standards, but also that the staff must seek truthful conclusions and refrain from organizational partisanship.

The operations research group manager must be careful not to overcommit his staff. In an effort to please, many groups undertake more projects than they can accomplish in a reasonable period of time. As a result, all the users become dissatisfied. An operations research group should have a systematic way to decide what projects to accept and how to allocate its own scarce professional resources to best serve the needs of the entire company.

Cooperation with users. The preceding sections emphasized the importance of working with line managers in the conduct of operations research projects. Here this subject is treated from the technical staff's point of view.

The group should always keep in sight the way an operations research model typically assists managers. In most applications, the model-building effort provides insights into the quantitative implications of specified data and assumptions. Ultimately, it is the managers who make the decisions and are held responsible for the outcomes. Hence these executives must assess the relative likelihood of various assumptions and weigh the risks associated with different courses of action. An operations researcher should avoid the trap of believing that his model is true reality.

When a corporate operations research staff is first establishing its reputation, the group will work under less than ideal cooperative arrangements with its users. The requesting organization may be pleased to see the project completed successfully, and even may pay for the project. Nevertheless, the user organization may not readily provide other necessary kinds of help, which often include the collection of data and careful managerial review of intermediate results; consequently, the effort may get bogged down waiting for essential assistance in the line organization. But when the operations research staff has progressed to where it can pick and choose from among several worthwhile projects, then a major selection criterion should be the willingness of the user organization to commit its *personnel time* to the project team. A good index of user interest and involvement is the extent to which it will allocate the time of its people to assist in the application.

22.5 Like It Will Be

Operations research has advanced so rapidly that speculating about even the near future is risky. But several developments are now underway that certainly will have a major impact over the years immediately ahead. We somewhat arbitrarily separate these into technical and technological advances.

Technical progress. Two avenues of research are particularly important for new applications of operations research to executive decision problems. The first is the development of efficient techniques for analyzing very large-scale problems, such as linear programming models containing thousands of constraints. The second is the development of practical methods for solving realistic combinatorial problems (as discussed in Chap. 13).

Contributions will continue to be made, of course, in the theory of operations research, including the development of improved nonlinear programming algorithms, multi-item inventory replenishment models, and statistical procedures for simulation experiments. Business applications including decision models in areas such as marketing, advertising, pricing, purchasing, personnel development, and finance also will receive more attention from management scientists. In addition, tremendous progress will be made in the application of operations research in other than profit-making enterprises.

Technological progress. Although the technical breakthroughs often occur independently of advances in computer hardware, the applications of the techniques to actual problems do depend significantly on the state of computer technology. (Linear programming models, for example, did not have widespread acceptance until comprehensive and easy-to-use computer programs were generally available. The same is true for simulation models.) The development of time-shared computing systems seems to be the most significant technological advance with regard to future operations research applications.

Time-sharing has already reduced the amount of effort required to build and test a model; and this mode of computing has markedly cut the turnaround time between successive trial runs. But the more important impact is the stimulus to building new types of models and attacking different types of managerial problems. Corporations in the avant-garde are constructing very detailed financial planning models and are continually running economic analyses of new action alternatives as they arise in managerial deliberations. Time-sharing now allows the decision-maker to perform sensitivity analysis on-line. Being able to execute hundreds of thousands of calculations in a matter of seconds and getting the results immediately is an impressive and important step forward in the science of executive decision making.

An inevitable future impact of time-sharing will be the development of operating systems for decision problems that relate to the scheduling and daily allocating of scarce resources, and to the supervision of production processes. The rate of progress and acceptance in these areas depends on the growth in the general availability of time-shared computing equipment and software systems that are appropriate to the needs of commercial installations.

Administrative science. The time is past when an operations researcher can build a mathematical model and remain impervious to the behavioral characteristics of the individuals affected and the organizational milieu. Visionaries among operations research professionals are fully aware that new developments such as those described above exert tremendous strains on the managerial fabric of a corporate organization. To enhance the adoption of these technical and technological advances by industry and government, management and behavioral scientists together will have to find ways by which executives can deal effectively with computerized systems as beneficial change agents.

Appendices

CONTENTS

APPENDIX **I**

Advanced Topics in
Network Algorithms

I.1 MAXIMUM FLOW THROUGH
A CAPACITATED NETWORK

In the development of sophisticated techniques to solve difficult network models, analysis of the following problem is of central importance: given a network with arc capacities, where Node 0 is the source of all flow and Node $p + 1$ is the sink, what is the maximum amount of flow that can be routed from source to sink? Formally, the model is described as

(1) $$\text{maximize } F$$

subject to

(2) $$\sum_{\substack{(0,\,j) \text{ in} \\ \text{network}}} x_{0j} = F \qquad \text{for } k = 0$$

(3) $$\sum_{\substack{(k,\,j) \text{ in} \\ \text{network}}} x_{kj} - \sum_{\substack{(i,\,k) \text{ in} \\ \text{network}}} x_{ik} = 0 \qquad \text{for } k = 1, 2, \ldots, p$$

(4) $$- \sum_{\substack{(i,\,p+1) \\ \text{in network}}} x_{i,\,p+1} = -F \quad \text{for } k = p + 1$$

(5) $$0 \leq x_{ij} \leq u_{ij} \quad \text{for all } (i, j) \text{ in network,}$$

where u_{ij} are nonnegative integers.

A simple method can be used to solve the problem. To make the basic idea of the algorithm transparent, assume

(6) $$u_{ij} = 1 \quad \text{for all } (i, j) \text{ in network.}$$

Once you see how to find a solution with (6), you will have no difficulty in understanding the minor modification required to solve the general case.

A3

Begin with any feasible flow. The steps in the technique either determine that the flow is maximal, or discover another solution with increased flow:

Step 1. Starting at Node 0, put a (+) on each arc $(0, j)$ without flow and **label** Node j with a check mark (✗). Put the mark (✗) on Node 0.

Step 2. Consider any Node j that is labeled (✗). Put a (+) on every flowless outward arc (j, k) *if* Node k is not labeled, and label Node k with (✗). Then put a (−) on every inward arc (k, j) with flow *if* Node k is not labeled, and label Node k with (✗). Finally, cross the check (✗) on Node j to indicate that the node also has been **spanned.**

Step 3. Continue with the operation in *Step 2* until Node p + 1 is labeled or all labeled nodes have been spanned. A **breakthrough** occurs as soon as Node p + 1 is labeled, because a **flow-augmenting path** has been discovered from Node 0 to Node p + 1. The path can be found by tracing back from Node p + 1 the arcs that have been marked with a (+) or a (−). Add a unit of flow on each arc with a (+) and remove the flow from each arc with a (−). Return to *Step 1.* If, however, Node p + 1 remains unlabeled at the termination of *Step 2*, then the current solution is maximal.

The method is carried out for the example in Fig. I.1. The initial routing has two units of flow.

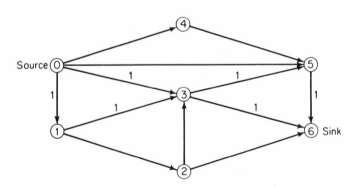

FIGURE I.1. Maximum Flow Example.

There are several ways to proceed. Follow the one below by making light pencil marks on Fig. I.1.

   (i) Scan Node 0: put + on arcs (0, 4) and (0, 5) and label Nodes 4 and 5 with (√). Mark Node 0 as (✗).

(ii) Scan Node 5: put − on arc (3, 5) and label Node 3 with (✓). Mark Node 5 with (✗).

(iii) Scan Node 3: put − on arc (1, 3) and label Node 1 with (✓). Mark Node 3 with (✗).

(iv) Scan Node 1: put + on arc (1, 2) and label Node 2 with (✓). Mark Node 1 with (✗).

(v) Scan Node 2: put + on arc (2, 6) and label Node 6 with (✓). A flow-augmenting path has been found.

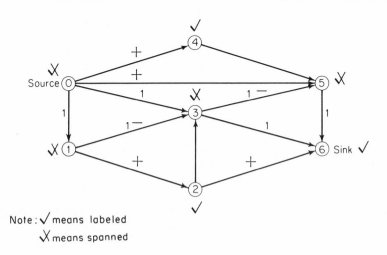

Note : ✓ means labeled
       ✗ means spanned

FIGURE I.2. Scanning
Process.

Check your work with the result in Fig. I.2. The solution therefore improves if you

(i) Add a unit of flow on the arcs (2, 6) and (1, 2).
(ii) Remove a unit of flow from arcs (1, 3) and (3, 5).
(iii) Add a unit of flow on arc (0, 5).

The revised solution is given in Fig. I.3 on the next page.

Verify that the flow is now maximal by repeating the steps of the algorithm. The sequence of nodes scanned will be Nodes 0, 4, and 5. It will not be possible to label any other node.

To remove the arc capacity restriction (6), the algorithm is modified in two respects. Put a (+) on every outward arc with less than capacity flow in the scanning process. Then, when a flow-augmenting path has been found, route as much flow as possible on the path, taking into account the amount of *unused* capacity on each (+) arc and the current level of flow on each (−) arc. Thus for the maximum flow problem (1) through (5) the algorithm now terminates according to the following stopping rule.

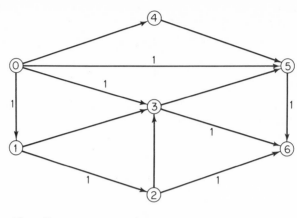

Flow = 3

One Unit: ⓪→①→②→⑥

One Unit: ⓪→③→⑥

One Unit: ⓪→⑤→⑥

FIGURE I.3. Maximum Flow Solution.

STOPPING RULE. Every arc from a spanned node to an unlabeled node is at its full capacity and every arc from an unlabeled node to a spanned node is at zero flow.

At each iteration, *Step 3* results either in one or more units of increased flow or in termination; therefore the algorithm is finite, since the maximum possible flow is bounded. It remains only to show that when the algorithm terminates, the solution in fact is optimal. To do this, partition all the nodes into two classes, say, C_0 and C_{p+1}. Put Node 0 in C_0 and Node p + 1 in C_{p+1}. Such a separation is called a **cut**, and we define the **cut capacity** as the sum of all the u_{ij} such that Node i is contained in C_0 and Node j in C_{p+1}.

The cut capacity for *any* partition provides a limit on the maximal value of flow possible. (If the cut capacity equals 0, then Node 0 literally is cut off from Node p + 1 and no flow is possible between source and sink.) Consequently, if a feasible flow equals any cut capacity, the flow must be optimal. Furthermore, because of the conservation of flow restrictions (2), (3), and (4), the value of F in any feasible routing must equal the sum of the flows along all arcs (i, j) minus the sum of the flows along all arcs (j, i), where Node i is contained in C_0 and Node j in C_{p+1}.

With the above observations, the optimality proof is at hand. Consider the feasible solution when the algorithm terminates. Define C_0 to be all the spanned nodes, and C_{p+1} the remaining nodes. According to the Stopping Rule, there is *no* flow from any node in C_{p+1} to any node in C_0, so the total flow equals the sum of the flows on all arcs from nodes in C_0 to nodes in C_{p+1}. *All* of these arcs contain flows at capacity levels; therefore the total flow in the solution equals the cut capacity, and no further improvement is possible.

The preceding argument is summarized by the fundamental result below.

MAX FLOW/MIN CUT THEOREM: The maximum flow F in the network structure (2) through (5) is equal to the minimal cut capacity relative to the source and sink.

A corollary result is that the algorithm results in integral values for all x_{ij}.

I.2 SOLUTION OF THE ASSIGNMENT MODEL

Recall the assignment model, discussed in detail in Sec. 6.4:

(1) $$\text{minimize} \sum_{i=1}^{n} \sum_{j=1}^{n} c_{ij} x_{ij}$$

subject to

(2) $$\sum_{j=1}^{n} x_{ij} = 1 \quad \text{for } i = 1, 2, \ldots, n$$

(3) $$\sum_{i=1}^{n} x_{ij} = 1 \quad \text{for } j = 1, 2, \ldots, n$$

(4) $$x_{ij} = 0 \text{ or } 1 \quad \text{for all } i \text{ and } j.$$

By the nature of the problem, a feasible solution contains only n variables equal to 1, whereas a *basic* solution includes $n + n - 1$ variables. Consequently, when the simplex algorithm for networks is applied to the assignment model (1) through (4), each basis contains $n - 1$ routes at zero level. This observation suggests that the special structure of the assignment model is not fully exploited by the simplex algorithm. In this section, three other approaches will be explained.

The first makes use of the maximum flow problem of the preceding section. The second combines the principles of the maximum flow and shortest-route algorithms. The third demonstrates a further connection between the assignment problem and the shortest-route problem. The methods will be illustrated by an example, which is first solved by the simplex algorithm to provide a basis for comparison. As you will learn in Sec. I.3, the three approaches are of additional significance because they generalize to other network optimization models.

Simplex algorithm. Consider the assignment problem shown in Fig. I.4. If you apply the procedure explained in the advanced material of Sec. 7.4 for calculating relative costs to assist in picking an initial basic solution, you obtain the amounts in Fig. I.5. A starting basis is exhibited in Fig. I.4. Notice that three routes (in the second row) are at zero level, indicating degeneracy. You can follow the iterations by examining Figs. I.6 through I.12, which contain the succession of improvement potentials and trial solutions. Observe that the value of the objective function does not change until the final solution.

[2] 1	[10]	[15]	[0]	1
[10] 0	[18] 1	[20] 0	[9] 0	1
[15]	[24]	[26] 1	[10]	1
[12]	[25]	[27]	[8] 1	1
1	1	1	1	

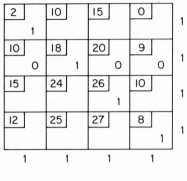

Total Cost = 54

FIGURE I.4. Assignment Model Initial Basic Solution.

	$c_{ij} - v_i - w_j$				v_i
	1	1	4	0	0
	0	0	0	0	9
	4	5	5	0	10
	3	8	8	0	8
w_j	1	9	11	0	

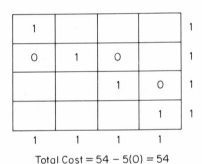

FIGURE I.5. Assignment Model Relative Costs: $c_{ij} - v_i - w_j$.

					v_i
	[2] $\underline{0}$	[10] 0	[15] −3	[0] 1	−8
	[10] $\underline{0}$	[18] $\underline{0}$	[20] $\underline{0}$	[9] $\underline{0}$	0
	[15] 1	[24] 0	[26] $\underline{0}$	[10] 5	6
	[12] −3	[25] −8	[27] −8	[8] $\underline{0}$	−1
w_j	10	18	20	9	

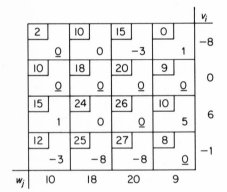

FIGURE I.6. Assignment Model Improvement Potentials for Initial Solution.

1				1
0	1	0		1
		1	0	1
			1	1
1	1	1	1	

Total Cost = 54 − 5(0) = 54

FIGURE I.7. Assignment Model Second Basic Solution.

					v_i
	[2] $\underline{0}$	[10] 0	[15] −3	[0] −4	−8
	[10] $\underline{0}$	[18] $\underline{0}$	[20] $\underline{0}$	[9] −5	0
	[15] 1	[24] 0	[26] $\underline{0}$	[10] $\underline{0}$	6
	[12] 2	[25] −3	[27] −3	[8] $\underline{0}$	4
w_j	10	18	20	4	

FIGURE I.8. Assignment Model Improvement Potentials for Second Solution.

1				1
	1	0		1
		1	0	1
0			1	1
1	1	1	1	

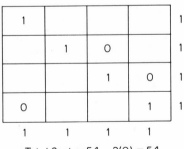

Total Cost = 54 − 2(0) = 54

FIGURE I.9. Assignment Model Third Basic Solution.

				v_i
2 / 0	10 / 2	15 / −1	0 / −2	−6
10 / −2	18 / 0	20 / 0	9 / −5	0
15 / −1	24 / 0	26 / 0	10 / 0	6
12 / 0	25 / −3	27 / −3	8 / 0	4
w_j: 8	18	20	4	

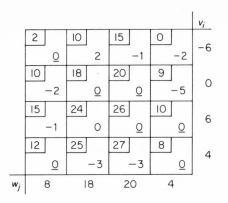

FIGURE I.10. Assignment Model Improvement Potentials for Third Solution.

	1			1
	0	1		1
		0	1	1
1			0	1
1	1	1	1	

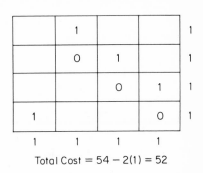

Total Cost = 54 − 2(1) = 52

FIGURE I.11. Assignment Model Optimal Basic Solution.

				v_i
2 / −2	10 / 0	15 / −3	0 / −4	−8
10 / −2	18 / 0	20 / 0	9 / −5	0
15 / −1	24 / 0	26 / 0	10 / 0	6
12 / 0	25 / −3	27 / −3	8 / 0	4
w_j: 8	18	20	4	

FIGURE I.12. Assignment Model Improvement Potentials for Optimal Solution.

Maximum flow approach. An alternative method is based on the maximum flow algorithm in the preceding section. It is also motivated by a consideration close in spirit to the suggestion in the advanced material of Sec. 7.4 (p. 228) for finding a good initial solution. The technique, in bare outline, consists of two steps:

Step 1. Given row constants v_i, for $i = 1, 2, \ldots, n$, and column constants w_j, for $j = 1, 2, \ldots, n$, yielding nonnegative relative costs $(c_{ij} - v_i - w_j) \geq 0$, determine whether a feasible solution exists using *only* routes with relative costs *equal* to 0. If so, stop, since the solution is optimal; otherwise go to *Step 2*.

Step 2. Revise v_i and w_j such that at least one *new* route has relative cost *equal* to 0. Return to *Step 1*.

The details of each step are explained with reference to the previous example. You can always begin *Step 1* with the constants used by the method for selecting an initial solution suggested in Sec. 7.4. (In the illustration, the relative costs are the entries in Fig. I.5.) However, in order to compare this approach with the simplex algorithm, it is convenient to start with the values indicated in Fig. I.13.

The maximum flow algorithm is employed in *Step 1* to find whether there exists a feasible solution using only routes with 0 entries in Fig. I.13. Tabular short-cuts

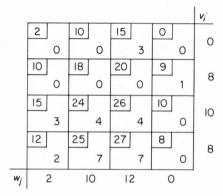

FIGURE I.13. Assignment Model Relative Costs: $c_{ij} - v_i - w_j$.

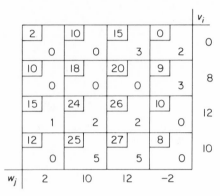

FIGURE I.14. Maximum Flow Algorithm Revised Relative Costs.

are available to carry out the procedure; but since the main purpose of this discussion is to make clear how the maximum flow model is of value, the exposition will not streamline the format to aid the calculations.

A network flow diagram comprised only of the routes with relative cost equal to 0 in Fig. I.13 is constructed in Fig. I.15. The node designation r_i corresponds

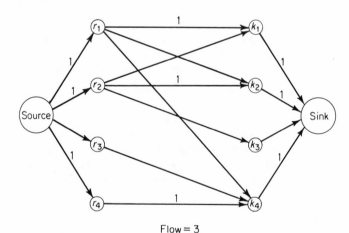

Flow = 3

FIGURE I.15. Network Flow for Assignment Model.

to Row i in Fig. I.13, and similarly k_j to Column j. All arcs out of the source node and into the sink node have capacity 1, corresponding to the row and column constraints of the problem.

If the maximum flow for the network were four, the corresponding routing would be an optimal assignment, since a unit of flow on arc (r_i, k_j) would imply $x_{ij} = 1$. A trial solution with three units of flow is exhibited in Fig. I.15. The maximum flow algorithm is carried out in Fig. I.16 to demonstrate that flow cannot be augmented in this network. Therefore you must go to *Step 2*.

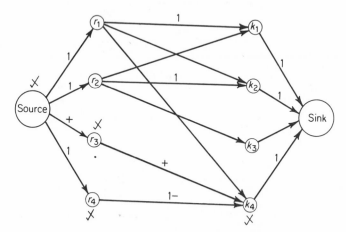

FIGURE I.16. Scanning for Augmented Flow.

The following rationale makes plausible a way to revise the v_i and w_j. Since the flow in Fig. I.16 is maximal but less than four units, it is necessary to introduce at least one new arc (r_i, k_j). Given the nature of the flow algorithm, it is reasonable to restrict attention to those arcs such that Node r_i is labeled but Node k_j is not. If such an arc is added, then the steps of the flow algorithm will continue and permit at least one more Node k_j to be spanned.

In altering the v_i and w_j, however, you should be careful not to destroy the equality $c_{ij} - v_i - w_j = 0$ for routes now having flow, as well as for those marked with $(+)$ in the spanning process. Otherwise, you may not be able to continue the scanning where you left off in *Step 1* (Fig. I.16). Also, the relation $c_{ij} - v_i - w_j \geq 0$ must be preserved for all i and j. A rule that achieves all these conditions is

(5)   (i) Add $\bar{c}$ to v_i if Node r_i is labeled,

(ii) Subtract $\bar{c}$ from w_j if Node k_j is labeled,

where

(6) $\bar{c} =$ smallest relative cost for arcs between every labeled Node r_i and *un*labeled Node k_j.

In Fig. I.16, Nodes r_3 and r_4 are labeled, whereas Nodes k_1, k_2, and k_3 are not; therefore in Fig. I.13 examine the entries at the intersection of Rows 3 and 4 and Columns 1, 2, and 3 to obtain

(7) $\bar{c} = $ minimum $(3, 4, 4, 2, 7, 7) = 2 = c_{41}.$

The revised v_i and w_j are shown in Fig. I.14 along with the new relative costs. Observe that arc (r_4, k_1) now has relative cost equal to 0, but arc (r_1, k_4) has a positive relative cost. The associated network appears in Fig. I.17. The maximum

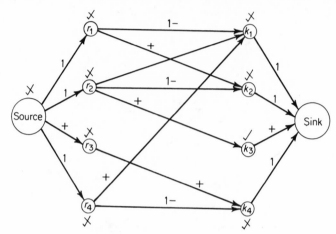

FIGURE I.17. Revised Network.

flow algorithm continues from Fig. I.16 and, in the process, labels Nodes $k_1, r_1, k_2, r_2, k_3,$ and finally the sink. The $(+)$ and $(-)$ signs on the arcs indicate the flow-augmenting path that produces the optimal solution in Fig. I.18.

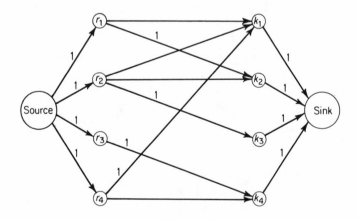

Flow = 4

FIGURE I.18. Final Solution.

We now recapitulate the algorithm. Starting with trial values for v_i and w_j in *Step 1*, apply the maximum flow algorithm to the associated network. If the resultant total flow equals n, the solution is optimal and you stop. Otherwise, proceed to *Step 2*, where you revise the v_i and w_j according to the rule in (5) and

(6). Return to *Step 1* with the resultant, somewhat altered, network: at least one new arc will have been added (where it is assumed the corresponding c_{ij} equals the value $\bar{c}$), and some *unused* arcs may have been dropped. Restart the maximum flow algorithm with the previous flow pattern. Again check for a total flow of n, and so forth.

Proof that the solution at termination is optimal is exactly the same as that given for the simplex method applied to the transportation model. Convergence in a finite number of iterations is established by noting that

(i) Each time *Step 2* occurs, at least one more node is spanned in the subsequent *Step 1*. Since the number of nodes is finite, *Step 2* eventually results in a breakthrough at the succeeding *Step 1*.

(ii) Only a finite number of breakthroughs can occur, because each results in increased flow, and total possible flow is bounded.

An implication of the convergence proof is that no more than $.5(n^2 + 3n - 2)$ applications of *Step 2* are required. This bound is typically far in excess of what actually occurs; however, you should note that the bound is considerably smaller than $\binom{2n-1}{n}$, which is the simplex algorithm bound calculated in terms of the number of basic solutions possible.

The network flow approach has a certain resemblance to the dual simplex method in that the dual constraints are satisfied at every iteration, but a feasible solution is not obtained until termination. In sharp contrast to both the standard and dual simplex methods, the network approach does *not* maintain a *basic* solution.

Minimal cost/maximum flow approach. To initiate *Step 1* of the previous approach, you had to find constants v_i and w_j such that all the relative costs $(c_{ij} - v_i - w_j)$ were nonnegative. You can assume without loss of generality that all $c_{ij} \geq 0$, since you can always add a positive constant c^* to *every* cost element. Then you can begin *Step 1* in the previous approach by letting $v_i = w_j = 0$. If you do so, the sequence of solutions turns out to be a minimal cost routing among all routings with the corresponding amount of flow. This point of view leads to another statement of the algorithm that provides a helpful insight in generalizing the method to more complex network problems. The idea is to increase total flow in such a way that the routing for each higher level of flow incurs minimal total cost. Thus, if F units of flow have been so routed, the method seeks a flow-augmenting path with least cost, and increases flow on this path. The technique for finding the path employs the shortest-route algorithm.

The approach is summarized below:

Step 1. Construct a new network based on the current solution as follows. Include each arc in the original network that currently is flowless, and let c_{ij} be the arc's path length. If flow occurs between Nodes r_i and k_j, add arc (k_j, r_i) and let its path length be $-c_{ij}$. It is possible to augment flow in the original network on *any* path between source and sink of the new network.

Step 2. Find a shortest path from the source to the sink in the new network. In the usual manner, increase flow on this path in the original network. If all the assignment model's constraints are satisfied, stop; otherwise, return to *Step 1.*

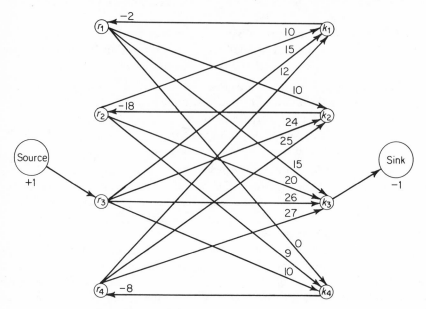

FIGURE I.19. Minimal Cost/Maximal Flow Network.

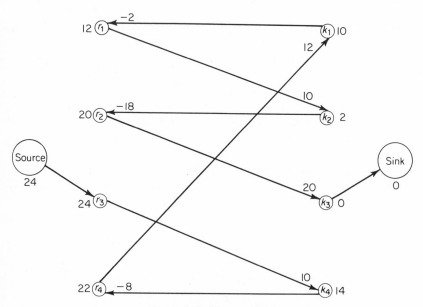

FIGURE I.20. Shortest Route.

The approach is illustrated for the example in Fig. I.4. Assume you have applied the algorithm to obtain the minimal cost routing for three units of flow. The solution is the same as that in Fig. I.15, and has a cost of 28 ($= 2 + 18 + 8$).

The new network constructed according to *Step 1* appears in Fig. I.19. Notice the source is connected only to Node r_3 and the sink to Node k_3, since the other such arcs are at capacity flow. The network contains arcs (k_1, r_1), (k_2, r_2), and (k_4, r_4) because the current solution has flow in the opposite direction. The remaining arcs have zero flow in the current solution.

The shortest-route algorithm of Sec. 7.6 is applied to the network and yields the result in Fig. I.20. Sending a unit of flow along the indicated path produces the optimal solution in agreement with Fig. I.18. Notice that a unit routed on arc (k_4, r_4) implies that flow is to be removed from arc (r_4, k_4) in the original network. Since the shortest path has length 24, the final solution has total cost of 52 ($= 28 + 24$). The length of the shortest routes from each Node r_i is an optimal value for $-v_i$ and similarly, the length from each Node k_j is an optimal value for w_j.

Shortest-route approach. In Sec. 6.5, you discovered how to convert a shortest-route problem into the format of an assignment model. In this chapter, you learned an efficient method for solving the shortest-route problem *without* making such a conversion. Now you will see how to solve the assignment model by putting it into the form of a shortest-route problem and then applying the shortest-route algorithm in Sec. 7.6.

The general idea is to solve a 1×1 assignment model, which is a trivial task. Then use the answer to solve a 2×2 model, and continue in the same fashion, adding one more row and column at each iteration until the $n \times n$ solution is obtained. Given the solution for a $p \times p$ problem, any remaining row and any remaining column can be chosen to form the $(p + 1) \times (p + 1)$ problem.

As before, the technique is explained in terms of the example in Fig. I.4. Suppose you have solved the 3×3 problem consisting of Rows 1, 2, and 4 and Columns 1, 2, and 4 of Fig. I.4. For convenience, the array is displayed in Fig. I.21, and the circled c_{ij} correspond to the optimal solution for that table. Notice that the solution is the same as that in Fig. I.15.

	(Col. 1)	(Col. 2)	(Col. 4)	
(Row 1)	②	10	0	1
(Row 2)	10	⑱	9	1
(Row 4)	12	25	⑧	1
	1	1	1	

FIGURE I.21. 3×3 Assignment Problem.

	(Col. 1)	(Col. 2)	(Col. 4)	(Col. 3)	
(Row 3)	15	24	10	26	1
(Row 1)	2	10	0	15	1
(Row 2)	10	18	9	20	1
(Row 4)	12	25	8	27	1
	1	1	1	1	

FIGURE I.22. 4×4 Assignment Problem.

To form the 4×4 problem, add the remaining third row and column of Fig. I.4, which gives Fig. I.22. Then calculate relative costs $(c_{ij} - v_i)$, where $v_i = 0$ for the new row and the other v_i are the values of c_{ij} for the optimal routes in the 3×3 problem. The result appears in Fig. I.23. Notice the table has the

	Node 1	2	3	4	v_i
Node 0	15	24	10	26	0
1	0	8	-2	13	2
2	-8	0	-9	2	18
3	4	17	0	19	8

FIGURE I.23. Relative Costs: $c_{ij} - v_i$.

same appearance as that for a shortest-route problem, such as Fig. 6.9 on p. 179. The network is drawn in Fig. I.24, using the node designations appearing in Fig. I.23.

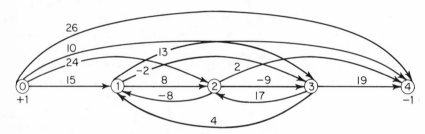

FIGURE I.24. Shortest Route Network for 4×4 Assignment Problem.

Apply the shortest-route algorithm to find a best path from Node 0 to Node 4 in Fig. I.24. The solution, exhibited in Fig. I.25, corresponds to the optimal solution to the original assignment problem.

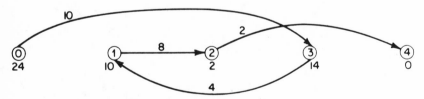

FIGURE I.25. Shortest Route from Node 0 to Node 4.

The only subtlety in demonstrating the validity of the approach is to establish that when the shortest-route network is drawn, the sum of the path lengths around every loop is nonnegative. Recall that such a condition is required for the shortest-route algorithm. Observe in Fig. I.24 that the only loops possible involve Nodes 1, 2, and 3, which correspond to the rows and columns considered in the 3 × 3 problem. As usual, the optimal solution to the 3 × 3 problem must remain optimal in terms of the relative costs in Fig. I.23. A loop among the Nodes 1, 2, and 3 is tantamount to a particular solution to the 3 × 3 problem; therefore no loop can have a negative cost, since the optimal 3 × 3 solution has zero cost in Fig. I.23.

I.3 ALGORITHMS FOR OTHER NETWORK MODELS

The techniques in the preceeding section generalize readily to other network optimization problems.

The only alteration needed to adapt the *maximum flow approach* to handle the standard transportation problem in Sec. 6.2 is to let the arc capacity from the source to Node r_i be S_i, and similarly the arc capacity from Node k_j to the sink be D_j. For this problem, the number of times *Step 2* is executed cannot exceed

$$(1) \qquad \sum_{i=1}^{m} S_i + \left(\sum_{i=1}^{m} S_i - 1 \right) \cdot [\text{minimum } (m, n) + 1].$$

Analogously, the only essential change required in the *minimal cost/maximum flow approach* to cover the general network optimization model (1) through (4) in Sec. 6.8 (pp. 192–193) is to revise *Step 1* so as to include each arc in the original network that at present has flow below capacity. (The statement concerning Nodes r_i and k_j applies to any Nodes i and j in the network.) As the advanced material at the end of Sec. 6.8 indicated, it may be necessary to transform the model initially so that there is only a single source and sink.

The *shortest-route approach* also can be extended to treat the standard transportation problem, which is not surprising since such a problem is conceptually equivalent to an assignment model.

CONTENTS

Probabilistic
Inventory Models with
Periodic Review

II.1 BACKGROUND SUMMARY

This chapter deals with dynamic single-item inventory models in which a reorder decision is allowed only at fixed intervals of time, such as every 10 days, or on each Monday. (Recall that the dynamic probabilistic model in Sec. 19.6 permitted a replenishment action to occur at any instant.) There are two main reasons for studying periodic (or discrete) review models: they are much more amenable to rigorous analysis than are continuous review models; and the theoretical results, which often do not require stationarity assumptions, lead to computable formulas. Both advantages will be illustrated in the sections to follow. In an actual application, if stationarity *is* assumed and the horizon is unbounded, then the selection of a continuous or a discrete review model rests primarily on which better represents reality. (As you will find in Sec. II.6, the corresponding numerical calculations to find an approximately optimal policy for a periodic review model are as simple as those in Sec. 19.6.)

You have already seen several examples of periodic review inventory models. Section 8.3 was devoted to a situation with deterministic demand and periodic reviews occurring over a finite horizon; the analysis was extended to the case of an unbounded horizon in Sec. 12.5, and to probabilistic demand in Secs. 17.4, 18.3, and 18.4. Chapter 9 demonstrated that if you are willing to make special cost assumptions, then you can derive the *form* of an optimal policy for deterministic demand, and thereby simplify the numerical optimization process. Now you will consider the analogous simplifications for the case of probabilistic demand.

II.2 TIMING AND UNFILLED DEMAND

Let the planning horizon comprise a finite number of periods. Assume that the integer λ (lambda) represents the **delivery lag**, so that an order placed in Period t arrives in Period $t + \lambda$. Further suppose the sequence of events within any Period t is

 (i) ordering decision
 (ii) delivery of any order due in from Period $t - \lambda$
 (iii) customer demand,

and let

$$p_t(q) = \text{probability that demand is } q \text{ in Period } t \quad (\text{where } q \geq 0).$$

Assume that demand in Period t is integer valued and independent of all previous demands.

It is meaningful to permit the value $\lambda = 0$, which is the case of **immediate delivery**. Observe the following difference between the continuous and discrete review models. When the value of the lag $L = 0$ in the continuous review model of Sec. 19.6, the analysis simplifies to the economic lot-size calculation in Sec. 19.5, since there is no need to protect against uncertain demand occurring over an interval of time. But in the periodic review model, even if $\lambda = 0$, one period's random demand occurs prior to the next opportunity to reorder. In general, a value for λ in the periodic review model corresponds to a value $(L = \lambda + 1)$ in the continuous review model.

Let

$i_t = $ level of inventory on hand at the *start* of Period t
$j_t = $ level of inventory on hand plus on order at the start of Period t
  prior to the ordering decision
$x_t = $ amount ordered in Period t
$k_t \equiv i_t + x_{t-\lambda} = $ level of inventory on hand after any delivery
      but before demand
$y_t \equiv j_t + x_t = $ level of inventory on hand plus on order in Period t
      after the ordering decision but before demand.

Then

(1)
$$j_t = \begin{cases} i_t & \text{for } \lambda = 0. \\ i_t + x_{t-\lambda} + \cdots + x_{t-1} & \text{for } \lambda > 0. \end{cases}$$

Figure II.1 displays the timing relationships among these quantities.

If $\lambda = 0$, then $j_t = i_t$, and hence $k_t = y_t$ is the total inventory available to meet demand in Period t. Consequently, the decision x_t has an immediate effect on the value of k_t.

If $\lambda > 0$, the situation is different, for then x_t will not affect the inventory position until Period $t + \lambda$, when the order arrives. By definition, $k_{t+\lambda} = i_{t+\lambda} + x_t$

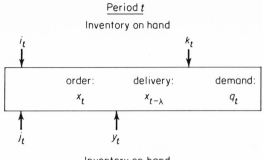

Figure II.1. Time Sequence and Inventory Quantities.

but the value of $i_{t+\lambda}$ depends in part on the next λ demands $q_t, q_{t+1}, \ldots, q_{t+\lambda-1}$. Let us see how.

Backlog case. If *all* unfilled demand is backlogged and eventually satisfied by future deliveries, then

$$(2) \qquad k_{t+\lambda} = (i_t + x_{t-\lambda} + \cdots + x_{t-1} + x_t) - (q_t + q_{t+1} + \cdots + q_{t+\lambda-1})$$
$$= y_t - (q_t + \cdots + q_{t+\lambda-1}) \qquad \text{(complete backlog: } \lambda > 0\text{).}$$

Explain why, using the definitions of $i_{t+\lambda}, j_t,$ and y_t. When $k_{t+\lambda}$ is negative, there is a corresponding backlog of demand at Period t + λ, prior to demand occurring in Period t + λ. Be sure you see that (2) implies $k_{t+\lambda}$ is completely determined by the ordering decision in Period t and the *cumulative* demand over λ successive periods, starting with Period t.

Given the probability distributions $p_t(q)$, you can easily obtain the probability distribution for cumulative demand over λ successive periods. Let

$$(3) \qquad p_{t, t+\lambda-1}(Q) = \text{probability that the cumulative demand}$$
$$(q_t + \cdots + q_{t+\lambda-1}) \text{ is } Q.$$

Then, because of (2), $p_{t, t+\lambda-1}(Q)$ also represents the probability that $k_{t+\lambda}$ has the value $(y_t - Q)$. You can compute $p_{t, t+\lambda-1}(Q)$ recursively by a **convolution** calculation,

$$(4) \qquad p_{t, u+1}(Q) = \sum_{q=0}^{Q} p_{u+1}(q) p_{t, u}(Q - q) \quad \text{for } Q = 0, 1, \ldots,$$

where $p_{t, t} \equiv p_t$, and (4) is applied successively for $u = t, \ldots, t + \lambda - 1$.

For many standard probability distributions, you can derive a formula to obtain $p_{t, t+\lambda-1}(Q)$ without having to perform all the recursive numerical calculations in (4). For example, if $p_t(q)$ is a Poisson distribution with mean $E[q_t] = m_t$:

$$(5) \qquad p_t(q) = \frac{(e^{-m_t})(m_t)^q}{q!} \quad \text{for } q = 0, 1, 2, \ldots,$$

then the distribution for cumulative demand is also Poisson with mean $(M = m_t + \cdots + m_{t+\lambda-1})$:

(6) $$p_{t,t+\lambda-1}(Q) = \frac{(e^{-M})(M)^Q}{Q!} \quad \text{for } Q = 0, 1, 2, \ldots.$$

An important special case of (3) and (4) arises if $p_t(q)$ is the same distribution for all t,

(7) $$p_t(q) \equiv p(q);$$

then

(8) $$p^\lambda(Q) \equiv p_{t,t+\lambda-1}(Q) = \sum_{q=0}^{Q} p(q) p^{\lambda-1}(Q-q),$$

where $p^\lambda(Q)$ is called the λ-*fold convolution* of $p(q)$. To illustrate, suppose $p(q)$ is a negative binomial distribution:

(9) $$p(q) = \binom{r-1+k}{r-1}(1-p)^r p^q \quad \text{for } q = 0, 1, 2, \ldots,$$

where $E[q] = rp/(1-p)$, $0 < p < 1$, and r is a positive integer. Then it can be shown that the λ-fold convolution is also a negative binomial distribution

(10) $$p^\lambda(Q) = \binom{\lambda r-1+k}{\lambda r-1}(1-p)^{\lambda r} p^Q \quad \text{for } Q = 0, 1, 2, \ldots,$$

where $E[Q] = \lambda rp/(1-p)$.

As another example of λ-fold convolutions, consider the probability distribution

(11) $$p(2) = .2 \qquad p(3) = .8.$$

Then the formula for λ-fold convolution (8) is

(12) $$p^2(Q) = \sum_{q=0}^{Q} p(q) p(Q-q),$$

so that

(13) $$\begin{aligned} p^2(4) &= p(2)p(2) = .04 \\ p^2(5) &= p(2)p(3) + p(3)p(2) = .32 \\ p^2(6) &= p(3)p(3) = .64. \end{aligned}$$

And continuing to $\lambda = 3$, you have

(14) $$p^3(Q) = \sum_{q=0}^{Q} p(q) p^2(Q-q),$$

so that

(15) $$\begin{aligned} p^3(6) &= p(2)p^2(4) = .008 \\ p^3(7) &= p(2)p^2(5) + p(3)p^2(4) = .096 \\ p^3(8) &= p(2)p^2(6) + p(3)p^2(5) = .384 \\ p^3(9) &= p(3)p^2(6) = .512. \end{aligned}$$

Lost demand case. Now suppose that $\lambda > 0$, but all unfilled demand is permanently lost; then the formula for $k_{t+\lambda}$ becomes complex. To see why, consider the case $\lambda = 2$. Specifically, verify that

$$k_{t+2} = \text{maximum}(k_{t+1} - q_{t+1}, 0) + x_t$$

(16)
$$= \text{maximum}\,[\text{maximum}(k_t - q_t, 0) + x_{t-1} - q_{t+1}, 0] + x_t$$

$$= \text{maximum}\,[\text{maximum}(i_t + x_{t-2} - q_t, 0) + x_{t-1} - q_{t+1}, 0] + x_t,$$

which is not *always* the same as the value in (2). In particular, note that k_{t+2} does not depend simply on y_t but on the separate components $(i_t + x_{t-2}, x_{t-1}, x_t)$, and similarly does not depend on the cumulative demand, but on the individual demands (q_t, q_{t+1}). As a consequence, the probability distribution for $k_{t+\lambda}$, given the value for y_t, is not directly related to $p_{t,t+\lambda-1}(Q)$.

To avoid the intricacies associated with this more complex situation, we postulate from here on that *all unfilled demand is completely backlogged*. If the penalty cost is relatively large, the resultant policy will be approximately optimal when unfilled demand is in fact lost. (When $\lambda = 0$, the lost sales case is nearly as easy to solve as the backlogged demand case, and the results will be indicated in the special material.)

II.3 FINITE HORIZON MODEL

Assume that the objective function is the discounted sum of each period's expected purchasing, inventory holding, and shortage costs. Specifically, let

(1) $c_t(x) = $ cost of ordering the amount x in Period t,

and suppose that this cost is actually incurred when the order is delivered in Period t + λ. Also, let

(2) $H_t(k, q) = $ inventory holding and shortage penalty cost incurred in Period t when k units are available for filling the demand q in Period t.

For example, $H_t(k, q)$ may be of the form

(3)
$$H_t(k, q) = \begin{cases} h_t(k - q) & \text{for } k - q \geq 0 \\ \pi_t(q - k) & \text{for } k - q < 0. \end{cases}$$

An important special case of (3) is when the two functions on the right of (3) are linear. Note that when k is negative, indicating a backlog condition before the demand q occurs, then the amount $(q - k)$ on which the penalty cost is assessed represents the sum of demand and the backlog. Hence the penalty cost is charged in each period that a unit of demand is backlogged, and not in just the period when the backlog first occurs. Recall when $\lambda = 0$, $k_t = y_t$ so that

(4) $\begin{array}{l}\text{expected holding and penalty} \\ \text{cost in Period t given } y_t = y\end{array} \equiv L_t(y) = \sum\limits_{q=0}^{\infty} H_t(y, q)p_t(q)$ $(\lambda = 0)$.

When $\lambda > 0$, recall that

(5) $k_{t+\lambda} = y_t - Q$ $(Q \equiv q_t + \cdots + q_{t+\lambda-1})$,

so that the level of y_t directly influences holding and penalty costs in Period t + λ. Consequently,

(6)
$$
\begin{array}{l}
\text{expected holding} \\
\text{and penalty cost} \\
\text{in Period } t + \lambda \\
\text{give } y_t = y
\end{array}
\equiv L_t(y) = \sum_{Q=0}^{\infty} \sum_{q=0}^{\infty} H_{t+\lambda}(y - Q, q) p_{t+\lambda}(q) p_{t,t+\lambda-1}(Q) \quad (\lambda > 0).
$$

According to (6), $L_t(y)$ is found by taking for each $(y - Q)$ the conditional expected value of $H_{t+\lambda}(y - Q, q)$ with respect to q, and then taking the unconditional expected value with respect to Q. If $H_t(k, q)$ has the form in (3), then (6) reduces to

(7) $L_t(y) = \begin{cases} \displaystyle\sum_{Q=0}^{y} h_{t+\lambda}(y - Q) p_{t,t+\lambda}(Q) + \sum_{Q>y} \pi_{t+\lambda}(Q - y) p_{t,t+\lambda}(Q) & \text{for } y \geq 0 \\[4mm] \displaystyle\sum_{Q=0}^{\infty} \pi_{t+\lambda}(Q - y) p_{t,t+\lambda}(Q) & \text{for } y < 0. \end{cases}$

Note that here $Q \equiv q_t + \cdots + q_{t+\lambda-1} + q_{t+\lambda}$; that is, the random variable q in (6) representing demand in Period $t + \lambda$ has been absorbed in the symbol Q in (7), and the second subscript on the convolution probability distribution has been increased by 1, accordingly. If all the $p_t(q)$ are identical, then $p_{t,t+\lambda}(Q)$ in (7) is the corresponding $(\lambda + 1)$-fold convolution, which would be denoted by $p^{\lambda+1}(Q)$.

Finally, assume inventory decisions are to be made in Periods $1, 2, \ldots, T$, which implies that the inventory system, itself, is to operate until the end of Period $T + \lambda$. [Note that $L_T(y)$ should be defined so as to indicate what happens at the end of Period $T + \lambda$ if any items remain in inventory or if there is a backlog.] Because the optimization occurs for decisions made in Periods $1, 2, \ldots, T$, it is convenient to let T denote the length of the planning horizon (rather than $T + \lambda$), and this convention is used hereafter.

The minimization problem involves finding an optimal order quantity $x_t(j_t)$ for each period and every possible j_t or, equivalently, an optimal value for $y_t(j_t) \geq j_t$. Leaving implicit in the notation below the dependence of y_t on j_t, and j_{t+1} on y_t, the expected value for a specified set of policies y_t, for $t = 1, 2, \ldots, T$, and initial level j, is

(8)
$$
E\left\{ \sum_{t=1}^{T} \alpha^{\lambda+t-1} [c_t(y_t - j_t) + L_t(y_t)] \right\},
$$

where the expectation is taken over all possible sequences of demand, and α is the usual one-period discount factor, where $0 < \alpha \leq 1$. Observe that the expression in (8) really ignores the costs in Periods $1, 2, \ldots, \lambda - 1$; this is legitimate, since these costs are beyond control. Also notice that the constant α^λ multiplies the whole expression, and can and will be dropped henceforth for simplicity. The dynamic programming recursion appropriate to finding optimal policies that minimize the expression in (8) is

(9)
$$
f_t(j) = \underset{y \geq j}{\text{minimum}} \left[c_t(y - j) + L_t(y) + \alpha \sum_{q=0}^{\infty} f_{t+1}(y - q) p_t(q) \right]
$$
$$
\text{for } t = 1, 2, \ldots, T
$$

$$
f_{T+1}(j) \equiv 0.
$$

The functions $f_t(j)$ are computed in the usual way for each possible j, starting with $t = T, T - 1, \ldots, 1$. (In practice, the range for q is truncated at a value $q^* < \infty$ such that the cumulative demand function at q^* is approximately 1. Similarly, the values for j are restricted to a range of interest.) Such a recursion is easily calculated on a high-speed electronic computer.

▶The implicit notation in (8) conceals the following details. Given any set of replenishment *rules* and j_1, the random demands induce a probability distribution on the j_t, for $1 < t \leq T$, and they, in turn, induce a probability distribution on the y_t, for $1 < t \leq T$. The expectation in (8) is over these induced probability distributions, so that the required minimization is really over replenishment *rules*.   ◀

*Lump-sum penalty cost example. The following example was considered in Sec. 19.4 (pp. 798-799) in the context of a single-period decision model:

$$p(q) = \frac{1}{2} \quad \text{for } q = 4, 8$$

(10)
$$c(x) = \begin{cases} 0 & \text{for } x = 0 \\ K + c \cdot x & \text{for } x > 0 \end{cases}$$

$$L(y) = \pi \sum_{q > y} p(q) = \begin{cases} \pi & \text{for } y \leq 3 \\ \dfrac{\pi}{2} & \text{for } y = 4, 5, 6, 7 \\ 0 & \text{for } y \geq 8, \end{cases}$$

where $K \geq 0$, $c \geq 0$, and $\pi > 0$.

Assume $\lambda = 0$, and that the demand distributions and cost functions are stationary, $\alpha = 1$, and $T = 2$. Apply (9) and check your results with those in Fig. II.2. (Refer to the calculations in Sec. 19.4 to verify the Period 2 policies.)

$$c = 1 \quad \alpha = 1 \quad T = 2$$

		K = 4.5 and π = 12			K = 1 and π = 5			
	$y_1(j)$	$f_1(j)$	$y_2(j)$	$f_2(j)$	$y_1(j)$	$f_1(j)$	$y_2(j)$	$f_2(j)$
$j \leq 0$	8	$13.5 + (8 - j)$	j	12	j	10	j	5
1	8	20.5	8	11.5	1	10	1	5
2	8	19.5	8	10.5	2	10	2	5
3	8	18.5	8	9.5	4	9.5	4	4.5
4	8	17.5	4	6	4	7.5	4	2.5
5	8	16.5	5	6	5	7.5	5	2.5
6	8	15.5	6	6	8	6.75	6	2.5
7	8	14.5	8	5.5	8	5.75	8	2
8	8	9	8	0	8	3.75	8	0

Figure II.2. Lump-Sum Penalty Cost Example.

▶The recursion in (9) can be applied with little or no modification to other inventory situations having different assumptions. For example, you can let the value of $(1 - \alpha)$ represent a probability that the inventoried item becomes completely obsolete. If the probability of survival changes over time, then you can use a value α_t instead of α. (The value of α_t can actually represent the combined effect of product survival and the discount factor.)

As another example, you can constrain the values of y_t and $x_t = (y_t - j_t)$ in the minimization in (9). Finally, under several conditions, such as postulating that only one order can be outstanding at any time, you can modify (9) so as to encompass a random lead time, that is, to permit the value of λ to vary probabilistically.

Note that the optimization in (9) has been expressed in terms of minimizing expected costs. Suppose each item purchased by the company's customers yields revenue r per unit, which is remitted to the company when the item is actually delivered to the customer. If $\alpha = 1$, this revenue can be ignored in the optimization process, because a policy that minimizes cost also maximizes profit, provided *all* demand is eventually satisfied, including unfilled demand at the end of Period T $+ \lambda$. But for $\alpha < 1$, unfilled demand diminishes the present value of revenue receipts, since the payment of r is postponed until the customer is supplied his item. To handle this consideration, let $L_t^*(y)$ represent the expected holding and penalty costs *exclusive* of revenue, and then define

(i) $$L_t(y) \equiv L_t^*(y) + (1 - \alpha)r \sum_{Q > y} (Q - y)p_{t, t+\lambda}(Q).$$

[Assume $L_T^*(y)$ includes the *cost* in Period T $+ \lambda + 1$ of filling any backlog existing at the end of Period T $+ \lambda$.]

Suppose unfilled demand *is* lost. If $\lambda = 0$ so that $j_t = i_t$, the appropriate dynamic programming recursion analogous to (9) is

(ii) $$f_t(j) = \operatorname*{minimum}_{y \geq j} \left[c_t(y - j) + L_t(y) + \alpha \sum_{q=0}^{y} f_{t+1}(y - q)p_t(q) + \alpha f(0) \sum_{q > y} p_t(q) \right],$$

which is computationally no more complex than (9). The no-backlog case for $\lambda > 1$ can formally be treated by the recursion

(iii)
$$\begin{aligned} f_t(k, x_{t-\lambda+1}, \ldots, x_{t-1}) = \operatorname*{minimum}_{x \geq 0} &\left[\alpha^\lambda c_t(x) + \sum_{q=0}^{\infty} H_t(k, q)p_t(q) \right. \\ &+ \alpha \sum_{q=0}^{k} f_{t+1}(k - q + x_{t-\lambda+1}, x_{t-\lambda+2}, \ldots, x) \\ &\left. + \alpha \sum_{q > k} f_{t+1}(x_{t-\lambda+1}, x_{t-\lambda+2}, \ldots, x) \right]. \end{aligned}$$

Write the appropriate recursion for $\lambda = 1$ and compare it to (ii).   ◀

II.4 FORM AND EXACT COMPUTATION OF OPTIMAL POLICIES

The model in the preceding section will be specialized by making these cost assumptions:

(1) $$c_t(x) = \begin{cases} 0 & \text{for } x = 0 \\ K_t + c_t x & \text{for } x > 0 \end{cases} \quad \text{and} \quad K_t \geq \alpha K_{t+1}$$

(2) $\quad L_t(y)$ is convex   and $(c_t - \alpha c_{t+1})y + L_t(y) \to \infty$ as $|y| \to \infty$,

where $K_t \geq 0$, $c_t \geq 0$, and $c_{T+1} \equiv 0$. For example, suppose $L_t(y)$ is given by (7) in the previous section, and $h_{t+1}(j) + \pi_{t+1}(-j)$ is a convex function for all j. Then $L_t(y)$ is convex and satisfies the assumptions in (2) provided $(c_t - \alpha c_{t+1})y + L_t(y) \to \infty$ as $|y| \to \infty$.

Define an inventory policy as being of the (s, S) type if for *every* Period t

(3)
$$y_t(j) = j \quad \text{and} \quad x_t(j) = 0 \qquad \text{for } j \geq s_t$$
$$y_t(j) = S_t \quad \text{and} \quad x_t(j) = S_t - j \quad \text{for } j < s_t.$$

Then we can demonstrate:

OPTIMALITY OF (s, S) POLICY. Given the model represented by the dynamic programming recursion (9) in Sec. II.3, in which (1) and (2) above hold, there is an optimal policy of the (s, S) type. Further, if all $K_t = 0$, then $s_t = S_t$.

An important implication of the theorem is that you can completely summarize an optimal policy for each period by specifying only two parameters (s_t, S_t) and without stating the precise level of inventory at the start $(t = 1)$. {The theorem remains true when the condition in (2) that $L_t(y)$ is convex is weakened to $-[(c_t - \alpha c_{t+1})y + L_t(y)]$ is *unimodal*, which was defined in Sec. 14.3.}

Calculation of an optimal policy. Our knowing that the form of an optimal policy is (s, S) greatly simplifies the optimization process in the recursion (9) above. Assume here that $S_t \geq 0$ for all t and $K_t > 0$ for at least one t. (The case of all $K_t = 0$ is treated later.)

To begin, suppose j is arbitrarily small so that the optimal $y_t(j) = S_t$. Then you can see by inspecting the dynamic programming recursion (9) that S_t is a minimizing value of y in

(4)
$$\underset{y}{\text{minimum}} \left[c_t y + L_t(y) + \alpha \sum_{q=0}^{\infty} f_{t+1}(y - q)\, p_t(q) \right]$$
$$\equiv \underset{y}{\text{minimum}} \left[g_t(y) \right] = g_t(S_t).$$

Given the (s, S) form of the policy, you can state that

(5)
$$f_t(j) = \begin{cases} g_t(S_t) + K_t - c_t j & \text{for } j < s_t \\ L_t(j) + \alpha \sum_{q=0}^{\infty} f_{t+1}(j - q)p_t(q) & \text{for } j \geq s_t. \end{cases}$$

Therefore s_t is the smallest value such that

(6)
$$L_t(s_t) + \alpha \sum_{q=0}^{\infty} f_{t+1}(s_t - q)p_t(q) \leq g_t(S_t) + K_t - c_t s_t,$$

or on rearranging terms, s_t is the smallest value such that

(7)
$$g_t(s_t) \leq g_t(S_t) + K_t$$

where, as in (4),

(8)
$$g_t(y) \equiv c_t y + L_t(y) + \alpha \sum_{q=0}^{\infty} f_{t+1}(y - q)p_t(q).$$

In summary, the algorithm for Period t can be stated as:

Step 1. Calculate $g_t(y)$ in (8) for all relevant y and let $S_t \geq 0$ satisfy minimum $g_t(y) = g_t(S_t)$.

Step 2. Let s_t be the smallest value such that $g_t(s_t) \leq g_t(S_t) + K_t$. (Note that s_t may be negative.)

Step 3. Calculate $f_t(j)$ according to (5).

Thus for each Period t the algorithm performs only a single minimization in *Step 1*, and not one for each j as in the recursion (9) for the general model in the preceding section. The algorithm begins with $t = T$, where $f_{T+1} \equiv 0$, and proceeds to $t = T - 1, T - 2, \ldots, 1$. The algorithm is illustrated below.

▶When all $K_t = 0$, you can omit *Step 2* since $s_t = S_t$ by the theorem. Further, if all the cost parameters as well as the demand distributions are stationary, then $S_t \geq S_{t+1}$. By making one further assumption about a terminating condition, *Step 1* can be considerably simplified—this approach is given in Sec. II.5.   ◀

Examples. The following examples serve two purposes: they demonstrate how the algorithm operates, and they give you an idea of how optimal policies behave when both $K_t > 0$ and the planning horizon is finite.

Assume that K_t and c_t are stationary, and that the holding and penalty cost function is also stationary and of the form

$$(9) \qquad H_t(y, q) = \begin{cases} h \cdot (y - q) & \text{for } y - q \geq 0 \\ \pi \cdot (q - y) & \text{for } y - q < 0, \end{cases}$$

where $c + h > 0$ and $\pi > c$. Further let

$$(10) \qquad \lambda = 0 \quad \text{and} \quad p_t(q) = p(q)$$

so that the demand too is stationary, and

$$(11) \quad L_t(y) \equiv L(y) = \begin{cases} \displaystyle\sum_{q=0}^{y} h \cdot (y - q)p(q) + \sum_{q>y} \pi \cdot (q - y)p(q) & \text{for } y \geq 0 \\ \displaystyle\sum_{q=0}^{\infty} \pi \cdot (q - y)p(q) & \text{for } y < 0. \end{cases}$$

Given all the stationarity assumptions, it is now more convenient to describe the stage variable in the dynamic programming relation in terms of "number of periods remaining until the end of the horizon," thereby yielding, analogously to (9) in the preceding section, the recursion

$$(12) \quad \begin{aligned} F_n(j) &= \underset{y \geq j}{\text{minimum}} \left[c(y - j) + L(y) + \alpha \sum_{q=0}^{\infty} F_{n-1}(j - q)p(q) \right] \\ F_0(j) &= 0. \end{aligned}$$

To help you remember that the recursion is now backward in time, the symbol F_n is employed instead of f_t.

To start, suppose

(13) $K = 24 \quad c = 1 \quad h = 2 \quad \pi = 10 \quad \alpha = 1 \quad \lambda = 0$

and that demand is deterministic:

(14) $p(3) = 1.$

Consequently,

(15) $L(y) = \begin{cases} 2 \cdot (y - 3) & \text{for } y \geq 3 \\ 10 \cdot (3 - y) & \text{for } y < 3. \end{cases}$

For any n, *Step 1* of the algorithm indicates you must calculate the function,

(16) $G_n(y) = cy + L(y) + \alpha \sum\limits_{q=0}^{\infty} F_{n-1}(y - q)p(q),$

which, given (14), simplifies to

(17) $G_n(y) = cy + L(y) + F_{n-1}(y - 3).$

Again, to help you remember that the recursion is now backward in time, the symbol G_n is employed instead of g_t.

To illustrate, let $n = 1$; then from (12), (13), (15), and (17),

$$G_1(6) = 6 + 2(6 - 3) + 0 = 12$$

(18) $$G_1(0) = 0 + 10(3) + 0 = 30$$

$$G_1(-2) = -2 + 10[3 - (-2)] + 0 = 48.$$

The entire function $G_1(y)$ is found in Fig. II.3. Accordingly, $S_1 = 3$ since $G_1(3) = 3$ is the minimum value for $G_1(y)$.

Going to *Step 2*, you can see that $s_1 = 1$ is the smallest value of s_1 such that

(19) $G_1(s_1) \leq G_1(3) + K = 27,$

since $G_1(1) = 21$ whereas $G_1(0) = 30$.

For any n, *Step 3* indicates you are to calculate

(20) $F_n(j) = \begin{cases} G_n(S_n) + K - cj & \text{for } j < s_n \\ L(j) + \alpha \sum\limits_{q=0}^{\infty} F_{n-1}(j - q)p(q) & \text{for } j \geq s_n. \end{cases}$

So for $n = 1$, verify that

(21) $F_1(j) = \begin{cases} 27 - j & \text{for } j < 1 \\ 10(3 - j) + 0 & \text{for } 1 \leq j < 3 \\ 2(j - 3) + 0 & \text{for } 3 \leq j; \end{cases}$

the complete function $F_1(j)$ is also shown in Fig. II.3.

Returning to *Step 1* for $n = 2$, you calculate $G_2(y)$ according to (17); for example,

$$G_2(6) = 12 + F_1(3) \quad = 12 + \ \ 0 = 12$$

(22) $$G_2(0) = 30 + F_1(-3) = 30 + 30 = 60$$

$$G_2(-2) = 48 + F_1(-5) = 48 + 32 = 80.$$

y and j	$G_1(y)$	$F_1(j)$	$G_2(y)$	$F_2(j)$	$G_3(y)$	$F_3(j)$	$G_4(y)$	$F_4(j)$	$G_5(y)$	$F_5(j)$	$G_6(y)$	$F_6(j)$	$G_7(y)$	$F_7(j)$
−3	57	30	90	39	99	54	114	75	135	90	150	105	165	126
−2	48	29	80	38	89	53	104	74	125	89	140	104	155	125
−1	39	28	70	37	79	52	94	73	115	88	130	103	145	124
0	30	27	60	36	69	51	84	72	105	87	120	102	135	123
1	21	20	50	35	59	50	74	71	95	86	110	101	125	122
2	12	10	40	34	49	47	64	62	85	83	100	98	115	113
3	3	0	30	27	39	36	54	51	75	72	90	87	105	102
4	6	2	26	22	41	37	56	52	77	73	92	88	107	103
5	9	4	19	14	43	38	56	51	71	66	92	87	107	102
6	12	6	12	6	39	33	48	42	63	57	84	78	99	93
7	15	8	17	10	37	30	52	45	67	60	88	81	103	96
8	18	10	22	14	32	24	56	48	69	61	84	76	105	97
9	21	12	27	18	27	18	54	45	63	54	78	69	99	90
10	24	14	32	22	34	24	54	44	69	59	84	74	105	95
11	27	16	37	26	41	30	51	40	75	64	88	77	103	92
12	30	18	42	30	48	36	48	36	75	63	84	72	99	87
13	33	20	47	34	55	42	57	44	77	64	92	79	107	94
14	36	22	52	38	62	48	66	52	76	62	100	86	113	99
15	39	24	57	42	69	54	75	60	75	60	102	87	111	96
Optimal Policies	(1,3)		(3,6)		(2,9)		(2,6)	(2,12)	(2,9)	(2,6)	(2,9)		(2,9)	(2,6) (2,12)

Data: $K = 24$ $c = 1$ $h = 2$ $\pi = 10$ $\alpha = 1$ $p(3) = 1$ $\lambda = 0$

Figure II.3. Deterministic Example.

The complete function $G_2(y)$ is given in Fig. II.3, where you can see that $S_2 = 6$. Continuing to *Step 2*, check that $s_2 = 3$ is the smallest value of s_2 such that

$$(23) \qquad G_2(s_2) \leq G_2(6) + K = 36,$$

since $G_2(3) = 30$ whereas $G_2(2) = 40$. The resultant values for $F_2(j)$ are indicated in Fig. II.3; to test your understanding, verify the values for $F_2(9)$, $F_2(6)$, $F_2(0)$, and $F_2(-2)$.

The values of $G_n(y)$ and $F_n(j)$ for $n = 3, 4, \ldots, 7$, also appear in Fig. II.3. Notice that these $G_n(y)$ and $F_n(j)$ are *not* convex. For example, there are local minima of both $G_4(y)$ and $F_4(j)$ at y and j equal to 3, 6, and 12. Observe that $F_n(j)$ decreases for $j < s_n$, and, as you would expect, increases for j sufficiently large, for then you incur a large inventory holding cost. But note that $F_n(j)$ does not always decrease for $s_n \leq j \leq S_n$. To illustrate, $F_4(3) = 51$ whereas $F_4(4) = 52$, even though (2, 9) is optimal for $n = 4$. Consequently, although it is optimal to order $(9 - j_4)$ if $j_4 < 2$, it is *more* costly to start with inventory $j_4 = 4$ than with $j_4 = 3$. In such an instance, it would be better for the company to get rid of one item, provided the associated cost of disposal were less than $1 (= 52 - 51)$.

The corresponding optimal values for (s_n, S_n) are shown at the bottom of

Fig. II.3. Notice that in certain periods there is more than one optimal policy. In fact, it can be shown that multiple optimal policies continue to be present for larger n. Specifically, for $k = 0, 1, 2, \ldots$, the optimal policies are

(24)

	$(2, 9)$ and $(2, 6)$	for $n = 5 + 3k$
	$(2, 9)$	for $n = 6 + 3k$
	$(2, 9), (2, 6),$ and $(2, 12)$	for $n = 7 + 3k,$

where n is the number of periods remaining until the end of the horizon. Despite this multiplicity of solutions for specific finite horizons, the unique optimal policy is easily shown to be $(2, 9)$ when the horizon is unbounded.

▶ If the disposal cost of x units is $d_t \cdot x$, then it is possible to modify an (s, S) policy as follows. If $j_t < s_t$, order $(S_t - j_t)$, where (s_t, S_t) are determined by (4) and (7). Otherwise, let y be the minimizing value in

(i)　$\displaystyle \operatorname*{minimum}_{y \le j} \left[d_t(j - y) + L_t(y) + \alpha \sum_{q=0}^{\infty} f_{t+1}(y - q) p_t(q) \right] = f_t(j)$ 　for $j \ge s_t$.

For the example in Fig. II.3 with $d_t = 0$, the modified policy leads to the same set of (s_t, S_t).　　　　　　　　　　　　　　　　　　　　　　　　　◀

As a second illustration, suppose the economic data are the same as in (13), except here consider $\alpha = 1, .9,$ and $.8$, and $\lambda = 0, 1, 2$, and assume the stationary demand distribution is now

(25)　　　　　　　　　　$p(2) = .2 \quad p(3) = .8.$

[Recall $p^{\lambda+1}(Q)$ were calculated in (13) and (15) of Sec. II.2.] The resultant optimal policies, which are unique, are shown in Fig. II.4. Notice that neither

	$\lambda = 0$			$\alpha = 1$	
	$\alpha = 1$	$\alpha = .9$	$\alpha = .8$	$\lambda = 1$	$\lambda = 2$
n	s_n, S_n, D_n	s_n, S_n, D_n	s_n, S_n, D_n	$s_{n-1}, S_{n-1}, D_{n-1}$	$s_{n-2}, S_{n-2}, D_{n-2}$
1	1,3,2	1,3,2	1,3,2	— —	— —
2	3,6,3	2,6,4	2,6,4	3,6,3	— —
3	2,8,6	2,8,6	2,8,6	5,9,4	6,9,3
4	2,11,9	1,6,5	1,6,5	5,11,6	8,11,3
5	2,6,4	2,6,4	2,6,4	4,13,9	8,14,6
6	2,9,7	2,8,6	1,6,5	5,9,4	7,16,9
7	2,9,7	2,6,4	2,6,4	5,11,6	7,12,5
8	2,9,7	2,8,6	2,6,4	4,12,8	8,14,6
9	2,9,7	2,8,6	2,6,4	5,9,4	7,14,7
10	2,9,7	2,8,6	2,6,4	5,11,6	7,14,7

Note: $D_n \equiv S_n - s_n$, n = number of periods remaining to end of horizon
Data: $K = 24$ $c = 1$ $h = 2$ $\pi = 10$ $p(2) = .2$ $p(3) = .8$

FIGURE II.4. Probabilistic Examples.

s_n, S_n, nor $D_n \equiv S_n - s_n$ is monotonic. Observe that as α gets smaller, both s_n and S_n get smaller, so that the ordering decision tends to be postponed and the order quantity diminished. In other words, the smaller the α, the greater the tendency to incur the replenishment expenses further into the future. Lastly, note that as λ gets larger, so do both s_n and S_n.

For a final example, consider the same economic data in (13), but let $h = 4$, and keep the same deterministic demand assumption in (14). As you can verify by applying the optimizing algorithm, the optimal policy (s_n, S_n) is

$$(26) \qquad \begin{array}{llll} (1, 3) & (1, 6) & (1, 9) & \text{for } n = 1, 3, 5, 7, \ldots \\ & (2, 6) & & \text{for } n = 2, 4, 6, \quad , \ldots, \end{array}$$

where n is the number of periods remaining to the end of the horizon. Observe not only the multiplicity of optimal policies when n is odd, but also the persistent oscillation of s_n between the values 1 and 2. Consequently, if n periods remain to the end of the horizon and if at the current period $j_n = 1$, you *do* order if n is even, but *do not* if n is odd. As shown in the special material below, $(2, 6)$ becomes the *unique* optimal stationary policy when the horizon is taken as unbounded.

▶Suppose for every n you let $S_n = 6$ in (26). Consider the case of inventory being at level 1 for the initial period. Then if you place an order immediately, so that in effect $s = 2$, the resultant sequence of order quantities is $(5, 0, 6, 0, 6, 0, 6, \ldots)$ and the sequence of ending inventory levels is $(3, 0, 3, 0, \ldots)$, regardless of whether $s = 1$ or 2 in the remaining periods. Consequently, the associated sequence of replenishment costs is

(ii) $K + 5c + 3h, \quad 0, \quad K + 6c + 3h, \quad 0, \quad K + 6c + 3h, \quad 0, \ldots$
$$(s = 2 \text{ at initial period}).$$

If instead you do not place an order at the initial period, so that in effect $s = 1$, then the resultant sequence of order quantities is $(0, 8, 0, 6, 0, 6, \ldots)$ and sequence of ending inventory levels is $(-2, 3, 0, 3, 0, \ldots)$, regardless of wh᷉ · $s = 1$ or 2 in the remaining periods. Therefore the associated sequence of replenis.   costs is

(iii) $2p, \quad K + 8c + 3h, \quad 0, \quad K + 6c + 3h, \quad 0, \quad K + 6c + 3h.$
$$(s - \quad \text{initial period}).$$

Consider the economic parameters of the example in (26), namely, $K = 24$, $c = 1$, $h = 4$, and $p = 10$. You can verify by *accumulating* the costs in (ii) and (iii) that placing an order in the initial period ($s = 2$) is better than postponing the order for one period ($s = 1$) if the horizon length T is even; it is worse if T is odd.

Now suppose the horizon is unbounded, and introduce the discount factor α. Then using $(s, S) = (2, 6)$ as a stationary policy results in the present value of all costs

(iv) $$\text{P.V.}[2] = K + 5c + 3h + \frac{\alpha^2(K + 6c + 3h)}{1 - \alpha^2},$$

and similarly using $(s, S) = (1, 6)$ results in

(v) $$\text{P.V.}[1] = 2p + \alpha(K + 8c + 3h) + \frac{\alpha^3(K + 6c + 3h)}{1 - \alpha^2}.$$

Thus

(vi) P.V.[1] $-$ P.V.[2] $= (2p - K - 5c - 3h) + \alpha(K + 8c + 3h) - \dfrac{\alpha^2(K + 6c + 3h)}{1 + \alpha}$

$$= 2p - \frac{K}{2} - \frac{3h}{2} > 0 \quad \text{for } \alpha = 1,$$

given the values of the cost parameters, so that $(s, S) = (2, 6)$ is better.   ◄

*Proof of "Optimality of (s, S) Policy". The proof that an (s, S) policy is optimal under the hypotheses stated in (1) and (2) above is of two-fold importance. Obviously such a proof is required in order to establish that the stated theorem is indeed correct; but this reason is the concern of technical specialists, and therefore does not justify our including the proof in an introductory text. The second reason is that the proof exemplifies what is called an inductive line of reasoning. This approach applied to dynamic programming recursions sometimes leads to insightful results, such as the *form* of an *optimal* policy. That is why the argument appears here. The case of all $K_t = 0$ is fully proved, and the argument for the more general case is only sketched.

To start the **inductive proof**, suppose for a given t that $g_t(y)$ in (8) is convex:

(27) $g_t(y + 1) - g_t(y) \geq g_t(y) - g_t(y - 1)$ for all integer y,

and $g_t(y) \to \infty$ as $|y| \to \infty$. As in *Step 1* of the algorithm, let S_t be the value of y that minimizes $g_t(y)$. These hypotheses on $g_t(y)$ and $K_t = 0$ establish the result in *Step 2* that $s_t = S_t$, and that the form of the optimal policy is to order $(S_t - j)$ if $j < s_t$, and not to order otherwise. To summarize so far, the inductive hypothesis that $g_t(y)$ is convex and $K_t = 0$ leads to the conclusion that the optimal policy is (s_t, S_t) with $s_t = S_t$.

The next part of the proof is to establish that $g_{t-1}(y)$ is convex and $g_{t-1}(y) \to \infty$ as $|y| \to \infty$.

Consider first $\leq s_t - 1$. Then from (5) and the fact that $s_t = S_t$,

(28) $f_t(j)$ ⁷ $(s_t) - c_t j = -c_t(s_t - j) + L_t(s_t) + \alpha \sum_{q=0}^{\infty} f_{t+1}(s_t - q) p_t(q)$,

and from (5), the expression (28) also is valid for $j = s_t$. Therefore, according to (28), if $j \leq s_t - 1$,

(29) $f_t(j + 1) - f_t(j) = -c_t = f_t(j) - f_t(j - 1)$,

so that $f_t(j)$ is convex for these integer values of j.

Consider next $j \geq s_t$. Then from (5) and the hypothesis that $g_t(y)$ is convex,

(30) $f_t(j + 1) - f_t(j) = g_t(j + 1) - g_t(j) - c_t \geq g_t(j) - g_t(j - 1) - c_t.$

If $j > s_t$, then simplifying the expression on the right of (30) gives

(31) $f_t(j + 1) - f_t(j) \geq f_t(j) - f_t(j - 1).$

If $j = s_t$, then since $y = s_t = S_t$ minimizes $g_t(y)$,

(32) $$g_t(s_t + 1) - g_t(s_t) - c_t \geq -c_t = f_t(s_t) - f_t(s_t - 1),$$

so that from (29), (30), (31), and (32), $f_t(j)$ is convex for *all* integer j.

Knowing that $f_t(j)$ is convex, it follows that $\alpha f_t(j - q)p_{t-1}(q)$ is convex for any q. Since the sum of convex functions is convex, you can conclude that

(33) $$g_{t-1}(y) \equiv c_{t-1}y + L_{t-1}(y) + \alpha \sum_{q=0}^{\infty} f_t(y - q)p_{t-1}(q)$$

is convex. Further, since $(c_{t-1} - \alpha c_t)y + L_{t-1}(y) \to \infty$ as $|y| \to \infty$ by assumption (2), so does $g_{t-1}(y)$, as can be shown. The inductive proof that $g_t(y)$ is convex for *all* t and $g_t(y) \to \infty$ for $|y| \to \infty$ is complete upon verifying that, for $t = T$ (the end of the horizon),

(34) $$g_T(y) \equiv c_T y + L_T(y)$$

is convex and $g_T(y) \to \infty$ as $|y| \to \infty$. These statements are indeed true by the assumptions in (2).

The same inductive line of reasoning can be used in the case where all $K_t \geq 0$, except that the assumption of convexity in (27) must be generalized to the postulate that $g_t(y)$ in (7) satisfies, for integer y,

(35) $$g_t(y + a) - g_t(y) + K_t \geq \frac{a}{b}[g_t(y) - g_t(y - b)] \qquad (K_t\text{-convexity}),$$

where a and b are arbitrary positive integers. The property in (35) is referred to as **K_t-convexity**. The inductive hypothesis is that (35) holds for a given t, and you can show that (35) implies that the form of an optimal policy for Period t is (s_t, S_t) as constructed by *Steps 1* and *2*. For the remainder of the proof, you must establish that $g_{t-1}(y)$ possesses the property of K_{t-1}-*convexity*.

II.5 CASE OF ZERO SETUP COSTS

Suppose the model in the preceding section is further specialized by eliminating the setup costs K_t, so that

(1) $$c_t(x) = c_t \cdot x \quad \text{for } x \geq 0,$$

where $c_t \geq 0$.

Further assume that if any items are left in inventory at the end of the horizon, they can be salvaged at the cost of c_{T+1} per unit, and if any demands are still backlogged, they must be filled at the same cost of c_{T+1} per unit. Note that here we let $c_{T+1} \geq 0$. Consequently, the general dynamic programming recursion (9) in Sec. II.3 is altered by setting

(2) $$f_{T+1}(j) = -c_{T+1}j.$$

The Optimality of (s, S) Policy Theorem still remains valid with this new assumption. For many situations, when all $K_t = 0$, you can obtain the common value of

$s_t = S_t$ by a procedure that is much simpler than that in the previous section. In fact, it amounts to solving a sequence of static or one-period models, which you studied in Sec. 19.4.

Of course assumption (2) can lead to different (s_t, S_t) values than would arise if you assume $f_{T+1} \equiv 0$, especially for periods near the end of the horizon. Explain why. But if the horizon T is fairly long, this ending assumption (2) usually has just a negligible effect on the ordering policy for the *current* period, especially when $\alpha < 1$, for then f_{T+1} is weighted by only $\alpha^{\lambda+T}$ in the T-period objective function. Indeed, if the horizon is unbounded and all the cost parameters as well as the demand probability distributions are stationary, then the determination of an optimal stationary policy is unaffected by assuming (2).

The approach is to consider

(3)　$\displaystyle\operatorname*{minimum}_{y}[(c_t - \alpha c_{t+1})y + L_t(y)]$　for $t = 1, 2, \ldots, T$　　　General Case,

and let

$$\bar{y}_t = \text{value of } y \text{ found in (3)}.$$

If

(4)　　　　　　　　　$\bar{y}_t \leq \bar{y}_{t+1}$　for all $t = 1, 2, \ldots, T - 1,$

then

(5)　　　　　　　　　　　$s_t = S_t = \bar{y}_t,$

and $\bar{y}_t$ is often referred to as an **optimal single critical number** for Period t.

The following observation argues for the plausibility of (5). Suppose the sequence of optimal single critical numbers $(s_t = S_t)$ is such that $s_t \leq s_{t+1}$ for all $t \leq T - 1$. Then the *incremental* cost of purchasing $(s_t - j)$ items instead of $(s_t - 1 - j)$ items in Period t is only $(c_t - \alpha c_{t+1})$, since this additional unit would otherwise be purchased in Period t + 1, regardless of demand in Period t given that $s_{t+1} \geq s_t$. Consequently, if $s_t \leq s_{t+1}$ for all $t \leq T - 1$, the optimization can be performed for $t = 1, 2, \ldots, T - 1$ on a period-by-period basis, where you minimize the sum of incremental purchase cost and expected holding-and-penalty cost. (Note the preceding argument breaks down when $s_t > s_{t+1}$. Then an additional unit ordered in Period t might not otherwise be purchased in Period t + 1—it *would* depend on the level of demand in Period t.) For $t = T$, the assumption (2) justifies employing $(c_T - \alpha c_{T+1})$ as the appropriate ordering cost.

The preceding paragraph in essence demonstrated that *if* $s_t \leq s_{t+1}$, for all $t \leq T - 1$, is indeed optimal, then the minimization in (3) provides the value for s_t. But we really want to establish the more operational proposition that if the inequalities in (4) hold, then (5) is optimal. This result is argued in the advanced material at the end of this section.

Suppose the holding and penalty cost functions are linear, so that

$$
(6) \quad L_t(y) =
\begin{cases}
\sum_{Q=0}^{y} h_{t+\lambda} \cdot (y - Q) p_{t,t+\lambda}(Q) + \sum_{Q>y}^{\infty} \pi_{t+\lambda} \cdot (Q - y) p_{t,t+\lambda}(Q) \\
\qquad\qquad\qquad\qquad\qquad\qquad\qquad\qquad\qquad \text{for } y \geq 0 \\
\sum_{Q=0}^{\infty} \pi_{t+\lambda} \cdot (Q - y) p_{t,t+\lambda}(Q) \qquad\qquad\qquad \text{for } y < 0.
\end{cases}
$$

Then $\bar{y}_t$ is the smallest integer such that

$$
(7) \quad \sum_{Q=0}^{\bar{y}_t} p_{t,t+\lambda}(Q) \geq \frac{\pi_{t+\lambda} - (c_t - \alpha c_{t+1})}{\pi_{t+\lambda} + h_{t+\lambda}} \qquad \underline{\text{Linear Cost—Nonstationary Case.}}
$$

How does $\bar{y}_t$ change as $\pi_{t+\lambda}$ increases? As $h_{t+\lambda}$ increases? How do the purchase costs affect the value of $\bar{y}_t$?

If in addition all the economic parameters and probability distributions are stationary, then (7) reduces to

$$
(8) \quad \sum_{Q=0}^{\bar{y}} p^{\lambda+1}(Q) \geq \frac{\pi - (1 - \alpha)c}{\pi + h} \quad \underline{\text{Linear Cost—Stationary Case.}}
$$

How do you think $\bar{y}_t$ is likely to change as the lag λ increases? In answering, you might think of what happens if the probability on the left-hand side of (8) is approximated by a cumulative Normal distribution. Suppose $\alpha = 1$. What effect does the purchase cost c have on $\bar{y}$? How reasonable, then, is this policy for, say, the last period in a finite horizon problem?

Therefore, the algorithm to find the optimal single critical numbers can be stated as:

Step 1. Calculate $\bar{y}_t$, for $t = 1, 2, \ldots, T$, according to (3)—or according to (7) or (8) if appropriate.

Step 2. Verify whether $\bar{y}_t \leq \bar{y}_{t+1}$, for all $t = 1, 2, \ldots, T - 1$. If so, let $s_t = S_t = \bar{y}_t$. Otherwise, apply the algorithm in Sec. II.4.

For many important cases, the inequalities in *Step 2* will always be satisfied. For example, the inequalities hold if you postulate full stationarity (8); then all the $\bar{y}_t$ are identical. Consequently, once inventory falls below the level $\bar{y}$ as specified by (8), you always order the amount demanded in the previous period. Further, in this case the value of $\bar{y}$ found by (8) is also optimal for an unbounded horizon and all values of α, where $0 \leq \alpha \leq 1$. We return to this point in the next section.

If you assume both the probability distribution of demand and the unit purchasing costs c_t are stationary, but that the penalty costs $\pi_{t+\lambda}$ in (7) are rising over time *relative* to $h_{t+\lambda}$, then all $\bar{y}_t \leq \bar{y}_{t+1}$. Give a verbal explanation of the reason why. Now, how much do you order in each period?

As was pointed out above, *Step 1* is no more complex than the optimization process required in the one-period (static) model of Sec. 19.4. In fact, when $\lambda = 0$ and $\alpha = 0$ in the model above, the two methods are identical.

▶The material at the end of Sec. II.3 pointed out that when $\lambda = 0$, the lost sales case could also be handled by a simple dynamic programming recursion. Assuming further that all the $K_t = 0$, a single-critical-number type of policy is optimal. If $L_t(y)$ is given by (6), and $\bar{y}_t$ is the smallest integer such that

(i) $\qquad \sum_{q=0}^{\bar{y}_t} p_t(q) \geq \dfrac{\pi_t - c_t}{\pi_t + h_t - \alpha c_{t+1}}$ Immediate Delivery—Linear Cost—Lost Sales Case,

then $\bar{y}_t$ is the optimal single critical number *provided* (4) holds.

We now prove the validity of the single-critical-number *algorithm*. Specifically, let $\bar{y}_t$ be a value of y such that

(ii) $\underset{y}{\text{minimum}}\ [(c_t - \alpha c_{t+1})y + L_t(y)] = (c_t - \alpha c_{t+1})\bar{y}_t + L_t(\bar{y}_t)$ for $t = 1, 2, \ldots, T$.

We show that if $\bar{y}_t \leq \bar{y}_{t+1}$, for $t = 1, 2, \ldots, T - 1$, then $s_t = S_t = \bar{y}_t$.

The argument can be established inductively. Start at $t = T$. Then by assumptions (1) and (2)

(iii) $\qquad f_T(j) \equiv \underset{y \geq j}{\text{minimum}}\ [c_T \cdot (y - j) + L_T(y) - \alpha \sum_{q=0}^{\infty} c_{T+1} \cdot (y - q)p_T(q)],$

where, as usual, $f_T(j)$ represents the expected cost of an optimal policy when entering inventory is j at Period T. Given that a single-critical-number policy is optimal for (iii), $(s_T = S_T)$ is a minimizing value of y found from

(iv) $\qquad\qquad\qquad \underset{y}{\text{minimum}}\ [c_T \cdot y + L_T(y) - \alpha c_{T+1} y],$

which agrees with (ii). Hence, $\bar{y}_T = s_T = S_T$, as claimed by the algorithm.

Consequently,

(v) $f_T(j) = \begin{cases} c_T \cdot (\bar{y}_T - j) + L_T(\bar{y}_T) - \alpha \sum_{q=0}^{\infty} c_{T+1} \cdot (\bar{y}_T - q)p_T(q) & \text{for } j \leq \bar{y}_T \\[2mm] L_T(j) - \alpha \sum_{q=0}^{\infty} c_{T+1} \cdot (j - q)p_T(q) & \text{for } j > \bar{y}_T. \end{cases}$

Define

(vi) $\qquad d_T(j) \equiv c_T \cdot (\bar{y}_T - j) + L_T(\bar{y}_T) + \alpha \sum_{q=0}^{\infty} c_{T+1} \cdot (\bar{y}_T - q)p_T(q)$

$\qquad\qquad\qquad \equiv -c_T j + d_T(\bar{y}_T).$

Given that $\bar{y}_T$ is derived from (iv), verify that

(vii) $\qquad\qquad\qquad \begin{aligned} d_T(j) &= f_T(j) \quad \text{for } j \leq \bar{y}_T \\ d_T(j) &\leq f_T(j) \quad \text{for } j > \bar{y}_T. \end{aligned}$

Hence,

(viii) $\qquad \underset{y \geq j}{\text{minimum}}\ [c_{T-1}(y - j) + L_{T-1}(y) + \alpha \sum_{q=0}^{\infty} d_T(y - q)p_{T-1}(q)]$

(ix) $\qquad \leq \underset{y \geq j}{\text{minimum}}\ [c_{T-1}(y - j) + L_{T-1}(y) + \alpha \sum_{q=0}^{8} f_T(y - q)p_{T-1}(q)]$

(x) $\qquad\qquad \equiv f_{T-1}(j),$

where, as usual, $f_{T-1}(j)$ represents the expected cost using of an optimal policy when entering inventory is j at Period T $-$ 1.

Substitute the expression (vi) into (viii) and check that for j sufficiently small in (viii), a minimizing value of y can be found from

(xi) $$\underset{y}{\text{minimum}}\ [c_{T-1}y + L_{T-1}(y) - \alpha c_T y].$$

By hypothesis, $\bar{y}_{T-1}$ is a solution to (xi).

Also, $\bar{y}_{T-1} \leq \bar{y}_T$ by assumption, and therefore $\bar{y}_{T-1} - q \leq \bar{y}_T$, for $q \geq 0$; a fortiori,

(xii) $$d_T(\bar{y}_{T-1} - q) = f_T(\bar{y}_{T-1} - q)\quad \text{for } q \geq 0.$$

We are now justified in writing (viii) and (ix) as:

(xiii)
$$c_{T-1}(\bar{y}_{T-1} - j) + L_{T-1}(\bar{y}_{T-1}) + \alpha \sum_{q=0}^{\infty} f_T(\bar{y}_{T-1} - q)p_{T-1}(q)$$
$$\leq \underset{y \geq j}{\text{minimum}}\ [c_{T-1}(y - j) + L_{T-1}(y) + \alpha \sum_{q=0}^{\infty} f_T (y - q)p_{T-1}(q)],$$

so that $\bar{y}_{T-1}$ is an optimal value of y in the right-hand expression in (xiii), for sufficiently small j; a fortiori, since a single-critical-number policy is optimal, $\bar{y}_{T-1} = s_{T-1} = S_{T-1}$, as was to be shown.

The correctness of the entire algorithm is established by continuing in the same fashion for $t = T - 2, T - 3, \ldots, 1$.   ◀

II.6 UNBOUNDED HORIZON MODEL

Here we postulate the cost assumptions made in Sec. II.4, except now we assume that the economic data and demand distributions are stationary over an unbounded horizon. Specifically, the cost assumptions are

(1) $$c(x) = \begin{cases} 0 & \text{for } x = 0 \\ K + cx & \text{for } x > 0 \end{cases}\quad \text{where } K \geq 0 \text{ and } c \geq 0$$

(2) $L(y)$ is convex

(3) $c(1 - \alpha)y + L(y) \to \infty \quad \text{as } |y| \to \infty.$

We can show the following proposition.

OPTIMALITY OF A STATIONARY (s, S) POLICY. Given the model represented by the dynamic programming recursion (9) in Sec. II.3 in which the economic parameters satisfy (1), (2), and (3), where $0 \leq \alpha \leq 1$, there is an optimal policy of the (s, S) type in which $s_t = s$ and $S_t = S$, for all t, over an unbounded horizon. Further, if all $K_t = K = 0$, then $s = S$.

{The theorem remains true when (2) is weakened to $-[c(1 - \alpha)y + L(y)]$ is *unimodal*, defined in Sec. 14.3.}

The numerical procedures for calculating an optimal (s, S) policy are involved —except when all $K_t = 0$—and are presented in the next section. In the remainder of this section, you will find a sensitivity analysis of optimal (s, S) policies to changes in the economic parameters and demand probability distributions. You will also see how to calculate the optimal $(s = S)$ when all $K_t = 0$, and how to compute a nearly optimal (s, S) policy using a Normal distribution approximation.

▶ For $\alpha < 1$, a unique solution exists to the dynamic programming functional equation

(i) $f(j) = \underset{y \geq j}{\text{minimum}} \left[c(y - j) + L(y) + \alpha \sum_{q=0}^{\infty} f(y - q)p(q) \right]$ $(0 \leq \alpha < 1)$,

which is the appropriate generalization of the finite horizon recursion (9) in Sec. II.3. Assuming the theorem applies so that the optimal form of the policy is (s, S), the function $f(j)$ must satisfy, for an optimal (s, S) policy,

(ii)

$$f(j) = K + c \cdot (S - j) + L(S) + \alpha \sum_{q=0}^{\infty} f(S - q)p(q) \quad \text{for } j < s$$

$$f(j) = L(j) + \alpha \sum_{q=0}^{\infty} f(j - q)p(q) \qquad\qquad \text{for } j \geq s.$$

For $\alpha = 1$, the analogous extremal equation is

(iii) $g(j) + \bar{g} = \underset{y \geq j}{\text{minimum}} \left[c(y - j) + L(y) + \sum_{q=0}^{\infty} g(y - q)p(q) \right]$,

where $\bar{g}$ represents the expected cost per period of an optimal policy. Assuming the theorem applies, the function $g(j)$ and $\bar{g}$ must satisfy, for an optimal (s, S) policy,

(iv)

$$g(j) + \bar{g} = c \cdot (s - j) + \bar{g} \qquad\qquad \text{for } j < s$$

$$g(j) + \bar{g} = L(j) + \sum_{q=0}^{\infty} g(j - q)p(q) \quad \text{for } j \geq s. \qquad \blacktriangleleft$$

Sensitivity analysis. Assume $\alpha = 1$ and that the expected holding and penalty cost function is

(4) $L(y) = \begin{cases} \sum_{Q=0}^{y} h \cdot (y - Q)p^{\lambda+1}(Q) + \sum_{Q > y} \pi \cdot (Q - y)p^{\lambda+1}(Q) & \text{for } y \geq 0 \\[2mm] \sum_{Q=0}^{\infty} \pi \cdot (Q - y)p^{\lambda+1}(Q) & \text{for } y < 0. \end{cases}$

Since all demands are eventually filled, $c_t = c$, and $\alpha = 1$, the value of c does not influence the optimality of a policy and therefore can be omitted in the discussion below. Further, you can normalize one of the cost parameters, say

(5) $h = 1$,

because a policy that is optimal for the costs (K, h, π) is also optimal for any multiple of the costs, such as $(2K, 2h, 2\pi)$.

Over a wide range of economic parameters and demand probability distributions,

(6)

$s, S, (S - s)$ increase as λ increases;

$S, (S - s)$ increase and s decreases as K increases;

s increases and $(S - s)$ decreases as π increases; and

s increases as $E[q]$ increases.

As the example in Fig. II.5 shows, S need not increase with π or $E[q]$, and $(S - s)$ need not increase with $E[q]$. A second illustration showing that $(S - s)$ need not increase with $E[q]$ is exhibited in Fig. II.6. Notice there is a moderate decrease in $(S - s)$ when $E[q]$ goes from 22 to 23 and a large decrease when $E[q]$ goes from 61 to 63.

Poisson Distribution
$K = 64$ $h = 1$ $\pi = 9$ $\lambda = 0$

$E[q]$	$s, S, S-s$
21	16,65,49
22	17,68,51
23	18,52,34
24	19,54,35
59	52,126,74
61	53,131,78
63	55,73,18
64	56,74,18

Poisson Distribution
$K = 64$ $h = 1$ $\lambda = 0$

$E[q]$	$\pi = 4$ $s, S, S-s$	$\pi = 99$ $s, S, S-s$
49	35,100,65	56,116,60
64	46,131,85	72,83,11

FIGURE II.5. Sensitivity Analysis.   FIGURE II.6. Variation in $(S - s)$.

The fact that $(S - s)$ does drop substantially as $E[q]$ gets large demonstrates a significant difference between the discrete review models in this appendix and the continuous review model in Chap. 19. In the continuous review case, as the mean demand rate increases, the order quantity $(S - s)$ always increases, but the interval between successive orders decreases. In the discrete review case, as $E[q]$ grows, eventually the probability is nearly 1 that a replenishment order is placed at every period. Consequently, the system *behaves* almost as if $K = 0$, that is, as if $s = S$.

▶ In the following special case, the optimal $(S - s)$ is precisely the EOQ formula (8) for the *deterministic* lot-size model in Sec. 19.5. Assume $\alpha = 1$, $\lambda = 0$, $p(q)$ is the exponential *density* function

(i) $$p(q) = me^{-qm} \quad \text{for } q \geq 0 \qquad E[q] = \frac{1}{m},$$

and $L(y)$ is given by (4), except that integrals are used instead of summations. Then the optimal values for s and S are determined by

(ii) $$S - s = \sqrt{\frac{2K \cdot E[q]}{h}} \qquad e^{-sm} = \left(\frac{h}{h + \pi}\right)[1 + m(S - s)]. \qquad ◀$$

Case of $K = 0$. If $K = 0$, then the calculation for the common value $s = S$ is identical to that in Sec. II.5. Specifically, if $L(y)$ is given by (4) above, then $\bar{y} = s = S$ is the smallest integer such that

(7) $$\sum_{Q=0}^{\bar{y}} p^{\lambda+1}(Q) \geq \frac{\pi - (1 - \alpha)c}{\pi + h} \quad (0 \leq \alpha \leq 1).$$

For more general $L(y)$, $\bar{y}$ is found by

(8) $$\text{minimum}_{y} [(1 - \alpha)cy + L(y)].$$

Case of $K > 0$. A complete algorithm to compute policies efficiently for an unbounded horizon is briefly sketched in the advanced material in the next section. For many practical situations, however, you can apply a very simple approximation procedure.

Assume the expected holding and penalty function is given by (4). Also let $\alpha = 1$, which is an adequate assumption for most applications of the model, as can be seen in Fig. II.7. This table indicates values for α when, say, the *annual* interest rate is i and there are 12, 52, 365 review intervals per year.

The technique uses a Normal distribution approximation in a manner analogous to that employed for the continuous review model in Sec. 19.6. Let

$$a = (1 + i)^{-1/T}$$

i	12	52	365
.01	.9992	.9998	.9999
.05	.9959	.9991	.9999
.15	.9884	.9973	.9996
.20	.9849	.9965	.9995
.25	.9816	.9957	.9994
.30	.9784	.9950	.9993

(9) $E[q] = M \quad \text{Var}[q] = V,$

so that

FIGURE II.7. Compound Discount Factors.

(10)
$$E[q_t + \cdots + q_{t+\lambda}] = (\lambda + 1)M$$
$$\text{Var}[q_t + \cdots + q_{t+\lambda}] = (\lambda + 1)V.$$

Define

(11)
$$u_s = \frac{s - (\lambda + 1)M}{\sqrt{(\lambda + 1)V}}$$

so that

(12) $$s = (\lambda + 1)M + u_s\sqrt{(\lambda + 1)V}.$$

Denote the *cumulative standardized Normal distribution* as

(13)
$$P_N(u) = \int_{-\infty}^{u} \frac{1}{\sqrt{2\pi}} e^{-.5t^2}\, dt$$

and the *standardized Normal loss integral* as

(14)
$$I_N(u) = \int_{u}^{\infty} (t - u)\frac{1}{\sqrt{2\pi}} e^{-.5^2} dt.$$

Both $P_N(u)$ and $I_N(u)$ are tabled in Fig. 19.6 (p. 819).

The approximation algorithm is as follows.

Step 1. Calculate

(15)
$$EOQ \equiv \sqrt{\frac{2KM}{h}}.$$

Step 2. Compute

(16)
$$R_N = \frac{h \cdot EOQ}{\pi\sqrt{(\lambda + 1)V}}$$

and find the value for u_s such that

(17) $$I_N(u_s) = R_N.$$

Step 3. If $M < .8888\ K/h$, then let (s, S) be determined by s in (12) and $S = s + EOQ$. Otherwise go to *Step 4*.

Step 4. Compute

$$(18) \qquad R = \frac{\pi}{h + \pi}$$

and find the value for v_s such that

$$(19) \qquad P_N(v_s) = R.$$

Define

$$(20) \qquad w_s = \text{minimum }(u_s, v_s)$$

and let (s, S) be determined by

$$(21) \qquad s = (\lambda + 1)M + w_s\sqrt{(\lambda + 1)V}$$

$$(22) \qquad S = (\lambda + 1)M + \text{minimum }[u_s\sqrt{(\lambda + 1)V} + EOQ, v_s\sqrt{(\lambda + 1)V}].$$

Justification for *Steps 1* and *2* involves mathematical arguments too advanced for an introductory text, but which are based on an analysis of how the expected cost function behaves as K and π increase. The calculation test $(M < .8888K/h)$ in *Step 3* establishes whether $(EOQ/M) > 1.5$ periods. If $(EOQ/M) \leq 1.5$, then *Step 4* calculates in (18) and (19) a Normal approximation to the optimal single-critical-number policy, as given by (7). The approximate s in (21) is the smaller of the trial s indicated by u_s in (17) and by v_s in (19). Similarly, the approximate S in (22) is the smaller of the trial S implied by u_s and the EOQ, and by v_s.

Several examples using the approximation are given in Fig. II.8. (The data employed permit you to compare the results with those in Fig. 19.7, p. 821, which exhibited a Normal approximation method for the continuous review model.) To see how the algorithm works, consider data for Case 1 in Fig. II.8:

$$(23) \qquad h = 1 \quad \pi = 9 \quad K = 32 \quad \lambda = 0 \quad M = 9 \quad V = 9.$$

According to *Step 1*,

$$(24) \qquad EOQ = \sqrt{\frac{2 \cdot 32 \cdot 9}{1}} = 24.$$

Then in *Step 2*,

$$(25) \qquad R_N = \frac{1 \cdot 24}{9\sqrt{9}} = .889,$$

and so from Fig. 19.6,

$$(26) \qquad u_s = -.75.$$

Since $9 < .8888(32/1)$,

$$(27) \qquad EOQ = S - s = 24 \qquad s = 9 - .75\sqrt{9} \approx 7 \qquad S = 31.$$

As Fig. II.8 shows, the optimal policy is $(7, 28)$.

Case	Varied Parameters	Normal Approximation			Optimal		
		s	S	$S-s$	s	S	$S-s$
1	None	7	31	24	7	28	21
	$\pi = 99$	12	36	24	13	33	20
	$K = 64$	5	39	34	6	37	31
	$\pi = 99$ $K = 64$	11	45	34	12	42	30
	$M = 16$	13	45	32	14	37	23
	$\lambda = 4$	45	69	24	45	68	23
	$V = 90$ (Neg. Bin.)	11	35	24	10	33	23
2	None	103	148	45	105	148	43
	$\pi = 9$	82	127	45	82	128	46
	$K = 32$	105	137	32	107	137	30
	$\pi = 9$ $K = 32$	86	118	32	85	117	32
	$M = 8$	56	88	32	58	90	32
	$\lambda = 0$	24	69	45	25	65	40
	$V = 16$ (Poisson)	91	136	45	92	131	39

Nonvaried Parameter Values:

Case 1: $h = 1$　$\pi = 9$　$K = 32$　$c = 0$　$\lambda = 0$　Poisson　$M = 9$　$V = 9$

Case 2: $h = 1$　$\pi = 99$　$K = 64$　$c = 0$　$\lambda = 4$　Negative Binomial　$M = 16$　$V = 48$

FIGURE II.8. Approximately Optimal (s, S) Policies.

Now suppose $M = V = 36$. Then

(28) $$EOQ = 48 \quad R_N = .889 \quad u_s = -.75.$$

Since $36 > .8888(32/1)$, calculate

(29) $$R = .9 \quad v_s = 1.3,$$

so that

(30) $$w_s = \text{minimum } (-.75, 1.3) = -.75.$$

Then

(31) $$s = 36 - .75(6) \approx 33$$
$$S = 36 + \text{minimum } [-.75(6) + 48, 1.3(6)] \approx 44,$$

which is the exactly optimal policy if the demand distribution is Poisson.

▶If there are a finite number of possible values for j, then the several techniques of successive approximation as well as the linear programming approach in Chap. 18 can be used to solve the functional equations (i) and (iii) in the advanced material at the beginning of this section. Since Secs. 18.3 through 18.5 analyze an inventory model by these means, no further illustrations are given here. Such solution methods are attractive when the purchase cost function, $c(y - j)$, and the expected holding and penalty cost function, $L(y)$, do *not* satisfy the assumptions of the model in Sec. II.4. When the theorem that the form of an optimal policy is (s, S) applies, you can reformulate the optimization model in such a way as to exploit the special structure when using successive approximations and linear programming techniques. Another optimizing technique is outlined below.   ◀

*II.7 MARKOV CHAIN ANALYSIS

Chapter 18 introduced Markov chains as a means of analyzing probabilistic dynamic structures. Here you will see how that approach can be applied to characterize the behavior of an inventory system operating under a stationary (s, S) type of policy. We can postpone making any assumptions about the cost structure until we discuss a method for finding optimal policies.

Recall that

y_t = level of inventory on hand plus on order in Period t
    after the ordering decision but before demand.

Given a specific (s, S) policy, not necessarily optimal, the probability distribution of demand induces a probability distribution on y_t. In particular, the transition law is

(1)
$$y_{t+1} = \begin{cases} y_t - q_t & \text{if } q_t \leq y_t - s \\ S & \text{otherwise,} \end{cases}$$

where $s \leq y_t \leq S$, according to the (s, S) policy.

Assuming the demand distribution is stationary, the implied matrix of one-period transition probabilities is shown in Fig. II.9. For expository convenience, the state $y = S$ has been designated as the last row and column. Observe two important features of this matrix. First, the probability entries do not depend on s and S separately, but only on their difference,

(2)
$$D \equiv S - s.$$

Second, the probability entries do not depend on λ.

Let

(3)
$$r(y) = \text{stationary probability of } y.$$

Then the values $r(y)$, for $y = s, s + 1, \ldots, S$, are uniquely characterized by the $D + 1$ linear equations,

(4) $$r(S - z) = \sum_{q=1}^{z} r(S - q)p(z - q) + r(S)p(z) \quad \text{for } 1 \leq z \leq D$$

y_t: \ y_{t+1}:	$S-1$	$S-2$	$\cdots$	s	S
$S-1$	$p(0)$	$p(1)$	$\cdots$	$p(D-1)$	$\sum_{q>D-1} p(q)$
$S-2$		$p(0)$	$\cdots$	$p(D-2)$	$\sum_{q>D-2} p(q)$
$\vdots$			$\ddots$	$\vdots$	$\vdots$
s				$p(0)$	$\sum_{q>0} p(q)$
S	$p(1)$	$p(2)$	$\cdots$	$p(D)$	$p(0) + \sum_{q>D} p(q)$

FIGURE II.9. Markov Transition Matrix for (s, S) Policy with $D \equiv S - s$.

$$(5) \qquad \sum_{z=0}^{D} r(S-1) = 1.$$

Give a verbal interpretation to the equations in (4). [The stationary equation for $r(S)$ has been omitted, since it is linearly dependent on the set of equations (4).]

The system (4) and (5) is easily solved, as you would guess after noticing the triangular structure in the first $(S-1)$ rows and columns of Fig. II.9. The approach is first to calculate recursively the quantities

$$(6) \qquad m(0) = \frac{p(0)}{1 - p(0)}$$

$$m(z) = \frac{p(z) + \sum_{q=0}^{z-1} p(z-q)m(q)}{1 - p(0)} \quad \text{for } z = 1, 2, \ldots, D,$$

and for any z let

$$(7) \qquad M(z) \equiv m(0) + m(1) + \cdots + m(z).$$

Then

$$(8) \qquad r(S-z) = \frac{m(z)}{1 + M(D)} \quad \text{for } 1 \le z \le D$$

$$r(S) = \frac{1 + m(0)}{1 + M(D)} \quad \text{for } z = 0.$$

As a check, substitute the quantities in (8) into the equations (4) for $z = 1, 2,$ and 3.

It can be shown that

$$(9) \qquad \begin{array}{l} \text{average number of periods} \\ \text{between successive} \\ \text{replenishments} \end{array} = 1 + M(D) \qquad \begin{array}{l} \text{probability of a} \\ \text{replenishment} \\ \text{occurring at any period} \end{array} = \frac{1}{1 + M(D)}.$$

To see how the algorithm works, consider the example

(10) $$p(q) = \frac{1}{3} \quad \text{for } q = 0, 1, 2.$$

Then, for $z = 0, 1, 2,$ and 3,

$$m(0) = \frac{\frac{1}{3}}{1 - \frac{1}{3}} = \frac{1}{2} \qquad m(1) = \frac{\frac{1}{3} + \frac{1}{3}(\frac{1}{2})}{1 - \frac{1}{3}} = \frac{3}{4}$$

(11) $$m(2) = \frac{\frac{1}{3} + \frac{1}{3}(\frac{1}{2}) + \frac{1}{3}(\frac{4}{3})}{1 - \frac{1}{3}} = \frac{9}{8}$$

$$m(3) = \frac{0 + 0(\frac{1}{2}) + \frac{1}{3}(\frac{3}{4}) + \frac{1}{3}(\frac{9}{8})}{1 - \frac{1}{3}} = \frac{15}{16}.$$

Suppose $D = 2$, so that

(12) $$M(2) = \frac{1}{2} + \frac{3}{4} + \frac{9}{8} = \frac{19}{8} \qquad 1 + M(2) = \frac{27}{8}.$$

Then

(13) $$r(S-1) = \frac{\frac{3}{4}}{\frac{27}{8}} = \frac{2}{9} \qquad r(S-2) = \frac{\frac{9}{8}}{\frac{27}{8}} = \frac{3}{9} \qquad r(S) = \frac{\frac{3}{2}}{\frac{27}{8}} = \frac{4}{9}.$$

Consider, instead, $D = 3$ and verify that

(14)
$$1 + M(3) = \frac{69}{16}$$

$$r(S-1) = \frac{4}{23} \qquad r(S-2) = \frac{6}{23} \qquad r(S-3) = \frac{5}{23} \qquad r(S) = \frac{8}{23}.$$

▶ It is also possible to develop the recursion (6) and the stationary probabilities (8) by recourse to a *renewal* type of argument. This approach is insightful as it will provide you with meaningful interpretations of the quantities $m(z)$ and $M(z)$ in (6) and (7) as well as a deeper understanding of the probabilistic behavior of an (s, S) type inventory rule.

Suppose in the current period a replenishment order is placed so that $y = S$. Then the next replenishment will not occur until cumulative demand *exceeds* D. The expected number of periods for this event can be found as follows.

Let

(i) Q_t = cumulative demand for t consecutive periods,

that is, $Q_t = q_1 + q_2 + \cdots + q_t$, and denote

(ii) $M(z)$ = expected number of periods that cumulative demand remains less than or equal to z.

To compute $M(z)$, define the **indicator function**

$$I_t(z) = \begin{cases} 1 & \text{if } Q_t \leq z \\ 0 & \text{otherwise,} \end{cases}$$

so that

(iii) $$M(z) = E\left[\sum_{t=1}^{\infty} I_t(z)\right] = \sum_{t=1}^{\infty} E[I_t(z)] = \sum_{t=1}^{\infty} P^t(z),$$

where $P^t(z)$ is the cumulative distribution function of the t-fold convolution of $p(q)$.

Let

$m(z) =$ expected number of periods that cumulative demand equals z,

and, consequently,

(iv) $M(z) = m(0) + m(1) + \cdots + m(z) = M(z - 1) + m(z).$

Then, from (iv),

(v) $m(z) = \sum_{t=1}^{\infty} P^t(z) - \sum_{t=1}^{\infty} P^t(z - 1) = \sum_{t=1}^{\infty} p^t(z),$

and $m(z)$ satisfies the so-called **renewal equation**

(vi) $m(z) = p(z) + \sum_{q=0}^{z} p(z - q)m(q),$

because

(vii)
$$
\begin{aligned}
m(z) &= \sum_{t=1}^{\infty} p^t(z) = p(z) + \sum_{t=2}^{\infty} p^t(z) \\
&= p(z) + \sum_{t=2}^{\infty} \sum_{q=0}^{z} p(z - q)p^{t-1}(q) \\
&= p(z) + \sum_{q=0}^{z} p(z - q) \sum_{t=1}^{\infty} p^t(q) = p(z) + \sum_{q=0}^{z} p(z - q)m(q).
\end{aligned}
$$

As you can verify, starting with $z = 0$, the renewal equation (vi) can be solved recursively according to the formulas in (6).

Since the next replenishment occurs in the period just after cumulative demand *exceeds D,*

(viii) $\begin{array}{l}\text{expected number of periods between} \\ \text{successive replenishments}\end{array} = 1 + M(D).$

Therefore the *fraction* of time that the system remains in the states $S - 1, S - 2, \ldots,$ $S - z$ during this interval is simply

(ix) $\sum_{q=0}^{z} r(S - q) = \dfrac{M(z)}{1 + M(D)}$ for $1 \le z \le D,$

so that

(x) $r(S - z) = \dfrac{m(z)}{1 + M(D)}$ for $1 \le z \le D.$

Since

(xi) $r(S) + \sum_{z=1}^{D} r(S - z) = 1,$

it follows that

(xii) $r(S) = \dfrac{1 + m(0)}{1 + M(D)}.$ ◄

Policy operating characteristics. Given the stationary distribution $r(y)$, the probability distributions of other system characteristics are easily computed. For example, define

$v(j) =$ stationary probability that the level of inventory on hand plus on order at the start of Period t *prior* to the ordering decision equals j.

Then

(15) $\qquad v(S - z) = \begin{cases} \dfrac{m(z)}{1 + M(D)} & \text{for } 0 \le z \le D \\[2ex] \dfrac{p(z) + \sum\limits_{q=0}^{D} p(z - q)m(q)}{1 + M(D)} & \text{for } z > D. \end{cases}$

As another example, define

$w(i) =$ long-run fraction of periods that the level of inventory on hand at the start of the period equals i.

Then

(16) $\quad w(i) = \dfrac{p^{\lambda+1}(S - i) + \sum\limits_{z=0}^{D} p^{\lambda+1}(S - i - z)m(z)}{1 + M(D)} \quad$ for $i = S, S - 1, S - 2, \dots.$

Note that $w(i)$ *does* depend on λ.

Because all demands are eventually filled,

(17) $\quad \begin{array}{l}\text{expected amount}\\ \text{ordered in any}\\ \text{period}\end{array} = E[q] \quad \begin{array}{l}\text{expected purchase}\\ \text{quantity } given \text{ a}\\ \text{replenishment occurs}\end{array} = E[q] \cdot [1 + M(D)].$

*Optimization. Given the cost assumptions of the model in Sec. II.6, expressed in (1) and (2), the objective function is simply

(18) $\qquad \dfrac{K}{1 + M(D)} + \sum\limits_{z=0}^{D} L(S - z)r(S - z),$

which represents the expected cost per period. The average purchase cost per period is a constant $cE[q]$, and therefore has been omitted from (18).

For the sake of completeness, we outline an algorithm for optimizing (18) by a search on D and S. A computationally attractive alternative is to solve an optimization model like those treated in Chap. 18, where the formulation exploits the (s, S) form of an optimal policy. Either successive approximations or linear programming can be applied as a solution technique to the appropriate formulation. To obtain an optimal (s, S) policy, you must minimize (18) with respect to D and S. The general algorithm is:

Step 1. Calculate lower and upper bounds on both s and S, and thereby determine lower and upper bounds for an optimal D.

Step 2. For each value of D between the upper and lower bounds found in *Step 1*, compute the stationary distribution $r(v)$, and find a corresponding optimal S by minimizing $\sum_{z=0}^{D} L(S - z)r(S - z)$.

Step 3. For each of the pairs of D and S obtained in *Step 2*, calculate the associated value of (18) and select a pair that gives the minimum for (18).

Further detail on the algorithm is given in the advanced material below. But we point out here that if $L(y)$ has the simple linear form (4) in Sec. II.6, then, in *Step 2*, an optimal S will be the smallest value such that

$$(19) \qquad \sum_{i=0}^{S} w(i) \geq \frac{\pi}{\pi + h},$$

where $w(i)$ is given in (16). Thus the system incurs no backlog for at least $\pi/(\pi + h)$ of the periods, or equivalently, incurs a backlog for no more than $h/(\pi + h)$ of the periods.

▶ The reason that all the possible values for D need to be tested in *Steps 2* and *3* is that as D gets progressively larger, the associated values of the objective function may exhibit local but not global minima.

The formulas developed above are easily generalized to encompass the discounted-stationary-cost case where $\alpha < 1$. Specifically, the only changes required are to compute

(i)
$$m(0) = \frac{\alpha p(0)}{1 - \alpha p(0)} \qquad\qquad \text{for } z = 0$$

$$m(z) = \frac{\alpha\left[p(z) + \sum_{q=0}^{z-1} p(z - q)m(q) \right]}{1 - \alpha p(0)} \qquad \text{for } 1 \leq z \leq D,$$

instead of (6), and

(ii)
$$\frac{K}{1 + M(D)} + \sum_{z=0}^{D} G(S - z)r(S - z),$$

where

(iii)
$$G(y) \equiv (1 - \alpha)cy + L(y),$$

instead of (18). Note that when $\alpha = 1$, (i) and (6) are identical, as are (ii) and (18). The analogue of (19) is

(iv)
$$\sum_{i=0}^{S} w(i) \geq \frac{\pi - (1 - \alpha)c}{p + h},$$

where $w(i)$ are computed in (16) using the values from (i).

Let (s, S) and $(\bar{s}, \bar{S})$ be the lower and upper bounds in *Step 1*, so that a lower bound for D is $(S - \bar{s})$ and an upper bound is $(\bar{S} - s)$. The bounds are determined by the following:

(v) S is the smallest integer that minimizes $G(y)$

(vi) $\bar{S}$ is the smallest integer not less than S for which
$$G(\bar{S} + 1) \geq G(S) + \alpha K$$

(vii) s is the smallest integer for which $G(s) \leq G(S) + K$

(viii) $\bar{s}$ is the smallest integer for which $G(\bar{s}) \leq G(S) + (1 - \alpha)K$.

Since $\sum_{z=0}^{D} L(S - z)r(S - z)$ is a convex function of S, the minimization operation in *Step 2* can be performed rapidly. A local minimum for this sum is also a global minimum, so that *given D*, you can let S be the smallest integer for which

(ix) $$\sum_{z=0}^{D} L(S + 1 - z)r(S + 1 - z) \geq \sum_{z=0}^{D} L(S - z)r(S - z).$$

When $\alpha < 1$, in certain cases you must record in *Step 2* any additional values for S that minimize the summation and then include these values in *Step 3*. This additional work ensures that you obtain an (s, S) policy that is optimal for *any* initial level of inventory on hand plus on order.   ◀

REVIEW EXERCISES

1 Consider an inventory model like that described in Sec. II.2. Assume $\lambda = 2$, the level of inventory at the start of Period 1 equals 10, and no replenishment orders are outstanding. Suppose the demands for the next 10 periods are

$$q_1 = 7 \quad q_2 = 7 \quad q_3 = 5 \quad q_4 = 8 \quad q_5 = 2$$
$$q_6 = 6 \quad q_7 = 3 \quad q_8 = 1 \quad q_9 = 9 \quad q_{10} = 7.$$

In each part below, find the values for $i_t, j_t, x_t, k_t,$ and y_t, for $t = 1, 2, \ldots , 10$, using the policy $(s, S) \equiv (9, 17)$.

(a) Assume the backlog case.

(b) Assume the lost demand case.

(c) Answer parts (a) and (b) for $\lambda = 1$ and $\lambda = 3$.

2 (a) Explain in detail the justification for (2) in Sec. II.2.

(b) Explain why $p_{t,t+\lambda-1}(Q)$ also represents the probability that $k_{t+\lambda}$ has the value $(y_t - Q)$.

(c) Explain in detail the justification for (16) in Sec. II.2.

*3 (a) Derive the convolution of Poisson distributions as given by (6) in Sec. II.2. (*Hint:* You may find it helpful to use an inductive proof.)

(b) Derive the convolution of negative binomial distributions as given by (10).

4 In each part below, use (4) and (8) in Sec. II.2 to find the indicated convolutions.

(a) Assume $p_1(q) = \frac{1}{3}$, for $q = 0, 1, 2$; $p_2(q) = \frac{1}{4}$, for $q = 0, 1, 2, 3$; $p_3(q) = \frac{1}{2}$, for $q = 2, 4$. Calculate $p_{1,2}(Q), p_{1,3}(Q),$ and $p_{2,3}(Q)$.

(b) Assume $p_t(0) = \frac{1}{2}, p_t(1) = \frac{1}{3}, p_t(2) = \frac{1}{6}$, for every t. Calculate $p^\lambda(Q)$ for $\lambda = 2, 3, 4$.

5 (a) Describe, verbally, the calculation in (4) of Sec. II.3.

(b) Explain how (7) follows from (6) when $H_t(k, q)$ has the form in (3).

(c) Rewrite (7) for the case that all the $p_t(q)$ are identical.

(d) Explain how j_{t+1} depends on y_t, given the backlog assumption.

(e) Explain why the term $\alpha^{\lambda+t-1}$ multiplies both $c_t(y_t - j_t)$ and $L_t(y_t)$ in (8). (*Hint:* review the definitions and economic assumptions.) Also explain why the text states that (8) ignores the holding and penalty costs in Periods $1, 2, \ldots , \lambda - 1$.

(f) Interpret $f_t(j)$ in (9), verbally, and state why the recursion is an appropriate representation of the optimization problem. Explain why it is legitimate to let j (the level of inventory on hand plus on order at the start of the period prior to the ordering decision) be the state variable.

*6 Apply (9) in Sec. II.3 to the data in (10) and check the results in Fig. II.2, for

(a) $K = 4.5$ and $\pi = 12$.
(b) $K = 1$ and $\pi = 5$.

*7 (a) Consider the model that maximizes profit, as described in the special material at the end of Sec. II.3. Justify (i) as the appropriate modification.

(b) Consider the model in which unfilled demand is lost, as described in the special material at the end of Sec. II.3. Justify (ii) and (iii) as the appropriate recursions for $\lambda = 0$ and $\lambda > 1$, respectively. Write the appropriate recursion for $\lambda = 1$, and compare it to (ii).

8 (a) Explain why (4) in Sec. II.4 yields an optimal S_t.

(b) Justify the expression for $f_t(j)$ in (5), given that the form of an optimal policy is (s, S).

(c) Explain why (6) and (7) determine an optimal s_t.

9 Consider the example (13) and (14) in Sec. II.4.

(a) Verify the calculations in (15), (18), (19), (21), and (23). What assumption is being made in (11) and (12) about unfilled demand at the end of the horizon?

(b) Perform the algorithm to find an optimal policy and $F_n(j)$ for $n = 3$, using the data for $n = 2$ in Fig. II.3. (Check your results with those in Fig. II.3.)

(c) Answer part (b) for $n = 7$, using the data for $n = 6$.

(d) Assume that the holding cost $h = 4$, instead of $h = 2$. Apply the algorithm for $n = 1, 2, 3, 4$, and check that your answer agrees with the policies given in (26).

10 Consider the example (13) and (25) in Sec. II.4. Verify the policy shown in Fig. II.4, for

(a) $\lambda = 0$, $\alpha = 1$, and $n = 1, 2, 3$.
(b) $\lambda = 1$, $\alpha = 1$, and $n = 2, 3, 4$.
(c) Give a plausible explanation of why S_n oscillates the way it does in Fig. II.4 for the case $\lambda = 0$ and $\alpha = 1$.

*11 (a) Give an economic interpretation of the assumption (2) in Sec. II.5 relating to the cost of excess inventory or unfilled demand at the end of the horizon.

*(b) Derive the formula for $\bar{y}_t$ given by (7) when the holding and penalty cost functions are linear, according to (6).

(c) Consider the formula for $\bar{y}_t$ given by (7). Describe how the value of $\bar{y}_t$ changes as $\pi_{t+\lambda}$ increases. As $h_{t+\lambda}$ increases. Explain how the purchase costs c_t and c_{t+1} affect the value of $\bar{y}_t$.

(d) Consider the formula for $\bar{y}$ given by (8). What effect does the purchase cost c have on $\bar{y}$ when $\alpha = 1$? Is the resultant policy "reasonable" for the last period in a finite horizon problem? Explain and indicate how the assumption in (2) gives rise to this result.

(e) Explain how you think $\bar{y}$ given by (8) is likely to vary when the delivery lag λ increases. [Suggestion: assume that $p(Q)$ can be well-enough approximated by a Normal distribution with mean 10 and variance 4. Suppose that the fraction on the right of (8) is .9. Use the tabled values in Fig. 19.6 to find $\bar{y}$ for $\lambda = 0, 1, 2$.]

(f) Suppose the penalty costs π_{t+1} in (7) are rising over time relative to $h_{t+\lambda}$ Show that all $\bar{y}_t \leq \bar{y}_{t+1}$, and verbally explain why. State how much you order in each period, assuming that initial inventory on hand plus on order at the start of the horizon is 0.

(g) Verify that when $\lambda = 0$ and $\alpha = 0$, the value of $\bar{y}_1$ is the same as that obtained in the one-period (static) model of Sec. 19.4. Be sure you compare the formulas for the linear holding and penalty cost case.

*12 Consider the lost-sales case model (where $\lambda = 0$) in the special material at the end of Sec. II.5. Examine the formula determining $\bar{y}_t$ in (i) and (7) and state whether $\bar{y}_t$ is larger in one case than in the other.

*13 Consider the proof of the single-critical-number *algorithm* in the special material at the end of Sec. II.5. Justify each step in the proof in detail.

14 In each part below, apply the Normal approximation algorithm described in Sec. II.6 to find a nearly optimal (s, S) inventory policy.

(a) Case 2 in Fig. II.8 (show the detailed calculations).
(b) The case $E[q] = 64$ and $\pi = 4$ in Fig. II.5. Do the same for $\pi = 99$.
(c) The case $E[q] = 21$ in Fig. II.6. Do the same for $E[q] = 23$. For $E[q] = 59$. For $E[q] = 64$.
(d) Verify that the test $M < .8888K/h$ in *Step 3* establishes whether $EOQ/M > 1.5$ periods.

*15 Consider the Markov analysis of an (s, S) policy, as given in Sec. II.7.

(a) Justify the validity of the entries in Fig. II.9. Explain why the number of rows and columns and an entry in the ith row and jth column are the same for the policies $(3, 8)$ and $(9, 14)$.
(b) Justify the statement that the values of the stationary probabilities $r(y)$ are determined by (4) and (5). Interpret the equations in (4) verbally. Write the equation for $r(S)$ and show that it is linearly dependent on the set of equations (4).
(c) Substitute the quantities in (8) into the equations (4) for $z = 1, 2,$ and 3, and check that the formulas for $r(S - z)$ do, in fact, satisfy the stationary equations.
(d) Consider the example (10). Verify the results in (14) for $D = 3$. Find the stationary probabilities for $D = 4$.
(e) Find the stationary probabilities $r(y)$, for $y = s, s + 1, \ldots, S$, for the policy $(2, 6)$, where $p(q) = \frac{1}{4}$, for $q = 0, 1, 2, 3$.
(f) Justify the validity of the formula for $v(i)$ given by (15).
(g) Justify the validity of the formula for $w(i)$ given by (16).
(h) Justify the validity of the expected cost formula given by (18).

16 Explain your understanding of the following terms:

immediate delivery	convolution
delivery lag	*inductive proof
continuous review model	*K-convexity
discrete (periodic) review model	optimal single critical number
backlog case	*indicator function
lost demand case	*renewal equation.

FORMULATION AND COMPUTATIONAL EXERCISES

17 Consider the formulas for the expected holding and penalty cost function $L_t(v)$ in (7) in Sec. II.3. Assume that the economic functions and probability distributions are stationary.

   (a) Rewrite (7) to exhibit the simplifications resulting from assuming stationarity.

   (b) Let $L(y|\lambda)$ denote your answer in part (a), where the symbol λ is introduced in the notation to stress the dependence on the delivery lag. Show that you can calculate $L(y|\lambda)$ recursively as follows:

$$L(y|\lambda) = \sum_{q=0}^{\infty} L(y - q|\lambda - 1)p(q) \quad \text{for } \lambda \geq 1.$$

   Also, interpret the recursion verbally.

18 Suppose the inventory holding and shortage penalty cost function $H_t(k, q)$, as defined by (2) in Sec. II.3, is calculated as h times the average level of inventory on hand during Period t weighted by the fraction of the period that inventory is on hand, plus π times the average level of shortage during Period t weighted by the fraction of the period that inventory is "negative." For simplicity, assume that the fraction of the period that inventory is on hand is the smaller of 1 and the ratio of

$$\frac{\text{inventory on hand at the start of period}}{\text{total demand}}.$$

If inventory on hand at the start of the period is "negative," assume the ratio equals 0. Write the appropriate formula for $H_t(k, q)$.

19 Consider the inventory model characterized by the dynamic programming recursion (9) in Sec. II.3. Assume the horizon $T = 2$; the demand distribution in each period is $p(2) = .2$ and $p(3) = .8$; the ordering cost is $K_t + x$ for $x > 0$; the delivery lag $\lambda = 0$; the inventory holding and shortage penalty cost is linear with $h = 6.7$ and $\pi = 26$; and $\alpha = .9$. (Assume there is no salvage value for inventory at the end of Period 2 and unfilled demand at that time remains unfilled forever.) Suppose $K_1 = 24$ and $K_2 = 5$, so that the proposition in Sec. II.4 on the optimality of an (s, S) policy does not apply. (Why?) Use (9) to calculate an optimal policy.

*20 Consider the data in Fig. II.4, and assume $\alpha = .8$. In each part below, use (ii) and the special material at the end of Sec. II.3 to find an optimal policy for $n = 1, 2, 3$.

   (a) Assume $\lambda = 0$.
   (b) Assume $\lambda = 1$.

21 *Uncertain Horizon.* Consider the inventory model yielding the recursion (9) in Sec. II.3. Suppose the horizon length for the inventory system is uncertain, because a much better substitute product may possibly be developed and marketed. Specifically, let β_t be the conditional probability that the item *will* be needed to satisfy demand in Period $t + \lambda + 1$, given that it *is* needed to meet demand in Period $t + \lambda$. Show the appropriate modification of (9). Explain verbally of how to implement an optimal policy found from this recursion.

22 *Perishable Commodity.* Consider the following modification of the inventory model in Sec. II.3. Assume that any item delivered in Period t perishes (cannot be used to meet demand) beyond Period t + 2. Also assume that the delivery lag $\lambda = 0$. Derive an appropriate dynamic programming recursion. Be sure to define all the symbols you employ.

*23 Consider a so-called (t, T) inventory policy, which is defined as: order the quantity T if the level of inventory on hand is smaller than t, and do not order otherwise. Assume delivery lag $\lambda = 0$. Suppose the probability distribution of demand is

$$p(0) = .2 \quad p(1) = .4 \quad p(2) = .3 \quad p(3) = .1,$$

and that unfilled demand is completely lost.

(a) Find the stationary probabilities for the states of the system when the policy is $(1, 2)$. Is $(2, 1)$.

(b) Assume that the ordering cost is $3 + 2T$; the holding cost, assessed on inventory at the end of the period, is 1 per unit; and the penalty cost for each unit of unfilled demand is 4. Based on your answers in part (a) is $(1, 2)$ or $(2, 1)$ the better policy?

*24 (k, Q) *Policy* (Exercise 40 in Chap. 19). Suppose you utilize a (k, Q) policy over an unbounded horizon, and assume unfilled demand is completely backlogged.

(a) Consider $(k, Q) \equiv (8, 5)$. Construct a Markov transition matrix for this policy, analogous to Fig. II.9. Label the rows and columns with their exact values.

(b) Determine the stationary probabilities $r(y)$ for part (a). (*Hint:* check the value of the column sums.)

*25 In each part below, find an optimal (s, S) policy, using the algorithm in Sec. II.7 and the calculations suggested in the special material at the end of that section. Consider the data in Fig. II.4, where

(a) $\lambda = 0$ and $\alpha = 1$.

(b) $\lambda = 0$ and $\alpha = .8$.

(c) $\lambda = 1$ and $\alpha = 1$.

*26 Use the algorithmic techniques at the end of Sec. II.7 to find an optimal (s, S) policy for the data below.

(a) Let $p(q) = \frac{1}{10}$, for $q = 1, 2, \ldots, 10$; $\alpha = 1$; $\lambda = 0$; $h = 5$; $\pi = 10$; $c = .1$; and $K = 5$.

(b) Rework part (a), letting $K = 10$.

(c) Rework part (a), letting $\alpha = .5$.

(d) Rework part (a), letting $p(q) = \frac{1}{5}$, for $q = 1, 2, \ldots, 5$, and $\lambda = 1$.

MIND-EXPANDING EXERCISES

27 *Uncertain Delivery Lag.* Consider the inventory model resulting in the dynamic programming recursion (9) in Sec. II.3. In that model, the delivery lag λ is assumed known. Suppose, instead, that λ is a random variable. Assume that there is never a "crossover"

in deliveries, that is, an order placed in Period t is never delivered *before* an order placed in an earlier period (it may be delivered in the *same* period). Also assume r_l, for $l = 0, 1, \ldots . N$, is the probability that *all* the orders that were placed l or more periods ago *and* have not yet been delivered arrive in Period t; every order arrives within N periods. (Note that r_l is assumed to be independent of the order *sizes* and the *number* of orders not yet delivered.) Finally, assume that the ordering cost $c_t(x)$ is incurred in Period t, when the order is placed. Show the appropriate modification of (9). [*Hint:* let the state of the system be $(i, x_1, \ldots, x_N)$, where i is the level of inventory on hand at the start of Period t, and x_l is the amount ordered l periods ago and not yet delivered. Note that if $x_l = 0$, then so do $x_{l+1}, \ldots, x_N$. Also define $L_t(k)$ as the expected holding and penalty cost in Period t, given that inventory on hand after delivery and before demand equals k.]

28 A military supply depot faces the following inventory problem. The demand for the item in Period t is $p_t(q)$, where $q = 0, 1, 2, \ldots$. The depot may purchase x new items from a vendor, and they are delivered immediately so that the delivery lag $\lambda = 0$. At the start of each period, the depot has in stock i "serviceable" items and k "reparable" items, where the former are items in good working order and the latter are items that can, at a cost, be put into good working order. For simplicity, assume that the repair action is also immediate. The depot's decision involves whether to repair items, to purchase new items from the vendor, or to scrap some of the available serviceables and reparables. Assume that the cost parameters are such that it is always optimal to scrap reparables before scrapping serviceables, to scrap reparables instead of storing them, and to repair before purchasing new items. The planning horizon is T periods.

Let y be the number of serviceable items *after* the decision to repair, purchase, or scrap. If demand q exceeds y, then the depot places an emergency order and pays a penalty price for doing so. Let $L_t(y)$ represent the expected holding and penalty cost in Period t, given that the depot's decision in Period t leads to the level y. Also assume that the demand q in Period t yields q reparables at the beginning of Period t + 1. Let the purchase cost function be $c_t(x)$, the repair cost be b_t per unit, and the scrap values be v_s and v_r per serviceable and reparable item, respectively. Assume the discount factor $\alpha = 1$. Formulate a dynamic programming recursion for finding an optimal policy. [*Hint:* let the state be (i, k) and distinguish the possibilities $y > i + k$, $i < y \leq i + k$, and $y \leq i$, as well as $q \leq y$ and $q > y$.]

*29 Assume the inventory policy is $(s, S) \equiv (3, 6)$ and $\lambda = 3$. Suppose all unfilled demand is lost. Explain why there is never more than one replenishment order outstanding. Construct a Markov transition matrix analogous to Fig. II.9. (*Suggestion:* define the state of the system by three numbers, namely, the amount of inventory on hand at the start of the period, the size of any order outstanding, and the number of periods between the present date and an outstanding order's due date.)

*30 Determine the probability distributions $r(y)$ and $v(j)$, as described in Sec. II.7, for a geometric demand distribution $p(q) = p(1 - p)^q$, where $q = 0, 1, \ldots$, and $0 < p < 1$.

*31 *Separable Markovian Decision Formulation.* Consider an inventory model satisfying the Optimality of a Stationary (s, S) Policy proposition in Sec. II.6. Assume the discount factor satisfies $0 \leq \alpha < 1$. The appropriate dynamic programming recursion is given by (i) in the special material. Suppose you have lower and upper bounds on optimal s and S, namely $\underline{s}$, $\bar{s}$, $\underline{S}$, $\bar{S}$; see (v) through (viii) in the special material ending Sec. II.7 for computational techniques of computing these bounds. Also suppose that there is only one optimal policy.

(a) Show how to adapt the *idea* in exercise 51, part (b), of Chap. 18 to characterize the extremal equations. (*Hint:* let the special state correspond to the $j = s - 1$, so that a replenishment order must be placed, and the system is moved to one of the states $j = \underline{S}, \ldots, \bar{S}$, at an appropriate cost. Notice that no replenishment order is placed for $j = \bar{s}, \ldots, \bar{S}$. The decisions at $j = \underline{s}, \ldots, \underline{s} - 1$, are either not to order, or to order up to the level that was used at state $j = s - 1$.)

(b) Write the primal linear programming model, analogous to that in (1) and (2) of Sec. 18.5, for the extremal equations in part (a). Determine the number of constraints and variables.

(c) Determine whether the simplifications in part (d) of exercise 51 in Chap. 18 can be applied here. If so, state the resultant number of equations and variables in the linear programming model of part (b) above.

CONTENTS

Advanced Techniques for Waiting Line Models †

III.1 PRELIMINARIES

This appendix provides additional results for rather simple queuing models, and, more importantly, introduces you to several useful mathematical techniques for treating such models. We begin by presenting two devices that are frequently employed in waiting line analysis. The first one is a generating function, and the second is a Laplace-Stieltjes transform.

Consider a random variable taking on the values $j = 0, 1, 2, \ldots$, with the associated probabilities $P_0, P_1, P_2, \ldots$. Define the **generating function** for this probability distribution as

$$(1) \qquad P^*(s) \equiv P_0 + sP_1 + s^2P_2 + \cdots = \sum_{j=0}^{\infty} s^j P_j,$$

where the variable s in (1) satisfies $-1 \leq s \leq 1$, but has no particular interpretative significance. Observe that

$$(2) \qquad P^*(1) = 1 \quad P^*(0) = P_0$$

$$(3) \qquad \frac{dP^*}{ds} = \sum_{j=0}^{\infty} js^{j-1}P_j,$$

so that

$$(4) \qquad \frac{dP^*}{ds} = \sum_{j=0}^{\infty} jP_j = E[j] \quad \text{for } s = 1.$$

Verify that

$$(5) \qquad \frac{d^nP^*}{ds^n} = n!P_n \quad \text{for } s = 0.$$

†This appendix requires a knowledge of elementary differential and integral calculus.

Consequently, by knowing $P^*(s)$, you can compute the expectation of the random variable according to (4), as well as the individual terms of the distribution according to (5).

As you can check by elementary algebraic manipulation, if

(6) $P_j = (1 - \rho)\rho^j$ (geometric distribution; $0 < \rho < 1$)

then

(7) $P^*(s) = \dfrac{1 - \rho}{1 - s\rho};$

if

(8) $P_j = \dfrac{\lambda^j e^{-\lambda}}{j!}$ (Poisson distribution),

then

(9) $P^*(s) = e^{-\lambda + \lambda s};$

if

(10) $P_j = \binom{n}{j} p^j (1 - p)^{n-j}$ (binomial distribution; $0 < p < 1$)

then

(11) $P^*(s) = [(1 - p) + ps]^n;$

and if

(12) $P_j = \binom{j+m-1}{j} p^j (1 - p)^m$ (negative binomial distribution; $0 < p < 1$)

then

(13) $P^*(s) = \left(\dfrac{1 - p}{1 - ps}\right)^m.$

When $m = 1$, (12) is simply the geometric distribution with $p = \rho$. Check that when you take the nth derivative of $P^*(s)$ in (7), (9), (11), and (13) and let $s = 0$, you obtain $n! P_n$ as stated in (5).

Next consider a nonnegative random variable x and let

(14) $G(t) \equiv P[x \leq t]$

be its distribution function. Define the **Laplace-Stieltjes transform** of $G(t)$ as

(15) $G^*(s) \equiv \displaystyle\int_0^\infty e^{-st} \, dG(t),$

where s is a real number contained in a bounded interval around 0, say, $-S < s < S$; here again s has no particular interpretative significance. Sometimes this transform is called a **moment generating function**, since

(16) $(-1)^n \cdot \dfrac{d^n G^*}{ds^n} = E[t^n]$ for $s = 0.$

To illustrate (15), suppose

(17) $G(t) = \displaystyle\int_0^t \mu e^{-\mu w} \, dw$ (exponential distribution);

then

(18)
$$G^*(s) = \frac{\mu}{\mu + s}.$$

If x and y are independent random variables, the Laplace-Stieltjes transform for the distribution function of their sum is equal to the product of the transforms for each of the distribution functions. Consequently, if

(19)
$$G(t) = \int_0^t \frac{\mu(\mu w)^{M-1} e^{-\mu w}}{(M-1)!} \, dw \qquad \text{(gamma distribution)},$$

which is the distribution of a sum of M identically and independently exponentially distributed variables, then

(20)
$$G^*(s) = \left(\frac{\mu}{\mu + s}\right)^M.$$

Or if you replace μ by $M\mu$ in (19), and thereby use the form for an Erlang distribution,

(21)
$$G(t) = \int_0^t \frac{(\mu M)(\mu M w)^{M-1} e^{-\mu M w}}{(M-1)!} \, dw \qquad \text{(Erlang distribution)},$$

which has

(22)
$$E[t] = \frac{1}{\mu} \quad \text{and} \quad \text{Var}[t] = \frac{1}{M\mu^2},$$

then

(23)
$$G^*(s) = \left(\frac{\mu M}{\mu M + s}\right)^M = \left(1 + \frac{s}{\mu M}\right)^{-M}.$$

A constant service time distribution can be viewed as the limiting case of $M \to \infty$ in (21); then $G^*(s) = e^{-s/\mu}$.

The next two sections analyze a single-server queuing system in which either the interarrival or the service time distribution is not exponentially distributed. (The case of both distributions being general is treated in the final section of this appendix.) The generating function and Laplace-Stieltjes transform provide the principal tools for deriving many of the important stationary operating characteristics. To specify the formulas for the steady-state probabilities, the queuing system's behavior will be described by a Markov chain. Hence you may find it helpful to reread pp. 752 through 756, which give several illustrative examples of Markov chains and the calculation of stationary probabilities.

III.2 SINGLE-SERVER MODEL WITH POISSON
INPUT AND GENERAL SERVICE DISTRIBUTION

In Sec. 20.5 you studied a system composed of a single server with interarrivals exponentially distributed and service times generally distributed (designated as $M/G/1$); formulas (29) through (32) gave the values for several long-run averages. You should review that material, including the proof at the end of the section.

Recall that this proof considered only those instants in time when a service had just been completed and the associated customer had departed. These are termed **regeneration points**, because at such instants the only information needed to predict the system's future is the *number* of customers then present; the detailed history of the system prior to these instants is not required. Consequently, the probabilistic behavior of the system at the regeneration points can be described by means of a so-called **imbedded Markov chain**. The adjective "imbedded" refers to the fact that the system is examined *only* at the regeneration points. The corresponding steady-state probabilities refer to such instants. An important fact is that it can be proved that for the $M/G/1$ system, these probabilities at regeneration points also represent the proportion of all time over an unbounded horizon that the system is in each state.

Continuing with the notation introduced in the advanced material ending Sec. 20.5, let n be the number of persons in the system immediately after a departure, say, at Time T, and n' the number of persons in the system immediately after the *next* departure, say, at Time T'. Let j be the number of arrivals during the next interval of service. Then, as was established in Sec. 20.5,

(1)
$$n' = \begin{cases} j & \text{if } n = 0 \\ n - 1 + j & \text{if } n > 0. \end{cases}$$

If the length of the next interval of service is h,

(2)
$$P\,[\,j \text{ arrivals}\,|\,\text{interval } h\,] = \frac{(\lambda h)^j e^{-\lambda h}}{j!},$$

given that the arrival process is Poisson with rate λ. (Note how the memoryless property of the exponential distribution is being used.) Therefore the unconditional probability is

(3)
$$P\,[\,j \text{ arrivals}\,] = \int_0^\infty \frac{(\lambda h)^j e^{-\lambda h}}{j!}\, dG(h) \equiv k_j,$$

where $G(h)$ is the distribution function for service time. As shown below, for certain $G(h)$, such as a gamma distribution, the value of k_j is easily derived by mathematical analysis. In general however, you can always calculate k_j by using standard methods of numerical integration.

The states of the imbedded Markov chain are characterized by the number of customers in the system at a regeneration point. Hence, given n, the probability of n' in (1) is provided by the probability of j arrivals, according to (3), and the resultant Markov chain in matrix form is

n' customers at Time T':

$$
\begin{array}{c}
 \\
(4) \quad n \text{ customers at} \\
\text{Time T:}
\end{array}
\quad
\begin{array}{cc}
 & \begin{array}{cccc} 0 & 1 & 2 & 3 \quad \cdots \end{array} \\
\begin{array}{c} 0 \\ 1 \\ 2 \\ 3 \\ \cdot \\ \cdot \\ \cdot \end{array} &
\left[\begin{array}{ccccc}
k_0 & k_1 & k_2 & k_3 & \cdots \\
k_0 & k_1 & k_2 & k_3 & \cdots \\
0 & k_0 & k_1 & k_2 & \cdots \\
0 & 0 & k_0 & k_1 & \cdots \\
\cdot & \cdot & \cdot & \cdot \\
\cdot & \cdot & \cdot & \cdot \\
\cdot & \cdot & \cdot & \cdot
\end{array} \right]
\end{array}
\quad
\begin{array}{l}
\text{(T and T' are} \\
\text{regeneration} \\
\text{points).}
\end{array}
$$

Steady-state analysis. Let

$P_r =$ stationary probability of r customers in the system at a regeneration point.

To ensure the existence of a steady-state distribution, assume that

(5)　　　　　　　　　$\rho \equiv \lambda E\,[\text{service time}] < 1.$

Then, given (4), the P_r must satisfy the steady-state equations

$$P_0 = P_0 k_0 + P_1 k_0$$

$$P_1 = P_0 k_1 + P_1 k_1 + P_2 k_0$$

(6)

$$\cdot$$

$$\cdot$$

$$P_r = P_0 k_r + P_1 k_r + P_2 k_{r-1} + \cdots + P_{r+1} k_0 = P_0 k_r + \sum_{j=1}^{r+1} P_j k_{r+1-j}.$$

Rearranging terms in (6) yields the recursive formulas

$$P_1 = \frac{P_0(1 - k_0)}{k_0}$$

$$P_2 = \frac{P_1(1 - k_1) - P_0 k_1}{k_0}$$

(7)

$$\cdot$$

$$\cdot$$

$$\cdot$$

$$P_{r+1} = \frac{P_r(1 - k_1) - \sum_{j=1}^{r-1} P_j k_{r+1-j} - P_0 k_r}{k_0}.$$

Notice that to actually compute the P_r using (7), you need to have the value of P_0, the probability that the server is idle. It will be shown below that

(8)　　　　　　　$P_0 = 1 - \rho,$　　where ρ is given by (5).

To prove (8) as well as to characterize the stationary probability distribution P_r, we derive the generating function for P_r. Take the expression for P_r in (6) and multiply both sides by s^r, giving

(9)　　　　　　$s^r P^r = s^r P_0 k_r + \sum_{j=1}^{r+1} s^r P_j k_{r+1-j}.$

Define the generating function $K^*(s) \equiv \sum_{j=0}^{\infty} s^j k_j$. Then sum the terms in (9) for $r = 0, 1, 2, \ldots$, to yield

$$P^*(s) = P_0 K^*(s) + \sum_{r=0}^{\infty} \sum_{j=1}^{r+1} s^r P_j k_{r+1-j}$$

$$= P_0 K^*(s) + \sum_{j=1}^{\infty} \sum_{r=j-1}^{\infty} s^r P_j k_{r+1-j}$$

(10)

$$= P_0 K^*(s) + \sum_{j=1}^{\infty} s^{j-1} P_j \sum_{i=0}^{\infty} s^i k_i$$

$$= P_0 K^*(s) + \frac{[P^*(s) - P_0] K^*(s)}{s},$$

so that

(11) $\quad P^*(s) = \dfrac{P_0 K^*(s)(1-s)}{K^*(s) - s}$ $\qquad$ (generating function for the probability distribution of the number of customers in system).

Hence, $P^*(s)$ has been expressed in terms of the generating function for k_j.

The function $K^*(s)$ can, in turn, be expressed by means of the Laplace-Stieltjes transform of $G(t)$ as follows:

$$K^*(s) = \sum_{j=0}^{\infty} s^j k_j = \sum_{j=0}^{\infty} s^j \int_0^{\infty} \frac{(\lambda h)^j e^{-\lambda h}}{j!} dG(h)$$

(12)
$$= \int_0^{\infty} e^{-\lambda(1-s)h} \, dG(h)$$

$$= G^*[\lambda(1-s)].$$

Notice that given (12),

(13) $$\frac{dK^*(s)}{ds} = -\lambda \frac{dG^*(z)}{dz}\bigg|_{z=\lambda(1-s)},$$

and therefore at $s = 1$, (13) yields the result

(14) $\qquad E\begin{bmatrix} \text{number of arrivals} \\ \text{in a service interval} \end{bmatrix} \equiv E[j] = \lambda E\,[\text{service time}] \equiv \rho,$

since $\dfrac{dG^*(z)}{dz}\bigg|_{z=0} = -(1)E[t]$ according to (16) in the preceding section.

To derive P_0, we take the limit of $P^*(s)$ in (11) as $s \to 1$. This gives, on applying l'Hospital's rule,

$$1 = \lim_{s\to 1} P^*(s) = \lim_{s\to 1} \frac{P_0 K^*(s)(1-s)}{K^*(s) - s}$$

(15)
$$= \frac{P_0}{1 - \dfrac{dK^*(1)}{ds}}.$$

Using (14), you can simplify (15) to

(16) $$1 = \frac{P_0}{1 - \rho},$$

and consequently the probability that the server is idle is $(\rho_0 = 1 - \rho)$, in accordance with (5).

By a similar approach, you can derive the Laplace-Stieltjes transform for the time spent in the system and the time spent in line. Assume the queue discipline is first come, first served. Consider a regeneration point. Let $U(t)$ be the distribution function for the time the departing customer has spent in the system. Then the number of customers he leaves behind is the number who arrived during the time he remained in the system, that is, after he entered. Therefore an alternative formula to (6) for P_r is

$$(17) \qquad P_r = \int_0^\infty \frac{(\lambda h)^r e^{-\lambda h}}{r!} \, dU(h),$$

so that

$$(18) \qquad P^*(s) = \sum_{r=0}^\infty s^r \int_0^\infty \frac{(\lambda h)^r e^{-\lambda h}}{r!} \, dU(h) = U^*[\lambda(1-s)].$$

Letting $[v \equiv \lambda(1-s)]$ and using (5) and (12), check that you can rewrite (11) as

$$(19) \qquad U^*(v) = \frac{(1-\rho)vG^*(v)}{v - \lambda + \lambda G^*(v)} \qquad \text{(transform for the distribution of time a customer spends in system).}$$

[This is sometimes called the **Pollaczek-Khintchine equation**, and it leads to formulas (32) in Sec. 20.5.]

Observe that taking the derivative with respect to s on both sides of (18) and setting $s = 1$ yield

$$(20) \qquad E \text{ [number of customers in system]} = \lambda E \text{ [time in system]},$$

as was stated in (33) of Sec. 20.5.

The time a customer spends in the system is the sum of the time he spends in line and the time he spends in service. Letting $W(t)$ represent the distribution function of the time he spends waiting in line, you can write

$$(21) \qquad U^*(v) = W^*(v) \cdot G^*(v).$$

Therefore from (19) you have

$$(22) \qquad W^*(v) = \frac{(1-\rho)v}{v - \lambda + \lambda G^*(v)} \qquad \text{(transform for the distribution of time a customer spends in line).}$$

Examples. The computational usefulness of the generating function (11) and the Laplace-Stieltjes transforms (19) and (22) depends on whether they represent distributions that are easily calculated.

To illustrate, suppose the service time distribution is

$$(23) \qquad G(t) = \int_0^t \frac{\mu(\mu w)^{M-1} e^{-\mu w}}{(M-1)!} \, dw \qquad \text{(gamma distribution; mean service time = M/\mu)}$$

so that, according to (20) in the preceding section,

$$(24) \qquad G^*(v) = \left(\frac{\mu}{\mu+v}\right)^M.$$

Then, from (12),

$$(25) \qquad K^*(s) = G^*[\lambda(1-s)] = \left[\frac{\mu}{\mu + \lambda(1-s)}\right]^M.$$

Letting

$$(26) \qquad p = \frac{\lambda}{\mu+\lambda},$$

you can write (25) as

$$(27) \qquad K^*(s) = \left(\frac{1-p}{1-ps}\right)^M,$$

so that from (13) in Sec. III.1, you can conclude

(28) $k_j = \binom{j+M-1}{j} p^j (1-p)^M$ (negative binomial distribution)

with

(29) $E[j] = \dfrac{Mp}{1-p} = \dfrac{M\lambda}{\mu} = \rho$ $\operatorname{Var}[j] = M\left[\left(\dfrac{\lambda}{\mu}\right)^2 + \dfrac{\lambda}{\mu}\right].$

Then from (11), after some manipulation,

(30)
$$P^*(s) = \frac{\left(1 - \dfrac{M\lambda}{\mu}\right)(1-s)}{1 - s\left(\dfrac{1-ps}{1-p}\right)^M} .$$

When $M = 1$ in (23), giving the exponential distribution, then (30) reduces after simplification to

(31) $P^*(s) = \dfrac{1-\rho}{1-\rho s}$ where $\rho = \dfrac{\lambda}{\mu},$

so that

(32) $P_r = (1-\rho)\rho^r$ (geometric distribution),

in accordance with (12) of Sec. 20.5 Further, when $M = 1$, you have from (19) that

(33) $U^*(v) = \dfrac{(1-\rho)v\left(\dfrac{\mu}{\mu+v}\right)}{v - \lambda + \lambda\left(\dfrac{\mu}{\mu+v}\right)} = \dfrac{\mu(1-\rho)}{\mu(1-\rho)+v},$

which is the transform of an exponential distribution with mean $\mu(1-\rho)$. Consequently, the waiting time density is

(34) $\mu(1-\rho)e^{-\mu(1-\rho)t}$ for $t \ge 0,$

in agreement with (19) of Sec. 20.5.

▶ If you want to express the service time distribution as an Erlang distribution according to (21) in Sec. III.1, then replace μ by μM in (24), (25), (26), and (30).

   In the case of constant service time of $1/\mu$—which can be treated formally as the limiting case of an Erlang distribution with $M \to \infty$—you have

(i) $k_j = \dfrac{\rho^j e^{-\rho}}{j!}$ (Poisson distribution),

where $\rho \equiv \lambda/\mu$, so that

(ii) $K^*(s) = e^{-\rho(1-s)}.$

Then

(iii) $P^*(s) = \dfrac{(1-\rho)e^{-\rho(1-s)}(1-s)}{e^{-\rho(1-s)} - s}$ (generating function for the probability distribution of the number of customers in an $M/D/1$ system).

It can be shown that (iii) implies

(iv) $P_r = (1-\rho)\sum_{i=1}^{r}(-1)^{r-i}e^{\rho i}\left[\dfrac{(i\rho)^{r-i}}{(r-i)!} + \dfrac{(i\rho)^{r-i-1}}{(r-i-1)!}\right]$ for $r > 0$

       $P_0 = 1 - \rho.$

Further

(v) $G^*(s) = e^{-s/\mu}$ (transform for constant service time distribution),

so that, by (22),

(vi) $W^*(v) = \dfrac{(1-\rho)v}{v - \lambda + \lambda e^{-s/\mu}}$ (transform for the distribution of time a customer spends in line for $M/D/1$).

It can be shown that (vi) implies

(vii)
$$W(t) = (1 - \rho)e^{\lambda t} \sum_{i=0}^{[\mu t]} \frac{(i\rho - \lambda t)^i}{i!} e^{-i\rho},$$

where $[\mu t]$ represents the integral part of μt.

For the sake of completeness, we mention how to find the steady-state probabilities for the case of constant service time $1/\mu$ and S servers (designated as $M/D/S$). Consider the system at instants $t, t + (1/\mu), t + (2/\mu), \ldots$, where the value of t is arbitrary, say, $t = 0$. If there are $j \le S$ customers in the system at Time T, then all of these will have been served by Time T $+ (1/\mu)$. Consequently, the number of customers, i, in the system at Time T $+ (1/\mu)$ is simply the number of arrivals, given by the Poisson distribution with parameter ρ. If instead of the above there are $j > S$ customers in the system at Time T, then the number at Time T $+ (1/\mu)$ is $j - S$ plus the number of arrivals. These observations lead to the Markov chain matrix describing the system's behavior at two instants spaced $1/\mu$ apart:

number in system at Time T $+ (1/\mu)$:

		0	1	2	$\cdots$	S	$S+1$	$S+2$	$\cdots$
	0	k_0	k_1	k_2	$\cdots$	k_S	k_{S+1}	k_{S+2}	$\cdots$
	1	k_0	k_1	k_2	$\cdots$	k_S	k_{S+1}	k_{S+2}	$\cdots$
	2	k_0	k_1	k_2	$\cdots$	k_S	k_{S+1}	k_{S+2}	$\cdots$
	$\cdot$								
number in	$\cdot$								
system	$\cdot$								
at Time T:	S	k_0	k_1	k_2	$\cdots$	k_S	k_{S+1}	k_{S+2}	$\cdots$
	$S+1$	0	k_0	k_1	$\cdots$	k_{S-1}	k_S	k_{S+1}	$\cdots$
	$S+2$	0	0	k_0	$\cdots$	k_{S-2}	k_{S-1}	k_S	$\cdots$
	$\cdot$								$\cdots$
	$\cdot$								$\cdots$
	$\cdot$								$\cdots$
	$2S$	0	0	0	$\cdots$	k_0	k_1	k_2	$\cdots$
	$\cdot$								
	$\cdot$								
	$\cdot$								

(viii)

where, as in (i),

(ix)
$$k_j = \frac{\rho^j e^{-\rho}}{j!} \quad \text{with } \rho = \frac{\lambda}{\mu}.$$

Numerical techniques for finding stationary probabilities for a Markov transition matrix can be applied to obtain P_r.

Unfortunately, an analysis of the multiple-server model with a general service time distribution (designated as $M/G/S$) is too involved to be included in this text.   ◀

III.3 SINGLE-SERVER MODEL WITH GENERAL INPUT
AND EXPONENTIAL SERVICE DISTRIBUTION

The approach to analyzing this model (designated as $GI/M/1$) is again to examine the system only at regeneration points. But in contrast to the method used in the preceding section, a regeneration point is defined here to be the moment immediately after an arrival.

Specifically, let n be the number of customers in the system in front of the person arriving at Time T, and let n' be the number of customers in front of the person arriving at Time T'. Let j be the number of customers served during this interval, including the person arriving at Time T if his service is completed by Time T'. Verify that

$$(1) \qquad\qquad n' = n + 1 - j,$$

and note that $0 \le n' \le n + 1$. If the length of the interval between two successive arrivals is h,

$$(2) \qquad P\,[\,j\ \text{services}\,|\,\text{interval}\ h\,] = \frac{(\mu h)^j e^{-\mu h}}{j!} \qquad \text{for}\ j \le n,$$

given that the service distribution is exponential with rate μ. (Note how the memoryless property of the exponential distribution is being used.) Therefore the unconditional probability is

$$(3) \qquad P\,[\,j\ \text{services}\,] = \int_0^\infty \frac{(\mu h)^j e^{-\mu h}}{j!}\,dF(h) \equiv k_j \quad \text{for}\ j \le n,$$

where $F(h)$ is the distribution function for interarrival times.

To represent the system in terms of an imbedded Markov chain, let the states be characterized as the number of customers in front of a person when he arrives. Hence, given n, the probability of n' in (1) is indicated by the probability of j departures, according to (3), and the resultant Markov chain in matrix form is

n' customers in front of a person
arriving at Time T':

		0	1	2	3	4	$\cdots$
	0	$1 - \sum_0$	k_0	0	0	0	$\cdots$
n customers	1	$1 - \sum_1$	k_1	k_0	0	0	$\cdots$
in front of	2	$1 - \sum_2$	k_2	k_1	k_0	0	$\cdots$
a person	3	$1 - \sum_3$	k_3	k_2	k_1	k_0	$\cdots$
arriving							
at Time T:							

(4) (T and T' are regeneration points), where we have defined the symbol

$$(5) \qquad \Sigma_q \equiv \sum_{j=0}^{q} k_j.$$

Steady-state analysis. Let

$P_r =$ stationary probability of r customers in front of a person arriving at a regeneration point.

To ensure the existence of a steady-state distribution, assume that

$$(6) \qquad \frac{1}{\rho} \equiv E \,[\text{interarrival time}] \, \mu > 1.$$

Then, given (4), the P_r must satisfy the steady-state equations

$$(7) \qquad P_r = \sum_{i=0}^{\infty} P_{i+r-1} k_i \quad \text{for } r \geq 1$$

$$(8) \qquad P_0 = \sum_{i=0}^{\infty} P_i (1 - \Sigma_i).$$

It is easily shown that a solution to (7) is of the form

$$(9) \qquad P_r = cs^r,$$

where the values of $c > 0$ and s are determined so that both (7) and (8) are satisfied.

To obtain s, substitute (9) into (7) to give

$$(10) \qquad cs^r = \sum_{i=0}^{\infty} cs^{i+r-1} k_i,$$

so that

$$(11) \qquad 1 = \sum_{i=0}^{\infty} s^{i-1} k_i = s^{-1} \sum_{i=0}^{\infty} s^i k_i.$$

Thus s must satisfy

$$(12) \qquad s = K^*(s),$$

where $K^*(s)$ is the generating function for k_j. Now

$$(13) \qquad K^*(s) = \sum_{j=0}^{\infty} s^j \int_0^{\infty} \frac{(\mu h)^j e^{-\mu h}}{j!} \, dF(h) = F^*[\mu(1-s)],$$

and therefore (12) can be written as

$$(14) \qquad s = F^*[\mu(1-s)],$$

so that it is only necessary to calculate the Laplace-Stieltjes transform of the interarrival distribution $F(h)$. It can be shown that there always exists a unique solution s_0 to (14) for which $0 < s_0 < 1$.

To obtain c, you can use (8), or equivalently, employ the equation that the probabilities must sum to 1:

$$(15) \qquad 1 = \sum_{i=0}^{\infty} cs_0^i = \frac{c}{1 - s_0},$$

so that $c = 1 - s_0$. Therefore,

(16) $P_r = (1 - s_0)s_0^r$ for $r = 0, 1, 2, \ldots$

[geometric distribution; mean $= s_0/(1 - s_0)$].

Note that $P_0 = 1 - s_0$.

Given that a newly arriving person finds n customers in front of him, the time he must spend in the system, including his own service, is described by a gamma density with distribution function

(17) $$U(t \mid n) = \int_0^t \frac{\mu(\mu w)^n e^{-\mu w}}{n!} \, dw,$$

since service times are exponentially distributed. Hence,

(18)
$$U(t) = \sum_{n=0}^{\infty} U(t \mid n)P_n = \int_0^t \mu(1 - s_0)e^{-\mu(1-s_0)w} \, dw$$
$$= 1 - e^{-\mu(1-s_0)t} \quad \text{[exponential distribution; mean } = 1/\mu(1 - s_0)\text{]}.$$

Consider the probability of r customers in the system at *any* Time T; then it can be proved that as Time T $\to \infty$, this probability tends to a limit:

(19)
$$P_0^* = 1 - \rho$$
$$P_r^* = \rho P_{r-1} = \rho(1 - s_0)s_0^{r-1} \quad \text{for } r = 1, 2, \ldots$$

$$E \text{ [number of customers in system]} = \frac{\rho}{1 - s_0},$$

where ρ is given by (6).

Thus you have observed an important result: $P_r^* = P_r$ *only* when $s_0 = \rho$, which occurs if the arrival distribution is Poisson, as is shown below. Otherwise, the proportion of all time over an unbounded horizon during which the system has r customers, namely P_r^*, does *not* equal the long-run fraction of regeneration points in which the system has r customers, namely P_r. Hence the systems $M/G/1$ and $GI/M/1$ differ essentially in this respect.

Examples. Suppose the interarrival distribution is

(20) $F(t) = \int_0^t \frac{\lambda(\lambda z)^{M-1}e^{-\lambda z}}{(M - 1)!} \, dz$ (gamma distribution; mean $= M/\lambda$).

Then

(21) $k_j = \int_0^{\infty} \frac{(\mu h)^j e^{-\mu h}}{j!} \cdot \frac{\lambda(\lambda z)^{M-1}e^{-\lambda z}}{(M - 1)!} \, dz = \binom{j + M - 1}{j} p^j (1 - p)^M$

(negative binomial distribution; $E[j] = M\mu/\lambda$),

where

(22) $$p = \frac{\lambda}{\mu + \lambda}.$$

Therefore,

(23) $K^*(s) = \left(\frac{1 - p}{1 - ps}\right)^M = \left(\frac{\rho}{1 + \rho - s}\right)^M$ where $\rho = \frac{\lambda}{\mu}$.

When $M = 1$ in (20), giving the exponential distribution, $(s_0 = \rho)$ is a solution to (12), and the steady-state distribution (14) and distribution of time a customer spends in the system (16) agree with the results in Sec. 20.5.

▶ If you want to express the interarrival time distribution as an Erlang distribution, where $M\lambda$ replaces λ in (20), then substitute $M\lambda$ for λ in (20), (21) and (22), and $M\rho$ for ρ in (23).

In the case of a constant arrival time (denoted as $D/M/1$),

(i) $$K^*(s) = e^{-(1-s)/\rho}.$$ ◀

*III.4 MULTIPLE-SERVER MODEL WITH GENERAL INPUT AND EXPONENTIAL SERVICE DISTRIBUTION

The derivation of steady-state probabilities for this model (denoted as $GI/M/S$) generalizes the approach used in the preceding section. In particular, it employs the instants of new arrivals as regeneration points. Although the details of the analysis are involved, the resulting formulas can be stated in a straightforward fashion, and are given here for completeness.

Analogously to (14) in Sec. III.3, let s_0 be the unique solution for $0 < s_0 < 1$ of the equation

(1) $$s = F^*[\mu S(1 - s)],$$

where F^* is the Laplace-Stieltjes transform of the interarrival distribution, and S is the number of servers. Define and calculate

(2) $$F_j^* \equiv F^*(\mu j) \quad \text{for } j = 0, 1, 2, \ldots, S$$

(3) $$C_j \equiv \left(\frac{F_1^*}{1 - F_1^*}\right) \cdot \left(\frac{F_2^*}{1 - F_2^*}\right) \cdots \left(\frac{F_j^*}{1 - F_j^*}\right)$$
$$\text{for } j = 1, 2, \ldots, S \quad \text{and } C_0 = 1$$

(4) $$D_j \equiv \sum_{k=j+1}^{S} \frac{\binom{S}{k}}{C_k(1 - F_k^*)} \left[\frac{S(1 - F_k^*) - 1}{S(1 - s_0) - 1}\right]$$
$$\text{for } j = 0, 1, 2, \ldots, S - 1$$

(5) $$M \equiv \left[\frac{1}{1 - s_0} + D_0\right]^{-1}.$$

To ensure the existence of stationary distributions, assume that $\lambda < \mu S$, where $1/\lambda$ is the mean interarrival time.

Then it can be proved that

(6) $$P_r = \begin{cases} \sum_{j=r}^{S-1} (-1)^{j-r}\binom{j}{r} \cdot MC_jD_j & \text{for } r = 0, 1, \ldots, S - 1 \\ Ms_0^{r-S} & \text{for } r = S, S + 1, \ldots. \end{cases}$$

Notice that for $r \geq S$, the form of P_r is geometric.

Using an approach similar to that in (17) and (18) in the preceding section, you can derive that

(7) $W(t) \equiv P$ [time a customer spends in line $\leq t$] $= 1 - \dfrac{Me^{-S\mu(1-s_0)t}}{1 - s_0}$

and

(8) $$E \text{ [time in line]} = \frac{M}{S\mu(1 - s_0)^2}.$$

The probability of r customers in the system at Time T tends, as Time $T \to \infty$, to the limit

(9)
$$P_0^* = 1 - \frac{\lambda}{S\mu} - \frac{\lambda}{\mu} \sum_{j=1}^{S-1} P_{j-1}\left(\frac{1}{j} - \frac{1}{S}\right)$$

$$P_r^* = \frac{\lambda P_{r-1}}{r\mu} \quad \text{for } r = 1, 2, \ldots, S - 1$$

$$P_r^* = \frac{\lambda P_{r-1}}{S\mu} \quad \text{for } r = S, S + 1, \ldots.$$

*III.5 SINGLE-SERVER MODEL WITH GENERAL
INPUT AND GENERAL SERVICE DISTRIBUTION

The key idea for analyzing this model (designated as $GI/G/1$) is to work directly with the distribution of the time spent in line. Let $F(h)$ and $G(h)$ be the distribution functions of interarrival and service times, respectively, and as usual, let $1/\lambda$ and $1/\mu$ be the corresponding means. To ensure the existence of limiting distributions assume that $\rho = \lambda/\mu < 1$.

Suppose the system begins at Time $t = 0$, when the first customer arrives. Define:

w_r = time that Customer r spends in line

s_r = service time for Customer r

a_r = interarrival time between Customer r and Customer r + 1.

Since the line is empty just before Time $t = 0$,

(1) $$W_1(t) \equiv P[w_1 \leq t] = \begin{cases} 0 & \text{for } t < 0 \\ 1 & \text{for } t \geq 0. \end{cases}$$

The w_r can be characterized recursively by

(2) $$w_{r+1} = \begin{cases} 0 & \text{if } a_r \geq w_r + s_r \\ w_r + s_r - a_r & \text{if } a_r < w_r + s_r. \end{cases}$$

Give a verbal interpretation of (2).

Then for $t > 0$,

(3) $W_{r+1}(t) \equiv P[w_{r+1} \leq t] = P[w_{r+1} = 0] + P[0 < w_{r+1} \leq t]$

$= P[w_r + (s_r - a_r) \leq 0] + P[0 < w_r + (s_r - a_r) \leq t]$

$= P[w_r + (s_r - a_r) \leq t].$

Note that s_r and a_r are independently distributed and the distribution of $(s_r - a_r)$

is independent of r. Let

$$(4) \qquad K(t) \equiv P[s_r - a_r \leq t] = \int_0^\infty G(t + h) \, dF(h) \quad \text{for } -\infty < t < \infty,$$

where, in any specific case, the integral on the right of (4) can be calculated by numerical methods.

Consequently, you can write (3) as a convolution of $K(h)$ and $W_r(h)$:

$$(5) \qquad W_{r+1}(t) = \int_0^\infty K(t - h) \, dW_r(h) \quad \text{for } t \geq 0.$$

Starting with (1), you can in principle use (5) to calculate all the distribution functions, $W_r(t)$, for $r = 2, 3, \ldots$.

Given that $\rho < 1$, the functions $W_r(t)$ approach a function $W(t)$ as $r \to \infty$, where $W(t)$ satisfies the so-called **Weiner-Hopf integral equation**:

$$(6) \qquad W(t) = \int_0^\infty K(t - h) \, dW(h) \quad \text{for } t \geq 0.$$

One way of calculating $W(t)$ is to perform the recursive computations implied by (5) up to a large value of r. For any t, $W_{r+1}(t) \geq W_r(t)$, so that the distribution functions converge monotonically from below. [Another approach is to use a discrete and finite approximation. For example, you may consider t only at Times 0, e, 2e, 3e, ..., Me; this method leads to a set of simultaneous linear equations for the approximate values of $W(t)$.] For special models, such as Erlang interarrival and service times (denoted by $E_n/E_m/1$), it is possible to apply advanced analytic methods for the solution of (6), and thereby derive explicit formulas for $W(t)$.

Operating characteristics. Having the distribution $W(t)$, you can find E[time in line], and then by multiplying this average by μ you will have the expected number of customers in the system in front of an entering customer. It also can be shown that as the system operates over an unbounded horizon, the limiting probability that the server is idle is $1 - \rho$. Note that this value may differ from that given by (16) in Sec. III.3. There the value $1 - s_0$ gives the probability that the server is idle *at a regeneration point* when a new customer enters; these two probabilities agree only when the arrival distribution is Poisson, for then $s_0 = \rho$.

REVIEW EXERCISES

1 In each part below, verify the indicated statement or formula involving the generating function $P^*(s)$, given by (1) in Sec. III.1. *Parts (e) and (f) are on p. A74.*

  (a) (2), (3), (4), and (5).
  (b) Geometric distribution (6) and (7).
  (c) Poisson distribution (8) and (9).
  (d) Binomial distribution (10) and (11).

(e) Negative binomial distribution (12) and (13).

(f) Check that when you take the nth derivative of $P^*(s)$ in (7), (9), (11), and (13) and let $s = 0$, you obtain $n!P_n$.

2 In each part below, verify the indicated statement or formula involving the Laplace-Stieltjes transform $G(t)$, given by (15) in Sec. III.1.

(a) Moment generating property (16).

(b) Exponential distribution (17) and (18).

(c) If x and y are independent random variables, the Laplace-Stieltjes transform for the distribution function of their sum is equal to the product of the transforms for each of the distribution functions.

(d) Gamma distribution (19) and (20).

(e) Erlang distribution (21) and (23), and the constant service time distribution.

3 Consider the single-server model with Poisson input and general service distribution, discussed in Sec. III.2.

(a) Give a detailed justification for (1), (2), and (3). Explain how the memoryless property of the exponential model is exploited in (2).

(b) Justify in detail the construction of the Markov chain matrix (4).

(c) Verify that the steady-state equations for the Markov matrix (4) are those given in (6).

(d) Perform the intermediate algebraic steps to verify that the steady-state probabilities P_r can be computed by the formulas in (7).

(e) Perform the intermediate algebraic steps to justify each equality for the generating function $P^*(s)$ in (10) and (11).

(f) Justify in detail the derivation of the Laplace-Stieltjes transform in (12).

(g) Perform the intermediate steps to justify the equality in (13).

(h) Justify in detail the equalities in (14).

(i) Perform the intermediate steps to justify the derivation of P_0 in (15) and (16).

(j) Justify in detail the derivation of the Pollaczek-Khintchine equation (19).

(k) Verify the derivation of (20).

(l) Justify in detail the equalities in (21) and (22) relating to the time a customer spends in the system, in line, and in service.

4 Consider the single-server model with Poisson input and Gamma service distribution, given by (23) in Sec. III.2.

(a) Verify the equalities in (25), and derive the form (27).

(b) Perform the intermediate steps to derive $P^*(s)$ in (30).

(c) Examine the exponential case $M = 1$; show how to obtain $P^*(s)$ in (31).

(d) Perform the intermediate steps to derive the transform for the waiting time density, given in (33).

*5 Consider the single-server model with Poisson input and Erlangian service, as discussed in the special material ending Sec. III.2.

(a) Rewrite (24), (25), (26), and (30), where you replace μ by μM.

(b) Examine the constant service case, in which $M \longrightarrow \infty$. Verify (i), (ii), and (iii).

6 Consider the single-server model in Sec. III.3 with general input and exponential service distribution.

   (a) Verify the transition relation (1).
   (b) Justify (2) and explain how the memoryless property of the exponential distribution is exploited.
   (c) Justify in detail the construction of the Markov chain matrix (4).
   (d) Verify that the steady-state equations for the Markov matrix are those given in (7) and (8).
   (e) Substitute the solution for P_r given in (9) into the stationary equations (7), and verify the derivation in (10), (11), and (12).
   (f) Justify in detail the derivation in (13) and (14).
   (g) Justify in detail the derivation of the service time distribution in (17) and (18).

7 Consider the single-server model with a gamma interarrival distribution and exponential service, given by (20) in Sec. III.3.

   (a) Verify the equalities in (21) and (23).
   (b) Show that when $M = 1$, a solution to (12) is $s_0 = \rho$, and the steady-state distribution (14) and distribution of time a customer spends in the system (16) agree with the results in Sec. 20.5.
   *(c) Give a detailed justification for (i), which pertains to the case of a constant arrival time and is discussed at the end of Sec. III.3.

8 Consider a single-server system with input as specified below and exponential service at mean rate $\mu = 10$. In each part, give explicit formulas for the probability that r customers are in the system and for the expected number of customers in the system at both regeneration points and at a Time T that is an arbitrarily long distance into the future.

   (a) Gamma input distribution, given by (20) in Sec. III.3, where $M = 1$ and $\lambda = 9$.
   (b) Rework part (a), letting $M = 2$.
   (c) Rework part (a), letting $M = 3$.
   (d) Rework part (a), letting $M = 2$ and $\lambda = 18$.
   *(e) Constant arrival time, where $\lambda = 9$.

9 Explain your understanding of the following terms:

   generating function
   Laplace-Stieltjes transform
   moment generating function
   regeneration point
   imbedded Markov chain
   Pollaczek-Khintchine equation
   *Weiner-Hopf integral equation.

Probability of a Busy Period: $P[n \geq S]$ for $M/M/S$ Model

ρ	S 1	2	3	4
.1	.1000			
.15	.1500	.0104		
.2	.2000	.0181		
.25	.2500	.0277		
.3	.3000	.0391		
.35	.3500	.0521		
.4	.4000	.0666		
.45	.4500	.0826	.0113	
.5	.5000	.1000	.0151	
.55	.5500	.1186	.0195	
.6	.6000	.1384	.0246	
.65	.6500	.1594	.0304	
.7	.7000	.1814	.0369	
.75	.7500	.2045	.0441	
.8	.8000	.2285	.0520	
.85	.8500	.2535	.0606	.0117
.9	.9000	.2793	.0700	.0143
.95	.9500	.3059	.0801	.0171
1.00		.3333	.0909	.0204

Note: $\rho = \lambda/\mu$ traffic intensity

λ = arrival rate

μ = service rate

S = number of servers

S

ρ	2	3	4	5	6	7	8	9	10
1.0	.3333	.0909	.0204						
1.2	.4499	.1411	.0370						
1.4	.5764	.2033	.0603	.0153					
1.6	.7111	.2737	.0906	.0258					
1.8	.8526	.3547	.1285	.0404	.0111				
2.0		.4444	.1739	.0597	.0180				
2.2		.5421	.2267	.0839	.0274				
2.4		.6471	.2870	.1135	.0399	.0125			
2.6		.7588	.3544	.1486	.0558	.0187			
2.8		.8766	.4286	.1895	.0754	.0270			
3.0			.5094	.2361	.0991	.0376	.0129		
3.2			.5964	.2885	.1271	.0508	.0184		
3.4			.6893	.3466	.1595	.0669	.0256		
3.6			.7877	.4103	.1965	.0862	.0346	.0127	
3.8			.8914	.4795	.2382	.1088	.0456	.0175	
4.0				.5541	.2847	.1351	.0590	.0237	
4.2				.6337	.3359	.1650	.0749	.0313	.0121
4.4				.7183	.3919	.1988	.0935	.0407	.0164
4.6				.8077	.4525	.2365	.1150	.0518	.0217
4.8				.9016	.5177	.2783	.1395	.0650	.0282
5.0					.5875	.3241	.1672	.0805	.0361

Note: $\rho = \lambda/\mu$ traffic intensity

λ = arrival rate

μ = service

S = number of servers

S

ρ	6	7	8	9	10	11	12	13	14	15
5.0	.5875	.3241	.1672	.0805	.0361	.0150				
5.2	.6616	.3740	.1982	.0983	.0455	.0196				
5.4	.7401	.4279	.2827	.1186	.0565	.0252	.0105			
5.6	.8227	.4859	.2706	.1415	.0694	.0319	.0137			
5.8	.9094	.5479	.3120	.1673	.0843	.0398	.0176			
6.0		.6138	.3569	.1959	.1012	.0492	.0224			
6.2		.6836	.4055	.2275	.1204	.0600	.0281	.0124		
6.4		.7572	.4576	.2622	.1420	.0725	.0349	.0158		
6.6		.8345	.5133	.2999	.1660	.0868	.0428	.0199		
6.8		.9155	.5725	.3408	.1925	.1029	.0520	.0248	.0112	
7.0			.6353	.3849	.2217	.1211	.0626	.0306	.0141	
7.2			.7015	.4322	.2536	.1413	.0746	.0373	.0177	
7.4			.7711	.4827	.2882	.1637	.0883	.0451	.0219	.0100
7.6			.8441	.5363	.3256	.1884	.1036	.0541	.0268	.0126
7.8			.9204	.5932	.3659	.2154	.1208	.0644	.0326	.0156
8.0				.6533	.4091	.2449	.1398	.0759	.0392	.0193
8.2				.7165	.4552	.2769	.1608	.0890	.0469	.0235
8.4				.7828	.5042	.3114	.1838	.1036	.0556	.0284
8.6				.8522	.5561	.3484	.2090	.1198	.0655	.0342
8.8				.9246	.6110	.3881	.2364	.1377	.0767	.0407
9.0					.6687	.4304	.2660	.1575	.0891	.0482
9.2					.7293	.4754	.2979	.1790	.1030	.0567
9.4					.7927	.5231	.3322	.2025	.1184	.0662
9.6					.8590	.5734	.3688	.2280	.1353	.0769
9.8					.9281	.6264	.4078	.2556	.1538	.0888
10.0						.6821	.4493	.2852	.1741	.1020

Note: $\rho = \lambda/\mu$ traffic intensity

λ = arrival rate

μ = service rate

S = number of servers

Selected References

•Operations Research•

INTRODUCTORY TEXTS AND SURVEYS

BOOKS

[1] Ackoff, Russell L., *Progress in Operations Research*, Vol. I, John Wiley & Sons, Inc., 1961.

[2] Ackoff, Russell L. and Patrick Rivett, *A Manager's Guide to Operations Research*, John Wiley & Sons, Inc., 1963.

[3] Ackoff, Russell L. and Maurice W. Sasieni, *Fundamentals of Operations Research*, John Wiley & Sons, Inc., 1968.

[4] Baumol, W. J., *Economic Theory and Operations Analysis*, Prentice-Hall, 1963.

[5] Boot, J. C. G., *Mathematical Reasoning in Economics and Management Science: Twelve Topics*, Prentice-Hall, 1967.

[6] Bowman, Edward H. and Robert B. Fetter, *Analysis for Production and Operations Management*, R. D. Irwin, 1967.

[7] Carr, Charles R. and Charles W. Howe, *Quantitative Decision Procedures in Management and Economics-Deterministic Theory and Applications*, McGraw-Hill, 1964.

[7a] Churchman, C. West, *The Systems Approach*, Delacorte Press, 1968.

[8] Churchman, C. West, Russell L. Ackoff, and E. Leonard Arnoff, *Introduction to Operations Research*, John Wiley & Sons, 1957.

[9] Fishburn, Peter C., *Decision and Value Theory*, John Wiley & Sons, 1964.

[10] Hertz, David B. and Roger T. Eddison, *Progress in Operations Research*, Vol. II, John Wiley & Sons, 1964.

[11] Hertz, David B., *New Power for Management-Computer Systems and Management Science*, McGraw-Hill, 1969.

[12] Hillier, Frederick S. and Gerald J. Lieberman, *Introduction to Operations Research*, Holden-Day, Inc., 1967

[13] Horowitz, Ira, *An Introduction to Quantitative Business Analysis*, McGraw-Hill, 1965.

[14] Miller, David W. and Martin K. Starr, *Executive Decisions and Operations Research*, Prentice-Hall, 1960.

[15] Teichroew, Daniel, *An Introduction to Management Science Deterministic Models*, John Wiley & Sons, 1964

[16] Theil, Henri, *Optimal Decision Rules for Government and Industry*, North Holland, 1964.

•Mathematical Programming•

LINEAR PROGRAMMING (Chaps. 2 through 5)

BOOKS

[1] Beale, E. M. L., *Mathematical Programming in Practice*, Pitman, 1968.

[2] Charnes, A. and W. W. Cooper, *Management Models and Industrial Applications of Linear Programming*, Volumes I and II, John Wiley & Sons, 1961.

[3] Dantzig, George B., *Linear Programming and Extensions*, Princeton University Press, 1963.

[4] Dorfman, Robert, Paul A. Samuelson, and Robert M. Solow, *Linear Programming and Economic Analysis*, McGraw-Hill, 1958.

[5] Gale, David, *The Theory of Linear Economic Models*, McGraw-Hill, 1960.

[6] Gass, Saul I., *Linear Programming: Methods and Applications*, McGraw-Hill, Third Edition, 1969.

[7] Graves, Robert L. and Philip Wolfe, *Recent Advances in Mathematical Programming*, McGraw-Hill, 1963.

[8] Hadley, G., *Linear Programming*, Addison-Wesley, 1962.

[9] Karlin, Samuel, *Mathematical Methods and Theory in Games, Programming and Economics*, Vol. I, Addison-Wesley, 1959.

[10] Koopmans, Tjalling C., *Activity Analysis of Production and Allocation. Proceeding of a Conference*, John Wiley & Sons, 1951.

[11] Kuhn, H. W. and A. W. Tucker, *Linear Inequalities and Related Systems*, Princeton University Press, 1956.

[12] Manne, Alan S., *Scheduling of Petroleum Refinery Operations*, Harvard University Press, 1956.

[13] Manne, Alan S. and Harry M. Markowitz, *Studies in Process Analysis Economy-Wide Production Capabilities*, John Wiley & Sons, 1963.

[14] Orchard-Hays, William, *Advanced Linear-Programming Computing Techniques*, McGraw-Hill, 1968.

[15] Vajda, S., *Mathematical Programming*, Addison-Wesley, 1961.

ARTICLES

[16] Bennett, John M., "An Approach to Some Structured Linear Programming Problems," *Operations Research*, Vol. 14 (1966), pp. 636–645.

[17] Dantzig, G. B. and Philip Wolfe, "Decomposition Principle for Linear Programs," *Operations Research*, Vol. 8 (1960), pp. 101–111.

[18] Fetter, Robert B., "A Linear Programming Model for Long Range Capacity Planning," *Management Science*, Vol. 7 (1961), pp. 372–378.

[19] Gilmore, P. C. and R. E. Gomory, "A Linear Programming Approach to the Cutting Stock Problem," *Operations Research*, Vol. 9 (1961), pp. 849–859.

[20] Gilmore, P. C. and R. E. Gomory, "A Linear Programming Approach to the Cutting Stock Problem—Part II," *Operations Research*, Vol. 11 (1963), pp. 863–888.

[21] Gilmore, P. C. and R. E. Gomory, "Multistage Cutting Stock Problems of Two and More Dimensions," *Operations Research*, Vol. 13 (1965), pp. 94–120.

[22] Lemke, C. E., "The Dual Method of Solving the Linear Programming Problem," *Naval Research Logistics Quarterly*, Vol. 1 (1954), pp. 36–47.

[23] Quandt, R. E. and H. W. Kuhn, "On Upper Bounds for the Number of Iterations in Solving Linear Programs," *Operations Research*, Vol. 12 (1964), pp. 161–165.

[24] Sakarovitch, M. and R. Saigal, "An Extension of Generalized Upper Bounding Techniques for Structured Linear Programs," *SIAM J. on Applied Mathematics*, Vol. 15 (1967), pp. 906–914.

[25] Sharpe, William F., "A Linear Programming Algorithm for Mutual Fund Portfolio Selection," *Management Science*, Vol. 13 (1967), pp. 499–510.

[25a] Zionts, Stanley, "The Criss-Cross Method for Solving Linear Programming Problems," *Management Science*, Vol. 15 (1969), pp. 426–445.

[26] Wagner, Harvey M., "A Linear Programming Solution to Dynamic Leontief Type Models," *Management Science*, Vol. 3 (1957), pp. 234–254.

[27] Wagner, Harvey M., "The Dual Simplex Algorithm for Bounded Variables," *Naval Research Logistics Quarterly*, Vol. 5 (1958), pp. 257–261.

DIRECTED READING

Section	References
4.7	[1], [23]
5.2	[6]
5.4	[2], [3], [10], [11]
5.8	[22]
5.10	[3], [24], [27]

NETWORK OPTIMIZATION (Chaps. 6, 7, and Appendix I)

BOOK

[28] Ford, L. R., Jr., and D. R. Fulkerson, *Flows in Networks*, Princeton University Press, 1962.

ARTICLES

[29] Balinski, M. L. and R. E. Gomory, "A Primal Method for the Assignment and Transportation Problems," *Management Science*, Vol. 10 (1964), pp. 578–593.

[30] Derman, Cyrus and Morton Klein, "Inventory Depletion Management," *Management Science*, Vol. 4 (1958), pp. 450–456.

[31] Eisemann, Kurt, "The Generalized Stepping Stone Method for the Machine Loading Model," *Management Science*, Vol. 11 (1964), pp. 154–176.

[32] Farbey, B. A., A. H. Land, and J. D. Murchland, "The Cascade Algorithm for Finding All Shortest Distances in a Directed Graph, "*Management Science*, Vol. 14 (1967), pp. 19–28.

[33] Hoffman, A. J. and H. M. Markowitz, "A Note on Shortest Path, Assignment, and Transportation Problems," *Naval Research Logistics Quarterly*, Vol. 10 (1963) pp. 375–379.

[34] Hu, T. C., "Revised Matrix Algorithms for Shortest Paths," *SIAM J. on Applied Mathematics*, Vol. 15 (1967), pp. 207–218.

[35] Hu, T. C., "A Decompositon Algorithm for Shortest Paths in a Network," *Operations Research*, Vol. 16 (1968), pp. 91–102.

[36] Jewell, W. S., "Warehousing and Distribution of a Seasonal Product," *Naval Research Logistics Quarterly*, Vol. 4 (1957), pp. 29–34.

[37] Jewell, W. S., "Optimal Flow through Networks with Gains," *Operations Research*, Vol. 10 (1962), pp. 476–499.

[38] Kelley, James E., Jr., "Critical-Path Planning and Scheduling: Mathematical Basis," *Operations Research*, Vol. 9 (1961), pp. 296–320.

[39] Klein, Morton, "A Primal Method for Minimal Cost Flows with Applications to the Assignment and Transportation Problems," *Management Science*, Vol. 14 (1967), pp. 205–220.

[40] Kuhn, H. W., "Variants of the Hungarian Method for Assignment Problems," *Naval Research Logistics Quarterly*, Vol. 3 (1956), pp. 253–258.

[41] Lagemann, J. J., "A Method for Solving the Transportation Problem," *Naval Research Logistics Quarterly*, Vol. 14 (1967), pp. 89–99.

[42] Orden, Alex, "The Transhipment Problem," *Management Science*, Vol. 2 (1956), pp. 276–285.

[43] Pierskalla, William P., "The Multidimensional Assignment Problem," *Operations Research*, Vol. 16 (1968), pp. 422–431.

[44] Pollack, Maurice and Walter Wiebenson, "Solutions of the Shortest-Route Problem—A Review," *Operations Research*, Vol. 8 (1960), pp. 224–230.

[45] Prager, William, "On the Caterer Problem," *Management Science*, Vol. 3 (1956), pp. 15–23.

[46] Rao, M. R. and S. Zionts, "Allocation of Transportation Units to Alternative Trips—A Column Generation Scheme with Out-of-Kilter Subproblems," *Operations Research*, Vol. 16 (1968), pp. 52–63.

[47] Rothschild, B., A. Whinston, and J. Kent, "Computing Two-Commodity Flows," *Operations Research*, Vol. 16 (1968), pp. 446–450.

[48] Szwarc, Wlodzimierz, "The Initial Solution of the Transportation Problem," *Operations Research*, Vol. 8 (1960), pp. 727–729.

[49] Wagner, Harvey M., "On a Class of Capacitated Transportation Problems," *Management Science*, Vol. 5 (1959), pp. 304–318.

[50] Williams, A. C., "A Treatment of Transpertation Problems by Decomposition," *SIAM J. on Applied Mathematics*, Vol. 10 (1962), pp. 35–48.

[51] Yaspan, A., "On Finding a Maximal Assignment," *Operations Research*, Vol. 14 (1966), pp. 646–651.

Directed Reading

INTEGER PROGRAMMING AND COMBINATORIAL MODELS
(Chap. 13)

Books

[51a] Hu, T. C., *Integer Programming and Network Flows*, Addison-Wesley, 1969.

[52] Muth, J. F. and G. L. Thompson, *Industrial Scheduling*, Prentice-Hall, 1963.

[53] Tonge, Fred M., *A Heuristic Program for Assembly Line Balancing*, Prentice-Hall, 1961.

[54] Weingartner, H. Martin, *Mathematical Programming and the Analysis of Capital Budgeting Problems*, Prentice-Hall, 1960.

Articles

[55] Alcaly, R. E. and A. K. Klevorick, "A Note on the Dual Prices of Integer Programs," *Econometrica*, Vol. 34 (1966), pp. 206–214.

[56] Allen, S. G., "Computation for the Redistribution Model with Set-up Charge," *Management Science*, Vol. 8 (1962), pp. 482–489.

[57] Balas, Egon, "An Additive Algorithm for Solving Linear Programs with Zero-One Variables," *Operations Research*, Vol. 13 (1965), pp. 517–546.

[58] Balas, Egon, "Discrete Programming by the Filter Method," *Operations Research*, Vol. 15 (1967), pp. 915–957.

[59] Balinski, M. L., "Integer Programming: Methods, Uses, Computation," *Management Science*, Vol. 12 (1965), pp. 253–313.

[60] Balinski, M. L. and R. E. Quandt, "On an Integer Program for a Delivery Problem," *Operations Research*, Vol. 12 (1964), pp. 300–304.

[61] Bellmore, M. and G. L. Nemhauser, "The Traveling Salesman Problem: A Survey," *Operations Research*, Vol. 16 (1968), pp. 538–558.

[62] Burt, O. R. and C. C. Harris, Jr., "Apportionment of the U.S. House of Representatives: A Minimum Range, Integer Solution, Allocation Problem" *Operations Research*, Vol. 11 (1963), pp. 648–652.

[63] Cooper, L. and C. Drebes, "An Approximate Solution Method for the Fixed Charge Problem," *Naval Research Logistics Quarterly*, Vol. 14 (1967), pp. 101–113.

[63a] Cabot, A. Victor and Arthur P. Hurter, Jr., "An Approach to Zero-One Integer Programming," *Operations Research*, Vol. 16 (1968), pp. 1206–1211.

[64] Crowston, W. and G. L. Thompson, "Decision CPM: A Method for Simultaneous Planning, Scheduling, and Control of Projects," *Operations Research*, Vol. 15 (1967), pp. 407–426.

[65] Dalton, R. E. and R. W. Llewellyn, "An Extension of the Gomory Mixed-Integer Algorithm to Mixed-Discrete Variables," *Management Science*, Vol. 12 (1966), pp. 569–575.

[66] Dantzig, G. B., D. R. Fulkerson, and S. M. Johnson, "On a Linear Programming, Combinatorial Approach to the Traveling Salesman Problem," *Operations Research*, Vol. 7 (1959), pp. 58–66.

[67] D'Esopo, D. A. and B. Lefkowitz, "Note on an Integer Linear Programming Model for Determining a Minimum Embarkation Fleet," *Naval Research Logistics Quarterly*, Vol. 11 (1964), pp. 79–82.

[68] Dwyer, P. S., "Use of Completely Reduced Matrices in Solving Transportation Problems with Fixed Charges," *Naval Research Logistics Quarterly*, Vol. 13 (1966), pp. 289–313.

[69] Efroymson, M. A. and T. L. Ray, "A Branch-Bound Algorithm For Plant Location," *Operations Research*, Vol. 14 (1966), pp. 361–368.

[70] Elmaghraby, Salah E., "The Machine Sequencing Problem—Review and Extensions," *Naval Research Logistics Quarterly*, Vol. 15 (1968), pp. 205–232.

[71] Freeman, Rauol J., "Computational Experience with a 'Balasian' Integer Programming Algorithm," *Operations Research*, Vol. 14 (1966), pp. 935–941.

[72] Gavett, J. W. and N. V. Plyter, "The Optimal Assignments of Facilities to Locations by Branch and Bound," *Operations Research*, Vol. 14 (1966), pp. 210–232.

[73] Geoffrion, Arthur M., "Integer Programming by Implicit Enumeration and Balas' Method," *SIAM Review*, Vol. 9 (1967), pp. 178–190.

[74] Giglio, Richard J. and Harvey M. Wagner, "Approximate Solutions to the Three-Machine Scheduling Problem," *Operations Research*, Vol. 12 (1964), pp. 305–324.

[75] Glassey, C. R., "Minimum Change-Over Scheduling of Several Products on One Machine," *Operations Research*, Vol. 16 (1968), pp. 342–352.

[76] Glover, Fred, "A Multiphase-Dual Algorithm for the Zero-One Integer Programming Problem," *Operations Research*, Vol. 13 (1965), pp. 879–919.

[77] Glover, Fred, "Stronger Cuts in Integer Programming," *Operations Research*, Vol. 15 (1967), pp. 1174–1177.

[78] Glover, Fred, "A New Foundation for a Simplified Primal Integer Programming Algorithm," *Operations Research*, Vol. 16 (1968), pp. 727–740.

[79] Glover, Fred, "Surrogate Constraints," *Operations Research*, Vol. 16 (1968), pp. 741–749.

[79a] Glover, Fred, "A Note on Linear Programming and Integer Feasibility," *Operations Research*, Vol. 16 (1968), pp. 1212–1216.

[80] Gomory, R. E., "An Algorithm for Integer Solutions to Linear Programs," pp. 269–302 in *Recent Advances in Mathematical Programming*, Robert L. Graves and Philip Wolfe (eds.), McGraw-Hill, 1963.

[81] Gomory, R. E., "On the Relation Between Integer and Noninteger Solutions to Linear Programs," *National Academy of Sciences*, Vol. 53 (1965), pp. 260–265.

[82] Gomory, R. E. and W. J. Baumol, "Integer Programming and Pricing," *Econometrica*, Vol. 28 (1960), pp. 521–550.

[83] Graves, G. W. and A. Whinston, "A New Approach to Discrete Mathematical Programming," *Management Science*, Vol. 15 (1968), pp. 177–190.

[84] Gutjahr, A. L. and G. L. Nemhauser, "An Algorithm for the Line Balancing Problem," *Management Science*, Vol. 11 (1964), pp. 308–315.

[85] Haldi, John and L. M. Isaacson, "A Computer Code for Integer Solutions to Linear Problems," *Operations Research*, Vol. 13 (1965), pp. 946–959.

[86] Held, M. and R. M. Karp, "A Dynamic Programming Approach to Sequencing Problems," *SIAM J. on Applied Mathematics*, Vol. 10, (1962), pp. 196–210.

[87] Held, M., R. M. Karp, and R. Shareshian, "Assembly-Line Balancing— Dynamic Programming with Precedence Constraints," *Operations Research*, Vol. 11 (1963), pp. 442–459.

[88] Hillier, Frederick S. and Michael M. Connors, "Quadratic Assignment Problem Algorithms and the Location of Indivisible Facilities," *Management Science*, Vol. 13 (1966), pp. 42–57.

[89] Hirsch, W. M. and G. B. Dantzig, "The Fixed Charge Problem," *Naval Research Logistics Quarterly*, Vol. 15 (1968), pp. 413–424.

[90] Ignall, Edward and Linus E. Schrage, "Application of the Branch and Bound Technique to Some Flow-Shop Scheduling Problems," *Operations Research*, Vol. 13 (1965), pp. 400–412.

[91] Karg, R. L. and G. L. Thompson, "A Heuristic Approach to Solving Traveling Salesman Problems," *Management Science*, Vol. 10 (1964), pp. 225–248.

[92] Kolesar, Peter J., "A Branch and Bound Algorithm for the Knapsack Problem," *Management Science*, Vol. 13 (1967), pp. 723–735.

[93] Koopmans, T. C. and M. Beckmann, "Assignment Problems and the Location of Economic Activities," *Econometrica*, Vol. 25 (1957), pp. 53–76.

[93a] Kortanek, K. O. and W. L. Maxwell, "On a Class of Combinatorial Optimizers for Multi-Product Single-Machine Scheduling," *Management Science*, Vol. 15 (1969), pp. 239–248.

[94] Kuehn, A. A. and M. J. Hamburger, "A Heuristic Program for Locating Warehouses," *Management Science*, Vol. 9 (1963), pp. 643–666.

[95] Kuhn, H. W. and W. J. Baumol, "An Approximative Algorithm for the Fixed-Charges Transportation Problem," *Naval Research Logistics Quarterly*, Vol. 9 (1962), pp. 1–15.

[96] Land, A. H. and A. G. Doig, "An Automatic Method of Solving Discrete Programming Problems," *Econometrica*, Vol. 28 (1960), pp. 497–520.

[97] Lawler, E. L., "The Quadratic Assignment Problem," *Management Science*, Vol. 9 (1963), pp. 586–599.

[98] Lawler, E. L. and D. E. Wood, "Branch-and-Bound Methods: A Survey," *Operations Research*, Vol. 14 (1966), pp. 699–719.

[99] Lemke, C. E. and K. Spielberg, "Direct Search Algorithms for Zero-One and Mixed-Integer Programming," *Operations Research*, Vol. 15 (1967), pp. 892–914.

[100] Levy, F. K., G. L. Thompson, and J. D. Wiest, "Multiship, Multishop, Work-load-Smoothing Program," *Naval Research Logistics Quarterly*, Vol. 9 (1962), pp. 37–44.

[101] Little, John D. C., K. G. Murty, D. W. Sweeney, and C. Karel, "An Algorithm for the Traveling Salesman Problem," *Operations Research*, Vol. 11 (1963), pp. 972–989.

[102] Manne, Alan S., "On the Job-Shop Scheduling Problem," *Operations Research*, Vol. 8 (1960), pp. 219–223.

[103] Manne, Alan S., "Plant Location under Economies-of-Scale—Decentralization and Computation," *Management Science*, Vol. 11 (1964), pp. 213–235.

[104] Mao, J. C. T. and B. A. Wallingford, "An Extension of Lawler and Bell's Method of Discrete Optimization with Examples from Capital Budgeting," *Management Science*, Vol. 15 (1968), pp. B-51–B-60.

[105] Markowitz, H. M. and Alan S. Manne, "On the Solution of Discrete Programming Problems," *Econometrica*, Vol. 25 (1957), pp. 84–110.

[106] Mizukami, Koichi, "Optimum Redundancy for Maximum System Reliability by the Method of Convex and Integer Programming, "*Operations Research*, Vol. 16 (1968), pp. 392–406.

[107] Moore, J. Michael, "An n Job, One Machine Sequencing Algorithm for Minimizing the Number of Late Jobs," *Management Science*, Vol. 15 (1968). pp. 102–109.

[108] Murty, Katta G., "Solving the Fixed Charge Problem by Ranking the Extreme Points," *Operations Research*, Vol. 16 (1968), pp. 268–279.

[109] Nemhauser, G. L. and Z. Ullmann, "A Note on the Generalized Lagrange Multiplier Solution to an Integer Programming Problem," *Operations Research*, Vol. 16 (1968), pp. 450–453.

[110] Pierce, John F., "Application of Combinatorial Programming to a Class of All-Zero-One Integer Programming Problems, "*Management Science*, Vol. 15 (1968), pp. 191–209.

[111] Reiter, Stanley and Gordon Sherman, "Discrete Optimizing," *SIAM J. on Applied Mathematics*, Vol. 13 (1965), pp. 864–889.

[112] Shapiro, Jeremy F., "Dynamic Programming Algorithms for the Integer Programming Problem I: The Integer Programming Problem Viewed as a Knapsack Type Problem," *Operations Research*, Vol. 16 (1968), pp. 103–121.

[113] Shapiro, Jeremy F., "Group Theoretic Algorithms for the Integer Programming Problem II: Extension to a General Algorithm," *Operations Research*, Vol. 16 (1968), pp. 928–947.

[114] Smith, R. D. and R. A. Dudek, "A General Algorithm for Solution of the n-Job, M-Machine Sequencing Problem of the Flow Shop," *Operations Research*, Vol. 15 (1967), pp. 71–82.

[114a] Spielberg, Kurt, "Algorithms for the Simple Plant-Location Problem with Some Side Conditions," *Operations Research*, Vol. 17 (1969), pp. 85–111.

[115] Tillman, F. A. and J. M. Liittschwager, "Integer Programming Formulation to Constrained Reliability Problems," *Management Science*, Vol. 13 (1967), pp. 887–899.

[116] Tonge, Fred M., "Assembly Line Balancing Using Probabilistic Combinations of Heuristics," *Management Science*, Vol. 11 (1965), pp. 727–735.

[117] Vergin, R. C. and J. D. Rogers, "An Algorithm and Computational Procedure for Locating Economic Facilities," *Management Science*, Vol. 13 (1967), pp. B-240–B-254.

[118] Wagner, Harvey M., "An Integer Linear-Programming Model for Machine Scheduling," *Naval Research Logistics Quarterly*, Vol. 6 (1959), pp. 131–140.

[119] Wagner, Harvey M., Richard J. Giglio, and R. George Glaser, "Preventive Maintenance Scheduling by Mathematical Programming," *Management Science*, Vol. 10 (1964), pp. 316–334.

[120] Watters, Lawrence J., "Reduction of Integer Polynomial Programming Problems to Zero-One Linear Programming Problems," *Operations Research*, Vol. 15 (1967), pp. 1171–1174.

[121] Weingartner, H. Martin, "Capital Budgeting of Interrelated Projects: Survey and Synthesis," *Management Science*, Vol. 12 (1966), pp. 485–516.

[122] Weingartner, H. Martin and David N. Ness, "Methods for the Solution of the Multi-Dimensional 0/1 Knapsack Problem," *Operations Research*, Vol. 15 (1967), pp. 83–103.

[123] Wiest, Jerome D., "A Heuristic Model for Scheduling Large Projects with Limited Resources," *Management Science*, Vol. 13 (1967), pp. B-359–B-377.

[124] Wilson, Robert B., "Stronger Cuts in Gomory's All-Integer Integer Programming Algorithm," *Operations Research*, Vol. 15 (1967), pp. 155–157.

[125] Young, R. D., "A Simplified Primal (All-Integer) Integer Programming Algorithm," *Operations Research*, Vol. 16 (1968), pp. 750–782.

[126] Zionts, S. "On an Algorithm for the Solution of Mixed Integer Programming Problems," *Management Science*, Vol. 15 (1968), pp. 113–116.

DIRECTED READING

Section	References
13.2	[3], [54], [56], [69], [72], [114a], [117], [121]
13.3	[59], [94], [111]
13.4	[55], [65], [77], [78], [80], [82], [85], [105], [124], [125]
13.5	[1], [96]
13.6	[61], [66], [91], [98], [101],
13.7	[57], [58], [71], [73], [79], [83], [99], [120]

NONLINEAR PROGRAMMING (Chaps. 14 and 15)

BOOKS

[127] Abadie, J. (ed.), *Nonlinear Programming*, John Wiley & Sons, 1967.

[128] Arrow, Kenneth J, Leonid Hurwicz, and Hirofumi Uzawa, *Studies in Linear and Non-Linear Programming*, Stanford University Press, 1958.

[129] Bracken, Jerome and G. P. McCormick, *Selected Applications of Nonlinear Programming*, John Wiley & Sons, 1968.

[130] Duffin, R. J., E. L. Peterson, and Clarence Zener, *Geometric Programming: Theory and Application*, John Wiley & Sons, 1967.

[131] Fiacco, A. V. and G. P. McCormick, *Nonlinear Programming, Sequential Unconstrained Minimization Techniques*, John Wiley & Sons, 1968.

[132] Hadley, G., *Nonlinear and Dynamic Programming*, Addison-Wesley, 1964.

[133] Künzi, Hans Paul, Wilhelm Krelle, and Werner Oettli, *Nonlinear Programming*, Blaisdell, 1966.

[134] Mangasarian, O. L., *Nonlinear Programming*, McGraw-Hill, 1969.

[135] Markowitz, Harry M., *Portfolio Selection Efficient Diversification of Investments*, John Wiley & Sons, 1959.

[136] Saaty, Thomas L. and Joseph Bram, *Nonlinear Mathematics*, McGraw-Hill, 1964.

[137] Wilde, D. J., *Optimum Seeking Methods*, Prentice-Hall, 1964.

[138] Wilde, D. J. and C. S. Beightler, *Foundations of Optimization*, Prentice-Hall, 1967.

[139] Zangwill, Willard I., *Non-Linear Programming—A Unified Approach*, Prentice-Hall, 1969.

[140] Zoutendijk, G., *Methods of Feasible Directions*, Elsevier, 1960.

ARTICLES

[141] Arrow, Kenneth J. and A. C. Enthoven, "Quasi-Concave Programming," *Econometrica*, Vol. 29 (1961), pp. 779–800.

[142] Baumol, W. J. and R. C. Bushnell, "Error Produced by Linearization in Mathematical Programming," *Econometrica*, Vol. 35 (1967), pp. 447–471.

[143] Baumol, W. J. and Philip Wolfe, "A Warehouse-Location Problem" *Operations Research*, Vol. 6 (1958), pp. 252–263.

[144] Beale, E. M. L., "On Quadratic Programming," *Naval Research Logistics Quarterly*, Vol. 6 (1959), pp. 227–243.

[145] Beale, E. M. L., "Note on A Comparison of Two Methods of Quadratic Programming," *Operations Research*, Vol. 14 (1966), pp. 442–443.

[146] Bernholtz, B., "A New Derivation of the Kuhn-Tucker Conditions," *Operations Research*, Vol. 12 (1964), pp. 295–299.

[147] Boot, J. C. G., "On Sensitivity Analysis in Convex Quadratic Programming Problems," *Operations Research*, Vol. 11 (1963), pp. 771–786.

[148] Brooks, R. and A. M. Geoffrion, "Finding Everetts' Lagrange Multipliers by Linear Programming," *Operations Research*, Vol. 14 (1966), pp. 1149–1153.

[149] Charnes, A. and W. W. Cooper, "Nonlinear Network Flows and Convex Programming Over Incidence Matrices," *Naval Research Logistics Quarterly*, Vol. 5 (1958), pp. 231–240.

[150] Charnes, A. and W. W. Cooper, "Programming with Linear Fractional Functionals," *Naval Research Logistics Quarterly*, Vol. 9 (1962), pp. 181–186.

[151] Cottle, Richard W., "Nonlinear Programs with Positively Bounded Jacobians," *SIAM J. on Applied Mathematics*, Vol. 14 (1966), pp. 147–158.

[152] Dantzig, George B., "Linear Control Processes and Mathematical Programming," *SIAM J. on Control*, Vol. 4 (1966), pp. 56–60.

[153] Dinkelbach, Werner, "On Nonlinear Fractional Programming," *Management Science*, Vol. 13 (1967), pp. 492–498.

[154] Dorn, W. S., "Self Dual Quadratic Programs," *SIAM J. of Applied Mathematics*, Vol. 9 (1961), pp. 51–54.

[155] Dorn, W. S., "Non-Linear Programming—A Survey," *Management Science*, Vol. 9 (1963), pp. 171–208.

[156] Duffin, R. J. and E. L. Peterson, "Duality Theory for Geometric Programming," *SIAM J. on Applied Mathematics*, Vol. 14 (1966), pp. 1307–1349.

[157] Everett, Hugh, III, "Generalized LaGrange Multiplier Method for Solving Problems of Optimum Allocation of Resources," *Operations Research*, Vol. 11 (1963), pp. 399–417.

[158] Frank, Marguerite and Philip Wolfe, "An Algorithm for Quadratic Programming," *Naval Research Logistics Quarterly*, Vol. 3 (1956), pp. 95–110.

[159] Fromovitz, Stan, "Non-Linear Programming with Randomization," *Management Science*, Vol. 11 (1965), pp. 831–846.

[160] Gaschütz, G. K. and J. H. Ahrens, "Suboptimal Algorithms for the Quadratic Assignment Problem," *Naval Research Logistics Quarterly*, Vol. 15 (1968), pp. 49–62.

[161] Geoffrion, Arthur M., "Strictly Concave Parametric Programming, Part I: Basic Theory," *Management Science*, Vol. 13 (1966), pp. 244–253.

[162] Geoffrion, Arthur M., "Strictly Convace Parametric Programming, Part II: Additional Theory and Computational Considerations," *Management Science*, Vol. 13 (1967), pp. 359–370.

[163] Geoffrion, Arthur M., "Reducing Concave Programs with Some Linear Constraints," *SIAM J. on Applied Mathematics*, Vol. 15 (1967), pp. 653–664.

[164] Geoffrion, Arthur M., "Solving Bicriterion Mathematical Programs," *Operations Research*, Vol. 15 (1967), pp. 39–54.

[165] Graves, Robert L., "A Principal Pivoting Simplex Algorithm for Linear and Quadratic Programming," *Operations Research*, Vol. 15 (1967), pp. 482–494.

[166] Hartley, H. O., "Non-Linear Programming by the Simplex Method," *Econometrica*, Vol. 29 (1961), pp. 223–237.

[167] Hartley, H. O. and R. R. Hocking, "Convex Programming by Tangential Approximation," *Management Science*, Vol. 9 (1963), pp. 600–612.

[168] Hu, T. C., "Minimum-Cost Flows in Convex-Cost Networks," *Naval Research Logistics Quarterly*, Vol. 13 (1966), pp. 1–9.

[169] Huard, Pierre, "Dual Programs," pp. 55–62, in *Recent Advances in Mathematical Programming*, Robert L. Graves and Philip Wolfe (eds.), McGraw-Hill, 1963.

[170] Hwang, C. L. and L. T. Fan, "A Discrete Version of Pontryagin's Maximum Principle," *Operations Research*, Vol. 15 (1967), pp. 139–146.

[170a] John, F., "Extremum Problems with Inequalities as Subsidiary Conditions," *Studies and Essays' (Courant Anniversary Volume)*, Interscience Publishers Inc., New York, 1948, pp. 187–204.

[171] Joksch, H. C., "Programming with Fractional Linear Objective Functions," *Naval Research Logistics Quarterly*, Vol. 11 (1964), pp. 197–204.

[172] Kelly, J. E., Jr., "The Cutting-Plane Method for Solving Convex Programs," *SIAM J. on Applied Mathematics*, Vol. 8 (1960), pp. 703–712.

[173] Kiefer, J., "Optimum Sequential Search and Approximation Methods under Minimum Regularity Assumptions," *SIAM J. of Applied Mathematics*, Vol. 5 (1957), pp. 105–136.

[174] Kortanek, K. O. and J. P. Evans, "Pseudo-Concave Programming and Lagrange Regularity," *Operations Research*, Vol. 15 (1967), pp. 882–891.

[175] Kriebel, Charles H., "Coefficient Estimation in Quadratic Programming Models," *Management Science*, Vol. 13 (1967), pp. B-473–B-486.

[176] Kuhn, H. W. and A. W. Tucker, "Nonlinear Programming," pp. 481–492, in *Proceedings of the Second Berkeley Symposium on Mathematical Statistics and Probability*, Jerzy Neyman (ed.), University of California Press, 1950.

[177] Lemke, C. E., "A Method of Solution for Quadratic Programs," *Management Science*, Vol. 8 (1962), pp. 442–453.

[178] Luenberger, David G., "Quasi-Convex Programming," *SIAM J. on Applied Mathematics*, Vol. 16 (1968), pp. 1090–1100.

[179] Mao, C. T. and C. E. Särndal, "A Decision Theory Approach to Portfolio Selection," *Management Science*, Vol. 12 (1966), pp. B-323–B-333.

[180] Martos, Bela, "Hyperbolic Programming," *Naval Research Logistics Quarterly*, Vol. 11 (1964), pp. 135–155.

[180a] McCormick, Garth P., "Anti-Zig-Zagging by Bending," *Management Science*, Vol. 15 (1969), pp. 315–320.

[181] Miller, Clair E., "The Simplex Method for Local Separable Programming," pp. 89–100, in *Recent Advances in Mathematical Programming*, Robert L. Graves and Philip Wolfe (eds.), McGraw-Hill, 1963.

[182] Moore, J. H. and A. B. Whinston, "Experimental Methods in Quadratic Programming," *Management Science*, Vol. 13 (1966), pp. 58–76.

[182a] Pierskalla, W. P., "Mathematical Programming with Increasing Constraint Functions," *Management Science*, Vol. 15 (1969), pp. 416–425.

[183] Rosen, J. B., "The Gradient Projection Method for Nonlinear Programming. Part I. Linear Constraints," *SIAM J. on Applied Mathematics*, Vol. 8 (1960), pp. 181–217.

[184] Rosen, J. B., "The Gradient Projection Method for Nonlinear Programming. Part II. Nonlinear Constraints," *SIAM J. on Applied Mathematics*, Vol. 9 (1961), pp. 514–532.

[185] Rosen, J. B. and J. C. Ornea, "Solution of Nonlinear Programming Problems by Partitioning," *Management Science*, Vol. 10 (1963), pp. 160–173.

[186] Roy, A. D., "Safety First in the Holding of Assets," *Econometrica*, Vol. 20 (1952), pp. 431–449.

[187] Sanders, J. L., "A Nonlinear Decomposition Principle," *Operations Research*, Vol. 13 (1965), pp. 266–271.

[188] Scarf, Herbert E., "The Approximation of Fixed Points of a Continuous Mapping," *SIAM J. on Applied Mathematics*, Vol. 15 (1967), pp. 1328–1343.

[189] Sengupta, J. K., G. Tintner, and C. Millham, "On Some Theorems of Stochastic Linear Programming with Applications," *Management Science*, Vol. 10 (1963), pp. 143–159.

[190] Sharpe, William F., "A Simplified Model for Portfolio Analysis," *Management Science*, Vol. 9 (1963), pp. 277–293.

[191] Theil, Henri and C. van de Panne, "Quadratic Programming as an Extension of Classical Quadratic Maximization," *Management Science*, Vol. 7 (1960), pp. 1–20.

[192] Topkis, Donald M. and Arthur F. Veinott, Jr., "On the Convergence of Some Feasible Direction Algorithms for Nonlinear Programming," *SIAM J. on Control*, Vol. 5 (1967), pp. 268–279.

[193] Tucker, A. W., "Linear and Nonlinear Programming," *Operations Research*, Vol. 5 (1957), pp. 244–257.

[194] van de Panne, C. and A. Whinston, "Simplicial Methods for Quadratic Programming," *Naval Research Logistics Quarterly*, Vol. 11 (1964), pp. 273–302.

[195] van de Panne, C. and A. Whinston, "A Comparison of Two Methods of Quadratic Programming," *Operations Research*, Vol. 14 (1966), pp. 422–441.

[196] Veinott, Arthur F., Jr., "The Supporting Hyperplane Method for Unimodal Programming," *Operations Research*, Vol. 15 (1967), pp. 147–152.

[197] Wagner, Harvey M., "Linear Programming and Regression Analysis," *Journal of the American Statistical Association*, Vol. 54 (1959), pp. 206–212.

[198] Wagner, Harvey M., "Non-linear Regression with Minimal Assumptions," *Journal of the American Statistical Association*, Vol. 57 (1962), pp. 572–578.

[199] Whinston, A., "Conjugate Functions and Dual Programs," *Naval Research Logistics Quarterly*, Vol. 12 (1965), pp. 315–322.

[200] Whinston, A. "The Bounded Variable Problem—An Application of the Dual Method for Quadratic Programming," *Naval Research Logistics Quarterly*, Vol. 12 (1965), pp. 173–179.

[201] Wolfe, Philip, "The Simplex Method for Quadratic Programming," *Econometrica*, Vol. 27 (1959), pp. 382–398.

[202] Wolfe, Philip, "A Duality Theorem for Nonlinear Programming," *Quarterly of Applied Mathematics*, Vol. 19 (1961), pp. 239–244.

[203] Wolfe, Philip, "Accelerating the Cutting Plane Method for Non-Linear Programming," *SIAM J. on Applied Mathematics*, Vol. 9 (1961), pp. 481–488.

[204] Zionts, S., "Programming with Linear Fractional Functionals," *Naval Research Logistics Quarterly*, Vol. 15 (1968), pp. 449–451.

[205] Zoutendijk, G., "Nonlinear Programming: A Numerical Survey," *SIAM J. on Control*, Vol. 4 (1966), pp. 194–210.

DIRECTED READING

Section	References
14.1	[135], [142], [179], [186], [190]
14.3	[137], [138], [173]
14.4	[137], [138]
14.5	[132], [136], [137], [139]
14.6	[1], [144], [145], [147]
14.7	[1], [3], [181]
14.8	[150], [153], [171], [180], [197], [198], [204]
14.9	[132], [139]
15.2	[158]
15.3	[139]
15.4	[128], [166], [167], [172], [183], [184], [196], [203]
15.6	[139], [140], [148], [192]
15.7	[128], [134], [141], [146], [154], [169], [170a], [174], [176], [178], [199], [202]
15.8	[3], [182], [191], [194], [195], [200], [201]
15.9	[129], [131], [139]
15.10	[3], [185], [187]
15.11	[3], [16], [17], [35], [46], [50]

STOCHASTIC PROGRAMMING (Chap. 16)

BOOKS

[206] Pratt, John W., Howard Raiffa, and Robert Schlaifer, *Introduction to Statistical Decision Theory*, McGraw-Hill, 1965.

[207] Raiffa, Howard, *Decision Analysis-Introductory Lectures on Choices Under Uncertainty*, Addison-Wesley, 1968.

ARTICLES

[208] Bowman, E. H., "Consistency and Optimality in Managerial Decision Making," *Management Science*, Vol. 9 (1963), pp. 310–321.

[209] Bracken, J. and R. M. Soland, "Statistical Decision Analysis of Stochastic Linear Programming Problems," *Naval Research Logistics Quarterly*, Vol. 13 (1966), pp. 205–225.

[210] Charnes, A., M. Kirby, and W. Raike, "Chance-Constrained Generalized Networks," *Operations Research*, Vol. 14 (1966), pp. 1113–1120.

[211] Charnes, A. and M. Kirby, "Some Special P-Models in Chance-Constrained Programming," *Management Science*, Vol. 14 (1967), pp. 183–195.

[212] Charnes, A. and W. W. Cooper, "Chance-Constrained Programming," *Management Science*, Vol. 6 (1959), pp. 73–79.

[213] Charnes, A. and W. W. Cooper, "Deterministic Equivalents for Optimizing and Satisficing Under Chance Constraints," *Operations Research*, Vol. 11 (1963), pp. 18–39.

[214] Charnes, A., W. W. Cooper and G. L. Thompson, "Critical Path Analyses via Chance Constrained and Stochastic Programming," *Operations Research*, Vol. 12 (1964), pp. 460–470.

[215] Charnes, A., Jacques Dreze, and Merton Miller, "Decision and Horizon Rules for Stochastic Planning Problems: A Linear Example,"*Econometrica*, Vol. 34 (1966), pp. 307–330.

[216] Cocks, K. D., "Discrete Stochastic Programming," *Management Science*, Vol. 15 (1968), pp. 72–79.

[217] Elmaghraby, Salah E., "An Approach to Linear Programming Under Uncertainty," *Operations Research*, Vol. 7 (1959), pp. 208–216.

[218] Elmaghraby, Salah E., "Allocation under Uncertainty when the Demand has Continuous d.f.," *Management Science*, Vol. 6 (1960), pp. 270–294.

[219] Evers, William H., "A New Model for Stochastic Linear Programming," *Management Science*, Vol. 13 (1967), pp. 680–693.

[220] Freund, R. J., "The Introduction of Risk into a Programming Problem," *Econometrica*, Vol. 24 (1956), pp. 253–263.

[221] Geoffrion, Arthur M., "Stochastic Programming with Aspiration or Fractile Criteria," *Management Science*, Vol. 13 (1967), pp. 672–679.

[222] Hartley, H. O. and A. W. Wortham, "A Statistical Theory for Pert Critical Path Analysis," *Management Science*, Vol. 12 (1966), pp. B-469–B-481.

[223] Hespos, R. F. and P. A. Strassmann, "Stochastic Decision Trees for the Analysis of Investment Decisions," *Management Science*, Vol. 11 (1965), pp. B-244–B-259.

[224] Hillier, Fredrick S., "Chance-Constrained Programming With 0–1 or Bounded Continuous Decision Variables," *Management Science*, Vol. 14 (1967), pp. 34–57.

[225] Kataoka, Schingi, "A Stochastic Programming Model," *Econometrica*, Vol. 31 (1963), pp. 181–196.

[226] Madansky, A., "Inequalities for Stochastic Linear Programming Problems," *Management Science*, Vol. 6 (1960), pp. 197–204.

[227] Madansky, A., "Methods of Solution of Linear Programs Under Uncertainty," *Operations Research*, Vol. 10 (1962), pp. 463–471.

[228] Mangasarian, O. L., "Nonlinear Programming Problems with Stochastic Objective Functions," *Management Science*, Vol. 10 (1964), pp. 353–359.

[229] Mangasarian, O. L. and J. B. Rosen, "Inequalities for Stochastic Nonlinear Programming Problems," *Operations Research*, Vol. 12 (1964), pp. 143–154.

[230] Miller, Bruce L. and Harvey M. Wagner, "Chance Constrained Programming with Joint Constraints," *Operations Research*, Vol. 13 (1965), pp. 930–945.

[231] Näslund, Bertil, "A Model of Capital Budgeting Under Risk," *J. of Business*, Vol. 39 (1966), pp. 257–271.

[232] Näslund, Bertil and Andrew Whinston, "A Model of Multi-Period Investment Under Uncertainty," *Management Science*, Vol. 8 (1962), pp. 184–200.

[233] Radner, Roy, "The Application of Linear Programming to Team Decision Problems," *Management Science*, Vol. 5 (1959), pp. 143–150.

[233a] Sengupta, J. K., "Safety-First Rules Under Chance-Constrained Linear Programming," *Operations Research*, Vol. 17 (1969), pp. 112–132.

[234] Symonds, G. H., "Stochastic Scheduling by the Horizon Method," *Management Science*, Vol. 8 (1962), pp. 138–167.

[235] Symonds, G. H., "Deterministic Solutions for a Class of Chance-Constrained Programming Problems," *Operations Research*, Vol. 15 (1967), pp. 495–512.

[235a] Symonds, G. H., "Chance-Constrained Equivalents of Some Stochastic Programming Problems," *Operations Research*, Vol. 16 (1968) pp. 1152–1160,

[236] Szwarc, W., "The Transportation Problem with Stochastic Demand," *Management Science*, Vol. 11 (1964), pp. 33–50.

[237] Thompson, G. L., "CPM and DCPM Under Risk," *Naval Research Logistics Quarterly*, Vol. 15 (1968), pp. 233–239.

[238] van de Panne, C., "Optimal Strategy Decisions for Dynamic Linear Decision Rules in Feedback Form," *Econometrica*, Vol. 33 (1965), pp. 307–320.

[239] van de Panne, C. and W. Popp, "Minimum-Cost Cattle Feed Under Probabilistic Protein Constraints," *Management Science*, Vol. 9 (1963) pp. 405–430.

[240] van Slyke, Richard and Roger Wets, "Programming Under Uncertainty and Stochastic Optimal Control," *SIAM J. on Control*, Vol. 4 (1966), pp. 179–193.

[241] Veinott, Arthur F., Jr., "Commentary on Part Two," pp. 313–321 in *Mathematical Studies in Management Science*, Arthur F. Veinott, Jr. (ed.), Macmillan Company, 1965.

[242] Walkup, David W. and R. J. B. Wets, "Stochastic Programs with Recourse," *SIAM J. on Applied Mathematics*, Vol. 15 (1967), pp. 1299–1314.

[243] Wets, R. J. B., "Programming Under Uncertainty: The Equivalent Convex Program," *SIAM J. on Applied Mathematics*, Vol. 14 (1966), pp. 89-105.

[244] Wets, R. J. B., "Programming Under Uncertainty: The Solution Set," *SIAM J. on Applied Mathematics*, Vol. 14 (1966), pp. 1143–1151.

[245] Williams, A. C., "A Stochastic Transportation Problem," *Operations Research*, Vol. 11 (1963), pp. 759–770.

[246] Williams, A. C., "On Stochastic Linear Programming," *SIAM J. on Applied Mathematics*, Vol. 13 (1965), pp. 927–940.

[247] Williams, A. C., "Approximation Formulas for Stochastic Linear Programming," *SIAM J. on Applied Mathematics*, Vol. 14 (1966), pp. 668–677.

DIRECTED READING

Section	References
16.2	[206], [207]
16.3	[222], [237]
16.4	[3], [226], [227], [228], [229], [242], [243], [244]
16.5	[211], [212], [213], [221], [230], [231], [232], [239]
16.6	[217], [218], [236], [245], [246], [247]
16.7	[215], [216], [241]
16.8	[238]

•Dynamic Programming•

THEORY AND APPLICATIONS (Chaps. 8, 10, and 17)

BOOKS

[1] Beckmann, Martin J., *Dynamic Programming of Economic Decisions*, Springer-Verlag, Berlin, 1968.

[1a] Bellman, Richard E., *Dynamic Programming*, Princeton University Press, 1957.

[2] Bellman, Richard E. and Stuart E. Dreyfus, *Applied Dynamic Programming*, Princeton University Press, 1962.

[3] Howard, Ronald A., *Dynamic Programming and Markov Processes*, The Massachusetts Institute of Technology Press, 1960.

[4] Jorgenson, D. W., J. J. McCall, and R. Radner, *Optimal Replacement Policy*, Rand McNally, 1967.

[5] Kemeny, John G. and J. Laurie Snell, *Finite Markov Chains*, D. Van Nostrand Company, 1960.

[6] Martin, J. J., *Bayesian Decision Problems and Markov Chains*, John Wiley & Sons, 1967.

[7] Nemhauser, George L., *Introduction to Dynamic Programming*, John Wiley & Sons, 1966.

[8] Sengupta, S. Sankar, *Operations Research in Sellers' Competition*, John Wiley & Sons, 1968.

ARTICLES

[9] Bellman, Richard, I. Glicksberg, and O. Gross, "The Theory of Dynamic Programming as Applied to a Smoothing Problem," *SIAM J. on Applied Mathematics*, Vol. 2 (1954), pp. 82–88.

[10] Bellman, Richard and Robert Kalaba, "On kth Best Policies," *SIAM J. on Applied Mathematics*, Vol. 8 (1960), pp. 582–588.

[11] Breiman, Leo, "Stopping-Rule Problems," pp. 284–319 in *Applied Combinatorial Mathematics*, Edwin F. Beckenbach (ed.), Wiley & Sons, 1964.

[12] Delfausse, J. and S. Saltzman, "Values for Optimum Reject Allowances," *Naval Research Logistics Quarterly*, Vol. 13 (1966), pp. 147–157.

[13] Derman, Cyrus and G. J. Lieberman, "A Markovian Decision Model for a Joint Replacement and Stocking Problem," *Management Science*, Vol. 13 (1967), pp. 609–617.

[14] Derman, Cyrus and Morton Klein, "Some Remarks on Finite Horizon Markovian Decision Models," *Operations Research*, Vol. 13 (1965), pp. 272–278.

[15] Eppen, Gary D., "A Dynamic Analysis of a Class of Deteriorating Systems," *Management Science*, Vol. 12 (1965), pp. 223–240.

[16] Eppen, Gary D. and Eugene F. Fama, "Solutions for Cash-Balance and Simple Dynamic-Portfolio Problems," *J. of Business*, Vol. 41 (1968), pp. 94–112.

[17] Gaver, D. P., Jr., "Models for Appraising Investments Yielding Stochastic Returns," *Management Science*, Vol. 11 (1965), pp. 815–830.

[18] Greenberg, H. J., "The Use of Branching in Dynamic Programming for Parametric Analysis, *Operations Research*, Vol. 15 (1967), pp. 976–977.

[19] Greenberg, H. J., "Dynamic Programming with Linear Uncertainty," *Operations Research*, Vol. 16 (1968), pp. 675–678.

[20] Kao, Richard C., "Note on Program Uncertainty in the Dynamic Programming Model," *Econometrica*, Vol. 30 (1962), pp. 336–342.

[21] Karp, Richard M. and Michael Held, "Finite-State Processes and Dynamic Programming," *SIAM J. on Applied Mathematics*, Vol. 15 (1967), pp. 693–718.

[22] Karush, William, "On a Class of Minimum-Cost Problems," *Management Science*, Vol. 4 (1958), pp. 136–153.

[23] Karush, William, "A General Algorithm for the Optimal Distribution of Effort," *Management Science*, Vol. 9 (1962), pp. 50–72.

[24] Karush, William and A. Vazsonyi, "Mathematical Programming and Employment Scheduling," *Naval Research Logistics Quarterly*, Vol. 4 (1957), pp. 297–320.

[25] Klein, Morton, "Inspection—Maintenance—Replacement Schedules under Markovian Deterioration," *Management Science*, Vol. 9 (1962), pp. 25–32.

[26] Klein, Morton, "Markovian Decision Models for Reject Allowance Problems," *Management Science*, Vol. 12 (1966), pp. 349–358.

[27] Kolesar, Peter, "Minimum Cost Replacement under Markovian Deterioration," *Management Science*, Vol. 12 (1966), pp. 694–706.

[28] Kolesar, Peter, "Randomized Replacement Rules which Maximize the Expected Cycle Length of Equipment Subject to Markovian Deterioration," *Management Science*, Vol. 13 (1967), pp. 867–876.

[29] Levitan, R. E., "The Optimum Reject Allowance Problem," *Management Science*, Vol. 6 (1960), pp. 172–186.

[30] Lieberman, Gerald J., "Lifo vs. Fifo in Inventory Depletion Management," *Management Science*, Vol. 5 (1958), pp. 102–105.

[30a] Lippman, Steven A., "Planning-Horizon Theorems for Knapsack and Renewal Problems with a Denumerable Number of Activities," *Operations Research*, Vol. 17 (1969), pp. 163–174.

[31] MacQueen, J. and R. G. Miller, Jr., "Optimal Persistence Policies," *Operations Research*, Vol. 8 (1960), pp. 362–380.

[32] Marschak, T. A. and J. A. Yahav, "The Sequential Selection of Approaches to a Task," *Management Science*, Vol. 12 (1966), pp. 627–647.

[33] McCall, John J., "The Economics of Information and Optimal Stopping Rules," *J. of Business*, Vol. 38 (1965), pp. 300–317.

[34] McCall, John J., "Maintenance Policies for Stochastically Failing Equipment: A Survey," *Management Science*, Vol. 11 (1965), pp. 493–524.

[35] McGuire, C. B., "Some Team Models of a Sales Organization," *Management Science*, Vol. 7 (1961), pp. 101–130.

[36] McNaughton, Robert, "Scheduling with Deadlines and Loss Functions," *Management Science*, Vol. 6 (1959), pp. 1–12.

[37] Mitten. L. G., "Composition Principles for Synthesis of Optimal Multi-Stage Processes," *Operations Research*, Vol. 12 (1964), pp. 610–619.

[38] Pierskalla, William P., "Optimal Issuing Policies in Inventory Management—I," *Management Science*, Vol. 13 (1967), pp. 395–412.

[39] Pierskalla, William P., "Inventory Depletion Management with Stochastic Field Life Functions," *Management Science*, Vol. 13 (1967), pp. 877–886.

[40] Randolph, Paul, "An Optimal Stopping Rule," *Operations Research*, Vol. 15 (1967), pp. 562–564.

[41] Root, James G., "Scheduling with Deadlines and Loss Functions on k Parallel Machines," *Management Science*, Vol. 11 (1965), pp. 460–475.

[42] Shapiro, Jeremy F. and Harvey M. Wagner, "A Finite Renewal Algorithm for the Knapsack and Turnpike Models," *Operations Research*, Vol. 15 (1967), pp. 319–341.

[43] Taylor, Howard M., "Markovian Sequential Replacement Processes," *Annals Mathematical Statistics*, Vol. 36 (1965), pp. 1677–1694.

[44] Taylor, Howard M., "Optimal Stopping in a Markov Process," *Annals Mathematical Statistics*, Vol. 39 (1968), pp. 1333–1344.

[45] Thompson, Gerald L., "Optimal Maintenance Policy and Sale Date of a Machine," *Management Science,* Vol. 14 (1968), pp. 543–550.

[46] Veinott, Arthur F., Jr. and Harvey M. Wagner, "Optimal Capacity Scheduling —I," *Operations Research*, Vol. 10 (1962), pp. 518–532.

[47] Veinott, Arthur F., Jr. and Harvey M. Wagner, "Optimal Capacity Scheduling —II," *Operations Research*, Vol. 10 (1962), pp. 533–546.

[48] White, Leon S., "Markovian Decision Models for the Evaluation of a Large Class of Continuous Sampling Inspection Plans," *Management Science,* Vol. 36 (1965), pp. 1408–1420.

[49] White, Leon S., "The Analysis of a Simple Class of Multistage Inspection Plans," *Management Science*, Vol. 12 (1966), pp. 685–693.

[50] White, Leon S., "Bayes' Markovian Decision Models for a Multiperiod Reject Allowance Problem," *Operations Research*, Vol. 15 (1967), pp. 857–865.

[50a] White, Leon S., "Shortest Route Models for the Allocation of Inspection Effort on a Production Line," *Management Science*, Vol. 15 (1969), pp. 249–259.

[51] Williams, A. C. and J. I. Nassar, "Financial Measurement of Capital Investments," *Management Science*, Vol. 12 (1966), pp. 851–864.

[51a] Wong, Peter J. and David G. Luenberger, "Reducing the Memory Requirements of Dynamic Programming," *Operations Research*, Vol. 16 (1968) pp. 1115–1125.

[52] Ying, Charles C., "Learning by Doing—An Adaptive Approach to Multiperiod Decisions," *Operations Research*, Vol. 15 (1967), pp. 797–812.

DIRECTED READING

Section	References
8.1	[1], [2]
10.2	[22], [23], [42]
10.5	[42]
10.6	[2], [46], [47]
10.7	[1], [2]
10.9	[2]
17.5	[12], [26], [29], [50]
17.7	[2], [3], [4], [45]

UNBOUNDED HORIZON AND
MARKOVIAN DECISION MODELS (Chaps. 11, 12, and 18)

ARTICLES

[53] Blackwell, D., "Discrete Dynamic Programming," *Annals Mathematical Statistics*, Vol. 33 (1962), pp. 719–726.

[54] Blackwell David, "Discounted Dynamic Programming," *Annals Mathematical Statistics*, Vol. 36 (1965), pp. 226–235.

[55] Brown, B., "On the Iterative Method of Dynamic Programming on a Finite Space Discrete Time Markov Process," *Annals Mathematical Statistics*, Vol. 36 (1965), pp. 1279–1285.

[56] Crabill, Thomas B., "Sufficient Conditions for Positive Recurrence and Recurrence of Specially Structured Markov Chains," *Operations Research*, Vol. 16 (1968), pp. 858–867.

[57] de Cani, John S., "A Dynamic Programming Algorithm for Embedded Markov Chains when the Planning Horizon Is at Infinity," *Management Science*, Vol. 10 (1964), pp. 716–733.

[58] de Ghellinck, Guy T. and Gary D. Eppen, "Linear Programming Solutions for Separable Markovian Decision Problems," *Management Science*, Vol. 13 (1967), pp. 371–394.

[59] Denardo, Eric V., "Contraction Mappings in the Theory Underlying Dynamic Programming," *SIAM Review*, Vol. 9 (1967), pp. 165–177.

[60] Denardo, Eric V., "Separable Markovian Decision Problems," *Management Science*, Vol. 14 (1968), pp. 451–462.

[61] Denardo, Eric V., "Computing a Bias-Optimal Policy in a Discrete-Time Markov Decision Problem," *Operations Research*, Vol. 17 (1969).

[62] Denardo, Eric V. and Bennett Fox, "Multichain Markov Renewal Programs," *SIAM J. on Applied Mathematics*, Vol. 16 (1968), pp. 468–487.

[63] Denardo, Eric V. and B. L. Miller, "An Optimality Condition for Discrete Dynamic Programming with no Discounting," *Annals Mathematical Statistics*, Vol. 39 (1968), pp. 1220–1227.

[64] Derman, Cyrus, "On Sequential Decisions and Markov Chains," *Management Science*, Vol. 9 (1962), pp. 16–24.

[65] Derman, Cyrus, "Optimal Replacement and Maintenance under Markovian Deterioration with Probability Bounds on Failure," *Management Science*, Vol. 9 (1963), pp. 478–481.

[66] Derman, Cyrus, "Markovian Sequential Control Processes—Denumerable State Space," *Journal of Mathematical Analysis and Applications*, Vol. 10 (1965), pp. 295–302.

[67] Derman, Cyrus, "Denumerable State Markovian Decision Processes—Average Cost Criterion," *Annals Mathematical Statistics*, Vol. 37 (1966), pp. 1545–1554.

[68] Derman, C. and R. E. Strauch, "A Note on Memoryless Rules for Controlling Sequential Decision Processes," *Annals Mathematical Statistics*, Vol. 37 (1966), pp. 276–279.

[69] Derman, Cyrus and Arthur F. Veinott, Jr., "A Solution to a Countable System of Equations Arising in Markovian Decision Processes," *Annals Mathematical Statistics*, Vol. 38 (1967), pp. 582–585.

[70] Fisher, L., "On Recurrent Denumerable Decision Processes," *Annals Mathematical Statistics*, Vol. 39 (1968), pp. 424–432.

[71] Fisher, Lloyd and Sheldon M. Ross, "An Example in Denumerable Decision Processes," *Annals Mathematical Statistics*, Vol. 39 (1968), pp. 674–675.

[72] Fox, Bennett "Markov Renewal Programming by Linear Fractional Programming," *SIAM J. on Applied Mathematics*, Vol. 14 (1966), pp. 1418–1432.

[73] Hoffman, A. J. and R. M. Karp, "On Nonterminating Stochastic Games," *Management Science*, Vol. 12 (1966), pp. 359–370.

[74] Jewell, William S., "Markov-Renewal Programming. I: Formulation, Finite Return Models," *Operations Research*, Vol. 11 (1963), pp. 938–948.

[75] Jewell, William S., "Markov-Renewal Programming. II: Infinite Return Models, Example," *Operations Research*, Vol. 11 (1963), pp. 949–971.

[76] MacQueen, J., "A Test for Suboptimal Actions in Markovian Decision Problems," *Operations Research*, Vol. 15 (1967), pp. 559–561.

[77] Manne, Alan S., "Linear Programming and Sequential Decisions," *Management Science*, Vol. 6 (1960), pp. 259–267.

[78] Miller, B. L, "Finite State Continuous Time Markov Decision Processes with a Finite Planning Horizon," *SIAM J. on Control*, Vol. 6 (1968), pp. 266–280.

[79] Ross, Sheldon, "Non-discounted Denumerable Markovian Decision Models," *Annals Mathematical Statistics*, Vol. 39 (1968), pp. 412–423.

[80] Shapiro, Jeremy F., "Turnpike Planning Horizons for a Markovian Decision Model," *Management Science*, Vol. 14 (1968), pp. 292–300.

[80a] Shapiro, Jeremy F., "Shortest Route Methods for Finite State Space Deterministic Dynamic Programming Problems," *SIAM J. Appl. Math.*, Vol. 16 (1968), pp. 1232–1250.

[81] Smallwood, Richard D., "Optimum Policy Regions for Markov Processes with Discounting," *Operations Research*, Vol. 14 (1966), pp. 658–669.

[82] Strauch, Ralph, "Negative Dynamic Programming," *Annals Mathematical Statistics*, Vol. 37 (1966), pp. 871–890.

[83] Veinott, Arthur F., Jr. "On Finding Optimal Policies in Discrete Dynamic Programming With no Discounting," *Annals Mathematical Statistics*, Vol. 37 (1966), pp. 1284–1294.

[84] Wagner, Harvey M., "On the Optimality of Pure Strategies," *Management Science*, Vol. 6 (1960), pp. 268–269.

[85] Wolfe, Philip and G. B. Dantzig, "Linear Programming in a Markov Chain," *Operations Research*, Vol. 10 (1962), pp. 702–710.

DIRECTED READING

Section	References
11.4	[42]
11.5	[78]
11.6	[3]
11.7	[3], [53], [54]
12.1	[53]
12.2	[3], [53], [54], [80a]
12.3	[3], [53]
12.6	[62], [75]
18.2	[14]
18.3	[3], [53], [54], [57], [59], [64], [66], [68], [74], [75] [80], [81]
18.4	[3], [53], [55], [57], [59], [62], [63], [64], [66], [67], [68], [69], [70], [71], [74], [75], [79], [80], [82], [83]
18.5	[61], [62], [72], [77], [84], [85]

•Inventory and Production Theory•

INTRODUCTORY SURVEYS AND
RESEARCH MONOGRAPHS (Chaps. 9, 19, and Appendix II)

BOOKS

[1] Arrow, Kenneth J., Samuel Karlin, and Herbert E. Scarf, (eds.), *Studies in the Mathematical Theory of Inventory and Production*, Stanford University Press, 1958.

[2] Arrow, Kenneth J., Samuel Karlin, and Herbert E. Scarf (eds.), *Studies in Applied Probability and Management Science*, Stanford University Press, 1962.

[3] Buchan, Joseph and Ernest Koenigsberg, *Scientific Inventory Management*, Prentice-Hall, 1963.

[4] Buffa, Elwood S., *Modern Production Management*, John Wiley & Sons, 1965.

[5] Buffa, Elwood S., *Production-Inventory Systems: Planning and Control*, Irwin, 1968.

[6] Elmaghraby, Salah E., *The Design of Production Systems*, Reinhold, 1966.

[7] Hadley, G. and T. M. Whitin, *Analysis of Inventory Systems*, Prentice-Hall, 1963.

[8] Holt, C. C., F. Modigliani, J. F. Muth, and H. A. Simon, *Planning Production, Inventories, and Work Force* Prentice-Hall, 1960.

[9] Naddor, Eliezer, *Inventory Systems*, John Wiley & Sons, 1966.

[10] Scarf, Herbert E., Dorothy Gilford, and Maynard W. Shelly (eds.), *Multistage Inventory Models and Techniques*, Stanford University Press, 1963.

[11] Starr, Martin K., *Production Management Systems and Synthesis*, Prentice-Hall, 1964.

[12] Starr, Martin K. and David W. Miller, *Inventory Control: Theory and Practice*, Prentice-Hall, 1962.

[13] Wagner, Harvey M., *Statistical Management of Inventory Systems*, John Wiley & Sons, 1962.

[14] Whitin, Thomson M., *The Theory of Inventory Management*, Second Edition, Princeton University Press, 1957.

DETERMINISTIC MODELS (Chap. 9)

ARTICLES

[15] Charnes, A., W. W. Cooper, and B. Mellon, "A Model for Optimizing Production by Reference to Cost Surrogates," *Econometrica*, Vol. 23 (1955), pp. 307–323.

[16] Eppen, G. D. and F. J. Gould, "A Lagrangian Application to Production Models," *Operations Research*, Vol. 16 (1968), pp. 819–829.

[16a] Eppen, Gary D., F. J. Gould, and B. Peter Pashigian, "Extensions of the Planning Horizon Theorem in the Dynamic Lot Size Model," *Management Science*, Vol. 15 (1969), pp. 268–277.

[17] Fabrycky, W. J. and J. Banks, "A Hierarchy of Deterministic Procurement Inventory Systems," *Operations Research*, Vol. 14 (1966), pp. 888–901.

[18] Hoffman, A. J. and W. Jacobs, "Smooth Patterns of Production," *Management Science*, Vol. 1 (1954), pp. 86–91.

[19] Hu, T. C. and W. Prager, "Network Analysis of Production Smoothing," *Naval Research Logistics Quarterly*, Vol. 6 (1959), pp. 17–23.

[20] Hwang, C. L., L. T. Fan, and L. E. Erickson, "Optimum Production Planning by the Maximum Principle," *Management Science*, Vol. 13 (1967), pp. 751–755.

[21] Johnson, S. M., "Sequential Production Planning over Time at Minimum Cost," *Management Science*, Vol. 3 (1957), pp. 435–437.

[22] Klein, Morton, "Some Production Planning Problems," *Naval Research Logistics Quarterly, Vol.* 4 (1957), pp. 269–286.

[23] Klein, Morton, "On Production Smoothing," *Management Science*, Vol. 7 (1961), pp. 286–293.

[24] Kortanek, K. O., D. Sodaro, and A. L. Soyster, "Multi-Product Production Scheduling via Extreme Point Properties of Linear Programming," *Naval Research Logistics Quarterly*, Vol. 15 (1968), pp. 287–300.

[25] Lippman, Steven A., Alan J. Rolfe, Harvey M. Wagner, and John S. C. Yuan, "Optimal Production Scheduling and Employment Smoothing with Deterministic Demands," *Management Science*, Vol. 14 (1967), pp. 127–158.

[26] Lippman, Steven A., Alan J. Rolfe, Harvey M. Wagner, and John S. C. Yuan, "Algorithms for Optimal Production Scheduling and Employment Smoothing," *Operations Research*, Vol. 15 (1967), pp. 1011–1029.

[27] Manne, Alan S., "Programming of Economic Lot Sizes," *Management Science*, Vol. 4 (1958), pp. 115–135.

[28] Manne, Alan S. and Arthur F. Veinott, Jr., "Optimal Plant Size with Arbitrary Increasing Time Paths of Demand," pp. 178–192 in *Investments for Capacity Expansion, Size, Location, and Time-Phasing*, Alan S. Manne (ed.), Massachusetts Institute of Technology Press, 1967.

[29] Nemhauser, G. L. and H. L. W. Nuttle, "A Quantitative Approach to Employment Planning," *Management Science*, Vol. 11 (1965), pp. B-155–B-165.

[30] Silver, Edward A., "A Tutorial on Production Smoothing and Work Force Balancing," *Operations Research*, Vol. 15 (1967), pp. 985–1010.

[31] Sobel, M. J., "Smoothing Start-Up and Shut-Down Costs in Sequential Production," *Operations Research*, Vol. 17 (1969), pp. 133–144.

[32] Veinott, Arthur F., Jr., "Production Planning with Convex Costs: a Parametric Study," *Management Science*, Vol. 10 (1964), pp. 441–460.

[33] Wagner, Harvey M., "A Postscript to 'Dynamic Problems in the Theory of the Firm,'" *Naval Research Logistics Quarterly*, Vol. 7 (1960), pp. 7–12.

[34] Wagner, Harvey, M. and Thomson M. Whitin, "Dynamic Problems in the Theory of the Firm," *Naval Research Logistics Quarterly*, Vol. 5 (1958), pp. 53–74.

[35] Wagner, Harvey M. and Thomson M. Whitin, "Dynamic Version of the Economic Lot Size Model," *Management Science*, Vol. 5 (1958), pp. 89–96.

[36] Zabel, Edward, "Some Generalizations of an Inventory Planning Horizon Theorem," *Management Science*, Vol. 10 (1964), pp. 465–471.

[37] Zangwill, Willard I., "A Deterministic Multi-Period Production Scheduling Model with Backlogging," *Management Science*, Vol. 13 (1966), pp. 105–119.

[38] Zangwill, Willard I., "A Deterministic Multiproduct, Multifacility Production and Inventory Model," *Operations Research*, Vol. 14 (1966), pp. 486–507.

[39] Zangwill, Willard I., "Production Smoothing of Economic Lot Sizes with Non-Decreasing Requirements," *Management Science*, Vol. 13 (1966), pp. 191–209.

DIRECTED READING

Section	References
9.3	[15], [21], [22], [32], [33], [34]
9.4	[15], [32], [16]
9.6	[27], [28], [33], [34], [35], [37], [38]
9.7	[16a], [33], [35], [36]
9.8	[18], [19], [23], [25], [26], [30], [31], [39]

PROBABILISTIC MODELS (Chap. 19 and Appendix II)

ARTICLES

[40] Arrow, Kenneth J., T. Harris, and J. Marschak, "Optimal Inventory Policy," *Econometrica*, Vol. 19, pp. 250–272.

[41] Beckmann, Martin J., "An Inventory Model for Arbitrary Interval and Quantity Distributions of Demand," *Management Science*, Vol. 8 (1961), pp. 35–57.

[42] Beckmann, Martin J., "Production Smoothing and Inventory Control," *Operations Research*, Vol. 9 (1961), pp. 456–467.

[43] Beebe, J. H., C. S. Beightler, and J. P. Stark, "Stochastic Optimization of Production Planning," *Operations Research*, Vol. 16 (1968), pp. 799–818.

[44] Beesack, Paul R., "A Finite Horizon Dynamic Inventory Model with a Stockout Constraint," *Management Science*, Vol. 13 (1967), pp. 618–630.

[45] Bellman, R., I Glicksberg, and O. Gross, "On the Optimal Inventory Equation," *Management Science*, Vol. 2, (1955), pp. 83–104.

[46] Bessler, S. A. and A. F. Veinott, Jr., "Optimal Policy for a Dynamic Multi-Echelon Inventory Model," *Naval Research Logistics Quarterly*, Vol. 13 (1966), pp. 355–389.

[47] Boylan, Edward S., "Existence and Uniqueness Theorems for the Optimal Inventory Equation," *SIAM J. on Applied Mathematics*, Vol. 14 (1966), pp. 961–969.

[48] Boylan, Edward S., "Multiple (s, S) Policies and the n-Period Inventory Problem," *Management Science*, Vol. 14 (1967), pp. 196–204.

[49] Chang, Yu Sang and Powell Niland, "A Model for Measuring Stock Depletion Costs," *Operations Research*, Vol. 15 (1967), pp. 427–447.

[50] Clark, A. J. and H. E. Scarf, "Optimal Policies for a Multi-Echelon Inventory Problem," *Management Science*, Vol. 6 (1960), pp. 475–490.

[51] d'Epenoux, F., "A Probabilistic Production and Inventory Problem," *Management Science*, Vol. 10 (1963), pp. 98–108.

[52] Dvoretzky, A., J. Kiefer, and J. Wolfowitz, "The Inventory Problem. I: Case of Known Distributions of Demand," *Econometrica*, Vol. 20 (1952), pp. 450–466.

[53] Evans, Richard V., "Inventory Control of a Multiproduct System with a Limited Production Resource," *Naval Research Logistics Quarterly*, Vol. 14 (1967), pp. 173–184.

[54] Falkner, Charles H., "Jointly Optimal Inventory and Maintenance Policies for Stochastically Failing Equipment," *Operations Research*, Vol. 16 (1968), pp. 587–601.

[55] Fenske, R. W., "Non-Stocking Criterion," *Management Science*, Vol. 14 (1968), pp. B-705–B-714.

[56] Fromovitz, Stan, "A Class of One-Period Inventory Models," *Operations Research*, Vol. 13 (1965), pp. 779–799.

[57] Fukuda, Yoichiro, "Optimal Disposal Policies," *Naval Research Logistics Quarterly*, Vol. 8 (1961), pp. 221–227.

[58] Gaver, D. P., "Operating Characteristics of a Simple Production-Inventory Control Model," *Operations Research*, Vol. 9 (1961), pp. 635–649.

[59] Geisler, Murray A., "A Test of a Statistical Method for Computing Selected Inventory Model Characteristics by Simulation," *Management Science*, Vol. 10 (1964), pp. 709–715.

[60] Geisler, Murray A., "The Sizes of Simulation Samples Required to Compute Certain Inventory Characteristics with Stated Precision and Confidence," *Management Science*, Vol. 10 (1964), pp. 261–286.

[61] Greenberg, Harold, "Stock Level Distributions for (s, S) Inventory Problems," *Naval Research Logistics Quarterly*, Vol. 11 (1964), pp. 343–349.

[62] Greenberg, Harold, "Time Dependent Solutions for the (s, S) Inventory Problem," *Operations Research*, Vol. 12 (1964), pp. 725–735.

[63] Hurter, A, P. and F. C. Kaminsky, "An Application of Regenerative Stochastic Processes to a Problem in Inventory Control," *Operations Research*, Vol. 15 (1967), pp. 467–472.

[64] Iglehart, Donald L., "Optimality of (s, S) Policies in the Infinite Horizon Dynamic Inventory Problem," *Management Science*, Vol. 9 (1963), pp. 259–267.

[65] Iglehart, Donald L., "The Dynamic Inventory Problem with Unknown Demand Distribution," *Management Science*, Vol. 10 (1964), pp. 429–440.

[66] Iglehart, Donald L. and Samuel Karlin, "Optimal Policy for Dynamic Inventory Process with Nonstationary Stochastic Demands," pp. 127–147 in *Studies in Applied Probability and Management Science*, K. J. Arrow, S. Karlin, and H. E. Scarf (eds.), Stanford University Press, 1962.

[66a] Ignall, Edward, "Optimal Continuous Review Policies for Two Product Inventory Systems with Joint Setup Costs," *Management Science*, Vol. 15 (1969), pp. 278–283.

[66b] Ignall, Edward and A. F. Veinott, Jr., "Optimality of Myopic Inventory Policies Policies for Several Substitute Products," *Management Science*, Vol. 15 (1969), pp. 284–304.

[67] Johnson, Ellis L., "Optimality and Computation of (σ, S) Policies in the Multi-Item Infinite Horizon Inventory Problem," *Management Science*, Vol. 13 (1967), pp. 475–491.

[68] Johnson, Ellis L., "On (s, S) Policies," *Management Science*, Vol. 15 (1968), pp. 80–101.

[69] Karlin, Samuel, "Dynamic Inventory Policy with Varying Stochastic Demands," *Management Science*, Vol. 6 (1960), pp. 231–258.

[70] Karlin, Samuel, "Optimal Policy for Dynamic Inventory Process to Stochastic Demands Subject to Seasonal Variations," *SIAM J. on Applied Mathematics*, Vol. 8 (1960), pp. 611–629.

[71] Kriebel, Charles H., "Team Decision Models of an Inventory Supply Organization," *Naval Research Logistics Quarterly*, Vol. 12 (1965), pp. 139–154.

[72] Kunreuther, Howard, "Scheduling Short-Run Changes in Production to Minimize Long-Run Expected Costs," *Management Science*, Vol. 12 (1966), pp. 541–554.

[73] Love, Robert F., "A Two-Station Stochastic Inventory Model with Exact Methods of Computing Optimal Policies," *Naval Research Logistics Quarterly*, Vol. 14 (1967), pp. 185–217.

[74] Maxwell, William L., "The Scheduling of Economic Lot Sizes," *Naval Research Logistics Quarterly*, Vol. 11 (1964), pp. 89–124.

[75] Modigliani, F. and F. E. Hohn, "Production Planning over Time and the Nature of Expectation and Planning Horizon," *Econometrica*, Vol. 23 (1955), pp. 46–66.

[76] Murray, G. R., Jr., and E. A. Silver, "A Bayesian Analysis of the Style Goods Inventory Problem," *Management Science*, Vol. 12 (1966), pp. 785–797.

[77] Neuts, Marcel F., "An Inventory Model with an Optional Time Lag," *SIAM J. on Applied Mathematics*, Vol. 12 (1964), pp. 179–185.

[78] Resh, M. and P. Naor, "An Inventory Problem with Discrete Time Review and Replenishment by Batches of Fixed Size," *Management Science*, Vol. 10 (1963), pp. 109–118.

[79] Roberts, Donald M., "Approximations to Optimal Policies in a Dynamic Inventory Model," pp. 207–229 in *Studies in Applied Probability and Management Science*, K. J. Arrow, S. Karlin, and H. E. Scarf (eds.), Stanford University Press, 1962.

[80] Scarf, Herbert E., "The Optimality of (S, s) Policies in the Dynamic Inventory Problem," pp. 196–202 in *Mathematical Methods in the Social Sciences*, K. J. Arrow, S. Karlin, and P. Suppes (eds.), Stanford University Press, 1960.

[81] Schrady, D. A., "A Deterministic Inventory Model for Reparable Items," *Naval Research Logistics Quarterly*, Vol. 14 (1967), pp. 391–398.

[82] Veinott, Arthur F., Jr., "Optimal Policy for a Multi-Product, Dynamic, Non-stationary Inventory Problem," *Management Science*, Vol. 12 (1965), pp. 206–222.

[83] Veinott, Arthur F., Jr., "Optimal Policy in a Dynamic, Single Product, Non-Stationary Inventory Model with Several Demand Classes," *Operations Research*, Vol. 13 (1965), pp. 761–778.

[84] Veinott, Arthur F., Jr., "The Optimal Inventory Policy for Batch Ordering," *Operations Research*, Vol. 13 (1965), pp. 424–432.

[85] Veinott, Arthur F., Jr., "The Status of Mathematical Inventory Theory," *Management Science*, Vol. 12 (1966), pp. 745–777.

[86] Veinott, Arthur F., Jr., "On the Optimality of (s, S) Inventory Policies: New Conditions and a New Proof," *SIAM J. on Applied Mathematics*, Vol. 14 (1966), pp. 1067–1083.

[87] Veinott, Arthur F., Jr. and Harvey M. Wagner, "Computing Optimal (s, S) Inventory Policies," *Management Science*, Vol. 11 (1965), pp. 525–552.

[88] Wagner, Harvey M., Michael O'Hagan, and Bertil Lundh, "An Empirical Study of Exactly and Approximately Optimal Inventory Policies," *Management Science*, Vol. 11 (1965), pp. 690–723.

[89] Wright, G. P., "Optimal Policies for a Multi-Product Inventory System with Negotiable Lead Times," *Naval Research Logistics Quarterly*, Vol. 15 (1968), pp. 375–401.

[90] Zabel, Edward, "A Note on the Optimality of (S, s) Policies in Inventory Theory," *Management Science*, Vol. 9 (1962), pp. 123–125.

Directed Reading

II.3   [45], [65], [69], [70], [82], [83]
II.4   [1], [40], [45], [47], [48], [52], [80], [86], [90]
II.5   [1], [45], [66], [69], [70], [83], [84]
II.6   [40], [47], [64], [67], [68], [79], [86], [88]
II.7   [51], [61], [62], [68]

•Waiting Line Theory•

INTRODUCTORY SURVEYS AND RESEARCH MONOGRAPHS (Chap. 20 and Appendix III)

BOOKS

[1] Benes, Václav E., *General Stochastic Processes in the Theory of Queues*, Addison-Wesley, 1963.

[2] Cox, D. R. and W. L. Smith, *Queues*, John Wiley & Sons, 1961.

[2a] Lee, Alec M., *Applied Queueing Theory*, St. Martin's Press, 1966.

[3] Morse, Philip M., *Queues, Inventories and Maintenance: The Analysis of Operations Systems with Variable Demand and Supply*, John Wiley & Sons, 1958.

[4] Prabhu, N. U., *Queues and Inventories: A Study of Their Basic Stochastic Processes*, John Wiley & Sons, 1965.

[5] Riordan, John, *Stochastic Service Systems*, John Wiley and Sons, 1962.

[6] Saaty, Thomas L., *Elements of Queueing Theory with Applications*, McGraw-Hill, 1961.

[7] Syski, R., *Introduction to Congestion Theory in Telephone Systems*, Oliver and Boyd, 1960.

[8] Takács, Lajos, *Introduction to the Theory of Queues*, Oxford University Press, 1962.

SPECIAL MODELS AND THEORY (Chap. 20 and Appendix III)

ARTICLES

[9] Ancker, C. J., Jr. and A. V. Gafarian, "Some Queuing Problems with Balking and Reneging—I," *Operations Research*, Vol. 11 (1963), pp. 88–100.

[10] Ancker, C. J., Jr. and A. V. Gafarian, "Some Queuing Problems with Balking and Reneging—II," *Operations Research*, Vol. 11 (1963), pp. 928–937.

[11] Avi-Itzhak, B., "Preemptive Repeat Priority Queues as a Special Case of the Multipurpose Server Problem—I," *Operations Research*, Vol. 11 (1963), pp. 597–609.

[12] Avi-Itzhak, B., "Preemptive Repeat Priority Queues as a Special Case of the Multipurpose Server Problem—II," *Operations Research*, Vol. 11 (1963), pp. 610–619.

[13] Avi-Itzhak, B., W. L. Maxwell, and L. W. Miller, "Queuing with Alternating Priorities," *Operations Research*, Vol. 13 (1965), pp. 306–318.

[14] Cinlar, Erhan and Ralph L. Disney, "Stream of Overflows from a Finite Queue," *Operations Research*, Vol. 15 (1967), pp. 131–134.

[15] Cobham, Alan, "Priority Assignment in Waiting Line Problems," *Operations Research*, Vol. 2 (1954), pp. 70–76.

[16] Evans, Richard V., "Queuing when Jobs Require Several Services which Need Not be Sequenced," *Management Science*, Vol. 10 (1964), pp. 298–315.

[17] Evans, Richard V., "Capacity of Queuing Networks," *Operations Research*, Vol. 15 (1967), pp. 530–536.

[18] Gaver, D. P., Jr., "Observing Stochastic Processes and Approximate Transform Inversion," *Operations Research*, Vol. 14 (1966), pp. 444–459.

[19] Gordon, W. J. and G. F. Newell, "Closed Queuing Systems with Exponential Servers," *Operations Research*, Vol. 15 (1967), pp. 254–265.

[20] Gordon, William J. and Gordon F. Newell, "Cyclic Queuing Systems with Restricted Length Queues," *Operations Research*, Vol. 15 (1967), pp. 266–277.

[21] Harris, Terrell J., "Duality of Finite Markovian Queues," *Operations Research*, Vol. 15 (1967), pp. 575–576.

[22] Hillier, Frederick S., "Economic Models for Industrial Waiting Line Problems," *Management Science*, Vol. 10 (1963), pp. 119–130.

[23] Jackson, James R., "Multiple Servers with Limited Waiting Space," *Naval Research Logistics Quarterly*, Vol. 5 (1958), pp. 315–321.

[24] Jackson, James R., "Queues with Dynamic Priority Discipline," *Management Science*, Vol. 8 (1961), pp. 18–34.

[25] Jackson, James R., "Jobshop-Like Queueing Systems," *Management Science*, Vol. 10 (1963), pp. 131–142.

[26] Jewell, William S., "A Simple Proof of: $L = \lambda W$," *Operations Research*, Vol. 15 (1967), pp. 1109–1116.

[27] Kabak, Irwin W., "Blocking and Delays in $M^{(n)}/M/c$ Bulk Queuing Systems," *Operations Research*, Vol. 16 (1968), pp. 830–840.

[27a] Keilson, Julian, "A Note on the Waiting-Time Distribution for the $M/G/1$ Queue with Last-Come-First-Served Discipline," *Operations Research*, Vol. 16 (1968), pp. 1230–1232.

[27b] Kendall, D. G., "Stochastic Processes Occurring in the Theory of Queues and Their Analysis by the Method of Imbedded Markov Chains," *Annals of Mathematical Statistics*, Vol. 24 (1953), pp. 338–354.

[28] Kleinrock, Leonard, "Optimum Bribing for Queue Position," *Operations Research*, Vol. 15 (1967), pp. 304–318.

[29] Kleinrock, Leonard and Roy P. Finkelstein, "Time Dependent Priority Queues," *Operations Research*, Vol. 15 (1967), pp. 104–116.

[30] Little, John D. C., "A Proof for the Queuing Formula: $L = \lambda W$," *Operations Research*, Vol. 9 (1961), pp. 383–387.

[31] Mitrany, I. L. and B. Avi-Itzhak, "A Many-Server Queue with Service Interruptions," *Operations Research*, Vol. 16 (1968), pp. 628–638.

[32] Moder, Joseph J. and Cecil R. Phillips, Jr., "Queuing with Fixed and Variable Channels," *Operations Research*, Vol. 10 (1962), pp. 218–231.

[33] Neuts, M. F., "The Busy Period of A Queue with Batch Service," *Operations Research*, Vol. 13 (1965), pp. 815–819.

[34] Neuts, M. F., "An Alternative Proof of a Theorem of Takács on the $GI/M/1$ Queue," *Operations Research*, Vol. 14 (1966), pp. 313–316.

[35] Oliver, Robert M., "An Alternate Derivation of the Pollaczek-Khintchine Formula," *Operations Research*, Vol. 12 (1964), pp. 158–159.

[36] Prabhu, N. U., "Transient Behavior of a Tandem Queue," *Management Science*, Vol. 13 (1967), pp. 631–639.

[37] Restrepo, Rodrigo A., "A Queue with Simultaneous Arrivals and Erlang Service Distribution," *Operations Research*, Vol. 13 (1965), pp. 375–381.

[38] Saunders, L. R., "Probability Functions for Waiting Times in Single-Channel Queues, with Emphasis on Simple Approximations," *Operations Research*, Vol. 9 (1961), pp. 351–362.

[39] Schrage, Linus E., "The Queue *M/G/*1 with Feedback to Lower Priority Queues," *Management Science*, Vol. 13 (1967), pp. 466–474.

[40] Schrage, Linus, E. "A Proof of the Optimality of the Shortest Remaining Processing Time Discipline," *Operations Research*, Vol. 16 (1968), pp. 687–690.

[41] Schrage, Linus E. and Louis W. Miller, "The Queue *M/G/*1 with the Shortest Remaining Processing Time Discipline," *Operations Research*, Vol. 14 (1966), pp. 670–684.

[42] Sobel, Matthew J., "Optimal Average Cost Policy for a Queue with Start-Up and Shut-Down Costs," *Operations Research*, Vol. 17 (1969), pp. 145–162.

[43] Wolff, Ronald W., "Problems of Statistical Inference for Birth and Death Queuing Models," *Operations Research*, Vol. 13 (1965), pp. 343–357.

[44] Young, John P., "Administrative Control of Multiple-Channel Queuing Systems with Parallel Input Streams," *Operations Research*, Vol. 14 (1966), pp. 145–156.

DIRECTED READING

Section	References
20.2	[7]
20.3	[8]
20.4	[7]
20.5	[2], [6], [8], [11], [12], [13], [15], [24], [26], [29] [30], [31], [35]
20.6	[2], [3], [5]
20.7	[2], [3], [6]
20.8	[9], [10]
III.1	[3]
III.2	[2], [4], [7], [27b]
III.3	[2], [4], [7], [27b] [34]
III.4	[1], [7], [8]
III.5	[1], [2], [8]

•Computer Simulation•

INTRODUCTORY SURVEYS AND APPLICATIONS (Chap. 21)

BOOKS

[1] Bonini, Charles P., *Simulation of Information and Decision Systems in the Firm*, Prentice-Hall, 1963.

[2] Conway, Richard W., William L. Maxwell, and Louis W. Miller, *Theory of Scheduling*, Addison-Wesley, 1967.

[3] Cyert, Richard M. and James G. March, *A Behavioral Theory of the Firm*, Prentice-Hall, 1963.

[4] Greenlaw, Paul S., Lowell W. Herron, and Richard H. Rawdon, *Business Simulation in Industrial and University Education*, Prentice-Hall, 1962.

[5] Hammersley, J. M. and D. C. Handscomb, *Monte Carlo Methods*, John Wiley & Sons, 1964.

[6] Kiviat, P. J., R. Villanueva, and H. M. Markowitz, *The Simscript II Programming Language*, Prentice-Hall, 1969.

[7] Meier, Robert C., William T. Newell, and Harold L. Pazer, *Simulation in Business and Economics*, Prentice-Hall, 1969.

[8] Mize, Joe H. and J. Grady Cox, *Essentials of Simulation*, Prentice Hall, 1968.

[9] Naylor, Thomas H., Joseph L. Balintfy, Donald S. Burdick, and Kong Chu, *Computer Simulation Techniques*, John Wiley & Sons, 1966.

[10] RAND Corporation, *A Million Random Digits with 100,000 Normal Deviates,*" The Free Press, 1955.

THEORY AND APPLICATIONS (Chap. 21)

ARTICLES

[11] Blake, K. and G. Gordon, "System Simulation with Digital Computers," *IBM Systems Journal*, Vol. 3 (1964), pp. 14–20.

[12] Burr, Irving, W., "A Useful Approximation to the Normal Distribution Function, with Application to Simulation," *Technometrics*, Vol. 9 (1967), pp. 647–651.

[13] Clark, Charles E., "Importance Sampling of Monte Carlo Analyses," *Operations Research*, Vol. 9 (1961), pp. 502–620.

[14] Cohen, Kalman J. and Edwin J. Elton, "Inter-Temporal Portfolio Analysis Based on Simulation of Joint Returns," *Management Science*, Vol. 14 (1967), pp. 5–18.

[15] Efron, R. and G. Gordon, "A General Purpose Digital Simulator and Examples of its Application: Part I—Description of the Simulator," *IBM Systems Journal*, Vol. 3 (1944), pp. 22–34.

[16] Ehrenfeld, S. and S. Ben-Tuvia, "The Efficiency of Statistical Simulation Procedures," *Technometrics*, Vol. 4 (1962), pp. 257–275.

[17] Fetter, R. B. and J. D. Thompson, "The Simulation of Hospital Systems," *Operations Research*, Vol. 13 (1965), pp. 689–711.

[18] Fishman, George S., "Problems in the Statistical Analysis of Simulation Experiments: The Comparison of Means and the Length of Sample Records," *Communications of the ACM*, Vol. 10 (1967), pp. 94–99.

[19] Fishman, George S., "The Allocation of Computer Time in Comparing Simulation Experiments," *Operations Research*, Vol. 16 (1968), pp. 280–295.

[20] Fishman, George S. and Philip J. Kiviat, "The Analysis of Simulation-Generated Time Series," *Management Science*, Vol. 13 (1967), pp. 525–557.

[21] Gafarian, A. V. and C. J. Ancker, "Mean Value Estimation from Digital Computer Simulation," *Operations Research*, Vol. 14 (1966), pp. 25–44.

[22] Ghare, P. M., "Multichannel Queuing System with Bulk Service," *Operations Research*, Vol. 16 (1968), pp. 189–192.

[23] Gordon, G., "A General Purpose Systems Simulator," *IBM Systems Journal*, (1962), pp. 18–32.

[24] Greenberger, Martin, "Method in Randomness," *Communications of the ACM*, Vol. 8 (1965), pp. 177–179.

[25] Hertz, David B., "Risk Analysis in Capital Investment," *Harvard Business Review*, Vol. 42 (1964), pp. 95–106.

[26] Hertz, David B., "Investment Policies that Pay Off," *Harvard Business Review*, Vol. 46 (1968), pp. 96–108.

[27] Hull, R. E. and A. R. Dobell, "Random Number Generators," *SIAM Review*, Vol. 4 (1962), pp. 230–254.

[28] Kabak, Irwin W., "Stopping Rules for Queuing Simulations," *Operations Research*, Vol. 16 (1968), pp. 431–437.

[29] Krasnow, Howard S. and Reino A. Merikallio, "The Past, Present, and Future of General Simulation Languages," *Management Science*, Vol. 11 (1964), pp. 236–267.

[30] MacLaren, M. Donald and George Marsaglia, "Uniform Random Number Generators," *Journal of the Association for Computing Machinery*, Vol. 12 (1965), pp. 83–89.

[31] Markowitz, H. M., "Simulating with Simscript," *Management Science*, Vol. 12 (1966), pp. B-396–B-405.

[32] Maxwell, W. L. and M. Mehra, "Multiple-Factor Rules for Sequencing with Assembly Constraints," *Naval Research Logistics Quarterly*, Vol. 15 (1968), pp. 241–254.

[33] McKenney, James L., "Simultaneous Processing of Jobs on an Electronic Computer," *Management Science*, Vol. 8 (1962), pp. 344–354.

[34] Nelson, Rosser T., "Queuing Network Experiments with Varying Arrival and Service Processes," *Naval Research Logistics Quarterly*, Vol. 13 (1966), pp. 321–347.

[35] Nelson, Rosser T, "Labor and Machine Limited Production Systems," *Management Science*, Vol. 13 (1967), pp. 648–671.

[36] Nelson, Rosser T., "Dual-Resource Constrained Series Service Systems," *Operations Research*, Vol. 16 (1968), pp. 324–341.

[37] Scheuer, Ernest and David S. Stoller, "On the Generation of Normal Random Vectors," *Technometrics*, Vol. 4 (1962), pp. 278–281.

[38] Shubik, Martin, "Bibliography on Simulation, Gaming Artificial Intelligence and Allied Topics," *Journal of the American Statistical Association*, Vol. 55 (1960), pp. 736–751.

[39] Taft, Martin Israel and Arnold Reisman, "Toward Better Curricula Through Computer Selected Sequencing of Subject Matter," *Management Science*, Vol. 13 (1967), pp. 926–945.

[40] Teichroew, Daniel and John F. Lubin, "Computer Simulation—Discussion of the Technique and Comparison of Languages," *Communications of the ACM*, Vol. 9 (1966), pp. 723–741.

[41] Tocher, K. D., "Review of Simulation Languages," *Operational Research Quarterly*, Vol. 16 (1965), pp. 189–218.

[42] Westlake, W. J., "A Uniform Random Number Generator Based on the Combination of Two Congruential Generators," *J. of ACM*, Vol. 14 (1967), pp. 337–340.

DIRECTED READING

Section	References
21.1	[1], [2], [3], [7], [8], [14], [17], [25], [26], [32], [33], [34], [35], [36]

21.4   [9]
21.5   [5], [9], [10], [12], [24], [27], [30], [37], [42]
21.6   [6], [9]
21.7   [5], [13], [16], [18], [19], [20], [21], [28]
21.8   [6], [9], [11], [15], [23], [29], [31], [40], [41]
21.9   [4], [7], [8], [38], [39]

Author Index

I1

Subject Index

I5